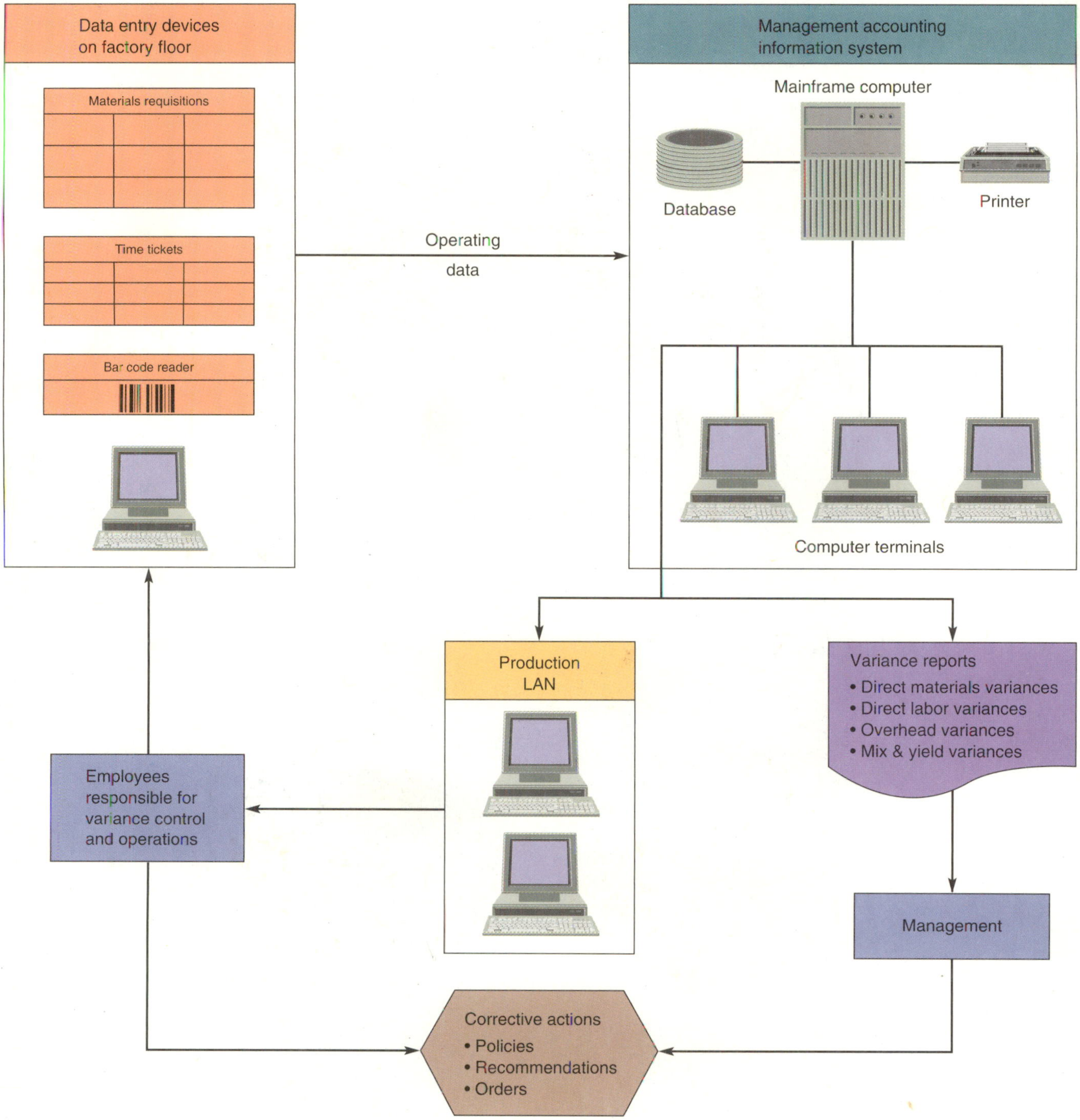

Data entry devices on factory floor

Materials requisitions

Time tickets

Bar code reader

Management accounting information system

Mainframe computer

Database

Printer

Computer terminals

Operating data

Production LAN

Variance reports
- Direct materials variances
- Direct labor variances
- Overhead variances
- Mix & yield variances

Employees responsible for variance control and operations

Management

Corrective actions
- Policies
- Recommendations
- Orders

The Operational Control System

D0215790

COST AND MANAGEMENT ACCOUNTING

Cost and Management Accounting: A Modern Approach

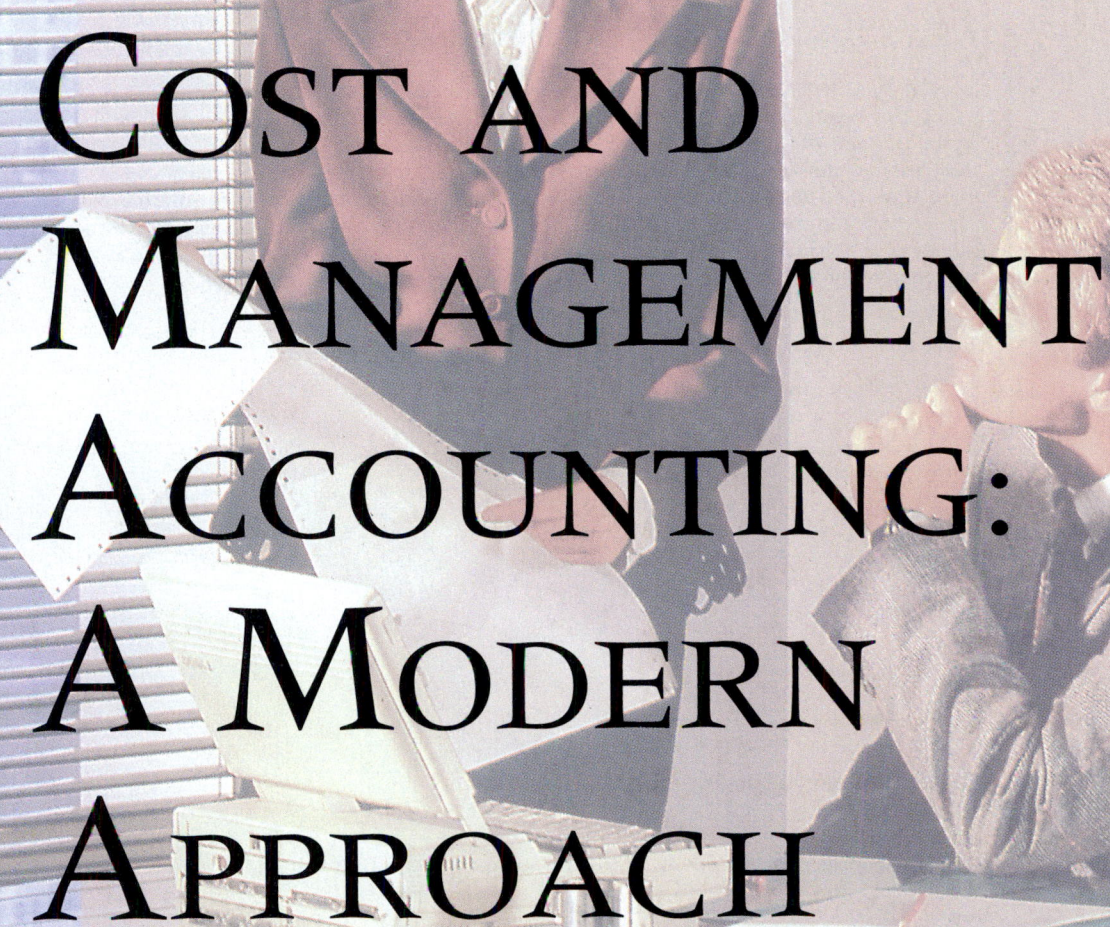

■ John G. Burch

UNIVERSITY OF NEVADA, RENO

Special Assistance from Michael F. Thomas,

UNIVERSITY OF NEVADA, RENO

WEST PUBLISHING COMPANY

SAINT PAUL ■ NEW YORK ■ LOS ANGELES ■ SAN FRANCISCO

COPYEDITOR	Patricia Lewis
COMPOSITION	Bi-Comp, Inc.
COVER DESIGN	K. M. Weber
INTERIOR DESIGN	K. M. Weber
PAGE LAYOUT	Diane Beasley
ARTWORK	Randy Miyake, Miyake Illustration and Design

WEST'S COMMITMENT TO THE ENVIRONMENT

In 1906, West Publishing Company began recycling materials left over from the production of books. This began a tradition of efficient and responsible use of resources. Today, up to 95% of our legal books and 70% of our college texts and school texts are printed on recycled, acid-free stock. West also recycles nearly 22 million pounds of scrap paper annually—the equivalent of 181,717 trees. Since the 1960s, West has devised ways to capture and recycle waste inks, solvents, oils, and vapors created in the printing process. We also recycle plastics of all kinds, wood, glass, corrugated cardboard, and batteries, and have eliminated the use of Styrofoam book packaging. We at West are proud of the longevity and the scope of our commitment to the environment.

Production, Prepress, Printing and Binding by West Publishing Company.

Library of Congress Cataloging-in-Publication Data

Burch, John G.
    Cost and management accounting : a modern approach / John G. Burch.
        p.   cm.
    Includes index.
    ISBN 0-314-02773-4
    1. Cost accounting. 2. Managerial accounting. I. Title.
HF5686.C8B773   1994
657'.42—dc20   93-27986
                                                    CIP

Microsoft Project is a registered trademark of Microsoft Corporation, Redmond, WA.
CA-Super Project for Windows is a registered trademark of Computer Associates International, Inc., Islandia, NY.
Project Scheduler 6 is a registered trademark of Scitor Corporation, Sunnyvale, CA.
Artemis Prestige for Windows is a registered trademark of Lucas Management Systems Inc., Houston, TX.
Open Plan 4.0 is a registered trademark of Welcom Software Technology, Houston, TX.
PARISS Enterprise is a registered trademark of Computer Aided Management Inc., Petaluma, CA.
Primavera Project Planner 5.0 is a registered trademark of Primavera systems, Inc., Bala Cynwyd, PA.
Project Workbench is a registered trademark of Applied Business Technology Corporation, New York, NY.
Lotus 1-2-3 is a registered trademark of Lotus Development Corporation, Cambridge, MA.
Material from Certified Management Accounting Examinations, Copyright © 1979–1991 by National Association of Accountants, now Institute of Management Accountants, is reprinted (or adapted) with permission.
Material from Uniform CPA Examinations, Questions and Unofficial Answers, Copyright © 1975–1992 by American Institute of Certified Public Accountants, Inc., is reprinted (or adapted) with permission.
Material from Certified Internal Auditor Examinations, Copyright © 1983–1990 by Institute of Internal Auditors, is reprinted (or adapted) with permission.

To Dr. A. J. Penz, distinguished professor, understanding mentor, and good friend

CONTENTS

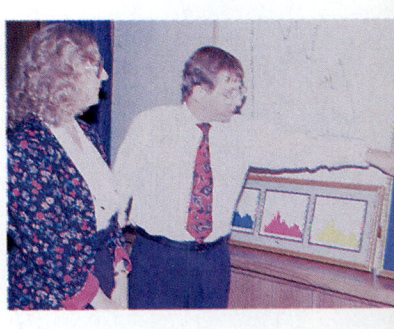

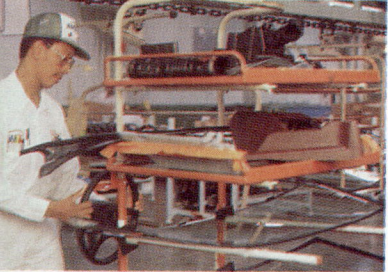

2 MOVING FROM TRADITIONAL TO MODERN MANUFACTURING ENVIRONMENTS   46

3 ENABLING TECHNOLOGIES FOR MODERN MANUFACTURING ENVIRONMENTS   91

Cost Accounting Systems   126

■ **PART II**

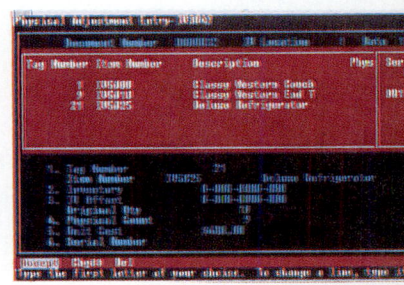

4 Building a Framework for Cost Accounting   128

5 The Job Order Cost Accounting System   170

6 THE PROCESS COST ACCOUNTING SYSTEM   221

▌7 THE STANDARD COST ACCOUNTING SYSTEM PART 1: SETTING STANDARDS 275

▌8 THE STANDARD COST ACCOUNTING SYSTEM PART 2: JOURNAL ENTRIES, COST VARIANCES, AND REPORTS 329

9 THE NEED FOR MULTIPLE OVERHEAD ACCOUNTS   399

10 THE ACTIVITY-BASED COSTING SYSTEM   444

COST MANAGEMENT SYSTEMS   492

■PART III

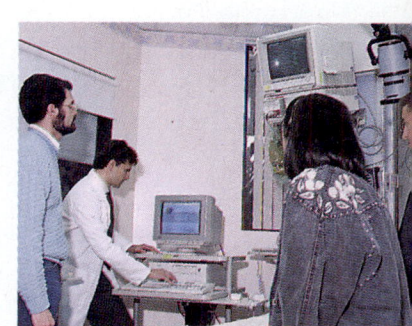

11 COST MANAGEMENT THROUGH ACTIVITY-BASED MANAGEMENT   494

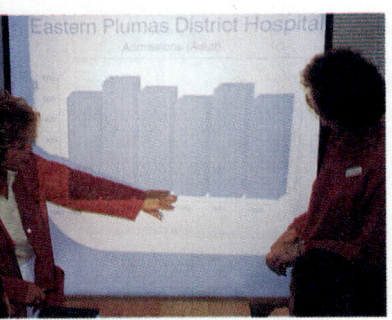

12 COST MANAGEMENT THROUGH A TOTAL QUALITY MANAGEMENT SYSTEM   551

15 THE THEORY OF CONSTRAINTS: EMPHASIZING THROUGHPUT   691

16 LINEAR PROGRAMMING: THE GRAPHICAL AND SIMPLEX METHODS   724

PROFIT MANAGEMENT SYSTEMS   778

■ **PART IV**

▌17 STRATEGIC PLANNING AND THE MASTER BUDGET   780

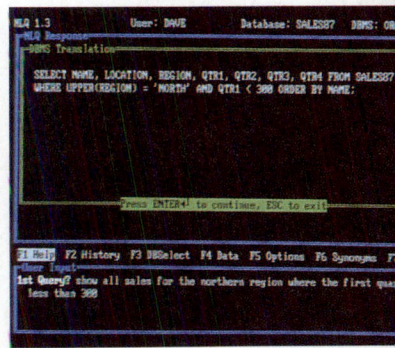

18 ANALYZING COST-VOLUME-PROFIT RELATIONSHIPS   833

19 MAKING SHORT-RUN PROFIT MANAGEMENT DECISIONS   875

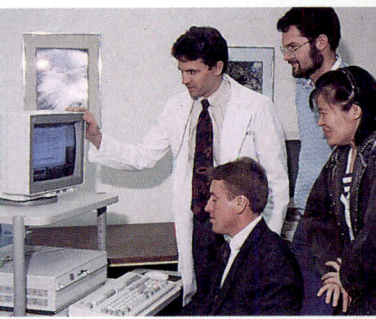

20 SEGMENTING THE ENTERPRISE FOR PROFIT PERFORMANCE EVALUATION 931

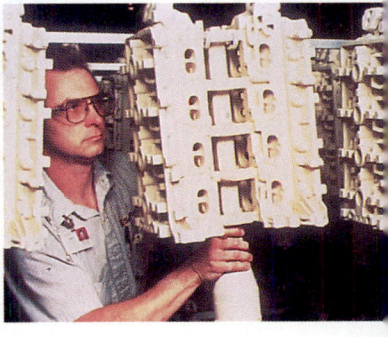

21 PRODUCT TRANSFERS WITHIN A COMPANY 1002

■ **PART V**   INVESTMENT MANAGEMENT SYSTEMS   1040

22 THE CAPITAL BUDGETING METHODOLOGY AND ITS FIRST STAGE   1042

23 CAPITAL BUDGETING METHODOLOGY: THE FINANCIAL ANALYSIS STAGE   1078

24 CAPITAL PROJECT IMPLEMENTATION MANAGEMENT   1136

PREFACE

During the last decade, new ways of doing business have swept through manufacturing and service industries, not only in the United States but throughout the world. "Global competition," "world-class," "continuous improvement," and "customer satisfaction" represent driving forces behind changes taking place in business and, to some extent, in government.

Organizations of all kinds have taken initiatives to harness these driving forces. These initiatives include just-in-time (JIT) methods, cellular and synchronous manufacturing, integrated computer-based information systems (ICBISs), electronic data interchange (EDI), activity-based costing (ABC), activity-based management (ABM), total quality management (TQM), cost management of logistics, life cycle analysis and target costing, quality function deployment (QFD), and throughput analysis. These new initiatives will cause substantial operating and cultural change throughout business and government, and one of the most important areas that must change is the management accounting system.

Not since the Industrial Revolution has management accounting been challenged to change, and even abandon, some traditional methods. From this challenge, great opportunities abound for management accountants who understand the new initiatives, master modern concepts and methods, and build on relevant traditional methods.

To succeed during this period of change and beyond, managers and workers need an array of timely, relevant information supplied by management accountants. Cost accounting systems are needed to produce accurate product and service costs. Cost management systems and performance measurements must be developed that enable managers and workers to evaluate activities, eliminate waste, improve quality, satisfy internal and external customers, and control costs throughout a company's value chain. Profit management systems must be installed to assist managers in planning, budgeting, and evaluating organizational segments. Investment systems must be set up that allow managers to perform strategic planning and make appropriate capital project decisions.

Indeed, managers and workers are turning to management accountants to provide them with this array of information. Now is the time for management accountants to welcome this opportunity, meet the challenge, and play an influential and supportive role that far exceeds that of their predecessors.

The purpose of this book is to provide aspiring management accountants with the vision, concepts, and methods necessary to fulfill their challenging new role.

THE AUDIENCE FOR THIS BOOK

This book's intended audience includes accounting and business juniors and seniors, MBAs, and others who need to understand the role of cost and management accounting in organizations. For accounting majors, this book redirects their focus from external to internal users. These students will be particularly concerned with the meaning and usability of information they provide management and other internal users, how the information is to be used, and how to prepare and present it in an attractive and understandable form.

This book is especially helpful for students aspiring to become professional accountants and endeavoring to obtain professional certifications, such as the CMA, CPA, and/or CIA. Students planning careers in management will find this book provides them with an understanding of management accounting information and its preparation, as well as the ability to use that information to make correct decisions.

This book contains more material than is normally covered in a one-semester course. For those schools still offering a traditional one-semester course titled *Cost Accounting,* instructors can select from a wide array of topics most suited to their objectives. This book is also tailor-made for a two-semester *Cost and Management Accounting* course. With its many modern topics and think-tank problems, it is also suitable for an MBA course. The result is a book that allows instructors to teach any of these courses in their own way and at their own pace.

ORGANIZATION OF THIS BOOK

One of the differentiating characteristics of this book is the logical sequencing of chapters so that topics are grouped into well-defined parts. First, the book presents a definitional and environmental foundation that addresses the new initiatives alluded to earlier. Then it describes cost accounting systems, followed by cost management systems, followed by profit management systems. Finally, a part on investment management systems wraps up the book. The major parts of this book include the following:

- *Part I: Management Accounting's Role in Modern Organizations.* This part enables students to understand the new environment in which they will be working and the reasons for it. Chapter 1 defines the modern management accountant, describes the challenge to provide an array of high-quality information, and presents ethical considerations. Chapter 2 provides a comprehensive treatment of world-class concepts and methods. Building off Chapter 2, Chapter 3 continues this theme by describing the kinds of information technology and systems required to support world-class initiatives and organizations.

- *Part II: Cost Accounting Systems.* Part II presents cost accounting systems, the cornerstone of the management accounting profession. This part ensures that students have comprehensive understanding of both traditional costing systems and activity-based costing, a relatively new costing system. Moreover, this part describes how construction companies and service firms as well as manufacturing organizations use cost accounting systems. Chapter 4 sets the stage for basic cost accounting systems design. Chapters 5 and 6 present job order and process costing systems with an emphasis on modern applications. Chapters 7 and 8 cover standard cost systems with Chapter 7 devoted solely to standard setting and budgeting issues. Chapter 8 provides a detailed treatment of variance analysis and reporting and their relevance to modern environments such as just-in-time (JIT) production processes. Chapters 9 and 10 present overhead accounting issues including service department allocations and activity-based costing. The unique cost management reporting perspective includes activity-based cost variances for JIT production cells and for service departments and overhead activities.

- *Part III: Cost Management Systems.* Part III provides a logical transition from Part II. Managers and workers need more than product and service costs; they need both financial and nonfinancial information to help them improve efficiency, effectiveness, and decision making so they can eliminate redundancy and waste, improve quality, and reduce, if not eliminate, constraints to throughput. This part covers concepts and methods that management accountants can use to supply such information. Chapter 11 employs work done in Chapter 10 to reengineer activities, benchmark, and develop performance measurements for continuous improvement. Chapter 12 provides detailed coverage of concepts and methods being used to install total quality management systems in forward-looking enterprises. Chapter 13 deals with techniques used to manage logistics costs. An array of advantages flow to companies that learn to make and deliver products and services faster than their competitors in terms of a target price and cost. Chapter 14 describes how to achieve such advantages through simultaneous engineering, quality function deployment, analysis of life cycle costs, and target costing. Numerous constraints inhibit enterprises from achieving maximum throughput. Chapter 15 gives practical steps that can overcome these constraints. Chapter 16 examines how companies can maximize profits and minimize costs in terms of various constraints.

- *Part IV: Profit Management Systems.* This part explains how management accountants can provide information that will help managers increase profits. The chapters center on the three decision-making functions of profit managers: planning, operational control, and performance evaluation. Chapter 17 begins the planning process by introducing strategic planning and developing master budgets for it. Chapter 18 applies cost-volume-profit (CVP) analysis to both budgeting and operational control to help managers reach target profits. Chapter 19 extends CVP analysis to enable managers to make short-run operational decisions. Chapter 20 presents profit performance evaluation methods and reports for responsibility accounting. Transferring products and services between responsibility centers can be a headache. Chapter 21 shows how to develop a viable transfer pricing system that helps ensure cooperation between responsibility center managers and achieve higher profits for the total enterprise.

- *Part V: Investment Management Systems.* In this part, the book concludes with a detailed coverage of capital project investment and implementation. Chapter 22 introduces capital budgeting by presenting a unique four-stage capital budgeting methodology. Detailed consideration is given to eliciting management judgments and estimating feasibility and benefit factors. Chapter 23 presents cash flow evaluation methods and sensitivity analysis. Chapter 24 concludes with capital project implementation and review methods applicable to modern management accounting systems. These include project management techniques, implementation, and postimplementation audits.

PEDAGOGICAL FEATURES

Each chapter includes many features that will help students understand concepts and methods. Among these features are the following:

- *Learning Objectives and Summary of Learning Objectives.* Learning objectives listed at the beginning of each chapter indicate what students will achieve by studying and applying chapter material. At the end of the main body of the chapter, a summary of chapter learning objectives reviews the main points of the chapter.

■ *Photographs*. At various points throughout the book, photographs are introduced to illustrate how some of the concepts and methods discussed in this book are being applied in the modern workaday world.

■ *Insights & Applications*. At appropriate points throughout each chapter are features titled *Insights & Applications*. For the most part, these are real-world applications that explain and reinforce concepts and methods presented in the main-line chapter material. They can spark students' interest and enliven class discussion.

■ *Important Terms*. Each chapter contains an important terms section, which lists and defines new or unique words or phrases that are introduced in that chapter. A list of *all* important terms is included at the back of the book.

■ *Exhibits*. This book is filled with exhibits that illustrate and clarify specific topics. Like the photographs and *Insights and Applications,* the exhibits provide students with a clearer understanding of the material and drive home major points made in the chapter.

■ *Demonstration Problems*. Several problems and their solutions are included just before the assignment material in each chapter to guide students in solving the chapter-specific and think-tank problems. These demonstration problems provide examples of how concepts and methods are used to solve various problems.

■ *Assignment Material*. The assignment material is composed of three elements: review questions, chapter-specific problems, and think-tank problems. The review questions require students to recall important chapter material and provide an excellent basis for outlining the chapters. The chapter-specific problems require students to apply what they learned in the chapter and, on occasion, in previous chapters to derive a solution. The think-tank problems require students to go beyond the bounds of the chapter material, possibly reviewing previous chapters, making assumptions, and researching specific topics, to create a feasible response, approach, or recommendation. Many problems are based on material from CMA, CPA, and CIA examinations.

An abundance and variety of exercises are included in each category. Those instructors who prefer a quantitative emphasis and specific recall will be quite comfortable with the chapter-specific problems and many of the review questions. Those who prefer a more analytical and discussion-oriented approach will welcome the think-tank problems, as well as some of the review questions. Obviously, many possibilities exist between the two extremes.

ANCILLARIES

A variety of ancillary materials is provided to adopters of *Cost and Management Accounting: A Modern Approach*. The following ancillaries are available:

■ *Solutions Manual*. This manual includes comprehensive answers to review questions, complete solutions to chapter-specific problems, and in-depth presentations for think-tank problems. In addition, *Let's Talk* boxes appear at appropriate points where additional comments and illustrations are needed.

■ *Instructor's Resource Manual*. This manual aids instructors in structuring the course to fit the interests and backgrounds of their students. It contains outlines, summaries, *Let's Talk* boxes, and transparency masters. A variety of icons and cartoons are available to introduce lecture material and stimulate interest.

■ *Student's Resource Manual*. This manual uses self-tests and demonstration problems to help students master the material in the book. For every chapter in the book, the manual also provides an outline and problem-solving tips.

- *Test Bank.* This ancillary, prepared by Ceil and Jerome Fewox of Trident Technical College, contains nearly 2,000 test items, including true/false, multiple-choice, and essay questions. All items are keyed to chapter learning objectives. This supplement is also available on *WESTEST,* a microcomputer test-generation package.
- *Transparency Acetates.* Selected transparencies of end-of-chapter solutions are available that contain detailed calculations. The transparencies are in a large type font that will ensure high-quality presentations.
- *Spreadsheet Templates and Instructions.* This ancillary enables students to use a Lotus 1-2-3 spreadsheet to solve selected in-text problems. This package also contains a section that assists novice users in learning the software package.
- *Astound Software.* This software is a multimedia presentation program that will allow instructors to display art, exhibits, solutions, and other elements from the text. The instructor can modify these materials or create entirely original transparencies. The software is available free to qualified adopters.
- *Check Figures.* Check figures are available in quantity to the instructor for in-class distribution.
- *Videotapes.* Videotapes depicting various management accounting issues and practices are available to qualified adopters.

ACKNOWLEDGMENTS

It is with great pleasure and gratitude that I acknowledge the many people whose expertise and support contributed to the development of this book. A project of this size could not have been completed without the assistance of many dedicated people.

I am indeed fortunate to have worked with a talented and committed team at West Educational Publishing. The enthusiasm with which this team accepted the challenge to create and market a breakthrough, top-of-the-line package is truly appreciated. Among those I would like to recognize and thank are:

- Robert Horan, editor, brought support, encouragement, and direction. Bob's ideas, experienced judgment, and managerial talents were forces that provided the basis for the completed project.
- Janine Wilson, development editor, provided a logical plan for the project's development. Her knowledge of manuscript development and production was valuable in coordinating the efforts of many people. Janine's willingness to listen during times of trouble will always be appreciated.
- Pat Lewis, copyeditor, brought a personal dedication to the superb copyediting of this manuscript. Her knowledge and ability to turn a "pumpkin into a golden carriage" are truly amazing. She is simply the best.
- Matthew Thurber, production editor, is to be congratulated for his extraordinary efforts to coordinate the many tasks necessary to convert bundles of paper into a beautiful book. Thanks for doing a great job and keeping the project on schedule.
- Ellen Stanton, promotion manager, is doing a terrific job in presenting a high-quality product to the marketplace. She has the ability to convey to prospective adopters the essence and major features of the total teaching package.

Thanks go to the reviewers who spent many hours evaluating each chapter. The quality of the material in this book is attributable to their thoughtful recommendations. The reviewers include the following:

C. Richard Aldridge
Western Kentucky University

Germain Böer
Vanderbilt University

Donald Bostrom
University of North Dakota

Marvin Bouillon
Iowa State University

Thomas Calderon
University of Akron

Frederick Cole
University of North Florida

Joanne Collins
California State University at Los Angeles

Harold Cook
Central Michigan University

Alan Deck
University of Southwestern Louisiana

Kenneth Eske
Naval Post Graduate School

Linda Ferreri
University of North Carolina at Charlotte

Margaret Gagne
University of Colorado at Colorado Springs

Robert Greenberg
Washington State University

John Hardy
Brigham Young University

William Harmon

Medhat Helmi
University of Alabama at Birmingham

James Holmes
University of Kentucky

Arley Howard
Western New Mexico University

Jai Kang
San Francisco State University

Il-woon Kim
University of Akron

Paul Krause
California State University at Chico

Leslie Kren
University of Wisconsin at Milwaukee

Ken Lavery
Purdue University—North Central

William Letzkus
University of Arkansas

James Mackey
California State University at Sacramento

Alan McNamee
University of New Mexico

Christina Moorcroft
Luther College

David Nix
Boise State University

Diane Pattison
University of San Diego

Shirley Polejewski
University of St. Thomas

Grover Porter
University of Alabama at Huntsville

Manash Ray
Lehigh University

Frederick Schaeberle
Western Michigan University

Jeffrey Schatzberg
University of Arizona

Robert Seay
Murray State University

Michael Shields
Memphis State University

Howard Toole
San Diego State University

Robert Zimmer
University of Denver

A special word of thanks is due to a number of colleagues and students for their contributions, suggestions, and encouragement. Thanks go to Phil Dooley, Missy Catuzzo, Steve Loomis, Erika Loomis, Scott Wahrer, Roy E. Gilbreath, Craig Parkhurst, Jeff Carleton, Recep Eksi, Kevin Brewer, Uma Mani, Vitalis C. Ozoude, Ping Ping Fu, Laurie Saint, and Bruce Honberger. Special thanks are due also to Cheryl Thomas, for her technical assistance.

Gratefully acknowledged is the help of the numerous companies that supplied photographs and technical information. These photographs provide the reader with significant insight into the text material.

Thanks are due to the American Institute of Certified Public Accountants, Institute of Certified Management Accountants, Institute of Internal Auditors, and many publishers and companies for their generous permission to quote from their publications. Problems from the Uniform CPA Examinations are designated (AICPA adapted); problems from the Certificate in Management Accounting examinations are designated (CMA adapted); and problems from the Certificate in Internal Auditing examinations are designated (CIA adapted).

I am especially grateful to Michael F. Thomas for his efforts in revising several chapters in Parts II and IV. His expertise in electronic spreadsheets and costing systems has been especially important to this project. Moreover, Mike has indicated total commitment to the future of this project.

Although Glenda Burch is not listed as an author, her substantial efforts and unwavering dedication to the completion of this project are without equal. She performed all the hard, thankless work of word processing, filing, organizing, ordering, researching, copying, mailing, and many other tasks not always evident to the casual observer. In this particular case, however, without her cooperation, support, and long hours of hard work, this project would not have seen the light of day.

ABOUT THE AUTHOR

John G. Burch is a professor of management accounting and computer information systems at the University of Nevada, Reno. He earned a B.S. in accounting from Louisiana Tech University and M.A. and Ph.D. degrees in accounting from the University of Alabama. Prior to his academic career, Burch owned and operated three businesses and held managerial positions in energy and construction companies.

Active in research, Professor Burch has written over 45 articles that have appeared in *Information Systems Management, Information Strategy: The Executive's Journal, Journal of Accounting and EDP, Management Accounting, Journal of Systems Management*, and *Business Horizons*.

Professor Burch has produced over 20 seminars dealing with information technology, accounting information systems, and entrepreneurship. He has served as a consultant to a number of organizations on management accounting and information system issues. Vitally interested in the expanding and challenging role of management accounting, Burch has conducted a large number of field studies in a variety of manufacturing and service firms across the country.

Then . . .

. . . And Now

ACCOUNTING TEXTBOOKS FROM WEST EDUCATIONAL PUBLISHING

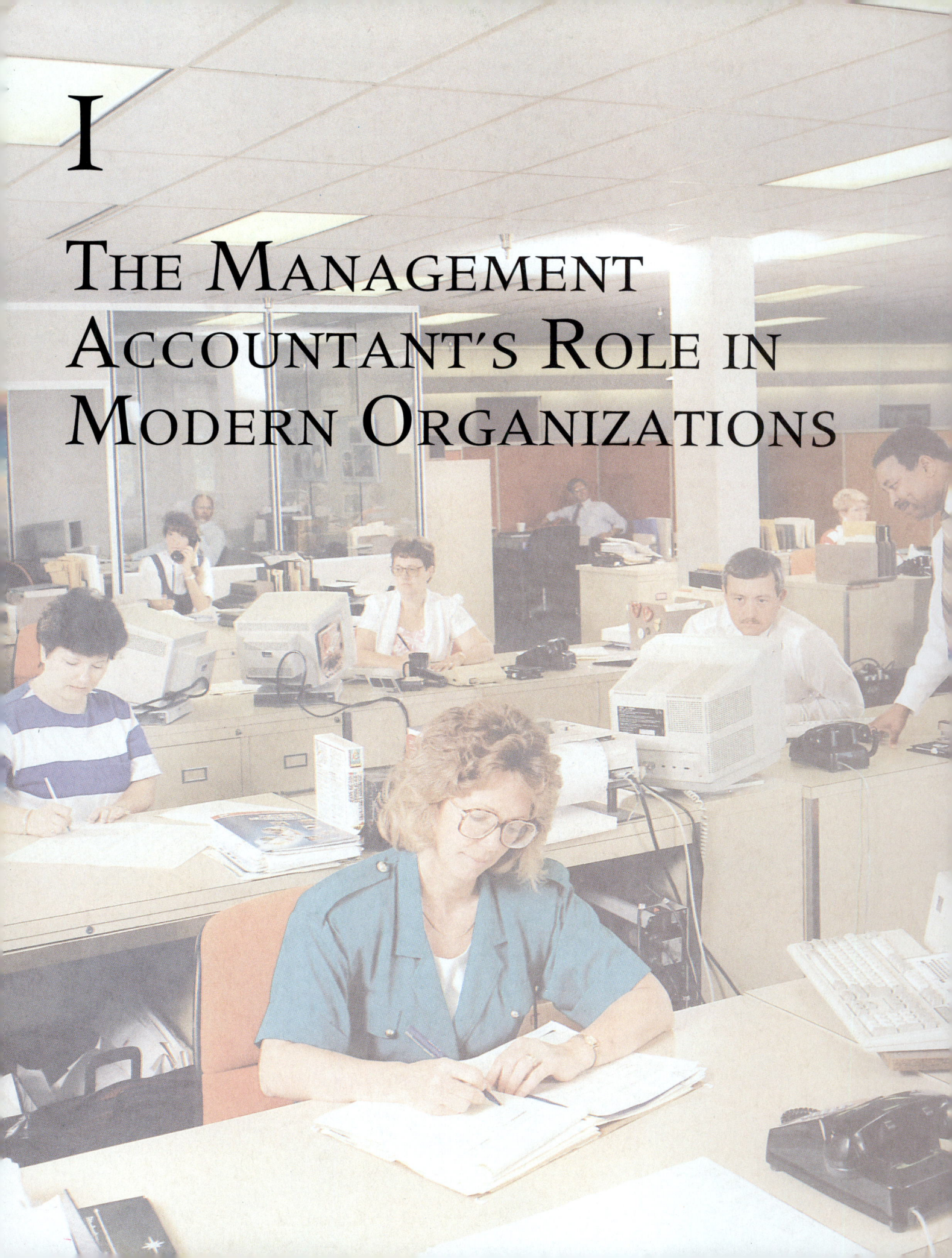

I

THE MANAGEMENT ACCOUNTANT'S ROLE IN MODERN ORGANIZATIONS

Today's management accountant is entering an environment substantially different from the environment pervasive before the 1990s. This new environment, which is still evolving, is influenced by all of the following:

- Sharpened awareness that financial accounting information is insufficient for managing organizations and that management accountants must correct this insufficiency
- Heightened concerns about ethical conduct
- Stiff worldwide competition and apprehension about the ability to compete
- Radical departure from how enterprises were managed and operations were performed in the past
- Pervasive use of information and manufacturing technologies

Before you come to grips with specific management accounting tools, the three chapters of Part I will help you to understand this new environment and to appreciate the need for such tools.

Chapter 1 introduces the broadening field of management accounting and describes the role played by management accountants in organizations, including standards of ethical conduct. Chapter 2 contrasts traditional manufacturing environments with world-class manufacturing (WCM) environments. Two WCM systems covered in Chapter 2 are just-in-time (JIT) and computer-integrated manufacturing (CIM). Chapter 3 explains the development of integrated computer-based information systems (ICBISs). It also covers manufacturing resource planning (MRP II) and the use of electronic data interchange (EDI) to create metacorporations. ▬▬

i
INTRODUCTION TO TYPES OF ORGANIZATIONS AND THE MANAGEMENT ACCOUNTANT

Management accountants provide information for internal users.

LEARNING OBJECTIVES

After studying this chapter, you should be able to:

1. Describe the four types of organizations that are served by management accounting.

2. Explain the relationship of management accounting to financial and cost accounting.

3. Present the major trends in the new manufacturing environment and discuss the role of modern management accountants in organizations.

4. Explain how to become a professional management accountant.

■INTRODUCTION

Management accounting is concerned with providing information to people within organizations who have the responsibility of planning, monitoring and controlling their operations, and evaluating performance to ensure the success of these organizations. Management accounting can be contrasted with **financial accounting,** which is concerned with providing financial statements to stockholders, creditors, investment analysts, and others who are outside organizations.

The present business environment of intense competition, both local and global, is leading modern enterprises to a renewed commitment to excellence. As part of this commitment, management accounting has also had to change. The focus of management accounting is to improve the information provided to those people who have to run the organization's operations. Indeed, American business and management accounting have been reborn.

The people who provide information to internal users (people within the company) to help them make better decisions are **management accountants.** The rise of management accountants to professional status has paralleled the growth and acceptance of their professional organization, the Institute of Management Accountants (IMA). The IMA provides management accountants with several important services:

- The Certified Management Accountant (CMA) program
- Standards of Management Accounting
- Standards of ethical conduct
- Continuing education programs
- Professional publications

The purpose of this chapter is to establish a framework for studying the remaining chapters. The chapter begins by describing the four types of organizations that management accountants work for. Next, it explains the relationship of management accounting to financial and cost accounting and the major trends taking place in the new manufacturing environment. Later sections examine the role of management accountants in organizations. And, finally, the chapter concludes with a discussion of the management accountant as a professional.

TYPES OF ORGANIZATIONS SERVED BY MANAGEMENT ACCOUNTANTS

Management accountants serve any of four types of organizations:

- Manufacturing organizations
- Merchandising firms (also called wholesalers and retailers)
- Profit-oriented service firms
- Not-for-profit service entities

LEARNING OBJECTIVE 1

Describe the four types of organizations that are served by management accounting.

Manufacturing Organization

A **manufacturing organization** is an enterprise that converts raw materials, which it purchases, into finished goods (i.e., products) through the use of labor, machines, technology, and various facilities. Within the manufacturing category are a wide variety of production characteristics that call for different management accounting systems.

MANUFACTURING COST ELEMENTS. The cost of a manufactured product is made up of the following manufacturing cost elements: direct materials, direct labor, and variable and fixed overhead. These cost elements can be assigned to an individual product's cost in two ways: direct tracing and allocation. For example, appliances (and their costs) can be directly traced to each house built by a building contractor. In contrast, the nails used are not traced to each house. Instead the total cost of nails is often divided **(allocated)** among all the houses built in a month. Cost elements that need to be allocated into a product's cost are called indirect product costs or overhead.

■ **Direct materials** are those materials (and their costs) that can be easily traced to (and costs charged to) the product. For example, cement is charged to the manufacture of concrete blocks, or so many yards of woolen cloth go into the manufacture of dresses and suits.

  Other materials may be an integral part of a finished product, but are directly traceable to the product only at great cost and effort. Such items include bolts used to connect pieces of steel together to make trucks or the glue that holds a box together. These materials are referred to as **indirect materials** and are included as part of overhead so they can be allocated into the product's cost.

■ **Direct labor,** also called **touch labor,** includes labor costs that are directly traceable to the products those people work on. Examples of employees who generate direct labor costs include machine operators, assembly line workers, carpenters, and bricklayers; that is, those people who are in direct contact with the production of the product. In service firms, direct labor includes, for example, surgeons, engineers, architects, and CPAs.

  Labor costs that cannot be traced directly to the products are called **indirect labor** and are treated as part of overhead. These costs include the wages of workers such as janitors, forklift operators, inventory clerks, and materials handlers.

■ **Overhead** includes all costs of manufacturing that are not directly traced to the product. Thus, overhead includes all the indirect costs of production such as indirect materials, indirect labor, factory utilities, plant building taxes and insurance, machinery repairs and maintenance, and factory depreciation.

  In planning, controlling, and evaluating overhead items, the management accountant must separate them into variable and fixed categories. For example, the more mobile homes a manufacturer plans to build, the more nails it will need. These are variable costs because the total amount needed increases with the number of homes planned. On the other hand, the factory's depreciation is the same each month (assuming a straight-line method) regardless of how many homes are planned. More will be said about how to distinguish between variable and fixed overhead costs in Chapter 7.

Overhead combined with direct labor is known as **conversion cost.** This term stems from the fact that direct labor costs and overhead costs are incurred in the conversion of direct materials into finished products. The combination of direct labor and direct materials is known as **prime cost.**

PROPORTION OF MANUFACTURING COST ELEMENTS IN TRADITIONAL AND AUTOMATED FACTORIES. Exhibit 1–1 shows how the proportions of manufacturing cost elements differ in traditional (labor-intensive) and automated (machinery-intensive) manufacturing environments. The percentages in the exhibit are approximations simply to show magnitude.

As enterprises introduce more automated machinery, workers are increasingly engaged in setup and supervisory functions rather than actually working directly on the product. Often, labor's main tasks are to load the machines and

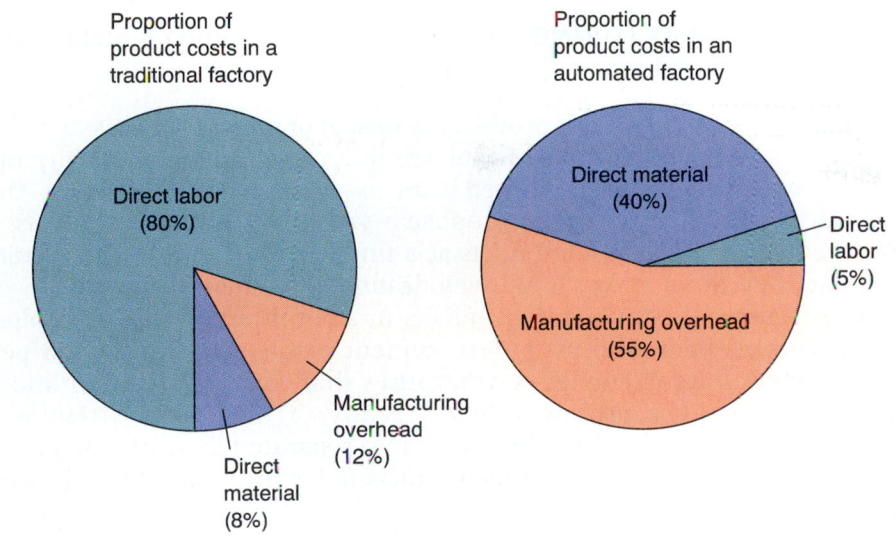

Proportion of product costs in a traditional factory

Proportion of product costs in an automated factory

Direct labor (80%)

Manufacturing overhead (12%)

Direct material (8%)

Direct material (40%)

Direct labor (5%)

Manufacturing overhead (55%)

■ EXHIBIT 1–1
Magnitude of Product Cost Elements in Traditional and Automated Factories

act as troubleshooters. Machines perform most of the tasks once performed by direct labor.

In traditional factories, product diversity is sufficiently small. Thus, the demands made by different products on the enterprise's overhead resources do not vary widely. But these conditions are no longer typical of automated factories where overhead is becoming a larger and larger share of total manufacturing costs. This creates a serious problem in trying to determine the real cost of a product because overhead represents indirect costs that have to be allocated (divided up) in some way.

If all cost elements could be directly traced to each product, then accurately calculating the product's cost and profitability would be relatively simple. The more costs that must be allocated, though, the less accurate the product's cost may be. With the increasing competition created by the substantial growth in international trade, accurate measurement of production costs has become a key variable in organizational survival. Consequently, management accountants are playing very important roles in new world-class manufacturing firms. The need for accurate product cost information to manage costs more effectively has led to the development of new allocation methods such as activity-based costing and activity-based management (Chapters 10 and 11).

DIRECT TECHNOLOGY AS A FOURTH MANUFACTURING COST ELEMENT.   Some management accounting authorities believe that a fourth manufacturing cost element called **direct technology** should be added to reflect the growing dependence of manufacturing on automation. This technology includes computers, software, and telecommunications, which control processes and provide the intelligence for machines, and various pieces of equipment and robots used to convert raw materials into finished products. Rather than lumping the costs for this technology into overhead, these costs could be traced and charged directly to the product.

Most technology costs these days are accounted for by depreciation and are included in overhead. The problem is that traditional depreciation methods are based on time, not production. When straight-line or accelerated methods (based on time periods like a month) are used, these technology costs are included in fixed overhead. By adopting a direct production-based depreciation method, such as units of production or machine hours, these costs can be matched more accurately with the products manufactured.

TYPES OF MANUFACTURING SYSTEMS.   Manufacturing systems can be divided into two broad types:

- **Job order systems** produce products as special orders. In some systems each order has one or more features that are different from those of any other order; a custom jeweler or printer is an example of such a system. Other manufacturing enterprises may produce a variety of standard products, but produce only one or a few products at a time; examples include a furniture manufacturer and a maker of oil well drilling equipment.
- **Process systems** manufacture products in a continuous stream. Appliance manufacturers, paint manufacturers, cement plants, flour mills, and petroleum refineries are examples of enterprises that convert materials into finished goods using a process system. Clearly, a job order system is not applicable in these firms because there is no separate job or unique product. Instead, a stream of homogeneous products flows through various processes and departments.

Merchandising Firm

A **merchandising firm** is a retailer or wholesaler that buys completed products for resale. Retailing activities involve the selling of goods to ultimate consumers for personal or household consumption. International Shoe Corporation, a manufacturing organization, buys leather and other raw materials and converts them into shoes that are sold in large quantities to wholesalers like Shiprite Distributors. Shiprite, in turn, sells shoes to retailers like Matilda's Shoe Store.

Merchandising Firm and Manufacturing Organization Financial Statements Compared

From an accounting viewpoint, the best way to differentiate merchandising firms from manufacturing organizations is to look at their respective financial statements. The financial statements prepared by a manufacturing organization are more complex than the statements prepared by a merchandising firm. The production process gives rise to many costs that do not exist in a merchandising firm.

BALANCE SHEETS COMPARED.   Exhibit 1–2 compares the current asset sections of a merchandising firm and a manufacturing firm. A merchandising firm has only one class of inventory. This is **merchandise inventory,** which is composed of products purchased from vendors awaiting resale to consumers. By contrast, manufacturing firms have three classes of inventory:

- **Raw materials** is the inventory of direct and indirect materials awaiting input to the production process. In traditional manufacturing enterprises, raw materials normally are stored in a stockyard or storeroom until requisitioned into the factory. In many firms, separate inventory records are kept for direct and indirect materials because they are controlled and accounted for differently.
- **Work-in-process** or **work-in-progress (WIP)** is the inventory account within the general ledger that is used to accumulate production costs while products are being manufactured. The ending balance shown on the balance sheet represents products only partially complete at the end of a period.
- **Finished goods** are products that are complete as to manufacturing but have not yet been sold to customers. This is the same as a retailer's merchandise inventory.

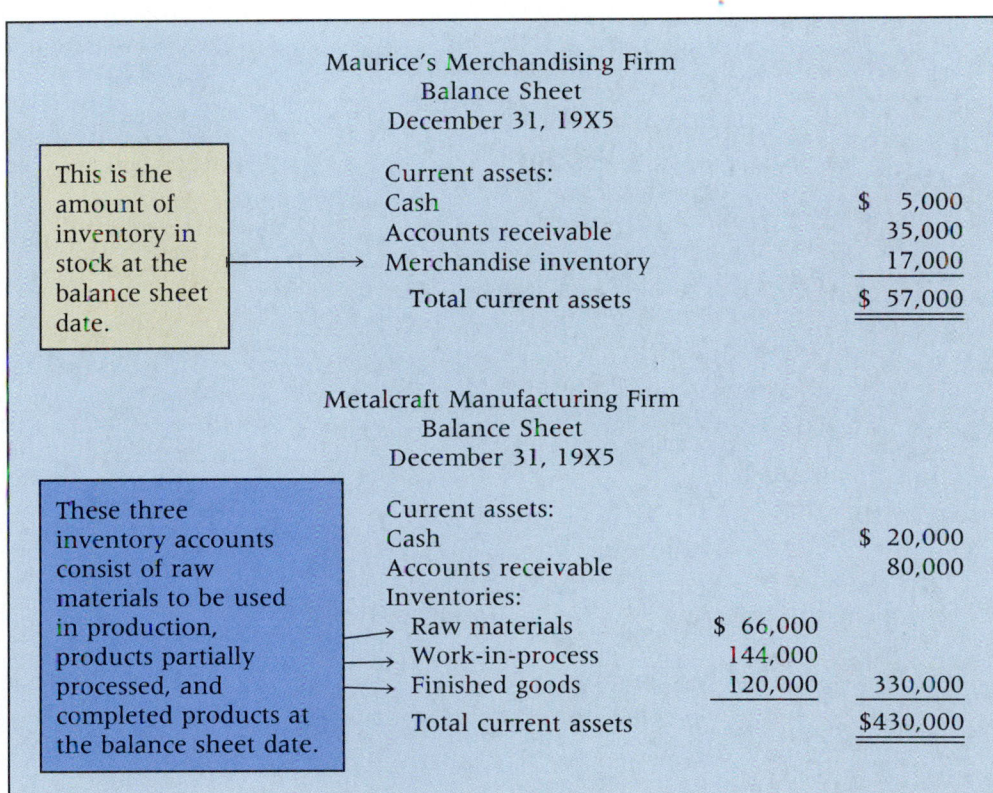

■EXHIBIT 1–2
Current Asset Data of the Balance Sheets of a Merchandising Firm and a Manufacturing Firm

Maurice's Merchandising Firm
Balance Sheet
December 31, 19X5

This is the amount of inventory in stock at the balance sheet date.

Current assets:	
Cash	$ 5,000
Accounts receivable	35,000
Merchandise inventory	17,000
Total current assets	$ 57,000

Metalcraft Manufacturing Firm
Balance Sheet
December 31, 19X5

These three inventory accounts consist of raw materials to be used in production, products partially processed, and completed products at the balance sheet date.

Current assets:		
Cash		$ 20,000
Accounts receivable		80,000
Inventories:		
Raw materials	$ 66,000	
Work-in-process	144,000	
Finished goods	120,000	330,000
Total current assets		$430,000

INCOME STATEMENTS COMPARED. Exhibit 1–3 compares the income statement of a merchandising firm to that of a manufacturing organization. The cost of goods sold for merchandising firms is simply the purchase cost of inventory items received from an outside supplier that have been sold. In contrast, the cost of goods sold in a manufacturing firm consists of many different costs that have been incurred in the process of manufacturing those products.

The income statement of a manufacturing firm is supported by a **Schedule of Cost of Goods Manufactured,** which reflects the cost of completed production work. This schedule includes the specific cost elements that have gone into the products a company has manufactured during a period. Basically, to determine the cost of goods manufactured, this statement adds the manufacturing costs incurred during the time period (e.g., a month) to the beginning work-in-process inventory and then subtracts the ending work-in-process inventory.

▌Reporting Finished Goods Inventory Information for Management in Merchandising and Manufacturing Firms

Finished goods for manufacturers are equivalent to merchandise for merchandising firms in that they both await customer sales. Management accountants can use electronic spreadsheets to generate both numerical and graphical sales information for people who manage and sell this inventory.

Assume that Ace Company wants to tie its TV commercials to shoe sales revenue. The electronic spreadsheet screen in Exhibit 1–4 and its accompanying bar and line graph depict this relationship clearly. Bear in mind that such information is useful for sales managers of both a merchandising firm and a manufacturing firm.

Exhibit 1–5 (see p. 12) shows a spreadsheet with data values ranging over six months for raw materials, work-in-process, and finished goods inventories at Achilles Company, a manufacturer of shoes. The accompanying stacked-line

EXHIBIT 1–3

Comparison of a Merchandising Firm Income Statement with a Manufacturing Firm Income Statement

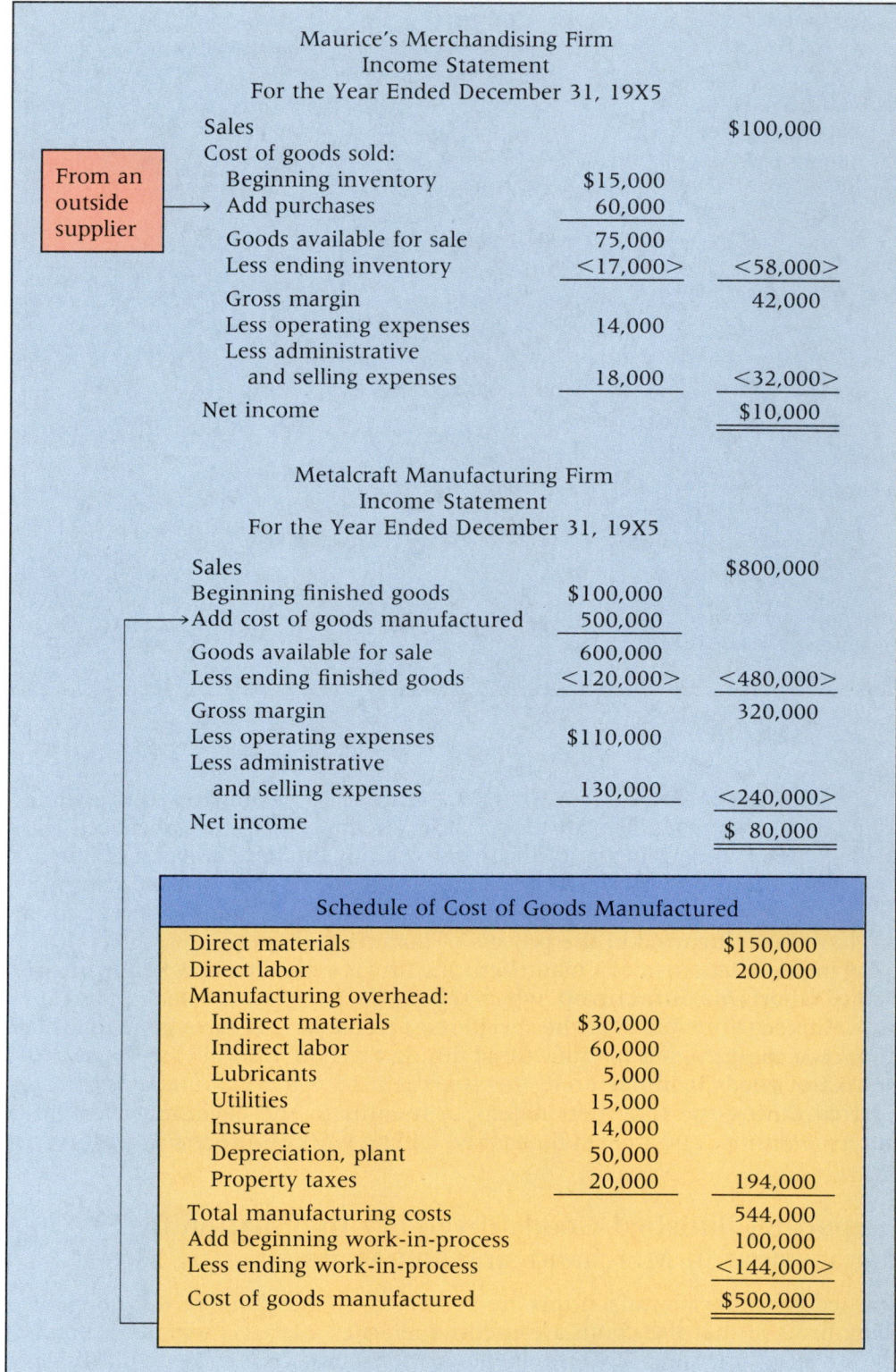

Maurice's Merchandising Firm
Income Statement
For the Year Ended December 31, 19X5

Sales		$100,000
Cost of goods sold:		
Beginning inventory	$15,000	
Add purchases	60,000	
Goods available for sale	75,000	
Less ending inventory	<17,000>	<58,000>
Gross margin		42,000
Less operating expenses	14,000	
Less administrative and selling expenses	18,000	<32,000>
Net income		$10,000

From an outside supplier

Metalcraft Manufacturing Firm
Income Statement
For the Year Ended December 31, 19X5

Sales		$800,000
Beginning finished goods	$100,000	
Add cost of goods manufactured	500,000	
Goods available for sale	600,000	
Less ending finished goods	<120,000>	<480,000>
Gross margin		320,000
Less operating expenses	$110,000	
Less administrative and selling expenses	130,000	<240,000>
Net income		$ 80,000

Schedule of Cost of Goods Manufactured

Direct materials		$150,000
Direct labor		200,000
Manufacturing overhead:		
Indirect materials	$30,000	
Indirect labor	60,000	
Lubricants	5,000	
Utilities	15,000	
Insurance	14,000	
Depreciation, plant	50,000	
Property taxes	20,000	194,000
Total manufacturing costs		544,000
Add beginning work-in-process		100,000
Less ending work-in-process		<144,000>
Cost of goods manufactured		$500,000

graph shows fluctuations in these data over time. As in all stacked-line graphs, the top line represents the total of all the lines, and each line takes as its zero point the data point on the line below it.

Various colors and patterns can be used in such graphs to differentiate categories of finished goods or merchandise inventory. Indeed, the computer and various software packages, including spreadsheet software, are strong management accounting tools that can be used to produce meaningful management information.

	A	B	C	D	E
1			January	February	March
2	30-second TV spots		40	60	50
3	Shoe sales revenue		$600	$800	$750
4	(in thousands)				

EXHIBIT 1–4
TV Ads and Sales Revenue

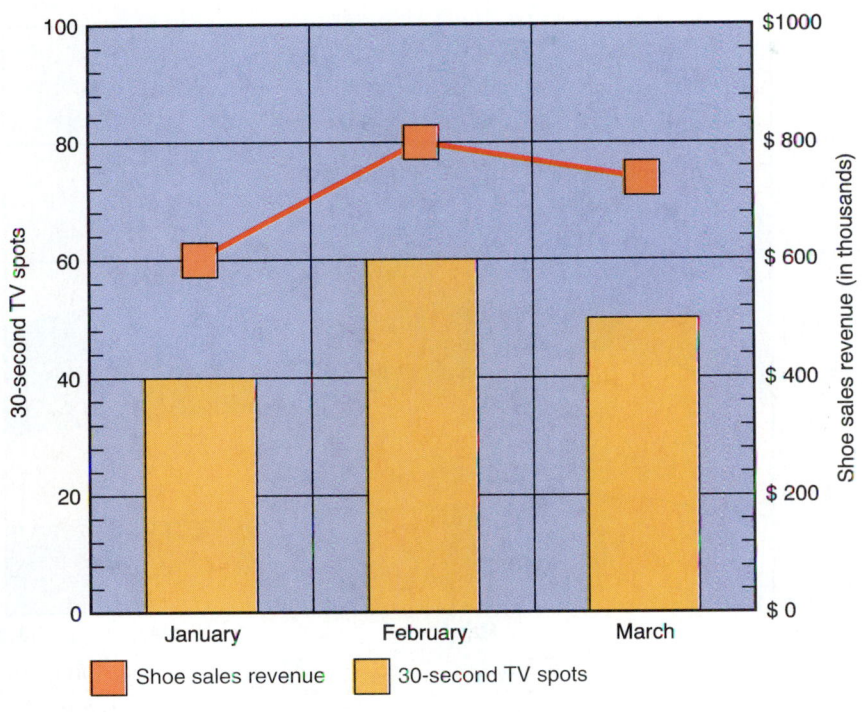

Profit-Oriented Service Firm

A **profit-oriented service firm** is an enterprise that sells knowledge, functions, or some other benefits, rather than products, to its customers. Examples of profit-oriented service firms are banks, law firms, advertising agencies, medical centers, and accounting firms. Unlike manufacturing and merchandising organizations, service firms do not have inventories. Nevertheless, a profit-oriented service firm needs management accounting just as much as a manufacturing or merchandising organization does. For example, when an advertising agency or accounting firm takes on a client or audit engagement, it should use the same basic techniques for cost accounting, cost management, and performance measurement that a manufacturing organization would use in costing and managing its production jobs. To the law or public accounting firm, a client is a job.

An income statement for Bighype Advertising Agency, a typical profit-oriented service firm, is shown in Exhibit 1–6. Bighype's balance sheet appears in Exhibit 1–7. A balance sheet for a typical service organization, such as Bighype Advertising Agency, is normally very simple compared to the balance sheets of manufacturing and merchandising organizations.

Not-for-Profit Service Entity

A **not-for-profit service entity** offers a benefit to its clients for free or for a minimal fee. Like profit-oriented service firms, not-for-profit service entities do not have inventories. Governmental agencies, some hospitals, and various charitable organizations are examples of not-for-profit service entities. Again, management accounting is just as important to not-for-profit service entities as

■ EXHIBIT 1-5
Inventory Report for Achilles Company

	A	B	C	D	E	F	G
1		January	February	March	April	May	June
2	Raw materials	400	500	450	400	375	350
3	Work-in-process	500	600	550	500	450	400
4	Finished goods	800	950	800	600	550	450

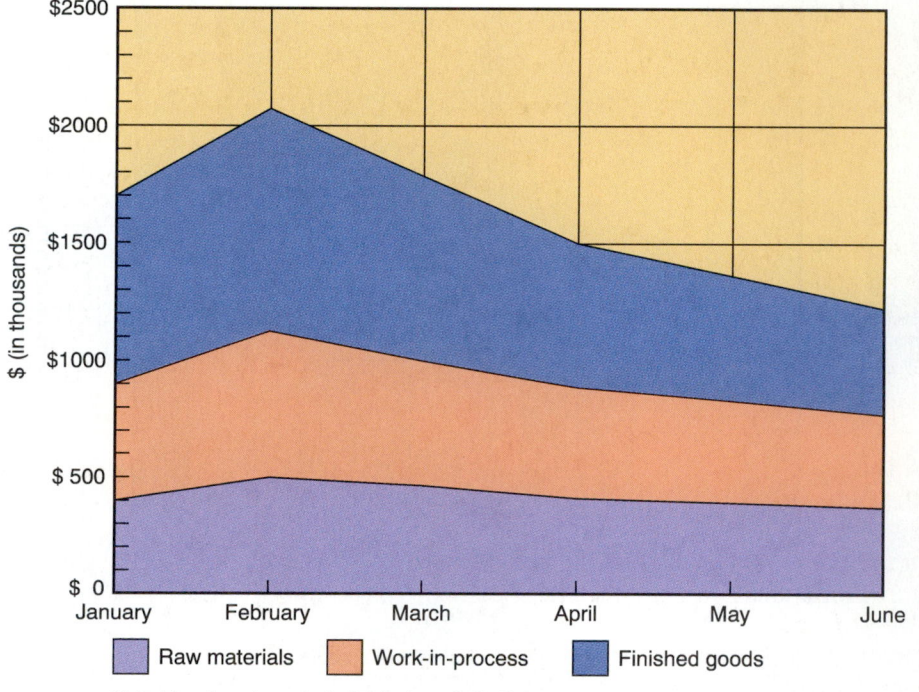

Note: The sharp increase in finished goods for February was due to a shipper's strike.

it is to other organizations. For example, costing various services, managing costs, and measuring performance for welfare cases, imprisonment, patient care, and the like are critical for the proper management of not-for-profit service entities. Just because they don't make a profit doesn't mean that these organizations should not be managed effectively and efficiently.

■ EXHIBIT 1-6
Income Statement for a Profit-Oriented Service Firm

Bighype Advertising Agency
Income Statement
For the Year Ended December 31, 19X3

Advertising revenue		$10,400,000
Cost of services rendered:		
Direct labor	$5,000,000	
Supplies	300,000	
Overhead	2,000,000	<7,300,000>
Gross margin on services		3,100,000
Operating expenses:		
Selling expenses	$ 500,000	
Administrative expenses	1,000,000	<1,500,000>
Income from operations		1,600,000
Interest expense		<50,000>
Income before taxes		1,550,000
Income taxes		<350,000>
Net income		$ 1,200,000

Bighype Advertising Agency
Balance Sheet
December 31, 19X3

ASSETS

Cash	$11,800,000
Accounts receivable	4,900,000
Prepaid rent	50,000
Prepaid insurance	40,000
Supplies	100,000
Other assets	80,000
Total assets	$16,970,000

LIABILITIES AND STOCKHOLDERS' EQUITY

Accounts payable	$ 1,000,000
Stockholders' equity	15,970,000
Total liabilities and stockholders' equity	$16,970,000

Another way of looking at not-for-profit service firms is to compare them with profit-oriented service firms. A CPA firm, for example, has direct control over its revenues. The partners set billing rates and choose their customers. Thus, they need management accounting information to help them better plan, control, and evaluate revenues. They also need information to control client (job) costs and profits.

Not-for-profit firms, such as a welfare agency, do not have the same level of direct control over "revenues." Revenues to the welfare agency are the funds provided by various governmental agencies. Nevertheless, the welfare agency has the same need to control client (job) costs as the CPA firm or a shoe manufacturer.

The real difference, from the management accountant's perspective, is only the amount of profit planned for. The shoe manufacturer, shoe retailer, and CPA firm all have positive profit goals. The not-for-profit service firm has a zero profit ("break-even") goal. The point is that each type of firm (merchandising, manufacturing, for-profit service, and not-for-profit service) needs the same basic management accounting information.

MANAGEMENT ACCOUNTING: A PERSPECTIVE

LEARNING
OBJECTIVE 2

Explain the relation-
ship of management
accounting to financial
and cost accounting.

Management accounting systems evolved in the late 1800s to provide inventory cost information. For nearly 90 years, management accounting, often referred to more narrowly as cost accounting, employed procedures designed primarily to accumulate inventory valuation information for preparing balance sheets and income statements. The accumulated information was used in reporting the financial position and the financial results of the organization's operations as a whole to external users. This information, although necessary and helpful to financial accountants, is not very helpful to managers running the day-to-day affairs of these organizations.

Today's management accountants are entering a new era. They are measuring and reporting on all major facets of their company's operations. Management accounting is no longer just a function that serves financial accounting, but has broadened its scope to serve a wide variety of users. Management accounting systems now provide information for managerial decisions involving all of the following:

- Production cost management (cost budgeting, cost accounting, and performance evaluation)
- Performance measurement and control over revenues and profits
- Investment planning, control, and capital project evaluation

Higher-quality products and services and total customer satisfaction are the driving forces behind today's service and manufacturing industries. Such an emphasis requires management accountants to identify and address many non-financial areas that measure quality, service, and cost as well as the usual financial areas. Emphasis is also placed on production lead time. **Lead time** (or **cycle time**) is the time a service or product takes to get through the process.

Management accountants not only need a knowledge of cost and management accounting, they also need a strong familiarity with all organizational activities, especially product and service development, production systems, and logistics. It is very difficult to measure what one does not understand. As a novelist once said, "The office is a very dangerous place from which to observe the world." A management accounting system that is comprehensive and relevant to the enterprise and management it serves will not by itself make an enterprise great. But an inadequate, irrelevant, and misleading management accounting system will keep the enterprise from becoming great or, worse, cause it to fail.

Management Accounting: No Longer Subservient to Financial Accounting

In the past, financial accountants, many of whom are certified public accountants (CPAs), "regard(ed) information from the financial accounts as the backbone of a management system."[1] **Financial accountants** record financial transactions and prepare balance sheets, income statements, and cash flow statements for stockholders, investment analysts, and other users external to the enterprise, all in accordance with generally accepted accounting principles (GAAP). Financial accounting's main purpose is to report to various interested parties what has happened to the enterprise in the past. Although the financial accounting function is important for external users and for financial stewardship and control, its value to the enterprise's management is limited. Management must know what their products and services cost and must understand the underlying causes of costs, in order to perform the following functions:

- Develop strategic plans for the enterprise
- Translate those plans into budgets
- Make day-to-day control decisions about operations
- Evaluate how well operations were performed and continually strive to improve performance
- Make an array of other special decisions for which financial accounting information may be irrelevant and, in some cases, misleading

As Johnson states, ". . . fixation on financial accounting, as the primary source of management accounting information, has kept managers, until recently, from attending to the . . . demand of global competition."[2]

Compliance with GAAP and the reporting requirements of the Internal Revenue Service (IRS), Securities and Exchange Commission (SEC), and Financial Accounting Standards Board (FASB) is a necessary part of doing business. But the financial accounting system that meets these reporting requirements is not

---

[1] H. Thomas Johnson, "Let's Return the Controller to Relevance: A Historical Perspective," in *Cost Accounting for the '90s: Responding to Technological Change Conference Proceedings,* ed. Alfred M. King and Norman E. Hadad (Montvale, N.J.: Institute of Management Accountants, formerly the National Association of Accountants, 1988), p. 195.

[2] Ibid., p. 198.

the chief source of the relevant information required to manage sources of competitiveness, customer value, and cost.[3]

> The only reason why management accountants should allow their measurements for management purposes to be the dog the GAAP tail wags is that dual measurement systems (i.e., a financial accounting system and a management accounting system) are uneconomically expensive. However, the cost of accumulating and processing data has been decreasing at an astounding rate. What was unfeasible 20, 10, or even 5 years ago is clearly feasible now.[4]

The Cost Accounting Function and Its Relationship to Financial and Management Accounting

Cost accounting is defined as "a technique or method for determining the cost of a project, process or thing. . . . This cost is determined by direct measurement, arbitrary assignment, or systematic and rational allocation."[5] The cost accounting system performs a vital function within an enterprise, providing information for two primary purposes:

- Valuing ending inventories and determining cost of goods sold for financial reporting purposes
- Costing products and services for management control purposes (planning, monitoring and controlling operations, and performance evaluation)

Today, some management accountants believe that separate cost accounting systems should be used for financial reporting and management reporting purposes. With computers and various information technologies available at relatively low costs, the creation of separate systems is now feasible.

Why two systems? As alluded to in the previous section, financial accounting needs inventory values and cost of goods manufactured and sold information for preparing the balance sheet and income statement. Such information is historical and aggregated. The same information for managers attempting to manage costs and improve productivity is "too dated, too aggregated, and too distorted to be relevant."[6]

> Costs get distributed to products by simplistic measures, usually direct labor based, that do not represent the demands made by each product on the firm's resources. While simplistic and aggregate product costing methods are adequate for financial reporting requirements—the methods yield values for inventory and the cost of goods sold that satisfy external reporting and auditing requirements—these methods systematically bias and distort product costs at the individual product level. . . .
>
> An organization's management accounting system must provide timely and accurate information to facilitate efforts to control costs, to measure and improve productivity, and to devise improved production processes. The management accounting system also needs to report accurate product costs so that pricing decisions, introduction of new products, abandonments of obsolete products, and responses to the appearance of rival products can be made with the best possible information on product resource demands. Finally, large decentralized organizations require systems to motivate and evaluate the performance of their managers. These systems should

[3] Ibid., p. 201.
[4] Gordon Shillinglaw, "Looking Back From the Future," in *Cost Accounting, Robotics, and the New Manufacturing Environment*, ed. Robert Capettini and Donald K. Clancy (Sarasota, Fla.: American Accounting Association, 1988), p. 9.12.
[5] "Management Accounting Terminology," *Statement on Management Accounting Number 2* (Montvale, N.J.: Institute of Management Accountants, formerly the National Association of Accountants, June 1, 1983), p. 25.
[6] H. Thomas Johnson and Robert S. Kaplan, "The Rise and Fall of Management Accounting," *Management Accounting*, January 1987, in *World-Class Accounting for World-Class Manufacturing*, ed. by Lamont F. Steedle (Montvale, N.J.: Institute of Management Accountants, formerly the National Association of Accountants, 1990), p. 4. Reprinted from *Management Accounting*. Copyright by Institute of Management Accountants, Montvale N.J.

■EXHIBIT 1–8
Cost Accounting's Integrating Relationship between Financial and Management Accounting

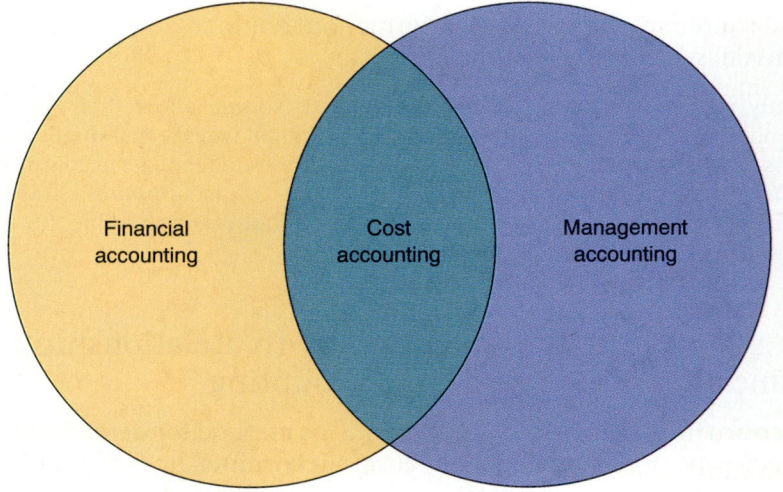

provide appropriate incentives and signals to managers working in different functions, with diverse products and processes, amid globally dispersed operations.[7]

Cost accounting, therefore, must serve both financial and management accounting. Cost accounting will continue to provide inventory values and cost of goods manufactured and sold in compliance with GAAP. Cost accounting will also be an integral part of the broader field of management accounting, providing product and service costing information that is more relevant to managers. This dual role is illustrated in Exhibit 1–8. The cost accounting function permits a linkage between financial and management accounting that results in a fully integrated information system—one part (financial accounting) serving external users and another part (management accounting) serving internal users. Whether two separate systems are required will depend on the information technology in use within a particular enterprise. For example, with the advent of sophisticated database management systems and integrated computer-based information systems, one system may be able to serve both the financial and management accounting objectives. This will be further discussed below and in the next two chapters.

LEARNING OBJECTIVE 3

Present the major trends in the new manufacturing environment and discuss the role of modern management accountants in organizations.

▌MAJOR TRENDS IN THE NEW MANUFACTURING ENVIRONMENT

Traditional methods of manufacturing, based on large blue-collar, muscle-power work forces, are giving way to new manufacturing practices. Manufacturing organizations today are focusing on several trends:

- High quality
- Customer service
- Low inventory
- Flexibility
- Automation
- Team concept
- Integrated computer-based information system (ICBIS)

For now, we will introduce these trends. In the next chapter, we will examine them in more detail because understanding them will put you in a good position to be a successful management accountant.

WHAT IS HIGH QUALITY? **High quality** is an elevated level of excellence in product reliability and performance. "Quality is job one" as the Ford commercial

[7] Ibid.

states. Indeed, it is the credo of many companies that are trying to compete in today's marketplace.

Rather than inspecting the product *after* it has been produced, companies are building quality into the product *before* it is produced; that is, in the design and prototyping stages (a prototype is the first full-scale functional model of a new product) of the product. This approach seems to make more sense than trying to ensure quality by employing after-the-fact inspection. At that time, it is very difficult to increase product quality without a great many engineering changes and much rework.

High quality requires coordination among everyone in the company—production people, engineers, marketing personnel, logistics people, service departments, and vendors. Quality output requires quality input and quality work in manufacturing a product or providing a service. Thus, quality starts with the vendor of raw materials, proceeds to work-in-process quality controls, and finally continues through delivery and service to the customer. Management accountants should play a significant role in developing quality control measures and implementing their use throughout this process.

Modern companies realize that they can provide *higher quality at a lower cost*. In the past, many companies believed that higher quality meant higher costs. Moreover, the way cost accounting information was used in performance evaluation contributed to this fallacy. For example, purchasing was typically evaluated with only a purchase price variance. Consider a situation in which the budgeted price for a direct material was $2 per pound. If the actual price was lower, then a "favorable price variance" resulted. Conversely, if the actual price was higher, there was an "unfavorable price variance." If the only performance evaluation criterion was "maximize favorable variances," then material quality could be sacrificed for lower price.

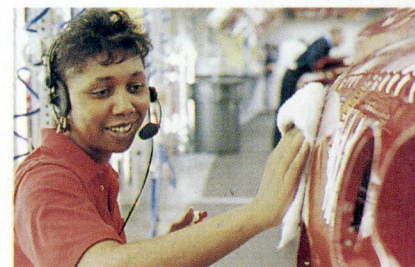

This evaluation motivated purchasers to buy raw materials from vendors at the lowest price. However, lower-quality materials often resulted in problems "down-the-line" such as excess scrap, rework, production schedule disruptions, field service, and product warranty claims. Purchasing was rarely held accountable for these costs. By motivating Purchasing to pursue only the "best price," the rest of the company incurred these costs of nonquality that often were far greater than the cost savings achieved by the lower purchase price.[8] As modern organizations change their emphasis to "total quality management" (covered in Chapter 12), the challenge to the management accountant is to identify and link these nonquality costs back to their real causes.

Quality that shows.

WHAT IS CUSTOMER SERVICE?   **Customer service** gets the right product to the right customer at the right time and at the right price. Customer service and satisfaction are paramount. How well customer service is being met can be measured in terms of the number of customer complaints. Keeping track of the number and kind of customer complaints provides information that indicates how well quality objectives are being met in addition to how well other operations are being performed. Many companies today are achieving 100 percent on-time delivery and zero customer complaints.

Giving the customers what they want.

WHAT IS LOW INVENTORY?   **Low inventory** is the minimum amount of raw materials, work-in-process, and finished goods necessary to meet production and marketing needs. Many companies regard large stocks of inventory as "evil" because they require storage and warehouse facilities and result in excessive handling costs. Moreover, inventory is more subject to obsolescence today than in the past because many competitors are bringing out new products almost

[8] Robert A. Howell and Stephen R. Soucy, "The New Manufacturing Environment: Major Trends for Management Accounting," *Management Accounting*, July 1987, in *World-Class Accounting for World-Class Manufacturing*, ed. Lamont F. Steedle (Montvale, N.J.: Institute of Management Accountants, formerly the National Association of Accountants, 1990), p. 14.

Controlling inventory.

overnight. By preparing detailed information about inventory, its location, and how often it's being used, management accountants can help management reduce inventory and the costs associated with holding it.

WHAT IS FLEXIBILITY? **Flexibility** is the ready capability to adapt to new, different, or changing requirements. The ability to set up and change production lines quickly increases production flexibility. This increased flexibility decreases lead times; that is, the time it takes to produce a product or complete a service from start to finish. Flexibility enables a company to offer a greater variety of products and get them into customers' hands quicker.

WHAT IS AUTOMATION? **Automation** is the implementation of highly technical machines that are designed to follow, with little human intervention, a predetermined sequence of operations or respond to computer-generated instructions. The implementation of automating technologies, such as robots and computer-controlled equipment, potentially enables companies to achieve higher quality, greater customer service, lower inventory, and flexibility. Thus, automation has the power to improve the overall competitiveness of organizations.

Simply automating outdated production processes, however, will not help but will only add to the existing problems. The first thing to do when considering automation is to analyze, redesign, and simplify the production process and *then* determine if automation will provide the benefits desired. In some cases, companies may achieve benefits by simply eliminating nonvalue-added activities,[9] such as inventory handling and storage.

Management accountants help identify nonvalue-added activities. Moreover, if an organization is considering automation, management accountants evaluate whether an investment in automated technologies will generate returns in excess of costs. Returns to the company are based on how automated technologies improve quality and customer service, decrease inventories, and provide flexibility, which are nonfinancial factors. Financial accountants may not have to deal with these factors for external reporting purposes, but to be helpful to managers, modern management accountants must provide both financial and nonfinancial information.

Automated welding line.

WHAT IS THE TEAM CONCEPT? The **team concept** fosters an organization of people who work together in a coordinated, cooperative manner to ensure the enterprise's success. The ultimate purpose of the team concept is to attract the best and brightest people to all segments of the enterprise.

Companies that are successfully competing on a global basis all share a common philosophy of providing the best possible products at the best possible price to their customers on time. To make this philosophy a reality requires a team approach in which all workers from top managers to production workers are directly involved.

The team concept is to a large extent based on a grass-roots, employee-directed movement whose results come from employee innovation. Companies encourage meaningful worker participation, which in turn heightens worker morale. Supervisory personnel and some middle management jobs are eliminated. Workers share in the benefits of their good work, continuous improvement, and own ideas. Top management commitment is absolutely critical, however, for the team concept to work.

Team concept in action.

[9] Nonvalue-added activities are discussed in detail in Chapter 2. These are "wasteful" activities that could be eliminated by redesigning the way the product is made or the service is applied.

INSIGHTS & APPLICATIONS

Self-Managing Teams

Worthington Industries and Chaparral Steel produce steel of superb quality—but have *no* quality inspectors. "Our people in the plants are responsible for their own product and its quality," says Chaparral's Gordon Forward. "We expect them to act like owners."

The modest-sized, task-oriented, semi-autonomous, mainly self-managing team should be the basic organizational building block. Structure kills. We need to radically reduce layers of management. We are being strangled by bloated staffs, made up of carping experts filling too many layers on the organization chart. Good intentions and brilliant proposals are deadened, delayed, sabotaged, massaged to death, or revised beyond recognition or usefulness by the over-layered structures at most large and all too many smaller firms.[10]

WHAT IS AN INTEGRATED COMPUTER-BASED INFORMATION SYSTEM AND ITS ROLE IN ORGANIZATIONS?   An **integrated computer-based information system (ICBIS)** is an enterprisewide interconnection of computers and related information technology that provides a multilevel, cross-functional flow of information to all managers and workers in the enterprise. Such information systems support the team concept and produce synergism rather than departments working against one another.

ICBISs are developed starting with manager and worker requirements. The information system is then designed to meet these requirements in the most efficient and effective manner possible. In this way, the information system can be designed to mirror the way the enterprise operates.

Lack of integration among an organization's segments or departments tends to create suboptimal behaviors. **Suboptimal behavior** results when a person attempts to optimize his or her own (limited) goals rather than those of the overall organization, and these goals are in conflict with each other. This often happens when department personnel consider only their own jobs while ignoring other departments affected by their actions. For example, a marketing manager may take orders for nonstandard products to the detriment of the production manager's job. For his part, the production manager may plan long production runs to minimize setups and changeovers. These behaviors result in unacceptable deliveries and excessively high inventories of some products and out-of-stock conditions for others.

As a final example, consider a common situation in decentralized, multinational companies. A manager of a large division buys parts from an outside supplier who quoted a lower price than an associated division of the manager's parent company. If the parts had been purchased from the associated division, however, the overall profits of the parent company would have been higher. By purchasing outside, the division manager maximized her division's profits, but the overall business suffered.

The preceding suboptimizing situations occur because of the "silo effect" in which each segment of the organization erects tall, cylindrical boundaries to seal itself off from other segments. Facilitated by an ICBIS, the other trends of high quality, customer service, low inventory, flexibility, automation, and the team concept can help to penetrate these artificial boundaries, reduce suboptimization, and build a goal congruent organization. **Goal congruence** is making decisions for the greater good. It is the opposite of suboptimal behavior.

Today, management accountants are involved in developing ICBISs for a variety of enterprises in which they are employed. Others are employed as

---

[10] From *Thriving on Chaos* by Tom Peters, copyright © 1987 by Excel, California Limited Partnership. Reprinted by permission of Alfred A. Knopf. Inc. pp. 349, 356, 425, 426, and 427.

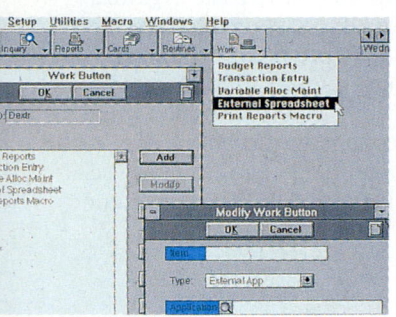

Modern management accountants make extensive use of computer systems.

information system consultants in CPA firms, such as Arthur Andersen (Andersen Consulting), Coopers & Lybrand, Deloitte & Touche, Ernst and Young, KPMG Peat Marwick, and Price Waterhouse.

Computers, magnetic and optical storage media, and telecommunications provide management accountants with the ability to design and install innovative ICBISs that significantly improve management accounting information. Transactions can be captured when they occur and the results communicated to management instantly. One of the major criticisms of management accounting in the past was after-the-fact reporting. For example, a report about variances in a production process prepared one month after the variances occurred will not be much help in correcting them because retracing variances to their root cause is very difficult after this much time has passed. Monitoring and controlling operations is a very short-term activity. Managers need to know immediately which operations are not performing as expected and why. Managers need to look at the task, operator, machine, and units affected and be able to determine what the cost consequences are *when* they occur; in other words, managers need information in real-time. The chief attribute of today's information technology is its ability to provide information in real-time.

MODERN MANAGEMENT ACCOUNTANTS

Essentially, the chief job of modern management accountants is to facilitate the foregoing trends and help managers to perform successfully. Modern management accountants also take an active role in the operation of the enterprise. A cut-and-dried standardized definition of the modern management accountant, however, is doomed because no two jobs are the same any more than two accountants or two enterprises are the same. Moreover, aspiring management accountants who view management accounting as a completed discipline are looking at the past, not the future. Like all other disciplines, such as medicine, law, and engineering, management accounting must change and adapt itself to a changing environment if it is to prosper.

In general terms, management accountants' key role in an enterprise, now and in the future, is to provide quality information to use in running the enterprise in an optimum manner. Further, management accountants play a consultative role in the management process. Today, companies need every tool available if they are to be viable competitors. The management accounting function is one of these critical tools.

Providing Quality Information

The nemesis of management is uncertainty. **Quality information** decreases uncertainty. The need for quality information has never been more apparent than in today's highly competitive global market.

Management accounting information is necessary for driving key strategic, operating, and financial decisions. By providing quality information, management accountants can help managers understand their businesses, and this knowledge in turn will enable managers to make the right decisions at the right time and thus become more competitive and productive.

Quality information that management accountants must keep in mind includes, but is not limited to, the following five attributes:

- Accuracy
- Relevancy
- Timeliness
- Fairness
- Usability

WHAT IS ACCURACY?   **Accuracy** means that information must be free from mistakes and errors. The information must correctly reflect the data on which it is based. If inaccuracies occur, management accountants quickly lose their credibility.

WHAT IS RELEVANCY?   **Relevancy** of information relates to the matter at hand or the purpose intended. The information must be applicable or pertinent to what is being considered. Authorities who stress the need for relevant management accounting information often say, "It's better to be approximately right than precisely wrong." For example, someone may state that the cost of product X is $4.197832 per unit, but if this cost figure is based on improper costing procedures, it is irrelevant and worse than useless because management may rely on it and reach incorrect decisions. Its precision (i.e., calculation to six decimal places) is contrived complexity. On the other hand, someone else may use costing procedures that are appropriate but require some degree of estimation to determine that the cost of product X is approximately $18.95. This $18.95 figure is far more relevant than the "precise" $4.197832 figure.

WHAT IS TIMELINESS?   **Timeliness** means getting information to managers and workers within the needed time frame. Obviously, this is a key attribute of quality information and one that has been missing in traditional financial and cost accounting systems. Information must be made available to the right people at the right time so they can react to it. Receiving a report about processes or operations one or two months after they occurred is normally of little benefit to managers. Managers need information today to make decisions for tomorrow. Yesterday's "information" rarely matters.

WHAT IS FAIRNESS?   **Fairness** means that information is impartial and free from self-interest, prejudice, or favoritism. The following are examples where fairness is lacking. A superintendent on a construction project may ask the management accountant to reassign costs arbitrarily to make some project items look good and others look bad. Or, performance measurements may be manipulated in favor of department A's inept manager so he will be able to retain his job. Or, product B, which was championed by the chief executive officer, is unprofitable, but costs are assigned to other products to make product B appear profitable.

WHAT IS USABILITY?   **Usability** is the final test of information quality. Managers and workers should be able to get information and understand it instantly without any special instructions. Too much detail or precision may actually obscure the substance of the information. For example, a report containing page after page of single-spaced computer printouts without meaningful headings and breaks may contain relevant, accurate, timely, and fair information but be so overwhelming in its volume and complexity that managers are discouraged from even looking at the information. Including numbers four or five places to the right of the decimal point for financial values, especially if the values are based on estimates to begin with, is misleading.

Divisional managers in a major coal company frequently complained that they spent three to four hours each week reviewing cumbersome accounting reports. The new management accountant analyzed the situation and eliminated accounting jargon and reduced the detail with no loss in substance. Now, managers can review the reports in 30 minutes per week.[11]

---

[11] Donald L. Madden and James R. Holmes, *Management Accountants: Responding to Change, an Exploratory Study* (Montvale, N.J.: Institute of Management Accountants, formerly the National Association of Accountants, 1990), p. 38.

■ EXHIBIT 1–9
Radar Chart Comparing Corporate Values with Industry Averages

Source: Adapted from Takashi Kanatsu, *TQC for Accounting: A New Role in Companywide Improvement* (Cambridge, Mass.: Productivity Press, 1990), p. 187. With permission.

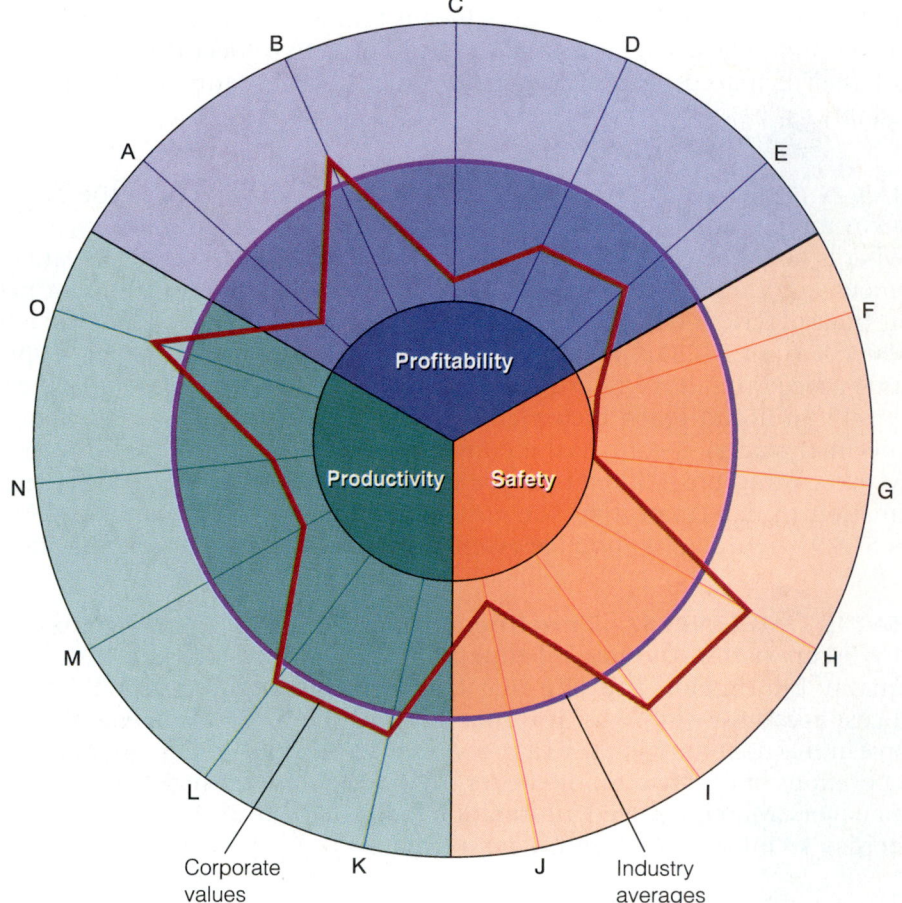

A: Earnings per share of common stock	F: Times interest earned	K: Sales per employee
B: Return on investment	G: Debt-to-equity ratio	L: Rate of profit to labor costs
C: Price-earnings ratio	H: Current ratio	M: Inventory turnover
D: Dividend yield rate	I: Quick ratio	N: Production lead time
E: Profit margin	J: Receivable turnover	O: Sales per square foot

If precise, detailed readings of information are critical, then conventional reports containing columns of numbers and meaningful headings and descriptions are appropriate. On the other hand, graphs can be used in a number of situations to turn thousands of numbers into a "picture" that will enable managers to quickly "see" the problem or situation.

Graphs, which are easily produced by computers, provide a way for management accountants to illustrate numerical data and convert them into information that can be quickly comprehended. Graphs make relationships between numbers visible by turning quantities into shapes, thus increasing the information's usability. Indeed, presenting information in graphical form reinforces the cliché that "a picture is worth a thousand computer printouts." For example, Exhibit 1–9 presents a sample radar chart that compares key success factors of a corporation with the industry average. The key success factors are profitability, financial safety, and productivity.

Management can see at a glance how well the corporation stacks up against the industry average. Profitability is low. Action must be taken to increase profits. Although the liquidity ratios are fairly strong, the corporation may have some problems servicing debt. Moreover, the collections on accounts receivable need substantial improvement. Labor performance is slightly better than the industry average. However, inventory turnover needs to be increased, and pro-

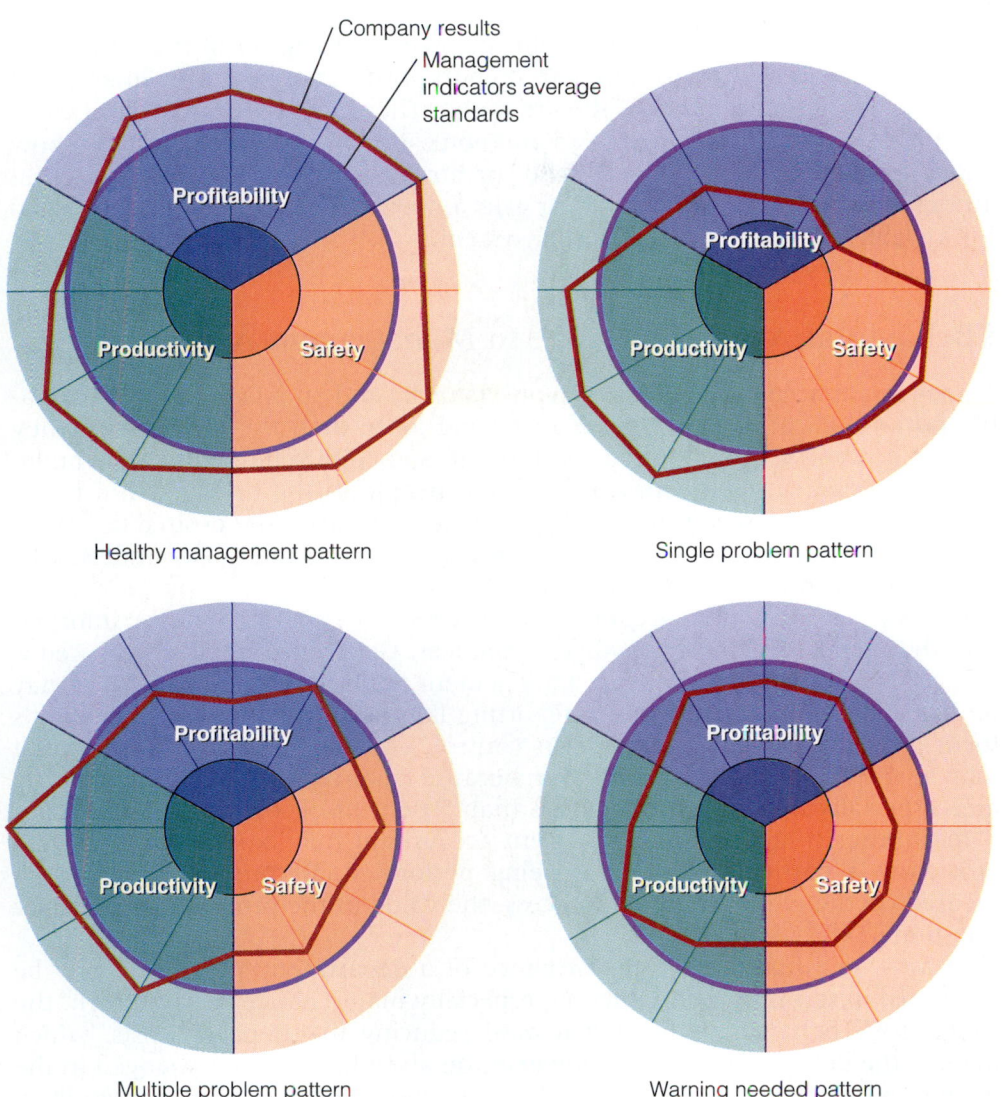

■ EXHIBIT 1–10
Performance Patterns for Management Action

Source: Takashi Kanatsu, *TQC for Accounting: A New Role in Companywide Improvement* (Cambridge, Mass.: Productivity Press, 1990), p. 192. With permission.

duction lead time needs to be decreased to bring these two productivity measurements in line with the industry. Sales per square foot of facilities (e.g., warehouses and sales outlets) is slightly above the industry average.

To extend the idea further, radar chart–based presentations can give rise to the four performance patterns shown in Exhibit 1–10:

■ Healthy management pattern, indicating above-average performance in all key success factor areas
■ Single problem pattern, signaling that more focus and action are needed in one key success factor area
■ Multiple problem pattern, signaling that a wider focus and coordinated action are needed in two key success factor areas
■ Warning needed pattern, signaling below-average performance in *all* key success factor areas and requiring across-the-board management action

▌ Getting Involved in the Enterprise's Operations

To become more helpful, management accountants are increasing their knowledge about operations and production processes of the enterprise. They're part of the work environment. They put on their hard hats and get out in the field or on the factory floor to gain insight into what's going on in the enterprise. They not only know *how* to gather and report information, but they understand the *what* and the *why* of what they're doing. There's no substitute for actually seeing how concrete is being mixed and poured on a construction project, how trucks are being assembled in a plant, or how patients are being processed in an emergency ward of a hospital to gain a deeper understanding of the need for a viable management accounting system.

▎Behavioral Aspects Relative to Management Accounting

Management accounting plays both an *informing* and an *influencing* role. Probably nothing dictates the behavior of people more than the information they receive or information reported about them. Someone yelling "fire" in a building will evoke survival behavior from the people in the building. If a fire is underway, the message is indeed appropriate and causes the desired behavior. Conversely, if there is no fire, then the message is wrong and causes undesirable, even dysfunctional, behavior.

Likewise, management accountants must be very careful about the information they report and the behaviors it produces. Generally, what is measured is what is considered important. A management accountant in Company A may be spending a great deal of time reporting labor cost. In turn, management's focus is directed to labor cost and its control. This intense focus on labor cost may be the wrong behavior, however, because labor cost may not be the critical area especially if labor represents less than 5 percent of total production costs.

In another company, a management accountant may be reporting on how efficiently a particular process is being performed. Because everyone is so focused on the efficiency of the process, the value of the process itself is never questioned.

In another situation, the performance of a department supervisor may be evaluated in terms of cost reduction, especially maintenance costs. In turn, the supervisor's behavior is directed toward reducing maintenance costs, which may be the behavior sought. If, however, oil and filters are not changed in the equipment as recommended, the savings in short-term costs may have disastrous consequences in the long term. New motors may have to be purchased because the old ones were not properly maintained.

An old saying in business is that "what gets measured gets done." For example, a newly hired management accountant, working for a mid-size manufacturer, found that past reports had focused almost entirely on measuring equipment maintenance costs. Therefore, maintenance personnel cut maintenance costs drastically. Equipment downtime problems were rampant. As an experiment, the management accountant developed a report focusing on efforts to improve equipment productivity. The resulting measure, equipment uptime, prompted a vastly different approach to managing the highly automated production facility. Replacing a somewhat negative measure with a positive measure changed behavior and led to a significant improvement in manufacturing productivity.

LEARNING OBJECTIVE 4

Explain how to become a professional management accountant.

▎BECOMING A PROFESSIONAL MANAGEMENT ACCOUNTANT

Authorities have identified four characteristics that a group must exhibit to be classified as a profession:

- A well-defined body of knowledge
- Competency in the knowledge area

- Strict admission criteria
- Adoption of standards of ethical conduct[12]

What Is the Certified Management Accountant Program?

The **certified management accountant (CMA)** certification program was developed to give management accounting status and to provide a means for management accountants to demonstrate their educational attainment and competency in specific areas of knowledge. The CMA certification program has identified the areas of knowledge in which management accountants should be proficient. The CMA is recognized as a professional, similar to a certified public accountant (CPA) or professional engineer (PE). The CMA designation is offered by the **Institute of Certified Management Accountants (ICMA).** The ICMA was established by the **Institute of Management Accountants (IMA),** formerly the National Association of Accountants (NAA), the largest management accounting organization in the world. The **Society of Management Accountants (SMA)** is the sponsoring organization in Canada.

The ICMA and SMA evaluate the credentials of candidates, administer the examination, grant certificates, and ensure that CMAs continue to meet the professional development requirements necessary to retain their certificates in good standing. Candidates must complete four steps to become a CMA:

1. File an application for admission with the ICMA or SMA and register for the CMA examination.
2. Pass all four parts of the CMA examination within a three-year period.
3. Meet the CMA experience requirement.
4. Comply with the *Standards of Ethical Conduct for Management Accountants.*

What will the CMA designation mean to you? The CMA program is actively supported by a wide range of companies. The CMA designation indicates that you are exceptionally well prepared for the challenges in your organization. Business leaders recognize this and therefore actively seek people who are CMAs. One need only look at the employment ads in the *Wall Street Journal, New York Times,* and other prominent business publications to see that the CMA appears frequently as a desired credential for employment.

Many companies also pay for review courses and examination fees through educational reimbursement programs. Several *Fortune 500* companies offer in-house development courses to help their employees prepare for the CMA examination.

Standards of Ethical Conduct for Management Accountants

The ***Standards of Ethical Conduct for Management Accountants*** is a written code of ethics that provides formal guidance to management accountants who must deal with ethical dilemmas in their work environment. A large number of business improprieties, such as insider trading, bribery, cover-ups, fraud, and other illegal and immoral acts have occurred throughout organizations. "Crime in business is a sad fact of life. And, unfortunately, more than 70 percent of all of the crimes encountered by businesses—fraud, embezzlement, bribery and conflicts of interest—are committed by people who work for them."[13] Because management accountants play a significant role in these organizations, both as a consultant to management and a provider of information, the IMA believed it was necessary to establish a set of standards of ethical conduct.

---

[12] Howard L. Siers and Robert B. Sweeney, "Ethics and the CMA," *Management Accounting,* April 1992, p. 47. Reprinted from *Management Accounting.* Copyright by Institute of Management Accountants, Montvale, N.J.

[13] Joseph T. Wells, "Fraud Becomes a Growth Industry," *New Accountant,* November 1990, p. 13.

INSIGHTS & APPLICATIONS

Demanding Ethical Behavior

Demand total integrity of the "squeaky clean" sort—in all dealings, with people, inside the firm and out. Eliminate Mickey Mouse rules that induce cheating and game playing, which then spread to all the firm's affairs.

Set absurdly high standards for integrity—and then live them, with no fuzzy margins. A deal made on a milestone which is subsequently missed is grounds for dismissal, especially when it involves support for another function, vendor, or customer. If a promise is not kept, if ethics are compromised, and if management behaves inconsistently, then the strategies necessary to survive today simply can't be executed.[14]

Management accountants have an obligation to the organizations they serve, their profession, the public, and themselves to maintain the highest standards of ethical conduct. In recognition of this obligation, the IMA has promulgated the following standards of ethical conduct for management accountants. Management accountants shall not commit acts contrary to these standards nor shall they condone the commission of such acts by others within their organizations. These ethical standards are in four areas:[15]

- Competence
- Confidentiality
- Integrity
- Objectivity

WHAT IS COMPETENCE?   **Competence** means that management accountants have requisite or adequate abilities to perform their work. Management accountants have a responsibility to:

- Maintain an appropriate level of professional competence by ongoing development of their knowledge and skills
- Perform their professional duties in accordance with relevant laws, regulations, and technical standards
- Prepare complete and clear reports and recommendations after appropriate analyses of relevant and reliable information

WHAT IS CONFIDENTIALITY?   Management accountants, due to the nature of their work, are entrusted with sensitive information. **Confidentiality** means that management accountants honor this trust. Management accountants have a responsibility to:

- Refrain from disclosing confidential information acquired in the course of their work except when authorized, unless legally obligated to do so
- Inform subordinates as appropriate regarding the confidentiality of information acquired in the course of their work and monitor their activities to assure that confidentiality is maintained
- Refrain from using or appearing to use confidential information acquired in the course of their work for unethical or illegal advantage either personally or through third parties

---

[14] Peters, op. cit., pp. 626–27.
[15] "Standards of Ethical Conduct for Management Accountants," *Management Accounting*, February 1991, p. 28. Reprinted from *Management Accounting.* Copyright by Institute of Management Accountants, Montvale, N.J.

INSIGHTS & APPLICATIONS

Dealing with Demands for Unethical Behavior

A project management accountant for a large construction firm was asked by the project manager to use petty cash to purchase a refrigerator and camping equipment for one of the inspectors to encourage favorable inspection decisions for work being performed. Such a request put the project management accountant in an ethical quandary. If she refused, she could lose her job. Or the inspector might give the project manager a "hard time" by refusing to approve any of the construction work, thus jeopardizing the company.

What to do? The project management accountant called company headquarters and talked to the controller about her ethical dilemma. Based on this situation, the company installed a telephone hot line so all project management accountants in the field can contact the controller at any time to discuss an ethical problem. The controller now gives advice and involves other top managers in reviewing and discussing written summaries of each case. These cases are, in turn, used for educational exercises for both newly hired and experienced project management accountants.

Top management of this company views open communication as one of the best ways to ensure continuing sensitivity to ethical dilemmas. They believe that ethical misconduct should not be tolerated, so any ethical problem is solved immediately and explicitly. They also think that a "look-the-other-way" climate invites ethical abuses.

WHAT IS INTEGRITY?   **Integrity** means management accountants are honest. Management accountants have a responsibility to:

- Avoid actual or apparent conflicts of interest and advise all appropriate parties of any potential conflict
- Refrain from engaging in any activity that would prejudice their ability to carry out their duties ethically
- Refuse any gift, favor, or hospitality that would influence or would appear to influence their actions
- Refrain from either actively or passively subverting the attainment of the organization's legitimate and ethical objectives
- Recognize and communicate professional limitations or other constraints that would preclude responsible judgment or successful performance of an activity
- Communicate unfavorable as well as favorable information and professional judgments or opinions
- Refrain from engaging in or supporting any activity that would discredit the profession

WHAT IS OBJECTIVITY?   **Objectivity** means that management accountants deal with data and conditions as perceived without distortion by personal feelings, prejudices, or interpretations. Management accountants have a responsibility to:

- Communicate information fairly and objectively
- Disclose fully all relevant information that could reasonably be expected to influence an intended user's understanding of the reports, comments, and recommendations presented[16]

Management accountants need to make these standards of ethical conduct an ongoing part of everyday performance. Every management accountant has a responsibility not only to *be* above reproach, but to establish the *perception* that he or she *is* above reproach and expects the same ethical standards from others.[17]

---

[16] Ibid.
[17] Laura L. Nash, *Good Intentions Aside: A Manager's Guide to Resolving Ethical Problems* (Boston: Harvard Business School Press, 1990), p. 4.

INSIGHTS & APPLICATIONS

Ethical Quandary at Precision Parts

Shirley Ford is a management accountant at Precision Parts (a hypothetical company), which is a maker of key components for rockets. She asked, "Where are the quality control and testing data for the order of valves going to NASA?"

"Don't worry," replied Harvey Haddox, production supervisor, "It's nothing. We haven't had any problems with these valves. Anyway, we're behind schedule. NASA needs the valves now. We can't afford to delay shipment."

"Are you sure? Can you guarantee me they're OK?" asked Shirley.

"Sure. No problem," replied Harvey. "Everything's going to be just fine."

Six months later, a rocket was launched at Cape Kennedy and exploded while in flight. Investigations into the disaster revealed the untested valves from Precision Parts did not operate properly, thus causing the explosion. The attempt to achieve a short-term goal by cutting corners and participating in various improprieties resulted in indictments and long-term problems for Precision Parts.

Dealing with Ethical Dilemmas

(handwritten margin notes: don't go outside organ., call Police—violates confident. Rule. Resign & include Reason ur Resign Ltr)

Good intentions do not necessarily resolve ethical dilemmas or provide automatic immunity from wrongdoing.[18] Among the more common ethical dilemmas for which management accountants should be on the lookout are the following:

- Cover-ups and misrepresentations in reporting
- Poor quality, ineptness, and improper operations
- Lockstep obedience to authority however improper it may be
- Conflict of interest
- Prejudice and favoritism
- Failure to speak up when unethical practices occur
- Exaggeration to achieve certain results
- Failure to be accountable and take responsibility for personal actions

The first professional credo, the Hippocratic oath, which was adopted by physicians in the fifth century B.C., states in part, "Never willingly do injury." Assessing whether an act deliberately causes injury to others can provide great insight into otherwise condoned wrongdoings. Indeed, a philosophy of never willingly doing injury to others is a good, effective way to deal with many ethical dilemmas. The consistent question to ask is, "Whom could my decisions or actions injure?" Several other questions will also provide guidance for dealing with ethical problems:

- Am I confident that my decisions or actions will be as proper over a long period of time as they seem now?
- Can I in good conscience defend these decisions or actions to my boss, my colleagues, my family, and society?
- What is the appearance of my decisions or actions if understood? If misunderstood?

Because ethics vary among people and organizations, tests can be devised to measure ethical activities. One test that helps determine if an unethical boundary has been crossed is to ask a simple question: What would a third party say about the matter? If this third party takes a negative position, what would that person find to criticize? If the disgruntled third party could find nothing to say, then there is a good chance that an unethical boundary has not been crossed. Another test of an ethical decision is whether the person making the decision

[18] Ibid., p. x.

INSIGHTS & APPLICATIONS

Juggling Costs at Premier Advertising Agency

Margie Johnson is the southwest district manager at Premier Advertising Agency (a hypothetical service company). She asks you, the district management accountant, to "charge the $50,000 consulting fees that I authorized for client A's account to client B's account. Don't worry, I'll take responsibility."

You know better. You're responsible for correctly assigning costs to the appropriate accounts. So, you make up your mind not to charge the $50,000 to client B's account. But how do you deal with this ethical dilemma?

You wait three days to restate Ms. Johnson's original request by saying, "Let me get this straight. You want me to charge the $50,000 in consulting fees that should be charged to client A to client B?" This question gets the ethical dilemma out in the open and increases ethical awareness. It also evokes second thoughts and gives Ms. Johnson a chance to change her mind without losing face.

---

would want the full details of the activity discussed in the local newspaper or aired on a television show viewed by family, friends, and employers.[19]

When faced with a significant ethical dilemma, a management accountant should follow the policies of the company that are pertinent to dealing with such a situation. If the policies do not help resolve the ethical dilemma, the management accountant should consider the following courses of action:

- Discuss the problem with the immediate superior except when it appears that the superior is involved, in which case the problem should be presented initially to the next higher managerial level. If a satisfactory resolution cannot be achieved when the problem is initially presented, submit the issues to the next higher managerial level. If the immediate superior is the chief executive officer, or the equivalent, the acceptable reviewing authority may be a group such as the audit committee, executive committee, board of directors, board of trustees, or owners. Contact with levels above the immediate superior should be initiated only with the superior's knowledge, assuming the superior is not involved.
- Clarify relevant concepts by confidential discussion with an objective adviser to obtain an understanding of possible courses of action.
- If the ethical conflict still exists after exhausting all levels of internal review, the management accountant may have no other recourse on significant matters than to resign from the organization and to submit an informative memorandum to an appropriate representative of the organization. Except where legally prescribed, communication of such problems to authorities or individuals not employed or engaged by the organization is not considered appropriate.[20]

SUMMARY OF LEARNING OBJECTIVES

The major goals of this chapter were to enable you to achieve four learning objectives:

Learning objective 1.   Describe the four types of organizations that are served by management accounting.

---

[19] Jerry L. Ford, "Working with Executive Management and Others," *Corporate Controller's Manual,* 2d ed., ed. Paul J. Wendell (Boston: Warren Gorham Lamont 1991), p. A4-5.
[20] "Standards of Ethical Conduct for Management Accountants," op. cit., p. 28.

There are four types of organizations:

- Manufacturing
- Merchandising
- Profit-oriented service
- Not-for-profit service

A manufacturing organization converts raw materials (inputs) into finished products (outputs). Merchandising firms sell their inventory "as is." Manufacturers and merchandisers are both in business to make a profit from the sale of inventory. Merchandisers have only one type of inventory—merchandise inventory. Manufacturers have three types of inventory:

- Raw materials (both direct and indirect materials) inventory
- Work-in-process inventory
- Finished goods inventory

A manufacturer has the following product costs:

- Direct materials
- Direct labor
- Overhead (variable and fixed)

The balance sheet for merchandisers displays inventory as merchandise inventory. The balance sheet for manufacturers shows all three inventories—raw materials, work-in-process, and finished goods.

The basic format of the income statement is the same for both the merchandiser and the manufacturer. The cost of goods sold for a manufacturer, however, is much more detailed than it is for a merchandiser. For a manufacturer, the cost of goods manufactured must be calculated. This figure is determined by first adding together direct materials, direct labor, and overhead. Then, the beginning balance of work-in-process inventory is added to this total, and the work-in-process ending balance is subtracted, yielding cost of goods manufactured. Cost of goods sold is then determined by adding the finished goods inventory beginning balance to the cost of goods manufactured, and then subtracting the ending finished goods inventory balance.

Profit-oriented service firms convert labor and other resource inputs into completed works, jobs, or benefits, such as demand deposit accounting services, legal defenses, advertisements, health care, audit reports, and blueprints, for a profit. Not-for-profit service firms also convert labor and other resources into completed works, jobs, or benefits. The output of both types of service firms may be tangible, such as a blueprint, or intangible, such as health care.

Learning objective 2.   Explain the relationship of management accounting to financial and cost accounting.

Financial accounting's focus is on providing financial statements to users outside the organization, such as stockholders, investment analysts, creditors, and various regulatory agencies. Financial accountants process financial data and aggregate it over some period of time. Their work is governed primarily by GAAP.

Cost accounting, serving its financial accounting objective, provides inventory valuations and cost of goods manufactured and sold for financial statements. In today's environment, however, where the objective is to maintain minimal inventories, the focus on inventory valuation is not as important as it once was. Cost accounting, serving its management accounting objective, provides detailed costs at the product or service level so managers can make informed decisions about cost control and productivity improvement. In this respect, the cost accounting function is an integral and important part of the broader field of management accounting.

Learning objective 3.   Present the major trends in the new manufacturing environment and discuss the role of modern management accountants in organizations.

The following major trends, which are occurring in manufacturing, merchandising, and service organizations, are increasing the role of the management accountant in running the firm:

- High quality
- Customer service
- Low inventory
- Flexibility
- Automation
- Team concept
- Integrated computer-based information system (ICBIS)

Management accountants do not have to adhere to GAAP in producing quality information for management. Quality information is based on the following attributes:

- Accuracy
- Relevancy
- Timeliness
- Fairness
- Usability

Management accountants get out of the office and go into the field or onto the factory floor to understand operations better. Only by understanding how enterprises work can management accountants produce high-quality information for management.

Information produced by management accountants influences behavior. Therefore, management accountants must be sure that what they are reporting achieves the correct behavior.

Learning objective 4.   Explain how to become a professional management accountant.

To become a professional management accountant, a person must:

- Pass an examination offered by the ICMA or SMA to qualified candidates and be designated as a CMA
- Adopt and abide by the standards of ethical conduct promulgated by the IMA
- Obtain adequate professional experience
- Maintain a program of continuing learning (certified professional education)

▌IMPORTANT TERMS

Accuracy   An attribute of quality information, which means that such information is free from mistake or error.

Allocation   One of the two ways a cost element can be assigned to a product cost. It is the dividing up of overhead (indirect) costs among the products made. The other, preferred, way to assign costs is to trace them directly to individual products.

Automation   The implementation of self-acting or self-regulating mechanisms. It is a technique of automatically controlling the operation of equipment, processes, or systems by mechanical or electronic devices that take the place of human observation, effort, and decision. Automation is a trend in modern organizations to help them become more efficient and effective.

Certified management accountant (CMA)   A professional management accountant who has demonstrated educational attainment and competency in specific areas of management accounting knowledge. People aspiring to become CMAs must qualify by passing a certification exam, gaining professional work experience, and maintaining certain continuing education requirements.

Competence   The ability to perform the work of a management accountant. It is a standard of ethical conduct that is integral in achieving the objectives of management accounting.

Confidentiality   The act of containing and protecting information from unauthorized disclosure. It is a standard of ethical conduct that is integral in achieving the objectives of management accounting.

Conversion cost   The total of direct labor and overhead costs; the cost necessary to transform direct materials into a finished good (product) or service.

Cost accounting   The information system for determining the cost of a project, process, product, service, or other cost object through the use of direct cost measurement and allocation techniques.

Customer service   Methods used to satisfy customer needs. It is a trend in modern organizations to get the right product or service to the right customer at the right time at the right price in order to meet or beat the competition.

Direct labor (touch labor)   People who work specifically on manufacturing a product or performing a service, and whose time can be directly traced to that product or service.

Direct materials   A substance that is a readily identifiable part of a product and whose cost is conveniently and directly traceable to that product.

Direct technology   Computers, software, and telecommunications equipment that control production processes, and production equipment and robots used in the manufacturing process.

Fairness   An attribute of quality information, which means that such information is equitable, impartial, and unbiased.

Financial accountants   People who process financial transactions and prepare financial statements for external reporting, which emphasize historical, custodial, and stewardship aspects of financial accounting. Financial accountants must adhere to generally accepted accounting principles (GAAP). A large number of financial accountants are certified public accountants (CPAs).

Financial accounting   The information system used to produce financial statements.

Finished goods   Product inventory items that are fully complete but not yet sold.

Flexibility   The ability of an organization to adapt to new, different, or changing requirements quickly and efficiently. It is a trend in modern organizations to offer new products or services to customers in a timely fashion or to change the mix of products or services rapidly.

Goal congruence   Making decisions that are in the best interests of the overall group or organization.

High quality   Methods and techniques used to design, develop, build, and deliver a product or service of elevated excellence. It is a trend in modern organizations to provide high-quality products and services to customers in order to be competitive.

Indirect labor   All manufacturing labor other than direct labor that is not directly traceable to the product or service.

Indirect materials   The raw materials that are not directly traced to a cost object (a product or service).

Institute of Certified Management Accountants (ICMA)   An organization established by the Institute of Management Accountants (IMA) and governed by a nine-member board of regents. The ICMA evaluates the credentials of candidates, administers the examination, grants certificates, and ensures that CMAs continue to meet the professional development requirements necessary to retain their certificates in good standing.

Institute of Management Accountants (IMA)   The largest management accounting association in the world, which was founded in 1919 as an educational organization. The IMA actively promotes management accounting; supports the certified management accountant program through the Institute of Certified Management Accountants; sponsors research reports and educational programs; and produces *Statements on Management Accounting,* conferences, technical information services, library services, and *Management Accounting* magazine.

Integrated computer-based information system (ICBIS)   The interconnection of computers and related information technology that provides a multilevel, cross-functional flow of information to all managers and workers throughout the enterprise.

Integrity   The quality or state of personal and professional honesty. It is a standard of ethical conduct that is integral in achieving the objectives of management accounting.

Job order systems   Production systems in which products or services are readily identified by individual units, jobs, or batches, each of which receives varying inputs of direct materials, direct labor, and overhead.

Lead time (cycle time)   The time it takes to convert a raw material to a finished product. Defined more broadly, it is the time it takes to convert an input to an output.

Low inventory   A sharp reduction in inventory levels while maintaining or even improving production lead times, delivery schedules, and customer service. It is a trend in modern organizations to reduce inventory in order to decrease or eliminate the costs of carrying inventory, including financial cost, obsolescence, shrinkage, storage costs, materials handling costs, record-keeping costs, insurance and tax obligations, slower lead times, and scrap.

Management accountants   Those people who are responsible for the management accounting system, and who perform cost, profit, and investment analyses.

Management accounting   An information system that includes the cost accounting system (i.e., product and service costing for management), the profit accounting system, and the investment accounting system. A system used to motivate, coordinate, and evaluate the effectiveness and efficiency of operations. A system that measures performance and produces quality information for managers to use as an aid in planning, controlling, and evaluating. (All definitions of management accounting are tentative, including this one, because the field of management accounting is dynamic and constantly adapting to changing needs and operations in organizations.)

Manufacturing organization   An enterprise engaged in converting raw materials to finished goods.

Merchandise inventory   The inventory of completed products awaiting sale to a firm's customers. *See also* finished goods.

Merchandising firm   An enterprise that sells products without changing their basic form.

Not-for-profit service entity   An organization engaged in a high or moderate degree of converting labor and resources into a service output for a small fee or for free. Such entities do not have a profit motive in offering their services.

Objectivity   The state of expressing or dealing with facts or conditions as perceived without distortion by personal feelings, prejudices, or interpretations. It is a standard of ethical conduct that is integral in achieving the objectives of management accounting.

Overhead   Any manufacturing cost that is indirectly traced (allocated) to the product or service.

Prime cost   The total of direct materials cost and direct labor cost.

Process systems   Production systems in which products are mass produced in a continuous manner through a series of stages called processes.

Profit-oriented service firm   An enterprise engaged in a high or moderate degree of conversion that results in service outputs that are sold for a profit.

Quality information   Data converted into meaningful form and substance that reduce uncertainty and contain the attributes of accuracy, relevancy, timeliness, fairness, and usability.

Raw materials   Direct and indirect materials waiting to be converted into finished goods.

Relevancy   An attribute of quality information, which means that such information is germane to the matter at hand or the issue under consideration.

Schedule of Cost of Goods Manufactured   A supporting report for the income statement that details the computation of the cost of goods produced during the period.

Society of Management Accountants (SMA)   The sponsoring organization of the CMA program in Canada.

Standards of Ethical Conduct for Management Accountants   Rules and principles adopted by the Institute of Certified Management Accountants (ICMA) to guide CMAs in their personal and professional life and work. The standards are competence, confidentiality, integrity, and objectivity.

Suboptimal behavior   Doing things (making decisions, taking actions) that benefit an individual or segment of an organization, but cause harm to others.

Team concept   The idea behind getting all employees in an organization actively involved in improving operations. It is a trend in modern organizations to operate the enterprise from the bottom up rather than from the top down and in a participative, democratic manner in order to improve morale, productivity, and quality.

Timeliness   An attribute of quality information, which means that managers and workers receive such information at the time they can use it to take action.

Usability   An attribute of quality information, which means that such information fits the cognitive style of the manager or worker receiving it.

Work-in-process or **work-in-progress (WIP)**   The inventory account for products undergoing a conversion process but not yet fully completed.

DEMONSTRATION PROBLEMS

■ **DEMONSTRATION PROBLEM 1**   *Schedule of cost of goods manufactured and an income statement for the Corerail Manufacturing Company.*

The following data pertain to the operations of the Corerail Manufacturing Company for the year 19X5. Corerail maintains separate accounts for direct and indirect materials within raw materials inventory.

Sales revenue	$1,000,000
Direct materials inventory, 01/01/X5	20,000
Direct labor	250,000
Depreciation, plant	50,000
Depreciation, factory equipment	30,000
Cutting tools used	12,000
Indirect labor	10,000
Utilities, plant	8,000
Supervisor salaries, plant	30,000
Indirect materials used	7,000
Property taxes, administrative offices	5,000
Administrative salaries	100,000
Salesperson salaries	150,000
Work-in-process inventory, 12/31/X5	20,000
Finished goods inventory, 01/01/X5	30,000
Property taxes, plant	11,000
Supplies, administrative offices	8,000
Finished goods inventory, 12/31/X5	40,000
Direct materials inventory, 12/31/X5	30,000
Work-in-process inventory, 01/01/X5	40,000
Direct materials purchases	120,000
Depreciation, administrative offices	60,000

Required:
Prepare a schedule of cost of goods manufactured and an income statement.

SOLUTION TO DEMONSTRATION PROBLEM 1

CORERAIL MANUFACTURING COMPANY
SCHEDULE OF COST OF GOODS MANUFACTURED
FOR THE YEAR ENDED DECEMBER 31, 19X5

Direct materials:		
Direct materials inventory, 01/01/X5	$ 20,000	
Purchases of direct materials	120,000	
Total direct materials available	140,000	
Less direct materials inventory, 12/31/X5	<30,000>	
Direct materials used		$110,000
Direct labor		250,000
Overhead:		
Depreciation, plant	$ 50,000	
Depreciation, factory equipment	30,000	
Supervisor salaries, plant	30,000	
Indirect labor	10,000	
Utilities, plant	8,000	
Indirect materials used	7,000	
Cutting tools used	12,000	
Property taxes, plant	11,000	
Total manufacturing overhead		158,000
Total manufacturing costs		$518,000
Work-in-process inventory, 01/01/X5		40,000
Less work-in-process inventory, 12/31/X5		<20,000>
Cost of goods manufactured		$538,000

CORERAIL MANUFACTURING COMPANY
INCOME STATEMENT
FOR THE YEAR ENDED DECEMBER 31, 19X5

Sales revenue		$1,000,000
Cost of goods sold:		
Finished goods inventory, 01/01/X5	$ 30,000	
Cost of goods manufactured	538,000	
Total goods available for sale	568,000	
Less finished goods inventory, 12/31/X5	<40,000>	
Cost of goods sold		<528,000>
Gross profit		$ 472,000
Selling and administrative expenses:		
Salesperson salaries	$150,000	
Administrative salaries	100,000	
Supplies, administrative offices	8,000	
Depreciation, administrative offices	60,000	
Property taxes, administrative offices	5,000	
Total selling and administrative expenses		<323,000>
Net income before taxes		$ 149,000

■ DEMONSTRATION PROBLEM 2   *Ethics.*

Dora Pliske is a newly hired management accountant who is facing the following unethical situations:

a. The company is in violation of environmental regulations.
b. An immediate superior has misstated inventory and refuses to correct it.
c. A cost report to be prepared by Dora will show very poor performance in the division where she works. Her boss wants her not to report certain costs.
d. Dora is prevented from gathering cost data on a pet project of the division manager.
e. Fearing that the division she works for will be discontinued, Dora is pursuing a position in another firm. The position calls for a management accountant with experience in world-class manufacturing, just-in-time (JIT) systems, computer-based information systems development, and activity-based costing. Dora does not have experience in any of these areas; however, wanting the job very badly, she states in the job application that she has the necessary experience. She even indicates that she worked on a systems project team that developed an integrated computer-based information system. She also states that she has installed an activity-based costing system.

Required:
Consider each situation separately. What action(s) should Dora take?

SOLUTION TO DEMONSTRATION PROBLEM 2

a. The proper action when the management accountant's immediate superior is involved is to present the matter to the next higher management level. If her immediate superior and the firm's chief executive officer know about the situation and refuse to correct it, then Dora should report the circumstances to the audit committee and/or the board of directors. Observing the standard of confidentiality, Dora should refrain from disclosing confidential information acquired in the course of her work, except when authorized, unless legally obligated to do so. In this case, a strong argument can be made that Dora is legally obligated. Moreover, such disclosure would not be in conflict with the confidentiality standard.
b. Apparently, Dora has discussed this problem with her immediate superior without resolution. Therefore, Dora should take the problem to the next higher management level. If Dora goes along with her immediate superior, then she is in conflict with the objectivity standard, which requires the fair and objective communication of information.

c. The management accountant must communicate unfavorable as well as favorable information and professional judgments or opinions.

d. Under the integrity standard, Dora should recognize and communicate professional limitations or other constraints that would preclude responsible judgment or successful performance of an activity.

e. The management accountant's responsibility under the competence standard is to maintain an appropriate level of professional competence through ongoing development of his or her knowledge and skills. Under the integrity standard, the management accountant should be honest and refrain from engaging in any activity that would discredit the profession. It appears that Dora is therefore in conflict with both the competence and the integrity standards.

REVIEW QUESTIONS

1.1 The following quotation is adapted from a letter by W. Michael Donovan, CMA, that appeared in *Management Accounting*, February 1992, p. 8:

> Wake up! Look at the world that is passing you by. Engineers and operations professionals can readily use the analytical tools of management accounting. Those are the people with whom we should be working. Recognize that CPAs have legal justification for their existence as suppliers of audits and tax advice. You will not overcome their position in the business world. Don't compete with them. Ignore them. The Institute of Management Accountants has made a fatal strategic error by even linking itself to the world of financial accountants. You must return to your engineering and costing roots and envision the organization as something totally different, the integration of strategy, finance, and economics within the world of engineering, cost, and operations.
>
> Look back and reread Kaplan's *The Rise and Fall of Management Accounting*, Hayes and Abernathy's *Managing Ourselves to Economic Decline*, Vollman and Miller's *The Hidden Factory*. You will see that their observations are linked to the everyday issues of operations and cost management, not to GAAP or the tax code.

Evaluate Mr. Donovan's comments. Do you believe they are justified? Why? Why not? Give your opinion as to the proper relationship between financial and management accounting.

1.2 Contrast financial and management accounting.

1.3 List and briefly describe the four types of organizations that management accountants serve.

1.4 List and define the cost elements of a manufacturing organization.

1.5 Define conversion cost and prime cost.

1.6 Is the proportion of direct labor cost increasing or decreasing in modern manufacturing organizations? Explain.

1.7 Is the proportion of overhead cost increasing or decreasing in automated factories? Explain.

1.8 Explain why some management accounting authorities believe that "direct technology" should be a direct cost element in automated factories.

1.9 List and briefly define the two broad types of manufacturing organizations.

1.10 Contrast merchandising firms and manufacturing organizations.

1.11 Describe how the income statement of a merchandising firm differs from the income statement of a manufacturing firm.

1.12 Of what value is the schedule of cost of goods manufactured? How does it tie into the income statement?

1.13 Describe how the balance sheet of a merchandising firm differs from the balance sheet of a manufacturing company insofar as current assets are concerned.

1.14 Contrast service firms and manufacturing companies. Can the same cost elements be used for both?

1.15 Is cost accounting a subset of management accounting or is management accounting a subset of cost accounting? Explain.

1.16 Is the body of knowledge of management accounting dynamic or static? Explain.

1.17 List the three managerial decision-making areas for which management accounting is the informational basis.

1.18 Define lead time.

1.19 Explain why financial accounting information is considered irrelevant for management.

1.20 Define cost accounting.

1.21 Explain how cost accounting serves financial accounting. Explain how cost accounting serves management accounting.

1.22 List and briefly describe the trends in the new manufacturing environment. Are the trends easily adaptable to service firms? Explain.

1.23 Define and give an example of suboptimal behavior.

1.24 Define quality information and list and describe its attributes.

1.25 Why is it important for the management accountant to get involved in the enterprise's operations?

1.26 "Management accounting plays both an *informing* and an *influencing* role." Explain this statement.

1.27 List the characteristics of a profession. Explain how the certified management accountant (CMA) exhibits these characteristics.

1.28 What are the four steps necessary to become a CMA?

1.29 List and summarize the areas of ethical standards.

1.30 Give three examples of ethical dilemmas that might affect the management accountant.

1.31 What questions should a management accountant ask himself or herself in dealing with ethical dilemmas?

▌CHAPTER-SPECIFIC PROBLEMS

These problems require responses based directly on concepts and techniques presented in the text.

1.32 *Financial and management accounting tasks.* Following is a list of tasks:

_____	Providing financial statements to stockholders and creditors.
_____	Preparing a balance sheet.
_____	Determining conversion costs of a product.
_____	Determining prime costs of a product.
_____	Preparing a schedule of cost of goods manufactured.
_____	Preparing reports for the Securities and Exchange Commission.
_____	Reporting lead time for a production process.

Required:
Insert the name of the kind of accountant, financial or management, who is most likely to perform each task.

1.33 *Schedule of cost of goods manufactured.* The CleanPac Company manufactures cleaning kits for PCs. Following are accounts from its year-end adjusted trial balance and other data:

	JANUARY 1	DECEMBER 31
Inventories:		
Finished goods	$40,000	$ 60,000
Work-in-process	16,000	14,000
Direct materials	9,000	15,000
Direct material purchases		240,000
Payroll costs:		
Production line workers		100,000
Material handling		50,000
Maintenance		30,000
Plant supervision		60,000
Sales salaries		120,000
Property taxes (70% for plant)		10,000

Depreciation (80% for plant)	90,000
Plant equipment repairs	20,000
Utilities (80% for plant)	16,000
Income taxes	50,000

Required:
Prepare the schedule of cost of goods manufactured for CleanPac.

1.34 *Schedules of cost of goods manufactured and cost of goods sold.* The following data are taken from the cost records of Lenox Company for June 19X8:

Maintenance, plant equipment	$ 4,000
Rent, plant facilities	30,000
Insurance, plant equipment	1,000
Insurance, office equipment	800
Direct labor cost	150,000
Purchase of direct materials	280,000
Depreciation, office equipment	5,000
Indirect materials cost	10,000
Indirect labor cost	50,000
Depreciation, plant equipment	22,000
Advertising expense	120,000
Sales salaries	100,000
Administrative salaries	150,000
Direct materials inventory, June 1	40,000
Direct materials inventory, June 30	20,000
Work-in-process inventory, June 1	60,000
Work-in-process inventory, June 30	80,000
Finished goods inventory, June 1	110,000
Finished goods inventory, June 30	85,000

Required:
a. Prepare a schedule of cost of goods manufactured for June 19X8.
b. Prepare the cost of goods sold section for Lenox's income statement for June 19X8.

1.35 *Schedules of cost of goods manufactured and cost of goods sold.* The following cost and inventory data are taken from the books of Starr Company for the year 19X6:

Costs incurred:	
Direct labor cost	$150,000
Direct material purchases	250,000
Indirect labor	70,000
Maintenance, plant equipment	15,000
Advertising expense	120,000
Insurance, plant equipment	2,000
Sales salaries	100,000
Property taxes, plant	40,000
Rent, plant	10,000
Indirect materials	8,000
Depreciation, office equipment	10,000
Depreciation, plant equipment	40,000

	JANUARY 1, 19X6	DECEMBER 31, 19X6
Inventories:		
Direct materials	$14,000	$30,000
Work-in-process	20,000	10,000
Finished goods	40,000	70,000

Required:
a. Prepare a schedule of cost of goods manufactured.
b. Prepare the cost of goods sold section of Starr Company's income statement for the year.

1.36 *Schedules of cost of goods manufactured, cost of goods sold, prime cost, and conversion cost.* Cost of goods sold for the Stables Corporation for the month of May 19X7 was $700,000. Work-in-process inventory at the end of May was 90% of work-in-process inventory at the beginning of May. Overhead is 80% of direct labor cost. During May, $250,000 of direct materials were purchased. Other data about Stables's inventory and production for May are as follows:

Beginning inventories, May 1:	
Direct materials	$ 45,000
Work-in-process	80,000
Finished goods	210,000
Ending inventories, May 31:	
Direct materials	$ 40,000
Work-in-process	?
Finished goods	210,000

Required:
a. Prepare a schedule of cost of goods manufactured for May.
b. Prepare a schedule to calculate the prime cost incurred during May.
c. Prepare a schedule to calculate the conversion cost charged to work-in-process during May.
d. Prepare a schedule of cost of goods sold for May.

1.37 *Direct materials purchased, direct labor costs, and cost of goods sold.* The following inventory data relate to the Manifold Company:

	ENDING	BEGINNING
Finished goods inventory	$95,000	$110,000
Work-in-process inventory	80,000	70,000
Direct materials inventory	95,000	90,000

Costs incurred during the period are as follows:

Cost of goods available for sale	$754,000
Total manufacturing costs	654,000
Manufacturing overhead	167,000
Direct materials used	193,000

Required:
Calculate direct materials purchased, direct labor costs, and cost of goods sold.

[AICPA adapted]

1.38 *Characteristics of quality information.* Following is a list of complaints about reports received from users of the accounting system:

_____	The cost of the new project was estimated at $500,000, almost 100% less than what it actually cost.
_____	The reports may contain good information, but they are so detailed and poorly prepared, we don't even look at them.
_____	We can't use these reports because we receive them 60 days too late.
_____	This report has nothing to do with the decision I'm trying to make.
_____	This report shows that all the property taxes and utility costs are being charged to my department. Why?

Required:
Insert the attributes of quality information most affected by these complaints.

THINK-TANK PROBLEMS

Although these problems are based on chapter material, reading extra material and using creativity may be required to develop workable solutions.

1.39 *Suboptimizing situation.* Gatestone Tire Company has invested millions of dollars in tire-making equipment. Jim Stoner, newly retired management accountant, had established a maintenance cost report emphasizing minimization of maintenance costs. Each year, the maintenance crews with the lowest maintenance costs received awards. But lately, most of the tire-making equipment is down 40% to 60% of the time. Suzy Wong was recently hired to replace Jim Stoner.

Required:
a. What do you believe is a major cause of Gatestone's excessive equipment downtime?
b. Describe the kind of reporting system you believe would be appropriate concerning equipment maintenance costs.

1.40 *Standards and ethical conduct.* Following is a list of situations that have ethical ramifications:

_____	Tracy Bickford, management accountant, accepted a golf cart from a potential vendor who wanted to persuade her to provide some favorable treatment.
_____	Tim Witherspoon, management accountant for Xorax Corporation, has become a major stockholder in Thompson Equipment, a major vendor of Xorax.
_____	Agnes Lee, management accountant for Miteson Industries, has compiled and provided sensitive pricing information to her friend at Bandig Company, a major competitor of Miteson.
_____	Benny Chemparathy, management accountant at Thorson Associates, has omitted some significant cost data in hopes that a new project will be accepted by senior management at Thorson. If accepted, this new project will be headed by Darcy Coffee, Benny's sister-in-law.
_____	Betty Wilkerson, management accountant at Bridgeton Corporation, has withheld some favorable performance information concerning a department managed by Teri Sanchez, a person Betty does not like.
_____	Tim Flores, newly hired management accountant for Tensas Industries, stated that he had been a management accountant for Ducet Cosmetics, a company located in France. Tim has never worked as a management accountant for Ducet or any other company.

Required:
Insert the ethical standard with which each of the preceding situations is in noncompliance. Some situations may be in conflict with more than one ethical standard.

1.41 *Ethical dilemma.* Cinco Manufacturing Company has received a loan from First Interstate Bank. A key stipulation in the loan agreement is that Cinco must maintain a gross margin of at least 30% of sales and net income of 15% of sales. The bank is to receive an income statement quarterly. Looking at this quarter's income statement, Joe Stearns, president of Cinco, notices that the gross margin is only 25% of sales while net income is 20% of sales. He tells Cory Martinez, accountant for Cinco, to shift some of the product costs included in cost of goods sold to the selling and administrative expenses section of the income statement so that the gross margin and net income figures will conform to the stipulation in the bank loan agreement.

Required:
a. What type of product cost would be easiest to reassign to the selling and administrative section?
b. Because Joe Stearns is not suggesting that any expenses be removed from the income statement, is there an ethical dilemma? If so, which ethical standards would be violated?
c. Write a short letter to convince the loan officer that the loan should not be terminated in spite of Cinco's noncompliance with the loan agreement stipulation.

1.42 *Ethical dilemma.* Masco Enterprises is a publicly owned corporation that makes various electronic control devices. Ken Polk has been the president and chief executive officer (CEO) of Masco for about five years. Martha Glakowski has been management accountant for about two years. Terry Brinker has been purchasing agent for about five years. Dianne Kim has been executive assistant to Ken Polk for about three years. Following is a conversation that Martha had with Ken recently:

"Good morning, Martha, come on in," said Ken, "Dianne said that you had a confidential matter to discuss. What's on your mind?"

"I've been reviewing our increased purchases from Aapex Electronics and wondered why our volume has tripled in the past year. When I spoke with Terry about this, he seemed a bit evasive and tried to dismiss the issue by stating that we can get one-day delivery on our orders," Martha responded.

"That's true," said Ken. "We get excellent delivery."

"But we could get the same electronic components from Stanley Products for 40% less. This cost differential would have saved us $900,000 so far this year," said Martha.

"Now look, Martha, we get quick delivery on some items, and who knows how much we are saving by not having to stock these components in advance or worry about them becoming obsolete. Is there anything else on your mind?"

"Well, Ken, as a matter of fact, there is," said Martha. "I ordered a Dun & Bradstreet credit report on Aapex and discovered that Tom Rasmussen is the principal owner. Isn't he your brother-in-law?"

"Sure he is. That's why we get good service," said Ken, a little heatedly. "Now, I've got a meeting with some people downtown. So, you'll have to excuse me."

"OK. Thanks for your time," said Martha.

As she left Ken's office, Martha wondered what her obligations were in this matter.

Required:
a. Which standards of ethical conduct may be violated?
b. What kind of cost information should Martha develop to help resolve any apparent conflicts? Evaluate this information's quality with respect to the five attributes of quality information.
c. Should Martha legally or ethically ignore the apparent conflict of interest?
d. What actions should Martha take?

1.43 *Ethical dilemma.* Zludge Products makes dyes and metal etching compounds. Steve Gould, a manager at Zludge, recently discovered that the company is using a nearby residential landfill to dump toxic waste. Steve has gathered sufficient documentation about Zludge's dumping of toxic waste. Steve has determined that he has three options:

■ Seek the advice of his boss, the controller
■ Anonymously release the information to the local newspaper and television station
■ Bring the information to the attention of an outside member of the board of directors

Required:
a. Does Steve have an ethical responsibility to take some action in the matter of the dumping of toxic waste?

b. Explain whether each of the three options that Steve has considered is proper.

c. Without prejudice to your answer in Requirement (b), assume that Steve sought the advice of the controller and discovered that he was involved in the dumping of toxic waste. Describe the steps that Steve should take in proceeding to resolve the conflict in this situation.

1.44 *Working in an unethical environment.* Following is an excerpt from a letter written by Nate Miles of the University of Idaho that appeared in *Management Accounting*, March 1992, p. 9.

> Unethical behavior usually occurs slowly in increments. As with any type of learning, unethical behavior is learned step by step. There are probably very few, if any, cases of those who go from performing judicious business one day to making major fabrications on financial statements or embezzling the next. It occurs more slowly and rationally for those involved, oftentimes beginning with the encouragement of an employer.
>
> . . . working in an environment where unethical behavior is encouraged, if it appears to serve the clients' or the firm's needs, is likely to wear down even the strongest people. Working for a firm [that] has this characteristic can be self-destructive where ethics are concerned.

Required:

Should an emphasis be placed on working in an ethical business environment? Is unethical behavior learned step by step? Describe a situation where unethical behavior is encouraged by an employer. Explain how working in an unethical environment may wear down even the most ethical person. Give an example of how unethical behavior can be self-destructive.

1.45 *Working in an unethical environment.* Tom Savin has recently been hired as a cost accountant by the Offset Press Company, a privately held company that produces a line of offset printing presses and lithograph machines. During his first few months on the job, Savin discovered that Offset has been recording some overhead costs as selling and administrative expenses. This understated manufacturing costs and the value of the (substantial) ending finished goods inventory. By increasing expenses, net income was understated. This practice has been going on since the start of the company, which is in its sixth year of operation. The effect in each year has been favorable, having a material impact on the company's tax position. No internal audit function exists at Offset, and the external auditors have not yet discovered the understated factory overhead.

Prior to the sixth-year audit, Savin had pointed out the practice and its effect to Mary Brown, the corporate controller, and had asked her to let him make the necessary adjustments. Brown directed him not to make the adjustments but to wait until the external auditors had completed their work and see what they uncovered.

The sixth-year audit has now been completed, and the external auditors have once more failed to discover the understated factory overhead. Savin again asked Brown if he could make the required adjustments and was again told not to make them. Savin, however, believes that the adjustments should be made and that the external auditors should be informed of the situation.

Since Offset Press Company has no established policies for resolving ethical conflicts, Savin is considering following one of the three alternative courses of action listed below.

1. Follow Brown's directive and do nothing further.
2. Attempt to convince Brown to make the proper adjustments and to advise the external auditors of her actions.
3. Tell the Audit Committee of the board of directors about the problem and give them the appropriate accounting data.

Required:

a. Explain whether or not each of the three alternative courses of action that Tom Savin is considering is appropriate. Refer to specific standards of *Standards of Ethical Conduct for Management Accountants* to support your answer.

b. Without prejudice to your answer in Requirement (a), assume that Tom Savin again approaches Mary Brown to make the necessary adjustments and is unsuccessful. Describe the steps that Savin should take in proceeding to resolve this situation.

[CMA adapted]

1.46 *Handling software license agreements.* Ward Corporation is a manufacturer of cleaning products with three wholly owned subsidiaries that are operated as separate divisions. Ward's corporate headquarters are located in an industrial park in a Chicago suburb. The Industrial Products Division is located in the same industrial park but in its own building. The other two divisions are located in Milwaukee and Indianapolis.

The corporation's operating and financial records are maintained on a mainframe computer at corporate headquarters. Each division has a small accounting department that submits operating and financial data to corporate headquarters on a regular basis.

The Profit Planning Department at corporate headquarters is responsible for preparing special analyses and reports for Ward. To facilitate its work, the Profit Planning Department has linked a microcomputer to the mainframe to download data. The special analyses are prepared using these data and a purchased spreadsheet software package.

Beth Simons recently joined the Industrial Products Division as an accounting analyst. Simons is proficient in the use of microcomputers and spreadsheet software. She has been given an assignment to work with Doug Laird, marketing manager of the Industrial Products Division, to develop analyses and reports. One week into the assignment, Simons suggested that the microcomputers used in the Marketing Department for word processing could be valuable analytical tools if spreadsheet software were acquired. Laird knows little about computers, but he has received some of the special analyses prepared by the Profit Planning Department at corporate headquarters. Laird wants Simons to try her idea but has suggested that she first borrow the software from the Profit Planning Department.

Simons has approached Tom Field, manager of Profit Planning, regarding the use of the software package. Field was very sympathetic to Simons's request, but the software is used extensively in his department. Therefore, he did not want to loan the original system disk. Furthermore, the software was copy-protected. However, Field did have a utility program that allowed him to make backup copies of most copy-protected software. Since there was no backup of the spreadsheet software, Field decided to make a copy and give it to Simons for her use. Simons indicated that she planned to use the software during regular business hours.

Upon giving the copy to Simons, Field said, "This is my only copy but you may borrow it for your use only. Don't give it to anyone else. Once you have tried the software for your assignment, you must return this copy to me. Industrial Product's Accounting or Marketing Department will have to purchase its own copy."

Field did not give Simons a copy of the licensing agreement that accompanied the original software package. The license agreement reproduced below was affixed to the original sealed disk package. While Simons was not aware of the specific provisions of the licensing agreement that pertained to the borrowed software, she knew that licensing agreements accompany computer software packages.

Software License Agreement

IMPORTANT: Please read this agreement before opening the envelope. Opening the disk envelope indicates the user's acceptance of the agreement to abide by these terms.

1. The software may be used on any compatible hardware that the purchaser owns or uses.
2. Backup copies of the software can be made provided that these copies are for exclusive use of the purchaser and only one copy of the software is in use at any one time.
3. No alterations to the software or the documentation are permitted.
4. The software may not be distributed to others on a permanent or temporary basis.

5. This license and the software may be transferred to another party provided that all copies of the software and documentation are transferred and the original party ceases to use the software after the transfer.

Required:

a. Based upon the stipulations enumerated in the license agreement for the spreadsheet software, did Tom Field violate the agreement when he:
   1. Made a copy of the software disk using the utility program?
   2. Gave Beth Simons the copy of the software disk he had made?
   Explain your answer in each case.

b. Without prejudice to your answer in Requirement (a), assume that Tom Field did violate the license agreement when he copied the software disk and gave it to Beth Simons. Identify the alternatives that Tom Field could have employed to determine the applicability of the spreadsheet software to the application of the Marketing Department of the Industrial Products Division without violating the license agreement.

c. Management accountants are expected to abide by the ethical standards set forth in the *Standards of Ethical Conduct for Management Accountants.* Were any of the standards violated by:
   1. Tom Field when he copied the software disk and gave Beth Simons the copy for her use?
   2. Beth Simons when she used the copy of the software to determine its usefulness in the applications for the Marketing Department of the Industrial Products Division?
   Explain your answer in each case being sure to identify the standard(s) that is (are) violated or explaining why no standards were violated.

[CMA adapted]

1.47 *Ethics and controls.* The Fore Corporation is an integrated food processing company that has operations in over two dozen countries. Fore's corporate headquarters are in Chicago, and the company's executives frequently travel to visit Fore's foreign and domestic facilities.

Fore has a fleet of aircraft that consists of two business jets with international range and six smaller turbine aircraft that are used on shorter flights. Company policy is to assign aircraft to trips on the basis of minimizing cost, but in practice the aircraft are assigned based on the organizational rank of the traveler. Fore offers its aircraft for short-term lease or for charter by other organizations whenever Fore itself does not plan to use the aircraft. Fore surveys the market often in order to keep its lease and charter rates competitive.

William Earle, Fore's vice-president of finance, has claimed that a third business jet can be justified financially. However, some people in the controller's office have surmised that the real reason for a third business jet was to upgrade the aircraft used by Earle. Currently, the people outranking Earle keep the two business jets busy, with the result that Earle usually flies in smaller turbine aircraft.

The third business jet would cost $11 million. A capital expenditure of this magnitude requires a formal proposal with projected cash flows and net present value computations using Fore's minimum required rate of return. If Fore's president and the Finance Committee of the board of directors approve the proposal, it will be submitted to the full board of directors. The board has final approval on capital expenditures exceeding $5 million, and has established a firm policy of rejecting any discretionary proposal that has a negative net present value.

Earle asked Rachel Arnett, assistant corporate controller, to prepare a proposal on a third business jet. Arnett gathered the following data:

- Acquisition cost of the aircraft, including instrumentation and interior furnishing
- Operating cost of the aircraft for company use
- Projected avoidable commercial airfare and other avoidable costs from company use of the plane
- Projected value of executive time saved by using the third business jet
- Projected contribution margin from incremental lease and charter activity
- Estimated resale value of the aircraft
- Estimated income tax effects of the proposal

When Earle reviewed Arnett's complete proposal and saw the large negative net present value figure, he returned the proposal to her. With a glare, Earle commented. "You must have made an error. The proposal should look better than that."

Feeling some pressure, Arnett went back and checked her computations; she found no errors. However, Earl's message was clear. Arnett discarded her projections and estimates that she believed were reasonable and replaced them with figures that had a remote chance of actually occurring, but were more favorable to the proposal. For example, she used first-class airfares to refigure the avoidable commercial airfare costs, even though company policy was to fly coach. She found revising the proposal to be distressing.

The revised proposal still had a negative net present value. Earle's anger was evident as he told Arnett to revise the proposal again and to start with a $100,000 positive net present value and work backward to compute supporting estimates and projections.

Required:
a. Explain whether Rachel Arnett's revision of the proposal was in violation of the *Standards of Ethical Conduct for Management Accountants*.
b. Did William Earle violate the *Standards of Ethical Conduct for Management Accountants* by telling Arnett specifically how to revise the proposal? Explain your answer.
c. What aspects of the projection and estimation process would be compromised in preparing an analysis for which a preconceived result is sought?
d. Identify specific internal controls that Fore Corporation could implement to prevent unethical behavior on the part of the vice-president of finance.

[CMA adapted]

2

MOVING FROM TRADITIONAL TO MODERN MANUFACTURING ENVIRONMENTS

Manufacturing cell at Caterpillar.

LEARNING OBJECTIVES

After studying this chapter, you should be able to:

1. Describe the traditional batch manufacturing environment.

2. Define the world-class manufacturing (WCM) environment.

3. List and describe the characteristics of WCM.

4. Describe just-in-time (JIT) manufacturing and computer-integrated manufacturing (CIM).

■ INTRODUCTION

There are various manufacturing industries ranging from processors of basic metals, chemicals, paper, and oil and gas to commercial products manufacturers and consumer products companies.[1] Within these industries there is also a variety of manufacturing environments, as depicted in Exhibit 2–1. As this exhibit clearly indicates, no single management accounting system will fit all industries and all manufacturing environments. Cost accounting methods and various performance measurement techniques need to be adapted to fit these different environments to be effective.[2]

> Today's manufacturing environment in the United States is turbulent and laced with uncertainty. Competition from abroad is constantly eroding both market share and profits of major American corporations. . . . They must change their manufacturing practices and regain a competitive edge in their markets or face entering the ranks of the displaced.
>
>   . . . To be successful, companies can no longer compete on a single dimension, such as cost. Instead, they must excel at . . . low cost, high quality, and high customer service. . . .
>
>   Managers seeking to prosper in this environment are turning to their management accounting system for new types of information. . . .[3]

This chapter examines manufacturing from the perspective of two different broad environments:

- The traditional batch manufacturing environment
- The world-class manufacturing (WCM) environment ━━

▍WHAT IS A TRADITIONAL BATCH MANUFACTURING ENVIRONMENT?

A **traditional batch manufacturing environment** is a PUSH system in which a subassembly or partially completed product is PUSHed to an area designated for work-in-process (WIP). The next department takes the subassemblies or partially completed products from their WIP locations, performs an operation on them, and then PUSHes the resulting work into the next WIP location. This procedure continues until the final product is completed, as shown in Exhibit 2–2.

Note the disjointed operations of the departments. The pipeline is not continuous between the three production departments. Each department is producing in large production runs, instead of producing just enough to meet the demand of the next department. This PUSH approach results in batches of WIP inventory being piled between departments throughout the plant. The cost accounting

LEARNING OBJECTIVE 1

Describe the traditional batch manufacturing environment.

Low-volume producers	versus	High-volume producers
Few products	versus	Many products
Long life cycle products	versus	Short life cycle products
Fabricators	versus	Assemblers
Job order systems	versus	Process systems
Long lead (cycle) time	versus	Short lead (cycle) time

■ EXHIBIT 2–1
Variety of Manufacturing Environments

---

[1] Robert A. Howell, James D. Brown, Stephen R. Soucy, and Allen H. Seed III, *Management Accounting in the New Manufacturing Environment* (Montvale, N.J.: Institute of Management Accountants, formerly the National Association of Accountants, 1987), p. 6. With permission.

[2] Ibid., p. 8.

[3] Carol J. McNair, William Mosconi, and Thomas F. Norris, *Beyond the Bottom Line: Measuring World Class Performance* (Homewood, Ill.: Dow Jones–Irwin, 1989), p. 1. With permission.

■ EXHIBIT 2–2
Traditional Batch Manufacturing Environment

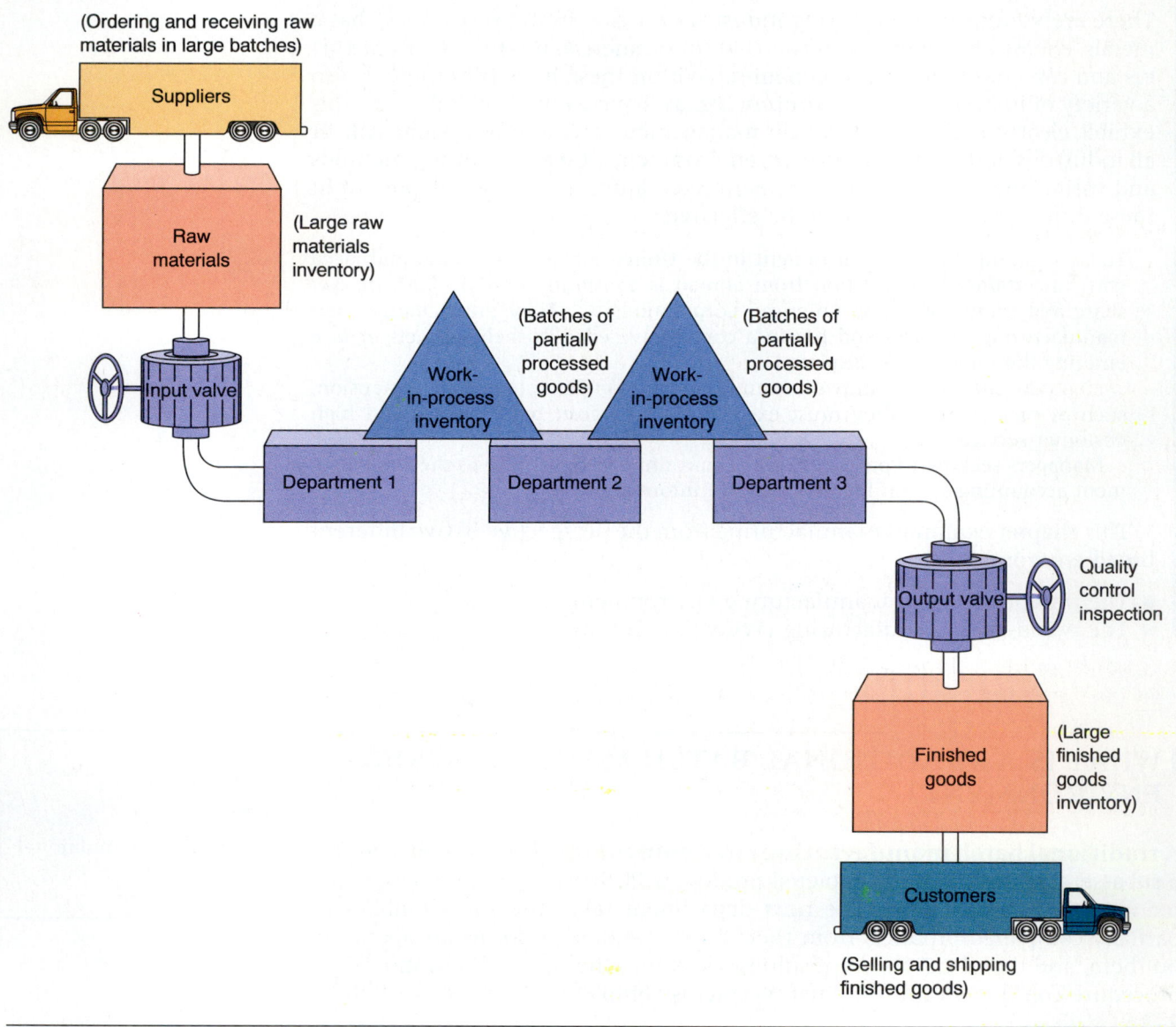

(Ordering and receiving raw materials in large batches)

Suppliers

Raw materials

(Large raw materials inventory)

Input valve

Department 1

Work-in-process inventory

(Batches of partially processed goods)

Department 2

Work-in-process inventory

(Batches of partially processed goods)

Department 3

Output valve

Quality control inspection

Finished goods

(Large finished goods inventory)

Customers

(Selling and shipping finished goods)

system has to accumulate and assign costs for these partially completed batches, thus adding complexity to the management accounting process.

Four problems have become apparent in traditional batch manufacturing:

- Suboptimizing behavior between organizational areas
- Producing and maintaining large inventories
- Producing products of subpar quality
- Striving for efficiency at the expense of effectiveness

▌Suboptimizing Behavior between Organizational Areas

Traditional areas of engineering, manufacturing, marketing, logistics, and customer service often operate in a suboptimizing manner, with little integration and communication between them. Engineering designs the product and PUSHes it into manufacturing, expecting manufacturing to make the product without any problems. Usually, however, a number of engineering changes have to be made before the product becomes manufacturable.

Manufacturing finally makes the product in large lot sizes so that enough parts are on hand to keep everyone busy, without considering marketing, logistics, and customer service. Meanwhile, marketing personnel are out trying to sell a product that they had little say in designing; logistics is trying to get the product to the customer on time; and service people are out trying to repair the product without input from anyone. Nor do the service people report back about the kinds of repairs they make to the engineering and manufacturing people who could correct the reasons for the repairs.

▎Producing and Maintaining Large Inventories

Traditional PUSH-type batch manufacturing environments drive products to lower average unit costs. The more products produced, the lower the average unit costs, but many products are left unsold, stacked up on factory floors and in large warehouses. Most companies produce more and more products to PUSH them into more and more warehouses. The more products produced, the greater the inventory asset, and therefore the better the balance sheet looks. So does the income statement, which shows a bigger income figure because of the lower unit costs.

For example, when a traditional batch manufacturer buys equipment, machine utilization is the focus. If the machine costs $500,000 and production is 100,000 units, then the machine's average unit cost is $5.00. If production is increased to 200,000 units, the machine's unit cost drops to $2.50. In many traditional manufacturers, minimizing the average product cost has been the key to a successful performance evaluation for managers. So, the incentive is to produce more and more units. The production people's attitude is "It's our job to make it. It's marketing's job to figure out how to sell it."

Although the financial statements may "look good," the PUSH approach results in large quantities of inventory sitting on shelves in massive warehouses. Over time, the storage of these products is costly. Even worse, many items become obsolete, damaged, or stolen.

▎Producing Products of Subpar Quality

Although workers are encouraged to make good-quality products, rarely are they penalized for producing poor-quality work. Under the traditional batch manufacturing system, workers do not have major responsibility for quality control during their work.

Quality control is in the hands of quality control inspectors who inspect products *after* they have been produced. Thus, inspection does not take place in the most timely fashion, making it difficult, if not impossible, to trace where production problems arose or defects occurred. The result is excessive scrap and rework over time because problems cannot be identified and prevented. Instead of preventing problems, the company maintains large WIP inventories to protect against line shutdowns or work delays. The emphasis of a PUSH system is on quantity rather than quality. Thus, workers PUSH poorly produced work to the next department, which also has little incentive to make corrections or improve quality.

▎Striving for Efficiency at the Expense of Effectiveness

Traditional batch manufacturers don't seem to strive for an optimized balance between efficiency and effectiveness. **Efficiency** means performing tasks to produce the best yield at the lowest cost from the resources available. It is *doing something right*. **Effectiveness** is the degree to which an objective or target is met. It is *doing the right thing.* Being the lowest-cost producer of products that nobody wants is efficient, but not effective. Killing a fly with a sledgehammer

Producing Quantity But Not Quality

At Marine Castings, a hypothetical company, workers were put on an incentive pay plan. Under the new incentive system, the workers produced 50 castings an hour instead of 30 castings an hour.

The workers were achieving good labor efficiency, but over 40 percent of the castings had to be scrapped because of poor quality.

The controller was the one who had insisted on the installation of an incentive system. The incentive system continued until the company went out of business.

is effective, but not efficient. Stressing efficiency over effectiveness, or vice versa, is suboptimal behavior.

One of the reasons for this suboptimal behavior is the use of financial accounting information (the average per unit cost of goods manufactured) for production performance evaluation. This causes a focus on "efficiency" as opposed to "effectiveness." As someone once said, "Nothing is more wasteful than doing with great efficiency that which is totally unnecessary."[4]

WHAT IS THE WORLD-CLASS MANUFACTURING ENVIRONMENT?

The **world-class manufacturing (WCM) environment** is a culture of problem prevention, continuous improvement, efficiency and effectiveness, and manufacturing excellence. In 1985, a presidential commission on industrial competitiveness concluded that the United States needed to drastically improve its ability to compete in world markets. Their recommendations, the report stated, needed to be implemented immediately to restore the competitive edge that American manufacturing had lost. At stake was nothing less than the world leadership needed to provide a standard of living for our people that they consider acceptable. As an executive said, "American manufacturers have to automate, integrate, or evaporate."

Why We Need Fundamental Changes in American Manufacturing

Fundamentally, the United States has had serious difficulties in four areas:

- Meeting foreign competition
- Being cost-effective against competitors
- Maintaining the level of domestic manufacturing activity for component parts
- Losing industries and companies that previously were considered the American manufacturing domain

At the root of these problems always seem to lie the issues of quality, customer satisfaction, responsiveness, and productivity. Let's take productivity as an example. The heyday of American manufacturing occurred between 1948 and 1964, when the United States recorded an average annual improvement in real output per worker hour of approximately 3.2 percent. Beginning in 1965, however, the annual increase began to drop, first to 2.4 percent, then by 1973

[4] Will Kaydos, *Measuring, Managing, and Maximizing Performance* (Cambridge, Mass.: Productivity Press, 1991), p. 17.

INSIGHTS & APPLICATIONS

Efficient Maybe, But Not Very Effective

Brooke is plant manager at Widgets, Incorporated. One day Brooke was talking to Marty, an engineer.

"You look tired," said Marty.

"You'd look tired too if you were working 12 to 15 hours a day," Brooke responded.

"Boy, business must be good," Marty replied.

"I wish that were true," said Brooke.

"Excuse me, Brooke, but if business is not good, why are you working 12 to 15 hours a day?" asked Marty.

"Well, headquarters has told us that we've got to decrease the unit cost of our products. The more we produce, the less fixed overhead we have to allocate to each one, lowering the unit cost," Brooke said confidentially.

"But if you're producing products that are not selling, what are you doing with them?" asked Marty, somewhat perplexed.

"Oh, we leased two warehouses and have another one under construction to stock the inventory," responded Brooke.

---

to below 1 percent, and finally in 1978 to negative levels. Across all industries, the U.S. productivity results were causing such a loss of jobs that the real problem could no longer be denied.

The commission report of 1985, without even mentioning WCM, was a clear call for implementing a WCM philosophy. Since then, numerous U.S. manufacturers have sought to achieve WCM status.

The Beginnings of World-Class Manufacturing in the United States

In the early 1980s, many U.S. companies began to seriously investigate the reasons why they were not competitive, particularly against the Japanese. Although they were looking for the very best in terms of world-class manufacturing practices, most firms found that their search ended in Japan, where the Toyota automobile company, the electronics industry, and other producers were taking a significant bite out of the market position of their U.S. counterparts. The idea was to learn from these new world-class competitors and to find out how they were able to compete and continually improve against more well-established American companies. The American firms found that continuous and simultaneous improvement in four competitive areas was the key:

- The lowest *total* cost (not lowest average cost per unit)
- The most consistent quality
- The most reliable delivery
- The most responsiveness to customers' needs

The difference was that the Americans had always regarded the relationship *among* these four areas as a *trade-off*. A manufacturer who wanted the lowest total cost, it was assumed, would have to trade off a certain amount of quality. Or, if greater reliability in customer deliveries was the goal, the manufacturer would require more time and be less responsive to customer needs.

Japanese manufacturers, on the other hand, believed and showed that simultaneous improvement in the competitive variables was possible and that one variable need not be sacrificed for another. If management insisted there would be no trade-off, the total picture would improve gradually with stability. The tool used to achieve this **continuous improvement,** *kaizen* in Japanese, was the elimination of waste in all parts of production, production support, worker involvement, and management practices.

Interestingly, the Japanese had developed this industrial culture largely through observing such American operations as supermarkets and studying

Henry Ford's automobile assembly concept of "taking the work to the worker, and not the worker to the work." Following World War II, the Japanese employed several American consultants to help them rebuild the industrial sector of their economy. The most notable consultant was Dr. W. Edwards (Ed) Deming who is considered by many to be the "father of world-class manufacturing." He is the capitalist revolutionary who sold Japan on the notion that quality drives profits *up* rather than *down*. The Deming Prize, a prestigious Japanese award, honors people for their contributions in the field of productivity and quality improvement.

Meanwhile, U.S. manufacturers sat idly by as the new competition emerged. Today, after a decade of WCM implementation by a few firms in this country, we are beginning to see signs of their success. Can this trend continue? As Tom Peters, the noted co-author of *In Search of Excellence,* says:

> In the end, Americans appear to have two choices . . . we can become a commodity producer of second rate goods, trying to make a profit by competing with the Indonesians on low wages, or . . . we can join the Japanese, the Germans, the Swiss and others, and become a nation that emphasizes high levels of value-added, awesome quality, and extraordinary service—not obtained through robotics, but through people—via training, self respect, self development and true partnership.

What role should the modern management accountant play in this process? Michael Thomas argues that we need to participate in designing new management systems based on the following "chain of causation" for production process control evaluation:

1. For the economic goals of the organization to be satisfied, the production process must function efficiently and effectively.
2. If appropriate responses are not made to problems as they occur, the production process will not function as specified in (1).
3. If the organizational members are not committed to their roles, or lack necessary control skills, they will not respond appropriately.
4. Commitment cannot be forced or bought. It must be designed into the jobs and roles assigned to people.
5. Appropriate information and training are necessary so that people will have the control skills required to identify and perform necessary control actions when needed. . . .

One key ingredient for success is *team involvement,* achieved through a systematic approach which considers the social system (people) to be a primary component of the total organization. *Thus, commitment results from having both the proper control skills and motivation to do the job right. Motivation results from rewards acceptable to the workers, and a performance evaluation system that allows workers to get rewarded. Proper evaluation requires information about the costs of production, problems that have happened, and whether they have been corrected.* [italics in original][5]

Maryann N. Keller, an automotive industry analyst and managing director of a brokerage firm, believes that the most profound change in the American auto industry in the past ten years was the realization that "quality can cost less because you design it in rather than inspect it in." The traditional American idea of quality is, as Keller says, to inspect it in; that is, you build a whole lot of widgets, inspect them, and separate the good from the bad. The bad can't be sold, but they cost a lot. Not only must all those inspectors be paid, but a bad widget takes the same amount of raw material, machinery, work time, and attention as a good widget does. That explains why, typically, about 25 percent of any manufacturing plant's budget goes for repair and rework. That's why so many manufacturers think quality costs more, but what actually costs is a lack of quality.

---

[5] Michael Thomas, et al., *Designing the Management Accounting System, Using ABC and Socio-Technical Systems Analysis, for a JIT Conversion at Ditch Witch* (Montvale, N.J.: Institute of Management Accountants, 1992), p. 4. With permission.

Some people feel that WCM cannot succeed in the United States as it has in Japan due to fundamental cultural differences. The Japanese, they say, have a sense of community effort that we individualistic Americans lack. Although differences exist, various Japanese firms that have set up production operations in the United States have achieved excellent results using WCM with American workers. It's been shown that the success of WCM is far more dependent on the culture developed *within the company* than on the culture of the nation as a whole.

In conclusion, for those who are still not convinced, consider the following WCM success stories from some very American companies:

- *Harley-Davidson.* This motorcycle manufacturer cut inventory by $20 million, setup time (the time required to prepare and adjust machines for an assigned task) by 75 percent, reduced its break-even point by 32 percent, increased inventory turns from 6 to 20, and reduced warranty claims and defects by 24 percent.
- *General Electric.* GE trimmed inventory 70 percent and raised labor productivity 35 percent.
- *Hewlett-Packard.* HP reduced the production space for a printer line from 10,000 square feet to 2,500 square feet. Product failures dropped 21 percent. The company also reduced inventory by 60 to 80 percent, cut product lead time (the time between the beginning and end of a process) by more than 50 percent, reduced floor space by 30 to 50 percent, and cut labor cost by 20 to 50 percent. Inventory turns went from 7.5 to 45.6 in nine months.
- *Cincinnati Milacron.* The Electronic Systems Division trimmed inventory by 60 percent, reduced lead time from 12 weeks to 4 weeks, reduced manufacturing costs by 24 percent, and lowered the cost of quality from 19 percent to 14 percent.
- *General Motors.* In GM's Bay City, Michigan plant of 1,850 employees, quality is up. Productivity is up 24 percent over 18 months. Customer-reported problems with the plant's products have been reduced by 54 percent, and the cost of making the products is 15 percent less. Absenteeism is 35 percent less than GM's corporate average.

Examples from almost every sector of Europe can also be cited. The following are some of the European companies that have attained WCM status:

- *Olivetti.* This typewriter manufacturer has reduced lead time from 20 days to 3 days.
- *Michelin.* This maker of tires has reduced setup time by 90 percent.
- *Farmitalia Carlo Erba.* This large pharmaceutical enterprise has reduced WIP inventory by 60 percent.

▌WHAT ARE THE CHARACTERISTICS OF WORLD-CLASS MANUFACTURING?

<table>
<tr><td>

Chapter 1 introduced seven trends in modern manufacturing environments:

- High quality
- Customer service
- Low inventory
- Flexibility
- Automation
- Team concept
- Integrated computer-based information systems (ICBISs)

</td><td>

LEARNING OBJECTIVE 3

List and describe the characteristics of WCM.

</td></tr>
</table>

These trends are also the characteristics of WCM, as Exhibit 2–3 shows. As modern manufacturers are discovering, they must aggressively pursue these characteristics if they are to achieve WCM status.

INSIGHTS & APPLICATIONS

Multinational Business: Ordering from the Japanese

For years, Generic Computer Company, a U.S. manufacturer of microcomputers, suffered from faulty components purchased from its suppliers. Ms. Peters, who just replaced the old purchasing manager, decided to switch to Gem Processing, a Japanese producer of computer chips. A little worried about their quality, she specified that defects must be limited to 1 percent of the quantity shipped.

When Gem Processing received its first order for 50,000 chips, the sales manager was very confused. The company strictly enforced its policy of "zero defects." But not wanting to offend his new American customer, the manager shipped 50,000 good chips in one box and 500 broken chips in another!

▌Achieving High Quality

Customers are demanding higher and higher quality. Those companies that can't or won't provide this quality will be out of business. When quality goes up, lead times go down, factors of production are more efficient, and waste is reduced, causing costs to drop, all at the same time. Quality is the number one priority and is practiced by everyone connected with the enterprise including top management, workers, and vendors. The aim is to make products right the first time and thus achieve zero defects. This eliminates the associated costs of scrap, rework, inspection, returns, and other costs of inadequate quality control. According to a WCM axiom, "Poor quality always costs something because if you don't do it right the first time you're going to have to do it over, and doing it over is more costly than doing it right the first time."

> There is an old cost axiom: The low quality producer is the low cost producer. The corollary is: The high quality producer is the high cost producer. The reason for this axiom is that we have accepted defects as a way of life.

▬ EXHIBIT 2–3
Characteristics of World-Class Manufacturing (WCM)

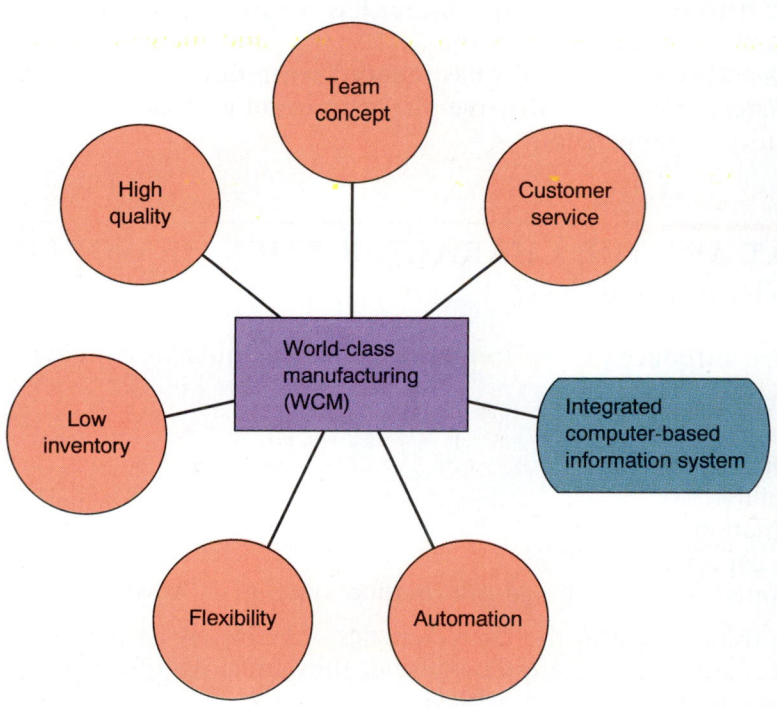

INSIGHTS & APPLICATIONS

Penny Wise and Pound Foolish

At Kadiddlehoppers, a shoe manufacturing company, productivity dropped like a rock through a wet cobweb. Shoes were sewn together, but it took an enormous quantity of thread and time. Eventually, things got so bad that a consultant was called in.

The consultant actually went down on the shop floor, unlike traditional accountants and managers (sorry for the sarcasm, but it's warranted), and asked the workers what went wrong. Sewing machine operators said the thread kept breaking, so they spent half their day rethreading the machines.

Some time earlier, a purchasing agent found a company that would sell thread a penny a bobbin cheaper than their regular supplier, and to save that penny a bobbin, the company's productivity was cut in half, not to mention the quality of the shoes.[6]

So to improve the quality of finished goods, we added product inspectors to the process. With that added cost, we could catch the defects and send them back for rework.

A good Japanese company designs a product for final production with high quality. They incur the costs up front in exhaustively designing the product and process. Once that product is released to the shop floor, there are no engineering changes and few, if any, process changes. There is little cost for warranty repairs or defects.[7]

In WCM enterprises, active quality control programs are pervasive. Quality-oriented charts, banners, posters, and slogans, such as "Quality Is Job One," abound.[8] In some plants, such as pharmaceutical companies, 100 percent quality is a given condition of doing business.[9]

The Japanese approach to achieving high quality and zero defects is that a discovered defect is a "gem." Their philosophy is that a defect didn't just happen. There is a cause and the defect can lead to the cause, which in turn can be eliminated. This insistence on ferreting out and eliminating causes of defects is based on the Japanese philosophy to "pursue the last grain of rice in the lunchbox."[10]

The road to high quality starts with vendors of raw materials. Building a long-term partnership with vendors of raw materials is a key to another axiom: "Good input produces good output, cuts costs, and increases productivity." More and more companies are hearing statements such as "Prices are only one component of total procurement costs, and the best prices often become the worst costs."

Careful supplier selection and certification and strong vendor relationships ensure that raw materials will be of highest quality. Selection and performance criteria include on-time deliveries, price competitiveness, and high quality. When these criteria are satisfied, little formal monitoring of vendor performance is needed, further reducing raw materials costs.[11]

---

[6] Adapted from an actual experience of Dr. W. Edwards (Ed) Deming while doing consulting work. The words are those of Dr. Deming; however, the name of the company is fictitious.

[7] Robert D'Amore, "Just-in-Time Systems," in *Cost Accounting, Robotics, and the New Manufacturing Environment*, ed. Robert Capettini and Donald K. Clancy (Sarasota, Fla.: American Accounting Association, 1988), p. 8.8.

[8] Allen H. Seed III, *Adapting Management Accounting Practice to an Advanced Manufacturing Environment* (Montvale, N.J.: Institute of Management Accountants, formerly the National Association of Accountants, 1988), p. 13. With permission.

[9] Ibid.

[10] Robert H. Hayes, "Why Japanese Factories Work," *Harvard Business Review*, July-August 1981, p. 61.

[11] C. J. McNair, William Mosconi, and Thomas Norris, *Meeting the Technology Challenge: Cost Accounting in a JIT Environment* (Montvale, N.J.: Institute of Management Accountants, formerly the National Association of Accountants, 1988), p. 67. With permission.

INSIGHTS & APPLICATIONS

Visual Controls and Mistake Proofing

Honda rejects only about one in 10,000 car seats it receives from Setex. Visual controls and simple *poka-yoke* (mistake proofing) devices help Setex prevent errors and assure that Honda gets the right number of defect-free seats on time.

Setex builds in lots of 30 and produces four lots, or 120 car seats, every eight hours. An electronic scoreboard automatically counts the number of seats in the shipment rack and informs shop-floor workers where they stand.

At one station, the jig won't release the seat frame until bolts are torqued down to the right specs. In the robotic welding area, if parts are loaded incorrectly onto the jig, the robot won't function.

In another mistake-proofing step, lights attached to eye sensors tip off operators if bolts are not torqued down properly to meet four different requirements for Japanese, American, European, and Canadian models. "This is not nonvalue-added inspection," operations manager Brian Briars insists. "It's in-process mistake-proofing."

At the final material-handling robot, a "cat whisker" (a thin sensor wire) detects the presence, absence or mislocation of a pivot nut used to attach the seat to the car. Seats without the nut don't get shipped.

Setex has borrowed many of its visual control and mistake-proofing ideas from Honda. "We still have lots to learn," says Briars. In fact, Honda and Setex are putting their heads together to design a non-destructive video imaging test for weld strength.[12]

Achieving Customer Service

The customer is the final judge as to whether or not a manufacturer has attained WCM status. Customers are the most important people for the enterprise. Obviously, they have a number of needs, or customer service factors, that must be satisfied. Some of the more significant factors are:

- Delivery of the right product in the right amount at the right time
- Product performance (doing what it is supposed to do)
- Product reliability
- Variety of product features
- Serviceability of the product
- Promptness and willingness to help customers

All WCM enterprises are market driven. They stay close to the customers to maintain a high level of customer service. In today's global market, unless customers are so delighted that they're not only willing to come back, but also are eager to bring their friends, the enterprise can close its doors, put up an "out-of-business" sign, and go fishing.

Achieving Low Inventory

As noted earlier, large raw materials, WIP, and finished goods inventories are a key characteristic of traditional PUSH-type batch manufacturing. In WCM environments, inventory is viewed as an evil, as something to eliminate. Inventory costs the company a lot of money and also camouflages problems. In WCM, the trend is, therefore, toward less inventory and smaller lot sizes, so as to move the product through the plant to the customer more quickly. The following are keys to achieving this WCM objective:

- For raw materials, vendors are needed who are in close proximity to the manufacturer and can make frequent deliveries of small lot sizes in standard containers with zero defects.
- For WIP, the manufacturer must produce zero defect products at high velocity and be able to make setups quickly.

[12] Brian Biars, "Flexible Manufacturing," *Productivity*, January 1992, p. 10. With permission.

Reasons for Having High Levels of Inventories	Reasons for Having Low Levels of Inventories
■ Long delay between when raw materials are ordered and delivered.	■ Raw materials arrive just at the time they are needed.
■ Vendor quality and delivery schedules force managers to order much more raw materials than are needed.	■ Vendors can be relied on to deliver quality materials in the right amount on time.
■ Inventory records are not frequently updated or are inaccurate so managers order more/less than needed.	■ All inventory transactions are processed in real-time and are accurate.
■ Hedge against future price increases and/or to take advantage of quantity discounts.	■ Raw materials prices are stable due to long-term contracts with suppliers.
■ Ordering, receiving, inspection, and/or setup costs are high.	■ Ordering, receiving, inspection, and setup costs are minimal.
■ The conversion process requires a long time.	■ Products move through the process efficiently (high-velocity production).
■ Large production volumes are needed due to poor quality (e.g., make 1,000 parts to get 800 good ones).	■ High quality results in zero defects.
■ Disruptions such as machine breakdowns or strikes are too frequent.	■ Production is not subject to disruptions.
■ Managers are rewarded for minimizing the average per unit production cost.	■ Managers are rewarded for minimizing the total costs of production throughout the plant.
■ Long delay times in delivering finished goods to customers.	■ Finished goods are delivered to customers overnight.
■ Customer demand is very uncertain.	■ Customer demand is known with a high degree of certainty.

■EXHIBIT 2–4
Reasons for Having High and Low Levels of Inventories

■ For finished goods, the manufacturer must know customer demand and be able to deliver products to customers quickly.

. . . inventories really camouflage a lot of manufacturing problems. One way we like to describe it is that inventories are evidence, and all your problems of manufacturing end up in inventory. Think about it. If you order too much, it ends up in inventory. If you've got a scheduling problem and it doesn't get fully processed, it's in your work-in-process inventory. If there are machine capacity differences within the manufacturing process, bottlenecks exist and work-in-process inventory builds in front of the bottleneck. If your customer orders don't match up with your production, it's in inventory. All your problems are in inventory.

. . . at Allen-Bradley, at the end of the day there is *no* work-in-process inventory or any finished goods inventory. The whole manufacturing process is cleared.[13]

High levels of inventory are generally traceable to poor management. Even a well-managed organization, however, normally needs some level of inventory to achieve excellent customer service and maximum operating efficiency. Only under ideal conditions would no WIP inventory be needed.[14] Exhibit 2–4 lists the reasons for having high and low levels of inventory.

Holding inventory incurs several costs including the following:

■ Cost of having money tied up in inventory. This is a cost of capital because this money could otherwise be invested in something that would generate a return to the enterprise.
■ Costs of deterioration, damage, shrinkage, spoilage, and obsolescence.
■ Costs of storage and handling.
■ Insurance premiums for the policies that are directly related to the value of the inventory.
■ Taxes assessed based on the value of the inventory.[15]

[13] Robert A. Howell, "World Class Manufacturing Controls: Management Accounting for the Factory of the Future," in *Cost Accounting, Robotics, and the New Manufacturing Environment,* ed. Robert Capettini and Donald K. Clancy, (Sarasota, Fla.: American Accounting Association, 1988), pp. 2.4 and 2.5.
[14] Charles D. Mecimore and James K. Weeks, *Techniques in Inventory Management and Control* (Montvale, N.J.: Institute of Management Accountants, formerly the National Association of Accountants, 1987), p. 9. With permission.
[15] Ibid., pp. 11–12.

Costs of not having finished goods inventory available when it is needed, or WIP to meet production schedules, are called **stockout costs** and include:

- Costs due to customers' ill will
- Costs of back ordering and special handling
- Costs incurred because of idle production capacity and schedule disruptions[16]

According to many accounting authorities, however, the main reason some manufacturers produce large quantities is because the financial accounting system makes management look very good to stockholders and creditors. Having high levels in the three inventories on the balance sheet (raw materials, WIP, and finished goods) increases assets. Moreover, the more finished goods produced, the less their per unit cost, and the greater the gross margin on the income statement. The better the financial statements look, the better management looks—at least in the stockholders' eyes.

Achieving Flexibility

Flexibility is the ability to be responsive to changing conditions. WCM environments provide the ability for both workers and equipment to meet changing customer demands. Setup times for machinery may be measured in minutes, whereas in traditional plants, days or weeks may be required. Customers want greater variety in products *and* want these products faster. Indeed, the rate of new product introduction has increased as product life cycles have shortened. The old Ford Model T assembly line approach was, "you can have it in any kind of color you want just as long as it's black." That approach is not competitive in today's market. More sophisticated consumers throughout the world expect products to be tailored to their specific needs. WCM enterprises are using flexible equipment and reducing setup times and lot sizes.

> . . . at Nissan, they take only 15 minutes to change the tools on a 3,200 ton press that bangs out steel parts. . . . In an older U.S. plant, it probably would have taken 4, 6, or 8 hours to change over that size press. . . . In terms of paint lines, they are able to make paint color changes in 15 seconds. . . . Think about that—a car that comes down the line; you want it red. The next one comes down the line behind it, and you want it blue. . . . They can do that.[17]

Underlying flexibility is reduction in **lead times,** or the time it takes to convert raw materials into finished goods. Reducing lead times allows the manufacturer to offer a variety of products and to deliver them to customers quicker. In service organizations, insurance companies are seeking ways to shorten the underwriting process, while banks are reducing the hours spent in the loan approval process. Reductions in lead time also lessen the risk that the product will be obsolete by the time it reaches the market. The corresponding reduction in WIP inventories means that the company can be more responsive to its customers and the market as a whole.

To achieve greater flexibility and reduction in manufacturing lead time, WCM organizations are changing their plant layouts. Most manufacturing plants have evolved in a piecemeal fashion. They also are predominantly organized by function (e.g., drilling, milling, finishing), resulting in a manufacturing flow that resembles a complicated maze. WCM enterprises are putting more emphasis on how products flow through the plant rather than thinking in terms of functional departments.

The mushroom concept also adds substantially to flexibility. The **mushroom concept** keeps processes and products standardized for as long as possible, creating a product structure that is diversified only at the final production stage. Rather than having specific subassemblies for specific products, subassemblies

---

[16] Ibid., p. 12.
[17] Howell, op. cit., p. 2.6.

"Hey look, I'd like to walk this plant. I'd like to start at the beginning where you bring in the raw material and walk through to the finished goods and the shipping dock."

They say, "Bob, you can't do that, it would take us all day."

"The product goes around and around, maybe it goes upstairs and downstairs, maybe it goes to another building (maybe the other building is across town) and then comes back into the first building.

"I can't get it in my head how it all works. Well, if I can't get it in my head while we're walking through, think about the people who are working there. Think about all the material that's moving from one location to another. It resembles a snake twisting back and forth, up and down."[18]

(and processes) are designed so they can be used in a larger variety of finished products. The goal is "all-purpose" subassemblies that can be used for many products. The result is that lead time for any given product can be reduced to the amount of time necessary for completing final assembly. The mushroom concept is presented in Exhibit 2–5.

Using Automation

Motorola's "Bandit" facility in Boca Raton, Florida, uses automation to produce a wide variety of pagers on demand. Benetton, the Italian sportswear company, has not only automated the knitting process, but also integrated its entire supply chain—from raw materials through the retail outlets that sell its wares. By doing so, it is able to respond rapidly to changing demands all over the world.[19]

More and more manufacturers are automating every day so they can achieve high quality, deliver customized products on time, minimize inventory, and increase flexibility. One of the most obvious characteristics of the WCM era is

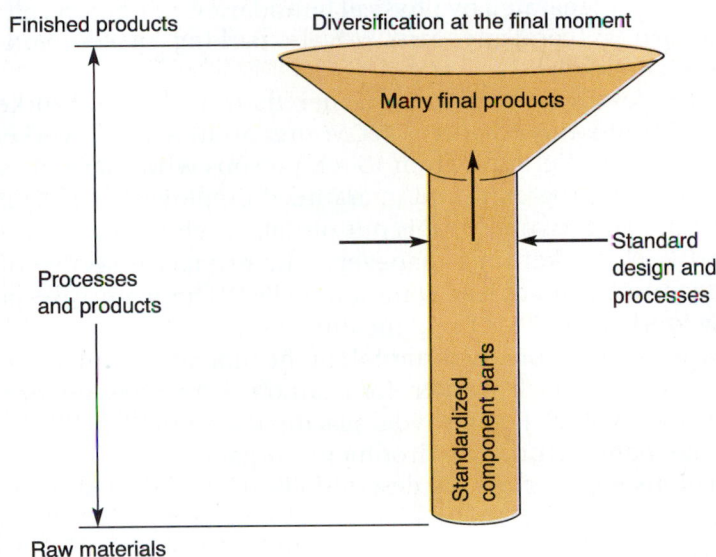

EXHIBIT 2–5

Structure of the Mushroom Concept

Adapted from: Giorgio Merli, *Total Manufacturing Management: Production Organization for the 1990s* (Cambridge, Mass.: Productivity Press, 1990), p. 240. With permission.

[18] Ibid., p. 2.6.
[19] Patricia E. Moody, ed., *Strategic Manufacturing: Dynamic New Directions for the 1990s* (Homewood, Ill.: Richard D. Irwin, 1990), p. 119.

INSIGHTS & APPLICATIONS

Just Like Baseball

In baseball, if the shortstop lets the ball go through his legs, typically the center fielder picks it up. He does not say, "If the shortstop messes up, I am not going to get the ball."

Running WCM factories is like running a baseball team. If an area is having a problem, we want the flexible work force to go in and fix the problem in order to keep the product flowing and achieve customer satisfaction.[20]

---

less direct labor, which is the result of both automation and the effort to use people's brains as well as their muscles. On the other hand, indirect labor has increased mostly to support the automated, technological environment.

Creating a Team Concept

In WCM, people are paid according to the number of tasks they can perform, rather than by their seniority or the number of parts they make. Master workers can perform every job. The more flexibility in the work force, the easier it is to move people around and handle bottlenecks.[21] For example, a worker at Nucor Steel may operate a crane today and a rolling mill tomorrow.

With the team concept, no one gets credit for producing finished goods until customers receive the products and are satisfied. The team concept discourages suboptimal behavior. The manufacturer does not want workers in one department producing a lot of unneeded parts just to make themselves look good.

Indeed, WCM organizations are managed differently from traditional organizations. In fact, installation of the team concept is considered a fundamental requirement for changing to a WCM organization. Autocratic management is out; participative management is in. The old-style foreman, who sat in a glass office and was master of the area surveyed (the "boss"), has given way to the foreman as team leader, coach, and facilitator. In some WCM enterprises, it is difficult to determine where the office ends and the factory begins, as managers and workers are not separated by physical boundaries.[22] Similarly, all traditional distinctions, such as company cars, private parking spaces, and executive restrooms, are eliminated.

Workers are viewed as a resource rather than as a cost. Workers *are* the company. To harness this resource, WCM organizations use worker-manager teams, quality circles (a group of four to ten persons who share the same work area), incentive pay programs, and guaranteed employment policies. Increasingly, the entire plant's work force is put on salary, eliminating a fundamental difference between workers and managers. The primary objective of all of this is to foster teamwork to achieve common goals.[23] The team is responsible for training new workers and for firing incompetents.

Although the team is more important than the individual, individual responsibility is still important. Each worker, for example, is responsible for the quality of his or her own work.[24] People avoid placing blame on others.

In traditional manufacturing environments, organization charts depict "pyramids" of positions with precise job descriptions at each level and large bureau-

[20] D'Amore, op. cit., p. 8.22.
[21] Ibid., p. 8.27.
[22] Seed, op. cit., p. 17.
[23] Ibid.
[24] Ibid.

INSIGHTS & APPLICATIONS

Rewards Drive Actions

Management needs to promote a company perspective rather than a departmental perspective. Everyone should be focused on profits in the broadest sense, and not on expenses. If the maintenance department thinks they have to work overtime to get a piece of equipment fixed, but that piece of equipme[nt] to the operation and, therefore, will get th[e] back on line, they'll spend the money and w[ill] "bat an eyelash." But if they look at their expen[se] [b]udget, and that's going to cause them to go into the red, and their boss is going to climb all over their backs for spending too much, then they're not going to work that overtime. People select an action because of the reward system in place. If the reward system is based on budget performance only, the system will yield dysfunctional results.[25]

---

cracies, as shown in Exhibit 2–6a. There is a sharp demarcation between line employees who are directly responsible for achieving an organization's goals and objectives and staff employees responsible for providing advice, guidance, and service to line employees. Boundaries between departments are precise, and management is exercised by authoritative levels and rules.

The preceding description of organizational structure is anathema to WCM. The pyramid is turned upside down as shown in Exhibit 2–6b. In a WCM environment, classical organization charts found in traditional management textbooks are irrelevant because the emphasis is not on boundaries between functions, job descriptions, and organizational levels. The idea is that *"many small brains used properly are better than a few large brains."* Line and staff functions tend to merge together, management hierarchies are flattened, and management is generally by consensus.

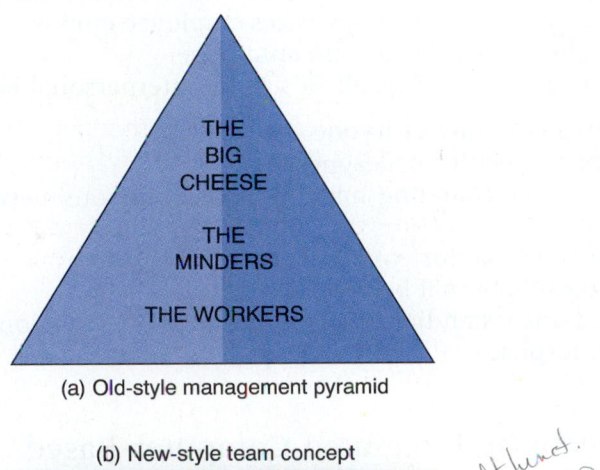

(a) Old-style management pyramid

(b) New-style team concept

■ EXHIBIT 2–6
The Old-Style Management Pyramid and the New Team Concept

Adapted from: Mark Louis Smith, "Production Planning Simplicity," in *Strategic Manufacturing: Dynamic New Directions for the 1990s,* ed. Patricia E. Moody (Homewood, Ill.: Business ONE Irwin, 1990), p. 256.

[25] Howell, op. cit., pp. 2.15 and 2.16.

INSIGHTS & APPLICATIONS

Turning the Pyramid Upside Down

Use a "reverse pyramid" organization chart, with front-line people "on top" and supervisors and middle managers (minders) below them in a support-and-facilitator role. The principal challenge is to empower people to take new initiatives. Dramatically shift reward and evaluation systems for middle managers in order to emphasize "making things happen" across formerly sacred functional boundaries. Middle managers are to be responsible for seeking out and battering down the very functional barriers that they were formerly paid to protect.[26]

A model for the team concept involves seven stages:

- *Orientation*. The team purpose and mandate are spelled out.
- *Trust building*. Rapport between team members is established and cultivated.
- *Goal and role clarification*. What each team member is to do is defined.
- *Commitment*. Necessary resources and tools are made available to team members so they can get the job done.
- *Implementation*. A schedule is prepared showing when activities must be performed.
- *High performance*. The work on activities is performed at maximum efficiency.
- *Renewal*. An effective and smooth transition is made from one project to another.[27]

The first four stages are the "creating stages." The last three stages are the "sustaining stages." The team concept requires large doses of communication, encourages meetings, and emphasizes employee empowerment. Employees call meetings. They virtually run the enterprise.

The team concept can result in several interpersonal benefits:

- Full participation by everyone
- Increased respect for colleagues
- Increased understanding and improved relations between employees and managers
- Reduced potential for conflict between work areas
- Decreased suboptimal behavior
- Increased understanding by everyone about the mission, goals, and strategies of the enterprise

Implementing Integrated Computer-Based Information Systems

Integrated computer-based information systems (ICBISs) connect information technology, including computers, software, and telecommunications, throughout the enterprise to gather data online and process it into relevant information for internal users in real-time. ICBISs are also used by financial accounting for transaction processing and for external reporting.

---

[26] From *Thriving on Chaos* by Tom Peters, copyright © 1987 by Excel, a California Limited Partnership. Reprinted by permission of Alfred A. Knopf, Inc., pp. 440, 442.

[27] R. Johansen, D. Sibbet, S. Benson, A. Martin, R. Mittman, and P. Saffo, *Leading Business Teams: How Teams Can Use Technology and Group Process Tools to Enhance Performance* (Reading, Mass.: Addison-Wesley, 1991), p. 216.

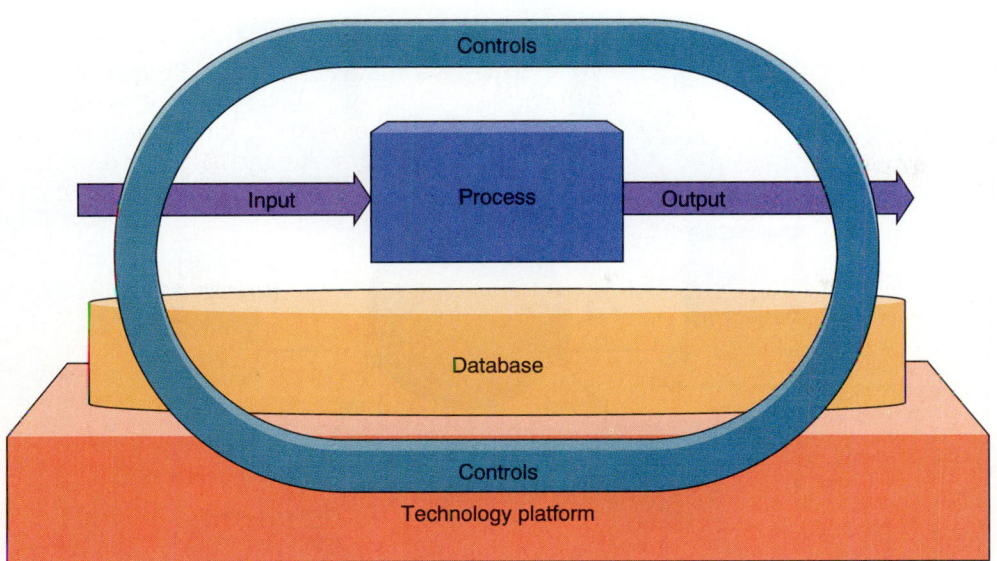

■■■ EXHIBIT 2–7
Components of an Integrated Computer-Based Information System (ICBIS)

OVERVIEW OF ICBISs.   ICBISs have six components:

■ Input
■ Process
■ Output
■ Database
■ Controls
■ Technology platform

Exhibit 2–7 shows how these components interrelate.

Input enters the data to be processed. The **process** component manipulates the data in accordance with accounting and operational procedures. **Output** is the information disseminated to internal and external users via printers, video screens, or electronic data interchange (discussed in the next chapter). The **database** is the repository of financial and management accounting and operational data stored on magnetic disk, optical disk, or magnetic tape. **Controls** are those physical devices and procedures that safeguard the information system from destruction, interruption, fraud, and inaccuracies. The **technology platform** supports the foregoing five components.

HOW TO PUT IT ALL TOGETHER TO FORM AN ICBIS.   If the entire telecommunications network is in the same room or building, it is commonly called a **local area network (LAN),** as illustrated in Exhibit 2–8. Typical hardware devices connected to form the LAN are workstations, printers, and magnetic disks containing accounting data.

If computer devices, such as microcomputers, minicomputers, mainframes, printers, and auxiliary storage devices, are distributed throughout a large area, possibly throughout the country or internationally, the network is termed a **wide area network (WAN).** Multinational enterprises typically need LANs connected together to form a WAN.

For example, assume that the WAN in Exhibit 2–9 is for Module Manufacturing Company's ICBIS. The company's corporate headquarters is located in Cleveland, Ohio. Part of the headquarters building is occupied by financial accounting, supported by LAN 1. Large amounts of both financial and management accounting data are transmitted to administration's LAN 2, which processes these data into long-range strategic planning information. Management accounting, through LAN 4, interacts with manufacturing personnel, supported

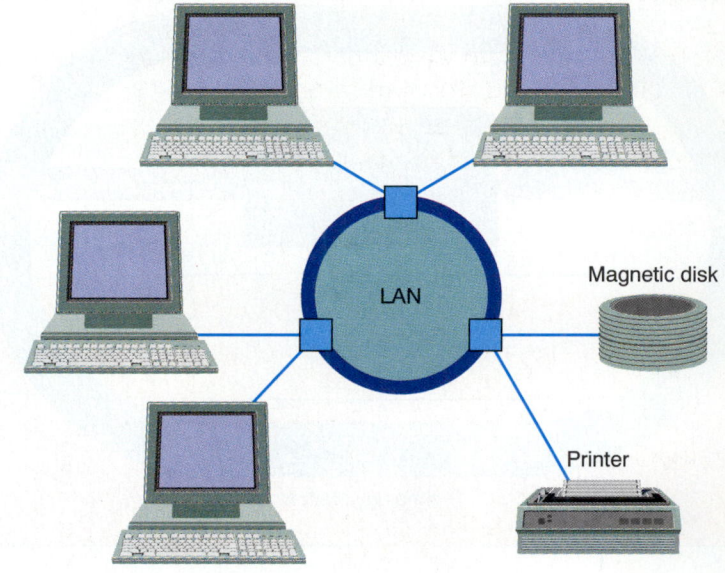

by LAN 3. Both of these LANs are located in Module's factory in Dallas, Texas. Management accounting also transmits manufacturing data to financial accounting's LAN. Financial accounting uses these and other manufacturing data to prepare various financial reports.

Various transmission media permit these LANs to be interconnected so that all areas of the company can communicate with each other and share computing resources. For example, LAN 1 and LAN 2 may be connected by telephone twisted pair wire. LANs 1 and 2 may be linked to LANs 3 and 4 by satellite. And, finally, LANs 3 and 4 may be linked by fiber optic cable. Today, many companies are developing ICBISs similar to the one used by Module Manufacturing Company.

The preceding characteristics are found in WCM environments. But WCM is not a project that ends at some point. It is a commitment by everyone in the organization, from top management to the workers on the shop floor, to a never-ending process of continuous improvement. It is truly an evolutionary journey rather than a revolutionary one, and no standard blueprint is available to implement it. Over and above any other factor, WCM implementation is dependent on the reeducation and rededication of people. People must learn a different pattern of thinking; in the process, all of them, including management accountants, will gain the confidence to implement new methods in their daily work. The commitment to these human factors and to WCM as a whole must clearly come from the highest levels of management.

<table>
<tr><td>

LEARNING OBJECTIVE 4
—

Describe just-in-time (JIT) manufacturing and computer-integrated manufacturing (CIM).

</td></tr>
</table>

▌JUST-IN-TIME MANUFACTURING

To achieve WCM status, many believe the production process must be redesigned as a JIT. Frequently called the "Toyota production system," **just-in-time (JIT) manufacturing** is a PULL-THROUGH system of production unlike the traditional batch manufacturing PUSH-THROUGH system. The JIT manufacturing system is a continuous, synchronized production flow process that can be compared to a pipeline, as depicted in Exhibit 2–10.

Unlike the PUSH manufacturing pipeline illustrated earlier in Exhibit 2–2, JIT can be viewed as a vacuum pipeline, or a PULL system; that is, products are made in response to downstream (end of the line) needs. As products are withdrawn at the finished goods end of the pipeline, raw materials are input

■ EXHIBIT 2–9
**Wide Area Network (WAN) for Module Manufacturing Company's
Integrated Computer-Based Information System (ICBIS)**

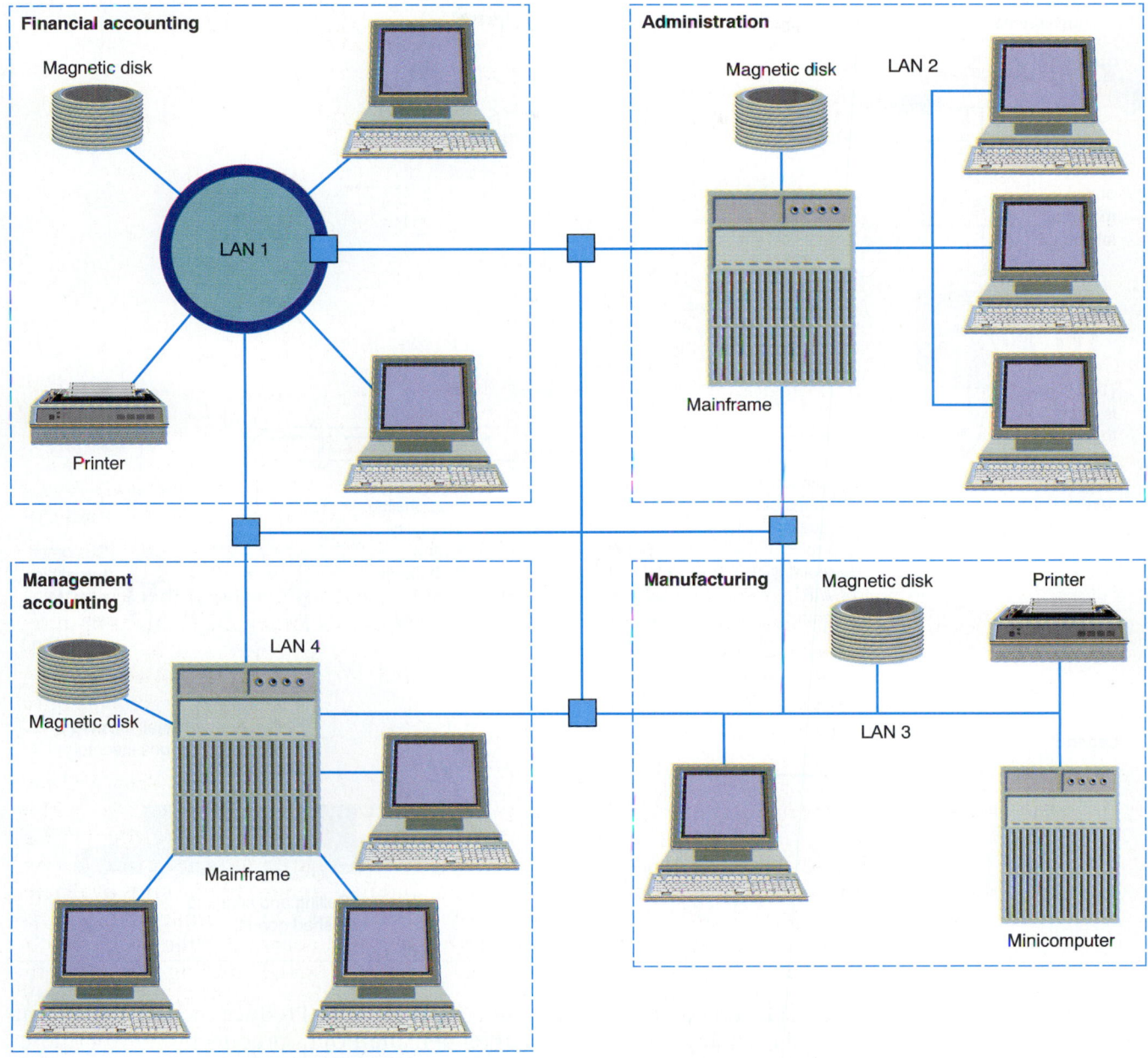

and drawn through the pipeline in a synchronized conversion process. Unlike traditional batch manufacturing systems in which products are based on a planned schedule and PUSHed downstream, JIT is based on the PULL of downstream operations.[28]

JIT manufacturing is dedicated to eliminating waste and producing the right products at the right time, as they are needed, rather than when they can be made.[29] In a JIT manufacturing system, production equals sales to the greatest extent possible; that is, products are not produced until they can be sold. The

[28] Mecimore and Weeks, op. cit., p. 133.
[29] McNair, Mosconi, and Norris, op. cit., (1988), pp. xiii and xiv.

■ **EXHIBIT 2–10**
Just-in-Time (JIT) Manufacturing System

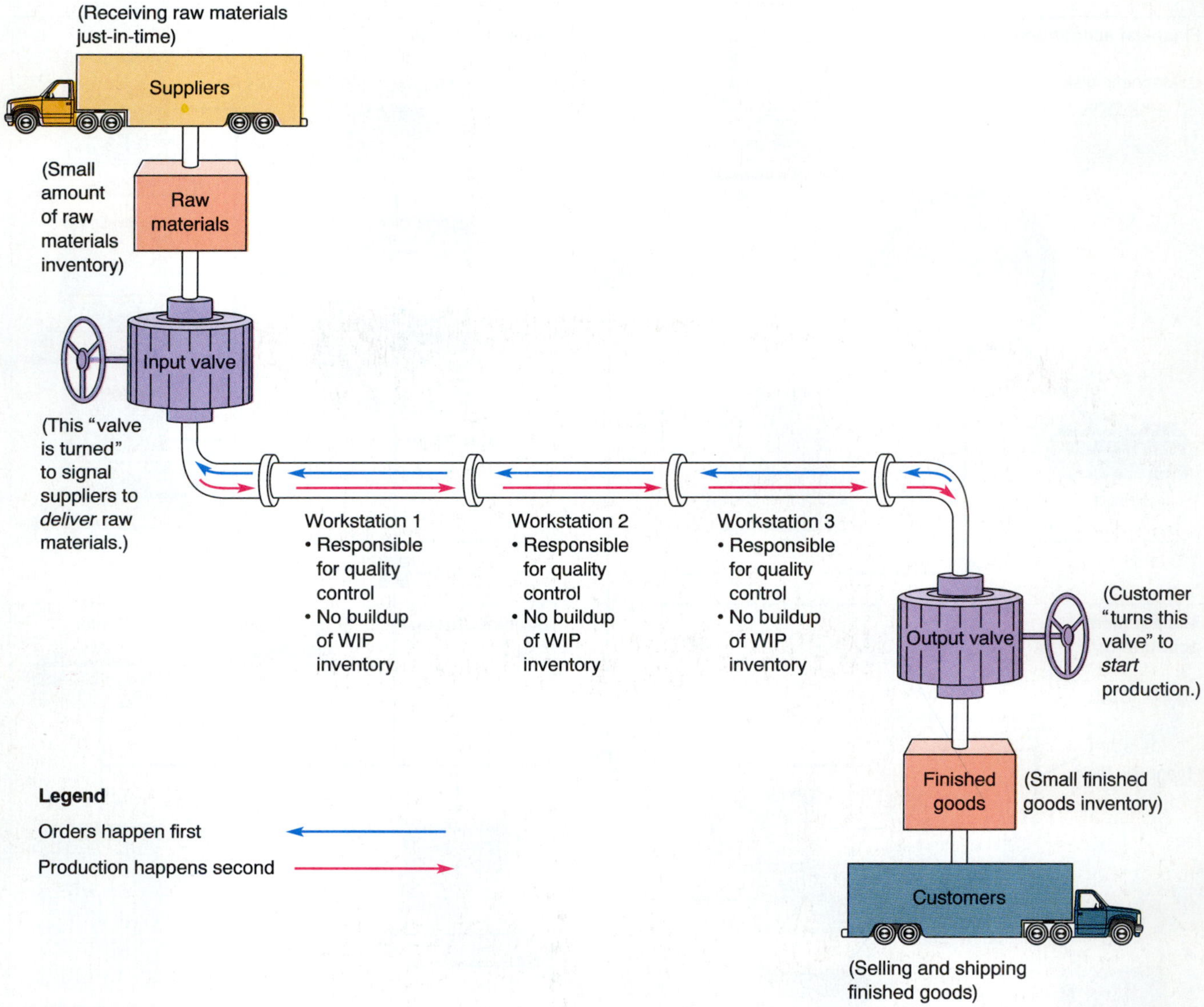

(Receiving raw materials just-in-time)

Suppliers

(Small amount of raw materials inventory)

Raw materials

Input valve

(This "valve is turned" to signal suppliers to *deliver* raw materials.)

Workstation 1
• Responsible for quality control
• No buildup of WIP inventory

Workstation 2
• Responsible for quality control
• No buildup of WIP inventory

Workstation 3
• Responsible for quality control
• No buildup of WIP inventory

Output valve

(Customer "turns this valve" to *start* production.)

Finished goods

(Small finished goods inventory)

Customers

(Selling and shipping finished goods)

Legend

Orders happen first ⟵

Production happens second ⟶

idea is: If you don't need it now, don't make it now. Produce each day only what is sold each day. In this way, market demand PULLs production. Furthermore, suppliers deliver small batches of raw materials, sometimes directly to the appropriate department just-in-time, or right-on-time, to meet production demands. These techniques reduce the need for expediters, dispatchers, inventory control people, large factory floor space, and warehouses. This approach results in lower raw materials, WIP, and finished goods inventories.

JIT manufacturing has been called a journey of continuous improvement— a management philosophy of doing business. JIT is, indeed, a journey that pursues seven objectives:

- Synchronized operations
- Zero inventories
- Zero setup time
- Zero lead time
- Zero defects
- Visual factory
- Computer-integrated manufacturing (CIM)

JIT Manufacturing at Honda.

No-Excuse Delivery

A visitor was touring a Toyota plant in Japan. The visitor watched as a worker opened a loading dock door to reveal a parked truck loaded with transmissions that were taken directly to the assembly line. Knowing that parts arrived on a tight schedule, the visitor asked his guide what would happen if the truck were late.

"Door open, truck there," the guide said.
"Suppose the truck broke down?" asked the visitor.
"Door open, truck there," the guide said.
"Suppose there is a traffic jam?" asked the visitor.
"Door open, truck there," the guide said.
The lesson soon learned by the visitor is that it is the vendor's duty to make sure the transmissions are there when needed.

▌Pursuing Synchronized Operations

Synchronized operations exist when input equals output, and tasks are coordinated, or synchronized, to the rate that finished goods are withdrawn at the end of the pipeline. For example, today's demand is 1,000 units. The first operation in production makes 1,000 units, and the last operation makes 1,000.

Vendors (or suppliers) play an important role in synchronized operations, because they are an integral part of the production process. In traditional PUSH systems, vendors are often given "freedom of the week" to make deliveries. If raw materials arrive sometime between Monday morning and Friday afternoon, they are counted as "on time." JIT has radically altered purchasing's notion of on-time delivery. Vendors are given the precise time *during a specific day* in which to show up. Early deliveries are penalized as much as late deliveries. The Honda plant in Marysville, Ohio, keeps *three hours* of raw materials on hand. The on-time delivery window at Toyota's assembly plant in Georgetown, Kentucky, is *one hour*.[30]

Physical layouts of plants also are changed to support a continuous, synchronized process. More and more support areas and people, such as purchasing, maintenance, engineering, and management accounting, are being moved out of remote offices and integrated into the production process on the factory floor. A total team approach is fostered.

The principle of synchronized operations is the foundation upon which JIT manufacturing systems are built. Grouping a variety of machines in the sequence required to make the product, and flowing one product at a time through them, is a major change in manufacturing philosophy. This new approach has made the old "one process" department found in traditional batch manufacturing systems practically obsolete. No longer are all of the punch presses in the punch press department, all of the lathes in the lathe department, and all of the milling machines in the milling department. Instead, these departments are replaced by a mixed lineup, usually U-shaped, of machines forming a workcenter. These U-shaped workcenters are often called "cells."

Exhibit 2–11 illustrates the difference between the traditional process and **cellular manufacturing,** also called "group technology." It is an often-used configuration in computer-integrated manufacturing (CIM). Cellular manufacturing uses a miniproduction line, usually conceptualized as a U-shaped loop (although it can take on any basic configuration). The main objective of cellular manufacturing is to minimize wait and move time by arranging machines sequentially. Two significant features of cellular manufacturing are:

- Production families
- Cross training

Manufacturing cell at Outboard Marine.

[30] Ernest Raia, "JIT Delivery: Redefining 'On-time,'" *Purchasing*, September 13, 1990, pp. 67–68.

■■■ EXHIBIT 2–11

Comparison between a Straight Production Line and a U-Shaped Production Cell

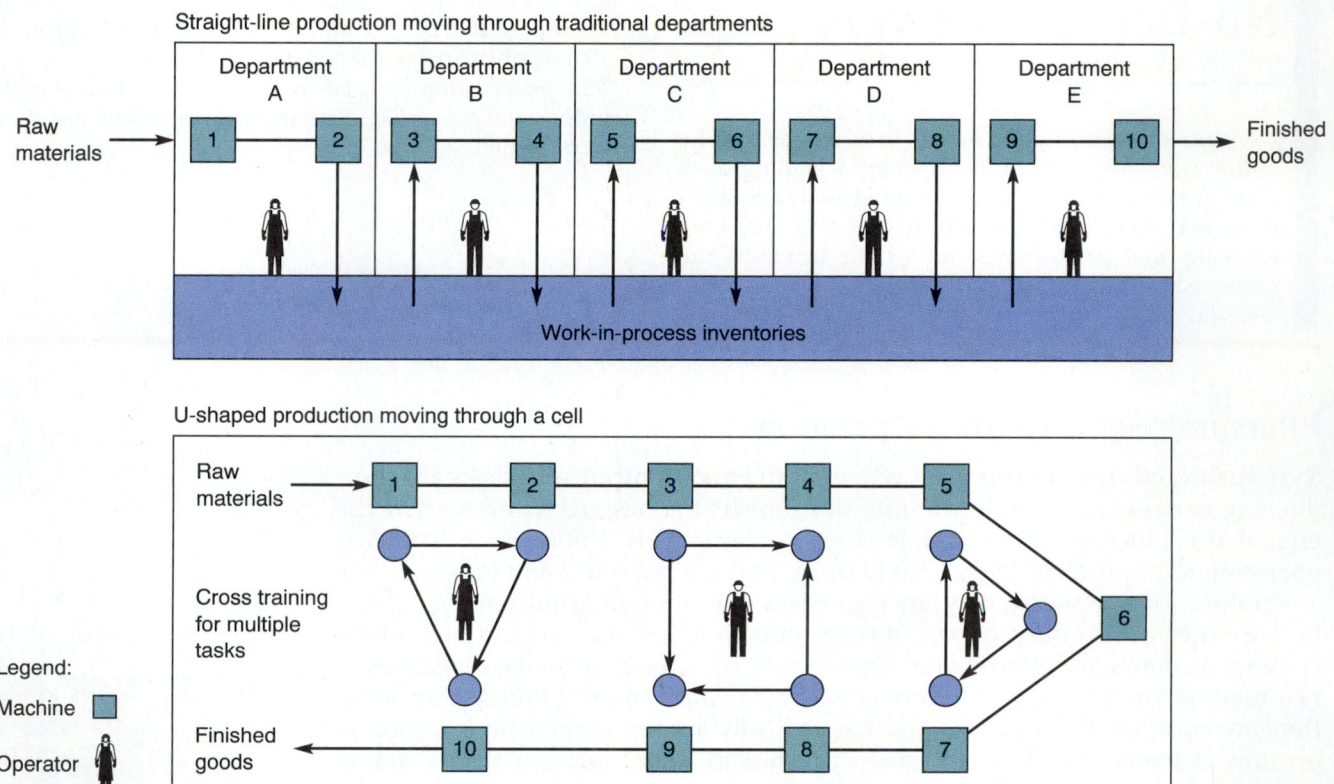

In a manufacturing plant that makes hundreds of different products, these products are divided into production families. Each **production family** follows the same production flow path of a particular synchronized manufacturing cell. One family's path may go from blanking to grinding to drilling to painting through a U-shaped loop that contains computer-controlled process-to-process devices that perform these tasks. The result is a miniproduction line for a specific family of products, as shown in Exhibit 2–12.

Cellular manufacturing often requires **cross training** of workers so they can perform a variety of tasks within the manufacturing cell. The company's pay structure for its production personnel can be used to motivate workers to take on additional training. A worker's pay level, for example, could be tied to the number of different tasks she is trained and certified to perform. Moreover, because workers are responsible for more things, they are less likely to be bored than workers in traditional plants who perform single-task work that is narrowly focused and repetitive. Cross training may therefore provide higher job satisfaction.

Cross training also provides production management with increased flexibility in the event of an absence, because another employee can fill in for the absent worker. This flexibility in staffing is extremely important to both CIM and JIT systems, where the lack of WIP inventories can quickly bring the production line to a halt in the event of a missing worker.

When it is technologically feasible to do so, it is advisable to create U-shaped production lines rather than the straight lines typically used by PUSH-type manufacturers. The U-shaped production line offers the following advantages:

■ Shorter lead times
■ Better response time

■■■EXHIBIT 2–12
A Cellular Manufacturing Configuration for Production Families from Independent Cells

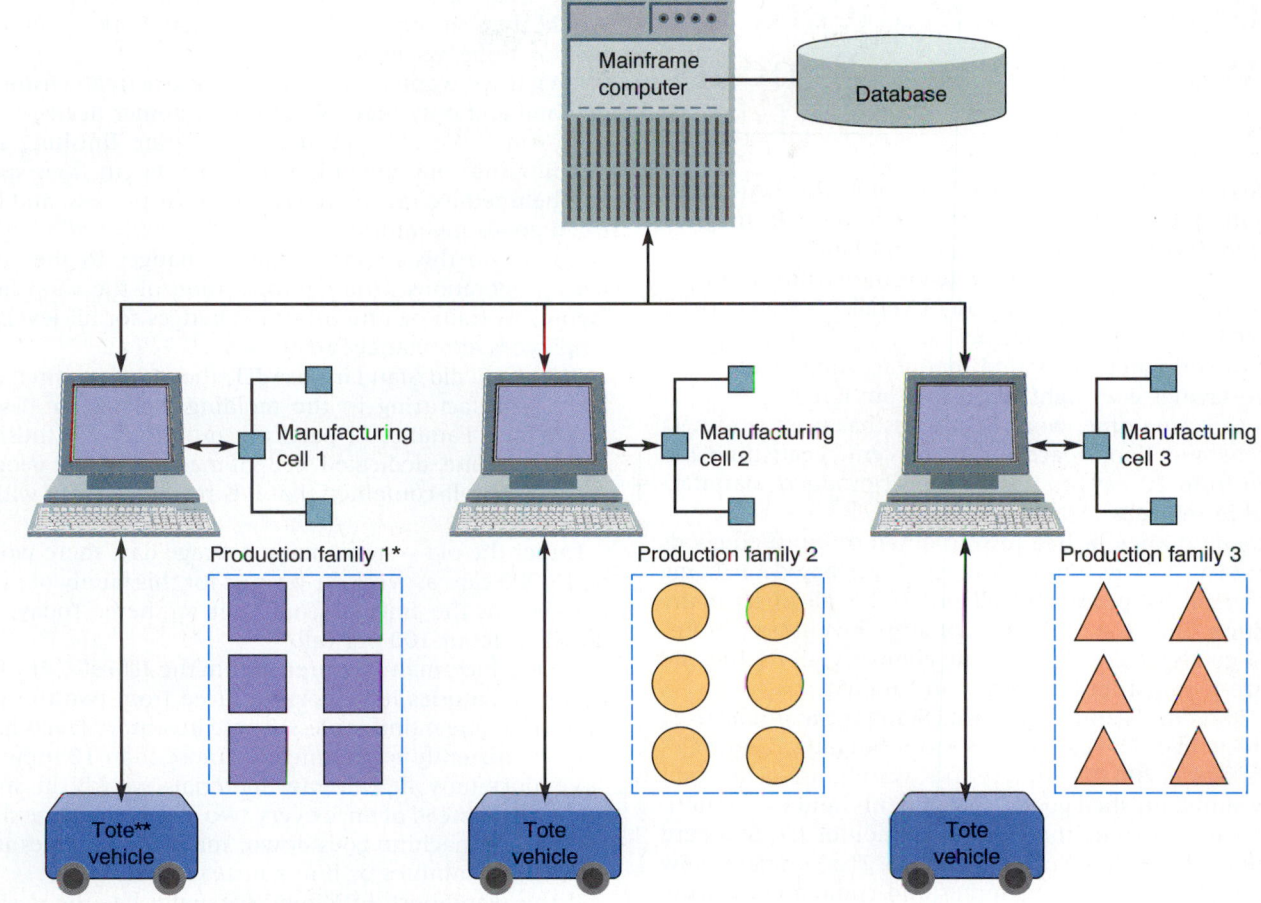

  * Representations of products in each production family
** Computer-controlled vehicles that transport raw materials to a manufacturing cell and finished goods from a manufacturing cell

- Less move time and material handling
- Minimum work-in-process inventory
- Less space
- Better coordination

The U-shaped line also has some disadvantages compared to the straight line:

- Possibility of having to increase the total number of machines
- Need for versatile personnel and cross training (some manufacturers do not consider this a disadvantage)

Usually, the advantages of the U-shaped production line decisively outweigh the disadvantages.

▎Pursuing Zero Inventories

In a traditional batch manufacturing process, large **buffers** of WIP inventories are often needed. If work stops in one department, the WIP inventory enables "downstream" departments to continue working. Thus, the WIP is said to provide a "buffer" (protection) from problems between departments.

INSIGHTS & APPLICATIONS

Becoming a Standard Way of Reaping Benefits

Standard Motor Products is reaping the benefits of introducing JIT cellular manufacturing to its molding and finishing operations in Long Island City, NY.

"We're avoiding hundreds of thousands of dollars a month in inventory costs overall for the five JIT 'cells' that we're operating," says Ray Donovan, manager of computer-integrated manufacturing at the firm. "That savings goes right to our bottom line."

At the same time, work-in-process has been cut by 94 percent and floor space by 66 percent. Lead time has fallen from 20 days to 4 days for all products manufactured in the cells.

Standard knew it had to slim down on finished goods inventory. But its reputation has been based on being able to fill 97 percent of all orders for all of its many products. But to do that, it kept large inventories in finished goods, at great cost to the company, in its 400,000 square-foot distribution center in Virginia.

In its Long Island City plant, Standard manufactured products in a 75-year-old, six-story building. Two miles away was a 200,000 square-foot warehouse. The company stored finished goods, components, and raw materials there. Following the implementation of JIT, Standard eliminated the New York warehouse. The company now makes and stores raw materials and components in the factory.

Before JIT procedures were instituted, Standard's molding facility was located in the factory's basement, while the assembly and packing operations were on the first floor. The molders would mold caps and rotors. Some went directly to the assembly and packing departments, while others were shipped to the warehouse. For those that went to the warehouse, the finisher would have to order them back when needed.

"The molders, and the finishers were not synchronized," said Donovan. The molder was manufacturing many different products. To avoid setting up a 300-ton molding machine for an order of 300 parts, he would make 3,000 parts—as much as 10 months' demand. This would then sit, unfinished, in the New York warehouse waiting to be assembled.

"What we wanted to do was work strictly to customer demand and only make what the customer needs," says Donovan. "We also wanted to integrate finishing and molding into one operation. This would cut floor space and help reduce raw materials, work-in-process, and finished goods inventories."

But to do this required radical changes in the company's operations, from configuration of the shop floor layout, to training and attitude changes for all levels of employees and management.

"Not only did Standard use JIT, they implemented cellular manufacturing in the molding department," says Donovan. "Families of parts are produced and finished entirely in one, dedicated 'cell' of machinery and people. A cell is so self-contained that it is really a factory within a factory."

Under the old system, on an average day, there would be 15,000 caps as work-in-process for this family of products before the finisher could get to them. Today, it's down to about 100 per cell.

On products manufactured within the JIT cells, finished goods inventories have been reduced from two to three months to one month or less. These inventory levels have been consistently maintained for more than 10 months.

Vendors now deliver raw materials weekly in small quantities instead of once every two months in large shipments. If a machine goes down, maintenance fixes it in a matter of minutes or hours instead of days.

If the warehouse in Virginia actually has the desired inventory level of a product and there is no customer demand, then that product will not be manufactured. Consequently, levels of inventory at that location are now beginning to be reduced.

Donovan believes any manufacturer can benefit from at least considering if JIT would help his operation. "Take a good look at your basic operation. See where the value added to a product really takes place," he says. "Then cut out the rest. That's how you save money."[31]

JIT proponents disagree with the buffer approach. They believe that the philosophy of using inventories to overcome work stoppages or defects is a way of ignoring production problems. JIT reduces inventories in order to recouple sequential workcenters into cells, forcing workers to solve problems, such as defects, as they arise. If a problem is not solved, it affects all workers, causing a large amount of disruption. In a JIT, everyone strives to eliminate problems, maintain production equipment, and increase quality to prevent a shutdown of operations.

[31] "Standard Motor Sees Big Savings with Just-in-Time Inventory," *Manufacturing Issues*, Vol. 3, No. 1, Winter 1992. © Grant Thornton, 1992, pp. 3–4. Reprinted by permission.

■ **EXHIBIT 2–13**
Kanban Card

Workcenter: Cleaning

Part number: X40C

Part name: Flange

Number of kanban
containers: 2

Container
capacity: 4 units

Preceding workcenter:

Forging

Subsequent workcenter:

Lathing

USING KANBANS TO REDUCE INVENTORIES.   **Kanban,** loosely translated from the Japanese, means "visible signal," "card," or "sign." It can be an electronic signal with a LAN. Kanban, as used in manufacturing, is an order for additional material, or a part to be produced, in either paper-based or computer-based form, sent from a using workcenter to a supplying workcenter (i.e., moving upstream). Under this PULL system, the *only* authorized production is that ordered by the kanban, as illustrated in Exhibit 2–13.

The kanban orders kanban containers to be filled. **Kanban containers** are receptacles that hold materials or parts for movement from one workcenter to another. In some plants, the kanban card is attached to the kanban container.

When all workcenters are interconnected through kanbans, PULL is created, and production is drawn "downstream" through the plant to the customer. The flow of kanbans is initiated by the last stage of the production process. In other words, nothing is made until it is needed for a specific customer order. Even the vendors are affected by the PULL, as they must deliver raw materials only when needed. Thus, plants controlled by kanbans are self-regulating, because each stage of production is activated by demand.[32]

Only in the most highly synchronized and automated factories are wait times between operations actually reduced to zero. In many operations, small buffers may be necessary to smooth production flow. Kanban containers specify the size of these buffers. Compared with the WIP inventories of traditional PUSH-type batch manufacturing, the capacity of a kanban container is truly minuscule, perhaps only two to five units. They are just big enough to permit the production line to continue operating smoothly despite minor interruptions at individual workcenters, such as a worker leaving his machine to go to the restroom or a brazing machine being shut down temporarily to replace an empty roll of solder. In a JIT environment, the product flow is visible, constant, and free of large WIP buffers.[33]

HOW DOES KANBAN WORK?   As an example, consider two machines in a workcenter. The JIT philosophy dictates that these machines should be physically close together, perhaps as part of a U-shaped workcenter or cell, as shown

[32] Giorgio Merli, *Total Manufacturing Management: Production Organization for the 1990s* (Cambridge, Mass.: Productivity Press, 1990), p. 46.
[33] McNair, Mosconi, and Norris, op. cit., (1988), p. 11.

■ EXHIBIT 2–14
The Kanban Containers in a U-Shaped Workcenter or Cell

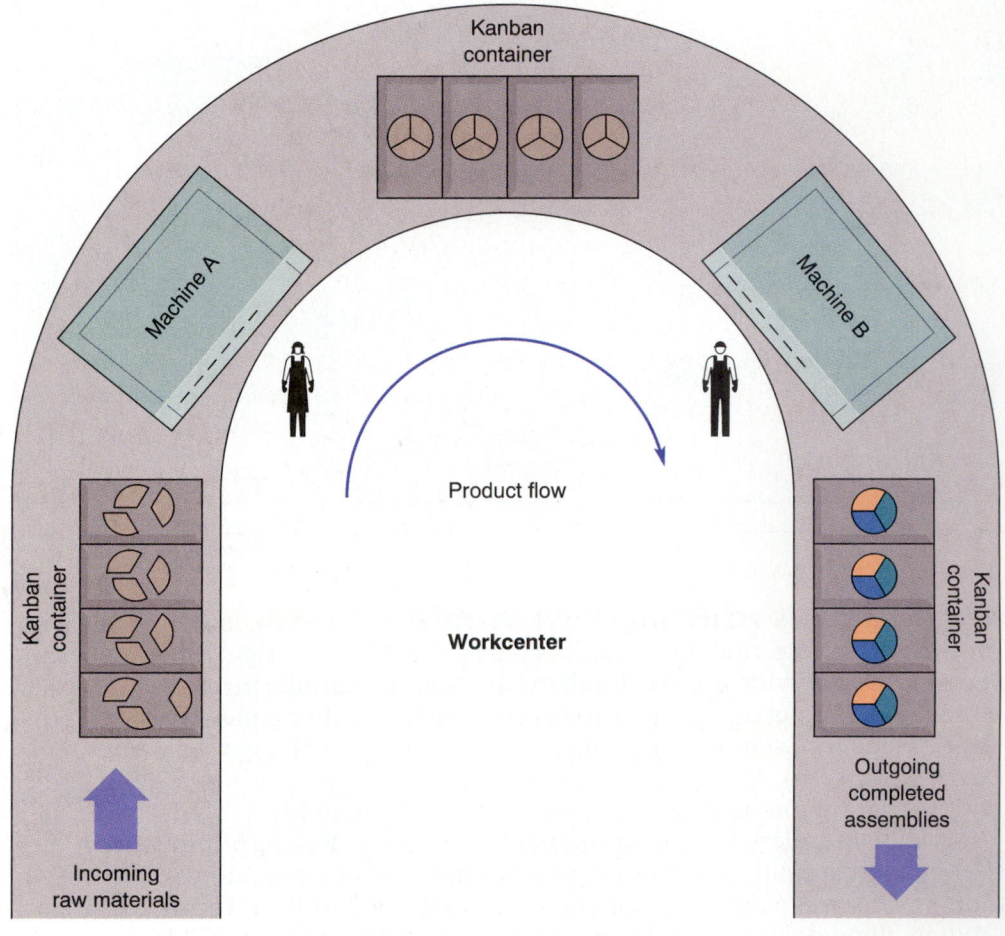

in Exhibit 2–14. Now, the workers at these two machines are able to communicate and coordinate their work. The worker at machine A can easily see when his co-worker at machine B will require another part. Also, and more importantly, the worker at machine B can immediately tell his co-worker if there is a problem with the quality of the parts coming from machine A. This prevents the buildup of large quantities of defective WIP—any problem always gets "nipped in the bud."

The kanban container between the two machines might hold four individual parts from machine A, perhaps in a bin with four divided cells for easy visual reference. As long as the kanban container is not full, the worker at machine A continues to produce parts, placing them in the kanban container. When the kanban container is full, that's it! Machine A stops producing until parts are needed again.

Having an idle worker may seem wasteful, but the reduction in WIP inventory and the elimination of defects that JIT provides are always worth it. When idle time occurs, the worker performs repairs and maintenance on the machine or engages in training activities. This reduces downtime and backlogs resulting from machine breakdowns and the need to get service people to fix it (usually from another department in a traditional factory). As the JIT line is fine-tuned and machine breakdowns are eliminated, each step can be synchronized to the point that workers are seldom idle and kanban container sizes can be further reduced.

As an example of such fine-tuning, consider the two machines A and B in Exhibit 2–14. If the step performed at machine A turned out to take half as long as machine B's, the machine A operator would be idle much of the time.

▬EXHIBIT 2–15
The Kanban Containers in a Y-Shaped Workcenter or Cell

This situation might be corrected by creating a Y-shaped layout, as in Exhibit 2–15. Here, machine A feeds two machine B's, resulting in better synchronization and a reduction or elimination of idle time.

Another option, which retains the original layout, would be to change the amount of work done by each operator until they have about the same amount to do (in terms of time). The worker currently at machine A might take on some of B's tasks, for example. In more automated facilities, a kanban container will have a mechanism that automatically shuts down upstream machines when it becomes full and then restarts them once the downstream machines catch up.

Pursuing Zero Setup Time

Setup time is the amount of time required to adjust equipment and to retool for the production of a different product. Setup time is one of the worst forms of waste in production because the entire company continues to incur costs while no value is being added to production (the worth, or value, of the product does not increase from this activity). In many JIT enterprises, setups take less than five minutes. Some JIT automobile manufacturers can change from one car model to another in two minutes, even though a complete retooling is required.

The reduction or elimination of WIP inventories is dependent on reducing setup times. Without a large buffer inventory, as in a traditional PUSH-type batch process, a lengthy setup at a JIT workcenter will bring the synchronized flow of the plant to a halt. A JIT system, therefore, seeks to reduce both the frequency and the time required to perform setups. For example, automatic calibration of equipment can be substituted for manual calibration. Some setup activities can be eliminated entirely by redesigning the products so that equipment (e.g., a drill press) does not have to be reset each time a different product is to be made.

■■■EXHIBIT 2–16
**Value-Added Time
and Nonvalue-Added
Time Make Up Total
Manufacturing Lead
Time**

Total manufacturing lead time	
Value-added time	Nonvalue-added time
• Time spent actually processing the raw materials into a finished product; that is, "time under the machine"	• Move time • Wait time • Inspection time

Pursuing Zero Lead Time

Lead time, also called **cycle time,** is how long it takes to produce a product or provide a service from start to finish. Lead time is composed of two kinds of times, summarized in Exhibit 2–16:

■ Value-added time
■ Nonvalue-added time

Value-added time represents activities performed by machines and people who work directly on making a product or providing a service. **Nonvalue-added time** comes from activities performed by people and machines that do not work on the product. Nonvalue-added time, which is wasted time, includes the following:

■ **Move time** is the amount of time it takes to transfer the product from one location to another. Moving material around is not only a nonvalue-added activity, it can result in misrouting or damaging the material. Reducing move time is largely a function of the plant layout. A straight-line layout is often the simplest, but may not be the best. Generally, a U-shaped cell is more effective and efficient, because it makes communication between workers easier and enables multiskilled workers to move from one workstation to the other, performing different tasks.
■ **Wait time** is the amount of time that the product sits around waiting for somebody to process it, move it, inspect it, rework it, or the amount of time finished products spend in storage waiting to be sold and shipped. Wait time is embodied in the queues of material just sitting at each workcenter. Is there value in having these large queues? No, the crew in the workcenter can only work on one order at a time. The objective is to reduce the queues by using kanbans and JIT principles. With these approaches, bottlenecks and imbalances are easier to see and deal with.
■ **Final inspection time** is the amount of time spent making sure the product is defect-free, or the amount of time actually spent reworking the product to an acceptable quality level. Reducing inspection time and rework is a function of the quality of raw material inputs, the quality of product design, and the quality of production.

Thus, the lead time formula is:

Lead time = Process time + Move time + Wait time + Inspection time

REDUCING LEAD TIME BY REDUCING NONVALUE-ADDED TIME. Nonvalue-added time is wasted time and is costly. Moving the product, waiting for something to happen to the product, and inspecting and reworking the product are wasteful, nonvalue-added activities. In many traditional PUSH-type batch manufacturing environments, the product is having value added to it only 5 percent of the time or less; 95 percent or more of the time the product is waiting, being moved, or being inspected and reworked.

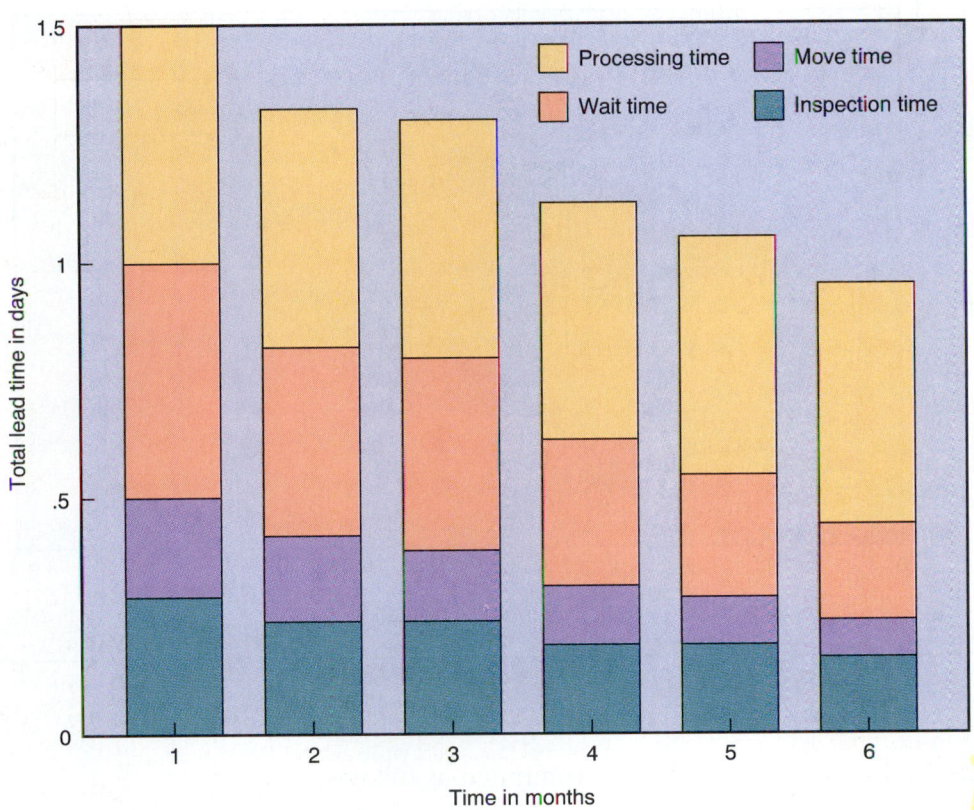

■EXHIBIT 2–17
Continuous Improvement as Illustrated by the Total Lead Time

If managers know what their lead time (or cycle time) is, they can improve it. Otherwise, they are managing by intuition. The management accountant is responsible for identifying and reporting on value-added and nonvalue-added times so that management can strip out nonvalue-added, useless activities and continuously improve operations. Management accountants can use two methods to help managers and workers focus on, and visualize, the progress (or lack of progress) in a continuous improvement campaign. Both methods emphasize that reducing nonvalue-added time is a continuous improvement campaign.

■ The **total lead time method** shows the absolute amount of each element in the lead time formula over time. The graph in Exhibit 2–17 shows clearly how well management has improved operations by decreasing nonvalue-added times over a six-month period.

■ The **lead time efficiency (LTE) ratio** is computed using the following formula:

$$\text{LTE ratio} = \frac{\text{Processing time}}{\text{Processing time} + \text{Move time} + \text{Wait time} + \text{Inspection time}}$$

This ratio is a simple and powerful measure of how well production efficiency is improving over time. Many companies have chosen the LTE ratio as a dominant measure of performance. For example, assume a company determines that it spends the following times manufacturing a product:

Processing time	4 hours
Move time	6 hours
Wait time	28 hours
Final inspection time	2 hours
Total lead time	40 hours

Continuous Improvement as Illustrated by the Lead Time Efficiency (LTE) Ratio

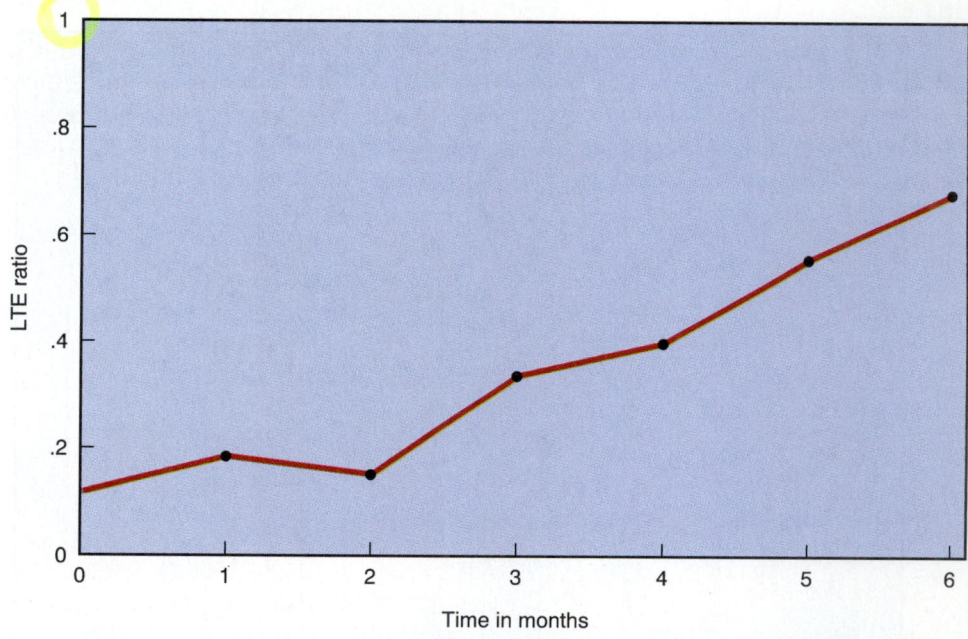

Time in months

The lead time efficiency ratio is computed as follows:

$$\text{LTE ratio} = \frac{4}{4 + 6 + 28 + 2}$$
$$= \underline{\underline{.10}}$$

More efficient manufacturers have increased their LTE ratios to as much as .60 and .70, with an ideal of 1.0 computed as:

$$\text{LTE ratio} = \frac{\text{Processing time}}{\text{Processing time} + 0}$$

The graph of the LTE ratio over time, as illustrated in Exhibit 2–18, indicates management's continuous improvement over a period of six months.

Traditional PUSH-type manufacturing, where performance evaluation stresses minimizing average per unit production cost, sends a loud and clear message: "Build more product!" This message encourages manufacturing to push more inventory into the pipeline to reduce fixed overhead cost per unit and to provide WIP buffers when defects and breakdowns are frequent. JIT manufacturing, on the other hand, sends a different message: "Focus on the process."

FOCUSING ON THE RIGHT THING.   Assume that Old Fashions Company does not consider value-added and nonvalue-added times, so the management accountant does not report total lead time or an LTE ratio. Instead, Old Fashions management tries *to make nonvalue-added activities more efficient.*

Old Fashions Company carries very large raw materials, WIP, and finished goods inventories. Management has not considered that reducing these inventories would also decrease lead time. Instead, the focus is on efficient handling and movement of these inventories, so management makes a large investment in automatic storage and material-handling equipment.

But having inventories in the first place results in large nonvalue-added costs. So, now Old Fashions Company has nonvalue-added costs in inventories, automatic equipment, and, possibly, additional people to service the equipment.

If managers had had the proper information based on total lead time or the LTE ratio, their original decision would have been different. They would have changed to a production process that does not require large inventories, and the large investments in automatic material-handling equipment would not be needed.

Pursuing Zero Defects

Zero defects means that there are no rejected materials, parts, or finished products, and no rework. It is a state of perfection and total quality. The idea of zero defects is the culmination of a problem prevention strategy.

While zero defects may seem an unattainable goal, it is important to believe that this level of quality can and will be achieved, no matter how difficult. The electronic components industry measures the level of manufacturing defects in items per *trillion* components produced.[34]

The journey toward zero defects is driven by **total quality management (TQM),** which focuses on preventing problems and "getting it right the first time." A TQM program is supported by the following techniques:

- Design of experiment (DOE)
- Total preventive maintenance (TPM)
- Statistical process control (SPC)
- Jidoka

As a general rule, over 40 percent of *all* quality problems originate in the design stage. The term **design of experiment (DOE)** is used to describe an ongoing program aimed at improving engineering's ability to create problem-free designs that meet customer requirements. DOE reviews various types of scientific experimentation, where the experiments are used to discover an unknown effect or to test a particular design feature.

The customer is not just the end user of the product once it has become a finished good. Every worker involved in the enterprise is thought of as "the customer." All these customers must be satisfied along the way, or the end customer will never be satisfied.

Total preventive maintenance (TPM) aims at extending equipment life and maximizing effectiveness throughout the machine's entire useful life. TPM motivates people to improve plant maintenance through small-group activities that range from the development of a maintenance system to education in basic housekeeping and problem-solving skills. Under TPM, the machine operator is frequently responsible for the maintenance of his own machine instead of assigning this responsibility to a repairs and maintenance department.

Statistical process control (SPC) uses statistical techniques, such as random sampling and control charts, to analyze a production process. The nature of this type of control is preventive. It seeks to catch problems before the process or activity can create defective products.

Jidoka is a Japanese term that means "stop *everything* when something goes wrong." This work ethic mandates that each person is responsible for finding and correcting his or her own errors before passing the product on to the next stage. If a defect is passed along, the worker who receives the defective product has the ability to stop the entire production line until the problem causing the defect is corrected. Such production line stoppages are very disruptive, so everyone works together to prevent problems from occurring, instead of trying to correct a problem after it occurs.

[34] Merli, op. cit., p. xxii.

INSIGHTS & APPLICATIONS

Implementing the Five S's

During a plant tour, the plant manager noticed two water bottles on the floor next to a full rack of bottles. The water service vendor explained that the two bottles were there to meet demand. The plant manager explained the plant's everything-in-its-place philosophy, and said she would have another rack built to hold enough bottles to meet demand.

A short time later, she noticed both racks filled and two bottles sitting on the floor. She waited for the water vendor to arrive, and as he watched, the plant manager smashed both bottles with a hammer.

The lesson: To implement the five S's, apply them to all aspects of plant operation, even water bottle storage.

Developing the Visual Factory

Production may be stopped manually or automatically by sensors installed on machines. JIT production facilities usually incorporate a visual control system, known in Japanese as **andon,** to help managers and workers know the status of production. Andon embodies the principle that "Problems must be seen in order to be solved." Indeed, as Yogi Berra said, "You can see a lot by observing."

Andon is the concept behind what some people call the **visual factory** where problems, abnormalities, defects, and all types of waste are immediately recognized at a single glance. The following five S's are fundamental to the visual factory:

The visual factory at Caterpillar.

- *Seiri* (organization) is distinguishing between needed and unneeded items. It is the elimination of unnecessary parts, adjustments, documents, and paper flow. It is an everything-in-its-place philosophy.
- *Seiton* (orderliness) is organizing the necessary items close to where they are needed and in such a way that any waste, nonvalue-added activity, or abnormality is apparent. Locations are clear and self-explanatory so that everyone knows what goes where. Nothing blocks access to fire extinguishers, hoses, and emergency exits.
- *Shitsuke* (discipline) means rules are followed precisely, including coming to work on time and wearing safety equipment. Following correct procedures becomes a habit. Instructions on how to do a job properly are clearly located on every machine.
- *Seiso* (cleanliness) ensures that tools, equipment, and the entire workplace are spotless. All dirt, oil, and scrap are eliminated.
- *Seiketsu* (standardization) results when the preceding S's are practiced. Because information is displayed for all to see, abnormalities are quickly recognized and eliminated, and a new state of efficiency is achieved.

The following are examples of visual controls displayed by computer screens, lights, and large graphs throughout the facility for all to see at a glance:

- Defect rates
- Inventory levels
- Planned production versus actual production
- Green, yellow, and red lights, indicating go, caution, or no-go conditions, to signify the state of quality at each workstation
- Kanban cards
- Display boards showing production stoppages and their causes
- Work assignments clearly posted for all to see
- Graphs showing improvement of teams, thus inspiring everyone to improve

Hewlett-Packard's Visual Factory

Simple graphs are everywhere in the Hewlett-Packard plant. Three large graphs are posted on a main wall near the center of the manufacturing floor. One shows JIT material flow. Another graph shows the total quality management (TQM) process. The third, centered between the others, shows a number of other performance measurements, such as lead times, level of WIP inventory, and several nonconformities (e.g., bent leads or missing parts). The plant is set up for visual management. Anyone, even a visiting class from a local college, can tour the plant and can readily "see" what's right and what's wrong.

The visual factory enables all managers, including senior management, who may know very little about specific operations, to see the status of production by merely walking through the plant and observing the easy-to-understand information displays. It is management by sight. This way, managers have a real-time picture of operations, so they can practice "preventive management" rather than "post-mortem management."

Computer-Integrated Manufacturing

The ultimate step toward full factory automation is **computer-integrated manufacturing (CIM).** CIM uses groups of technologies that are integrated plantwide and are controlled by an ICBIS, as shown in Exhibit 2–19. CIM

■■ EXHIBIT 2–19

A Computer-Integrated Manufacturing (CIM) System

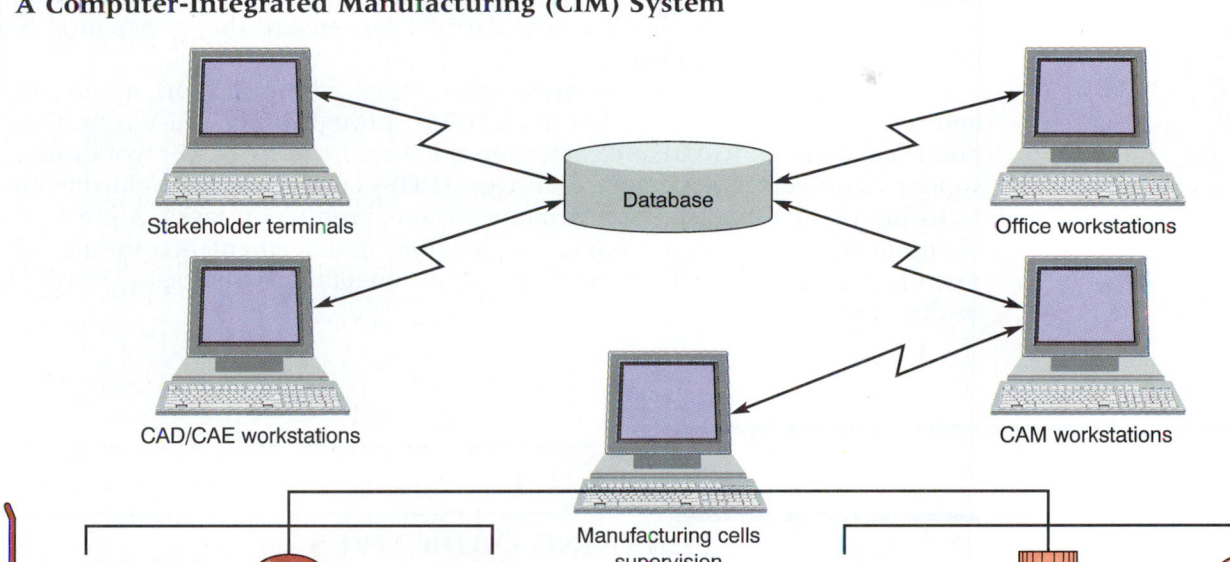

represents a major step toward "peopleless, lights-out" factories. Typically, manufacturers will convert to JIT to gain simplicity and synchronous operations and then will go to full CIM-JIT. Indeed, many experts consider JIT a prerequisite for CIM.

A CIM enterprise is integrated from the factory floor to the executive suite. Even customers, vendors, and carriers are part of the system, which includes the following major users:

- Stakeholders (customers, vendors, carriers)
- Office personnel
- Engineering
- Computer-aided manufacturing
- Manufacturing cells

Stakeholders are the people or organizations who have a vested interest in the manufacturer's success. A fairly steady stream of electronic information flows between the stakeholders and the manufacturer. Such a connection eliminates the need for paper flows, such as purchase orders and invoices.

Customers look to the manufacturer for a dependable source of products or services. They can be connected to the manufacturer by an ICBIS so messages and transactions can occur electronically. Customers can get information about products, prices, and deliveries. They can place orders and then track them—all electronically. In turn, the manufacturer receives information about customers' purchase plans and also receives performance information that indicates how well customers are being serviced.

The same arrangement exists between the manufacturer and its vendors, but in reverse because the manufacturer is the buyer rather than the seller. Vendors stay in close touch with the manufacturer to ensure that raw materials are delivered just-in-time.

Carriers transport raw materials from suppliers to the manufacturer and finished products from the manufacturer to customers. By being integrated into the system through the ICBIS, these carriers can ensure that a synchronized flow of goods is maintained.

Office personnel in different areas (marketing, administration, accounting, and so forth) are linked together in an ICBIS through LANs and WANs. Computer-aided design (CAD) and computer-aided engineering (CAE) workstations support engineers in design of experiment (DOE) tasks. Computer-aided manufacturing (CAM) workstations facilitate various production tasks. A great deal of interaction takes place among engineering, management accounting, and manufacturing. More will be said about these "enabling technologies" of WCMs in the next chapter.

SUMMARY OF LEARNING OBJECTIVES

The major goals of this chapter were to enable you to achieve four learning objectives:

Learning objective 1.   Describe the traditional batch manufacturing environment.

The traditional batch manufacturing environment is a PUSH system in which the product is produced in accordance with available capacity and moved along the production line in large batches. Inspection generally occurs at the end of the process. The following are characteristics of a traditional batch manufacturing environment:

- Suboptimizing behavior between organizational areas working at cross-purposes
- Producing and maintaining large raw materials, WIP, and finished goods inventories

- Producing products of subpar quality and performing a great deal of rework and repairs
- Striving for efficiency at the expense of effectiveness

Learning objective 2.   Define the world-class manufacturing (WCM) environment.

The WCM environment seeks to develop within enterprises a culture of problem prevention, continuous improvement, efficiency and effectiveness, and manufacturing excellence. Companies that don't achieve WCM status will have difficulty:

- Meeting foreign competition
- Being cost-effective against competitors
- Maintaining a high level of manufacturing activity
- Surviving as viable businesses

Practicing continuous improvement is one of the keys to attaining WCM status. Continuous improvement can result in the following:

- Lowering costs
- Improving quality
- Increasing customer satisfaction

Learning objective 3.   List and describe the characteristics of WCM.

WCM has seven major characteristics:

- *High quality.* The product works as intended without defect or deficiencies.
- *Customer service.* Customer service factors are used to achieve complete customer satisfaction.
- *Low inventory.* Minimal amounts of inventory are ordered, processed, stored, and handled.
- *Flexibility.* The manufacturing process can adapt quickly to changes in demand.
- *Automation.* Self-acting and self-regulating technologies are used to perform a large variety of tasks.
- *Team concept.* Workers and managers work together in a cooperative manner for the overall success of the enterprise.
- *Integrated computer-based information system (ICBIS).* A system in which various information technologies are used to connect all functions throughout the enterprise.

Learning objective 4.   Describe just-in-time (JIT) manufacturing and computer-integrated manufacturing (CIM).

JIT manufacturing is a PULL system that is demand based. Its objectives include the following:

- Synchronized operations
- Zero inventories
- Zero setup time
- Zero lead time
- Zero defects
- Visual factory
- Computer-integrated manufacturing (CIM)

The ultimate JIT uses computer-integrated manufacturing (CIM) to fully integrate information technologies, production technologies, and functions throughout the enterprise and beyond. Typically, the CIM-JIT enterprise is connected electronically to its stakeholders, such as customers, suppliers, and carriers.

Cellular manufacturing (usually U-shaped) is a configuration often used by JIT manufacturers. Two significant features of cellular manufacturing are production families and cross training.

IMPORTANT TERMS

Andon   A visual control system located on the shop (factory) floor in full view of workers and managers.

Buffer   Stockpiles of WIP inventory between operations or departments in traditional production systems to protect departments from problems arising in previous departments.

Cellular manufacturing   A layout of production resources in the form of a cell, usually U-shaped, to manufacture production families and facilitate cross training.

Computer-integrated manufacturing (CIM)   A full integration of information and production technologies, which is the culmination of JIT.

Continuous improvement   The uninterrupted striving to advance or make better the entire enterprise, especially the engineering, manufacturing, marketing, logistics, and service functions. The ultimate aim of continuous improvement is complete customer satisfaction.

Controls   A component of ICBISs that includes physical devices and procedures to protect the system from a host of threats and abuses.

Cross training   A process by which workers are trained to perform a wide array of tasks.

Cycle time   *See* lead time.

Database   A component of ICBISs that serves as a repository for all financial accounting, management accounting, and operational data.

Design of experiment (DOE)   A technique used to develop problem-free designs and meet customer requirements.

Effectiveness   The degree to which an objective or target is met.

Efficiency   The degree to which inputs are used in relation to a given level of outputs. The fewer inputs used in producing a set number of products, the greater production efficiency becomes.

Final inspection time   The amount of time spent to make sure the product (or service) is defect-free or the amount of time actually spent reworking the product to an acceptable quality level.

Flexibility   The ability to adapt quickly to changing conditions.

Input   A component of ICBISs that captures and enters data into the system for processing.

Jidoka   A technique used to stop the entire production process when a problem-causing defect occurs. The production process is stopped until the problem causing the defect is corrected.

Just-in-time (JIT) manufacturing   A PULL system of production that produces in accordance with downstream needs.

Kanban   A computerized or hard-copy signal to produce the next product or subassembly, or to order the direct materials for the next product, used in a JIT production process.

Kanban container   A standard-size container used in JIT manufacturing to achieve synchronized operations and minimum inventories.

Lead time (cycle time)   The time it takes to complete a product or service from start to finish.

Lead time efficiency (LTE) ratio   A way management accountants report lead time improvement, or lack of improvement, over time in ratio form.

Local area network (LAN)   A network in which all the devices of an ICBIS are located in the same office or building.

Move time   The amount of time it takes to transfer a product from one location to another.

Mushroom concept   A production process design that keeps processes and products standardized for as long as possible and creates a product structure that is diversified only at the final production stage.

Nonvalue-added time   The time spent on activities that are not part of the process. These times are categorized as move time, wait time, and inspection time.

Output   A component of ICBISs that generates information for end users.

Process   A component of ICBISs that manipulates data in accordance with accounting and operational procedures.

Production family   A group of like products that are manufactured in a synchronized production cell.

Setup time   The amount of time required to adjust equipment and make tool changes for the production of a different product.

Stakeholders   Those who have a vested interest in the manufacturer's success, such as customers, suppliers, and carriers.

Statistical process control (SPC)   Statistical techniques used to monitor and control the production process.

Stockout costs   The costs of not having inventory when needed, including customers' ill will and the costs of back ordering, special handling, and production line disruptions.

Synchronized operations   A method by which production and the movement of products are coordinated to the rate at which products are withdrawn from finished goods.

Technology platform   A component of ICBISs that includes all the computer hardware, computer software, and telecommunications devices necessary to support input, process, output, database, and controls.

Total lead time method   A way management accountants report lead time improvement, or lack of improvement, over time. It presents the total lead time in absolute amounts.

Total preventive maintenance (TPM)   A technique employed to maximize equipment performance and extend equipment life.

Total quality management (TQM)   A broad method that prevents problems from occurring. TQM employs four techniques: design of experiment (DOE), total preventive maintenance (TPM), statistical process control (SPC), and jidoka.

Traditional batch manufacturing environment   A production approach characterized by suboptimal behavior, large raw materials, WIP, and finished goods inventories, subpar-quality products, and efficiency-oriented procedures.

Value-added time   The time spent directly on the production of a product or the provision of a service. It is process time.

Visual factory   A management approach in which various graphical displays, video screens, signal lights, and markers are used to indicate problems, abnormalities, and all types of waste at a single glance.

Wait time   The amount of time that the product sits around waiting for somebody to process it, move it, or inspect it, or the amount of time finished products spend in storage waiting to be sold and shipped.

Wide area network (WAN)   A network in which all the devices of an ICBIS are dispersed over long distances.

World-class manufacturing (WCM) environment   Seeks to develop within manufacturing organizations a culture of problem prevention, continuous improvement, efficiency and effectiveness, and manufacturing excellence.

Zero defects   The absence of deficiencies in operations and products.

DEMONSTRATION PROBLEMS

■ **DEMONSTRATION PROBLEM 1**   *Reducing nonvalue-added activities through JIT raw materials delivery systems.*

Maxco is a PUSH-type manufacturer of sports equipment. Its current materials movement program is illustrated in the figure to the right:

Marv Chen has read that Apple Computer reduced its vendors from 400 to 75, and IBM Corporation cut its vendors from 640 to 32. He understands that such a program calls for stipulating prices and acceptable quality levels in long-term agreements with vendors, thus eliminating negotiations for each purchase transaction. He also understands that Hewlett-Packard specifies in its contracts that a vendor cannot miss a four-hour delivery window more than three times in a year; otherwise, the contract is up for renewal. Because of synchronized deliveries and long-term arrangements, Apple, IBM, and Hewlett-Packard have reduced most nonvalue-added activities associated with all inventories: raw materials, work-in-process, and finished goods.

Required:

a. Marv Chen believes he can emulate these WCMs by eliminating materials handling, inspection, and warehouse costs. Draw a diagram showing how materials movement will be handled at Maxco if Mr. Chen's goal is achieved.

b. Ronald Hartman, Maxco's controller, doesn't like Marv Chen's plan. He argues that the price of raw materials will increase by 10 percent. Maxco is currently spending $10,000,000 annually on the purchase of raw materials. Marv counters by stating that the emphasis is on the total cost of operations, not just on the purchase of raw materials. Marv has collected the following cost data for nonvalue-added activities:

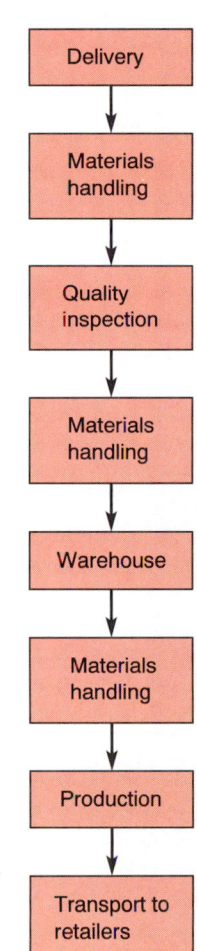

Materials handling	$ 4,000 per day
Inspection	2,000 per day
Warehousing	5,000 per day
Rework because of poor-quality raw materials	3,000 per day
Total cost per day	$14,000 per day

Maxco works 300 days per year. Manufacturers that have moved from traditional methods have experienced the following average results:

80% decrease in materials handling
90% decrease in inspection
90% decrease in warehousing
80% decrease in rework

From these data, compute the cost savings Mr. Chen's plan will achieve, assuming a 10 percent increase in the purchase price of raw materials.

SOLUTION TO DEMONSTRATION PROBLEM 1

a.

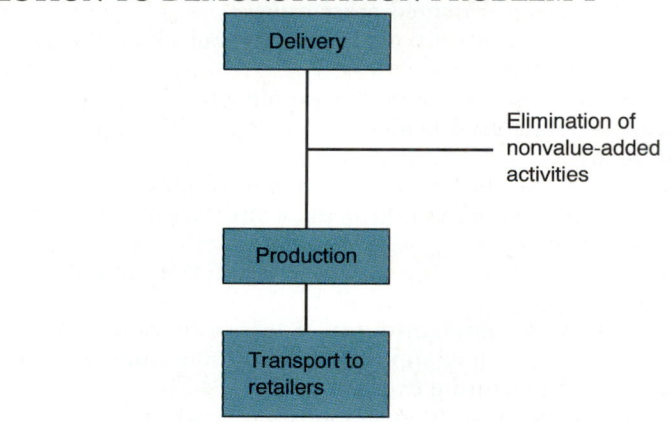

b.

	CURRENT COST		COST IF NEW PLAN IS IMPLEMENTED
Materials handling	$ 4,000	at 20%	$ 800
Inspection	2,000	at 10%	200
Warehousing	5,000	at 10%	500
Rework	3,000	at 20%	600
Totals	$14,000		$2,100

Cost per year under traditional activities @ $14,000/day	$4,200,000
Cost per year under Mr. Chen's plan @ $2,100/day	<630,000>
Annual cost savings of Mr. Chen's plan	$3,570,000

Cost savings of Mr. Chen's plan	$3,570,000
Less price increase due to Mr. Chen's plan	<1,000,000>
Annual net cost savings of Mr. Chen's plan	$2,570,000

■ DEMONSTRATION PROBLEM 2   *Cost savings from the mushroom concept.*

Western Electronics produces switching equipment used by telephone companies. The parts list that records all the parts used in switching equipment fills four volumes totaling 1,200 pages. A typical part, a screw, is described as follows:

PART NUMBER	DESCRIPTION	WHERE USED
B476594-94F-QH4	1/4" Brass Phillips screw	C489857-44G-LL3 T66430-28H-TA1

Jim Arcaro, an engineer, recently analyzed the screws used by Western Electronics in the manufacture of switching equipment. He found 20 separately designated screws that are virtually indistinguishable. He made similar discoveries concerning other parts, components, and subassemblies that are used to make Western Electronics' finished goods.

Marjorie Lankowski, management accountant, figured the only way to understand how raw materials for Western's products are used was to go out on the assembly floor and observe what was taking place.

Jim met Marjorie and said, "Let's take a walk."

"For what?" asked Marjorie.

"You see that plate that goes on our QFI switching element?" asked Jim.

"Yes. I'm familiar with it from the thousands of materials requisitions I process each year," said Marjorie.

"Well, it takes five different screws to hold that plate. But they're virtually the same. What's worse, follow me and I'll show you what an operator has to do to mount the plate," said Jim.

Jim and Marjorie took a 15-minute walk. They went out of the building, across the street, and into another building to get the five screws. On the way back, they talked to a few people, and about 20 minutes later they were back where they started.

"All of this just to get five screws to mount a plate? It seems wasteful to me," said Marjorie.

"You want to see something that's even more wasteful?" said Jim.

"I can't imagine. What?" said Marjorie.

Jim pulled a blueprint of one of the switching devices and showed Marjorie even more screws that were exactly the same as the ones they had just gotten, except that they were a tiny bit longer. Jim also showed plates that were the same except that one called for six holes, another seven, and so forth; each required differently designated screws that were all exactly the same functionally.

"Why haven't you told anybody?" asked Marjorie.

"I have. I've been telling my boss that if we changed some of our designs, we could standardize much of our raw materials and also our production process and yet still be able to offer a variety of switching devices. Most of the differences in the switching equipment are in the electronic components mounted, not in the production process itself. But I'm just about ready to give up," said Jim.

"Don't give up yet. I think we'll be able to make some changes after I've made some reports to senior management," said Marjorie.

Required:
Discuss how Western Electronics could save money by following the mushroom concept.

SOLUTION TO DEMONSTRATION PROBLEM 2
First, the engineering analysis of all parts used in Western's manufacturing operations should continue. Second, where possible, all redundant parts should be eliminated. For example, the 20 separately designated screws that are functionally the same can be reduced to *one*. Other parts and subassemblies would come under the same kind of analysis. The variability in the finished switching equipment would come primarily from electrical components, and even those components could be subjected to standardization. Cost savings would occur from the following:

- Less record keeping
- Less ordering and stocking
- Less time in getting the right parts to the right job
- Fewer tools needed because of standardized parts and subassemblies
- Better inventory control

■ DEMONSTRATION PROBLEM 3   *Plant layout.*
Diesel Parts, Inc., makes injection equipment used in diesel motors. The following diagram details the flow of the 12-stage process used to produce this equipment:

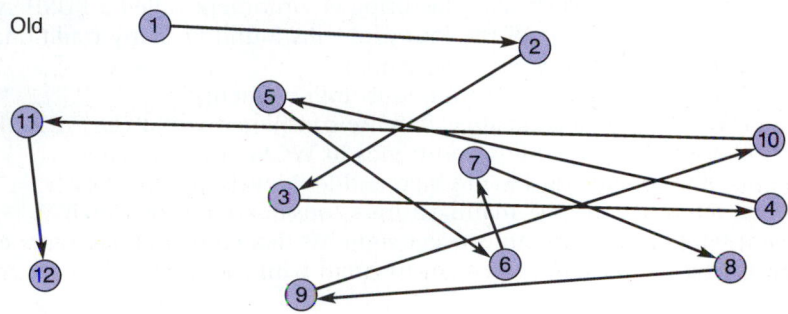

Required:
a. Redesign the current plant layout to gain efficiencies.
b. Discuss the possible benefits of your new design.

SOLUTION TO DEMONSTRATION PROBLEM 3

a.

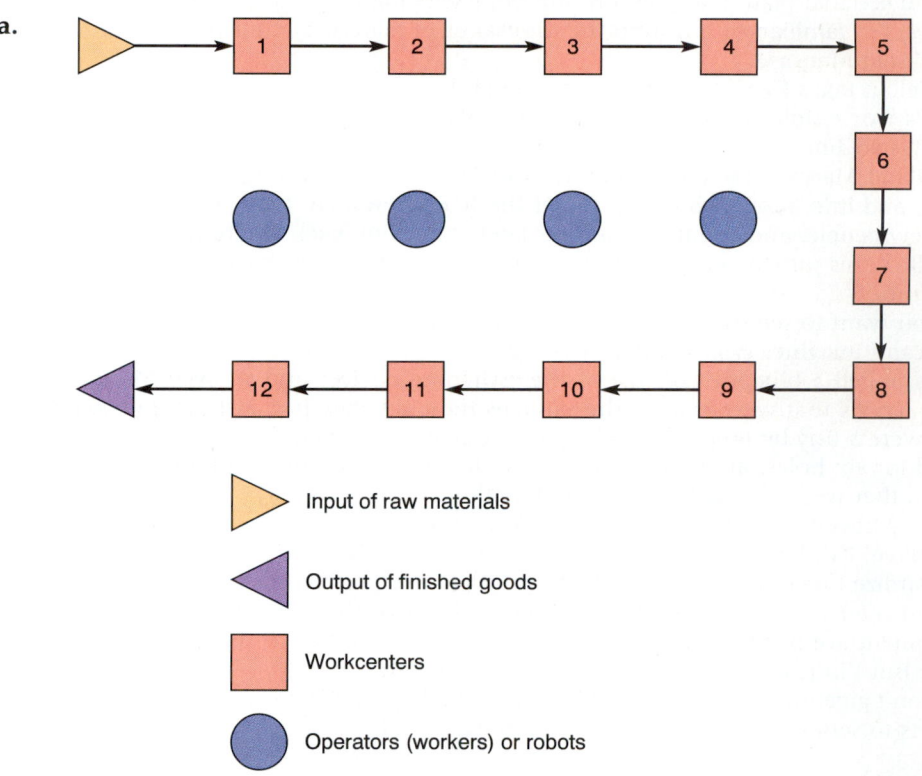

▷ Input of raw materials

◁ Output of finished goods

■ Workcenters

● Operators (workers) or robots

b. In the original layout, it appears that operations are not synchronized, with long movements of WIP between workstations. Probably, to keep everyone working, large WIP buffers are present as well. With the large physical distances between operations, workers probably do not communicate, coordinate their activities, or worry very much about WIP quality.

The new U-shaped production cell can employ a kanban system, electronic sensing devices, cross-trained workers, and robots. These JIT techniques should reduce raw materials storage, work-in-process inventory, finished goods inventory and lead times between the 12 operations. Diesel now uses end-unit demand to trigger production. Thus, the products are PULLed through the production cells. The visual factory concept can be used to indicate lead times, defect rates, kanbans, and work assignments.

▍REVIEW QUESTIONS

2.1 List and give an example of the two different manufacturing environments discussed in the chapter.
2.2 Why is a traditional batch manufacturing environment called a PUSH system?
2.3 List and give an example of the four problems found in many traditional PUSH-type batch manufacturing environments.
2.4 What Japanese word means continuous improvement?
2.5 Name three American companies that are considered world-class manufacturers.
2.6 List and briefly describe the seven trends in WCM environments.
2.7 What are the reasons for having high and low levels of inventory?
2.8 Why do many world-class manufacturers consider inventory "evil"?
2.9 Explain why the mushroom concept supports flexibility and decreases costs.
2.10 Contrast the old-style management pyramid with the new-style team concept.

2.11 List and give an example of the six components of an ICBIS.

2.12 Explain why telecommunication networks, especially LANs, can facilitate the team concept.

2.13 Why is JIT referred to as a PULL system?

2.14 List and briefly explain the seven objectives of JIT.

2.15 Explain how kanbans support synchronized operations.

2.16 What are the major differences between Exhibits 2–2 and 2–10?

2.17 Differentiate between value-added and nonvalue-added times. Give an example of each.

2.18 What is the lead time formula?

2.19 What is an ideal LTE ratio? Explain your answer.

2.20 List and briefly explain the four techniques that support a total quality management (TQM) system.

2.21 List and briefly explain the five S's.

2.22 What is the purpose of the visual factory? What makes up a visual factory?

2.23 What is a kanban and how does it differ from a kanban container?

2.24 List the users integrated by an ICBIS supporting a computer-integrated manufacturing (CIM) environment.

2.25 Why is cross training important in manufacturing cells?

2.26 List the advantages and disadvantages of a U-shaped production line compared to a straight production line.

CHAPTER-SPECIFIC PROBLEMS

These problems require responses based directly on concepts and techniques presented in the text.

2.27 *Comparing PUSH-type and PULL-type manufacturers.* Following is a list of characteristics:

_____	Large raw materials inventory.
_____	Very small WIP inventory.
_____	Warehouses full of finished goods.
_____	Focus on efficiency at the expense of effectiveness.
_____	Suboptimizing behavior between organization areas.
_____	Kanban system.

Required:
Insert the appropriate type of manufacturer in the space next to the characteristic.

2.28 *Whether to produce at or above demand.* Fixed costs are $200,000. If 50,000 units are produced during the period, the fixed cost per unit is $4. If 100,000 units are produced, the fixed cost per unit is $2. But demand for the period is 20,000 units. If production equals demand, then the fixed cost per unit skyrockets to $10.

Required:
Describe a situation where it would be both efficient and effective to produce at the maximum capacity of 100,000 units. Describe a situation where it would be both efficient and effective to produce at 20,000 units.

2.29 *The mushroom concept at work.* Kitchenhelper makes dishwashers. Currently, it makes four different-colored doors for the dishwashers. It costs $10 per door for direct labor to paint the doors. The painting facility costs $100,000. Moreover, because different colors are currently a factory-controlled variable, finished goods are always out of balance due to the wrong color being in stock. This problem adds $8 per dishwasher for inventory warehousing costs. Matthew Gilland, newly hired design engineer, has recommended eliminating the painting process. His idea is to include colored plastic sheets for all Kitchenhelper's offered colors in the shipping box. The consumer selects the desired color, inserts the sheet into the door, and discards the rest. Matthew says, "Designs should be standard throughout the early part of the procurement and manufacturing process, with all variability added as late as possible."

Required:
Justify Matthew Gilland's recommendation.

2.30 *Total vendor costs.* Vendor A's price for a key raw material is $50 per unit. Daily usage averages 1,000 units. In any month (25 days worked each month), vendor A averages 10 days' late deliveries. The cost of idle time caused by late deliveries is $40,000 per day. Vendor B's price for the same raw material is $65 per unit with zero late deliveries.

Required:
Which vendor do you recommend? Justify your answer.

2.31 *Components of ICBISs.* Following are some functions performed by ICBISs:

_____	Displaying a radar chart showing profitability, safety, and productivity measures.
_____	Storage of cost and performance data.
_____	Bar code readers that scan subassemblies during production.
_____	Transmission of kanban data throughout the production facility.
_____	Passwords for authorized users.
_____	An algorithm that converts raw data into production reports.

Required:
Insert the name of the appropriate ICBIS component in the space provided.

THINK-TANK PROBLEMS

Although these problems are based on chapter material, reading extra material, reviewing previous chapters, and using creativity may be required to develop workable solutions.

2.32 *Quality control inspection.* "We have an excellent quality control system, because we inspect the finished goods as soon as they come off the production line. Products that don't pass inspection are sent back to the beginning of the production line for rework. A few, however, are scrapped," said Jerry Sellers, production manager at Orico, a manufacturer of semiconductors.

Required:
Explain what's wrong with Mr. Sellers' quality control system. Why may such a system result in excessive scrap and rework? Describe a more effective way to ensure that good products go into finished goods.

2.33 *Behavioral ramifications.* The management accountant at Ultrix Optical Company devised the following direct labor incentive program:

NUMBER OF LENSES PRODUCED PER DAY	AMOUNT OF DAILY BONUS
10–20	$ 0
21–40	10
41–60	50
61–80	100

To decrease packaging and delivery time, random inspections are made by the shipping department. The performance of the shipping department is measured on the number of shipments made per day.

Required:
What kind of behavior does the direct labor incentive program engender? Should inspection responsibility be placed with the shipping department? Explain your answer. Will the present system be beneficial to Ultrix? Explain your answer.

2.34 *Is the lowest price the best price?* Chauncey's is a new franchisor specializing in turkey sandwiches. Wholesaler A has quoted a price 30 percent less than Wholesaler B's price for rolls of turkey. The cost of turkey rolls is 15 percent of the cost of making the sandwiches.

Required:

Describe the kind of analysis, both financial and nonfinancial, that should be performed before a decision is made on which wholesaler will supply the turkey rolls to Chauncey's.

2.35 *Redesign plant layout and product flow.* Tour De Frame makes frames for racing bicycles. The current plant layout and product flow are as follows:

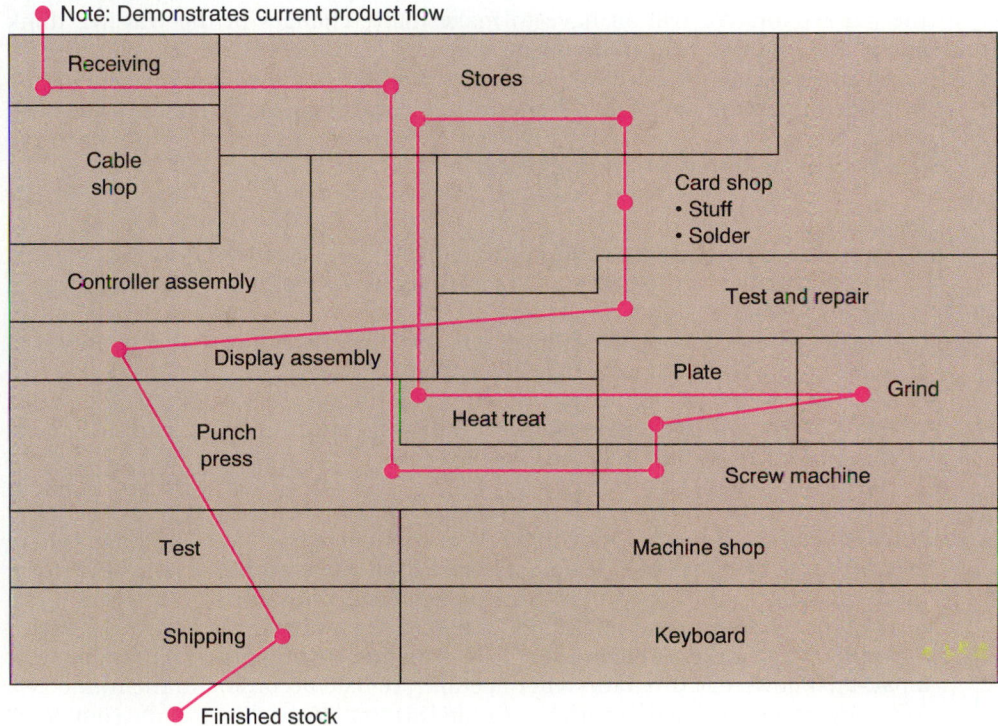

Source: C. J. McNair, William Mosconi, and Thomas Norris, *Meeting the Technology Challenge: Cost Accounting in a JIT Environment* (Montvale, N.J.: Institute of Management Accountants, formerly the National Association of Accountants, 1988), p. 83. With permission.

The zigzag path followed in the assembly of the bicycle frames is typical of many major production facilities in the United States. The result is an overwhelming percentage of nonvalue-added time in production. In the plant layout shown here, 99 percent of the time is spent in nonvalue-added activities and 1 percent of it in actual productive processing. The process and accounting in this traditional assembly layout are so complex that one manager noted, "If you put raw material in, eventually it will belch out as product at the end. Everything in the middle is something of a black box."

Required:

a. Redesign the plant layout and product flow at Tour De Frame in a way that will reduce nonvalue-added activities.

b. Write a report stating how you would convert Tour De Frame to a world-class manufacturer.

c. Assume the following annual costs:

- Receiving $400,000
- Storage   900,000
- Test and repair   300,000

State how you would go about reducing these costs. Make any assumptions you deem necessary.

2.36 *Discussing just-in-time.* The management at Megafilters, Inc., has been discussing the possible implementation of a just-in-time (JIT) production system at its Illinois plant, where oil filters and air filters for heavy construction equipment and large, off-the-road vehicles are manufactured. The metal stamping department at the Illinois plant has already instituted a JIT system for controlling raw materials inventory, but the remainder of the plant is still discussing how to proceed with the implementation of this concept. Some of the other department managers have grown increasingly cautious about the JIT process after hearing about the problems that have arisen in the metal stamping department.

Robert Goertz, manager of the Illinois plant, is a strong proponent of the JIT production system and recently made the following statement at a meeting of all departmental managers. "Just-in-time is often referred to as a management philosophy of doing business rather than a technique for improving efficiency on the plant floor. We will all have to make many changes in the way we think about our employees, our suppliers, and our customers if we are going to be successful in using just-in-time procedures. Rather than dwelling on some of the negative things you have heard from the metal stamping department, I want each of you to prepare a list of things we can do to make a smooth transition to the just-in-time philosophy of management for the rest of the plant."

Required:
a. The JIT management philosophy emphasizes objectives for the general improvement of a production system. Describe several important objectives of this philosophy.
b. Discuss several actions that Megafilters, Inc., can take to ease the transition to a JIT production system at the Illinois plant.
c. In order for the JIT production system to be successful, Megafilters, Inc., must establish appropriate relationships with its vendors, employees, and customers. Describe each of these relationships.

[CMA adapted]

2.37 *Discussing cross training.* Part of WCM is the concept of cross training, where production workers are able to operate more than one type of machine or perform more than one type of operation. This concept fosters flexibility in the work force. Under what circumstances might this flexibility be required? Is it always desirable?

To motivate workers to learn new jobs, a manufacturing firm might implement a pay-for-knowledge program, where people are paid according to the number of jobs they've been trained to perform. Could this strategy backfire on the company? How? If you were in charge of the payroll department at such a company, how would you structure the pay of manufacturing workers?

2.38 *Discussing bold goals.* Tom Peters lists eight bold goals in *Thriving on Chaos: Handbook for a Management Revolution:*

- Productivity: Increased by 100% to 200%
- Quality: Defects reduced by 95%
- Product development cycles: Shortened 75% to 80%
- Lead time: Reduced 90%
- Inventory: Reduced 90%
- Layers of management: Reduced 75%
- Span of control: Increased by a factor of 5 to 10
- Continuous learning: Training budget increased by 200% to 300%

Required:
Write a proposal spelling out how each of these goals can be achieved. Also, explain the synergism that may exist among the goals. As an example, consider these issues and any others you think important:

- Will continuous learning help increase productivity?
- Will the reduction in the layers of management increase span of control and help shorten product development cycles?
- How will a reduction in inventory improve quality?
- How will continuous learning improve quality and reduce lead time?

3

ENABLING TECHNOLOGIES FOR MODERN MANUFACTURING ENVIRONMENTS

Integrated computer-based information system.

LEARNING OBJECTIVES

After studying this chapter, you should be able to:

1. Describe how integrated computer-based information systems (ICBISs) are developed.

2. Explain how material requirements planning (MRP)

and manufacturing resource planning (MRP II) systems are used to integrate and improve operations.

3. Show how electronic data interchange (EDI) is used to form metacorporations.

■ INTRODUCTION

Modern organizations, including manufacturing enterprises, merchandising businesses, and service firms, are investing heavily in information technology to help coordinate operations and improve performance. The U.S. Chamber of Commerce reports that investment in information technology now constitutes over 50 percent of all U.S. capital investment and is increasing at a rate of 15 percent annually.[1] The purpose of this chapter is to introduce you to this enabling information technology and to describe how it is used. ━━

▌HOW TO DEVELOP AN INTEGRATED COMPUTER-BASED INFORMATION SYSTEM

In general terms, developing an integrated computer-based information system (ICBIS) entails two broad tasks:

- Enterprisewide modeling
- Implementing a technology platform

▌Creating an Enterprisewide Model with an Entity Relationship Diagram

The modeling tool used to create an enterprisewide model of a firm is an **entity relationship diagram (ERD). Enterprisewide models** show all major entities of a company and the relationships among these entities. An **entity** in an ERD is a person, place, object, event, activity, process, or concept about which data are recorded. The purpose of an ERD is to show which entities interact with each other and how they fit together to form the enterprise. It is a road map of the information flows.

The ERD is a popular enterprisewide modeling tool used by management accountants and systems consultants working for the "Big Six" accounting firms. Symbols used to develop ERD models are demonstrated in Exhibit 3–1. The ERD displayed in Exhibit 3–2 is an enterprisewide model of a manufacturer upon which its ICBIS is based.[2] In this ERD, most relationships are many-to-many (M : N), although the double arrows are not shown.

This enterprisewide model pulls together the following financial accounting entities:

- General ledger entity
- Sales order entity
- Accounts receivable entity
- Accounts payable entity
- Purchase order entity
- Payroll entity

Management accounting entities include the following:

- *Cost accounting entity.* This entity provides costs for manufactured products and helps to ensure that the costs assigned to each product accurately reflect the material, labor, and overhead that are required to make it. The cost accounting entity also provides data on the cost of goods manufactured and inventories for financial accounting's general ledger entity.
- *Inventory entity.* This entity maintains beginning and ending financial and nonfinancial data about raw materials, WIP, and finished goods.

---

[1] Robert D. Boyle and John J. Burbridge, Jr., "Who Needs a CIO?" *Information Strategy: The Executive's Journal,* Summer 1991, p. 14.
[2] John G. Burch, *Systems Analysis, Design, and Implementation* (Boston: boyd & fraser, 1992).

INSIGHTS & APPLICATIONS

Failing to Unleash the Power of Information

Knowledge is power, and information provides knowledge. An individual with information cannot help but take responsibility.

A plant manager at a one-billion dollar food-processing company is asked about a new bonus plan. He has surprisingly little to say. I probe, and am stunned to learn that he has never been privy to information on the profitability of the facility that he runs. How can he manage? How can he be motivated to improve? No one really knows the score. In fact, a detailed corporate study had just revealed that an all-time favorite, a product thought to be a "cash cow," had in fact been losing money for years.

To deal with the new strategic requirements for success, all the tools to induce and support action-taking must be available at the front line. Therefore, we must:

- Share virtually all information with everyone.
- Decentralize information systems.
- Provide training to help people understand how to use this newly available information.[3]

◼EXHIBIT 3–1
ERD Symbols and Their Meanings

Meaning	Symbol
An entity is a person, place, object, event, or concept about which data are recorded. Some of the entities in a manufacturing company include plant and equipment, material requirements planning, and cost accounting. In a bank, entities are customers, employees, accounts, branches, loans, and so on. A rectangle is used to represent an entity on an ERD.	
A relationship is the abstraction of a set of associations that hold between different entities. Relationships are represented by a diamond-shaped box with lines connected to related entity types. The diamond-shaped box contains a verb that explains the relationship. The verb contained in the diamond allows an analyst to explain the relationship between entities explicitly. This explanation makes the ERD understandable by all levels of personnel within an organization. A relationship also contains lines from the diamond to the related entities. The lines with proper notation show the occurrences between entities. Relationships can be one-to-one (one:one), one-to-many (one:M), or many-to-many (M:N).	

■ EXHIBIT 3–2
Enterprisewide Model

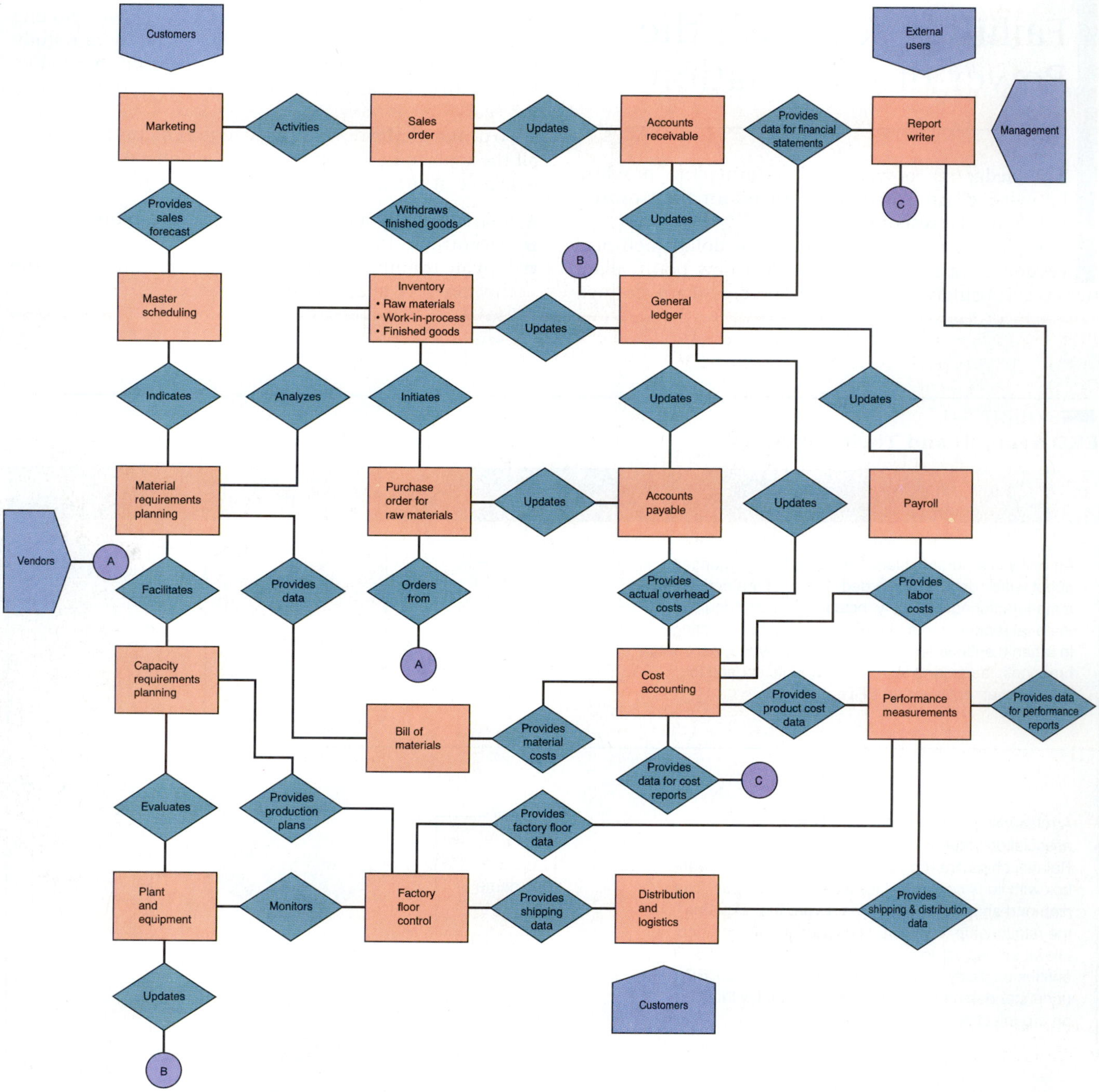

- *Plant and equipment entity.* This entity provides both a record of available production resources and depreciation data for product costing.
- *Performance measurements entity.* This entity includes a wide array of performance evaluations, such as the lead time efficiency (LTE) ratio discussed in the previous chapter. Performance measurements should support the continuous improvement philosophy of WCM, leading to reduced inventories, increased quality, decreased setup times, greater productivity, and improved customer service.
- *Report writer entity.* This entity provides other reports to meet the informational needs of managers.

Integrated with mangement accounting are engineering and manufacturing entities, such as the following:

- *Master scheduling entity.* This entity reflects management's overall production plans based on sales forecasts.
- *Material requirements planning entity.* This entity provides production scheduling and inventory planning and control.
- *Capacity requirements planning entity.* This entity identifies production load for the factory floor by time period, product, and operation.
- *Bill of materials entity.* This is an explosion list of all items required to make a particular product, in terms of quantity, quality, and cost.

Obviously, the modern management accountant cannot alone construct the ERD or design the ICBIS. The point is that the management accountant is part of an information systems team. Thus, management accountants need to understand the terminology, ideas, and ultimately the environment in which they will work. One fundamental objective is to make sure that the accounting entities are properly linked to the marketing, manufacturing, and logistics entities in an efficient and effective manner.

Implementing an Enterprisewide Technology Platform

Three major areas of technology are used to implement an enterprisewide technology platform, based on the enterprisewide model of a manufacturing firm:

- Computer processors and their peripherals
- Local area networks (LANs)
- Bar code scanners

Exhibit 3–3 shows how these technologies are put together to form an ICBIS for the manufacturing enterprise.

Designing an enterprisewide technology platform.

THE COMPUTER PROCESSORS AND THEIR PERIPHERALS. The ICBIS uses three types of processors:

- Mainframes
- Minicomputers
- Microcomputers (or workstations)

Popular peripherals for mainframes and minicomputers include large high-volume printers and magnetic disk packs. Popular peripherals for microcomputers, or workstations, include the following:

- Video disks
- Magnetic disks
- Touch screens
- Mice
- Graphical user interfaces
- Hand-held wands

ICBISs permit the functional specialization of these processors. For example, the forte of the mainframe is its ability to process large volumes of data and its enterprisewide integrity and control. The minicomputer possesses the same capabilities on a smaller scale. Also, the minicomputer is often used as a front-end processor and connector to the mainframe.

The advantages of the microcomputer are its graphics and user friendliness. Data from the mainframe or minicomputer are downloaded to individual workstations as needed for local processing. The microcomputer then displays the results in both tabular and graphical form, as desired by the user. Thus, in an ICBIS, the mainframe and minicomputer process and manage giga- or tera-bytes of data, print large volumes of output, and control interactions throughout

■ EXHIBIT 3–3
Technology Platform That Forms an ICBIS and Supports the Enterprisewide Model

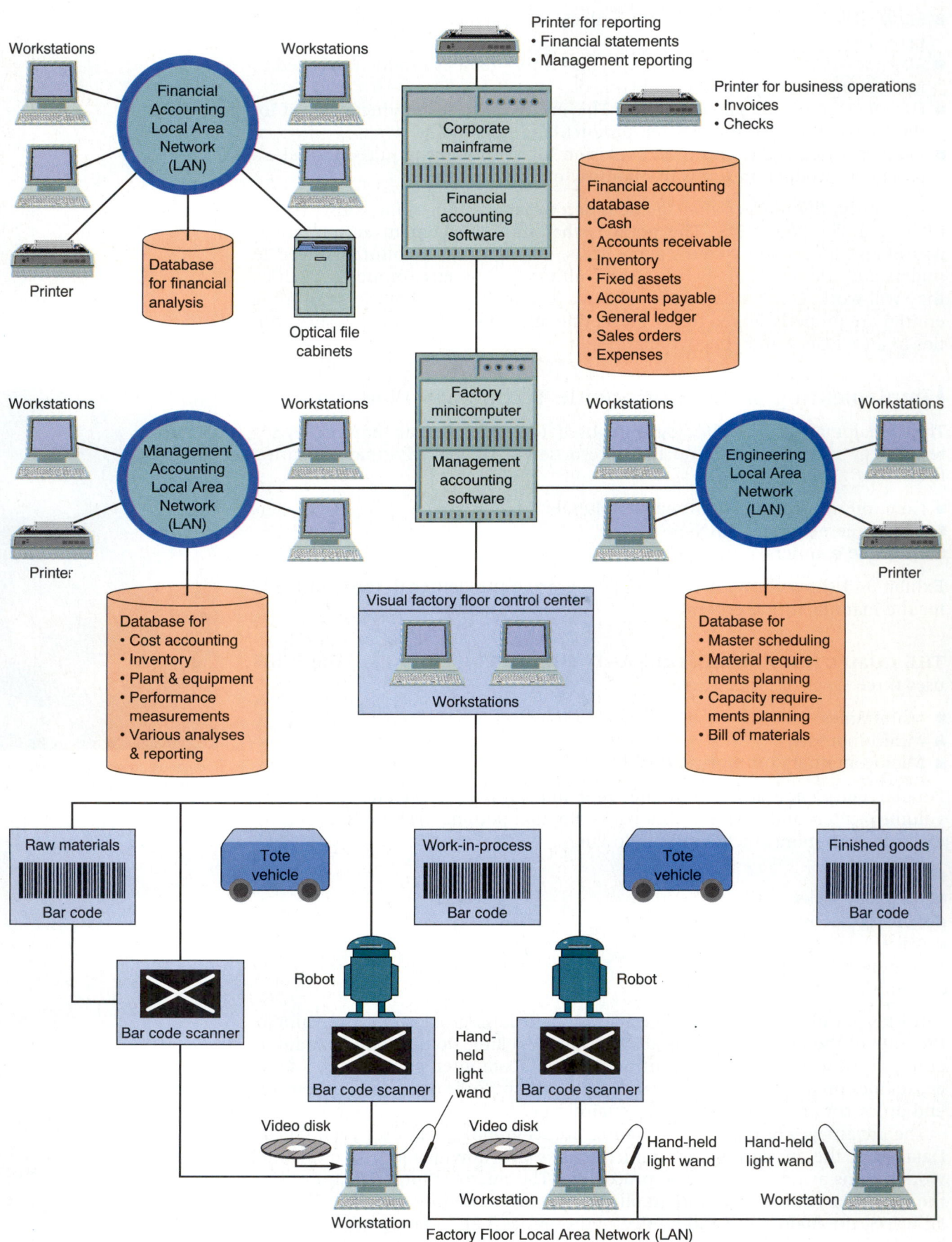

the enterprisewide network. Workstations, on the other hand, provide users with the ability to perform specific applications, make database queries, and generate a variety of graphical displays and reports.

LOCAL AREA NETWORKS.   Local area networks (LANs) connect processors and their peripherals for processing within each major function serviced by the ICBIS. These major functions are as follows:

LAN system.

- *The Financial Accounting Local Area Network (LAN).* This LAN is composed of various workstations, printer(s), optical file cabinets, and a magnetic disk database. The workstations enable users to perform financial accounting tasks. The financial accounting database is controlled by the mainframe, which also prints all critical financial reports and documents, some of which may be confidential. Workstations in the financial accounting LAN, however, are connected to the financial accounting database for uploading and down-loading data under strict input, processing, output, and database controls.

  Data required for local processing are stored in optical file cabinets and magnetic disks. An optical file cabinet is composed of optical disks and optical cards that are read by a low-power laser beam. They feature very high density storage, resistance to change, and immunity to electromagnetic influences that can destroy data on magnetic tapes, disks, or hard drives. Consequently, optical file cabinets are very useful for storing vital documents over a long period of time. The database that stores data for financial analysis (e.g., spreadsheet applications) is supported by a magnetic disk.

- *The Management Accounting Local Area Network (LAN).* This LAN consists of workstations, printer(s), and a database stored on magnetic disk. It performs cost accounting; raw materials, work-in-process, and finished goods inventory costing and control; plant and equipment control and depreciation accounting; performance measurements reporting; and various other management analyses and reports. It transmits data, such as cost of goods manufactured and inventory values, to the financial accounting LAN. Data for much of management accounting processing come from the factory floor LAN. The management accounting LAN also interacts with the engineering LAN.

- *The Engineering Local Area Network (LAN).* This LAN performs many of the manufacturing functions, such as master scheduling, material requirements planning, capacity requirements planning, and the bill of materials. The engineering LAN depends on both the management accounting LAN and the factory floor LAN to transmit a great deal of cost, performance, and production data to it. The engineering LAN also receives budget data and sales forecasts from corporate headquarters to facilitate its scheduling and planning functions.

- *The Factory Floor Local Area Network (LAN).* This LAN controls manufacturing operations. It also uses bar code scanners to collect manufacturing data that are transmitted to both the management accounting LAN and the engineering LAN. Bar coding is a key piece of technology used on the factory floor. In traditional systems, data are often captured either by pen or through manual key entry, but with **bar coding,** data can be identified and captured automatically. Letters, numbers, and special characters are encoded into a series of parallel bar and space patterns, called **bar codes.**

WHAT ARE BAR CODE SCANNERS AND HOW ARE THEY USED?   **Bar code scanners** (also called **readers**) are optical and electronic devices that scan bar code symbols and output the bar-coded data as electrical signals suitable for computer processing. Five generic types of bar code–reading equipment are now in use:

- Hand-held light wands
- Stationary fixed-beam scanners

- Stationary moving-beam scanners
- Hand-held lasers
- Imaging array readers[4]

The primary criteria for selecting an appropriate scanning device include cost, speed, and the need for online capability.

With a fully integrated bar code network in place, accounting reports that once lagged production by days and weeks can be generated in a matter of minutes via either a printer or a monitor display. This timely information allows management to monitor and control critical areas, identify problems and inefficiencies, and take corrective action before big problems occur.

Bar coding effectively eliminates the need for source documents. Bar-coded labels are directly imprinted on, or physically attached to, direct materials, WIP components, and finished goods. When these labels are scanned by a reading device, the underlying data are immediately transmitted to the computer. The data are processed to meet the needs of various entities throughout the ICBIS, such as the inventory, cost accounting, and factory floor control activities. Immediate input and processing of data result in real-time processing information for daily or even hourly planning and operational control. The real-time processing also provides better information than has been traditionally available for performance evaluation.

In highly automated factories, robots electronically scan bar-coded components on a moving conveyor line and are instructed by the computer to complete an assembly or perform a certain process. Direct laborers ("hands-on" production workers) interact with workstations through touch screens or hand-held light wands. At the start of their shifts, production workers pass a hand-held wand over their ID cards. This procedure tells the ICBIS that the employee is at work at a particular time, workstation, and job. This input in turn triggers the factory floor control center to tell the production worker what particular task, product, or job is to be undertaken and alerts the worker about any special notices or procedures currently in effect.

The engineering LAN has already transmitted a specific bill of materials that describes all the materials required to manufacture a product. Using the electronic bill of materials, the factory floor LAN electronically orders needed components from an automated stockroom or directly from a vendor. If the components are in an automated stockroom, they are loaded on an unmanned tote vehicle that is guided by the computer to the appropriate worker or robot.

At the employee workstation, a high-resolution color monitor delivers special instructions or updated procedures. When the employee completes a particular task, product, or job, he or she registers the work with the factory floor control center by pressing several buttons on a keyboard or touching a series of icons (symbols) on the touch-screen monitor. The system automatically notifies an inspector for approval and quality assurance. On approval, the employee begins work on another task, product, or job.

If employees want or need additional information about the process they're about to start or have already begun, they can access help screens that will display interactive and moving video images stored on video disks. The video images serve as tutorials and demonstrations on how a particular task is performed. If these demonstrations are not sufficient, or a tool or component is missing, the worker notifies the factory floor control center by pressing an alert button. A visual signal on a computer monitor automatically alerts an operator in the glass-encased control room, and a graph pinpoints the signal's source. After determining the location and nature of the problem, the control room operator will take whatever steps are necessary to correct the problem, such as dispatching an engineer to the workstation or ordering delivery of a needed tool or component.

---

[4] Arjan T. Sadhwani and Thomas Tyson, *Financial Managers' Guide to Selecting and Implementing Bar Codes* (Montvale, N.J.: Institute of Management Accountants, formerly the National Association of Accountants, 1990), Chapter 2. With permission.

Bar Coding at Xerox

Bar coding is an integral part of a sophisticated inventory control system at the Xerox Corporation copier assembly plant in Webster, New York. Within this site is a fully automated high-rise storehouse that handles over 1,000 transactions per day and deals with over 55,000 parts annually.

Timely scanning of bar-coded information is essential for Xerox's sophisticated material requirements planning (MRP) system that determines the quantity, frequency, and location of parts replenishment of all of its assembly lines and workstations. When warehoused parts are needed, pallets are automatically withdrawn from the high-rise and robotically delivered to material handlers. These handlers withdraw the required boxes, prepare a master replenishment ticket, and attach bar-coded routing tags to every box in the replenishment. Fixed scanners on another series of conveyors direct the boxes to appropriate assembly modules according to information encoded on the bar code label.

In the automated assembly module, handlers place all boxed parts in uniform, bar-coded tote bins which are then automatically routed to individual assembly workstations or assigned buffer areas. By scanning empty bins, the system is able to replace needed parts at individual stations automatically. In the console assembly module, handlers place part boxes in carts that are dedicated to particular assembly grid locations. Radio-directed drivers of forklifts transport these carts to the work-in-process grids. They then physically place the part boxes in the more than 350 individual workstation flow lines.

At Xerox, bar coding is looked upon as a naturally evolving productivity improving factor that enhances material requirements planning (MRP) and complements the philosophies of JIT. With the help of bar coding, records integrity has been improved, purchase lot sizes have been minimized, and parts can be accurately retraced to the date and source of supply if quality problems should develop. Bar coding has helped allow workstation cycle counts to consistently reconcile to within one percent accuracy levels, a criterion that Xerox must fulfill in order to avoid the taking of complete physical inventories that used to require annual two-week plant shutdowns.[5]

Bar coding fully complements JIT and CIM by helping to reduce waste and improving data integrity. The use of bar coding at Xerox is the subject of the accompanying sample case.

USING MATERIAL REQUIREMENTS PLANNING AND MANUFACTURING RESOURCE PLANNING SYSTEMS TO INTEGRATE AND IMPROVE OPERATIONS

Material requirements planning, better known by its acronym **MRP,** was one of the first computer-based technologies to hit the factory floor in the United States. MRP is a materials scheduling procedure geared toward maintaining adequate inventory levels and having items available when they are needed.[6] MRP begins with a schedule for finished goods that is converted into a schedule of requirements for the subassemblies, parts, and raw materials that will be needed to produce the finished goods in the specified time frame.

The primary inputs of MRP are (1) a **bill of materials (BOM),** which contains a listing of all the subassemblies, parts, and raw materials that are needed to produce one unit of a finished product; (2) a **master production schedule,** which states which finished products are to be produced, when they are needed, and what quantities are needed; and (3) an **inventory records file,** which tells how much raw materials inventory is on hand and how long it will take to receive more raw materials from vendors or suppliers.

---

[5] Excerpted from Thomas Tyson and Arjan T. Sadhwani, ''Bar Codes Speed Factory Floor Reporting,'' *Management Accounting*, April 1988, pp. 41–46. Reprinted from *Management Accounting.* Copyright by Institute of Management Accountants, Montvale, N.J.

[6] Carol J. McNair, William J. Mosconi, and Thomas F. Norris, *Beyond the Bottom Line: Measuring World Class Performance* (Homewood, Ill.: Dow Jones–Irwin, 1989), p. 15. With permission.

■ EXHIBIT 3–4
The MRP II and MRP Process

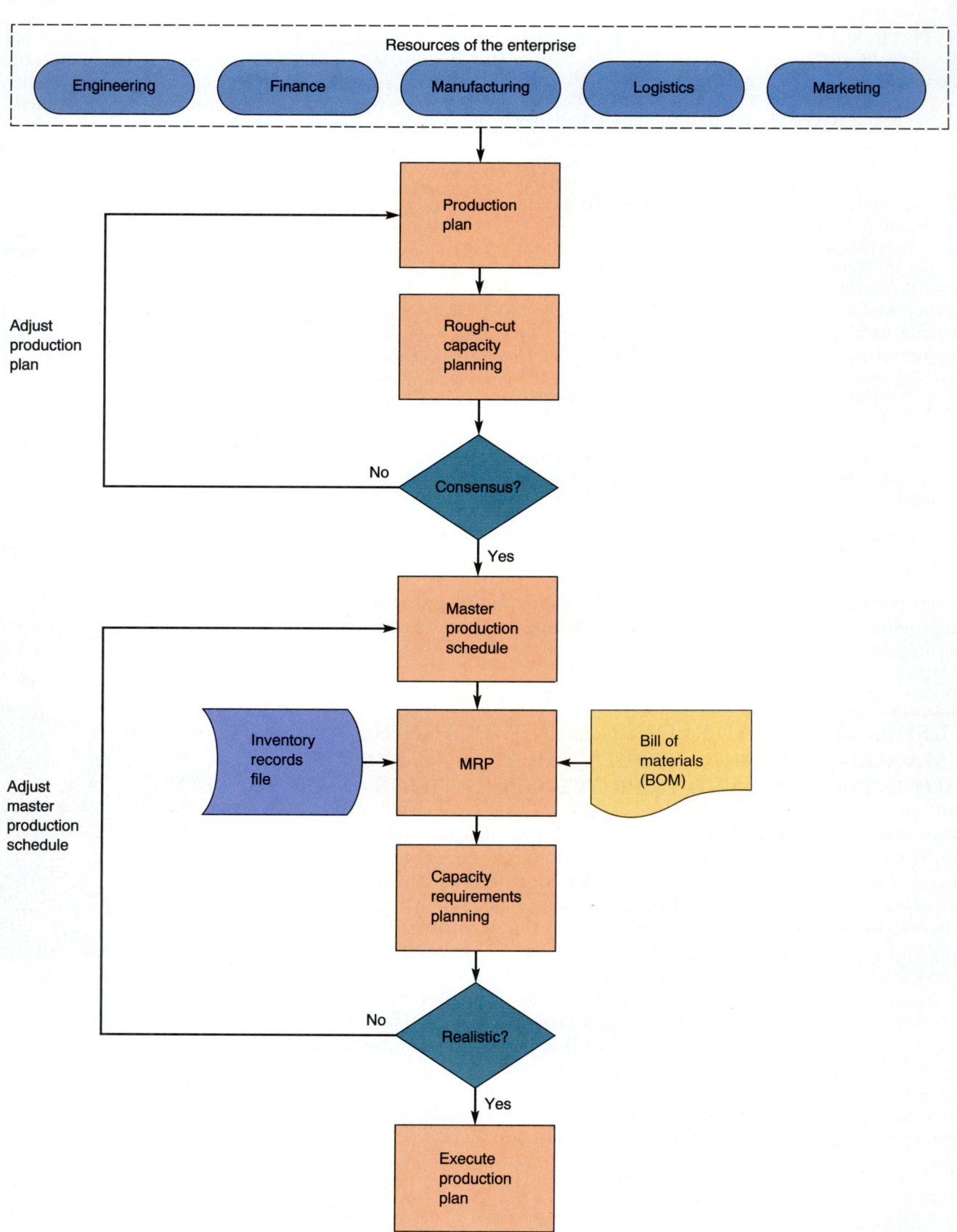

One of the most important features of MRP is its ability to help managers in **capacity requirements planning,** which is a process of determining short-term capacity requirements, such as machines and personnel. A master production schedule may appear realistic on the surface, but on further analysis, the capacity and resources required may turn out to be unrealistic. If so, the time and quantities in the master production schedule will have to be adjusted.

Manufacturing resource planning (MRP II) expands MRP into a broader approach for planning and scheduling the resources (e.g., engineering, finance, manufacturing, logistics, marketing) of the enterprise. Too often, the various areas of the enterprise are fragmented and uncoordinated without an integrated and timely flow of information. A major purpose of MRP II, supported by an ICBIS, is to *integrate* these areas in order to focus on and achieve the goals of the enterprise.

Still, the main element of MRP II is MRP, as Exhibit 3–4 shows. The process begins with demands from all the resource areas. They work together to develop a coordinated production plan, so each area will know what role it has to play. For example, finance will know the amount and timing of funds that will be needed to support the production plan. Often, however, the initial production plan will have to be revised until a consensus is reached.

Once a consensus is reached, a master production schedule is prepared. Then, capacity requirements planning is done to see if short-term available resources can meet the master production schedule. If capacity is not sufficient, the master production schedule will have to be adjusted until it corresponds to available capacity. At this point, orders are released and production begins.

What Are the Modules of MRP II Software?

The software modules that make up the MRP II system are presented in Exhibit 3–5. Notice that a module titled electronic data interchange (EDI) appears as both a customer and a vendor interface module. EDI will be discussed in the last major section of this chapter. Indeed, an increasing number of MRP II software vendors are offering EDI modules that enable companies to integrate their MRP II systems with their vendors' and customers' MRP II systems.

Also notice that the MRP II modules are similar to the entities in the enterprisewide model presented earlier in this chapter. Some companies are using MRP II software as the foundation for their ICBISs. One can build an ICBIS without the MRP II software, but unless the company has special needs that have to be customized, using an off-the-shelf package, such as MRP II, is generally the better way to go.

Computer-based MRP II system in action.

Comparing MRP II and Just-in-Time Manufacturing

Some people believe that an inherent conflict exists between MRP II and just-in-time (JIT) manufacturing. As a matter of fact, MRP II can be used as a key tool for implementing and supporting JIT manufacturing. MRP II does come into conflict with JIT when MRP II is used to support traditional batch manufacturing environments. For example, managers in a traditional environment may say, "We will have so much scrap, so let's plan on it." Thus, scrap is factored into MRP II, planned for, and purchased.

Scrap, not MRP II, is totally contrary to JIT management philosophy. If managers continue to use MRP II in the traditional way, then MRP II will be blamed for the conflict with JIT and WCM. As companies make progress in implementing JIT, however, vendors of MRP II software will drop some features and add others. For example, some MRP II vendors have added a kanban master file to their database to define every standard kanban container used in the plant. Kanban containers are controlled by reading bar code labels on the containers.

■ EXHIBIT 3–5
Modules of a Manufacturing Resource Planning (MRP II) Software System

Adapted from: Alan D. Luber, *Solving Business Problems with MRP II* (Bedford, Mass.: Digital Press, 1991), p. 6. With permission.

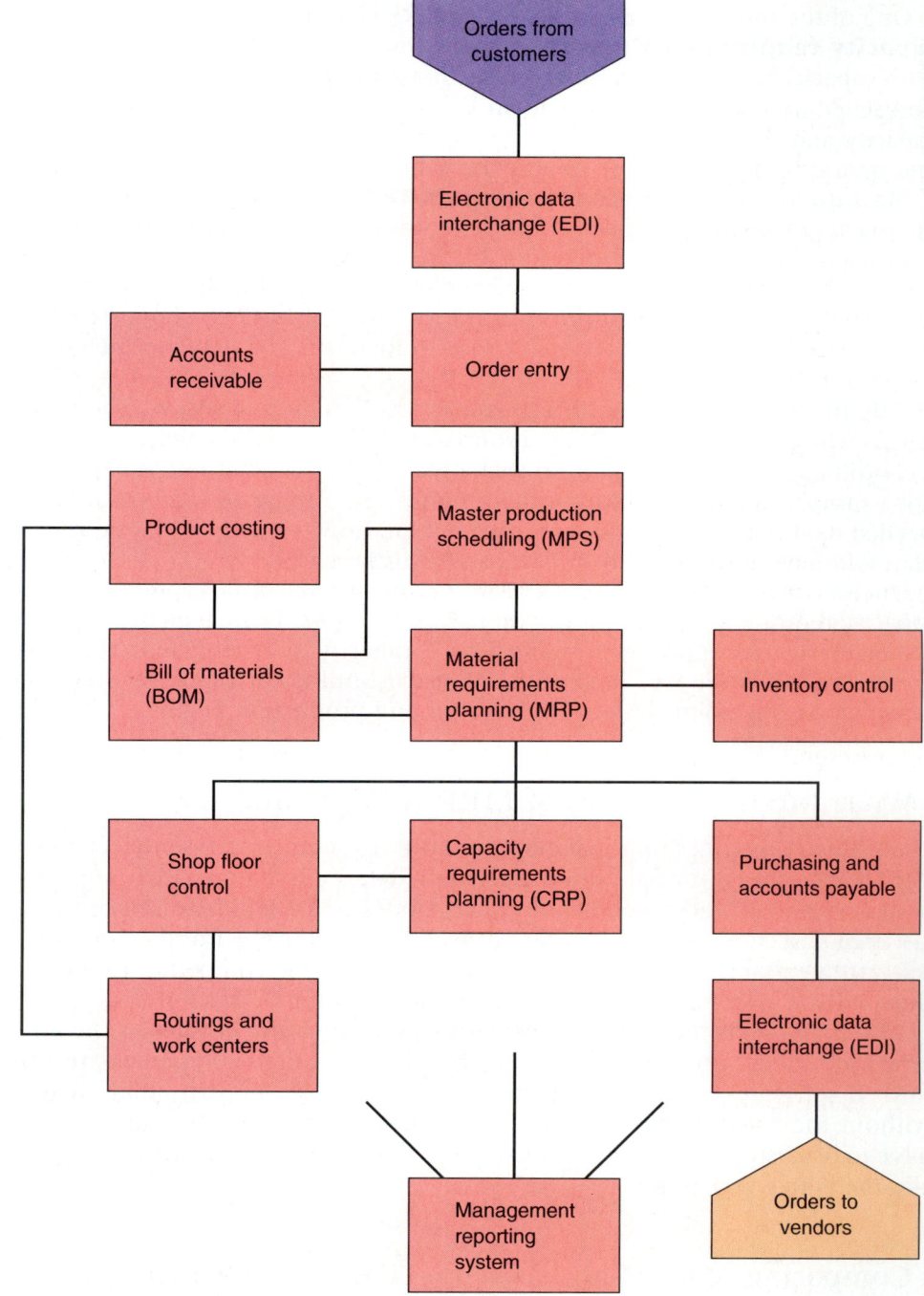

Solving Problems with MRP II

Any manufacturing environment presents a number of problems that must be solved in order to achieve success. The following are some typical problems solved with MRP II:

■ Material shortages
■ Poor quality
■ Poor customer service
■ Poor productivity

INSIGHTS & APPLICATIONS

Material Shortages Problems at Widgets, Unlimited

Jim McAdams, plant manager at Widgets, Unlimited, was mad. For the fourth consecutive month, material shortages had caused him to miss his plant output quota. Andrea Thomas, chief executive officer (CEO), was on his back, making his life miserable. Jim had had enough. He went to Elizabeth Heichler's office to get to the bottom of the problem.

"You're the management accountant, Elizabeth. Why do we continue to have these shortages? I want you to investigate the shortages and tell me what's causing them," said Jim, still fuming from his encounters with Andrea.

"I'll get right on it," said Elizabeth.

A five-day paper chase ensued. After tracking down each of the shortages, Elizabeth reported the following results to Jim:

- Two shortages were caused by lost shop orders.
- Four parts were never ordered because they weren't listed on the bill of materials.
- Three shortages occurred because purchase orders had not been rescheduled in coordination with production rescheduling.
- Six parts were "stolen" by production control to fill shortages on other, more critical jobs.
- A large order of parts was never delivered by a vendor who has a poor record of delivering orders on time.

- A large order of parts from another vendor had to be returned because of poor quality.

Jim shook his head in disbelief. "I hoped that your investigation would help solve this problem," said Jim. "But the way we're going now, I'm not sure that the same things won't happen next month and the next. We've got to do something to coordinate our work so the right hand will know what the left hand is doing."

"I agree," said Elizabeth, "and I believe I have a solution. I've taken the liberty of looking into a system called manufacturing resource planning, or MRP II for short. It will help us coordinate the entire manufacturing process, as well as integrate our operations with our vendors and customers."

"Will it help us eliminate material shortages?" said Jim.

"Yes, I believe it will," Elizabeth responded. "For example, MRP II contains a material requirements planning software module, dubbed MRP, that is employed to prevent material shortages. Its database stores detailed, permanent records of the quantity and need date of every requirement, as well as the quantity and due date of every scheduled receipt."

"Well, I'm for giving MRP II a try," said Jim." We'll hold some meetings to see what the others think about it."

"Yes, there's a lot of work to be done before we can even think about installing MRP II. We've got a lot of changes to make, both operationally and culturally, before we acquire an MRP II package," said Elizabeth.

"I totally agree," said Jim. "I worked for a company that tried to install a system before they got their basic operations squared away. Installing a system over bad operations just causes more problems," said Jim.

SOLVING THE MATERIAL SHORTAGES PROBLEM WITH MRP II.   Many enterprises spend more time and money identifying material shortages than on any other problem. By solving material shortages problems, a company can make significant progress in solving other problems, such as poor quality, poor customer service, and poor productivity.[7]

SOLVING THE QUALITY PROBLEM WITH MRP II.   Vendors should be selected on the basis of price, quality, and delivery. The *low-price* vendor may not be the *low-cost* vendor if late deliveries and poor quality cause increased costs.[8] The above sample case is an aid to a better understanding of the quality problem.

With an MRP II system, a company can rate vendors on the basis of price, quality, and delivery. The following formula provides a simple calculation of quality:

---

[7] Reprinted with permission from *Solving Business Problems with MRP II*, by Alan D. Luber, Copyright © 1991 Digital Press/Digital Equipment Corporation, 129 Parker Street, Maynard, MA 01754.

[8] Ibid., p. 115.

INSIGHTS & APPLICATIONS

The Quality Problem at Nordstrand Technologies

Linda Helgerson, manager of customer service at Nordstrand Technologies, had been receiving an unusual number of complaints from customers about product quality. The number of failures within the warranty period had quadrupled within the last three months, and the entire management team was concerned about the lack of success in solving the problem.

The source of the problem was discovered by a phone call from a vendor's representative who volunteered that his company had shipped defective parts on purchase order numbers 5392 and 5486.

"That's great news," said Roger Kaplan, manager of quality control. "Now all we have to do is purge all the bad parts in the stockroom, and on the factory floor and replace all bad parts out in the field."

Unfortunately, the task was not as easy as it sounded. Nordstrand did not keep detailed records that would enable anyone to determine whether any parts from the two purchase orders were in the stockroom, WIP, or finished goods, or which customers had received products that contained the defective parts.

The company took a costly approach to solving the problem. It scrapped $100,000 worth of parts in the stockroom. All WIP inventory was reworked to replace parts that might be defective. The company's field service group called on all customers who might have received shipments containing defective parts.

Nevertheless, the corrective actions were only about 60 percent effective, and the 60 percent solution cost the company more than $500,000. A better solution would have been to prevent the "junk" from getting in the company in the first place.

$$\text{Quality performance rating} = \frac{\text{Number of parts passing inspection}}{\text{Number of parts inspected}} \times 100\%$$

A perfect quality rating is 100 percent. The quality rating is stored in a vendor master file in the MRP II database. Records in the master file can be viewed online.[9] Exhibit 3–6 is an example of what users see on the screens of their workstations. In this exhibit, the quality performance rating of Precision Instruments has been improving steadily. So far in the current quarter, Precision enjoys a 100 percent quality performance rating with only one late shipment. Precision is providing this performance while supplying the company at a favorable price variance of 8.7 percent.

The vendor performance rating, especially incoming inspection, is at odds with JIT philosophy, however, because incoming inspection is a nonvalue-added activity and should be eliminated. JIT purchasing programs focus on eliminating the need for incoming inspection by developing long-term, single-source relationships with quality vendors. Certain vendors are certified and allowed to deliver directly to production, sometimes referred to as "ship-to-production-line" privileges. This eliminates inspecting, counting, handling, and storing activities, along with all the raw materials stockrooms. In fact, there are no raw materials stockrooms in JIT manufacturing. Certified vendors, though, are subject to periodic audits to retain their certification privileges.[10]

SOLVING THE CUSTOMER SERVICE PROBLEM WITH MRP II.   Customer service, as the previous chapter observed, is paramount in WCM. It entails getting the right product to the customer as needed. Next to missed shipments, not being able to provide customers with accurate delivery dates at the time of order entry is the most common cause of poor customer service.[11] Not being

---

[9] Ibid.
[10] Ibid., p. 145.
[11] Ibid., p. 171.

INSIGHTS & APPLICATIONS

Saturn's Vendor Relationships

The goal at GM's Tennessee-based Saturn Corporation is to build cars that compete globally. Part of the strategy is to maintain tight control over all incoming materials. This strategy has led to vendor agreements and long-term relationships.

Saturn spends six to eight months identifying and selecting *prospective* vendors. Then on-site evaluations are made of vendor personnel and facilities. Then Saturn conducts an in-depth analysis of each vendor's financial, quality, and delivery capabilities. Once selected, vendors must show *continuous improvement* as a world-class organization. These certified vendors are computer-linked through an electronic data interchange (EDI) system to handle transactions automatically.

"Quality is the number-one requirement," says Alan Perriton, Director of Materials Management for Saturn. "No exceptions. If a vendor stubs his toe, we work with him. If he continues to fail on a long-term basis, we consider the option to replace him."

"Fewer vendors means establishing better long-term relationships with those that understand Saturn. They become members of the family and are located physically at the plant," says Perriton.[12]

---

able to meet customer needs can jeopardize the success of any company, as the sample case on the next page illustrates.

Many companies are unable to provide customers with accurate delivery dates for one of two reasons:

- They are unable to calculate how much finished goods inventory is available-to-promise (ATP) to customers in a given time period.
- They do not have real-time access to ATP information at the time of order entry.[13]

■EXHIBIT 3–6
Vendor Performance Inquiry Screen

Vendor Performance Inquiry

Vendor Code: 964   Name: Precision Instruments

	Current Quarter	Year to Date	1994	1993	1992
Number of parts inspected	200	800	1000	1200	900
Number of parts rejected	0	10	20	50	50
Quality performance rating	100%	98.7%	98.0%	95.8%	94.4%
Total number of parts received	200	790	980	1150	850
Number of late shipments	1	3	6	10	12
Total dollars purchased	$42,000	$160,000	$195,000	$228,000	$166,500
Total dollars at standard	$46,000	$172,000	$200,000	$218,000	$156,000
Variance from standard	8.7%	7.0%	2.5%	<4.6%>	<6.7%>

---

[12] Condensed from "Saturn's Strategic MRO Buy," *Purchasing*, May 16, 1991, pp. 23, 27. With permission.
[13] Luber, op. cit., p. 172.

INSIGHTS & APPLICATIONS

Failing to Provide Customer Service at Monroe Technologies

Orders at Monroe Technologies were down for the sixth consecutive month. Dan Andreotti, manager of customer service, became concerned about the trend and decided to get at the root cause.

"Carla, this is Dan Andreotti at Monroe Technologies. How are you today?"

"Just fine," said Carla Cooper, buyer at Marconi Electronics, Monroe's largest customer. "To what do I owe the pleasure?"

"Well, Carla, I've been reviewing our records, and I see that you've been doing less than the usual volume of business with us over the last six months. Can you help me understand why?"

"Like many other manufacturers, Dan, we're implementing a JIT program. To implement JIT successfully, we need vendors who can provide us with accurate delivery dates. We need to know precisely when you can deliver the parts. General lead times won't do."

"Well, who in the world can do that?" asked Dan, exasperated.

"Your biggest competitor, that's who! Eight months ago they installed an MRP II system that links everything together—order entry with inventory with manufacturing planning and so forth."

"We weren't aware of your new JIT system," said Dan.

"We invited all chief executive officers (CEOs) of our major vendors. Yours never showed up."

There was nothing more Dan could say. He thanked Carla for the information and promised to investigate the matter further.

At the next management meeting, things became a little heated.

"Frankly, I don't recall receiving an invitation from anyone to participate in a JIT, or whatever you call it, program. For years, we've been quoting general lead times and that's been good enough," said Henry Halper, Monroe's CEO.

"It's not good enough anymore," Dan responded.

"Well, can't we provide our customers with more accurate delivery dates?" asked Henry.

"We've tried to do it with manual methods, but every attempt has met with failure," said Tres Sanjiv, management accountant.

"Why is that?" Henry asked.

"To provide customers with accurate delivery dates, our order entry clerks have to search every order manually to determine the status of finished goods inventory. If an item is not in stock, the order entry clerk then has to contact the master scheduler to determine when the next production run is scheduled. Moreover, two or more order entry clerks could commit the same inventory to two or more different customers, and no one would be the wiser until it's too late."

"Why do we continue with such a system, or better stated, lack of a system?" asked Henry.

"Henry, if you recall, I presented you with a proposal on MRP II over a year ago," said Tres.

"MRP II," Henry reflected. "Oh, that's a materials research planning software package that you tried to sell me on."

"Actually, MRP II means manufacturing resource planning. I've certainly been wanting to implement MRP II to help solve our material shortages and inventory problems. It would also provide capabilities that would enable us to become vendors for JIT customers," said Tres.

"Well, maybe it's high time I got behind you on this, Tres. Tell me more about this MRP II software package you've been looking at and . . . ."

MRP II systems use information about booked sales orders (i.e., orders that are committed), on-hand inventory, and scheduled production to calculate how much finished goods inventory is ATP in a given time period. The ATP quantity for the current week is calculated as follows:

$$ATP = (\text{On-hand balance} + \text{Master schedule}) - \text{Booked orders}$$

The ATP quantity for any future week n is calculated as follows:

$$ATP (\text{Week } n) = \text{Master schedule (Week } n) - \text{Booked orders (Week } n)$$

SOLVING THE PRODUCTIVITY PROBLEM WITH MRP II. MRP II systems should make the people who use them more productive. This means that the same number of people should be able to produce more, or that fewer people should be able to produce the same amount of work. The productivity problem is an issue at Thor Manufacturing, as the following sample case explains.

Solving the Productivity Problem at Thor Manufacturing

Jeff Norris, controller at Thor Manufacturing, scrutinized the request for $3 million for a computer system, telecommunication network, and MRP II system.

"I'm sick and tired of reviewing appropriations that are supposed to increase productivity. In the past three years, I've approved six major appropriation requests that were supposed to reduce inventory and salaried employees. My gosh, we ought to be down to zero inventory and no salaried employees."

"But this new system will help us achieve a CIM environment and become a world-class manufacturer," said Kathleen Sullivan, plant manager.

"I'm sorry, I don't believe any of it. Three years ago, we had 100 salaried employees whose main job was expediting. Today, we have 125 expediters on the payroll. Each of these people costs the company about $70,000 a year in salary and benefits. And they all add cost, not value. What happened to all that productivity promised three years ago?"

"Well, that's what we're trying to . . . ," said Kathleen.

"Oh, don't get me wrong," Jeff interrupted. "The way we currently operate, we couldn't get the work done without these people. But we won't survive much longer if we continue to operate this way. Salaried headcount has to be reduced."

"That's exactly what we're trying to do with CIM; turn our operations around and not only survive but flourish," said Kathleen.

"Well, please be more specific. How do you plan to improve productivity with CIM, MRP II, and all this other stuff you've been talking about?" asked Jeff.

"I will list a few examples for you, just to give you an idea," said Kathleen. "We could, for example, improve productivity in production services."

"How so?"

"Few people would think that MRP II would reduce headcount in production services, but MRP II's bill of materials module provides online access. So, rather than copying and distributing updated hard copies of bills of materials whenever an engineering change becomes effective, as we're doing now, we can do it electronically and save over 800,000 paper copies per year, as well as the labor required to make those copies."

"OK, but that's not worth $3 million," Jeff responded.

"There's more. For example, we have 14 clerks who do nothing but match sales invoices with purchase orders and packing slips to make sure invoices are correct and valid. MRP II provides electronic three-way matching of invoices, purchase orders, and packing slips.

"Also, look at all the nonvalue-added costs in purchasing and storing of raw materials. Our buyers and purchasing clerks spend more than half of their time placing purchase orders. To convert a plant requisition for raw materials into a purchase order, the buyer must select the vendor, determine price, and complete a purchase order request form. The buyer submits the request form to a purchasing clerk. After the purchase order is generated, a clerk compares the purchase order to the purchase order request form to make sure that no typing errors occurred. Finally, the clerk inserts the purchase order in an envelope and mails it to the vendor. MRP II, on the other hand, automatically generates purchase orders. And if we acquire an EDI module, we can eliminate all paperwork. As we move more and more to JIT, we can eliminate the purchasing function and raw materials stockroom altogether."

"Wait a minute," Jeff interrupted. "I can see how much of the purchasing function can be eliminated, but I can't see eliminating the raw materials stockroom. In theory, JIT manufacturing eliminates the need for stockrooms by synchronizing the flow of material so perfectly that the vendor delivers raw materials directly to the production line or cell precisely when they are needed. In our operation, I don't believe this state of perfection will be achieved for two reasons:

- The stockroom acts as a buffer for in-transit lead time variances for our vendors that are remotely located.
- The stockroom acts as a buffer for our inability to determine precisely where and when raw materials are needed.

You must bear in mind that part of our operation is job order manufacturing in which we make custom-ordered products. With this kind of manufacturing, we are unable to achieve an assembly line style of production suited to predictable, synchronized material flow."

"That's true," Kathleen responded, "but our stockroom costs are running close to $4 million per year. Therefore, minimizing the cost of operating the stockroom is important. We can do this in two ways:

- Automatically providing a picklist showing the location and quantities of materials based on the bill of materials for forthcoming production
- Permitting stockkeepers to enter completed picklists without having to enter individual inventory transactions for each item issued to manufacturing"

"I see what you mean. We're doing a lot of nonvalue-added manual work now. When I was in the service, we called this 'monkey work.' But what about our expediters, Kathleen?"

"There's no doubt that expediting is one of our highest nonvalue-added costs, as it is in many other companies. To help reduce, if not eliminate expediting, we must prevent material shortages. By shifting the emphasis from expediting to material shortages prevention, an MRP II system would make it possible for us to eliminate most of our expediters."

"I'll believe it when I see it," said Jeff. "But you've opened my eyes to a lot of things today. I am certainly willing to pursue your proposal further with an open mind."

"That's all anyone can ask," said Kathleen.

INSIGHTS & APPLICATIONS

Electronic Data Interchange: A Challenge and an Opportunity

The past year has been a tough one. Our company went through two mergers and one reorganization and has a new CEO. But things finally seem to be returning to normal. I don't usually have that tight feeling in my stomach when I pull into the parking lot in the morning, and I rarely have a headache when I pull out at the end of the day.

Then it happens—just when I think things are going smoothly, the vice president of marketing, Sharon Majors, comes into my office late on a Friday afternoon. "You're not going to believe this," she starts off. "I just got back from a trip to St. Louis with our Midwest sales representative. Our last stop was MaxTech. I scheduled it so we could spend as much time with them as they would give us."

"MaxTech is our company's largest customer. Last year their orders represented around 40% of sales and more than 50% of profits. Because they represent such a sig-

nificant portion of our business, everyone in our organization works hard to meet their requirements."

Sharon continues, "When we got to MaxTech, they had set up a meeting for us. In addition to the people I had expected to meet, their chief information officer and a couple of MIS staff were there, too. Soon after the meeting started, I found out what was up. MaxTech has decided that they want to streamline some of their internal operations. They have decided to implement an EDI system and want us to be one of their test vendors. They chose us because we have been so cooperative in the past."

I don't hear the last sentence because I am shuffling through my list of acronyms trying to decipher EDI. Finally, I remember that EDI stands for electronic data interchange. My hazy recollection is that EDI has something to do with computers communicating with other computers.

"When do they want us to do this?" I ask, hoping for an answer sometime in the next century.

"They're not firm on their dates yet, but it sounds like they would like a pilot test about six to eight months from now, followed by full implementation in 12 months."

"Six to eight months!" I say. Here we are again, thrown back into the crisis mode that we had operated in for so much of the past year. "Okay, I guess we will need to get going soon, I'll set up a meeting for early next week." As I drive home that night both my stomach and my head are hurting again.[14]

LEARNING OBJECTIVE 3

Show how electronic data interchange (EDI) is used to form metacorporations.

MOVING TO ELECTRONIC DATA INTERCHANGE AND METACORPORATIONS

Electronic data interchange (EDI) is a computer-to-computer communications system that enables a number of business transactions, such as ordering, shipping, billing, and paying, to be conducted between companies electronically. Such a system is illustrated in Exhibit 3–7.

New terms like **metacorporation,** also called **hypercorporation** or **virtual company,** refer to corporations that are relationship driven. To form a metacorporation, a manufacturer establishes long-term relationships with vendors, customers, bankers, and carriers; the result is a comprehensive economic entity that is held together by relationships supported by the enabling technology of EDI.

The shift to metacorporations has already occurred in a number of industries. For example, General Motors, its suppliers, customers, carriers, and banks are linked together through EDI to form a metacorporation. Virtually no paper, such as invoices, purchase orders, bills of lading, and checks, flows between the various entities.

---

[14] Jack M. Cathey, "Electronic Data Interchange: What a Controller Should Know," *Management Accounting,* November 1991, p. 47. Reprinted from *Management Accounting.* Copyright by Institute of Management Accountants, Montvale, N.J.

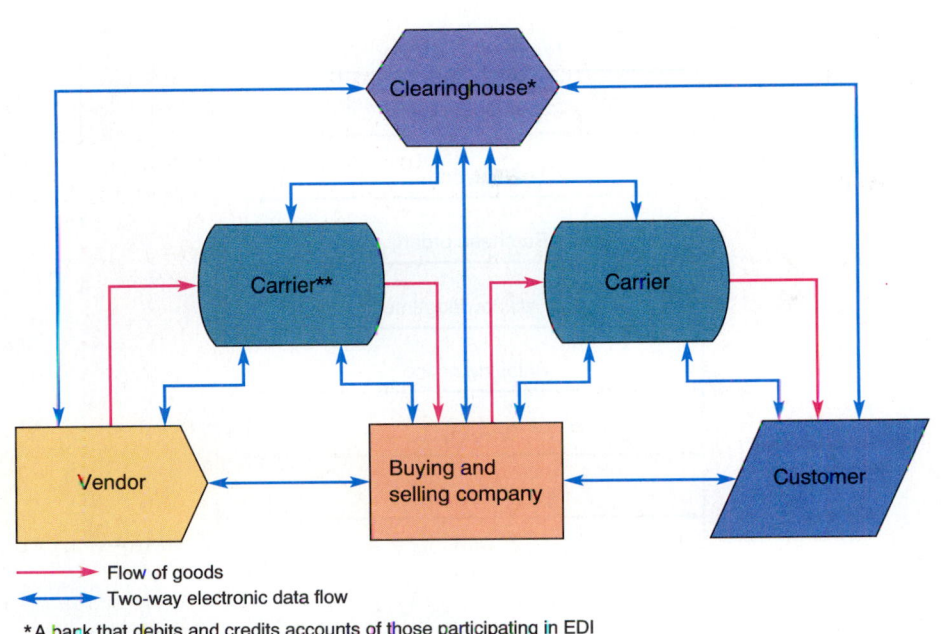

Flow of goods
Two-way electronic data flow
*A bank that debits and credits accounts of those participating in EDI
**A freight company that physically transports the goods

. . . relationships among companies in the next century will be profoundly symbiotic. Symbiosis captures the essence of a new business landscape where organizations will be defined more by their relationships than by organizational boundaries.[15]

TURNING ADVERSARIES INTO PARTNERS

Most innovation in the future will demand that historically *adversarial* relations:

- between many functions in the firm
- between labor and management
- between suppliers and the firm
- between distributors and the firm
- between customers and the firm

be replaced by *cooperative* relations.[16]

How Electronic Data Interchange Works

Direct computer-to-computer links take advantage of the speed and accuracy of electronic communication. The cost of such a connection is justified by the high volumes of data and speed of delivery. Moreover, a clearinghouse component, like a full-service bank, can significantly reduce the bookkeeping functions for all participants. Clearinghouses with expertise in EDI can pay freight bills and invoices, audit these payments, protect against duplicate payments, and reformat data and transmit them directly to subscribers' computers for reconciliation and management reports.[17]

Many transaction sets have been defined under the X.12 standard (maintained by the ANSI Accredited Standards Committee). The most comprehensively covered business activity is the purchasing activity. Exhibit 3–8 shows the major EDI transaction sets that can pass between vendors and customers.[18]

---

[15] Paul Saffo, "Computers Spell the Doom of Corporations As We Know Them," *Infoworld,* July 8, 1991, p. 45.

[16] Peters, op. cit., p. 337.

[17] John Burch, "EDI: The Demise of Paper," *Information Executive,* Winter 1989, p. 52.

[18] Trevor I. Richards, "Implementing EDI: The Three Key Steps," *Interact,* September 1991, pp. 44–45. With permission.

■EXHIBIT 3–8
**Major EDI
Transactions**

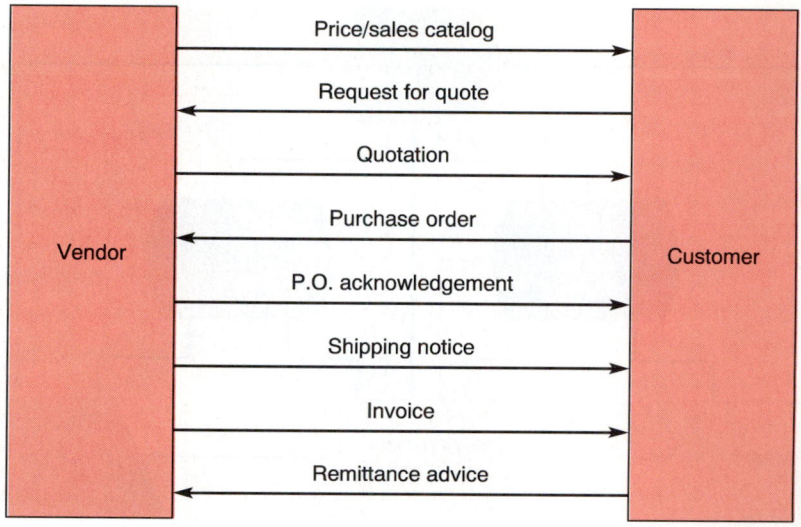

What Are the Benefits of Electronic Data Interchange?

EDI brings with it many substantial benefits. The most obvious is survival. A number of enterprises have said to their vendors, "No EDI, no business." Texas Instruments' global EDI system provides connections that enable its vendors to access data anywhere in the system. Vendors wishing to do business with TI must become EDI trading partners in the fullest sense of the word. TI's EDI system has reduced procurement costs by 80 percent. Other companies are including EDI as a high-priority criterion in selecting vendors.[19]

Management accountants should take the lead in exploring EDI for their organizations.[20] The use of EDI leads to a host of benefits, such as the following:

■ *Reduction in paperwork.* EDI eliminates mountains of paperwork and thereby reduces the chance of human error. Data are entered once and that's it. There's no need to recopy the information just so different clerks throughout the transportation pipeline can reenter the same data five or six times. Moreover, once the data are in the database, models can be applied to convert them into meaningful information for management.

■ *Cost savings.* Eliminating the printing and storage costs of paper forms are two other advantages of EDI. Bank charges for lockboxes are reduced. Companies can also make significant cuts in clerical personnel because EDI eliminates the need to "key" data, open envelopes, and carry mailbags to and from the post office.

A trade association estimates that EDI can reduce domestic automakers' manufacturing and marketing expenses by over $200 per car. For an automaker like General Motors, this cost savings would amount to around $2 billion a year. General Motors is developing a pan-European EDI system modeled after its U.S.-based system to link vendors, factories, and distributors. Toyota uses EDI to deliver an automobile with colors and accessories to customer specifications within five days after an order is placed.

■ *Better integration.* By using EDI, vendors will know in advance what parts and quantities the purchaser needs. Marketing in turn will know its customer needs better. This integration leads to a synchronized flow of operations and the ability to implement JIT techniques.

---

[19] Cathey, op. cit., p. 48.
[20] Martha M. Heidkamp, "Reaping the Benefits of Financial EDI," *Management Accounting* May 1991, p. 43. Reprinted from *Management Accounting.* Copyright by Institute of Management Accountants, Montvale, N.J.

INSIGHTS & APPLICATIONS

Reaping EDI Benefits at Cummins Engine Company

Cummins Engine Company is a satisfied EDI user. Martha Heidkamp spearheaded the EDI implementation at Cummins when she served as project team leader.

Martha Heidkamp says that Cummins has received the following benefits from implementing EDI:

- Reduced costs
- Improved accuracy
- Increased timeliness

She states that these benefits are brought about by not rekeying data. Over 70 percent of computer input for one company is output from another company's computer. For example, a vendor ships goods to a customer. The supplier creates an invoice, prints it, and mails a copy to the customer. When the invoice arrives, it is matched against receiving documents, then approved for payment and keyed in the accounts payable system. How much simpler it is if the supplier sends an invoice to the customer's computer.[21]

- *Improved inventory control.* "The inventory reduction is worth a lot of money, and we expect a 7- to 14-day reduction in the order cycle by eliminating manual processing and mail lag," says Garlan Crossno, director of special projects for Wal-Mart stores. The company has been able to cut inventory by over 15 percent with EDI. Moreover, Wal-Mart can lose millions if its stores run out of popular items during the height of a season. EDI ensures that such losses do not occur.
- *Increased automation.* EDI supports automation from the accounting office to the shop floor. All clerical and bookkeeping tasks are automated. Moreover, combining EDI with bar codes facilitates new manufacturing procedures, such as JIT, CIM, and MRP II.

Combining Electronic Data Interchange and Bar Coding

By combining EDI with bar-coding technologies, companies can increase the accuracy and the speed of the data collection process. EDI takes care of order processing and shipping, and bar coding tracks production from raw materials to WIP to finished goods. The sample case on the next page explains how these technologies are combined.

Supporting the Team Concept through Information Technology

As discussed in Chapter 2, the team concept plays a primary role in world-class manufacturing. Information technology, especially as applied in LANs, EDI, and telecommunications, supports team members any time and any place, whether they are in the same or different locations, on the road with a portable PC, or working at a vendor's, or customer's, location.

The term **groupware** refers to information technology that supports the team concept. Groupware applications include the following:

- Electronic calendars and scheduling systems
- Videoconferencing and screen sharing
- Electronic mail (called E-mail)
- Electronic bulletin boards and FAX messaging

[21] Ibid.

INSIGHTS & APPLICATIONS

Combining EDI and Bar Coding at Pillowtex

Pillowtex Corporation is one of the largest manufacturers of bed pillows. Within its product line are standard-, queen-, king-, and jumbo-size down and fiber-filled pillows. Pillowtex also produces a vast array of synthetic decorative pillows and fashion items. On average, Pillowtex produces approximately 1.5 million pillows per month.

At Pillowtex, EDI and bar coding were combined in order to make Pillowtex a quick-response manufacturer and to shorten lead times.

Before Pillowtex automated its production capabilities, inventory was tracked manually. Shop floor personnel packed finished goods into containers and then were responsible for updating a written order list as each container was packed and completed. As the order was shipped, the written order list was sent to a data entry function where another individual would double check the written list and key in the data at a terminal to update the inventory system.

By combining EDI and bar coding technologies, Pillowtex can track orders through every stage of the manufacturing process, from picking raw materials through shipment of the finished product to the customer. The implementation of this technology has enabled the company to move to a JIT manufacturing system which effectively allows it to meet unique retailer requirements with minimal disruption to company processes.[22]

- Voice mail
- Online, integrated databases

These groupware elements permit people to work together even though they are geographically separated.

One of the most serious challenges an enterprise faces is how to shorten the length of time it takes to make something happen or get the job done. The activity in question could be as simple as getting an agreement on the time and place of a team meeting or as complex as the process that converts a market demand into a commercial product. Problems arise and opportunities are missed when an enterprise is unable to move information in a timely manner and coordinate activities. Groupware offers a way to reduce this dilemma.

Enabling technologies are changing the role of management accountants in world-class enterprises. No longer will they be able to remain isolated from the rest of management, locked behind the closed doors of a distant accounting office. The management accountants of the future (and of the present) will be team members, an integral part of the management team. As such, an under-

INSIGHTS & APPLICATIONS

Involve Everyone in Everything

Involve all personnel at all levels in all functions in virtually everything; for example, quality improvement programs and 100 percent self-inspection; pro-

ductivity improvement programs; measuring and monitoring results; budget development, monitoring, and adjustment; layout of work areas; assessment of new technology; recruiting and hiring; making customer calls and participating in customer visit programs.

Be guided by the axiom: There are no limits to the ability to contribute on the part of a properly selected, well-trained, appropriately supported, and, above all, committed person. Surviving depends on quality, flexibility, and constant innovation, which in turn depends on people.[23]

---

[22] Adapted from Lawrence Klein and Randy M. Jacques, "'Pillow Talk' for Productivity," *Management Accounting*, February 1991. Reprinted from *Management Accounting*. Copyright by Institute of Management Accountants, Montvale, N.J.

[23] Peters, op. cit., pp. 342–344.

standing of new enterprise environments will be part of their critical, professional information base. Management accountants will need a detailed understanding of the production and computer-based information technologies available and will have to make sure that these are linked to the accounting system.

The purpose of this first part of the text has been to provide that understanding. Part II of the text will look at the design of cost accounting systems and how they fit into these new technologies.

▌ SUMMARY OF LEARNING OBJECTIVES

The major goals of this chapter were to enable you to achieve three learning objectives:

Learning objective 1. Describe how integrated computer-based information systems (ICBISs) are developed.

Generally, the first thing that systems consultants do when developing an ICBIS is to create an enterprisewide model of the firm using an entity relationship diagram (ERD). Once all user requirements have been defined, various information technologies, including computer hardware, software, and telecommunication devices, are installed in accordance with the enterprisewide model and user requirements.

Learning objective 2. Explain how material requirements planning (MRP) and manufacturing resource planning (MRP II) systems are used to integrate and improve operations.

MRP is an information system used to perform capacity requirements planning and to handle ordering of raw materials, parts, and subassemblies. Inputs to MRP include the following:

- Master production schedule
- Bill of materials (BOM)
- Inventory records file

The master production schedule indicates the timing and quantity of finished products. These finished products are exploded using the bill of materials. The exploded view of a BOM is usually a drawing or list showing separately, but in proper sequence and relationship, the various raw materials, parts, and subassemblies of a finished product. Then inventory records are used to prepare a material requirements plan to indicate the quantity and timing for ordering or producing raw materials, parts, and subassemblies.

MRP II expands MRP to include resource and production planning. Many authorities view MRP II software as a major enabling technology for the WCM methods of JIT and CIM, and as a foundation for ICBIS. The following problems are eliminated or reduced through MRP II software:

- Material shortages
- Poor quality
- Poor customer service
- Poor productivity

The key to solving these problems is to identify and eliminate their root causes. MRP II helps do just that.

Learning objective 3. Show how electronic data interchange (EDI) is used to form metacorporations.

EDI permits different companies to communicate with one another online and in real-time with little human intervention. Companies can buy, sell, deliver, charge, and pay without preparing various documents and mailing them. In this way, trading partners can be linked together to form a metacorporation.

Most projections indicate that a substantial portion of business transactions will be conducted using EDI by the year 2000. Many authorities believe that by the turn of the century, over 75 percent of the *Fortune 1000* companies and their customers and vendors will be connected via EDI. Thus, the question is not whether to do EDI, but rather when and how. Enterprises that implement EDI now will position themselves strategically for greater success in the future.

IMPORTANT TERMS

Bar code scanners (readers)   Devices used to read bar code labels. Bar code scanners are available in a variety of sizes, features, and price ranges to meet the needs of different applications. Five types of scanners are commonly in use: hand-held light wands, stationary fixed-beam scanners, stationary moving-beam readers, hand-held lasers, and imaging array readers.

Bar codes   Symbols that can be processed electronically to identify numbers, letters, or special characters.

Bar coding   A process of preparing and reading bar codes for online, real-time data input.

Bill of materials (BOM)   A listing of all the subassemblies, parts, and raw materials that are needed to produce one unit of a finished product.

Capacity requirements planning   A process of determining short-term capacity requirements, such as machines and personnel.

Electronic data interchange (EDI)   A computer-to-computer communication network (using standards set by the American National Standards Institute) that enables trading partners, such as buying and selling companies, vendors, customers, banks, and carriers, to carry on business transactions electronically.

Enterprisewide model   A visual description of all the major entities that comprise a company and the relationships among these entities. Preparing an enterprisewide model is one of the first steps systems consultants perform when developing an ICBIS.

Entity   A person, place, object, event, activity, process, or concept about which data are recorded.

Entity relationship diagram (ERD)   A very popular modeling tool used by systems consultants to create an enterprisewide model. It is also used for other modeling tasks.

Groupware   Information technology, including both hardware and software, that supports the team concept by enabling team members to interact with one another no matter the time or location.

Inventory records file   A storage medium that tells how much raw materials inventory is on hand and how long it will take to receive more raw materials from the vendor.

Manufacturing resource planning (MRP II)   A comprehensive software system that contains a number of modules that support WCM objectives and can serve as a foundation for ICBISs. MRP II expands MRP to include planning and scheduling for all the resources of the enterprise.

Master production schedule   A document that states which finished products are to be produced, when they are needed, and what quantities of raw materials are needed.

Material requirements planning (MRP)   A software system that helps determine the quantity of raw materials on hand, the quantity on order, and future material requirements. Early on, MRP was a stand-alone system. Today, it is a module in the MRP II software system.

Metacorporation (hypercorporation or **virtual company)**   A business enterprise composed of a manufacturing, merchandising, or service firm and its vendors, customers, banks, and carriers that are integrated via telecommunication and computer technologies to carry on business electronically and in a synchronized, cooperative fashion.

DEMONSTRATION PROBLEMS

■ **DEMONSTRATION PROBLEM 1**   *Development of ICBIS to handle EDI and JIT.*
Lobeam, Incorporated makes headlights for automobile manufacturers. Recently, Major Motors, Lobeam's largest customer, held a meeting with all of its vendors. The purpose of the meeting was conversion to EDI and JIT. Vendors that do not convert to EDI and JIT within 12 months will no longer be able to do business with Major Motors.

"From the accounting office to order entry or even to all of us here on mahogany row, today's most effective business enterprises must share information," Daniel F. Burtraw, Major Motors' CEO, stated emphatically. "It's absolutely critical for efficient and accurate work and data flow that all of our vendors integrate with us electronically. Over the last decade, many in our industry have created islands of automation and data banks of information. It's up to us at Major Motors to be an industry leader and integrate these islands into a unified whole for operations, reporting, and analysis. We expect the same initiative from our vendors."

Lobeam has responded to this challenge by giving Ping Fu, senior management accountant, the responsibility for developing the ICBIS design to support EDI and JIT. Ping has defined the major entities of the new system as follows:

- Electronic data interchange (EDI)
- General ledger (GL)
- Accounts receivable (AR)
- Accounts payable (AP)
- Payroll (PR)
- Assets and depreciation (AD)
- Customer orders and shipping (COS)
- Purchase orders and receiving (POR)
- Manufacturing resource planning (MRP II)
- Cost management (CM)
- Cost accounting (CA)
- Performance measurement (PM)

So far Ping hasn't really made much progress. All these entities have been in place and functional at Lobeam for quite some time. Her task now is to map out which entities relate to each other, then make certain that people in financial accounting, management accounting, production, and engineering all agree with her concept of these relationships. Only then can true integration be achieved, allowing efficient EDI implementation with Lobeam's vendors and customers. The improved, real-time data flow of the ICBIS will be instrumental in making JIT a reality on the production floor and elsewhere.

Ping's been advised by Dave Hall, the operations supervisor of Lobeam's computer-aided manufacturing group, that decentralized processing using microcomputer workstations should be sufficient for the ICBIS. He feels that the latest generation of microcomputers is able to provide a high level of performance, rivaling that of the minicomputers of just a few years ago. Linking them together with local area networks (LANs) according to functional areas such as production–engineering, financial accounting, and management accounting will allow sharing of common databases.

Required:
Prepare an entity relationship diagram (ERD) for the entities Ping has identified at Lobeam. Be sure to illustrate how EDI connections to vendors and customers relate to the rest of your ERD. Next, using the suggestions Ping received from Dave Hall, make a conceptual sketch of a computer technology platform that will satisfy the relationships of your ERD. Be sure to show where you would expect to find software modules that correspond to the various entities; that is, show which entities correspond to the various elements (LANs, workstations, databases, and so forth) of your technology platform.

SOLUTION TO DEMONSTRATION PROBLEM 1

After working with and interviewing people in production, engineering, and financial accounting, Ping and her project team members prepare an entity relationship diagram on page 116 that models the new enterprisewide ICBIS. Note how EDI connections from customers initiate actions by the customer orders and shipping (COS) entity, while other EDI connections to vendors are provided data by the purchase orders and receiving (POR) entity.

Ping presented this enterprisewide ERD to people in various areas of the firm to make sure that all parties were in agreement with it. After reaching a consensus, Ping and her project team members prepared a conceptual illustration of a technology platform design for the ICBIS that will support EDI and JIT, as shown on page 117. Again, Ping was careful to include the EDI connections. Her design is based on three microcomputer LANs and also shows how future JIT implementation on the production floor will be connected to the ICBIS.

■ ERD Model for the New Enterprisewide ICBIS

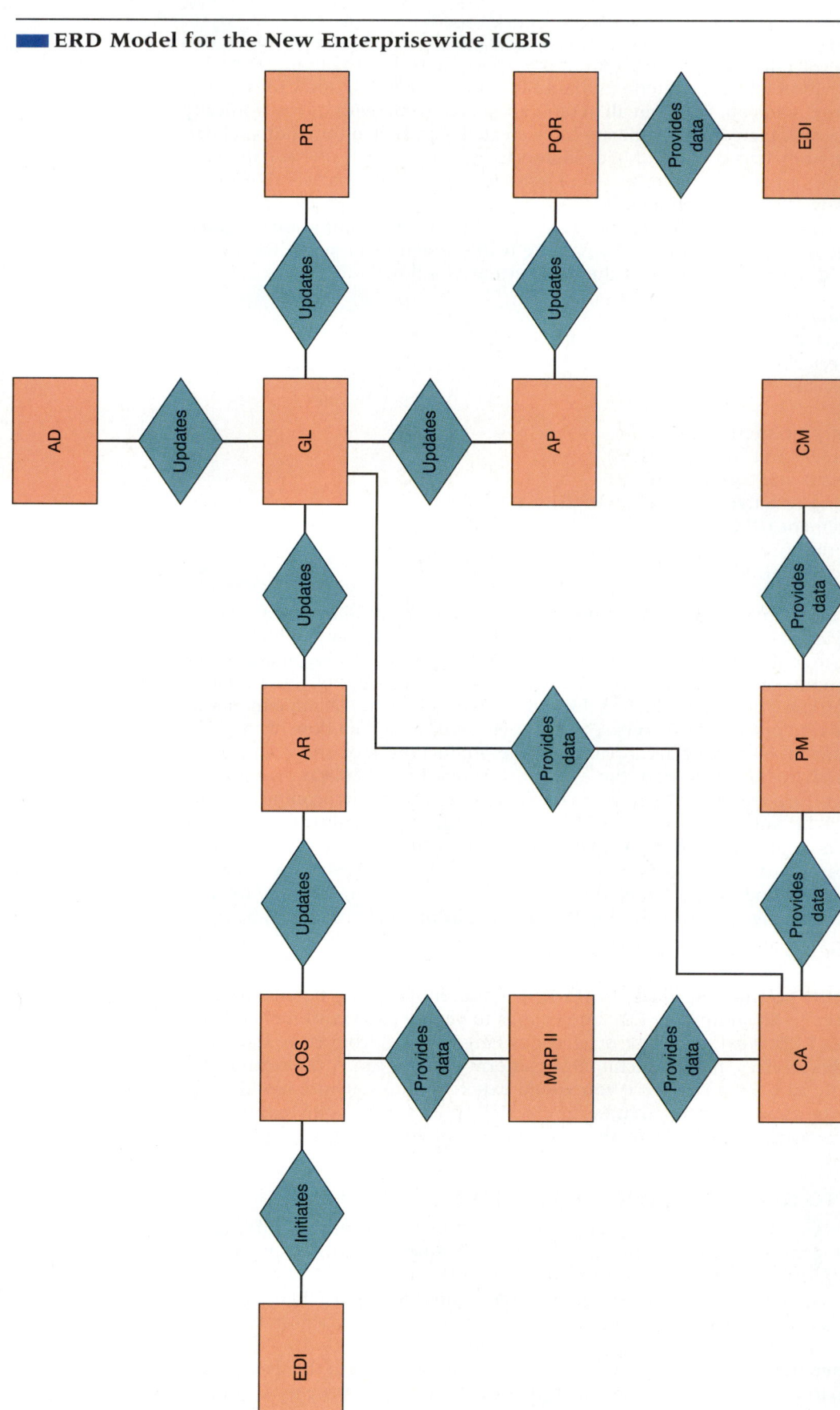

Technology Platform Design for the New Enterprisewide ICBIS

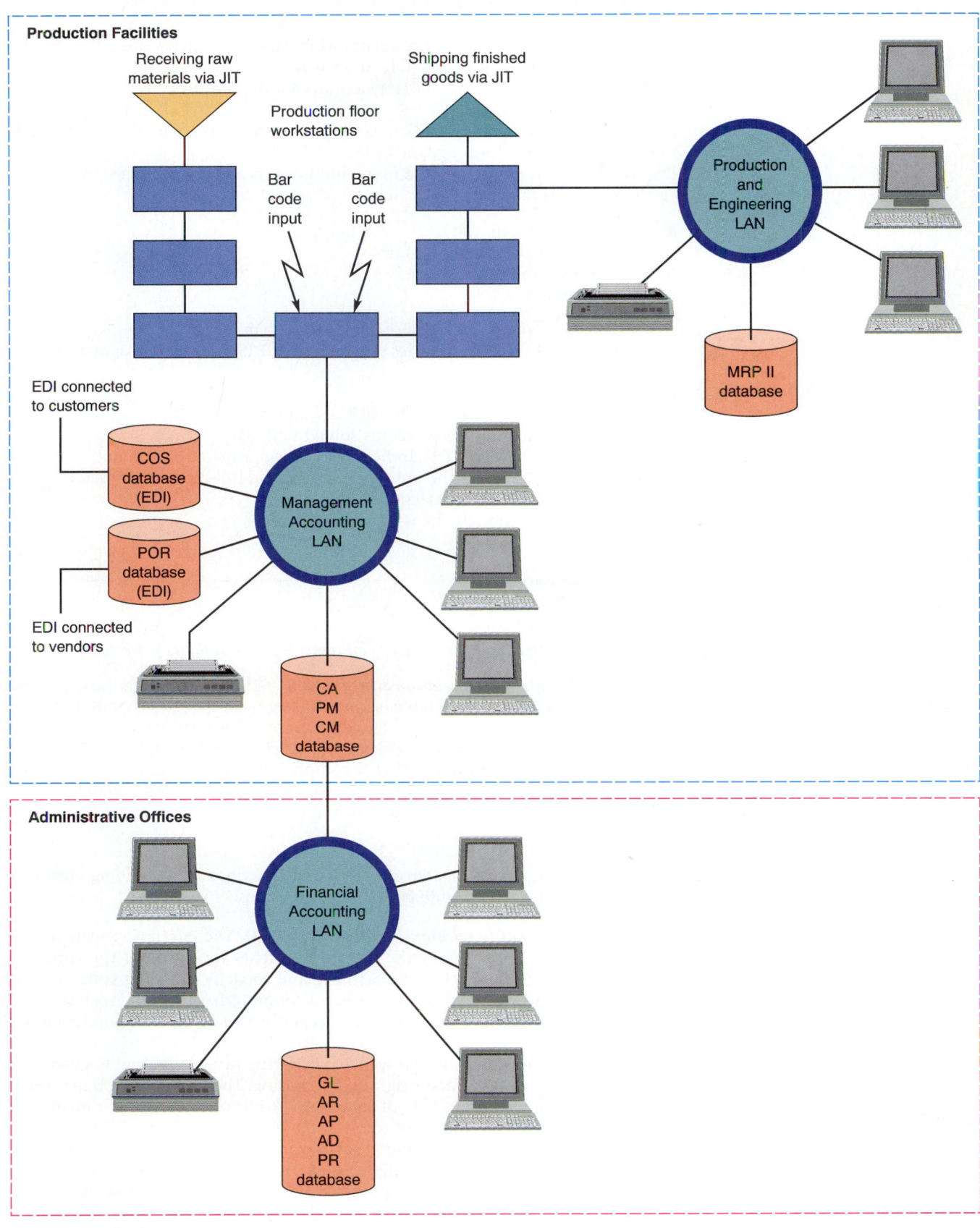

Production Facilities

Receiving raw materials via JIT

Shipping finished goods via JIT

Production floor workstations

Bar code input

Bar code input

Production and Engineering LAN

MRP II database

EDI connected to customers

COS database (EDI)

POR database (EDI)

EDI connected to vendors

Management Accounting LAN

CA PM CM database

Administrative Offices

Financial Accounting LAN

GL AR AP AD PR database

REVIEW QUESTIONS

3.1 What is the purpose of an entity relationship diagram (ERD)? How do management accountants use it in developing an ICBIS?

3.2 List and briefly describe the management accounting entities.

3.3 Define a bill of materials.

3.4 Name three popular processors (i.e., computers) and six peripherals used in building a technology platform for an ICBIS.

3.5 Briefly describe how each of the following LANs is used, and discuss why these LANs are interconnected:

- The financial accounting LAN
- The management accounting LAN
- The engineering LAN
- The factory floor LAN

3.6 List the five generic types of devices for reading bar codes.

3.7 Discuss the value of using bar codes as part of an ICBIS that supports a manufacturing enterprise.

3.8 Define MRP and MRP II.

3.9 List the modules that make up an MRP II system.

3.10 List and briefly explain four problems solved with MRP II.

3.11 Define EDI. Explain how EDI can be used to form a metacorporation.

3.12 Name and briefly describe the entities comprising a full-blown EDI system.

3.13 What are the major EDI transactions?

3.14 List and briefly describe the benefits of EDI.

CHAPTER-SPECIFIC PROBLEMS

These problems require responses based directly on concepts and techniques presented in the text.

3.15 *Modeling with an entity relationship diagram (ERD).* Customers purchase air compressors made to order. Each customer is assigned a specific account. Purchase orders are prepared by customers. Each purchase order must contain an account designation. The plant manager reviews the purchase orders and releases a work order to start work-in-process. After a compressor is completed, it is transferred to finished goods and inspected by the plant manager. The plant manager then releases the compressor for shipment to the customer.

Required:
Construct an entity relationship diagram that describes the foregoing customer order process. The ERD should contain eight entities.

3.16 *Modeling with an entity relationship diagram (ERD).* The Pitout Company manufactures machines that remove the pits from peaches for canning. The company is considering integrating its manufacturing and capacity planning systems. Currently, manufacturing is controlled through a computerized material requirements planning (MRP) system. Capacity planning is performed by the combined expertise of a group of analysts.

The manufacturing process involves five departments: Marketing, Engineering, Production Control, Manufacturing, and Purchasing. The Engineering Department is responsible for preparing bills of materials. A bill of materials is similar to a recipe; it lists all the parts that are necessary to make a "peach pitter." For example, each peach pitter requires ten general parts. To make one of the ten general parts requires another five parts. The Engineering Department makes sure that all bills of materials are current in the computer system. Each individual inventoried part necessary to put together a peach pitter is also recorded in the computer system. If the part must be manufactured, the manufacturing operations (called a routing) are stored in the computer separate from the part. If the part must be purchased, the price and lead time are included with the part. The quantity on hand is, of course, maintained for each part.

The manufacturing process is started by a forecast from the Marketing Department. For example, the Marketing Department might forecast that 20 peach pitters will be sold during the next quarter. This forecast is entered into the computer. The computer then produces a listing, based on the bill of materials, showing which parts must be purchased and which parts must be manufactured. This listing is called the Material Requirements Planning Master Report (MRPMR). Purchase and manufacture dates based on part lead times are included on the listing. The Purchasing Department uses the MRPMR for purchased parts to begin the purchasing process.

The Production Control Department uses the MRPMR for manufactured parts to schedule the production of manufactured parts. The Production Control Department issues work orders based on the MRPMR to communicate with the Manufacturing Department to actually produce the peach pitters. The company wants to make sure that it has enough capacity, in terms of people and equipment, to produce its peach pitters. If Pitout waits until a forecast is made and an MRPMR is generated, there won't be enough time to buy new manufacturing equipment and hire new people to facilitate the manufacturing process. An industrial engineer, working with a financial analyst and a marketing analyst, examines past peach pitter production and long-range marketing to plan future capacity requirements. The analysts use computer simulations to assist them in their decision making, but there is no link between the MRP system and the capacity planning system.

Required:
Model the production system described above with an entity relationship diagram.

3.17 *Quality performance rating.* The number of parts passing an inspection point is 11,400, and the number of parts inspected at this point is 12,000.

Required:
Calculate the quality performance rating.

3.18 *Vendor performance analysis.* Following are data collected on Unicore, a vendor for the company where you work as a management accountant.

	CURRENT YEAR	19X5	19X4
Number of parts inspected	1,000	1,200	1,100
Number of parts rejected	100	72	44
Quality performance rating	?	?	?
Total number of parts received	?	?	?
Number of late shipments	10	7	5
Total dollars purchased	$60,000	$70,800	$65,340
Total dollars at standard	$50,000	$60,000	$55,000
Variance from standard	?	?	?

Required:
Calculate the values for the question marks. Is vendor performance improving or getting worse? What action would you take concerning this vendor's performance?

3.19 *Available-to-promise (ATP).* Tranplex has 40 ten-inch valves on hand and a master schedule of 100 ten-inch valves. Booked orders are for 20 ten-inch valves.

Required:
Calculate ATP for Tranplex's ten-inch valves.

3.20 *Converting MRP II modules to an ERD model.* Take the modules of the MRP II software system illustrated in the chapter and convert them into an entity relationship diagram (ERD).

3.21 *Identify costs and benefits of a bar code system.* Here are some formulas that help quantify data entry costs:

- Filling-in-forms cost per day = Number of forms filled in per day × Characters per form × Writing time per character × Labor rate
- Keying cost per day = Number of characters keyed per day × Keying time per character × Labor rate
- Scanning cost per day = Number of characters scanned per day × Scanning time per character × Labor rate
- Errors per day = Number of characters per day × Error percentage
- Error correction cost per day = Number of errors per day × Correction time per error × Labor rate
- Rekeying cost per day to correct errors = Number of errors per day × Rekeying time per error × Labor rate

Viking Transport Company's management accountant has collected the following data:

- 2,000 paper forms processed daily
- 100 characters per paper form
- 2 seconds writing time per character
- $.005 per second labor rate for filling in forms
- 840,000 characters keyed per day
- 0.5 seconds keying time per character
- $.003 per second labor rate for keying
- 1,040,000 characters scanned per day
- .002 seconds scanning time per character
- $.0002 per second labor rate for scanning
- 10 percent error rate
- 5 minutes to trace and correct an error
- $.008 per second labor rate to trace and correct an error
- 0.5 seconds rekeying time per error
- $.003 per second labor rate for rekeying
- 300 working days per year

Required:
Calculate the annual savings from using a bar code system for data entry rather than a manual system based on filling in forms and keying. Calculate the annual cost of errors using manual methods.

▎THINK-TANK PROBLEMS

Although these problems are based on chapter material, reading extra material, reviewing previous chapters, and using creativity may be required to develop workable solutions.

3.22 *Processors and their peripherals.* Following is a list of various functions:

_____	Processing large volumes of data in a centralized, secure location.
_____	Front-end processor connected to the mainframe.
_____	Displaying a pleasing graphical and icon interface for system users.
_____	Pointing the cursor at certain areas on a screen and clicking for processing.
_____	A scanning device that can be held in an employee's hand for reading bar codes.
_____	A storage device that holds large quantities of data, both numbers and images, that cannot be easily erased.
_____	A storage device that holds large quantities of magnetized data that can be easily read from and written to.

Required:
Insert the name of the appropriate computer processor or peripheral in the space next to each function.

3.23 *Building an ICBIS.* Sunnydale, a wholesale food distributor for fast-food restaurants, is planning to develop a system that will allow its customers to place orders and retrieve account data via terminals. Sunnydale has traditionally taken orders over the telephone, but it has decided to install an order-entry network to reduce the cost of supporting its growing customer base and to serve as a foundation for new customer services. To anchor the network, Sunnydale is thinking about installing a minicomputer at the warehouse and one at the company's data center in its headquarters four blocks away.

Customers place orders from their terminals connected to the warehouse computer, which activates screens, formats transactions, generates shipping information, and acts as a front-end to the data center computers. The data center processes the orders, updates the database, and transmits order-filling instructions to the warehouse.

Required:
Develop a technology platform for Sunnydale.

3.24 *Building a network.* Buggy-Wash, a nationwide car wash company, intends to install a voice, data, and video network that will permit centralized supervision of remote sites. Buggy-Wash's central headquarters, where centralized supervision will be conducted, is located in Chicago. Car wash sites are scattered throughout the country.

Required:
Design a network using a telephone line for voice communications. Use a very small aperture terminal (VSAT) satellite system for transmission of data and video images. The processor at central headquarters is a mainframe. Each car wash site has a personal computer workstation that is used to transmit data to the computer at headquarters and also to perform stand-alone processing for local needs. Each car wash site also contains headsets, hand-held monitors, video cameras, and sensors.

3.25 *Organizational maps.* In *Thriving on Chaos: Handbook for a Management Revolution,* Tom Peters gives two "organizational maps." The Structured and Hierarchical

---

▬▬Structured and Hierarchical Organizational Map

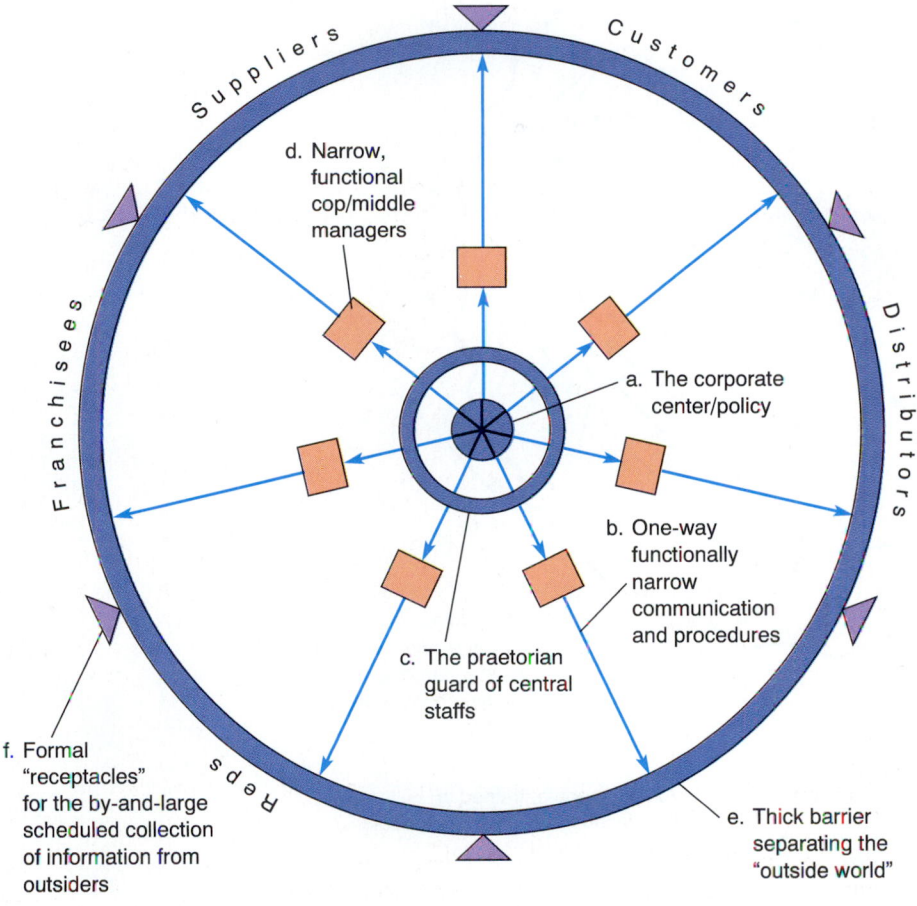

Organizational Map is shown on page 121; the Flexible and Adaptive Organizational Map is shown below.

Neither organizational map looks like a traditional organization chart that one finds in management textbooks with a square box at the top labeled "President" or "Chief Executive Officer." Both organizational maps include stakeholders, such as suppliers and customers, and both layouts are circular, moving from customers, vendors, and others in toward the corporate chieftains at each circle's center. But beyond the circular scheme, the two bear little resemblance.

The structured and hierarchical organizational map has a very tiny circle. This is the traditional out-of-touch corporate hub. Communication is downward and via the chain of command. Within the tiny circle lie the "brains of the organization." Next are the functionally narrow cop/middle managers. First and foremost, middle managers are guardians of their functional turfs. The middle manager serves as a filter of information coming from the bottom and the top. Indeed, the flow of information, what there is of it, is hierarchical.

The flexible and adaptive organizational map is radically different from the structured and hierarchical organizational map. According to Peters, it is also the one found in today's more innovative, world-class enterprises, including the following:

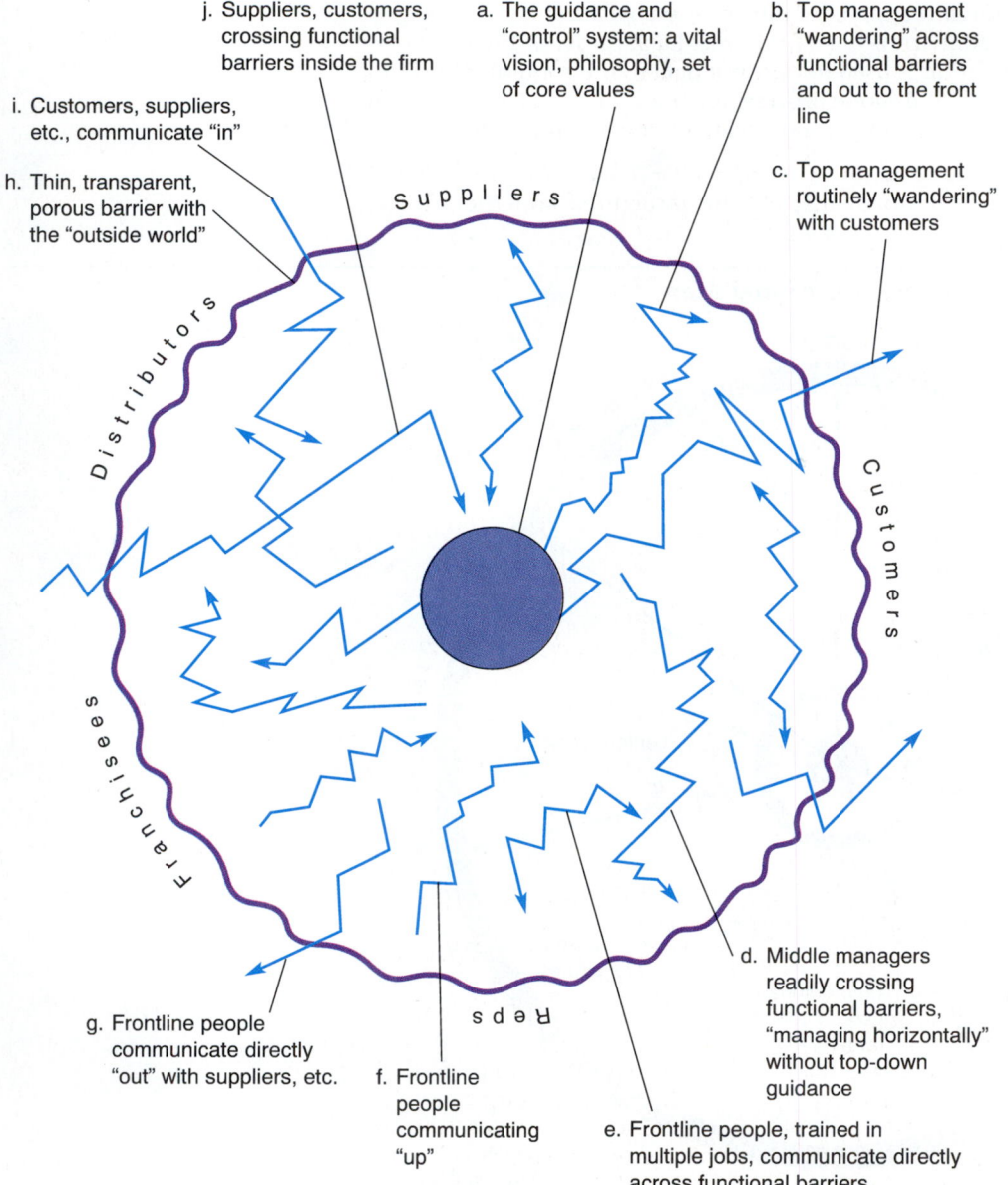

j. Suppliers, customers, crossing functional barriers inside the firm

a. The guidance and "control" system: a vital vision, philosophy, set of core values

b. Top management "wandering" across functional barriers and out to the front line

i. Customers, suppliers, etc., communicate "in"

c. Top management routinely "wandering" with customers

h. Thin, transparent, porous barrier with the "outside world"

Suppliers

Distributors

Customers

Franchisees

Reps

g. Frontline people communicate directly "out" with suppliers, etc.

f. Frontline people communicating "up"

e. Frontline people, trained in multiple jobs, communicate directly across functional barriers

d. Middle managers readily crossing functional barriers, "managing horizontally" without top-down guidance

■■■ **Flexible and Adaptive Organizational Map**

- Nucor
- Chaparral
- Worthington Industries
- The Limited
- Benetton
- The Gap
- Intel
- Motorola
- Microsoft
- Neutrogena
- ServiceMaster
- Weaver Popcorn
- Johnsonville Foods

Workers wander in and managers wander out. Customers and suppliers and other stakeholders are also connected to operations. The flexible and adaptive organizational map applies to any kind of organization. The flow of information is both vertical and horizontal, and internal and external. Middle managers are paid to make things happen among functional areas. Functional barriers do not exist. Frontline workers are trained in multiple jobs and routinely communicate with other frontline workers in other functional areas as well as communicating directly with vendors and customers.

Required:
a. Which organizational map will enable enterprises to be more competitive? Explain your answer.
b. Which organizational map fosters the team concept? Explain your answer.
c. Explain how the following terms apply to the flexible and adaptive organizational map:

  - Electronic data interchange
  - Groupware
  - Enterprisewide modeling

d. Describe how an ICBIS supports the flexible and adaptive organizational map.
e. Research the information system's literature and discuss how the following terms relate to and support the flexible and adaptive organizational map:

  - Interoperability
  - Cooperative and enterprisewide processing
  - Client/server
  - End-user computing
  - Downsizing

f. Which organizational map is supported by MRP II? Explain your answer.
g. Describe how the flexible and adaptive organizational map can improve the following:

  - Productivity
  - Quality
  - Product development cycles
  - Customer service
  - Management effectiveness

3.26 *Working together.* It's 7:30 A.M., time for the morning quiz at Eaton Corporation's factory. Ten frontline workers, each representing work teams, sit around a board-room table. "What were our sales yesterday?" asks a supervisor at the head of the table. A worker, glancing at a computer printout, replies that they were $625,275. "And in the month." From another worker comes the response: $6,172,666. The staccato review continues on to other vital information: the cost of materials and supplies used the day before; the cost of labor, shipping, and utilities; the amount of defects and scrap; customer delivery; and so forth.

Out on the shop floor minutes later, a worker tells the plant manager how to save over $5,000 a year on welding electrodes. Other workers over the past year have come up with hundreds of ways to save money. Such ideas on improving operations have caused profits to increase 30 percent over the previous year. Workers in turn are rewarded for their suggestions. Eaton stresses *kaizen,* the Japanese term for continuous improvement. The workers' attitude is: If the company can't make money, you can't expect to have a job very long.

A team of workers built two automated machines on the shop floor for $80,000 and $93,000 each rather than the $350,000 and $250,000, respectively, that outside vendors would have charged. The machines do the most tedious work and allow workers to handle more challenging jobs. The workers operate in teams and are more or less their own bosses.

One team called the "Scrap Attack" has been struggling to achieve a 50 percent reduction in scrap metal. Along the way, the team has encountered other questions, such as why dies on one press lasted 25 percent longer than the same dies that forge the same gears on other presses. The team finally discovered that one press operator preheated the dies before using them, extending their life. Now that practice has been adopted throughout the plant at a savings of $50,000 a year.

Both financial and nonfinancial information is shared with all employees. The workers believe that access to this information gives everyone a sense of direction and makes them appreciate their accomplishments.[24]

Required:

a. Explain the reason for the early-morning boardroom exercise conducted by supervisors and frontline workers.
b. Why are Eaton workers motivated to provide suggestions to improve operations?
c. Discuss how an ICBIS and the visual factory concept can support the management style at Eaton.
d. Which of the two organizational maps in Problem 3.25 applies to Eaton? Explain your answer.
e. A few years ago, Eaton was not nearly as competitive and profitable as it is today. Give your opinion as to why Eaton has enjoyed this turnaround.

3.27 *Designing an ICBIS for a university.* State University has decided to hire you to develop and install a new ICBIS. The new ICBIS should support online student registration and all other major activities of the university.

Required:

Using your knowledge of how a university works and material from the chapter, develop an entity relationship diagram and a technology platform for State University.

---

[24] Adapted from Thomas F. O'Boyle, "A Manufacturer Grows Efficient by Soliciting Ideas from Employees," *The Wall Street Journal,* Friday, June 5, 1992, pp. A1, A4.

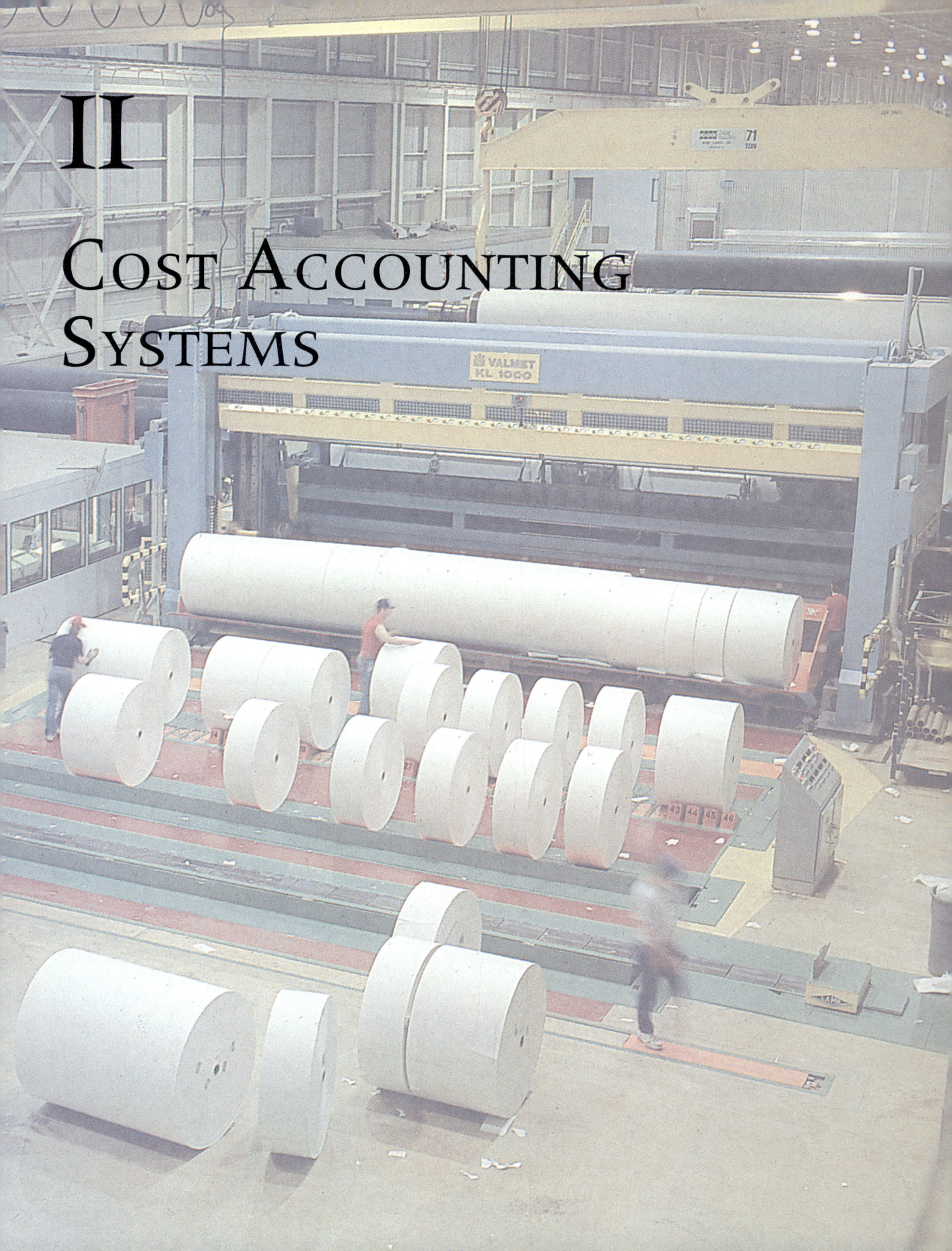

II

COST ACCOUNTING SYSTEMS

No single costing system is suitable for all enterprises. All costing systems should, however, provide the following:

- Reasonably accurate costs of cost objects, such as products and services
- Performance evaluation, planning, and operational control information
- Inventory valuation for financial statements and tax reports

Chapter 4 introduces concepts, calculations, and journal entries involved in designing costing systems. The two traditional types of manufacturing systems and their corresponding costing systems are compared. The three cost measurement methods are identified and integrated with the two costing systems.

Once the framework for tracing and assigning costs to cost objects has been set in Chapter 4, subsequent chapters examine specific costing systems. The job order costing system is presented in Chapter 5. This chapter contrasts traditional and world-class job order costing systems and ends with a detailed example of a computerized system for the construction industry. The chapter examines issues of scrap, rework, and spoilage in traditional and world-class costing systems.

The process costing system is the subject of Chapter 6, which examines two types of production flows (FIFO and weighted-average) and presents the calculations for both process systems. The issue of different input usage flows found in most modern manufacturing processes is addressed. The chapter also includes an analysis of traditional and modern approaches of accounting for spoilage.

The standard costing system is covered in Chapters 7 and 8. Chapter 7 deals with the issues of budgeting input costs, developing cost equations to predict total manufacturing costs, and creating standard cost cards for products. Chapter 8 covers journal entries required in both standard job order and process cost accounting systems, traditional cost variance analysis, and management reports. This chapter ends with a comparison of just-in-time systems from backflush costing to activity-based cost variance reporting.

One of the thorniest problems in developing any costing system is allocating overhead costs to cost objects. One traditional approach is to allocate costs from service departments to production departments and then apply overhead from production departments to the cost objects using a predetermined overhead rate, usually based on some measure of volume. This two-stage process for handling overhead costs is covered in Chapter 9.

The activity-based costing system, a relatively new and revolutionary costing system, is treated in Chapter 10. While traditional job order, process, and standard cost accounting systems are typically volume based, activity-based costing systems are activity driven. What drives these activities may or may not be correlated to the volume produced. This chapter ends with examples of how activity-based costing is used in two different service industries (hospitals and railroads). ▬▬

4

BUILDING A FRAMEWORK FOR COST ACCOUNTING

Parts come to the line on a JIT basis at Nissan Motor Manufacturing Corporation U.S.A.

LEARNING OBJECTIVES

After studying this chapter, you should be able to:

1. Understand how manufacturing cost elements flow through a production process, and describe the nine basic journal entries used to record these cost flows.

2. Describe the main records and procedures necessary to account for and control materials.

3. Illustrate the records and procedures used to account for labor.

4. Explain why overhead costs are accumulated and then applied to products and services.

5. Relate the two types of cost accounting systems to the two types of manufacturing systems identified in Chapter 1, and to the three ways of measuring a product's cost.

■ INTRODUCTION

All cost accounting systems (CASs) satisfy one overall goal—to determine the cost of products or services. Companies use cost information for many purposes:

■ To evaluate how well the organization is doing relative to its budget
■ To facilitate continuous improvement
■ To derive the value of inventory and cost of goods manufactured and sold for financial reporting
■ To value inventory for taxation
■ To price products or bid on contracts for various jobs
■ To determine product or job profitability
■ To decide whether to make or buy certain components

Contrary to popular belief, there is no such thing as the one "true product cost." All product and service costs are based on assumptions, estimates, allocations, and averages. It is up to the management accountant to choose the costing procedures that best fit the production system and management's needs for cost control and then aim for costs that are approximately accurate. Remember the "relevancy" attribute of quality information from Chapter 1: "It's more important to be approximately right than precisely wrong." The purpose of this chapter is to create a framework for the design of CASs. Subsequent chapters will expand on this framework, designing CASs for more sophisticated traditional and modern manufacturing systems. ■━━

❙ MANUFACTURING COST ACCOUNTING SYSTEMS BASICS

Before a framework can be built, a foundation must be laid. Thus, it is necessary to review some basic terminology from Chapter 1.

❙ Overview of the Four Manufacturing Cost Elements

First, there are four **manufacturing cost elements,** or inputs into a production process. These are the resources used in making a product or providing a service.

■ Direct materials (DM)
■ Direct labor (DL)
■ Variable overhead (VOH)
■ Fixed overhead (FOH)

Direct materials and direct labor costs are relatively easy to measure. If these were the only cost elements, determining product or service costs would be fairly straightforward. But management accountants must deal with overhead. Accounting for overhead costs causes a lot of trouble. It has been called the "albatross around the management accountant's neck." Some regard overhead as a big "glob" of costs, or a "black hole," that swallows up everything from depreciation of buildings and equipment to utilities and janitors' wages.

In accounting for overhead costs, the management accountant will ultimately have to answer the question, "How much overhead should be included in the cost of the product or service?" In Chapter 1, this was called overhead "allocation." Because this chapter will only build a framework for CAS design, the more complex overhead allocation issues will be deferred until Chapters 7 through 10. To keep the basic ideas and cost flows simple, fixed and variable overhead will be combined into one **total overhead (TOH)** account.

Overview of the Three Inventories in Manufacturing Enterprises

In traditional enterprises, three inventories are involved in the manufacturing process from the time materials are purchased through the sale of completed products to the customer:

- Raw materials inventory (RMI)
- Work-in-process inventory (WIP)
- Finished goods inventory (FGI)

Direct and indirect materials are first stored in RMI, usually a stockyard, warehouse, or storeroom, until they are needed in production. When production begins, and manufacturing inputs start to be used, their costs are accumulated in WIP. In other words, when manufacturing inputs enter the "front door" of the factory, their costs should be transferred from RMI to WIP. When the product is completed and leaves through the "back door" of the factory, the product's cost is removed from WIP and transferred to FGI. Finally, when the product is sold, its cost is removed from FGI and added to cost of goods sold (COGS).

Historically, it was not always feasible to use a **perpetual inventory system,** which records each product's cost of goods sold when it is actually sold. Instead, a **periodic inventory system** was used. The cost of goods sold journal entry was not made until the financial accountant wanted to prepare financial statements. At this time a physical inventory was taken, and the cost of the inventory "no longer on hand" became the cost of goods sold.

Many modern enterprises use point-of-sale equipment to record cost of goods sold in a perpetual manner. Electronic cash registers are linked directly to a minicomputer within a LAN, so that as sales are recorded, the sales price can be read from the minicomputer's magnetic disk, and cost of goods sold and inventory "relief" information can be recorded. In large grocery stores and department stores with customer checkout aisles, bar code scanners are built into the counter surface. In stores with point-of-sale registers located within departments, electronic hand-held wands are often used to read bar codes.

Bar code technology is also used in world-class manufacturing to record the receipt of raw materials, their transfer to the shop floor (WIP), and the completion and shipping of the product to retail outlets. If the manufacturer is linked to its suppliers and customers via EDI, receipts and shipments can be electronically recorded "in the books" of all three enterprises. With a JIT system, there may not be any RMI or FGI; instead, materials go directly to WIP, and the product is shipped from WIP directly to the customer.

Work-in-process inventory.

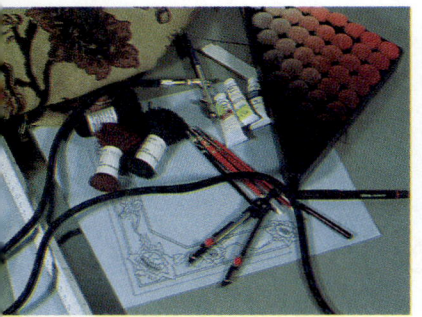

Finished goods inventory ready for the customer.

Overview of Traditional Cost Accounting Systems

The two traditional manufacturing systems introduced in Chapter 1 are job order and process systems. Each has a similarly named CAS. These are summarized in Exhibit 4–1.

A **job order cost accounting system (JOCAS)** is used in organizations whose products or services are readily identified by individual jobs, units, or projects. Commonly, the firm provides a special product or service that is tailored to customer specifications. No two orders are necessarily alike, nor do all orders always pass through the same departments or workcenters.

A "job" may consist of a single identifiable unit, such as a house, ship, or audit engagement. In a law firm, a job may be a client or a case. A job may also consist of a relatively small batch of identical or similar products (or services) covered by a single job or production order, such as an order to print 1,000 copies of a brochure. Indeed, many nonmanufacturing firms, as well as manufacturing enterprises, use JOCASs.

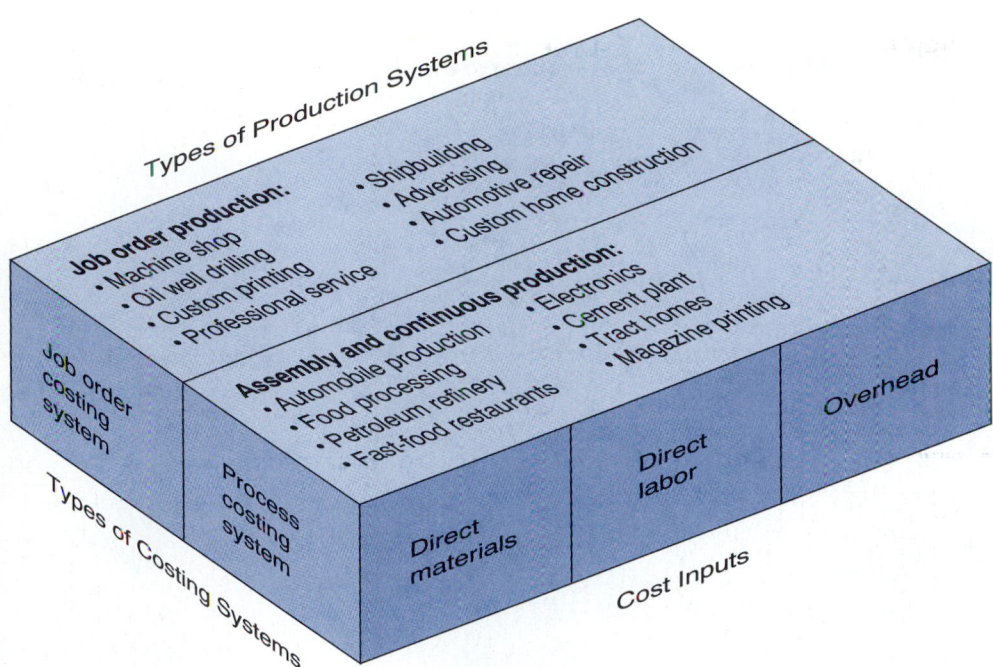

A **process cost accounting system (PCAS)** is used by organizations whose products or services are mass-produced in a continuous flow of production, such as in a cement plant or petroleum refinery. Costs are accumulated by departments, instead of by jobs, with an average cost per unit calculated by dividing the total costs by the number of products made.

Some manufacturing processes are a combination of job order and process systems. A **hybrid cost accounting system** is used in organizations that blend custom-order production and continuous-flow production. Often they produce a relatively wide variety of closely related standardized products. For example, an automobile manufacturer makes automobiles in a continuous flow, but each automobile may be customized with a special combination of motor, transmission, radio, air conditioner, and so forth.

A hybrid cost accounting system can be used when relatively large batches of homogeneous products are made. In this type of process, each batch is often a variation of a basic design that requires a specific sequence of operations. For example, a company that makes suits may have a basic design, but each batch of suits will vary. One batch uses wool, while another batch uses a mixed fabric (e.g., wool and polyester). One batch may require special stitching, another machine stitching. Such a process needs a hybrid cost accounting system; that is, part JOCAS and part PCAS. World-class manufacturers who have redesigned their production processes using the "mushroom concept" (illustrated in Exhibit 2–5) often use hybrid cost accounting systems.

▌HOW PRODUCT COSTS FLOW THROUGH A MANUFACTURING PROCESS

The general model that outlines product cost flows is demonstrated using T-accounts in Exhibit 4–2. The cost flows and journal entries are explained below. This general model applies to all types of cost accounting systems.

Within the CAS framework, there are nine basic journal entries. In this section, they will be organized according to the three types of events they record. These events involve:

■ EXHIBIT 4–2
General Model of How Product Costs Flow through a Manufacturing Process

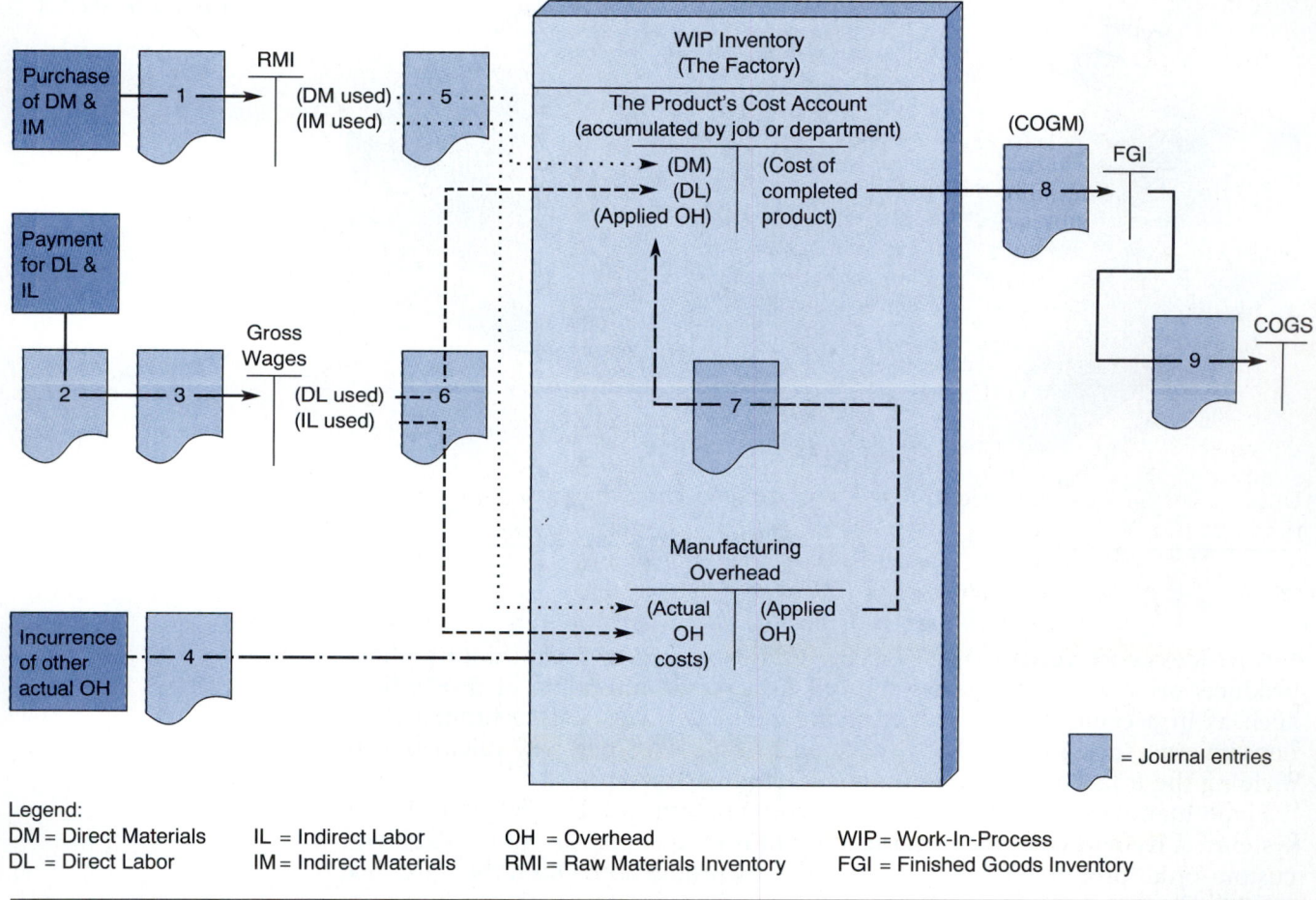

Legend:
DM = Direct Materials   IL = Indirect Labor   OH = Overhead   WIP = Work-In-Process
DL = Direct Labor   IM = Indirect Materials   RMI = Raw Materials Inventory   FGI = Finished Goods Inventory

- Obtaining the manufacturing cost elements
- Using these elements in production
- Valuing and transferring completed output to FGI and COGS.

In the following sections, materials, labor, and overhead cost accounting will be considered separately, and in more detail.

▌Cost Flows and Journal Entries for Obtaining Cost Elements

In traditional manufacturing systems, when direct and indirect materials are obtained and added into the raw materials inventory (possibly a storeroom or stockyard), their costs are debited (added) to the raw materials inventory account. Journal entry 1 in Exhibit 4–2 records this event:

JOURNAL ENTRY 1: Purchase of Raw Materials

| Raw Materials Inventory | debit | |
| Accounts Payable | | credit |

When direct and indirect labor are incurred, their costs also have to be paid for and recorded in a "temporary holding account" similar to the accounting for raw materials purchases. Raw materials are held in an inventory until used in making various products. Analogously, labor costs are held in a temporary account until it can be determined how much labor was used (how many hours worked) on each product. The labor holding account is called **gross wages.** Journal entry 2 records the purchase of (payment for) factory labor:

JOURNAL ENTRY 2: Recording Paychecks

Gross Wages	debit	
Wages and Payroll Withholdings Payable		credit

As all employers have discovered, the costs of their employees are more than just the sum of the employees' wages. Just as amounts must be withheld from employees' pay, the employer must pay for payroll-related taxes and fringe benefits. When the payroll accountant records paychecks, she also records this "employer's payroll burden." Journal entry 3 records the employer's burden:

JOURNAL ENTRY 3: Employer's Payroll Burden

Gross Wages	debit	
Employer's Payroll Burden Payable		credit

Usually journal entries 2 and 3 credit specific current liability accounts rather than the two accounts shown above. The specific accounts and calculations for employee withholdings and the employer's burden will be illustrated in the section "Accounting for Labor."

Like raw materials and factory labor, when other indirect production costs are incurred, they also have to be journalized into a temporary holding account. Later, in the section "Accounting for Overhead Costs and Cost Allocations," four reasons for this will be presented. The purpose here is only to create a foundation for understanding the basic cost flows and journal entries. To demonstrate this basic journal entry, assume that two other overhead costs were incurred: factory utilities and machinery depreciation. Journal entry 4 records these costs:

JOURNAL ENTRY 4: Incurring Other Overhead Costs

WIP–Manufacturing Overhead (Utilities)	debit	
WIP–Manufacturing Overhead (Depreciation)	debit	
Utilities Payable		credit
Accumulated Depreciation–Factory Equipment		credit

Each of these four basic journal entries recorded a similar event—the acquisition of manufacturing inputs (cost elements). Thinking in terms of these similarities will make it easier to learn the journal entries. In each journal entry, a cost element was *purchased,* and its *holding account debited.* As manufacturing inputs are obtained, each is "stored," or held temporarily, until needed (or actually used) in the manufacturing process. Using the general ledger account titles above, we can see that:

- Raw materials are held in the raw materials inventory account.
- Factory labor costs (wages, payroll taxes, and fringe benefits) are held in the gross wages account.
- Other indirect production costs are held in the manufacturing overhead account within WIP inventory.

The costs of these inputs were *credited to the accounts where they "came from":* raw materials came from accounts payable; factory wages came from wages and benefits payable; and overhead items came from such accounts as utilities payable, accumulated depreciation, indirect materials (IM) in raw materials inventory, and indirect labor (IL) in gross wages.

Cost Flows and Journal Entries for Using Cost Elements in Making a Product

When cost elements are *used* in making a product, their *holding accounts are credited and WIP is debited.* For example, as materials are issued to WIP, and thus are removed from raw materials, the raw materials inventory account is credited. Because all raw materials are issued into the factory, WIP must be debited. In conceptualizing WIP inventory, think of it as the CAS's general ledger account for the factory. Remember from Chapter 1 that all the activities in making a product occur within the factory "walls." Therefore, all the costs of these activities should be charged (debited) into the WIP inventory account within the cost accounting system.

The general ledger account for WIP is really a **control account.** A control account contains two or more **subsidiary general ledger accounts.** These subsidiary accounts represent subsets of the control account. Thus, a control account is just a summary, or total, of its subsidiary accounts. In financial accounting courses, accounts receivable and accounts payable were set up as control accounts, with each customer or supplier set up alphabetically as a subsidiary account. WIP inventory is no different. In building the framework, two subsidiary accounts exist within WIP:

- A subsidiary account for the *cost of the product*
- A subsidiary account for the indirect factory costs (*overhead*)

In Chapters 5 and 6, the subsidiary account for the product's cost will be expanded into many accounts. These will be called "jobs" in a JOCAS (Chapter 5) or "departments" if a PCAS is used (Chapter 6). In Chapters 7 through 10, the overhead account will be expanded. Right now, though, just one subsidiary account will be used for the product's cost, and one subsidiary account for overhead.

JOURNAL ENTRY 5: Requisition of Raw Materials

WIP–Product Cost (DM)	debit	
WIP–Manufacturing Overhead (IM)	debit	
Raw Materials Inventory		credit

Direct materials can be specifically identified with a product, so these costs are directly traced (debited) to that product in WIP. Indirect materials, by definition, are not directly traceable to a product, so those costs must be assigned to overhead. Once all the overhead costs are accumulated into this account, they can be applied to individual products. This will be discussed in journal entry 7 below.

Accounting for the use of labor is similar to accounting for materials: direct labor is debited to the product's subsidiary account, and indirect labor to overhead.

JOURNAL ENTRY 6: Distributing Gross Wages

WIP–Product Cost (DL)	debit	
WIP–Manufacturing Overhead (IL)	debit	
Gross Wages		credit

By the time the sixth journal entry is made, two types of events have occurred. All of the manufacturing inputs have been purchased and their cost elements recorded in holding accounts. Secondly, the direct cost elements have been used in making the product, and their costs recorded in the product's WIP subsidiary ledger account. Four indirect cost elements have been "purchased" by factory workers to use in production activities. These have been debited to the overhead subsidiary account in WIP, as shown in the following T-account:

WIP Inventory-Manufacturing Overhead

Journal Entry 4 (Utilities)	
Journal Entry 4 (Depreciation)	
Journal Entry 5 (IM)	
Journal Entry 6 (IL)	

Now that all the indirect costs have been grouped together, they can be divided up among ("applied" to) the products. Journal entry 7 records this event:

Journal Entry 7: Applying Overhead

| WIP–Product Cost (Applied OH) | debit | |
| WIP–Manufacturing Overhead | | credit |

Applied overhead is a particular type of allocated overhead. It is the amount of overhead cost actually added to, or "applied" to, the cost of a product. Other types of overhead allocations will be discussed in Chapters 9 and 10. Why do actual overhead costs need to be accumulated in a separate subsidiary account, just to be allocated into the cost of the product made? In other words, why can't the indirect costs be directly debited into the product's subsidiary account? The answer is that indirect costs are not directly traceable to a specific product. In order to assign these costs to products, they must first be grouped together somehow and then allocated to the products made. Remember from Chapter 1 that there are two ways to assign cost elements to products—direct tracing and allocation.

For example, assume that one of the overhead costs paid this month is the annual factory insurance bill. Only one-twelfth should be applied to the cost of the products made this month. If this bill is directly debited to the product's cost account, the cost of this month's product will be greatly overstated!

As a second example, assume two houses are built this month. One house is twice the size of the other. How much overhead should be allocated to the cost of each house? While the answer will have to wait until Chapters 9 and 10, the point is that overhead must first be accumulated in a temporary holding account and then allocated somehow into the costs of the products.

Notice the similarity in the three "usage" journal entries. As cost elements are used, they are *debited to the WIP–Product Cost subsidiary account and credited to the account where they come from.* Direct materials come from RMI, direct labor comes from gross wages, and applied overhead comes from the overhead subsidiary account. In summary, there are four rules for journalizing the acquisition and use of manufacturing cost elements:

- When cost elements are purchased, debit their holding accounts.
- When cost elements are used, credit their holding accounts, and debit WIP inventory.
- When cost elements are used in making a product and debited to WIP, a subsidiary WIP account *always* must be debited: the product's cost account for direct materials and direct labor, or overhead for indirect costs such as indirect materials and indirect labor.
- When overhead is used in making a product (applied to the product's cost via an overhead allocation), debit the product's subsidiary WIP account, and credit the overhead subsidiary WIP account.

The following conventions are used in recording account titles within the journal entries:

- Subsidiary accounts are separated from their control accounts by *dashes.*
- Posting references are shown in *parentheses.*

For example, to show that the product's cost account is a subsidiary account within WIP, these two account titles are separated with a dash. However, when direct materials, direct labor, and applied overhead are journalized into the WIP account for the product's cost, they are not journalized into separate, special subsidiary accounts within it. When a series of journal entries results in various debits to an account, it is a good idea to include posting references. These references, shown in parentheses, make it easier to analyze the costs that have gone into that account.

For example, notice how the posting references in the overhead T-account on page 135 facilitate an understanding of what its cost elements are. Similarly, the posting references in the WIP–Product Cost T-account in the next section provide a simple picture of its cost elements. The convention of using dashes for subsidiary accounts and parentheses for posting references will be used throughout this text in all journal entries.

Cost Flows and Journal Entries for Completed Products

Once overhead has been allocated into the cost of the products, and they have been completed, they are ready to ship to FGI or directly to the customer (as in a JIT). By now, the cost of the product has been accumulated in the "WIP–Product Cost" account. When the product "leaves the back door of the plant," its cost can be taken out of its WIP subsidiary account, as shown in the credit side of the following T-account:

WIP–PRODUCT COST SUBSIDIARY ACCOUNT

Journal Entry 5 (DM)	Cost of
Journal Entry 6 (DL)	completed
Journal Entry 7 (Applied OH)	product
Ending Balance 0	

The following journal entries are made if finished goods are shipped to, and later sold from, a retail outlet:

JOURNAL ENTRY 8: Cost of Goods Manufactured and Transferred to Finished Goods Inventory

Finished Goods Inventory	debit	
WIP–Product Cost		credit

JOURNAL ENTRY 9: Cost of Goods Sold

Cost of Goods Sold	debit	
Finished Goods Inventory		credit

In some enterprises, such as JITs, completed products are shipped directly to the customer. In these situations, there is no FGI, so journal entries 8 and 9 are replaced with a single journal entry recording the shipment and cost of goods sold as follows:

JOURNAL ENTRIES 8 AND 9 COMBINED: Recording Completed Production Shipped Directly to the Customer

Cost of Goods Sold	debit	
WIP–Product Cost		credit

A Comprehensive Example of Cost Flows and Journal Entries

The following *Insights & Applications* illustrates all nine journal entries and the cost flows they represent. They should be compared with Exhibit 4–2.

INSIGHTS & APPLICATIONS

The Monks of Glen Abbey: A Comprehensive Journal Entry Example

The Glen Abbey monastery, located a few miles west of Toronto, is known for its fine wines. The monks of Glen Abbey have been producing this wine for well over 100 years; they use the proceeds to fund the costs of the monastery and the missionary work they perform throughout the world.

For years, the monks were never concerned about the costs of producing their wines because sales climbed steadily along with the wine's reputation for quality. With the lowering of trade barriers between the United States and France, however, French wine sales have begun to erode the monks' market share. In addition, the California wines have been improving in quality and declining in price. Both of these market problems have resulted in declining sales and profits for the Glen Abbey monks.

Wanting to do something, they hired a recent management accounting graduate to develop a simple CAS to keep track of their costs. The first thing she did was to buy a microcomputer, which came with a spreadsheet software program. She used the spreadsheet software to construct a journal entry program.

The second thing she did was to take inventory. Raw materials consisted of various fruits, pectins, yeasts, crates, bottles, corks, and labels. From an analysis of the checking account, this year's beginning RMI balance was $20,000; the year-end balance was $25,000; and purchases were $105,000. She found that $90,000 worth of direct materials were transferred to the wine casks. The WIP-Product Cost beginning balance was $190,000; and the ending balance $200,000. FGI at the beginning of the year was $100,000; and at year-end $300,000.

The checking account also showed that the monks paid $400,000 in gross wages and another $50,000 in payroll taxes. Most of the gross wages were for pickers and stompers as the monastery has its own orchards and vineyards and produces wine in the old European way. Only $30,000 of the total costs of labor was for indirect laborers.

The checking account also showed that other indirect factory costs, all paid for, amounted to $220,000 for the year. But, only $200,000 of the total overhead was applied to the cost of making wine. There was no depreciation to be recorded as the casks were made of oak cut from Glen Abbey's land (which was donated to the monks), nor were there any unpaid bills at the end of the year.

The new management accountant prepared the T-account analysis shown in Exhibit 4–3 (see below and on p. 138) to help her in preparing summary journal entries for the year. She then input these amounts into her spreadsheet program to construct the journal entries shown in Exhibit 4–4 (see p. 138).

T-Accounts	Explanations	■ EXHIBIT 4–3

T-Accounts for Cost Flows at Glen Abbey

RAW MATERIALS INVENTORY

Beginning Balance	$ 20	
Purchases	$105	Use $100
Ending Balance	$ 25	

Each of the three debit amounts was given in the narrative. The $105,000 in purchases is recorded in journal entry (JE) 1. $100,000 must have been used (see JE 5) for the ending balance to be $25,000. Note that all amounts are in thousands.

GROSS WAGES

Gross Wages	$400	
Employer's Burden	$ 50	Distribution: $450
Ending Balance	$ 0	

Both the wages and employer's burden amounts were given (JE 2, 3). All wage costs are distributed to WIP accounts (JE 6).

WIP–MANUFACTURING OVERHEAD

Indirect Materials	$ 10	
Indirect Labor	$ 30	
Other	$220	Applied $200
Ending Balance	$ 60	

If DM = $90,000 of the $100,000 of raw materials used, then $10,000 must be IM (JE 5). IL and other overhead costs were given (JE 6, 4), as was applied overhead (JE 7), so the ending balance could be calculated.

Continued

■ EXHIBIT 4–3
T-Accounts for Cost Flows at Glen Abbey
—Continued

WIP–PRODUCT COST

Beginning Balance	$190		
DM	$ 90		
DL	$420		
Applied OH	$200	COGM	$700
Ending Balance	$200		

The beginning and ending balances were given. DM (JE 5) and applied overhead (JE 7) were also given. Total labor costs = $450,000 of which IL = $30,000. DL must be $420,000 (JE 6). Once DL has been calculated, cost of goods manufactured can be calculated (JE 8).

FINISHED GOODS INVENTORY

Beginning Balance	$100		
COGM	$700	COGS	$500
Ending Balance	$300		

The beginning and ending balances are given. Knowing COGM = $700,000 from JE 8, then cost of goods sold can be calculated (JE 9).

■ EXHIBIT 4–4
Journal Entries for Glen Abbey's Wine Production

SPREADSHEET PROGRAM TO REPORT GLEN ABBEY'S SUMMARY JOURNAL ENTRIES
For the Year Ended 1993

Ref	General Ledger Account Titles	dr's	cr's
	PURCHASE (ACQUISITION) OF RAW MATERIALS:		
1:	Raw Materials Inventory	$105,000	
	Accounts Payable		$105,000
	PREPARING (RECORDING) PAYCHECKS:		
2:	Gross Wages	$400,000	
	Wages & Payroll Withholdings Payable		$400,000
	EMPLOYER'S PAYROLL TAXES & BENEFITS (BURDEN):		
3:	Gross Wages	$ 50,000	
	Employer's Payroll Burden Payable		$ 50,000
	OTHER OVERHEAD COSTS INCURRED:		
4:	WIP–Manufacturing Overhead (Other OH costs)	$220,000	
	Cash		$220,000
	REQUISITION OF RAW MATERIALS INTO THE FACTORY:		
5:	WIP–Product Cost (DM)	$ 90,000	
	WIP–Manufacturing Overhead (IM)	$ 10,000	
	Raw Materials Inventory		$100,000
	DISTRIBUTING GROSS WAGES TO PRODUCTS:		
6:	WIP–Product Cost (DL)	$420,000	
	WIP–Manufacturing Overhead (IL)	$ 30,000	
	Gross Wages		$450,000
	APPLYING OVERHEAD:		
7:	WIP–Product Cost (Applied Overhead)	$200,000	
	WIP–Manufacturing Overhead		$200,000
	PRODUCTS COMPLETED:		
8:	Finished Goods Inventory	$700,000	
	WIP–Product Cost		$700,000
	PRODUCTS SOLD (INVENTORY RELIEF JOURNAL ENTRY ONLY):		
9:	Cost of Goods Sold	$500,000	
	Finished Goods Inventory		$500,000

JOURNAL ENTRY RECORDING CONVENTIONS:

1. Use a dash to separate a control account from a subsidiary account.
2. Use parentheses for a posting reference within a general ledger account.

RECORDS AND PROCEDURES FOR MATERIALS

Direct materials can be economically assigned to products or services (generally, services do not consume large quantities of raw materials). Indirect materials typically include items not physically identifiable with, or conveniently traceable to, products or services, such as staples, glue, supplies, and lubricating oil. Direct materials costs include the invoice price plus other costs such as delivery, sales tax, duty, and containers and pallets (net of return refunds). Purchase discounts taken reduce direct materials costs. Material-related costs should also be included in the cost of direct materials. Consistent with the definition of an asset (RMI inventory is a current asset), all costs of obtaining and preparing an asset for productive use should be capitalized into its cost. The allocation of material-related costs will be discussed in later chapters because several methods are available. Material-related costs include purchasing costs, receiving costs, incoming inspection costs, storage and handling costs prior to entering production, and issuing costs for materials entering production.

Material storage, handling, and moving costs *after* material has entered production are not considered material-related costs. These are costs incurred while actually making the product and, therefore, should be included in WIP.

Receiving Materials

A major concern of all companies is that the materials paid for are actually received. When shipments arrive at the receiving dock, workers inspect the materials for quality, and the quantity count is entered in the **receiving report.** Exhibit 4–5 presents an example of a report screen displayed on the receiving dock's computer terminal.

In traditional enterprises, a Purchasing Department agent prepares a **purchase order,** which authorizes the supplier to ship raw materials and bill the company upon their delivery. Usually, the purchase order is a multipart form. The original is sent to the supplier along with a copy to use as a **shipping**

**EXHIBIT 4–5
Receiving Report**

Receiving Report		
Number	Date	
Vendor/Shipper		
Carrier		
Bill of Lading Number	Purchase Order Number	
Freight Terms	☐ Prepaid ☐ Collect	
Container Type and Quantity	___Bags ___Pallets ___Cartons ___Rolls ___Drums ___Other	Weight ___

Item Number	Quantity	Unit of Measure	Item Description

Remarks	Received by: ___

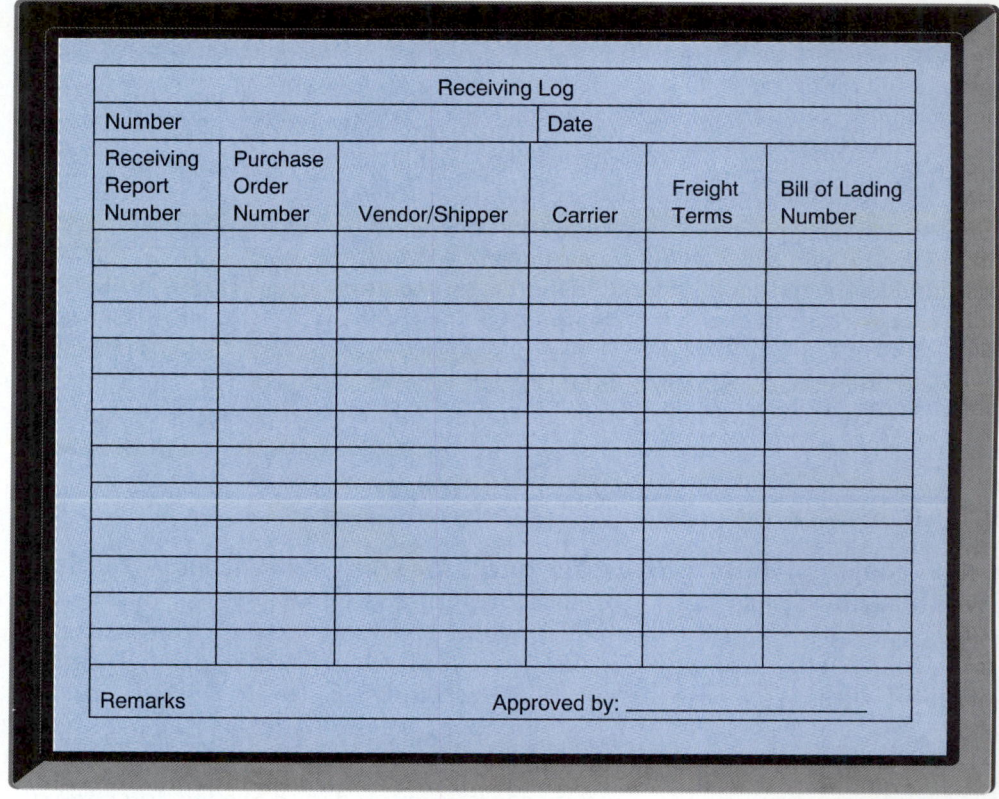

Receiving Log					
Number			Date		
Receiving Report Number	Purchase Order Number	Vendor/Shipper	Carrier	Freight Terms	Bill of Lading Number
Remarks			Approved by: _____		

advice. This copy is returned with the shipment to facilitate identification (by purchase order number) and payment. Once received, the shipping advice can be kept by the inventory supervisor and used to control inventory levels.

When the purchase order is prepared, another copy is sent to the inventory supervisor to inform him that the shipment is ordered and when it is scheduled to arrive. Upon receipt, the dock worker or inventory clerk uses this copy as the receiving report. It is then forwarded to the Accounts Payable Department for payment. Meanwhile, Accounts Payable has also received another copy of the purchase order so that they know when to expect the bill and prepare payment. Thus, the purchase order and the receiving report are the *source documents* necessary for payment within the CAS.

Consider all the costs involved in purchasing multipart forms, preparing them, mailing and delivering them, handling them, and filing them! Modern purchasing methods attempt to reduce or eliminate these nonvalue-added costs by computerizing purchase order preparation and filling. The ultimate system, virtually eliminating all paper processing costs, is EDI.

The **receiving log,** shown in Exhibit 4–6, summarizes receiving reports and is the primary record for identifying missing documents. It is useful for controlling the payment of freight bills and for summarizing receiving activity. A copy of the receiving log, attached to the receiving reports, should be sent daily to the Accounts Payable Department. A copy should also be sent to the Purchasing Department so that they can verify that all purchase orders were filled.

In addition to determining the quantity received, the Receiving Department is also responsible for inspecting incoming materials for the proper specifications. Some materials such as bricks or lumber can be visually inspected while materials such as electronic components may require test equipment. If items are damaged or do not meet specifications, the quantities are not entered on the receiving report and the damaged items are prepared for return to vendors.

Rejected Material Report			
Number	Date of Report		Date of Receipt
Receiving Report Number		Purchase Order Number	
Vendor			
Quantity	Unit of Measure	Item Number	Item Description
Reason for Rejection			
Disposition	☐ Return to Vendor ☐ Other _____		
	Return Authorization Number _____		

The **rejected material report,** presented in Exhibit 4–7, identifies material to be returned to the vendor. The Purchasing Department uses this information to evaluate vendor performance.

Using Materials Requisitions to Issue Materials to Work-in-Process

A **materials requisition** is a document that authorizes the transfer of raw materials from RMI to production. An example of a materials requisition terminal screen display appears in Exhibit 4–8. Note that it is for a JOCAS, as the requisition is for direct materials to use on job 12. A similar materials requisition is used to release direct materials to WIP for a PCAS (except that a department name would be used instead of a job number).

A requisition for indirect materials is identical to one for direct materials except that it shows an overhead account number instead of a job order number or department name. Indirect materials, such as glue, nails, grease, and screws, must be controlled and accounted for the same as direct materials. Normally, when the factory needs such indirect materials, a materials requisition is initiated by the requesting production department. For example, the machine maintenance foreman may requisition a barrel of grease to perform maintenance work on various machines. While the cost of the grease is charged to the overhead account, management knows where the barrel is. If no materials requisitions were used for indirect materials, workers could just "walk off with" whatever nails, screws, bolts, saw blades, and the like they might need. Then the company would have no way of identifying which machines, and production activities, are overusing supplies.

Using materials at Deere & Company.

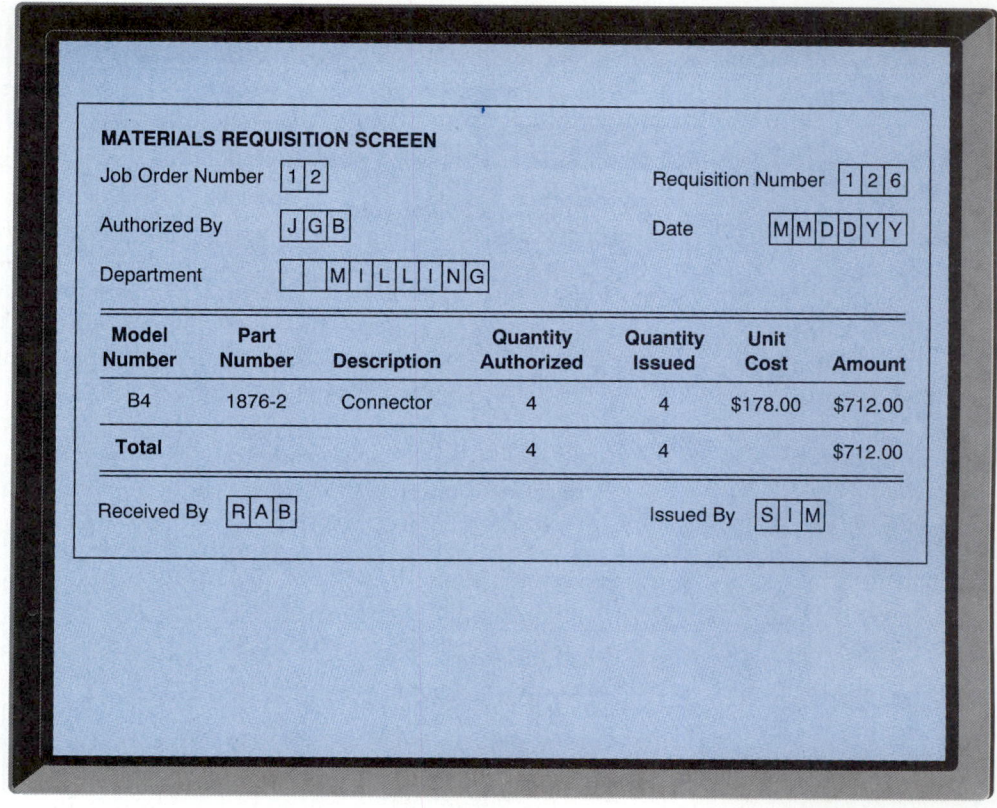

The materials requisition is usually prepared by the factory floor control supervisor or by a central scheduling department. In a paper-based system, authority for requisitioning and issuing materials is evidenced by signatures or initials. In a computer-based system, such authority is exercised by passwords or other built-in security measures. Materials requisitions are the *source documents* used to record materials issued to production in journal entry 5.

❙Accounting for Materials

The RMI account is a control account in the general ledger. A separate record for each type of material is maintained in a **materials subsidiary ledger** (also called a **materials inventory master file**). A typical record layout found in this subsidiary ledger, or master file in a computerized inventory records system, is illustrated in Exhibit 4–9. Each record identifies specific items in materials inventory by:

- Model number (or item number)
- Part number
- Description (or name)
- Unit cost
- Quantity received from vendor (also often indicated by a unit of measure, such as pounds, gallons, or feet)
- Purchase order number
- Date received
- Quantity issued to production
- Materials requisition number
- Job order number or department number to which direct materials are charged

- Date issued to production
- Quantity on hand after the most current issue
- Reorder quantity, which will trigger a purchase order when the quantity on hand is equal to or less than a minimum level
- Order quantity, which is the amount to order from the vendor each time the item is ordered

In most companies, these records are stored on magnetic disk for computerized processing. This represents an automated perpetual inventory system because individual item records have balances that are kept current. Perpetual inventory systems are used for all inventory accounts (RMI, WIP, and FGI). The materials records are continuously updated online as transactions take place. As soon as a materials item is received from a vendor or released to production, the transaction is keyed in via a terminal, which in turn updates the records stored on magnetic disk. In highly automated systems, bar codes are attached to all inventory items so that each item can be tracked throughout the production process. Such automation provides a true perpetual inventory system.

Thus, at any time during the year, the debit balance in each inventory account represents the updated balance at that time. Physical counts are still taken periodically, and the perpetual records are adjusted, if necessary, to show the balances indicated by the physical count.

ACCOUNTING FOR LABOR

Direct laborers are production workers who work directly on the product or service. The time they work on a product or service, and their costs, can be identified with, and assigned to, specific products or services in an economically

> **LEARNING OBJECTIVE 3**
>
> Illustrate the records and procedures used to account for labor.

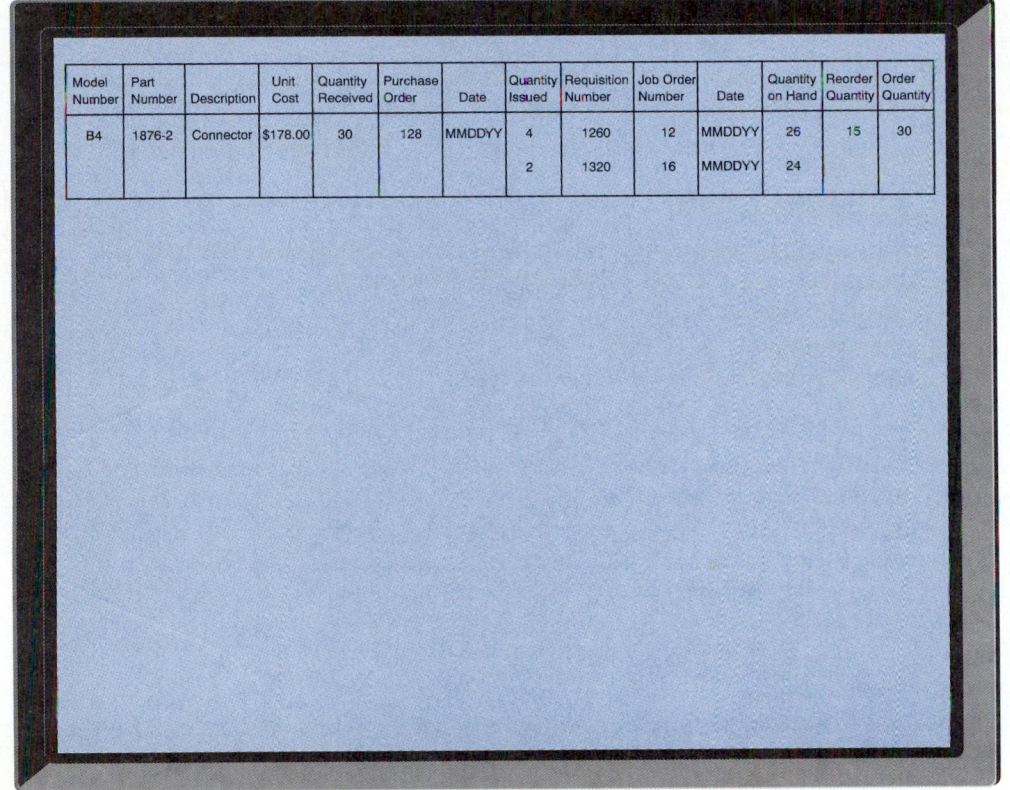

Model Number	Part Number	Description	Unit Cost	Quantity Received	Purchase Order	Date	Quantity Issued	Requisition Number	Job Order Number	Date	Quantity on Hand	Reorder Quantity	Order Quantity
B4	1876-2	Connector	$178.00	30	128	MMDDYY	4	1260	12	MMDDYY	26	15	30
							2	1320	16	MMDDYY	24		

■EXHIBIT 4–9
Record Layout for Materials

feasible way. Indirect laborers do not work directly on making a product, but instead provide some type of support service. Examples of indirect laborers include materials handlers within the factory who move WIP from one workstation or department to another; and custodians, repairs and maintenance personnel, and security guards.

Probably the most important aspect of the accounting system, at least in the eyes of the workers, is the payroll system. From their point of view, the most important job of the accountant is to have accurate paychecks ready on time. Accurate and timely output from the CAS are two characteristics of high-quality information. In accounting for labor costs, then, the objectives of a payroll system should be to:

- Ensure accurate and prompt payment to employees
- Maintain records of employees' earnings in accordance with a variety of governmental requirements
- Correctly withhold and pay various payroll-related taxes to the appropriate government agencies
- Journalize labor costs to the proper general ledger accounts

Calculating the Gross Labor Rate

The following costs are included in direct and indirect labor:

- Basic compensation
- Individual production efficiency bonuses
- Group production efficiency bonuses
- Sick leave credit
- Health insurance
- Vacation pay
- Union dues paid by the employer
- Pension costs
- Employer's share of Federal Insurance Contributions Act (FICA) taxes
- Workers' compensation insurance
- State or federal unemployment compensation insurance

Payroll and human resource department costs and most profit sharing plan costs usually are not treated as direct labor costs; instead, they are accounted for separately. Also, the following items usually are not considered part of direct labor costs:

- Wage continuation plans
- Contributions to Supplemental Unemployment Benefit (SUB) plans
- Membership dues in health clubs and country clubs
- Safety-related items
- Company-sponsored cafeteria
- Recreational facilities

EMPLOYEE WITHHOLDINGS.   Two basic kinds of withholdings are deducted from employee paychecks:

MANDATORY	VOLUNTARY
Federal income taxes	Union dues
State income taxes	Health insurance
Local income taxes	Retirement plans
Social Security taxes	Special deductions

Each employment situation is unique, though. Consequently, some items that are listed as voluntary may be required. For example, many labor unions

INSIGHTS & APPLICATIONS

The Glen Abbey Monks' Payroll Plan

Continuing the example used to illustrate the basic journal entries earlier, the new management accountant also needs to set up a payroll accounting system. Glen Abbey employs 25 workers in wine production operations. Each employee works 40 hours per week, 50 weeks per year. Each receives a one-week paid vacation (the monastery is closed one week a year for a retreat).

The local area around Glen Abbey is populated by retirees and upper-middle-class families who work in the greater Toronto area. The Glen Abbey employees are all highly trained and experienced union members, mostly from Michigan, and are subject to U.S. employment-related taxes.

The labor costs paid by employees and Glen Abbey (as the employer) are detailed in Exhibit 4–10 (see below). The column titled "Employees" represents the amounts *withheld from an employee's paycheck*. The amounts in the "Employer" column represent items paid by Glen Abbey as its *employer's payroll burden. These items are payable in addition to the employee's gross wage.*

Using her new microcomputer system and spreadsheet software, the management accountant linked the spreadsheet program for Exhibit 4–10 to a program that calculates individual payroll withholdings summaries for Internal Revenue Service reporting, and to the journal entry program already developed.

After she completed the spreadsheet programs, the management accountant asked the workers and monks to review them for accuracy and completeness. They were so impressed that the report in Exhibit 4–10 became an annual report prepared for each worker. Until this time, the workers had no idea that Glen Abbey was paying an extra dollar per hour (on average) to employ them!

EXHIBIT 4–10
Calculations of Employees Withholdings and Employer Payroll Burden

SPREADSHEET PROGRAM TO CALCULATE GLEN ABBEY'S PAYROLL RATE, EMPLOYEE WITHHOLDINGS, AND EMPLOYER BURDEN
For the Year Ended 1993

Payroll Items:	Percentages	Employees	Employer
BASIC WAGE RATE		$8.00	$8.00
		* Items Paid By: *	
Federal Income Taxes Withheld	15.00%	$1.20	
State Income Taxes Withheld	5.00%	$0.40	
Social Security Taxes (FICA)	7.50%	$0.60	$0.60
Federal Unemployment Tax (FUTA)	0.50%		$0.04
State Unemployment Tax (SUTA)	1.50%		$0.12
** Union Dues	0.50%	$0.04	$0.04
** Health Insurance	0.50%	$0.04	$0.04
** Vacation Liability	2.00%		$0.16
TOTAL BURDEN ITEMS:			
Employees	28.50%	($2.28)	
Employer	12.50%		$1.00
NET PAY RATE FOR EMPLOYEES		$5.72	
GROSS LABOR RATE FOR EMPLOYER			$9.00

** Notes:

Percentages are based on the basic wage rate paid to employees
Union dues: both employee and employer pay 1/2%
Health insurance: both employee and employer pay 1/2%

Vacation liability percentage: vacation (weeks/yr)	1
divided by work year	÷50
= Vacation percentage:	2.00%

require that employees' union dues be withheld from their paychecks. Some companies require that all employees contribute to a retirement plan. Further, income tax rates change with different levels of income, and Social Security taxes have a maximum limit on the amount to be withheld per employee per year. Special deductions can include savings plans, charitable contributions, and employee loans. The Glen Abbey illustration is oversimplified, but will allow the basic understanding necessary for building the CAS framework.

EMPLOYER-PAID PAYROLL COSTS.   The employer pays these payroll-related costs in addition to the wages paid to employees. The employer's burden is also composed of mandatory and voluntary items:

MANDATORY	VOLUNTARY
■ Federal unemployment taxes	■ Vacation time
■ State unemployment taxes	■ Health insurance
■ Local unemployment taxes	■ Retirement plans
■ Social Security taxes	■ Other fringe benefits
■ Workers' compensation insurance	

Like Social Security tax withholdings, unemployment tax liabilities are often subject to some maximum amount per employee per year. The Social Security tax is equal to that withheld from employees. In other words, the employer must match the amounts withheld from employees' paychecks. The voluntary items are unique to each company. Again, the Glen Abbey illustration is an oversimplification.

The vacation accrual requires further explanation. In determining a gross labor rate to use for assigning labor costs to products, the rate should include all the payroll-related costs involved. If an employee earns two weeks of vacation time and works 50 weeks per year, then the vacation time should be allocated over the "work" time that can be assigned to product costs. Two of 50 weeks equals 4 percent. If a worker earns three weeks of vacation and works 49 weeks per year, then the allocation percentage is 6.12 percent (3/49).

LABOR-RELATED JOURNAL ENTRIES.   The two journal entries recording the paychecks and the employer's burden are reproduced below:

JOURNAL ENTRY 2: Recording Paychecks

Gross Wages	debit	
Wages and Payroll Withholdings Payable		credit

JOURNAL ENTRY 3: Employer's Payroll Burden

Gross Wages	debit	
Employer's Payroll Burden Payable		credit

There are at least three ways to account for employee withholdings and the employer's burden within the two current liability accounts used in journal entries 2 and 3:

■ Individual line items (shown in Exhibit 4–10) could be treated as posting references within the two liability accounts.
■ Individual line items could be set up as separate subsidiary ledger accounts within each liability account. With this method, "Wages and Payroll Withholdings Payable" and "Employer's Payroll Burden Payable" become control accounts in the CAS.
■ The two liability accounts could be replaced with separate liability accounts for each line item.

All the journal entries throughout this text use the third option to make it easier to remember the various liabilities created by labor and who is responsible

■EXHIBIT 4–11
Journal Entries for Glen Abbey's Payroll and Employer's Burden

SPREADSHEET PROGRAM TO REPORT GLEN ABBEY'S SUMMARY JOURNAL ENTRIES
For the Year Ended 1993

** JOURNAL ENTRIES FOR RECORDING PAYCHECKS AND EMPLOYER'S BURDEN ONLY **

Ref	General Ledger Account Titles	dr's	cr's	Notes:
	PREPARING (RECORDING) PAYCHECKS:			
2:	Gross Wages	$400,000		
	FIT Withholdings Payable		$ 60,000	+$GROSS WAGES*0.15
	SIT Withholdings Payable		$ 20,000	+$GROSS WAGES*0.05
	FICA Taxes Payable		$ 30,000	+$GROSS WAGES*0.075
	Union Dues Payable		$ 2,000	+$GROSS WAGES*0.005
	Health Insurance Payable		$ 2,000	+$GROSS WAGES*0.005
	Wages Payable		$286,000	GROSS WAGES − WITHHOLDINGS
	EMPLOYER'S PAYROLL TAXES & BENEFITS (BURDEN):			
3:	Gross Wages	$ 50,000		SUM(EMPLOYER BURDEN)
	FICA Taxes Payable		$ 30,000	= withheld from paychecks
	FUTA Taxes Payable		$ 2,000	+$GROSS WAGES*0.005
	SUTA Taxes Payable		$ 6,000	+$GROSS WAGES*0.015
	Union Dues Payable		$ 2,000	+$GROSS WAGES*0.005
	Health Insurance Payable		$ 2,000	+$GROSS WAGES*0.005
	Vacation Payable		$ 8,000	+$GROSS WAGES*0.02

JOURNAL ENTRY RECORDING CONVENTIONS:

1. Use a dash to separate a control account from a subsidiary account.
2. Use parentheses for a posting reference within a general ledger account.

for them (i.e., which are deducted from paychecks versus paid separately by the employer). Exhibit 4–11 presents the payroll-related journal entries for Glen Abbey, using the third option format. From now on, these journal entries will replace journal entries 2 and 3 as originally demonstrated in Exhibit 4–4.

HOW MANY PAYROLL JOURNAL ENTRIES NEED TO BE MADE?   Some accountants combine these two journal entries together, because the information for them is obtained at the same time, and they are prepared together. Further, note that as soon as these journal entries debit the gross wages account, this account will be credited for the same amount when labor costs are distributed to products in journal entry 6. Because the gross wages account is simply a "clearing account" (i.e., it will never contain a balance after all three journal entries are posted), some accountants want to combine all three journal entries together.

This results in one very large compound journal entry that reduces the CAS to six basic journal entries. In many computerized payroll systems, the gross wages account does not exist. Until you have developed substantial knowledge and experience in making these journal entries, however, it is strongly recommended that they be kept as three separate journal entries.

TRADITIONAL PAYROLL BURDEN ACCOUNTING.   Chapter 1 noted that the more costs that can be directly traced to a product, and the less overhead allocated to it, the more accurate the product's cost will become. If all cost elements can be directly traced, the result will be an objectively accurate product cost everyone can accept. Overhead allocations are subjective, though, and depend on the methods chosen by the management accountant. Consider this logic in the treatment of the employer's payroll burden.

In more sophisticated, modern CASs, these costs are included in the Gross Wages account and are directly traced to each worker. Thus, as labor time is directly traced to products, so are the employer's burden costs. To illustrate this using the Glen Abbey example, the total gross labor rate is $9 per hour ($8 wage rate + $1 per hour in employer payroll taxes and fringe benefits). Glen Abbey employed 25 workers last year, each working 40 hours per week for 50 weeks. A total of 50,000 labor hours were worked, and $450,000 was debited to gross wages (see journal entries 2 and 3 in Exhibit 4–11). Of the 50,000 hours, 46,666.67 were direct labor (@ $9 = $420,000), and 3,333.33 hours were indirect labor (@ $9 = $30,000), as shown in journal entry 6 of Exhibit 4–4 earlier.

Historically, though, the $1 per hour employer burden has been included in (debited to) overhead. This procedure was considered satisfactory when the amount withheld and the employer's payroll taxes were relatively low. For example, in 1957, the employer's burden only averaged about 15 percent in the United States. By the mid-1980s, it had grown to 37 percent, and it continues to grow with the skyrocketing costs of pensions and health insurance.

Including these benefits in overhead was also considered satisfactory when our economy included many manufacturers with highly labor-intensive operations. All overhead was allocated to products using the labor hours directly traced to them (a method discussed in the next section). Thus, the end result was the same; eventually, these costs got into the product's cost. In modern world-class manufacturing, however, most overhead costs result from the direct technology cost elements (buildings, machinery and robotic operations, and computerized information systems). If overhead is allocated using something other than labor hours worked on the product (e.g., machine hours), then an incorrect amount of this overhead item (the employer's payroll burden) will be included in the cost of the product.

It is important for modern management accountants to be aware of practices such as including payroll taxes and fringe benefits in overhead, because they are still pervasive in many traditional CASs. Why haven't these systems been updated? Reasons suggested by some accounting authorities include a lack of knowledge of current alternatives, an already existing CAS that lacks relevance, and the costs of modifying the CAS. By failing to make the CAS as relevant as possible, management accountants may appear to be out-of-touch with the CAS users and unreceptive to their needs. Further, this may violate the competence standard of ethical conduct.

▍Manual Payroll Systems

One key activity that helps achieve the payroll system objectives is **timekeeping.** The timekeeping process may be performed manually or electronically. Some plants use time clocks. The time clock stamps employees' starting and quitting times on their clock cards (time cards). If the factory has many departments, the time cards can be color coded for easier separation. In any event, the clock cards serve as the *source documents* in accounting for the total hours employees work during a day or shift.

Time tickets, such as the one in Exhibit 4–12, are often used in conjunction with clock cards. Time tickets are used primarily to assign direct labor to a specific product or to charge indirect labor to overhead. An entry is made on the time ticket every time a worker starts or stops work on a specific product or performs an overhead task. For example, J. R. Lantz filled in the job number, department, and start and stop times. The payroll accountant can then fill in the rate and cost information when preparing payroll (to support journal entries 2, 3, and 6). In this way, time tickets serve as the *source documents* for recording

Time Ticket							
Employee Name: J. R. Lantz					Date: MMDDYY		
Employee Number: 1274					Shift: Swing		
Job Number	Department	Time Started	Time Stopped	Time Elapsed	Rate	Amount	Approval
127–X	Painting	8:00	12:00	4	$15.00	$ 60.00	JC
145–B	Finishing	1:00	4:00	3	$15.00	$ 45.00	AD
Total Direct Labor Cost				7		$105.00	
	Maintenance	4:00	5:00	1	$15.00	$ 15.00	ES
Total Indirect Labor Cost				1		$ 15.00	
Total Labor Cost				8		$120.00	

the labor distribution in journal entry 6. In some companies, time tickets are used only for direct labor.

Automated Systems

In an automated setting, time clocks, clock cards, and time tickets are eliminated. Direct labor hours are recorded by bar code scanners. Each task and its time are recorded and assigned automatically. The accounting procedure is the same, except the collection of data is instantaneous and there is no flow of paper. Entries are made electronically. The Scott Paper Company case on the next page gives an excellent description of an automated timekeeping and attendance system.

ACCOUNTING FOR OVERHEAD COSTS AND COST ALLOCATIONS

Overhead costs are not easily or economically traceable to products or services. These cost elements are indirect costs because they are either "common costs" (benefiting more than one product), or they are not important enough to account for on a direct basis. The following guidelines may help to distinguish between direct and indirect costs:

- If a cost can be easily traced to a product or service using source documents such as material requisitions and time tickets, then it is a direct cost.
- If a cost must be allocated in order to be assigned to a product, then it is an indirect cost with respect to that cost object.

Indirect production costs create a problem in measuring the cost of a particular product or service. This problem is overcome by a two-step approach, which

LEARNING OBJECTIVE 4

Explain why overhead costs are accumulated and then applied to products and services.

INSIGHTS & APPLICATIONS

Automating Timekeeping and Attendance at Scott Paper Company

When Scott Paper, a leading manufacturer and marketer of sanitary tissue paper products, replaced traditional time clocks with an automated time and attendance system at its largest plant, it gained unexpected savings. Now, instead of collecting time cards by hand from the 2,500 employees, making calculations manually, and then keying the numbers into the payroll system, Scott collects the time and attendance data by bar code readers. The data are calculated electronically and are fed automatically into the payroll system. In addition to tracking straight time, overtime, holiday pay, and so on, the system is programmed to take into account many very complex work rules and schedules. The system has dramatically reduced the demand on payroll and accounting resources.

The system feeds information automatically to corporate payroll, cost accounting, inventory, administrative, and manufacturing systems. By translating its accepted procedures into user-defined tables, Scott was able to retain the policies and pay rules that had evolved over years. The time and attendance software can accommodate thousands of different schedules and pay practices, as well as flextime or shift rotation policies.[1]

begins by accumulating overhead costs in a special subsidiary WIP account. Typically, these costs include the following:

- Indirect materials such as supplies that are not identified with specific products or services
- Indirect labor such as supervision, expediting, materials handling, inspection, maintenance, and clerical work within the plant
- Other overhead items including depreciation, rent, insurance, taxes, utilities, small tools, and repairs

The first step debits actual overhead costs to the WIP subsidiary ledger account. Once overhead costs are grouped together, they can be applied to the product's cost according to some formula, usually involving an overhead rate. This rate is used with a cost element that is directly traced to the product. Direct labor costs, direct labor hours, and machine hours are examples of frequently used bases for applying overhead. Choosing the best basis for applying overhead (its "cost driver") will be discussed in detail in Chapters 7, 9, and 10. Applying overhead costs to products or services is the second step in this two-step approach.

For example, if the product required four machine hours to make and the overhead rate is $10 per machine hour, then $40 of overhead would be *applied to the cost of the individual product* ($10 per Mhr worked in making the product multiplied by the 4 Mhr needed). In the Glen Abbey illustration, the overhead rate is $4.2857 per direct labor hour. Since 46,666.67 direct labor hours were worked last year, $200,000 of overhead was applied *in total throughout the year* to the cost of making wine ($4.2857 × 46,666.67 DLhr = $200,000 rounded). This overhead allocation was made in journal entry 7 of Exhibit 4–4.

A separate subsidiary ledger account for overhead is needed for four reasons:

- Overhead represents the indirect product costs that cannot be directly traced to the cost of the product (the other subsidiary account).
- Many overhead costs are incurred and paid for at different times than these cost elements are used in the manufacturing process. For example, the prop-

---

[1] Claire Barth, "Automating Time and Attendance," *Management Accounting*, June 1992, pp. 14–15. Reprinted from *Management Accounting*. Copyright by Institute of Management Accountants, Montvale, N.J.

erty taxes and insurance on the factory building may be paid annually in December. It would not be fair to charge the entire annual costs only to products made in December, which would happen if these costs were directly debited into the product's WIP subsidiary account.

■ Both of the previous reasons lead to the conclusion that overhead costs need to be first put into a "holding account." Then, after they are grouped ("pooled") together, they can be *applied* by some systematic method into the cost of the products.

■ Because overhead represents the indirect costs of making a product, they need to be separately accounted for to satisfy the cost management objectives of the CAS (planning, control, and evaluation).

Using this two-step method to account for overhead creates two related problems, however. First, the CAS needs the most accurate overhead rate possible. Second, the CAS needs an overhead application basis that is accurate enough for management cost control needs. The first issue is discussed in the next section. The second issue is discussed in detail in Chapters 9 and 10. It involves setting up multiple overhead accounts, each with its own separate journal entry 7.

This second issue is probably the most important topic in CAS design. No longer can modern manufacturers, professional service organizations (lawyers, doctors, hospitals), and governmental entities continue to record all overhead into a single account and use just one overhead rate based on direct labor hours (the traditional, and still too common, method of overhead allocation). As Exhibit 4–13 shows, labor is becoming a relatively small cost element compared to materials and overhead.

LEARNING OBJECTIVE 5

Relate the two types of cost accounting systems to the two types of manufacturing systems identified in Chapter 1, and to the three ways of measuring a product's cost.

▌COST MEASUREMENT ISSUES

The last topic in creating a CAS framework deals with the question, "which costs to use?" Here the concern is with how to calculate or measure the product's cost. This is a different issue from choosing between a JOCAS and a PCAS. Job order and process costing choices involve how to organize the product's costs. The

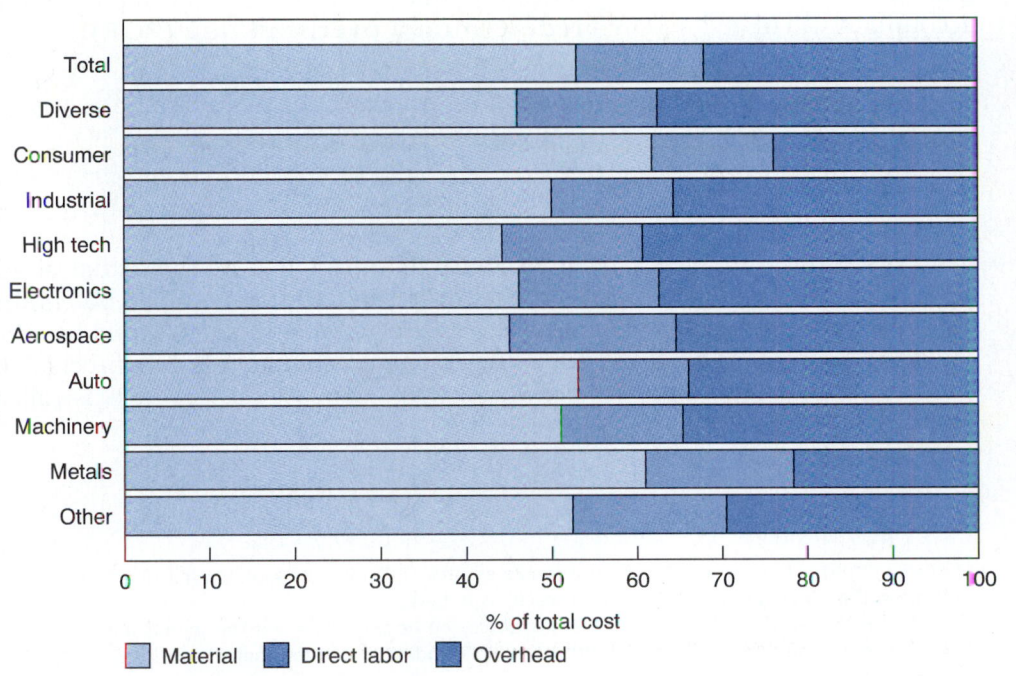

■EXHIBIT 4–13
Product Cost Breakdown

Source: Robert A. Howell, James D. Brown, Stephen R. Soucy, and Allen H. Seed III, *Management Accounting in the New Manufacturing Environment* (Montvale, N.J.: Institute of Management Accountants, formerly the National Association of Accountants; and Arlington, Tex.: Computer Aided Manufacturing-International, 1987), p. 11. With permission.

management accountant is asking, "Should the cost elements be traced to jobs or processes?" The cost measurement issue is, "How should the cost of each manufacturing input be measured?"

This may not appear to be an important issue, but it is. Typically, the first response is, "Use the actual costs of direct materials, direct labor, and total overhead." This cost measurement method is called actual costing. Managers who need current cost information for product pricing decisions find this method unsatisfactory, however. Consider the first overhead problem: develop the most accurate overhead rate possible. The most accurate rate is to take the total actual overhead cost and divide it by the total actual direct labor hours worked (if labor is the base for allocating overhead).

Using the Glen Abbey case, from journal entries 4 through 6 in Exhibit 4–4, total actual overhead for the year was $260,000. For the year, 46,667 (rounded) direct labor hours (DLhr) were worked. The management accountant could calculate a total overhead (TOH) actual overhead rate (AOR) using the following formula:

$$\text{TOH AOR} = \frac{\text{Total actual annual overhead cost}}{\text{Total actual annual direct labor hours}}$$

$$\$5.57/\text{DLhr} = \frac{\$260,000}{46,667 \text{ Direct labor hours}}$$

The problem with calculating an *actual* overhead rate is that the cost and hours are not known until *after* the year is over. Managers who need current cost information to set sales prices *throughout* the year cannot wait until year-end to find out how much overhead should be included in the cost of the product (so that an adequate sales price can be set). At year-end, not even the Glen Abbey monks can go back to a customer who bought a bottle of wine in March and say to him, "We're sorry, we didn't include overhead in our cost, and you owe us another $5.57!"[2]

To solve the problem of not having timely information (one of the attributes of high-quality information in CAS design), the new management accountant for Glen Abbey suggested that an estimated overhead rate be used. Such a rate can be "predetermined" at the beginning of the year and used to apply overhead throughout the year. With a good estimate of overhead, and good cost control over it, estimated and actual overhead costs for the year will be the same, and the amount applied will equal the amount spent. So, the management accountant calculated a TOH **predetermined overhead rate (POR)**:

$$\text{TOH POR} = \frac{\text{Total budgeted annual overhead cost}}{\text{Total budgeted annual direct labor hours}}$$

$$\$4.29/\text{DLhr (rounded)} = \frac{\$257,000}{60,000 \text{ Direct labor hours}}$$

If she used the estimated rate of $4.29/DLhr[3] multiplied by the actual direct labor hours worked to allocate overhead throughout the year, and 60,000 hours were worked and $257,000 spent, then all the actual overhead would be allocated to the products by year-end. Using actual direct materials and direct labor costs, with an *estimated applied overhead amount*, to cost the products is called **normal costing.**

---

[2] Assuming it takes one direct labor hour to make a bottle. Even if it took only a half-hour, the monks probably still can't get another $2.785 from each customer!
[3] The TOH POR was closer to $4.2857/DLhr, as discussed on page 150, but the monks didn't like that much precision, and told her to use $4.29 for the POR and $200,000 for applied overhead.

What Are the Purposes of Predetermined Overhead Rates?

PORs are used instead of actual overhead rates for four related purposes:

- To calculate an appropriate amount of overhead to be included in the cost of products or services.
- To enable overhead allocation to be made in a timely manner, rather than waiting until total actual overhead costs and hours worked become known at the end of the year.
- To provide timely product cost information for journal entries transferring completed products from WIP to FGI, and from FGI to COGS.
- To normalize the overhead charge: PORs smooth out uncontrollable fluctuations in actual overhead costs that are unrelated to activity or volume levels. Actual overhead rates, if calculated monthly, for example, often vary due to seasonal factors.

While normal costing solves the problem of untimely product cost information, it can cause another problem at year-end if total actual overhead (debits in the overhead account) does not equal total applied overhead (the credits). At year-end, a surplus debit balance in the overhead account represents **underapplied overhead;** a credit balance represents **overapplied overhead.** Consider Glen Abbey's overhead account balance at year-end:

WIP–MANUFACTURING OVERHEAD

JE 5 (IM)	$ 10,000	
JE 6 (IL)	$ 30,000	
JE 4 (Other OH)	$220,000	Applied $200,000
Ending Balance	$ 60,000	

Actual overhead costs incurred during the year will seldom equal applied overhead costs. The difference occurs because overhead costs were under- or overapplied during the period. Glen Abbey has $60,000 of underapplied overhead. In other words, the cost of its products is understated because not enough ("under") overhead was allocated ("applied") into those costs with journal entry 7. With normal costing, overhead is applied using the TOH POR of $4.29 per DLhr. Only 46,667 DLhr were worked during the year, so only $200,000 ($4.29/DLhr × 46,667 DLhr, rounded) was applied to the cost of wine.

Why is the allocation $60,000 less than the total actual overhead costs? For Glen Abbey, there are two reasons. First, when the TOH POR was calculated, only $257,000 was budgeted for overhead. In actuality, $3,000 more was spent. Second, the TOH POR was calculated using 60,000 *budgeted* DLhr. But, only 46,667 DLhr were *actually* worked. The difference of 13,333 hours at $4.29 per DLhr is $57,000 (rounded). More was spent than was budgeted, and fewer hours were worked than were budgeted. Therefore, less overhead ended up being applied than was actually spent.[4]

Disposing of Underapplied and Overapplied Overhead Costs

Because the products' costs are understated, when they are sold, their cost of goods sold on the income statement also will be understated. This must be corrected for external reporting purposes because both GAAP and federal tax

[4] In Chapters 8 and 9, these two differences will be formally calculated and labeled as unfavorable overhead spending and usage cost variances. Unfavorable cost variances mean more was spent than should have been. Thus, the products are undercosted. Underapplied overhead = unfavorable overhead cost variances = understated product costs (COGS in the income statement).

regulations require that the financial statements reflect actual costs. Thus, any balance at year-end in the overhead account needs to be *closed out* along with the revenue and expense accounts.

Disposition of under- or overapplied overhead depends on the significance ("materiality") of the amount involved. If the amount is small, it is closed to the cost of goods sold account. When underapplied overhead is closed, it causes cost of goods sold to increase, because not enough overhead costs were originally applied to production. Conversely, closing overapplied overhead causes cost of goods sold to decrease, because too much overhead costs were applied to production throughout the year.

If the amount of under- or overapplied overhead is significant, the applied overhead costs for all the products that were worked on during the year should be corrected. Thus, the ending overhead balance should be prorated among the following year-end account balances where the products' costs are located in the CAS:

- Work-in-process inventory (unfinished products)
- Finished goods inventory (finished but unsold products)
- Cost of goods sold (finished and sold products)

A substantial amount of under- or overapplied overhead means that the year-end ending balances in these accounts are quite different from what they would have been if overhead had been applied using an actual overhead rate and the actual hours worked. The under- or overapplied amount is prorated among these ending inventory balances in order to restate them so that they include all the actual overhead costs incurred throughout the year. Exhibit 4–14 demonstrates how Glen Abbey's underapplied overhead costs are prorated among its ending inventory balances (from Exhibit 4–3). Had the amount been over-

---

EXHIBIT 4–14
Prorating Underapplied Overhead Costs to Affected Accounts

Manufacturing overhead:			Account balances:	
Actual	$260,000		Work-in-process	$200,000
Less applied	<200,000>		Finished goods	300,000
Underapplied	$ 60,000		Cost of goods sold	500,000

1. Determine proportional relationships:

Balance		Proportion	Percentage
Work-in-process	$ 200,000	$200,000 ÷ $1,000,000	20%
Finished goods	300,000	$300,000 ÷ $1,000,000	30%
Cost of goods sold	500,000	$500,000 ÷ $1,000,000	50%
Total	$1,000,000		100%

2. Determine amount of adjustment needed:

	Percentage ×	Underapplied OH =	Adjustment Amount
Work-in-process	20%	$60,000	$12,000
Finished goods	30%	60,000	18,000
Cost of goods sold	50%	60,000	30,000

3. Prepare the journal entry to close the manufacturing overhead control account and prorate the adjustment amount to the affected accounts:

Prorating Underapplied Overhead

WIP–Product Cost (Applied OH)	12,000	
Finished Goods Inventory	18,000	
Cost of Goods Sold	30,000	
WIP–Manufacturing Overhead		60,000

applied, the accounts debited and credited in the journal entry would be reversed.

Most companies close out the balance to the cost of goods sold account. This approach offers the advantages of simplicity and expediency. Its disadvantage is some loss of accuracy in costing compared to the proration approach, which applies overhead costs to where they would have gone in the first place had the POR been totally accurate. Most companies believe that the greater accuracy simply isn't worth the extra effort that proration requires, especially when the dollar amounts are not material.

Evolving to Standard Cost Accounting Systems

Normal costing provides more timely product cost information than actual costing. Normal costing presents two problems, however: (1) a POR has to be calculated, based on estimates for the upcoming year; and (2) all the actual overhead may not be applied throughout the year, resulting in an ending overhead account balance that must be dealt with. The use of a POR, though, provides a second important benefit in terms of cost management information. A significant difference between actual and applied overhead signals a problem to management. In Glen Abbey's situation, more was spent on overhead than budgeted, and a lot fewer hours were worked than budgeted.

The use of a POR, or budgeted overhead rate, allows the CAS to produce information about production cost problems. These are called cost variances and are the subject of Chapters 8 and 9. This is such a major strength of the CAS that it should not be limited to just the overhead cost element. In other words, budgeted rates (and quantities) should be used to cost products for all cost elements: direct materials, direct labor, and overhead (not just for overhead as in normal costing). To satisfy the management accounting objective of the CAS, normal costing evolved into a **standard cost accounting system (SCAS).**

In an SCAS, journal entries 5 through 7 use a budgeted price, called a standard price (SP), for each cost element, multiplied by the amount of each input that should have been used (the standard quantity allowed, or SQA). By using standard costs instead of actual costs in measuring the cost of a product, any problems (cost variances) can be determined and reported to management through the SCAS.

For example, in the Glen Abbey case, the new management accountant discovered two overhead problems. These problems only became evident because she decided to use normal costing that applied overhead with a budgeted rate (the POR). Only an estimated ("should be") amount of overhead was credited to the overhead account, and any difference between it and the actual overhead spent (the debits to the overhead account), became an ending account balance that the management accountant brought to the attention of the monks.

In an SCAS, a budgeted rate is used for all inputs, making this type of management control information available for direct materials and direct labor. After the management accountant prepared the overhead analysis, the monks were pleased with it, but were upset by the labor costs. Apparently, they had budgeted to spend only $8.50 per DLhr on production labor costs (the actual labor rate the accountant calculated was $9.00 per DLhr as shown in Exhibit 4–10). Also, they figured that only 45,000 DLhr should have been worked, not the 46,667 actually worked.

In an SCAS, the $8.50 budgeted labor rate times 45,000 DLhr is used as the amount to charge products in journal entry 6 (the labor distribution journal entry). Using an SCAS, then, less labor cost would have been added to the products' costs than was debited to the gross wages account. This would be similar to the underapplied overhead situation in that more was spent on labor than should have been, as was true for overhead.

With overhead, the overspending resulted in an ending balance that could be reported in terms of its cost variances. Similarly, by not using the actual

■ EXHIBIT 4–15
Cost Elements, Cost Measurement, and Cost Accounting Systems

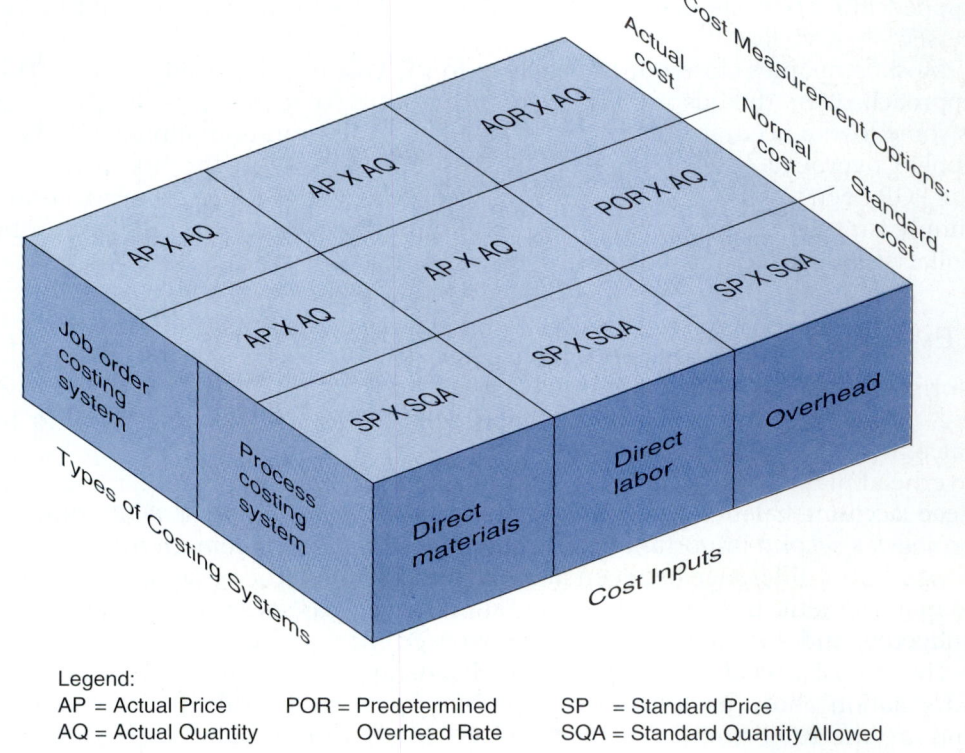

Legend:
AP = Actual Price   POR = Predetermined   SP   = Standard Price
AQ = Actual Quantity   Overhead Rate   SQA = Standard Quantity Allowed

costs of labor in measuring the products' costs, an SCAS could also report cost variances about labor (i.e., the labor rate was more than budgeted [$9.00 versus $8.50], and more hours were worked last year than should have been [46,667 versus 45,000], so total labor cost was higher than it should have been).

After the new management accountant saw this, she decided next year to change Glen Abbey's CAS from a normal costing system to an SCAS. How to do this is the subject of Chapters 7 and 8. First, though, Chapters 5 and 6 will look at JOCASs and PCASs. With either system, cost elements can be measured by using actual cost, normal cost, or standard cost. The following will help in distinguishing between these three cost measurement choices:

■ Actual costing uses the actual price (AP) times the actual quantity (AQ) of each cost element in measuring the product's cost.
■ Normal costing uses the actual cost of direct materials and direct labor, but an estimated overhead cost based on a predetermined overhead rate times the actual number of the inputs used to apply overhead (POR × AQ).
■ An SCAS uses a budgeted (standard) rate or price (SP) times only the amount of each input that should have been used (SQA).

The choices faced by the modern management accountant in setting up the CAS framework are summarized in Exhibit 4–15.

▌SUMMARY OF LEARNING OBJECTIVES

The major goals of this chapter were to enable you to achieve five learning objectives:

Learning objective 1. Understand how manufacturing cost elements flow through a production process, and describe the nine basic journal entries used to record these cost flows.

The first phase of the cost flows is the purchase of raw materials, factory labor, and indirect production costs (overhead). The CAS journalizes these cost elements into "temporary holding" accounts until they are used in the factory (journal entries 1–4). RMI is a tangible holding account in that physical materials are stored in it. Gross Wages, the holding account for factory labor costs, is the most temporary of the three; payroll-related costs go into it (debited) in journal entries 2 and 3, but it is cleared out through the labor distribution journal entry 6. The overhead account accumulates actual overhead costs throughout the year (journal entries 4–6), while overhead is being applied to production.

The second phase of the cost flows involves the use of cost elements in production. As manufacturing inputs are used, they are removed from their temporary holding accounts (credited) in the CAS (journal entries 5–7). The production process is WIP, so these cost elements are debited to it when directly traceable to products being made or when overhead is applied into the products' cost.

The third phase of the cost flows involves both the movement of completed products from WIP to FGI in journal entry 8 and the products' removal from FGI when sold in journal entry 9. The formal journal entries are presented in Demonstration Problem 1.

Learning objective 2.   Describe the main records and procedures necessary to account for and control materials.

Materials represent a major cost element in many organizations. Thus, they require careful control. First, the manufacturer should prepare (either manually, via a computer system, or with EDI) a purchase order properly authorizing the purchase and all its terms. Second, the materials should be received properly, which involves accurate counting and inspecting before storage in RMI. (A JIT system usually eliminates these activities.) A receiving report is then prepared. In addition, a receiving log is prepared showing all materials received during the day. Rejected materials are listed in a rejected material report.

When production needs materials from RMI, a materials requisition is prepared to release materials from RMI to WIP. Each item of direct materials is recorded in a direct materials subsidiary ledger, which can often take the form of a computerized materials record (Exhibit 4–9). In modern, world-class manufacturing, bar code systems can be used to track materials into and out of RMI and through WIP.

Learning objective 3.   Illustrate the records and procedures used to account for labor.

Factory labor costs have two components: the employees' gross wage rate and the employer's payroll burden. Recording paychecks (journal entry 2) involves a number of mandatory and voluntary withholdings. Records of these withholdings must be maintained for governmental tax reporting. Because amounts withheld from employee paychecks are owed to other entities, they are credited to current liability accounts.

Similarly, the employer owes governmental taxing agencies, insurance companies, pension plans, and so forth, additional amounts that are also journalized to current liabilities (credits in journal entry 3); these costs are included (debited) in the factory labor cost account called Gross Wages. Once all factory labor-related costs are added to the Gross Wages account, they are distributed to the manufacturing activities that used the labor (debits to WIP in journal entry 6).

Accounting for labor can be done manually or electronically. The key activity is timekeeping. In a manual system, the main document is the time ticket. Automated systems use bar codes to perform timekeeping. The data are input without using any documents and are then automatically transmitted to payroll, cost accounting, inventory, administrative, and manufacturing systems.

Learning objective 4.   Explain why overhead costs are accumulated and then applied to products and services.

As actual overhead costs are incurred, they are journalized (debited) into a temporary holding account in WIP. This is done because these cost elements cannot be directly traced to products that use them. The only alternative is to group them together, so that they can be divided up (applied) in some way and finally added into the product's cost.

In order to apply overhead to the product's cost, some basis for allocation is needed that can be directly traced to the product. Common bases for overhead allocation are direct labor hours worked on the product, machine hours, direct labor cost, and direct materials cost. Once the basis is selected, an overhead rate can be calculated and used to apply overhead.

One type of rate, an actual overhead rate, is calculated at year-end by dividing the total actual overhead cost by the total basis volume (e.g., total actual direct labor hours or machine hours). This AOR is then multiplied by the hours worked on each product to determine how much overhead is applied to its cost (journal entry 7). The major problem with this method is that the management accountant has to wait until the end of the year to obtain the information needed to calculate the AOR.

Therefore, CASs have evolved from actual costing to normal costing that use a predetermined overhead rate. The POR is calculated just like the AOR, but the calculation is made at the beginning of the year using budgeted overhead cost and hours. Applying overhead by using a POR times the actual hours worked on a product usually results in an ending balance in the overhead account at year-end. This over- or underapplied overhead needs to be written off to COGS or, if it is significant, prorated across the products made (ending balances in WIP and FGI and in COGS).

Learning objective 5. Relate the two types of cost accounting systems to the two types of manufacturing systems identified in Chapter 1, and to the three ways of measuring a product's cost.

Manufacturing operations that make products individually or in small unique batches are called job order systems. The corresponding CAS is a JOCAS, in which cost elements are directly traced (and overhead applied) to each job. Operations that make one product, or very similar products, in large batches through mass production methods are called process systems. A PCAS traces costs to departments and then calculates an average cost per product.

With either a JOCAS or a PCAS, there are three ways to measure the cost elements. Actual costing charges the products with the actual cost (actual price times actual quantity) of each input in journal entries 5–7. Normal costing uses the *actual* cost of direct materials and direct labor, but uses an *estimated* overhead charge based on a POR. An SCAS charges all three cost elements to the products based on their budgeted costs (standard price times standard quantity allowed for each input). SCASs provide the best cost management information because they allow production problems (cost variances) to be identified.

IMPORTANT TERMS

Actual costing A cost measurement method that bases the product's cost on the actual cost (AP × AQ) of all manufacturing cost elements.

Applied overhead The amount of overhead allocated to the product's cost.

Control account A general ledger account that has two or more subsidiary accounts within it.

Gross wages A temporary holding account in the CAS used to accumulate all payroll-related costs until they are distributed to products (direct labor) and overhead (indirect labor).

Hybrid cost accounting system A CAS that combines the characteristics of a JOCAS and PCAS.

Job order cost accounting system (JOCAS) A cost accounting system used in organizations whose products or services are readily identified by individual jobs, units, or projects.

Manufacturing cost elements The four resources input into the process of making a product or providing a service are direct materials, direct labor, variable overhead, and fixed overhead.

Materials requisition A document or computer program using screen displays that authorizes materials to be transferred from RMI to WIP.

Materials subsidiary ledger (materials inventory master file) A file that contains individual records for each (usually direct) material item.

Normal costing A cost measurement method that bases the product's cost on the actual cost (AP × AQ) of direct materials and direct labor, but uses an estimated amount of applied overhead (POR × AQ).

Overapplied overhead The amount by which the total applied overhead exceeds the actual overhead.

Periodic inventory system   A method of accounting for inventory relief transactions that backs into the amount used (sold) by periodically taking a physical inventory and using the inventory balances to calculate how much inventory was removed during that time period.

Perpetual inventory system   A method of accounting for (recording) inventory transactions when they occur so that all inventories are current at all times.

Predetermined overhead rate (POR)   A rate used in applying overhead to production. It is established at the beginning of an accounting period, using estimated amounts, to facilitate the averaging of overhead costs over all production.

Process cost accounting system (PCAS)   A cost accounting system used in organizations whose products or services are mass-produced in a continuous flow of production.

Purchase order   A document, computer program screen display, or electronic signal within an EDI network that authorizes the purchase and shipment of raw materials, specifying all the terms and conditions of the order.

Receiving log   A document that summarizes receiving reports and is the primary record for identifying missing documents.

Receiving report   A report about an order of raw materials received.

Rejected material report   A document that identifies material to be returned to the vendor.

Shipping advice   Usually, a copy of a purchase order sent with raw materials shipments by the vendor to facilitate the recording of their receipt and payment to the vendor.

Standard cost accounting system (SCAS)   A CAS that uses standard costs (SP × SQA) for all cost elements to measure the cost of the product.

Subsidiary general ledger accounts   Accounts within the CAS that are subsets of a control account, usually representing specific items that management wants controlled separately.

Time tickets   Documents used for timekeeping and for assigning labor to a specific department or job, or to overhead.

Timekeeping   A method of accounting for the number of hours employees work.

Total overhead (TOH)   The combination of variable and fixed overhead within one general ledger account.

Underapplied overhead   The amount by which the total actual overhead exceeds the applied overhead.

▌DEMONSTRATION PROBLEMS

■ DEMONSTRATION PROBLEM 1   *T-accounts and journal entries for a CAS using normal costing.*

Using the annual information below for Topper, Inc., prepare T-accounts for RMI, gross wages, the two subsidiary accounts for WIP, and FGI (the format from Exhibit 4–3 will be used so as to relate cost flows to their corresponding journal entries), and prepare the journal entries for each event using normal costing.

1. Raw materials beginning balance is zero, and the ending balance is $20,000. Purchases made on account are $100,000.
2. There is a $200,000 factory payroll for the year, with the following withholding rates: federal income taxes 10%, state income taxes 5%, Social Security taxes 7.5%, pension plan 2%, health insurance 1.5%.
3. Topper's payroll tax burden and fringe benefits rates are as follows: federal unemployment tax rate = 0.8% and the state's = 5.4%; fringe benefits include vacation pay (2 weeks when 50 weeks are worked in a year), Topper's contribution to a pension plan of 5.0%, and its contribution to the health insurance plan of 3.3%.
4. Other actual overhead costs, paid on account, are $88,000. Factory equipment depreciation equals $200,000.
5. Direct materials requisitioned equal $75,000.
6. $175,000 of the total gross wages represents direct labor.
7. Overhead allocation assuming a POR of 200% of direct labor cost.
8. Completed production = ? The beginning WIP balance is $500,000, and the ending balance is $100,000.
9. Inventory relief for product sales = ? The beginning and ending FGI balances are $100,000 and $300,000, respectively.

SOLUTION TO DEMONSTRATION PROBLEM 1

T-accounts with explanations and journal entry references:

T-Accounts

RAW MATERIALS INVENTORY

Beginning Balance	$ 0	
Purchases	$ 100	Used $80
Ending Balance	$ 20	

Explanations

Each of the three debit amounts is given in the narrative. The $100,000 in purchases is recorded in JE 1. $80,000 must have been used (see JE 5) for the ending balance to be $20,000. Note that all amounts are in thousands.

GROSS WAGES

Gross Wages	$ 200	
Employer's Burden	$ 52	Distribution: $252
Ending Balance	$ 0	

Both the wages and employer's burden amounts are calculated in JE 2 and JE 3. All wage costs are distributed to WIP accounts (JE 6).

WIP–MANUFACTURING OVERHEAD

Indirect Materials	$ 5	
Indirect Labor	$ 77	
Other	$ 288	Applied $350
Ending Balance	$ 20	

If DM = $75,000 of the $80,000 of raw materials used, then $5,000 must be IM (JE 5). IL is $77,000 if gross wages are $252,000 and DL is $175,000 (JE 6). Other overhead costs are given (JE 4). Applied overhead is calculated in JE 7 @ 200% of DL$.

WIP–PRODUCT COST

Beginning Balance	$ 500	
DM	$ 75	
DL	$ 175	
Applied OH	$ 350	COGM $1,000
Ending Balance	$ 100	

The beginning and ending balances are given. DM (JE 5), DL (JE 6), and applied overhead (JE 7) are posted. With these postings, cost of goods manufactured can be calculated (JE 8).

FINISHED GOODS INVENTORY

Beginning Balance	$ 100	
COGM	1,000	COGS $800
Ending Balance	$ 300	

The beginning and ending balances are given. Knowing COGM = $1,000,000 from JE 8, then COGS can be calculated (JE 9).

SOLUTION TO DEMONSTRATION PROBLEM 1 (*Continued*)

Journal entries:

Ref	General Ledger Account Titles	dr's	cr's	Notes:
	PURCHASE (ACQUISITION) OF RAW MATERIALS:			
1:	Raw Materials Inventory	$100,000		given
	Accounts Payable		$100,000	all RMI purchases are charged
	PREPARING (RECORDING) PAYCHECKS:			
2:	Gross Wages	$200,000		
	FIT Withholdings Payable		$20,000	+$GROSS WAGES*0.1
	SIT Withholdings Payable		$10,000	+$GROSS WAGES*0.05
	FICA Taxes Payable		$15,000	+$GROSS WAGES*0.075
	Pension Plan Payable		$4,000	+$GROSS WAGES*0.02
	Health Insurance Payable		$3,000	+$GROSS WAGES*0.015
	Wages Payable		$148,000	GROSS WAGES − WITHHOLDINGS

Continued

—Continued

EMPLOYER'S PAYROLL TAXES & BENEFITS (BURDEN):			
3: Gross Wages	$52,000		SUM (EMPLOYER BURDEN)
FICA Taxes Payable		$15,000	= withheld from paychecks
FUTA Taxes Payable		$1,600	+$GROSS WAGES*0.008
SUTA Taxes Payable		$10,800	+$GROSS WAGES*0.054
Pension Plan Payable		$10,000	+$GROSS WAGES*0.05
Health Insurance Payable		$6,600	+$GROSS WAGES*0.033
Vacation Payable		$8,000	+$GROSS WAGES*0.04
OTHER OVERHEAD COSTS INCURRED:			
4: WIP–Manufacturing Overhead (Other OH costs)	$88,000		amounts given
WIP–Manufacturing Overhead (Depreciation)	$200,000		
Accounts Payable		$88,000	amounts charged
Accumulated Depreciation–Factory. Equipment		$200,000	
REQUISITION OF RAW MATERIALS INTO THE FACTORY:			
5: WIP–Product Cost (DM)	$75,000		given
WIP–Manufacturing Overhead (IM)	$5,000		"plug" to balance
Raw Materials Inventory		$80,000	calculate from T-account
DISTRIBUTING GROSS WAGES TO PRODUCTS:			
6: WIP–Product Cost (DL)	$175,000		given
WIP–Manufacturing Overhead (IL)	$77,000		"plug" to balance
Gross Wages		$252,000	gross pay + employer burden
APPLYING OVERHEAD:			
7: WIP–Product Cost (Applied Overhead)	$350,000		POR = 200% of DL$
WIP–Manufacturing Overhead		$350,000	DL$ = $175,000 (given)
PRODUCTS COMPLETED:			
8: Finished Goods Inventory	$1,000,000		COGM calculated within T-account
WIP–Product Cost		$1,000,000	
PRODUCTS SOLD (INVENTORY RELIEF JOURNAL ENTRY ONLY):			
9: Cost of Goods Sold	$800,000		COGS calculated within T-account
Finished Goods Inventory		$800,000	

JOURNAL ENTRY RECORDING CONVENTIONS:

1. Use a dash to separate a control account from a subsidiary account.
2. Use parentheses for a posting reference within a general ledger account.

■ **DEMONSTRATION PROBLEM 2**   *Cost of goods sold with normal costing.*

Using the information from Demonstration Problem 1, prepare a combined COGM and COGS statement for Topper, Inc. (the ending overhead balance is not significant).

SOLUTION TO DEMONSTRATION PROBLEM 2

Topper, Inc.
Cost of Goods Manufactured and Sold Statement
For the Year Ended 12/31/XX

Direct materials used:		
Raw materials inventory beginning balance	$ 0	
Add raw materials purchases	100,000	
Less raw materials inventory ending balance	<20,000>	
Raw materials used	80,000	
Less indirect materials used	<5,000>	
DIRECT MATERIALS USED	$ 75,000	
DIRECT LABOR USED	175,000	
APPLIED MANUFACTURING OVERHEAD	350,000	
MANUFACTURING COSTS INCURRED THIS PERIOD	$ 600,000	

Continued

—Continued

Add beginning work-in-process inventory	500,000
Less ending work-in-process inventory	<100,000>
COST OF GOODS MANUFACTURED	$1,000,000
Add underapplied overhead (minus overapplied OH)	20,000
Add beginning finished goods inventory	100,000
Less ending finished goods inventory	<300,000>
COST OF GOODS SOLD	$ 820,000

The COGM format from Chapter 1 is modified to calculate direct materials used when no separate subsidiary account is kept for it within the CAS. If there is a subsidiary account for it, then DM used can be calculated as in Chapter 1. With no subsidiary account for DM, RMI used has to be computed first; then indirect materials used are subtracted to yield only the direct materials used. Remember that RMI, and therefore RMI used, includes both direct and indirect materials.

With normal costing, the overhead included in the production costs within WIP is applied overhead. In actual costing, as was demonstrated in Chapter 1, the total actual overhead is included in the product costs. Thus, each overhead cost element can be separately listed in the COGM Statement, as was done in Chapter 1.

With normal costing, if the over- or underapplied balance is insignificant, then it is written off to COGS. Underapplied overhead results in the products' costs being understated. So, COGS is also understated. Thus, underapplied overhead is an addition to COGS. Note the ending balance in the T-account (Demonstration Problem 1). To "zero out" the overhead account, it has to be credited (underapplied overhead is an ending debit balance), which means COGS has to be debited (increased).

■ **DEMONSTRATION PROBLEM 3** *PORs and the WIP–Manufacturing Overhead account in normal costing.*

While budgeting at the beginning of the year, it was decided that overhead is caused by the usage of machinery, and this is to be the basis for applying overhead to the products' costs. The following data about annual overhead are available:

OVERHEAD COSTS	BUDGETED	ACTUAL
Indirect materials	$ 31,000	$ 25,000
Indirect labor	45,000	48,000
Depreciation	105,000	100,000
Utilities	4,500	5,000
Miscellaneous	9,500	22,000
Totals	$195,000	$200,000
Machine hours for entire plant:	65,000 Mhr	100,000 Mhr

Required:

a. Calculate the POR.
b. Determine how much overhead was applied in total for the entire year.
c. Calculate the ending balance in the overhead account at year-end, properly labeled as over- or underapplied.
d. Assuming that the ending overhead balance is not significant, which general ledger account should it be written off to in the year-end closing journal entry?
e. If the ending overhead balance is significant, what should be done with it?

SOLUTION TO DEMONSTRATION PROBLEM 3

a. $\dfrac{\text{Budgeted TOH} = \$195,000}{\text{Budgeted machine hours} = 65,000} = \$3.00/\text{Mhr}$

b. 100,000 Mhr × $3.00/Mhr = $300,000.

c. Actual TOH of $200,000 (debits) − Applied TOH of $300,000 (credits) = Overapplied overhead of $100,000 (ending credit balance).

d. Cost of goods sold.

e. It should be allocated to the products worked on during the year, which are in the ending balances of WIP and FGI and in COGS. The easiest way to make this allocation is by prorating the ending overhead balance proportionately to the balances in those three accounts (WIP, FGI, COGS).

▍REVIEW QUESTIONS

4.1 What is a CAS? How does it differ from management and financial accounting systems? (See Chapter 1.)

4.2 What is the overall goal of a CAS? Why is this goal important?

4.3 Why is there "no one, true product cost"?

4.4 Define (using one sentence each) the four manufacturing inputs.

4.5 Give three examples of:

- Direct materials costs
- Direct labor costs
- Overhead costs

4.6 Distinguish between a direct cost and an indirect cost.

4.7 The inventory account that contains all manufacturing costs while products are being made is _____.

4.8 The inventory account that contains all materials received until they are required in production is called _____.

4.9 Completed output waiting to be sold is in which inventory account?

4.10 Explain the differences between a periodic and a perpetual inventory system.

4.11 When matching a cost system with a production process, which type of production process is appropriate for each of the following?

- A PCAS
- A JOCAS

4.12 What is a hybrid cost accounting system? What types of production processes might use a hybrid CAS?

4.13 Describe the three types of basic journal entries in a CAS.

4.14 Why are the purchases of cost elements debited to "temporary holding accounts"?

4.15 Why is the use of each of the cost elements debited to the same general ledger account in a CAS?

4.16 When making the three journal entries for the use of cost elements, what do the credits in these journal entries have in common?

4.17 In journalizing COGM and COGS, where does the product's cost come from?

4.18 What is the difference between a control and a subsidiary account?

4.19 In the journal entries to record direct materials and direct labor usage, why is there a debit to the overhead account?

4.20 What effect does making the overhead allocation journal entry have on the total balance in the WIP control account?

4.21 What is "applied overhead"?

4.22 List two reasons why actual overhead costs have to be accumulated and grouped together before they can be assigned to the cost of products.

4.23 List four rules for making basic CAS journal entries.

4.24 Distinguish between a subsidiary account and a posting reference. What are the recording and posting conventions used for each in this text?

4.25 Two types of costs (actual and applied) are included in the overhead accounts. Which type is debited to overhead? Which type is credited to overhead?

4.26 What source document is used for recording each of the following journal entries?

- Raw materials purchased
- Raw materials issuances into the factory
- Direct labor distribution to individual products

4.27 Explain the purpose of each of the following documents. Which department originates each document? Which departments receive copies of each document?

- Purchase order
- Receiving report
- Receiving log
- Rejected material report
- Materials requisition
- Time tickets

4.28 What are the key fields in a perpetual inventory system's materials record?

4.29 List four objectives of a payroll system.

4.30 What costs should be included in the gross labor rate used to charge factory labor to products?

4.31 Distinguish between mandatory and voluntary withholdings. Give examples of each.

4.32 Distinguish between mandatory and voluntary employer payroll costs. Give examples of each.

4.33 List three different ways to account for the current liabilities created by factory labor.

4.34 Present four reasons why a subsidiary ledger account for overhead is needed.

4.35 When choosing a cost system, we have three options for calculating the cost of our product. Which option would you choose in each of the following cases?

a. We want to use the actual direct input costs, but an estimated cost for the indirect input costs.

b. We want to use the budgeted costs of each manufacturing input.

c. We want to use the actual costs of each manufacturing input.

4.36 What is the purpose of a predetermined overhead rate? Give an example.

4.37 How does an AOR differ from a POR?

4.38 What amounts are used in the numerator and denominator of a POR?

4.39 Explain how overhead may be underapplied or overapplied.

4.40 When the amount of underapplied overhead is significant, the entry to close the overhead account at year-end will most likely require debits to which general ledger accounts?

CHAPTER-SPECIFIC PROBLEMS

These problems require responses based directly on concepts and techniques presented in the text.

4.41 *Classification of costs.* Following are typical items found in a manufacturing enterprise:

a. Subassemblies purchased from vendors including invoice price plus shipping costs.

b. Individual production efficiency bonuses.

c. Workers' compensation insurance.

d. Contributions to health insurance plans.

e. Glue used to hold components together.

f. Wages for inspection and maintenance.

g. Factory rent.

h. Factory insurance and taxes.

i. Supervisory salaries.

j. Welding supplies.

Required:
Classify the preceding items as direct materials, direct labor, or manufacturing overhead.

4.42 *T-accounts, schedule of cost of goods manufactured and sold, and income statement.*
Baker Company, a manufacturer, had these beginning and ending inventories at the end of its current year:

Raw materials	$22,000	$30,000
WIP–Product Cost	40,000	48,000
Finished goods	25,000	18,000

During the year, the following transactions occurred:

1. Direct materials purchased	$300,000
2. Indirect materials and supplies purchased	50,000
3. Direct labor wages	120,000
4. Indirect factory labor wages	60,000
5. Property taxes on factory building	15,000
6. Depreciation on factory building	5,000
7. Property taxes and depreciation on salesroom and office (shared on a 50%–50% basis)	15,000
8. Utilities (60% to factory, 20% to salesroom, and 20% to office)	50,000
9. Indirect materials issued to factory	40,000
10. Payroll taxes and fringe benefits paid	46,800
11. Factory overhead applied on the basis of 120% of direct labor costs	?
12. Sales salaries	40,000
13. Office salaries	24,000
14. Sales on account	730,000
15. Over- or underapplied overhead is deducted from or added to cost of goods sold.	

Required:
a. Prepare T accounts for the factory-related items and post the data.
b. Prepare a cost of goods manufactured statement.
c. Prepare a cost of goods sold statement.

[AICPA adapted]

4.43 *Journal entries.* Using the Baker Company information in the previous problem and the information below, prepare the nine basic journal entries for Baker's CAS.

a. The factory payroll is subject to the following withholding rates: federal income taxes 10%, state income taxes 5%, Social Security taxes 7.5%, pension plan 2%, health insurance 1.5%.
b. Baker Company's payroll tax burden and fringe benefits rates are as follows: federal unemployment tax rate = 0.8% and the state's = 5.4%; fringe benefits include vacation pay (2 weeks when 50 weeks are worked in a year), Baker's contribution to a pension plan of 5.0%, and its contribution to the health insurance plan of 3.3%.

4.44 *T-accounts and journal entries using normal costing.* Using the annual information below for Carson, Inc., prepare the journal entries for each event using normal costing. Post the journal entries to T-accounts for RMI, gross wages, the two subsidiary accounts for WIP, and FGI.

a. Raw materials beginning balance is $10,000, and the ending balance is $20,000. Purchases made on account are $200,000.
b. There is a $300,000 factory payroll for the year, with the following withholding rates: federal income taxes 15%, state income taxes 5%, Social Security taxes 7.5%, pension plan 5%, health insurance 2%.
c. Carson's payroll tax burden and fringe benefits rates are as follows: federal unemployment tax rate = 1% and the state's = 5%; fringe benefits include vacation pay (3 weeks when 49 weeks are worked in a year, round to whole dollars), Carson's contribution to a pension plan of 5%, and its contribution to the health insurance plan of 2%.
d. Other actual overhead costs, paid on account, are $100,000. Factory equipment depreciation equals $400,000.
e. Direct materials requisitioned equal $175,000.
f. $250,000 of gross wages represents direct labor.
g. Carson, Inc., uses a POR of 260% of direct labor cost.
h. The beginning WIP balance is $200,000 of which $5,000 is in the overhead subsidiary account. The ending balance in the product cost subsidiary account is $280,000.
i. The beginning and ending FGI balances are $75,000 and $100,000, respectively.

4.45 *T-accounts and journal entries using normal costing.* Using the annual information below for Jansen Skiwear (a New York City company), prepare the journal entries for each event. Post the journal entries to T-accounts for RMI, gross wages, the two subsidiary accounts for WIP, and FGI.

a. RMI beginning balance is 5,000, and the ending balance is $7,500. Purchases made on account are $80,000.

b. There is a $100,000 factory payroll for the year, with the following withholding rates: federal income taxes 28%, state income taxes 6%, city income tax 1%, Social Security taxes 7.5%, union dues 2%, health insurance 1%.

c. Jansen's payroll tax burden and fringe benefits rates are as follows: federal unemployment tax rate = 0.7% and the state's = 2.5%; fringe benefits include vacation pay (4 weeks when 48 weeks are worked in a year, round to whole dollars), Jansen's contribution to a pension plan of 5%, and its contribution to its health insurance plan of 5%.

d. Other actual overhead costs, paid on account, are $90,000. Factory equipment depreciation equals $200,000.

e. Direct materials requisitioned equal $65,000.

f. $75,000 of gross wages represents the 1,000 direct labor hours worked this year.

g. Jansen Skiwear uses a POR of $350 per direct labor hour.

h. The beginning WIP balance is $20,000 (all in the product costs subsidiary account) and the ending balance is $20,000.

i. The beginning and ending FGI balances are $75,000 and $30,000, respectively.

4.46 *Calculation of pretax income.* Carley Products has no work-in-process or finished goods inventories at the close of business on December 31, 19X5. The balances of Carley's accounts as of December 31, 19X5, are as follows:

Cost of goods sold	$2,040,000
General selling and administrative expenses	900,000
Sales	3,600,000
Actual factory overhead	700,000
Factory overhead applied	648,000

Required:
Calculate Carley's income before income taxes for 19X5.

[CMA adapted]

4.47 *Determination of predetermined overhead rates and their application.* Two companies have prepared the following estimated data for the year 19X4:

	COMPANY A	COMPANY B
Predetermined overhead rate based on	Machine hours	Direct labor cost
Estimated overhead costs	$100,000	$120,000
Estimated machine hours	50,000	–0–
Estimated direct labor cost	–0–	$ 80,000

$\frac{100,000}{50,000} = 2.00$

The actual results for each company are as follows:

	COMPANY A	COMPANY B
Actual overhead costs incurred	$95,000	$130,000
Actual machine hours	47,000	–0–
Actual direct labor cost	–0–	$ 89,000

Required:
a. Calculate the amount of overhead costs applied for both companies. Are these amounts over- or underapplied?

b. Explain why overhead costs are estimated and distinguish between actual overhead costs and applied overhead costs.

4.48 *Calculation of over- or underapplied overhead.* Woodman Company applies factory overhead on the basis of direct labor hours. Budget and actual data for direct labor and overhead for the year are as follows:

	BUDGET	ACTUAL
Direct labor hours	600,000	550,000
Factory overhead costs	$720,000	$680,000

Required:
Calculate the amount of applied overhead costs for the year. Is the amount over- or underapplied?

[CMA adapted]

4.49 *Allocation of over- or underapplied overhead.* Worley Company has underapplied overhead of $45,000 for the year. Before disposition of the underapplied overhead, selected year-end balances from Worley's accounting records were:

Sales	$1,200,000
Cost of goods sold	720,000
Direct materials inventory	36,000
Work-in-process inventory	54,000
Finished goods inventory	90,000

Under Worley's CAS, over- or underapplied overhead is prorated to appropriate inventories and COGS based on year-end balances.

Required:
What amount of cost of goods sold should Worley report in its year-end income statement? Round proration ratios to five decimal places.

[AICPA adapted]

4.50 *Calculation of direct materials, labor, and over- or underapplied overhead costs.* Summit Company provided the inventory balances and manufacturing cost data shown below for the month of January:

	JAN. 1	JAN. 31
Direct materials inventory	$30,000	$40,000
Work-in-process inventory	15,000	20,000
Finished goods inventory	65,000	50,000

	MONTH OF JANUARY
Factory overhead applied	$150,000
Cost of goods manufactured	515,000
Direct materials used	190,000
Actual factory overhead	144,000

Under Summit's CAS, any over- or underapplied overhead is closed to the cost of goods sold account at the end of the calendar year.

Required:
a. What was the total amount of direct materials purchases during January?
b. How much direct labor cost was incurred during January?
c. What would cost of goods sold be if under- or overapplied overhead costs were closed to cost of goods sold?
d. What would cost of goods sold be if under- or overapplied overhead costs were allocated to inventories and cost of goods sold? Round proration ratios to four decimal places.

[AICPA adapted]

THINK-TANK PROBLEMS

Although these problems are based on chapter material, reading extra material, reviewing previous chapters, and using creativity may be required to develop workable solutions.

4.51 *Definition of costs.* A portion of the costs incurred by business organizations is designated as "direct labor cost." As used in practice, the term "direct labor cost" has a wide variety of meanings. Unless the meaning intended in a given context is clear, misunderstanding and confusion are likely to ensue. If a user does not understand the elements included in direct labor cost, erroneous interpretations of the numbers may occur and could result in poor management decisions.

The National Association of Accountants has issued *Statement on Management Accounting (SMA) Number 4C*, "Definition and Measurement of Direct Labor Cost," to assist management accountants in dealing with problems that may arise in interpreting and understanding direct labor costs. Along with providing a conceptual definition of direct labor cost, this Statement describes how direct labor costs should be measured. Measurement of direct labor costs involves two aspects: (1) the quantity of labor effort that is to be included, that is, the types of hours or other units of time that are to be counted; and (2) the unit price by which each of these quantities is multiplied to arrive at a monetary cost.

Required:
a. Distinguish between direct labor and indirect labor.
b. Explain why some nonproductive labor (e.g., coffee breaks, personal time) is treated as direct labor while other nonproductive labor (e.g., downtime, training) is treated as indirect labor.
c. The following are labor cost elements that a company has classified as direct labor, manufacturing overhead, or either direct labor or manufacturing overhead, depending upon the situation:

- *Direct labor.* Includes cost production efficiency bonuses and certain benefits for direct labor workers, such as FICA (employer's portion), group life insurance, vacation pay, and workers' compensation insurance.
- *Manufacturing overhead.* Includes the cost of wage continuation plans, the company-sponsored cafeteria, the personnel department, and recreational facilities.
- *Direct labor or manufacturing overhead.* Includes maintenance expense, overtime premiums, and shift premiums.

Explain the possible rationale used by the company in classifying the cost elements in each of these categories.

[CMA adapted]

4.52 *Determination of overhead applied and total manufacturing costs.* Helper Corporation manufactures one product. You have obtained the following information for the year ended December 31 from the corporation's books and records:

- Total manufacturing costs added to product costs during the year were $1,000,000 based on actual direct materials, actual direct labor, and factory overhead applied using an actual direct labor dollars-based POR.
- COGM was $970,000.
- Factory overhead was applied at 75% of direct labor dollars. Applied factory overhead for the year was 27% of the total manufacturing costs.
- Beginning WIP on January 1 was 80% of ending WIP on December 31.

Required:
a. How can cost personnel at Helper Corporation determine the amount of overhead applied given no direct labor cost figure?
b. How much direct labor was incurred?
c. How much direct materials were used?
d. What is the ending work-in-process inventory?

[AICPA adapted]

4.53 *Discussion of overhead rates.* Moss Manufacturing has just completed a major change in its quality control (QC) process. Previously, products were reviewed by QC inspectors at the end of each major process, and the company's ten QC inspectors were charged as direct labor to the operation or job. In an effort to improve efficiency and quality, a computer video QC system was purchased for $250,000. The system consists of a minicomputer, 15 video cameras, other peripheral hardware, and software.

The new system uses cameras stationed by QC engineers at key points in the production process. Each time an operation changes or a new operation begins, the cameras are moved, and a new master picture is loaded into the computer by a QC engineer. The camera takes pictures of the units in process, and the computer compares them to the picture of a "good" unit. Any differences are sent to a QC engineer who removes the bad units and discusses the flaws with the production supervisors. The new system has replaced the ten QC inspectors with two QC engineers.

The operating costs of the new QC system, including the salaries of the QC engineers, have been included as factory overhead in calculating the company's plantwide factory overhead rate, which is based on direct labor dollars.

The company's president is confused. His vice president of production has told him how efficient the new system is, yet the factory overhead rate has increased significantly. The computation of the rate before and after automation follows:

	BEFORE	AFTER
Budgeted overhead	$1,900,000	$2,100,000
Budgeted direct labor	1,000,000	700,000
Budgeted overhead rate	190%	300%

"Three hundred percent," lamented the president. "How can we compete with such a high factory overhead rate?"

Required
a. Define factory overhead, and cite three examples of typical costs that would be included in factory overhead.
b. Explain why companies develop factory overhead rates.
c. Explain why the increase in the overhead rate should not have a negative financial impact on Moss Manufacturing.
d. Explain how Moss Manufacturing could change its overhead accounting system to eliminate confusion over product costs.

[CMA adapted]

4.54 *Inventory ERD.* Would a traditional manufacturing company prefer a periodic or a perpetual inventory system? What if the company is a JIT manufacturer? Diagram an ERD for a perpetual inventory system in a JIT environment.

4.55 *Quality information and payroll accounting systems.* Apply the characteristics of quality information to the design of a payroll system.

4.56 *EDI for the monks of Glen Abbey.* Refer to the Glen Abbey case within the chapter. Glen Abbey's major retail distributor, located in Chicago, wants to install an EDI system linking its suppliers and distribution outlets. As the new management accountant for Glen Abbey, discuss the problems and potential benefits of installing an EDI system.

4.57 *Spreadsheet applications.*
a. Create a spreadsheet program to summarize the basic CAS journal entries.
b. Create a spreadsheet program that will output a payroll report similar to the one in Exhibit 4–10.
c. Create a spreadsheet program that will produce a COGM and a COGS report.

5

THE JOB ORDER COST ACCOUNTING SYSTEM

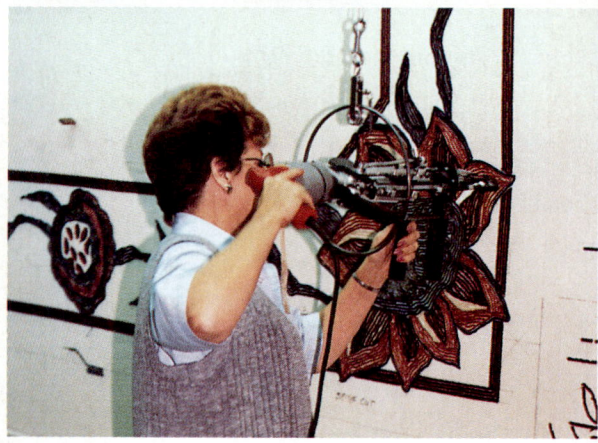

Raw materials converted to a customized carpet by Carousel Carpet Mills.

LEARNING OBJECTIVES

After studying this chapter, you should be able to:

1. Explain how to design a job order cost accounting system (JOCAS).

2. Illustrate the cost flows and prepare journal entries for a normal JOCAS.

3. Demonstrate how to account for scrap, reworked units, and spoilage in a normal JOCAS.

4. Describe how an integrated computer-based information system (ICBIS) can support a JOCAS.

5. Discuss how costs are estimated for construction projects and how work item software is used.

■ INTRODUCTION

A **job** is an individual product, a small and unique batch of products, a project, a case, or a client. Its distinguishing characteristic is that materials and labor can be directly traced to it, along with the basis for applying overhead. The basic purpose of a job order cost accounting system (JOCAS) is to provide information about the cost of a job.

But a world-class JOCAS is much more than that. It is designed and used to provide vital information to management for planning and estimating, monitoring and controlling daily shop floor operations, and evaluating performance. After demonstrating how to design and implement a JOCAS, this chapter explores how the system can aid management in ways other than just costing products or services. ■

▌DESIGNING THE JOB ORDER COST ACCOUNTING SYSTEM

A JOCAS has three main informational inputs:

- Materials requisitions
- Time tickets
- Information on the volume of the predetermined overhead rate's basis (machine hours, direct labor hours or cost, and so forth)

Notice that the third informational input means that this will be a normal JOCAS, not an actual or standard cost system. Designing a standard JOCAS will be discussed in Chapter 8.

The key record that details the costs of each job is the job cost sheet. A **job cost sheet** (also called a **job order cost record**) is used to accumulate and summarize all direct materials, direct labor, and applied overhead costs for each job order. The *only* difference between the basic CAS in Chapter 4 and a JOCAS is in the subsidiary ledger accounts of WIP. Instead of having one subsidiary ledger account for the cost of the product ("WIP–Product Cost"), each job has its own subsidiary account.

▌Setting Up the WIP General Ledger and Subsidiary Accounts

Exhibit 5–1 illustrates the WIP inventory subsidiary ledger system for a JOCAS. The WIP general ledger account remains a control account, as in any basic CAS. Because it is the control account for all production costs, its balance equals the sum of all actual manufacturing costs incurred. These costs are subtotaled by jobs and overhead. In other words, each job and overhead are accounted for as separate WIP subsidiary ledger accounts. The sum of their ending balances equals the balance in WIP.

In Exhibit 5–1, each job performed by the Earnest and Oldham accounting firm represents one of their clients. Manufacturers and construction companies maintain the same kind of accounts. In manufacturing firms, individual products or small batches of unique products are treated as jobs. In construction companies, projects such as an office building, mini-mall, house, or bridge are jobs. For the accounting firm, job 1572 is an audit of Clarksdale's financial accounting system. Job 1644 is an activity-based overhead allocation system for Mercy Hospital (covered in detail in Chapter 10). Job 1711 is the implementation of an ICBIS and EDI for Taylor Manufacturing.

LEARNING OBJECTIVE 1

Explain how to design a job order cost accounting system (JOCAS).

Building a JOCAS for automobile repairs at Sport Haus.

■EXHIBIT 5–1
Cost Flows and Journal Entries for a Normal JOCAS

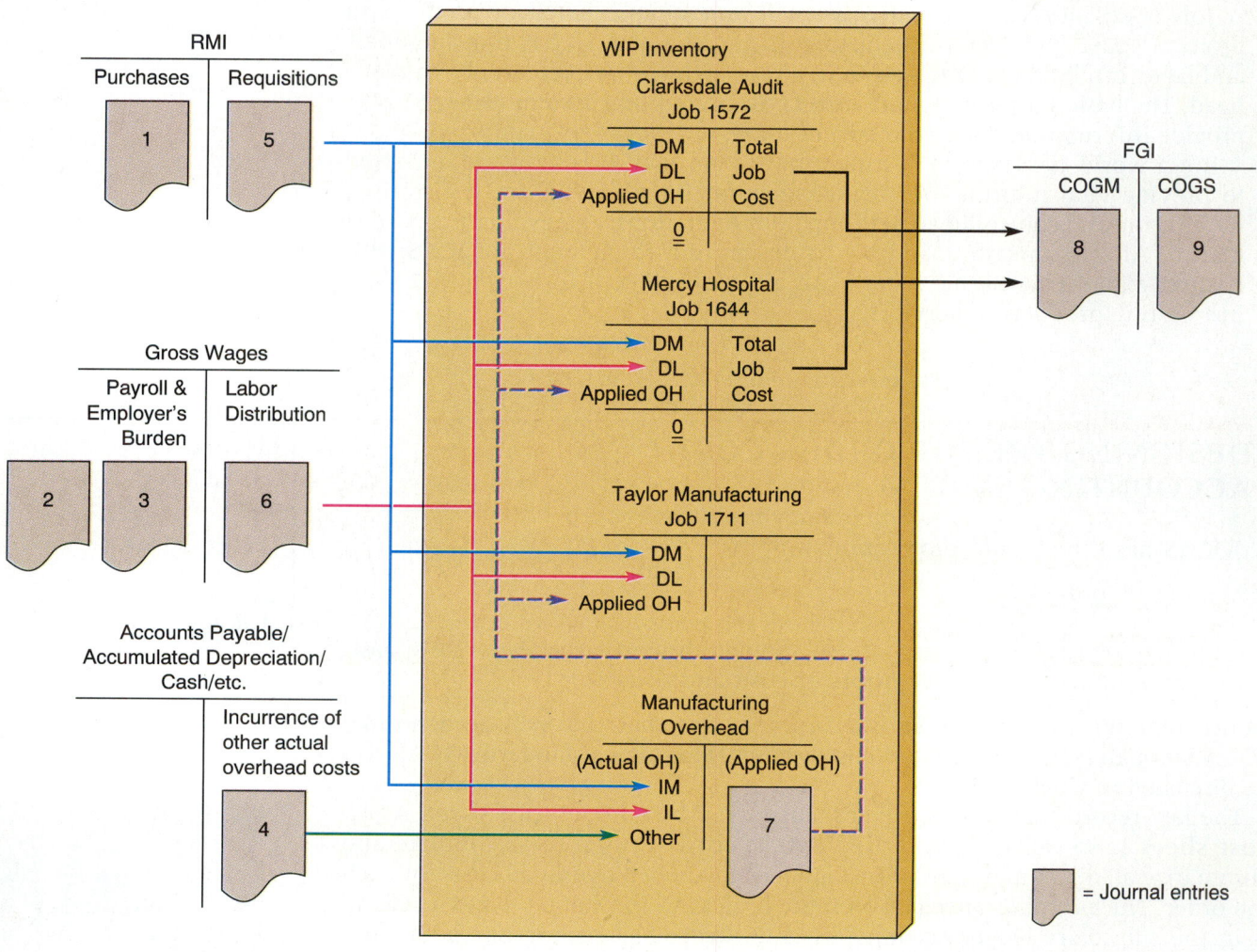

The WIP inventory subsidiary ledger accounts are periodically reconciled to the WIP inventory control account in the general ledger. This reconciliation provides an internal control feature for the JOCAS by helping to ensure the proper recording of costs.

Setting Up and Using Job Cost Sheets

As Exhibit 5–2 illustrates, each job order is assigned a unique job number to keep track of jobs and their costs as they progress toward completion. The top portion of the job cost sheet used at Milacron Company includes a job order number, contract price, customer name and address, description of job, and schedule. The rest of the record contains cost data. The bottom of the record summarizes the total manufacturing costs assigned to the job, marketing and administrative expenses directly traceable to the job, its contract price, and profit (or loss).

The job cost sheet for job 897 shows a contract price of $18,000 for the manufacture of five 24-inch sluice valves for Deephole Mining. Direct materials and direct labor costs are assigned to the job as work is performed. Data about

[Handwritten notes in margin: Subledgers detail give you COGS, WIP, FGI by totals of JOC sheet. OH applied @ end of Jobs]

Milacron Company		Job Order Number: 897	
1200 Industrial Drive		Contract Price: $18,000.00	
Reno, NV 89557			

				Date ordered:	02/05/X5
For:	Deephole Mining			Date promised:	02/26/X5
Product:	24" Sluice valves			Date started:	02/06/X5
Specification:	Beveled flanges			Date completed:	02/23/X5
Quantity:	5				

Direct Materials

Date	Requisition Number	Cost	Total
02/06	612	$3,450.00	
02/15	643	1,200.00	
02/18	651	400.00	
			$5,050.00

Direct Labor

Date	Hours	Cost	Total
02/06	10	$ 100.00	
02/13	60	600.00	
02/18	40	400.00	
02/23	30	300.00	
	140		$1,400.00

Applied Overhead

Date	For	Cost	Total
02/23	$12.00 x 500 machine hours	$6,000.00	$6,000.00

Directed materials	$ 5,050.00	Contract price		$18,000.00
Direct labor	1,400.00	Manufacturing cost	$12,450.00	
Applied overhead	6,000.00	Marketing cost	1,400.00	
Total manufacturing cost	$12,450.00	Administrative cost	800.00	
		Cost to make and sell		<14,650.00>
Unit cost ($12,450.00 ÷ 5) =	$ 2,490.00	Profit		$ 3,350.00

direct materials are gathered from materials requisitions. Data on direct labor costs are obtained from time tickets. Overhead costs are applied to the job using a POR based on machine hours. The management accountant at Milacron also includes applicable marketing and administrative costs associated with each job. These costs are *not* charged to WIP because they are not costs of *making the job*. They are costs of selling it and all aspects of its administration. Marketing and administrative costs are treated as expenses for financial and tax reporting. To help in identifying which *non*manufacturing costs are directly traceable to jobs, modern CASs include subsidiary ledger systems by job for related engineering, research and development, purchasing, marketing, and administrative activities.

The job cost sheet serves as the source record for the WIP subsidiary ledger accounts. In many manual JOCASs, it is the subsidiary ledger sheet. In computerized JOCASs, it is the report, or status screen display, from a job file or record in the database.

When a job is completed, costs posted to the job cost sheet are totaled to determine the total manufactured cost of the job (the cost of goods manufactured). This amount is used to credit the appropriate WIP subsidiary ledger account and to debit finished goods inventory when the job is completed and leaves the factory. If the job's product is directly shipped or sold to the customer upon completion, there is no FGI, and the debit is directly to COGS.

How Do Data Flow in a JOCAS?

The flow of the inputs, documents, and records is summarized in Exhibit 5–3. This flow diagram provides a visual summary of the overall operations in a normal JOCAS. In a manual JOCAS, completed job cost sheets are transferred to a FGI subsidiary ledger file and then, when sold, to a permanent COGS file for long-term storage. These job cost sheets are useful for planning and control purposes as well as for bidding on future jobs. If a particular job was very

Designing a computerized patient record at Eastern Plumas District Hospital.

■ EXHIBIT 5–3
The Flow of Data in a Normal JOCAS

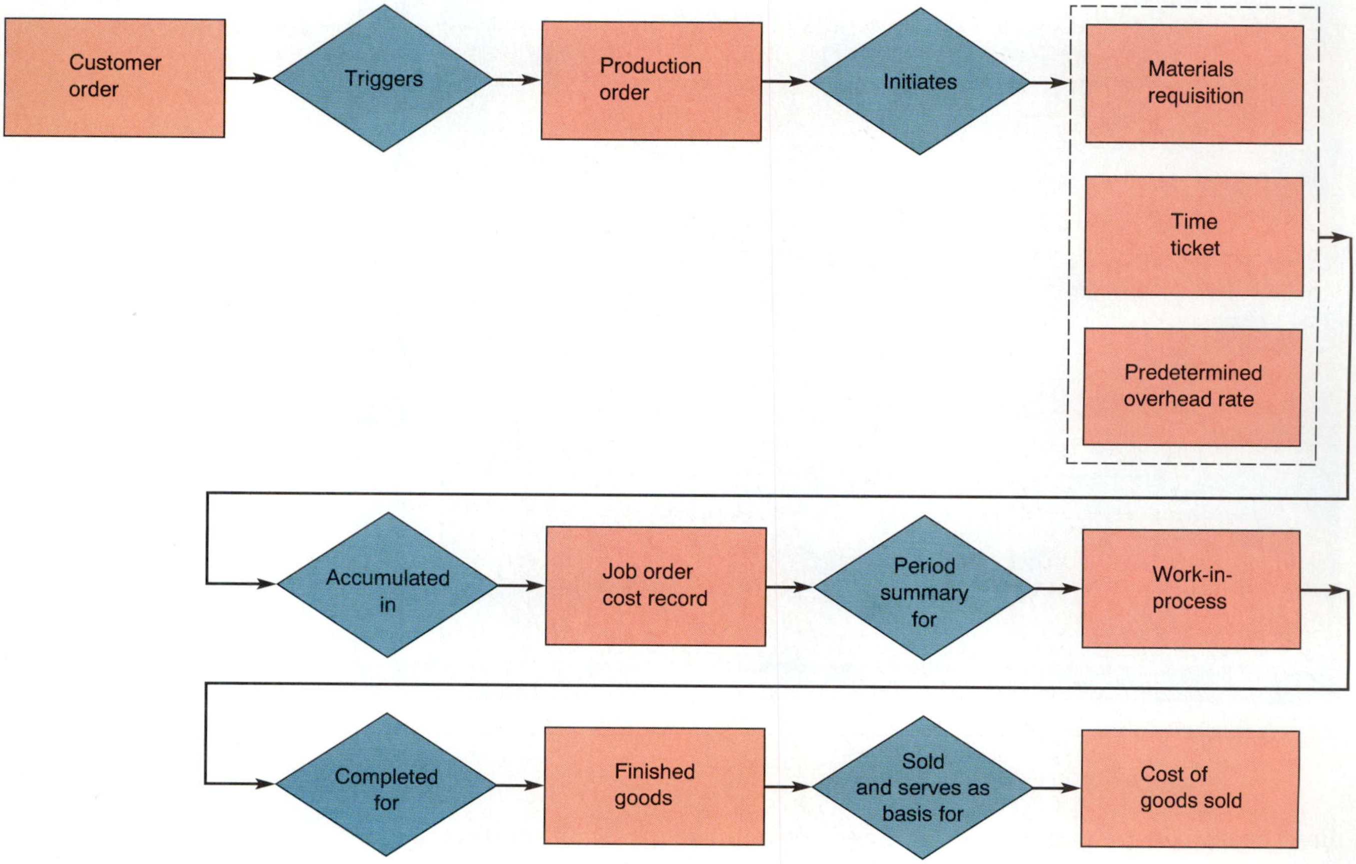

profitable, management may decide to pursue similar jobs in the future. If a job was unprofitable, the job cost sheet may provide the reasons why. In some instances, management may decide to produce some products that have not yet been ordered. If these products are not sold fairly quickly, management may decide to reduce prices or offer discounts. Having ready access to cost records for such products provides management with guidance as to how much prices can be reduced and still make a profit.

LEARNING OBJECTIVE 2

Illustrate the cost flows and prepare journal entries for a normal JOCAS.

▎JOURNAL ENTRIES FOR A NORMAL JOCAS

Thus far, the discussion has established the general outline of a JOCAS. This section describes the flow of production costs through the JOCAS and shows the journal entries that account for these costs. The following presentation records a single month's activity (May) for Oilwell Compressors, Inc., a company that manufactures a variety of air compressors and oil pumps used in producing and refining crude oil. The journal entries will be presented in order of the cost elements (DM, DL, and OH) instead of in journal entry number order to facilitate linking topics to Chapter 4.

On May 1, there was one unfinished production job, job 11, which was started in April. During April, $71,000 was charged to job 11 for direct materials ($50,000), direct labor ($20,000), and applied overhead ($1,000). This is labeled as its beginning balance in the exhibits that follow.

Accounting for Materials Costs

The beginning balance in RMI is $10,000. During May, Oilwell Compressors, Inc., purchased $100,000 of materials, including $80,000 for direct materials and $20,000 for indirect materials. The purchase is recorded as in any basic CAS (journal entry 1 for the basic CAS in Exhibit 4–4 in Chapter 4):

JOURNAL ENTRY 1: Purchase of Raw Materials

Raw Materials Inventory	$100,000	
Accounts Payable		$100,000

During May, the factory floor requisitioned $70,000 in raw materials from the storeroom for use in production. Direct materials equaled $60,000 and indirect materials, $10,000. In a basic CAS, the requisition of materials to production is recorded in journal entry 5:

BASIC CAS JOURNAL ENTRY 5: Requisition of Raw Materials

WIP–Product Cost (DM)	$60,000	
WIP–Manufacturing Overhead (IM)	$10,000	
Raw Materials Inventory		$70,000

The breakdown of direct materials by job from the material requisitions is presented in Exhibit 5–4. In a JOCAS, the "WIP–Product Cost" subsidiary

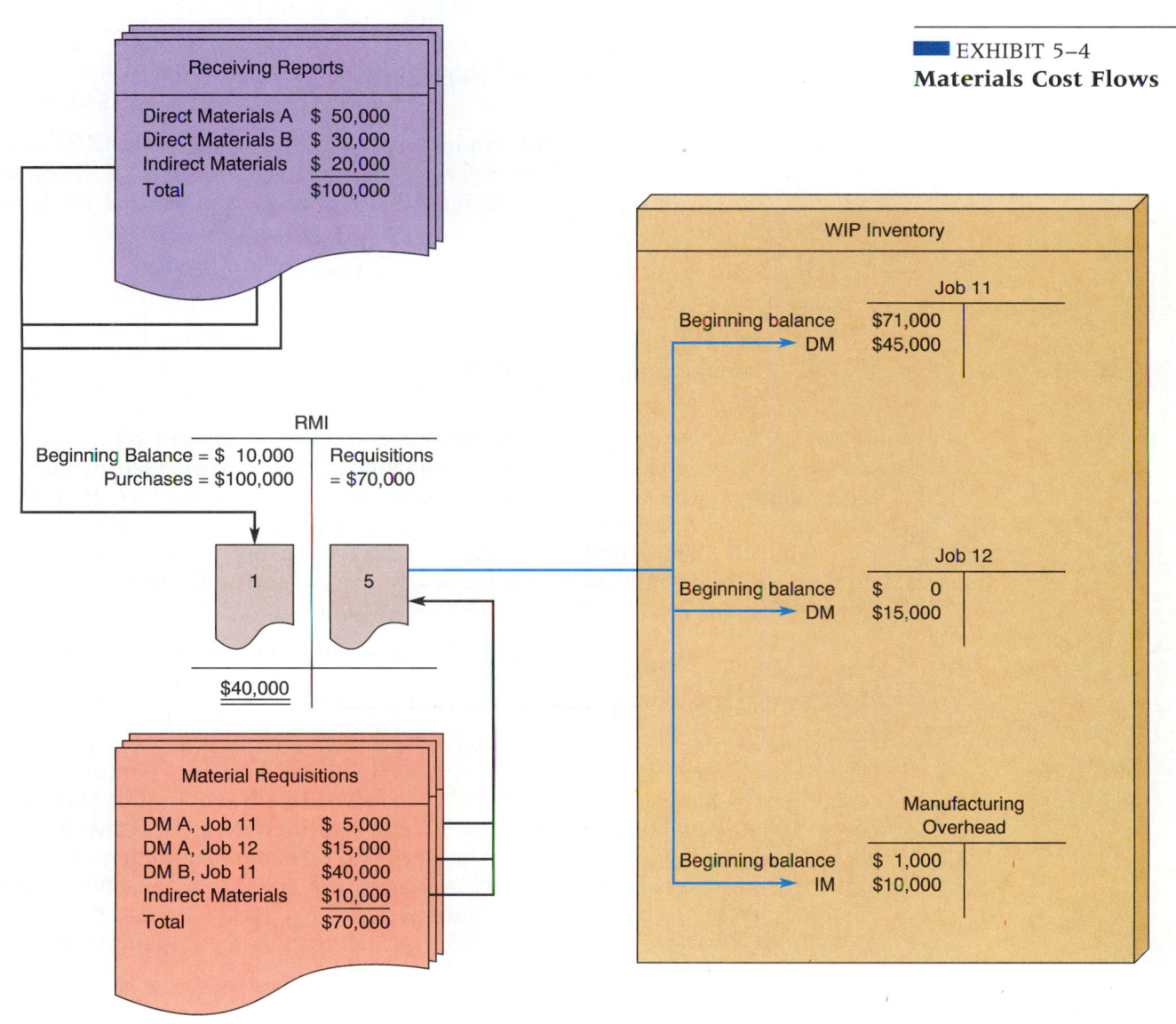

■■ EXHIBIT 5–4
Materials Cost Flows

Receiving Reports

Direct Materials A	$ 50,000
Direct Materials B	$ 30,000
Indirect Materials	$ 20,000
Total	$100,000

RMI

Beginning Balance = $ 10,000	Requisitions
Purchases = $100,000	= $70,000

1

5

$40,000

Material Requisitions

DM A, Job 11	$ 5,000
DM A, Job 12	$15,000
DM B, Job 11	$40,000
Indirect Materials	$10,000
Total	$70,000

WIP Inventory

Job 11

Beginning balance	$71,000
DM	$45,000

Job 12

Beginning balance	$ 0
DM	$15,000

Manufacturing Overhead

Beginning balance	$ 1,000
IM	$10,000

account is replaced with individual subsidiary accounts for each job. This changes journal entry 5 to:

JOCAS Journal Entry 5: Requisition of Raw Materials

WIP–Job 11 (DM)	$45,000
WIP–Job 12 (DM)	$15,000
WIP–Manufacturing Overhead (IM) *(only 1 MFG OH acct)*	$10,000
Raw Materials Inventory	$70,000

In Exhibit 5–4, $10,000 of raw materials issued to production was not directly traceable to any specific job and was charged to overhead as indirect materials. These costs remain in the overhead account until applied to the individual job cost sheets by use of a POR. At the end of May, $40,000 of raw materials remained in RMI and is reported as a current asset on Oilwell Compressors' May 31 balance sheet.

Accounting for Labor Costs

As work is performed, time tickets are generated daily. These tickets are used to trace labor costs directly to specific jobs (assume $40,000) and to identify indirect labor costs going to the overhead subsidiary account ($20,000). In a basic CAS, the labor distribution journal entry is:

Basic CAS Journal Entry 6: Distributing Gross Wages

WIP–Product Cost (DL)	$40,000
WIP–Manufacturing Overhead (IL)	$20,000
Gross Wages	$60,000

The amount charged to WIP–Product Cost represents the direct labor costs of specific jobs. The JOCAS's payroll system provides a summary of the direct labor by job for journal entry 6. Using the Exhibit 5–5 information, the labor distribution journal entry becomes:

JOCAS Journal Entry 6: Distributing Gross Wages

WIP–Job 11 (DL)	$30,000
WIP–Job 12 (DL)	$10,000
WIP–Manufacturing Overhead (IL)	$20,000
Gross Wages	$60,000

The labor costs charged to the overhead subsidiary account represent the indirect labor costs for May. Such costs include janitorial work, security guards, and maintenance. As in the case of indirect materials, the indirect labor costs charged to overhead will remain there until applied to the jobs through the use of a POR. Finally notice that, like material purchases (journal entry 1), the "purchase" of labor-related costs (journal entry 2 for payroll and journal entry 3 for the employer's burden) is the same as in any basic CAS.

Accounting for Actual Overhead Costs

As actual overhead costs are incurred, they are charged to WIP–Manufacturing Overhead in the same way as in any basic CAS. To illustrate, assume Oilwell Compressors incurred two cash overhead costs during the month of May, rent on the factory building of $10,000 and factory utilities of $2,000. Oilwell Compressors also recognized $25,000 in depreciation on factory equipment, $17,000 in accrued property taxes on factory buildings, and $6,000 of prepaid insurance expired on factory buildings and equipment.

In both a basic CAS and a JOCAS, journal entry 4 records these items as follows:

■■■ EXHIBIT 5–5
Labor Cost Flows

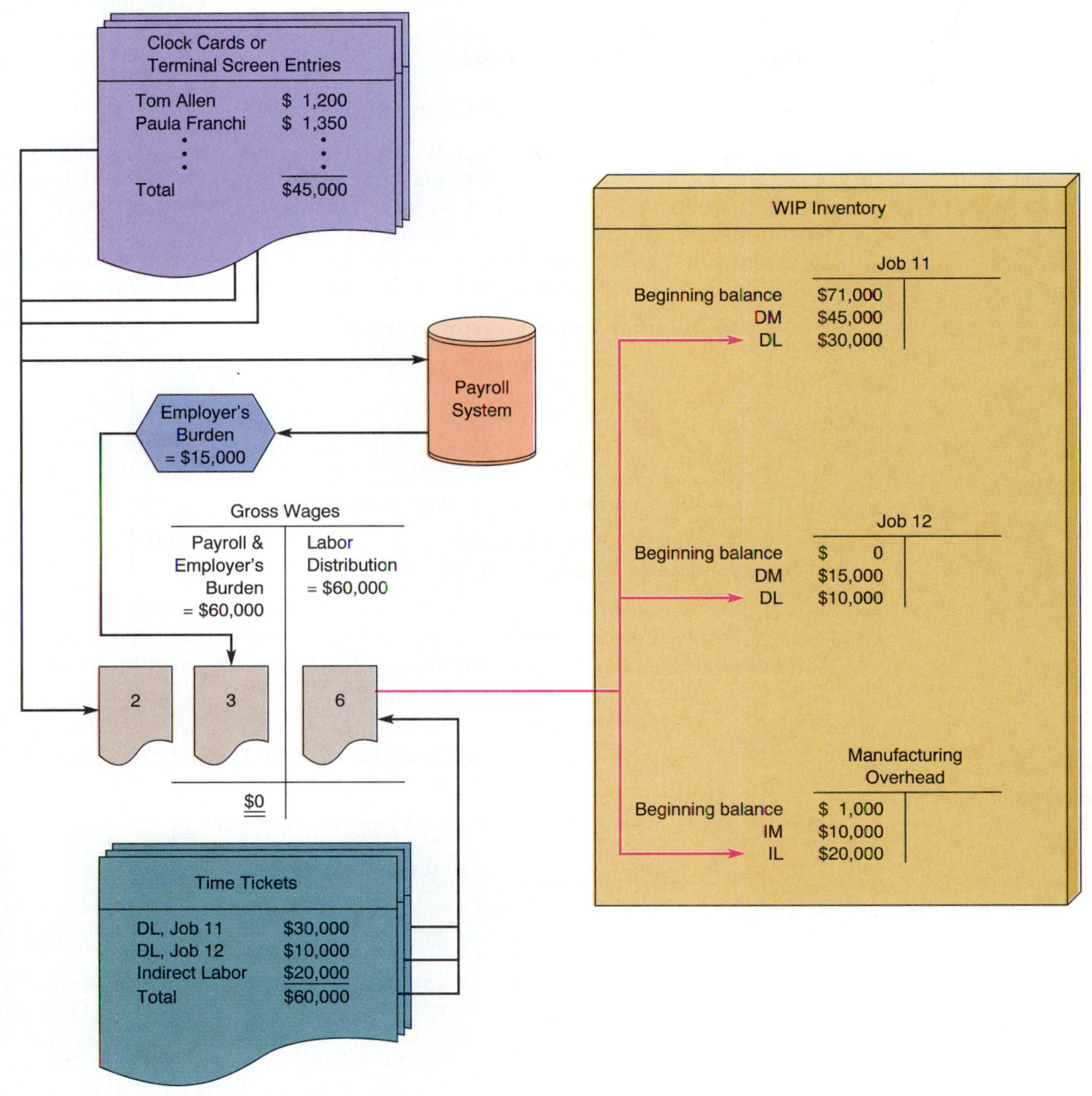

JOURNAL ENTRY 4: Incurring Other Overhead Costs

WIP–Manufacturing Overhead (Rent)	$10,000	
WIP–Manufacturing Overhead (Utilities)	$ 2,000	
WIP–Manufacturing Overhead (Depreciation)	$25,000	
WIP–Manufacturing Overhead (Taxes)	$17,000	
WIP–Manufacturing Overhead (Insurance)	$ 6,000	
Cash		$12,000
Accumulated Depreciation–Equipment		$25,000
Property Taxes Payable		$17,000
Prepaid Insurance		$ 6,000

All actual overhead costs are recorded directly into the overhead acount as they are incurred throughout the period. Thus, there are really a series of different journal entries, originating from different databases, at different times throughout May. This is illustrated in Exhibit 5–6.

▌Accounting for Applied Overhead

At the beginning of the year, Oilwell Compressors budgeted a POR of $10 per machine hour. During May, 5,400 machine hours (Mhr) were worked on job 11, and 4,000 Mhr were worked on job 12. Therefore, $54,000 ($10/Mhr × 5,400 Mhr) of overhead is applied to job 11 and $40,000 ($10/Mhr × 4,000 Mhr) to job 12. Journal entry 7 records the applied overhead of $94,000 ($54,000 + $40,000) transferred from the overhead account to the jobs:

JOCAS JOURNAL ENTRY 7: Applying Overhead

WIP–Job 11 (Applied OH)	$54,000	
WIP–Job 12 (Applied OH)	$40,000	
WIP–Manufacturing Overhead		$94,000

Compare this to the basic CAS overhead application journal entry:

BASIC CAS JOURNAL ENTRY 7: Applying Overhead

WIP–Product Cost (Applied OH)	$94,000	
WIP–Manufacturing Overhead		$94,000

As Exhibit 5–6 shows, overhead is applied to each job's subsidiary account, rather than to the single subsidiary account for all products created in the basic CAS of Chapter 4. Before preceding any farther, review the usage journal entries

---

 EXHIBIT 5–6
Overhead Cost Flows

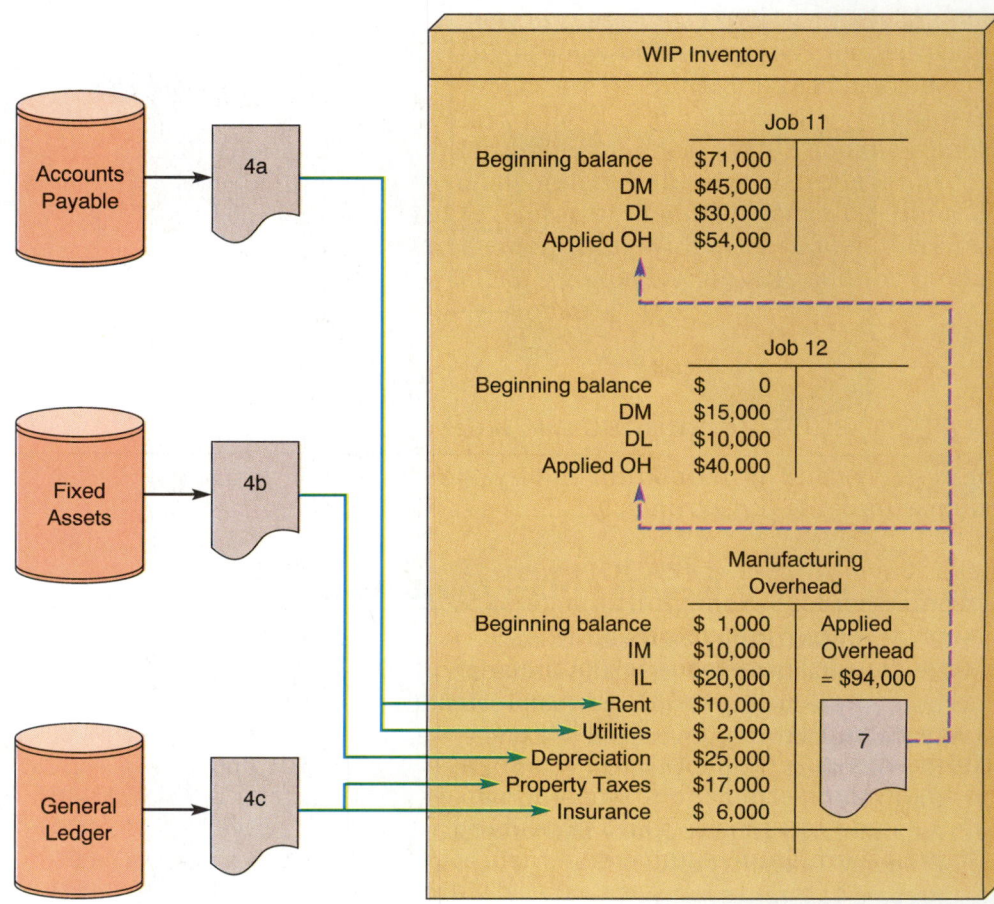

(JEs 5–7). These are the only journal entries that have changed from the basic CAS presented in Chapter 4. But the only change is that the subsidiary account titled "Product Cost" is replaced by subsidiary accounts for each job. The journal entries recording the acquisition of manufacturing cost elements have not changed.

The last issue to consider in overhead application is when to make journal entry 7. In this illustration, Oilwell Compressors uses a machine hour basis for its POR. Usually, the information on machine hours worked per job is accumulated throughout the month, and a summary month-end adjusting journal entry is made to apply overhead. This information can be summarized and a journal entry made at any time, though, including in real-time, based on bar code scanning, for an ICBIS JOCAS. If a job is completed before the end of the posting period (e.g., the month), journal entry 7 should be made upon job completion. For example, assume job 11 was completed on May 20. Then the overhead application journal entry would be prepared at that time when the management accountant obtains the machine usage information.

With a different application base this journal entry may be made at another time. What if the POR basis is direct labor hours or cost? If the factory workers are paid weekly, then journal entry 7 can be prepared along with the labor-related journal entries (journal entry 2 for the paychecks and journal entry 3 for the employer's burden).

Accounting for Cost of Goods Manufactured and Sold

Oilwell Compressors, Inc., completed job 11 during May. Job 12 was still in process. The cost flows and ending WIP subsidiary account balances for May are shown in Exhibit 5–7. The total costs charged to job 11 are as follows:

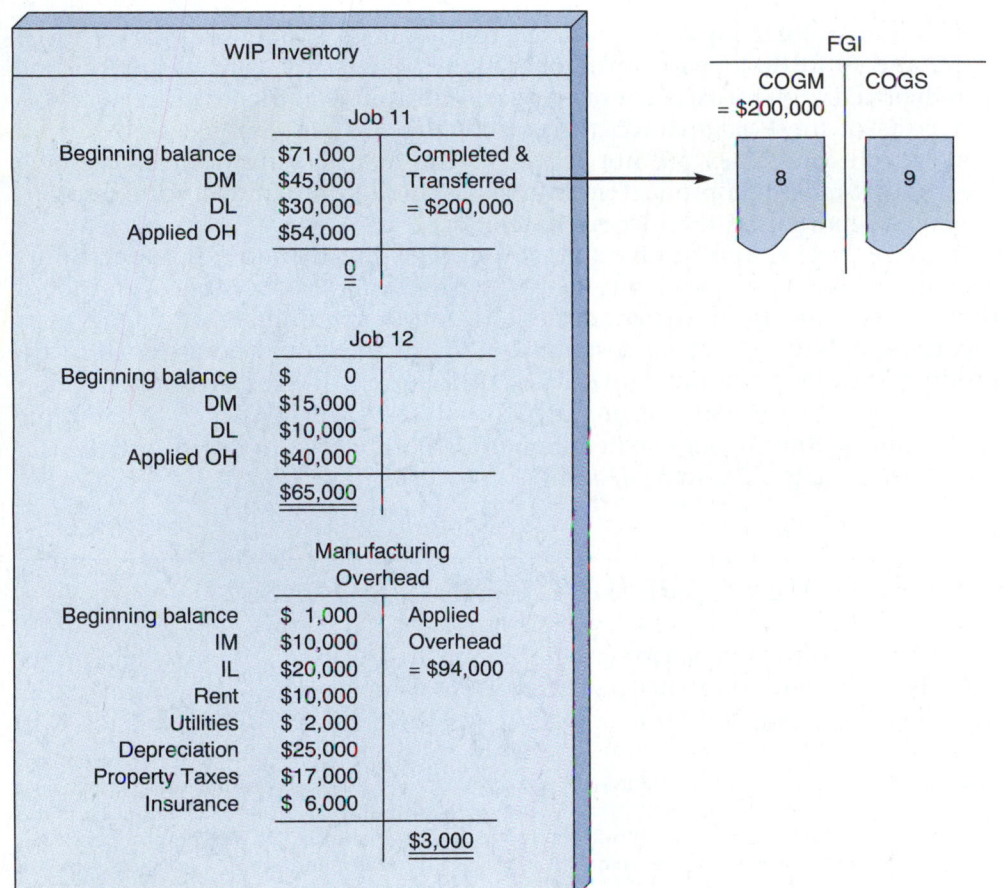

■ EXHIBIT 5–7
Completed Job Cost Flows and Ending Work-In-Process Balances

Beginning balance, May 1	$ 71,000
Direct materials added in May	45,000
Direct labor added in May	30,000
Applied overhead in May	54,000
Total costs incurred on job 11	$200,000

Journal entry 8 transfers job 11 costs from the factory to finished goods:

JOURNAL ENTRY 8: Cost of Goods Manufactured and Transferred to Finished Goods

Finished Goods Inventory–Job 11	$200,000	
WIP–Job 11		$200,000

When job 11 is sold, journal entry 9 records the removal of this job from FGI:

JOURNAL ENTRY 9: Cost of Goods Sold

Cost of Goods Sold–Job 11	$200,000	
Finished Goods Inventory–Job 11		$200,000

Notice that in both journal entries, FGI and COGS have subsidiary accounts to track which jobs have been completed and sold. Not all JOCASs track transfers to finished goods and sales by job. Consider a machining shop that makes batches of screws, bolts, nails, and the like. When transferred to FGI and when sold, all size 4 screws may be stored together in a bin, regardless of whether they were produced in May as job 11 or in July as job 45. Tracking FGI and COGS by job may not be possible in this situation.

Accounting for Nonmanufacturing Costs

In addition to incurring property taxes, rent, utilities, supervisor salaries, insurance, and so forth, as part of the operations of its plant, Oilwell Compressors also incurred similar costs generated by administrative and sales office activities. The costs of these *non*manufacturing activities are not charged to overhead, however, because they are not related to the manufacture of products. Only the costs of making a product go into WIP. These nonmanufacturing costs are expenses reported on the income statement.[1]

Because these administrative and sales costs go directly into expense accounts, they have no effect on the costing of Oilwell's *production* for May, even though they may be directly traceable to the jobs. A growing number of management accountants believe that all costs of the enterprise should be assigned to the product, including administrative, sales, distribution, and research and development costs. As in the earlier example of the job cost sheet (Exhibit 5–2), administrative and selling costs are added to manufacturing costs to determine the *total costs to make, sell, and deliver the job.*

SPREADSHEET APPLICATIONS IN JOCASs

Spreadsheet software has two common uses in JOCASs. As for any basic CAS, spreadsheet programs can be created for journal entries. The May journal entries for Oilwell Compressors, Inc., are presented in Exhibit 5–8. These should be

[1] Traditionally, management accountants have called expenses "period costs" to differentiate them from "product cost" elements (DM, DL, OH). This distinction can be misused by management, though, in that direct costs of distribution (logistics), advertising, and sales for a particular job may never be associated with the total cost of making, selling, and delivering the job. As a result, the job's profitability may be understated by traditional CASs.

■ EXHIBIT 5–8
JOCAS Journal Entries for Oilwell Compressors, Inc.

SPREADSHEET PROGRAM TO RECORD OILWELL COMPRESSORS, INC.
JOURNAL ENTRIES
For May 1993

Ref	General Ledger Account Titles	dr's	cr's
	PURCHASE (ACQUISITION) OF RAW MATERIALS:		
1:	Raw Materials Inventory	$100,000	
	Accounts Payable		$100,000
	PREPARING (RECORDING) PAYCHECKS:		
2:	Gross Wages	$45,000	
	FICA Payable		?
	FIT Payable		?
	Wages Payable		?
	EMPLOYER'S PAYROLL TAXES & BENEFITS (BURDEN):		
3:	Gross Wages	$15,000	
	FICA Payable		?
	FUTA Payable		?
	SUTA Payable		?
	OTHER OVERHEAD COSTS INCURRED:		
4:	WIP–Manufacturing OH (Rent)	$10,000	
	WIP–Manufacturing OH (Utilities)	$2,000	
	WIP–Manufacturing OH (Depreciation)	$25,000	
	WIP–Manufacturing OH (Property Taxes)	$17,000	
	WIP–Manufacturing OH (Insurance)	$6,000	
	Cash		$12,000
	Accumulated Depreciation		$25,000
	Accrued Property Taxes Payable		$17,000
	Prepaid Insurance		$6,000
	REQUISITION OF RAW MATERIALS INTO THE FACTORY:		
5:	WIP–Job 11 (DM)	$45,000	
	WIP–Job 12 (DM)	$15,000	
	WIP–Manufacturing OH (IM)	$10,000	
	Raw Materials Inventory		$70,000
	DISTRIBUTING GROSS WAGES TO JOBS:		
6:	WIP–Job 11 (DL)	$30,000	
	WIP–Job 12 (DL)	$10,000	
	WIP–Manufacturing OH (IL)	$20,000	
	Gross Wages		$60,000
	OVERHEAD ALLOCATION TO JOBS:		
7:	WIP–Job 11 (Applied OH)	$54,000	
	WIP–Job 12 (Applied OH)	$40,000	
	WIP–Manufacturing OH		$94,000
	JOBS COMPLETED:		
8:	Finished Goods Inventory–Job 11	$200,000	
	WIP–Job 11		$200,000
	JOBS SOLD (INVENTORY RELIEF JOURNAL ENTRY ONLY):		
9:	Cost of Goods Sold–Job 11	$200,000	
	Finished Goods Inventory–Job 11		$200,000

■ EXHIBIT 5-9
Oilwell Compressors, Inc., Job Cost Report for May

OILWELL COMPRESSORS, INC.
WIP INVENTORY AND JOB COSTS SUMMARY
For the Month of May 1993

COSTS	JOB 11	JOB 12	MFG OH	TOTALS
Direct Materials: Beginning Balance	$50,000	$0		$50,000
Direct Materials: Added	45,000	15,000		60,000
Subtotal	$95,000	$15,000		$110,000
Direct Labor: Beginning Balance	20,000	0		20,000
Direct Labor: Added	30,000	10,000		40,000
Subtotal	$50,000	$10,000		$60,000
Applied OH–Beginning Balance	1,000	0		1,000
Applied OH–Added	54,000	40,000	<$94,000>	0
Subtotal	$55,000	$40,000		$95,000
Overhead–Beginning Balance			1,000	
Indirect Materials			10,000	
Indirect Labor			20,000	
Rent			10,000	
Utilities			2,000	
Depreciation			25,000	
Property Taxes			17,000	
Insurance			6,000	
Actual OH–Added			90,000	
TOTAL JOB COSTS:	$200,000	$65,000	<$3,000>	$262,000
Less: Completed Jobs	<200,000>			<200,000>
WIP INVENTORY BALANCE	$0	$65,000	<$3,000>	$62,000

Note: Individual columns add (sum) *across* into the Totals column. The totals for each cost element ($110,000, $60,000, and $95,000) are not meant to add *down* into the Total Job Costs ($262,000). This is why each cost element's total is double-underlined.

compared with the basic CAS journal entries in Exhibit 4–4 and Demonstration Problem 1 in Chapter 4. Again, verify that the only journal entries that are different are the usage journal entries (JEs 5–7).

A second common application of spreadsheet software is in creating WIP summary reports showing the costs incurred on each job. The report program designed by Oilwell Compressors' management accountant is linked to the journal entry program. It is illustrated in Exhibit 5–9. The beginning and ending balances in the report can be verified by comparing them to the T-account balances shown in Exhibit 5–7.

LEARNING OBJECTIVE 3

▬

Demonstrate how to account for scrap, reworked units, and spoilage in a normal JOCAS.

SCRAP AND JOCAS

Scrap refers to fragments of material removed during the production or construction process. Metal fragments, odd pieces of lumber, cloth remnants, and meat trimmings are examples of scrap. Scrap is sometimes collected, inventoried, and either reused or sold to scrap dealers.

When the quantity and value of scrap are relatively high, it should be stored in a designated place (such as RMI) under the supervision of a storekeeper. A typical entry removes the market value less any disposal costs (the net realizable value or NRV) from the job's cost in WIP:

SCRAP METHOD 1: Inventory at NRV

| RMI–Scrap Material | debit | |
| WIP–Job 102 | | credit |

When the scrap is sold, the entry would be:

SCRAP METHOD 1: Sale of Scrap

| Cash (or accounts receivable) | debit | |
| RMI–Scrap Material | | credit |

To minimize accounting for scrap, often no entry is made until the scrap is actually sold. At that time, the entry would be:

SCRAP METHOD 2: Only Records Sale

| Cash (or accounts receivable) | debit | |
| Scrap Sales | | credit |

The second method is expedient and reasonable when scrap value is small. The amount accumulated in the scrap sales account may be closed directly to income summary and included on the income statement as other income. It is also advantageous because the cost of scrap remains in the job's cost. Those who support this method argue that since the job causes the scrap (i.e., without the job, there would be no scrap), this scrap should be budgeted as part of the cost of the job. JIT proponents argue that scrap is a nonvalue-added cost and that the production process should be changed to eliminate it. By including scrap in the cost of every job where it is created, management will be better aware of its costs. If scrap is taken out of the job's cost, as in the first method, set up in inventory, and then resold, management may not be motivated to eliminate it (or so the argument goes).

Proponents of the first method argue that if the scrap can be resold, its net realizable value should be removed from the cost of the job. Leaving it there overstates the job's cost and understates its profitability. Besides, they argue, the reasons for scrap are long run: as yet, there are no suppliers available who can deliver materials cut to size (so that there is no scrap from material use), or changing the direct technology cost elements (machines that cause scrap through cutting operations and the like) is not currently feasible. Whether scrap is included or excluded from the job's cost will not change management's motivation to eliminate it.

Obviously, the management accountant is faced with a choice in accounting methods for scrap. As long as the amounts of scrap are relatively small, accounting entries are not a major consideration. However, many manufacturers are discovering that scrap is a growing and serious problem. In dealing with scrap accounting, the management accountant should remember that what is important is an effective scrap performance measurement system that keeps scrap to a minimum, eliminates it entirely, or converts it to a profitable product. Timely scrap reports and performance measurements are the key to reducing scrap and managing its costs.

REWORKED UNITS AND TRADITIONAL JOCASs

Reworked units are defective products that are fixed so that they can be sold as acceptable finished units through regular marketing channels. Rework should be done only if incremental revenue is expected to exceed incremental costs. Otherwise, if possible, the defective units should be sold as irregulars without the reworking.

Defective units occur for several reasons including:

- Low-quality raw materials
- Faulty and poorly maintained machinery
- Poor workmanship
- Inadequate training and poor supervision
- Outdated methods and processes

World-class manufacturers work diligently to eliminate these problems, so the modern management accountant needs to provide information on rework costs within the CAS.

Traditional Accounting for Normal Rework

In traditional manufacturing firms, management expects some level of rework within all the jobs. If rework is common to all the jobs, each job should bear a fair share of the rework costs. However, solely due to random fluctuations, some jobs will incur more or less rework than others. Consequently, rework costs should not be directly charged to the jobs, but should instead be included in budgeted overhead and the POR. By allocating rework to all jobs through the POR, these costs will be more equitably spread across all production.

For example, assume that a clothing manufacturer receives an order for 1,000 men's suits. The POR includes a budgeted amount for reworking defective units. One hundred suits are defective and reworked at a total cost of $280 for direct materials, $790 for direct labor, and 100 machine hours of overhead applied at $4 per machine hour. The following entry records the rework:

JOURNAL ENTRY FOR NORMAL REWORK

WIP–Manufacturing Overhead (Rework)	$1,470	
RMI		$280
Gross Wages		$790
WIP–Manufacturing Overhead		$400

Note that all the source documents (material requisitions, time tickets, machine hour reports) must identify the cost elements used on rework. If the source documents do not clearly identify that this is rework, the costs could easily be charged into the job.

It may seem strange that overhead is both debited and credited. In effect, the CAS is applying overhead to itself. This occurs because the POR includes an allowance for rework, and it creates credits in the overhead account when used to apply overhead to jobs. Then, when rework is done, its actual costs have to be debited to overhead where the credits are, so that the debits and credits are matched in the same account. This creates yet another problem, however. Unquestionably, the rework used overhead, so some overhead should be included in its cost. But how much? $4 per machine hour? The $4/Mhr POR includes an allowance for spreading rework over all good suits made in the various jobs worked on during the year. Should these reworked suits be charged with even more rework cost through the POR? Probably not. In other words, the POR should be reduced by the amount of rework cost included in it when it is used to apply overhead to reworked suits! This means that two PORs are needed, one for normal work and one for rework.

This accounting method also creates another, potentially more serious problem. When rework is included in the overhead budget and not in the cost of the jobs, it may effectively be "buried" with all the other overhead items (indirect materials and labor, rent, utilities, depreciation, insurance, taxes, janitorial services, repairs and maintenance, and so forth). The JIT advocate argues that rework, like scrap, is a nonvalue-added activity that should be identified, "brought out into the open," and analyzed, so that it can be prevented in the future. Is an accounting method available that will do this and also be simple to implement and explain? Some modern management accountants believe so. Because this method treats rework and spoilage in the same way, it is discussed later in the section dealing with spoilage.

Traditional Accounting for Reworked Units for a Special Job or Unusual Conditions

The same clothing manufacturer receives a *special* order for 1,000 suits, with the agreement that any rework costs are chargeable to the job and billable to the customer. During production, 100 suits need to be reworked. In requisitioning additional materials, workers charge them to the job, as is done with any direct materials in journal entry 5. Workers charge their direct labor time to the job, and overhead is applied to it based on the total machine hours worked.

The problem, though, is that the POR of $4/Mhr has to be reduced by the amount included in it for rework. Since this rework is not debited to overhead, the regular amount of applied overhead representing normal rework should not be credited from the overhead account and charged to this job. The rework costs are already included in the job's cost. Thus, this method includes rework costs directly in the job's cost. It is used when the customer agrees to pay for the rework costs, or when the rework is a result of special circumstances unique to the job. In other words, this method is used for rework costs that are not considered common to all jobs or expected because of the condition of the equipment, raw materials, and/or work force.

SPOILAGE AND TRADITIONAL JOCASs

Spoilage refers to a rejected job or specific units within a job. A spoiled job or unit is so defective that it is not reworked to bring it up to specifications. In a JOCAS, the treatment of spoilage is basically the same as for rework.

Preparing a Spoilage Report

Exhibit 5–10 illustrates a spoilage report, which is prepared when defective products are removed from production. For cost management purposes, spoilage reports should be prepared and reported daily. In highly automated environments, these spoilage reports are made continuously.

Normal Spoilage Attributable to All Jobs

Normal spoilage, like normal rework, is expected under present conditions. Since this spoilage is expected on all jobs, the budgeted overhead includes an amount for normal spoilage, just as it does for normal rework. The POR spreads normal spoilage costs over all jobs through the overhead application journal entry. This means that, as with normal rework costs, when normal spoilage occurs, the costs of these products have to be debited to overhead.

Based on the *Insights & Applications* on the next page, the following entry is made to account for the actual normal spoilage cost incurred on these two jobs:

SPOILAGE JOURNAL ENTRY: **Normal Loss**

WIP–Manufacturing Overhead (Spoilage)	$1,286	
WIP–Job 101		$ 66
WIP–Job 106		$1,220

INSIGHTS & APPLICATIONS

Problems at Majordomo Catering

Majordomo is a catering company that provides food and service for weddings, banquets, parties, and special events. Each catered affair represents a separate job. Regardless of the job, there is always some spoilage. In calculating the POR for the forthcoming period, Majordomo's management accountant includes an allowance for normal spoilage. One of Majordomo's catering jobs is for a political rally (job 101). Its job cost sheet is displayed in Exhibit 5–11. Majordomo also catered a fancy wedding that called for mountain lilies to be flown from Hawaii to Lubbock, Texas. The job cost sheet for this job (job 106) is presented in Exhibit 5–12.

Normal Spoilage Caused by a Specific Job

If spoilage is not expected but is occasionally experienced on specific jobs, its estimated cost should *not* be included in calculating the POR. Why? In this case, the spoilage is caused by the extraordinary specifications of a particular job instead of being associated with standard conditions and specifications that affect all jobs. Chances are, this type of spoilage cannot be estimated at the beginning of the year. Majordomo, for example, does not know exactly what kinds of catering jobs it will have and, thus, the peculiar spoilage that might be associated with any one job. For the wedding (job 106), the total cost of the mountain lilies was $4,000. This normal spoilage cost, which is solely attributable to the wedding, remains with this job's cost. It is treated as just another direct material cost element.

■ EXHIBIT 5–10
A Spoilage Report

Spoilage Report				
Number			Date	
Part number:		Part name:		
Quantity spoiled:		Last completed operation number:		
Description of defect:				
Cause of defect	☐ Operator ☐ Material	☐ Vendor ☐ Other	Operation number responsible for defect:	
	☐ Machine		Inspector's signature: _____	
	Direct materials	Direct labor	Overhead	
Unit standard cost				
Total standard cost				

EXHIBIT 5–11
Majordomo Job Number 101 Cost Sheet

Job Order Cost Report

Job number: 101
Job name: Foghorn Political Rally

Date: MM/DD/YY
Location: Marquis Hotel

Direct materials	$10,000
Direct labor ($10.00 x 120 DLhr)	1,200
Overhead ($5.40 x 120 DLhr)	648
Total cost	11,848
Normal spoilage:	
1 turkey	$30.00
1 ham	36.00
Total actual normal spoilage cost	$66.00

(The turkey and ham were discovered to be spoiled before the cooking process began. Total cost accumulated to this point was $66.00)

EXHIBIT 5–12
Majordomo Job Number 106 Cost Sheet

Job Order Cost Report

Job number: 106
Job name: Deeppockets Wedding

Date: MM/DD/YY
Location: Happy Valley Church

Direct materials	$200,000.00
Direct labor ($10.00 x 5,000 DLhr)	50,000.00
Overhead ($5.40 x 5,000 DLhr)	27,000.00
Total cost	$277,000.00
Normal spoilage associated with all jobs:	
20 pounds of shrimp	$ 100.00
30 pounds of steak	120.00
Breakage	1,000.00
Total actual spoilage cost	$ 1,220.00

(The shrimp and steak were spoiled before the cooking process began. Breakage was determined after the wedding. The costs for this spoilage represent costs accumulated to the point of inspection.)

Normal spoilage caused by this job:

Mountain lilies	$4,000.00

(The lilies were spoiled after the wedding. They are valueless but require no disposal cost. The cost accumulated to this point for lilies is $4,000.00.)

Accounting for Abnormal Spoilage in Traditional JOCASs

Abnormal spoilage is the amount of spoilage in excess of the expected level of spoilage. Abnormal spoilage should be written off as a loss (expense) of the time period. For example, Majordomo catered a banquet (job 310) that incurred normal spoilage expected of all jobs of $2,000 and abnormal spoilage of $10,000 due to faulty refrigeration. The entry for this situation is:

SPOILAGE JOURNAL ENTRY: Abnormal Loss

WIP–Manufacturing Overhead (Spoilage)	$ 2,000	
Loss from Abnormal Spoilage	$10,000	
WIP–Job 310		$12,000

ACCOUNTING FOR REWORK AND SPOILAGE IN WORLD-CLASS JOCASs

To summarize the traditional CAS accounting for rework and spoilage:

- If rework and spoilage are "normal" occurrences, expected across all jobs due to the condition of the production process and the nature of the products, these costs should be budgeted for and included in the POR. When these costs occur, they should be debited to overhead. When overhead is applied to the jobs, the POR puts these costs back into the jobs, spreading the costs evenly throughout the year to all jobs.
- If unique rework and spoilage are attributable to a specific job, and not to the general operating conditions of the enterprise, these costs should remain within the job. If the company budgets for normal rework and spoilage, including them in the POR, then these amounts must be removed from the POR when overhead is applied to the rework and the job.
- Abnormal, unexpected spoilage costs should not be charged to the job. These costs should be written off (debited) to a loss account.

WCM managers ask, "Why bury the costs of rework and spoilage in overhead or in a completely separate, isolated expense account?" These are nonvalue-added costs that need to be measured, and their activities need to be identified in accordance with the Japanese philosophy that a defect is a gem to be understood so it can be prevented in the future. The JOCAS, then, should specifically measure, identify, and report the cost of all rework and spoilage.

Thus, modern job cost reports for WCMs are expanded to include budget and cost variance information about the job. This is illustrated in the last two sections of the chapter (see Exhibits 5–15 and 5–22). If all rework and spoilage costs are left within the job's cost, the job cost report can specifically identify them, and their causes, for management's attention. Further, through the use of an ICBIS, this information can be immediately available for daily operations control.

What are the accounting effects of leaving rework and spoilage costs within the job? First, the job cost report has to include budget and variance information to help measure the significance of these costs. For example, in a traditional CAS, normal rework and spoilage have to be budgeted for anyway. Rather than putting them in overhead, though, why not just budget for them within the jobs directly? If a job results in abnormal rework or spoilage, it will not have been budgeted for and will show up as a cost overrun (unfavorable cost variance) on the job cost report. If normal rework and spoilage costs are not included in overhead, the special journal entries described above do not have to be made. This actually simplifies the CAS and at the same time provides better information for management control.

Secondly, there is a potential effect on net income. When normal rework and spoilage are included in overhead and the POR, job costs are "smoothed."

All jobs are charged equally, regardless of random fluctuations between them (some have more or less rework and spoilage than others). Smoothing job costs smooths COGS and net income. But, if all rework and spoilage are left in individual jobs, this smoothing effect will not happen. Net income will be subject to the random fluctuations between jobs. In other words, instead of moving the fluctuations to overhead, they remain in the jobs and affect net income when the jobs are sold.

Traditional CAS theory argues that it is more important to smooth earnings because this gives a truer picture of the firm's profitability. Attaching these costs to specific jobs is not appropriate because the costs were caused by overall operating conditions, not by the individual jobs. The WCM management accountant counters this argument by pointing out that if the fluctuations are truly random and normal across all jobs, then the effect of not smoothing cannot be significant. The fluctuations will, for the most part, be relatively small (these costs will be fairly even across jobs). When a fluctuation is significant because a job results in an unusually high rework or spoilage cost, this job should be singled out for special attention. Only by keeping these nonvalue-added costs within the jobs will management be able to identify and eliminate them.

What about abnormal rework and spoilage? Under traditional CAS methods, these are expensed against net income in the time period they occur (within the month). If these costs remain in the job, and the job is sold, they will still "hit the income statement," not as an expense, but as a cost of the job (COGS). The net income effect is the same. But what if the job was not finished this month? The traditional approach would still expense these costs this month. The WCM approach would keep the costs in the job until it is completed and sold, thus matching the revenues from the job against all of its costs.

What's the "bottom line"? With increasing global competition, the WCM firm needs information on all nonvalue-added costs. The firm must measure these costs, identify the jobs where they were created, and ascertain the underlying causes. Whether these costs are added to every job through a POR, or specifically budgeted for within each job, they end up in the job's cost. Is it better to identify these costs through an overhead cost analysis or through a job cost analysis? Scrap, rework, and spoilage have become extremely serious problems for many traditional manufacturers. The modern management accountant must address the issue of how best to account for these costs in designing a world-class JOCAS.

INSTALLING AN ICBIS FOR A JOCAS

Many companies now apply computer technology to support their JOCASs. For example, the *Insights & Applications* feature on the following page introduces how Viking Boat Company uses an ICBIS to support its JOCAS.

Necessary Features of JOCAS Software

Different software packages have different features and are customized for different situations. The key to acquiring the best software is to match the needs of the enterprise with the capabilities of the software package. The following list of common features can serve as a guide for comparing the capabilities of different software packages:

- *User-friendly.* The software package should provide online help, menus, and tutorials. The system should be simple enough that it will not overwhelm the average user.

> **LEARNING OBJECTIVE 4**
>
> ▬
>
> Describe how an integrated computer-based information system (ICBIS) can support a JOCAS.

INSIGHTS & APPLICATIONS

Viking Boat Company's New ICBIS

The Viking Boat Company is located in West Palm Beach, Florida. Viking takes in about 100 boat construction jobs per month. Some are huge projects, lasting up to six months and producing revenue up to $500,000. Viking also has a large service area that performs a substantial number of repair jobs. Both of these areas, construction and service, fit into the categories for a JOCAS.

Viking's management accountant has acquired a JOCAS software package that will track, bill, and charge costs to construction and repair jobs. It is integrated into the financial accounting software, as shown in Exhibit 5–13. The advantage of this ICBIS is that transactions entered into one module simultaneously update a specific job as well as other accounting files. For example, when employee time tickets are entered into the payroll module, the hours spent on each job are automatically posted to the job cost sheet. The worker's paycheck is also calculated and prepared. In another example, when a part is taken from materials inventory, the cost is charged to the job cost sheet and WIP, and RMI is automatically reduced.

EXHIBIT 5–13
Viking Boat Company's ICBIS JOCAS

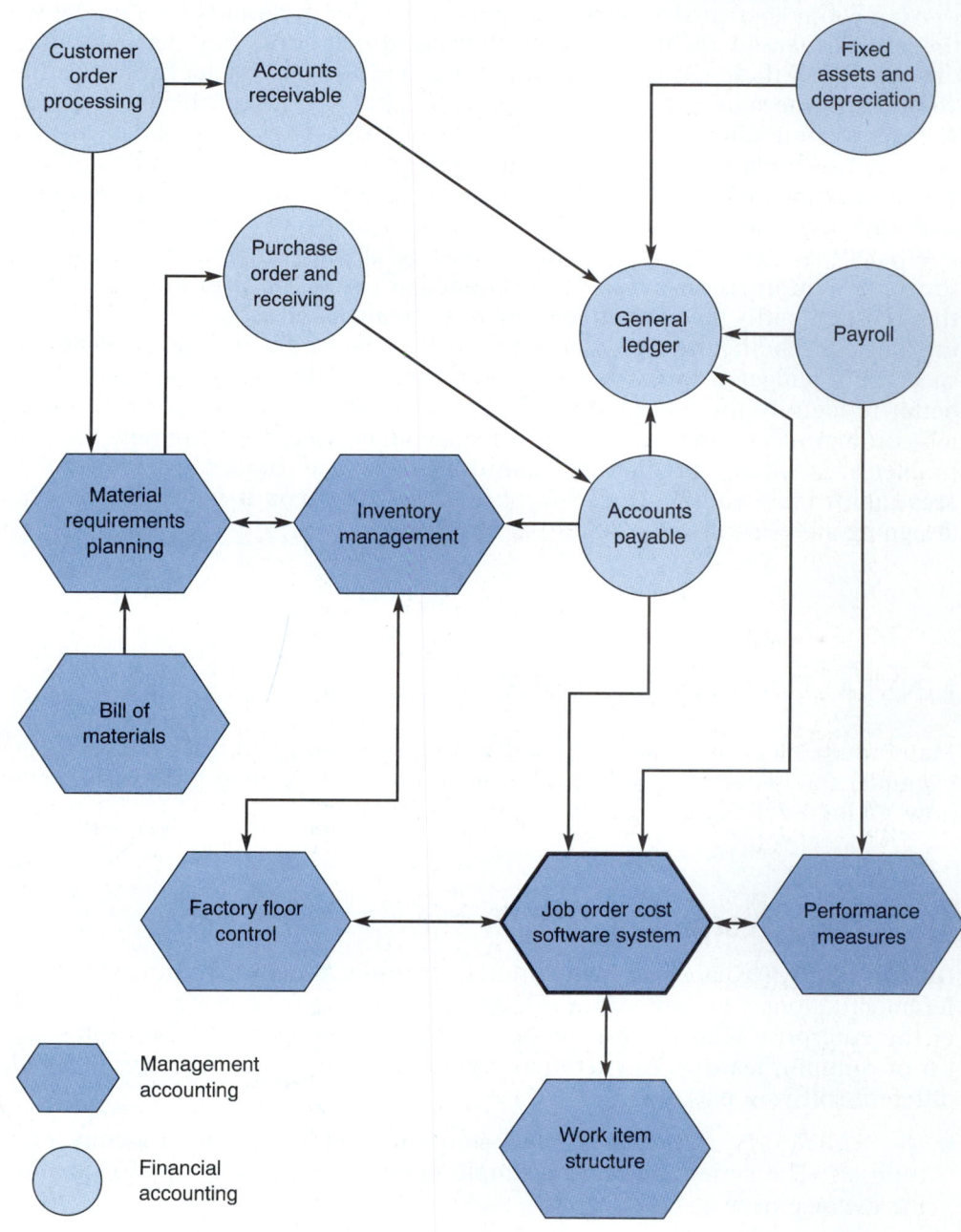

- *Internal controls.* The package should have internal controls, such as input, processing, output, and database controls.
- *Flexibility.* The software should permit each job to be set up according to the work ordered by the customer.
- *Break down by work areas.* The software should have the ability to break down a job into departments, workcenters, or cells to measure work performed and costs for each work area.
- *Integration.* The software should be easily integrated with other accounting tasks. For example: integration with payroll for entering labor costs and determining labor performance; integration with inventory for entering material costs and updating quantity on hand; integration with accounts payable and with purchasing for ordering materials and other items; integration with accounts receivable for producing customer invoices and recording receipts; and integration with the general ledger for preparing journals and monthly financial statements.
- *WIP reporting.* WIP reports keep management abreast of progress on various jobs and also can show at a very early date when costs (such as scrap, rework, and spoilage) are getting out of control.
- *Prebilling data.* Management should be provided with a prebilling worksheet to review before customer invoices are prepared and mailed.
- *Job scheduling.* This feature produces information including start and due dates, percent completion, and a list of open and closed jobs.
- *Job profitability.* This feature computes costs incurred and profit margin for each job.
- *New-job estimating.* This feature provides cost information that aids management in bidding for new jobs.

The Technology Platform for Viking's ICBIS

The network backbone and computer hardware platform for Viking's ICBIS are presented in Exhibit 5–14. The network transmission medium is fiber optic and the fiber distributed data interface (FDDI) standard supported by the American National Standards Institute (ANSI). Fiber optic's main advantage to Viking is

■■■ EXHIBIT 5–14
The Technology Platform for Viking's ICBIS JOCAS

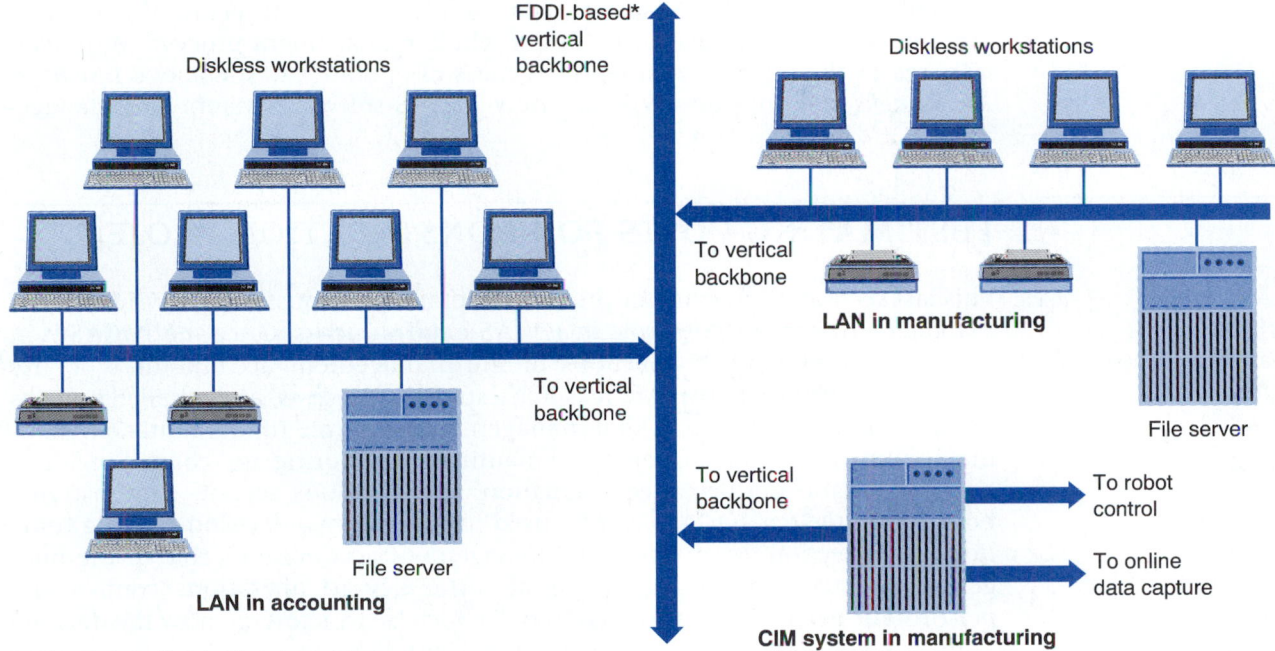

* FDDI stands for fiber distributed data interface

INSIGHTS & APPLICATIONS

Viking Boat Company's New JOCAS as a Management Tool

John Silver, CEO of Viking said, "One of the advantages of our new computerized system is that it gives me work-in-progress on all jobs, both construction and service, any time I want this information. I can see exactly what we have in a job; that is, in materials, labor, overhead, and any subcontracted work, by simply entering job numbers via my workstation. I also like the job order reports that I get upon completion of a job. (See Exhibit 5–15 for an example of the job 147F report.) I use these reports to help analyze performance, to bid on future jobs, and to determine product line profitability."

Teri Crusoe, marketing manager, said, "We have also improved customer relations. We're customer-oriented, and we have fewer billing disputes. We can send interim bills on major jobs so the customer knows how work is progressing. We also disclose a lot more detail in the bills to explain precisely what was done."

Marcy Gulliver, financial accountant, said, "On the productivity side, it has streamlined the work flow in our office by cutting the time we spend on billing almost in half. We also get customer revenues much faster, which has almost eliminated our need to obtain short-term loans. Moreover, the integration feature eliminates all the manual entries we used to make for each account. This feature not only increases productivity but reduces data-entry errors."

Homer Dreyfus, yard foreman, said, "I really like the system's flexibility in specifying the precise work the customer wants. I meet with the customer and enter the instructions in detail via my workstation. The tasks are grouped to departments, such as yard, electrical, mechanical, paint shop, and so forth. The exact assignment is keyed into the system. When the customer receives a bill, he sees what he told me to do and exactly what he is being charged for. Another feature I like is the graphics that give me performance and utilization information at a glance. I particularly like the trend of performance measures, such as labor utilization, machine utilization, and units rejected. I can use this information to analyze performance over one or more jobs, which might otherwise be obscured by the complexities of various job orders."

Sylvia Torrence, service and repair foreman, said, "The new system simplifies service work and repair jobs. We are able to assign the right parts to the right customer. This used to be a nightmare. Now, we know exactly what parts were used on each job. Since there is a tie to inventory, we can tell if we have the parts on hand before we start a job. We can track a job from the time a customer walks in the door until she leaves with a paid receipt. The work to be performed is entered on the keyboard, and a job cost sheet is set up and printed. Then, a mechanic takes the proper copy and begins the job. Parts are charged to the job cost sheet by the inventory clerk, and labor is entered from the mechanic's time clock tickets. We used to spend hours totaling up the parts and labor for each job. Now, we can hand the customer a computer-generated bill as soon as the job is completed."

its resistance to electrical interference from production equipment and lightning from thunderstorms, which are prevalent in Florida.

A computerized JOCAS is more than simply a historical record of what happens at Viking. It is a major tool in the whole management process. Moreover, it increases the efficiency and effectiveness of operations. The above *Insights & Applications* describes how Viking's new JOCAS software system aids management.

LEARNING OBJECTIVE 5

Discuss how costs are estimated for construction projects and how work item software is used.

ESTIMATING COSTS FOR CONSTRUCTION PROJECTS

This last section of the chapter presents a detailed demonstration of the modern management accountant's role in JOCAS environments. Once the JOCAS is in place, one of the main functions of the management accountant is to use information from it to prepare feasibility studies, forecasts, and detailed budgets for specific jobs. Remember that management has three fundamental decision-making functions (from Chapter 1): planning, monitoring and controlling daily operations, and performance evaluation. The previous section demonstrated how computerized JOCASs can be used in the last two decision-making functions. This section emphasizes the management accountant's role in the budgeting process. Since budgeting is also the key to operations control and performance evaluation, this section will conclude by showing how the detailed budget is tied to the other two managerial functions.

Closed Job Order Report

Job order number:	147F		Workcenter 4		Report date:	10/14/X5

Customer:	Water Sports	Product ordered:	28' Neptune Ski Rig
Order number:	19743M	Quantity ordered:	1
Contract number:	27948	Date ordered:	09/01/X5
Contract price:	$30,000.00	Date promised:	10/12/X5
		Date started:	09/03/X5
		Date completed:	10/13/X5

Cost inputs	Estimated	Actual	Under/<over>
Materials:			
Purchased parts	$ 6,500.00	$ 7,000.00	$ <500.00>
Manufactured stock	3,000.00	3,000.00	0.00
Total	$ 9,500.00	$10,000.00	$ <500.00>
Direct labor:			
Production	$ 2,600.00	$ 2,500.00	$ 100.00
Setup	200.00	500.00	<300.00>
Rework	400.00	1,000.00	<600.00>
Total	$ 3,200.00	$ 4,000.00	$ <800.00>
Applied overhead:			
Fixed	$ 4,200.00	$ 4,000.00	$ 200.00
Variable	1,600.00	2,000.00	<400.00>
Total	$ 5,800.00	$ 6,000.00	$ <200.00>
Total manufacturing costs	$18,500.00	$20,000.00	$<1,500.00>

Memo:	Contract price		$30,000.00
	Total manufacturing cost charged to the job	$20,000.00	
	Administrative cost	2,000.00	
	Selling cost	3,000.00	
	Total cost to make and sell		<25,000.00>
	Profit (loss)		$ 5,000.00

(Rework: The $1,000 for rework labor was caused by a bent shaft that had to be removed and replaced.)

Two points need to be emphasized first, though. Budgeting is perhaps the most demanding, frustrating, and important task of the management accountant. It is "crystal ball gazing" into the future. But unlike the fortune teller, if the management accountant prepares a "bad" budget, the customer (management) will come back and complain. Also, unlike fortune telling, modern budgeting does not involve magic but uses statistical techniques that are often complex and sometimes difficult to explain to managers relying on the budget. Good budgeting is not easy, but it is becoming the critical skill the modern management accountant needs to develop if businesses are to compete successfully in today's global, highly competitive, and economically risky environment.

The second point is that the management accountant cannot do this alone. As the first three chapters pointed out, the modern management accountant is part of the management team. The following demonstration is a real-world situation you can expect to encounter if you pursue a career in management accounting with world-class enterprises.

Elements in Estimating Costs

Three main elements are applicable to estimating construction costs:

$$\text{Bid price} = \text{Target profit} + \text{Estimated costs}$$

The **bid price** is the amount of money the owner must pay the general contractor to build the project. The bid price is similar to the price charged by a manufacturer for a product. Unlike the manufacturer, however, the general contractor usually does not have a chance to raise or lower its price. A bid for the project gives the general contractor "one shot" to win the contract.

Indeed, estimating costs and preparing bid prices are the lifeblood of general

Housing project under construction.

contractors.[2] Carelessness and overestimating costs can mean the loss of a project. On the other hand, omissions and underestimating costs can financially cripple the general contractor. The bid price of a project should be high enough to enable the general contractor to complete the project with a reasonable profit, yet low enough to win the contract.

Cost estimates may be divided into at least two different types:

- Preliminary cost estimates
- Detailed cost estimates

In either case, cost estimation requires knowledge and experience with the work required to build the project. Just as important is an accurate JOCAS database from previous projects of similar type and size.[3]

Preliminary Cost Estimates

A **preliminary cost estimate** (also called **conceptual, approximate,** or **budget estimate**) is a ballpark estimate of what the costs could be to build the project, including the target profit. Usually, a preliminary cost estimate is given to the prospective owner, prior to designing the project, to enable the prospective owner to decide whether design should continue and construction take place.

REDUCING THE PROJECT TO BASIC PARAMETERS. An architect will reduce a building to square feet of area or cubic feet of volume. An engineer will multiply the number of cubic yards of concrete in an airport runway by an average estimated cost per cubic yard to determine the probable cost of an airport runway job. Other basic parameters may be number of cars in a parking garage, number of linear feet of a pipeline, number of miles of an electrical transmission line, or number of barrels of oil processed per hour. It is the responsibility of the management accountant to record these basic parameters in the cost database from previous projects.

The following equation can be used to weight cost data from previous projects:

$$UC = \frac{A + 4B + C}{6}$$

where:

UC = Estimated unit cost
A = Minimum unit cost of previous projects
B = Average unit cost of previous projects
C = Maximum unit cost of previous projects

To illustrate, a general contractor is preparing a preliminary cost estimate for a parking garage that is to contain 135 parked cars. Exhibit 5–16 presents cost data from eight previously constructed parking garage projects. From these data, the estimated unit cost of the proposed parking garage project is:[4]

$$UC = \frac{\$2,987.30 + 4(\$3,803.94) + \$4,375.80}{6}$$

$$= \$3,763.14 \text{ estimated unit cost}$$

[2] Leo Diamant, *Construction Estimating for General Contractors* (New York: John Wiley & Sons, 1988), p. 1.
[3] R. L. Peurifoy and G. D. Oberlender, *Estimating Construction Costs*, 4th ed. (New York: McGraw-Hill, 1989), p. 2. With permission.
[4] Ibid., 425.

Project	Cost	Number of Cars	Unit Cost per Car
1	$466,560	150	$3,110.40
2	290,304	80	3,628.80
3	525,096	120	4,375.80
4	349,920	90	3,888.00
5	259,290	60	4,321.50
6	657,206	220	2,987.30
7	291,718	70	4,167.40
8	711,414	180	3,952.30
Simple average			$3,803.94

■■EXHIBIT 5–16
Cost Data from Eight Previously Constructed Parking Garage Projects

Source: R. L. Peurifoy and G. D. Oberlender, *Estimating Construction Costs,* 4th ed. (New York: McGraw-Hill, 1989), p. 425. With permission.

The preliminary cost estimate for the 135-car parking garage project is:

$$\begin{array}{l}\$508,023.90 \text{ preliminary}\\ \quad\quad\quad \text{cost estimate}\end{array} = \$3,763.14 \text{ estimated unit cost} \times 135 \text{ cars}$$

Before the target profit can be added to the preliminary cost estimate, it needs to be adjusted for all of the following:

■ Time
■ Location
■ Size

ADJUSTING THE PRELIMINARY COST ESTIMATE FOR TIME. Cost data from previous projects will be unreliable unless an adjustment is made for the time differences between the two projects. The adjustment should represent the relative increase or decrease in costs due to factors such as labor rates, material costs, equipment costs, interest rates, and inflation.

Various organizations publish indices that show economic trends over time. The *Engineering News Record* (*ENR*) publishes indices of construction costs annually. The estimator and management accountant can use the change in value of an index between any two years to calculate an equivalent compound interest rate. This rate can be used to adjust past cost data for future projects.

For example, using the indices shown in Exhibit 5–17, an equivalent compound interest rate can be calculated based on the change in the cost index during the three-year period:

$$\frac{378}{358} = (1 + i)^3$$
$$i = \underline{1.83\%}$$

■■EXHIBIT 5–17
Indices for Building Construction Projects

Year	Index
3 years ago	358
2 years ago	359
1 year ago	367
Current year	378

Source: R. L. Peurifoy and G. D. Oberlender, *Estimating Construction Costs,* 4th ed. (New York: McGraw-Hill, 1989), p. 426. With permission.

If an $843,500 project completed last year is to be used to prepare a preliminary cost estimate for a project three years from now, that cost should be adjusted for four years:[5]

$$\text{Estimated project cost} = \$843,500 \times (1 + 0.0183)^4$$
$$= \underline{\$906,960}$$

ADJUSTING THE PRELIMINARY COST ESTIMATE FOR LOCATION. Previous cost data also cannot be used reliably unless an adjustment is made

[5] Ibid., 426.

Preliminary Cost Estimate for the New Business Building

Terrence Mason has been asked by the university Board of Regents to provide a preliminary cost estimate for a new business building with 62,700 square feet of floor area. He will use the time, location, and size indices from the previous examples.

The new business building is to be constructed three years from now in city B. A similar building that cost $2,197,500 and contained 38,500 square feet was completed two years ago in city E. Using these data, Terrence prepares the following preliminary cost estimate for the new business building.[6]

$$\text{Preliminary cost estimate} = \frac{\text{Previous cost} \times \text{Time adjustment} \times}{\text{Location adjustment} \times \text{Size adjustment}}$$

$$= \$2,197,500 \times (1 + 0.0183)^5$$

$$\times \frac{1,170}{1,240} \times \frac{62,700}{38,500}$$

$$= \$2,197,500 \times 1.095 \times 0.944 \times 1.629$$

$$= \$3,700,300 \text{ (rounded up)}$$

for the difference between the locations of the two projects. This adjustment represents the relative difference in the costs of materials, labor, and equipment at the two locations.

The *Engineering News Record* (*ENR*) also publishes location cost indices, such as the one shown in Exhibit 5–18. To illustrate, cost data from a $387,200 project completed in city A are used to prepare a preliminary cost estimate for a proposed project in city D. The project's cost should be adjusted as follows:

$$\text{Estimated project cost} = \$387,200 \times \frac{1,105}{1,025}$$

$$= \$417,420$$

ADJUSTING THE PRELIMINARY COST ESTIMATE FOR SIZE. Further, cost data from a previous project will not be reliable unless they are adjusted for the difference in size of the two projects. In many projects, cost is directly proportional to size. The adjustment is a simple ratio of the size of the proposed project to the size of the previous project. For example, if the size of the previous project was 40,000 square feet with a cost of $1,600,000 and the size of the proposed project is 60,000 square feet, then:

$$\text{Estimated project cost} = \$1,600,000 \times \frac{60,000 \text{ sq. ft.}}{40,000 \text{ sq. ft.}}$$

$$= \$2,400,000$$

COMBINING THE ADJUSTMENTS. The above *Insights & Applications* illustrates how adjustments are combined in preparing a preliminary cost estimate.

Detailed Cost Estimates

A **detailed cost estimate** (also called **final** or **definitive cost estimate**) measures each cost element involved, contingencies, and target profit. When the preliminary cost estimate is made, only general design information will be available, and in some cases no design information at all. Detailed cost estimates, on the other hand, are usually prepared from a complete set of blueprints, technical specifications, and contract documents prior to submitting the bid price to the owner. In addition, the general contractor will often visit the pro-

◼EXHIBIT 5–18
Location Indices for Construction Costs

Location	Index
City A	1,025
City B	1,170
City C	1,260
City D	1,105
City E	1,240

Source: R. L. Peurifoy and G. D. Oberlender, *Estimating Construction Costs,* 4th ed. (New York: McGraw-Hill, 1989), p. 427. With permission.

[6] Adapted from ibid., pp. 427–428.

posed project site to observe factors that can influence the cost of construction, such as available space for storage of materials, control of traffic, security, and existing underground utilities.[7]

STEPS FOR PREPARING A DETAILED COST ESTIMATE.

When participating in the preparation of a detailed cost estimate, the management accountant should be involved in 11 steps:

Step 1. *Review the scope of the project.* Consider the effect of location, security, traffic, available storage space, underground utilities, and other factors on costs.

Step 2. *Review all bidding requirements, technical specifications, and conditions of the contract.* This step includes understanding instructions to bidders, bid forms, insurance and bond requirements, various regulatory requirements, general contractor's obligations, quality control, measurement and payment terms, and contract closeout.

Step 3. *Prepare a checklist of all work items necessary.* This entails making sure that all work items required to build the project are included. Before completing the detailed cost estimate, both the estimator and the management accountant, and then the general contractor, should check this list to make sure that no items have been omitted. Omission of a work item could cause the general contractor to suffer a substantial loss. A common error in construction cost estimating is to omit a work item completely or count one twice.

Step 4. *Determine materials quantities.* The quantity of materials in the project can be accurately determined from the blueprints (or drawings). The estimator may also add an appropriate percentage for waste (scrap). For example, a 5 percent waste might be added to the volume of mortar that is calculated for bricklaying. With proper data on scrap in the JOCAS database, the management accountant can provide this type of information.

The materials quantities estimates are extremely important in construction work because they often establish the quantities and costs for direct labor and equipment. For example, the quantity of concrete material for piers might be calculated as 20,000 cubic yards. The labor and equipment hours, and their costs, to place the concrete would also be based on the 20,000 cubic yards.[8]

Step 5. *Estimate labor costs.* This step determines cost of construction (direct) labor by the following equation:

$$\text{Direct labor cost} = \frac{\text{Quantity}}{\text{Direct labor production rate}} \times \text{DL rate}$$

Direct labor rates vary considerably with the locations of projects and with the various types of crafts. If, for example, the direct labor rate for bricklayers is \$18/DLhr and the production rate is 80 bricks laid per hour, a work item calling for 1,600,000 bricks would cost \$360,000 for direct labor:

$$\text{Direct labor cost} = \frac{1,600,000 \text{ bricks}}{80 \text{ bricks laid per hour}} \times \$18/\text{DLhr}$$
$$= \underline{\underline{\$360,000}}$$

The management accountant should verify that the rate includes all applicable payroll burden items, as discussed in Chapter 4.

The bidding process. Courtesy of Krump Construction Company.

[7] Ibid., p. 4.
[8] Ibid., pp. 9–10.

Step 6. Estimate equipment costs. This step uses the following equation to estimate equipment costs:

$$\text{Equipment costs} = \frac{\text{Quantity}}{\text{Equipment production rate}} \times \frac{\text{Equipment}}{\text{rate}}$$

The equipment rate usually includes the cost per hour for acquiring and operating the equipment, excluding labor. Computing this rate for leased equipment is usually straightforward, based on a contractual amount per hour. The general contractor will also pay for the operator, fuel, lubricants, and all repairs. When the equipment is purchased, computing the cost per hour becomes quite involved.

Cost Items Include:	*Additional Considerations:*
■ Depreciation	■ Estimated life of equipment
■ Maintenance and repairs	■ Estimated salvage value
■ Interest charges	■ Capacity of crankcase
■ Fuel and lubrication	■ Time between oil changes
■ Tires	■ Horsepower of engine
■ Shipping and freight from one project to another	■ Cost of tires
	■ Life of tires
■ An operating factor (i.e., the percentage of time the equipment is doing productive work)	■ Cost of repairing tires
	■ Cost of fuel
	■ Cost of lubricating oil
	■ Cost of repairs

Because of these complexities, some general contractors use standard costs gathered from industry publications. For example, the standard cost to own and operate a 160-horsepower diesel engine crawler-type tractor is $42 per Mhr, assuming operations of 2,000 productive hours per year. Thus, if this tractor can fill 10 cubic yards of dirt per hour, and it is used to fill 40,000 cubic yards of dirt, equipment costs for this work item are:

$$\text{Equipment costs} = \frac{40,000 \text{ cubic yards}}{10 \text{ cubic yards per hour}} \times \$42/\text{Mhr}$$
$$= \underline{\$168,000}$$

Step 7. Obtain subcontractors' bids. On many projects, a significant amount of work is performed by subcontractors who specialize in particular work items. Examples are site preparation, excavation, piles and caissons, marine work, paving and surfacing, painting, and roofing. The estimator provides a set of drawings and specifications to potential subcontractors and requests a bid price from them for their particular work.

Step 8. Estimate overhead costs. Some general contractors divide overhead into two categories:

■ Project overhead
■ General overhead

Project overhead includes costs that can be directly traced to a project: salaries of the project manager, superintendents, and field office personnel; utilities, supplies, engineering, tests, permits; and the like. General overhead is the percentage share of the costs incurred at the central office or headquarters of the general contractor. Since the cost of general overhead is incurred in operating all the projects built by the general contractor, it is reasonable to allocate a percentage of this cost to each project. This amount may be based on the duration of the project, cost of the project, complexity of the project, or a combination of all three. Traditionally, most contractors base the general overhead allocation on the project's cost. For example, if total construction for the forthcoming year is estimated at $12,000,000 and annual general overhead is estimated at $1,200,000, the amount of general overhead applied to a project is 10 percent ($1,200,000 annual general overhead ÷ $12,000,000 total annual value of construction projects).

If project A's estimated cost is $400,000, general overhead will be $40,000 ($400,000 × 10%). If project A is unique and complex, however, a higher percentage of general overhead may be charged to it, such as 15 to 20 percent. If project B is a common project with little complexity, a lower percentage of general overhead may be charged to it, such as 5 to 10 percent or less.

Surveying the project.

Step 9. Estimate contingency costs. Generally, a project will involve some unforeseen work that develops during construction, such as excavation work that must be redone due to a severe rainstorm. Caution must be used in assigning contingency costs. Contingency costs that are too low may not be sufficient to cover the actual contingencies, reducing the profits realized from the project. Contingency costs that are too high may prevent the bid from being competitive and accepted.

Step 10. Determine insurance and bond costs. Insurance usually includes basic builder's risk insurance and various liability insurance policies. The main bond is the contractor's performance bond. Normally, costs for insurance and bonds are fairly easy to determine with a high level of accuracy from insurance agents.

Step 11. Determine the target profit. This amount is subject to considerable variation, depending on the size of the project, the extent of risk and complexity involved, the desire of the general contractor to get the project, the amount of competition, and other factors. A general contractor, for example, might include a 3 to 6 percent profit on a $1,000,000 highway paving project when the risk is low and competition is high. On the other hand, the same general contractor might include 20 to 30 percent profit or more on a bridge project that spans a river in the Rocky Mountains and calls for the application of untested technology.

ORGANIZING THE WORK ITEMS FOR THE DETAILED COST ESTIMATE AND COMPUTING THE BID PRICE.   Two basic approaches have evolved to organize work items for estimating. One approach uses a work breakdown structure (WBS), which identifies work items by their location on a project. For example, a general contractor bidding for an electric power project involving one substation at Sacramento and another at San Francisco may organize the work items under three groups:

- Substation at Sacramento
- Substation at San Francisco
- Transmission line connecting the two substations

The other approach uses the Construction Specification Institute (CSI) division of work items. Building construction contractors organize their estimates to closely follow the CSI's 16 major divisions recognized as the industry standard. A typical summary of an estimate for a building construction project is illustrated in Exhibit 5–19. Each major division is subdivided into smaller work items. For example, the work required for division 2 sitework is subdivided into nine work items, as shown in Exhibit 5–20.

Regardless of whether the WBS or CSI system is selected, a code number is assigned to each work item. This same code should be used in accounting and keeping track of each work item during construction. It often becomes part of the general ledger account number in both manual and computerized JOCASs. For example, if WIP is general ledger account 140, and this is job 3, a coding

■ EXHIBIT 5–19
Example of a Building Construction Project Bid Summary Using CSI Organization of Work Items

Source: R. L. Peurifoy and G. D. Oberlender, *Estimating Construction Costs,* 4th ed. (New York: McGraw-Hill, 1989), p. 6. With permission.

Item	Division	Material	Labor	Subcontract	Total
1	General requirement	$ 16,435	$ 36,355	$ 4,882	$ 57,672
2	Sitework	15,070	20,123	146,186	181,379
3	Concrete	97,176	51,524	0	148,700
4	Masonry	0	0	212,724	212,724
5	Metals	212,724	59,321	0	272,045
6	Wood and plastics	38,753	10,496	4,908	54,157
7	Thermal and moisture	0	0	138,072	138,072
8	Doors and windows	36,821	32,115	0	68,936
9	Finishes	172,587	187,922	0	360,509
10	Specialties	15,748	11,104	9,525	36,377
11	Equipment	0	0	45,729	45,729
12	Furnishings	0	0	0	0
13	Special construction	0	0	0	0
14	Conveying systems	0	0	0	0
15	Mechanical	0	0	641,673	641,673
16	Electrical	0	0	354,661	354,661
	Total direct costs	$605,314	$408,960	$1,558,360	$2,572,634
	Material tax (5%)	30,266			2,602,900
	Labor tax (18%)		73,613		2,676,513
	Contingency (2%)			53,530	2,730,043
	Bonds/insurance			34,091	2,764,134
	Profit (10%)			276,414	3,040,548
				Bid price =	$3,040,548

■ EXHIBIT 5–20
Division 2 Estimate for Sitework

Source: R. L. Peurifoy and G. D. Oberlender, *Estimating Construction Costs,* 4th ed. (New York: McGraw-Hill, 1989), p. 7. With permission.

Cost Code	Description	Quantity	Material	Labor	Subcontract	Total
2110	Clearing	Lump sum	$ 0	$ 0	$ 3,694	$ 3,694
2220	Excavation	8,800 cubic yards	0	11,880	9,416	21,296
2250	Compaction	950 cubic yards	0	2,223	722	2,945
2294	Handwork	500 square yards	0	1,750	0	1,750
2281	Termite control	Lump sum	0	0	3,475	3,475
2372	Drilled piers	1,632 linear feet	14,580	2,800	14,524	31,904
2411	Foundation drains	14 each	490	1,470	0	1,960
2480	Landscape	Lump sum	0	0	8,722	8,722
2515	Paving	4,850 square yards	0	0	105,633	105,633
			$15,070	$20,123	$146,186	$181,379

system to record the subcontractor payment for clearing sitework might be G/L account 143-02-110, detailed as follows:

COST ELEMENT DESCRIPTION	G/L ACCOUNT NUMBER
WIP Inventory	140-xx-xxx
Job 3	xx3-xx-xxx
Sitework	xxx-02-xxx
Clearing	xxx-xx-110

USING COMPUTERS FOR COST ESTIMATING AND COST MANAGEMENT.

Preparing cost estimates and bids requires a great deal of historical data and computations. A historical database can be developed that contains detailed cost data for each work item for completed projects. The data stored in the database can be organized in a WBS or CSI system format with an appropriate cost code for each work item. Such data are extremely valuable for estimating the costs of future projects.

A computer system can be used to organize, store, and retrieve data and to perform the many calculations necessary to prepare bids. The data can be adjusted to reflect unique project conditions as previously demonstrated. The most common computer application for cost estimating is the electronic spreadsheet. Spreadsheet programs can be used to prepare these adjustments, the numerous price extension calculations, and the bid summary of an estimate.

An electronic digitizer connected to the computer system can be used to obtain the quantities of materials from the construction drawings of the project. A digitizer pen traces the lines on the drawings to obtain data such as square yards of paving, linear feet of pipe, or number of windows. Using a digitizer to calculate the material quantities automates the process and provides data in an organized form.

Using Work Item Software for Estimating

A work item software package, based on WBS or CSI, is an ideal tool to prepare cost estimates for bidding, monitoring performance, and helping to estimate the next similar job. To illustrate, Teri Simmons, management accountant for Roland Construction Company, uses a CSI-based work item software package installed on her workstation. The controlling (or parent) module and the two submodules are shown in Exhibit 5–21. This work item breakdown structure is used to estimate and record costs for the sitework job that Roland is bidding on.

Because the upper module in the exhibit is the controlling or parent module (i.e., sitework), the percent of total job costs is 100 percent. The estimated costs for the sitework job are composed of direct materials, direct equipment, direct labor, and applied overhead. Since equipment normally represents a large cost of construction work, this cost element is separated for more accurate cost estimating and more effective cost control. Examples of direct equipment are bulldozers, scrapers, motor graders, and paving machines.

Using Work Item Software for Operations Control and Performance Evaluation

Notice that the cost elements occur under three categories:

EXHIBIT 5–21
CSI-Based Work Item Structure for Estimating Construction Costs

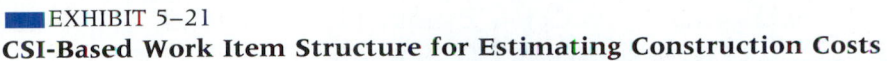

2.0		Sitework		Percent of Job:	100%
		Estimated Costs	Actual Costs	Cost Variances	
Materials:		$ 100,000			
Direct equipment:		$ 800,000			
Direct labor:		$ 300,000			
Applied overhead:		$ 200,000			
Total:		$1,400,000			

2110		Clearing		Percent of Job:	20%
		Estimated Costs	Actual Costs	Cost Variances	
Materials:		$ 20,000			
Direct equipment:		$160,000			
Direct labor:		$ 60,000			
Applied overhead:		$ 40,000			
Total:		$280,000			

2220		Excavation		Percent of Job:	80%
		Estimated Costs	Actual Costs	Cost Variances	
Materials:		$ 80,000			
Direct equipment:		$ 640,000			
Direct labor:		$ 240,000			
Applied overhead:		$ 160,000			
Total:		$1,120,000			

- Estimated costs
- Actual costs
- Cost variances

The estimated costs were used for bidding purposes and now become the benchmarks for monitoring operations and evaluating performance. The actual costs are costs incurred while performing the job. The cost variances are the differences between estimated costs and actual costs. Reports of cost variances enable management to identify problems and measure their seriousness (a $5 variance is not important, but a $50,000 variance is). The cost variances will also aid in future bidding on similar jobs, because they show the amount under- or overbid on the job's work items.

After the estimating process is complete, Teri Simmons has two important tasks while the job is under construction:

- Accumulate costs, report percent of completion, and calculate cost variances
- Keep all the work item data up to date to use as input for bidding on other similar jobs

Exhibit 5–22 shows how data are updated as the job progresses toward completion. The work item structure may be updated daily or weekly. The sitework project is 10 percent complete, clearing is 30 percent complete, and excavation is 5 percent complete. Actual costs incurred to this point are posted, and cost variances calculated, to aid management in monitoring operations and ultimately, when the job is complete, in evaluating the job's profitability.

Figures in parentheses indicate unfavorable cost variances; figures not in parentheses indicate favorable cost variances. To date, there is a total unfavorable cost variance of $4,000. According to the detailed reports, management should investigate direct equipment costs for clearing, direct materials costs for excavation, and applied overhead.

■ EXHIBIT 5–22
CSI-Based Work Item Structure for Monitoring Operations

2.0	Sitework	Percent of Completion: 10%	Percent of Job: 100%

	Estimated Costs	Actual Costs	Cost Variances
Materials:	$ 100,000	$ 9,500	($ 100,000x.10)–$ 9,500 = $ 500
Direct equipment:	$ 800,000	$ 84,000	($ 800,000x.10)–$ 84,000 = $<4,000>
Direct labor:	$ 300,000	$ 26,500	($ 300,000x.10)–$ 26,500 = $ 3,500
Applied overhead:	$ 200,000	$ 24,000	($ 200,000x.10)–$ 24,000 = $<4,000>
Total:	$1,400,000	$144,000	($1,400,000x.10)–$144,000 = $<4,000>

2110	Clearing	Percent of Completion: 30%	Percent of Job: 20%

	Estimated Costs	Actual Costs	Cost Variances
Materials:	$ 20,000	$ 3,200	($ 20,000x.30)–$ 3,200 = $ 2,800
Direct equipment:	$160,000	$57,000	($160,000x.30)–$57,000 = $<9,000>
Direct labor:	$ 60,000	$14,100	($ 60,000x.30)–$14,100 = $ 3,900
Applied overhead:	$ 40,000	$14,800	($ 40,000x.30)–$14,800 = $<2,800>
Total:	$280,000	$89,100	($280,000x.30)–$89,100 = $<5,100>

2220	Excavation	Percent of Completion: 5%	Percent of Job: 80%

	Estimated Costs	Actual Costs	Cost Variances
Materials:	$ 80,000	$ 6,300	($ 80,000x.05)–$ 6,300 = $<2,300>
Direct equipment:	$ 640,000	$27,000	($ 640,000x.05)–$27,000 = $ 5,000
Direct labor:	$ 240,000	$12,400	($ 240,000x.05)–$12,400 = $ <400>
Applied overhead:	$ 160,000	$ 9,200	($ 160,000x.05)–$ 9,200 = $<1,200>
Total:	$1,120,000	$54,900	($1,120,000x.05)–$54,900 = $ 1,100

SUMMARY OF LEARNING OBJECTIVES

The major goals of this chapter were to enable you to achieve five learning objectives:

Learning objective 1.   Explain how to design a job order cost accounting system (JOCAS).

A JOCAS has three main informational inputs:

- Materials requisitions
- Time tickets
- Information on the volume of the predetermined overhead rate's basis

Costs accumulated from these inputs are charged to the job, project, or case by posting costs to its job cost sheet. Direct materials are assigned to each job through materials requisitions. Direct labor is traced through time tickets. Overhead is applied to each job using a POR.

Job cost sheets serve as WIP subsidiary ledger accounts. Completed job cost records for jobs not yet delivered to customers are transferred to FGI subsidiary ledger accounts. When jobs are sold, the appropriate costs are transferred from the finished goods account to the cost of goods sold account. Corresponding FGI subsidiary ledger accounts are closed. Completed job cost sheets are maintained in a database for management analysis and to serve as a guide for bidding on future jobs.

Learning objective 2.   Illustrate the cost flows and prepare journal entries for a normal JOCAS.

The cost flows and journal entries are identical to those for any basic CAS, presented in Chapter 4, except that the three journal entries for cost element usage debit specific jobs rather than the WIP subsidiary account called "Product Cost." The "Product Cost" subsidiary account is replaced by separate subsidiary accounts for each job. Thus, when journal entries 5–7 record the usage of direct materials, direct labor, and applied overhead, the debits are to individual job cost sheets.

To review the cost flows, first cost elements are purchased. When raw materials, factory labor, and indirect manufacturing costs are obtained, their costs are debited (charged) to temporary holding accounts in the JOCAS (journal entries 1–4). These are RMI, gross wages, and overhead, respectively.

When raw materials and factory labor are used in the production process, their costs are removed (credited) from their holding accounts and charged (debited) to the jobs and overhead account as described above (journal entries 5–6). In a normal JOCAS, overhead is applied using a POR in journal entry 7. The journal entry is made when the job is completed, or more frequently, depending on how long it takes to complete the job and the basis used for the POR.

When jobs are completed and all their costs accumulated in their subsidiary WIP accounts, the jobs are transferred to FGI and, when sold, to COGS. Journal entries 8 and 9, recording COGM and COGS, may show subsidiary ledger accounts by job for FGI and COGS. This depends on whether individual jobs are tracked through FGI and sold separately. The journal entry formats are illustrated in Demonstration Problem 1.

Learning objective 3.   Demonstrate how to account for scrap, reworked units, and spoilage in a normal JOCAS.

Scrap and spoilage reports should be given to management in a timely fashion. Scrap also should be returned to the storeroom to be held for sale or for reuse. Typically, scrap is not assigned any cost. When it is sold, the proceeds are recorded as miscellaneous income. Sometimes, the net realizable value (NRV) is significant. In that case, the scrap is inventoried, with the NRV credited from the job's cost. Then, when the scrap is sold, no miscellaneous income is recognized.

When rework and spoilage are expected ("normal") and attributable to the overall condition of the production process, rather than caused by specific jobs, traditional CAS methods require that the budgeted costs for rework and spoilage be included in budgeted overhead and the POR. This allows these costs to be spread more evenly over all jobs, smoothing job costs and net income. The cost to rework defective units or the cost of rejected products (spoilage) is then charged to overhead.

If, on the other hand, rework and rejects are caused by extraordinary specifications or unusual conditions of a particular job, or the customer agrees to pay for these costs, the rework should be charged to the job. Abnormal spoilage, though, is written off to a loss (expense) account under traditional methods. In any case, the vast majority of rework and reject costs are not associated with specific jobs in a traditional CAS.

WCM managers, though, may prefer a different accounting for rework and spoilage. They argue that the costs should remain in the jobs where the rework and spoilage occurred. This eliminates the need to make special journal entries removing the costs from the jobs and "burying" them in the overhead account along with many other indirect cost elements. If these costs are truly random and common to all jobs, COGS and net income should not be materially affected. More importantly, if the job cost sheets include budget and cost variance data (as in Exhibits 5–15 and 5–22), the JOCAS can provide valuable information that will help managers deal with these problems.

Learning objective 4.   Describe how an integrated computer-based information system (ICBIS) can support a JOCAS.

More and more companies are installing computerized information networks that integrate data collection and information reporting throughout the firm. These ICBISs contain job order costing software as well as a host of other software, such as materials requirements planning, work item modules, performance measures, and inventory control. These modules are integrated with financial accounting modules to form an ICBIS.

Integrating the modules increases the effectiveness and efficiency of operations. Specifically, timely information is available for controlling operations from online, real-time access to job cost sheets via workstation terminals. Expanding the job cost sheet to include budget and cost variance information will provide better accountability for performance evaluation. Finally, this type of information is critical to budgeting similar projects in the future.

With or without ICBISs, spreadsheet software has become a common tool for reporting and analyzing job costs as well as for preparing budgets for jobs. Spreadsheet programs can be linked together, further increasing efficiency in processing information in modern JOCASs.

Learning objective 5.   Discuss how costs are estimated for construction projects and how work item software is used.

For any given project, the cost estimator and the management accountant must work together to estimate the direct costs for materials, labor, and equipment with reasonable accuracy. The bid price can then be determined by adding the costs for subcontract work, overhead, contingencies, insurance and bonds, and a target profit. The bid price of a project should be high enough to allow the contractor to complete the project with a reasonable profit, yet low enough to be competitive.

Cost estimates can be divided into:

■ Preliminary cost estimates
■ Detailed cost estimates

All cost estimates based on previous cost data should be adjusted for:

■ Time
■ Location
■ Size

A work item software program is a special tool that management accountants can add to their JOCAS. It provides a systematic way for firms to bid on jobs. If a job is awarded, the management accountant can also use the work item software for other purposes:

■ To accumulate actual costs
■ To report variances
■ As input to electronic spreadsheets for financial analysis
■ As a basis for bidding on future similar jobs

IMPORTANT TERMS

Abnormal spoilage   Spoilage that is unexpected and in excess of normal spoilage.

Bid price   The amount of money the owner must pay the general contractor to build a project.

Detailed cost estimate (final or **definitive cost estimate)**   A forecast of direct materials, direct labor, equipment, subcontractor work, overhead, contingencies, insurance and bonds, and profit, for a project based on a complete set of contract documents, technical specifications, drawings, and site visits.

Job   A job is an individual product, a small batch of unique products, a client, or case, or any other project that materials, labor, and the POR's basis can be directly traced to.

Job cost sheet (job order cost record)   A record set up for each job started into production, which serves as a means for accumulating the direct materials, direct labor, and overhead costs chargeable to the job. It is used as a means for computing unit costs. Job cost sheets are often the subsidiary ledger accounts in WIP for product costs.

Normal spoilage   Rejected products that are expected, and budgeted for, under present conditions.

Preliminary cost estimate (conceptual, approximate, or **budget estimate)**   A ballpark estimate of what costs could be to build a project, including the target profit.

Reworked units   Defective products that are fixed and sold as acceptable finished units.

Scrap   Fragments of material removed during the production or construction process.

Spoilage   A rejected job or products within a job. Spoiled jobs or units are discarded and are sometimes sold for disposal value.

DEMONSTRATION PROBLEMS

■ DEMONSTRATION PROBLEM 1   *Journal entries for a normal JOCAS.*

Using the annual information below for Topper, Inc., prepare the journal entries for each event using a normal JOCAS. (Note: this is the same problem as Demonstration Problem 1 in Chapter 4. It is repeated to facilitate comparisons between journal entries in a basic CAS and in a JOCAS.)

1. Raw materials beginning balance is zero, and the ending balance is $20,000. Purchases made on account are $100,000.
2. There is a $200,000 factory payroll for the year, with the following withholding rates: federal income taxes 10%, state income taxes 5%, Social Security taxes 7.5%, pension plan 2%, health insurance 1.5%.
3. Topper's payroll tax burden and fringe benefits rates are as follows: federal unemployment tax rate = 0.8% and the state's = 5.4%; fringe benefits include vacation pay (2 weeks when 50 weeks are worked in a year), Topper's contribution to a pension plan of 5.0%, and its contribution to the health insurance plan of 3.3%.
4. Other actual overhead costs, paid on account, are $88,000. Factory equipment depreciation equals $200,000.
5. Direct materials requisitioned equal $75,000.
6. $175,000 of factory labor costs represents direct labor.
7. Overhead allocation assuming a POR of 200% of direct labor cost.

New information:

8. The direct materials were for two jobs: job 31 = $50,000 and job 42 = $25,000. (See item 5 above)
9. Job 31 had $100,000 of direct labor, and job 42 had $75,000. (See item 6 above)
10. Job 31 had a beginning balance of $650,000. It was the only job completed and sold.
11. FGI and COGS accounts do not have subsidiary accounts for each job.

Study note: Verify that the only journal entries that have changed from the Chapter 4 solution are the three cost element usage journal entries (JEs 5–7), and that COGS has changed to $1,000,000 due to the sale of job 31.

SOLUTION TO DEMONSTRATION PROBLEM 1

Ref	General Ledger Account Titles	dr's	cr's	Notes:
	PURCHASE (ACQUISITION) OF RAW MATERIALS:			
1:	Raw Materials Inventory	$100,000		given
	Accounts Payable		$100,000	all RMI purchases are charged
	PREPARING (RECORDING) PAYCHECKS:			
2:	Gross Wages	$200,000		given
	FIT Withholdings Payable		$20,000	+$GROSS WAGES*0.1
	SIT Withholdings Payable		$10,000	+$GROSS WAGES*0.05
	FICA Taxes Payable		$15,000	+$GROSS WAGES*0.075
	Pension Plan Payable		$4,000	+$GROSS WAGES*0.02
	Health Insurance Payable		$3,000	+$GROSS WAGES*0.015
	Wages Payable		$148,000	GROSS WAGES − WITHHOLDINGS
	EMPLOYER'S PAYROLL TAXES & BENEFITS (BURDEN):			
3:	Gross Wages	$52,000		SUM(EMPLOYER BURDEN)
	FICA Taxes Payable		$15,000	= withheld from paychecks
	FUTA Taxes Payable		$1,600	+$GROSS WAGES*0.008
	SUTA Taxes Payable		$10,800	+$GROSS WAGES*0.054
	Pension Plan Payable		$10,000	+$GROSS WAGES*0.05
	Health Insurance Payable		$6,600	+$GROSS WAGES*0.033
	Vacation Payable		$8,000	+$GROSS WAGES*0.04
	OTHER OVERHEAD COSTS INCURRED:			
4:	WIP–Manufacturing Overhead (Other OH costs)	$88,000		amounts given
	WIP–Manufacturing Overhead (Depreciation)	$200,000		
	Accounts Payable		$88,000	amounts charged
	Accumulated Depreciation–Factory Equipment		$200,000	
	REQUISITION OF RAW MATERIALS INTO THE FACTORY:			
5:	WIP–Job 31 (DM)	$50,000		given
	WIP–Job 42 (DM)	$25,000		given
	WIP–Manufacturing Overhead (IM)	$5,000		"plug" to balance
	Raw Materials Inventory		$80,000	calculate from T-account
	DISTRIBUTING GROSS WAGES TO PRODUCTS:			
6:	WIP–Job 31 (DL)	$100,000		given
	WIP–Job 42 (DL)	$75,000		given
	WIP–Manufacturing Overhead (IL)	$77,000		"plug" to balance
	Gross Wages		$252,000	gross pay + employer burden
	OVERHEAD ALLOCATION TO PRODUCTS:			
7:	WIP–Job 31 (Applied Overhead)	$200,000		POR = 200% of DL$
	WIP–Job 42 (Applied Overhead)	$150,000		
	WIP–Manufacturing Overhead		$350,000	DL$ = $175,000 (given)
	PRODUCTS COMPLETED:			
8:	Finished Goods Inventory	$1,000,000		COGM calculated within T-account
	WIP–Job 31		$1,000,000	
	PRODUCTS SOLD (INVENTORY RELIEF JOURNAL ENTRY ONLY):			
9:	Cost of Goods Sold	$1,000,000		COGS calculated within T-account
	Finished Goods Inventory		$1,000,000	

JOURNAL ENTRY RECORDING CONVENTIONS:

1. Use a dash to separate a control account from a subsidiary account.
2. Use parentheses for a posting reference within a general ledger account.

■ **DEMONSTRATION PROBLEM 2**   *Accounting for scrap, rework, and spoilage.*

Waste Management Company has a traditional CAS. During the month of April, it incurred some significant scrap, rework, and spoilage costs. As the new management accountant, you have been asked to prepare the journal entries necessary to record these costs. You have found the following information:

Scrap: From the Accounts Receivable Department, receipts issued for the sale of scrap equal $5,000. You check with the shop floor foreman and find that the scrap could not be identified as coming from any particular jobs. Although workers collect scrap after each job and set it aside, no records are kept as to how much came from any job.

Rework: Rework occurred on two jobs during the month. Job 25 rework required $500 in direct materials and $1,000 in direct labor. The shop foreman believed that this was just normal rework that occurs due to the type of production process in place. He did believe, though, that this amount was a bit curious. Job 28 rework costs were due to the special nature of the job. These costs were not significant, however, being only $75 in direct materials and $100 in direct labor.

Spoilage: Forty products made in job 27 were rejected by quality control inspection. From talking to the shop floor foreman, you learn that up to 25 rejects were considered normal for this job. The rest were considered beyond normal expectations. This job was not unique relative to any other job, according to the foreman. From the job cost sheet, the direct materials and direct labor costs per unit on this job were $10 and $12, respectively.

From the JOCAS records, you also found that normal rework and spoilage were included in the overhead budget. The POR is based on budgeted direct labor cost of $600,000 for the year. The budgeted overhead included:

Indirect materials	$ 20,000
Indirect labor	40,000
Depreciation	100,000
Factory utilities	50,000
Normal rework	60,000
Normal spoilage	30,000
Total budgeted overhead	$300,000

SOLUTION TO DEMONSTRATION PROBLEM 2

SCRAP JOURNAL ENTRY:

Cash	$5,000	
Scrap Sales		$5,000

Comment: Since the scrap could not be identified with specific jobs, those jobs' costs could not be credited (reduced) and the market value set up in a subsidiary RMI account. If this is a significant amount, since workers collect scrap after each job, possibly the JOCAS should be changed to trace scrap directly to jobs.

REWORK JOURNAL ENTRY:

WIP–Manufacturing Overhead (Rework)	$1,900	
RMI		$ 500
Gross Wages		$1,000
WIP–Manufacturing Overhead		$ 400

Comment: The regular POR is 50% of direct labor cost (total budgeted overhead of $300,000 divided by budgeted direct labor cost of $600,000). However, this POR cannot be used in allocating overhead to the reworked products because it includes an allowance for rework. Normal rework is included in the overhead budget to spread its costs over the good products made. Therefore, the amount of the normal rework in the POR has to be deducted from it to yield a "rework allowance–free" POR. Since normal rework is 10% of direct labor cost ($60,000 ÷ $600,000), the adjusted POR should be 40% of direct labor cost, and the applied overhead should be $400.

Should there be a special journal entry for the abnormal rework on job 28? This is not clear in the problem. Since direct material and direct labor are incurred on the job, whether for regular production or for abnormal rework, these costs are debited to the job. Assuming that this happened in the normal course of recording material requisitions and time tickets, no new journal entry is needed. However, if no special journal entry was separately made for the abnormal rework, it is likely that the regular 50% POR was used in applying overhead to the job. Therefore, the applied overhead is overstated. The correct POR to use on the rework direct labor costs is 40%, not 50%, so the following journal entry may be necessary:

ADJUSTING JOURNAL ENTRY: To Correct Applied OH

WIP–Manufacturing Overhead	$10	
WIP–Job 28 (Applied Overhead)		$10

The overhead applied to the $100 of direct labor cost for the rework should not have been $50 (using the 50% POR), but rather $40 (based on the 40% POR).

If the abnormal rework was separately tracked in the JOCAS and a separate journal entry was made for these costs, it would be:

REWORK JOURNAL ENTRY: Abnormal Rework

WIP–Job 28 (Abnormal Rework)	$215	
RMI		$ 75
Gross Wages		$100
WIP–Manufacturing Overhead		$ 40

SPOILAGE JOURNAL ENTRY:

WIP–Manufacturing Overhead (Spoilage)	$700	
Loss from abnormal spoilage	$420	
WIP–Job 27		$1,120

The calculations for normal (charged to overhead) and abnormal spoilage (written off to a loss account) are:

COST ELEMENT	NORMAL	ABNORMAL
Direct materials	$250	$150
Direct labor	300	180
Applied overhead	150	90
Totals	$700	$420

Also notice that in applying overhead to all units worked on in the jobs, spoiled and rejected as well as good products, the normal 50% of direct labor cost POR is used. Does it make sense to allocate spoilage to spoiled units? Should some type of adjustment to the spoilage costs be made? These issues are considered in Think-Tank Problem 5.57.

■ **DEMONSTRATION PROBLEM 3** *Estimating the cost of hauling lumber to a job.*
Lumber is usually loaded by laborers directly onto flatbed trucks, hauled to the job, and stacked according to size. A laborer is able to load lumber at an average rate of 3,000 feet board measure (FBM) per hour. The laborer unloads the truck at the same average rate. A truck will transport lumber at 2,000 FBM per load. The job site is 2 miles from the lumberyard, and the truck will travel at an average speed of 20 miles per hour.

The truck driver (who is also a laborer) and a laborer will be used to load, transport, and unload the lumber. The costs are:

Truck @ $10.58 per hour

Truck driver @ $8.10 per hour

Laborer @ $7.50 per hour

The job calls for the transportation of 40,000 FBM of lumber.[9]

---

[9] Ibid., pp. 45–46.

Required:

a. Calculate the total time for the job.

b. Calculate the total cost for the job and the cost per 1,000 FBM.

SOLUTION TO DEMONSTRATION PROBLEM 3

a. Rate of loading/unloading truck, 2 × 3,000 =   6,000 FBM/hr

Time to load truck, 2,000 ÷ 6,000 =	0.33 hr
Time to unload truck, 2,000 ÷ 6,000 =	0.33 hr
Travel time, round trip, 4 miles ÷ 20 MPH =	0.20 hr
Total time per load	0.86 hr

Number of trips per hour, 1 ÷ 0.86 =	1.16
Quantity hauled, 1.16 × 2,000 =	2,320 FBM/hr
Total time for the job, 40,000 ÷ 2,320 =	17.2 hr

An alternative approach to calculating the total time for the job:

Number of truckloads required, 40,000 ÷ 2,000 =	20
Round-trip time per load, 0.86 hours	
Total time for the job, 20 × 0.86 =	17.2 hr

b. Total cost for the job is:

Truck, 17.2 hours @ $10.58 =	$181.98
Truck driver, 17.2 hours @ $8.10 =	139.32
Laborer, 17.2 hours @ $7.50 =	129.00
Total cost	$450.30

Cost per 1,000 FBM, $450.30 ÷ 40 = $11.26

REVIEW QUESTIONS

5.1 List and briefly describe the three main informational inputs to the normal JOCAS. Why is this information important and how is it used?

5.2 What is the purpose of the job cost sheet?

5.3 What information does the job cost sheet contain, and how does management use these records?

5.4 Outline the format of the job cost sheet and explain the purpose of each of its elements.

5.5 Although marketing and administrative costs are not normally charged to jobs, explain why such costs may be included in the job cost sheet.

5.6 Describe the flow of data in a JOCAS.

5.7 Which basic CAS journal entries change in a normal JOCAS?

5.8 Which basic CAS journal entries do not change in a normal JOCAS?

5.9 Why do some journal entries change, but others do not?

5.10 Which general ledger account titles change from a basic CAS? Why?

5.11 Explain why JOCASs are equally applicable to manufacturing, service, and construction organizations. Describe the types of manufacturing organizations in which JOCASs are not applicable.

5.12 What is scrap?

5.13 How is scrap accounted for in a traditional JOCAS?

5.14 How is scrap accounted for in a world-class JOCAS?

5.15 What are reworked units?

5.16 How are reworked units accounted for if rework is considered a normal result of the overall production system?

5.17 How is rework accounted for when it is a unique result of special jobs?

5.18 What adjustment has to be made to the regular POR when allocating overhead costs to special rework unique to a particular job?

5.19 How is rework accounted for in a world-class JOCAS?

5.20 Distinguish between normal and abnormal spoilage.

5.21 Describe the accounting procedure for normal spoilage in a traditional JOCAS.

5.22 What is the traditional JOCAS accounting procedure for abnormal spoilage?

5.23 How are the traditional procedures for spoilage accounting changed in a world-class JOCAS?

5.24 Describe how computers are used for cost estimating and cost management.

5.25 Explain the purpose of work item software and describe how it is used.

5.26 Explain why construction companies often add direct equipment as a fourth cost element. Do you recommend that highly automated manufacturers do the same? Explain why or why not.

5.27 Explain how service organizations can also use work item software.

5.28 Explain how work item software aids management in monitoring and controlling jobs.

5.29 List and briefly describe the necessary features of a JOCAS software system.

5.30 List and briefly describe the three main elements applicable to estimating construction costs.

5.31 Explain why cost estimating is the lifeblood of the construction industry.

5.32 Explain the purpose of a preliminary cost estimate.

5.33 Explain why it is helpful in cost estimating to reduce the project to its basic parameters.

5.34 Explain how costs of previous projects are adjusted so that they can be used in cost estimating.

5.35 What is the purpose of a detailed cost estimate? Distinguish a detailed cost estimate from a preliminary cost estimate.

5.36 List and briefly describe the steps for preparing a detailed cost estimate.

5.37 Briefly describe the two methods used to organize work items for preparing the cost estimate and computing a bid price.

CHAPTER-SPECIFIC PROBLEMS

These problems require responses based directly on concepts and techniques presented in the text.

5.38 *Making the appropriate journal entry.* Freeflow Company manufactures pipe and uses a normal JOCAS. During May, the following jobs were started (no other jobs were in process), and the following costs were incurred:

	JOB X	JOB Y	JOB Z	TOTALS
Materials requisitioned	$10,000	$20,000	$15,000	$45,000
Direct labor	5,000	4,000	2,500	11,500
	$15,000	$24,000	$17,500	$56,500

In addition, estimated overhead of $600,000 and direct labor costs of $150,000 were budgeted for the year. Overhead is applied on the basis of direct labor cost.

Required:
Make the appropriate journal entries to record the initiation of all jobs.

[CIA adapted]

5.39 *Normal JOCAS journal entries.* Using the information from the previous problem, and the additional information below, make the remaining journal entries for Freeflow's normal JOCAS.

- Raw materials purchases were $45,000 and requisitions were $50,000.
- There was a $20,000 factory payroll for May, with the following withholding rates: federal income taxes 10%, state income taxes 5%, Social Security taxes 7.5%, pension plan 2%, health insurance 1.5%.
- Freeflow's payroll tax burden and fringe benefits rates are as follows: federal unemployment tax rate = 0.8% and the state's = 5.4%; fringe benefits include vacation pay (2 weeks when 50 weeks are worked in a year), Freeflow's contribution into a pension plan of 5.0%, and to their health insurance plan of 3.3%.

■ Overhead costs include $4,000 in an accrual of utilities owed and factory equipment depreciation of $20,000. At the end of April, there was a $3,000 under-applied overhead account balance.

■ Jobs X and Y were started in April, incurring direct materials costs of $20,000 and $5,000 respectively that month. They also incurred direct labor costs in April of $6,000 and $4,000 respectively. Jobs X and Z were completed in May. Job X was sold. Both FGI and COGS contain subsidiary accounts for jobs.

5.40 *Job cost reports.* Using the information from the preceding problem, manually prepare a May WIP inventory and job cost report for Freeflow Company. Use the format in Exhibit 5–9.

5.41 *Calculating direct materials costs charged to a job.* For the month of April, the following debits (credits) appeared in the general ledger WIP inventory control account:

APRIL		
1	Balance	$ 24,000
30	Direct materials	80,000
30	Direct labor	60,000
30	Factory overhead	54,000
30	To finished goods	<200,000>

The JOCAS applies overhead to production using a POR of 90% of direct labor cost. Job 100, the only job still in process at the end of April, has been charged with factory overhead of $4,500.

Required:
Calculate the amount of direct materials charged to job 100.

[AICPA adapted]

5.42 *Journal entries in a normal JOCAS.* The following information for Abram's Jeans, Inc., a manufacturer based in San Jose, California, has been obtained from the various databases in its ICBIS JOCAS during the month of August:

1. Raw materials purchases made on account are $50,000.
2. There is a $100,000 factory payroll for the month with the following withholding rates: federal income taxes 15%, state income taxes 3%, Social Security taxes 7.5%, pension plan 1%, health insurance 1.5%.
3. Abram's payroll tax burden and fringe benefits rates are as follows: federal unemployment tax rate = 0.6% and the state's = 4.7%; fringe benefits include vacation pay (3 weeks when 49 weeks are worked in a year), Abram's contribution to a pension plan of 2.0%, and its contribution to the health insurance plan of 3.0%. Round all amounts to whole dollars.
4. Other actual overhead costs, paid on account, are $36,000. Factory equipment depreciation equals $70,000.
5. Raw materials requisitioned equal $80,000. Direct materials for job 14 are $50,000; and for job 26, $25,000.
6. Job 14 incurred $40,000 of direct labor costs, while job 26 incurred $20,000.
7. Overhead is allocated using a POR of $100 per machine hour. Job 14 used 1,000 Mhr in August, while job 26 used 750 Mhr. The beginning overhead account balance = $4,000 (underapplied). debit
8. Job 26 was completed and sold during August. It had a beginning balance in its job cost sheet of $5,000 in direct materials, $10,000 in direct labor, and 200 Mhr.

Required:
Prepare all the journal entries to record August activity.

5.43 *Job cost reports.* Using the information from the preceding problem, manually prepare an August WIP inventory and job cost report for Abram's Jeans. Use the format in Exhibit 5–9.

5.44 *Calculating cost of goods manufactured and overhead.* The Hamilton Company uses a JOCAS. Factory overhead is applied to production at a predetermined rate of 150% of direct labor cost. Any over- or underapplied factory overhead is closed to the cost of goods sold account at the end of each month. Additional information is available as follows:

Job 101 was the only job in process at January 31, with accumulated costs as follows:

Direct materials	$4,000
Direct labor	2,000
Applied factory overhead	3,000
	$9,000

Jobs 102, 103, and 104 were started during February.

Direct materials requisitions for February totaled $26,000.

Direct labor cost of $20,000 was incurred for February.

Actual factory overhead for February was $32,000.

The only job still in process on February 28 was job 104, with costs of $2,800 for direct materials and $1,800 for direct labor.

Required:
a. What was the cost of goods manufactured for February?
b. What was the amount of over- or underapplied overhead closed to the cost of goods sold account at February 28?

[AICPA adapted]

5.45 *Calculating the total manufacturing costs of a job.* Tillman Corporation uses a JOCAS and has two production departments, M and A. Budgeted manufacturing costs for the year are as follows:

	M	A
Direct materials	$700,000	$100,000
Direct labor	200,000	800,000
Manufacturing overhead	600,000	400,000

The actual direct materials and direct labor costs charged to job 432 during the year were as follows:

Direct materials		$25,000
Direct labor:		
Department M	$ 8,000	
Department A	12,000	20,000

Tillman applies overhead to production orders on the basis of direct labor cost, using separate departmental PORs determined at the beginning of the year based on the annual budget. Thus, there are two overhead application journal entries.

Required:
Calculate the total production costs associated with job 432.

[AICPA adapted]

5.46 *Journal entries for spoilage.* The D. Hayes Cramer Company manufactures product C, which has costs per unit of $1 for materials, $2 for labor, and $3 for overhead. During the month of May, 1,000 units of product C were spoiled. These units could be sold for scrap at $.60 each. The 1,000 units all came from job 1236.

The accountant said that any one of the following entries could be made for these 1,000 lost or spoiled units:

1.	Spoiled goods	$600	
	WIP–Materials		$100
	WIP–Labor		$200
	WIP–Overhead		$300

2.	Spoiled goods	$ 600	
	Manufacturing expenses	$5,400	
	WIP–Materials		$1,000
	WIP–Labor		$2,000
	WIP–Overhead		$3,000

3.	Spoiled goods	$ 600	
	Loss on spoiled goods	$5,400	
	WIP–Materials		$1,000
	WIP–Labor		$2,000
	WIP–Overhead		$3,000

4.	Spoiled goods	$ 600	
	Receivable	$5,400	
	WIP–Materials		$1,000
	WIP–Labor		$2,000
	WIP–Overhead		$3,000

Required:
a. Indicate the circumstances under which each of these four solutions would be appropriate.
b. Discuss any problems you see in the general ledger account titles used. Recommend correct account titles.
c. Recommend the appropriate journal entries if a world-class JOCAS were used.

[AICPA adapted]

5.47 *Estimating cost of equipment.* The ideal output of a backhoe is 180 cubic yards per hour. On a particular job, the average volume of a 1-cubic yard bucket is .8 cubic yards, with the bucket actually operating only 45 minutes per hour. The total cost of the backhoe, including the operator, is $100 per hour. The job calls for the excavation of 10,800 cubic yards.

Required:
Calculate the number of hours and the total cost to do the job.

5.48 *Estimating labor costs.* An ironworker works 10 hours per day, 6 days per week. A base wage of $15.80 per hour is paid for all straight-time work, 8 hours per day, 5 days per week. An overtime rate of time and one-half is paid for all hours over 8 hours per day, Monday through Friday, and double time is paid for all Saturday work. The Social Security tax is 7.51%, and the unemployment tax is 3% of actual wages. The rate for worker's compensation insurance is $5.50 per $100.00 of base wages, and the public liability and property damage insurance rate is $3.25 per $100.00 of base wages. Fringe benefits are $1.27 per hour.

Required:
a. Calculate the average hourly cost to hire an ironworker.
b. If there are five ironworkers in a crew and the crew can place 6,500 pounds of reinforcing steel per day, calculate the labor cost per pound.

5.49 *Estimating the cost of excavating a trench.* A proposed job calls for excavating a trench 3 feet wide, 6 feet deep, and 2,940 feet long in ordinary earth. A ladder-type trenching machine will be used, and there will be no obstructions to retard the progress of the trenching machine.

The average speed of the trenching machine is 40 feet per hour. The cost to transport the trenching machine to and from the job is $1,260.00. The trenching machine costs $86.25 per hour. The following additional resources will be required to perform the job:

Utility truck @ $12.50 per hour
Machine operator @ $16.50 per hour
Truck driver @ $5.10 per hour

Two laborers @ $6.90 per hour each
Foreman @ $17.30 per hour

Required:
Estimate the total cost and the cost per linear foot for excavating the trench.

5.50 *Estimating the cost of handling bricks.* Upon arrival at the job, 60,480 bricks are to be unloaded. This stockpile of bricks will be loaded on a tractor that transports the bricks around the perimeter of the structure where the bricks will be laid. The tractor can transport 1,600 bricks per hour. At the perimeter, laborers, using brick tongs, can carry an average of 8 bricks per load to the brick masons for laying. The average time for a trip is 45 seconds. The costs are as follows:

Tractor $19.00 per hour
Operator $9.50 per hour
Laborers $7.50 per hour

Required:
Calculate the cost per brick for handling 60,480 bricks.

5.51 *Estimating the cost of a building.* The management accountant at Tyler Builders is to provide a cost estimate for a proposed building project. The job will consist of a building that contains 32,500 square feet of floor area. The building is to be constructed three years from now in city A. A similar building that contained 48,300 square feet was completed last year in city C for a cost of $3,308,550.

Required:
The management accountant has kept time and location indices like those presented in the chapter. Using these indices, estimate the cost of the building under consideration.

5.52 *Estimating the cost of a building.* Following are cost data of completed projects stored in a database:

PROJECT	TOTAL COST	SQUARE FEET
1	$147,300	1,580
2	153,700	2,900
3	128,100	2,100
4	118,400	1,850
5	135,700	2,300

Required:
Calculate the weighted unit cost per square foot for the above project data and determine the cost of a project consisting of 2,700 square feet.

THINK-TANK PROBLEMS

Although these problems are based on chapter material, reading extra material, reviewing previous chapters, and using creativity may be required to develop workable solutions.

5.53 *Calculation of dollar balances and application of overhead.* Constructo, Inc., is a manufacturer of furnishings for infants and children. The company uses a normal job order costing system. Constructo's WIP inventory at April 30, 19X4, consisted of the following jobs:

JOB NUMBER	ITEMS	UNITS	ACCUMULATED COST
CBS102	Cribs	20,000	$ 900,000
PLP086	Playpens	15,000	420,000
DRS114	Dressers	25,000	250,000
			$1,570,000

The company's finished goods inventory, using the FIFO method, consisted of five items:

ITEM	QUANTITY AND UNIT COST	ACCUMULATED COST
Cribs	7,500 units @ $64 each	$ 480,000
Strollers	13,000 units @ $23 each	299,000
Carriages	11,200 units @ $102 each	1,142,400
Dressers	21,000 units @ $55 each	1,155,000
Playpens	19,400 units @ $35 each	679,000
		$3,755,400

Constructo applies factory overhead on the basis of direct labor hours. The company's factory overhead budget for the fiscal year ending May 31, 19X4, totals $4,500,000, and the company plans to expend 600,000 direct labor hours during this period. Through the first 11 months of the year, a total of 555,000 direct labor hours were worked, and total factory overhead amounted to $4,273,500.

At the end of April, the balance in Constructo's RMI account, which includes both raw materials and purchased parts, was $668,000. Additions to and requisitions from RMI during the month of May included the following:

	RAW MATERIALS	PURCHASED PARTS
Additions	$242,000	$396,000
Requisitions:		
Job CBS102	51,000	104,000
Job PLP086	3,000	10,800
Job DRS114	124,000	87,000
Job STR077 (10,000 strollers)	62,000	81,000
Job CRG098 (5,000 carriages)	65,000	187,000

During the month of May, Constructo's factory payroll consisted of the following:

ACCOUNT	HOURS	COST
CBS102	12,000	$122,400
PLP086	4,400	43,200
DRS114	19,500	200,500
STR077	3,500	30,000
CRG098	14,000	138,000
Indirect	3,000	29,400
Supervision		57,600
		$621,100

The following are the jobs that were completed and the unit sales for the month of May:

JOB NUMBER	ITEMS	QUANTITY COMPLETE
CBS102	Cribs	20,000
PLP086	Playpens	15,000
STR077	Strollers	10,000
CRG098	Carriages	5,000

ITEMS	QUANTITY SHIPPED
Cribs	17,500
Playpens	21,000
Strollers	14,000
Dressers	18,000
Carriages	6,000

Required:
a. Describe when it is appropriate for a company to use a job order cost system.
b. Calculate the dollar balance in Constructo's WIP inventory account as of May 31, 19X4.

c. Calculate the dollar amount related to the playpens in Constructo's finished goods inventory as of May 31, 19X4.

d. Explain the proper accounting treatment for over- or underapplied overhead balances when using a job order cost system.

[CMA adapted]

5.54 *Application of overhead and cost of goods manufactured.* Valpor Company employs a normal JOCAS. Manufacturing overhead is applied on the basis of machine hours using estimated manufacturing overhead costs of $1,200,000 and an estimated activity level of 80,000 Mhr. Valport's policy is to close the over/under application of manufacturing overhead to cost of goods sold.

Operations for the year ended November 30, 19X5, have been completed, and all of the accounting entries have been made for the year except the application of manufacturing overhead to the jobs worked on during November, the transfer of costs from WIP to finished goods for the jobs completed in November, and the transfer of costs from finished goods to cost of goods sold for the jobs sold during November. Jobs N11-007, N11-013, and N11-015 were completed during November 19X5. All completed jobs except job N11-013 had been turned over to customers by the close of business on November 30, 19X5.

Summarized data that have been accumulated from the accounting records as of October 31, 19X5, and for November 19X5, are as follows:

WORK-IN-PROCESS		NOVEMBER 19X5 ACTIVITY		
JOB NUMBER	BALANCE 10/31/X5	DIRECT MATERIALS	DIRECT LABOR	MACHINE HOURS
N11-007	$ 87,000	$ 1,500	$ 4,500	300
N11-013	55,000	4,000	12,000	1,000
N11-015	–0–	25,600	26,700	1,400
D12-002	–0–	37,900	20,000	2,500
D12-003	–0–	26,000	16,800	800
Totals	$142,000	$95,000	$80,000	6,000

OPERATING ACTIVITY	ACTIVITY THROUGH 10/31/X5	NOVEMBER 19X5 ACTIVITY
Manufacturing overhead incurred		
Indirect materials	$ 125,000	$ 9,000
Indirect labor	345,000	30,000
Utilities	245,000	22,000
Depreciation	385,000	35,000
Total incurred overhead	$1,100,000	$96,000
Other items		
Material purchases*	$965,000	$98,000
Direct labor costs	$845,000	$80,000
Machine hours	73,000	6,000

ACCOUNT BALANCES AT BEGINNING OF FISCAL YEAR	12/01/X4
Materials inventory*	$105,000
Work-in-process inventory	60,000
Finished goods inventory	125,000

* Material purchases and materials inventory consist of both direct and indirect materials. The balance of the materials inventory account as of November 30, 19X5, is $85,000.

Required:

a. Valport Company uses a predetermined overhead rate to apply manufacturing overhead to its jobs. When overhead is accounted for in this manner, there may be over- or underapplied overhead.

1. Explain why a business uses a predetermined overhead rate to apply manufacturing overhead to its jobs.
2. How much manufacturing overhead would Valport have applied to jobs through October 31, 19X5?
3. How much manufacturing overhead would Valport apply to jobs during November 19X5?
4. Determine the amount by which the manufacturing overhead is over- or underapplied as of November 30, 19X5. Be sure to indicate whether the overhead is over- or underapplied.
5. Over- or underapplied overhead must be eliminated at the end of the accounting period. Explain why Valport's method of closing over- or underapplied overhead to the cost of goods sold is acceptable in this case.

b. Determine the balance in Valport Company's finished goods inventory at November 30, 19X5.
c. Prepare a Schedule of Cost of Goods Manufactured for Valport Company for the year ended November 30, 19X5.

[CMA adapted]

5.55 *Calculating and applying overhead in a JOCAS.* Baehr Company's fiscal year runs from July 1 to June 30. The company uses a normal job order costing system for its production costs. A predetermined overhead rate based upon direct labor hours is used to apply overhead to individual jobs. A flexible budget of overhead costs was prepared for the fiscal year as follows:

DIRECT LABOR HOURS

	100,000	120,000	140,000
Variable overhead costs	$325,000	$390,000	$455,000
Fixed overhead costs	216,000	216,000	216,000
Total overhead	$541,000	$606,000	$671,000

Although the annual ideal capacity is 150,000 direct labor hours, company officials have determined 120,000 direct labor hours to be normal capacity for the year.

The following information is for November. Job 87-50 was completed and sold during November. During October, job 87-50 incurred $20,850 in direct materials and 3,000 direct labor hours.

Inventories, November 1:
Raw materials and supplies	$ 10,500
WIP (job 87-50)	54,000
Finished goods	112,500

Purchases of raw materials and supplies:
Raw materials	$135,000
Supplies	15,000
	$150,000

Materials and supplies requisitioned for production:
Job 87-50	$ 45,000
Job 87-51	37,500
Job 87-52	25,500
Supplies	12,000
	$120,000

Factory direct labor hours:
Job 87-50	3,500
Job 87-51	3,000
Job 87-52	2,000
	8,500

Labor costs:

Direct labor wages	$ 51,000
Indirect labor wages (4,000 hours)	15,000
Supervisory salaries	6,000
	$ 72,000

Building occupancy costs (heat, light, depreciation, etc.):

Factory facilities	$ 6,500
Sales offices	1,500
Administrative offices	1,000
	$ 9,000

Factory equipment costs:

Power	$ 4,000
Repairs and maintenance	1,500
Depreciation	1,500
Other	1,000
	$ 8,000

Required:
a. What is the predetermined overhead rate to be used in applying overhead to individual jobs during the fiscal year?
b. Prepare all possible journal entries for the JOCAS.
c. Manually prepare a WIP inventory and job cost report for November using the format in Exhibit 5–9.
d. Without prejudice to your answer to Requirement (a), assume the POR is $4.50 per direct labor hour.
  1. What is the total cost of job 87-50?
  2. What was the applied overhead cost to job 87-52 during November?
  3. What were the total amounts of overhead costs applied to jobs during November?
  4. What were the actual overhead costs incurred during November?

[CMA adapted]

5.56 *Analyzing cost flows and inventories with a JOCAS.* Targon, Inc., manufactures lawn equipment. A job order costing system is used because the products are produced in batches rather than on a continuous basis. The balances in selected general ledger accounts for the 11-month period ended November 30, 19X5, were as follows:

Materials inventory	$ 32,000
WIP inventory	1,200,000
Finished goods inventory	2,785,000
Overhead control	2,260,000
Cost of goods sold	14,200,000

The following additional information is also available:

1. The WIP inventory at November 30 consisted of two jobs:

JOB NUMBER	UNITS	ITEMS	TOTAL COST AS OF NOVEMBER 30
105	50,000	Estate sprinklers	$ 700,000
106	40,000	Economy sprinklers	500,000
			$1,200,000

2. The finished goods inventory at November 30 consisted of five separate items in stock:

ITEMS	QUANTITY AND UNIT COST	TOTAL COST
Estate sprinklers	5,000 units @ $22 each	$ 110,000
Deluxe sprinklers	115,000 units @ $17 each	1,955,000
Brass nozzles	10,000 gross @ $14 per gross	140,000
Rainmaker nozzles	5,000 gross @ $16 per gross	80,000
Connectors	100,000 gross @ $5 per gross	500,000
		$2,785,000

3. Manufacturing overhead cost is applied to jobs on a basis of direct labor hours. For 19X5, management estimated that the company would work 400,000 direct labor hours and incur $2,400,000 in manufacturing overhead cost.
4. A total of 367,000 direct labor hours were worked during the first 11 months of the year (through November 30).

Items (5) through (10) below summarize the activity that took place in the company during December 19X5.

5. A total of $708,000 in raw materials was purchased during the month.
6. Raw materials were drawn from inventory and charged as follows:

JOB NUMBER	QUANTITY AND ITEMS	MATERIAL CHARGED
105	See above	$210,000
106	See above	6,000
201	30,000 gross rainmaker nozzles	181,000
202	10,000 deluxe sprinklers	92,000
203	50,000 ring sprinklers	163,000
—	Indirect materials	20,000
		$672,000

7. The payroll during December was as follows:

JOB NUMBER	HOURS	TOTAL COST
105	6,000	$ 62,000
106	2,500	26,000
201	18,000	182,000
202	500	5,000
203	5,000	52,000
Indirect labor	8,000	84,000
Sales and administration	—	120,000
		$531,000

8. Other costs incurred in the factory during December were:

Depreciation	$62,500
Utilities	15,000
Insurance	1,000
Property taxes	3,500
Maintenance	5,000
	$87,000

9. Jobs completed during December and the number of good units transferred to the finished goods warehouse were as follows:

JOB NUMBER	QUANTITY	ITEMS
105	50,000 units	Estate sprinklers
106	40,000 units	Economy sprinklers
201	30,000 gross	Rainmaker nozzles
203	50,000 units	Ring sprinklers

10. Finished products were shipped to customers during December as follows:

ITEMS	QUANTITY
Estate sprinklers	16,000 units
Deluxe sprinklers	32,000 units
Economy sprinklers	20,000 units
Ring sprinklers	22,000 units
Brass nozzles	5,000 gross
Rainmaker nozzles	10,000 gross
Connectors	26,000 gross

Required:

a. Determine the amount of under- or overapplied overhead for the year 19X5.

b. What is the appropriate accounting treatment for this under- or overapplied overhead balance? Explain your answer.

c. Determine the dollar balance in the WIP inventory account as of December 31, 19X5. Show all computations in good form.

d. For the estate sprinklers only, determine the dollar balance in the finished goods inventory account as of December 31, 19X5. Assume a FIFO flow of units. Show all computations in good form.

[CMA adapted]

5.57 *Accounting for scrap, rework, and spoilage.* Recommend a new scrap, rework, and spoilage policy for Waste Management's JOCAS in Demonstration Problem 2. Discuss how the raw data will be obtained to administer the new method. Using the information from April, prepare all journal entries required by your new plan. Consider job 28. Is it wrong to use the lower POR on all rework if some of it must have been normal? How about rework? Should the POR include any allowances for scrap, rework, or spoilage?

5.58 *Design considerations for a world-class JOCAS.* Consider the characteristics of quality information and WCMs discussed in the first two chapters. What implications do these characteristics have for the design of a JOCAS?

5.59 *Spreadsheet programs for JOCASs.* Create a spreadsheet program for JOCAS reporting using the format in Exhibit 5–9. Use the information from Demonstration Problem 1 to create a job order cost report for Topper, Inc. Job 31 incurred $150,000 in direct labor last year.

5.60 *Spreadsheet programs for JOCASs.* Using the spreadsheet program created in Problem 5.59, input the data for Freeflow's May transactions in Problems 5.38 and 5.39, and print a monthly report.

5.61 *Spreadsheet programs for JOCASs.* Using the spreadsheet program created in Problem 5.59, input the data for Abram's Jeans' August transactions in Problem 5.42 and print a monthly report.

6

THE PROCESS COST ACCOUNTING SYSTEM

Getting ready to package the finished product at Adolph Coors Company.

LEARNING OBJECTIVES

After studying this chapter, you should be able to:

1. Describe the flow of products and their cost elements through continuous processing systems, and prepare the journal entries to record these events.

2. Explain equivalent units of production (EUP), and calculate EUP for each cost element in beginning and ending inventories and in the spoilage.

3. Describe the six steps for departmental cost accounting in a PCAS.

4. Demonstrate the differences in calculating product costs between FIFO and weighted-average methods.

Building a job.

Manufacturing a stream of homogeneous items.

■ INTRODUCTION

Process cost accounting systems (PCASs) are used in mass production environments where homogeneous products flow continuously through processes (departments), such as grinding, mixing, molding, and canning. Examples include beer, cement, flour, dairy products, and paint. As partially completed products move from process to process (department to department), their costs are accumulated within each process and then transferred with the products.

Job order cost accounting systems (JOCASs), on the other hand, are used in industries such as construction, printing, consulting, and some furniture manufacturing companies where each job or batch of products is relatively unique and easily identified. As jobs move through production, costs are accumulated within the job until it is completed.

As with the basic CAS (Chapter 4) and the JOCAS (Chapter 5), perpetual inventory systems with subsidiary ledgers for RMI, WIP, and FGI are generally used in a PCAS. In a JOCAS, direct materials, direct labor, and applied overhead costs are directly traced (journalized) to individual job order cost records. As direct materials are requisitioned for production, their costs move with them out of the RMI subsidiary ledger into the job's subsidiary ledger account in WIP. As jobs are completed, their costs move with them out of the factory (WIP subsidiary ledger account) into FGI. The job cost sheets also move with them, leaving the WIP subsidiary ledger system and becoming the FGI subsidiary ledger system.

The subsidiary ledger system in a PCAS does not accumulate WIP costs by job. Instead WIP subsidiary ledgers are created for each process or department. The FGI subsidiary ledger system is basically the same. Each different type of product (milk, cheese, cream, butter, and so forth) has its own FGI subsidiary ledger account.

Basically, in process costing, WIP costs are accumulated in a particular workcenter, cell, or department for an entire period, such as a month, then this total is divided by the number of units produced during the period. The basic formula for calculating the product's cost in a PCAS is:

$$\text{Unit cost} = \frac{\text{Total department costs}}{\text{Total units produced}}$$

Because each product is indistinguishable from any other product, each bears the same average cost as any other unit during the period.

The basic CAS presented in Chapter 4 is an example of a one-process manufacturing operation. Cost elements are journalized to a single WIP subsidiary account (Product Costs). In multiple-process manufacturing, a WIP subsidiary ledger account is required for each process. The output of process 1 becomes a direct material input into process 2; then the output of process 2 becomes one of the direct materials input into process 3, and so forth.

In a PCAS, instead of using job cost sheets, a **department production cost report** is used to provide a summary of the number of units moving through the department during the period along with their costs. The key differences between a JOCAS and PCAS are summarized in Exhibit 6–1. ▬

JOCAS	PCAS
• Uniquely identifiable jobs are worked on during each period, with each job normally requiring different levels of production resources.	• Identical products are produced on a continuous basis or for long periods of time.
• Costs are accumulated by individual jobs.	• Costs are accumulated by departments.
• The job cost sheet is the record controlling the accumulation of costs by jobs.	• The department production cost report is the key document showing the accumulation of costs by a department.
• Unit costs are computed by job on the job cost sheet.	• Unit costs are calculated by department on the department production cost report.

■EXHIBIT 6–1
Differences between a JOCAS and PCAS

UNDERSTANDING THE FLOW OF UNITS AND COSTS

Costs flow from one department to another as the units being manufactured move through the departments. The PCAS objective is to determine the departmental costs of products so that these costs can be combined to yield the total COGM. The processing departments can be configured in an unlimited number of ways as can the computer technology that supports them, the flow of products through them, and the flow of costs.

LEARNING
OBJECTIVE 1
—
Describe the flow of products and their cost elements through continuous processing systems, and prepare the journal entries to record these events.

What Are the Different Processing and Cost Flows?

Normally most process production flows follow one of two basic configurations:

■ Sequential
■ Parallel

In addition to the flow of goods through these processes, modern plants also integrate computer technology to control processes, collect and process production cost data, and provide various performance measurement reports. The technology is linked together in a network, with computing resources distributed out to where workers and managers need them.

SEQUENTIAL PROCESSING. Sequential processing centers or departments and the supporting computer technology platform are illustrated in Exhibit 6–2. Partially completed products flow from left to right, undergoing different kinds of processing in each processing center. Direct materials, direct labor, and applied overhead costs are traced to each center. Process center 2 receives the partially processed units from process center 1 together with the costs from process center 1. Process center 2 adds its own direct materials, direct labor (if materials and labor are added in process 2), and applied overhead costs. Process center 3 receives the further processed, but still incomplete, units and their costs from process center 2. Process center 3 then adds direct materials, direct labor, and applied overhead costs incurred in its process. The finished products and their total costs are finally transferred out of process center 3 to FGI. The costs of finished goods that are sold are then transferred to the COGS

Controlling paper machines at Boise Cascade

■EXHIBIT 6-2
Sequential Process Flow with Its Supporting Computer Technology Platform

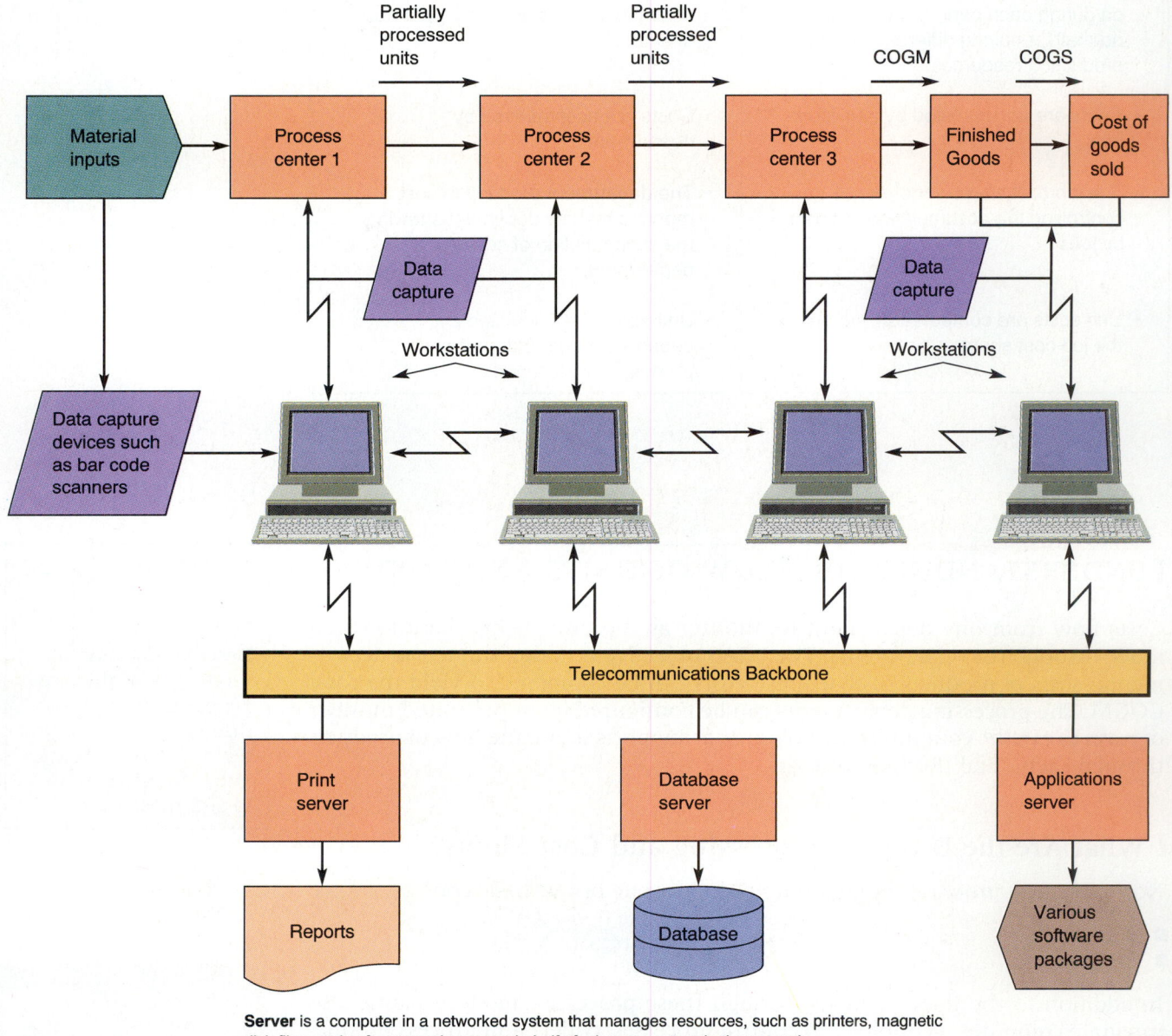

Server is a computer in a networked system that manages resources, such as printers, magnetic disk files, and software packages, on behalf of other computers in the network.

account. Meanwhile, the computer technology platform has collected and processed all the data generated by the total operation.

PARALLEL PROCESSING. In **parallel processing,** different products go through different processing centers or departments, depending on the nature of the product. Exhibit 6-3, illustrates this processing configuration, which is used in companies such as oil refineries. An oil refinery, for example, inputs crude oil into process center A where its output is refined further into several end products. In Exhibit 6-3, process center A performs a ''cracking'' process in which the heavy hydrocarbons in the crude oil are broken up by heat into direct materials for process centers B1 and B2, which produce gasoline. Process

■ EXHIBIT 6–3

Parallel Process Flow with Its Supporting Computer Technology Platform

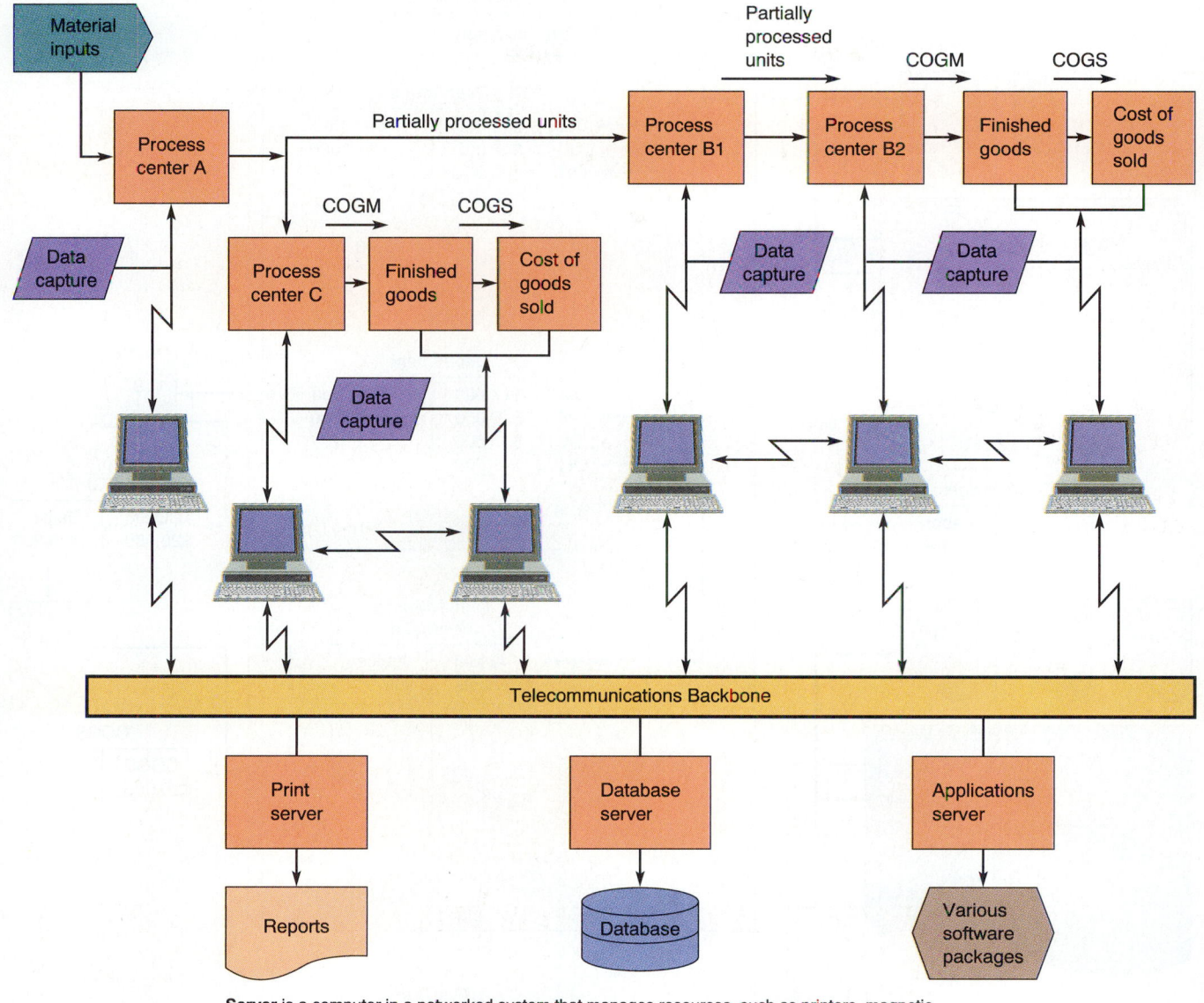

Server is a computer in a networked system that manages resources, such as printers, magnetic disk files, and software packages, on behalf of other computers in the network.

center C processes the materials from A into kerosene. Other joint products (not shown in the exhibit) derived from crude oil are naphtha, benzene, and paraffin. Costing joint products is illustrated in the last section of this chapter.

▌ A Simple Example of the Physical Flow of Units in a PCAS

Exhibit 6–4 presents the physical flow of units, with their cost flows, for processing 10,000 gallons of milk at Model Dairies during May. Direct materials ($10,000), direct labor ($2,000), and applied overhead ($5,000) are used in department 1, where the 10,000 gallons of raw milk are pasteurized. In depart-

■ EXHIBIT 6-4
Sequential Process Cost Flows at Model Dairies

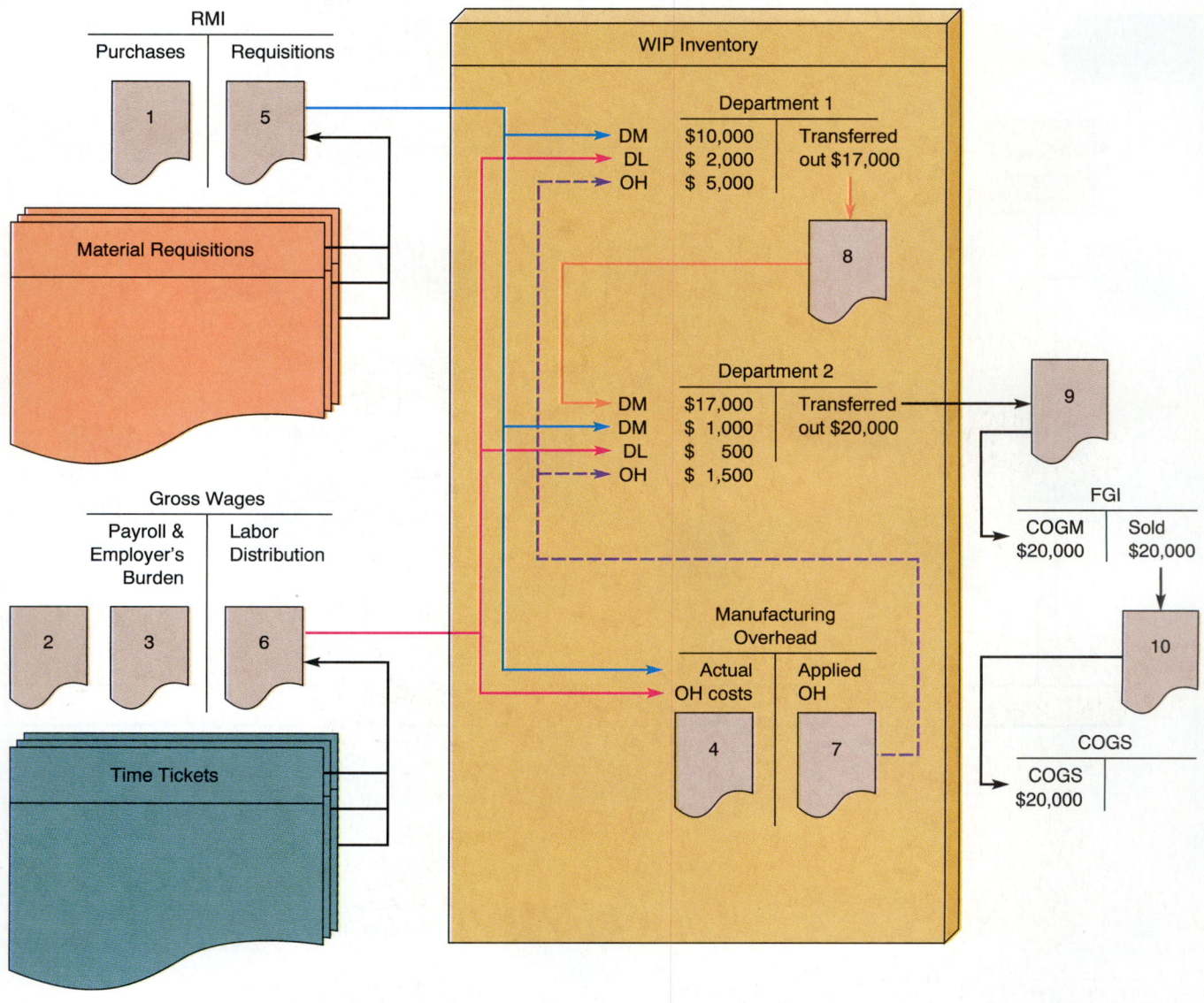

ment 2, where packaging takes place, the pasteurized milk from process 1 is input as a direct material (transferred from process 1 at an average cost of $1.70 per gallon, or $17,000 in total for 10,000 gallons). Milk cartons are requisitioned from RMI ($1,000), and direct labor ($500) and applied overhead ($1,500) are incurred. These four costs are accumulated and divided by production volume to give an average cost per gallon of $2.00 ($20,000 divided by 10,000 gallons). The cartons of milk are transferred to cold storage (FGI at $20,000), awaiting delivery to customers (retail grocery stores). Then, when the milk is delivered, the COGS account is debited for $20,000 and FGI is credited for $20,000.

The PCAS journal entries that are different from those in a JOCAS are shown in Exhibit 6–5. Journal entries 1–4 recording the acquisition of cost elements (DM, DL, actual OH costs) are the same as in a basic CAS (reference Exhibit 4–4) and in a JOCAS (reference Exhibit 5–8).

When recording the usage of inputs, though, PCAS journal entries 5–7 debit WIP–*Department* instead of WIP–*Job* as in a JOCAS. A new journal entry is

EXHIBIT 6–5
Model Dairies PCAS Journal Entries

PARTIAL SPREADSHEET PROGRAM TO RECORD MODEL DAIRIES JOURNAL ENTRIES
For May 1995

Ref	General Ledger Account Titles	dr's	cr's
REQUISITION OF RAW MATERIALS INTO THE FACTORY:			
5:	WIP–Department 1 (DM)	$10,000	
	WIP–Department 2 (DM)	$1,000	
	WIP–Manufacturing Overhead (IM)	?	
	Raw Materials Inventory		?
DISTRIBUTING GROSS WAGES TO PRODUCTS:			
6:	WIP–Department 1 (DL)	$2,000	
	WIP–Department 2 (DL)	$500	
	WIP–Manufacturing Overhead (IL)	?	
	Gross Wages		?
APPLYING OVERHEAD TO PRODUCTS:			
7:	WIP–Department 1 (Applied OH)	$5,000	
	WIP–Department 2 (Applied OH)	$1,500	
	WIP—Manufacturing Overhead		$6,500
WIP TRANSFER FROM DEPARTMENT 1 TO DEPARTMENT 2:			
8:	WIP–Department 2 (DM from Dept. 1)	$17,000	
	WIP–Department 1		$17,000
PRODUCTS COMPLETED:			
9:	Finished Goods Inventory–Milk	$20,000	
	WIP–Department 2		$20,000
PRODUCTS SOLD (INVENTORY RELIEF JOURNAL ENTRY ONLY):			
10:	Cost of Goods Sold–Milk	$20,000	
	Finished Goods Inventory–Milk		$20,000

JOURNAL ENTRY RECORDING CONVENTIONS:
1. Use a dash to separate a control account from a subsidiary account.
2. Use parentheses for a posting reference within a general ledger account.

needed to transfer work-in-process between departments (new journal entry 8 in the PCAS). The journal entries to record the movement of completed products out of the factory and into finished goods inventory, and to record the sale of finished products, have been renumbered. Note that the subsidiary ledger systems for FGI and COGS are not set up by job number (because there are no jobs in a process costing system). Instead, they are set up by type of finished product (milk, butter, cream, cheese, and so on for Model Dairies).

The important point to remember in designing the PCAS general ledger system is that WIP subsidiary accounts are departments rather than jobs. This is the only fundamental difference in assigning product costs between a PCAS and a JOCAS.

In most traditional process systems, though, each department has beginning and ending inventories of partially completed units on its assembly line for any month. This complicates the calculation of the costs of WIP transferred between departments for PCAS journal entry 8. An "equivalent units of production" calculation is needed, as explained in the next section. In JIT processes, where a cell produces the same subassembly over and over again (by kanban), there are no beginning and ending inventories within the cell, so the need to calculate equivalent units does not exist.

LEARNING OBJECTIVE 2

Explain equivalent units of production (EUP), and calculate EUP for each cost element in the beginning and ending inventories and in the spoilage. (This learning objective will be continued on page 232.)

DETERMINING EQUIVALENT UNITS OF PRODUCTION

In the Model Dairies' example, all 10,000 gallons of milk were started and completed during May. But this situation is usually rare. In most traditional process systems, four types of events happen in any accounting period (i.e., a month):

- Products are started in the previous period (beginning WIP) and completed in the current period.
- Products are started in the current period and completed in the period.
- Products are started in the current period but are not completed by the end of the period (ending WIP).
- Products are spoiled (rejected) or reworked during the period.

What Is the Equivalent Units of Production Calculation and Why Is It Needed?

Indeed, when beginning and ending inventories and spoilage exist, a calculation known as **equivalent units of production (EUP)** must be performed to measure how much production (work) was really done during the period. EUP represents the amount of completed output that could have been produced if all the work performed during the period had been for units both started and completed. It is an adjustment for the partial effort in beginning and ending inventories and in spoilage. In other words, EUP is how many units that could have been started, fully processed, and completed with the amount of inputs (costs) used during the month. EUP is divided into the total costs to obtain the cost per equivalent unit produced. This changes the basic formula for calculating unit cost to:

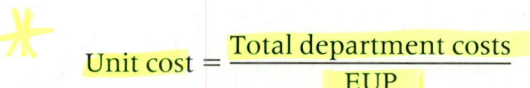

$$\text{Unit cost} = \frac{\text{Total department costs}}{\text{EUP}}$$

Returning to the Model Dairies example, assume that 10,000 gallons of milk were started during May in department 1, but only 9,000 were completed. The last 1,000 units were only 60 percent complete at the end of the month (thus, there were 1,000 gallons in ending WIP for department 1 in May). It is important to recognize that the $17,000 incurred in the department resulted in more than 9,000 gallons worth of milk production. Thus, the unit cost of the 9,000 gallons completed and transferred to department 2 is not $1.89 per gallon ($17,000 divided by 9,000 transferred gallons). Using this unit cost will overstate the cost of the 9,000 gallons transferred to department 2 and will result in no cost being associated with the 1,000 partially processed gallons left over at the end of May in ending WIP inventory.

Work was done on the ending WIP, so cost should be associated with it by the PCAS. But, how much? Ending WIP contained 1,000 gallons 60 percent complete, which is equivalent to the amount of work needed to fully complete 600 gallons (1,000 units 60 percent complete *is equivalent to* 600 units 100 percent complete). The formula for EUP is:

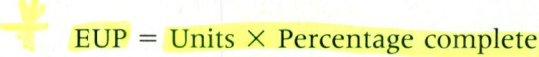

$$\text{EUP} = \text{Units} \times \text{Percentage complete}$$

In department 1 during May, Model Dairies could have made 600 gallons of completely processed milk (pasteurized and ready to transfer to department 2) with the amount of work done on the ending WIP. This amount is *in addition to* the 9,000 gallons completed and transferred. Thus, Model Dairies pasteurized 9,000 gallons completely plus 1,000 gallons only 60 percent, *or equivalently,* the company did enough work to have made 9,600 gallons of fully pasteurized (completed) milk.

The $17,000 in input costs used (recorded in journal entries 5–7) was enough to produce 9,600 gallons from start to finish (i.e., "from scratch"). On average, then, it cost $1.77 (rounded) per gallon to pasteurize milk in department 1 during May ($17,000 divided by 9,600 EUP). The total department 1 cost of the 9,000 gallons transferred out should be $15,930 ($1.77 per gallon times 9,000 gallons).

Computing Equivalent Units of Production

The preceding example just considered the EUP for ending WIP. The EUP calculation is needed for each subset (or group) of partially completed units in the department for the month:

- The partially completed products in beginning WIP
- The partially completed products in ending WIP
- The partially completed products that are rejected during the month (spoilage)

Additionally, the EUP calculation has to be performed for each cost element that is input into the process at a different time, or in different amounts, from the other inputs. To demonstrate, consider again Model Dairies' ending WIP of 1,000 gallons in department 1. Those gallons were 60 percent complete. In other words, they were 60 percent through the department 1 process. But since all the raw milk was added at the beginning of the process, these 1,000 gallons were really 100 percent complete *with respect to the amount (and cost) of raw milk input.* Further complicating the unit cost calculation, only one-half of the direct labor needed to fully process these gallons had been incurred up to this point. So, the 1,000 gallons were only 50 percent complete *with respect to direct labor.* Finally, assume that overhead costs are used up uniformly throughout the process. Then, if the ending WIP was 60 percent "down-the-line", these 1,000 gallons were 60 percent complete *with respect to overhead.*

Because each cost element is input in differing amounts and at differing times, separate EUP and unit cost calculations have to be performed for each cost element. The management accountant for Model Dairies created a spreadsheet program to perform all these calculations and determine the cost to make a gallon of pasteurized milk in department 1 for May. Exhibit 6–6 shows the output from this program.

There was no beginning WIP or spoilage, so these can be ignored at this time. They will be addressed in the next section. In interpreting the program's output, each cost element should be considered separately. First, consider the direct materials column (DM Added) of the program's Solution Section:

- In total, 10,000 gallons of raw milk were input into the process at a cost of $10,000. Of these, 9,000 gallons were fully processed (completed), plus there were another 1,000 gallons in ending WIP (1,000 gallons times 100 percent complete for the raw milk direct material). In total, EUP for raw milk equals 10,000 gallons. Dividing the $10,000 cost by 10,000 EUP results in a $1.00 per gallon average cost for raw milk.

Second, consider the direct labor column (DL Added):

- Enough labor was used (and cost incurred) to process the 9,000 gallons that were completed, plus 500 EUP in the ending WIP (1,000 gallons times 50 percent complete for labor). The $2,000 incurred on labor was enough to equivalently produce 9,500 completely processed gallons, yielding a unit cost for direct labor of $0.21 per gallon (rounded).

Third, consider the overhead column (Applied OH):

- Enough overhead was incurred to fully process the 9,000 gallons completed, plus another 600 EUP in ending WIP (1,000 gallons times 60 percent complete for overhead). The $5,000 in applied overhead was enough to equivalently

■■■ EXHIBIT 6–6
Model Dairies Department 1 Unit Cost

PCAS FOR MODEL DAIRIES
SPREADSHEET PROGRAM TO CALCULATE DEPARTMENT 1'S COST PER EUP
For May 1995

DATA SECTION:

	Units	DM Added	DL Added	Applied OH
Beginning WIP Inventory	0			
Beginning WIP %Complete				
Beginning WIP Cost		$0	$0	$0
Units Started	10,000			
Costs Added		$10,000	$2,000	$5,000
Ending WIP Inventory	1,000			
Ending WIP %Complete		100.00%	50.00%	60.00%
Units Completed	9,000			
Output Loss	0			
Output Loss %Complete				

SOLUTION SECTION:

MODEL DAIRIES
DEPARTMENT 1 COST REPORT
MAY 1995

EUP:	Units	DM Added	DL Added	Applied OH	Totals
Units Completed	9,000	9,000	9,000	9,000	
Less Beginning WIP	0	0	0	0	
Add Ending WIP	1,000	1,000	500	600	
Add Output Loss	0	0	0	0	
UNITS STARTED	10,000				
EQUIVALENT UNITS		10,000	9,500	9,600	
COST PER EUP:					
Beginning WIP Cost		$0	$0	$0	$0
Costs Added This Month		10,000	2,000	5,000	17,000
COSTS INCURRED		$10,000	$2,000	$5,000	$17,000
UNIT COSTS		$1.00	$0.21	$0.52	$1.73

produce 9,600 completely processed gallons, yielding a unit cost for overhead of $0.52 per gallon (rounded).

In total, then, the cost of fully processing a gallon of raw milk into pasteurized milk within department 1 during May was $1.73 (the sum of the three inputs' unit costs).

Note that this example included the ending WIP percentage complete for each cost element. If information is only available from the shop floor as to the stage of completion of beginning WIP, ending WIP, or spoilage, then the management accountant will have to figure out what percentage complete each input is at these stages. In other words, the management accountant must answer the question, "If the ending WIP is 60 percent processed, what percentage complete is each cost element at that stage of the process?" This is the second of the six steps involved in departmental cost accounting in a PCAS.

LEARNING
OBJECTIVE 3
—
Describe the six steps
for departmental cost
accounting in a PCAS.

▌STEPS IN PREPARING THE PCAS JOURNAL ENTRY 8 FOR DEPARTMENT TRANSFERS

The best way to learn how to set up and perform the steps necessary in preparing journal entry 8 is to go through, in detail, steps 2 through 5 in the six-step approach to departmental cost accounting. This section will highlight all six steps. In the next section, steps 2 through 5 will be demonstrated.

The Six-Step Approach to Departmental Cost Accounting

Step 1. *Journalize the acquisition and use of the cost elements.* As in any basic CAS, journal entries 1–7 must be prepared and posted to the appropriate subsidiary ledger accounts in RMI and WIP.

Step 2. *Summarize the flow of cost elements and calculate the inputs' percentage complete.* Units must be identified, such as those started in this period and those still in process from the previous period. This determines the number of units "to account for." Units are "accounted for" according to whether they are transferred to the next process (department) or to finished goods (if this is the last department in the factory), are still in process (ending WIP), or were spoiled. The total units "accounted for" must agree with the total units "to account for." Then, the percentage complete of each cost element for the partially completed units must be determined.

Step 3. *Compute equivalent units of production.* EUP must be calculated for each cost element in each subset of units only partially processed during the month (i.e., beginning WIP, ending WIP, and spoilage). If all direct materials are at the same degree of completion, a single direct materials calculation can be made. If multiple direct materials are used and are placed into production at different points, EUP calculations will be needed for each direct material. For example, in making vegetable soup, a tomato stock may be introduced at the beginning of the process, vegetables added at the 30 percent stage of completion, and cans brought in for packaging at the end of the process.

Step 4. *Compute unit production costs.* Once costs are accumulated by the processing centers or departments, and the period's output is determined in terms of EUP, unit production costs are computed by dividing the department's costs by its output expressed in EUP.

Step 5. *Calculate the costs of completed and transferred output, ending WIP, and spoilage.* In this step, total production costs are assigned to units transferred out, ending WIP inventory, and spoiled units. Journal entry 8 is prepared to record the transfer of products to the next department (or to FGI if this is the last department). In a normal PCAS, journal entry 8 is prepared from a department production cost report.

Step 6. *Prepare cost management reports analyzing whether department costs were within budget.* A variety of management control reports can be prepared. In a normal PCAS, departmental costs can be compared against budgeted costs, similar to the job cost reports in Exhibits 5–15 and 5–22 in the previous chapter. In a standard PCAS, standard costs can be used to prepare detailed cost variance reports by department. These types of reports will be illustrated in Chapter 8.

Cost Flows within a Department: FIFO versus Weighted-Average Methods

So far, two production flows *between* departments (processes) have been identified: sequential and parallel processing. The question is, "Which department (WIP subsidiary ledger account) is debited for the costs of WIP transferred out of department X?" The calculation of EUP or unit costs is the same for sequential and parallel processes.

A new question, which does affect the calculation of EUP and unit cost, now needs to be addressed: "How does production flow *through* a particular department?" Most PCASs are based on one of two types of product flows:

first-in, first-out (FIFO) and weighted-average (WA). Differences occur only when beginning WIP exists.

Beginning WIP in a department means that some processing costs are "leftover" from last month. Last month's ending WIP is this month's beginning WIP. With a FIFO flow, the first units worked on are the first units completed. Production flows through a department as if on an assembly line or a JIT. Product 1 is started, then product 2, then product 3, and so forth. Product 1 is finished first, followed by product 2, then 3, and so forth. This production flow allows the PCAS to separate last month's production effort, and costs, from this month's. Thus, with a **first-in, first-out (FIFO) cost flow method,** department production cost reports can be prepared that isolate last month's costs from this month's, promoting cost trend analyses from month to month.

Some production processes within a department do not work on one product after another. For example, in the oil refinery mentioned earlier, when crude oil is input into the cracking process, it is mixed up with crude oil already in the processing tank. The output from this process is a mixture of leftover crude input last month (beginning WIP) and new crude input this month. Because last month's and this month's "work" are commingled, so are the costs in the PCAS. The best the PCAS can do is to compute a weighted- (or moving) average unit cost across the two months. This means that with a **weighted-average (WA) cost flow method,** beginning WIP (and its costs) are averaged with work (and costs) done this month in calculating EUP and unit costs. *Thus, the only difference between the FIFO and WA methods is whether beginning WIP is separately accounted for or averaged in with this month's work.*

LEARNING OBJECTIVE 2

Explain equivalent units of production (EUP), and calculate EUP for each cost element in the beginning and ending inventories and in the spoilage.

PRODUCT COSTING FOR FIRST-IN, FIRST-OUT (FIFO) PROCESS FLOWS

The Pretty Pots example on the next page demonstrates steps 2 through 5 using a FIFO process flow. The data for Pretty Pots' production of clay pottery during July are included in the example.

Step 2: Summarize the Flow of Cost Elements and Calculate the Inputs' Percentage Complete

Panel (a) of Exhibit 6–7 is called an **input usage flow diagram.** This is a line chart that maps how and when inputs are added into a process or department. To calculate EUP, the management accountant needs to know how much of each input is in the product. Review the Model Dairies example at the beginning of the chapter. Ending WIP was 1,000 gallons, 100 percent complete for raw milk, 50 percent complete for direct labor, and 60 percent complete for overhead. To obtain these percentages, the management accountant needs to know the **input usage flows;** that is, how much of an input is added into the process and when. Roy Potter's line chart provides a simple map of these input usage flows for Pretty Pots Molding Department. *Preparing the input usage flow diagram is step 2 of the six steps in process costing.*

Reviewing the input usage flow diagram in Exhibit 6–7a, notice that all direct materials (Mud-X and water) are added at the beginning of processing. Thirty percent of the direct labor is added over the first one-fourth (25 percent) of the process. This is the mixing operation in Roy Potter's notes. One-half of the direct labor is used over just 10 percent of the process (the mold removal and inspection operation). The last 20 percent of the direct labor used in the department is required during the last 40 percent of processing (curing). Overhead is used up uniformly throughout the department's operations.

With his input usage flow diagram, Roy Potter can now calculate how much of each input is in the beginning and ending WIP, as well as the spoiled pots

INSIGHTS & APPLICATIONS

Pretty Pots Production Data for the Molding Department

Pretty Pots uses two processes, Molding and Firing, to manufacture clay flowerpots. Each pot is processed through both departments. From the firing process, the clay flowerpots are transferred to finished goods. In the Molding Department, a raw clay mixture known as Mud-X is started at the beginning of the process and mixed with water for two hours. The smooth liquefied clay is injected into molds where excess moisture is vaporized. Once the clay has set, the molds are removed, and the pots inspected. Sometimes, the clay has too much or too little moisture, causing the pots to collapse or crack, resulting in spoilage.

After the clay pots are cured, they are transferred to the Firing Department where they are subjected to extreme heat. After firing is completed, the pots are glazed and/or handpainted and then transferred to the finished goods warehouse.

Roy Potter, the management accountant, obtained the following information from the PCAS about Molding Department production data for July:

	COSTS	UNITS
Beginning work-in-process:		50
Direct materials	$ 75	
Direct labor	27	
Applied overhead	60	
Total beginning WIP cost	$162	
Units started during July		150
Units completed and transferred to Firing during July		145
Ending work-in-process		30
Spoilage during July		25
Input costs incurred during July:		
Direct materials (Mud-X)	$150	
Direct labor	354	
Applied overhead	492	
Total costs added to process	$996	

Realizing that he needed more information, Roy went to see the production manager to find out how the molding process worked. The production manager walked Roy through the department, showing him how pots are made. The process wasn't as simple as Roy expected, so, he took some notes:

■ During the first 25 percent of the process, clay and water are mixed. They are put into a big drum at the beginning of processing. The mixing process uses 30 percent of the department's labor time.

■ During the next 25 percent of the process, injection and molding take place. No labor is involved in this operation.

■ The next 10 percent of the process involves mold removal and inspection (MR&I). This is a labor-intensive operation, requiring 50 percent of the department's labor time.

■ The last 40 percent of the process is curing. This operation uses 20 percent of the labor needed to make pots in the Molding Department.

Now Roy understood the process better. He had observed the various operations involved, how much of each cost element was used in each operation, and when it was input. He then went back to his office and drew a simple line chart of the Molding Department's process. This line chart is shown in Exhibit 6–7a. He took the line chart back to the production manager to verify its correctness. With the line chart, Roy now had a simple method to calculate the percentage complete of beginning and ending WIP and spoilage for each cost element. With the percentage complete information, he could then write a spreadsheet program to calculate EUP and provide a department production cost report.

■■■ EXHIBIT 6–7
**Input Usage Flow
Diagram**

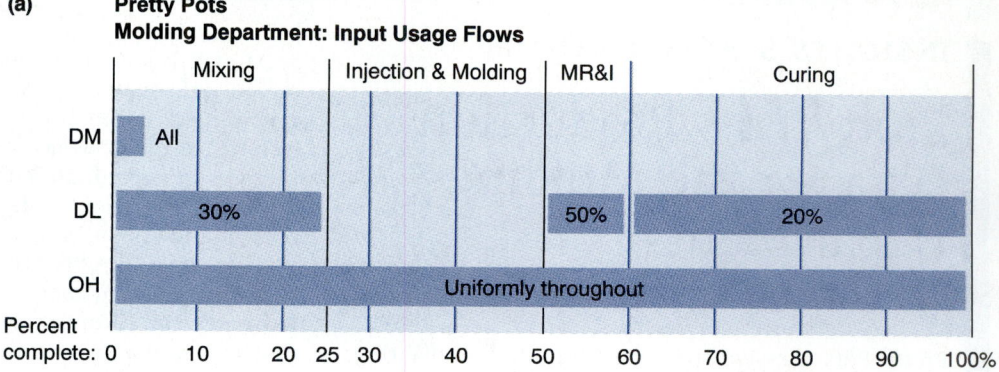

(a) **Pretty Pots
Molding Department: Input Usage Flows**

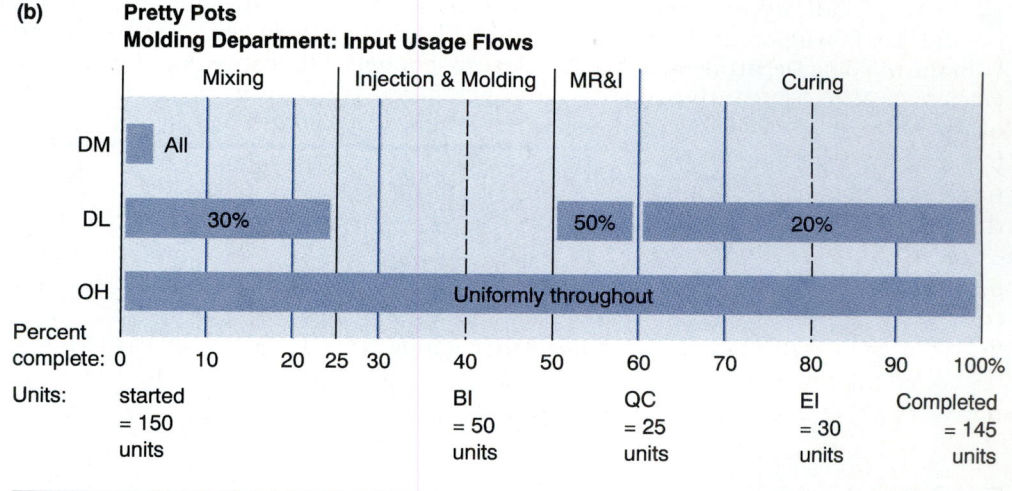

(b) **Pretty Pots
Molding Department: Input Usage Flows**

for any month. All he has to do for a given month is to draw two dashed vertical lines where beginning and ending inventories are, and add the number of pots for each to the bottom of the diagram. Roy did this from the PCAS information for July in panel (b) of Exhibit 6–7. At the beginning of the month (BI), there were 50 pots 40 percent complete (i.e., they were 40 percent of the way down the assembly line). At the end of the month (EI is ending WIP on the input usage flow diagram), there were 30 pots 80 percent complete. Spoilage is identified when the pots are 60 percent complete (QC stands for quality control inspection in the diagram); 25 pots were rejected during July.

HOW MUCH OF EACH COST ELEMENT (ITS PERCENTAGE COMPLETE) IS IN BEGINNING WIP? The beginning WIP percentage complete for each input can be determined by noting how much of the input is in a pot by the time it is 40 percent "down-the-line." Since all direct materials are added at the beginning, 100 percent of Mud-X and water are already in each pot comprising the beginning WIP. No more Mud-X or water has to be added to finish these pots in July. All the direct materials were added in June. In other words, the beginning WIP is 100 percent complete with respect to direct materials.

How much of the direct labor is in the beginning WIP? The answer is 30 percent. This amount was input by the time the pots are 25 percent down-the-line, and no more labor is used between that time and the point where the beginning WIP is. So, the beginning WIP is 30 percent complete with respect to direct labor.

Since overhead is added uniformly throughout the process, if the pots are 40 percent down-the-line, 40 percent of the overhead required to complete them has already been added. The beginning WIP is 40 percent complete with respect to overhead.

Roy Potter constructed a spreadsheet program to calculate EUP given the number of pots and their percentage complete for each input. The program, shown in Exhibit 6–8, is the same one used in the Model Dairies illustration (Exhibit 6–6). Roy uses the Data Section to input each month's information. The percentage complete information for each cost element in the beginning WIP pots is in the second line (row) of the Data Section (the "Beginning WIP %Complete" line). The Solution Section is the formal report, which is automatically updated each time new raw data are input into the Data Section.

HOW MUCH OF EACH COST ELEMENT (ITS PERCENTAGE COMPLETE) IS IN THE SPOILED POTS REJECTED AT QC?   Many traditional production processes have quality control (QC) inspection points throughout the process. In JITs, quality control is the responsibility of each cell worker when performing each operation within the cell. Thus, rejects (spoilage) can occur at any stage of production. If pots are rejected at the end of a process, calculating the EUP for each cost element is simple. Because each rejected pot is complete by the time it reaches the end of the process, 100 percent of all inputs are already in the pot; that is, it is 100 percent complete with respect to all cost elements.

But what if a pot is rejected part way through a process, such as at the 60 percent stage of completion in the Molding Department? How much of each cost element is in one of these rejected pots? Roy Potter used his input usage flow diagram in Exhibit 6–7b to determine the percentage complete of each cost element. Since all direct materials are added at the beginning, spoilage (the rejected pots) is 100 percent complete with respect to direct materials.

Molding Department's EUP at Pretty Pots

PCAS FOR PRETTY POTS
SPREADSHEET PROGRAM TO CALCULATE MOLDING DEPARTMENT'S EUP
For July 1995

DATA SECTION:

	Units	DM Added	DL Added	Applied OH
Beginning WIP Inventory	50			
Beginning WIP %Complete		100.00%	30.00%	40.00%
Beginning WIP Cost		$75	$27	$60
Units Started	150			
Costs Added		$150	$354	$492
Ending WIP Inventory	30			
Ending WIP %Complete		100.00%	90.00%	80.00%
Units Completed	145			
Output Loss	25			
Output Loss %Complete		100.00%	80.00%	60.00%
Cost Method	1 (1 = FIFO, 2 = WA)			

SOLUTION SECTION: FIFO

PRETTY POTS
MOLDING DEPARTMENT COST REPORT
JULY 1995

EUP:	Units	DM Added	DL Added	Applied OH
Units Completed	145	145	145	145
Less Beginning WIP	<50>	<50>	<15>	<20>
Add Ending WIP	30	30	27	24
Add Output Loss	25	25	20	15
UNITS STARTED	150			
EQUIVALENT UNITS		150	177	164

By the time a pot gets 60 percent through the department, 80 percent of the direct labor needed to make a pot already has been used (added to it). Thirty percent was incurred by the time the pots were 25 percent processed. By the time these pots were 60 percent of the way through the department, another 50 percent of labor was added. In total, then, spoilage is 80 percent complete with respect to direct labor.

Since overhead is added uniformly throughout the process, if pots are rejected when they are 60 percent through the department, then spoilage is 60 percent complete with respect to overhead. In Exhibit 6–8's Data Section, Roy Potter entered these percentages in the line labeled "Output Loss %Complete."

HOW MUCH OF EACH COST ELEMENT (ITS PERCENTAGE COMPLETE) IS IN ENDING WIP?   The ending WIP is 80 percent complete with its processing in the Molding Department. Since all direct materials are added at the beginning, 100 percent of the direct materials are already in these pots. No more direct materials have to be added next month to finish them. Thus, they are 100 percent complete with respect to direct materials. If the ending WIP is 80 percent processed through the department, then these pots are 80 percent complete with respect to overhead because overhead is added uniformly throughout the process.

Calculating the direct labor percentage complete is harder, however. Looking at the input usage flow diagram in Exhibit 6–7b, it is easy to see that 80 percent of direct labor is added by the time the pots are 60 percent of the way through the department. But, how much is added between the 60 percent and 80 percent stages of completion? Assuming the last 20 percent of labor is added uniformly over the last 40 percent of processing in the department, the amount added between 60 and 80 percent can be calculated using simple linear interpolation.

First, the amount of labor added between the 60 and 80 percent stages of completion can be intuitively determined. This is one-half of the processing (curing) during which 20 percent of labor is used. One-half of 20 percent is *10 percent.* Alternatively, 20 percent of labor is added over 40 percent of the department's processing. Therefore, one-half percent of labor is added for each percent of processing. If 20 percent more processing is done, then *10 percent* more labor is used. Using linear interpolation to verify this intuition:

$$\text{Percent added} = \frac{\begin{array}{c}\text{Distance from starting point} \\ \text{of line segment to units}\end{array}}{\text{Length of line segment}} \times \begin{array}{c}\text{Input added over} \\ \text{line segment}\end{array}$$

$$10\% = \frac{60\% \text{ to } 80\% = 20\% \text{ distance}}{40\%} \times 20\%$$

The labor added to the pots in ending WIP is 90 percent of what is needed to fully make a pot. Eighty percent was added by the time processing reached QC, and another 10 percent of labor was added during the curing process. In total, then, the ending WIP is 90 percent complete with respect to direct labor. These percentages are in the Data Section line "Ending WIP %Complete" (Exhibit 6–8).

Before completing step 2, Roy Potter used the input usage flow diagram to verify that all pots have been accounted for. Since there were 50 pots in beginning WIP and 150 pots started in July, two hundred pots could have been completed. In accounting for these 200 pots, 145 were completed, 30 were in ending WIP, and 25 pots were spoiled (rejected at QC). This internal control check is formally shown in the spreadsheet's Solution Section "Units" column. The "Units Started" of 150 pots is a summation of that column. This result is visually compared to the Data Section entry for units started to make sure they agree. Step 2 is now finished. The rest of the PCAS calculations are relatively simple.

Step 3: Calculate FIFO EUP

EUP is calculated for each subset of pots (beginning and ending WIP, spoilage) for each input. If there are three subsets of pots and three cost elements, then nine EUP calculations need to be made. The EUP formula is:

$$EUP = Units \times Percentage\ complete$$

In the Solution Section of the spreadsheet program in Exhibit 6–8, each of these nine EUP calculations can be verified by looking at the spreadsheet cells for the three middle columns (DM Added, DL Added, Applied OH) and the three rows for the partially completed pots (Less Beginning WIP, Add Ending WIP, Add Output Loss). Output loss refers to rejected pots (spoilage).

Why are the beginning WIP pots subtracted from the pots completed? Remember that *FIFO accounts for last month's work and costs separately from this month's.* Consider Mud-X (the DM Added column in the spreadsheet's Solution Section). Even though 145 pots were completed in July, were 145 pots' worth of Mud-X needed in July? No, 50 pots were leftover from June (the July beginning WIP). All the Mud-X needed to make these pots was added in June, and no more was needed in July. In other words, to complete 145 pots in July, given a fully completed beginning WIP with respect to direct materials, only 95 pots' worth of Mud-X had to be requisitioned in July. In addition to this 95 pots' worth of Mud-X needed to complete the 145 pots, another 30 pots in ending WIP and 25 rejects also were 100 percent complete with respect to direct materials. In total, enough direct materials were used in July to fully process 150 pots (145 − 50 = 95, 95 + 30 + 25 = 150 EUP for direct materials).

Before proceeding, the definition of EUP should be reviewed to see if it makes sense. This same logic should be verified with the other cost elements (the DL Added and Applied OH columns in the Solution Section of Exhibit 6–8).

Step 4: Calculate Cost per Unit (per EUP)

This is really a cost per EUP. This calculation is added to the bottom of the spreadsheet program as shown in Exhibit 6–9. In July, $150 worth of direct materials were requisitioned into the Molding Department. This was enough to make 150 pots, so the cost of Mud-X per pot was $1 in July.[1] Remember, *FIFO only considers July's effort (work or resources used) and costs.* That is why the beginning WIP EUP was subtracted from the completed pots in the EUP calculation, and why beginning WIP cost is not considered in the cost per unit calculation here. (*The work, as measured in EUP, is for the same time period as the costs. Both are only for July.*) To emphasize that Beginning WIP Cost should not be included in the Cost Per EUP, Roy entered "n/a" in the cells for the Beginning WIP Cost line.

Because each cost element is used up in a different way throughout the Molding Department, separate EUP and cost per EUP calculations are necessary. Whenever two cost elements have identical usage flows, their EUP will be the same. Whenever cost elements have different usage flows, they must be accounted for individually.

The good news is that the formula is always the same, only the numeric values change. This is why process costing is an ideal application for spreadsheet software. The EUP formula, for example, can be entered into one cell and then copied to all the other spreadsheet cells where other EUP calculations are to be performed. If separate data and report (solution) sections are properly created in the program, then each month's raw data can be input, and the program will update the results for that month. In other words, the modern management

---

[1] Water comes from a stream outside the factory and is free. The only direct material that has to be purchased is Mud-X.

EXHIBIT 6–9
Molding Department's Unit Cost at Pretty Pots

[handwritten marginalia: To calc. wkt costs + EUP ⓑ WIP (units) are not added in because it was acct. for prev. mo.) just as End. will be added to this mo.]

PCAS FOR PRETTY POTS
SPREADSHEET PROGRAM TO CALCULATE MOLDING DEPARTMENT'S COST PER UNIT
For July 1995

DATA SECTION:

	Units	DM Added	DL Added	Applied OH
Beginning WIP Inventory	50			
Beginning WIP %Complete		100.00%	30.00%	40.00%
Beginning WIP Cost		$75	$27	$60
Units Started	150			
Costs Added		$150	$354	$492
Ending WIP Inventory	30			
Ending WIP %Complete		100.00%	90.00%	80.00%
Units Completed	145			
Output Loss	25			
Output Loss %Complete		100.00%	80.00%	60.00%
Cost Method	1	(1 = FIFO, 2 = WA)		

[handwritten: Step 2]

SOLUTION SECTION: FIFO

PRETTY POTS
MOLDING DEPARTMENT COST REPORT
JULY 1995

EUP:	Units	DM Added	DL Added	Applied OH	Totals
Units Completed	145	145	145	145	
Less Beginning WIP	<50>	<50>	<15>	<20>	
Add Ending WIP	30	30	27	24	
Add Output Loss	25	25	20	15	
UNITS STARTED	150				
EQUIVALENT UNITS		150	177	164	
COST PER EUP:					
Beginning WIP Costs		n/a	n/a	n/a	n/a
Costs Added This Month		$150	$354	$492	$996
COSTS INCURRED		$150	$354	$492	$996
UNIT COSTS		$1.00	$2.00	$3.00	$6.00

[handwritten: Step 3] *[handwritten: Step 4]*

accountant needs to know how to create "template" programs that are reusable month after month. Creating such a program for process costing was relatively simple for Roy Potter, the management accountant for Pretty Pots.

Step 5: Calculate the Costs of Completed Output, Ending WIP, and Spoilage

Roy Potter calls the final section of his spreadsheet program "Cost Allocations." It is added to the bottom of the program and is shown in Exhibit 6–10. Again, only one formula is needed for virtually all the cells in this section of the spreadsheet:

$$\frac{\text{Total cost of an input item}}{\text{for a particular subset of units}} = \text{EUP} \times \text{Cost per unit}$$

Remembering that EUP = Units × Percentage complete for a cost element leads to the conclusion that there is only *one basic formula in process costing:*

$$\text{Units} \times \text{Percentage complete for a cost element}$$

■EXHIBIT 6–10
**Molding Department's
FIFO Cost Report at
Pretty Pots**

SOLUTION SECTION: FIFO

PRETTY POTS
MOLDING DEPARTMENT COST REPORT
JULY 1995

EUP:	Units	DM Added	DL Added	Applied OH	Totals
Units Completed	145	145	145	145	
Less Beginning WIP	<50>	<50>	<15>	<20>	
Add Ending WIP	30	30	27	24	
Add Output Loss	25	25	20	15	
UNITS STARTED	150				
EQUIVALENT UNITS		150	177	164	
COST PER EUP:					
Beginning WIP Cost		n/a	n/a	n/a	n/a
Costs Added This Month		$150	$354	$492	$996
COSTS INCURRED		$150	$354	$492	$996
UNIT COSTS		$1.00	$2.00	$3.00	$6.00
COST ALLOCATIONS:					
UNITS COMPLETED:	145	n/a	n/a	n/a	n/a
Beginning WIP Costs	50	$75	$27	$60	$162
Costs To Complete Beg. WIP		0	70	90	160
Started This Month	95	95	190	285	570
COSTS TRANSFERRED OUT		$170	$287	$435	$892
ENDING WIP INVENTORY	30	$30	$54	$72	$156
OUTPUT LOSS	25	$25	$40	$45	$110
COSTS ACCOUNTED FOR:		$225	$381	$552	$1,158

note that BWP & costs added during current mo. are added back in

= carry over costs

Step 5

This formula yields EUP. When calculating the total cost of an input item, the cost per unit value is attached to the formula:

Total cost of an input
item for a particular = Units × Percentage complete for a cost element × Cost per unit
subset of units

To verify this, consider the DM Added column in the Cost Allocations section for ending WIP. There are 30 pots in ending WIP, 100 percent complete with respect to direct materials, multiplied by the direct materials cost of $1 per pot. For the direct labor cost in the output loss (spoilage), there are 25 spoiled pots, 80 percent complete with respect to direct labor, multiplied by the direct labor cost of $2 per pot (total direct labor cost in spoilage is $40).

The Units Completed subsection needs further elaboration. FIFO accounts for each month's work and costs separately. The 145 completed pots involved 50 pots from beginning WIP (started but not finished last month) plus 95 pots started and completed this month. This is shown in the "Units" column. The 50 pots have a beginning WIP cost (costs incurred last month) of $75 for direct materials, $27 for direct labor, and $60 in applied overhead. These 50 pots needed some more inputs to finish them in July. How many?

Costs to complete the   Units × (1 − %Complete last month)
beginning WIP units = × Cost per unit

To illustrate, the direct materials costs to complete the beginning WIP is zero. The beginning WIP was 100 percent complete with respect to direct materials last month, so no more direct materials had to be added in July.

Direct materials costs
to complete the   = 50 units × (1 − 100%) × $1.00 per unit
beginning WIP units   = 50 units × (1 − 1.00) × $1.00 per unit
                                     = $0

For direct labor, these 50 pots were 30 percent complete last month (this month's beginning WIP percentage complete). Therefore, only 70 percent of the required labor to make a pot had to be added in July. The 50 pots times 70 percent labor needed in July times July's labor cost of $2.00 per pot equals $70.

Direct labor costs
to complete the   = 50 units × (1 − 30%) × $2.00 per unit
beginning WIP units   = 50 units × (1 − 0.30) × $2.00 per unit
                                     = $70

For applied overhead:

Applied overhead costs
to complete the   = 50 units × (1 − 40%) × $3.00 per unit
beginning WIP units   = 50 units × (1 − 0.40) × $3.00 per unit
                                     = $90

These costs are shown in the Costs to Complete line just below the Beginning WIP Costs line in the Units Completed subsection of Cost Allocations in Exhibit 6–10. In total, the beginning WIP had a cost from June of $162. Another $160 (in direct labor and overhead) was needed to finish them in July.

The 95 pots started and completed in July had 100 percent of each cost element added in July times the July cost per pot for each input item. This is the same basic formula used for the ending WIP and spoilage.

Costs for 95 pots started and completed in July:

Direct materials: 95 pots × 100% complete × $1.00 per pot = $ 95
Direct labor: 95 pots × 100% complete × $2.00 per pot = $190
Applied overhead: 95 pots × 100% complete × $3.00 per pot = $285

Costs for 30 pots in ending WIP inventory:

Direct materials: 30 pots × 100% complete × $1.00 per pot = $30
Direct labor: 30 pots × 90% complete × $2.00 per pot = $54
Applied overhead: 30 pots × 80% complete × $3.00 per pot = $72

Costs for 25 pots rejected (spoiled):

Direct materials: 25 pots × 100% complete × $1.00 per pot = $25
Direct labor: 25 pots × 80% complete × $2.00 per pot = $40
Applied overhead: 25 pots × 60% complete × $3.00 per pot = $45

Before making the journal entry to record the pots transferred from the Molding Department to the Firing Department, Roy Potter performed one more internal control check. Have all the costs in WIP-Molding Department been accounted for? The beginning WIP cost was $162, costs added in July were $996, which equals $1,158 to account for. The cost of the pots transferred to Firing was $892, the cost of ending WIP was $156, and the cost of the spoiled pots was $110. The costs accounted for sum to the same $1,158. Therefore, all costs have been accounted for, and Roy Potter is ready to make journal entry 8 to record the transfer of the 145 completed pots from Molding to Firing.

The costs calculated in the preceding example were based on a FIFO flow of pots through the Molding Department. If a WA flow is appropriate, the costs could be different. Consequently, before making journal entry 8, the differences between the FIFO cost per unit and the WA cost per unit should be discussed.

PRODUCT COSTING FOR WEIGHTED-AVERAGE (WA) PROCESS FLOWS

LEARNING OBJECTIVE 4

Demonstrate the differences in calculating product costs between FIFO and weighted-average methods.

In a FIFO flow, last month's work and costs can be separated from this month's. Last month's effort (the beginning WIP) is backed out of the EUP calculation, and last month's (July's beginning WIP) cost is separately treated in the Cost Allocations section of the department's production cost report. In a WA flow, however, the units worked on last month cannot be separated from the units worked on this month. Because the units in beginning WIP and the units started this month are mixed together, their costs cannot be separately accounted for and, instead, must be averaged together. This is the only difference between FIFO and WA: *in FIFO, the beginning WIP is separately accounted for, but in WA it is averaged in with this month's work and costs.*

To illustrate, study the WA department production cost report for the Molding Department in Exhibit 6–11. In the EUP section, the beginning WIP EUP is not subtracted from the completed units (line 2). EUP includes last month's work on the beginning WIP with this month's work on all the products.

EXHIBIT 6–11 Molding Department's Weighted-Average Cost Report at Pretty Pots

SOLUTION SECTION: WA

PRETTY POTS
MOLDING DEPARTMENT COST REPORT
JULY 1995

EUP:	Units	DM Added	DL Added	Applied OH	Totals
Units Completed	145	145	145	145	
Less Beginning WIP	<50>	n/a	n/a	n/a	
Add Ending WIP	30	30	27	24	
Add Output Loss	25	25	20	15	
UNITS STARTED	150				
EQUIVALENT UNITS		200	192	184	
COST PER EUP:					
Beginning WIP Costs		$75	$27	$60	$162
Costs Added This Month		150	354	492	996
COSTS INCURRED		$225	$381	$552	$1,158
UNIT COSTS		$1.13	$1.98	$3.00	$6.11
COST ALLOCATIONS:					
UNITS COMPLETED:	145	$163	$288	$435	$886
Beginning WIP Costs		n/a	n/a	n/a	n/a
Costs To Complete Beg. WIP		n/a	n/a	n/a	n/a
Started This Month		n/a	n/a	n/a	n/a
COSTS TRANSFERRED OUT		$163	$288	$435	$886
ENDING WIP INVENTORY	30	$34	$54	$72	$159
OUTPUT LOSS	25	$28	$40	$45	$113
COSTS ACCOUNTED FOR:		$225	$381	$552	$1,158

Thus, in the Cost Per EUP section, the beginning WIP costs are also included in the Costs Incurred. The work on all the units is combined, and the costs for all this work are combined. The resulting unit cost is an average cost of work done last month with work done this month.

Under Cost Allocations, the same formula used with FIFO is used with WA to calculate the total costs:

$$\text{Units} \times \text{Percentage complete for a cost element} \times \text{Cost per unit}$$

The total cost of the completed units is straightforward with WA. There is no distinction between, or separate accounting for, beginning WIP and the rest of the units completed. To illustrate, the total cost of direct materials in the completed pots during July was $163 (145 pots times 100 percent complete times $1.13 per pot for direct materials).[2] The same is true for each cost in this section. The cost of pots transferred to the Firing Department for journal entry 8 is $886 (145 pots times $6.11 each).

▌Comparing the Department Production Cost Reports

The FIFO and WA calculations for EUP, cost per unit, and cost totals are compared in Exhibit 6–12. FIFO accounts for beginning WIP separately, whereas WA does not. This single difference between the two methods leads to the six

[2] Roy Potter formatted his spreadsheet to display the unit costs to the penny, and all other costs displayed in whole dollars. The program stores all calculations to 15 significant places, however. While this feature eliminates many rounding errors, some users may be confused. For example, the unit cost for DM Added is really $1.125 and the DM Added cost for the completed pots is $163.125. Multiplying the rounded $1.13 by 145 pots, however, equals $163.85, which may cause some confusion for spreadsheet novices as they will expect to see $164 in this spreadsheet cell. They may also expect to see $287 for the DL Added into the units completed. You should understand that $288 is correct. Spreadsheets also create addition errors because of formatting to whole dollars, as seen in the Costs Accounted For, DL Added.

▌▌ EXHIBIT 6–12
Comparing the FIFO and Weighted-Average Methods

SOLUTION SECTION: FIFO   WA

PRETTY POTS
MOLDING DEPARTMENT COST REPORT
JULY 1995

EUP:	Units	DM Added	DL Added	Applied OH	Totals	Units	DM Added	DL Added	Applied OH	Totals
Units Completed	145	145	145	145		145	145	145	145	
Less Beginning WIP	<50>	<50>	<15>	<20>		<50>	n/a	n/a	n/a	
Add Ending WIP	30	30	27	24		30	30	27	24	
Add Output Loss	25	25	20	15		25	25	20	15	
UNITS STARTED	150					150				
EQUIVALENT UNITS		150	177	164			200	192	184	
COST PER EUP:										
Beginning WIP Cost		n/a	n/a	n/a	n/a		$75	$27	$60	$162
Costs Added This Month		$150	$354	$492	$996		150	354	492	996
COSTS INCURRED		$150	$354	$492	$996		$225	$381	$552	$1,158
UNIT COSTS		$1.00	$2.00	$3.00	$6.00		$1.13	$1.98	$3.00	$6.11
COST ALLOCATIONS:										
UNITS COMPLETED:	145	n/a	n/a	n/a	n/a	145	$163	$288	$435	$886
Beginning WIP Costs	50	<$75>	$27	$60	$162		n/a	n/a	n/a	n/a
Costs To Complete Beg. WIP		0	70	90	160		n/a	n/a	n/a	n/a
Started This Month	95	95	190	285	570		n/a	n/a	n/a	n/a
COSTS TRANSFERRED OUT		$170	$287	$435	$892		$163	$288	$435	$886
ENDING WIP INVENTORY	30	$30	$54	$72	$156	30	$34	$54	$72	$159
OUTPUT LOSS	25	$25	$40	$45	$110	25	$28	$40	$45	$113
COSTS ACCOUNTED FOR:		$225	$381	$552	$1,158		$225	$381	$552	$1,158

lines being different in the FIFO and WA reports as described next:

- *Less Beginning WIP* (EUP section, line 2). With FIFO the beginning WIP EUP is subtracted so that it can be separately accounted for. With WA it is not backed out and, thus, is included in EUP totals.
- *Beginning WIP Costs* (Cost Per EUP section, line 1). Beginning WIP cost is separately accounted for with FIFO, but is included with this month's costs in WA.
- *The four lines under Units Completed* (Cost Allocations section, Costs Transferred Out). With FIFO the cost of the units completed has to be separated between last month's cost and this month's cost (to complete the beginning WIP and the units both started and completed). Since last month and this month are combined with WA, no separate accounting is needed.

When the department production cost report is prepared manually, WA involves fewer calculations and is easier. When the reports are prepared with spreadsheet software, though, both methods can be run from the same program. Furthermore, the program can be used again in subsequent months simply by inputting a new month's raw data in the Data Section. The six lines of differences noted above can be dealt with by using an "If-Then" statement. For example, in the EUP section, the beginning WIP line can read, "If FIFO, subtract the beginning WIP EUP, if not, then input n/a." In this way, one program can be used with multiple departments, some with FIFO flows and some with WA flows.[3]

Comparing the FIFO and WA Information

By separately accounting for this month's costs, FIFO allows across-month cost comparisons (trend analysis). Exhibit 6–12 can be used to demonstrate this. This month's unit cost ($6.00, FIFO) is less than the average cost over the last two months ($6.11, WA). Costs must have decreased from last month. But, by how much? Look at the beginning WIP cost for direct materials. The $75 cost was for 50 pots, which were 100 percent complete with respect to direct materials. Last month's direct materials cost per EUP must have been $1.50 per pot ($75 = 50 pots times 100 percent complete times $1.50 unit cost). This month the direct materials only cost $1.00 per pot.

A similar calculation shows that direct labor went up. Last month, it cost $1.80 per pot ($27 = 50 pots times 30 percent complete times $1.80 unit cost). Workers got a raise effective July 1st. Overhead cost did not change because it is applied using a POR that does not change from month to month.[4]

SPOILAGE ACCOUNTING AND JOURNAL ENTRY 8

Spoilage has to be accounted for within journal entry 8, when the cost of the 145 completed pots is transferred from the Molding Department to the Firing Department. In traditional PCASs, normal spoilage is allocated to all the good pots made. In this way, the costs of rejects can be averaged into the cost of the salable pots. This is the same logic used in a JOCAS. The question is, "How much spoilage cost should be included in the cost of the good pots transferred to Firing?"

As in a traditional JOCAS, abnormal and normal spoilage are accounted for differently in a traditional PCAS. Abnormal spoilage is credited out of the WIP–Molding Department subsidiary ledger account and debited to a loss account. Normal spoilage is averaged over all the pots made. In a traditional

---

[3] Using one program for both can also facilitate doing multiple homework problems.
[4] Unless, of course, management chooses to change it because circumstances have changed. This will be discussed in Chapter 7.

JOCAS, normal spoilage is budgeted for and included in the POR. This can also be done in the PCAS. Then the cost of normal spoilage will be debited to overhead. The calculation of normal and abnormal spoilage, and journal entry 8, is shown below as Method 1 in the section titled Preparing Journal Entry 8 for Transfers.

Normal spoilage can also just be allocated over the good pots each month rather than being included in the overhead budget and the POR. Conceptually, this is a better approach than Method 1 in that the POR allocates spoilage to good pots as well as to pots that will eventually be spoiled. This does not happen in Method 2, as illustrated following Method 1.

Calculating Normal and Abnormal Spoilage

Refer to the input usage flow diagram in Exhibit 6–7b. Fifty pots in beginning WIP went through inspection (QC is at the department's 60 percent stage of completion), along with all 150 of the pots started in July. In total, 200 pots were inspected in July.[5] Assume management considers a 10 percent failure rate (reject or spoilage rate) of the pots inspected to be normal. The first 20 pots rejected in July are normal output loss (NOL), and any excess is abnormal output loss (AOL).

Total spoilage is allocated between normal and abnormal as follows:

$$\text{Normal spoilage cost} = \frac{\text{NOL units}}{\text{Total spoilage}} \times \text{Output loss cost}$$

and

$$\text{Abnormal spoilage cost} = \frac{\text{AOL units}}{\text{Total spoilage}} \times \text{Output loss cost}$$

Pretty Pots Molding Department's spoilage in July is calculated as follows (using FIFO):

$$\text{Normal spoilage cost} = \frac{20 \text{ units}}{25 \text{ units}} \times \$110$$
$$= \underline{\underline{\$88}}$$

$$\text{Abnormal spoilage cost} = \frac{5 \text{ units}}{25 \text{ units}} \times \$110$$
$$= \underline{\underline{\$22}}$$

Preparing Journal Entry 8 for Transfers

In a traditional PCAS, using Method 1, which charges normal spoilage to overhead, the journal entry to record spoilage and transferred pots is:

JOURNAL ENTRY 8: Transfers between Departments (Method 1: Normal Spoilage to Overhead)

WIP–Firing Department (pots)	$892	
WIP–Manufacturing Overhead (Spoilage)	$ 88	
Loss from Abnormal Spoilage	$ 22	
WIP–Molding Department		$1,002

[5] The last 30 pots started, which were not finished and in ending WIP, passed through QC during July.

Before the Method 2 journal entry is made, the normal spoilage has to be allocated between the ending WIP and the pots transferred, because it has to be spread over all the good units that passed inspection. Of the 200 pots inspected, 25 were rejected; consequently, 175 passed.

$$\text{To ending WIP cost} = \frac{30 \text{ units}}{175 \text{ units}} \times \$88$$

$$= \underline{\$15} \text{ (rounded)}$$

$$\text{To transferred pots} = \frac{145 \text{ units}}{175 \text{ units}} \times \$88$$

$$= \underline{\$73} \text{ (rounded)}$$

JOURNAL ENTRY 8: Transfers between Departments (Method 2: Normal Spoilage to Good Pots)

WIP–Firing Department (pots)	$965	
Loss from Abnormal Spoilage	$ 22	
WIP–Molding Department		$987

With either method, the management accountant should verify that all costs have been correctly accounted for:

	Method 1		Method 2	
Good pots finished	$892		$892	
+ NOL (method 2)	0		73	
Costs to Firing Department		$ 892		$ 965
Ending WIP good pots	$156		$156	
+ NOL (method 2)	0		15	
Ending WIP total cost		$ 156		$ 171
+ Overhead (NOL, method 1)		$ 88		$ 0
+ AOL (to loss account)		$ 22		$ 22
Total costs accounted for		$1,158		$1,158

Journal Entry 8 for World-Class Manufacturing

Proponents of WCM, JIT, and TQM believe all spoilage is a nonvalue-added cost that should be accounted for separately and should not be allocated to the good output. These management accountants journalize all spoilage to a cost variance, as can be done in a JOCAS:

JOURNAL ENTRY 8: Transfers between Departments (WCM: All Spoilage to Cost Variance)

WIP–Firing Department (pots)	$892	
WIP–Molding Department Spoilage Cost Variance	$110	
WIP–Molding Department		$1,002

This spoilage is then reported to management in a special report along with the other cost variances of the Molding Department in July.

Through the concept of continuous improvement, world-class manufacturers are striving to eliminate spoilage, but to help achieve this goal, they need a performance measurement system. A performance measurement system, among other things, measures the production process and lets managers and workers know how well they are progressing toward the goal of zero defects. In these manufacturing environments, the goal is to drive spoilage or rework to insignificant levels in the short run (while eliminating them entirely in the long run).

In the meantime, spoilage and rework are still a significant part of production in many manufacturing firms. Thus, the purpose of this discussion, and the corresponding discussion in the last chapter for JOCASs, has been to explain how to account for such costs of spoilage when they do occur. By accounting for and spotlighting these costs, the management accountant can make management aware of their magnitude. Thus, managers can, at the very least, use this information to start on the road to total quality management.

JOINT AND BY-PRODUCT COSTING IN A PCAS

This section discusses situations in which a process or department produces more than one type of product (output). Depending on the monetary significance of the products, they can be joint products, or one is the main product and the other a by-product.

Joint costs are those costs incurred in a single operation that yields two or more products or services simultaneously. **Joint products** are two or more products (or services) that:

- Have relatively significant sales values, and
- Are not separately identifiable as individual products until their split-off point

The **split-off point** is the production juncture where the joint products and by-products become individually identifiable. For example, in mining gold, the leaching process yields both gold and silver. If both have significant sales value, they are joint products.

By-products are incidental products of a joint process that:

- Have minor sales value as compared with the sales value of the major product or products, and
- Are not separately identifiable as individual products until their split-off point

By-products are often disposed of for small amounts of revenue or are recycled in the production process. Current market values for gold are around $400 per ounce, compared to around $4 per ounce for silver. Many mining companies therefore treat silver (and the other ores that are leached out of the mining process) as a by-product. At one time, silver was accounted for as a joint product—and may be again in the future.

Contrarily, many products once considered by-products now make significant contributions to the enterprise's profits and have been reclassified as joint products. For example, shavings and wood chips, once considered by-products of lumber mills, are now sold to paper mills as raw materials for making paper products.

Joint costs are incurred up to the split-off point. The following are examples of industries where joint costs are common:

- Meat packing
- Lumber
- Dairy
- Food processing
- Petroleum
- Chemical

Joint products receive some pro rata share of the department's joint production costs prior to split off, generally according to some arbitrary cost allocation formula. By-products are not assigned any of the prior joint costs. By-products are inventoried at their net realizable value, as is scrap held for sale in Chapter 5. By-products' net realizable values are deducted from the joint costs prior to allocating them between the joint products.

At the split-off point, several products emerge, and the management accountant has to allocate the costs incurred up to that time among the joint products. The arbitrary methods usually selected to allocate these joint costs are based on some physical measure or on the joint products' relative sales values at the split-off point. In practice, many variations of these allocation methods are used.

The Physical Measure Method

Under the **physical measure method,** the total production costs incurred in the joint process are allocated to the various joint products according to the ratios of their physical output measurement. Product output measurements include units, liters, pounds, tons, gallons, or square feet. The cost allocated under this method may bear no relation to the costs incurred or the revenue generated by the various products.

The Relative Sales Value Method

Under the **relative sales value method,** joint costs are allocated among the various joint products in proportion to their anticipated sales values; that is, the expected market prices of the products when they are sold. The relative sales value method is probably the most widely used method.

This method is based on the assumption that costs should be allocated on the basis of a product's ability to "bear" them. Thus, products with the largest sales value should absorb most of the costs. The sales value used in this method is often the value at the split-off point. In situations where products are sold without additional processing, the relative sales value is the market price of each product times the quantity produced.

When products can be processed further into a refined or new product, but a market exists for them as they are, the sales value used for joint cost allocation purposes is the amount that could have been received if the products had been sold before being processed further. When joint products that have no market at the split-off point are processed further, a relative sales value must be assigned at the split-off point. The most widely used method in this situation is to estimate the sales value of the finished product and reduce it by the production costs incurred to complete the product after the split-off point (its net realizable value).

The New Horizons example on the following page shows how the physical measure and relative sales value methods are used. New Horizons manufactures two chemicals, both of which are sold at the split-off point.

ALLOCATING JOINT COSTS BY THE PHYSICAL MEASURE METHOD.   In this case, a pound is the physical measurement unit. Thus, 40 percent of the joint costs would be allocated to Xyclog, because the 4,000 pounds of Xyclog obtained is 40 percent of the total number of usable pounds resulting from the process. The proportion of joint costs allocated to Zonia is 60 percent for similar reasons. Computations are as follows:

PRODUCT	POUNDS	RATIO	ALLOCATED JOINT COSTS	COST PER POUND
Xyclog	4,000	40%	$160,000	$40
Zonia	6,000	60%	240,000	40
	10,000	100%	$400,000	

Note that the physical measurement method results in identical costs per pound for both products. This outcome implies that the benefits accruing from a pound of each product are identical. Identical benefits, however, will accrue

INSIGHTS & APPLICATIONS

New Horizons Chemical Company

Assume that New Horizons manufactures Xyclog and Zonia by processing fuzzy pears, a newly discovered fruit from the Amazon. New Horizons sells Xyclog to a pharmaceutical company as a raw material, which is used as the main ingredient for a hair restorer product. Zonia is sold to a cosmetic firm that uses it as a prime ingredient for lip gloss. Management at New Horizons has considered processing both Xyclog and Zonia further into consumer products but has not elected to do so at this time. Therefore, Xyclog and Zonia are considered finished goods as far as New Horizons is concerned.

For every 11,000 pounds of fuzzy pears put into process, 4,000 pounds of Xyclog and 6,000 pounds of Zonia are produced. The remaining 1,000 pounds is waste for which there is no value. Production costs for processing 11,000 pounds of fuzzy pears are $400,000.

only if the products are homogeneous. If the unit sales prices of the joint products are relatively close to each other, the products would be considered homogeneous, and the physical measurement method would be acceptable to most management accountants.

ALLOCATING JOINT COSTS BY THE RELATIVE SALES VALUE METHOD.   Assume that the sales price for Xyclog is $50 per pound and the sales price for Zonia is $100 per pound. This substantial difference in sales price indicates that the products are not homogeneous. Note that the following calculations provide costs per unit that are in proportion to the sales prices:

PRODUCT	POUNDS	MARKET PRICE	SALES VALUE	RATIO	ALLOCATED JOINT COSTS	COST PER POUND
Xyclog	4,000	$ 50	$200,000	25%	$100,000	$25
Zonia	6,000	100	600,000	75%	300,000	50
	10,000		$800,000	100%	$400,000	

The relative sales value method results in identical gross margin ratios for the joint products, in contrast to the physical measurement method where they have the same cost per pound. The relative sales value method implies that the benefits accruing to a dollar of sales from each product are identical.

SUMMARY OF LEARNING OBJECTIVES

The major goals of this chapter were to enable you to achieve four learning objectives:

Learning objective 1.   Describe the flow of products and their cost elements through continuous processing systems, and prepare the journal entries to record these events.

Units can flow through production in many different ways, but the following are two common product flow configurations:

- Sequential
- Parallel

In a sequential configuration, products flow from one processing department to another in a serial fashion. Costs are transferred from one WIP subsidiary account to another as the units are transferred between departments, with the cost of finished goods being transferred from the last WIP subsidiary account to FGI.

In a parallel product flow, two or more products go through two or more processing departments or centers. These different processes may be carried out simultaneously, or one process may run for a while and then another starts. The flow of costs reflects the flow of units in parallel processing just as it does in sequential processing.

When an enterprise has more than one processing center and different process flow configurations, computer technology becomes an effective and efficient ally for the management accountant. Workstations in each processing center are connected in a network that covers the entire process across all processing centers. By facilitating the prompt entering and processing of data, the network can help coordinate production activities through generating online real-time reports of results. The journal entries for a normal PCAS are illustrated in the demonstration problems that follow.

Learning objective 2.   Explain equivalent units of production (EUP), and calculate EUP for each cost element in the beginning and ending inventories and in the spoilage.

If no partially completed units are rejected, or remain in WIP inventory at either the beginning or the end of the period, the unit production cost for that process can be computed very easily. The total production costs are simply divided by the number of units completed during the period. There is no need for EUP calculations.

When some units have only been partially completed during the period, as is often the case, EUP must be calculated because a partially completed unit must carry a production cost that is a fraction of the production cost of a completed whole unit. To compute EUP, the actual number of units is multiplied by their stage of completion. For example, the EUP for 500 units 30 percent complete are 150 units. Because cost elements can be input into the process at different stages and in varying amounts, EUP calculations are separately required for each cost element in each of the subsets of partially completed units (beginning and ending WIP and spoilage).

Spreadsheet programs are particularly helpful in EUP calculations because the same formula is used over and over again:

$$\text{EUP} = \text{Units} \times \text{Percentage complete for each cost element}$$

If two cost elements are input into a department in exactly the same quantities and at the same times, they will have the same equivalent units. The EUP calculations are illustrated in the demonstration problems that follow.

Learning objective 3.   Describe the six steps for departmental cost accounting in a PCAS.

Step 1 involves journalizing the acquisition and use of the cost elements through journal entries 1–7. Step 2 summarizes the flow of cost elements and production in the department by preparing an input usage flow diagram. In step 3, EUP are calculated for each cost element in each subset of units only partially processed during the month (beginning WIP, ending WIP, and spoilage). Step 4 entails computing unit production costs. Once costs are accumulated by the processing centers or departments, and the period's output is determined in terms of EUP, unit production costs are computed by dividing the department's costs by its output expressed in EUP. Step 5 calculates the costs of completed and transferred output, ending WIP, and spoilage. In this step, total production costs are assigned to units transferred out, ending WIP inventory, and spoiled units.

Journal entry 8 is prepared to record the transfer of products to the next department (or to FGI if this is the last department). In a normal PCAS, journal entry 8 is prepared from a departmental production cost report. Step 6 concerns preparing cost management reports analyzing whether department costs were within budget. A variety of management control reports can be prepared. In a normal PCAS, departmental costs can be compared against budgeted costs, similar to the job cost reports prepared in Exhibits 5–15 and 5–22 in the last chapter. Special spoilage and rework cost reports can be prepared if these costs are properly accounted for. In a standard PCAS, standard costs can be used to prepare detailed cost variance reports by department.

Learning objective 4.   Demonstrate the differences in calculating product costs between FIFO and weighted-average methods.

If a beginning WIP inventory exists, then some production costs were charged to it in the previous accounting period. These production costs can either (1) be averaged with the current costs in calculating the unit production cost to be used this period, or (2) remain attached to the specific units in the beginning WIP inventory. The first alternative is performed by the weighted-average (WA) cost flow method. The second alternative is performed by the FIFO cost flow method.

If there is no beginning WIP, the FIFO and WA methods yield the same product costs. The separate accounting for last month's work and costs with FIFO results in three calculation differences in the two methods' production reports. In calculating EUP, beginning WIP EUP is subtracted from completed output with FIFO, but not with WA. In determining the cost to use with EUP, only this month's costs added to the department are used with FIFO because this method includes only this month's work in its EUP. With the WA method, EUP includes last month's work in the beginning WIP, so its cost includes the beginning WIP cost.

The third difference occurs in computing the cost of the completed output. FIFO requires separate calculations for the costs to complete the beginning WIP and the costs of the units both started and completed. These are then added to the beginning WIP cost to yield the cost of the completed output. Since the WA method does not account for beginning WIP separately, the average unit cost is simply multiplied by the total units completed, without regard to whether they came from beginning WIP or units started this period.

IMPORTANT TERMS

By-products   Incidental outputs of a joint process.

Department production cost report   A PCAS report of the units produced in a department during a specified period together with their EUP and related costs.

Equivalent units of production (EUP)   The number of units that could have been fully produced (made from "scratch," or started and completed) during a period with the amount of each cost element input into that department or process.

First-in, first-out (FIFO) cost flow method   A method used to account for cost flows in a PCAS in which EUP and unit costs relate only to work done during the current period.

Input usage flows   The flow of cost elements in a process or department. They represent when and how much of direct materials, direct labor, and overhead are added to the process.

Input usage flow diagram   A line chart that summarizes how and when cost elements are added into production. It maps input usage flows throughout production.

Joint costs   Those costs incurred in a single process that yields two or more products or services simultaneously.

Joint products   Two or more products resulting from a joint process. Each joint product has substantial revenue-generating ability.

Parallel processing   A method of arranging processing departments or centers in which, after a certain point, some units may go through different processing departments.

Physical measure method   A procedure used to allocate joint costs to the various joint products in proportion to their physical output measurement.

Relative sales value method   A procedure used to allocate joint costs to the various joint products in proportion to their anticipated sales values.

Sequential processing   A method of arranging processing departments in which all units flow serially from one department to another.

Split-off point   The point at which the outputs of a joint process are first identifiable or can be separated as individual products.

Weighted-average (WA) cost flow method   A method used to account for cost flows in a PCAS that computes an average cost per EUP. To compute this average, beginning inventory units and costs are combined with current production and costs.

DEMONSTRATION PROBLEMS

■ **DEMONSTRATION PROBLEM 1**   *Journal entries to record cost elements acquisition and usage, and transfers between departments in a normal PCAS.*

Using the annual information below for Topper, Inc., prepare the journal entries for each event. (Note: this is the same problem as Demonstration Problem 1 in Chapters 4 and 5. It is repeated to facilitate comparisons between journal entries in a basic CAS, JOCAS, and PCAS.)

1. Raw materials beginning balance is zero, and the ending balance is $20,000. Purchases made on account are $100,000.
2. There is a $200,000 factory payroll for the year, with the following withholding rates: federal income taxes 10%, state income taxes 5%, Social Security taxes 7.5%, pension plan 2%, health insurance 1.5%.
3. Topper's payroll tax burden and fringe benefits rates are as follows: federal unemployment tax rate = 0.8% and the state's = 5.4%; fringe benefits include vacation pay (2 weeks when 50 weeks are worked in a year), Topper's contribution to a pension plan of 5.0%, and its contribution to the health insurance plan of 3.3%.
4. Other actual overhead costs, paid on account, are $88,000. Factory equipment depreciation equals $200,000.
5. Direct materials requisitioned equal $75,000.
6. $175,000 of factory labor costs represents direct labor.
7. Overhead allocation assuming a POR of 200% of direct labor cost.

New information:

8. The direct materials were for two departments: A = $50,000 and B = $25,000
9. Department A incurred $100,000 of direct labor, and department B incurred $75,000.
10. Departments A and B had no beginning WIP or ending WIP balances.
11. All Department B production was completed and transferred to FGI.

Study note: Verify that the only journal entries that have changed from the Chapter 4 and 5 solutions are the three cost element usage journal entries (5–7). These now debit WIP–*Department* instead of WIP–*Job* as in a JOCAS. Journal entry 8 is unique to the PCAS.

SOLUTION TO DEMONSTRATION PROBLEM 1

Ref	General Ledger Account Titles	dr's	cr's	Notes:
	PURCHASE (ACQUISITION) OF RAW MATERIALS:			
1:	Raw Materials Inventory	$100,000		given
	Accounts Payable		$100,000	all RMI purchases are charged
	PREPARING (RECORDING) PAYCHECKS:			
2:	Gross Wages	$200,000		given
	FIT Withholdings Payable		$20,000	+$GROSS WAGES*0.1
	SIT Withholdings Payable		$10,000	+$GROSS WAGES*0.05
	FICA Taxes Payable		$15,000	+$GROSS WAGES*0.075
	Pension Plan Payable		$4,000	+$GROSS WAGES*0.02
	Health Insurance Payable		$3,000	+$GROSS WAGES*0.015
	Wages Payable		$148,000	GROSS WAGES − WITHHOLDINGS
	EMPLOYER'S PAYROLL TAXES & BENEFITS (BURDEN):			
3:	Gross Wages	$52,000		SUM (PAYROLL BURDEN)
	FICA Taxes Payable		$15,000	= withheld from paychecks
	FUTA Taxes Payable		$1,600	+$GROSS WAGES*0.008
	SUTA Taxes Payable		$10,800	+$GROSS WAGES*0.054
	Pension Plan Payable		$10,000	+$GROSS WAGES*0.05
	Health Insurance Payable		$6,600	+$GROSS WAGES*0.033
	Vacation Payable		$8,000	+$GROSS WAGES*0.04
	OTHER OVERHEAD COSTS INCURRED:			
4:	WIP–Manufacturing Overhead (Other OH costs)	$88,000		amounts given
	WIP–Manufacturing Overhead (Depreciation)	$200,000		
	Accounts Payable		$88,000	amounts charged
	Accumulated Depreciation-Factory Equipment		$200,000	
	REQUISITION OF RAW MATERIALS INTO THE FACTORY:			
5:	WIP–Department A (DM)	$50,000		given
	WIP–Department B (DM)	$25,000		given

Continued

—Continued

WIP–Manufacturing Overhead (IM)	$5,000		"plug" to balance
Raw Materials Inventory		$80,000	calculate from T-account
DISTRIBUTING GROSS WAGES TO PRODUCTS:			
6: WIP–Department A (DL)	$100,000		given
WIP–Department B (DL)	$75,000		given
WIP–Manufacturing Overhead (IL)	$77,000		"plug" to balance
Gross Wages		$252,000	gross pay + employer burden
APPLIED OVERHEAD TO PRODUCTS:			
7: WIP–Department A (Applied Overhead)	$200,000		POR = 200% of DL$
WIP–Department B (Applied Overhead)	$150,000		
WIP Manufacturing Overhead		$350,000	DL$ = $175,000 (given)
WIP TRANSFER FROM DEPARTMENT A TO DEPARTMENT B:			
8: WIP–Department B (DM transferred from A)	$350,000		sum of input costs added
WIP–Department A		$350,000	
PRODUCTS COMPLETED:			
9: Finished Goods Inventory	$600,000		sum of input costs added +
WIP–Department B		$600,000	costs transferred from dept A

JOURNAL ENTRY RECORDING CONVENTIONS:
1. Use a dash to separate a control account from a subsidiary account.
2. Use parentheses for a posting reference within a general ledger account.

■ **DEMONSTRATION PROBLEM 2**   *Equivalent units calculations.*

Lollipops, Inc., a confectioner, produces lollipops in three departments. The first department makes secret centers. The second department inserts the secret centers into a candy mold and adds a powdered candy mix, heating and cooling it to produce a hard candy, inspecting it, and then inserting a stick. The third department wraps and boxes the lollipops.

The following information is available about the production process, units worked on, and costs for Department 2 during the month of April:

Direct material 1:	Secret centers transferred in from Department 1 are all added at the start of production.
Direct material 2:	40% of the materials (candy mix) added within Department 2 are input uniformly over the first 40% of processing. Another 35% is added uniformly until processing is 50% complete. The last 25% of materials added (sticks) occurs over the last 20% of processing.
Direct labor:	75% is incurred uniformly throughout the first half of processing. Another 15% occurs uniformly over the next 30% of processing, with the last 10% added during the last one-fifth of the process.
Overhead:	Overhead items are added uniformly throughout the entire process.
Quality control inspection:	Lollipops are inspected at the 70% completion point. A reject rate of 10% of the units inspected is considered normal.

DATA SECTION:

	Units	DM Trans in	DM Added	DL Added	Applied OH
BEG WIP INV	20				
BEG %COMPLETE	30%	(Beginning WIP is 30% down the assembly line)			
BEG WIP COST		$400	$24	$135	$55
UNITS STARTED	100				
COSTS ADDED		$800	$421	$1,676	$203
END WIP INV	20				
END %COMPLETE	60%				
UNITS COMPLETED	85				
OUTPUT LOSS	15				

Required:

Calculate both FIFO and WA equivalent units.

SOLUTION TO DEMONSTRATION PROBLEM 2: Lollipops, Inc., Department 2 Input Usage Flow Diagram.

Lollipops, Inc., Department 2 Input Usage Flow Diagram.

Note: DM-TI is the direct materials transferred in from Department 1
DM-A is the direct materials added within Department 2

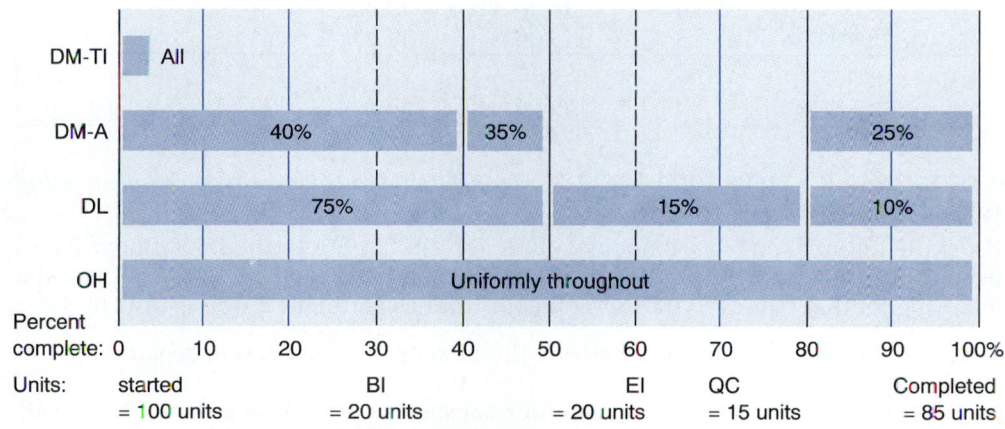

Percentage Complete Calculations

Units:	DM-TI	DM-A	DL	OH
BI:	100%	$\frac{30\%}{40\%} \times 40\% = \underline{30\%}$	$\frac{30\%}{50\%} \times 75\% = \underline{45\%}$	30%
EI:	100%	$40\% + 35\% = \underline{75\%}$	$75\% + \left[\frac{10\%}{30\%} \times 15\%\right] = \underline{80\%}$	60%
QC:	100%	$40\% + 35\% = \underline{75\%}$	$75\% + \left[\frac{20\%}{30\%} \times 15\%\right] = \underline{85\%}$	70%

DATA SECTION:

	Units	DM Trans in	DM Added	DL Added	Applied OH
BEG WIP INV	20				
BEG %COMPLETE		100.00%	30.00%	45.00%	30.00%
BEG WIP COST		$400	$24	$135	$55
UNITS STARTED	100				
COSTS ADDED		$800	$421	$1,676	$203
END WIP INV	20				
END %COMPLETE		100.00%	75.00%	80.00%	60.00%
UNITS COMPLETED	85				
OUTPUT LOSS	15				
LOSS %COMPLETE		100.00%	75.00%	85.00%	70.00%
COST METHOD	1	(1 = FIFO, 2 = WEIGHTED-AVERAGE)			

SOLUTION SECTION: FIFO

LOLLIPOPS, INC.
DEPARTMENT 2 COST REPORT
APRIL 1994

EQUIVALENT UNITS	Units	DM Trans in	DM Added	DL Added	Applied OH
UNITS COMPLETED	85	85.00	85.00	85.00	85.00
LESS: BEG WIP	<20>	<20.00>	<6.00>	<9.00>	<6.00>
ADD: ENDING WIP	20	20.00	15.00	16.00	12.00
ADD: OUTPUT LOSS	15	15.00	11.25	12.75	10.50
UNITS STARTED	100				
EQUIVALENT UNITS		100.00	105.25	104.75	101.50

SOLUTION SECTION: Weighted-Average

LOLLIPOPS, INC.
DEPARTMENT 2 COST REPORT
APRIL 1994

EQUIVALENT UNITS	Units	DM Trans in	DM Added	DL Added	Applied OH
UNITS COMPLETED	85	85.00	85.00	85.00	85.00
LESS: BEG WIP	<20>	n/a	n/a	n/a	n/a
ADD: ENDING WIP	20	20.00	15.00	16.00	12.00
ADD: OUTPUT LOSS	15	15.00	11.25	12.75	10.50
UNITS STARTED	100				
EQUIVALENT UNITS		120.00	111.25	113.75	107.50

■ **DEMONSTRATION PROBLEM 3** *Transferring costs between departments using WA and FIFO cost flow methods.*

Using the information from Demonstration Problem 2, prepare the Department 2 production cost report for April using both the FIFO and WA methods. Then prepare the following journal entries to transfer lollipops from Department 2 to Department 3:

1. Both FIFO and WA journal entries with all spoilage treated as a department cost variance.
2. Using the WA cost values only with normal spoilage treated as a cost of overhead.
3. Using the WA cost values only with normal spoilage allocated to the good lollipops passing inspection.

SOLUTION TO DEMONSTRATION PROBLEM 3: FIFO Report:

SOLUTION SECTION: FIFO

LOLLIPOPS, INC.
PRODUCTION DEPARTMENT 2 COST REPORT
APRIL 1994

EQUIVALENT UNITS:	Units	DM Trans in	DM Added	DL Added	Applied OH	Totals
UNITS COMPLETED	85	85.00	85.00	85.00	85.00	
LESS: BEG WIP	<20>	<20.00>	<6.00>	<9.00>	<6.00>	
ADD: ENDING WIP	20	20.00	15.00	16.00	12.00	
ADD: OUTPUT LOSS	15	15.00	11.25	12.75	10.50	
UNITS STARTED	100					
EQUIVALENT UNITS		100.00	105.25	104.75	101.50	
COST/EQUIVALENT UNIT:						
BEGINNING WIP COSTS		n/a	n/a	n/a	n/a	n/a
COSTS ADDED THIS MONTH		$800	$421	$1,676	$203	$3,100
COSTS INCURRED		$800	$421	$1,676	$203	$3,100
UNIT COSTS		$8.00	$4.00	$16.00	$2.00	$30.00
COST ALLOCATIONS:						
UNITS COMPLETED:	85	n/a	n/a	n/a	n/a	n/a
BEG WIP COSTS	20	$400	$24	$135	$55	$614
COSTS TO COMPLETE		0	56	176	28	260
STARTED THIS MONTH	65	520	260	1,040	130	1,950
COSTS TRANSFERRED OUT		$920	$340	$1,351	$213	$2,824
ENDING WIP INV:	20	$160	$60	$256	$24	$500
OUTPUT LOSS:	15	$120	$45	$204	$21	$390
COSTS ACCOUNTED FOR:		$1,200	$445	$1,811	$258	$3,714

SOLUTION TO DEMONSTRATION PROBLEM 3: WA Report.

SOLUTION SECTION: WA

LOLLIPOPS, INC.
PRODUCTION DEPARTMENT 2 COST REPORT
APRIL 1994

EQUIVALENT UNITS:	Units	DM Trans in	DM Added	DL Added	Applied OH	Totals
UNITS COMPLETED	85	85.00	85.00	85.00	85.00	
LESS: BEG WIP	<20>	n/a	n/a	n/a	n/a	
ADD: ENDING WIP	20	20.00	15.00	16.00	12.00	
ADD: OUTPUT LOSS	15	15.00	11.25	12.75	10.50	
UNITS STARTED	100					
EQUIVALENT UNITS		120.00	111.25	113.75	107.50	
COST/EQUIVALENT UNIT:						
BEGINNING WIP COSTS		$400	$24	$135	$55	$614
COSTS ADDED THIS MONTH		800	421	1,676	203	$3,100
COSTS INCURRED		$1,200	$445	$1,811	$258	$3,714
UNIT COSTS		$10.00	$4.00	$15.92	$2.40	$32.32
COST ALLOCATIONS:						
UNITS COMPLETED:	85	$850	$340	$1,353	$204	$2,747
BEG WIP COSTS		n/a	n/a	n/a	n/a	n/a
COSTS TO COMPLETE		n/a	n/a	n/a	n/a	n/a
STARTED THIS MONTH		n/a	n/a	n/a	n/a	n/a
COSTS TRANSFERRED OUT		$850	$340	$1,353	$204	$2,747
ENDING WIP INV:	20	$200	$60	$255	$29	$544
OUTPUT LOSS:	15	$150	$45	$203	$25	$423
COSTS ACCOUNTED FOR:		$1,200	$445	$1,811	$258	$3,714

SOLUTION TO DEMONSTRATION PROBLEM 3: Journal entries for transfers.

1a. FIFO:

WIP–Department 3 (DM from Dept. 2)	$2,824	
WIP–Department 2 Spoilage Cost Variance	$ 390	
WIP–Department 2		$3,214

1b. WA:

WIP–Department 3 (DM from Dept. 2)	$2,747	
WIP–Department 2 Spoilage Cost Variance	$ 423	
WIP–Department 2		$3,170

2.

WIP–Department 3 (DM from Dept. 2)	$2,747	
WIP–Manufacturing Overhead (Spoilage)	$ 282	
Loss from Abnormal Spoilage	$ 141	
WIP–Department 2		$3,170

3.

WIP–Department 3 (DM from Dept. 2)*	$3,029	
Loss from Abnormal Spoilage	$ 141	
WIP–Department 2		$3,170

* Note: All NOL is added to transferred out lollipops because the EI units have not yet been inspected and, therefore, are not part of the good lollipops passing inspection.

NOL and AOL Calculations:

$$NOL = 10\% \times [20 \text{ units (BI)} + 100 \text{ units (started)} - 20 \text{ units (EI)} = 100 \text{ units}]$$
$$\underline{\underline{= 10 \text{ units}}}$$

$$AOL = 15 \text{ units rejected} - 10 \text{ units (NOL)} = \underline{\underline{5 \text{ units}}}$$

$$\text{Normal spoilage cost} = \frac{10 \text{ units}}{15 \text{ units}} \times \$423$$
$$= \underline{\underline{\$282}}$$

$$\text{Abnormal spoilage cost} = \frac{5 \text{ units}}{15 \text{ units}} \times \$423$$
$$= \underline{\underline{\$141}}$$

REVIEW QUESTIONS

6.1 Compare a process and a job order production environment.

6.2 Compare the WIP subsidiary ledger system in a JOCAS and in a PCAS.

6.3 What is the basic formula for computing unit cost in a PCAS?

6.4 How does the basic CAS in Chapter 4 compare to a PCAS?

6.5 What is the purpose of a department production cost report?

6.6 List the key differences between a JOCAS and PCAS.

6.7 What is the basic objective of a PCAS?

6.8 Describe the physical flow of units and the flow of costs in a sequential processing configuration.

6.9 Describe the physical flow of units and the flow of costs in a parallel processing configuration.

6.10 Give an example of a product line that is made sequentially and one made in a parallel process.

6.11 How is WIP transferred into a subsequent department accounted for within the receiving department?

6.12 Which PCAS journal entries are the same as those in a JOCAS?

6.13 Which PCAS journal entries are different from those in a JOCAS?

6.14 What new journal entry is required in a PCAS, and why?

6.15 What is the one difference in recording cost element usage journal entries in a PCAS as compared to a JOCAS?

6.16 What is the difference between PCAS and JOCAS subsidiary ledger systems for FGI and COGS?

6.17 What is meant by EUP? Why is it necessary to use EUP to determine the actual production for a period?

6.18 What four events usually happen in traditional PCASs?

6.19 How does the existence of partially completed output in a department change the basic PCAS formula for calculating unit cost?

6.20 What is the formula for EUP? Give an example calculation.

6.21 List and briefly describe the six steps in a PCAS.

6.22 Contrast "units to be accounted for" and "units accounted for." Why is this distinction important?

6.23 Why is it important to ascertain how products flow through a department?

6.24 Explain a FIFO flow. Give an example product that would be produced in this way.

6.25 Explain a WA cost flow. Give an example product that would be produced in this way.

6.26 What can be said about the FIFO and WA cost flow methods when there is no beginning WIP in a department? Why is this true?

6.27 What is an input usage flow? Why is it important in calculating EUP?

6.28 What is an input usage flow diagram, and why is it important?

6.29 What is linear interpolation, and why is it important in determining a cost element's percentage complete for a specific subset of products?

6.30 What is the formula for linear interpolation? Give an example calculation.

6.31 What is the difference between WA and FIFO EUP?

6.32 Why is beginning WIP EUP subtracted from units completed in FIFO, but not in WA?

6.33 Explain why multiple EUP may have to be calculated for direct materials.

6.34 When will different cost elements have the same EUP?

6.35 List two versions of the formula for calculating the total cost of an input item in a particular subset of units.

6.36 What is the total cost formula for FIFO costs to complete the beginning WIP this month?

6.37 What is the one basic difference between FIFO and WA, and what effect does it have on the production department cost reports?

6.38 From the standpoint of cost control, why is the FIFO method superior to the WA method?

6.39 How can last month's unit cost be calculated from this month's FIFO cost report? Give an example.

6.40 Differentiate between normal and abnormal spoilage. Explain how both should be reported for management purposes.

6.41 How are the amounts of normal and abnormal spoilage determined at an inspection point?

6.42 What is the justification for spreading the cost of spoiled units over the remaining good units?

6.43 When does normal spoilage have to be allocated between ending WIP and good units transferred out of the department?

6.44 Define:

- Joint costs
- Joint products
- Split-off point
- By-products

Give an example of a situation in which all these terms come into play.

6.45 Describe two methods of allocating joint costs to joint products.

6.46 What are the implications for the joint products' unit costs and profit from using these two methods?

CHAPTER-SPECIFIC PROBLEMS

These problems require responses based directly on concepts and techniques presented in the text.

6.47 *Calculating equivalent units of production.* Xanadu produces multimedia computers. Its sales for May are 125,000 units. The following additional data are provided:

	NUMBER OF UNITS
Beginning inventory:	
Work-in-process	–0–
Finished goods	37,500
Budgeted inventory at May 31:	
Work-in-process (75% processed)	8,000
Finished goods	30,000

Required:

Calculate the number of equivalent units of production (EUP) for Xanadu for May assuming all inputs are added uniformly throughout production.

6.48 *Calculating equivalent units of production.* The Lodi Company uses a process costing system to account for the costs of its only product, Wizmo. Production begins in the Fabrication Department where units of raw material are molded into various connecting parts. After fabrication is complete, the units are transferred to the Assembly Department. No material is added in the Assembly Department. After assembly is complete, the units are transferred to the Packaging Department where packing material is placed around the units. After the units are ready for shipping, they are sent to the shipping area. At the end of the period, June 30, the following inventory of Wizmo is on hand:

No unused raw material or packing material.
Fabrication Department:
   300 units, one-third complete as to raw materials and
   one-half complete as to conversion costs (DL + OH).
Assembly Department:
   1,000 units, two-fifths complete as to conversion costs.
Packaging Department:
   100 units, three-fourths complete as to packing material and
   one-fourth complete as to conversion costs.
Shipping area:
   400 units.

Required:
a. Calculate the number of equivalent units of raw material in all inventories at June 30.
b. Calculate the number of equivalent units of Fabrication Department conversion costs in all inventories at June 30.
c. Calculate the number of equivalent units of packing material in all inventories at June 30.

[AICPA adapted]

6.49 *FIFO and WA equivalent units of production.* The Rally Company uses the FIFO method in its process costing system. All direct materials are introduced at the beginning of the process in the Milling Department. The following data are available for the month of July:

	UNITS
Beginning WIP (40% complete as to conversion costs)	500
Started	2,000
Transferred to the Finishing Department	2,100
Ending WIP (25% complete as to conversion costs)	400

Direct labor and overhead are added into the process uniformly, so they are combined together as conversion costs for EUP calculations.

Required:
a. What are the EUP for the month of July?
b. Using the same data, what are the EUP under the WA method?

[AICPA adapted]

6.50 *Calculating FIFO equivalent units of production.* The Assembly Department is the second process of Elgin Company's production cycle. On May 1, beginning WIP contained 25,000 units that were 60% complete as to overhead. During May, 100,000 units were transferred in from the first process. On May 31, ending WIP contained 20,000 units that were 80% complete as to overhead; 100,000 units were completed. Direct materials are added at the end of the process. Direct labor is added uniformly over the last half of the process. Spoilage occurs at the 75% stage of completion. Overhead is added uniformly throughout the process.

Required:
Using the FIFO cost flow method, calculate the EUP at May 31.

6.51 *Calculating WA EUP.* Using the information from the preceding problem, calculate the weighted-average EUP.

6.52 *Production cost report using the WA method.* You have just been hired as the cost accountant for Digitech Corporation. This position has been vacant for one month. Fred Sotheby, manager of Digitech's tax department, has performed some computations for last month's information. However, he confesses that he doesn't remember a great deal about cost accounting. Fred took the following costs and units for last month (July 1994) from the financial statements:

	UNITS	COSTS
Work-in-process (50% complete as to labor and overhead)	300,000	$ 660,960
Finished goods	200,000	1,009,800

Materials are added at the beginning of production, and overhead is applied to each product at the rate of 60% of direct labor costs. Labor and overhead are incurred uniformly throughout the process. There was no finished goods inventory at the beginning of last month. A review of Digitech's inventory cost records provides you with the following information:

	UNITS	DIRECT MATERIALS COSTS	DIRECT LABOR COSTS
Work-in-process, 07/01/94 (80% complete as to labor and overhead)	200,000	$ 200,000	$ 315,000
Units started in production	1,000,000		
Units completed in July	900,000		
Costs for July		1,300,000	1,995,000

Required:
a. Prepare a production cost report for July.
b. Prepare the journal entry to correct the recorded amounts for finished goods and work-in-process inventory.

[AICPA adapted]

6.53 *Production cost report in second department using the WA method.* Lakeview Corporation manufactures plastic toys that require operations in three separate departments: Molding, Assembling, and Finishing. Additional materials are added during the assembly process. The company uses the WA method, and the following information is available for the Assembling Department for the month of June 1994.

Beginning inventory (degree of completion: transferred in 100%; direct materials, 100%; direct labor, 60%; overhead, 50%)	2,000 units
Transferred in from Molding	10,000 units
Ending inventory (degree of completion: transferred in, 100%; direct materials, 90%; direct labor, 70%; overhead, 35%)	4,000 units
Transferred to Finishing	8,000 units

COSTS	BEGINNING INVENTORY	CURRENT PERIOD
Transferred in	$32,000	$160,000
Direct materials	20,000	96,000
Direct labor	7,200	36,000
Overhead	5,500	18,000

Required:
Prepare a production cost report for the Assembling Department for June 1994.

[AICPA adapted]

6.54 *Weighted-average and FIFO methods.* The Belltone Company assembles cellular telephones in a one-process operation. Belltone combines DL and OH into conversion costs. Data for May follow:

	UNITS
Beginning WIP inventory:	
Direct materials (100% complete)	10,000
Conversion costs (75% complete)	10,000

Continued

Units started during May		70,000
Ending WIP inventory:		
Direct materials (100% complete)		12,000
Conversion costs (40% complete)		12,000
Costs of beginning WIP inventory:		
Direct materials	$ 12,000	
Conversion costs	14,000	$ 26,000
Costs of current period:		
Direct materials	$ 86,000	
Conversion costs	100,000	186,000
		$212,000

Required:

a. Assuming the WA method, prepare a production cost report for May.

b. Assuming the FIFO method, prepare a production cost report for May.

6.55 **FIFO and WA production reports.** Marshall Manufacturing produces a single product in two production departments: Department A and Department B. The following data pertain to production in both departments for the month of June:

	DEPARTMENT A	DEPARTMENT B
Beginning WIP inventory	2,000	1,000
Units started	6,000	—
Units transferred to B	5,000	—
Units transferred to finished goods		4,000
Ending WIP inventory	3,000	2,000
Cost data:		
Direct materials	$32,000	$ —
Conversion costs	37,000	25,500
Beginning WIP inventory costs:		
Transferred in*	—	11,000
Direct materials	8,000	
Conversion costs	5,000	6,000

*Also called prior department costs.

In Department A, the direct materials are added at the beginning of the process, and the beginning WIP inventory is three-fifths complete as to conversion costs (DL + OH), while ending WIP inventory is two-thirds complete. No additional direct materials are added in Department B. Conversion costs are incurred uniformly throughout both departments. The beginning WIP inventory in Department B is 75% complete and the ending WIP inventory is 25% complete as to conversion costs.

Required:

Determine the value of WIP inventory as of June 30 and the cost of goods transferred to finished goods inventory using the WA and FIFO cost flow methods.

[AICPA adapted]

6.56 **Converting the form of units, adding materials, and accounting for spoilage.** Portland Chemical Company manufactures one product called LawnCare. Process Center A and Process Center B are required to produce this product. Physical production data for March are as follows:

- Units transferred:
  - From Process Center A to Process Center B: 2,200 pounds
  - From Process Center B to finished goods: 900 gallons
- Units spoiled in Process Center B: 100 gallons
- Inventory data:

	PROCESS CENTER A		PROCESS CENTER B	
	BEGINNING	ENDING	BEGINNING	ENDING
Units	200	300	200	300
Degree of completion as to conversion costs	½	½	½	⅔

For each unit of Process Center A output, two units of raw material X are put in at the start of processing. For each unit of Process Center B output, three cans of raw material Y are put in at the end of processing and two pounds of Process Center A output are put in at the start. Spoilage generally occurs in Process Center B at the start of the process.

Work-in-process accounts are maintained for materials, conversion costs (DL + OH), and prior department costs. Portland uses the FIFO cost flow method for inventory evaluation for Process Center A and the WA cost flow method for inventory valuation for Process Center B.

Required:
Determine the EUP for Process Center A and Process Center B.

[AICPA adapted]

6.57 *Weighted-average method versus the FIFO method.* Kristina Company, which manufactures quality paint sold at premium prices, uses a single production department. Production begins with the blending of various chemicals, which are added at the beginning of the process, and ends with the canning of the paint. Canning occurs when the mixture reaches the 90% stage of completion. The gallon cans are then transferred to the Shipping Department for crating and shipment. Labor and overhead are added continuously throughout the process. Factory overhead is applied on the basis of direct labor hours at the rate of $3 per hour.

Prior to May, when a change in the process was implemented, WIP inventories were insignificant. The change in the process enables greater production but results in material amounts of WIP for the first time. The company has always used the WA method to determine equivalent production and unit costs. Now, production management is considering changing from the WA method to the FIFO method.

The following data relate to actual production during the month of May:

COSTS FOR MAY	
Work-in-process inventory, May 1 (4,000 gallons 25% complete):	
Direct materials–chemicals	$ 45,600
Direct labor ($10 per hour)	6,250
Factory overhead	1,875
May costs added:	
Direct materials–chemicals	228,400
Direct materials–cans	7,000
Direct labor ($10 per hour)	35,000
Factory overhead	10,500

UNITS FOR MAY	GALLONS
Work-in-process inventory, May 1 (25% complete)	4,000
Sent to Shipping Department	20,000
Started in May	21,000
Work-in-process inventory, May 31 (80% complete)	5,000

Required:
a. Prepare a schedule of equivalent units for each cost element for the month of May using the:
   1. WA method.
   2. FIFO method.

b. Calculate the cost (to the nearest cent) per equivalent unit for each cost element for the month of May using the:
   1. WA method.
   2. FIFO method.
c. Discuss the advantages and disadvantages of using the WA method versus the FIFO method, and explain under what circumstances each method should be used.

[CMA adapted]

6.58 *Transferred-in and conversion costs per EUP using the WA method.* The following data pertain to the Malone Company:

	UNITS	COSTS
Beginning WIP inventory	5,000	$ 6,300
Units transferred in	35,000	58,000
Units completed	37,000	
Ending WIP inventory	3,000	

	TRANSFERRED IN COSTS	DIRECT MATERIALS COSTS	CONVERSION COSTS	TOTAL COSTS
Beginning WIP	$ 2,900	$ —	$ 3,400	$ 6,300
Transferred in	17,500	25,500	15,000	58,000
	$20,400	$25,500	$18,400	$64,300

Conversion costs (DL + OH) were 20% complete as to beginning WIP inventory and 40% complete as to ending WIP inventory. All direct materials are added at the end of the process. The WA method is used.

Required:
a. Calculate the cost per EUP for conversion costs, rounded to the nearest penny.
b. Calculate the portion of the total costs of ending WIP inventory attributable to transferred in costs.

[AICPA adapted]

6.59 *Calculating abnormal spoilage.* A company that manufactures baseballs begins operations on January 1. Each baseball requires three elements:

■ A hard plastic core
■ Several yards of twine that are wrapped around the plastic core
■ A piece of leather to cover the baseball

The plastic core is started down a conveyor belt and is automatically wrapped with twine to the approximate size of a baseball, at which time the leather cover is sewn to the wrapped twine.

Finished baseballs are inspected, and defective ones are pulled out. Defective baseballs cannot be economically reworked and are destroyed. Normal spoilage is 3% of baseballs that *pass* inspection. Costs for the first week of operations are:

Direct materials cost	$ 840
Conversion costs (DL + OH)	315
	$1,155

During the week, 2,100 baseballs were completed, and 2,000 passed inspection. There was no ending WIP inventory.

Required:
Calculate abnormal spoilage cost.

[CIA adapted]

6.60 *The FIFO method for spoilage.* Sedco Manufacturing manufactures product A in three processes, each of which is done by a different department. The Finishing

Department is the last process before product A is completed and transferred to finished goods inventory.

All materials needed to complete product A are added at the beginning of the process in the Finishing Department, and spoiled units, if any, occur only at this point. Conversion costs (DL + OH) are incurred uniformly throughout the process. The company uses the FIFO cost flow method in its cost accounting system and has accumulated the following data for October for the Finishing Department:

1. Production of Product A:
   - Beginning WIP inventory
     (conversion work is ¾ complete)   10,000
   - Transferred from preceding depart-
     ments during October   40,000
   - Completed and transferred to finished
     goods inventory during October   35,000
   - Ending WIP inventory
     (conversion work is ½ complete)   10,000

2. Cost of beginning WIP inventory:
   - Costs from preceding departments $ 38,000
   - Costs added in Finishing Department
     prior to October 1:
       Direct materials   21,500
       Conversion costs   81,000
                                                _____
                                                $140,500

3. Units transferred to the Finishing Department during October had costs of
   $140,000 assigned from preceding depart-
   ments.

4. During October, the Finishing Department
   incurred the following costs:
       Direct materials $ 70,000
       Conversion costs   292,500
                                               _____
                                               $362,500

Required:

a. Prepare a production cost report for the Finishing Department using the FIFO method.

b. Even though the problem states that spoilage occurs at the beginning of the process, prepare a production cost report for the Finishing Department assuming that spoilage occurs at the end of the process.

6.61 *Assigning costs to transferred units, ending WIP, and abnormal spoilage.* The Babbage Company uses a process costing system in its three-department operation. A unit of product passes through molding, assembly, and finishing before it is transferred to finished goods. Finishing Department data for May follow:

	UNITS
Beginning WIP	1,400
Units transferred in from the Assembly Department	14,000
Units spoiled	700
Units transferred to finished goods inventory	11,200

Direct materials are added at the beginning of the processing in the Finishing Department without changing the number of units being processed. Beginning WIP inventory was 70% complete as to conversion costs (DL + OH).

Ending WIP inventory was 40% complete as to conversion costs. All spoilage was discovered at final inspection before the units were transferred to finished goods; 560 of the units spoiled were within the limit considered normal.

The Babbage Company uses the WA method. The equivalent units and the current costs per EUP for each cost factor are as follows:

	EUP	CURRENT COSTS PER EUP
Transferred in	15,400	$5
Direct materials	15,400	1
Conversion costs	13,300	3
Total cost per EUP		$9

Required:

a. Calculate the cost of production transferred to the finished goods inventory.
b. Calculate the costs assigned to WIP inventory on May 31.
c. What are the total costs transferred in from the Assembly Department during May if the total costs of prior departments included in the WIP of the Finishing Department on May 1 amounted to $6,300?
d. What is the cost associated with abnormal spoilage?
e. To what account are abnormal spoilage costs usually charged?

[CMA adapted]

THINK-TANK PROBLEMS

Although these problems are based on chapter material, reading extra material, reviewing previous chapters, and using creativity may be required to develop workable solutions.

6.62 *Equivalent units of production and unit costs.* Wood Glow Manufacturing Company produces a single product, a wood refinishing kit that sells for $17.95. The final processing of the kits occurs in the Packaging Department. An internal quilted wrap is applied at the beginning of the packaging process. A compartmented outside box printed with instructions and the company's name and logo is added when units are 60% through the process. Conversion costs, consisting of direct labor and applied overhead, occur evenly throughout the packaging process. Conversion activities after the addition of the box involve package sealing, testing for leakage, and final inspection. Rejections in the Packaging Department are rare and may be ignored. The following data pertain to the activities of the Packaging Department during the month of October:

■ Beginning WIP inventory was 10,000 units, 40% complete as to conversion costs.
■ 30,000 units were started and completed in the month.
■ There were 10,000 units in ending WIP, 80% complete as to conversion costs.

The Packaging Department's October costs were:

Quilted wrap	$80,000
Outside boxes	50,000
Direct labor	22,000
Applied overhead	
($3 per direct labor dollar)	66,000

The costs transferred in from prior processing were $3 per unit. The cost of goods sold for the month was $240,000, and the ending finished goods inventory was $84,000. Wood Glow uses the FIFO method of inventory valuation.

Wood Glow's controller, Mark Brandon, has been asked to analyze the activities of the Packaging Department for the month of October. Brandon knows that in order to properly determine the department's unit cost of production, he must first calculate the EUP.

Required:

a. Prepare an EUP schedule for the October activity in the Packaging Department. Be sure to account for the beginning WIP inventory, the units started and completed during the month, and the ending WIP inventory.
b. Determine the cost per equivalent unit of the October production.
c. Assuming that the actual overhead incurred during October was $5,000 more

than the overhead applied, describe how the value of the ending WIP inventory could be determined.

[CMA adapted]

6.63 *Production cost report using WA and FIFO methods.* Deterra, Inc., uses three departments to produce a detergent. The Finishing Department is the third and last step before the product is transferred to storage.

All materials needed to give the detergent its final composition are added at the beginning of the process in the Finishing Department. Any lost units occur only at this point and are considered to be normal.

The company uses FIFO costing. The following data for the Finishing Department for October have been made available:

Production data:
In process, October 1	
(labor and factory overhead, ¾ complete)	10,000 gallons
Transferred in from preceding department	40,000 gallons
Finished and transferred to storage	35,000 gallons
In process, October 31	
(labor and factory overhead, ½ complete)	10,000 gallons

Additional data:
Work-in-process inventory, October 1:	
Cost from preceding department	$ 38,000
Cost from this department:	
Materials	21,500
Labor	39,000
Factory overhead	42,000
Total work-in-process inventory, October 1	$140,500
Transferred in during October	$140,000
Cost added in this department:	
Materials	$ 70,000
Labor	162,500
Factory overhead	130,000
Total costs added	$362,500
Total costs to be accounted for	$643,000

Required:
a. Prepare a production cost report for the Finishing Department for October using the FIFO method.
b. Prepare a production cost report for the Finishing Department for October using the WA method. (Carry unit cost calculations to three decimal places, and round up the digit "5" in the fourth decimal place.)

[AICPA adapted]

6.64 *Accretion and production cost reports for two departments using the FIFO and WA methods.* The Crews Company produces a chemical agent for commercial use. The company accounts for production in two cost centers: (1) Cooking and (2) Mix-Pack. In the first cost center, liquid substances are combined in large cookers and boiled. After the batch is cooked, it is transferred to Mix-Pack, the second cost center, where a quantity of alcohol equal to the liquid measure of the batch is added. Following this, the batch is mixed and bottled in one-gallon containers.

Material is added at the beginning of production in each cost center, and labor is added equally during production in each cost center. The FIFO method is used in the Cooking Department and the WA method in the Mix-Pack Department.

The following information is available for the month of October:

	COOKING	MIX-PACK
Work-in-process, October 1:		
Materials	$ 996	$ 114

Labor	100	60
Overhead	80	48
Prior department cost	0	426
Month of October:		
Materials	$39,600	$15,276
Labor	10,050	16,000
Overhead	8,040	12,800

Inventory and production records show that Cooking had 1,000 gallons, 40% processed, on October 1 and 800 gallons, 50% processed, on October 31; Mix-Pack had 600 gallons, 50% processed, on October 1 and 1,000 gallons, 30% processed, on October 31.

Production reports for October show that Cooking started 40,000 gallons into production and completed and transferred 40,200 gallons to Mix-Pack, and Mix-Pack completed and transferred 80,000 one-gallon containers of the finished product to the distribution warehouse.

Required:

a. Prepare a production cost report for the Cooking Department.

b. Prepare a production cost report for the Mix-Pack Department.

[AICPA adapted]

6.65 *Normal and abnormal spoilage.* Romano Foods, Inc., manufactures Roman Surprise Fresh Frozen Pizzas, which are 12 inches in diameter and retail for $4.69 to $5.99, depending upon the topping. The company employs a PCAS in which the product flows through several processes. Joe Corolla, Vice President of Production, has had a long-running disagreement with the controller, Sue Marshall, over the handling of spoilage costs. Corolla resists every attempt to charge production with variance responsibilities unless they are favorable. Spoilage costs have not been significant in the past, but in November, the Mixing Department had a substantial amount of spoilage. Traditionally, Romano Foods has treated 10% of good output as normal spoilage. The department input 120,000 units of ingredients, and 13,000 dough units were rejected at inspection. Marshall is concerned about the abnormal spoilage and wants Corolla to take corrective steps. Corolla, on the other hand, maintains that the Mixing Department is operating properly. He has prepared the following report for the Mixing Department to support his contention.

Romano Foods–Mixing Department
Production Cost Report
Month Ended November 30, 19X8

INPUT UNITS	TOTAL COST	GOOD OUTPUT UNITS	10% NORMAL SPOILAGE	ABNORMAL SPOILAGE	GOOD UNIT COST
120,000	$45,360	107,000	12,000	1,000	$0.42

Budgeted unit cost	$0.435
Actual cost per good unit	0.420
Favorable variance	$0.015

COST RECONCILIATION

Cost of 107,000 good units @ $0.42 each	$44,940
Abnormal spoilage (charge to purchasing for buying inferior materials):	
1,000 units @ $0.42 each	420
Total cost	$45,360

Required:

a. Revise Joe Corolla's production cost report for November 19X8 by calculating:

1. The number of units of normal spoilage.

2. The number of units of abnormal spoilage.
3. The total and unit costs of the Mixing Department's production of good units in November.
4. The total and unit costs of abnormal spoilage.

b. Prepare the journal entry to transfer costs for the Mixing Department for November to the Assembly Department.

c. Describe how Joe Corolla's production cost report shows the performance of the Mixing Department to be less favorable than that shown in the revised report.

[CMA adapted]

6.66 *Equivalent units of production cost per unit, normal spoilage, and ending WIP costs.* Ranka Company manufactures high-quality leather products. The company's profits have declined during the past nine months. Ranka has used unit cost data (which were developed 18 months ago) in planning and controlling its operations. In an attempt to isolate the causes of poor profit performance, management is investigating the manufacturing operations of each of its products.

One of Ranka's main products is fine leather belts. The belts are produced in a single, continuous process in the Bluett Plant. During the process, leather strips are sewn, punched, and dyed. Buckles are attached by rivets when the belts are 70% complete as to direct labor and overhead (conversion costs). The belts then enter a final finishing stage to conclude the process. Labor and overhead are applied continuously during the process.

The leather belts are inspected twice during the process: (1) just before the buckles are attached (70% point in the process) and (2) at the conclusion of the finishing stage (100% point in the process). Ranka uses the WA method to calculate its unit costs.

The leather belts produced at the Bluett Plant sell wholesale for $9.95 each. Management wants to compare the current manufacturing costs per unit with the prices on the market for leather belts. Top management has asked the Bluett Plant to submit data on the cost of manufacturing the leather belts for the month of October. These data will be used to evaluate whether modifications in the production process should be initiated or whether an increase in the selling price of the belts is justified. The cost per equivalent unit being used for planning and control purposes is $5.35 per unit.

On October 1, the WIP inventory consisted of 400 partially completed units. The belts were 25% complete as to conversion costs. The costs included in the inventory on October 1 were as follows:

Leather strips	$1,000
Conversion costs	300
	$1,300

During October, 7,600 leather strips were placed in production. A total of 6,800 good leather belts were completed. A total of 300 belts were identified as defective at the two inspection points—100 at the first inspection point (before the buckle is attached) and 200 at the final inspection point (after finishing). The quantity of defective belts was considered normal. In addition, 200 belts were removed from the production line when the process was 40% complete as to conversion costs because they had been damaged as a result of a malfunction during the sewing operation. This malfunction was considered an unusual occurrence, so the spoilage was classified as abnormal. Defective (spoiled) units are not reprocessed and have zero salvage value. The WIP inventory on October 31 consisted of 700 belts that were 50% complete as to conversion costs.

The costs charged to production during October were as follows:

Leather strips	$20,600
Buckles	4,550
Conversion costs	20,700
Total	$45,850

Required:

a. What are the EUP for the leather strips for October?

b. What is the cost per EUP for the buckles?

c. What are the total production costs to account for in October?

d. What is the total cost per EUP?

e. What is the total cost of normal spoilage?

f. What is the total ending WIP inventory cost?

g. What is the average cost per unit for finished goods?

h. If the 300 defective belts (normal spoilage) were reworked and management wanted to be sure that the incremental costs did not exceed the cost of producing new units, how would the rework costs be accounted for?

[CMA adapted]

6.67 *Weighted-average method, normal spoilage, and abnormal spoilage.* APCO Company manufactures various lines of bicycles. Because of the high volume of each type of product, the company employs a process cost system using the WA method to determine unit costs. Bicycle parts are manufactured in the Molding Department and transferred to the Assembly Department, where they are partially assembled. After assembly, the bicycles are sent to the Packing Department.

Cost per unit data for the 20-inch dirt bike has been completed through the Molding Department. Annual cost and production figures for the Assembly Department are as follows:

PRODUCTION DATA

Beginning inventory	3,000 units (100% complete as to transferred in; 100% complete as to assembly materials; 80% complete as to conversion, DL + OH)
Transferred in during year	45,000 units (100% complete as to transferred in)
Transferred out to Packing during year	40,000 units
Ending inventory	4,000 units (100% complete as to transferred in; 50% complete as to assembly materials; 20% complete as to conversion)

COST DATA

	TRANSFERRED IN	DIRECT MATERIALS	CONVERSION COSTS
Beginning inventory	$ 82,200	$ 6,660	$ 11,930
Current period	1,237,800	96,840	236,590
Totals	$1,320,000	$103,500	$248,520

Defective bicycles are identified at an inspection point when the assembly process is 70% complete; all assembly materials have been added by this point of the process. The normal rejection percentage for defective bicycles is 5% of the bicycles reaching the inspection point. Any defective bicycles over and above the 5% quota are considered as abnormal. All defective bikes are removed from the production process.

Required:

a. Compute the number of defective bikes considered to be:

1. A normal amount of defective bikes.

2. An abnormal amount of defective bikes.

b. Compute the weighted-average EUP for the year for:

1. Bicycles transferred in from the Molding Department.

2. Bicycles produced with regard to assembly material.

3. Bicycles produced with regard to assembly conversion.

c. Compute the cost per equivalent unit for the fully assembled dirt bike.

d. Compute the amount of the total production cost of $1,672,020 that will be associated with the following items:

1. Normal defective units.

2. Abnormal defective units.
3. Good units completed in the Assembly Department.
4. Ending WIP inventory in the Assembly Department.

e. Describe how the applicable dollar amounts for the following items would be presented in the financial statements:
1. Normal defective units.
2. Abnormal defective units.
3. Completed units transferred to the Packing Department.
4. Ending WIP inventory in the Assembly Department.

f. Discuss some potential reasons why spoilage might occur in this company. Which of these reasons would you consider important enough to correct and why? How might you attempt to correct these problems?

[CMA adapted]

6.68 *Inventory costing using the WA and FIFO methods.* In attempting to verify the costing of the December 31, 19X4, inventory of WIP and finished goods recorded on Spirit Corporation's books, the auditor finds:

Finished goods, 200,000 units	$1,009,800
Work-in-process, 300,000 units, 50% complete as to labor and factory overhead	660,960

Materials are added to production at the beginning of the manufacturing process, and factory overhead is applied at the rate of 60% of direct labor cost. Spirit's inventory cost records disclosed zero finished goods on January 1, 19X4, and the following additional information for 19X4:

	UNITS	DIRECT MATERIALS COST	DIRECT LABOR COST
Work-in-process, January 1 (80 percent complete as to labor and factory overhead)	200,000	$ 200,000	$ 315,000
Units started in production:	1,000,000		
Materials cost		$1,300,000	
Labor cost			$1,995,000
Units completed	900,000		

Required:
a. What are the EUP for labor under the WA method?
b. What are the EUP for labor under the FIFO method?
c. What is the unit cost for overhead using the WA method?
d. What is the unit cost for overhead using the FIFO method?
e. What is the cost per EUP for labor using the WA method?
f. What is the cost per EUP for labor using the FIFO method?
g. What is the total cost for the ending inventory of finished goods using the WA method?
h. What is the cost assigned to the 300,000 units in ending WIP inventory using the WA method?
i. What is the cost of finished goods in ending inventory per the books?
j. Prepare the necessary journal entry to state the WIP and finished goods inventories correctly, using the WA method.

[AICPA adapted]

6.69 *Comprehensive problem.* Ballinger Paper Products manufactures a high-quality paper box. The Box Department applies two separate operations—cutting and folding. The paper is first cut and trimmed to the dimensions of a box form by one machine group. One square foot of paper is equivalent to four box forms. The trimmings from this process have no scrap value. Box forms are then creased and folded (i.e., completed) by a second machine group. Any partially processed boxes in the department are cut box forms that are ready for creasing and folding. These partially processed boxes are considered 50% complete as to labor and overhead.

During June, the Materials Department purchased 1,210,000 square feet of unprocessed paper for $244,000. Conversion costs (DL + OH) for the month were $226,000. A quantity equal to 30,000 boxes was spoiled during paper cutting, and 70,000 boxes were spoiled during folding. All spoilage has a zero salvage value, is considered abnormal, and cannot be reprocessed. Ballinger applies the WA method to all inventories. Inventory data for June follow:

		JUNE 1			JUNE 30
INVENTORY	PHYSICAL UNITS	UNITS ON HAND	COST		UNITS ON HAND
Materials Department: paper	square feet	390,000	$76,000		200,000
Box Department: boxes cut, not folded	number	800,000	55,000*		300,000
Finished goods: completed boxes	number	250,000	18,000		50,000

*$35,000 materials + $20,000 conversion costs.

Required (round unit costs to the nearest cent):
a. What is the cost of paper available in June?
b. What is the number of units transferred out of the Materials Department?
c. What is the cost of units transferred out of the Materials Department?
d. What is the number of units transferred out of the Box Department?
e. What is the total number of units transferred from finished goods to cost of goods sold?
f. What is the number of EUP for direct materials and conversion costs, respectively, for the Box Department under the WA method?
g. What is the number of EUP for direct materials and conversion costs, respectively, for the Box Department under the FIFO method?
h. What are the unit direct materials and conversion costs, respectively, assuming the WA method for June for the Box Department?
i. What is the total unit cost for June for the Box Department?
j. What are the number of total completed units and their material costs, respectively, for the Box Department?
k. What are the total completed units and their conversion costs, respectively, in the Box Department?
l. How many units are available in finished goods, and what is their cost?
m. What is the unit cost for finished goods?
n. What is the cost of units sold for June?

[AICPA adapted]

6.70 *Joint costs.* In its three departments, Amaco Chemical Company manufactures several products:

1. In Department 1, the raw materials amanic acid and bonyl hydroxide are used to produce Amanyl, Bonanyl, and Am-Salt. Amanyl is sold to others who use it as a raw material in the manufacture of stimulants. Bonanyl is not salable without further processing. Although Am-Salt is a commercial product for which there is a ready market, Amaco does not sell this product, preferring to submit it to further processing.
2. In Department 2, Bonanyl is processed into the marketable product, Bonanyl-X. The relationship between Bonanyl used and Bonanyl-X produced has remained constant for several months.
3. In Department 3, Am-Salt and the raw material Colb are used to produce Colbanyl, a liquid propellant that is in great demand. As an inevitable part of this process, Demanyl is also produced. Demanyl was discarded as scrap until it was discovered that it is useful as a catalyst in the manufacture of glue; for two years, Amaco has been able to sell all of its production of Demanyl.

In its financial statements, Amaco states inventory at the lower of cost (on the FIFO basis) or market. Unit cost of the items most recently produced must therefore be computed. Costs allocated to Demanyl are computed so that after allowing for packaging and selling cost of $0.04 per pound, no profit or loss will be recognized on sales of this product. Certain data for October 19X2 follow:

RAW MATERIALS

	POUNDS USED	TOTAL COST
Amanic acid	6,300	$5,670
Bonyl hydroxide	9,100	6,370
Colb	5,600	2,240

CONVERSION COSTS (LABOR AND OVERHEAD)

	TOTAL COST
Department 1	$33,600
Department 2	3,306
Department 3	22,400

PRODUCTS

	POUNDS PRODUCED	INVENTORIES (POUNDS) SEPTEMBER 30	INVENTORIES (POUNDS) OCTOBER 31	SALES PRICE PER POUND
Amanyl	3,600			$ 6.65
Bonanyl	2,800	210	110	
Am-Salt	7,600			6.30
Bonanyl-X	2,755			4.20
Colbanyl	1,400			43.00
Demanyl	9,800			.54

Required:
Prepare the following schedules for October 19X2. Supporting computations should be prepared in good form. Round answers to the nearest cent.
a. Cost per pound of Amanyl, Bonanyl, and Am-Salt produced using the WA method.
b. Cost per pound of Amanyl, Bonanyl, and Am-Salt produced using the relative sales value method.
c. Cost per pound of Colbanyl produced. Assume that the cost per pound of Am-Salt produced was $3.40.

[AICPA adapted]

6.71 *Joint costs.* Multiproduct Corporation is a chemical manufacturer that produces two main products (Pepco-1 and Repke-3) and a by-product (SE-5) from a joint process. If Multiproduct had the proper facilities, it could process SE-5 further into a main product. The ratio of output quantities to input quantity of direct materials used in the joint process remains consistent with the processing conditions and activity level.

Multiproduct currently uses the physical method of allocating joint costs to the main products. The FIFO inventory method is used to value the main products. The by-product is inventoried at its net realizable value, and the net realizable value of the by-product is used to reduce the joint production costs before the joint costs are allocated to the main products.

Jim Simpson, Multiproduct's controller, wants to implement the relative sales value method of joint cost allocation. He believes that inventoriable costs should be based on each product's ability to contribute to the recovery of joint production costs. The net realizable value of the by-product would be treated in the same manner as with the physical method.

Data regarding Multiproduct's operations for November 19X6 follow:

| | MAIN PRODUCTS | | BY-PRODUCT |
	PEPCO-1	REPKE-3	SE-5
Finished goods inventory in gal- lons on November 1, 19X6	20,000	40,000	10,000
November sales in gallons	800,000	700,000	200,000
November production in gallons	900,000	720,000	240,000
Sales value per gallon at split- off point	$2.00	$1.50	$0.55*
Additional processing costs after split-off	$1,800,000	$720,000	—
Final sales value per gallon	$5.00	$4.00	—

*Disposal and selling costs of $0.05 per gallon will be incurred to sell the by-product.

The joint production costs amounted to $2,640,000 for November 19X6.

Required:
a. Describe the relative sales value method, and explain how it accomplishes Jim Simpson's objective.
b. Assuming Multiproduct Corporation adopts the relative sales value method for internal reporting purposes:
   1. Calculate how the joint production cost for Novemer 19X6 would be allocated.
   2. Determine the dollar values of the finished goods inventories for Pepco-1, Repke-3, and SE-5 as of November 30, 19X6.
c. Multiproduct Corporation plans to expand its production facilities to enable it to further process SE-5 into a main product. Discuss how the allocation of the joint production costs under the relative sales value method will change when SE-5 becomes a main product.

[CMA adapted]

6.72 *Distinguish between joint costs and other costs and discuss allocation methods.* The Harbison Company manufactures two sizes of plate glass, which are produced simultaneously in the same manufacturing process. Since the small sheets of plate glass are cut from large sheets that contain flaws, the joint costs are allocated equally to each good sheet, large and small, produced. The difference in after-split-off costs for large and small sheets is material.

In 19X1, the company decided to increase its efforts to sell the large sheets because they produce a larger gross margin than the small sheets. Accordingly, the amount of the fixed advertising budget devoted to large sheets was increased, and the amount devoted to small sheets was decreased. No changes in sales prices were made, however.

By mid-year, the production scheduling department had increased the monthly production of large sheets in order to stay above the minimum inventory level. However, it also had cut back the monthly production of small sheets because the inventory ceiling had been reached.

At the end of 19X1, the net result of the change in product mix was a decrease of $112,000 in gross margin. Although sales of large sheets had increased 34,500 units, sales of small sheets had decreased 40,200 units.

Required:
a. Distinguish between joint costs and each of the following:
   1. After-split-off costs.
   2. Fixed costs.
   3. Prime costs.
   4. Indirect costs.
b. Discuss the propriety of allocating joint costs for general-purpose financial statements on the basis of:
   1. Physical measures, such as weights or units.
   2. Relative sales or market value.
c. In developing weights for allocating joint costs to joint products, why is the relative sales value of each joint product usually reduced by its after-split-off costs?

d. Identify the mistake that the Harbison Company made in deciding to change its product mix, and explain why the change caused a smaller gross margin for 19X1.

[AICPA adapted]

6.73 Allocation of joint costs. Doe Corporation grows, processes, cans, and sells three main pineapple products—sliced pineapple, crushed pineapple, and pineapple juice. The outside skin is cut off in the Cutting Department and processed as animal feed. The skin is treated as a by-product. Doe's production process is as follows:

> Pineapples first are processed in the Cutting Department. The pineapples are washed, and the outside skin is cut away. Then the pineapples are cored and trimmed for slicing. The three main products (sliced, crushed, juice) and the by-product (animal feed) are recognizable after processing in the Cutting Department. Each product is then transferred to a separate department for final processing.
>
> The trimmed pineapples are forwarded to the Slicing Department where they are sliced and canned. Any juice generated during the slicing operation is packed in the cans with the slices.
>
> The pieces of pineapple trimmed from the fruit are diced and canned in the Crushing Department. Again, the juice generated during this operation is packed in the can with the crushed pineapple.
>
> The core and surplus pineapple generated from the Cutting Department are pulverized into a liquid in the Juicing Department. An evaporation loss equal to 8% of the weight of the good output produced in this department occurs as the juices are heated.
>
> The outside skin is chopped into animal feed in the Feed Department.

Doe Corporation uses the net realizable value (relative sales value) method to assign costs of the joint process to its main products. The by-product is inventoried at its market value.

A total of 270,000 pounds entered the Cutting Department during May. Processing data and costs for May are summarized in the following schedule:

MAY PROCESSING DATA AND COSTS

DEPARTMENT	COSTS INCURRED	PROPORTION OF PRODUCT BY WEIGHT TRANSFERRED TO DEPARTMENTS	SELLING PRICE PER POUND OF FINAL PRODUCT
Cutting	$60,000	—	None
Slicing	4,700	35%	$.60
Crushing	10,580	28	.55
Juicing	3,250	27	.30
Animal feed	700	10	.10
Total	$79,230	100%	

Required:
a. How many net pounds of pineapple juice were produced in May?
b. What is the net realizable value of pineapple slices at the split-off point?
c. What is the total amount of separable costs for the three main products?
d. What is the total amount of joint costs for the Cutting Department to be assigned to each of the three main products in accordance with Doe's policy?
e. How much of the joint costs is allocated to crushed pineapple?
f. What is the gross margin for the pineapple juice?

6.74 Complex EUP calculations. Lovers Delight makes speciality candies. One of its products, a heart-shaped lollipop containing two secret centers and sticks, is manufactured within three departments. Department 1 makes secret centers. Department 2 inserts the secret centers into a candy mold and adds a powered candy mix, heating and cooling it to produce a hard candy, inspecting it, and then inserting the sticks. Department 3 wraps and boxes the lollipops.

The following information is available about the production process, units worked on, and costs for Department 2 during the month of April:

Direct material 1: Secret centers transferred in from Department 1 are all added at the start of production.

Direct material 2:   15% of the materials (candy mix) added within Department 2 are input uniformly over the first 30% of processing. Another 60% is added uniformly until processing is 60% complete. The last 25% of materials added (sticks) occurs over the last 40% of processing.

Direct labor: All of the direct labor is incurred uniformly throughout the first 80% of processing.

Overhead: Overhead items are added uniformly throughout the entire process.

*Quality control
inspection:*   Lollipops are inspected at the 72% completion point. A reject rate of 5% of the units inspected is considered normal.

DATA SECTION:

	Units	DM Trans In	DM Added	DL Added	Applied OH
BEG WIP INV	10				
BEG %COMPLETE	20%	(Beginning WIP Inventory is 20% down the assembly line)			
UNITS STARTED	120				
END WIP INV	20				
END %COMPLETE	50%	(Ending WIP Inventory is 50% down the assembly line)			
UNITS COMPLETED	80				

Required:
a. Calculate EUP assuming a FIFO cost flow.
b. Calculate EUP assuming a WA cost flow.

7

THE STANDARD COST ACCOUNTING SYSTEM PART 1: SETTING STANDARDS

Computers help calculate and track standard costs.

LEARNING OBJECTIVES

After studying this chapter, you should be able to:

1. Describe the role of the modern management accountant and the CAS in cost management.

2. Define the components of a standard cost card, and list its benefits for cost management.

3. Calculate the standard price and quantity for direct materials and direct labor, and understand the issues involved in these calculations.

4. Calculate the standard costs for variable and fixed overhead, and understand the issues involved in setting these standards.

5. Discuss the need for a manufacturing cost equation.

■ INTRODUCTION

What does the management accountant do? The management accountant provides a product: information. Who are the management accountant's customers? People within organizations. Thus, management accounting is concerned with providing information for organizational members.

In running a business or providing a service, people in different specialties within the enterprise must make many different types of decisions. In doing so, they use cost accounting system (CAS) information. The fact that CAS information is used inside the organization has three implications:

1. People inside the company need more detailed and specific information than do people outside the firm who make investment decisions about the firm as a whole.
2. Because so many different types of decisions are made within a company, cost management reporting formats have to be more flexible than the somewhat more rigid formats used for financial accounting.
3. When CAS information is used within the firm, no externally imposed rules and procedures are required as is the case when financial accounting reports are prepared.

The two preceding chapters presented cost accounting systems that mainly accumulated actual costs, either by job (JOCAS) or by department (PCAS). When production costs were assigned to jobs or departments, the actual direct materials and direct labor costs were used with an estimated amount of overhead (normal costing). The difference between actual and applied overhead (over/under applied ending overhead account balance) was closed to COGS at year-end. Thus, all actual costs ended up in COGS. Actual costs are required for financial and tax reporting purposes.

But, if this is all the information a CAS reports, it is not as useful as it could be in budgeting, controlling operations, and evaluating performance.[1] Benchmarks, or standards, are needed to compare against actual costs. This need for more detailed information, which can be reported in various ways (flexibility), was demonstrated in the discussions of the ICBIS and construction cost estimates in Chapter 5, where job order cost reports were expanded to include budget, actual, and variance information.

The purpose of the remaining chapters in Parts II and III of this text is to investigate the CAS's role in modern cost management. This chapter examines the basis for creating standards. The next chapter shows how these standards can be used in designing a standard cost accounting system (SCAS) for cost management reporting. The following chapters build off this basic cost management framework, addressing more sophisticated aspects of modern cost management. ▬

<table>
<tr><td>

LEARNING OBJECTIVE 1

─

Describe the role of the modern management accountant and the CAS in cost management.

</td></tr>
</table>

▌THE COST MANAGEMENT ENVIRONMENT AND THE ROLE OF THE MANAGEMENT ACCOUNTANT

One of the most difficult transitions the traditional management accountant will have to make is to remember that management accounting does not just provide information to managers. With the advent of new types of manufacturing technologies, many workers are required to perform cost management tasks that have traditionally been thought of as belonging within the roles of managers.

---

[1] Usability is one of the five characteristics of high-quality information discussed in Chapter 1.

For example, JIT production lines and quality circles (dedicated production cells) require workers who make the product to also be involved in quality control and testing. When problems occur, workers should communicate with each other, even when they are in different departments or cells, and coordinate activities to solve the problems. Workers in these new production environments must now perform two types of tasks: (1) make the product and (2) control the production process. The latter has traditionally been considered management's task.

Before accountants can figure out what kind of information workers and managers need, they should understand the types of decisions made. Some decisions are automatic (e.g., taking a breath versus not breathing), while others are semiautomatic (e.g., getting up when the alarm clock sounds versus pressing the "snooze" control for a few more minutes of sleep). Many decisions concerning cost management require thought, reasoning, and a choice of a specific action.

In making such decisions, the decision makers, whether workers or managers, have two objectives. First, each person in an organization needs to make good decisions individually. Second, each person needs to communicate and coordinate actions with others in the organization who might be affected. This second objective involves "group" decision making.

❚ Decision Making, Rationality, and Goal Congruence

This section will set out some definitions and ideas that will be used throughout the remaining chapters to help evaluate what management accountants do and why. A **decision** is a choice of actions between two or more problem solution alternatives. A **problem** is simply the difference between what a person wants and what that person has. It is the difference between goals and reality. In cost management, a problem is called a **cost variance;** it is the difference between budgeted costs and actual costs. Technically speaking, a cost variance is the financial result of a problem.

Cost variance reports are simply reports about the problems of a department or JIT cell. Reporting about problems is part of the management accountant's role under a management-by-exception control philosophy. **Management-by-exception** involves focusing attention on one's problems. The basic premise is, "I don't need control information about what's going right. I don't need to fix those things. Instead, tell me about my problems. Identify and isolate them for me so that I can correct them and prevent them in the future."

Implementing this control philosophy, however, requires a balancing act by the management accountant, especially in world-class enterprises. Reporting cost variances to the shop floor can result in a short-run focus on achieving standards, but attention may not be given to improving on those standards. As Chapters 1 and 2 pointed out, *kaizen*, the philosophy of continuous improvement, is a fundamental characteristic of world-class enterprises. Instead of focusing only on what is wrong, the WCM shop floor believes nothing is right and everything can be improved. The implication for the modern management accountant is that reports (at least annually) measuring the improvement in standards over time are just as important as short-run reporting about cost variances. The long-run focus is especially necessary in planning and group decision-making activities. The short-run focus on achieving current standards is important in both operational control and performance evaluation.[2]

---

[2] This topic will be discussed further in the "Revising Standards" section later in this chapter. Cost variance reports are discussed in Chapter 8. Other types of reports for long-run total quality management are discussed in Chapter 12.

Not all decisions are "good" decisions. Simply stated, a good decision is a "rational" decision. **Rational decisions** are goal-directed decisions. Thus, good (rational) decisions are actions (choices) that lead to accomplishing goals. Goals differ from objectives. Objectives are long-range statements of what is wanted; goals are short-run targets that if accomplished will lead to the realization of an objective. Goals are for a specified time period, and goal-related performance can be measured. Reporting this information is one of the management accountant's tasks.

For example, an accounting major may have the objective of becoming a certified management accountant (a CMA). One goal is passing the CMA exam. Successfully finishing this course, as it is part of the educational base needed to become a CMA, is rational, because it leads to realizing this goal. But rational decision making is not an end in itself. Consider the example on the next page.

In the Johnson Foundry example, it's rational to cancel the maintenance because this will lead to the goal of remaining within budget. However, cancelling maintenance is not in the best interests of the company in the long run.

This is an example of what is called a "myopic focus" on short-run profits. Overemphasis on short-run profits (like minimizing cost variances) is not always in the best interests of the organization. Instead, the firm wants workers and foremen to make goal-congruent decisions and take actions that lead to its goals. Choices that lead to an individual's goals, but not to the organization's goals, are called suboptimal or dysfunctional. This issue, first discussed in Chapter 1, is probably the key problem faced by the management accountant in designing an SCAS for cost management.

The role of the management accountant in this case is to provide enough flexibility and detail in performance reports so that suboptimal behavior does not occur. For example, a Johnson Foundry report for Mike Himes's department showing a budget of $100,000 and actual expenditures of $100,000, with no cost variance, would not be professionally ethical. The cost variance report should show a $5,000 "unfavorable" variance for labor usage (assume that was the real problem) and a $5,000 "favorable" variance for maintenance. Thus, both problems, if they occurred, would be reported.

Good decisions are rational decisions, but because each manager is a member of a larger organization, rationality must be tempered with goal congruence and ethics throughout all of the managers' and workers' decision-making functions. These include planning (for the future), monitoring and controlling (the present), and evaluating (past performance). The role of the management accountant, then, is to provide information that helps people in an organization (individually and as team members) to plan, control, and evaluate their areas of responsibility better.

The Standard Cost Accounting System's Role in Responsibility Accounting

Responsibility accounting has two aspects: functional and behavioral. From the functional perspective, **responsibility accounting** is concerned with measuring how well organizational members are achieving the organization's goals. From the behavioral perspective, responsibility accounting systems are a subset of the organizational control system. The control system's role is to provide the rewards that will motivate individuals to make goal-congruent decisions.

THE FUNCTIONAL SIDE OF RESPONSIBILITY ACCOUNTING. As explained earlier, people within organizations share two common decision-making objectives (individual and group), and they all have three decision-making functions (planning, control, and evaluation). The specific types of

Goal-Congruent versus Suboptimal Behavior at Johnson Foundry

Mike Himes is one of the factory foremen at Johnson Foundry. His budget to produce 1,000 casings this week is $100,000. Every Friday afternoon, maintenance work on the production machinery should be done, which costs $5,000. There have been some cost variances this week, and Mike is considering canceling the maintenance work. Because he is evaluated with cost variance reports, saving the $5,000 in maintenance costs will get him back within his budget. What should he do?

decisions they make, though, depend on their responsibilities. By looking at the management hierarchy, three basic responsibility levels can be identified:

■ **Cost centers.** Cost center employees are responsible for planning, controlling, and evaluating activities that create costs. A factory foreman, or a JIT cell's work team, are good examples. Mike Himes is responsible for budgeting, controlling, and evaluating the costs of his department. His responsibilities are to hit a production quota,[3] produce quality output, and do this within budgeted costs (minimize cost variances).[4] He does not have any responsibilities for sales and marketing decisions, though. Thus, this responsibility level is not concerned with revenue (and profit) creation, but only with cost management.

■ **Profit centers.** Profit center managers are one step above cost center managers in the firm's hierarchy. These managers have an added level of responsibility. In addition to controlling costs, they also are responsible for generating revenues. A product line manager is a good example. At this level, obtaining budgeted revenues, while containing costs within budget, leads to the achievement of target profits.

■ **Investment centers.** Investment center managers can be considered the top management in a firm. The new responsibility added at this level is over investment decisions. At this level, responsibilities include obtaining budgeted profits, capital budgeting, and financing asset acquisitions.[5]

Since all three levels must ultimately be concerned with cost management, the SCAS has a multiple reporting obligation. In other words, there are multiple users, with different information needs. How cost variance reports can be designed to serve these different needs will be illustrated in the next chapter. All levels need to be involved in the setting of standards, though. This process has many behavioral implications that require the involvement of all workers and all levels of management, from the shop floor worker to the CEO.

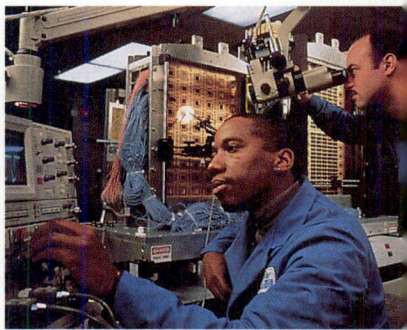

Responsibility centers at Cray Research.

BEHAVIORAL DIMENSIONS TO RESPONSIBILITY ACCOUNTING.   If the responsibility accounting system is to function properly in its motivational role, it must be accepted by the people being evaluated. This means that employees

---

[3] In a process system, this quota may be in terms of production runs. In a job order system, it refers to production volume within each job. In a JIT, it means keeping the kanban containers full or, if all containers are full, keeping the production process running smoothly within the cell.

[4] This is not to imply that cost variance minimization is, or should be, *the* primary responsibility used in evaluating his performance. If it is, the possibility for suboptimal behavior exists, as the Johnson Foundry example illustrated. Actually, Mike Himes's cost variances are the result of production problems. Thus, minimizing cost variances results from minimizing production problems. This will be discussed in greater detail later and in the next chapter.

[5] Profit center management accounting is covered in Part IV of this text, and investment centers are covered in Part V.

must internalize the company's goals as their own. Proper motivation also requires a reward system that employees believe will allow them to satisfy their individual needs if they make decisions in the best interests of the firm (goal-congruent behavior). To distribute these rewards, firms need to evaluate performance. This need, in turn, creates five criteria for the responsibility accounting system:

- *The planning criterion: participative budgeting.* First, it must communicate the organization's objectives and goals to the employees, allowing them to participate in setting their own goals consistent with the company's.
- *The operational control criterion: decision usefulness.* Second, it should provide timely, relevant information so that managers can make the best individual and group decisions possible on a day-to-day basis. In other words, it should be a high-quality information system.
- *The short-run performance evaluation criterion: management-by-exception.* Third, it should evaluate performance by comparing planned outcomes against actual results.
- *The long-run performance evaluation criterion: continuous improvement.* Fourth, it should evaluate long-run improvement in standards over time.
- *The overall performance evaluation criterion: controllability.* Fifth, it should distinguish (for proper performance evaluation) those activities over which a worker, manager, or JIT cell team has been given control.

The organization designs control systems by recognizing the following linkages:

- *Control* requires that people in the organization be properly motivated to take actions that will lead to the firm's goals.
- *Motivation* requires knowing what organizational members want and providing a reward system to give it to them.
- The *reward system* requires an evaluation system.
- The *evaluation system* requires organizational goals to use as benchmarks in measuring performance.
- *Performance measurement* requires the assignment of responsibilities.
- *Responsibility* requires controllability over the factors measured and evaluated.
- *Controllability* requires the ability to influence both the standards that represent the goals to be accomplished and actual events (decisions) related to those goals.

What is the role of the responsibility accounting system within the firm's control system? It is only one part of the overall control system. The motivation to control operations comes from employees knowing that they will receive acceptable rewards for making goal-congruent decisions. This is the role of the reward system. To successfully motivate employees to accept the organization's goals as their own, the budgeting process must communicate the firm's goals and allow the employees to participate in setting the standards used in their performance evaluations. The accounting system must also evaluate performance in a way that is acceptable to the people being evaluated. Performance should be evaluated against the standards set, and employees should only be evaluated on the activites they control. The motivation to control operations comes from employees accepting the legitimacy of the planning and evaluation components of the responsibility accounting system, which they perceive as being linked to an adequate reward system.

▌Ethical Considerations within the Management Accountant's Role in Control

Ethics concern right and wrong behavior. Because management accountants are professionals, they should practice a code of ethics. The Institute of Management Accountants (IMA) has published "Standards of Ethical Conduct for Management Accountants" (SMA #1C, 1983).[6] Management accountants are also members of an organization, the company employing them. Thus, they also have an ethical responsibility to it. According to the IMA, ethical behavior is evidenced in four areas: competence, objectivity, confidentiality, and integrity.

If management accountants are competent, they will design responsibility accounting systems that are based on participative budgeting, distinguish between controllable and uncontrollable costs, and report variances in an understandable and useful way. Objectivity requires disclosing the information needed by employees to make goal-congruent decisions (completeness and fairness). Because this is confidential financial information, the management accountant also has the ethical responsibility to maintain that confidentiality. Information should not be used for personal gain at the expense of the firm. Integrity means avoiding actual or apparent conflicts of interest professionally or as a member of the company. Controllability of standards and variances are important considerations when designing the SCAS.

STANDARDS AND THE STANDARD COST CARD

A **standard cost** is the budgeted cost of a particular input item (cost element) used in making one unit of a product. For example, how much should be spent on chocolate used in a one-pound box of chocolate candies? Obviously, this depends on the price of chocolate and the quantity of chocolate needed.

Each cost element has its own standard cost. The standard costs for a particular product are summarized on a **standard cost card,** such as the one displayed in Exhibit 7–1.

LEARNING OBJECTIVE 2

Define the components of a standard cost card, and list its benefits for cost management.

The Components of a Standard Cost

A **standard price** is the amount of money budgeted for one unit of an input item. In Exhibit 7–1, for example, the standard price of raw (bulk) chocolate is projected at $1.50 per pound.

A **standard quantity** is the budgeted amount of an input item needed to make one unit of output. In Exhibit 7–1, SweetTooth budgets one and one-third pounds of raw chocolate as the amount that should be needed to produce a one-pound box of chocolates.

Standard prices, quantities, and costs are related. Standard price multiplied by standard quantity equals standard cost. Each manufacturing input item should have its own standard cost. The sum of all inputs' standard costs is the **standard absorptive manufacturing cost (SAMC)** for the product. In absorption costing, each individual product includes an allocation of fixed manufacturing overhead. This will be discussed in the last section of this chapter.

$SP \times SQ = SC$

---

[6] Refer back to Chapter 1 for the detailed discussion of ethical behavior.

Standard Cost Card for One-Pound Box of Chocolate Candies

Items	Standard Price	Standard Quantity	Standard Cost
Chocolate	$1.50/lb.	1⅓ lb./box	$2.00/box
Wrapping paper	$0.10/sq. ft.	6 sq. ft./box	$0.60/box
Direct labor	$4.00/DLhr	1 DLhr/box	$4.00/box
Variable overhead	$0.30/DLhr	1 DLhr/box	$0.30/box
Fixed overhead	$2.92/DLhr	1 DLhr/box	$2.92/box
Standard absorptive manufacturing cost (SAMC)			$9.82/box

EXHIBIT 7–1
The Standard Cost Card for SweetTooth, Inc.'s One-Pound Box of Chocolate Candies

The standard absorptive manufacturing cost for SweetTooth's one-pound box of chocolates is $9.82 per box.

Standard Cost Card Benefits

The use of a standard cost card provides benefits for both decision-making objectives of a cost center manager (individual and group decision making). It also provides benefits for each of the three decision-making functions (planning, controlling, evaluating). In individual planning decisions, attention is focused on each component of the product's cost (prices versus quantities for each manufacturing input). The need for coordination and communication in obtaining these budgeted amounts (the group decision-making objective) becomes obvious.

In performance evaluation, standard costs provide the benchmarks for measuring cost overruns. By calculating separate price and usage variances for each manufacturing input, variances can be reported to the proper managers (those having control over the variance). Reporting only the controllable variances to each manager is an example of how the management-by-exception philosophy is implemented within a responsibility accounting system.

Both evaluation and daily operational control are facilitated by calculating and reporting variances to the people responsible. For example, the purchasing department is most likely responsible for price variances for materials. When the department prepares purchase orders, any difference between the standard and actual purchase price can be noted on the purchase order with an explanation of why it will occur. This feedforward information can alert management of a problem before it actually affects profits. Once informed, management may be able to take other actions (communication, coordination, and group decisions) that may prevent the problem from adversely affecting operations and profits.

Similarly, line managers probably are responsible for direct material and direct labor usage variances. Some companies have computer systems that report usage variances directly to the workers and line managers as each product (or batch of products) is worked on in their department or JIT cell. Such online, real-time feedback not only allows workers to see the effects of their efforts, but also makes it possible to detect the underlying causes of any usage variances at the source. This information can also be used in a feed-forward mode to alert subsequent operations of any potential problems that can affect them.

Standard cost cards also provide benefits in other areas besides cost management. Profit center managers, knowing the SAMC of a product, have a better idea of the adequacy of its planned sales price and profit. Cost accountants also can use standard costs to run the cost accounting system more efficiently. The next chapter discusses how standards are used in the SCAS journal entries, as well as in calculating variances and reporting for control and evaluation.

LEARNING OBJECTIVE 3

Calculate the standard price and quantity for direct materials and direct labor, and understand the issues involved in these calculations.

SETTING DIRECT MATERIALS AND DIRECT LABOR STANDARDS

Before standards can be used, they have to be created. The first question the management accountant should ask is, "Which costs do we want to include within the direct materials and labor standards?" How a firm budgets for particular costs will determine the general ledger accounts that will have to be debited and credited when these costs are incurred. Thus, it will affect how certain costs are reported and controlled.

Budgeting the Standard Price of Direct Materials

The **direct material standard price** is its budgeted **net** delivered purchase price. For example, the standard price of raw chocolate for SweetTooth's one-pound box of chocolates is $1.50 per pound. This is calculated as follows:

Gross purchase price	$1.37/lb.
Less purchase discount of 5%	<0.07>
Net purchase price	$1.30/lb.
Add freight-in	0.20/lb.
Standard price for chocolate	$1.50/lb.

Standard prices can be stable or unstable, and easy or hard to budget, depending on the supply environment of the enterprise. For example, seafood prices for a restaurant located on the wharf at San Francisco can vary daily. In contrast, a fast-food restaurant franchisee may have a long-term contract with its franchisor and very stable prices to use as standards. Characteristically, WCMs using JITs negotiate long-term supply contracts with vendors, possibly administered through an EDI system.

As prices change, it is important to adjust standards and sales prices if possible. To illustrate, the budgeted price for a lobster dinner charged to customers at the San Francisco Bay Inn is $25, based on a standard price of $5 per lobster at the wharf. If the actual wholesale price increases to $7, the restaurant will want to adjust the price of the meal to $27.

Standard direct material prices can be important in service enterprises as well as in merchandising and manufacturing firms. For example, to justify a request for increased funding, a welfare agency may want to identify the standard direct materials and labor needed for each case. These direct materials may include multiple file folders, special forms, photocopies, and the like. Direct labor can include special travel time to a client's home and meetings with other agencies to coordinate day-care services or special education and training courses. A children's dentist may budget rubber gloves, bite-wing X-rays, and lollipops in the cost of each patient.

Budgeting the Standard Price of Direct Labor

Standard direct labor at Honda of America Manufacturing, Inc.

The price of labor includes more than just the gross wage rate paid to workers. To employ workers, companies must incur payroll and fringe benefits costs. Because the costs can be directly traced to, and are directly caused by, individual workers, payroll burden and fringe benefits should be included in the standard price. This is consistent with the accounting for labor costs in any CAS. In journal entry 2, the total (gross) wages are charged to the gross wages clearing account in the general ledger. Journal entry 3 adds the employer's payroll taxes and fringe benefits into the gross wages account. Thus, when direct labor is assigned to product costs (via jobs or departments), it includes both labor-related costs.

Because cost elements should be budgeted and accounted for in the same way, the direct labor standard price for SweetTooth's one-pound box of chocolates is calculated as follows:

Budgeted gross wage rate	$3.00/DLhr
Add payroll taxes and fringe benefits (10⅓% and 23%, respectively)	1.00/DLhr
Standard price for direct labor	$4.00/DLhr

Labor rates, payroll taxes, and fringe benefits costs are fairly stable in most enterprises. In union shop manufacturers, multiyear union contracts provide specific wage rates and certain fringe benefits costs for up to three years. In WCMs and JITs, many enterprises have long-term employment agreements, bonuses, and profit-sharing plans. In service firms, such as a CPA firm, the annual salaries of various accountants are broken down into an hourly rate, with time cards (or logs) used to trace hours worked directly on each client engagement. The hourly rates plus burden costs determine in part the billing rates charged to clients by CPA firms, legal firms, engineering firms, and the like. In nonprofit service agencies, such as a grant administration office of a state government, standard direct labor prices can be used to calculate how much the state can bill the grant program for administration costs.

Budgeting Direct Materials Standard Quantities

Production processes (both the equipment and the people) are seldom perfect. This means that not all of the materials or labor input into production will find its way into the product. The amount of a particular input that is lost during production is called scrap. There are two kinds of scrap: anticipated (normal) and excess (abnormal). Notice in Exhibit 7–1 that SweetTooth budgeted for one and one-third pounds of raw chocolate to be input into a one-pound box of chocolates. This was because 25 percent of the raw chocolate put into the process is lost during production (25 percent of 1⅓ pounds is ⅓ pound, so the result is exactly one pound of completed output—a finished one-pound box of chocolates).

The standard quantity is *not* the amount of an input required to be in the product when it is complete and ready to sell. This amount is called an **output specification** (also called an **engineering** or **marketing specification**). An output specification is the amount of an input that must be in the completed product for it to be salable. In contrast, a standard quantity is the amount of that input that must be placed *into* the production process at the beginning, so that salable output can result.

To budget standard quantities properly, the output specification and normal scrap rate (more generally, the normal input loss percentage) must be known. The following formula is used to calculate standard quantity:

$$\text{Standard quantity} = \frac{\text{Output specification}}{(1 - \text{Normal scrap percentage})}$$

$$= \frac{1 \text{ lb. per box}}{(1 - 25\%)}$$

$$= \frac{1 \text{ lb. per box}}{(1 - .25)}$$

$$= 1\tfrac{1}{3} \text{ lb. per box}$$

Many people when budgeting standard quantities mistakenly focus on the product (the output) rather than on the input item. Continuing the SweetTooth example, the *error* that results goes like this:

1. One pound of chocolate is needed in the final product.
2. Since normal input loss equals 25 percent, *this means 25 percent of one pound (the output specification) or one-fourth pound will be lost.*
3. Therefore, one and one-fourth pounds (the standard quantity) of raw chocolate should be purchased per box of chocolates.

To demonstrate this error to the managers and workers responsible for budgeting these costs, the management accountant might want to present the following simple "proof":

Amount to input (standard quantity)	1.25 lb.
Less normal input loss @ 25%	<.31> lb.
Amount in finished product (output specification)	0.94 lb.

Not enough chocolate is in the box! The problem is that the 25 percent that is lost is lost from the input, not from the output. Or, to put it differently, the output is three-fourths of the amount *input* into the production process at the beginning. If managers have trouble with this, the management accountant might draw them a simple picture like this:

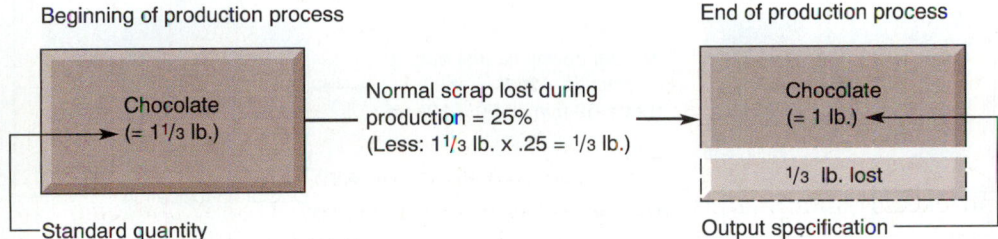

Budgeting Direct Labor Standard Quantities

Normal input loss also exists for labor. This can be thought of as "downtime." Notice that the standard quantity for direct labor in Exhibit 7–1 was one hour per box of chocolates. However, only 48 minutes of direct labor time is needed to make a box. The 48 minutes can be labeled "productive time." On average, 12 minutes per hour are needed for activities other than directly working on the product. Thus, SweetTooth needs to input 60 minutes of "paid" labor time to make a box of chocolates. The 12 minutes per hour downtime is a 20 percent loss of this input. It is calculated as follows:

Downtime per day:	
■ Two 15 minute breaks	30 minutes/day
■ Setup time in morning	25 minutes/day
■ Cleanup time at night	20 minutes/day
■ Miscellaneous downtime	21 minutes/day
Total downtime per day	96 minutes/day

The 96 minutes per day is 20 percent of an eight hour day. As a result, 20 percent of paid direct labor time (on average) is not available for producing chocolates. The 48 minutes of direct productive time needed to make a box is an output specification. Given a 20 percent normal input loss ratio:

$$\text{Standard quantity} = \frac{\text{Output specification}}{(1 - \text{Normal input loss percentage})}$$

$$= \frac{48 \text{ minutes per box}}{(1 - 20\%)}$$

$$= 60 \text{ minutes per box}$$

In other words, the standard labor quantity is the amount of time that should be purchased and input into the production process so that enough productive time is available to make one box of chocolates. Relating the direct labor standard quantity to paid time produces the following equation:

$$\text{Paid time} = \text{Downtime} + \text{Productive time}$$

$$60 \text{ minutes per box} = 12 \text{ minutes} + 48 \text{ minutes}$$

The standard quantity calculation for direct labor can be shown in the same manner used to illustrate direct materials. Both are presented in Exhibit 7–2.

■■EXHIBIT 7–2
Standard Quantities and Normal Input Loss

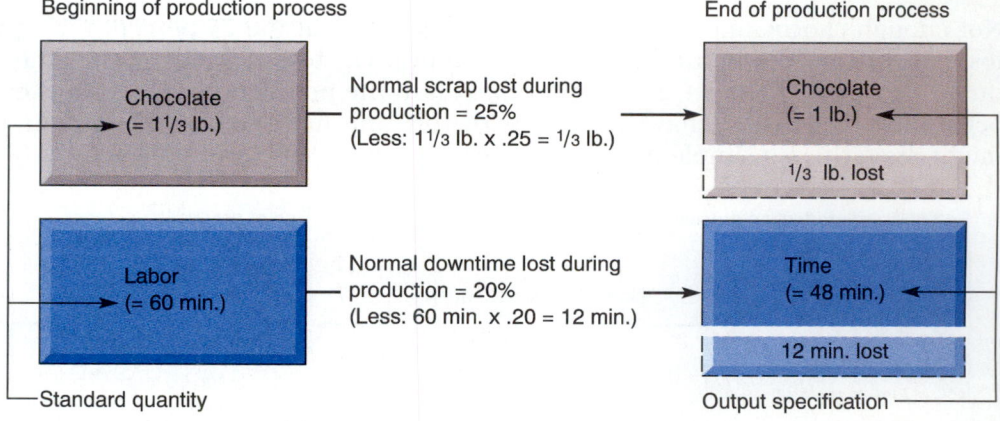

Theoretical versus Practical Standards

The degree of difficulty in achieving a standard is known as *tightness*. The more difficult a standard is to attain, the tighter it is said to be. Tight standards can promote positive behavior if they motivate employees to strive for excellence through continuous improvement. Alternatively, they can cause dysfunctional behavior if they are too difficult or impossible to achieve. Standards that are too loose, however, may not motivate employees to perform at their best because such standards can be achieved too easily. Moreover, such standards do not support continuous improvement.

Implicit in the setting of standard quantities is the concept of an acceptable level of performance corresponding to management's goals. That is, does management want to maintain the status quo or build a world-class enterprise? Because standards are goals that are used to judge actual performance, a key question is, "Just how demanding should standards be?" Should they assume theoretical perfection, or should they assume various factors that prevent perfect performance, at least in the short run?

THEORETICAL STANDARDS.   **Theoretical standards** (often called **ideal standards**) are based on the best performance possible under existing operating conditions and with existing equipment. Such standards assume an ideal situation in which both people and equipment work at peak efficiency 100 percent of the time and in which it is possible to produce with no waste. The standards may include allowances for rest periods and personal needs of employees but usually do not include any allowances for scrap, lost time, or any nonvalue-added activities. An ideal standard quantity for raw chocolate would not include the one-third pound normally lost in production (normal scrap) that was included in SweetTooth's box of chocolates. An ideal standard quantity for direct labor would not include setup and cleanup time and may or may not include bathroom time.

The standards are set as goals toward which employees work for continuous improvement, a concept of world-class manufacturing. Variances from theoretical standards will probably always be unfavorable, but continuous improvement will result in these variances becoming smaller over time.

INSIGHTS & APPLICATIONS

Emphasizing the Achievable

Put a 5-foot-10-inch person into 6 feet 3 inches of water, and odds are he'll learn to swim. He may sputter and spit a bit, but he can always hop up off the bottom and get air. Put that same person in 7 feet 4 inches of water, and you may have a dead body on your hands.

The 6 feet 3 inches of water forces the 5-foot-10-inch person to stretch. The stretching provides a sense of accomplishment. It's challenging, but achievable. Field Marshal Bernard Montgomery and General George Patton, although different in style, had something in common. Both inherited winless and dispirited armies. And both rapidly reversed these armies' fortunes using exactly the same technique to begin the turnaround. Both focused on the instantly "doable." A first "stretch goal" was to demand spotless uniforms and to launch an intensive physical fitness program. Both officers were able to convert demoralized losers into winners.[7]

PRACTICAL STANDARDS. Practical standards (also called currently attainable standards) are tight but achievable standards. They do not tolerate abnormal scrap and downtime, although they allow for normal machine downtime, employee rest periods, and currently necessary, but nonvalue-added activities. They are closely akin to theoretical standards in that they are future oriented and are used as a basis for continuous improvement. Unlike theoretical standards, practical standards can be achieved and even surpassed on occasion when operations are being performed at high levels of efficiency. They are within the achievable range of most employees, yet difficult enough that when they are attained employees feel as though something of value has been accomplished. The standard quantities budgeted for SweetTooth's box of chocolates are practical standards.

Employees are motivated by practical standards, especially if they've had input into their development, and will normally put forth their best efforts to achieve them. Moreover, practical standards can serve several purposes. In addition to indicating abnormal variances in costs, they can also be used in estimating and planning, whereas theoretical standards do not allow for normal inefficiencies and therefore may result in unrealistic budgeting data.

Variances from practical standards are very useful to management because they provide information about how well operations are *improving.* Generally, such standards have also been considered to be more useful than theoretical standards in determining how effectively and efficiently present operations are being carried out.

Some authorities, however, believe practical standards demand too little because such standards may be based more on the past than the future. Certain inefficiencies may be built into the standards. Therefore, some managers believe theoretical standards are more useful for continuous improvement because of their future orientation.

Such managers do not want to include costs for idle capacity, setup times, material movement, inspection, and other nonvalue-added activities in an SCAS. When nonvalue-added activities are built into the standard quantities, the existence of waste may never be questioned. The goal is zero waste and inventory. Management may never achieve such a lofty goal, but by pursuing it, substantial cost savings will occur.

PRODUCTIVITY IMPROVEMENT, STANDARDS, AND NONVALUE-ADDED ACTIVITIES.   Whether ideal or practical standards are used, the mod-

[7] From *Thriving on Chaos* by Tom Peters, Copyright © 1987 by Excel, a California Limited Partnership. Reprinted by permission of Alfred A. Knopf, Inc.

ern management accountant needs to report improvements in productivity. With ideal standards, the change in variances over time measures the movement toward the theoretical optimum. While ideal standards will almost always result in unfavorable usage variances, continuous improvement is evidenced by a reduction in the variances over time. In other words, as actual productivity improves, the difference between the ideal standard quantity and actual results will decrease.

When practical standards are used, reporting the change (reduction) over time in standard quantities and costs, as nonvalue-added activities are eliminated from them, will provide the same type of information to management. For example, as the amount of raw chocolate lost in production goes down, the standard quantity can be reduced. A decreasing standard quantity over time signals continuous improvement.

Care has to be taken in interpreting measurements developed with practical standards. Where, for example, are the nonvalue-added activities and costs in the direct materials standard quantity for SweetTooth, Inc.? They are in the inefficiencies in production that cause a normal scrap rate of 25 percent. Eliminating this scrap can save SweetTooth $0.50 per box (the standard price of $1.50 per pound multiplied by the one-third pound normally lost).

Where are the nonvalue-added activities in direct labor? They are potentially in the output specification and the downtime. As with materials, the labor time lost due to setup and cleanup may be eliminated by redesigning the production process. Many firms have reported significant savings through changing operations from traditional batch production processes involving multiple functional departments to JITs. Harley-Davidson cut inventory by $20 million, increased inventory turns from 6 to 20, decreased setup times by 75 percent, and reduced warranty claims and defects by 24 percent.[8] The "Ditch Witch" example on the next page provides another example of the benefits that can be realized from JIT conversions.

PRODUCTIVITY IMPROVEMENTS, STANDARDS, AND LEARNING CURVES. The second avenue for labor productivity improvement for SweetTooth, Inc., is in the output specification of 48 minutes per box of chocolates. As workers become more experienced, learning takes place. Learning how to do the job better usually results in doing it faster, at least over the short run. As experience increases, then, the amount of productive time needed goes down. Practically speaking, it currently takes 48 minutes of productive time to make a box of chocolates. Ideally, however, an experienced worker should be able to make a box in 45 minutes. The ideal output specification would be 45 minutes, but the practical output specification is 48 minutes.

How does the modern management accountant measure the effects of learning on the standard labor quantity? In production and operations management, formulas are available for measuring and predicting the effects of learning over time. For example, consider a general contractor who builds expansion bridges for the federal interstate highway system. As each bridge is finished, workers become more efficient. The engineer calculates that the learning curve is a 10 percent reduction in total direct labor time for the next bridge each time one is finished.

Using this information with the standard labor cost for the first bridge, the management accountant can budget the standard labor cost for the second and subsequent bridges to be bid. To illustrate, 10,000 manhours were budgeted for the productive time to build the first bridge. Normal downtime is 20 percent. Therefore, the standard labor quantity for the first bridge was 12,500 manhours. Using the 10 percent learning curve projection, the second bridge should only

---

[8] Peter Reid, *Well Made in America, Lessons from Harley-Davidson on Being the Best* (New York: McGraw-Hill, 1990), provides interesting, in-depth reading. Other examples, cited in Chapter 2, include General Electric, Hewlett-Packard, Cincinnati Milacron, General Motors, and Michelin.

INSIGHTS & APPLICATIONS

The JIT Conversion at Charles Machine Works, Inc.

The Charles Machine Works, Inc. manufactures the industry's most complete line of "Ditch Witch" underground construction equipment. This equipment is used to install underground power and communications cable, water distribution systems, natural gas lines, oil field gathering lines, and the like. At Ditch Witch, most component parts, subassemblies, and final products, are manufactured in different departments within the plant. Ditch Witch has recognized the interdependent nature of these processes and the need for coordination and communication across departments in improving control over subassembly quality and product cost.

In answer to this need for one subassembly process, the cylinder assembly line was converted from a traditional multi-department, batch production process into a dedicated JIT production cell. . . . There were *three goals for the conversion:* (1) better control over shop floor inventories, (2) reduction of scrap and rework, and (3) better product cost information.

A number of benefits have already been realized from the conversion. NT II machine setup time has been reduced 92% when the machine has to be adjusted for length and diameter changes (100% reduction when only the length is changed). The standard labor time for barrel assembly has been reduced 43%. The real time and cost savings, though, are in the total elapsed time to produce a cylinder, which could have been days counting all the warehouse moves and material handling time now eliminated. The focused factory cell also has resulted in the discovery and correction of problems before large inventories of parts are built-up, which would have had to be inspected, and possibly reworked or scrapped when problems were finally discovered during cylinder assembly. Not only is there a virtual elimination of the number of parts to be inspected, the number of people who used to be involved have been significantly reduced. Most importantly, the number of problems requiring rework have been reduced because the same people who make the cylinder components also now assemble and test the cylinder.

Quality control and productivity improvement should continue in the long run because of the workers' feelings of being a team member which have been developed throughout the conversion process. The project provided additional benefits during the design and conversion processes by linking "people" needs with technical needs. Equal emphasis is given to identifying production process steps and problem causes and effects, as well as to the training, motivation, and coordination needed to "get the job done right the first time."[9]

---

require 90 percent of the productive time budgeted for the first bridge, or 9,000 manhours of productive time and 11,250 manhours as the standard quantity.

REVISING STANDARDS.   Learning raises the issue of how frequently standards should be revised. In many traditional enterprises, goals are set and budgets prepared annually. Consider the standards and cost variances that the SCAS would produce at Carslaw International (see p. 290).

Setting and revising standards, whether theoretical or practical, can foster significant improvements in making a product or rendering a service in future periods. The setting of standard costs should, therefore, include the following:

- A careful selection of materials based on both price and quality
- A comprehensive study and evaluation of all activities
- An engineering study of equipment and other manufacturing facilities

The careful setting of standards is likely to uncover inefficiencies in operations. By reducing or eliminating these, the total enterprise will benefit.

To achieve maximum effectiveness, standards must be accepted by those who will carry them out. Employees should believe that standards are both fair and achievable, or they will tend to sabotage, ignore, or circumvent them. Participation in the standard-setting process will encourage acceptance of standards and increase understanding of their measures, meanings, and purposes by those affected.

[9] M. Thomas, et al., *Designing the Management Accounting System, Using ABC and Socio-Technical Systems Analysis, for a JIT Conversion Project at Ditch Witch* (Montvale, N.J.: The Institute of Management Accountants, 1992), pp. i–ii. With permission.

Carslaw International

Carslaw International is a multinational enterprise (MNE) with operations in England, Canada, New Zealand, and the United States. Charles Carslaw, founder and CEO, located at the U.S. corporate headquarters, is concerned over the implementation of an ICBIS wide area network (WAN) linking the foreign operations together.

Currently, labor standards are set annually. All U.S. employees are scheduled to get a raise on July 1. The average annual labor rate is used as the standard price. Thus, throughout the first half of the year, there are favorable labor rate variances, because the actual rate is less than the annual average used as the standard. After the raises go into effect, however, the second half of the year shows unfavorable labor rate variances, simply because actual wage rates are now greater than the annual average.

Clyde Newman, CFO, has suggested that more frequent standard revisions be included as part of the ICBIS con-version. He has complained that although the current SCAS reports that these variances are preplanned and expected (so management can focus attention on real production problems), they clutter up the cost variance report, diminishing its usefulness and reducing overall information quality. Clyde suggests that standards should be revised as frequently as circumstances dictate. As economic conditions change in a foreign operation, the revised standards will flow through the ICBIS, providing updated information to the MRP II, the production LANs, and the marketing LANs. He also argues that organizational flexibility will be improved because response time to changing conditions will be reduced.

Charles is afraid, though, that if standards are frequently revised, it will be harder to obtain information about whether the annual and long-range goals are being achieved. The CEO strongly supports *kaizen*.

Clyde has, therefore, developed a report that compares current standards against those used in the annual plan, noting differences in standard prices and quantities. The report program can be run from corporate headquarters' LAN, on demand, for any foreign or domestic operation. A second report, comparing standard cost changes quarterly and annually, shows improvement over time.

SETTING VARIABLE AND FIXED OVERHEAD STANDARDS

The activities that cause short-run variable overhead costs are often different from those causing fixed overhead items. For example, the cost of nails for a general contractor depends on the number and size of houses built. But, the cost of a supervisor for a tract home subdivision, many permits and fees, bonds, and insurance may be a set amount for the project. Because variable and fixed overhead costs are caused by different activities, they should be accounted for separately. This is necessary for identifying controllability accurately and assigning responsibility in performance evaluation. It also facilitates more effective and efficient budgeting.

Thus, a high-quality responsibility accounting system needs to identify the different activities that cause both variable and fixed overhead. As a first step, variable and fixed overhead will be separated here. Chapter 9 will discuss the need for multiple variable and fixed overhead accounts for production and nonproduction (support services) departments. Finally, Chapters 9 and 10 will look at multiple overhead accounts and allocations for all the overhead activities involved in production.

Choosing Bases to Budget and Apply Variable Overhead Costs to Products or Services

In any CAS, overhead is accumulated in a separate WIP subsidiary ledger account and periodically applied to products. Whether journal entry 7 applies overhead to jobs (JOCAS) or products in a department (PCAS), the amount is determined by multiplying an overhead rate by the base's volume. For example, in a normal JOCAS, overhead might be applied at a rate of $5 per direct labor hour times the actual number of hours worked on a job. If 20 direct labor hours are worked on a job, a normal JOCAS would apply $100 of overhead to its cost. A normal JOCAS uses a predetermined (budgeted) overhead rate (a POR), or in other words, a standard price.

In an SCAS, the standard price for overhead is the POR. For variable overhead (VOH), the VOH POR is calculated by the following formula:

$$\text{VOH POR} = \frac{\text{Estimated VOH costs}}{\text{Estimated direct labor hours}}$$

This VOH POR uses direct labor hours as the basis for estimating and applying overhead to products. Refer back to the SweetTooth box of chocolates in Exhibit 7–1. SweetTooth management set a standard price for variable overhead (a VOH POR) of $0.30 per direct labor hour. One direct labor hour per box was budgeted as the standard labor quantity, so the standard cost for variable overhead was $0.30 per box. A variety of bases can be used for estimating and applying variable overhead costs to products or services. Typical bases include the following:

- Direct labor cost
- Direct labor hours
- Machine hours
- Units of product on a basis of weight or volume
- Direct materials weight or volume

In choosing the proper base to use, the management accountant's primary goal is to select a base that represents a cause-effect relationship between the overhead costs and the activities that cause these costs. For example, if the overhead costs in question are predominantly related to the supervision and use of labor, then the proper base probably is direct labor cost or direct labor hours.

Although these two bases have been widely used by traditional enterprises, in recent years increased automation has led to a trend away from them. In automated environments, these two bases are unlikely to have a strong cause-effect relationship to the incurrence of manufacturing overhead. In labor-intensive operations, however, these labor bases may be the most appropriate bases to use. If the overhead costs are predominantly related to operation of machinery, a machine hour base is more appropriate. If the overhead costs relate to the handling of materials, then the direct materials cost base may be best, and so forth.

VOH POR USING A DIRECT LABOR DOLLAR BASE.   Applying overhead as a percentage of direct labor cost is one of the oldest methods. Estimated overhead costs are divided by the estimated dollar amount of direct labor and converted to a percentage. Variable overhead may be applied as, for example, 200 percent of the product or service direct labor cost. Stated differently, VOH may be applied at the rate of $2 for every $1 of labor cost traced directly to a product or service.

The direct labor dollar base is simple and easy to use. All the data necessary to use this method are available from the payroll system. If more VOH is incurred by the more highly skilled and paid employees, the VOH POR should be based on direct labor costs. If varying wage rates reflect differences in the speed or quality of work, it may be proper to assume that higher-paid workers use more VOH items. Budgeting VOH in this way, the direct labor cost-based VOH POR properly applies proportionately different amounts of overhead costs when these different workers are used on a job or service.

VOH POR USING A DIRECT LABOR HOUR BASE. If the major factor of production is labor, and overhead is caused uniformly by all types of employees, then the direct labor hour method represents a better base for budgeting and applying variable overhead costs. Like the direct labor dollar base, it is easy to use. But unlike the direct labor dollar base, the direct labor hour base makes use of a time factor. Therefore, it overcomes a major objection of the direct labor dollar base, because operations taking the same time should incur, and are costed with, the same overhead, although the workers may be receiving different rates of pay. But as stated earlier, when the different rates of pay accurately reflect different skills, quality, or different speeds of operation, it may be proper to budget and apply more overhead costs for the higher-paid direct labor. In this situation, the direct labor dollar base is more appropriate. Like the direct labor dollar base, the direct labor hour base should not be used in operations where direct labor plays a minor role in production.

VOH POR USING A MACHINE HOUR BASE. In operations where machinery is the major factor of production, the major components of VOH may be maintenance and power, while the major components of fixed overhead may be depreciation and insurance. In these environments, the machine hour base is normally the best basis for budgeting and applying variable overhead costs. The drawback to using this base is that the machine hours expected and actually used may not be readily available. This drawback can be overcome by installing timing devices on the machinery. Machinery manufacturer specifications and engineering studies can also assist in determining a standard machine time (a standard quantity).

VOH POR USING A UNIT OF PRODUCT BASE. Application of VOH costs on the basis of the number of units of product made or the number of service jobs rendered during the period is the simplest method for applying overhead, although it may not be the best method for budgeting VOH costs. The VOH POR is computed as follows:

$$\text{VOH cost per unit (or job)} = \frac{\text{Estimated VOH costs}}{\text{Estimated number of units of products or services}}$$

The unit of product base is limited to situations where only one product or a few closely related products (a product family) using the same overhead activities are produced. If this is not the case, the unit of product base is not recommended.

Two popular variations of the unit of product base are the:

- Weight base
- Volume base

The weight base is used in applying overhead in mining and certain other industries where the natural unit of output is ounces, pounds, or tons. The volume base for applying overhead costs is sometimes used by water, pipeline, petroleum companies, or other enterprises that measure output in gallons, barrels, bushels, and the like. The volume base is also used in companies that produce a single product packaged in various sized containers easily differentiated by volume.

VOH POR USING A DIRECT MATERIALS COST BASE. In some companies, VOH involves costs related to the purchase, inspection, storage, and movement of materials. A VOH POR using direct materials weight or volume is calculated as follows:

$$\begin{array}{c}\text{VOH cost per some}\\\text{unit of measure (e.g.,}\\\text{pounds, tons, gallons,}\\\text{barrels)}\end{array} = \frac{\begin{array}{c}\text{Estimated direct materials}\\\text{handling overhead costs}\end{array}}{\begin{array}{c}\text{Estimated weight (or volume)}\\\text{of direct materials}\end{array}}$$

Overhead application based on weight, volume, or other physical output is simple and useful where only one product or a few closely related products are produced. They can be used, however, only when output can be measured in one common denominator, such as pounds, tons, gallons, bushels, barrels, and so forth. Even then they provide accurate estimates only when actual overhead activities are closely related to that physical base.

Estimating Variable Overhead and Fixed Overhead

Once the cause-effect linkage of overhead activities to overhead costs is determined (the VOH POR's denominator basis), total variable overhead and total fixed overhead (FOH) can be budgeted. To do this, however, the management accountant must understand cost behavior patterns. This understanding needs to be communicated to all those involved in the standard-setting process.

CLASSIFYING COSTS ACCORDING TO THEIR BEHAVIOR PATTERNS. Cost behavior is the movement of total cost in response to changes in volume or activity, such as an increase or decrease in amount of units produced or direct labor hours worked. Four general types of cost behavior patterns exist:

- Variable cost
- Fixed cost
- Mixed cost
- Step cost

Management accountants relate these costs to a narrow band of volume or level of activity called the **relevant range.** Within these bands, the assumptions about cost behavior patterns are valid. Exhibit 7–3 presents graphical examples of these cost behavior patterns.

VARIABLE COSTS.   Variable costs increase *in total* in direct proportion to increases in volume or level of activity. If the level of activity doubles, then the variable cost will double as well. If the level of activity decreases by 20 percent, then the variable cost will decrease by 20 percent. Direct materials and direct labor are examples of variable costs.

For variable costs to change in total in direct proportion to changes in the level of volume or activity, they must be *constant on a per unit basis.* To illustrate, Sporty Car Company installs one engine for each car it produces. The engines cost $300 each. On a per car basis, the cost remains constant at $300. But the *total cost* of engines changes in direct proportion to the number of cars produced. If 200 cars are produced, the total engine cost will be $60,000 (200 cars × $300 per engine).

As long as Sporty acquires 100 to 300 engines, the band of the relevant range, the cost per engine will be $300. Should Sporty acquire less than 100 or more than 300 engines, the cost per unit may be different because of such things as quantity discounts or surcharges on minimal orders. This is why knowledge of the relevant range is important in budgeting variable costs. The standard price may change outside the relevant range.

FIXED COSTS.   Fixed costs are costs that remain constant *in total* for a period of time regardless of volume or level of activity. To continue with the Sporty Car

Costs for manufacturing facilities are fixed no matter how many cars are produced. Courtesy of Saturn.

■■ EXHIBIT 7–3
Cost Behavior Patterns

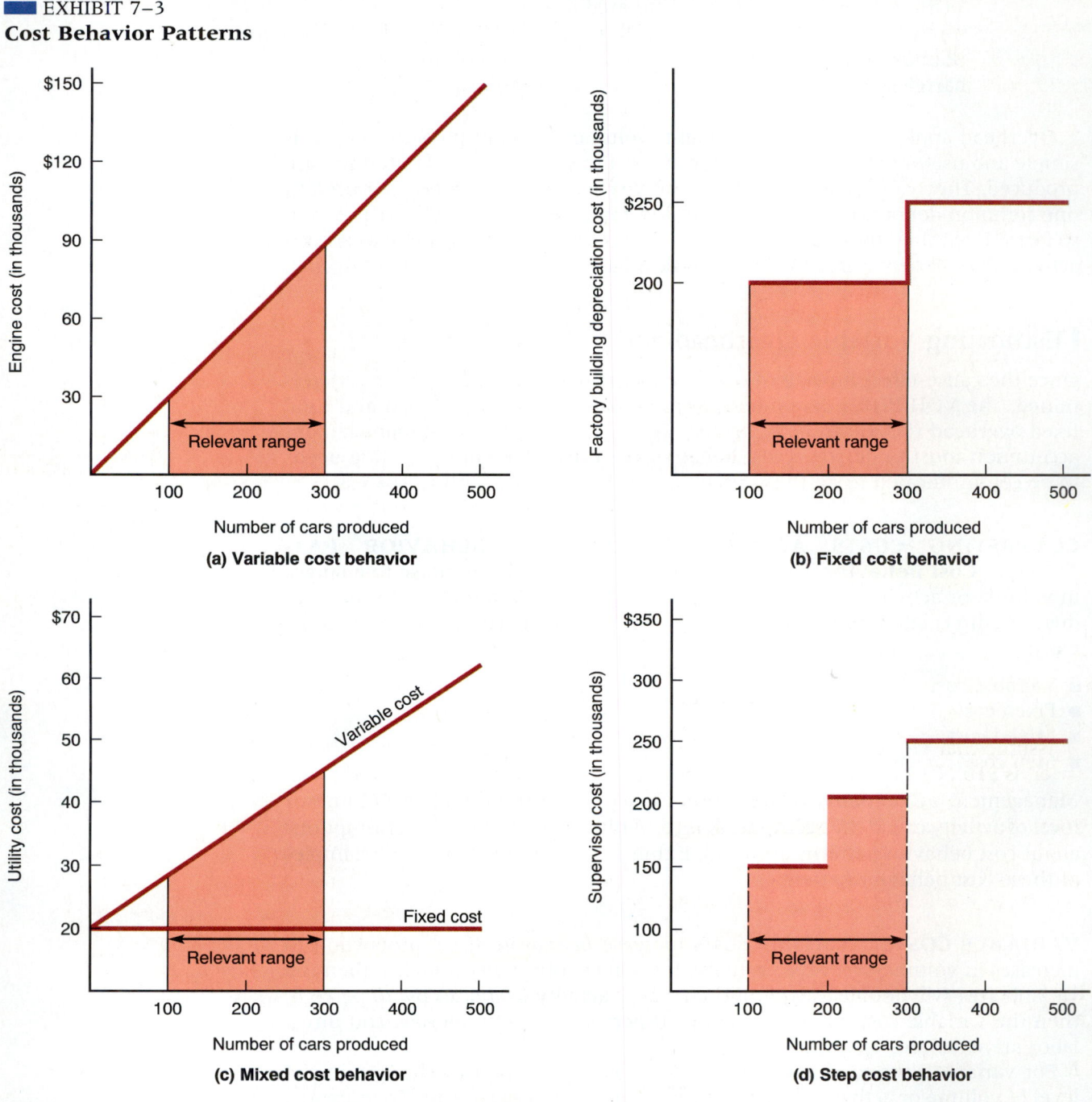

(a) **Variable cost behavior**

(b) **Fixed cost behavior**

(c) **Mixed cost behavior**

(d) **Step cost behavior**

Company example, assume that the firm builds a factory to handle production volume of between 100 and 300 cars. The total cost of the factory is $1,000,000, and it has a useful life of five years with no salvage value. If the building is depreciated on a straight-line basis, the depreciation is $200,000 per year.

Because fixed costs remain constant *in total*, the amount of cost computed on a *per unit* basis will get progressively smaller the greater the number of cars produced. Assume factory depreciation is the only fixed overhead cost. If Sporty manufactures only 100 cars in a year, the $200,000 factory building depreciation cost will result in an FOH standard cost of $2,000 per car. If 200 cars are produced, the FOH standard cost will decrease to $1,000 per car.

The management accountant concentrates on the behavior of fixed costs within the relevant range. Fixed costs are based on an expected band of volume or level of activity. Outside this band, fixed costs in total can increase or decrease just as variable costs per unit can.

As long as Sporty's manufacturing activity level stays within the relevant range of 100 to 300 cars produced per year over the next five years, the budgeted FOH cost of $200,000 stemming from factory building depreciation will remain constant. If the activity level increases beyond 300 cars produced per year, the building will have to be expanded, increasing factory building depreciation.

Other fixed costs may also increase. For example, production volume beyond the relevant range may require that another production shift be added, calling for another supervisor and additional insurance.

MIXED COSTS.   **Mixed costs** are composed of both variable and fixed cost components. Utility cost is a good example of a mixed cost. Generally, it consists of a fixed service charge plus a variable charge for usage beyond a certain amount. Telephone charges, for example, have a fixed cost per month plus long-distance toll charges.

The cost behavior in the mixed cost graph can be described by the following equation:

$$Y = TFC + (VCU \times X)$$

where Y is total cost, and:

$$TFC = \text{Total fixed costs}$$
$$VCU = \text{Variable cost per unit}$$
$$X = \text{Volume or activity level in units}$$

In some operations, design may be a mixed cost.

Assume that an overhead item, for example, the rent on a mainframe computer, is $10,000 per month plus $100 per hour of central processing time used, and the enterprise plans on 70 hours of central processing unit (CPU) time. Then the budgeted rent is computed as follows:

Monthly computer rent = $10,000 + ($100 per CPU hour × 70 CPU hours)
                      = $10,000 + $7,000
                      = $17,000

If the company does not use the computer during a month, the rent is calculated as follows:

Monthly computer rent = $10,000 + ($100 per CPU hour × 0 hours)
                      = $10,000 + $0
                      = $10,000

STEP COSTS.   **Step costs** are costs that are constant in total only over small ranges of volume within the relevant range. Supervisory payroll can be a step cost. As the work force is increased, an additional supervisor must be hired for each specified increment of workers. Step costs are difficult to incorporate in the budgeted overhead amount for calculating PORs. Usually, the management accountant assumes they are variable or fixed. If the steps are very narrow, as in Exhibit 7–3d, little budgeting accuracy may be lost by treating them as variable costs. If, on the other hand, the steps are wide, treating this cost element as a fixed cost may be sufficiently accurate for budgeting overhead.

The modern management accountant is a member of a team, getting out of the office and onto the shop floor to obtain the information necessary from the

Supervision is usually a step cost. Courtesy of Saturn.

Saturn's world-class finishes involve process inspection, which is often a step cost.

people who know. Shop floor personnel can be expected to know the activities that cause variable and fixed overhead. With the help of the management accountant, engineers, and others, overhead standard prices (PORs) and standard quantities can be estimated. This can be done through direct observation and/or special engineering studies by the team.

Historically, some traditional enterprises expected the management accountant to identify a basis for budgeting and applying overhead and to prepare the overhead standards independently. Financial accounting systems dominated the attention of accountants. In these systems, direct materials, direct labor, and total overhead were separately accounted for, but variable and fixed overhead did not need to be differentiated.[10] To satisfy external reporting requirements, the primary goal became the selection of a base that resulted in a reasonable application of overhead. Many times a simple base to measure, such as direct labor hours, was chosen. As long as all the overhead was applied in some systematic fashion to all the products, then GAAP was satisfied.

Being isolated in the accounting department and lacking the necessary information about overhead activities and their "cost drivers" (bases), the management accountant was forced to prepare estimated costs from historical cost information using quantitative techniques. Since these techniques still appear on the professional certification exams, they will be reviewed in the following section.

▎Quantitative Methods for Estimating Variable and Fixed Overhead Costs from Historical Data

In traditional CASs, having only one total overhead account resulted in overhead being treated as a mixed cost. Thus, the management accountant had to calculate an equation to predict total overhead, such as the equation previously used to predict mainframe computer rental cost. The following methods can be used to estimate the relationship between volume or level of activity and total overhead costs:

- Scattergraph method
- High-low method
- Regression methods

THE SCATTERGRAPH METHOD.   The **scattergraph method** (also called **scatterplot** or **scatter diagram**) of identifying variable and fixed overhead costs consists of plotting data on a graph and fitting a line to the data by visual inspection. To illustrate, assume that maintenance costs for Moran Industries have been compiled as shown in Exhibit 7–4. This data sample consists of 12 monthly observations of maintenance costs and production volume. While the management accountant believed that machine usage (hours used) caused overhead, no information was available from the traditional CAS on this base. Further, believing that production volume caused machine usage, the management accountant used this as the basis for building an overhead cost equation and budgeting overhead costs. These data will be used to demonstrate the scattergraph method as well as the high-low and regression methods.

The type of correlation between maintenance cost and production volume can be understood from the patterns of the observations on the graph. The patterns, and the types of correlations they indicate, are illustrated in Exhibit 7–5.

---

[10] This is one of the reasons why only the total overhead POR was calculated in Chapter 4. In modern CASs required in WCMs, multiple VOH and FOH accounts are necessary. These refinements will be incorporated into CAS design in Chapters 9 and 10.

Month	Units of Product Produced	Maintenance Cost Incurred
January	500	$ 700
February	700	960
March	600	750
April	750	900
May	650	780
June	850	1,050
July	800	950
August	650	800
September	750	880
October	750	920
November	700	900
December	550	700

■ EXHIBIT 7–4
Compilation of Maintenance Cost Incurred over Twelve Months at Moran Industries

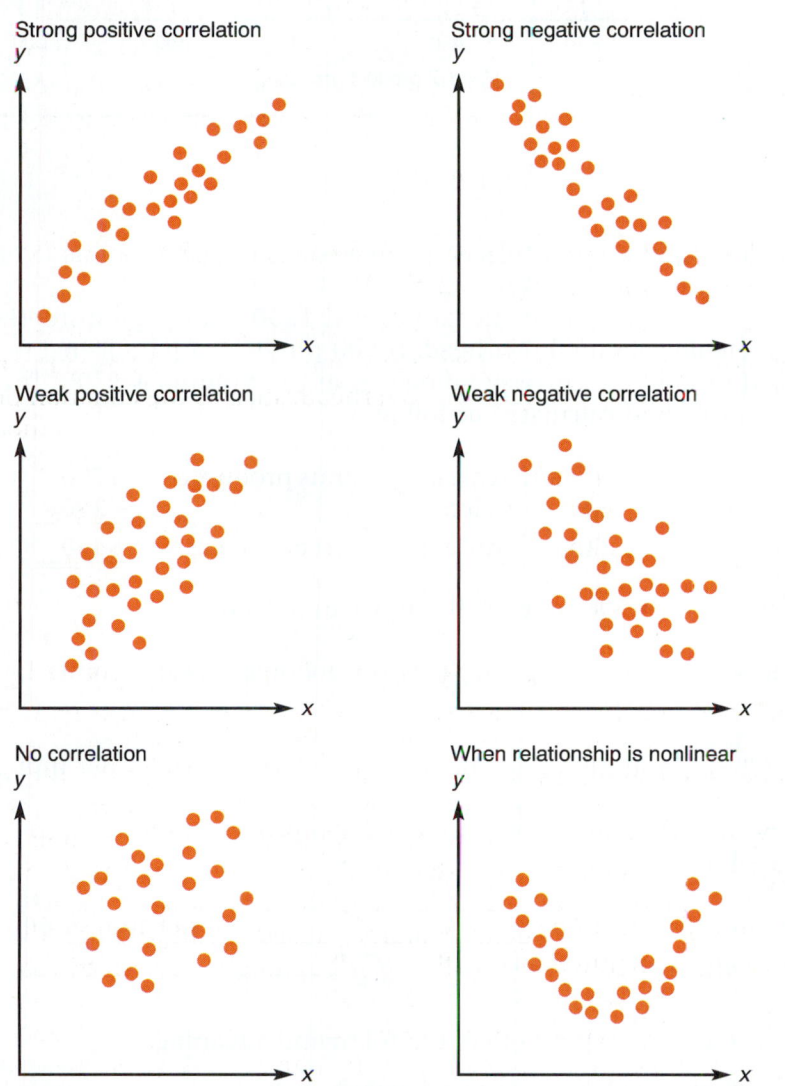

Strong positive correlation

Strong negative correlation

Weak positive correlation

Weak negative correlation

No correlation

When relationship is nonlinear

■ EXHIBIT 7–5
Types of Correlation between Data

Source: Takashi Kanatsu, *TQC for Accounting: A New Role in Companywide Improvement* (Cambridge, MA: Productivity Press, 1990), p. 203. With permission.

The line fitted to the data by visual inspection in Exhibit 7–6 can be expressed as a linear equation. Total maintenance cost is plotted on the vertical, or *y*, axis. The units produced are plotted on the horizontal, or *x*, axis. The average variable cost per product is represented by the slope of the line, and the total fixed costs are represented by the point where the line intersects the cost axis (the inter-

**A Completed
Scattergraph
Identifying Variable
and Fixed Cost
Elements for
Maintenance Cost at
Moran Industries**

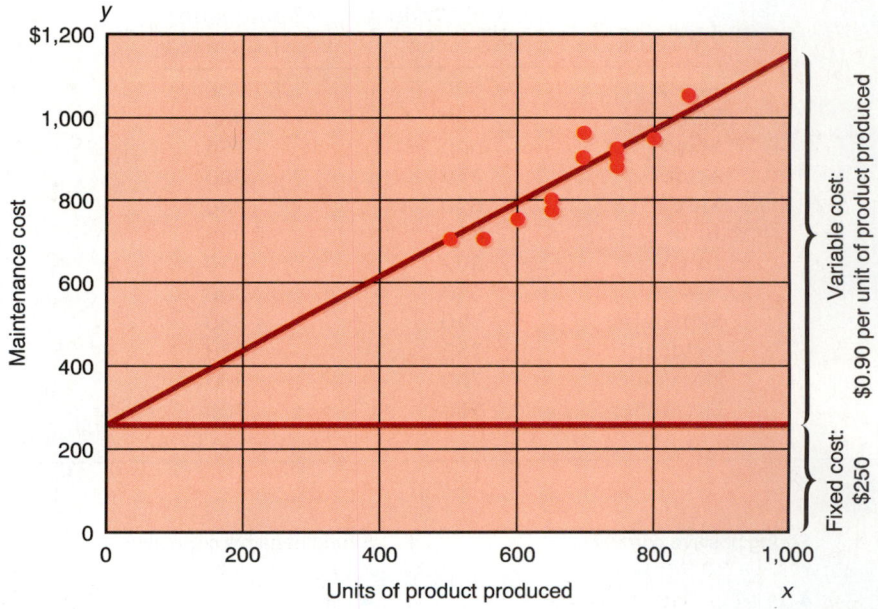

See prev. PS:

cept). Generally, the line is placed so that the number of points falling above and below it are approximately equal.

Because the line intersects the cost axis at $250, that amount represents the fixed cost element in total overhead. If 500 products are budgeted to be made in the next month, the corresponding cost at this volume is $700. The variable cost element is then calculated as follows:

Total maintenance cost at 500 units produced	$700
Less the fixed cost element	<250>
Total estimated variable maintenance cost	$450

$450 ÷ 500 units = $0.90 per unit produced

Thus, the scattergraph method yields the following cost formula for maintenance:

Total monthly maintenance cost = $250 + $0.90 per unit

For a month with a production quota of 600 products, total maintenance cost is estimated as:

Total monthly maintenance cost = $250 + ($0.90 per unit × 600 units)
Total monthly maintenance cost = $790

The scattergraph method offers the following advantages:

- It is relatively quick and easy to develop.
- A deviation in cost behavior is easily spotted, and that observation can be ignored when visually fitting the line.
- The resulting cost equation may be good enough for the intended use (e.g., the cost to be estimated is relatively unimportant, and the decision made from this information would not be seriously affected by more sophisticated analyses).

The disadvantage is that different people given the same data will probably draw different lines and, thus, have different estimates of variable and fixed costs.

THE HIGH-LOW METHOD.   The **high-low method** uses only two observations from the data, at the high and low levels of volume or activity.[11] Variable cost per unit (the slope) is equal to the difference in cost divided by the difference in volume or activity. In Exhibit 7–4, June was the month with the highest production volume, while January was the lowest.

$$\text{Variable rate} = \frac{\text{High observation cost} - \text{Low observation cost}}{\text{High observation volume} - \text{Low observation volume}}$$

$$= \frac{\$1,050 - \$700}{850 \text{ units} - 500 \text{ units}}$$

$$= \$1.00 \text{ per unit produced}$$

This formula indicates that *two points* are being chosen, each of which is a volume-cost pair. These two points are chosen on the basis of highest and lowest volume, not on the basis of highest and lowest cost. Activity volume is used to determine high and low points because the activity is expected to drive (cause) maintenance costs.

Having determined that the variable rate is $1 per unit, the management accountant can now calculate the total fixed overhead cost (the intercept). This is done by taking total cost at *either* the high or low point and deducting the total variable cost calculated for that volume. In the following calculation, total cost at the high point of volume or activity is used:

$$\text{Fixed cost element} = \text{Total cost} - \text{Variable cost element}$$

$$= \$1,050 - (\$1.00 \text{ per unit} \times 850 \text{ units})$$

$$= \$200$$

The cost of maintenance can now be estimated using the following cost equation from the high-low method:

Monthly maintenance cost = $200 + $1.00 per unit produced

If 600 products are planned for a month, then the high-low cost equation yields the following estimated cost:

Total monthly maintenance cost = $200 + ($1.00 per unit × 600 units)
Total monthly maintenance cost = $800

Exhibit 7–7 shows the relationships graphically. Maintenance cost is known as the **dependent variable** because the amount of maintenance cost incurred during a period will be dependent on the level of volume or activity for the period. As the level of volume or activity increases, maintenance cost will also increase. The level of volume or activity is called the **independent variable** because it is used to predict the amount of maintenance cost that will be incurred during a period.

The advantages of the high-low method include the following:

---

[11] The high-low method is the "slope-intercept method of calculating a straight line" learned in elementary school.

■EXHIBIT 7–7

High-Low Method of Identifying Variable and Fixed Cost Elements for Maintenance Cost at Moran Industries

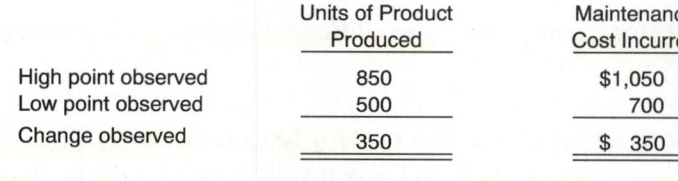

	Units of Product Produced	Maintenance Cost Incurred
High point observed	850	$1,050
Low point observed	500	700
Change observed	350	$ 350

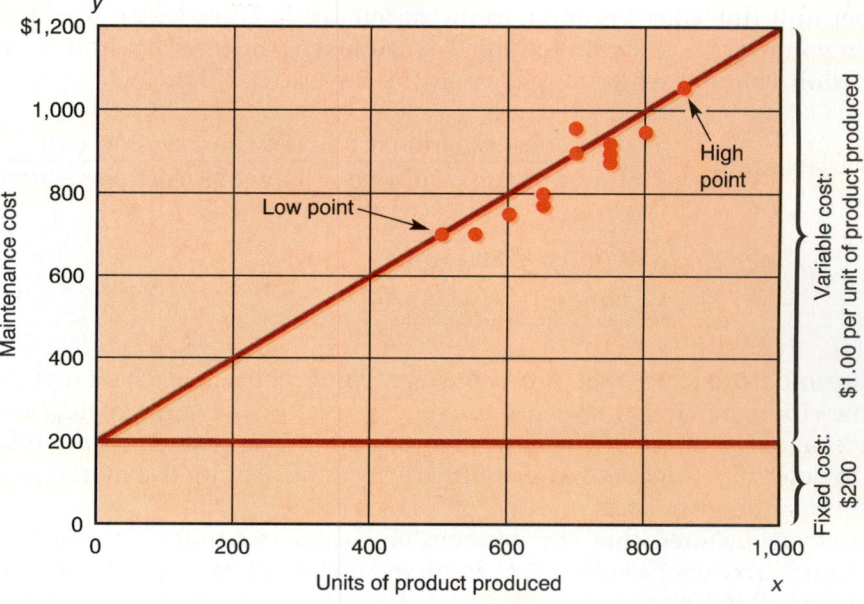

■ It is easy to calculate.
■ It is easy to understand.
■ It is objective (everyone will calculate the same cost equation).

But there are two disadvantages:

■ It uses only two data points, so if either data point is extreme, the results will be skewed, and estimated costs may not be accurate.
■ Only one independent variable is considered (this is also a disadvantage of the scattergraph method).[12]

THE UNIVARIATE LEAST SQUARES REGRESSION METHOD.   The most statistically precise method of fitting the data to a linear equation is the **least squares method.** The regression line is based on the same type of cost equation used in the previous methods. To illustrate, refer back to the data in Exhibit 7–4. These data are entered into a hand-held business calculator. The calculations involve solving simultaneous equations for two variables. The slope (variable maintenance cost per unit) and the intercept (the total fixed maintenance cost) values from the calculator are used in the cost formula:

Monthly maintenance cost = $161.08 + $1.01 per unit produced

If 600 products are expected to be produced next month, the expected maintenance cost will be:

Monthly maintenance cost = $161.08 + ($1.01 per unit × 600 units)
= $767.08

The increased statistical precision of the least squares method is an advantage over the other two methods. If the calculations are done manually, this method

[12] Maryanne M. Mowen, *Accounting for Costs as Fixed and Variable* (Montvale, N.J.: Institute of Management Accountants, formerly the National Association of Accountants, 1986), p. 13. With permission.

will take more time, which can be a disadvantage, depending on the importance of the cost estimate and the amount of time available.

COMPARING THE METHODS' PREDICTED COSTS.   Exhibit 7–8 compares the cost equations and cost estimates from the three methods. The differences between the predicted costs do not appear to be significant, due in part to the small amount of maintenance costs per month.

Which method is better? For a very simple and relatively unimportant cost, the quickest method may be best. However, with the availability of LANs, microcomputer software (like spreadsheet programs), and even hand-held calculators, regression analysis may not require any more time than the other two methods, and by accessing SCAS database information, it may even be faster.

CORRELATION ANALYSIS.   A second reason for the closeness of the cost predictions in Exhibit 7–8 is the high positive correlation between production volume (the independent, predictor variable) and monthly maintenance cost (the dependent variable being predicted).

Correlation analysis measures how well production volume predicts monthly maintenance cost. The coefficient of correlation, r, is a statistic that evaluates how closely production volume and monthly maintenance cost move together. If monthly maintenance cost rises as production volume rises, there is a positive correlation. If monthly maintenance cost falls as production volume rises, there is a negative correlation. When there is no discernible pattern, there is no correlation. Refer back to Exhibit 7–5 for graphical illustrations.

The values for r can range from -1 (perfect negative correlation) to 1 (perfect positive correlation). Values close to zero denote no correlation. Continuing

---

■■EXHIBIT 7–8

Comparison of Cost Equations and Predictions for the Scattergraph, High-Low, and Least Squares Methods

Scattergraph Method:

Total monthly maintenance cost = $250 + $0.90 per unit

Budgeting total overhead for 600 products:

Total monthly maintenance cost = $250 + ($0.90 per unit × 600 units)
= $790.00

High-Low Method:

Total monthly maintenance cost = $200 + $1.00 per unit produced

Budgeting total overhead for 600 products:

Total monthly maintenance cost = $200 + ($1.00 per unit × 600 units)
= $800.00

Least Squares Regression Method:

Total monthly maintenance cost = $161.08 + $1.01 per unit produced

Budgeting overhead for 600 products:

Total monthly maintenance cost = $161.08 + ($1.01 per unit × 600 units)
= $767.08

the Moran Industries monthly maintenance cost example, r equals 0.939, indicating that production volume and maintenance cost are highly positively correlated.

If r is squared, it denotes the percentage of variation in the dependent variable explained by the independent variable. The coefficient of determination, r^2, ranges from zero (no variation is explained) to 1 (all variations in the dependent variable are explained by the independent variable). In this example, r^2 is 0.881; that is, 88.1 percent of the variation in the dependent variable is explained by the independent variable. It can be concluded that the independent variable, production volume, is a good predictor of maintenance cost, at least for Moran Industries.

STANDARD ERROR OF THE ESTIMATE. The standard error of the estimate, S_e, indicates the degree of dispersion of actual observations from estimated values. It indicates the *average* difference between actual observations and expected results. Putting it another way, S_e is the measure of the scatter of the actual observations about the regression line.

When each actual value of the dependent variable falls on the regression line, the standard error of the estimate is zero, indicating that the regression equation provides perfect estimations for that set of data. As the standard error of the estimate increases, the strength of the relationship between the two variables declines, and the regression equation will produce progressively less precise cost estimates.

MULTIPLE REGRESSION ANALYSIS. Often, overhead is caused by more than one independent variable ("cost driver"). Moran Industries' maintenance cost might be predicted even more accurately if the cost equation contained two predictor variables, such as production volume and age of the machinery. **Multiple regression analysis** is a statistical method that creates cost equations containing multiple predictor variables. The maintenance cost equation for Moran Industries could be:

Monthly maintenance cost = \$110.56 + \$0.71 per unit produced
+ \$0.84 per each additional month of age

When overhead costs are caused by multiple factors, this method should produce a more reliable cost prediction, evidenced by a higher coefficient of determination and a smaller standard error of the estimate. This advantage may, or may not, be greater than the effort involved in using this method, which requires computer software. If the statistical program is loaded into a microcomputer or is available within a LAN, this method may be as efficient as least squares or any other.

Another potential advantage of multiple regression is that the total overhead cost equation can be programmed for budgeting purposes. In the Moran Industries example, only maintenance cost is being predicted, but the equations for all the overhead costs could be combined into one for computer calculations in the cost accounting entity.[13] As part of the management accountant's group decision-making role, the individual cost equations may provide more useful information to the shop floor during the budgeting process. As those responsible for various overhead costs prepare their budgets and standards, the information can be input into the budgeting program. As enterprises develop more sophisticated technology platforms and ICBISs, data for the separate equations will be needed for the manufacturing resource planning entity (MRP II).

---

[13] The cost accounting entity, displayed in an entity relationship diagram, includes programs to budget overhead costs. This was discussed in Chapter 3.

Understanding the Ramifications of Using Statistical Estimating Methods

A variety of software packages exist that can perform regression calculations quickly and easily. Entering data into a computer without understanding how the method works and what its ramifications are, however, may lead to misapplications or wrong conclusions.

It is important to understand that the regression equation is based on a relational situation, not necessarily a causal one. The predictor variables used should make sense to those responsible for budgeting, controlling, and evaluating various overhead costs. For example, an MIT statistics professor can very accurately predict whether the Boston Celtics will win a basketball game at home based on the stage of the moon.[14]

If the analysis indicates a predictive relationship between the independent and dependent variables, can the management accountant, and the users of CAS output, assume that the sampled data are relevant to the future? This raises the issue of the relevant range of production volumes over which a univariate or multivariate linear equation may provide accurate estimated costs.

Should the parameters of the equations be adjusted for changing economic factors expected during the time period budgeted? Prices and labor rates may change over time, as may the technology being used. Both manufacturers and service companies are automating their operations as they shift toward capital-intensive production. Increased automation means increased investment in equipment, which results in higher fixed overhead costs (depreciation or lease charges, insurance, property taxes, and the like). Investments also grow each year because of the continuing investment in new technology by world-class enterprises as they develop computer-integrated manufacturing, robotics, ICBISs, and EDI systems.

Direct labor costs, which traditionally have been treated as strictly variable, are becoming more fixed. Union contracts, company policies, and government regulations are factors tending to make direct labor a fixed cost. Many workers are paid on the basis of a salary, which is a fixed compensation paid on a regular basis (e.g., weekly, biweekly, or monthly). Implementation of JIT and cellular manufacturing also results in direct labor becoming a fixed cost.[15]

Another question that arises is whether the sample is truly representative of the overhead activity or process being budgeted. Data sampling is critical to the effective use of estimating methods. Carelessly collected data may lead to erroneous cost relationships and "bad" decisions. Although statistical sampling is beyond the scope of this book, several important considerations in collecting data are presented here:

- During the data collection period, the process or activity from which the data are collected should not undergo significant changes. For example, a change in a maintenance activity from a primarily manual process to a machine-intensive process would lead to two sets of fundamentally different observations.
- If data are drawn from more than one activity, the underlying characteristics of the different activities must be the same. For example, if some maintenance

---

[14] This (probably fictitious) statement was made in the bar on an episode of the "Cheers" television show.

[15] Data relevance also depends on a number of statistical properties and problems such as serial (auto) correlation, heteroscedasticity and multicollinearity. To cope with the modern environment, the management accountant needs to be familiar with many knowledge areas. In this case, consulting a statistics text is appropriate.

costs are incurred in a U-shaped manufacturing cell with cross-trained workers, and some from a sequential, department-based manufacturing process with no cross training of workers, sample data from the two activities will probably give substantially different results.

■ A sufficient number of observations must be collected. If proper sampling techniques are used, such as simple random sampling, a sample size of 20 to 40 observations from a very large population is normally adequate.

■ Each observation must be produced by a random process (e.g., simple random sample).

Although regression methods yield mathematically better results, these methods must be used with caution. Often, equations and complex calculations give both the management accountant and shop floor personnel a false impression of accuracy. For example, a scattergraph may be as good as the least squares method for analyzing cost behavior. By actually plotting the data, the management accountant gains a perspective on cost behavior that he or she would not get from simply outputting a regression equation from a computer program. Indeed, data should always be graphed before any quantitative or statistical method is considered.

Completing the Standard Cost Card

The overhead budgeting process just described results in an equation for predicting total overhead costs. After adjusting the equation parameters for any changing factors that are relevant, the VOH and FOH PORs can be calculated. To illustrate, refer back to the SweetTooth one-pound box of chocolate candies standard cost card in Exhibit 7–1. Assume that the overhead cost equation is:

Budgeted annual total overhead cost = $58,400/year + $0.30/DLhr

THE VARIABLE OVERHEAD STANDARD COST CARD LINE. Because SweetTooth, Inc., produces *handmade* chocolate confections, the shop floor personnel and the management accountant discovered that the direct labor hours worked on each product cause the amount of VOH costs incurred. Direct labor usage is the independent variable and the basis for overhead application to the products. The variable cost component of overhead is the slope of the total overhead cost equation. Thus, it is the VOH POR and the standard price for variable overhead. Since one direct labor hour is budgeted for each box, this is the standard quantity.

THE FIXED OVERHEAD STANDARD COST CARD LINE. The annual production quota is 20,000 one-pound boxes of chocolates. The intercept of the total overhead cost equation is $58,400 per year. The intercept is the budgeted fixed overhead cost. Dividing it by the production quota yields the fixed overhead standard cost:

$$\text{Fixed overhead standard cost} = \frac{\text{Budgeted FOH cost}}{\text{Production quota}}$$

$$= \frac{\$58,400}{20,000 \text{ boxes}}$$

$$= \underline{\$2.92 \text{ per box}}$$

Because direct labor hours are used to apply variable overhead, this basis is also used to apply fixed overhead to the products. Working backwards, the FOH standard cost is divided by the standard quantity to calculate the FOH POR (standard price.)[16]

ABSORPTION VERSUS VARIABLE COSTING

Two different views exist as to whether fixed production costs should be included in the standard product cost. The pervasive view for *external reporting* is that product costs should include *all* production costs:

- Direct materials
- Direct labor
- Overhead, both variable and fixed

For *internal reporting,* the pervasive view is that product costs should include only variable costs:

- Direct materials
- Direct labor
- Variable overhead

Defining the Opposing Costing Methods

Absorption costing (also called **full costing**) treats *all* costs of production as product costs, regardless of whether they are variable or fixed. Absorption costing is currently required for tax purposes and for external reporting under GAAP. Absorption costing is also required in government contracting. The defense industry, for example, uses absorption costing.

Some management accounting authorities believe that absorption costing is appropriate for internal reporting in automated plants and service organizations because of the higher level of fixed costs and lower levels of variable costs. In fact, in highly automated environments, the only variable cost is direct materials because it is the only cost element that is volume-dependent. Therefore, the allocation of all fixed costs, in this case labor and overhead, would lead to better product-related decisions. Consequently, many management accountants in automated environments use absorption costing, especially those who work for aerospace, computer, and scientific equipment manufacturers. At the Charles Machine Works, Inc., makers of "Ditch Witch" underground trenching equipment, the SAMC is used to cost subassemblies produced in JIT cells, as well as in pricing them for field repair work.[17]

Variable costing (sometimes called **direct costing**) is a management accounting tool used to provide management with information about *cost, volume, and profit* relationships in a form that is easy to understand. Under variable costing, only the variable costs are included in the product's standard cost. All

---

[16] Standard price times standard quantity equals standard cost. Therefore, standard cost divided by standard quantity equals standard price. A different approach to preparing the FOH line is to directly calculate the standard price. If the production quota is 20,000 boxes per year, and the standard direct labor quantity is 1 DLhr per box, then 20,000 DLhr will be budgeted for the year. This is the volume of the overhead basis and the denominator volume of the FOH POR:

$$\text{FOH POR} = \frac{\$58,400 \text{ budgeted FOH cost}}{20,000 \text{ budgeted direct labor hours}}$$

$$= \underline{\$2.92/\text{DLhr}}$$

The FOH POR multiplied by the direct labor standard quantity equals the FOH standard cost.

[17] Thomas, et al., op cit.

fixed production costs are written off to COGS in total. The key advantage of variable costing is that the method facilitates profit planning, cost management, and decision making. To illustrate, at Ditch Witch the standard variable cost is used for costing rejected subassemblies during final assembly. This allows the SCAS to provide information on the costs of internal failures. The labor and related overhead standard costs involved in replacing a bad subassembly plus the standard variable cost of the subassembly is the cost to correct this failure. If enough failures occur over time, and management is considering purchasing subassemblies (outsourcing) rather than continuing to make them, the standard variable cost provides relevant information for that decision.[18] The Ditch Witch SCAS is an example of the need for flexibility in the design of modern high-quality information systems.[19] That system reports both the standard variable cost and the SAMC.

Advantages of a Standard Cost Card

The standard cost card for SweetTooth's one-pound box of chocolates (Exhibit 7–1) provides a number of benefits:

- Separate standard prices and quantities are required for each cost element. This emphasizes the need for coordination, communication, and group decision-making in the standard-setting process. Participation by those who are responsible for controlling the costs can increase their motivation to make goal-congruent decisions and seek continuous improvements.
- Separate standard prices and quantities provide information for daily operational control if used in a real-time mode to calculate cost variances. This information needs to be available to the shop floor as production problems happen.
- Standard prices and quantities are needed for cost variance calculations used in performance evaluation. Calculating and reporting cost variances are covered in the next chapter.
- The SAMC is useful in setting sales prices by profit center managers. The sales price has to be high enough to cover the variable costs of making a product as well as covering ("absorbing") a fair share of the fixed overhead.
- The SAMC is useful in making journal entries in the SCAS. An SCAS may be more efficient to operate than an actual or normal CAS. How to use standard costs in journal entries is discussed in the next chapter.

LEARNING OBJECTIVE 5

Discuss the need for a manufacturing cost equation.

Disadvantages of Standard Absorptive Manufacturing Cost

There are two problems with absorption costing. First, the SAMC cannot be used to budget total production costs. To do this, the variable and fixed costs need to be separately accounted for. Variable costs need to be known on a per unit basis and fixed costs in total. These relationships are captured in the product's cost equation.

BUDGETING TOTAL MANUFACTURING COSTS. In the SweetTooth box of chocolates example (Exhibit 7–1), the total overhead cost equation was:

Budgeted annual total overhead cost = $58,400/year + $0.30/DLhr

---

[18] Ibid.
[19] Flexibility is a characteristic of world-class systems, as discussed in Chapter 1. Flexibility allows for more relevant and usable information, two characteristics of high-quality information, also discussed in Chapter 1.

A similar equation needs to be created for all the manufacturing costs involved in making the box of chocolates. The variable standard cost is $6.90 per box, which includes:

- The standard raw chocolate cost of $2.00/box
- The standard wrapping paper cost of $0.60/box
- The standard direct labor cost of $4.00/box
- The standard variable overhead cost of $0.30/box

The budgeted fixed overhead cost in total (from the overhead cost equation) is $58,400 per year. Combining these amounts into a cost equation to predict the total manufacturing costs for this product:

$$\text{Budgeted annual manufacturing cost for one-pound boxes of chocolates} = \$58,400/\text{yr} + \$6.90/\text{box}$$

The usefulness of the cost equation becomes apparent when budgeting for one box to be produced in a year and then for 10,000 boxes in a year:

If one box is all that is produced:

$$\text{Budgeted annual manufacturing cost for one-pound boxes of chocolates} = \$58,400/\text{yr} + \$6.90/\text{box}$$
$$= \$58,400 + (\$6.90 \times 1 \text{ box})$$
$$= \underline{\$58,406.90}$$

If 10,000 boxes are produced:

$$\text{Budgeted annual manufacturing cost for one-pound boxes of chocolates} = \$58,400 + (\$6.90 \times 10,000 \text{ boxes})$$
$$= \underline{\$127,400}$$

What happens if the standard absorptive manufacturing cost is used to budget total production costs?

If one box is all that is produced:

$$\text{Budgeted annual manufacturing cost for one-pound boxes of chocolates} = \$9.82/\text{box} \times 1 \text{ box}$$
$$= \underline{\$9.82}$$

If 10,000 boxes are produced:

$$\text{Budgeted annual manufacturing cost for one-pound boxes of chocolates} = \$9.82/\text{box} \times 10,000 \text{ boxes}$$
$$= \underline{\$98,200}$$

In budgeting costs, cost behavior patterns must be known for accurate budgets to result. The problem with using an absorption cost is that the fixed overhead appears to be a variable cost on the standard cost card. The management accountant must communicate this, properly explaining cost behaviors and budgeting to the shop floor personnel involved in planning decisions. Obviously, the fixed costs in total will be incurred regardless of the production volume (within the relevant range). If one box of candy is all that will be made next year, $58,400 of fixed overhead still will be incurred. If the sales price is to recapture all the costs of production, then it will have to be set above $58,406.90![20]

CHOICE OF A PRODUCTION VOLUME FOR FIXED OVERHEAD STAN-DARD COST. The second problem with using an absorption cost (i.e., includ-

---

[20] Budgeting total costs is discussed in more detail in Chapter 17.

ing fixed overhead in the standard cost of the product) is with the production volume used in calculating the FOH standard cost. There are four commonly used production volumes:

- Theoretical capacity
- Practical capacity
- Normal capacity
- Expected annual capacity

The **theoretical capacity** (also referred to as **ideal capacity**) is the production volume that could be achieved under 100 percent operating efficiency. It is the estimated absolute maximum production potential at all times. There are no delays, shutdowns on weekends or holidays, or machine breakdowns. Theoretical capacity cannot be achieved in a real-world situation and, accordingly, is seldom used. It is an ideal standard. Although it has been recommended as a target of *kaizen,* continuous improvement, in world-class enterprises, it is an unrealistic assumption in many organizations.

Practical capacity is a feasible level of output. The practical capacity of a plant or department is the theoretical capacity less ordinary, regular, and unavoidable operating interruptions. The level of efficiency indicated by practical capacity is difficult but not impossible to achieve.

Normal capacity is the long-term (usually three to ten years) average output of the enterprise. It takes into consideration idle time brought about by year-to-year fluctuations and economic cycles. It represents the practical capacity less the estimated idle capacity. An advantage of using normal capacity in calculating the fixed overhead standard cost is that it represents a level of activity that the enterprise can reasonably expect to achieve on average over some long-range planning period.

Expected annual capacity is the level of activity budgeted for the upcoming year. Expected annual capacity will result in product or service costs that more closely reflect their actual annual costs if costs are properly controlled. The 20,000 boxes of chocolates in the SweetTooth, Inc., example is the production quota based on the sales forecast for the year.

Which capacity measure should the management accountant use to set the FOH standard cost? The answer is the capacity measure that best motivates management and workers to achieve the goals of the company. Motivation, though, depends on the individual personalities involved. Additionally, enterprises have short-run and long-range goals. So, there is no simple answer. To illustrate some of the problems involved, Exhibit 7–9 presents the FOH standard costs for SweetTooth, Inc., using the four different production volumes.

The larger the volume (denominator), the smaller the FOH standard cost, and the less fixed overhead cost included (applied) in each product's, job's, or service's SAMC. Theoretical capacity, which is the absolute capacity, provides the largest denominator.

From a short-term viewpoint, the standard cost from expected annual capacity is probably closest to the "true" product cost if the annual production quota is achieved. This standard cost will probably be most relevant to marketing managers setting sales prices because it reflects the amount of fixed overhead that will need to be covered in the sales price, given the current annual sales forecast and production quota. With expected annual capacity, a pricing problem may develop between years, however. If next year the sales forecast drops

■■■EXHIBIT 7–9
Fixed Overhead Standard Costs Using Various Production Volumes for SweetTooth, Inc.'s One-Pound Box of Chocolate Candies

	Budgeted FOH Cost	÷	Production Volume	=	Standard FOH Cost
Expected:	$58,400	÷	20,000 boxes	=	$2.92/box
Normal:	$58,400	÷	25,000 boxes	=	$2.34/box
Practical:	$58,400	÷	30,000 boxes	=	$1.95/box
Theoretical:	$58,400	÷	35,000 boxes	=	$1.67/box

because of worsening economic conditions, the FOH standard cost will increase. Some marketing managers may interpret this as an increase in fixed overhead costs and attempt to raise prices at just the time when economic events suggest otherwise.

From a long-term viewpoint, the normal capacity probably provides the "truest" total product cost as it represents the long-range average fixed overhead cost per unit. However, if sales prices are based on the SAMC, they will be too low in years when the sales forecast is less than "normal" and too high in years when expected sales exceed the long-run normal volume.

Generally, the use of theoretical and practical capacity may result in underpricing products. Further, some management accountants believe that there is little sense in using these volumes if they represent more products than can be sold. Considering behavioral (motivational) issues, they also believe that in many cases theoretical capacity may demand too much. At the other extreme, normal and expected annual capacity demand too little, because unit costs are calculated at a capacity level based on anticipated sales demand with no regard for available capacity. Finally, some authorities argue that fixed overhead standard costs should be based on practical or theoretical capacity because these volumes stress a fuller utilization of available resources and a *kaizen* philosophy of continuous improvement.

The volume ultimately chosen will depend on the consensus of upper management, shop floor personnel, and the management accountant. The management accountant's role is to assure that relevant costing, pricing, and motivational issues are considered so that the decision is a rational, goal-directed one.

The SweetTooth box of chocolates is a very simple example. If different overhead items are caused by different cost elements (i.e., direct labor hours, machine hours, direct materials, and so forth), then the management accountant may want to have separate cost card lines for each subset of overhead. For example, RMI costs may be allocated based on direct materials purchases. Materials purchasing department costs may be allocated using the number of purchase orders projected. Indirect materials and indirect labor may use a direct labor hour basis. Electricity may be caused by machine hours worked. All this does is add complexity to the standard cost card. Now, there will be multiple standard cost card lines for the different elements of overhead.[21]

Notice that there are already multiple lines for direct materials (raw chocolate and wrapping paper). Similarly, in a standard PCAS, there are multiple production departments. Each department's direct labor may have a separate standard cost and cost card line. As products become more complex, they will have many individual cost elements and standard cost card lines. For example, how many different direct materials, labor, and overhead items go into the making of an automobile or a jet aircraft? At one time, the controller of a major soft drink company reported that 27 different PORs were used in measuring the standard cost of one of their soft drinks!

The standard-setting process, and budgeting in general, is not an easy task. Effective budgeting, however, is fundamental in designing an effective responsibility accounting system. The standards set affect prices and profits. They affect the motivation of organizational members to achieve the firm's goals by affecting how performance is evaluated. If standards are too tight or too loose, daily operational control activities may not happen, and continuous, long-run productivity improvement may not result. Without a doubt, the modern management accountant's role in the standard-setting process is one of the most difficult aspects of his or her job.

---

[21] These issues are considered in depth in Chapters 9 and 10 and in Part III of the text.

SUMMARY OF LEARNING OBJECTIVES

The major goals of this chapter were to enable you to achieve five learning objectives:

Learning objective 1. Describe the role of the modern management accountant and the CAS in cost management.

The modern management accountant is part of a team that plans for the future, monitors and controls the present, and evaluates past performance. Planning requires communication and coordination across functional levels within an organization and across hierarchical levels. It starts with top management communicating objectives and goals. The management accountant works with different responsibility centers (cost, profit, investment) to establish budgets reflecting these goals. Cost management is concerned with establishing standard costs, which motivate organizational members to control operations and strive for continuous improvement.

Control and performance evaluation require that standards be used as benchmarks in identifying problems and their resultant cost variances. The cost variance information should be reported in a timely and understandable way to those having responsibility and control over the variances. Operational control is facilitated by reporting cost variances in a real-time mode. Performance evaluation will more likely be accepted by those being evaluated if they participated in setting the standards and believe the standards are attainable. Of course, any performance evaluation method must lead to rewards acceptable to those being evaluated. Thus, the CAS is only one component of the organization's control system.

Traditionally, a management-by-exception philosophy has been used. This results in reporting cost variances. WCMs, and their management accountants, though, believe that the improvement in standards over time should also be reported and used in performance evaluation to promote *kaizen,* continuous improvement.

Learning objective 2. Define the components of a standard cost card, and list its benefits for cost management.

A standard cost is the budgeted cost for a manufacturing input item (cost element) to make one product, or used in providing a service. Each cost element has its own standard cost. The sum of all cost elements' standard costs is the standard absorptive manufacturing cost (SAMC). The standard cost of any input item is calculated by multiplying its standard price by its standard quantity. The standard price is the budgeted price to obtain one unit of that input (i.e., the budgeted price per pound for raw chocolate, or the budgeted price for one hour of direct labor time). A standard quantity is the budgeted amount of an input to make one product or provide a service.

Standard cost cards provide five benefits in cost management. First, setting standards focuses individuals and groups on prices and quantities. Their efforts to eliminate non-value-added activities and learn how to do things better promote *kaizen.* Second, standards provide the basis for performance evaluation. Third, operational control is promoted by real-time reporting of variances from standards to those responsible for controlling the activities causing the variances. Fourth, profit center managers need the standard absorptive manufacturing cost to set sales prices. Fifth, the SAMC can be used in running the SCAS.

Learning objective 3. Calculate the standard price and quantity for direct materials and direct labor, and understand the issues involved in these calculations.

The standard price is the net delivered purchase price budgeted for direct materials. The direct labor standard price (rate) includes both the budgeted wage rate and the employer's payroll taxes and fringe benefits associated with an hour of labor time. The standard quantity for materials and labor is calculated with the following formula:

$$\text{Standard quantity} = \frac{\text{Output specification}}{(1 - \text{Normal input loss percentage})}$$

Normal input loss is the anticipated scrap rate for direct materials and downtime for direct labor. This standard quantity formula results in a practical standard. A theoretical, or ideal, standard quantity does not include any allowance for normal input loss.

Ideal standards provide a benchmark for measuring continuous improvement over time, but may not motivate employees if they do not believe the standards are attainable. For example, if the technology (equipment) is not perfect, some material loss may always result. This is outside the control of the workers, and they may not accept the use of an ideal standard to evaluate their performance as legitimate. Similarly, an ideal standard for labor time may not include any allowance for necessary control activities that the organization really wants the workers to do. Further, ideal standards may lead to unrealistic budgets.

If the standard quantities include too much loss, though, they may be so loose that attaining them does not support continuous improvement. Management and workers also may come to accept normal loss as a condition that cannot be changed, inhibiting continuous improvement. When workers have been allowed to participate in continuous improvement activities, companies have realized tremendous increases in productivity.

Learning objective 4.   Calculate the standard costs for variable and fixed overhead, and understand the issues involved in setting these standards.

Separate standard costs should be calculated for variable and fixed overhead because they are caused by different decisions. Variable overhead is caused by short-run activities such as the number of purchase orders that will have to be issued in the upcoming year (for purchasing department costs), the machine time planned (for electricity and equipment repairs and maintenance), or the production quota (for VOH costs such as indirect materials and labor). Thus, determining cause-effect relationships is the first step in budgeting VOH costs.

Fixed overhead is often caused by long-run decisions, such as the size of the factory (building depreciation, insurance, and taxes) or the equipment and computer technologies in place (equipment depreciation, insurance, taxes, and salaries of support labor). Identifying the individual FOH items is the first step in budgeting these costs.

Once the causal bases for VOH and FOH are identified, their total costs can be budgeted. Usually, the same basis is used for applying VOH and FOH to individual products. For example, if VOH is caused by machine usage, then this basis may be used to apply VOH and FOH to products. Thus, both the VOH and FOH PORs are calculated using budgeted VOH and FOH divided by budgeted machine hours. The standard quantity for VOH and FOH will then be the standard machine time for making a product.

Obtaining this information requires the coordinated and cooperative efforts of many organizational members. When these group activities and decisions do not occur, the management accountant may have to estimate VOH and FOH costs individually using historical cost data from the CAS. In many traditional CASs, quantitative methods have been used to extrapolate historical data. These methods include the scattergraph, high-low method, univariate (least squares) regression, and multivariate regression.

In budgeting total overhead with these quantitative methods, the management accountant must understand the differences between variable, fixed, mixed, and step costs. Also, the resulting overhead cost equations may have to be adjusted for changes in costs and technology over time. Finally, an understanding of the various statistical problems associated with these methods is required.

Learning objective 5.   Discuss the need for a manufacturing cost equation.

Although standard cost cards offer a number of benefits for budgeting and provide motivation to control costs, if based on absorption costing, they cannot be used to budget total manufacturing costs. This costing method includes a fixed overhead standard cost for each product. Fixed overhead does not behave in the same manner as VOH. It is constant in total, whereas VOH is constant per unit. To budget total overhead and the total costs of manufacturing a product (or providing a service), fixed and variable costs need to be accounted for separately. This is accomplished by creating a cost equation as the second output of the cost budgeting process. When the cost equation is combined with the standard cost card (the first output of the cost budgeting process), the management accountant will have the necessary information to budget costs and report on cost management activities.

▌IMPORTANT TERMS

Absorption costing (full costing) A costing method that includes all costs of production, both variable and fixed, in the cost of an individual product or service.

Cost behavior How costs change with changes in the activity volumes that cause those costs. The four basic patterns are variable, fixed, mixed, and step costs.

Cost centers A responsibility center in which the manager has the authority to incur costs and is evaluated on the basis of how well these costs are controlled.

Cost variance The difference between a standard cost and an actual cost. It is the financial measure of a problem.

Cost variance reports Reports from an SCAS that compare standard and actual costs.

Decision The choice between two or more alternatives.

Dependent variable A variable that is predicted by an independent variable.

Expected annual capacity The level of activity (output) budgeted for the forthcoming year.

Fixed costs Costs that are constant in total, but decrease per unit as some activity basis (such as production volume) increases.

High-low method A statistical technique that uses some measure of activity (an independent variable) to predict cost (a dependent variable) based on the highest and lowest observations from a sample of activity-cost observations.

Independent variable An activity that can be used to predict something else, such as a cost, that depends upon its occurrence.

Investment centers Parts of an enterprise whose members are responsible for making investment decisions. These centers are usually considered to be the highest level of management in the organization's hierarchy.

Least squares method A statistical technique for predicting cost that uses all the cost-activity observations from a sample to create a univariate regression equation.

Management-by-exception A philosophy of reporting and control based on the belief that managers only need information about what is going wrong within their responsibility centers, such as a cost variance report. Its goal is to focus attention on problems.

Mixed costs Costs that are part variable and part fixed.

Multiple regression analysis A statistical technique that predicts something (a dependent variable) by creating an equation that uses more than one predictor (independent) variable.

Normal capacity The long-term, average output of the total enterprise.

Output specification (engineering or marketing specification) The amount of an input (cost element) that should be in a completed product or service. It is also sometimes called an engineering or marketing specification.

Practical capacity A feasible level of output of a department or plant, which is theoretical capacity less ordinary, regular, and unavoidable operating interruptions.

Practical standards (currently attainable) These are achievable goals that can be accomplished with effort.

Problem The difference between what is desired and what actually occurs. In cost accounting, it is a cost variance.

Profit centers Responsibility centers of an enterprise whose members are responsible for cost management and revenue generation, but not for investment decisions.

Rational decisions Alternative choices that lead to accomplishing a goal. Decisions can be rational but also dysfunctional if they are not congruent with the goals of the organization.

Relevant range The range of activity (such as production volume) over which variable costs are assumed to be constant per unit and fixed costs constant in total.

Responsibility accounting An information system that reports on how well organizational members are achieving the firm's goals.

Scattergraph method (scatterplot or scatter diagram) A method of estimating a cost equation by visually drawing a line through a plot (graph) of observations.

Standard absorptive manufacturing cost (SAMC) The sum of all the standard costs in making a product or providing a service, including the standard fixed overhead cost.

Standard cost How much is budgeted for a particular input item (cost element) to make one product or provide a service (i.e., one unit of output).

Standard cost card A document that reports the individual standard costs in making a product. Each product or service should have its own standard cost card.

Standard price The budgeted price for one unit of an input, i.e., the budgeted net delivered purchase price for direct materials, or the budgeted wage rate plus fringe benefits per hour, or the VOH POR and FOH POR.

Standard quantity The budgeted amount of a cost element to make one product or render a service.

Step costs Costs that are constant in total (fixed), but only over a short segment of the relevant range.

Theoretical capacity (ideal capacity) The estimated absolute maximum potential output of a department or plant for a period.

Theoretical standards (ideal standards) Standards based on the best performance possible under existing operating conditions and with existing equipment.

Variable costs Costs that are constant per unit but increase in total with changes in some activity basis such as production volume.

Variable costing (direct costing) A costing method that includes only variable manufacturing costs in the cost of a product.

❙ DEMONSTRATION PROBLEMS

■ DEMONSTRATION PROBLEM 1 *Preparing the standard cost card and manufacturing cost equation.*

As the new management accountant, you are required to prepare a standard cost card for the Donchalikeit Candy Company's three-pound box of chocolates. You have gathered the following information from the purchasing agent and personnel manager:

Chocolate costs	$1.50/lb.
Wrapping paper costs	$0.10/square-foot sheet
Direct labor costs	$6.00/DLhr

Historically, one-third of all chocolate input into the production process is lost during production. One square foot of wrapping paper can make (produce) six cups (for chocolates). There are 30 cups in a three-pound box of chocolates. Eighteen minutes of productive labor time is needed to make a box of candy. Employees work eight hours a day and are allowed two 15-minute breaks plus 18 minutes to clean up each day. Budgeted production volume is 17,833 boxes per year.

There are two overhead subsidiary general ledger accounts within WIP inventory, one for the entire factory's variable overhead and one for the entire factory's fixed overhead. Machine usage is the cost driver for both overhead accounts. Forty-five minutes of machine time are budgeted to produce one box. The controller obtained the following annual overhead information from her SCAS LAN, intending to use the high-low method to perform a total overhead cost analysis:

YEAR	MACHINE HOURS	COSTS
1988	8,000	$54,000
1989	7,500	61,000
1990	7,500	60,500
1991	10,000	61,750
1992	7,000	60,500
1993	11,000	67,000
1994	12,000	65,500

Required:

a. Prepare the standard cost card for a box of chocolates.

b. Calculate the manufacturing cost equation.

SOLUTION TO DEMONSTRATION PROBLEM 1

a. The standard cost card for Donchalikeit's three-pound box of chocolate candies:

Standard Cost Card for 3-Pound Box of Chocolate Candies

ITEMS	STANDARD PRICE	STANDARD QUANTITY	STANDARD COST
Chocolate	$1.50/lb.	4½ lb./box	$ 6.75/box
Wrapping paper	$0.10/sq. ft.	5 sq. ft./box	$ 0.50/box
Direct labor	$6.00/DLhr	⅓ DLhr/box	$ 2.00/box
Variable overhead	$1.00/Mhr	¾ Mhr/box	$ 0.75/box
Fixed overhead	$4.00/Mhr	¾ Mhr/box	$ 3.00/box
Standard absorptive manufacturing cost (SAMC)			$13.00/box

Calculation of direct materials standard quantity:

$$\text{Standard quantity} = \frac{\text{Output specification}}{(1 - \text{Normal scrap percentage})}$$

$$= \frac{3 \text{ pounds per box}}{(1 - \frac{1}{3})}$$

$$= 4.5 \text{ pounds per box}$$

Calculation of direct labor standard quantity:

$$= \frac{18 \text{ minutes per box}}{[1 - (48 \text{ minutes per day} \div 480 \text{ minutes})]}$$

$$= 20 \text{ minutes per box}$$

Calculation of VOH POR:

$$\text{Variable rate} = \frac{\text{High observation cost} - \text{Low observation cost}}{\text{High observation volume} - \text{Low observation volume}}$$

$$= \frac{\$65,500 - \$60,500}{12,000 \text{ machine hours} - 7,000 \text{ machine hours}}$$

$$= \$1.00 \text{ per machine hour}$$

Calculation of total fixed overhead (*using the low point*):

$$\text{Fixed cost element} = \text{Total cost} - \text{Variable cost element}$$
$$= \$60,500 - (\$1.00 \text{ per Mhr} \times 7,000 \text{ Mhr})$$
$$= \$53,500$$

Calculation of FOH standard cost:

$$\text{Fixed overhead standard cost} = \frac{\text{Budgeted FOH cost}}{\text{Production quota}}$$

$$= \frac{\$53,500}{17,833 \text{ boxes}}$$

$$= \$3.00 \text{ per box}$$

Calculation of FOH POR:

$$\text{FOH POR} = \frac{\text{FOH standard cost of \$3.00 per box}}{\text{FOH standard quantity of ¾ Mhr per box}}$$

$$= \$4.00/\text{Mhr}$$

b. Manufacturing cost equation:

Annual production costs
for Donchalikeit's 3-pound = $53,500/year + $10.00/box
boxes of chocolates

(The slope of the equation is the sum of the standard variable costs: chocolate, wrapping paper, direct labor, and variable overhead.)

REVIEW QUESTIONS

7.1 Why is it appropriate to think of cost accounting as having a product and customers? What is the CAS's product? Who are its customers?

7.2 What are the three differences between CAS output and financial reports?

7.3 Why are actual total manufacturing costs needed from a CAS?

7.4 Why are benchmarks (standards) needed from a CAS?

7.5 What new tasks are required of workers in modern production processes?

7.6 List the two decision-making objectives of all organizational members.

7.7 Define, and give an example of, a decision. Relate it to a problem.

7.8 Define a cost variance as it relates to a production problem.

7.9 How do cost variance reports implement a management-by-exception control philosophy?

7.10 Is management-by-exception contrary to world-class manufacturing?

7.11 Are rational decisions always goal congruent? Create an example.

7.12 Can management-by-exception reporting lead to myopic focusing by shop floor personnel?

7.13 List the three decision-making functions of enterprise members.

7.14 What is the SCAS's role in responsibility accounting?

7.15 Distinguish between the three functional responsibility levels of management.

7.16 Explain the five criteria an SCAS must meet to be a high-quality responsibility accounting system.

7.17 What role does the SCAS play in control motivation?

7.18 In designing an SCAS, what ethical considerations arise?

7.19 Define a standard cost and its components.

7.20 What is the difference between a standard cost and a standard absorptive manufacturing cost?

7.21 List five benefits of a standard cost card.

7.22 Make up a product and calculate the standard price for one of its direct materials.

7.23 Are standard prices only useful in manufacturing enterprises?

7.24 Using the example product from Question 7.22, calculate the standard labor rate.

7.25 How does an output specification differ from a standard quantity?

7.26 What is the formula for a standard quantity based on an output specification?

7.27 Discuss the relationships between paid time, downtime, and productive time.

7.28 What is the difference between an ideal and a practical standard? Give an example of how they would be different for direct labor.

7.29 List four reasons why practical standards support a high-quality SCAS.

7.30 What factors should be considered in determining how tight standards should be set? Discuss some of the problems that may occur when standards are set too tight or too loose.

7.31 Explain why ideal standards support continuous improvement. Explain why practical standards may not support continuous improvement.

7.32 Create an example of a nonvalue-added item that is included in a practical direct material standard quantity.

7.33 How do learning curves affect the direct labor standard quantity?

7.34 How often would you revise a standard cost card?

7.35 Why should VOH and FOH be budgeted for separately?

7.36 What is the relationship between the VOH POR and the standard VOH price?

7.37 List five common causes of VOH. Give an example of a VOH item that could be caused by each of these activities (bases for applying VOH to products).

7.38 In choosing an overhead budgeting and application base, what is the primary goal in SCAS design?

7.39 Why are CASs moving away from a direct labor application base for overhead?

7.40 Distinguish between and give an example of each of the four types of cost behavior patterns.

7.41 Why is a relevant range important in budgeting variable and fixed costs?

7.42 Create an example of a mixed cost. Make up some values and predict its total cost for some particular volume you made up.

7.43 How does a step cost differ from a fixed cost?

7.44 Describe the four quantitative methods for analyzing past total overhead costs. Rank order them in terms of quality predictions. Why is your order valid?

7.45 What is the difference between a dependent and an independent variable?

7.46 How do you determine the standard quantity for VOH and FOH?

7.47 What is the formula for a FOH standard cost based on budgeted production volume? Make up an example.

7.48 Explain the difference between a standard variable manufacturing cost and a standard absorptive manufacturing cost.

7.49 List two disadvantages of using a standard absorptive manufacturing cost in the budgeting process.

7.50 Distinguish between the four commonly used production volumes in the FOH standard cost. Which would you choose for a high-quality SCAS?

CHAPTER-SPECIFIC PROBLEMS

These problems require responses based on concepts and techniques presented in the text.

7.51 *Standard cost card.* Define, relate and create a simple example of the components of a standard absorptive manufacturing cost.

7.52 *Ideal versus practical standards.* Can ideal and practical standard quantities differentially affect cost management and operational control motivations? Do you think the difference between them is really important in designing a high-quality SCAS?

7.53 *VOH allocation bases.* Cite an example variable overhead cost that could result from each of the five common allocation bases. Why are the bases appropriate for your examples?

7.54 *Direct materials and labor standard costs.* The production of one five-gallon container of Quikill insecticide requires the use of direct materials as follows:

	MATERIAL A	MATERIAL B
Output specification	6 lb.	2 lb.
Allowance for waste	5%	10%
Purchase price per pound	$3.50	$5.00
Purchase discount	10%	5%
Delivery costs per pound	$0.85	$1.25

One container of Quikill also requires one direct labor hour in Department 1 and two direct labor hours in Department 2. These are the productive times required in each department.

	DEPARTMENT 1	DEPARTMENT 2
Estimated hourly wages per employee	$10.50	$13.12
Fringe benefits	25%	25%
Downtime (minutes per day):		
Setup	15	5
Cleanup	15	25
Breaks	30	30

Required:
Calculate the standard cost card lines for direct materials and direct labor.

7.55 *Direct materials and labor standard costs.* The production of one seven-gallon container of Quikill insecticide requires the use of direct materials as follows:

	MATERIAL X	MATERIAL Y
Output specification	4 lb.	3 lb.
Allowance for waste	10%	5%
Purchase price per pound	$6.50	$8.25
Purchase discount	2%	4%
Delivery costs	$0.63	$0.08

One container of Quikill also requires one and one-half direct labor hours in Department 1 and three direct labor hours in Department 2.

1½hr   3hr

	DEPARTMENT 1	DEPARTMENT 2
Estimated wages per employee	$8.75	$12.25
Fringe benefits	20%	30%
Downtime (minutes per day):		
Setup	20	30
Cleanup	25	30
Breaks	30	30

Required:
Calculate the standard cost card lines for direct materials and direct labor.

7.56 *Preparing a standard cost card.* You are required to prepare a standard cost card for the Donchalikeit Candy Company's one-pound box of chocolates. You have gathered the following information from the purchasing agent and personnel manager:

Chocolate costs	$1.50/lb.
Wrapping paper costs	$0.10/square-foot sheet
Direct labor costs	$4.00/DLhr

The controller has prepared the following annual total overhead analysis for use with the high-low method:

OH analyses

YEAR	DIRECT LABOR HOURS	COSTS
1988	8,000	$54,000
1989	12,000	62,000
1990	7,500	60,500
1991	10,000	61,750
1992	7,000	60,500
1993	11,000	62,500
1994	7,500	61,000

Historically, one-fourth of all chocolate input into the production process is lost during production. One square foot of wrapping paper can make (produce) five cups (for chocolates). There are 30 cups in a one-pound box of chocolates. Ninety-six minutes of a day's labor are nonproductive time, and 12 minutes of productive time is needed to make a box of candy. Budgeted production volume is 20,000 boxes per year.

Required:
Calculate the manufacturing cost equation and prepare the standard cost card for a box of candy. Round all calculations to the nearest cent.

7.57 *Preparing a standard cost card.* You are required to prepare a standard cost card for the Donchalikeit Candy Company's basic lollipop. A completed lollipop has 4 ounces of candy mix in it and takes 36 minutes of productive time to make. Twenty percent of the candy mix input gets spilled before the lollipop is formed. Candy mix costs $1.60 per pound. Laborers are paid $6 per hour and work eight hours per day. They are allowed two 15-minute breaks each day, 5 minutes to setup in the morning, 5 minutes to cleanup at night, and 8 minutes for other miscellaneous activities.

The controller has prepared the following annual total overhead analysis. Overhead is caused by machine usage, and the standard quantity for machine time is one-half hour per lollipop. Annual production volume is budgeted at 10,000 lollipops.

YEAR	MACHINE HOURS	COST
1988	12,500	$62,500
1989	12,000	62,000
1990	6,500	56,500
1991	10,000	61,750
1992	7,250	50,500
1993	11,000	62,750
1994	7,500	61,000

Required:
a. Prepare the standard cost card for a basic lollipop.
b. Calculate the manufacturing cost equation. Use the high-low method.

7.58 *Questions about VOH and FOH standards.* Describe the four capacity measures. What effect does the capacity used to develop and apply overhead costs have on product costs? Explain your answer to each of the following questions:

1. The numerator in the predetermined overhead rate is:
   a. Estimated overhead costs.
   b. Volume or level of activity.
   c. Actual overhead costs.
   d. Service department costs.
2. There are several alternative activity bases for overhead. Which activity base is not commonly used?
   a. Direct labor cost.
   b. Direct labor hours.
   c. Machine hours.
   d. Sales value.
3. Which capacity measure (production volume) results in the lowest fixed overhead standard cost?
   a. Theoretical capacity.
   b. Practical capacity.
   c. Normal capacity.
   d. Expected annual capacity.
4. In a labor-intensive company where more overhead costs are incurred by the more highly skilled and paid employees, which activity base would be appropriate for budgeting a VOH POR?
   a. Direct labor hours.
   b. Direct labor dollars (cost).
   c. Machine hours.
   d. Sales value.

7.59 *Determination of the overhead rates.* Tastee-Treat Company prepares, packages, and distributes six frozen vegetables in two different sized containers. The different vegetables and different sizes are prepared in large batches. The company employs a job order costing system. Manufacturing overhead is assigned to batches by a predetermined rate on the basis of direct labor hours. The manufacturing overhead costs incurred by the company during two recent years (adjusted for changes using current prices and wage rates) are presented below:

	19X3	19X4
Direct labor hours worked	2,760,000	2,160,000
Manufacturing overhead costs incurred (adjusted for changes in current prices and wage rates):		
Indirect labor	$11,040,000	$ 8,640,000
Employee benefits	4,140,000	3,240,000
Supplies	2,760,000	2,160,000
Power	2,208,000	1,728,000
Heat and light	552,000	552,000
Supervision	2,865,000	2,625,000
Depreciation	7,930,000	7,930,000
Property taxes and insurance	3,005,000	3,005,000
Total overhead costs	$34,500,000	$29,880,000

Required:

a. Determine the total overhead cost equation using the high-low method.
b. What will the total overhead be for a 2,300,000 direct labor hour level of activity in 19X5?
c. Calculate the VOH, FOH, and TOH PORs.
d. Repeat Requirements (a–c) using your professional judgment instead of the high-low method. Employee benefits are proportionately related to indirect labor and supervision.

[CMA adapted]

7.60 *Regression analysis.* The Pilot Shop is a catalog business that provides a wide variety of aviation products to pilots throughout the United States. Maynard Shephard, the recently hired management accountant, has been assigned the task of developing a cost function to forecast shipping costs. The previous management accountant had forecast Shipping Department costs each year by plotting cost data against direct labor hours for the most recent 12 months and visually fitting a straight line through the points. The results have not been satisfactory.

After discussions with the Shipping Department personnel, Shephard decided that shipping costs may be more closely related to the number of orders filled. Shephard based his conclusion on the fact that ten months ago the Shipping Department added some automated equipment.

Furthermore, Shephard believed that using linear regression analysis would improve the forecasts of shipping costs. Weekly cost data for the Shipping Department have been accumulated for the last 25 years and adjusted for inflation. Shephard ran two regression analyses of the data, one using direct labor hours and one using the number of cartons shipped. The information obtained from the two linear regressions follows:

	EQUATION 1	EQUATION 2
Equation	SC = 804.3 + 15.68DL	SC = 642.9 + 3.92NR
Coefficient of correlation	.604	.854
Coefficient of determination	.365	.729
Standard error of the estimate	2.652	1.884

The meanings of the notations used in the equations are as follows:

SC = Total Shipping Department costs
DL = Total direct labor hours
NR = Number of cartons shipped

Required:

a. Identify which cost function the Pilot Shop should adopt for forecasting total Shipping Department costs and explain why.
b. If the Pilot Shop projects that 600 cartons will be shipped in the coming week, calculate the total Shipping Department cost using the appropriate regression equation.

c. Explain why linear regression analysis is better than a scatter diagram of the data points for forecasting total Shipping Department costs.

[CMA adapted]

7.61 *Cost behavior patterns.* Review the following graphs. The vertical axes of the graphs represent total cost, and the horizontal axes represent activity or production volume. Choose the appropriate cost behavior pattern for each of the ten cost elements that follow.

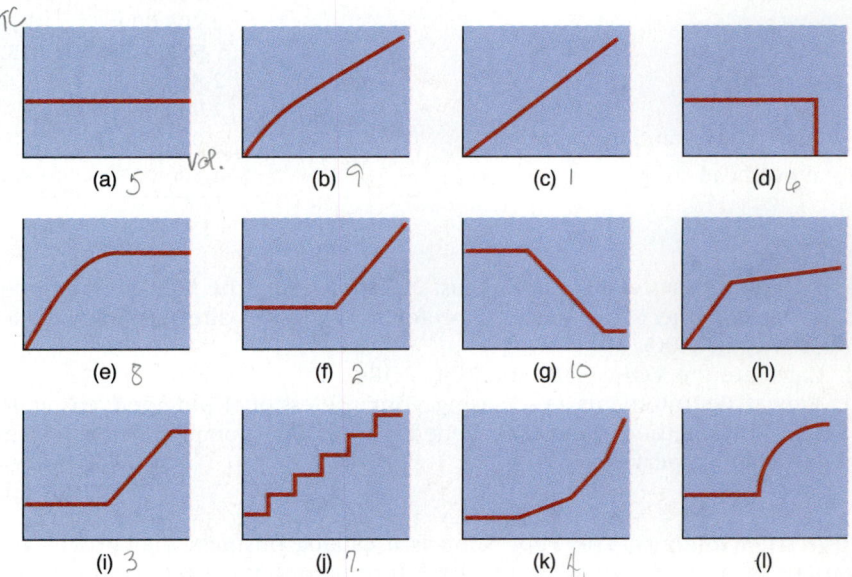

(a) 5   (b) 9   (c) 1   (d) 6

(e) 8   (f) 2   (g) 10   (h)

(i) 3   (j) 7.   (k) 4.   (l)

_____ 1. Depreciation of equipment, where the amount of depreciation charged is computed by the machine hours method.

_____ 2. Electricity bill—a flat fixed charge, plus a variable cost after a certain number of kilowatt hours are used.

_____ 3. City water bill, which is computed as follows:

First 1,000,000 gallons or less	$1.000 flat fee
Next 10,000 gallons	0.003 per gallon used
Next 10,000 gallons	0.006 per gallon used
Next 10,000 gallons	0.009 per gallon used

_____ 4. Cost of lubricant for machines, where cost per unit decreases with each pound of lubricant used (for example, if one pound is used, the cost is $10; if two pounds are used, the cost is $19.98; if three pounds are used, the cost is $29.94; with a minimum cost per pound of $9.25).

_____ 5. Depreciation of equipment, where the amount is computed by the straight-line method. When the depreciation rate was established, it was anticipated that the obsolescence factor would be greater than the wear and tear factor.

_____ 6. Rent on a factory building donated by the city, where the agreement calls for a fixed fee payment unless 200,000 labor hours are worked, in which case no rent needs to be paid.

_____ 7. Salaries of repair crew, where one repair person is needed for every 1,000 hours of machine time or less (that is, 0 to 1,000 hours requires one repair person, 1,001 to 2,000 hours requires two, and so on).

_____ 8. Federal unemployment compensation taxes for the year, where the labor force is constant in number throughout the year (average annual salary is $10,000 per worker). Only the first $4,200 earned is subject to tax.

_____ 9. Cost of raw material used.

_____ 10. Rent on a factory building donated by the county, where the agreement calls for rent of $100,000 less $1 for each direct labor hour worked in excess of 200,000 hours, but a minimum rental payment of $20,000 must be paid.

[AICPA adapted]

7.62 *High-low method.* Joel Corporation has gathered the following data on the cost of electricity and direct labor hours worked for the past six months:

MONTH	COST OF ELECTRICITY	DIRECT LABOR HOURS
January	$ 15,000	3,000
February	14,000	2,200
March	17,000	2,800
April	20,000	3,800
May	17,500	2,700
June	18,300	2,900
Totals	$101,800	17,400

Required:
Using the high-low method, calculate the overhead cost equation for electricity.

7.63 *High-low method for estimating costs.* The Tahoe Hotel's guest-days of occupancy and custodial supplies costs over the last six months were as follows:

MONTH	GUEST-DAYS OF OCCUPANCY	CUSTODIAL SUPPLIES COST
January	4,400	$ 8,000
February	6,800	9,000
March	8,200	11,200
April	10,800	12,800
May	12,400	14,200
June	9,400	11,800

Required:
a. Using the high-low method, determine the cost equation for custodial supplies cost.
b. What amount of custodial cost would you expect to be incurred at an occupancy level of 11,500 guest-days?

7.64 *High-low method and scattergraph method.* The following data relating to units shipped and total shipping cost have been collected by the management accountant at the Clarkson Company:

MONTH	UNITS SHIPPED	TOTAL SHIPPING COST
March	400	$2,000
April	700	2,800
May	500	1,900
June	600	2,500
July	800	3,000
August	900	3,750
September	300	1,800
October	490	2,100

Required:
a. Using the high-low method, determine the cost equation for shipping costs.
b. For the scattergraph method, do the following:
   1. Prepare a scattergraph using the data given. Fit a line to your plotted data points by visual inspection.
   2. Using the data from your scattergraph, determine the approximate variable cost per unit shipped and the approximate fixed cost per month.

7.65 *Simple regression analysis.* The management accountant finds that the intersection of the line of best fit for total overhead with the *y*-axis is $10,000. The slope of the regression line is .20. The independent variable, direct labor cost, amounts to $600,000 for the month.

Required:
What is the estimated total overhead for the month?

7.66 Simple regression analysis. The management accountant at Gilland Company derived the following cost relationship from a regression analysis of the company's monthly manufacturing overhead costs:

$$\text{Monthly manufacturing overhead costs} = \$90,000 + \$10/\text{Mhr}$$

The standard error of the estimate of the regression line is $5,000. The standard time required to manufacture one six-unit case of Gilland's single product is four machine hours. Gilland applies manufacturing overhead to production on the basis of machine hours, and its normal annual production is 60,000 cases.

Required:
a. Estimate the total manufacturing overhead cost for a month in which scheduled production is 5,000 cases.
b. What is Gilland's predetermined fixed manufacturing overhead rate?
c. What is the VOH standard cost?

7.67 Variable and fixed costs estimating methods. Barco has a separate maintenance department that performs all routine and major repair work on the company's machines. The maintenance cost is primarily a function of machine hours worked in various production departments. The maintenance cost incurred and the actual machine hours worked during the first six months of 19X3 are as follows:

MONTH	MAINTENANCE COST (Y)	MACHINE HOURS (X)
January	$4,000	900
February	4,000	1,000
March	2,000	500
April	6,000	1,500
May	5,000	1,200
June	3,000	600

Required:
a. Draw a scattergraph depicting the preceding data.
b. Compute the VOH POR for maintenance cost per machine hour and fixed maintenance cost per month using the high-low method.
c. Compute VOH POR for maintenance cost per machine hour and fixed maintenance cost per month using the least squares method from a calculator or spreadsheet program.

7.68 Regression analysis. In preparing the annual profit plan for the coming year, Wilkens Company wants to determine the cost behavior pattern of its maintenance costs. Wilkens has decided to use linear regression. The prior year's data regarding maintenance hours and costs and the results of the regression analysis are as follows:

MONTH	HOURS OF ACTIVITY	MAINTENANCE COSTS
January	480	$ 4,200
February	320	3.000
March	400	3,600
April	300	2,820
May	500	4,350
June	310	2,960
July	320	3,030
August	520	4,470

Continued

—*Continued*

	90	4,260
September	70	4,050
October	350	3,300
November	340	3,160
December	4,800	$43,200
Totals		
	400	$ 3,600
Avera per hour		$ 9.00
Ave		684.65
		7.2884
a error of *a*		49.515
b error of *b*		.12126
error of the		
ate		34.469
		.99724

sion equation $Y = a + bX$, the letter "*b*" is *best* described

Required:
a. In the able.
   as a(r able.
   1. I cient.
   2. determination.
   in the standard regression equation is *best* described as a(n):
   t variable.
   variable.
   coefficient.
   coefficient.
   ent of determination.
   n the data derived from the regression analysis, 420 maintenance
   a month would mean the maintenance cost (rounded to the nearest
   vould be budgeted at:
   80.
   600.
   ,790.
   3,746.
   $3,756.
e percentage of the total variance that can be explained by the regression
quation is:
1. 99.724%.
2. 69.613%.
3. 80.982%.
4. 99.862%.
5. Some amount other than those given above.

[CMA adapted]

THINK-TANK PROBLEMS

Although these problems are based on chapter material, reading extra material, reviewing previous chapters, and using creativity may be required to develop workable solutions.

7.69 Accounting for production problems with cost variances. Define a cost variance, and create an example of how a production problem causes multiple cost variances. Make up some simple costs, and demonstrate how the total cost variance from your example problem can be calculated and reported to the shop floor. What type of technology platform and ICBIS would you design to support shop floor operational control, performance evaluation, and future budgeting?

7.70 CAS ERD and motivation. If an entity relationship diagram of the control process was prepared, what would be its entities, given the goal of supporting a *kaizen*

motivation? What role does the SC~~s~~ play in the motivation cause-effect chain?

7.71 High-quality information. Consider ~~t~~ ~~~~characteristics of high-quality information, the two decision-making objective~~s~~ ~~~~d the three decision-making functions
of all employees. How can a standard c~~d~~ ~~~~rd support a high-quality SCAS?

7.72 Statistical analysis of overhead. Discuss th~~e~~ ~~~~cations of using statistical methods to analyze past overhead costs. Why a~~~~ ~~~~ methods used? What would
you do to overcome these potential problem~~s~~ ~~~~igning a high-quality SCAS?

7.73 Standards in nonmanufacturing enterprises. E~~~~ ~~~~w an SCAS is applicable
in an enterprise that routinely manufactures th~~~~ ~~~~ducts or performs the
same services. Are standard costs applicable to c~~~~ ~~~~at make an array of
unique products or perform one-of-a-kind service~~s~~ ~~~~rd costs useful for
construction companies, consultants, repair shops,

7.74 Participation of workers in setting standards. Reid Cor~~~~ ~~~~rsified man-
u~~~~facturing firm, has been experiencing decreasing profi~~t~~ ~~~~are for the
past two years. The company president, Kristin Johnson,~~~~ ~~~~agement
accounting consultant to report on the operations of three ~~~~turing
plants. The consultant has made several visits to each of the~~~~ ~~~~ntly
compiled his findings in a report to Johnson. The consult~~~~ ~~~~he
levels of employee participation vary considerably througho~~~~
and presented the following examples:

- At the western plant, where small appliances are manufacture~~d~~ ~~~~
  system was recently implemented. The steps used by the pl~~~~
  establish the standards provided for employee participation at al~~l~~
  the process. Despite these efforts, the employee perception is t~~~~
  standards were imposed by top management to satisfy some over~~~~
  goal.
- At the southern plant, where heavy equipment is assembled, stop but~~~~
  been installed on the assembly line to allow workers to correct problem~~~~
  diately. This enables the employees to have greater control over thei~~r~~
  and, as a consequence, the workers perceive greater involvement in all~~~~
  of decision making.
- At the northern plant, a metal-stamping facility, costs have risen and prod~~~~
  quality has declined to the point where the products are no longer competitiv~~~~
  The employees have little sense of commitment to the company as most job~~~~
  are routine and uninteresting. The plant is experiencing high employee turnover~~~~
  and excessive absenteeism. Some plant workers have suggested that the formation of quality circles might improve the situation.

Required:
a. Describe four factors that generally determine the level of employee participation in an organization's control systems.
b. Recommend ways to modify the standard cost system at the western plant in
   order to increase employee participation and gain wider acceptance of the
   standards.
c. Other than those mentioned above, describe the benefits that have accrued to
   the southern plant from the installation of the stop buttons on the assembly
   line. (Review *Jidoka* in Chapter 2.)
d. Explain how the northern plant and its employees could benefit from the
   introduction of quality circles.

[CMA adapted]

7.75 Characteristics of a standard cost system. Some executives believe that it is
extremely important to manage "by the numbers." This form of management
requires that all employees with departmental or divisional responsibilities spend
time understanding the company's operations and how they are reflected in the
company's financial reports. As a manager's comprehension of the financial
reports and the activities that they represent increases, his or her subordinates
will become more attuned to the meaning of financial reports and the important

signposts that can be detected in them. Companies utilize a variety of numerical measurement systems including standard costs, financial ratios, human resource forecasts, and operating budgets.

Required:
a. 1. Discuss the characteristics that should be present in a standard cost system in order to encourage positive employee motivation.
   2. Discuss how a standard cost system should be implemented to positively motivate employees.
b. The use of variance analysis often results in management-by-exception.
   1. Explain the meaning of management-by-exception.
   2. Discuss the behavioral implications of management-by-exception.
c. Explain how employee behavior could be adversely affected when "actual to budget" comparisons are used as the basis for performance evaluation.

[CMA adapted]

7.76 *Advantages and disadvantages of a standard cost system.* Mark-Wright, Inc. (MWI) is a specialty frozen-food processor located in the midwestern states. Since its founding in 1992, MWI has enjoyed a loyal local clientele that is willing to pay premium prices for the high-quality frozen foods it prepares from specialized recipes. In the last two years, the company has experienced rapid sales growth in its operating region and has had many inquiries about supplying its products on a national basis. To meet this growth, MWI expanded its processing capabilities, which resulted in increased production and distribution costs. Furthermore, MWI has been encountering pricing pressure from competitors outside its normal marketing region.

As MWI desires to continue its expansion, Jim Condon, CEO, has engaged a consulting firm to assist the company in determining its best course of action. The consulting firm concluded that, while premium pricing is sustainable in some areas, if sales growth is to be achieved, MWI must make some price concessions. Also, in order to maintain profit margins, costs must be reduced and controlled. The consulting firm recommended the institution of a standard cost system that would also facilitate a flexible budgeting system to better accommodate the changes in demand that can be expected when serving an expanding market area.

Condon met with his management team and explained the recommendations of the consulting firm. Condon then assigned the task of establishing standard costs to his management team. After discussing the situation with their respective staffs, the management team met to review the matter.

Jane Morgan, purchasing manager, advised that meeting expanded production would necessitate obtaining basic food supplies from other than MWI's traditional sources. This would entail increased raw material and shipping costs and may result in lower-quality supplies. Consequently, these increased costs would have to be made up by the processing department if current cost levels are to be maintained or reduced.

Stan Walters, processing manager, countered that the need to accelerate processing cycles to increase production, coupled with the possibility of receiving lower-grade supplies, can be expected to result in a slip in quality and a greater product rejection rate. Under these circumstances, per unit labor utilization cannot be maintained or reduced, and forecasting future unit labor costs becomes very difficult.

Tom Lopez, production engineer, advised that if the equipment is not properly maintained and thoroughly cleaned at prescribed daily intervals, it can be anticipated that the quality and unique taste of the frozen-food products will be affected. Jack Reid, vice president of sales, stated that if quality cannot be maintained, MWI cannot expect to increase sales to the levels projected.

When Condon was apprised of the problems encountered by his management team, he advised them that if agreement could not be reached on appropriate standards, he would arrange to have the standards set by the consulting firm and everyone would have to live with the results.

Required:
a. 1. List the major advantages of using a standard cost system.

2. List disadvantages that can result from using a standard cost system.

b. 1. Identify those who should participate in setting standards and describe the benefits of their participation in the standard-setting process.

2. Explain the general features and characteristics associated with the introduction and operation of a standard cost system that make it an effective tool for cost control.

c. What could be the consequences if Jim Condon, CEO of MWI, has the standards set by the outside consulting firm?

[CMA adapted]

7.77 *Standard costs and ethics.* Quincy Farms is a producer of items made from local farm products that are distributed to supermarkets. For many years, Quincy's products have had strong regional sales on the basis of brand recognition; however, other companies have begun marketing similar products in the area, and price competition has become increasingly important. Doug Gilbert, the management accountant, is planning to implement a standard cost system for Quincy and has gathered considerable information from his co-workers on production and material requirements for Quincy's products. Gilbert believes that the use of standard costing will allow Quincy to improve cost control and make better pricing decisions.

Quincy's most popular product is strawberry jam. The jam is produced in ten-gallon batches, and each batch requires six quarts of good strawberries. The fresh strawberries are sorted by hand before entering the production process. Because of imperfections in the strawberries and normal spoilage, one quart of berries is discarded for every four quarts of *acceptable* berries. Three minutes is the standard direct labor time for the sorting that is required to obtain one quart of acceptable strawberries. The acceptable strawberries are then blended with the other ingredients; blending requires 12 minutes of direct labor time per batch. After processing, the jam is packaged in quart containers. Gilbert has gathered the following information from Joe Adams, Quincy's cost accountant, relative to processing the strawberry jam:

- Quincy purchases strawberries at a cost of $0.80 per quart. All other ingredients cost a total of $0.45 per gallon.
- Direct labor is paid at the rate of $9.00 per hour.
- The total cost of material and labor required to package the jam is $0.38 per quart.

Adams has a friend who owns a strawberry farm that has been losing money in recent years. Because of good crops, there has been an oversupply of strawberries, and prices have dropped to $0.50 per quart. Adams has arranged for Quincy to purchase strawberries from his friend and hopes that $0.80 per quart will put his friend's farm in the black.

Required:

a. Develop the standard cost for the direct cost components of a ten-gallon batch of strawberry jam. The standard cost should identify the following for each direct cost component of a batch of strawberry jam:
   1. Standard quantity.
   2. Standard rate.
   3. Standard cost per batch.

b. Citing the specific standards of competence, confidentiality, integrity, and/or objectivity from *Standards of Ethical Conduct for Management Accountants*, explain why Joe Adams's behavior regarding the cost information provided to Doug Gilbert is unethical.

[CMA adapted]

7.78 *Regression analysis.* Elisko, Inc., is a major book distributor that ships books throughout the United States. Elisko's Shipping Department consists of a manager plus ten other permanent positions—four supervisors and six loaders. The four supervisors and six loaders provide the minimum staff and frequently must be supplemented by additional workers, especially during the weeks when the volume of shipments is heavy. Thus, the number of people shipping the orders frequently averages over 30 per week, i.e., 10 permanent employees plus 20 temporary workers. The temporary workers are hired through a local agency.

Elisko must use temporary workers to maintain a minimum daily shipment rate of 95% of orders presented for shipping. The loss of efficiency from using temporary workers is minimal, and the $10.00 per hour cost of temporary workers is less than the $15.00 per hour for the loaders and $22.50 per hour for the supervisors on Elisko's permanent staff. The agency requires Elisko to utilize each temporary worker for at least four hours each day.

Jim Locter, shipping manager, schedules temporary help based on forecasted orders for the coming week. Supervisors serve as loaders until temporary help is needed. A supervisor stops loading when the ratio of loaders to supervisors reaches 7 : 1. Locter knows that he will need temporary help when the forecasted average daily orders exceed 300. Locter has frequently requested from two to four extra temporary workers per day to guard against unexpected rush orders. If there was not enough work, he would dismiss the extra people at noon after four hours of work.

The agency has not been pleased with Locter's practice of overhiring and has notified Elisko that it is changing its policy. From now on, if a person is dismissed before an eight-hour assignment is completed, Elisko will still be charged for an eight-hour day plus mileage back to the agency for reassignment. This policy will go into effect the following week.

Paula Brand, general manager, called Jim Locter to her office when she received the notice from the agency. She told Locter, "Your staffing has to be better. This penalty could cost us up to $300–$500 per week in labor cost for which we receive no benefit. Why can't you schedule better?"

Locter replied, "I agree that the staffing should be better, but I can't do it accurately when there are rush orders. By being able to lay off people at noon, I have been able to adjust for the uncertain order schedule without cost to the company. Of course, the agency's new policy changes this."

Locter and Brand contacted Elisko's controller, Mitch Berg, regarding the problem of how to estimate the number of people needed each week. Berg realized that Locter needed a quick solution until he could study the work flow. Berg suggested a regression analysis using the number of orders shipped as the independent variable and the number of workers (permanent plus temporary) as the dependent variable. Berg indicated that data for the past year were available and that the analysis could be done quickly on the Accounting Department's microcomputer.

Berg completed the two regression analyses presented below. The first regression was based on the data for the entire year. The second regression excluded the weeks when only the 10 permanent employees were used; these weeks were unusual and appeared to be out of the relevant range.

Regression Equation
$$W = a + bS$$

Where: W = Total workers (permanent plus temporary)
        S = Orders shipped

	REGRESSION 1 (DAILY DATA FOR 52 WEEKS)	REGRESSION 2 (DAILY DATA FOR 38 WEEKS)
a	5.062	0.489
b	0.023	0.028
Standard error (S_e) of the estimate for W	2.012	0.432
95% confidence for W	3.943	0.848
Coefficient of determination (r^2)	0.962	0.998
Standard error of coefficient (S_b)	0.0007	0.0002

Locter was not familiar with regression analysis and, therefore, was unsure of how to implement this technique. He wondered which regression data he should employ, i.e., which one was better. When Locter recognized that the regression was based on actual orders shipped by week, Berg told him he could use the forecasted shipments for the week to determine the number of workers needed.

Required:

a. Using Regression 1 based on data from a full year, calculate the number of temporary workers Jim Locter would plan to hire for a forecast indicating 1,200 shipments per day.
b. Which of the two regressions appears to be better? Explain your answer.
c. Explain the circumstances under which Jim Locter can use the regression in his planning for temporary workers.
d. Explain whether the regression analysis that Elisko employed in this situation could be improved. If it cannot be improved, explain why.

[CMA adapted]

7.79 *Spreadsheet program for standard cost card.* Refer to the spreadsheet program in Exhibit 8–11. It contains a current standard cost card and a manufacturing cost equation. Create a spreadsheet program to produce this part of the report. Use the information in Problems 7.56 and 7.57 to test the program.

8

THE STANDARD COST ACCOUNTING SYSTEM PART 2: JOURNAL ENTRIES, COST VARIANCES, AND REPORTS

LEARNING OBJECTIVES

After studying this chapter, you should be able to:

1. Discuss the role of a standard cost accounting system (SCAS) in responsibility accounting.

2. Explain the meaning of a cost variance, and calculate and interpret the variable costs' spending variances.

3. Calculate and interpret the variable costs' usage variances.

4. Calculate and interpret the fixed overhead variances.

5. Prepare the journal entries for an SCAS, and the cost variance report.

6. Design a high-quality SCAS with management reports useful for operational control and performance evaluation.

Standard cost for direct materials, direct labor, and overhead at Saturn.

■ INTRODUCTION

Chapters 4, 5, and 6 presented actual and normal JOCASs and PCASs. These cost accounting systems are mainly based on actual costs. By themselves, however, actual costs are not particularly useful to management in controlling daily operations and evaluating performance. For these decision-making needs, actual costs should be compared against standard costs.

The standard costs, prices, and quantities and the standard manufacturing cost equation reside in the SCAS LAN database. This information is accessed by the production LAN's MRP II system as needed in shop floor operational planning and control. The SCAS also includes a report generator that, in world-class enterprises, can provide real-time cost variance information as well as summary reports. In this way, the SCAS can provide high-quality information for its cost management objective.

In addition, standard costs can be used in the SCAS journal entries to represent the product's cost in WIP, FGI, and COGS. Some enterprises use standard costs and cost variances strictly as planning, controlling, and evaluating techniques. Cost variance information is available within the JOCAS or PCAS LAN, but actual costs are used in the journal entries. An example of a JOCAS that reported cost variances was discussed in Chapter 5 (see Exhibit 5–22). Other companies enter standard costs in the general ledger accounts and journalize cost variances.

As explained in the last chapter, when actual costs and standard costs differ, the difference is a cost variance. A cost variance can be either favorable or unfavorable. A **favorable cost variance** results when actual costs are less than standard costs. An **unfavorable cost variance** occurs when actual costs are greater than standard costs. Although variances are excellent devices for gauging economic and operating performance, management accountants must take care to ensure that they are used properly and do not cause counterproductive behavior. ▬

<table>
<tr><td>

LEARNING OBJECTIVE 1

Discuss the role of a standard cost accounting system (SCAS) in responsibility accounting.

</td></tr>
</table>

COST VARIANCE REPORTING, RESPONSIBILITY ACCOUNTING, AND MOTIVATION

A standard cost developed jointly by management and employees responsible for the costs can be a motivating influence for employees and result in higher productivity. Generally, people are more motivated to do a good job if they clearly understand what is expected of them and believe they will be rewarded for their efforts.

Using cost variances as fault-finding devices and placing too much reliance on them in evaluations may, however, motivate people to engage in counterproductive acts such as delayed maintenance, bickering over cost allocations, or even falsifying data. Indeed, most people's needs are too diverse and changeable to be satisfied by a single evaluation criterion, such as a cost variance. Rewards for learning additional skills, reducing spoilage, increasing equipment uptime, and suggesting successful improvements, to name just a few, are part of the evaluation-reward-motivation systems of many world-class enterprises.

Cost management, through control of shop floor activities, is an important component in a firm's success and profitability. In assigning responsibility to the individuals in a position to exercise control over those costs, shop floor employees become cost-conscious as they become aware of results. The cost-consciousness tends to reduce costs and encourage improvement in performance in all activities of the organization.

The SCAS, however, should not be used as an excuse to conduct "witch hunts." The focus should be on supporting the production process by helping workers solve problems and achieve the standards they participated in setting. Spending too much time investigating previous period cost variances and blaming people can often bring about results contrary to those intended.

Ideal and Practical Standards

In describing the SCAS's role as a responsibility accounting system, it is important first to consider how the standards are set. Because standards are goals that are used to judge actual performance, a key question is, "Just how demanding should standards be?" Should they assume theoretical perfection, or should they assume various factors that prevent perfect performance? Standards can be based on ideal or practical operating conditions. For example, a small unfavorable variance implies very good performance if ideal standards are set, while the same variance implies average performance, at best, if practical standards are used. A small unfavorable variance from an ideal standard may not lead to further investigation, whereas the same variance based on practical standards may lead to investigation and corrective action.

Ideal standards are set as goals toward which employees work for continuous improvement, a concept of world-class manufacturing. Variances from these standards will probably always be unfavorable, but continuous improvement will result in the variances becoming smaller over time. Thus, the SCAS, when using ideal standards, will have to output trend analysis reports, often in graphic form. By showing the reduction in cost variances over time (i.e., movement toward the ideal standards), these reports can provide long-range, continuous improvement information.

Practical standards are tight but achievable. They do not tolerate abnormal waste and lost time, although they allow for normal machine downtime, employee rest periods, and the like. Both favorable and unfavorable variances result from the use of these standards. Generally, they have been considered to be most useful in determining how effectively and efficiently *present* operations are being carried out.

These standards can be met or surpassed by actual performance, but only if high efficiency is achieved. They are indeed within the achievable range of most employees, yet difficult enough that employees feel as though they have accomplished something of value when the standards are attained. Employees are motivated by practical standards, especially if they've had input into their development, and will normally put forth their best efforts to achieve them.

If management is trying to compete against world-class enterprises, however, cost variances from practical standards may not provide the kind of performance information the firm needs. Enterprises using standards that typically ignore continuous improvement and have avoidable inefficiencies built in will not be able to compete against world-class enterprises that are continually striving to eliminate waste and inefficiencies of all kinds.

The best standard for today's competitive environment is one that seeks to *improve future performance*. Long-run continuous improvement is measured by the movement toward ideal standards. When *ideal standards* are used to calculate cost variances, the *reduction in cost variances over time* signals this improvement. An enterprise that uses *practical standards* also needs long-range graphical trend analysis of the *change in standards*. The difference between ideal and practical standards is the long-run continuous improvement goal. Thus, this difference should be decreasing over time.

Managing by Exception

The use of standard costs makes possible the concept of management-by-exception. In traditional and world-class, manufacturing and nonmanufacturing, profit and nonprofit enterprises, the most important scarce resource is time.

Computers are used for managing by exception and tracking cost variances.

This is especially true in JITs that need to respond quickly to changing customer needs and production problems that can lead to *jidoka* (defined in Chapter 2). Thus, shop floor personnel must be able to distinguish between variances that can be ignored and those that should be investigated. To make this distinction, managers set upper and lower limits of acceptable variances from standard. So long as cost variances remain within the limits set, no special attention is needed. When an unfavorable cost variance falls outside the limits, the people responsible are expected to determine its cause. Whenever possible, immediate corrective action is taken to eliminate the cause and bring operations back in line with standard.

If the variance is favorable, management can reward superb performance and learn why this favorable variance occurred. A favorable variance, however, is not always indicative of good performance. It may mean that an error was made in setting the standard or that another type of problem exists. For example, purchasing inferior quality materials for a price less than standard can create a favorable cost variance. Using less materials than the standard quantity also results in a favorable variance. However, both of these events may be real problems! Therefore whether a variance is unfavorable or favorable, it should be investigated if it falls outside the limits.

Even if a variance never exceeds the limits, managers may still want a variance report when variances consistently come close to the limits. A variance that is close to the limits period after period may indicate that the standard is inappropriate or that the performance regarding that standard needs an occasional check by management.

Even very large variances may be out of management's control, however. Utility, payroll tax, and insurance rates are typical examples. Such variance-causing items may be included on the variance report for information purposes, but do not necessarily require follow-up by management beyond adjusting the standard prices.

Further, managers may view some variances as more significant than others depending on what they measure. Certain items, such as usage of direct materials in some operations, may be deemed so critical that any deviation from standard should be reported and investigated. Also, in certain operations, any variance should always be investigated whether it falls outside the limits or not. For example, anything dealing with equipment maintenance warrants careful scrutiny. Preventive maintenance keeps equipment fine-tuned to run more efficiently. Equipment that is not properly maintained uses more oil and fuel (or electricity) to run and can entail major costs when it breaks down.

Reporting Variances

The key objective of variance analysis and reporting is to isolate off-standard performance quickly and correct it. The operational control loop is illustrated in Exhibit 8–1. Steps necessary to install this operational control loop include the following:

Step 1. Set the standards, prepare the standard cost card, and develop the budgeted manufacturing cost equation. This step was covered in Chapter 7.

Step 2. Collect operating data and measure actual performance. With the use of computers, automated production equipment, and online data collection and entry devices, measurement may be real-time, whereas in manual-based systems, measurement may be monthly.

Step 3. Process operating data and calculate variances.

Step 4. Report variances to the managers and workers who are responsible for them and have authority to take corrective action. The key for corrective action and operational control is the timely arrival of variance information and immediate action by managers and operating personnel. Variances occur as operations are performed. Therefore, the quicker the

■ EXHIBIT 8–1
Operational Control Loop

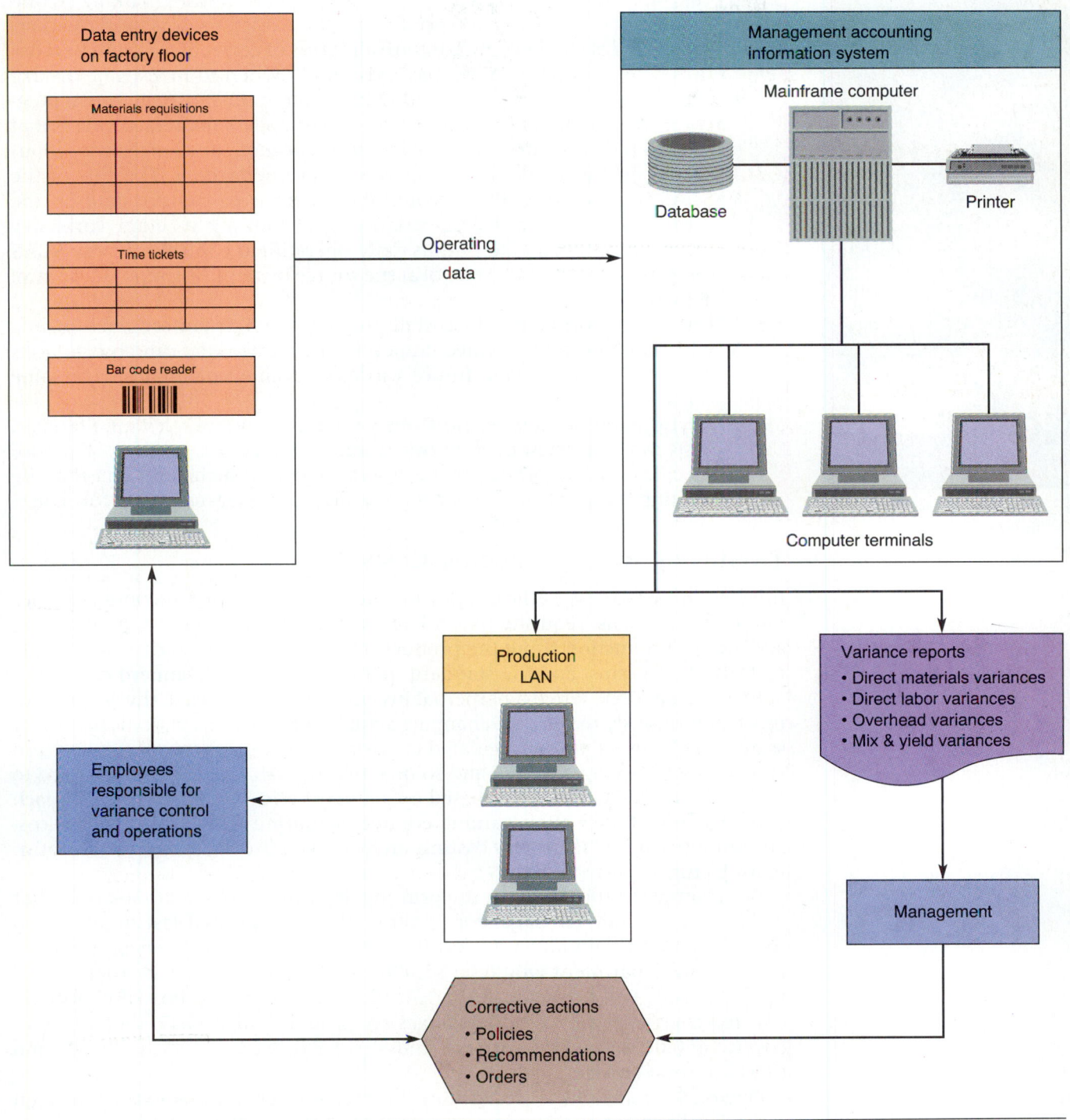

variances are reported, the sooner corrective action can be taken, if warranted. For example, if an operation is using excessive amounts of direct materials and the variance indicating this abnormal usage is not reported until a month after the fact, management may not know about the problem and therefore can take no corrective action during that month. Cost control must be applied at the place and time where the cost variance originates.

Step 5. Determine the significance of each variance. Some variances require investigation, others do not. In turn, investigation may or may not reveal the need for corrective action.

Step 6. Take appropriate corrective actions. Setting new policies, making recommendations, and giving specific orders to supervisors and workers involved directly in operations are all forms of corrective action. Because no set rules or parameters may exist about when to investigate or take corrective action, managers and workers often must use their own judgment. A fundamental characteristic of world-class manufacturing is that control (i.e., investigation, problem identification, and corrective action) occurs on the shop floor as operations are performed. The role of the SCAS as a responsibility accounting system is to capture data on the sources and causes of cost variances and indicate whether corrective actions have been taken. In its daily operational control role, the SCAS reinforces the need for control at the source by requiring input on control activities.

Step 7. Change performance, if possible, to bring actual performance in line with standard performance. Supervisors and workers can change tasks and activities to prevent future variances from occurring from the same causes.

Step 8. Revise standards if those previously set are no longer relevant. Standard costs must be revised when prices, rates, operations, product or service specifications, or other circumstances change to such an extent that the existing standards no longer represent a good measure of performance.

Reducing Record-Keeping Costs

Information-processing efficiency is increased when record-keeping costs are reduced. Materials requisitions and labor time tickets can be prepared in advance of production using the production LAN's bill of materials, MRP and/or MRP II programs, and the standard quantities from the standard cost cards.

In an actual CAS, when a perpetual inventory system is used, the accountant must continuously recalculate changing actual unit costs. In a periodic inventory system, RMI costs may be calculated by assuming some inventory flow pattern (FIFO, LIFO, moving average, and so on). In an SCAS, costs can be assigned to WIP, FGI, and COGS accounts based on standard prices and quantities for each cost element. Rather than valuing completed output by performing the cost allocations required in process costing, an SCAS will use the standard absorptive manufacturing cost (SAMC).

For example, if the SAMC in the printing department of a textbook publisher is $5 per book and the pages for 1,000 books were printed last month, then the journal entry amount transferring printed pages from this department to the binding department would be $5,000 (see Exhibit 6–4 and journal entry 8 in the PCAS). For a JOCAS, if the SAMC for a one-pound box of chocolate-covered cherries is $6.50 and 100 boxes are produced in job 247, then the job's cost is $650.00 for journal entries 8 and 9 (see Exhibit 5–1 and the COGM and COGS journal entries).

Obviously, some of the clerical time and record-keeping costs saved through such simplification is offset by time spent in deriving standards, keeping them current, and calculating and reporting cost variances. The real cost savings occur in the long run, during the implementation of the SCAS when inefficiencies may be identified and corrected and waste uncovered, and later when variances are reported, investigated, and corrected.

Computer networks are used to report variances.

LEARNING OBJECTIVE 2

Explain the meaning of a cost variance, and calculate and interpret the variable costs' spending variances.

SCAS COST VARIANCE FORMULAS

Generically speaking, there are only two types of cost variances: spending (price) variances and efficiency (usage) variances. In this section, the spending vari-

INSIGHTS & APPLICATIONS

Nulife's Variance Analysis

Nulife purchases large volumes of a special compound from a pharmaceutical company that it mixes with water to produce a health drink called Tigerade. The standard costs for direct materials, direct labor, and overhead to produce one case of Tigerade are presented in Exhibit 8–2. This exhibit also includes the manufacturing cost equation and actual production and cost data for July.

EXHIBIT 8–2
The Standard Cost Card for Nulife's Tigerade Sports Drink

Standard Cost Card for One Case of Tigerade

Items	Standard Price	Standard Quantity	Standard Cost
Direct materials	$1.00/lb.	3 lb./case	$3.00/case
Direct labor	$10.00/DLhr	2 DLhr/case	$20.00/case
Variable overhead	$1.50/DLhr	2 DLhr/case	$3.00/case
Fixed overhead (based on a production quota of 10,000 cases per month)	$0.60/DLhr	2 DLhr/case	$1.20/case
Standard absorptive manufacturing cost (SAMC)			$27.20/case

Monthly Tigerade manufacturing costs = $12,000/month + $26.00/case

Actual Production Data and Costs for July

Items	Actual Costs	Actual Quantities
Direct materials	$1.10/lb.	40,000 lb. purchased
		30,000 lb. requisitioned
Direct labor	$9.50/DLhr	17,500 DLhr worked
Variable overhead	$25,000	
Fixed overhead	$12,100	
Actual output		9,000 cases of Tigerade

ances for the variable manufacturing costs (direct materials, direct labor, and variable overhead) will be illustrated first. Next, the usage variances will be calculated for the variable manufacturing costs, followed by the spending and usage variances for fixed overhead. Finally, alternative methods for calculating overhead variances will be considered. The Nulife Sports Drink Company will be used to illustrate these calculations:

Spending Variances for Variable Costs

The basic formula for a variable cost spending variance is:

Variable cost spending variance
$$= \text{Actual quantity purchased} \times (\text{Standard price} - \text{Actual price})$$
$$= AQp \times (SP - AP)$$

DIRECT MATERIALS PRICE VARIANCE. The direct materials standard price is usually based on either the expected price during the period the standard

The cost of direct materials must be controlled. Courtesy of Saturn.

is in effect or on the price existing at the time the standard is set. Normally, this group decision-making activity involves the purchasing department aided by the management accountant.

Many factors influence the price paid for materials, such as quantities purchased, delivery method used, quantity discounts, and rush orders. Serious study should be given to handling and storage procedures to determine whether they are the most efficient possible. Such analysis should indicate the most economical quantities to purchase, the best delivery method at the lowest cost, and the most economical ways of storing and handling in-plant materials.

The **direct materials price variance** measures the difference between what is paid for a given quantity of materials and what should have been paid according to the standard price that has been set. The formula used to compute this variance is:

$$\text{Direct materials price variance} = AQp \times (SP - AP)$$

In July, Nulife incurred the following price variance for Tigerade's direct materials:

Direct materials price variance
$$= 40,000 \text{ pounds purchased} \times (\$1.00/\text{lb.} - \$1.10/\text{lb.})$$
$$= <\$4,000> \text{ unfavorable}$$

Explaining the price variance calculation is relatively simple. Forty thousand pounds were purchased at an average price that is $0.10 per pound higher than the standard price. Ten cents per pound multiplied by the 40,000 pounds purchased results in a cost overrun of $4,000—in other words, an unfavorable spending variance of $4,000.[1] While explaining the calculation to shop floor personnel is relatively easy, identifying the cause of the variance may be more difficult.

Generally, the purchasing agent has control over the prices paid for materials and, therefore, is responsible for purchase price variances. This is the first person who should be consulted in attempting to identify the cause of the variance. In Nulife's case, the unfavorable price variance resulted from the pharmaceutical company unexpectedly raising its price $0.10 per pound. The purchasing agent has negotiated a price of $1.05 per pound for the next six months. The new direct materials standard price will be $1.05 per pound next period. In a high-quality SCAS, the explanation for any price variance is recorded on the purchase order. This information is then available as soon as it is known for input into the SCAS database and for use by the MRP II LAN and the marketing LAN in updating sales prices (if possible).

Caution must be exercised to make sure that the purchasing agent is not buying poor-quality material, at a lower cost, to realize a favorable price variance. The poor-quality material will cause problems later in production. Also, the purchasing agent may increase the purchase order quantity to obtain a lower unit cost. Large inventories, however, require large automated stockrooms and sophisticated inventory tracking systems, which drive up nonvalue-added costs. Maintaining these systems generates even more nonvalue-added activities and costs. Thus, if this purchasing price variance is the only performance evaluation criterion for the purchasing agent, he or she may be motivated into these dysfunctional decisions.

In some instances, however, someone other than the purchasing agent may be responsible for a direct materials price variance. The production manager,

[1] If the cost variance is negative, it is unfavorable. If it is positive, it is favorable since the actual price must be lower than the standard price. Some accountants calculate the variance by subtracting standard price from actual price (reversing the order of the prices within the parentheses). A negative result would then be a favorable variance. Thus, it is important to always label a variance as "favorable" or "unfavorable."

for example, may schedule production in such a way as to require overnight delivery of materials, thus driving up the price paid for them. The following are several additional reasons why actual direct materials prices may differ from standard direct materials prices:

- Change of vendor
- Change of lot size
- Change in price by vendor
- Change in specifications
- Change in the marketplace

Two considerations relevant to the design of a high-quality SCAS become obvious. First, the SCAS needs to capture data on the cause of the variance when it first becomes known. Second, once the cause has been identified, its source has to be input into the SCAS so that responsibility can be properly assigned for performance evaluation. If the source and cause of cost variances are not captured within the SCAS, then it cannot provide accurate and relevant information for operational control and performance evaluation. In that case, the SCAS may not lead to proper evaluation and rewards and, therefore, may not promote the desired motivations and goal-congruent behaviors for daily control activities.

DIRECT LABOR RATE VARIANCE.   The development of a standard direct labor cost requires identifying the direct labor classification needed for the operation and the wage rate paid for that labor skill. Rates for labor are often determined by union negotiations or by the prevailing rate in the area where the company is located. The key objective is to match the operations with the labor classifications called for.

The **direct labor rate variance** measures any deviation from standard in the average hourly rate paid to employees plus the average hourly payroll taxes and fringe benefits paid for them. The formula used to compute this variance for July's production of Tigerade at Nulife is:

Direct labor rate variance
$$
\begin{aligned}
&= \text{Actual DLhr worked} \times (\text{Standard rate} - \text{Actual rate}) \\
&= \text{AQp} \times (\text{SP} - \text{AP}) \\
&= 17{,}500 \text{ DLhr worked} \times (\$10.00/\text{DLhr} - \$9.50/\text{DLhr}) \\
&= \$8{,}750 \text{ favorable}
\end{aligned}
$$

The same basic formula is used for both the direct materials and the direct labor spending variances. The difference between the standard price (rate) and the actual price (rate) is multiplied by the quantity purchased. For direct labor, the hours purchased always equal the hours worked because labor is actually "purchased" (paid for) after it is used. Similarly, with a JIT purchasing system, the quantity of materials used and purchased is equal.

As with the direct materials price variance, this variance's calculation is relatively simple to explain. The average labor rate (including the direct labor wage rate plus employer payroll taxes and fringe benefits) was 50 cents per hour less than budgeted. For the 17,500 DLhr actually worked (i.e., for the actual quantity purchased), this resulted in a cost savings of $8,750.

In many companies, the rate paid workers is set by union contract. Therefore, in such instances, rate variances tend to be small. The way workers are used can lead to rate variances, however. Skilled employees with high hourly rates of pay can be assigned tasks that require little skill and call for low hourly rates of pay. Such misuse of workers will result in unfavorable direct labor rate variances because the actual hourly rate of pay will exceed the standard rate authorized for the particular task being performed. Also, poor scheduling of

The cost of direct labor must be controlled. Courtesy of Saturn.

work may cause unfavorable rate variances. In addition, workers may have to be paid excess rates during peak seasonal periods in order to obtain the necessary work force.

In the Nulife example, just the opposite situation happened during July. The favorable rate variance resulted from hiring part-time help. Total actual labor cost was $166,250. These temporary workers earned a lower hourly wage rate and cost Nulife less in payroll taxes and fringe benefits than the company would have spent if it had used regular workers and paid them overtime. The result was an average savings of 50 cents per hour when the total direct labor costs were averaged over the total hours worked.

VARIABLE OVERHEAD SPENDING VARIANCE. The **variable overhead spending variance** is the amount budgeted for the number of direct labor hours worked minus the actual VOH costs incurred. This variance is usually the responsibility of the person or persons in charge of such VOH cost items as indirect labor, utilities, maintenance, supplies, and so forth. These costs should be in line with the amount of work performed. For the Nulife case, the VOH spending variance is:

Budgeted costs based on actual hours worked (17,500 DLhr × $1.50/DLhr)	$26,250
Less actual variable overhead costs	<25,000>
Variable overhead spending variance	$ 1,250 favorable

While this "formula" may look different from the formula used for direct materials and labor, it is really the same, just in an unfactored form. To illustrate this, the "actual VOH price" is $1.43 per DLhr (rounded). A price per DLhr must be calculated to compare against the standard price (VOH POR), which is also per DLhr. The quantity used in the formula must then be DLhr as well. Using the basic formula:

$$\text{VOH spending variance} = AQp \times (SP - AP)$$
$$= 17{,}500 \text{ DLhr worth of VOH items purchased}$$
$$\times (\$1.50/\text{DLhr} - \$1.43/\text{DLhr})$$
$$= \underline{\$1{,}225 \text{ favorable}}$$

The $25.00 difference between these two versions of the formula is due to a rounding error in using the $1.43 average price per DLhr worked. The actual average VOH price per DLhr is $1.42857. Thus, using the unfactored format originally presented avoids this rounding error. The unfactored format can be used for all three variable cost spending variances.[2] In many SCASs, only the total actual VOH costs may be recorded, not the individual actual prices and rates. In these situations, the unfactored format may be simpler and more accurate. With the implementation of an ICBIS, though, fields within computer database records usually exist for storing the unit prices. Also, calculation of

The cost of variable overhead must be controlled. Courtesy of Bobcat, Inc.

---

[2] Unfactoring the basic formula:

Variable cost spending variance	$= AQp \times (SP - AP)$
	$= (AQp \times SP) - (AQp \times AP)$
	$= (AQp \times SP) - \text{Actual cost}$
For direct materials:	$= (40{,}000 \text{ lb.} \times \$1.00/\text{lb.}) - \$44{,}000$
	$= \underline{<\$4{,}000> \text{ unfavorable}}$
For direct labor:	$= (17{,}500 \text{ DLhr} \times \$10.00/\text{DLhr}) - \$166{,}250$
	$= \underline{\$8{,}750 \text{ favorable}}$

unit prices and rates may make the information more usable for the shop floor, where people think in terms of per pound and per hour prices.

The favorable VOH spending variance for Tigerade could have been caused by cost decreases in variable overhead items or the efficient use of these items, or both. To better understand why this is true, consider how the VOH line in the standard cost card is calculated. While total VOH is budgeted by using a DLhr basis, VOH items are *not* really purchased by the labor hour. Lubricating oil may be purchased in 50-gallon drums; drill bits and saw blades by the box of one dozen; and nails, tacks, brackets, and the like in 25-pound boxes. To apply all the VOH items to individual products, they are averaged over the activity basis that causes their use (i.e., direct labor hours for Tigerade). Since the VOH applied is computed by using a standard price (VOH POR) based on direct labor hours, the average actual VOH costs are also averaged over the actual direct labor hours worked to calculate an average VOH price per DLhr for the variance comparison.

Thus, the average actual VOH price per DLhr worked results from the prices of the VOH items purchased and the amount used for the hours actually worked. If the price for certain VOH items is less than budgeted and/or the amount used is less than budgeted for a DLhr, then this variance will be favorable. The variance itself, however, does not provide insight into which factors caused it.

The management accountant should break down the VOH spending variance into the elements comprising it. Exhibit 8–3 illustrates how the variance is presented as a line-by-line analysis. This more complete analysis is much more useful to managers who are responsible for different elements. Although the total VOH spending variance may be small and favorable, such a report is usually necessary. For example, a small favorable VOH spending variance may be the result of large individual favorable and unfavorable overhead item variances offsetting one another.

The second column in Exhibit 8–3 is titled "Flexible Budget for 17,500 DLhr Actually Worked." A **flexible budget** is a budget amount calculated using the actual hours worked. It is an "after-the-fact" budget prepared by using the cost equation and the hours actually worked. This is necessary because variable costs exist. Variable costs change in total with changes in production volume and the number of hours worked.

For example, in preparing the original budget for Tigerade, the production quota was 10,000 cases. Using the standard quantity for direct labor (2 DLhr per case), 20,000 DLhr were originally budgeted to be worked, and $30,000 of VOH was budgeted in total (VOH POR of $1.50 per DLhr multiplied by 20,000

Detailed Comparison of Flexible
Variable Overhead Budget Costs with
Actual Variable Overhead Costs
For the Month Ended July 31

Variable Overhead Elements	Flexible Budget for 17,500 DLhr Actually Worked	Less: Actual VOH Costs	VOH Spending Variance	
Indirect labor (17,500 DLhr × $0.70)	$12,250	$13,250	<$1,000>	U
Utilities (17,500 DLhr × $0.25)	4,375	2,400	1,975	F
Maintenance (17,500 DLhr × $0.55)	9,625	9,350	275	F
Total (17,500 DLhr × $1.50)	$26,250	$25,000	$1,250	F

EXHIBIT 8–3
Detailed Analysis of the Variable Overhead Spending Variance for Nulife Corporation

Explanation of variances:

- Indirect labor variance of $1,000 U is caused by a raise in pay.
- Utilities variance of $1,975 F is due to an earlier policy to conserve energy.
- Maintenance variance of $275 F is caused by a new expert maintenance system.

DLhr budgeted). The original budgeted $30,000 cannot be compared to the $25,000 actually spent, though, because this amount was spent in working only 17,500 direct labor hours. Of course, if fewer hours are worked, less total VOH should be spent.

For a valid comparison, the budget has to be adjusted to what it should be for the DLhr actually worked. For 17,500 DLhr, only $26,250 in VOH should have been spent (VOH POR of $1.50 per DLhr multiplied by 17,500 actual DLhr worked). This is the "flexible" budget amount that should be compared against the actual VOH costs incurred for the same 17,500 DLhr worked. The spending variance formula automatically adjusts for this by comparing (AQp × SP) to actual cost. This can be seen in the unfactored format of the variance formula.

<table>
<tr><td>

LEARNING OBJECTIVE 3

Calculate and interpret the variable costs' usage variances.

</td></tr>
</table>

Usage Variances for Variable Costs

As with the variable costs spending variances, there is one basic formula for the variable costs' efficiency variances:

Variable cost usage variance
= Standard price × (Standard quantity allowed − Actual quantity used)
= SP × (SQA − AQu)

The **standard quantity allowed (SQA)** is the total amunt of an input item that should have been used for the actual production volume. The formula for SQA is:

$$SQA = \text{Standard quantity} \times \text{Actual output}$$

For example, if one case of Tigerade (in Exhibit 8–2) is made, then:

$$SQA_{\text{Direct materials}} = 3 \text{ lb. per case} \times 1 \text{ case} = \underline{3 \text{ lb.}}$$

$$SQA_{\text{Direct labor}} = 2 \text{ DLhr per case} \times 1 \text{ case} = \underline{2 \text{ DLhr}}$$

$$SQA_{\text{VOH}} = 2 \text{ DLhr per case} \times 1 \text{ case} = \underline{2 \text{ DLhr}}$$

If ten cases of Tigerade are made, then:

$$SQA_{\text{Direct materials}} = 3 \text{ lb. per case} \times 10 \text{ cases} = \underline{30 \text{ lb.}}$$

$$SQA_{\text{Direct labor}} = 2 \text{ DLhr per case} \times 10 \text{ cases} = \underline{20 \text{ DLhr}}$$

$$SQA_{\text{VOH}} = 2 \text{ DLhr per case} \times 10 \text{ cases} = \underline{20 \text{ DLhr}}$$

If 9,000 cases of Tigerade (the actual output) are made, then:

$$SQA_{\text{Direct materials}} = 3 \text{ lb. per case} \times 9,000 = \underline{27,000 \text{ lb.}}$$

$$SQA_{\text{Direct labor}} = 2 \text{ DLhr per case} \times 9,000 = \underline{18,000 \text{ DLhr}}$$

$$SQA_{\text{VOH}} = 2 \text{ DLhr per case} \times 9,000 = \underline{18,000 \text{ DLhr}}$$

The more cases of Tigerade produced, the more direct materials, direct labor, and VOH items will be used. These are variable costs. The SQA calculation is a flexible budget adjustment for quantities.

In July, 9,000 cases of Tigerade were produced. There were no beginning or ending WIP inventories, or output loss. If partial effort exists in beginning or ending WIP, or in output loss, the partial effort needs to be accounted for by computing equivalent units of production (EUP) for each cost element. This is a standard PCAS. To illustrate, assume an ending WIP inventory in July of 200 cases, 100 percent complete with respect to direct materials, 50 percent complete for direct labor, and 25 percent complete for VOH. The EUPs for July are:

$$\text{EUP for direct materials} = 9{,}000 \text{ completed cases} + (100\% \times 200 \text{ cases})$$
$$= \underline{9{,}200 \text{ EUP}}$$

$$\text{EUP for direct labor} = 9{,}000 \text{ completed cases} + (50\% \times 200 \text{ cases})$$
$$= \underline{9{,}100 \text{ EUP}}$$

$$\text{EUP for VOH} = 9{,}000 \text{ completed cases} + (25\% \times 200 \text{ cases})$$
$$= \underline{9{,}050 \text{ EUP}}$$

Then:

$$\text{SQA}_{\text{Direct materials}} = 3 \text{ pounds per case} \times 9{,}200 \text{ EUP} = \underline{27{,}600 \text{ pounds}}$$

$$\text{SQA}_{\text{Direct labor}} = 2 \text{ DLhr per case} \times 9{,}100 \text{ EUP} = \underline{18{,}200 \text{ DLhr}}$$

$$\text{SQA}_{\text{VOH}} = 2 \text{ DLhr per case} \times 9{,}050 \text{ EUP} = \underline{18{,}100 \text{ DLhr}}$$

Throughout the remainder of this chapter, we will continue to ignore the existence of partial effort in beginning WIP, ending WIP, and/or output loss (spoilage). This is to emphasize the concepts and calculations involved in an SCAS. In reality, though, it is important to remember the need for EUP calculations in process system SCASs.

DIRECT MATERIALS USAGE VARIANCE. The **direct materials usage variance** measures the difference between the actual quantity of materials used in production and the quantity that should have been used (SQA). The formula used to compute this variance is:

$$\text{Direct materials usage variance} = \text{SP} \times (\text{SQA} - \text{AQu})$$

For the Tigerade example:

$$\text{Direct materials usage variance} = \$1.00/\text{lb.} \times (27{,}000 \text{ lb.} - 30{,}000 \text{ lb.})$$
$$= \underline{<\$3{,}000> \text{ unfavorable}}$$

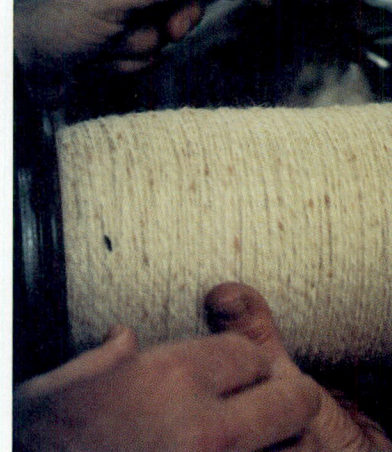

Usage of direct materials must be controlled.

Like the spending variances, this usage variance is fairly easy to explain. For the 9,000 cases of Tigerade that were produced in July, only 27,000 pounds of direct materials should have been used. But, 30,000 pounds were used. If there is no price variance, then the extra 3,000 pounds used cost Nulife an extra $3,000. This cost overrun is an unfavorable usage variance. But also like the spending variances, the variance by itself does not indicate its underlying cause(s). This information needs to be obtained from the people responsible for direct materials usage.

Generally, the production manager is responsible for the direct materials usage variance because he or she is in charge of how direct materials are used. In instances where direct materials are substandard, the responsibility may lie with the purchasing department. Other causes include the following:

- Incorrect machine settings or lack of proper tools
- Failure to keep machines and tools in good working condition
- Inexperienced or inefficient workers
- Fatigue caused by pressure to complete a rush order
- Changes in production or quality control methods

- Inadequate blueprints or errors in specifications
- Variations in yield from materials
- Failure to return excess materials to the storeroom

In the Tigerade example, the variance was due to inexperienced workers and improper supervision at mixing vat 3. A total of 3,000 pounds of compound was spilled on the floor and wasted.

The direct materials standard quantity is affected by the desired size, shape, and quality of the finished product, as well as by the kind and quality of the direct materials used to make the product. An allowance for normal spoilage is included in determining practical standard quantities. The tighter the standard, the smaller the allowance for scrap. When appropriate direct materials standard quantities are in effect, control over material losses, waste, and scrap is facilitated, because any usage variance from what was determined to be a reasonable amount can be traced to its source, as was done in the Tigerade example.

Given the kind and quality of direct materials, physical quantity estimates are made in terms of weight, size, volume, or other measure. The standard quantities and quality of direct materials needed to make the product are compiled in its bill of materials within an MRP or MRP II program. The actual quantities are input via bar code scanning devices, or materials requisitions in nonautomated SCASs.

Usage of direct labor must be controlled. Courtesy of Saturn.

DIRECT LABOR EFFICIENCY VARIANCE. The **direct labor efficiency variance** measures the productivity of direct labor. The basic formula used to compute this variance is the same as that used for the direct materials usage variance:

$$\text{Direct labor efficiency variance} = SP \times (SQA - AQu)$$

During July, the direct labor efficiency variance for Tigerade was:

$$\text{Direct labor efficiency variance} = \$10/\text{DLhr} \times (18{,}000 \text{ DLhr} - 17{,}500 \text{ DLhr})$$
$$= \underline{\underline{\$5{,}000 \text{ favorable}}}$$

Explaining this variance to shop floor personnel, 500 direct labor hours less than expected (the SQA) were worked. At a budgeted labor rate of $10 per DLhr, this resulted in a cost savings of $5,000 (a favorable usage variance). The Tigerade production manager explained that this efficiency was due to the high spirit of the temporary workers. But remember the cause of the direct materials usage variance—by working so fast, they also wasted 3,000 pounds of Tigerade mix.

This observation provides the management accountant with insights into some of the characteristics required in a high-quality SCAS:

- For operational control, it is important that the SCAS captures input data about the sources and causes of cost variances. By having shop floor personnel input these data as operations take place, their attention is focused on the need to identify production problems and control them at the source.
- In assigning responsibility for cost variances, these source and cause data are critical. To ensure proper performance evaluation and the rewards necessary for proper employee motivation, the SCAS needs to report the sources and causes of cost variances and whether corrective actions have been taken.
- As the Tigerade example shows, one decision (activity) may result in more than one cost variance. In other words, cost variances can be related; they are not necessarily financial measures of independent problems. For July production of Tigerade, the hiring of temporary workers resulted in three cost variances: an unfavorable direct materials usage variance of $3,000; a

favorable direct labor rate variance of $8,750; and a favorable direct labor efficiency variance of $5,000.

The direct labor efficiency variance is vital for management's review, because increasing productivity in labor-intensive processes is a key to reducing production costs. Generally, this variance is the responsibility of supervisors and workers. In some instances, however, an unfavorable direct labor efficiency variance may stem from areas not controlled by them, such as the following:

- Faulty equipment or materials
- Machine breakdowns
- Lack of materials
- Changes in production processes

Factors that cause the variance to occur can be identified by careful analysis of the operations, which must include discussion with individuals involved in specific areas of the organization. Two important factors used to determine the direct labor standard quantities are:

- Specific operations to be performed
- Amount of labor time to be spent on each operation

Both factors are measured by engineering, production, and management accounting personnel.

Each operation performed by either employees or equipment should be determined. Examples of labor operations are bending, lifting, turning, reaching, moving materials, setting up for a new production run, cleaning up, and reworking. All of these operations will affect the time needed to produce a product. Thus, such operations should be evaluated to determine which are adding value and which can be eliminated or reduced.

Some organizations conduct time and motion studies. During such studies, unusual times due to abnormal conditions should be eliminated. Some industries have developed predetermined times based on standard time and motion studies. Using these data reduces the cost of developing standards for a specific company in one of those industries. Care must be taken, however, to make sure the operations and labor of the company match the operations and labor on which the data were gathered.

Plant layout, equipment conditions, and the workplace should be analyzed, and an effort should be made to improve these to the best practical level (maybe even close to an ideal level). In conjunction with studying and setting direct materials and direct labor standards, purchasing and expediting materials should be studied so that employees have the right materials (quality and quantity) at the right place at the right time. Moreover, employees should be properly trained *before* being put on the job and should have quick access to complete instructions *after* being put there.

If direct labor standards are based on a work environment that is conducive to maximum efficient and effective operations, variations of actual from standard become valid indicators of what *really* should be occurring. A poor workplace that is unsuitable for both people and efficient operations will most likely lead to variances whose underlying causes cannot be easily traced.

The direct labor efficiency variance, however, can encourage costly actions by employees. For example, employees may rush through a process wasting costly materials to improve labor efficiency as happened at Nulife during July.

The direct labor efficiency variance may have little relevance in a highly automated plant that has few employees. For example, some companies, such as Allen-Bradley, manufacture over $100 million worth of products per year and employ only three to five workers.

VARIABLE OVERHEAD EFFICIENCY VARIANCE. The **variable overhead efficiency variance** is a measure of the excess VOH used solely because the

Use of variable overhead must be controlled. Courtesy of Bobcat, Inc.

actual direct labor hours worked differed from the standard hours allowed. The assumption is that if more direct labor hours are worked, then more VOH items are used (VOH is a variable cost). This variance can be computed using the following formula (the same basic formula used with the direct materials and labor efficiency variances):

$$\text{VOH efficiency variance} = SP \times (SQA - AQu)$$

During July, the VOH efficiency variance for Tigerade production was:

$$\begin{aligned}\text{VOH efficiency variance} &= \$1.50/\text{DLhr} \times (18{,}000 \text{ DLhr} - 17{,}500 \text{ DLhr})\\ &= \underline{\underline{\$750 \text{ favorable}}}\end{aligned}$$

The assumption that more labor usage means more VOH items are used is questionable. For example, the temporary workers at Nulife in July wasted 3,000 pounds of Tigerade mix by working too fast. Did they also use excess VOH items such as supplies? The VOH efficiency variance does not really answer this question, but from looking at the VOH spending variance, it appears that excess usage of indirect items was not a problem. Again, this highlights the major disadvantage of traditional cost variance analysis. Variances alone do not provide information about their real underlying causes.

Whether favorable or unfavorable, the responsibility for this variance lies with the manager in charge of labor for the period (if labor causes VOH usage). Other bases, such as machine hours, can also be used to budget VOH and measure its variances.

Fixed Overhead Cost Variances

With each of the variable cost elements, there are fundamentally only two kinds of cost variances, spending and usage. This is also true for fixed overhead, but the formulas for the FOH cost variances differ from the variable cost variances because this cost element behaves differently. It is a fixed cost, not a variable cost.

FIXED OVERHEAD BUDGET VARIANCE. The **fixed overhead budget variance** is the difference between budgeted fixed overhead costs and actual fixed overhead costs:

$$\text{Fixed overhead budget variance} = \text{Budgeted FOH} - \text{Actual FOH}$$

In the Nulife Tigerade example, the following FOH budget variance resulted in July:

$$\begin{aligned}\text{Fixed overhead budget variance} &= \$12{,}000 - \$12{,}100\\ &= \underline{\underline{<\$100> \text{ unfavorable}}}\end{aligned}$$

During July, $100 more was spent on FOH items than was budgeted ($12,000 from its manufacturing cost equation in Exhibit 8–2). The unfavorable FOH spending (budget) variance is the responsibility of the various people who have control over the different items that comprise the total budgeted FOH costs. Generally, managers have only limited ability to control FOH costs in the short run, however. Fixed overhead costs are incurred to provide production capacity. In other words, FOH exists because of the production process (the factory) and its size. The bigger the factory, the larger its fixed costs (usually), such as building depreciation, insurance, property taxes, and the costs of heating and air conditioning. Because different people are responsible for different components of FOH, the SCAS should report this variance on a line-item basis, similar to the reporting of the VOH spending variance (see Exhibit 8–3). Exhibit 8–4 illustrates a line-by-line FOH budget variance report.

Any control that is to be exerted over FOH must take place when managers are preparing the annual budget, modifying it during the year, and/or planning capacity changes. Fixed overhead items, therefore, are usually not subject to as much day-to-day, or even month-to-month, control as are variable cost items.

FIXED OVERHEAD PRODUCTION VOLUME VARIANCE.   This variance is usually called the **fixed overhead volume variance,** or just the volume variance. It is a usage variance in that it measures how well the factory as a whole was used. Since the costs of the factory are FOH costs, this is an FOH usage variance. It can be calculated by either of two formulas:[3]

Fixed costs are difficult to control in the short term. Courtesy of Honda of America Manufacturing, Inc.

FOH volume variance

$$= \text{FOH standard cost} \times (\text{Actual output} - \text{Production quota})$$

or: $$= \text{FOH standard price} \times (\text{SQA} - \text{Budgeted DLhr})$$

The second formula more closely resembles the formula for variable cost usage variances and may be easier to learn because of its similarity to the other usage variance formulas. First, the basis for applying FOH has to be known. This information is in the standard cost card (Exhibit 8–2 for Tigerade). Fixed overhead is applied to cases of Tigerade based on the DLhr worked. Thus, the standard hours allowed (SQA) and the budgeted DLhr need to be calculated in

[3] These two formulas are actually the same. One version is in terms of outputs (production volume), and the other is in terms of inputs (the basis used to apply FOH to products, i.e., direct labor hours in the Tigerade example).

■ **EXHIBIT 8–4**

Detailed Analysis of the Fixed Overhead Spending (Budget) Variance for Nulife Corporation

Detailed Comparison of
Budgeted Fixed Overhead Costs with
Actual Fixed Overhead Costs
For the Month Ended July 31

3 ✗

Fixed Overhead Elements	Budget for July	Less: Actual FOH Costs	FOH Budget Variance
Supervisor salaries	$ 6,000	$ 6,500	<$500> U
Depreciation	4,000	4,000	–0–
Insurance	1,500	1,000	500 F
Property taxes	500	600	< 100> U
Totals	$12,000	$12,100	<$100> U

Explanation of variances:
■ Supervisor salaries variance of $500 U is due to a raise in pay.
■ Insurance variance of $500 F is caused by an unexpected reduction in premium due to an improvement in the employee safety program.
■ Property taxes variance of $100 U is caused by a new taxing formula passed by the city council this month.

order to use this version of the volume variance formula. The budgeted DLhr for July were 20,000.[4] Using DLhr and the FOH POR in this formula:

$$\text{FOH volume variance} = \$0.60/\text{DLhr} \times (18,000 \text{ DLhr} - 20,000 \text{ DLhr})$$
$$= \underline{\underline{<\$1,200> \text{ unfavorable}}}$$

If the FOH POR (standard price for FOH) is based on machine hours, then the standard machine hours allowed and the budgeted machine hours would be used.

The first version of this variance formula may be easier to explain, however. To illustrate, the FOH volume variance for Tigerade is calculated as:

$$\text{FOH volume variance} = \$1.20/\text{case} \times (9,000 \text{ cases} - 10,000 \text{ cases})$$
$$= \underline{\underline{<\$1,200> \text{ unfavorable}}}$$

The FOH volume variance measures how efficiently the entire plant is used. Using the output-based formula, 10,000 cases of Tigerade were budgeted for July production. The FOH cost budgeted was $12,000 (reference the cost equation in Exhibit 8–2). Thus, only $1.20 of FOH cost had to be absorbed by each case (this is the FOH standard cost). In other words, if the sales price is increased by $1.20 per case, and 10,000 cases are produced and sold, Nulife will receive extra sales revenues of $12,000 that can be used to pay for the FOH. One of the benefits of a standard *absorptive* manufacturing cost is that it serves as an aid to adequate sales price setting.[5]

In July, however, Nulife produced only 9,000 cases of Tigerade, not the 10,000 planned for. Thus, there were 1,000 cases not produced and not sold. Because these cases were not sold, Nulife cannot recover the extra $1.20 from each needed to pay for the FOH costs. The 1,000 cases not produced, multiplied by the $1.20 FOH standard cost, equals $1,200 (10 percent of the $12,000 budgeted FOH). This $1,200 of sales revenues is needed to pay for the last $1,200 of FOH costs. Since the revenues are not there, the remainder of the FOH will have to be paid for out of the profits made on the 9,000 cases produced and sold. Total profits will be $1,200 less than they should have been for the 9,000 cases sold, because the production quota was not met. Because the plant was not used as efficiently as planned, profits went down. This is equivalent to the lower profits that result from inefficient use of labor or materials (their usage variances). The plant is just another manufacturing resource, like materials and labor, and using it inefficiently creates a usage variance just like the other manufacturing inputs.

The usefulness and interpretation of the FOH volume variance depend on the volume used in calculating the FOH standard cost. In the Nulife situation, expected capacity was used. Nulife could have used normal, practical, or theoretical capacity (refer back to Exhibit 7–9). If any of these three options had been chosen, the usefulness and interpretation of the FOH volume variance would have been different.

---

[4]   Budgeted DLhr = *SQ* × *Production quota* = 2 DLhr/case × 10,000 cases budgeted to be produced

This calculation should be compared to the calculation of SQA:

$$\text{SQA} = SQ \times Actual\ output = 2 \text{ DLhr} \times 9,000 \text{ cases actually produced}$$

Note that these formulas calculate the same thing: how many labor hours should be worked. The difference is that the first calculation is done at the beginning of the year (when only production quota is known), and the second is done at the end of the year using the actual volume (i.e., a flexible budget calculation).

[5] Note that if variable costing is used instead of absorption costing, FOH is not applied to the cost of each product. With variable costing, there is no FOH volume variance.

For example, WCM proponents might use theoretical capacity in determining the FOH standard cost. The difference between this maximum productive capacity and the actual output measures how much of the plant is idle. While this may be by design, a continuous improvement philosophy means that the volume variance should get smaller over the years. Here is yet another example of how a high-quality SCAS should report long-run trends in variances.

When expected capacity is used to set the FOH standard cost, an unfavorable volume variance is due to lower than budgeted production. This is often caused by a lack of sales orders. Lack of sales orders may be caused by one or a combination of the following:

- High prices for the product
- Low quality of the product
- Inadequate advertising and lack of aggressive sales campaigns
- Inability to deliver when customers want the product
- Economic recession

Some other causes of unfavorable volume variances *are* controllable by plant management:

- Poor job scheduling
- Excessive employee absenteeism
- Shortage of direct materials and supplies due to poor planning
- Breakdown of machines due to poor preventive maintenance
- Inadequate training or supervision of workers

COMBINING THE OVERHEAD VARIANCES.   In the preceding discussions, two variances (spending and usage) were calculated for each cost element (direct materials, direct labor, VOH, and FOH). Note that for overhead, spending and usage variances were separately calculated for VOH and FOH, resulting in a total of four overhead cost variances. These were separately calculated because the variances are controlled by different people (responsibility centers).

In traditional CAS designs, though, VOH and FOH were not separately accounted for. In Chapters 4, 5, and 6, VOH and FOH were combined into just one total overhead (TOH) account, and only one TOH POR was used to apply overhead to products. Unless VOH and FOH are separated in the SCAS, calculating four overhead variances is difficult.

Consequently, in many traditional SCASs, fewer than four overhead variances were prepared for management. Presenting all four overhead variances is called "four-way analysis of overhead." Sometimes only three overhead variances are calculated ("three-way" analysis), or only two variances ("two-way" analysis), or just one TOH cost variance ("one-way" analysis).

These simpler presentations result in less useful information and degrade the quality of the SCAS. Nevertheless, these methods still often appear on professional accounting certification exams (CPA, CMA, CIA), so they will be briefly illustrated here. There are two "tricks" to remember in performing three-way, two-way, or one-way overhead analysis. First, four overhead variances have already been calculated. In three-way analysis, two variances are added together. In two-way analysis, three of the four overhead variances are added together. In one-way analysis, all four overhead variances are added together.

The second "trick" is to know which variances to calculate first. This involves two steps. The first variance to calculate is the **total overhead variance.** This is the sum of the four variances and represents the one-way method. The total overhead variance is the difference between the TOH applied to production and the TOH actually incurred:[6]

---

[6] Review Chapter 4 (Exhibit 4–15) for a discussion of overhead application with actual, normal, and standard costing. The TOH POR is the sum of the VOH POR and the FOH POR (see the Tigerade standard cost card in Exhibit 8–2).

$$\text{TOH applied} = \text{TOH POR} \times \text{SQA}$$

For Tigerade,

$$\text{TOH applied} = \$2.10/\text{DLhr} \times 18,000 \text{ DLhr}$$
$$= \underline{\$37,800}$$

The actual TOH in July equaled $37,100 (VOH of $25,000 plus FOH of $12,100 as shown in Exhibit 8–2). The difference is $700 favorable. This can be verified by adding together the four overhead cost variances:

$$
\begin{array}{rrl}
\text{VOH spending variance} = & \$1,250 & \text{favorable} \\
\text{VOH efficiency variance} = & 750 & \text{favorable} \\
\text{FOH budget variance} = & <\ 100> & \text{unfavorable} \\
\text{FOH volume variance} = & <1,200> & \text{unfavorable} \\
\hline
\text{TOH variance} = & \$\ \ 700 & \text{favorable} \\
\end{array}
$$

The second variance to calculate is the FOH volume variance. This variance is one of the cost variances in two-way, three-way, and four-way analysis. Knowing the TOH variance and the FOH volume variance, two- and three-way analysis can be quickly performed.

In two-way analysis, the two variances are the FOH volume variance and the "everything else" variance. This is simply the difference between the TOH variance and the FOH volume variance and is often labeled the "TOH budget variance":

$$
\begin{array}{rrl}
\text{TOH variance} = & \$\ \ 700 & \text{favorable} \\
\text{Less FOH volume variance} = & -<1,200> & \text{unfavorable} \\
\hline
\text{TOH budget variance} = & \$1,900 & \text{favorable} \\
\end{array}
$$

This is also the sum of "everything else" (VOH spending and efficiency, and FOH budget variances).

To prepare three-way analysis, calculate the VOH efficiency variance. The three cost variances are the FOH volume variance, the VOH efficiency variance, and "everything else" (the sum of the VOH spending and FOH budget variances, which is often called the TOH spending variance).

▌Summary of Cost Variance Formulas

Cost variance analysis is really not as difficult as it may seem at this moment. There are only two types of cost variances, spending and usage. There are four kinds of manufacturing inputs: direct materials, direct labor, variable overhead, and fixed overhead. Since each has its own spending and usage variance, there are eight cost variances in total. All of the variable costs, though, use the same formula for their spending variances. They also use the same formula for their usage variances. The fixed overhead variances' formulas are a little different. The formulas are summarized in Exhibit 8–5.

The cost variances also can be combined into a general model approach to cost variance analysis. This is accomplished by grouping the direct materials variances together, then the direct labor, VOH, and FOH variances. The general model also includes the total cost variance for each input. Exhibit 8–6 (see p. 350) presents this general model approach for Nulife's Tigerade variances for direct materials and direct labor during July. Exhibit 8–7 (see p. 351) illustrates the variable and fixed overhead cost variances for Tigerade.

COST VARIANCE ANALYSIS		
Types of Cost Variances	Spending	Usage
Inputs: Direct materials Direct labor Variable overhead†	$AQp(SP - AP)$*	$SP(SQA** - AQu)$
Fixed overhead† (Spending = "Budget" usage = "Volume")	Budgeted FOH − AC	$SP_{FOH}(SQA - \text{Budgeted DLhr})$ or $SC_{FOH}(\text{Actual output} - \text{Budgeted output})$

* AP can be calculated if not known: AP x AQ = AC. Thus, AP = AC ÷ AQ.

** SQA = SQ x Actual output.

† This is four-way overhead cost variance analysis (2 VOH cost variances + 2 FOH cost variances).

Note: Whether four-way, three-way, or two-way, the TOH cost variance =

$\text{Applied TOH} - AC_{TOH}$

$(SP_{TOH} \times SQA) - AC_{TOH}$

In four-way: TOH cost variance = VOH spending + FOH budget + VOH usage + FOH volume

In three-way: TOH cost variance =   TOH spending   +   +

In two-way: TOH cost variance =   TOH budget   +

(Hint: In two-way and three-way, always calculate TOH cost variance and FOH volume.)

■EXHIBIT 8–5
Cost Variance Formulas

SCAS JOURNAL ENTRIES

LEARNING OBJECTIVE 5

Prepare the journal entries for an SCAS, and the cost variance report.

SCASs can be used in job order, process, and JIT systems. Jobs, departments, or cells (in a JIT) are debited with the costs of the manufacturing inputs used. The journal entries in an SCAS, versus a normal JOCAS or PCAS, differ in two basic ways, however:

■ In an SCAS, the *cost amounts used are not the same* as in a PCAS or JOCAS. Instead of recording actual costs, all cost elements are recorded at **standard cost allowed (SCA).** SCA is the standard cost for each input multiplied by production volume. To demonstrate, the standard cost for direct materials in Tigerade (Exhibit 8–2) is $3 per case. If 10 cases are produced, the SCA is $30 for direct materials, and this is all that will be charged to its cost for direct materials. For production of 10 cases, the direct labor SCA is $200. The VOH and FOH SCAs for 10 cases are $30 and $12, respectively. Either of two formulas can be used to calculate SCA:[7]

$$\text{SCA} = \text{Standard cost} \times \text{Actual output}$$
$$= \text{Standard price} \times \text{Standard quantity allowed (SQA)}$$

[7] The first formula is in terms of outputs, and the second in terms of inputs. They can be reconciled as follows:

$$\text{Standard cost} = \text{Standard price} \times \text{Standard quantity}$$

and:

$$\textit{SCA} = \textit{Standard cost} \times \textit{Actual output}$$

therefore:

$$\text{SCA} = (SP \times SQ) \times \text{Actual output}$$
$$= SP \times (SQ \times \text{Actual output})$$
$$= SP \times SQA$$

Exhibit 4–15 compares the different cost measurements used in actual, normal, and standard costing.

■ EXHIBIT 8–6
Analysis of Direct Materials and Direct Labor Variances for Nulife Corporation

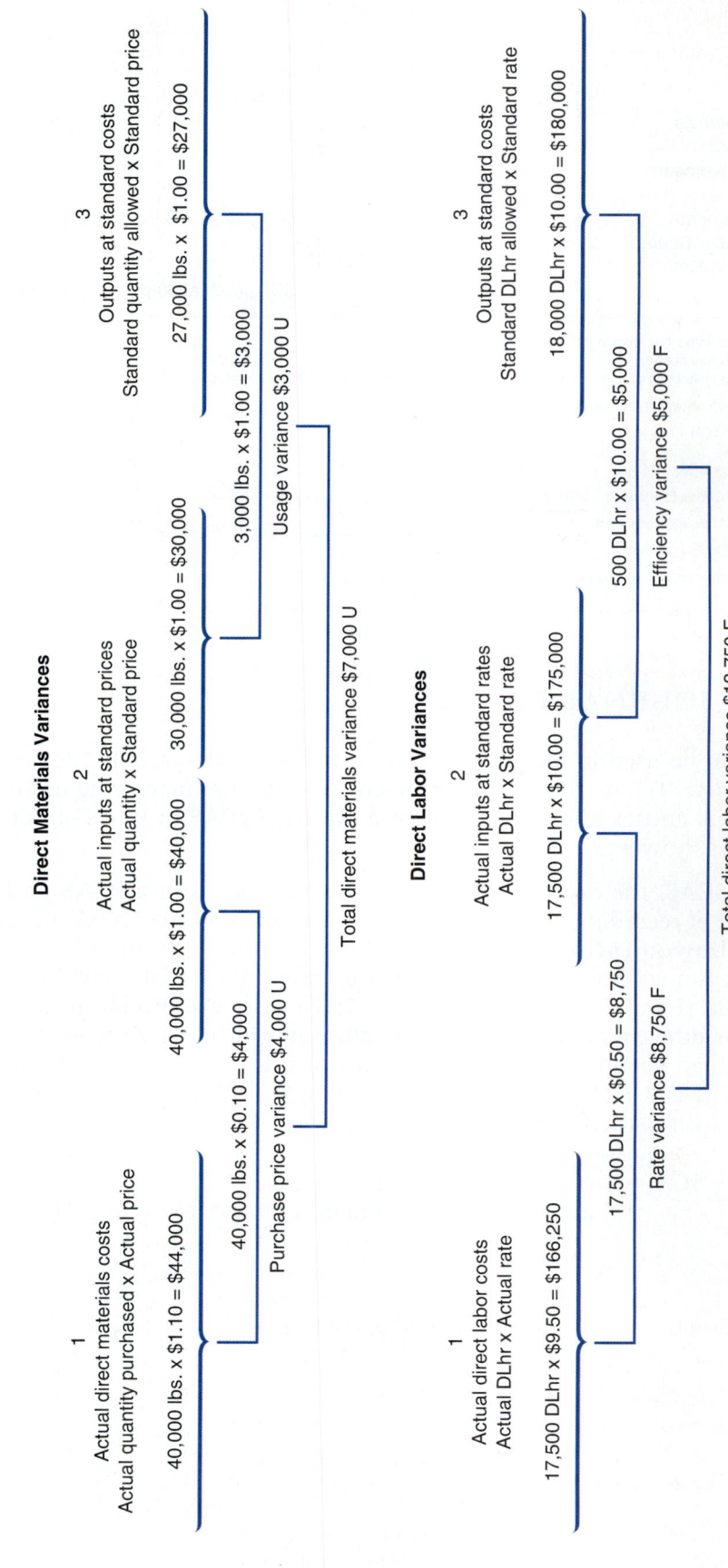

Direct Materials Variances

1	2	3
Actual direct materials costs Actual quantity purchased × Actual price	Actual inputs at standard prices Actual quantity × Standard price	Outputs at standard costs Standard quantity allowed × Standard price
40,000 lbs. × $1.10 = $44,000	40,000 lbs. × $1.00 = $40,000 30,000 lbs. × $1.00 = $30,000	27,000 lbs. × $1.00 = $27,000

40,000 lbs. × $0.10 = $4,000

Purchase price variance $4,000 U

3,000 lbs. × $1.00 = $3,000

Usage variance $3,000 U

Total direct materials variance $7,000 U

Direct Labor Variances

1	2	3
Actual direct labor costs Actual DLhr × Actual rate	Actual inputs at standard rates Actual DLhr × Standard rate	Outputs at standard costs Standard DLhr allowed × Standard rate
17,500 DLhr × $9.50 = $166,250	17,500 DLhr × $10.00 = $175,000	18,000 DLhr × $10.00 = $180,000

17,500 DLhr × $0.50 = $8,750

Rate variance $8,750 F

500 DLhr × $10.00 = $5,000

Efficiency variance $5,000 F

Total direct labor variance $13,750 F

Analysis of Overhead Variances for Nulife Corporation

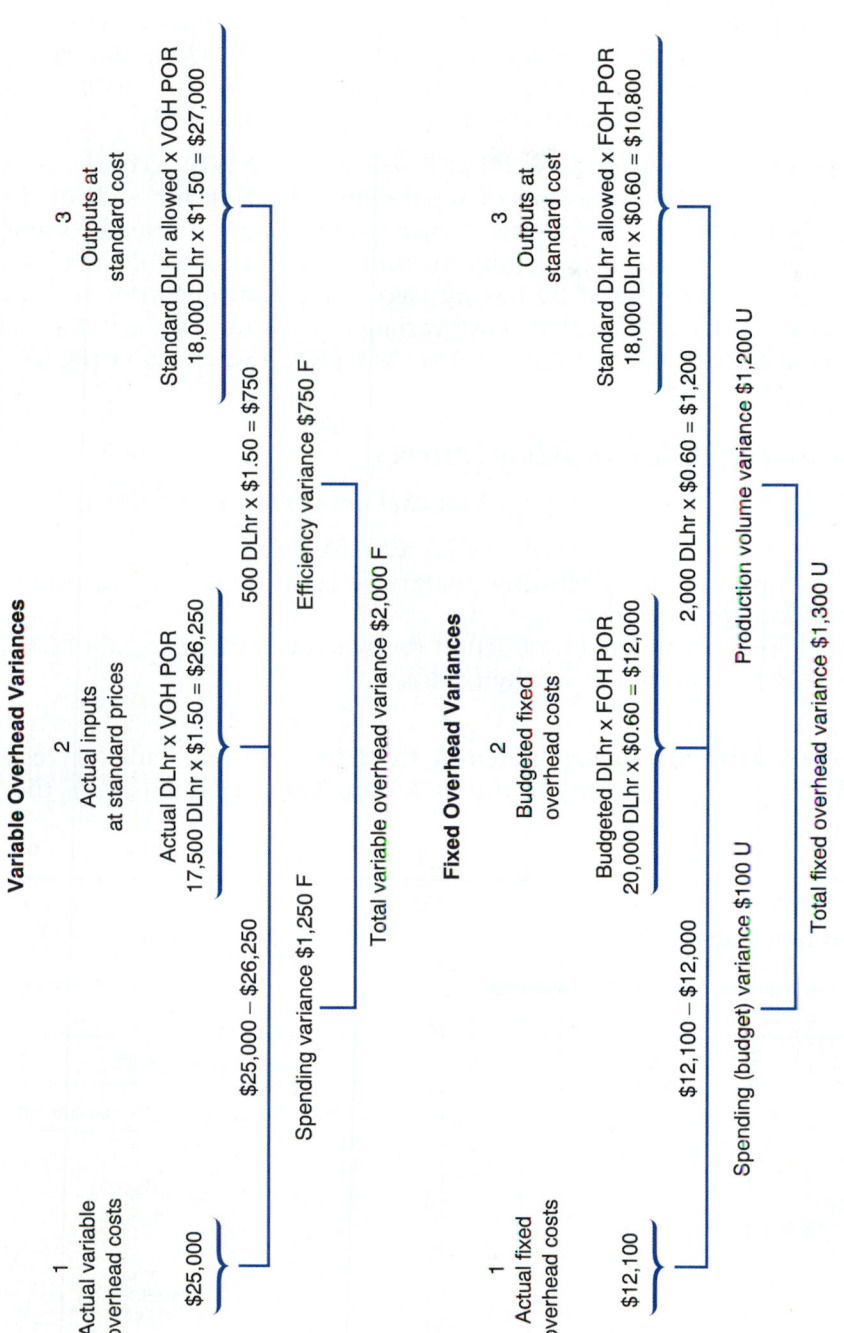

In an SCAS, the total production cost assigned to 10 cases of Tigerade is $272. This is calculated by simply summing the SCA for each input item or by the following formula:

$$\text{Total production cost} = \text{SAMC} \times \text{Actual production volume}$$
$$= \$27.20/\text{case} \times 10 \text{ cases}$$
$$= \underline{\underline{\$272.00}}$$

■ The second difference between normal and SCAS journal entries is related to the first. Since all inputs, and production volume in total, are costed at standard, then the difference between SCA and actual cost also is journalized.

In other words, each cost variance is journalized into its own subsidiary account. Actual and normal cost systems have two "levels" of general ledger subsidiary accounts, product costs and overhead. SCASs have three "levels" of subsidiary accounts. This is highlighted in Exhibit 8–8.

In Exhibit 8–8, separate VOH and FOH subsidiary WIP accounts are created, consistent with the discussion of separately budgeting for each of these cost elements in Chapter 7. Chapter 7 also pointed out the need to assign cost variances to responsibility centers for proper performance evaluation. This is illustrated in Exhibit 8–8 by having two production departments (A and B), each with its own subsidiary cost variance account. This exhibit should be compared to Exhibits 4–2 (basic CAS), 5–1 (JOCAS), and 6–4 (PCAS).

❙ Standard PCAS Journal Entries

In Chapter 4, three basic types of journal entries were identified:

- ■ Purchasing inputs (materials, labor, and overhead)
- ■ Using inputs in manufacturing (materials requisitions, labor distribution, and overhead applications)
- ■ Transferring completed production (between departments in a PCAS, to FGI for COGM, and to COGS when sold)

PURCHASING MANUFACTURING INPUTS. Journal entry 1 records the purchase of raw materials. In the SCAS for Nulife (Exhibit 8–2), the journal

---

◼◼EXHIBIT 8–8
WIP General Ledger System Comparisons

Subsidiary Accounts	Actual and Normal Cost Systems	Standard Cost Systems

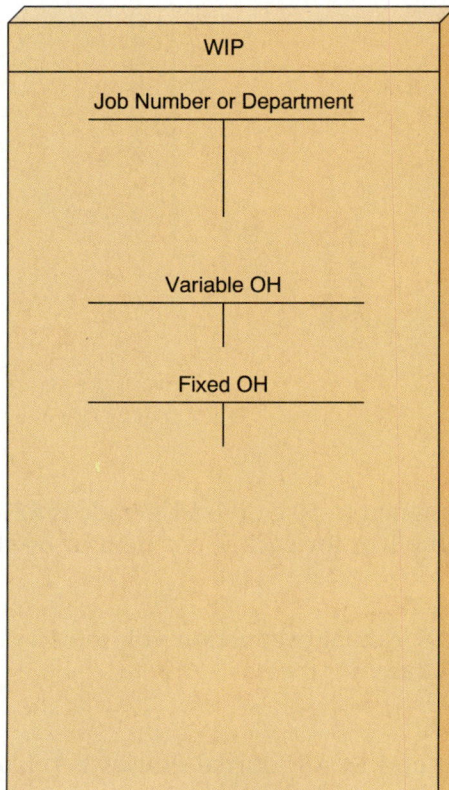
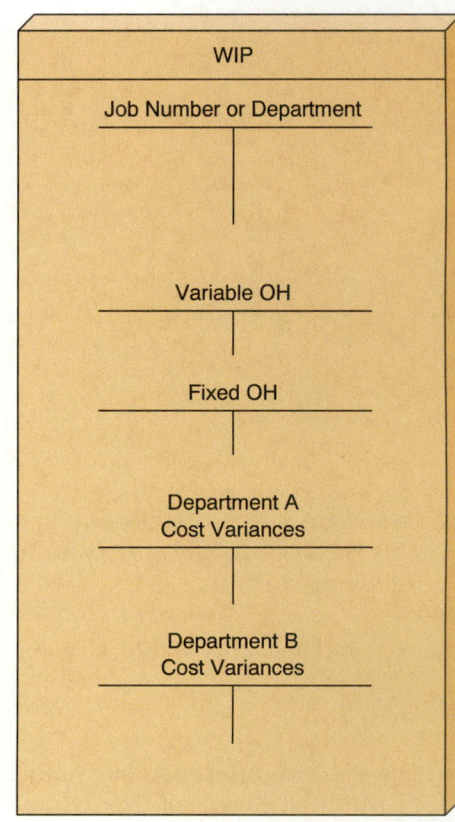

Level 1: Product costs

(Separate accounts for each job or department)

Level 2: Overhead

(Separate VOH and FOH accounts)

Level 3: Cost variances

(Separate accounts for each responsibility center)

entry to record the purchase of Tigerade drink mix (its direct material) is:

Journal Entry 1: Direct Materials Purchases

RMI–Tigerade Mix	$40,000	
(SP × AQp = $1.00/lb. × 40,000 lb.)		
RMI–Tigerade Mix Price Variance	$ 4,000	
[AQp × (SP − AP) = 40,000 lb. ×		
($1.00/lb. − $1.10/lb.)]		
Accounts Payable		$44,000
(AP × AQp = $1.10/lb. × 40,000 lb.)		

Tigerade mix, being a special direct material, has its own subsidiary ledger account within RMI. The price variance is recorded when the materials that create it are received.

An *unfavorable cost variance is debited* to the cost variance account. An unfavorable cost variance is a cost overrun. Paying for this increased cost reduces (credits) cash. If cash is credited, then the cost variance account must be debited. Conversely, a *favorable cost variance is a credit* amount within the journal entries. Favorable variances are cost savings. Saving costs increases (debits) cash. Thus, the cost variance account is credited.

The information explaining the variance should be available from the purchase order for entry into the SCAS. If a record field is established for the explanation, or a general ledger coding system is created to identify its cause, then the cause can be input and reported. The ability to capture and report information on the causes of cost variances is a characteristic of a high-quality SCAS.

Journal entries 2 and 3 recording payroll and the employer's related liabilities are the same in all CASs. In recording actual overhead costs (journal entry 4), separate WIP subsidiary accounts are created for VOH and FOH. Assume that the $25,000 in actual VOH costs (Exhibit 8–2) represents utilities costs for July that are paid for in cash and that the $12,100 of FOH represents July's factory depreciation. Journal entry 4 to record these costs is:

Journal Entry 4: Other Overhead Costs Incurred

WIP–VOH (Utilities)	$25,000	
WIP–FOH (Depreciation)	$12,100	
Cash		$25,000
Accumulated Depreciation		$12,100

USING MANUFACTURING INPUTS IN PRODUCTION.   Journal entries 5–7 record the issuance of materials, labor, and the application of overhead to production departments. When the journal entries for assigning these costs were made in a normal PCAS, each department was charged with the materials and labor costs directly traced to it and with the overhead applied to it. This resulted in multiple subsidiary accounts (one for each department) being debited in journal entries 5–7.

In a process costing SCAS, though, each department's usage is journalized separately. To illustrate, instead of having one journal entry 5 for direct materials used in Departments A *and* B, a separate journal entry is made just for Department A's usage. Another journal entry is made to record direct materials usage in Department B. Preparing individual journal entries for each department's usage of direct materials, direct labor, and applied overhead facilitates the recording and control of each department's cost variances. To demonstrate using the Tigerade example, assume that the costs shown in Exhibit 8–2 are only for Department A:

JOURNAL ENTRY 5: Direct Materials Requisitions

WIP–Department A (DM) (SP × SQA = $1.00/lb. × 27,000 lb.)	$27,000	
WIP–Department A DM Usage Variance [SP × (SQA − AQu) = $1.00/lb. × (27,000 lb. − 30,000 lb.)]	$ 3,000	
RMI − Tigerade Mix (SP × AQu = $1.00/lb. × 30,000 lb.)		$30,000

Because the price variance was already recorded in journal entry 1 when the direct materials were purchased, materials enter RMI at their standard price. Thus, when these materials are requisitioned into the production department, they are taken out of (credited to) RMI at standard price.

Notice that the usage of direct labor and overhead are recorded by a different method. These were journalized (debited) into their "temporary holding accounts" at their actual costs. When these inputs are used in production, they are removed (credited) from their holding accounts at actual cost. The SCA is debited to WIP (as was done above for direct materials), and both the spending and usage variances are recorded in journal entries 6 and 7:

JOURNAL ENTRY 6: Direct Labor Distribution

WIP–Department A (DL) (SP × SQA = $10.00/DLhr × 18,000 DLhr)	$180,000	
WIP–Department A DL Rate Variance [AQ × (SP − AP) = 17,500 DLhr × ($10.00/DLhr − $9.50/DLhr)]		$ 8,750
WIP–Department A DL Efficiency Variance [SP × (SQA − AQ) = $10.00 DLhr × (18,000 DLhr − 17,500 DLhr)]		$ 5,000
Gross Wages (Actual cost = AP × AQ = $9.50/DLhr × 17,500 DLhr)		$166,250

JOURNAL ENTRY 7a: VOH Applied

WIP–Department A (VOH Applied) (SP × SQA = $1.50/DLhr × 18,000 DLhr)	$27,000	
WIP–Department A VOH Spending Variance [(AQ × SP) − AC = (17,500 DLhr × $1.50/DLhr) − $25,000]		$ 1,250
WIP–Department A VOH Efficiency Variance [SP × (SQA − AQ) = $1.50/DLhr × (18,000 DLhr − 17,500 DLhr)]		$ 750
WIP–VOH (Actual cost)		$25,000

JOURNAL ENTRY 7b: FOH Applied

WIP–Department A (FOH Applied) (SP × SQA = $0.60/DLhr × 18,000 DLhr)	$10,800	
WIP–Department A FOH Budget Variance (Budgeted FOH − Actual FOH = $12,000 − $12,100)	$ 100	
WIP–Department A FOH Volume Variance [SP × (SQA − Budgeted DLhr) = $0.60/DLhr × (18,000 DLhr − 20,000 DLhr)]	$ 1,200	
WIP–FOH (Actual cost)		$12,100

In the above journal entries, each Department A cost variance has its own subsidiary account. When this is compared to Exhibit 8–8, it is clear that the Exhibit 8–8 cost variance accounts for Departments A and B are actually control accounts. The reason for having individual subsidiary accounts for each department's cost variances is that some of the variances may not be the responsibility of the department's manager. By having separate variance accounts in the general ledger system, the account balances can be reported to the responsibility center that really caused each variance.

JOURNAL ENTRIES FOR COMPLETED PRODUCTION. The production costs have been debited to the department's subsidiary ledger account at SCA. Thus, when output is transferred to the next department or to FGI, and then to COGS, SCA is the amount to use in journal entries 8–10:[8]

JOURNAL ENTRY 8: Transferring Output to Department B

WIP–Department B (SAMC × Actual output = $27.20/case × 9,000 cases)	$244,800	
WIP–Department A		$244,800

To demonstrate the transfer of finished goods from the factory to finished goods inventory, assume that Tigerade is moved from Department A to FGI:

JOURNAL ENTRY 9: Cost of Goods Manufactured

FGI–Tigerade	$244,800	
WIP–Department A		$244,800

Finally, the journal entry to record COGS is:

JOURNAL ENTRY 10: Cost of Goods Sold

COGS–Tigerade	$244,800	
FGI–Tigerade		$244,800

▌Standard JOCAS Journal Entries

Traditionally, SCASs have been used more in PCASs than in JOCASs. However, the need for effective and efficient cost management is just as crucial in job order systems as it is in process systems. This was first demonstrated in Chapter 5 in the illustration of construction cost budgeting and control (Exhibits 5–21 and 5–22).

In job order enterprises (e.g., construction, print shops), in for-profit services

---

[8] The sum of the standard costs allowed for all the cost elements is equal to the standard absorptive manufacturing cost multiplied by actual production volume.

(CPAs, engineers, and lawyers), and in certain merchandising firms (such as distribution centers), the need for cost control is fast becoming a serious management concern. This is also true in nonprofit services, such as hospitals and government services. With increasing public and national concern over health care cost management, the role of the modern management accountant is becoming more important. Standard costing and cost variance analysis can have a significant impact on cost management in the economy's service sector.

Whether cost variances are journalized within the SCAS or just calculated and reported within a normal JOCAS, information about them is essential for proper cost management. One advantage of journalizing cost variances is that the subsidiary accounts provide the basis for reporting this information. The cost variances are isolated within separate accounts, and a formal record exists within the SCAS for both short-run cost variance reports and long-run trend analyses.

In designing the general ledger system for WIP, level 1 subsidiary accounts are established by department in a PCAS and by job in a JOCAS. This only creates a difference in journal entries 5–7 representing the use of manufacturing cost elements in production. Continuing the Tigerade example, assume the 9,000 cases produced in July was just one job order (482) and that there are still two production departments. As with the PCAS journal entries above, the costs incurred in Exhibit 8–2 are for Department A. In a standard JOCAS, these journal entries become:

JOURNAL ENTRY 5: Direct Materials Requisitions

WIP–Job 482 (Department A DM) (SP × SQA = \$1.00/lb. × 27,000 lb.)	\$27,000	
WIP–Dept. A DM Usage Variance (Job 482) [SP × (SQA − AQu) = \$1.00/lb. × (27,000 lb. − 30,000 lb.)]	\$ 3,000	
RMI–Tigerade Mix (SP × AQu = \$1.00/lb. × 30,000 lb.)		\$30,000

JOURNAL ENTRY 6: Direct Labor Distribution

WIP–Job 482 (Department A DL) (SP × SQA = \$10.00/DLhr × 18,000 DLhr)	\$180,000	

WIP–Dept. A DL Rate Variance (Job 482)
    [AQ × (SP − AP) = 17,500 DLhr ×
        (\$10.00/DLhr − \$9.50/DLhr)]
		\$ 8,750

WIP–Dept. A DL Efficiency Variance (Job 482)
    [SP × (SQA − AQ) = \$10.00/DLhr ×
        (18,000 DLhr − 17,500 DLhr)]
		\$ 5,000

Gross Wages
    (Actual cost = AP × AQ = \$9.50/DLhr ×
        17,500 DLhr)
		\$166,250

JOURNAL ENTRY 7a: VOH Applied

WIP–Job 482 (VOH Applied) (SP × SQA = \$1.50/DLhr × 18,000 DLhr)	\$27,000	

WIP–Dept. A VOH Spending Variance
      (Job 482)
    [(AQ × SP) − AC =
      (17,500 DLhr × \$1.50/DLhr) − \$25,000]
		\$ 1,250

Continued

—Continued

WIP–Dept. A VOH Efficiency Variance (Job 482) [SP × (SQA − AQ) = $1.50/DLhr × (18,000 DLhr − 17,500 DLhr)]	$ 750	
WIP–VOH (Actual cost)		$25,000

JOURNAL ENTRY 7b: FOH Applied

WIP–Job 482 (FOH Applied) (SP × SQA = $0.60/DLhr × 18,000 DLhr)	$10,800	
WIP–Dept. A FOH Budget Variance (Job 482) (Budgeted FOH − Actual FOH = $12,000 − $12,100)	$ 100	
WIP–Dept. A FOH Volume Variance (Job 482) [SP × (SQA − Budgeted DLhr) = $0.60/DLhr × (18,000 DLhr − 20,000 DLhr)]	$ 1,200	
WIP–FOH (Actual cost)		$12,100

The amounts calculated are the same as in a standard PCAS. There are only two differences in the general ledger account titles:

- The WIP subsidiary accounts for product costs are organized by jobs instead of by departments.
- The department cost variance accounts have posting references for cost variances caused within specific jobs.

Why are posting references needed for the cost variance subsidiary accounts? Consider the dilemma faced by the Department A manager. His department worked on seven different jobs during the month, and his direct labor usage variances stemmed from a number of different sources and causes. To understand which jobs created which labor usage variances, the manager needs to know cost variance information by job. A high-quality SCAS has to capture this information. This is the role of the posting references for jobs. Through a screen display or a hard-copy report, the Department A Direct Labor Efficiency Variance account can provide this information. An example of a departmental report for direct materials usage variances by job is presented in Exhibit 8–9.

Some cost variances, however, may not be directly traceable to specific jobs. If a job does not have any unique (direct) fixed overhead costs budgeted for it, the FOH budget variance may only apply to the month's activities of the department as a whole. Thus, the FOH budget variance would be calculated monthly for the department, as in a standard PCAS. Similarly, the FOH volume variance may or may not be attributable to individual jobs. It may also have to be calculated for the department as a whole on a monthly basis. JOCAS and PCAS SCAS journal entries are compared in Exhibit 8–10 (see p. 359).

Disposition of Variance Account Balances

The balances in the subsidiary ledger cost variance accounts can be disposed of in one of three ways:

- Transferred with the products to FGI and/or COGS
- Closed to the cost of goods sold account at year-end
- Closed to COGS, FGI, and WIP accounts at year-end

As jobs or processes are completed, the variances created by this work theoretically can be transferred with the completed output to FGI and then to COGS.

■■■ EXHIBIT 8–9
A Weekly Summary of Direct Materials Usage Variances

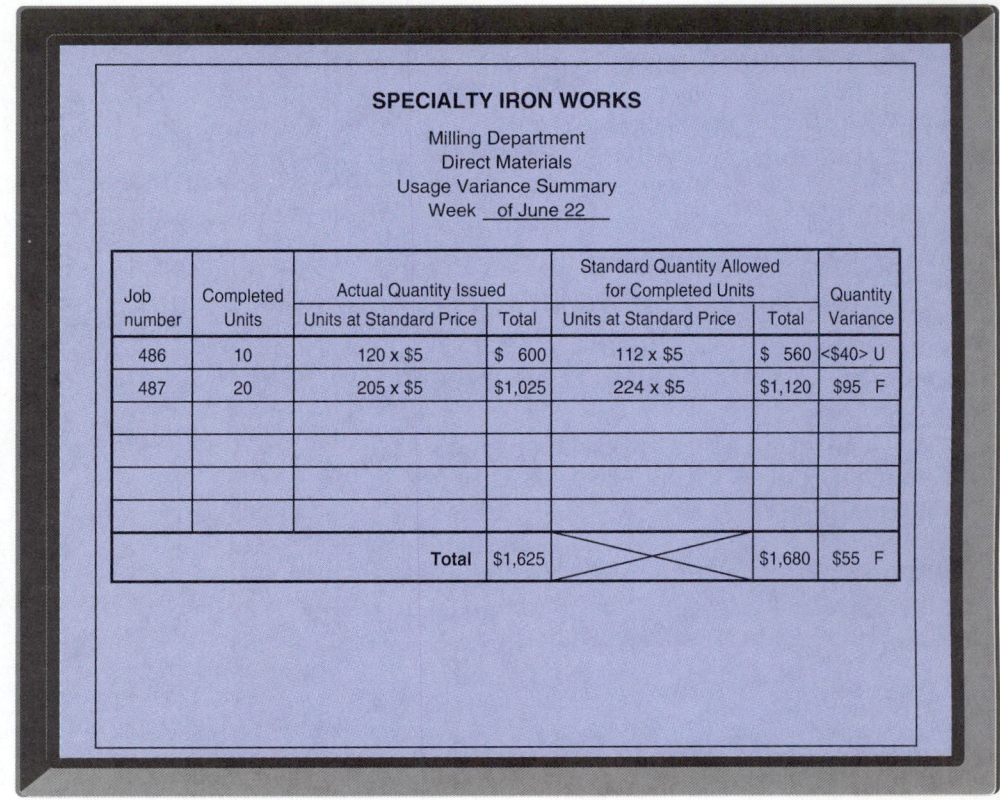

SPECIALTY IRON WORKS

Milling Department
Direct Materials
Usage Variance Summary
Week ___of June 22___

Job number	Completed Units	Actual Quantity Issued		Standard Quantity Allowed for Completed Units		Quantity Variance
		Units at Standard Price	Total	Units at Standard Price	Total	
486	10	120 x $5	$ 600	112 x $5	$ 560	<$40> U
487	20	205 x $5	$1,025	224 x $5	$1,120	$95 F
	Total		$1,625		$1,680	$55 F

This has the effect of establishing an actual cost system. If the balances are insignificant, they can be closed to COGS as jobs are sold or at the end of each reporting period for interim financial statement preparation.

On the other hand, the balances can be left in these subsidiary accounts until year-end. Then, these account balances can be disposed of in the same manner as an ending over- or underapplied overhead balance is disposed of in a normal CAS.[9] If they are significant, they should be prorated between the year-end balances in WIP, FGI, and COGS. If they are insignificant, they can be written off directly to COGS.

When overhead is applied to products (jobs or departments), the total actual overhead costs are credited to the VOH and FOH subsidiary accounts.[10] The difference between the overhead applied and the actual overhead costs is journalized to four overhead cost variance accounts. In a normal CAS, this difference is not journalized to special cost variance accounts. Instead, it remains in the overhead account. In other words, over- and underapplied overhead is the sum of the four overhead cost variances. Therefore, it is consistent to treat the disposition of cost variance account balances in the same manner as the ending overhead account balance in a normal CAS.

▌REPORTING COST VARIANCES

A high-quality SCAS possesses the following characteristics:

■ *Information is timely.* For operational control, cost variance information needs to be available in a real-time mode.

[9] The disposition of the ending overhead account balance was discussed in Chapter 4.
[10] Journal entries 7a and 7b should be reviewed to verify this.

■■■■EXHIBIT 8–10
Job Order and Process SCAS Journal Entries Compared

JE#	JOURNAL ENTRY	JOCAS	FORMULAS	PCAS
1	DIRECT MATERIALS PURCHASES	dr: RMI-Tigerade Mix cr: A/P RMI-Tigerade Mix Price CV	$SP \times AQp$ $AC = AP \times AQp$ $AQp(SP - AP)$	SAME SAME SAME
2	WAGES (Paychecks)	Same as actual and normal CASs		SAME
3	PAYROLL TAXES & FRINGE BENEFITS	Same as actual and normal CASs		SAME
4	OTHER OVERHEAD COSTS	dr: WIP-VOH (Utilities) dr: WIP-FOH (Depreciation) cr: Cash cr: Accumulated Depreciation	Actual Cost Actual Cost Actual Cost Actual Cost	SAME
5	DM REQUISITIONS	dr: WIP-Job 482 (Dept A DM) cr: RMI-Tigerade Mix WIP-Dept A DM Usage CV (Job 482)	$SP \times SQA$ $SP \times AQu$ $SP(SQA - AQu)$	WIP-Dept A (DM) SAME WIP-Dept A DM Usage CV
6	LABOR DISTRIBUTION	dr: WIP-Job 482 (Dept A DL) cr: Gross Wages WIP-Dept A DL Rate CV (Job 482) WIP-Dept A DL Usage CV (Job 482)	$SP \times SQA$ $AC = AP \times AQ$ $AQ(SP - AP)$ $SP(SQA - AQ)$	WIP-Dept A (DL) SAME WIP-Dept A DL Rate CV WIP-Dept A DL Usage CV
7a	VOH APPLIED	dr: WIP-Job 482 (VOH applied) cr: WIP-VOH WIP-Dept A VOH Spending CV (Job 482) WIP-Dept A VOH Efficiency CV (Job 482)	$SP \times SQA$ $AC = AP \times AQ$ $AQ(SP - AP)$ $SP(SQA - AQ)$	WIP-Dept A (VOH applied) SAME WIP-Dept A VOH Spending CV WIP-Dept A VOH Efficiency CV
7b	FOH APPLIED**	dr: WIP-Job 482 (FOH applied) cr: WIP-FOH WIP-Dept A FOH Budget CV (Job 482) WIP-Dept A FOH Volume CV (Job 482)	$SP \times SQA$ Actual Cost Budgeted Cost-AC $SC(AO - BO)$	WIP-Dept A (FOH applied) SAME WIP-Dept A FOH Budget CV WIP-Dept A FOH Volume CV
8	COMPLETED PRODUCTION	dr: FGI-Job 482 cr: WIP-Job 482	$SCA = SAMC \times AO$ $SCA = SAMC \times AO$	FGI-Product WIP-Dept A
9	PRODUCTS SOLD	dr: COGS-Job 482 cr: FGI-Job 482	$SCA = SAMC \times AO$ $SCA = SAMC \times AO$	COGS-Product FGI-Product

** Note: AO = Actual output, BO = Budgeted output (production quota)

■ *Relevant information is reported.* For operational control, the SCAS needs to capture information on the real sources and causes of cost variances and on whether the problems causing them have been corrected. For performance evaluation, cost variances need to be assigned to the responsibility centers where they were created.

■ *The reports and screen displays need to present information in a usable format.* The SCAS should present information in a manner consistent with the way its users think about it. The SCAS should also help users assess the significance of the cost variances.

▌Multiuser Report Format

In world-class enterprises with computerized SCASs, multiple reporting formats can be designed to satisfy these needs. In simpler environments, however, a management accountant may have to make do with access to spreadsheet programs. This is the situation Rod Sterling, the management accountant found himself in at Nulife. Realizing that the cost variance information had multiple users, he prepared the spreadsheet program shown in Exhibits 8–11 and 8–12. Exhibit 8–11 contains the top half of the program. This information includes a data section for both the standard costs and actual costs and quantities used in making Tigerade during July. It also includes the standard cost card and manufacturing cost equation. Exhibit 8–12 contains the report that Rod Sterling believes is most useful to shop floor personnel, upper management, and financial accounting for journal entry preparation.[11]

Rod includes the data sections and standard cost card information in the copies sent to both the shop floor personnel and upper management. This is to alert them to the normal input loss budgeted in the practical standards. A 10 percent normal spoilage rate is allowed for direct materials. Although only 2.7 pounds of Tigerade mix are actually needed to make a case, 3.0 pounds are allowed for input (the standard quantity). The normal spoilage costs Nulife $0.30 per case. There is also a 10 percent loss of labor time. Only 1.8 DLhr of productive time are needed to make a case of Tigerade, but the standard quantity is 2.0 DLhr because of breaks, setup time, and cleanup time. Nulife shop floor personnel have worked hard to reduce setup time to a minimum. Even though the 10 percent labor time lost costs Nulife $2 per case, management does not believe any additional efficiencies could be realized. To reduce standard labor

[11] Nulife uses a standard PCAS.

EXHIBIT 8–11
Data and Standard Cost Card for Tigerade

DATA SECTION: STANDARD COSTS

Manufacturing Inputs	Price	Output Quantity	Loss%
Direct Materials	$1.00 per lb.	2.70 lb.	10.00%
Direct Labor	$10.00 per DLhr	1.80 DLhr	10.00%
Variable Overhead	$1.50 per DLhr		
Fixed Overhead	$0.60 per DLhr		
Normal Production Volume (in units)		10,000	

SOLUTION SECTION: STANDARD COST CARD & MANUFACTURING COST EQUATION

NULIFE SPORTS DRINK, INC.
TIGERADE
STANDARD COST CARD

Manufacturing Inputs	Standard Prices	Standard Quantities	Standard Costs
Direct Materials	$1.00/lb.	3.00 lbs./case	$3.00/case
Direct Labor	$10.00/DLhr	2.00 DLhr/case	$20.00/case
Variable Overhead	$1.50/DLhr	2.00 DLhr/case	$3.00/case
Fixed Overhead	$0.60/DLhr	2.00 DLhr/case	$1.20/case
STANDARD ABSORPTIVE MANUFACTURING COST (SAMC)			$27.20/case

Monthly Tigerade Production Costs = $12,000 per month + $26.00/case

DATA SECTION: ACTUAL COSTS FOR JULY

Direct Materials	Actual DM Price	$1.10	DM Purchased	40,000
Direct Labor	Actual DL Rate	$9.50	DM Used	30,000
Variable Overhead	Actual VOH Cost	$25,000	Actual Hours	17,500
Fixed Overhead	Actual FOH Cost	$12,100	Actual Output	9,000

■EXHIBIT 8–12
Tigerade Cost Variance Report for July

NULIFE SPORTS DRINK, INC.: TIGERADE
COST VARIANCES REPORT
For July 1995

MANUFACTURING INPUTS:		PER UNIT	TOTAL UNITS	TOTAL COSTS	VARIANCE PERCENTAGE	JOURNAL ENTRIES
DIRECT MATERIALS:	STANDARD PRICE	$1.00		$40,000		dr RMI
	−ACTUAL PRICE	<$1.10>		<$44,000>		cr A/P
	PRICE VARIANCE	<$0.10>	40,000	<$4,000>	−10.00%	dr CV
	STANDARD QUANTITY	3.00	27,000	$27,000		dr WIP
	−ACTUAL QUANTITY	<3.33>	<30,000>	<$30,000>		cr RMI
	USAGE VARIANCE	<0.33>	<3,000>	<$3,000>	−11.11%	dr CV
DIRECT LABOR:	STANDARD RATE	$10.00		$175,000		
	−ACTUAL RATE	<$9.50>		<$166,250>		cr GW
	RATE VARIANCE	$0.50	17,500	$8,750	5.00%	cr CV
	STANDARD QUANTITY	2.00	18,000	$180,000		dr WIP
	−ACTUAL QUANTITY	<1.94>	<17,500>	<$175,000>		
	USAGE VARIANCE	0.06	500	$5,000	2.78%	cr CV
VARIABLE OVERHEAD:	STANDARD RATE	$1.50		$26,250		
	−ACTUAL RATE	<$1.43>		<$25,000>		cr VOH
	RATE VARIANCE	$0.07	17,500	$1,250	4.76%	cr CV
	STANDARD QUANTITY	2.00	18,000	$27,000		dr WIP
	−ACTUAL QUANTITY	<1.94>	<17,500>	<$26,250>		
	USAGE VARIANCE	0.06	500	$750	2.78%	cr CV
FIXED OVERHEAD:	BUDGETED COSTS			$12,000		
	−ACTUAL COSTS	<$1.34>		<$12,100>		cr FOH
	BUDGET VARIANCE	<$0.01>	9,000	<$100>	−0.83%	dr CV
	APPLIED	$1.20	9,000	$10,800		dr WIP
	−BUDGETED	$1.20	<10,000>	<$12,000>		
	VOLUME VARIANCE	<$0.13>	<1,000>	<$1,200>	−10.00%	dr CV
COST VARIANCE TOTALS:	APPLIED	$27.20	9,000	$244,800		
	−ACTUAL	<$26.37>	9,000	<$237,350>		
	COST VARIANCE	$0.83	9,000	$7,450	3.04%	

NOTES: POSITIVE COST VARIANCES are FAVORABLE (negative = unfavorable).
   Per unit usage, fixed overhead, and cost variance totals are per unit of output.
   Per unit price variances equal total price variance divided by pounds purchased or DLhr worked.
   All per unit and percentage amount spreadsheet cells are formatted for two decimal places.

cost, the productive time required will have to be reduced (e.g., through learning or production process redesign).

The report shown in Exhibit 8–12 is sent to multiple users. Upper management wants to know the effects of the cost variances on profits. Therefore, Rod Sterling includes a total costs column. In total, profits from July Tigerade production and sales are $7,450 above budget (a net favorable total cost variance). Although the shop floor is excited about this, upper management is not. This favorable variance is only $0.83 per case and only 3.04 percent of SCA. Upper management is more interested in the number of significant individual cost variances and whether these problems are now under control.

The shop floor personnel are more interested in the per unit column information, because this is how they usually think about production activities. For example, the purchasing agent is worried about the $0.10 per pound direct materials price variance as it is 10 percent over the standard price.[12] Similarly, the shop floor is concerned about the direct materials usage variance and the FOH volume variance. The direct labor usage variance was 0.33 lbs. per case (11.11 percent over the 3 lb. per case SQ). The FOH volume variance averaged $0.13 per case ($1,200 ÷ 9,000 cases actually produced; $1,200 ÷ $12,000 = 10 percent over budget). Both, however, were caused by the temporary employees and are not expected to recur again in August. The shop floor personnel are worried that the favorable direct labor variances may not occur again. These were also caused by the temporary help. Their concern is justified because without the favorable direct labor variances, the total cost variance for July would have been unfavorable.

In reviewing the total costs column, the shop floor was excited over the large favorable direct labor variances, as many people might be over an extra $8,750 and $5,000 in profits. Upper management was not overly impressed, however, and reminded the shop floor personnel that looking at the absolute dollar value of a cost variance can be misleading. From Nulife's point of view, as a multimillion dollar operation, neither the $8,750 nor the $5,000 was significant, representing variances over standard of only 5 percent and 2.78 percent, respectively.[13]

Rod Sterling, though, was proud. He recognized that:

- Shop floor personnel often think on a per unit basis, and he provided this information to them.
- Upper management wanted information on the total costs and effect of the variances on total profits. The report also contained this information.
- Both users need information on the significance of the cost variances, and the percentage of standard cost column provides that information to help them keep a proper perspective.

Finally, Rod thought that the last column noting which general ledger accounts should be debited and credited provided useful information to general ledger accounting personnel. All they have to do is "pull" the total costs from the report for each account. Each of the amounts in the total costs column should be verified by referring back to the journal entries presented in the previous section on standard PCAS journal entries. This last column was only included on the copy printed for financial accounting.

The controller wanted an explanation of how Rod Sterling calculated the total actual costs shown in the cost variance totals section at the bottom of the report. The total actual costs of $237,350 includes five amounts:

- Actual direct labor costs of $166,250
- Actual VOH costs of $25,000
- Actual FOH costs of $12,100
- Actual direct materials used multiplied by its standard price (30,000 lb. × $1.00/lb. = $30,000)
- Plus or minus the direct materials price variance. A favorable variance is subtracted as it represents a cost savings. An unfavorable variance is added. Thus, the $4,000 unfavorable variance is added to the total actual costs.

Celebrating his perceived success that Friday night at the local pub, Rod ran

---

[12] This is why she worked hard to negotiate a new contract with Nulife's supplier of Tigerade mix beginning in August.

[13] The percentages can be calculated by dividing the total cost variance into the appropriate standard costs. For example, the 5 percent DL rate variance is $8,750 ÷ $175,000. The DL usage variance of 2.78 percent is $5,000 ÷ $180,000. The corresponding per unit amounts can also be used, but rounding errors sometimes result.

into an old college friend, Linda Onestepahead. Linda earned a masters degree in management accounting and was now CFO of Eaton Corporation.[14] After a few moments of discussing their relative successes, Rod was no longer so proud of himself. He realized that he still had a great deal to do if Nulife's SCAS was to be transformed into a high-quality responsibility accounting system. Not wanting to wait until Monday morning, he excused himself, went home, and began working on an entity relationship diagram (see Chapter 3) and technology platform for a new ICBIS.

Accounting for Loss

One suggestion Linda made to Rod could be immediately incorporated into the cost variance report. At Eaton, she reports nine cost variances for each department. The additional cost variance is for total output loss (normal and abnormal spoilage) consistent with the presentations of world-class accounting for spoilage in Chapters 5 and 6.

Rod realized that no additional changes are needed to account for input loss. Normal input loss is accounted for within the standard quantities for direct materials (scrap) and direct labor (downtime). Abnormal input loss equals the direct materials, direct labor, and variable overhead usage variances.

PRODUCTION MIX AND YIELD VARIANCES

In the Nulife case, only one type of direct material and one class of direct labor were involved in the production of Tigerade. Many enterprises, however, use a combination of several direct materials and various classifications of direct labor to manufacture products. When a company uses more than one direct material in its product, one goal is to combine the materials in such a way as to produce the desired product quality in the most economical manner. Some direct materials can be substituted for others without affecting product quality.

Direct labor, in some instances, can also be combined in many different ways to produce the same product. Some combinations will be more expensive than others, and some will be less expensive. In situations like this, the direct materials usage variances are related, as are the direct labor efficiency variances. One type of material may have a favorable variance, while another has an unfavorable variance because of substituting one for the other. To better understand the net total usage variance from substitutions, the usage variances for direct materials, as well as for direct labor, need to be combined and reorganized into two summary variances:

- Mix variance
- Yield variance

The Mylantic Chemical Company case on the following page illustrates the direct materials and direct labor mix and yield variances. These variances will be calculated for Mylantic's "cash cow" product, which is Alphachem.

Direct Materials Mix and Yield Variances

The **direct materials mix variance** results when direct materials are mixed in a ratio different from the standard direct materials formula. The **direct materials yield variance** is the result of obtaining an output different from the one expected based on the total quantities of direct materials placed in process. Together, these variances make up the direct materials usage variance.

---

[14] Review Problem 3.26.

INSIGHTS & APPLICATIONS

Mylantic Chemical Company

Mylantic's Alphachem product consists of three types of direct materials. The standard direct materials costs for a 100-pound bag of Alphachem are as follows:

TYPE OF MATERIAL	STANDARD RATIO	STANDARD POUNDS	STANDARD PRICE PER POUND	TOTAL STANDARD MATERIALS COSTS
X	40%	50	$5	$250
Y	40%	50	8	400
Z	20%	25	4	100
	100%	125		$750

Weighted-average standard direct materials price per pound of input ($750 ÷ 125) $6.00

The standard direct labor costs for a 100-pound bag of Alphachem are:

CLASS OF DIRECT LABOR	STANDARD RATIO	STANDARD HOURS	STANDARD RATE PER HOUR	TOTAL STANDARD LABOR COSTS
A	20%	1 hour	$10	$10
B	80%	4 hours	6	24
	100%	5 hours		$34

Weighted-average standard direct labor rate per hour ($34 ÷ 5 hours) $6.80

During the past week, 120,000 pounds of materials (composed of 46,000 pounds of X, 44,000 pounds of Y, and 30,000 pounds of Z) were placed in process. Nine hundred bags of Alphachem were produced. A total of 3,800 direct labor hours were worked (composed of 950 of A and 2,850 of B).

Exhibit 8–13 presents the calculations of the direct materials mix and yield variances.

The direct materials mix variance is similar to a spending variance in that it measures how much money is saved (or extra money spent) by changing the mix of direct materials. Less than the expected amount of Y and too much X and Z were actually mixed together in the process. Because X and Z are cheaper per pound than Y, the resulting average standard price from changing the mix creates a favorable variance of $18,000.

The direct materials yield variance is the combined usage variance that results from changing the mix ratios, in other words, from inputting the actual quantities of each direct material. Inputting 120,000 pounds in total should have yielded more output than 900 bags of Alphachem. Only 112,500 pounds should have been input for this actual production volume.

The total direct materials mix variance of $18,000 favorable plus the total direct materials yield variance of $45,000 unfavorable equals the total direct materials usage variance of $27,000 unfavorable for all three materials. The trade-off of materials (changing the mix) cost Mylantic $27,000.

Direct Materials Usage Variances:

Material	SP	×	(SQA			−	AQu)	=	Usage Cost Variance
X	$5/lb.	×	[(50 lb. × 900 bags =	45,000 lb.)	−	46,000 lb.]		=	< $5,000> U
Y	$8/lb.	×	[(50 lb. × 900 bags =	45,000 lb.)	−	44,000 lb.]		=	8,000 F
Z	$4/lb.	×	[(25 lb. × 900 bags =	22,500 lb.)	−	30,000 lb.]		=	< 30,000> U
Totals				112,500 lb.		120,000 lb.			<$27,000> U

Direct Materials Mix Variance:

Direct materials mix variance = AQ × (SP − WAP)

Where:

$$SP = \text{Weighted-average standard price}$$
$$WAP = \text{Weighted-average standard price for the pounds input}$$

$$= \frac{(\$5 \times 46{,}000 \text{ lb.}) + (\$8 \times 44{,}000 \text{ lb.}) + (\$4 \times 30{,}000 \text{ lb.})}{46{,}000 \text{ lb.} + 44{,}000 \text{ lb.} + 30{,}000 \text{ lb.}}$$

$$= \frac{\$702{,}000}{120{,}000 \text{ lb.}}$$

$$= \$5.85 \text{ per average pound}$$

$$\text{Direct materials mix variance} = AQ \times (SP - WAP)$$
$$= 120{,}000 \text{ lb.} \times (\$6.00/\text{lb.} - \$5.85/\text{lb.})$$
$$= \$18{,}000 \text{ favorable}$$

Direct Materials Yield Variance:

$$\textbf{Direct materials yield variance} = \textbf{SP} \times \textbf{(SQA} - \textbf{AQu)}$$
$$= \$6.00/\text{lb.} \times (112{,}500 \text{ lb.} - 120{,}000 \text{ lb.})$$
$$= <\$45{,}000> \text{ unfavorable}$$

Direct Labor Mix and Yield Variances

The **direct labor mix variance** shows the change in the average standard labor rate from changing the combination of higher- and lower-paid workers. The **direct labor yield variance** presents the results of using more or fewer total direct labor hours than the standard allowed. The sum of these variances equals the direct labor efficiency variance. Exhibit 8–14 presents the calculations of Mylantic's direct labor mix and yield variances.

As far as the unfavorable direct labor mix variance of $760 is concerned, Mylantic spent an extra $760 by using the actual mix of direct labor rather than the standard. A greater proportion of more expensive labor (Class A) than specified in the standard mix was used. The standard mix is 20 percent of Class A and 80 percent of Class B (1 hour of A and 4 hours of B). The actual mix of direct labor used was 25 percent of Class A and 75 percent of Class B. This drove up the average standard labor rate to $7.00, producing this unfavorable labor spending variance.

In spite of substituting a greater proportion of Class A labor than required at standard, a favorable direct labor yield variance of $4,760 occurred. The total actual direct labor hours of 3,800 were less than the total 4,500 standard direct labor hours allowed for the actual output produced. By working more type A labor hours, fewer type B labor hours were needed, creating this favorable net usage variance. The total direct labor mix variance of $760 unfavorable plus the total direct labor yield variance of $4,760 favorable results in a total direct labor efficiency variance of $4,000 favorable.

EXH
Direct
and Y
for Myl.
Alphachem

366

EXHIBIT 8–14
Direct Labor Mix and
Yield Variances for
Mylantic's Alphachem

Direct Labor Usage Variances:

Labor Type	SP	× (SQA		−	AQu) =	Usage Cost Variance
A	$10/DLhr ×	[(1 DLhr/bag × 900 bags =	900 DLhr) −		950 DLhr] =	<$500> U
B	$6/DLhr ×	[(4 DLhr/bag × 900 bags =	3,600 DLhr) −		2,850 DLhr] =	4,500 F
Totals			4,500 DLhr		3,800 DLhr	$4,000 F

Direct Labor Mix Variance:

$$\text{Direct labor mix variance} = AQ \times (SP - WAP)$$

Where:

$$SP = \text{Weighted-average standard price}$$
$$WAP = \text{Weighted-average standard price for the hours worked}$$
$$= \frac{(\$10 \times 950 \text{ DLhr}) + (\$6 \times 2,850 \text{ DLhr})}{950 \text{ DLhr} + 2,850 \text{ DLhr}}$$
$$= \frac{\$26,600}{3,800 \text{ DLhr}}$$
$$= \underline{\$7.00 \text{ per average DLhr}}$$

$$\text{Direct labor mix variance} = AQ \times (SP - WAP)$$
$$= 3,800 \text{ DLhr} \times (\$6.80/\text{DLhr} - \$7.00/\text{DLhr})$$
$$= \underline{<\$760> \text{ unfavorable}}$$

Direct Labor Yield Variance:

$$\text{Direct labor yield variance} = SP \times (SQA - AQu)$$
$$= \$6.80/\text{DLhr} \times (4,500 \text{ DLhr} - 3,800 \text{ DLhr})$$
$$= \underline{\$4,760 \text{ favorable}}$$

LEARNING OBJECTIVE 6

Design a high-quality SCAS with management reports useful for operational control and performance evaluation.

STANDARD COST ACCOUNTING SYSTEMS IN JIT PROCESSES

With the advent of world-class manufacturing and JIT conversions, many modern management accountants are rethinking the design of SCASs. Should the SCAS be designed as a process, job order, or hybrid cost system? In part, this depends on:

- The products' cycle times (lead times)
- The information needs of the shop floor personnel and how they want cost variance information displayed
- The sophistication of the information system

For example, since products are made one-at-a-time in a JIT, the management accountant may want to track input costs to each one, as if it were a job. This makes sense only if the product has a relatively long production lead time. If product production lead times are relatively short, however, treating production cells as departments (or processes) and tracking input costs to them within a PCAS design may be more appropriate. Even though products are pulled through the cells one-at-a-time, tracking costs to each product, as in a JOCAS, may not be feasible.

In considering shop floor information needs, production workers may only want variance information expressed in quantities, such as the "Per Unit" column information in Exhibit 8–12's report. When a JIT philosophy of continuous improvement is employed, all variances are considered significant, warranting special attention. Thus, there is no need to convert a direct materials or direct labor usage variance from pounds per unit, or hours per unit, into dollars or percentages of standard. In such situations, journalizing cost variances may not be a value-added activity. A simpler SCAS can be used, such as a backflush CAS discussed below.

Before deciding what type of SCAS to use, the sophistication of the total information system must be considered. If the enterprise has a highly automated production process with a sophisticated ICBIS, bar coding and reading on the shop floor, and a visual factory, then variance information is available within a real-time mode.[15] The SCAS may not add any new information that is useful in daily operational control activities.

In contrast, if there is no other production control system, then the SCAS may have to calculate, journalize, and report cost variance information. A simple SCAS, such as a backflush system, may not provide the information needed for operational control. At the other end of the SCAS design continuum is a sophisticated SCAS that can report cost variances by production activities within each JIT cell. This SCAS will also be illustrated below.

The modern management accountant cannot design an SCAS in isolation from the other information subsystems within the enterprise. Whatever SCAS is chosen must be congruent with the information needs of the firm, the other information gathering and reporting systems (e.g., MRP or MRP II, EDI, visual factory), the technology platform available, and the reward systems used. Simpler SCASs are not always better SCASs. The challenge facing the modern management accountant is to look beyond the SCAS to the whole information system. "Does the entire information system satisfy the needs of the enterprise?" is the question that the management accountant must ask and answer.

Backflush Cost Accounting System

All the cost systems previously developed, from the basic CAS in Chapter 4 through the standard PCAS and JOCAS in this chapter, track input costs throughout the production process. A **backflush cost accounting system (BCAS)** does not. There is no WIP account within this system's general ledger. WIP is replaced with a **raw-in-process (RIP)** general ledger account. RIP, however, includes only the raw materials purchased. Direct labor and overhead costs are journalized into a "Conversion Costs" account. Costs are not taken out of these accounts until the product is completed (the COGM journal entry 8 in a JOCAS, or 9 in a PCAS). In this way, costs are "flushed out of the general ledger" when production is completed.[16] Exhibit 8–15 illustrates the basic differences between a traditional PCAS and a JIT using a BCAS. A BCAS differs from the more traditional systems in four ways:

- Raw materials are debited to RIP instead of RMI.
- Direct labor and overhead are debited to Conversion Costs (DL + OH) instead of Gross Wages and WIP–Overhead.
- No input usage journal entries are made as production takes place. The use of materials, labor, and overhead is recorded "after-the-fact" in the COGM journal entry.
- Cost variances are not journalized in the BCAS.

July's COGM journal entry for Tigerade production at Nulife using a BCAS becomes:

[15] These characteristics of WCMs and enabling technologies were covered in Chapters 2 and 3.
[16] George Foster and Charles Horngren, "Cost Accounting and Cost Management in a JIT Environment," *Emerging Practices in Cost Management,* ed. by Barry Brinker (Boston: Warren Gorham Lamont, 1990), p. 207. With permission.

JOURNAL ENTRY 9: Cost of Goods Manufactured

FGI–Tigerade (SAMC × Actual output = $27.20/case × 9,000 cases)	$244,800	
RIP (RMI standard cost × Actual output = $3.00/case × 9,000 cases)		$ 27,000
Conversion Costs (Standard conversion costs × Actual ouptut = $24.20/case × 9,000 cases)		$217,800

Exhibit 8–16 contrasts the cost data flows for a traditional PCAS and a BCAS where no FGI is maintained in a JIT. Here, the "trigger point" for recording input usage is the COGS journal entry. COGS, instead of FGI, is debited at SCA.

FOCUSING ON OUTPUT. A BCAS focuses first on the output of an organization and then works backward when assigning costs to FGI or units sold. The term "backflush" comes from the technique of delaying journal entries until products are completed (or as late as sales in some BCASs), when costs finally are flushed through the accounting system. This approach is opposite to traditional cost accounting systems, which accumulate costs through WIP, beginning with the issuance of raw materials into production.

Traditional cost accounting systems are set up in terms of inputs, such as the amount of direct labor input into WIP. The backflush system is based on output, which means that credit is not given unless the product is completed with good quality. Under the backflush method, product cost accumulation is not tracked as products move through successive work cells.

Because the major checkpoint is on output and yield of input, the management accountant prepares a daily activity report of a day's production. A com-

---

◼ EXHIBIT 8–15
Traditional PCAS and JIT BCAS Compared

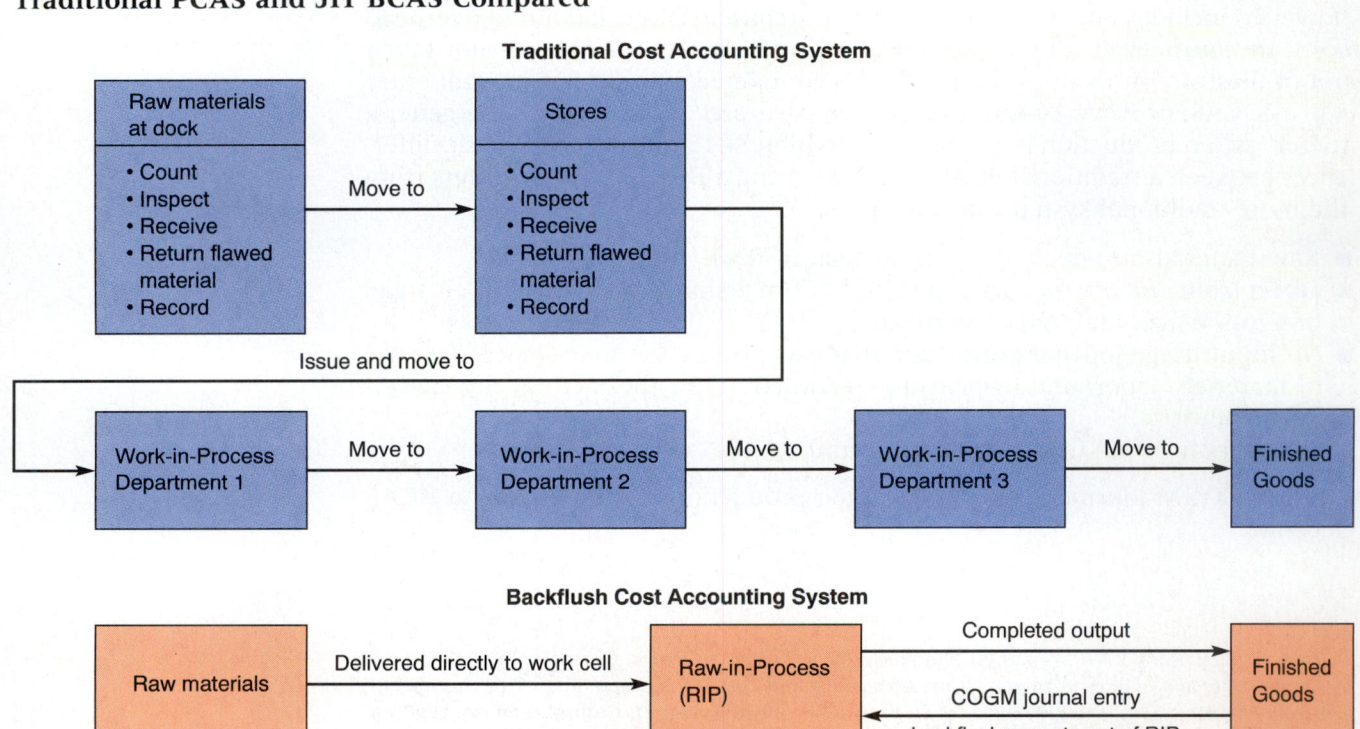

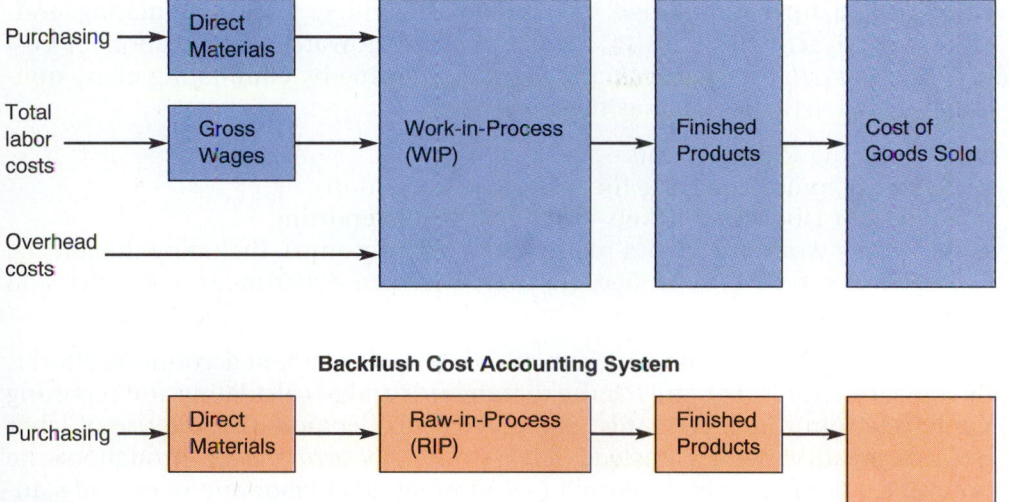

**Data Flows in
Traditional and
Backflush Cost
Accounting Systems**

mon base such as pounds may be used for physical factory floor day-to-day
measurement and comparison. This measurement basis should be in terms that
production people readily understand and relate to. An illustration of a material
yield report for product A is presented in Exhibit 8–17.

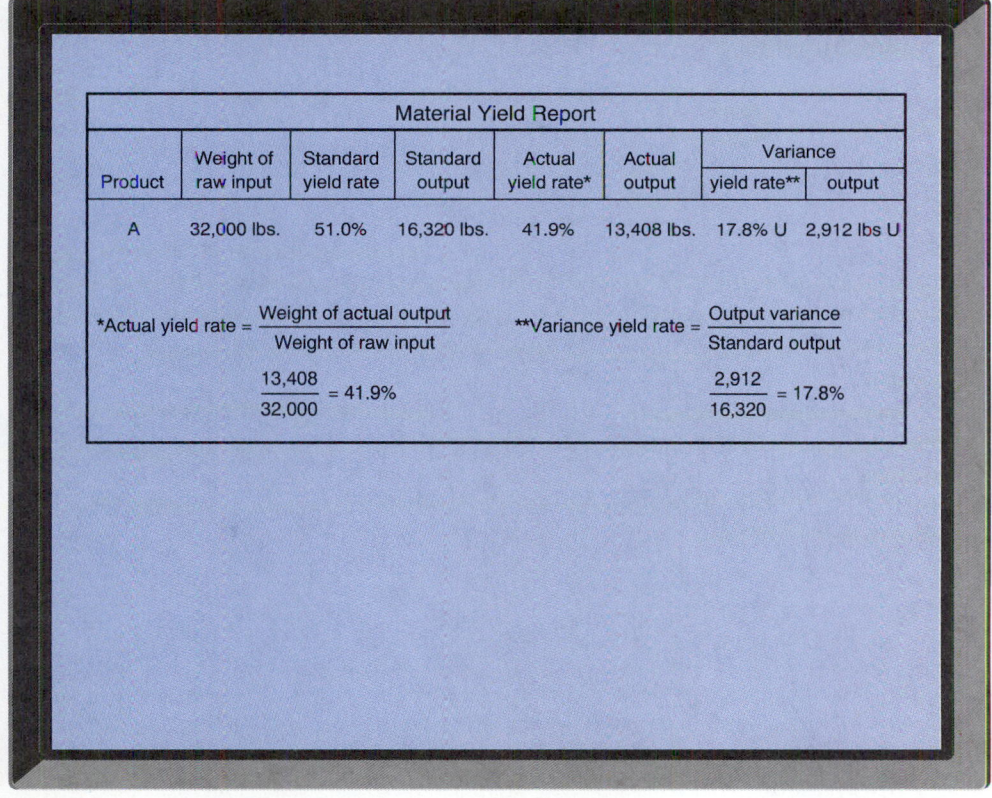

**Materials Yield
Analysis Report**

BCAS ADVANTAGES AND DISADVANTAGES. The JIT philosophy is to simplify and further improve value-added activities, while eliminating non-value-added activities. It also implies a move toward simplification of cost accounting systems. BCASs simplify cost accounting by eliminating many non-value-added activities such as the following:

- Maintaining RMI accounts
- Preparing and accounting for materials requisitions
- Filling out labor time tickets and direct labor reporting
- Recording work orders and maintaining WIP accounts, including the journal entries to record input usage, transfers between departments (or cells), and cost variances

In many traditional companies, much of the management accounting effort is devoted to setting labor and overhead standards and to calculating and reporting variances from these standards. Some JIT firms deemphasize the use of labor and overhead variances. Instead, they stress *total performance* throughout the enterprise. For example, Motorola has eliminated all labor and overhead standards. The benefits reported include reduced dysfunctional decison making within production departments.[17]

One of the SCAS design criteria faced by the modern management accountant is the trade-off between more sophisticated cost tracking and reporting versus the extra cost involved in obtaining, processing, and reporting this information. For example, when direct labor is a relatively small component of the total manufacturing cost of a product, the extra costs and effort involved in direct labor reporting may not be justified in terms of better cost management decisions. At Harley-Davidson, direct labor represents less than 5 percent of the SAMC. Consequently, reporting labor costs and variances was not seen as a value-added activity.[18]

For products with short production lead times, JIT manufacturing results in a very high-velocity level of output. The short lead times make it hard to track each piece moving through the process without an ICBIS and automated operations.[19] Consequently, under backflush costing, product cost accumulation is not tracked as products move through successive work cells.

While BCASs can reduce paperwork and CAS cost, these systems also can have disadvantages:

- They may only work well in production processes with extremely low levels of inventories. When significant RMI and WIP exist, GAAP for financial reporting requires that these inventories be valued and their ending balances reported as current assets.
- By not tracking the use of manufacturing input costs and the movement of WIP through the manufacturing process, certain audit trails are lost. Other information systems need to be in place to provide information for reconciling the RIP and Conversion Costs accounts. Cost elements are debited to these accounts using their actual costs, but removed from these accounts (credited) at SCA.
- The reconciliation process can be further complicated if RIP and Conversion Costs do not contain separate subsidiary ledger accounts for the different products.
- Information about production problems and the cost variances they may create is still needed. Although a visual factory may provide some of this

[17] Ibid., p. 204.

[18] William Turk, ''Management Accounting Revitalized: The Harley-Davidson Experience,'' *Journal of Cost Management*, Winter 1990, pp. 28–39.

[19] C. J. McNair, William Mosconi, and Thomas Norris, *Meeting the Technology Challenge: Cost Accounting in a JIT Environment* (Montvale, N.J.: Institute of Management Accountants, formerly the National Association of Accountants, 1988), p. 47.

information, other information systems may be needed to identify the priority areas for continuous improvement.[20]

■ Since only the good output is debited to FGI and credited to RIP and Conversion Costs, spoilage and the cost variances it creates require separate accounting.

In summary, a BCAS may provide a simpler, less costly CAS. The benefits in terms of the cost savings from these systems must be considered in light of the information needs of the enterprise. In mature JITs with operations under control, production problems and their cost variances may be so infrequent and insignificant that formal SCAS reporting becomes a nonvalue-added activity. In one JIT conversion and SCAS redesign, these considerations led the organization to reject a BCAS in favor of a more sophisticated SCAS that formally tracks and journalizes cost variances within JIT cells by their underlying sources and causes. Such a system can be considered to be at the other end of the SCAS design continuum.[21] This type of system is illustrated in the following section.

Production Activity-Based SCAS for JIT Manufacturing Cells

In this final example, production activities and their costs within a JIT cell form the basis for organizing the standard cost card, as well as for reporting activity-based cost variances. This is illustrated in the Newmount case on the next page.

LESSON 1: THE MANAGEMENT ACCOUNTANT MUST BE PART OF THE TEAM.   The situation at Newmount described above is not unusual.[22] One interesting sidelight, though, was that many production workers sought the job of the problem investigator. It was reserved for someone who had knowledge of all the machine operations and had demonstrated the ability to get along with all the different workers in the various production departments. When Newmount's upper management decided to solve these problems, the head of liaison engineering recommended redesigning the cylinder assembly process into a linked set of three JIT cells. It was also decided to redesign the cost accounting system to provide better information for control and evaluation of production activities. Thus, a control team was created that included the head of liaison engineering, each production department foreman, the vice president of production, a systems design analyst, the cost accounting manager, and an outside management accounting specialist associated with the Institute of Management Accountants.

Once the plan was developed, the foremen and plant vice president were replaced by the factory workers who were going to become cell workers. The idea was that the people who would have to run the operation should design and create it, including the cost management system. Newmount hoped that by designing and creating the cost management system as part of the production redesign, the workers would be more motivated to accept it as their own and use, maintain, and improve it. Throughout the process, the systems analyst, cost accounting manager, and management accounting specialist were just part of the team, going to work each day wearing blue jeans and hard hats (a nice

---

[20] Michael Thomas and James Mackey, "Activity-Based Cost Variances for Just-in-Times," forthcoming in *Management Accounting*.

[21] If a BCAS can be considered the simplest type of CAS, then the SCAS discussed next may be classified as the most complex.

[22] The case described here is abstracted from Michael Thomas, et al., *Designing the Management Accounting System, Using ABC and Socio-Technical Systems Analysis, for a JIT Conversion at Ditch Witch* (Montvale, N.J.: The Institute of Management Accountants, 1992). Some of the facts have been changed to allow better linkage with previous text materials. With permission.

Newmount Engine Manufacturing

Newmount produces specialty engines used in construction and agricultural equipment. Because Newmount has always been committed to product excellence and customer service, it has historically made virtually all its own component parts for its engines. Newmount has one factory located in the midwestern United States that was built in 1975.

All the component parts and the final engine assemblies are produced in a traditional shop floor design. Lately, Newmount has been experiencing significant problems in one of its component lines, the cylinder assembly process. Cylinder barrels and rods are constructed in operations that involve five different departments. During the manufacturing process, the barrels and rods move back and forth between departments and the warehouse 11 times. The steps in this process are listed in Exhibit 8–18.

Direct materials and labor cost variances are used to evaluate the performance of each production department. This has led to a "pounds-in-the-bucket" production mentality among the workers, who concentrate on beating their production quotas. One way to do this is by not inspecting the barrels and rods after each department has finished with them. The savings in inspection time makes the workers look good in terms of favorable labor and material usage variances.

Of course, this has also resulted in large WIP inventories in the warehouse, a lack of coordination and synchronization in the amount produced within each department, and significant scrap. The scrap results from final cylinder assembly workers scrapping barrels whenever they discover a problem. The workers have no incentive to attempt to fix the barrels because this rework would result in unfavorable materials and labor usage variances in final assembly. These workers do not feel that they should be penalized for problems caused by other workers in previous departments.

The accounting system is also very traditional with just one plantwide overhead account and one predetermined total overhead rate based on direct labor hours. When a significant number of scrapped barrels accumulated, someone from liaison engineering was notified to investigate. Liaison engineering was set up as an indirect cost, and all its costs were debited to the one total overhead account of the factory. Thus, there was no tracking of the costs of scrap or rework.

■ EXHIBIT 8–18

Steps in Barrel and Rod Subassembly Processes at Newmount Engine Manufacturing

Barrel subassembly:

1. Issue barrel stock (20′ bars of honed tubing) from warehouse to NT II bar lathe in Machinery Department 1.
2. Cut barrels to length on NT II machine.
3. Move barrels to warehouse.
4. Move barrels from warehouse to mill station in Machinery Department 2.
5. Mill barrel threads.
6. About half the time, milled barrels are returned to warehouse and then subsequently moved back to Machinery Department 2's drill station. About half the time, milled barrels can be moved directly to the drill station.
7. Drill barrels.
8. Move barrels back to warehouse.
9. Move barrels and fittings from warehouse to Welding Department.
10. Weld fittings onto barrels.
11. Move barrel subassembly to warehouse.
12. Move barrel subassembly and barrel ends from warehouse to welding.
13. Weld barrel end onto barrel subassembly.
14. Move completed barrels to warehouse.

Rod Subassembly:

1. Issue bushing stock from warehouse to NC lathe.
2. Fabricate bushing (cut to length and drill hole in stock).
3. Move bushing to warehouse.
4. Issue rod material from warehouse to saw.
5. Cut rods to length.
6. Move rods to warehouse.
7. Issue rods from warehouse to NC lathe.
8. Machine rod threads.
9. Move threaded rods to warehouse.
10. Issue rods and bushings from warehouse to Welding.
11. Weld rods and bushings into finished rods.
12. Move finished rod assemblies to warehouse.

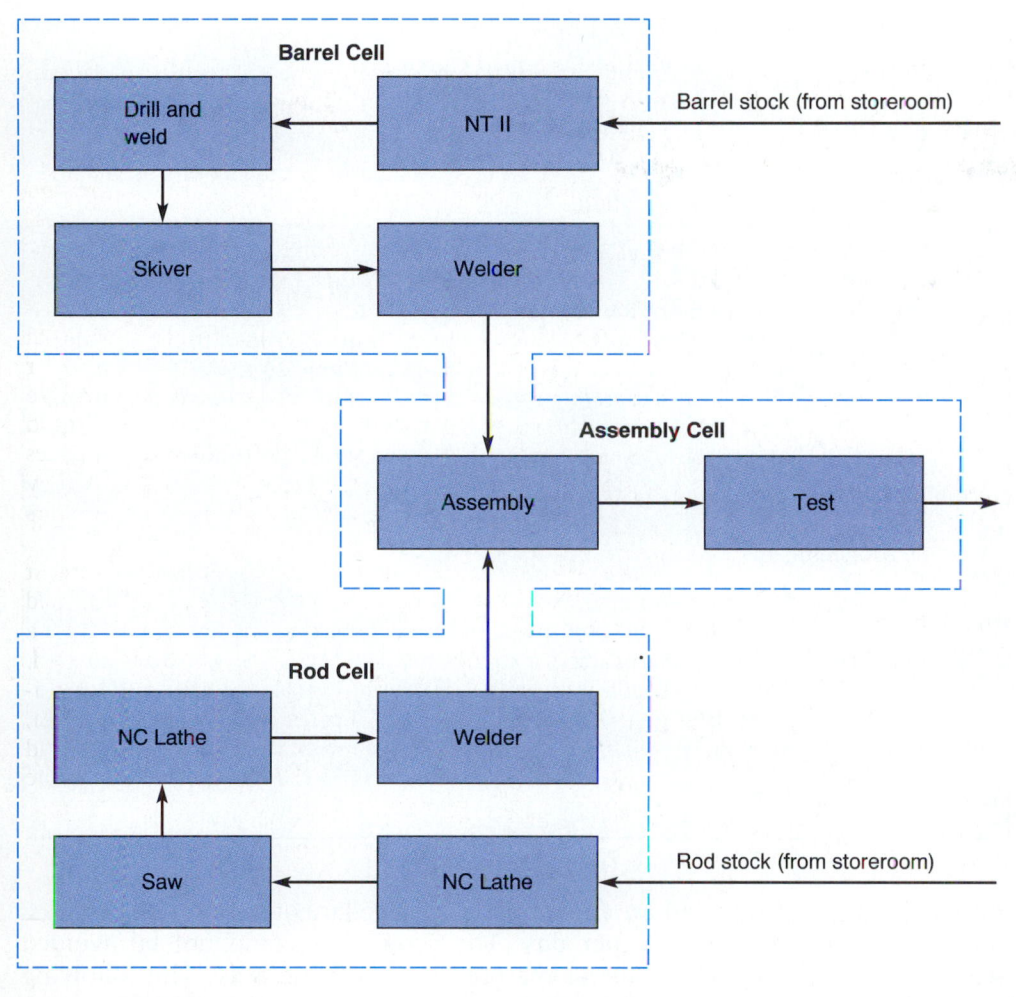

■■■■EXHIBIT 8–19
Physical Layout of Cylinder Cells at Newmount

change from three-piece suits and wing-tip shoes or high heels!). Exhibit 8–19 shows the three new JIT cells.

LESSON 2: CHANGING OVERHEAD TO DIRECT CELL ACTIVITIES COSTS.

While redesigning the machine operations, the cell workers wanted to know the costs of each machine task. This information could be used to measure the costs of scrap and rework, as well as providing benchmarks for productivity improvement over time (i.e., these are nonvalue-added activities). By summing the costs of each machine operation, the cost of making a cylinder barrel could be developed.

Since a kanban system controlled cylinder production, each cylinder kanban could be treated as a job. Thus, the team believed that a JOCAS would best provide the actual costs of making a cylinder. They discovered, however, that many production problems (causing cost variances) were cell related. Such problems, and their cost variances, should not be treated as a cost of a particular cylinder (job) in the accounting system. Since 35,000 of the anticipated 40,000 cylinders to be produced in a year were identical, the planners concluded that a standard PCAS should be used. Only part of the barrel cell's standard cost card is illustrated in Exhibit 8–20.

Any of the overhead costs that were directly related to labor time were included within the worker's standard price. For example, in the operating, inspecting, and move time allowed for "Machine Operation 1" of the standard cost card, the $10.65 per hour standard labor rate included a gross wage rate of $8.00 plus fringe benefits and payroll taxes of $2.65 per hour. The labor

■■■ EXHIBIT 8–20
Partial Standard Cost Card for Newmount's Cylinder Barrel

Partial Standard Cost Card
4-Inch Cylinder Barrel Subassembly
(Part #151-018-1000)

Part Number/ Step Number	Description	Standard Price	Standard Quantity	Standard Cost
Machine Operation 1: Cut Barrel Stock on NT II				
151-018-1010	Barrel stock	$59/20' rod	.01695 rod	$1.00
01	Delivery from Raw Materials	$14.75/20'	.01695 rod	0.25
02	NT II machine cost	$1.00/min	3 min	3.00
02	NT II power cost	$.025/KWhr	20 KWhr	0.50
02	Direct labor (operating time)	$10.65/DLhr	1.14 min	0.20
02	Direct labor (inspection)	$10.65/DLhr	1.14 min	0.20
03	Direct labor (move barrel)	$10.65/DLhr	.57 min	0.10
Subtotal: Machine Operation 1 Standard Cost				$5.25
..				
..(Other Machine operations)				
..				
..				
Subtotal: Standard variable cost/barrel				
	Direct materials			$ 3.00
	Direct labor			3.25
	Machinery			14.75
Barrel's incremental standard cost				$21.00

standard quantity included an allowance for miscellaneous time (e.g., breaks, setup, cleanup) of one hour per day. The scrap that could not be avoided was included in the barrel's direct material standard quantity. The following illustrates the standard quantity calculations:

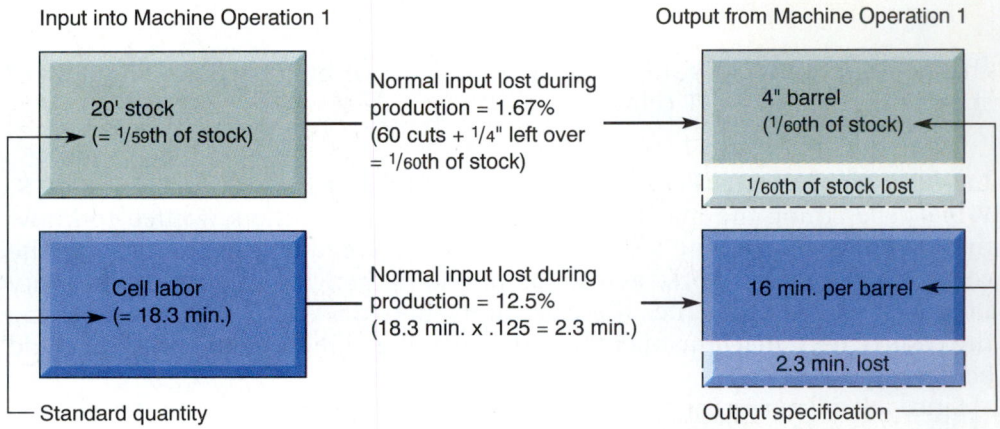

One important aspect was separately including the cost of inspection time after each machine operation within the barrel's standard cost. World-class manufacturing and JIT philosophies recognize the need for quality control when tasks are performed. The costs of "direct technology" (the costs of operating the machines) were also treated as direct costs within the cell. For example, machinery depreciation was based on operating time (depreciation was changed from a straight-line method to a rate per minute), as was machinery power cost.

LESSON 3: USE STANDARD ACTIVITY-BASED COSTS TO CALCULATE COST VARIANCES. Within the barrel cell (Exhibit 8–19), there are 4 machine operations. Each machine operation is considered as an activity. The activity-based standard costs now become the basis for computing cost variances and reconciling the actual costs incurred within the barrel cell each week. As a problem occurred, the cell worker coded it by activity for input into the cost management system. Having workers code the sources and causes and whether the problem has been corrected for input into the SCAS is not a new idea.[23] For example, one completed barrel had to be scrapped during the week. From the standard cost card, its incremental standard cost was $21.00. Also, one partially completed barrel had to be scrapped after it was cut in Machine Operation 1. From the standard cost card, the cost of processing the barrel to this stage should be $5.25 (this production activity's standard cost). These are the third and fourth cost variances shown on the weekly report in Exhibit 8–21.

The control team at Newmount Engine Manufacturing believed it was important to understand the costs of production problems. Thus, when calculating and reporting cost variances, each variance was identified in terms of the activity that caused it. At the same time, cost variances could still be summarized in terms of materials, labor, and overhead, as in a traditional SCAS. To trace cost variances to their underlying problems, however, the cell workers needed to identify those problems and code the input information by activity for the cost management system. Because cost variances were coded and reported in terms of production activities, the Newmount cell workers called this an "activity-based cost variance reporting system."

[23] R. DeWelt, "Integrating Cost Accounting with Inventory Control and MRP," *APICS Conference Proceedings*, 1975, pp. 277–86; S. Hanson, "Integrating Shop Floor Control and Standard Cost Accounting," *APICS Conference Proceedings*, 1980, pp. 365–68; and D. Nelleman, "Closing the Financial Loop: Shop Floor Controls," *APICS Conference Proceedings*, 1980, pp. 308–12.

EXHIBIT 8–21
Weekly Cost Variance Report: June 24–28

	Direct Materials	Factory Supplies	Direct Labor	Machinery	Total Costs
Actual Output (251 barrels):					
(A) Standard cost allowed for 251 barrels:	$753.00	$30.12	$835.83	$3,702.25	$5,321.20
Per unit (Direct cell costs only)					$21.20
Cost Variances:					
Drill and weld breakdown		5.00	10.65		15.65
Reskive barrel			.30	1.00	1.30
Scrapped one barrel	3.00		3.25	14.75	21.00
Scrapped partial barrel after NT II operation	1.25		.50	3.50	5.25
(B) Total cost variances	$ 4.25	$ 5.00	$ 14.70	$ 19.25	$ 43.20
Percentage of standard costs	0.6%	16.6%	1.8%	0.5%	0.8%
Per unit					$0.17
(C) Actual Costs Incurred:	< 757.25>	< 35.12>	< 852.00>	< 3,721.50>	< 5,365.87>
Percentage of standard costs					100.8%
Per unit					$21.38
(D) Unexplained Cost Variances Remaining: (negative amount is unfavorable)					
(D = A + B − C)	$ 0.00	$ 0.00	<$ 1.47>	$ 0.00	<$ 1.47>
Percentage of standard costs			<0.2%>		0.03%

| SUMMARY OF LEARNING OBJECTIVES

The major goals of this chapter were to enable you to achieve six learning objectives:

Learning objective 1.   Discuss the role of a standard cost accounting system (SCAS) in responsibility accounting.

Three responsibility accounting concepts are critical in designing an SCAS. First, standards must be designed jointly by management and operational personnel. Management involvement is needed to assure that the enterprise's goals are incorporated into the standards. Operational personnel must be involved so that they clearly understand what is expected. When employees participate in setting the standards used to evaluate their performance, they are more likely to accept the standards as legitimate and internalize the expected performance.

Standards and cost variances should not be the only basis for performance evaluation, though. In world-class enterprises, employees are rewarded for additional skills learned, preventive maintenance, suggestions for improvements, and the like. Primarily, an SCAS should provide the information needed to help people identify problems and correct them as soon as possible. The learning that results from control activities can prevent problems from happening in the future.

The second concept concerns the tightness of the standards. If ideal standards are set, unfavorable variances will be common. Small unfavorable variances can signal excellent performance. With practical standards, both favorable and unfavorable variances may suggest abnormal operating conditions. The SCAS should also report trend analysis over time for continuous improvement evaluation.

The third concept involves implementing the management-by-exception philosophy. Two issues are involved. First, when should variances be reported? To support quality control throughout the production process, variance information needs to be available on the shop floor in real time. An ICBIS and visual factory control system, with terminals at workstations, can provide immediate feedback and feedforward information to the workers. The input coding activities to identify the sources and causes of cost variances when they happen is the key idea for SCAS design in promoting effective and efficient operational control.

The second issue involves which variances should be investigated. Some variances are investigated only if they fall outside preset control limits. Random fluctuations in labor time are often expected causing minor favorable and unfavorable variances that can be ignored. Other variances, such as problems with materials quality or machine breakdowns, are investigated whenever they occur and regardless of their significance. Exhibit 8–1 highlights the operational control loop and the steps involved in designing an SCAS for responsibility accounting.

Learning objective 2.   Explain the meaning of a cost variance, and calculate and interpret the variable costs' spending variances.

The two basic types of cost variances are spending and usage. Cost variances compare standard prices and quantities against actual prices and quantities. Favorable variances result from actual costs being less than standard costs. When actual costs exceed standard costs, unfavorable variances result. The terms favorable and unfavorable refer to the effect on planned profits due to the cost variance. Favorable variances mean actual profits are greater than planned profits for the actual production volume. Unfavorable variances mean that actual profits are less than planned profits. In this way, variances measure the difference between planned and actual profits because of the activities that created those variances. Exhibit 8–5 summarizes the cost variance formulas and Demonstration Problem 1 presents the calculations and journal entries.

Spending variances for variable cost elements are calculated with the following formula:

Variable cost spending variance
$$= \text{Actual quantity purchased} \times (\text{Standard price} - \text{Actual price})$$

A favorable direct materials spending (price) variance means the actual purchase price of direct materials is less than the standard price. Similarly, a favorable direct labor rate variance means the actual labor rate is less than the standard rate. The analysis of overhead variances can be performed by calculating one total overhead variance, or by calculating two, three, or four variances. Four-way overhead variance analysis provides better information than the other methods. Using the four-way method, separate spending and usage variances are calculated for VOH and FOH. The VOH spending variance has a limited interpretation in that it includes both price and usage problems.

Learning objective 3. Calculate and interpret the variable costs' usage variances.

The variable costs' usage variances can be calculated with the following formula:

Variable cost usage variance
= Standard price × (Standard quantity allowed − Actual quantity used)

An unfavorable direct materials usage variance results from the actual quantity of materials used being greater than the standard quantity allowed (SQA). SQA is the total quantity of a manufacturing input that should have been used for the actual output. If the actual labor hours worked exceed the standard labor hours allowed, an unfavorable labor efficiency variance results. The VOH efficiency variance measures the difference between the SQA of the overhead application basis and the actual quantity used. To clarify this, let the POR's basis be machine usage. If more machine hours were used than should have been for the actual production volume (the standard machine hours allowed), an unfavorable VOH efficiency variance results. The assumption is that if more machine hours are worked, more variable overhead items are used. This may, or may not, be true.

Learning objective 4. Calculate and interpret the fixed overhead variances.

The four-way method of analyzing overhead cost variances provides separate FOH spending and usage variances. The FOH spending variance is called the budget variance. It measures the difference between the total budgeted FOH and the total actual FOH costs. In budgeting, control, and evaluation, fixed costs need to be considered as total costs, not as per unit costs. The per unit fixed cost is not stable over the relevant range. As production volume increases, the FOH per unit decreases. Fixed costs are stable (i.e., they have predictive usefulness) when measured as total costs. The formula for the FOH budget variance is:

FOH budget variance = Budgeted FOH cost − Actual FOH cost

The FOH usage variance (the volume variance) is a gauge of how well the factory is used. In interpreting this variance, FOH represents the costs of having the factory (the productive capacity) available for use. If the production quota is met, the factory is used as efficiently as planned. If the production quota is not obtained, the factory is not used as efficiently as planned when the FOH standard cost and the product's sales price were determined.

The interpretation of the FOH volume variance depends on the production volume used in the FOH standard cost. The explanation above is valid when the production quota (the expected capacity) is used in preparing the standard cost card. The FOH volume variance formula is:

FOH volume variance = FOH standard cost × (Actual output − Budgeted output)

Exhibit 8–5 provides a variation of this formula, using the FOH POR basis (i.e., using units of input such as direct labor hours, instead of the above formula which uses units of output).

Learning objective 5. Prepare the journal entries for an SCAS, and the cost variance report.

The cost variance calculations can be prepared and reported separately from the journal entries in an SCAS or both can be done together, as illustrated in Demonstration Problem 1. Cost elements are journalized into inventories using their standard costs. For example, direct materials are debited to RMI at their standard prices. When used, direct materials, direct labor, VOH and FOH are journalized into WIP at their standard costs allowed (standard price × SQA, or standard cost × actual output). Actual costs are credited to accounts payable (for direct materials purchased), gross wages (for direct labor), and the VOH and FOH control accounts. The differences between the standard costs (debited) and the actual costs (credited) are recorded in separate subsidiary ledger accounts for the cost variances.

SCAS reports present cost variances in three ways. Cost variances per unit facilitate use by operations personnel who often think about prices per pound, wage rates per hour, and pounds or hours per unit of product. Cost variance amounts reported in total dollars measure the difference between planned and actual profits, useful in profitability evaluations by upper management. Finally, cost variances as a percentage of standard help upper management and operations personnel judge their significance.

Learning objective 6. Design a high-quality SCAS with management reports useful for operational control and performance evaluation.

The modern management accountant has two roles in operational control and performance evaluation. First, an SCAS should provide the information wanted by different people in the firm. Second, if this is not perceived by the management accountant as the best (optimal) information, he or she must educate and demonstrate how different information can lead to better decisions. This second role is critical to the long-run success of the firm and its quest toward continuous improvement. Many traditional SCASs were designed primarily from a financial accounting perspective. Consequently, the historical usefulness of SCASs in operational control and performance evaluation has been quite limited.

Even in world-class enterprises, an SCAS may operate independently of the control system, or as an integral component of it. For example, a simple backflush accounting system does not report information about cost variance problems for shop floor control or performance evaluation. Consequently, it cannot provide information useful in future planning activities. A separate information system is needed if control information is desired. On the other end of the SCAS design continuum is a production activity-based cost variance reporting system. This SCAS, using cause-effect coding of cost variances, provides online, real-time information for operational control, as well as for performance evaluation and future budgeting.

For effective and efficient operational control, the SCAS should report the sources and causes of cost variances. Capturing information on the underlying activities that cause cost variances can provide valuable information both for short-run corrective actions as well as for long-run continuous improvement programs. For example, favorable variances are not necessarily "good news." A favorable direct materials spending variance may occur because substandard materials are purchased. When laborers use substandard materials, other variances result, such as unfavorable direct materials, direct labor, and VOH usage variances. Thus, one underlying cause of a particular variance also may be the cause of a number of other variances. In understanding production problems, these cause-effect chains must be identified. Developing a database of historical cause-effect chains and the costs of corrective actions can aid in future operational control decisions.

IMPORTANT TERMS

Backflush cost accounting system (BCAS) An SCAS that records input acquisitions at actual cost and output at standard cost. RMI is replaced with RIP, WIP is not used, and direct labor and overhead costs are debited to a Conversion Costs account. Input usage is recorded through the COGM or COGS journal entry, resulting in input costs being flushed backward out of the general ledger.

Direct labor efficiency variance This cost variance is the difference between the standard direct labor hours allowed and direct labor hours used, multiplied by the standard rate per direct labor hour. It measures the difference between planned and actual production labor costs due to labor efficiency being more or less than what it should have been for the actual output.

Direct labor mix variance This variance measures the difference in the average standard price of labor from assigning workers to activities in a manner different from planned. Thus, it is a spending variance.

Direct labor rate variance   This variance reports the difference between the standard direct labor rate and the actual direct labor rate per hour, multiplied by the actual direct labor hours worked. It measures the difference in labor costs from budget due to changes in wage rates and/or payroll taxes and fringe benefits.

Direct labor yield variance   This variance presents the difference between planned and actual profits from the use of a different mix of labor than originally planned. Thus, it is a usage variance.

Direct materials mix variance   This variance measures the change in the average standard price from mixing direct materials in a ratio different from the standard direct materials formula. Thus, it is a price variance.

Direct materials price variance   This variance reports the difference between the standard price and the actual price, multiplied by the actual quantity of direct materials purchased. It measures the difference in direct materials costs from budget due to price differences from standard.

Direct materials usage variance   This variance is the difference between the standard quantity allowed and the actual quantity of direct materials used, multiplied by the standard price. It measures the difference in direct materials cost from the standard cost allowed due to usage of direct materials.

Direct materials yield variance   This variance is the result of obtaining an output different from the one expected based on the total quantities of direct materials used. It measures the impact on planned profits from the difference between the total quantity of materials that should have been used with the standard mix and the actual total quantity of direct materials used. Thus, it is a usage variance.

Favorable cost variance   A favorable variance results when actual costs are less than standard costs allowed. A spending variance is favorable when the actual price of an input item is less than its standard price. A favorable usage variance results when the actual quantity used is less than that input's standard quantity allowed.

Fixed overhead budget variance   This variance is the difference between the budgeted fixed overhead costs and the actual fixed overhead costs.

Fixed overhead volume variance   This variance measures the difference between budgeted profits and actual profits created by producing a different volume than planned.

Flexible budget   A budget that is prepared using the actual production volume rather than the production quota. It can be used to compare actual and ''should be'' variable costs for the same level of production.

Raw-in-process (RIP)   The general ledger account for raw materials purchased in a BCAS. Raw materials costs are removed from this account at the completion or sale of the products.

Standard cost allowed (SCA)   The total cost of an input that should have been incurred for the actual output. It is calculated by multiplying an input's standard cost and actual production volume, or by multiplying standard price and standard quantity allowed for that input.

Standard quantity allowed (SQA)   The total amount of an input item that should have been used given the actual output produced. It is the result of multiplying an input's standard quantity by the actual production volume.

Total overhead variance   This is simply the sum of the four overhead cost variances. It is also the difference between the total overhead costs applied and the total overhead costs actually incurred.

Unfavorable cost variance   An unfavorable variance results when actual costs are greater than standard costs. An unfavorable spending variance occurs when the actual price of a cost element is greater than its standard price. When the actual input quantity is greater than its standard quantity allowed, an unfavorable usage variance results.

Variable overhead efficiency variance   This variance measures the difference between the standard quantity allowed of the basis used to apply VOH costs and the actual quantity used. When direct labor hours are used to apply VOH, then an unfavorable labor usage variance causes an unfavorable VOH usage variance.

Variable overhead spending variance   This variance is the difference between the VOH standard price multiplied by the actual quantity of the overhead application basis used and the actual total VOH costs. It measures the difference between total actual VOH cost and the VOH cost that should have been incurred given the number of direct labor hours worked (or the actual quantity of the basis used to apply overhead if it is something other than direct labor hours).

DEMONSTRATION PROBLEMS

DEMONSTRATION PROBLEM 1 *Calculating cost variances and preparing SCAS journal entries.*

Armando Corporation manufactures electronic video and audio equipment. Each of its products is made in a separate department. One of its newer products, CD Players, is built in the CD Player Department. CD Players are made one-at-a-time in quality circles. To further control quality and reduce inventory costs, the department operates on a JIT basis. Thus, there are no beginning or ending WIP inventories. Armando has two overhead accounts (variable and fixed), and direct labor hours is the cost driver for both. Armando uses an SCAS with monthly cost variance reports issued for each department.

Two data sections follow. The CD Player standard absorptive manufacturing cost is $93. Normal production volume requires 2,400 direct labor hours per month.

DATA SECTION: STANDARD COSTS

Manufacturing Inputs	Price	Output Quantity	Loss%
Direct Materials	$1.35 per lb.	19.00 lb.	5.00%
Direct labor	$9.00 per DLhr	3.60 DLhr	10.00%
Variable Overhead	$5.00 per DLhr		
Fixed Overhead	$2.50 per DLhr		
Normal Production Volume (in units)		600	

DATA SECTION: ACTUAL COSTS FOR JULY

Direct Materials	ACTUAL DM PRICE	$1.38	DM PURCHASED	18,000
Direct Labor	ACTUAL DL RATE	$9.15	DM USED	9,500
Variable Overhead	ACTUAL VOH COST	$9,650.00	ACTUAL HOURS	2,100
Fixed Overhead	ACTUAL FOH COST	$7,000.00	ACTUAL OUTPUT	500

Required:

Prepare the journal entries to record direct materials purchases, usage of direct materials and labor, and applied VOH and FOH. Also record the cost of CD Players completed.

SOLUTION TO DEMONSTRATION PROBLEM 1

JOURNAL ENTRY 1: Recording the Purchase of Direct Materials

RMI–CD Player Direct Materials (SP × AQp = $1.35/lb. × 18,000 lb.)	$24,300	
RMI–CD Player Direct Materials Price Variance [AQp × (SP − AP) = 18,000 lb. × ($1.35/lb. − $1.38/lb.)]	$ 540	
Accounts Payable (AP × AQp = $1.38/lb. × 18,000 lb.)		$24,840

Before preparing the input usage journal entries, the following calculations are needed:

$$\text{SQ}_{\text{Direct materials}}: 19 \text{ lb.} \div (1.00 - .05) = \underline{20 \text{ lb. per unit}}$$

$$\text{SQ}_{\text{Direct labor}}: 3.60 \text{ DLhr} \div (1.00 - .10) = \underline{4 \text{ DLhr per unit}}$$

$$\text{SQA}_{\text{Direct materials}}: 20 \text{ lb. per unit} \times 500 \text{ units} = \underline{10,000 \text{ lb.}}$$

$$\text{SQA}_{\text{Direct labor}}: 4 \text{ DLhr per unit} \times 500 \text{ units} = \underline{2,000 \text{ DLhr}}$$

JOURNAL ENTRY 5: Direct Materials Requisitions

WIP–CD Player Department (DM) (SP × SQA = $1.35/lb. × 10,000 lb.)	$13,500	
WIP–CD Player Direct Materials Usage Variance [SP × (SQA − AQu) = $1.35/lb. × (10,000 lb. − 9,500 lb.)]		$ 675
RMI–CD Player Direct Materials (SP × AQu = $1.35/lb. × 9,500 lb.)		$12,825

JOURNAL ENTRY 6: Direct Labor Distribution

WIP–CD Player Department (DL) (SP × SQA = $9.00/DLhr × 2,000 DLhr)	$18,000	
WIP–CD Department Direct Labor Rate Variance [AQ × (SP − AP) = 2,100 DLhr × ($9.00/DLhr − $9.15/DLhr)]	$ 315	
WIP–CD Department Direct Labor Efficiency Variance [SP × (SQA − AQ) = $9.00/DLhr × (2,000 DLhr − 2,100 DLhr)]	$ 900	
Gross Wages (Actual cost = AP × AQ = $9.15/DLhr × 2,100 DLhr)		$19,215

JOURNAL ENTRY 7a: VOH Applied

WIP–CD Department (VOH Applied) (SP × SQA = $5.00/DLhr × 2,000 DLhr)	$10,000	
WIP–CD Department VOH Spending Variance [(AQ × SP) − AC = (2,100 DLhr × $5.00/DLhr) − $9,650]		$ 850
WIP–CD Department VOH Efficiency Variance [SP × (SQA − AQ) = $5.00/DLhr × (2,000 DLhr − 2,100 DLhr)]	$ 500	
WIP–VOH (Actual cost)		$ 9,650

JOURNAL ENTRY 7b: FOH Applied

WIP–CD Department (FOH Applied) (SP × SQA = $2.50/DLhr × 2,000 DLhr)	$ 5,000	
WIP–CD Department FOH Budget Variance (Budgeted FOH − Actual FOH = $6,000 − $7,000)**	$ 1,000	
WIP − CD Department FOH Volume Variance [SP × (SQA − Budgeted DLhr) = $2.50/DLhr × (2,000 DLhr − 2,400 DLhr)]	$ 1,000	
WIP–FOH (Actual cost)		$ 7,000

** Note on calculating the budgeted FOH: The budgeted FOH can be determined by multiplying the FOH POR by the budgeted direct labor hours. The FOH POR was originally calculated by dividing the budgeted FOH cost by the budgeted direct labor hours. Alternatively, once the direct labor standard quantity is known, the FOH standard cost can be calculated ($2.50/DLhr × 4 DLhr per unit = $10.00 per unit). Working backward, the $10.00 per unit FOH standard cost resulted from dividing budgeted FOH cost by the 600-unit production quota.

JOURNAL ENTRY 9: Cost of Goods Manufactured

FGI–CD Players	$46,500	
WIP–CD Player Department		$46,500
(Standard cost × Actual output = $93 per unit × 500 units)		

■ **DEMONSTRATION PROBLEM 2** *Preparing the standard cost card, manufacturing cost equation, and cost variance report.*

Using the two data sections from Demonstration Problem 1, (a) prepare the standard cost card and manufacturing cost equation using the format from Exhibit 8–11, and (b) prepare a cost variance report using the format from Exhibit 8–12.

SOLUTION TO DEMONSTRATION PROBLEM 2

a.

Armando Corporation
CD Player
Standard Cost Card

Manufacturing Inputs	Standard Prices	Standard Quantities	Standard Costs
Direct materials	$1.35/lb.	20.00 lb./unit	$27.00/unit
Direct labor	$9.00/DLhr	4.00 DLhr/unit	$36.00/unit
Variable overhead	$5.00/DLhr	4.00 DLhr/unit	$20.00/unit
Fixed overhead	$2.50/DLhr	4.00 DLhr/unit	$10.00/unit
Standard absorptive manufacturing cost (SAMC)			$93.00/unit

Monthly CD Player production costs = $6,000 per month[a] + $83.00/unit[b]

NOTES: [a] FOH standard cost $= \dfrac{\text{Budgeted FOH}}{\text{Production quota}}$

$10/unit $= \dfrac{\text{Budgeted FOH}}{600 \text{ units}}$

Budgeted FOH = $6,000 per month

[b] Σ standard variable manufacturing costs

SOLUTION TO DEMONSTRATION PROBLEM 2

b.

ARMANDO CORPORATION: CD PLAYER DEPARTMENT
COST VARIANCES REPORT
For July 1994

MANUFACTURING INPUTS:		PER UNIT	TOTAL UNITS	TOTAL COSTS	VARIANCE PERCENTAGE
DIRECT MATERIALS:	STANDARD PRICE	$1.35		$24,300	
	−ACTUAL PRICE	<$1.38>		<$24,840>	
	PRICE VARIANCE	<$0.03>	18,000	<$540>	−2.22%
	STANDARD QUANTITY	20.00	10,000	$13,500	
	−ACTUAL QUANTITY	<19.00>	<9,500>	<$12,825>	
	USAGE VARIANCE	1.00	500	$675	5.00%
DIRECT LABOR:	STANDARD RATE	$9.00		$18,900	
	−ACTUAL RATE	<$9.15>		<$19,215>	
	RATE VARIANCE	<$0.15>	2,100	<$315>	−1.67%
	STANDARD QUANTITY	4.00	2,000	$18,000	
	−ACTUAL QUANTITY	<4.20>	<2,100>	<$18,900>	
	USAGE VARIANCE	<0.20>	<100>	<$900>	−5.00%

Continued

—Continued

VARIABLE OVERHEAD:	STANDARD RATE	$5.00		$10,500	
	−ACTUAL RATE	<$4.60>		<$9,650>	
	RATE VARIANCE	$0.40	2,100	$850	8.10%
	STANDARD QUANTITY	4.00	2,000	$10,000	
	−ACTUAL QUANTITY	<4.20>	<2,100>	<$10,500>	
	USAGE VARIANCE	<0.20>	<100>	<$500>	−5.00%
FIXED OVERHEAD:	BUDGETED COSTS			$6,000	
	−ACTUAL COSTS	<$14.00>		<$7,000>	
	BUDGET VARIANCE	<$2.00>	500	<$1,000>	−16.67%
	APPLIED	$10.00	500	$5,000	
	−BUDGETED	$10.00	<600>	<$6,000>	
	VOLUME VARIANCE	<$2.00>	<100>	<$1,000>	−16.67%
VARIANCE TOTALS:	APPLIED	$93.00	500	$46,500	
	−ACTUAL	<$98.46>	500	<$49,230>	
	COST VARIANCE	<$5.46>	500	<$2,730>	−5.87%

NOTES: POSITIVE COST VARIANCES are FAVORABLE (negative = unfavorable).
Per unit usage, fixed overhead, and cost variance totals are per unit of output.
Per unit price variances equal total price variance divided by pounds purchased or DLhr worked.
All per unit and percentage amount spreadsheet cells are formatted for two decimal places.

▌REVIEW QUESTIONS

8.1 Explain how an SCAS is applicable in an enterprise that routinely manufactures the same products or performs the same services. Are standard costs and cost variances applicable to companies that make an array of unique products or perform one-of-a-kind services? Are standard costs and cost variances useful for construction companies, consultants, repair shops, and hospitals?

8.2 What is the difference between an SCAS and a normal or actual CAS?

8.3 How does a favorable variance differ from an unfavorable variance?

8.4 What is meant by the term "management-by-exception"? Explain how it is used in an SCAS. Discuss how it may be misused.

8.5 Why is it important to consider how standards are set? Which type of standards do you believe will better motivate employees, ideal or practical? Why?

8.6 Is it important to present trend analyses of standards and/or variances over time? Why isn't it sufficient to just report cost variances each period?

8.7 Do favorable variances always represent "good" performance? Do unfavorable variances always represent "bad" performance?

8.8 List and very briefly describe the steps in variance analysis and operational control.

8.9 What is the "key" factor for operational control?

8.10 In world-class enterprises, when are operational control actions taken?

8.11 Should the SCAS provide feedforward information in support of operational control? Explain your answer.

8.12 How can an SCAS reduce record-keeping costs?

8.13 Distinguish between the two basic types of cost variances.

8.14 List the four formulas for the eight cost variances.

8.15 What are three possible underlying causes of direct materials price variances?

8.16 What are three possible underlying causes of direct labor rate variances?

8.17 Explain a VOH spending variance. Why is it important to break down this variance into its individual items?

8.18 Define and give an example of a flexible budget.

8.19 What is meant by the term "standard quantity allowed"?

8.20 Which responsibility center is customarily held responsible for an unfavorable direct materials usage variance? What are three possible underlying causes of direct materials usage variances?

8.21 What are three possible underlying causes of direct labor efficiency variances? Why is it important to investigate this variance?

8.22 Explain three characteristics that a high-quality SCAS should possess.

8.23 Explain the VOH efficiency variance.

8.24 What is the difference between the FOH budget and volume variances? Are these really spending and usage variances?

8.25 How does the production volume used in determining the FOH standard cost affect the interpretation of the FOH volume variance?

8.26 What are the differences between the two-way variance analysis method and the three-way variance analysis method?

8.27 The total production overhead variance can be divided into two, three, or four variances. No matter how many variances are isolated, one is always the:

    a. Flexible budget variance.
    b. Fixed overhead volume variance.
    c. Variable overhead efficiency variance.
    d. Variable overhead spending variance.

8.28 Explain the two basic differences between SCAS journal entries and PCAS or JOCAS journal entries.

8.29 In designing the SCAS general ledger system for WIP, what type of accounts are cost variances? Why are cost variance accounts organized by responsibility center?

8.30 Identify two differences between the journal entries in a standard PCAS and in a standard JOCAS.

8.31 How should variances of significant amounts be treated at the end of the accounting period?

    a. Reported as a different charge or credit.
    b. Allocated among work-in-process inventory, finished goods inventory, and cost of goods sold.
    c. Charged or credited to cost of goods manufactured.
    d. Allocated among cost of goods manufactured, finished goods inventory, and cost of goods sold.

8.32 Why do cost variances need to be reported in total, per unit, and as a percentage of standard? How are these different calculations useful to different people within the enterprise?

8.33 Distinguish between:

    ■ Direct materials mix variance
    ■ Direct materials yield variance

Explain the purpose of each. Together, what variance do they comprise?

8.34 Distinguish between:

    ■ Direct labor mix variance
    ■ Direct labor yield variance

Explain the purpose of each. Together, what variance do they comprise?

8.35 How does a BCAS differ from a traditional SCAS?

8.36 How does a production activity–based SCAS differ from a traditional SCAS?

8.37 Why is it important to identify cost variances in terms of the underlying activities that create them?

CHAPTER-SPECIFIC PROBLEMS

These problems require responses based directly on concepts and techniques presented in the text.

8.38 *Entry in the accounts for direct materials variances.* At Timken Company during August direct materials were purchased for $650 (at $5 per square foot). Their standard price is $4. In project 738A, 1,000 square feet of materials were used. According to standards, 900 square feet should have been used.

Required:

Calculate the direct materials cost variances and make the journal entries.

8.39 *Entry in the accounts for direct labor variances.* Project 738A at Timken Company (see the previous problem) also required 50 direct labor hours to complete at a rate of $10 per hour, when it should have taken only 45 hours at a rate of $12 per hour.

Required:
Make the journal entries for the direct labor usage on project 738A.

8.40 *Solving for the actual direct materials purchase price.* Information on Kennedy Company's direct materials costs includes:

Standard price	$3.60
Actual quantity purchased	1,600
Standard quantity allowed	1,450
Materials purchase price variance, favorable	$240

Required:
Calculate the actual purchase price rounded to the nearest penny.

[AICPA adapted]

8.41 *Solving for the standard and actual direct labor rates.* Goodman Company's direct labor costs are as follows:

Standard direct labor hours	30,000
Actual direct labor hours	29,000
Direct labor efficiency variance, favorable	$4,000
Direct labor rate variance, favorable	$5,800
Total gross wages	$110,200

Required:
a. What was Goodman's standard direct labor rate?
b. What was Goodman's actual direct labor rate?

[AICPA adapted]

8.42 *Direct materials and labor variances.* Arrow Industries employs a standard cost system. Arrow has established the following standards for the prime costs of its Hunters' Bow product line:

	STANDARD QUANTITY	STANDARD PRICE	STANDARD COST
Direct materials	8 lb.	$1.80/lb.	$14.40
Direct labor	0.25 DLhr	$8.00/DLhr	2.00
			$16.40

During November, Arrow purchased 160,000 pounds of direct materials at a total cost of $304,000. The total factory wages for November were $42,000, 90% of which were for direct labor. Arrow manufactured 19,000 Hunters' Bows during November using 142,500 pounds of direct materials and 5,000 direct labor hours.

Required:
a. What was the direct materials purchase price variance for November?
b. What was the direct materials usage variance for November?
c. What was the direct labor rate variance for November?
d. What was the direct labor efficiency variance for November?

[CMA adapted]

8.43 *Direct labor variances (including mix and yield).* Landeau Manufacturing Company has a process cost accounting system. A monthly analysis compares actual results with both a monthly plan and a flexible budget. Standard direct labor rates used in the flexible budget are established at the time the annual plan is formulated and held constant for the entire year. Standard direct labor rates in effect for the fiscal year ending June 30 and standard hours allowed for the output in April are:

	STANDARD DL RATE PER HOUR	STANDARD DLhr ALLOWED FOR OUTPUT
Labor class III	$8.00	500
Labor class II	$7.00	500
Labor class I	$5.00	500

The wage rates for each labor class increased on January 1 under the terms of a new union contract negotiated in December of the previous fiscal year. The standard wage rates were not revised to reflect the new contract. The actual direct labor hours worked and the actual direct labor rates per hour experienced for the month of April were:

	ACTUAL DIRECT LABOR RATE PER HOUR	ACTUAL DIRECT LABOR HOURS
Labor class III	$8.50	550
Labor class II	$7.50	650
Labor class I	$5.40	375

Required:
a. What is the total direct labor variance?
b. What is the direct labor rate variance?
c. What is the direct labor efficiency variance?
d. What is the direct labor yield variance? (Round all standard prices to four decimal places.)
e. What is the direct labor mix variance for April?

[CMA adapted]

8.44 *Applied overhead and overhead usage variances.* Union Company uses a standard cost accounting system. The following overhead costs and production data are available for August:

Standard fixed overhead rate per DLhr	$1
Standard variable overhead rate per DLhr	$4
Budgeted monthly DLhr	40,000
Actual DLhr worked	39,500
Standard DLhr allowed for actual production	39,000
Overall production overhead variance, favorable	$2,000

Required:
a. What should be the amount of applied overhead for August?
b. Calculate the VOH efficiency variance.
c. Calculate the FOH volume variance.

[AICPA adapted]

8.45 *Spending variance using the three-way variance analysis method.* The following information is available from the Tyro Company:

Actual overhead costs incurred	$15,000
Actual fixed overhead costs incurred	$7,200
Budgeted fixed overhead costs	$7,000
Actual hours worked	3,500
Standard hours allowed	3,800
Variable overhead rate per DLhr	$2.50

Required:
Assuming that Tyro uses a three-way variance analysis method, what is the spending variance?

[AICPA adapted]

8.46 *Fixed overhead production volume variance using the two-way variance analysis method.* Information on Ripley Company's overhead costs for the January production activity is as follows:

Budgeted fixed overhead	$75,000
Standard fixed overhead rate per DLhr	$3
Standard variable overhead rate per DLhr	$6
Standard DLhr allowed for actual production	24,000
Actual total production overhead incurred	$220,000

Required:
Using the two-way variance analysis method, calculate the FOH production volume variance for January. Will the three-way variance analysis method produce the same FOH production volume variance? Explain.

[AICPA adapted]

8.47 *Flexible budget controllable variance.* Universal Company uses a standard cost system and has prepared the following budget at normal capacity for the month of January:

Direct labor hours	24,000
Variable factory overhead	$48,000
Fixed factory overhead	$108,000
Total factory overhead per DLhr	$6.50

Actual data for January were as follows:

Direct labor hours worked	22,000
Total factory overhead	$147,000
Standard DLhr allowed for capacity attained	21,000

Required:
Using the two-way variance analysis method, calculate the flexible budget controllable variance for January.

[CMA adapted]

8.48 *VOH and FOH variances and journal entries.* Based on a monthly normal volume of 50,000 units (100,000 direct labor hours), Raff Company's standard cost system contains the following overhead costs for department A:

Variable	$6 per unit
Fixed	8 per unit

The following information pertains to the month of March:

Units actually produced	38,000
Actual DLhr worked	80,000

Actual overhead incurred:

Variable	$250,000
Fixed	384,000

Required:
a. Calculate the VOH spending variance for March.
b. What is the VOH efficiency variance?
c. Determine the FOH budget variance.
d. Calculate the FOH volume variance for March.
e. Prepare the journal entries to record VOH and FOH.

[AICPA adapted]

8.49 *Four production overhead variances and journal entries.* Derf Company applies overhead on the basis of direct labor hours in department B. Two direct labor hours are required for each product unit. Planned production for the period was set at 9,000 units. Manufacturing overhead was budgeted at $135,000 for the period; 20% of this cost is fixed. The 17,200 hours worked during the period resulted in production of 8,500 units. Variable manufacturing overhead costs incurred were $108,500, and fixed manufacturing overhead costs were $28,000. Derf Company uses a four-variance method for analyzing manufacturing overhead.

Required:
a. Calculate the VOH spending variance for the period.
b. Calculate the VOH efficiency variance for the period.
c. Calculate the FOH spending (budget) variance for the period.
d. Calculate the FOH production volume variance for the period.
e. Prepare the journal entries to record VOH and FOH.

[CMA adapted]

8.50 *Four production overhead variances and journal entries.* Franklin Glass Works'
production budget for the year ended November 30, 19X4, in department C was
based on 200,000 units. Each unit requires two standard hours of labor for completion. Total overhead was budgeted at $900,000 for the year, and the fixed overhead
rate was estimated to be $3 per unit. Both fixed and variable overhead are applied
to the product on the basis of direct labor hours. The actual data for the year
ended November 30, 19X4, are as follows:

Actual production in units	198,000	Actual variable overhead	$352,000
Actual direct labor hours	440,000	Actual fixed overhead	$575,000

Required:
a. What were the standard hours allowed for actual production for the year ended
   November 30, 19X4?
b. What was the VOH efficiency variance for the year?
c. What was the VOH spending variance for the year?
d. What was the FOH spending variance for the year?
e. What was the FOH applied to Franklin's production for the year?
f. What was the FOH production volume variance for the year?
g. Prepare the VOH and FOH journal entries.

[CMA adapted]

8.51 *Multiple direct materials, mix and yield variances.* Energy Modification Company
produces a gasoline additive, Gas Gain. This product increases engine efficiency
and improves gasoline mileage by creating a more complete burn in the combus-
tion process. Careful controls are required during the production process to ensure
that the proper mix of input chemicals is achieved and that evaporation is controlled. Loss of output and efficiency may result if the controls are not effective.
The standard cost of producing a 500-liter batch of Gas Gain is $135. The standard
materials mix and related standard cost of each chemical used in a 500-liter batch
are as follows:

CHEMICAL	STANDARD INPUT QUANTITY (LITERS)	STANDARD PRICE PER LITER	TOTAL COST
Echol	200	$.200	$ 40.00
Protex	100	.425	42.50
Benz	250	.150	37.50
CT-40	50	.300	15.00
Totals	600		$135.00

The quantities of chemicals purchased and used during the current production
period are shown in the schedule below. A total of 140 batches of Gas Gain were
manufactured during the current production period. Silly Willy, the controller of
Energy Modification Company, determines its costs and chemical usage variations
at the end of each production period.

CHEMICAL	QUANTITY PURCHASED (LITERS)	TOTAL PURCHASE PRICE	QUANTITY USED (LITERS)
Echol	25,000	$ 5,365	26,600
Protex	13,000	6,240	12,880
Benz	40,000	5,840	37,800
CT-40	7,500	2,220	7,140
Totals	85,500	$19,665	84,420

Required:
a. What is the direct materials purchase price variance for Echol?
b. What is the direct materials purchase price variance for Protex?
c. What is the direct materials purchase price variance for Benz?
d. What is the direct materials purchase price variance for CT-40?
e. What is the direct materials usage variance for Echol?
f. What is the direct materials usage variance for Protex?
g. What is the direct materials usage variance for Benz?
h. What is the direct materials usage variance for CT-40?
i. What is the direct materials mix variance?
j. What is the direct materials yield variance?

[CMA adapted]

8.52 *Comprehensive direct labor variance analysis.* Mountain View Hospital has adopted a standard cost accounting system for evaluation and control of nursing labor. Diagnosis Related Groups (DRGs), instituted by the U.S. government for health insurance reimbursement, are used as the output measure in the standard cost system. A DRG is a patient classification scheme that treats hospitals as multiproduct firms; inpatient treatment procedures are related to the numbers and types of patient ailments treated. Mountain View Hospital has developed standard nursing times for the treatment of each DRG classification, and nursing labor hours are assumed to vary with the number of DRGs treated within a time period.

The nursing unit on the fourth floor treats patients with four DRG classifications. The unit is staffed with registered nurses (RNs), licensed practical nurses (LPNs), and aides. The standard nursing hours and salary rates for the nursing unit are as follows:

STANDARD HOURS

DRG CLASSIFICATION	RN	LPN	AIDE
1	6	4	5
2	26	16	10
3	10	5	4
4	12	7	10

STANDARD HOURLY RATES	
RN	$12.00
LPN	8.00
Aide	6.00

The results of operations for the fourth-floor nursing unit for the month of May 19X4, are presented below:

ACTUAL NUMBER OF PATIENTS	
DRG 1	250
DRG 2	90
DRG 3	240
DRG 4	140
	720

	RN	LPN	AIDE
Actual hours	8,150	4,300	4,400
Actual salary	$100,245	$35,260	$25,300
Actual hourly rate	$12.30	$8.20	$5.75

The time accountant for Mountain View Hospital calculated the following standard times for the fourth-floor nursing unit for May 19X4:

DRG CLASSIFICATION	NUMBER OF PATIENTS	STANDARD HOURS/DRG			TOTAL STANDARD HOURS		
		RN	LPN	AIDE	RN	LPN	AIDE
1	250	6	4	5	1,500	1,000	1,250
2	90	26	16	10	2,340	1,440	900
3	240	10	5	4	2,400	1,200	960
4	140	12	7	10	1,680	980	1,400
					7,920	4,620	4,510

Since the hospital does not have data to calculate variances by DRG, it calculates labor variances, using a flexible budgeting approach, for each reporting period by labor classification (RN, LPN, aide). Labor mix and labor yield variances are also calculated since one labor input can be substituted for another labor input. The variances are used by nursing supervisors and hospital administration to evaluate the performance of nursing labor.

Required:
a. Calculate the total flexible budget variance for the fourth-floor nursing unit of Mountain View Hospital for May 19X4, indicating how much of this variance is attributed to:
   1. Labor efficiency.
   2. Rate differences.
b. 1. Calculate the labor mix variance for the fourth-floor nursing unit of Mountain View Hospital. (Use whole hours and whole cents in all calculations.)
   2. Explain the significance of the labor mix variance calculated in Requirement (b)1.
c. 1. Calculate the labor yield variance for the fourth-floor nursing unit of Mountain View Hospital. (Use whole hours and whole cents in all calculations.)
   2. Interpret the meaning of the labor yield variance calculated in Requirement (c)1.

[CMA adapted]

8.53 *Comprehensive direct materials and labor variances analysis.* Dash Company adopted a standard cost system several years ago. The standard costs for the prime costs of its single product are as follows:

Direct materials (8 kilograms × $5.00/kg) $40.00
Direct labor (6 hours × $8.20/hr) $49.20

The operating data for November are:

- In-process beginning inventory: None.
- In-process ending inventory: 800 units, 75% complete as to labor; material is issued at the beginning of processing.
- Units completed: 5,600 units.
- Budgeted output: 6,000 units.
- Purchases of materials: 50,000 kilograms.
- Total actual direct labor costs: $300,760.
- Actual hours of labor: 36,500 hours.
- Direct materials usage variance: $1,500 unfavorable.
- Total direct materials variance: $750 unfavorable.

Required:
a. Calculate the direct labor efficiency variance for November.
b. Calculate the direct labor rate variance for November.
c. Calculate the actual kilograms of direct materials used in production during November.

d. Calculate the actual price paid per kilogram of direct materials during November.

e. Calculate the total amounts of direct materials and labor costs transferred to the finished goods account for November.

f. Calculate the total amount of direct materials and labor costs in the ending balance of WIP inventory at the end of November.

[CMA adapted]

8.54 Direct materials, labor, and overhead variances. Eastern Company manufactures special electrical equipment and parts. Eastern employs a standard cost accounting system with separate standards established for each product.

A special transformer is manufactured in the Transformer Department. Production volume is measured by direct labor hours in this department, and a flexible budget system is used to plan and control department overhead.

Standard costs for the special transformer are determined annually in September for the coming year. The standard cost of a transformer for the year was computed at $67 as follows:

Direct materials

Iron	5 sheets × $2	$10
Copper	3 spools × $3	9
Direct labor	4 hours × $7	28
Variable overhead	4 hours × $3	12
Fixed overhead	4 hours × $2	8
Total		$67

Overhead rates were based upon normal and expected monthly capacity for the year, both of which were 4,000 direct labor hours. Practical capacity for this department is 5,000 direct labor hours per month. Variable overhead costs are expected to vary with the number of direct labor hours actually used.

During October, 800 transformers were produced. This was below expectations because a work stoppage occurred during contract negotiations with the labor force. Once the contract was settled, the department scheduled overtime in an attempt to catch up to expected production levels.

The following costs were incurred in October:

DIRECT MATERIALS	DIRECT MATERIALS PURCHASED	DIRECT MATERIALS USED
Iron	5,000 sheets @ $2.00/sheet	3,900 sheets
Copper	2,200 spools @ $3.10/spool	2,600 spools

Direct labor:
   Regular time: 2,000 hours @ $7.00
                        1,400 hours @ $7.20

   Overtime: 600 of the 1,400 hours were subject to overtime premium. The total overtime premium of $2,160 is included in variable overhead in accordance with company accounting practices.

   Variable overhead: $10,000
   Fixed overhead: $ 8,800

Required:

a. When is the most appropriate time to record any variance of actual direct materials price from standard? Explain your answer.

b. Calculate the direct labor rate variance.

c. Calculate the total direct materials usage variance.

d. Calculate the VOH spending variance.

e. What are the number of hours used to calculate the VOH efficiency variance?

f. Calculate the FOH spending variance.

g. Calculate the FOH production volume variance.

[CMA adapted]

8.55 Comprehensive problem for direct materials, labor, and overhead variances. Gelltite Corporation manufactures a basic line of draperies with the following standard costs:

Direct materials (20 yards × $1.35 per yard) $27
Direct labor (4 hours × $9.00 per hour)   36
Factory overhead (applied at ⅚ of direct labor.
   Ratio of variable costs to fixed costs: 2 to 1)   30
Total standard cost per unit of output $93

Standards are based on normal monthly production involving 2,400 direct labor hours (600 units of output).

The following information pertains to the month of July:

Direct materials purchased (18,000 yards × $1.38 per yard) $24,840
Direct materials used   9,500 yards
Direct labor (2,100 hours × $9.15 per hour) $19,215
Actual factory overhead $16,650

500 units of the product were actually produced in July.

Required:
a. Calculate the predetermined VOH rate per direct labor hour.
b. Calculate the budgeted FOH costs based on normal activity.
c. Calculate the direct materials price variance (isolated at time of purchase).
d. Calculate the direct materials usage variance for July.
e. Calculate the direct labor rate variance for July.
f. Calculate the direct labor efficiency variance for July.
g. Calculate the total budgeted overhead costs.
h. Calculate the total applied factory overhead costs.
i. Calculate the FOH production volume variance.

[AICPA adapted]

8.56 *Comprehensive flexible budgeting and variance analysis.* Cain Company has an automated production process, and consequently, machine hours are used to describe production activity. A full absorption costing system is employed by the company. The annual profit plan for the coming fiscal year is finalized in April of each year. The profit plan for the fiscal year ending May 31 called for 6,000 units to be produced, requiring 30,000 machine hours. The full absorption costing rate for the fiscal year was determined using 6,000 units of planned production.

Cain develops flexible budgets for different levels of activity for use in evaluating performance. A total of 6,200 units was actually produced during the fiscal year requiring 32,000 machine hours. The schedule presented below (in both columns) compares Cain Company's actual costs for the fiscal year with the profit plan and the budgeted costs for two different activity levels. Cain uses the three-way variance analysis method. The report below is in thousands of dollars.

| | | FLEXIBLE BUDGETS FOR | | |
ITEM	PROFIT PLAN (6,000 UNITS)	31,000 Mhr	32,000 Mhr	ACTUAL COSTS
Direct material				
G27 aluminum	$ 252.0	$ 260.4	$ 268.8	$ 270.0
M14 steel alloy	78.0	80.6	83.2	83.0
Direct labor				
Assembler	273.0	282.1	291.2	287.0
Grinder	234.0	241.8	249.6	250.0
Manufacturing overhead				
Maintenance	24.0	24.8	25.6	25.0
Supplies	129.0	133.3	137.6	130.0
Supervision	80.0	82.0	84.0	81.0
Inspector	144.0	147.0	150.0	147.0
Insurance	50.0	50.0	50.0	50.0
Depreciation	200.0	200.0	200.0	200.0
Total cost	$1,464.0	$1,502.0	$1,540.0	$1,523.0

Required:
a. Calculate the actual cost of direct materials used in one unit of product.
b. Calculate the cost of direct materials that should be processed per machine hour.
c. Calculate the budgeted direct labor cost for each unit produced.
d. Calculate the variable manufacturing overhead rate per machine hour in a flexible budget formula.
e. Calculate the FOH production volume variance for the year.
f. Calculate the overhead spending variance for the year.
g. Calculate the VOH efficiency variance for the year.
h. How much overhead was applied to finished goods?
i. What is the total overhead variance?
j. Using the flexible budget formula, calculate the total budgeted manufacturing costs (in thousands of dollars) for an output of 6,050 units.

[CMA adapted]

| THINK-TANK PROBLEMS

Although these problems are based on chapter material, reading extra material, reviewing previous chapters, and using creativity may be required to develop workable solutions.

8.57 *Allocation of variances.* Tolbert Manufacturing Company uses a standard cost system in accounting for the cost of production of its only product, product A. The standards for the production of one unit of product A are as follows:

■ Direct materials: 10 feet of item 1 at $0.75 per foot and 3 feet of item 2 at $1 per foot.
■ Direct labor: 4 hours at $3.50 per hour.
■ Manufacturing overhead: Applied at 150% of standard direct labor costs.

There was no inventory on hand at the beginning of the year. Material price variances are isolated at purchase. Following is a summary of costs and related data for the production of product A during the year:

■ 100,000 feet of item 1 were purchased at $0.78 per foot.
■ 30,000 feet of item 2 were purchased at $0.90 per foot.
■ 8,000 units of product A were produced, which required 78,000 feet of item 1; 26,000 feet of item 2; and 31,000 hours of direct labor at $3.60 per hour.
■ 6,000 units of product A were sold.

Required:
a. What should be the total debits to the materials inventory account for the purchase of item 1?
b. What should be the total debits to the WIP inventory account for direct labor?
c. What is the balance in the direct materials usage variance account for item 2?
d. If all standard variances are allocated to cost of goods sold and inventory accounts, what is the amount of direct materials usage variance for item 2 to be allocated to the materials inventory account?
e. If all standard variances are allocated to cost of goods sold and inventory accounts, what would be the amount of direct materials price variance of item 1 to be allocated to the materials inventory account?

[AICPA adapted]

8.58 *Comprehensive analysis of variances.* Allglow Company is a cosmetics manufacturer specializing in stage makeup. The company's best-selling product is Skin-Klear, a protective cream used under the stage makeup to protect the skin from frequent makeup use. SkinKlear is packaged in three sizes—8 ounces, one pound, and three pounds—and regularly sells for $21 per pound. The standard cost per pound of SkinKlear, based on Allglow's normal monthly production of 8,000 pounds, is as follows:

COST ITEM	QUANTITY	STANDARD COST	TOTAL COST
Direct materials			
Cream base	9.0 oz.	$ .05/oz.	$0.45
Moisturizer	6.5 oz.	.10/oz.	0.65
Fragrance	.5 oz.	1.00/oz.	0.50
			$ 1.60
Direct labor*			
Mixing	.5 hr	$4.00/hr	$2.00
Compounding	1.0 hr	5.00/hr	5.00
			7.00
Variable overhead**	1.5 hr	$2.10/hr	3.15
Total standard cost per pound			$11.75

* Direct labor dollars include employee benefits.
** Applied on the basis of direct labor hours.

Based on these standard costs, Allglow prepares monthly budgets. Following are the budgeted performance and the actual performance for May 19X6, when the company produced and sold 9,000 pounds of SkinKlear:

CONTRIBUTION REPORT FOR SKINKLEAR
FOR THE MONTH OF MAY 19X6

	BUDGET	ACTUAL	VARIANCE
Units	8,000	9,000	1,000F
Revenue	$168,000	$180,000	$12,000F
Direct material	12,800	16,200	3,400U
Direct labor	56,000	62,500	6,500U
Variable overhead	25,200	30,900	5,700U
Total variable costs	$ 94,000	$109,600	$15,600U
Contribution margin	$ 74,000	$ 70,400	$ 3,600U

Barbara Simmons, Allglow's president, was not pleased with these results; despite a sizable increase in the sales of SkinKlear, the product's contribution to the overall profitability of the firm decreased. Simmons has asked Allglow's cost accountant, Brian Jackson, to prepare a report that identifies the reasons why the contribution margin for SkinKlear has decreased. Jackson has gathered the following information to help in the preparation of the report:

MAY 19X6 USAGE REPORT FOR SKINKLEAR

COST ITEM	QUANTITY	ACTUAL COST
Direct materials		
Cream base	84,000 oz.	$ 4,200
Moisturizer	60,000 oz.	7,200
Fragrance	4,800 oz.	4,800
Direct labor		
Mixing	4,500 hr	18,000
Compounding—manual	5,300 hr	26,500
Compounding—mechanized	2,700 hr	13,500
Compounding—idle	900 hr	4,500
Variable overhead		30,900
Total variable cost		$109,600

While doing his research, Jackson discovered that the Manufacturing Department had mechanized one of the manual operations in the compounding process on an experimental basis. The mechanized operation replaced manual operations that represented 40% of the compounding process.

The workers' inexperience with the mechanized operation caused increased usage of both the cream base and the moisturizer; however, Jackson believed these inefficiencies would be negligible if mechanization became a permanent part of the process and the workers' skills were improved. The idle time in compounding was traceable to the fact that fewer workers were required for the mechanized process. During this experimental period, the idle time was charged to direct labor rather than overhead. The excess workers could either be reassigned or laid off in the future. Jackson also was able to determine that all of the variable manufacturing overhead costs over standard could be traced directly to the mechanization process.

Required:

a. Prepare an explanation of the cost variances included in the $3,600 unfavorable variance between the budgeted and actual contribution margin for SkinKlear during May 19X6 by calculating the following variances:
   1. Material price variance.
   2. Material quantity variance.
   3. Labor efficiency variance.
   4. Variable overhead efficiency variance.
   5. Variable overhead spending variance.
b. Allglow Company must decide whether to continue the mechanization of the compounding operation in the SkinKlear manufacturing process that was mechanized on an experimental basis. Calculate the variable cost savings that can be expected to arise in the future from the mechanization. Explain your answer.

[CMA adapted]

8.59 *Motivational aspects and benefits of a standard cost system.* Terry Travers is the manufacturing supervisor of the Aurora Manufacturing Company, which produces a variety of plastic products. Some of these products are standard items that are listed in the company's catalog, while others are made to customer specifications. Each month, Travers receives a performance report displaying the budget for the month, the actual activity for the period, and the variance between budget and actual. Part of Travers's annual performance evaluation is based on her department's performance against budget. Aurora's purchasing manager, Bob Christensen, also receives monthly performance reports and is evaluated in part on the basis of these reports.

Last month's reports have just been distributed on the 21st of this month, when Travers met Christensen in the hallway outside their offices. Scowling, Travers began the conversation, "I see we have another set of monthly performance reports hand-delivered by that not very nice junior employee in the budget office. He seemed pleased to tell me that I was in trouble with my performance again."

Christensen: "I got the same treatment. All I ever hear about are the things I haven't done right. Now, I'll have to spend a lot of time reviewing the report and preparing explanations. The worst part is that the information is almost a month old, and we spend all this time on history."

Travers: "My biggest gripe is that our production activity varies a lot from month to month, but we're given an annual budget that's written in stone. Last month, we were shut down for three days when a strike delayed delivery of the basic ingredient used in our plastic formulation, and we had already exhausted our inventory. You know about that, of course, since we asked you to call all over the country to find an alternate source of supply. When we got what we needed on a rush basis, we had to pay more than we normally do."

Christensen: "I expect problems like that to pop up from time to time—that's part of my job—but now we'll both have to take a careful look at the report to see where charges are reflected for that rush order. Every month, I spend more time making sure I should be charged for each item reported than I do making plans for my department's daily work. It's really frustrating to see charges for things I have no control over."

Travers: "The way we get information doesn't help either. I don't get copies of the reports you get, yet a lot of what I do is affected by your department and by most of the other departments we have. Why do the budget and accounting people assume that I should only be told about my operations even though the president regularly gives us pep talks about how we all need to work together as a team?"

Christensen: "I seem to get more reports than I need, and I am never asked to comment until top management calls me on the carpet about my department's shortcomings. Do you ever hear comments when your department shines?"

Travers: "I guess they don't have time to review the good news. One of my problems is that all the reports are in dollars and cents. I work with people, machines, and materials. I need information to help me this month solve this month's problems—not another report of the dollars expended last month or the month before."

Required:

a. Based upon the conversation between Terry Travers and Bob Christensen, describe the likely motivation and behavior of these two employees resulting from Aurora Manufacturing Company's variance reporting system.

b. Both employees and companies should benefit from properly implemented variance reporting systems.

   1. Describe the benefits that can be realized from using a variance reporting system.

   2. Based on the situation presented above, recommend ways for Aurora Manufacturing Company to improve its variance reporting system so as to increase employee motivation.

[CMA adapted]

8.60 *Developing standard costs and explaining the causes of variances.* ColdKing Company is a small producer of fruit-flavored frozen desserts. For many years, ColdKing's products have had strong regional sales on the basis of brand recognition. However, other companies have begun marketing similar products in the area, and price competition has become increasingly important. John Wakefield, the company's management accountant, is planning to implement a standard cost system for ColdKing and has gathered considerable information from his co-workers on production and material requirements for ColdKing's products. Wakefield believes that the use of standard costing will allow ColdKing to improve cost control and make better pricing decisions.

ColdKing's most popular product is raspberry sherbet. The sherbet is produced in ten-gallon batches, and each batch requires six quarts of good raspberries. The fresh raspberries are sorted by hand before entering the production process. Because of imperfections in the raspberries and normal spoilage, one quart of berries is discarded for every four quarts of acceptable berries. Three minutes is the standard direct labor time for the sorting required to obtain one quart of acceptable raspberries. The acceptable raspberries are then blended with the other ingredients; blending requires 12 minutes of direct labor time per batch. After blending, the sherbet is packaged in quart containers. Wakefield has gathered the following pricing information:

■ ColdKing purchases raspberries at a cost of $.80 per quart. All other ingredients cost a total of $.45 per gallon.

■ Direct labor is paid at the rate of $9.00 per hour.

■ The total cost of direct materials and direct labor required to package the sherbet is $.38 per quart.

Required:

a. Develop the standard cost for the direct cost components of a ten-gallon batch of raspberry sherbet. The standard cost should identify the:

   1. Standard quantity.

   2. Standard rate.

   3. Standard cost per batch for each direct cost component of a batch of raspberry sherbet.

b. As part of the implementation of a standard cost system at ColdKing, John Wakefield plans to train those responsible for maintaining the standards in the use of variance analysis. Wakefield is particularly concerned with the causes of unfavorable variances.

   1. Discuss the possible causes of unfavorable direct materials price variances,

and identify the individual(s) who should be held responsible for these variances.

2. Discuss the possible causes of unfavorable direct labor efficiency variances, and identify the individual(s) who should be held responsible for these variances.

[CMA adapted]

8.61 *Ethical considerations in SCAS design.* Chapter 1 identified four ethical standards for management accountants. What are the implications of each standard in designing a high-quality SCAS?

8.62 *Accounting for loss.* Review the procedures involved in accounting for scrap, rework, and spoilage presented in Chapters 5, 6, and 7. Given the goal of designing a high-quality SCAS, create a policy to account for all three types of loss. Demonstrate how this policy works through an illustration of the journal entries in a PCAS and JOCAS.

8.63 *High-quality information and SCAS design.* Consider each characteristic of high-quality information presented in Chapter 1. What implications does each have in the design of a high-quality SCAS for use in either a process or job order situation?

8.64 *SCAS for JIT.* Design the WIP general ledger system for a JIT SCAS. The cost accounting system should be a high-quality system. Consider whether cost variance information is really needed. If so, how should the cost variances be calculated and reported? If you do not think cost variances information is needed, then what information should be provided by the SCAS, to whom, and how?

8.65 *Backflush systems and production activity–based SCASs.* In the chapter it was argued that these two types of SCASs represent opposite ends on a continuum of SCAS design sophistication. Do you agree? Why? Discuss the benefits and limitations of each type of SCAS.

8.66 *Cost variances, journal entries, and reports.* Another product Armando Corporation makes is a turntable (Armando Corporation was introduced in Demonstration Problems 1 and 2). The turntable also is made in its own department. As with CD Players, there are no beginning or ending WIP inventories. The department has two overhead accounts (variable and fixed) and direct labor hours is the cost driver for both. Armando uses a standard cost system with monthly cost variance reports issued for this department.

The turntable's standard absorptive manufacturing cost (SAMC) is $44. Fixed overhead in the department is budgeted at $120,000 per month. Following are the data for standard costs and actual activity during May:

DATA SECTION: STANDARD COSTS

Manufacturing Inputs	Price	Output Quantity	Loss%
Direct Materials	$3.00	3.80	5.00%
Direct Labor	$9.00	1.80 DLhr	10.00%
Variable Overhead	$2.00 per DLhr		
Fixed Overhead	$5.00 per DLhr		
Normal Production Volume (in units)			

DATA SECTION: ACTUAL COSTS FOR MAY

Direct Materials	Actual DM Price	$2.98	DM Purchased	50,000
Direct Labor	Actual DL Rate	$9.36	DM Used	41,500
Variable Overhead	Actual VOH Cost	$41,000	Actual Hours	21,000
Fixed Overhead	Actual FOH Cost	$117,000	Actual Output	10,000

Required:
a. Calculate the cost variances for direct materials, direct labor, VOH and FOH, and the total monthly cost variance for the department.
b. Journalize the cost variances and completed production transferred to FGI.

c. Prepare a report that presents the cost variances in total, per unit, and as a percentage of standard.

8.67 *SCAS spreadsheet reports.* Refer to the previous problem. Create a spreadsheet program that reports monthly cost variances. It should report each cost variance per unit, in total, and as a percentage. The report should also include both Data Sections and the Standard Cost Card. Use the format from Exhibits 8–11 and 8–12.

8.68 *Cost variances, journal entries, and reports.* Logan Boris Company is a subsidiary of Ben Logan Golf Club Corporation. Logan Boris makes metal woods and different types of irons, each in separate departments. The company maintains two overhead accounts (variable and fixed), and direct labor hours is the cost driver for both. All subsidiaries of Ben Logan use a standard cost system with annual cost variance reports issued to corporate headquarters for each subsidiary company.

The standard absorptive manufacturing cost for a metal wood is $32 (the Data Section for the standard cost card is shown below). Last year, Logan Boris had a production quota of 10,000 metal woods, but produced 11,000.

The actual costs for last year were:

Utilities: $500 for the sales office, $11,000 for the factory ($4,000 was considered a fixed cost).

Insurance: $500 for the office, $2,000 for the factory.

Depreciation: Factory = $10,000 (straight-line basis), office = $900.

Salaries: Sales office = $50,000, factory supervision = $25,000.

Advertising: $100,000.

Finished clubs delivery expense: $10,000.

Direct materials purchased: 50,000 pounds at $1.90/lb.

Gross wages: Direct labor = $193,200 (23,000 DLhr worked), $35,000 indirect.

Materials used: Direct materials = 35,000 lb., factory supplies = $20,000, office supplies = $1,000.

DATA SECTION: STANDARD COSTS

Manufacturing Inputs	Price	Output Quantity	Loss%
Direct Materials	$2.00	2.50 lb.	16.67%
Direct Labor	$8.00	1.60 DLhr	20.00%
Variable Overhead	$3.00 per DLhr		
Fixed Overhead	$2.00 per DLhr		
Normal Production Volume (in units)		10,000	

Required:
a. Calculate the cost variances for direct materials, direct labor, VOH and FOH, and the total annual cost variance for the department.
b. Journalize the cost variances and completed production transferred to FGI.
c. Prepare a report that presents the cost variances in total, per unit, and as a percentage of standard. To avoid rounding errors, input one-sixth as the normal input loss percentage (instead of 16.67%) shown in the Data Section.

8.69 *SCAS spreadsheet reports.* Refer to the previous problem. Create a spreadsheet program that reports annual cost variances. It should report each cost variance per unit, in total, and as a percentage. The report should also include both Data Sections and the Standard Cost Card. Use the format from Exhibits 8–11 and 8–12.

9

THE NEED FOR MULTIPLE OVERHEAD ACCOUNTS

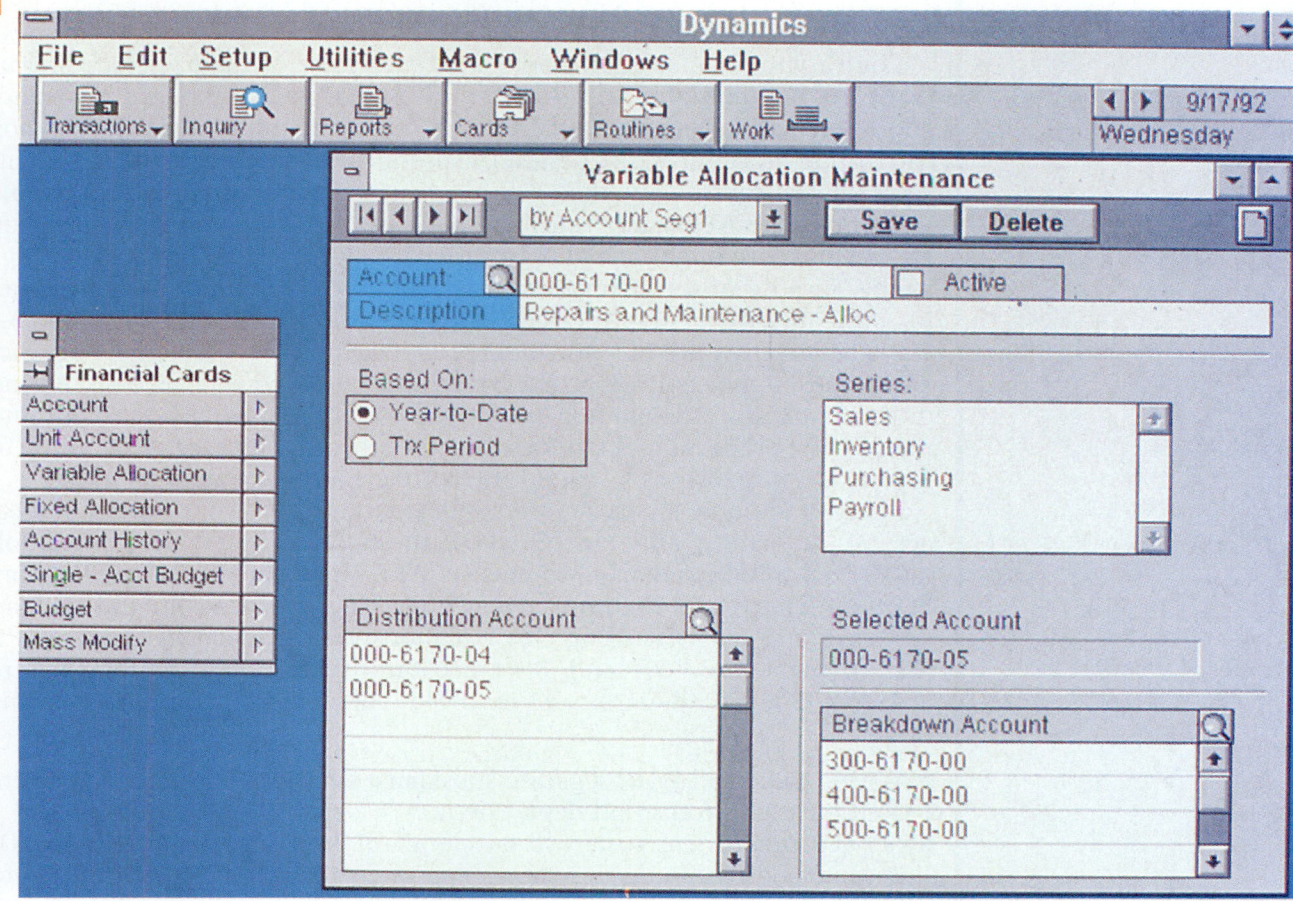

Computer systems are used to allocate overhead. Courtesy of Great Plains Software.

LEARNING OBJECTIVES

After studying this chapter, you should be able to:

1. Discuss the need for multiple overhead accounts within WIP.

2. Describe how the general ledger system for WIP can be designed to provide more accurate product cost information and cost management information.

3. Explain how to allocate service department costs to production departments, and describe the different methods that can be used.

4. Design an SCAS that includes cost variances for both production and service departments.

■ INTRODUCTION

As Chapter 4 pointed out, all CASs satisfy one overall goal, to determine the cost of products or services. The cost of a product or service is used for many purposes:

- Evaluate how well the organization is doing relative to its budget
- Facilitate continuous improvement
- Derive the value of inventory and cost of goods manufactured and sold for financial reporting
- Value inventory for taxation
- Price products or bid on contracts for various jobs
- Determine product or job profitability
- Decide whether to make or buy certain components

Contrary to popular belief, there is no such thing as the one "true product cost." All product and service costs are based on assumptions, estimates, allocations, and averages. It is up to the management accountant to choose the costing procedures that best fit the production system and management's need for cost control, and then aim for costs that are approximately accurate. Remember the "relevancy" attribute of high-quality information from Chapter 1: "It's more important to be approximately right than precisely wrong."

The purpose of this chapter is to provide the theory and tools necessary for designing more sophisticated CASs to account for overhead. If all costs could be directly traced to individual products, the "true cost" of the products would be known and objectively measurable. However, all costs are not directly traceable. As manufacturers become more capital intensive (automated), the proportion of indirect costs (overhead) increases. Accounting for overhead is the albatross around the management accountant's neck.

Many traditional manufacturers still maintain only one total overhead account and one plantwide TOH POR to apply all the overhead into jobs (JOCAS) or production departments (PCAS). The need for separate VOH and FOH subsidiary WIP accounts when budgeting overhead for the standard cost card and manufacturing cost equation was discussed in Chapter 7. In this chapter, the VOH and FOH accounts within WIP become control accounts. The CAS design issues involved will be identified in the following order:

- Within VOH and FOH, separate subsidiary overhead accounts will be created for each production department.
- Service department costs will be identified, and separate VOH and FOH accounts created for each service department. **Service departments** provide services to production departments.[1] Because their costs are not directly traceable to products, they are part of the plant's total overhead.
- For service department costs to be included in the cost (and the sales price) of products, they have to be allocated to the production departments' VOH and FOH accounts. This means that two sets of overhead allocations have to be made. First, service department costs are allocated into the overhead accounts of production departments. Second, the production departments' overhead, which now includes the service department costs, is allocated (applied) to the products. This is illustrated in Exhibit 9–1.[2]
- Different methods for making the first set of allocations (service department-to-production overhead accounts) will be examined.
- Finally, cost variances are designed into the CAS for better cost management information. ▬

[1] Service departments have a staff, rather than a line, responsibility.
[2] Notice in the exhibit that the term *allocated* is used for the assignment of service department costs to production departments. But, the term *applied* is used to describe the assignment of production department overhead costs to the final cost objects; that is, the products manufactured or services performed by the organization.

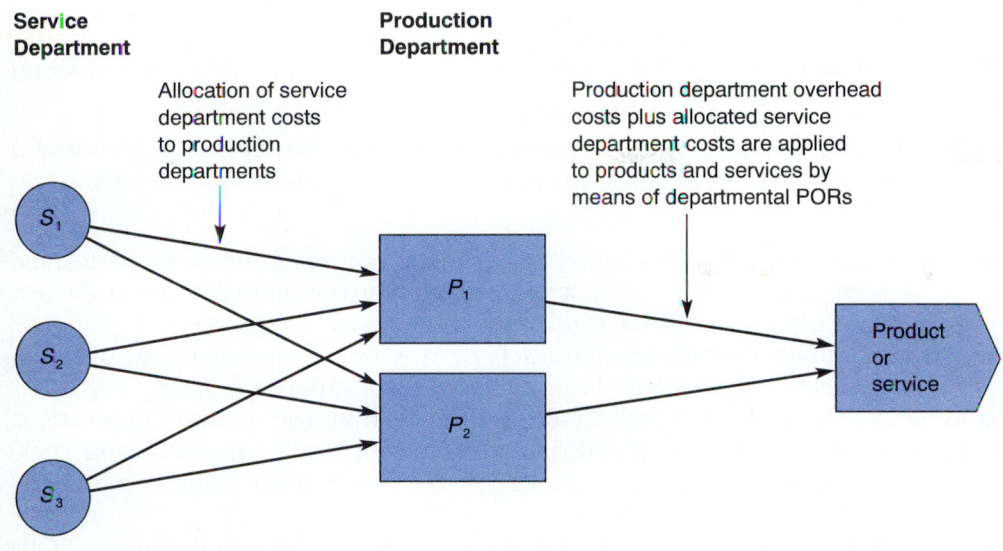

Service Department

Production Department

Allocation of service department costs to production departments

S_1 S_2 S_3

P_1 P_2

Production department overhead costs plus allocated service department costs are applied to products and services by means of departmental PORs

Product or service

■■■ ■ EXHIBIT 9–1
Overhead Cost Allocations with Service Departments

PLANTWIDE VERSUS MULTIPLE PREDETERMINED OVERHEAD RATES

The management accountant can develop a single plantwide TOH POR. Or, instead of using one plantwide blanket rate, the TOH POR may be subdivided into two or more component PORs. The following examples demonstrate both situations.

LEARNING OBJECTIVE 1

Discuss the need for multiple overhead accounts within WIP.

Plantwide Total Predetermined Overhead Rate

Assume that Cerro Company makes only one product and uses one TOH POR for the entire plant's overhead, rather than separate rates for VOH and FOH costs. Cerro estimates 100,000 machine hours as the level of activity, $340,000 VOH costs, and $400,000 FOH costs. The single plantwide TOH POR for Cerro is calculated as follows:

Total estimated VOH costs	$340,000
Total estimated FOH costs	400,000
Estimated TOH costs	$740,000
Divided by estimated level of activity in machine hours	÷100,000 Mhr
Single plantwide TOH POR per machine hour	$7.40

For each machine hour used during the period on a job (JOCAS) or in a production department (PCAS), the TOH POR will apply $7.40 of overhead to the products in journal entry 7.

Multiple Predetermined Overhead Rates

In a simple one-product company such as Cerro's, a single plantwide TOH POR may be sufficient. In highly diversified companies, a single plantwide TOH POR may result in misinformation that leads to wrong decisions. Therefore, the goals in subdividing the TOH POR are to provide more useful cost management information and more accurate product or service costing. The TOH POR can be subdivided in a number of different ways:

- Separate rates for applying VOH and FOH
- Separate rates for each production department
- Separate rates for different machines

In complex operations, a single plantwide TOH POR may not be sufficient.

■ Separate rates for each product line or service class
■ Separate rates for applying material-related, labor-related, and machine-related overhead costs

In deciding whether to use multiple PORs, the management accountant should analyze both the operations and the kinds of products made or services performed:

■ When there are important differences in the nature of the work performed in different areas of the plant, separate PORs for these areas, such as departments, JIT cells, and/or machines, should be used.
■ When significantly different products or services use resources in different ways, separate PORs should be used for each product or service.
■ When products differ substantially in their relative use of direct materials, a more accurate allocation of materials-related overhead costs (such as purchasing, receiving, storing, and handling) may result from using a materials-related POR.
■ In special situations, similar arguments can be made for using separate PORs for applying different labor-related and machine-related overhead.

Departmental Overhead Rates

The power department provides motors to the assembly department at Saturn.

Normally, however, the best way to begin designing the overhead accounting system is to set up separate PORs for production departments. No matter how diverse the products or services, they will receive a fairer share of the overhead if separate production department PORs are used. For example, if product X flows through three departments, it will be charged its appropriate share of overhead costs within each department, assuming a proper activity application base is chosen. If product Y flows through two departments, it likewise will be charged its appropriate share of overhead costs from only these departments.

Indeed, the management accountant can use various combinations. The aim is to search for the most accurate basis for applying overhead costs to products or services. But there is a practical limit to the extent overhead rates can be subdivided. At some point, further subdivision leads to an insignificant change in product or service costs and does not provide more useful cost management information. Each company must decide on the number of overhead rates after experimenting with different methods. A balance should be struck between the need for more detailed accuracy on the one side and the time and cost of preparing and applying multiple overhead rates on the other side. The accompanying Starfire Company case on the next page illustrates the differing results from using departmental PORs versus a single plantwide overhead rate.

What is learned from the Starfire case?

■ If departmental TOH PORs are used, the applied overhead costs more closely reflect the different amounts and types of machine and labor work performed on the two products.
■ If a plantwide TOH POR based on machine hours is used, too much of the *Painting Department's overhead* is applied to car bodies and too little to truck bodies. Labor usage causes Painting Department overhead. Car bodies require only 4 hours of painting labor, while truck bodies require 14 hours. In other words, less Painting Department overhead should be included in the cost of a car body than in the cost of a truck body. But, when machine hours are used to apply overhead, the opposite situation results. Applying overhead based on machine hours results in 12 machine hours worth of overhead being applied to car bodies and only 5 machine hours worth of overhead being applied to truck bodies. Thus, more Painting Department overhead is applied to car bodies than to truck bodies.
■ An even more serious miscosting occurs when the plantwide TOH POR is based on direct labor hours. The majority of the plant's overhead is caused

INSIGHTS & APPLICATIONS

Starfire Company's Use of Departmental versus Plantwide Overhead Rates

Starfire has two production departments: Assembly and Painting. Assembly work is performed by robots, and depreciation, utilities, and maintenance make up a large part of this department's overhead costs. Painting and special detail work are performed manually by skilled workers.

Starfire makes two products: fiberglass bodies for its Starfire miniature automobile and for its customized miniature truck line. Car bodies require 12 machine hours in Assembly and 4 direct labor hours in Painting. Truck bodies require 5 machine hours in Assembly and 14 direct labor hours in Painting. Total budgeted overhead is $800,000 for the Assembly Department and $177,500 for the Painting Department. Departmental and plantwide POR calculations follow:

	ASSEMBLY DEPARTMENT	PAINTING DEPARTMENT
Estimated annual overhead	$800,000	$177,500
Estimated annual direct labor hours (DLhr)	–0–	50,000
Estimated annual machine hours (Mhr)	80,000	5,000

Departmental TOH PORs:

Assembly: $800,000 ÷ 80,000 Mhr = $10.00 per Mhr

Painting: $177,500 ÷ 50,000 DLhr = $ 3.55 per DLhr

Total plantwide overhead costs: $800,000 + $177,500 = $977,500

Plantwide overhead rate using Mhr: $977,500 ÷ 85,000 Mhr = $11.50 per Mhr

Plantwide overhead rate using DLhr: $977,500 ÷ 50,000 DLhr = $19.55 per DLhr

OVERHEAD APPLIED:	CAR BODIES	TRUCK BODIES
Using departmental overhead rates:		
Assembly	$10.00 × 12 Mhr = $120.00	$10.00 × 5 Mhr = $ 50.00
Painting	$ 3.55 × 4 DLhr = 14.20	$ 3.55 × 14 DLhr = $ 49.70
Totals	$134.20	$ 99.70
Using plantwide overhead rates:		
Based on Mhr	$11.50 × 12 Mhr = $138.00	$11.50 × 5 Mhr = $ 57.50
Based on DLhr	$19.55 × 4 DLhr = $ 78.20	$19.55 × 14 DLhr = $273.70

The direct materials cost per unit for truck bodies is $100, and the direct labor cost is $50. Adding the various overhead amounts to these prime costs gives the total product cost under each method. The following calculations show the product costs and the profit or loss for truck bodies assuming a selling price of $300 per unit:

	DEPARTMENTAL RATES	PLANTWIDE RATE (Mhr)	PLANTWIDE RATE (DLhr)
Direct materials	$100.00	$100.00	$100.00
Direct labor	50.00	50.00	50.00
Overhead	99.70	57.50	273.70
Total cost	<$249.70>	<$207.50>	<$423.70>
Selling price	300.00	300.00	300.00
Profit (loss)	$ 50.30	$ 92.50	<$123.70>

by machine usage in the Assembly Department. Car bodies require 12 machine hours whereas truck bodies only require 5 machine hours. Obviously, more *Assembly Department overhead* should be applied to car bodies than to truck bodies. However, since car bodies require less direct labor hours of work than do truck bodies, less overhead is applied to car bodies than to truck bodies!

■ Use of *either plantwide TOH POR* ignores the different causes of overhead in the two departments, as well as the different amounts of those activities used in each department. Using a machine hour base, too much Painting Department overhead is applied to car bodies, and too little to truck bodies. Car bodies are cross-subsidizing truck bodies. When a direct labor base is used, though, truck bodies are cross-subsidizing car bodies. Truck bodies absorb some of the overhead that car bodies should have been charged. Cross-subsidization occurs when too much overhead is applied to one product, while too little is applied to other products.

Use of the product costs generated from plantwide TOH PORs may cause management to make wrong decisions about truck bodies (and car bodies). The product cost produced by a plantwide TOH POR based on machine hours will make management think that truck bodies are more profitable than the product line actually is. This belief may motivate management to employ more resources to produce more truck bodies, thereby diverting resources from other more profitable products.

If the plantwide TOH POR based on direct labor hours is used, management may think that truck bodies should be eliminated because this product line appears to be generating a significant loss. The more accurate product cost is generated by the departmental overhead rates because they more closely reflect truck bodies' utilization of different overhead resources in each department. Thus, decisions based on the product costs produced by the departmental overhead rates should be better decisions.

Predetermined Variable and Fixed Overhead Rates

To support management analysis of overhead costs, it is usually desirable to calculate two PORs, a variable overhead (VOH) rate and a fixed overhead (FOH) rate. Generally, separate VOH and FOH rates provide managers with more useful information than just developing one TOH POR for VOH and FOH costs combined. Budgeting separate VOH and FOH PORs was introduced in Chapter 7. The last section of this chapter will illustrate an allocation method using separate VOH and FOH PORs.

Many traditional CASs were designed primarily for financial reporting needs. Cost management information was viewed as less important. With respect to accounting for overhead, just one TOH subsidiary account was designed into the WIP general ledger system. Overhead costs were debited into this account in journal entries 4, 5, and 6. Overhead was applied to products in total using one plantwide TOH POR in journal entry 7. This type of overhead accounting was illustrated for a basic CAS in Chapter 4 (Exhibit 4–2), for a JOCAS in Chapter 5 (Exhibit 5–1), and for a PCAS in Chapter 6 (Exhibit 6–4). Similarly, the Starfire Company example above, which illustrated separate overhead accounts for each production department, did not have separate VOH and FOH accounts within the departments.

In the discussion that follows, VOH and FOH will not be separated to avoid overly complicating the calculations. Furthermore, the techniques that follow are usually used with total overhead on professional accounting certification exams. Nevertheless, even though the VOH and FOH accounts are not separate in the CAS examples that follow, their separation is important for standard cost card calculations and overhead budgeting, as well as in cost control through four-way overhead cost variance analysis.

Service Department PORs

LEARNING OBJECTIVE 2

Describe how the general ledger system for WIP can be designed to provide more accurate product cost information and cost management information.

Production departments (also called **operating departments, cells,** or **workcenters**) are where the central purposes of the organization are carried out. Examples include the surgery department in a hospital, the shoe department in a retail store, and the assembly department in a manufacturing enterprise.

Service departments, by contrast, do not engage directly in production activities. Rather, they provide assistance and support that facilitate the activities of the production departments. Examples include the human resources department, purchasing, storeroom, maintenance, computing center, engineering, internal auditing, and cafeteria. Although service departments do not engage directly in the producing activities of the organization, their costs are part of the cost of manufacturing products or providing services.

Because service department costs cannot be directly traced to products being manufactured or services (for the customer) performed by the company, these costs must be allocated to the production departments' overhead accounts. The service department costs then become part of the budgeted overhead costs of the production departments. In this manner, they are included with the other overhead costs of the production department in calculating the departmental TOH POR. In total, these "all-inclusive" departmental PORs, therefore, ultimately apply all the plant's overhead to the products when the PORs are used in the overhead application journal entry 7.

This type of CAS design results in a three-stage overhead allocation process:

■ *Stage one: Overhead cost assignments.* As overhead costs are incurred, they are debited to the proper service and production department overhead accounts. This is called **primary cost assignment.** Some costs can be directly traced to each service and production department, including the following:

a. Salaries, employment taxes, and fringe benefits of the production department foremen and managers of the service departments

b. Indirect materials requisitioned by production departments and all materials used by service departments

c. Depreciation of machinery within production departments and other equipment, furniture, and fixtures of service departments

d. Wages, employment taxes, and fringe benefits of workers within service departments

Stage one primary cost assignment directly traces costs to service departments. It also directly traces as many VOH and FOH costs as is possible to the production departments. These are properly considered direct costs to the departments even though they may be indirect (overhead) costs *with respect to individual products.* A cost element can be directly traceable to one cost object (such as a department) and still be an indirect cost with respect to another cost object (such as a job). Thus, these costs are labeled as direct VOH costs (DVOH) and direct FOH costs (DFOH).

■ *Stage two: Service department overhead cost allocations.* Once overhead costs are accumulated in the service and production department overhead accounts within WIP, the service department costs can be allocated to the production department overhead accounts so that they can be included in the departmental TOH PORs. This is called **secondary cost allocation.** The management accountant must use a reasonable allocation base for secondary cost allocations. The allocation base for each service used must bear a relationship to the costs of the services being rendered. Ideally, this is a cause-and-effect relationship. If, for example, the costs of operating the human resources department tend to vary with the number of people employed, this service department's costs can be allocated according to the number of employees working in each production department. As another example, the purchasing department's costs may be allocated to production department overhead accounts on the basis of the number of purchase orders processed for each

The design department provides a service for the production department at Carousel Carpet Mills, Inc.

Weather forecasting and flight planning is a service to airlines. Courtesy of PRC, Inc.

■ EXHIBIT 9–2
Possible Stage Two Allocation Bases for Service Department Costs

Service Departments	Possible Allocation Bases
Cafeteria	Number of employees
Medical infirmary	Periodic survey of cases handled, number of employees
Airport ground services	Number of flights
Occupancy services	Square footage
Materials handled	Volume handled, number of requisitions
Power	Kilowatt hours used, number of machines
Computing center	Number of reports, computer time
Human resources	Number of employees, turnover of labor, periodic survey of time spent
Custodial	Square footage
Repairs and maintenance	Number of machines, number of repair calls
Laundry	Pounds of laundry, number of items processed

producing department. Some common bases used in allocating service department costs are presented in Exhibit 9–2.

■ *Stage three: Overhead cost application.* Finally, once the overhead costs are accumulated in the proper overhead accounts (stage one), and service department costs allocated to production department overhead accounts (stage two), the departmental PORs can be developed for applying overhead to the products (stage three). As with secondary cost allocations, the management accountant must choose a basis for the PORs, hopefully derived from a cause-and-effect relationship between the department's overhead cost incurrence and the products made. Choosing the proper basis for the POR was discussed in Chapter 7 as part of preparing the standard cost card lines for VOH and FOH.

In summary, any overhead costs that can be specifically associated with a production or service department should be directly assigned to it. For example, the costs of computer supplies are charged directly to the computing center. Lease payments on computer equipment also are charged directly to the computing center. Food costs are charged directly to the cafeteria.

The service department costs should be allocated according to some measure that has a cause-and-effect or benefit relationship. Thus, such items as building depreciation, insurance, and taxes are commonly allocated on the basis of square feet of floor space occupied. Plant heating and cooling costs may be allocated on cubic feet of space occupied. Costs of lighting may be allocated on the basis of kilowatt hours. Inspection costs may be allocated on the basis of direct labor hours and so on.

Stage two allocates all overhead to production department overhead accounts. In stage three, overhead is applied from the production department overhead accounts to the products produced or services rendered by the company, using departmental PORs. Refer to Exhibit 9–1 to verify this.

The computing center services the entire organization. Courtesy of Novell.

LEARNING OBJECTIVE 3

Explain how to allocate service department costs to production departments, and describe the different methods that can be used.

■ **METHODS OF PERFORMING SERVICE DEPARTMENT SECONDARY COST ALLOCATIONS**

Four common methods exist for allocating service department costs to production department overhead accounts. The first three methods are illustrated here, assuming there is one total overhead account for each service department and production department. The fourth method, illustrated in the next section of this chapter, uses separate VOH and FOH accounts for each service and production department. The first three methods discussed, in order of increasing sophistication, are as follows:

- Direct method
- Step method
- Reciprocal method

The Direct Method

The **direct method** is widely used for allocating service department costs. This method allocates each service department's total costs directly to the production departments' overhead accounts. This method's major weakness is that it ignores any service rendered by one service department to another. For example, Birchtree Manufacturing makes white-water rafting products such as canoes, kayaks, and rafts. These products are made in two production departments, Assembly and Finishing. The plant has four service departments, each with its own subsidiary ledger account within WIP–Manufacturing Overhead. These services include the Human Resources Department, Occupancy Services, the Computing Center, and the Engineering Department.

Obviously, each of the four service departments occupies space and should be allocated some occupancy costs (building depreciation, property taxes and insurance, heating and air conditioning, and so forth). The Human Resources and Engineering Departments also use computer services. To determine the "real costs" of each service more accurately, inter-service department cost allocations should be made. The Human Resources Department's cost should include some allocation of Occupancy Services costs and Computing Center costs. The direct method, however, ignores this inter-service department usage in determining the costs of each service allocated in stage two, secondary cost allocations.

With the direct method, the primary costs of operating each service department are allocated directly to the production departments. This method is the simplest and quickest way to allocate service costs. The number of secondary cost allocations is equal to the number of service departments. Exhibit 9–3 illustrates the direct method cost allocation worksheet. Each department's primary costs are shown as the first line. The secondary cost allocations to production departments are made using the following bases:

The variable costs of a hospital's staff cafeteria are allocated to those using it from a sign-in sheet at the beginning of the line. Courtesy Washoe Medical Center.

DEPARTMENT	ALLOCATION BASE	PERCENTAGE	SERVICE DEPARTMENT ALLOCATION
Human Resources	*Budgeted payroll:*		
Assembly	$60,000	75%	$165,000
Finishing	20,000	25%	55,000
Total	$80,000	100%	$220,000
Occupancy Services	*Square feet:*		
Assembly	14,000 square feet	70%	$105,000
Finishing	6,000 square feet	30%	45,000
Total	20,000 square feet	100%	$150,000
Computing Center	*Expected reports:*		
Assembly	40 reports	40%	$ 72,000
Finishing	60 reports	60%	108,000
Total	100 reports	100%	$180,000
Engineering	*Budgeted machine hours:*		
Assembly	2,000 machine hours	80%	$ 80,000
Finishing	500 machine hours	20%	20,000
Total	2,500 machine hours	100%	$100,000

The budgeted Human Resources cost of $220,000 is allocated to Assembly and Finishing on the basis of 75 percent and 25 percent, respectively, using

■■EXHIBIT 9–3
Cost Allocation Worksheet for the Direct Method

Birchtree Manufacturing
Allocation of Service Department Costs

	Service Departments				Production Departments		
	Human Resources	Occupancy Services	Computing Center	Engineering	Assembly	Finishing	Total
Stage one primary cost assignment:							
Total DVOH and DFOH costs	$220,000	$150,000	$180,000	$100,000	$170,000	$ 50,000	$870,000
Stage two service department cost allocations:							
Human Resources	<220,000>				$165,000	$ 55,000	
Occupancy Services		<150,000>			105,000	45,000	
Computing Center			<180,000>		72,000	108,000	
Engineering				<100,000>	80,000	20,000	
Total overhead costs allocated to production departments TOH accounts	$ –0–	$ –0–	$ –0–	$ –0–	$592,000	$278,000	$870,000
Stage three overhead cost application:							
Budgeted Mhr					÷2,000 Mhr		
Budgeted DLhr						÷10,000 DLhr	
Departmental TOH PORs					$ 296.00/Mhr	$ 27.80/DLhr	

payroll dollars as the allocation base. Since the major purpose of Human Resources is to service employees, the Human Resources costs are allocated to these production departments on the basis of their payroll amounts.

Because Assembly occupies 14,000 square feet of the building versus 6,000 square feet occupied by Finishing, it seems equitable to allocate 70 percent ($105,000) of the budgeted occupancy costs to Assembly. Thirty percent ($45,000) of budgeted occupancy costs is allocated to Finishing.

The Computing Center expects to process 40 reports for Assembly and 60 reports for Finishing. So, 40 percent of the Computing Center's budgeted costs of $180,000 is allocated to Assembly and 60 percent to Finishing.

Management has determined that there is a cause-and-effect relationship between Engineering costs and machine hours. Therefore, 80 percent ($80,000) of Engineering's budgeted costs ($100,000) is allocated to Assembly. The remaining $20,000, or 20 percent, is allocated to Finishing.

The Step Method

Some companies use the **step method,** which allows for limited recognition of services rendered by service departments to other service departments. This method is more complex than the direct method because a sequence of allocations must be chosen. The sequence often begins with the department that renders the most services to other service departments. The sequence continues in a step-by-step fashion and ends with the allocation of the costs of the service department that renders the lowest percentage of its services to other service departments.

Where reciprocal (inter-service department) relationships exist, first allocating the service department providing the most service to the other service departments will generally result in the best step allocation. The deficiency in the step method is that it recognizes only one-way inter-service department use. Once a service department's costs are allocated to other service and production departments, a subsequent service department's costs are not allocated back to the original service. To illustrate, using the Birchtree Manufacturing example, the following order of service department allocations has been determined:

1. Human Resources
2. Computing Center
3. Occupancy Services
4. Engineering

Using this order, the Human Resources service is allocated first. Its costs are allocated to the remaining service centers and to the production departments. The Computing Center's costs are allocated next. These costs now include the primary costs of the Computing Center (from stage one) plus an allocation of Human Resources costs (from stage two). Human Resources, having already been allocated, does not receive an allocation of Computing Center costs even though it uses computing services. This means that the "real" total cost of Human Resources is understated because it does not include any Computer Center costs. To minimize this costing error from not making any "backward" allocations of subsequent service center costs to previous service centers, the biggest service is allocated first, with smaller services allocated subsequently.[3] The cost allocation worksheet for the step method is illustrated in Exhibit 9–4.

The base used to allocate budgeted Human Resources costs is payroll dollars. The payroll dollars associated with the other departments, along with the amounts of Human Resources costs allocated to each department, are as follows:

DEPARTMENT	BUDGETED PAYROLL	PAYROLL PROPORTION	×	AMOUNT TO BE ALLOCATED	=	AMOUNT ALLOCATED
Computing Center	$ 50,000	50/200		$220,000		$ 55,000
Occupancy Services	40,000	40/200		220,000		44,000
Engineering	30,000	30/200		220,000		33,000
Assembly	60,000	60/200		220,000		66,000
Finishing	20,000	20/200		220,000		22,000
	$200,000	200/200				$220,000

The step method allocates the $220,000 of budgeted Human Resources costs to each department using its services, regardless of whether the user is another service department or a production department. Thus, 25 percent ($55,000) of Human Resources costs is allocated to the Computing Center because it represents 25 percent ($50,000 ÷ $200,000 shown in the Payroll Proportion column above) of Birchtree's budgeted factory payroll costs *for the departments that are to receive an allocation under the step method.*

The second department to have its costs allocated is the Computing Center. A reasonable base is computer time or number of reports. Because the reports all require about the same amount of work and the number of reports is easier to measure than computer time, number of reports is used as the allocation base. The expected number of reports for each department and their proportion of the total for the departments *receiving an allocation of Computing Center costs under the step method,* together with the amounts of budgeted Computing Center costs allocated to its users, follow:

[3] In some situations, a certain service department allocation order must be used, regardless of the relative amounts of services provided. This is true in Medicare reimbursement claims by hospitals. All hospitals are required by law to use the same allocation order. Technically, however, the most accurate allocations result from ordering services by the amount of services provided to the other service departments. This order may not always be the same as ordering service departments from highest to lowest budgeted cost.

◼ EXHIBIT 9–4
Cost Allocation Worksheet for the Step Method

Birchtree Manufacturing
Allocation of Service Department Costs

	Service Departments			Production Departments			
	Human Resources	Computing Center	Occupancy Services	Engineering	Assembly	Finishing	Total
Stage one primary cost assignment:							
Total DVOH and DFOH costs	$220,000	$180,000	$150,000	$100,000	$170,000	$ 50,000	$870,000
Stage two service department cost allocations:							
Human Resources	<220,000>	55,000	44,000	33,000	66,000	22,000	
		235,000					
Computing Center		<235,000>	47,000	164,500	9,400	14,100	
			241,000				
Occupancy Services			<241,000>	41,000	140,000	60,000	
				338,500			
Engineering				<338,500>	270,800	67,700	
Total overhead costs allocated to production departments TOH accounts	$ –0–	$ –0–	$ –0–	$ –0–	$656,200	$213,800	$870,000
Stage three overhead cost application:							
Budgeted Mhr					÷2,000 Mhr		
Budgeted DLhr						÷10,000 DLhr	
Departmental TOH PORs					$328.10/Mhr	$21.38/DLhr	

DEPARTMENT	NUMBER OF REPORTS	PROPORTION	× AMOUNT TO BE ALLOCATED	= AMOUNT ALLOCATED
Human Resources	100	n/a	n/a	n/a
Occupancy Services	200	200/1,000	$235,000	$ 47,000
Engineering	700	700/1,000	235,000	164,500
Assembly	40	40/1,000	235,000	9,400
Finishing	60	60/1,000	235,000	14,100
Totals	1,100	1,000/1,000		$235,000

Notice that the Human Resources Department receives computer reports. These reports are not included in the allocation proportions, however, because no Computing Center costs are allocated "backward" to Human Resources when using the step method.

The Occupancy Services costs are allocated next because this department provides more services to more departments than Engineering, the remaining service department. Occupancy Services costs are generally allocated on the basis of floor space occupied by the departments, although in some situations, a cubic measure may be more appropriate, such as for heating cost in a plant where ceilings are of varying heights. The square footage occupied by each department and the proportions for the departments *receiving an allocation of occupancy costs*, as well as the amount of budgeted Occupancy Services costs allocated to each, follow:

DEPARTMENT	AREA IN SQUARE FEET	PROPORTION	×	AMOUNT TO BE ALLOCATED	=	AMOUNT ALLOCATED
Human Resources	1,000	n/a		n/a		n/a
Computing Center	900	n/a		n/a		n/a
Engineering	4,100	4,100/24,100		$241,000		$ 41,000
Assembly	14,000	14,000/24,100		241,000		140,000
Finishing	6,000	6,000/24,100		241,000		60,000
Totals	26,000	24,100/24,100				$241,000

The budgeted Occupancy Services costs are allocated over a base consisting only of the area occupied by departments that have not yet been allocated. Although Human Resources occupies 1,000 square feet and the Computing Center occupies 900 square feet, no costs are allocated back to these departments. Thus, their areas are not included in the base for allocating Occupancy Services costs, which is 24,100 square feet rather than 26,000 square feet.

Engineering is the last service department to be allocated. Consequently, its costs are allocated only to the production departments. Budgeted Engineering costs, which now include the costs allocated to this department from previous services, are allocated to the production departments as follows:

DEPARTMENT	MACHINE HOURS	PROPORTION	×	AMOUNT TO BE ALLOCATED	=	AMOUNT ALLOCATED
Assembly	2,000	2,000/2,500		$338,500		$270,800
Finishing	500	500/2,500		338,500		67,700
Totals	2,500	2,500/2,500				$338,500

Compare the budgeted overhead allocated to the two production departments with the direct method (Exhibit 9–3) and the step method (Exhibit 9–4). The step method, being more accurate, allocated more service departments' overhead to the Assembly Department than did the direct method. The direct method understated Assembly Department overhead costs. This means that the Finishing Department absorbed more service departments' overhead than it should have. Consequently, the direct method resulted in the Finishing Department cross-subsidizing the Assembly Department (i.e., the Finishing Department's overhead account includes service department costs that should be assigned to the Assembly Department).

The Reciprocal Method

Like the step method, the **reciprocal method** recognizes that services rendered by certain service departments are used, in part, by other service departments. This method, therefore, allocates services back-and-forth among all departments using the services. Instead of the one-way allocations performed under the step method, this method performs two-way (reciprocal) allocations. The reciprocal method's advantage over the step method is that it recognizes all interrelationships among departments and, therefore, produces more accurate service department cost allocations.

The first step in making reciprocal allocations is to determine the share of each service department's costs that is to be allocated to the other service departments and to the production departments. A spreadsheet program can be used to calculate these percentage shares. Exhibit 9–5, which will be used as a starting point for reciprocal cost allocations, shows each Birchtree Manufacturing department's proportionate usage of the other departments' services.

The percentages in Exhibit 9–5 are used to derive simultaneous equations for calculating the costs of the services rendered. When there are few departments and interrelationships, simultaneous equations can be solved by hand.

■EXHIBIT 9–5
Summary of Bases and Percentage Allocations for Reciprocal Method

Birchtree Manufacturing
Share Calculations for Cost Allocations

	Cost Allocation Base							
	Payroll Dollars		Reports		Square Feet		Machine Hours	
Department	Amount	Percent	Amount	Percent	Amount	Percent	Amount	Percent
Human Resources	n/a	n/a	100	9.1	1,000	3.8	–0–	0.0
Computing Center	$ 50,000	25.0	n/a	n/a	900	3.5	–0–	0.0
Occupancy Services	40,000	20.0	200	18.2	n/a	n/a	–0–	0.0
Engineering	30,000	15.0	700	63.6	4,100	15.8	n/a	n/a
Assembly	60,000	30.0	40	3.6	14,000	53.8	2,000	80.0
Finishing	20,000	10.0	60	5.5	6,000	23.1	500	20.0
Totals	$200,000	100.0	1,100	100.0	26,000	100.0	2,500	100.0

If a large number of variables are present, the simultaneous equations will be too complex to solve without the aid of a computer.

With the method of simultaneous equations, the relationships among departments are expressed as a system of linear equations, with one equation for each department. Exhibit 9–6 summarizes the percentages of service department cost allocations from Exhibit 9–5. The percentages in the vertical columns, shown as negative amounts, represent credits to the overhead accounts indicated at the top of the columns. The charges (debits) to other service departments' overhead accounts and to the production departments' overhead accounts are the percentage of the service used multiplied by its cost from the reciprocal solution. The stage one TOH costs of each department are shown in the last column of Exhibit 9–6. The following symbols represent the total cost associated with the departments indicated:

SERVICE DEPARTMENT	PRODUCTION DEPARTMENT
X_1 = Human Resources	X_5 = Assembly
X_2 = Computing Center	X_6 = Finishing
X_3 = Occupancy Services	
X_4 = Engineering	

Then, X_1, the cost associated with Human Resources, is expressed as:

$$X_1 = 0.091X_2 + 0.038X_3 + 0X_4 + 0X_5 + 0X_6 + \$220,000$$

This expression indicates that the cost of Human Resources is its DVOH and DFOH cost of $220,000 plus stage two allocations from the Computing Center and Occupancy Services.

■EXHIBIT 9–6
Summary of Services Rendered Recognizing Reciprocal Relationships

Birchtree Manufacturing
Proportion of Cost to be Allocated to Other Departments

Department Rendering Service

Department Receiving Service	X_1 Human Resources	X_2 Computing Center	X_3 Occupancy Services	X_4 Engineering	X_5 Assembly	X_6 Finishing	Total DVOH and DFOH Costs
Human Resources	—	−0.091	−0.038	0.00	0.00	0.00	$220,000
Computing Center	−0.25	—	−0.035	0.00	0.00	0.00	180,000
Occupancy Services	−0.20	−0.182	—	0.00	0.00	0.00	150,000
Engineering	−0.15	−0.636	−0.158	—	0.00	0.00	100,000
Assembly	−0.30	−0.036	−0.538	−0.80	—	0.00	170,000
Finishing	−0.10	−0.055	−0.231	−0.20	0.00	—	50,000
Totals	−1.00	−1.000	−1.000	−1.00	0.00	0.00	$870,000

Similarly, the cost of the Computing Center is expressed as:

$$X_2 = 0.25X_1 + 0.035X_3 + 0X_4 + 0X_5 + 0X_6 + \$180{,}000$$

This expression indicates that the Computing Center is to be charged with 25 percent of the cost of Human Resources and 3.5 percent of Occupancy Services plus its DVOH and DFOH costs of $180,000. Formatting all the equations:

$$
\begin{aligned}
X_1 &= (0.091)X_2 + (0.038)X_3 + (0.000)X_4 + (0.00)X_5 + (0.00)X_6 + \$220{,}000 \\
X_2 &= (0.250)X_1 + (0.035)X_3 + (0.000)X_4 + (0.00)X_5 + (0.00)X_6 + \$180{,}000 \\
X_3 &= (0.200)X_1 + (0.182)X_2 + (0.000)X_4 + (0.00)X_5 + (0.00)X_6 + \$150{,}000 \\
X_4 &= (0.150)X_1 + (0.636)X_2 + (0.158)X_3 + (0.00)X_5 + (0.00)X_6 + \$100{,}000 \\
X_5 &= (0.300)X_1 + (0.036)X_2 + (0.538)X_3 + (0.80)X_4 + (0.00)X_6 + \$170{,}000 \\
X_6 &= (0.100)X_1 + (0.055)X_2 + (0.231)X_3 + (0.20)X_4 + (0.00)X_5 + \$\ 50{,}000
\end{aligned}
$$

The total cost variables X_1 through X_6 appear on the left-hand side of the equations, one variable for each equation. On the right-hand side of each equation are the cost variables for each of the remaining departments, multiplied by the appropriate proportions from Exhibits 9–5 and 9–6.

Using a spreadsheet program to solve this system of equations, the secondary cost allocations of service department costs to the producing departments' overhead accounts are shown in Exhibit 9–7a. Note that the Assembly Department's budgeted total overhead equals $656,682, while $213,318 is budgeted for the Finishing Department. The TOH PORs are shown in Exhibit 9–7b.

Neither of the production departments renders services to any of the service departments. Thus, the production departments are not involved in the "vicious circle" of reallocations. The term *vicious circle* refers to the fact that where service departments are interrelated, it is impossible to know the total cost of department A until the allocation of department B is complete, but the allocation of department B cannot be made until it has received its share of department A's cost.[4]

[4] The vicious circles of reallocations created by solving simultaneous equations results in a "circular" (CIRC) error message appearing in the spreadsheet.

■EXHIBIT 9–7
Reciprocal Method Overhead Cost Allocations

(a) Reciprocal Allocations

Service Departments	Variable Name	Reciprocal Allocation Amounts	Formulas
Human Resources	X1	= $252,261	0.091*CC+0.038*OS+220,000
Computing Center	X2	= $251,684	0.25*HR+0.035*OS+180,000
Occupancy Services	X3	= $246,259	0.2*HR+0.182*CC+150,000
Engineering	X4	= $336,819	0.15*HR+0.636*CC+0.158*OS+100.000

Producing Departments			
Assembly	X5	= $656,682	0.3*HR+0.036*CC+0.538*OS+0.8*E+170,000
Finishing	X6	= $213,318	0.1*HR+0.055*CC+0.231*OS+0.2*E+50,000
TOTAL BUDGETED OVERHEAD		= $870,000	

(b) TOH POR Calculations

Assembly Department:

$$\text{TOH POR} = \frac{\$656{,}682 \text{ Budgeted TOH}}{2{,}000 \text{ Mhr}} = \$328.34 \text{ per Mhr}$$

Finishing Department:

$$\text{TOH POR} = \frac{\$213{,}318 \text{ Budgeted TOH}}{10{,}000 \text{ DLhr}} = \$21.33 \text{ per DLhr}$$

Compare the total budgeted overhead to be included in each production department's TOH POR using the direct method (Exhibit 9–3), the step method (Exhibit 9–4), and the reciprocal method (Exhibit 9–7). Earlier, the comparison of the direct and step methods indicated that the direct method resulted in the Finishing Department cross-subsidizing the Assembly Department because too much service department costs were allocated to Finishing, while Assembly was undercosted. Now, comparing the step and reciprocal methods reveals that the step method apparently results in the same cross-subsidization costing problem. However, the magnitude of this problem has been greatly reduced. The difference between the step and reciprocal methods' allocations of total service department costs to the production departments' overhead accounts is insignificant.

<table>
<tr><td>

LEARNING OBJECTIVE 4

Design an SCAS that includes cost variances for both production and service departments.

</td></tr>
</table>

∎ RESPONSIBILITY ACCOUNTING AND SERVICE DEPARTMENT ALLOCATIONS

Seldom, if ever, will overhead costs applied during a period equal the actual overhead costs recorded in the same period. The reason for this disparity is that the actual level of activity is above or below the budgeted level, and/or actual overhead costs are different from estimated overhead costs. Consequently, in some periods actual overhead costs exceed applied overhead costs, and overhead is underapplied. In other periods, applied overhead costs exceed actual overhead, and overhead is overapplied. Several factors can produce under- or overapplied overhead:

■ *Actual and estimated variable overhead cost per unit difference.* If the actual VOH rate is greater than the VOH POR, variable overhead costs will be underapplied. If the actual VOH rate is less than the VOH POR, variable overhead costs will be overapplied. The rate differences can be caused by spending more on VOH items than budgeted or by using more of the overhead allocation base (e.g., direct labor hours or machine hours) than the standard quantity allowed (SQA). In the discussion of the four-way overhead variance analysis method in Chapter 8, these differences were identified as VOH spending and efficiency variances.

■ *Actual and estimated total fixed overhead costs difference.* A difference between total actual and total estimated FOH costs will cause under- or overapplied fixed overhead. Actual FOH costs may differ from estimated FOH costs for several reasons: rent may have increased, new equipment may have been purchased, taxes may have increased, and so forth. These differences are measured by calculating the FOH budget variance.

■ *Actual activity and expected capacity difference.* Fixed overhead costs will be under- or overapplied if actual production volume differs from the production quota. Possible reasons for a difference between actual and budgeted output were presented in the last chapter. This difference is measured by the FOH volume variance.

The need for overhead cost variance analysis becomes even greater when service departments are present. For proper responsibility accounting and cost management, overhead cost variances need to be traced back to where they are caused. In other words, overhead cost variances for service departments, as well as for production departments, are needed.

Cost variance analysis is very difficult, if not impossible, for two reasons, when percentages are used to allocate total service department costs. First, VOH and FOH are combined into one TOH account, but four-way overhead variance analysis cannot be performed without separate VOH and FOH costs. Second, the percentages based on relative usage normally are recalculated when making actual overhead cost allocations throughout the year.

To illustrate, Birchtree Manufacturing's use of percentages based on the relative usage of services created two problems in evaluating performance. These problems resulted from two events during the year:

- The Computing Center hired three people not planned for originally. This increased its payroll from $50,000 budgeted to $150,000.
- The Human Resources Department spent $280,000 instead of the $220,000 budgeted.

In many traditional CASs, the percentages used to allocate a service department's costs are recalculated based on actual data. These recalculated percentages for the Human Resources Department are shown in Exhibit 9–8. Upon seeing the actual overhead cost allocations from the Human Resources Department to the other departments, Birchtree's management made the following performance evaluations:

- Occupancy Services, Engineering, Assembly, and Finishing personnel all received bonuses at year-end equal to 10 percent of the favorable cost variances reported in Exhibit 9–8.
- The Computing Center personnel did not receive any bonuses because more Human Resources costs were allocated to their overhead account than was expected when the TOH PORs were prepared.

What happened? First, assume that by keeping their payroll costs at budget, Occupancy Services, Engineering, Assembly, and Finishing used the same amount of Human Resources services as planned. Although they used exactly the amount of services budgeted, all of these departments were rewarded because the amount of overhead allocated to each was less than budgeted, *solely due to Computing Services having a larger payroll than originally budgeted.* This created the illusion that the departments saved Birchtree some money. Birchtree management rewarded them for something they did not do!

Second, the Computing Services personnel were penalized for being allowed to hire three people. Computing Services may, or may not, have used more Human Resources services than it should have used. But, the CAS does not capture this information. As a result of recalculating the Human Resources allocation percentages based on actual payroll costs, the Computing Services Center is apparently cross-subsidizing the other departments. Both a motivational and an ethical dilemma have resulted.

The problem of a potentially incorrect performance evaluation was caused by recalculating the percentages used to allocate service department costs. Using percentages based on actual payroll costs may not produce a high-quality CAS. Birchtree management also experienced another problem stemming from the

---

■■ EXHIBIT 9–8
**Actual Percentages for Birchtree's Human Resources Department's
Actual Overhead Cost Allocations**

	Original Allocations (See Exhibits 9–4 and 9–5)			Revised Allocations (Using actual costs)			
	Budgeted Payroll a	Allocation Percentages b	Budgeted Allocations c	Actual Payroll d	Actual Percentages e	Actual Costs Allocated f	Cost Variances g = c − f
Computing Center	$50,000	25%	$ 55,000	$150,000	50.00%	$140,000	<$85,000>U
Occupancy Services	40,000	20%	44,000	40,000	13.33%	37,333	6,667 F
Engineering	30,000	15%	33,000	30,000	10.00%	28,000	5,000 F
Assembly	60,000	30%	66,000	60,000	20.00%	56,000	10,000 F
Finishing	20,000	10%	22,000	20,000	6.67%	18,667	3,333 F
Totals	$200,000	100%	$220,000	$300,000	100.00%	$280,000	<$60,000>U

amount of Human Resources costs allocated. Originally, the budgeted costs of $220,000 were allocated to the user departments. When many traditional CASs recalculate the percentages, they also allocate the actual costs of the services along with these new percentages.

In other words, since the Human Resources Department actually spent $280,000, the CAS allocated this amount to the other departments. The CAS did not capture the spending variance created by this service department, nor did the CAS assign the variance to the proper responsibility center. Instead, the CAS allocations buried this cost overrun in the users' accounts! Thus, Birchtree management, not knowing any better, rewarded the Human Resources Department personnel for not showing any cost variances.[5]

A high-quality CAS will separate VOH and FOH, creating separate accounts and overhead allocations for each department's VOH and FOH. The system used at Birchtree did not. Exhibit 9–9 illustrates the design of a WIP general

[5] When the Computing Services employees found out that everyone got bonuses but them, they quickly figured out why. If the three new people had not been hired, then none of the rewards everyone else received at the expense of Computing Services would have happened. The three new computer people were ostracized and finally quit Birchtree even though they had promising careers. On their way out, they sabotaged the CAS allocation program, which they saw as the real reason for their lost jobs.

■EXHIBIT 9–9
General Ledger System Comparisons: Overhead Accounts for Production Departments and Service Departments

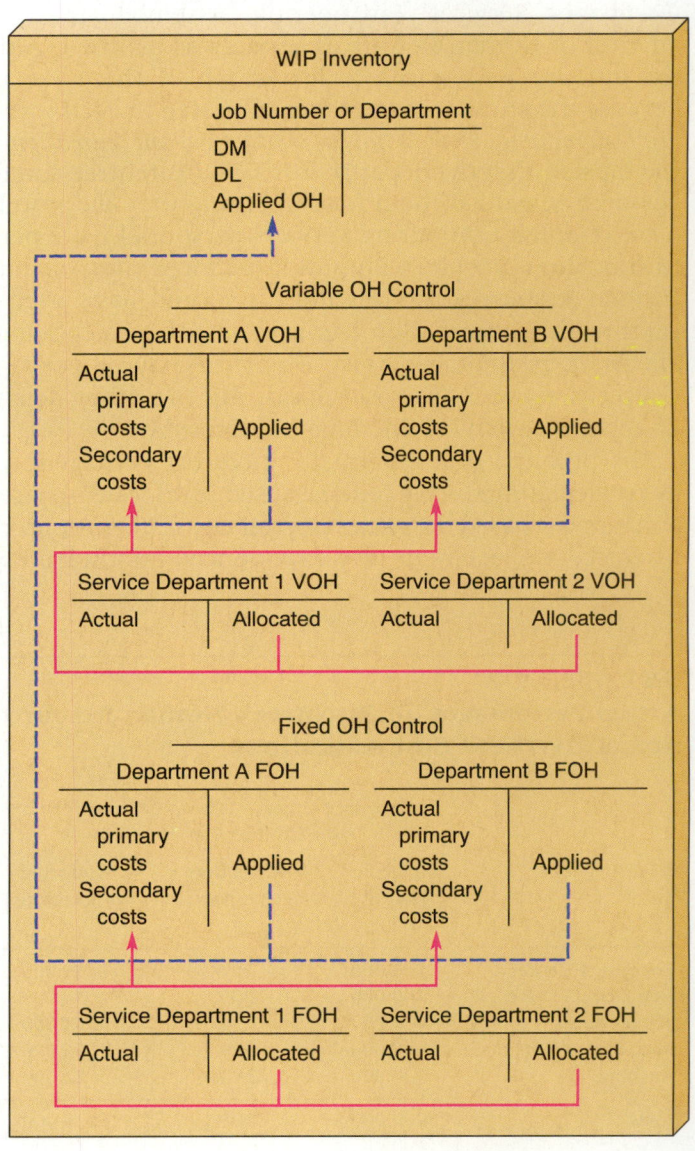

Subsidiary Accounts

Level 1: Product Costs
(Separate accounts for each job or department)

Level 2a: VOH Control

(Separate VOH subsidiary accounts for each production department)

(Separate VOH subsidiary accounts for each service department)

Level 2b: FOH Control

(Separate FOH subsidiary accounts for each production department)

(Separate FOH subsidiary accounts for each service department)

Actual and Normal Cost Systems

WIP Inventory

Job Number or Department
DM
DL
Applied OH

Variable OH Control

Department A VOH | Department B VOH
Actual primary costs / Secondary costs | Applied | Actual primary costs / Secondary costs | Applied

Service Department 1 VOH | Service Department 2 VOH
Actual | Allocated | Actual | Allocated

Fixed OH Control

Department A FOH | Department B FOH
Actual primary costs / Secondary costs | Applied | Actual primary costs / Secondary costs | Applied

Service Department 1 FOH | Service Department 2 FOH
Actual | Allocated | Actual | Allocated

INSIGHTS & APPLICATIONS

St. John's Hospital

St. John's Hospital is a relatively small rural hospital located in central Iowa. Its three profit centers are Outpatient Services, Obstetrics, and General Services.[6] The hospital calls these billing centers. It has three services: Cafeteria, Administration, and Laundry. The management accountant, Prasid Kalari, has designed a normal JOCAS in which each patient is treated as a job. Even though a normal CAS is used, rather than a standard CAS, cost variances are prepared and reported annually. The CAS has separate VOH and FOH accounts for each billing center and service center.

Variable service department costs are allocated using a budgeted rate. For example, variable costs of the Cafeteria (meals) are allocated using a budgeted meal rate multiplied by the number of meals eaten in the other responsibility centers. Administration variable costs (files, insurance claims, and so forth) are allocated based on the files processed multiplied by a budgeted rate per file. Laundry variable costs are allocated using the number of loads of laundry processed for each revenue center multiplied by its budgeted rate per load.

The logic behind using a budgeted rate (instead of a percentage) is that these costs are variable. The stable relationship for expressing a variable cost is on a per unit (rate) basis. For example, it should cost so much per meal, or file processed, or load of laundry washed and dried.

The fixed costs of each service are allocated based on percentages. These percentages are calculated from the maximum capacity usage of each service, rather than the actual or budgeted usage, as is done in many traditional CASs. Prasid's rationale is that fixed costs represent the costs of having a certain amount of capacity available. The size of each user of a service, such as the Cafeteria, determines how big that service should be and, therefore, its fixed costs. Allocating the fixed costs by using relative size percentages of the users, in effect, charges the users a flat fee for having the service available. Prasid Kalari prepared a flowchart for making budget allocations at the beginning of an accounting period (BOP) to set PORs and for making end-of-period (EOP) actual overhead cost allocations for performance evaluation. The flowchart is shown in Exhibit 9–10 (see p. 418).

When services are allocated using the step method, the Cafeteria is first, then Administration, and, finally, Laundry. The secondary cost allocation bases for these three services are meals served, files processed, and loads of laundry, respectively. The basis for each billing center's POR is patient-days for the stage three overhead application to the patients' bills (i.e., to these individual jobs).

---

ledger system that has individual VOH and FOH accounts for production and service departments. Compare this exhibit to Exhibit 8–8.

A high-quality CAS also recognizes that VOH and FOH are caused by different activities, even for the same department. Thus, VOH and FOH should be allocated differently. The above Saint John's Hospital example has a high-quality CAS for overhead responsibility accounting.

Budget Allocations for VOH PORs

In developing the service departments' budgets, Prasid felt it was important to involve all those responsible for the costs and their control. Accordingly, each department head had to coordinate plans with the others, sharing information so that the budgeting process could be efficiently and effectively performed. For example, the heads of the three billing centers and the other two service departments provided the Cafeteria manager with the meals they expected to eat given their budgeted patient-days for the upcoming year. Similarly, the budgeted files and the budgeted loads of laundry also were determined, based on the budgeted patient days for the billing centers.

In allocating the fixed service center costs, Prasid obtained information about the size of the various departments from the head of hospital administration. With this information, the various department heads prepared their DVOH and DFOH budgets. Prasid then collected the budget information and input it into the Data Section of his spreadsheet program shown in Exhibit 9–11 (see p. 419). The Data Section for Budget Allocations has two parts, one for VOH and one for FOH. The first line of each part ("Budgeted DVOH" and "Budgeted

---

[6] Refer to Chapter 7 for definitions of investment, profit, and cost centers.

◼◼ EXHIBIT 9–10
Service Department Cost Allocations: Step Method

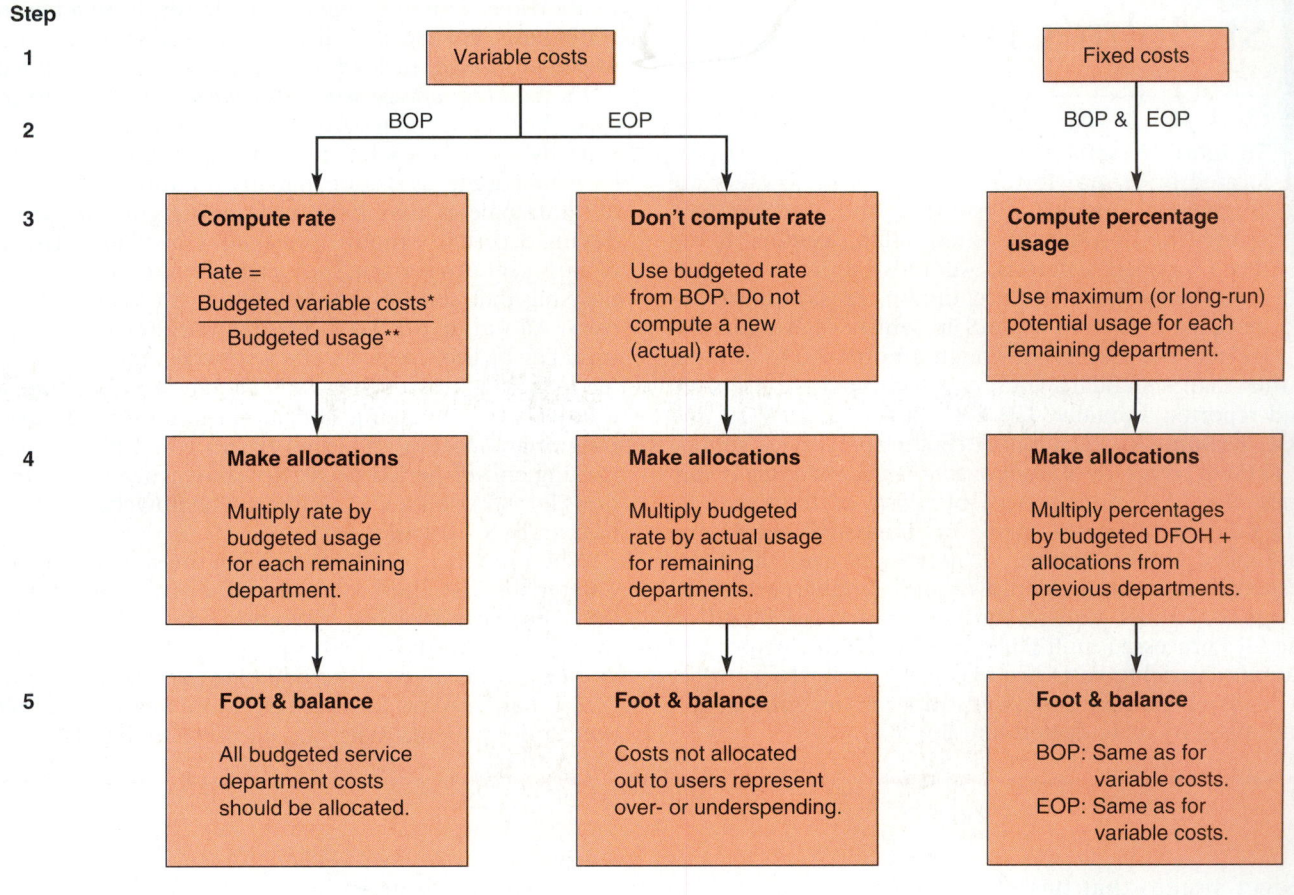

*DVOH + allocations from previous departments.
**For remaining departments only.
(**Foot** means to total a column of numbers.)

DFOH'') represent the budgeted direct variable and fixed costs of each service department along with the budgeted DVOH and DFOH for each billing center.

The Cafeteria can be used to demonstrate how the VOH service department rates are calculated in the Solution Section for VOH Allocations. From line two in the Data Section, the Cafeteria manager is budgeting to serve 37,500 meals (1,000 to Administration, 500 to Laundry personnel, none to outpatients, 6,000 to OB patients, and 30,000 to general patients). She budgeted variable food preparation costs of $71,250 for this volume of meals (line one in the Data Section). Dividing this budgeted DVOH by the budgeted meals produces the Meal Rate shown in the Solution Section. The meals' variable costs should be $1.90 per meal. Using this budgeted meal rate, the cafeteria's variable meal costs can be allocated to the other departments based on the number of meals each has planned:

USER OF CAFETERIA SERVICES	MEAL RATE ×	BUDGETED MEALS	= VOH ALLOCATION
Administrative Services	$1.90/meal ×	1,000	$ 1,900
Laundry Services	$1.90/meal ×	500	950
Outpatient	$1.90/meal ×	–0–	–0–
Obstetrics	$1.90/meal ×	6,000	11,400
General	$1.90/meal ×	30,000	57,000
Variable cafeteria costs to be allocated	$1.90/meal ×	37,500	$71,250

■■■ EXHIBIT 9–11
St. John's Hospital Step Method Allocations: Budget Allocations for PORs

DATA SECTION: BUDGET ALLOCATIONS AT BEGINNING OF PERIOD (BOP)

| | SERVICE DEPARTMENTS | | | BILLING DEPARTMENTS | | |
	CAFETERIA	ADMIN	LAUNDRY	OUTPATIENT	OB	GENERAL
BUDGETED DVOH	$71,250	$8,100	$38,300	$12,000	$15,000	$251,700
BUDGETED MEALS	37,500	1,000	500	0	6,000	30,000
BUDGETED FILES		20,000	1,500	3,000	900	14,600
BUDGETED LOADS			10,000	1,200	300	8,500
BUDGETED PATIENT-DAYS				6,000	3,000	50,000
BUDGETED DFOH	$48,000	$33,040	$59,520	$26,958	$99,738	$344,744
CAPACITY MEALS	50,000	1,000	500	0	8,500	40,000
CAPACITY FILES		20,000	2,000	4,000	6,000	8,000
CAPACITY LOADS			12,000	1,560	360	10,080

SOLUTION SECTION: BUDGET ALLOCATIONS AT BEGINNING OF PERIOD (BOP)

| | | SERVICE DEPARTMENTS | | | BILLING DEPARTMENTS | | |
VOH ALLOCATIONS:		CAFETERIA	ADMIN	LAUNDRY	OUTPATIENT	OB	GENERAL
BUDGETED DVOH		$71,250	$8,100	$38,300	$12,000	$15,000	$251,700
MEAL RATE	$1.90						
MEAL ALLOCATION		<71,250>	1,900	950	0	11,400	57,000
FILE RATE	$0.50						
FILE ALLOCATION			<10,000>	750	1,500	450	7,300
LAUNDRY RATE	$4.00						
LAUNDRY ALLOCATION				<40,000>	4,800	1,200	34,000
TOTAL VOH		$0	$0	$0	$18,300	$28,050	$350,000
VOH POR/PATIENT-DAY					$3.05	$9.35	$7.00
FOH ALLOCATIONS:							
BUDGETED DFOH		$48,000	$33,040	$59,520	$26,958	$99,738	$344,744
MEAL CAPACITIES		100%	2%	1%	0%	17%	80%
MEAL ALLOCATION		<48,000>	960	480	0	8,160	38,400
FILE CAPACITIES			100%	10%	20%	30%	40%
FILE ALLOCATION			<34,000>	3,400	6,800	10,200	13,600
LAUNDRY CAPACITIES				100%	13%	3%	84%
LAUNDRY ALLOCATION				<63,400>	8,242	1,902	53,256
TOTAL FOH		$0	$0	$0	$42,000	$120,000	$450,000
FOH POR/PATIENT-DAY					$7.00	$40.00	$9.00
TOH BUDGETED		$0	$0	$0	$60,300	$148,050	$800,000
TOH POR/PATIENT-DAY					$10.05	$49.35	$16.00

The File Rate and Laundry Rate are calculated in a similar way. The File Rate is $0.50 per file processed, and the Laundry Rate is $4.00 per load.[7] As with the meal allocations, these rates are multiplied by the budgeted number of files and loads of laundry, respectively, in each user department to receive an allocation under the step method. Using the budgeted rates for the services multiplied by the budgeted amount of services to be provided, all the variable service department costs are allocated into the VOH accounts of the three billing

[7] *File Rate:* $8,100 in DVOH Administrative Services costs plus an allocation of $1,900 from the Cafeteria, divided by 20,000 budgeted files to be processed by the remaining user departments. *Laundry Rate:* $38,300 in DVOH costs plus a Cafeteria allocation of $950 and an Administration Services allocation of $750, divided by 10,000 budgeted loads of laundry.

departments. Once the total VOH for each billing department is known, the VOH PORs can be prepared. Each outpatient is billed $3.05 for VOH, each OB patient is billed $9.35 per day, and each patient in the General Wing of St. John's Hospital is billed $7.00 per day.

Budget Allocations for FOH PORs

Fixed service department costs are allocated to producing departments (billing centers in the hospital) based on the relative size of each user. To demonstrate this, the number of meals that could be eaten by each user department _if operating at full capacity_ is used to determine "relative size ratios" for each user department. For the cafeteria, these ratios are as follows:

USER OF CAFETERIA SERVICES	CAPACITY MEALS	RELATIVE SIZE RATIO	CAFETERIA FOH ALLOCATION
Administrative Services	1,000 meals	2%	$ 960
Laundry Services	500	1%	480
Outpatient Treatment	–0–	–0–	–0–
Obstetrics	8,500	17%	8,160
General	40,000	80%	38,400
Totals	50,000 meals	100%	$48,000

With these relative size ratios, the cafeteria's budgeted fixed costs ($48,000) can be allocated to the various users of this service. Combining the VOH and FOH allocations, each user is contracting to receive a particular service for a mixed cost.[8] The FOH allocations represent the fixed cost of having this service available for its users. The VOH allocations represent the incremental cost of using one more unit of that service. The allocated costs of the Cafeteria that should be used by the other departments in budgeting their OH costs are as follows:

USER OF CAFETERIA SERVICES	FIXED COST	+	VARIABLE COST
Administrative Services	$960/year	+	$1.90/meal
Laundry Services	$480/year	+	$1.90/meal
Outpatient Treatment	n/a		n/a
Obstetrics	$8,160/year	+	$1.90/meal
General	$38,400/year	+	$1.90/meal

In effect, each user is contracting for a specific amount of service at a contracted cost (expressed by the Cafeteria's cost equation for each user). These budgeted (contracted) amounts will be used in the actual overhead cost allocations and cost variances presented in the following sections.

Actual Variable Cost Allocations

Each user of a service contracts to buy that service for a specific price, such as $1.90 per meal for the Cafeteria. As shown in the Data Section for Actual Cost Allocations in Exhibit 9–12, the actual variable and fixed costs, along with the actual usage of each service, are input. The first two amounts under the "Cafeteria" column are the actual variable Cafeteria costs and the actual meals served. From these two amounts, the actual variable cost of a meal is $2.00 ($80,000 ÷ 40,000 meals). However, the users only contracted to pay $1.90 per meal, and that is all they should have to pay. It is the Cafeteria manager's responsibility to control these costs. If more is spent in preparing meals than

---

[8] A mixed cost is part variable and part fixed, and is usually represented by a linear equation over the relevant range. See Chapter 7 on budgeting VOH and FOH costs for more information.

■■ EXHIBIT 9–12

St. John's Hospital Step Method Allocations: Year-End Actual Costs Allocations

DATA SECTION: ACTUAL COST ALLOCATIONS AT END OF PERIOD (EOP)

	SERVICE DEPARTMENTS			BILLING DEPARTMENTS		
	CAFETERIA	ADMIN	LAUNDRY	OUTPATIENT	OB	GENERAL
ACTUAL DVOH	$80,000	$6,210	$38,600	$11,050	$15,000	$177,885
ACTUAL MEALS	40,000	1,000	400	0	8,600	30,000
ACTUAL FILES		18,000	1,280	4,000	1,500	11,220
ACTUAL LOADS			10,000	1,500	500	8,000
ACTUAL PATIENT-DAYS				6,500	4,000	45,000
ACTUAL DFOH	$50,000	$31,040	$59,520	$30,000	$143,000	$340,000

SOLUTION SECTION: ACTUAL COST ALLOCATIONS AT END OF PERIOD (EOP)

		SERVICE DEPARTMENTS			BILLING DEPARTMENTS		
VOH ALLOCATIONS:		CAFETERIA	ADMIN	LAUNDRY	OUTPATIENT	OB	GENERAL
ACTUAL DVOH		$80,000	$6,210	$38,600	$11,050	$15,000	$177,885
MEAL RATE	$1.90						
MEAL ALLOCATION		<76,000>	1,900	760	0	16,340	57,000
FILE RATE	$0.50						
FILE ALLOCATION			<9,000>	640	2,000	750	5,610
LAUNDRY RATE	$4.00						
LAUNDRY ALLOCATION				<40,000>	6,000	2,000	32,000
TOTAL VOH		$4,000	<$890>	$0	$19,050	$34,090	$272,495
LESS: PATIENT CHARGES					<19,825>	<37,400>	<315,000>
ENDING VOH BALANCE		$4,000	<$890>	$0	<$775>	<$3,310>	<$42,505>
FOH ALLOCATIONS:							
ACTUAL DFOH		$50,000	$31,040	$59,520	$30,000	$143,000	$340,000
MEAL CAPACITIES		100%	2%	1%	0%	17%	80%
MEAL ALLOCATION		<48,000>	960	480	0	8,160	38,400
FILE CAPACITIES			100%	10%	20%	30%	40%
FILE ALLOCATION			<34,000>	3,400	6,800	10,200	13,600
LAUNDRY CAPACITIES				100%	13%	3%	84%
LAUNDRY ALLOCATION				<63,400>	8,242	1,902	53,256
TOTAL FOH		$2,000	<$2,000>	$0	$45,042	$163,262	$445,256
LESS: PATIENT CHARGES					<45,500>	<160,000>	<405,000>
ENDING FOH BALANCE		$2,000	<$2,000>	$0	<$458>	$3,262	$40,256
ENDING TOH BALANCE		$6,000	<$2,890>	$0	<$1,233>	<$48>	<$2,249>

was budgeted, this "spending" variance should remain within the Cafeteria VOH account.

The number of meals eaten, however, is the responsibility of the user departments. Therefore, their allocated actual variable meal costs are calculated as the budgeted meal rate multiplied by the *actual* meals eaten.[9] In this way, the users assume responsibility for the usage of services (i.e., the number of meals they actually ate), and the provider of the service assumes responsibility for the cost of providing that service.

To illustrate this for the cafeteria costs, there was a $0.10 per meal unfavorable variable cost spending variance ($1.90/meal standard rate versus the $2.00/

[9] Allocating overhead using a predetermined rate and the actual volume used is a feature of a normal CAS. A standard CAS uses SQA, not the actual volume. These topics were discussed in Chapter 4 ("Cost Measurement Issues") and Chapter 8 ("Variable Costs Usage Variances," and "SCAS Journal Entries").

meal actual rate) for each of the 40,000 actual meals served. This $4,000 unfavorable spending variance is the responsibility of the Cafeteria manager, and this allocation method keeps the spending variance within the Cafeteria's VOH account.[10] The $4,000 ending (debit, underapplied) overhead balance in the Cafeteria's VOH account is shown on the "Ending VOH Balance" line of the Solution Section for VOH Allocations in Exhibit 9–12.[11]

What type of variances should make up the ending VOH account balances? There are two VOH cost variances, spending and usage (efficiency):

- Each department should have a spending variance only for its own direct VOH costs.
- Each department should have a usage variance if it used more or less of a service allocated to it. The usage of each service can generate its own usage variance. For example, as illustrated in the "Service Department Cost Variances" section below, the Outpatient VOH account balance of <$775> can be composed of up to four cost variances: a DVOH spending variance and usage variances for each of the three services it used (Cafeteria, Administration, and Laundry). While the Laundry Department's VOH account balance is zero, this total could be comprised of three different cost variances: a DVOH spending variance, a usage variance for meals eaten, and a usage variance for files processed.

Actual Fixed Cost Allocations

Actual fixed service department costs are not really allocated to the using departments. Instead, the budgeted FOH is allocated. During the budgeting process, the departments using services contracted to pay for these services as a mixed cost. Using a *budgeted* VOH rate, users pay for the actual meals eaten, files processed, or loads of laundry done. With respect to the fixed costs of having a service available, each user contracted to pay a fair share of the *budgeted* fixed cost. From the users' perspective, they should only have to pay the budgeted rate (multiplied by the actual amount of services used) and the budgeted fixed cost. Accordingly, they should only have to pay the budgeted fixed cost agreed to in the service's cost equation developed as part of the POR and budgeting process. In other words, only the budgeted fixed cost should be allocated to the users of a service. Any difference between the actual FOH and budgeted FOH should remain in the service's FOH account as an FOH budget (spending) variance.

To illustrate this for the Cafeteria's fixed costs, the ending balance in its FOH account is $2,000. From the FOH Allocations in the Solution Section in Exhibit 9–12, actual fixed cafeteria costs were $50,000 against a budget of $48,000. The $2,000 unfavorable FOH budget variance is the responsibility of the Cafeteria manager, and, as with a VOH spending variance, this amount remains in the Cafeteria's account. It is not allocated to the users and buried in the cost of their overhead. In Administration, $33,040 was budgeted for primary (direct) fixed costs. Actual DFOH was $31,040, yielding a $2,000 favorable FOH budget variance for Administration. This variance (overapplied overhead is a credit balance) remains in the Administration FOH account. For Laundry, $59,520 was budgeted and spent for DFOH, so that service center has no ending FOH account balance.

---

[10] The formula for a variable cost spending variance from Chapter 8 is $AQp \times (SP - AP)$. For the cafeteria, 40,000 actual meals eaten $\times$ ($1.90/meal − $2.00/meal) = <$4,000> unfavorable. An unfavorable variance is a debit to the overhead account, as it represents an extra cost. An unfavorable variance represents underapplied overhead.

[11] In Exhibit 9–12, the lines titled "Less: Patient Charges" represent the VOH and FOH applied. In the case of a hospital, rather than applying overhead to individual products (as in a manufacturing firm), overhead is billed to patients.

In summary, by allocating the same amounts at both the beginning of the year and the end of the year, any FOH spending variance remains in the service center FOH account responsible for it. Which cost variances comprise the ending FOH account balance?

■ Under this allocation procedure, the ending FOH account balances contain only one cost variance for *service departments*, the FOH budget variance for the service's DFOH.

■ The ending FOH account balances in *producing departments* can be made up of two FOH cost variances, the DFOH budget variance of the production department and an FOH volume variance if actual patient-days are different from the amount budgeted.

There is no FOH volume variance for the service departments because an FOH POR is not used to allocate service department FOH to other services and production departments. A service's FOH is allocated using the lump-sum amounts budgeted for each user. There is an FOH volume variance, though, in the production department FOH accounts because a rate (FOH POR) is used to apply FOH to individual products. FOH needs to be absorbed into each products' cost and sales price so that total sales revenues are sufficient to pay for the total FOH costs. The FOH POR is multiplied by the volume of its basis in allocating FOH to products. If more products are made than budgeted, more FOH will be allocated than budgeted (resulting in a favorable volume variance).

Service Department Cost Variances

In reconciling the ending overhead account balances and breaking down the balances into their underlying cost variances, Prasid Kalari prepared the analyses shown in Exhibits 9–13 and 9–14 (see p. 424 and p. 426). Exhibit 9–13 contains the cost variances for the service departments that are discussed in the following paragraphs.

CAFETERIA COST VARIANCES.   The Cafeteria's DVOH spending variance has already been illustrated, as has the DFOH budget variance. These two variances are calculated as follows:

$$\text{DVOH spending variance} = AQp \times (SP - AP)$$
$$= 40{,}000 \text{ meals} \times (\$1.90/\text{meal} - \$2.00/\text{meal})$$
$$= <\$4{,}000> \text{ unfavorable}$$

$$\text{DFOH budget variance} = \text{Budgeted DFOH} - \text{Actual DFOH}$$
$$= \$48{,}000 - \$50{,}000$$
$$= <\$2{,}000> \text{ unfavorable}$$

A service department's overhead account balances are made up of its direct (primary) costs spending variances and usage variances for any services allocated to it. Since the Cafeteria is the first service department, no previous service costs are allocated to it. Its overhead account ending balances can only consist of the two variances above, totaling <$6,000>.[12]

ADMINISTRATION COST VARIANCES.   Administration's VOH account balance can be made up of two cost variances, the DVOH spending variance and

---

[12] You may be confused because Exhibit 9–13 presents unfavorable cost variances in brackets (i.e., as negative amounts, such as the $6,000 for the Cafeteria). But, Exhibit 9–12 shows the $6,000 ending balance in the Cafeteria's account without brackets. The reason for the different presentation is that unfavorable cost variances are debit balances in the general ledger. Debit balances are normally presented as positive (unbracketed) values. Also remember that ending debit balances in overhead accounts are underapplied overhead.

■■EXHIBIT 9–13
St. John's Hospital Step Method Allocations: Cost Variance Analysis of Year-End Service Department Overhead Accounts

	QUANTITIES	COSTS PER UNIT	TOTALS
Cafeteria:			
Variable costs should have totaled:		$1.90	$76,000
Actual variable costs for 40,000 meals:		<$2.00>	<$80,000>
Overspent (Unfavorable Spending Variance):		<$0.10>	<$4,000>U
Actual direct fixed costs should not have been different from budget. Overspent by:			<$2,000>U
TOTAL NET UNFAVORABLE SPENDING VARIANCE:			<$6,000>U
Administration:			
Direct Variable Costs should have totaled:		$0.405	$7,290
Actual Direct Variable Costs for 18,000 files:		<$0.345>	<$6,210>
Underspent (Favorable Spending Variance):		$0.060	$1,080 F
Standard Quantity Allowed (meals per file):	900		
Actual meals eaten:	<1,000>		
Unfavorable Meal Usage Variance	<100>	$1.90	<$190>U
Net Favorable Variable Cost Variance:			$890 F
Favorable Direct Fixed Costs Spending Variance:			$2,000 F
TOTAL NET FAVORABLE COST VARIANCE:			$2,890 F
Laundry Services:			
Direct Variable Costs should have totaled:		$3.83	$38,300
Actual Direct Variable Costs (10,000 Loads):		<$3.86>	<$38,600>
Unfavorable Direct VOH Spending Variance:		<$0.03>	<$300>U
Standard Quantity Allowed (meals per load):	500		
Actual meals eaten:	<400>		
Favorable Meal Usage Variance:	100	$1.90	$190 F
Standard Quantity Allowed (files per load):	1,500		
Actual files processed:	<1,280>		
Favorable File Usage Variance:	220	$0.50	$110 F
Net Variable Costs Variance:			$0
Direct Fixed Costs Spending Variance:			$0
TOTAL NET COST VARIANCE:			$0

a Cafeteria usage variance. Its FOH balance consists of only one variance, the DFOH budget variance.

$$\text{DVOH spending variance} = AQp \times (SP - AP)$$
$$= 18{,}000 \text{ files} \times (\$0.405/\text{file} - \$0.345/\text{file})$$
$$= \$1{,}080 \text{ favorable}$$

The $0.50 budgeted file rate (Exhibit 9–12) consists of $0.405 per file for DVOH ($8,100 ÷ 20,000 budgeted files) and $0.095 per file for variable meal costs ($1,900 ÷ 20,000 files). The actual DVOH rate is $6,210 ÷ 18,000 actual files ($0.345). These calculations are shown in the Administration section of Exhibit 9–13.

$$\text{Meal usage variance} = SP \times (SQA - AQu)$$
$$= \$1.90/\text{meal} \times (900 \text{ meals} - 1{,}000 \text{ meals})$$
$$= \$<190> \text{ unfavorable}$$

The standard quantity of meals per file is 0.05 (1,000 budgeted meals ÷

20,000 budgeted files). This manager budgeted 1,000 meals to be eaten if 20,000 files are planned to be processed. Thus, 20 files should be processed for each meal eaten. Since 18,000 files were actually processed, only 900 meals (the SQA) should have been eaten.

$$\begin{aligned} \text{DFOH budget variance} &= \text{Budgeted DFOH} - \text{Actual DFOH} \\ &= \$33,040 - \$31,040 \\ &= \underline{\$2,000 \text{ favorable}} \end{aligned}$$

LAUNDRY SERVICES COST VARIANCES.   As the third service department in the step method allocation order, Laundry Services' VOH account balance can consist of three variances: its DVOH spending variance and usage variances for each of the two services allocated to it. Its FOH balance consists of the DFOH budget variance.

$$\begin{aligned} \text{DVOH spending variance} &= \text{AQp} \times (\text{SP} - \text{AP}) \\ &= 10,000 \text{ loads} \times (\$3.83/\text{load} - \$3.86/\text{load}) \\ &= \underline{<\$300> \text{ unfavorable}} \end{aligned}$$

The budgeted DVOH rate is \$3.83 (\$38,300 budgeted DVOH ÷ 10,000 budgeted loads). The actual DVOH laundry rate is \$3.86 per load (\$38,600 ÷ 10,000 loads).

$$\begin{aligned} \text{Meal usage variance} &= \text{SP} \times (\text{SQA} - \text{AQu}) \\ &= \$1.90/\text{meal} \times (500 \text{ meals} - 400 \text{ meals}) \\ &= \underline{\$190 \text{ favorable}} \end{aligned}$$

The standard quantity of meals per load of laundry is 0.05 meals per load (500 budgeted meals ÷ 10,000 budgeted loads). If 10,000 actual loads of laundry were done, 500 meals should have been eaten.

$$\begin{aligned} \text{Files usage variance} &= \text{SP} \times (\text{SQA} - \text{AQu}) \\ &= \$0.50/\text{file} \times (1,500 \text{ files} - 1,280 \text{ files}) \\ &= \underline{\$110 \text{ favorable}} \end{aligned}$$

The number of files that should have been processed for the loads of laundry actually done (SQA) is 1,500 (SQ of 0.15 files per load multiplied by the 10,000 actual loads). The SQ for files is 1,500 budgeted files ÷ 10,000 budgeted loads. There is no FOH ending balance for Laundry Services because its budgeted and actual DFOH are \$59,520.

Production Department Cost Variances

Exhibit 9–14 (see p. 426) reports the overhead cost variances for each of the billing departments. The VOH variances can include a direct VOH spending variance for each billing department and usage variances for each service allocated to it. The FOH variances include a direct FOH budget variance and a volume variance for each billing department. These variances are calculated below.

OUT-PATIENT OVERHEAD COST VARIANCES

$$\begin{aligned} \text{DVOH spending variance} &= \text{AQp} \times (\text{SP} - \text{AP}) \\ &= 6,500 \text{ patient-days} \times \\ &\quad (\$2.00/\text{patient-day} - \$1.70/\text{patient-day}) \\ &= \underline{\$1,950 \text{ favorable}} \end{aligned}$$

■ EXHIBIT 9–14

St. John's Hospital Step Method Allocations: Cost Variance Analysis of Year-End Billing Department Overhead Accounts

	QUANTITIES	COSTS PER UNIT	TOTALS
Out-Patient:			
Direct VOH costs should have totaled:		$2.00	$13,000
Actual Direct VOH costs for 6,500 patients:		<$1.70>	<$11,050>
Favorable DVOH Spending Variance:		$0.30	$1,950 F
Standard Quantity Allowed (files per patient-day):	3,250		
Actual files processed:	< 4,000>		
Unfavorable File Usage Variance:	<750>	$0.50	<$375>U
Standard Quantity Allowed (loads per patient-day):	1,300		
Actual loads done:	<1,500>		
Unfavorable Laundry Usage Variance:	<200>	$4.00	<$800>U
Net Favorable Variable Costs Variance:			$775 F
Unfavorable Direct FOH Spending Variance			<$3,042>U
Actual Patient-days:	6,500		
Budgeted Patient-days:	<6,000>		
Favorable FOH Volume Variance:	500	$7.00	$3,500 F
Net Favorable FOH Cost Variance:			$458 F
TOTAL NET FAVORABLE COST VARIANCE:			$1,233 F
Obstetrics:			
Direct VOH costs should have totaled:		$5.00	$20,000
Actual Direct VOH costs for 4,000 patients:		<$3.75>	<$15,000>
Favorable DVOH Spending Variance:		$1.25	$5,000 F
Standard Quantity Allowed (meals per patient-day):	8,000		
Actual meals eaten:	<8,600>		
Unfavorable Meal Usage Variance:	<600>	$1.90	<$1,140>U
Standard Quantity Allowed (files per patient-day):	1,200		
Actual files processed:	<1,500>		
Unfavorable File Usage Variance:	<300>	$0.50	<$150>U
Standard Quantity Allowed (loads per patient-day):	400		
Actual loads done:	<500>		
Unfavorable Laundry Usage Variance:	<100>	$4.00	<$400>U
Net Variable Costs Variance:			$3,310 F
Unfavorable Direct FOH Spending Variance:			<$43,262>U
Actual Patient-days:	4,000		
Budgeted Patient-days:	<3,000>		
Favorable FOH Volume Variance:	1,000	$40.00	$40,000 F
Net Unfavorable FOH Cost Variance:			<$3,262>U
TOTAL NET FAVORABLE COST VARIANCE:			$48 F
General:			
Direct VOH costs should have totaled:		$5.034	$226,530
Actual Direct VOH costs for 45,000 patients:		<$3.953>	<$177,885>
Favorable DVOH Spending Variance:		$1.081	$48,645 F
Standard Quantity Allowed (meals per patient-day):	27,000		
Actual meals eaten:	<30,000>		
Unfavorable Meal Usage Variance:	<3,000>	$1.90	<$5,700>U
Standard Quantity Allowed (files per patient-day):	13,140		
Actual files processed:	<11,220>		
Favorable File Usage Variance:	1,920	$0.50	$960 F

Continued

—Continued

	QUANTITIES	COSTS PER UNIT	TOTALS
Standard Quantity Allowed (loads per patient-day):	7,650		
Actual loads done:	<8,000>		
Unfavorable Laundry Usage Variance:	<350>	$4.00	<$1,400>U
Net Favorable Variable Costs Variance:			$42,505 F
Favorable Direct FOH Spending Variance:			$4,744 F
Actual Patient-days:	45,000		
Budgeted Patient-Days:	<50,000>		
Unfavorable FOH Volume Variance:	<5,000>	$9.00	<$45,000>U
Net Unfavorable FOH Cost Variance:			<$40,256>U
TOTAL NET FAVORABLE COST VARIANCE:			$2,249 F

The budgeted DVOH of $12,000 (Exhibit 9–11) ÷ 6,000 budgeted patient-days equals the $2.00 per patient-day budgeted rate. The actual rate is $11,050 ÷ 6,500 actual patient-days ($1.70).

$$\text{File usage variance} = SP \times (SQA - AQu)$$
$$= \$0.50/\text{file} \times (3,250 \text{ files} - 4,000 \text{ files})$$
$$= <\$375> \text{ unfavorable}$$

For outpatient treatments, planning called for 3,000 files to be processed for 6,000 patient-days (Exhibit 9–11), yielding a standard quantity of 0.5 files per patient-day and an SQA of 3,250 files for the 6,500 actual patient-days.

$$\text{Laundry usage variance} = SP \times (SQA - AQu)$$
$$= \$4.00/\text{load} \times (1,300 \text{ loads} - 1,500 \text{ loads})$$
$$= <\$800> \text{ unfavorable}$$

From the budgeted information in the Data Section of Exhibit 9–11, the loads of laundry planned (1,200) for the budgeted patient-days (6,000) yields a standard quantity of 0.2 loads per patient-day. For the actual 6,500 patient-days incurred, then, 1,300 loads should have been done.

$$\text{DFOH budget variance} = \text{Budgeted DFOH} - \text{Actual DFOH}$$
$$= \$26,958 - \$30,000$$
$$= <\$3,042> \text{ unfavorable}$$

$$\text{FOH volume variance} = \text{FOH POR} \times$$
$$\quad (\text{Actual patient-days} - \text{Budgeted patient-days})$$
$$= \$7.00/\text{patient-day} \times (6,500 - 6,000)$$
$$= \$3,500 \text{ favorable}$$

The volume variance arises because FOH has to be absorbed into the cost of each patient-day. In other words, the FOH has to be billed to all the patients by breaking it down into a rate per patient-day. This is absorption costing. The FOH volume variance only arises with absorption costing. There are no volume variances for the service departments' FOH allocations because a rate is not needed to allocate service department FOH to the production departments' FOH accounts.

Why is an FOH POR needed for production departments in applying FOH to products (stage three allocations), but not needed for service-to-production department (stage two) allocations? The number of departments receiving a service's FOH allocation is known. Therefore, a lump-sum amount can be allocated to each. If the number of patient-days could be known with certainty, then a lump-sum amount of FOH could be applied to each department. But, because sales and production volumes are not known when budgeting, an FOH POR must be calculated based on the estimated volumes. When the estimated and actual volumes do not agree, an FOH volume variance results.

OBSTETRICS AND GENERAL OVERHEAD COST VARIANCES. The cost variances of the Obstetrics and General Billing departments are calculated in the same way as for the Outpatient Treatment center, and, therefore, will not be reproduced here.[13] The VOH account for Obstetrics contains four cost variances: the DVOH spending variance ($5,000 favorable) and a meal usage variance ($1,140 unfavorable), file usage variance ($150 unfavorable), and laundry usage variance ($400 unfavorable). The DFOH budget variance for Obstetrics is $43,262 unfavorable, and the FOH volume variance is $40,000 favorable.

The same variances exist in the VOH and FOH accounts for the General Wing of St. John's Hospital. These variances include a DVOH spending variance ($48,645 favorable), meal usage variance ($5,700 unfavorable), file usage variance ($960 favorable), laundry usage variance ($1,400 unfavorable), direct FOH budget variance ($4,744 favorable), and FOH volume variance ($45,000 unfavorable).

Standard Cost Accounting Systems for Service Department Allocations

Prasid Kalari developed a normal JOCAS for St. John's Hospital, but cost variances were calculated and reported annually. An SCAS could have been used. How would an SCAS differ from the normal JOCAS used by Kalari? In an SCAS, cost variances are journalized into separate subsidiary WIP accounts for each responsibility center. These "level three" accounts within WIP were first introduced in Chapter 8 (Exhibit 8–8). When service departments are present, each will have its own cost variance accounts just like the production departments' cost variance accounts.

In journalizing service department VOH cost variances, the stage two amounts allocated to production departments are calculated by using the budgeted rates multiplied by the standard quantity of the service allowed, rather than the actual quantity of the service used. Accordingly, instead of including the usage variances for services within the using department's VOH account balance, these can be journalized to that department's cost variance accounts if using an SCAS. When the actual amount of a service is used to allocate VOH, the usage variance remains within the user's VOH and FOH accounts as ending under- or over-applied overhead.

As long as cost variances are properly calculated and reported to the correct responsibility centers, whether or not they are journalized into special accounts (as with an SCAS) is not critical for effective cost management. The important attribute of a high-quality overhead accounting system is that the cost variances are reported to the proper responsibility centers. This reporting should be timely enough to allow corrective actions and operational control. It is unlikely that St. John's annual reporting will promote operational control actions if cost variances are only reported annually.

---

[13] It probably is a good idea to go back to Exhibits 9–12 and 9–14 and work through the cost variance calculations.

SUMMARY OF LEARNING OBJECTIVES

The major goals of this chapter were to enable you to achieve four learning objectives:

Learning objective 1.   Discuss the need for multiple overhead accounts within WIP.

Overhead represents the indirect costs of making a product or providing a service. These costs, which are becoming a more significant portion of the total manufacturing costs as enterprises automate processes, need to be accounted for in a way that promotes accurate product costing and cost management. Traditionally, CASs were designed primarily for financial reporting. All overhead items were (and still are in many manufacturers) journalized into one TOH account, and one TOH POR was created to apply these costs to production.

To understand and control overhead, and to measure the costs of making a product more accurately, multiple overhead accounts are needed. Each overhead account should have a POR that applies that overhead based on the activities that cause it.

Separate overhead accounts can be created for VOH and FOH and for each production and service department. This allows overhead costs and their cost variances to be directly traced to responsibility centers. In addition to facilitating control over these costs, separate PORs can more accurately apply VOH and FOH based on their different causes.

Accumulating primary costs in departmental overhead accounts is the first stage in overhead accounting. The second stage involves secondary overhead cost allocations from service departments to other service and production departments using those services. Variable and fixed service costs should be allocated using a basis that represents their usage. Once all overhead costs have been allocated into production department VOH and FOH accounts, then (stage three) these costs can be applied to products as they pass through the production departments.

Learning objective 2.   Describe how the general ledger system for WIP can be designed to provide more accurate product cost information and cost management information.

WIP consists of two "levels" of subsidiary accounts in a normal PCAS or JOCAS. These are the product cost accounts (jobs or production departments) and overhead accounts. Product costs are level one accounts. Overhead accounts are level two accounts. SCASs add a third level of subsidiary accounts, as discussed in Learning Objective 4.

The overhead accounts consist of two control accounts, one for VOH and one for FOH. Within the VOH and FOH control accounts, there are separate accounts for each production and service department. Using multiple overhead accounts enables these costs to be accumulated according to the departments that are responsible for their management and control.

Using proper allocation techniques (summarized in the next learning objective), a more accurate product cost can result. By analyzing the ending balances in each overhead account, the CAS can also provide cost variance information to promote cost management.

Learning objective 3.   Explain how to allocate service department costs to production departments, and describe the different methods that can be used.

Four methods can be used for making secondary (stage two) overhead cost allocations between service department accounts and production department overhead accounts:

- The direct method allocates each service department independently to production departments. This method is the simplest of the four, but it provides the least accurate allocations when reciprocal usage between service departments exists.
- The step method improves upon the direct method by making one-way allocations of certain services to other service departments. Once a service has been allocated no other services can be allocated "back" to it. This method reduces the cross-subsidization costing problem that occurs with the direct method, but does not eliminate it. Eliminating the problem requires simultaneous allocations between service departments.

■ The reciprocal method, using simultaneous equations, allocates service department costs back-and-forth between services. Accordingly, it is considered to provide the most accurate product cost. The allocations can be performed with a fairly simple spreadsheet program, although the circular error problem may require the use of matrix algebra or linear programming as the number of services increases.

■ The reciprocal method allocates service costs based on the percentages of services used by other departments. For better cost management information, separate allocations should be made for VOH and FOH. The variable service costs should be allocated with a budgeted rate (summarized under the next objective). The fixed service costs should be allocated using percentages based on the relative size of each user in terms of the service rendered. These relative size ratios are calculated using the maximum amount of the service that could be requested by each user if it is operating at full production capacity.

Learning objective 4.   Design an SCAS that includes cost variances for both production and service departments.

An SCAS adds a third level of subsidiary accounts to WIP. These are for departmental cost variances. Both service departments and production departments should have cost variance accounts.

To calculate overhead cost variances properly, service department variable costs should be allocated using a POR. By using a POR, the DVOH spending variance can be isolated within the responsibility center's VOH account. Fixed overhead should be allocated using relative size ratios. This allows the DFOH budget variance to be isolated within the departmental overhead account responsible for controlling the cost of that service.

Within a normal CAS, service department variable costs are allocated using the actual quantity of the service instead of the SQA. This moves the services' usage variances to the VOH accounts of the departments using those services. The ending balances in the VOH accounts of each service and production department will then include that department's DVOH spending variance, as well as usage variances for each service used by it. The ending over- and underapplied overhead balances in each service and production department's account are analyzed in terms of the overhead cost variances that make up those ending balances.

With an SCAS, the variances are journalized into the variance accounts for each department. Thus, VOH and FOH cost variances are moved out of the service and production department VOH and FOH accounts. With an SCAS, then, there are no ending over- or underapplied overhead account balances.

IMPORTANT TERMS

Direct method   A cost allocation technique that allocates service department costs directly to production departments without making any inter-service department allocations. It is the simplest, but least accurate, of the secondary (stage two) cost allocation methods.

Primary cost assignment   In stage one, overhead costs are initially assigned to the service and production departments' VOH and FOH accounts.

Production departments (operating departments, cells, or workcenters)   The areas where the central purposes of the organization are carried out; that is, where work is performed directly on products manufactured or services are performed for customers.

Reciprocal method   A cost allocation technique that considers all interrelationships of the departments and reflects these relationships in simultaneous equations. This is considered to provide the most accurate allocations of the three methods.

Secondary cost allocation   Stage two involves allocating service department costs to other service and production departments. Once all service department costs are allocated to production department overhead accounts, they are included in the departmental PORs.

Service departments   Areas or segments of the organization that do not engage directly in production activities, but are used to provide assistance and support for production departments.

Step method   A cost allocation technique that allows for limited recognition of services rendered by service departments to other service departments. It provides more accurate PORs and product costs than the direct method, but it is not as accurate as the reciprocal method.

DEMONSTRATION PROBLEMS

■ DEMONSTRATION PROBLEM 1   *Allocation of budgeted service department costs by the direct method.*

Use the information from St. John's Hospital in Exhibit 9–11 to calculate VOH and FOH PORs for each of its three billing departments. Allocate the variable service department costs using a budgeted rate for each service based on budgeted cost of the service and budgeted demand. The FOH allocations should be based on relative size ratios. Discuss the differences that result from the direct method and the step method.

SOLUTION TO DEMONSTRATION PROBLEM 1

The solution is presented below and on top of the next page. The same spreadsheet program used for the step method in Exhibit 9–11 can be used for the direct method. The difference between the two methods is that with the direct method, no service department costs are allocated to other service departments.

This is reflected in the Data Section by inputting zero meals and zero files for Administration and Laundry Services. As can be seen in the VOH and FOH Solution Sections, no service department costs are allocated to other services. Instead they are directly allocated to the billing departments.

Because no Cafeteria or Administrative Services costs were allocated to other service departments, the meal rate increased. It now represents a rate based just on the meals eaten in the billing departments. The file and laundry rates decreased from the step method rates, for the same reason (no inter-service allocations). No previous service department costs are included in the direct method rates for these (subsequent) services. The FOH allocations also changed from the step method amounts for the same reason.

The ultimate effect on the VOH, FOH, and TOH PORs appears negligible in this example. But, this may not always be the case. If these allocations are done manually, then the direct method, which is easier, may provide accurate enough PORs and product costs. Alternatively, if a spreadsheet program is used, it takes no more time to input the raw data necessary for the step method. Since it produces more accurate cost allocations and PORs, the step method seems the logical choice.

A word of caution is in order. The spreadsheet program is formatted to display all allocations rounded to the nearest whole dollar. The rate cells are formatted to display dollars and cents. For example, the meal rate is $1.979167. When doing these calculations manually, using $1.98 will produce slightly different amounts. Additionally, this formatting choice appears to create some minor addition errors. For example, the Outpatient VOH and FOH really sum to $59,947 (rounded). But, $17,910 + $42,038 = $59,948. The modern management accountant understands that this is not an addition error in the program, and is not bothered by this. It is simply a rounding problem created by the formatting option used and is of no real consequence.

DATA SECTION: BUDGET ALLOCATIONS AT BEGINNING OF PERIOD (BOP)

	SERVICE DEPARTMENTS			BILLING DEPARTMENTS		
	CAFETERIA	ADMIN	LAUNDRY	OUTPATIENT	OB	GENERAL
BUDGETED DVOH	$71,250	$8,100	$38,300	$12,000	$15,000	$251,700
BUDGETED MEALS	36,000	0	0	0	6,000	30,000
BUDGETED FILES		18,500	0	3,000	900	14,600
BUDGETED LOADS			10,000	1,200	300	8,500
BUDGETED PATIENT-DAYS				6,000	3,000	50,000
BUDGETED DFOH	$48,000	$33,040	$59,520	$26,958	$99,738	$344,744
CAPACITY MEALS	48,500	0	0	0	8,500	40,000
CAPACITY FILES		18,000	0	4,000	6,000	8,000
CAPACITY LOADS			12,000	1,560	360	10,080

SOLUTION SECTION: BUDGET ALLOCATIONS AT BEGINNING OF PERIOD (BOP)

VOH ALLOCATIONS:		SERVICE DEPARTMENTS			BILLING DEPARTMENTS		
		CAFETERIA	ADMIN	LAUNDRY	OUTPATIENT	OB	GENERAL
BUDGETED DVOH		$71,250	$8,100	$38,300	$12,000	$15,000	$251,700
MEAL RATE	$1.98						
MEAL ALLOCATION		<71,250>	0	0	0	11,875	59,375
FILE RATE	$0.44						
FILE ALLOCATION			<8,100>	0	1,314	394	6,392
LAUNDRY RATE	$3.83						
LAUNDRY ALLOCATION				<38,300>	4,596	1,149	32,555
TOTAL VOH		$0	$0	$0	$17,910	$28,418	$350,022
VOH POR/PATIENT-DAY					$2.98	$9.47	$7.00
FOH ALLOCATIONS:							
BUDGETED DFOH		$48,000	$33,040	$59,520	$26,958	$99,738	$344,744
MEAL CAPACITIES		100%	0%	0%	0%	18%	82%
MEAL ALLOCATION		<48,000>	0	0	0	8,412	39,588
FILE CAPACITIES			100%	0%	22%	33%	44%
FILE ALLOCATION			<33,040>	0	7,342	11,013	14,684
LAUNDRY CAPACITIES				100%	13%	3%	84%
LAUNDRY ALLOCATION				<59,520>	7,738	1,786	49,997
TOTAL FOH		$0	$0	$0	$42,038	$120,949	$449,013
FOH POR/PATIENT-DAY					$7.01	$40.32	$8.98
TOH BUDGETED		$0	$0	$0	$59,947	$149,367	$799,035
TOH POR/PATIENT-DAY					$9.99	$49.79	$15.98

■ **DEMONSTRATION PROBLEM 2**   *Allocation of budgeted service department costs by the step method.*

Using the following new raw data for St. John's Hospital, calculate VOH and FOH PORs for each of its three billing departments. Allocate the variable service department costs using a budgeted rate for each service based on the budgeted cost of the service and budgeted demand. The FOH allocations should be based on relative size ratios.

St. John's Hospital Step Method Allocations
Budget Allocations for PORs

DATA SECTION: BUDGET ALLOCATIONS AT BEGINNING OF PERIOD (BOP)

	SERVICE DEPARTMENTS			BILLING DEPARTMENTS		
	CAFETERIA	ADMIN	LAUNDRY	OUTPATIENT	OB	GENERAL
BUDGETED DVOH	$75,000	$8,000	$5,000	$15,280	$5,600	$35,120
BUDGETED MEALS	30,000	900	400	0	8,000	20,700
BUDGETED FILES		25,625	1,500	3,800	8,000	12,325
BUDGETED LOADS			11,000	2,000	2,000	7,000
BUDGETED PATIENT-DAYS				6,000	3,000	48,000
BUDGETED DFOH	$60,000	$17,500	$20,000	$39,766	$99,696	$315,038
CAPACITY MEALS	50,000	1,000	500	0	8,500	40,000
CAPACITY FILES		35,000	3,500	7,000	10,500	14,000
CAPACITY LOADS			12,000	2,400	2,400	7,200

SOLUTION TO DEMONSTRATION PROBLEM 2

DATA SECTION: BUDGET ALLOCATIONS AT BEGINNING OF PERIOD (BOP)

	SERVICE DEPARTMENTS			BILLING DEPARTMENTS		
	CAFETERIA	ADMIN	LAUNDRY	OUTPATIENT	OB	GENERAL
BUDGETED DVOH	$75,000	$8,000	$5,000	$15,280	$5,600	$35,120
BUDGETED MEALS	30,000	900	400	0	8,000	20,700
BUDGETED FILES		25,625	1,500	3,800	8,000	12,325
BUDGETED LOADS			11,000	2,000	2,000	7,000
BUDGETED PATIENT-DAYS				6,000	3,000	48,000
BUDGETED DFOH	$60,000	$17,500	$20,000	$39,766	$99,696	$315,038
CAPACITY MEALS	50,000	1,000	500	0	8,500	40,000
CAPACITY FILES		35,000	3,500	7,000	10,500	14,000
CAPACITY LOADS			12,000	2,400	2,400	7,200

SOLUTION SECTION: BUDGET ALLOCATIONS AT BEGINNING OF PERIOD (BOP)

VOH ALLOCATIONS:		SERVICE DEPARTMENTS			BILLING DEPARTMENTS		
		CAFETERIA	ADMIN	LAUNDRY	OUTPATIENT	OB	GENERAL
BUDGETED DVOH		$75,000	$8,000	$5,000	$15,280	$5,600	$35,120
MEAL RATE	$2.50						
MEAL ALLOCATION		<75,000>	2,250	1,000	0	20,000	51,750
FILE RATE	$0.40						
FILE ALLOCATION			<10,250>	600	1,520	3,200	4,930
LAUNDRY RATE	$0.60						
LAUNDRY ALLOCATION				<6,600>	1,200	1,200	4,200
TOTAL VOH		$0	$0	$0	$18,000	$30,000	$96,000
VOH POR/PATIENT-DAY					$3.00	$10.00	$2.00
FOH ALLOCATIONS:							
BUDGETED DFOH		$60,000	$17,500	$20,000	$39,766	$99,696	$315,038
MEAL CAPACITIES		100%	2%	1%	0%	17%	80%
MEAL ALLOCATION		<60,000>	1,200	600	0	10,200	48,000
FILE CAPACITIES			100%	10%	20%	30%	40%
FILE ALLOCATION			<18,700>	1,870	3,740	5,610	7,480
LAUNDRY CAPACITIES				100%	20%	20%	60%
LAUNDRY ALLOCATION				<22,470>	4,494	4,494	13,482
TOTAL FOH		$0	$0	$0	$48,000	$120,000	$384,000
FOH POR/PATIENT-DAY					$8.00	$40.00	$8.00
TOH BUDGETED		$0	$0	$0	$66,000	$150,000	$480,000
TOH POR/PATIENT-DAY					$11.00	$50.00	$10.00

■ **DEMONSTRATION PROBLEM 3** *Allocation of actual service department costs by the step method.*

Using the following new raw data for St. John's Hospital, allocate actual service department costs to each of its three billing departments. Allocate the actual variable service department costs using a budgeted rate for each service (based on the budgeted cost of the service and budgeted demand from Demonstration Problem 2) and actual demand. The FOH allocations should be based on relative size ratios.

St. John's Hospital Step Method Allocations
Year-End Actual Costs Allocations

DATA SECTION: ACTUAL COST ALLOCATIONS AT END OF PERIOD (EOP)

	SERVICE DEPARTMENTS			BILLING DEPARTMENTS		
	CAFETERIA	ADMIN	LAUNDRY	OUTPATIENT	OB	GENERAL
ACTUAL DVOH	$80,000	$5,200	$5,000	$15,000	$10,000	$25,000
ACTUAL MEALS	39,250	800	450	0	8,000	30,000
ACTUAL FILES		18,000	1,280	4,000	1,500	11,220
ACTUAL LOADS			10,000	1,500	500	8,000
ACTUAL PATIENT-DAYS				6,500	4,000	45,000
ACTUAL DFOH	$60,000	$17,000	$22,000	$41,766	$95,000	$340,000

SOLUTION TO DEMONSTRATION PROBLEM 3

DATA SECTION: ACTUAL COST ALLOCATIONS AT END OF PERIOD (EOP)

	SERVICE DEPARTMENTS			BILLING DEPARTMENTS		
	CAFETERIA	ADMIN	LAUNDRY	OUTPATIENT	OB	GENERAL
ACTUAL DVOH	$80,000	$5,200	$5,000	$15,000	$10,000	$25,000
ACTUAL MEALS	39,250	800	450	0	8,000	30,000
ACTUAL FILES		18,000	1,280	4,000	1,500	11,220
ACTUAL LOADS			10,000	1,500	500	8,000
ACTUAL PATIENT-DAYS				6,500	4,000	45,000
ACTUAL DFOH	$60,000	$17,000	$22,000	$41,766	$95,000	$340,000

SOLUTION SECTION: ACTUAL COST ALLOCATIONS AT END OF PERIOD (EOP)

VOH ALLOCATIONS:		SERVICE DEPARTMENTS			BILLING DEPARTMENTS		
		CAFETERIA	ADMIN	LAUNDRY	OUTPATIENT	OB	GENERAL
ACTUAL DVOH		$80,000	$5,200	$5,000	$15,000	$10,000	$25,000
MEAL RATE	$2.50						
MEAL ALLOCATION		<98,125>	2,000	1,125	0	20,000	75,000
FILE RATE	$0.40						
FILE ALLOCATION			<7,200>	512	1,600	600	4,488
LAUNDRY RATE	$0.60						
LAUNDRY ALLOCATION				<6,000>	900	300	4,800
TOTAL VOH		<$18,125>	$0	$637	$17,500	$30,900	$109,288
LESS: PATIENT CHARGES					<19,500>	<40,000>	<90,000>
ENDING VOH BALANCE		<$18,125>	$0	$637	<$2,000>	<$9,100>	$19,288
FOH ALLOCATIONS:							
ACTUAL DFOH		$60,000	$17,000	$22,000	$41,766	$95,000	$340,000
MEAL CAPACITIES		100%	2%	1%	0%	17%	80%
MEAL ALLOCATION		<60,000>	1,200	600	0	10,200	48,000
FILE CAPACITIES			100%	10%	20%	30%	40%
FILE ALLOCATION			<18,700>	1,870	3,740	5,610	7,480
LAUNDRY CAPACITIES				100%	20%	20%	60%
LAUNDRY ALLOCATION				<22,470>	4,494	4,494	13,482
TOTAL FOH		$0	<$500>	$2,000	$50,000	$115,304	$408,962
LESS: PATIENT CHARGES					<52,000>	<160,000>	<360,000>
ENDING FOH BALANCE		$0	<$500>	$2,000	<$2,000>	<$44,696>	$48,962
ENDING TOH BALANCE		<$18,125>	<$500>	$2,637	<$4,000>	<$53,796>	$68,250

▌REVIEW QUESTIONS

9.1 What is the overall goal of all CASs?

9.2 Why it is impossible in most situations to design a CAS that provides the true cost of a product or service?

9.3 Is overhead becoming a more or less significant component of the cost of products or services? Why?

9.4 Why do many traditional manufacturing firms only have one TOH account?

9.5 What is the difference between a service department and a production department? Give several examples of both.

9.6 Explain why service department costs are allocated to production departments.

9.7 List five different ways to break down the TOH POR.

9.8 Give four reasons for designing multiple PORs within a CAS.

9.9 Why are departmental predetermined overhead rates usually preferable to a plant-wide blanket rate?

9.10 Can the use of one TOH POR create product cost cross-subsidies?

9.11 Do separate VOH and FOH PORs provide better product costs? Can they provide better cost management information?

9.12 What is the purpose of primary cost allocation? What is the purpose of secondary cost allocation?

9.13 Distinguish between the three stages in overhead cost allocation.

9.14 List three criteria for choosing an overhead allocation basis.

9.15 Develop possible allocation bases for the costs of the service departments identified in Review Question 9.5.

9.16 Describe the direct service department cost allocation method, and list its advantages and disadvantages.

9.17 Describe the step method, and list its advantages and disadvantages.

9.18 Describe the reciprocal method, and list its advantages and disadvantages.

9.19 Why is a spreadsheet program useful in performing reciprocal service department allocations?

9.20 What are "vicious circles of allocations" and how can one know whether they exist within a spreadsheet program?

9.21 What factors can cause under- or overapplied overhead?

9.22 How can cost variance analysis of overhead costs aid cost management when service departments are present?

9.23 Discuss two reasons why cost variance analysis is difficult when percentages are used to allocate service department total costs.

9.24 What types of level two WIP accounts should be designed into a high-quality CAS?

9.25 Why is group decision making and coordination important in budgeting VOH PORs?

9.26 How can some costs be direct costs of a department but indirect costs of a product?

9.27 A high-quality CAS develops budgeted rates for variable service department costs. Why?

9.28 How is a budgeted variable rate for a service department developed?

9.29 Why are relative size ratios used to allocate fixed service department costs?

9.30 How is a relative size ratio calculated?

9.31 Can cost equations represent contracts between the providers of services and the users of services?

9.32 How are budgeted rates used to allocate actual service department variable costs?

9.33 Describe how the allocation of variable service department costs can isolate spending and usage variances in the proper responsibility centers.

9.34 Which variances appear in the ending VOH account balances of service and producing departments?

9.35 Why are actual fixed service department costs *not* allocated to the departments using that service?

9.36 How can fixed service department costs be allocated so that their spending variances are properly assigned to responsibility centers?

9.37 Which variances comprise the ending FOH balances of service and production department FOH accounts?

9.38 Why are FOH PORs needed for production departments but not for service departments?

9.39 What design changes would be made for an SCAS (versus a normal CAS)?

9.40 How many cost variance accounts should be included in a high-quality SCAS?

CHAPTER-SPECIFIC PROBLEMS

These problems require responses based directly on concepts and techniques presented in the text.

9.41 *Multiple-choice questions concerning service department allocations.*

1. Allocation of service department costs to production departments is necessary to:

   a. Predict costs.
   b. Coordinate production activity.
   c. Determine predetermined overhead rates.
   d. All of the above.

2. The overhead cost allocation method that usually starts with the service department rendering services to the greatest number of other service departments and progresses in descending order to the service department rendering service to the smallest number of other service departments is the:

   a. Step method.
   b. Direct method.
   c. Reciprocal method.
   d. Partial method.

3. The overhead cost allocation method that allocates service department costs without consideration of services rendered to other service departments is the:

   a. Direct method.
   b. Reciprocal method.
   c. Step method.
   d. POR method.

4. The most accurate method for allocating service department costs is the:

   a. Step method.
   b. Direct method.
   c. Reciprocal method.
   d. None of the above.

5. The method that recognizes service provided by one service department to another but does not recognize reciprocal interdepartmental service is the:

   a. Direct method.
   b. Reciprocal method.
   c. Simultaneous equation method.
   d. Step method.

6. The janitorial department provides cleaning services to all departments of a large store. Management wishes to allocate the janitorial costs to the various sales departments that benefit from this service. What would be the most reasonable allocation base for janitorial services?

   a. Sales of each department.
   b. Number of employees in each department.
   c. Square footage of each department.
   d. Number of inventory items.

7. The function of a cost allocation base is to:

   a. Estimate service department costs.
   b. Allocate costs.
   c. Develop a cost object.
   d. Divide conversion costs.

8. Why are predetermined overhead rates used?

a. To budget overhead costs.
b. To smooth seasonal variability of overhead costs.
c. Allow timely product and service costing.
d. Both (b) and (c).

9. It is proper to allocate variable and fixed elements of overhead costs by individual predetermined overhead rates for:

a. Service departments to production departments.
b. Production departments to the final output units of products and services.
c. Both (a) and (b).
d. None of the above.

9.42 *Departmental predetermined overhead rates.* Tillman Corporation has two production departments, M and A. Budgeted manufacturing costs for the year were as follows:

	DEPARTMENT M	DEPARTMENT A
Direct materials	$700,000	$100,000
Direct labor	200,000	800,000
Manufacturing overhead	600,000	400,000

The actual material and labor costs charged to job 432 during the year were as follows:

Direct materials		$25,000
Direct labor:		
Department M	$ 8,000	
Department A	12,000	$20,000

Tillman applies manufacturing overhead to production orders on the basis of direct labor cost using departmental rates predetermined at the beginning of the year based on the annual budget.

Required:
Determine the total annual manufacturing costs associated with job 432.
[AICPA adapted]

9.43 *Allocation of service department costs by the direct and step methods.* Thomas Manufacturing Company has two producing departments, Fabrication and Assembly, and three service departments, General Factory Administration, Factory Maintenance, and Factory Cafeteria. A summary of costs and other data for each department prior to allocation of service department costs for the year ended June 30, 19X2, follows:

	PRODUCING DEPARTMENTS		SERVICE DEPARTMENTS		
	FABRICATION	ASSEMBLY	GENERAL FACTORY ADMINISTRATION	FACTORY MAINTENANCE	FACTORY CAFETERIA
Direct labor costs	$1,950,000	$2,050,000	$90,000	$82,100	$87,000
Direct materials costs	3,130,000	950,000	—	65,000	91,000
Factory overhead costs	1,650,000	1,850,000	70,000	56,100	62,000
Direct labor hours	562,500	437,500	31,000	27,000	42,000
Number of employees	280	200	12	8	20
Square footage occupied	88,000	72,000	1,750	2,000	4,800

The costs of General Factory Administration, Factory Maintenance, and Factory Cafeteria are allocated on the basis of direct labor hours, square footage occupied, and number of employees, respectively. Round all final calculations to the nearest dollar.

Required:
a. Assuming that Thomas Manufacturing Company elects to distribute service department costs directly to the producing departments without inter-service

department cost allocation, compute the amount of Factory Maintenance costs that would be allocated to production departments.

b. Assuming the same policy of allocating service department costs to producing departments only, compute the amount of General Factory Administration costs that would be allocated to production departments.

c. Assuming that Thomas Manufacturing Company elects to distribute service department costs to other service departments (starting with the service department with the greatest total costs) as well as to the producing departments and that once a service department's costs have been allocated, no subsequent service department costs are recirculated back to it, compute the total costs for the production departments after the allocation of service department costs.

[AICPA adapted]

9.44 *Allocation of service department costs by the step and reciprocal methods.* Departments A, B, and C provide services to each other and to production departments Y and Z in the following manner:

TOTAL COST		SERVICE DEPARTMENTS			PRODUCTION DEPARTMENTS	
		A	B	C	Y	Z
$100,000	A	—	15%	5%	55%	25%
75,000	B	10%	—	9%	18%	63%
60,000	C	—	—	—	30%	70%
$235,000						

Required:
Make the proper cost allocations using the step method.

9.45 *Reciprocal allocations.* You have been provided with the following equations, which represent total costs for each department (D_1 through D_5) at Crystal-Glo Corporation:

$D_1 = (0.00)D_2 + (0.00)D_3 + (0.00)D_4 + (0.00)D_5 + \$22,000$
$D_2 = (0.25)D_1 + (0.04)D_3 + (0.00)D_4 + (0.00)D_5 + \$18,000$
$D_3 = (0.20)D_1 + (0.40)D_2 + (0.00)D_4 + (0.00)D_5 + \$15,000$
$D_4 = (0.15)D_1 + (0.30)D_2 + (0.36)D_3 + (0.00)D_5 + \$14,400$
$D_5 = (0.40)D_1 + (0.30)D_2 + (0.60)D_3 + (0.00)D_4 + \$65,000$

Required:
Use the reciprocal method to allocate costs between the five departments. Primary costs are given in dollars.

9.46 *Allocation of service department costs using the direct, step, and reciprocal methods.* Hartwell Company distributes service department overhead costs directly to producing departments without allocation to the other service departments. Information for the month of January follows:

	MAINTENANCE	UTILITIES
Overhead costs incurred	$18,700	$9,000
Service provided to:		
Maintenance Department	—	10%
Utilities Department	20%	—
Producing Department A	40%	30%
Producing Department B	40%	60%

Required:
a. Under the direct method, what should be the amount of Utilities Department costs allocated to Producing Department B for January?
b. Under the step method, how much of Hartwell's Utilities Department cost is allocated between Departments A and B?

c. Under the reciprocal method, what would be the formula to determine the total maintenance costs?

d. Under the reciprocal method, what would be the formula to determine the total utilities costs?

[AICPA adapted]

9.47 *Allocation of service department costs using the direct method.* A hospital has a $100,000 expected utility bill this year. The Janitorial, Accounting, and Orderlies Departments are service functions to the Operating, Hospital Rooms, and Laboratories Departments. Floor space is assigned to each department as follows:

DEPARTMENT	SQUARE FOOTAGE
Janitorial	1,000
Accounting	2,000
Orderlies	7,000
Operating	4,000
Hospital Rooms	30,000
Laboratories	6,000
	50,000

Required:
How much of the $100,000 will eventually become the Hospital Rooms Department total costs, assuming a direct allocation based on square footage?

[CIA adapted]

9.48 *Service department allocations with separate VOH and FOH PORs.* Illinois Electric produces electricity from the Chicago River. The electricity is carried over electric lines to four branch stations. Using the information below and the step method, calculate VOH and FOH PORs based on DLhr for each branch station.

DATA SECTION: BUDGETED VARIABLE AND FIXED OVERHEAD COSTS

| | ELECTRIC COSTS | BRANCHES | | | |
		ROCKFORD	PEORIA	HAMMOND	KANKAKEE
BUDGETED DIRECT VOH	$6,000	$25,000	$30,000	$20,000	$ 15,000
BUDGETED USAGE (KWhr)	30,000	8,000	9,000	7,000	6,000
BUDGETED DIRECT LABOR HOURS		266,000	3,180	107,000	8,100
BUDGETED DIRECT FOH	$9,000	$130,000	$145,000	$90,000	$150,000
CAPACITY USAGE (KWhr)	50,000	10,000	20,000	12,000	8,000

9.49 *Service department allocations with separate VOH and FOH PORs.* During July, the Maintenance Department of WonderWorks, Inc., budgeted variable costs of $9,000 and fixed costs of $4,500. The Maintenance Department serves three production departments: Grinding, Polishing, and Assembly. Maintenance direct labor hours are used to allocate its overhead to the production departments. The following information is available:

	GRINDING	POLISHING	ASSEMBLY	
Budgeted DLhr (Maint.)	300	200	400	=900
Capacity DLhr	500	600	400	
Primary VOH	$3,000	$4,000	$5,000	
Primary FOH	$6,000	$7,000	$8,000	
Budgeted machine hours	1,000	800	2,000	

Required:
Calculate the VOH and FOH PORs for each production department using machine hours as the PORs' allocation basis.

9.50 *Single and separate allocations of budgeted service department costs.* During April, the Accounts Receivable Department budgeted $20,000 in variable costs and $50,000 in fixed costs. Credit sales of the four retail branches are used to allocate these costs. Budgeted credit sales information includes the following:

	UPTOWN	DOWNTOWN	EASTSIDE	WESTSIDE
Budgeted for April	$20,000	$100,000	$40,000	$40,000
Maximum potential sales	75,000	120,000	60,000	45,000

Required:
a. Determine the budgeted costs to be allocated to each store assuming total Accounts Receivable costs are allocated based on one rate.
b. Determine the budgeted costs to be allocated to each store using a separate variable cost rate and relative size ratios for fixed costs.

THINK-TANK PROBLEMS

Although these problems are based on chapter material, reading extra material, reviewing previous chapters, and using creativity may be required to develop workable solutions.

9.51 *Ethical considerations in overhead allocation.* In Chapter 1, four ethical standards for management accounting were identified. What are the implications of each in designing an overhead allocation system?

9.52 *High-quality information about overhead.* Consider each characteristic of high-quality information presented in Chapter 1. What implications does each have for the design of a high-quality CAS for reporting overhead?

9.53 *Service departments and JITs.* Design a WIP general ledger system for a JIT. The CAS should be high quality. Consider the value of service department allocations to JIT cells and the need for service department cost variance information. If you do not believe allocations should be made to JIT cells or believe that cost variance information is not needed, then what information should be provided by the CAS, to whom, and how?

9.54 *Backflush systems and service departments.* Review backflush systems in Chapter 8. If services exist, can a high-quality backflush system be designed to account for them?

 9.55 *Spreadsheet programs for budgeted service department allocations.* Construct a spreadsheet program that will perform step method allocations for calculating VOH and FOH PORs. Variable service department costs should be allocated based on the budgeted rates developed. Fixed costs should be allocated using relative size ratios. Test your program using the information from Demonstration Problem 2.

 9.56 *Spreadsheet programs for actual service department cost allocations.* Construct a spreadsheet program that will perform step method allocations for actual VOH and FOH costs. Test the program using the information from Demonstration Problems 2 and 3.

 9.57 *Spreadsheet programs for direct method allocations.* Using the information from Demonstration Problems 2 and 3, construct a spreadsheet program that will perform direct method allocations for budgeted and actual service department costs. Variable and fixed costs should be allocated separately as was done in Demonstration Problem 1.

 9.58 *Comprehensive allocation of costs.* Barnes Company has two service departments and three production departments, each producing a separate product. For a number of years, Barnes has allocated service department costs to the production departments on the basis of the annual sales revenue dollars. In a recent audit report, the internal auditor stated that the distribution of service department costs on the basis of annual sales dollars would lead to serious inequities. The auditor suggested that maintenance and engineering service hours would be a better service cost allocation basis. For illustrative purposes, the following information was appended to the audit report:

	SERVICE DEPARTMENTS		PRODUCTION DEPARTMENTS		
	MAINTENANCE	ENGINEERING	PRODUCT A	PRODUCT B	PRODUCT C
Maintenance hours used	—	400	800	200	200
Engineering hours used	400	—	800	400	400
Department direct costs	$12,000	$54,000	$80,000	$90,000	$50,000

Required:

a. Using the direct method, how much maintenance cost is allocated to the Engineering Department?

b. Using the direct method, how much maintenance cost is allocated to Department C?

c. Using the direct method, how much engineering cost is allocated to Department A?

d. Using the step method and allocating maintenance first, how much maintenance cost is allocated to the Engineering Department?

e. Using the step method and allocating maintenance first, how much maintenance cost is allocated to Department B?

f. Using the step method and allocating maintenance first, how much engineering cost is allocated to Department B?

g. Using the step method and allocating maintenance first, how much engineering cost is allocated to Department C?

h. Using the step method, what is the total amount of service department costs allocated to Department A?

[CIA adapted]

9.59 *Comprehensive allocation of costs.* The managers of Rochester Manufacturing are discussing ways to allocate the cost of service departments such as Quality Control and Maintenance to the production departments. To aid them in this discussion, the controller has provided the following information:

	QUALITY CONTROL	MAINTENANCE	MACHINING	ASSEMBLY	TOTAL
Budgeted overhead costs before allocation	$350,000	$200,000	$400,000	$300,000	$1,250,000
Budgeted machine hours	—	—	50,000	—	50,000
Budgeted direct labor hours	—	—	—	25,000	25,000
Budgeted hours of service:					
Quality Control	—	7,000	21,000	7,000	35,000
Maintenance	10,000	—	18,000	12,000	40,000

Required:

a. If Rochester Manufacturing uses the direct method of allocating service department costs, what would be the total service costs allocated to the Assembly Department?

b. Using the direct method, what would be the total amount of overhead allocated to each machine hour?

c. Using the step method and beginning with Quality Control, what is the amount of maintenance costs allocated to the Assembly Department?

d. Using the reciprocal method, what is the total amount of Quality Control costs (rounded to the nearest dollar) allocated to other departments?

[CMA adapted]

9.60 *Development of predetermined overhead rates.* Marfrank Corporation is a manufacturing company with six functional departments—Finance, Marketing, Personnel, Production, Research and Development (R&D), and Information Systems—each administered by a vice president. The Information Systems Department (ISD) was established in 19X3 when Marfrank decided to acquire a new mainframe computer and develop a new information system.

While systems development and implementation is an ongoing process at Marfrank, many of the basic systems needed by each of the functional departments were operational at the end of 19X4. Thus, calendar year 19X5 is considered the first year when the ISD costs can be estimated with a high degree of accuracy. Marfrank's president wants the other five functional departments to be aware of the magnitude of the ISD costs by reflecting the allocation of ISD costs in the reports and statements prepared at the end of the first quarter of 19X5. The allocation of ISD costs to each of the departments was based on their actual use of ISD services.

Jon Werner, vice president of ISD, suggested that the actual costs of ISD be allocated on the basis of pages of actual computer output. He suggested this basis because all of the departments use reports in evaluating their operations and making decisions. The use of this basis resulted in the following allocation:

DEPARTMENT	PERCENTAGE	ALLOCATED COST
Finance	50%	$112,500
Marketing	30	67,500
Personnel	9	20,250
Production	6	13,500
R&D	5	11,250
Totals	100%	$225,000

After the quarterly reports were distributed, the Finance and Marketing Departments objected to this allocation method. Both departments recognized that they were responsible for most of the output in terms of reports, but they believed that these output costs might be the smallest of ISD costs and requested that a more equitable allocation basis be developed.

After meeting with Werner, Elaine Jergens, Marfrank's controller, concluded that ISD provided three distinct services—systems development, computer processing represented by central processing unit (CPU) time, and report generation. She recommended that a predetermined rate be developed for each of these services from budgeted annual activity and costs. The ISD costs would then be assigned to the other functional departments using the predetermined rate times the actual activity used. Any difference between actual costs incurred and costs allocated to the other departments would be absorbed by ISD.

Jergens and Werner concluded that systems development could be charged on the basis of hours devoted to systems development and programming, computer processing based on CPU time used for operations (exclusive of database development and maintenance), and report generation based on pages of output. The only cost that should not be included in any of the predetermined rates would be purchased software; these packages were usually acquired for a specific department's use. Thus, Jergens concluded that purchased software would be charged at cost to the department for which it was purchased. In order to revise the first quarter allocation, Jergens gathered the information on ISD costs and services shown on the next page:

Information Systems Department Costs

	ESTIMATED ANNUAL COSTS	ACTUAL FIRST QUARTER COSTS	PERCENTAGE DEVOTED TO		
			SYSTEMS DEVELOPMENT	COMPUTER PROCESSING	REPORT GENERATION
Wages and benefits					
Administration	$100,000	$ 25,000	60%	20%	20%
Computer operators	55,000	13,000		20	80
Analysts/programmers	165,000	43,500	100		
Maintenance					
Hardware	24,000	6,000		75	25
Software	20,000	5,000		100	
Output supplies	50,000	11,500			100
Purchased software	45,000	16,000*	—	—	—
Utilities	28,000	6,250		100	
Depreciation					
Mainframe computer	325,000	81,250		100	
Printing equipment	60,000	15,000			100
Building improvements	10,000	2,500		100	
Total department costs	$882,000	$225,000			

*Note: All software purchased during the first quarter of 19X5 was for the benefit of the Production Department.

Information Systems Department Services

	SYSTEMS DEVELOPMENT	COMPUTER OPERATIONS (CPU)	REPORT GENERATION
Annual capacity	4,500 hours	360 CPU hours	5,000,000 pages
Actual usage during first quarter, 19X5			
Finance	100 hours	8 CPU hours	600,000 pages
Marketing	250	12	360,000
Personnel	200	12	108,000
Production	400	32	72,000
R&D	50	16	60,000
Total usage	1,000 hours	80 CPU hours	1,200,000 pages

Required:
a. 1. Develop predetermined rates for each of the service categories of ISD—systems development, computer processing, and report generation.
   2. Using the predetermined rates developed in Requirement (a)1, determine the amount each of the other five functional departments would be charged for services provided by ISD during the first quarter of 19X5.
b. With the method proposed by Elaine Jergens for charging the ISD costs to the other five functional departments, there may be a difference between ISD's actual costs incurred and the costs assigned to the five user departments.
   1. Explain the nature of this difference.
   2. Discuss whether Jergens's proposal will improve cost control in ISD.
   3. Explain whether Jergens's proposed method of charging user departments for ISD costs will improve planning and control in the user departments.

[CMA adapted]

10

THE ACTIVITY-BASED COSTING SYSTEM

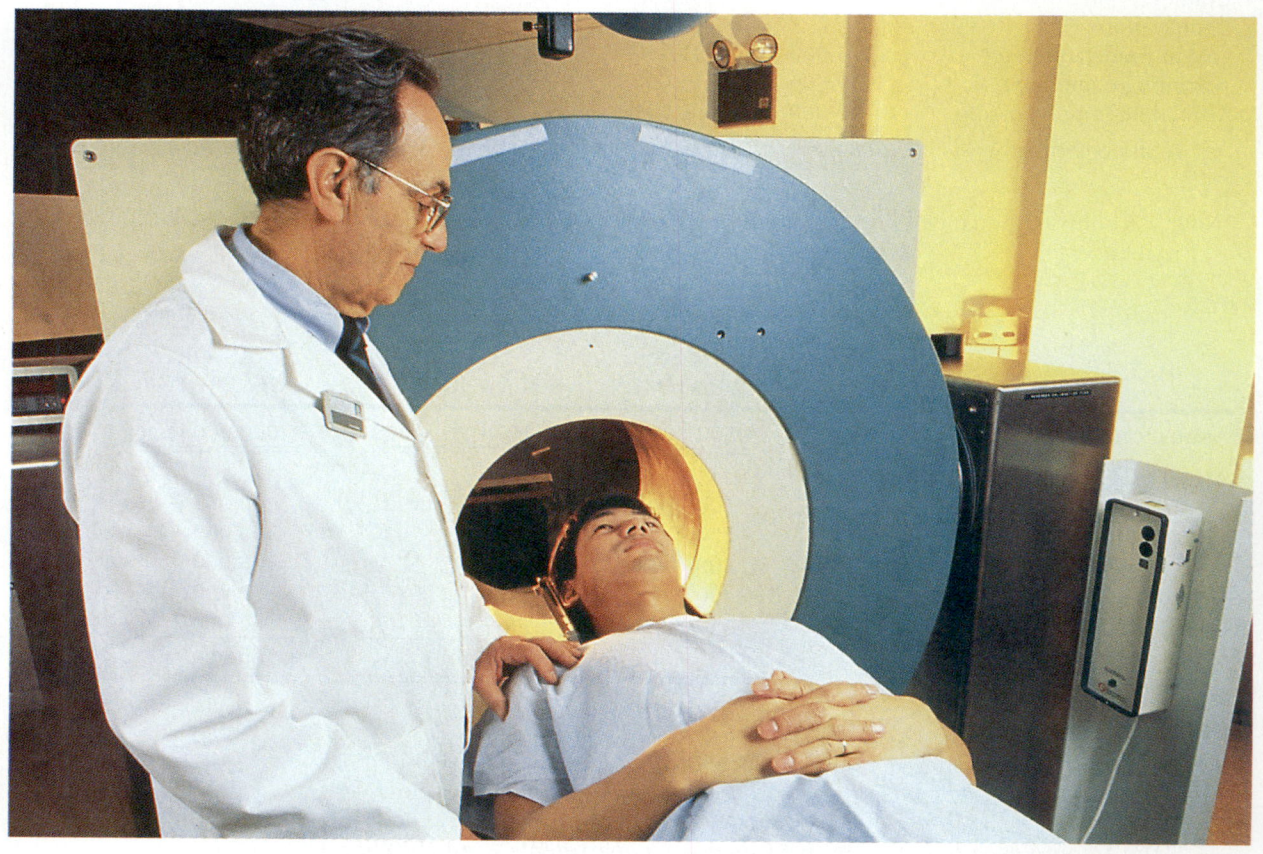

Activity-based costing systems are used in hospitals.

LEARNING OBJECTIVES

After studying this chapter, you should be able to:

1. Define activity-based costing systems.

2. Contrast traditional volume-based costing systems with activity-based costing systems.

3. Explain how to develop activity-based costing systems.

4. Discuss how activity-based costing systems are used in service organizations.

■ INTRODUCTION

In general terms, the traditional volume-based costing system is shown on the left in Exhibit 10–1 (see p. 446), and the activity-based costing system is shown on the right. Both costing systems use a conventional two-stage process for assigning overhead costs to products, services, jobs, projects, or other cost objects.

Under the traditional volume-based costing system, the second-stage cost driver is usually a predetermined overhead rate (POR) or multiple PORs with direct labor hours, direct labor dollars, machine hours, or materials dollars as the base (or denominator). The more units of a particular product that are produced, the more overhead costs are applied to the units. No matter what base is used, they all apply overhead costs in strict proportion to production volume.

The idea behind activity-based costing is that cost objects, which can be products, services, jobs, units, batches, customers, or anything the management accountant is trying to cost, consume activities. In turn, activities consume resources. Activity drivers measure the activities consumed, and resource drivers measure the resources consumed.

Activity-based costing systems try to determine what is *really* driving costs and charge a cost object for only the overhead it actually consumes. If, for example, 1,000 units of product A and 100 units of product B are produced, the traditional volume-based costing system will apply 10 times the overhead costs to product A relative to product B. But product A may not have used 10 times the overhead costs. Product B, being a more complex product with many special features, may have actually consumed most of the overhead costs because it required more support, such as setups, engineering changes, material purchasing, storing, handling, and so forth.

The accuracy of costing systems has become a matter of serious concern in some firms. Managers believe that their costing systems are grossly underestimating the cost of low-volume products and overestimating the cost of high-volume products. Production managers believe that certain products are not "earning their keep" because they are difficult to produce and thus place severe demands on resources and activities. But, with traditional volume-based costing systems, these difficult-to-produce products are reported as the *most* profitable. Managers in some construction firms, as well as in other firms that bid on customized jobs, are also concerned by the failure of their costing systems in developing winning bids. Examples of companies that have implemented activity-based costing systems are Caterpillar, General Dynamics, General Motors, Hewlett-Packard, Martin Marietta, and Siemans.

The concept of activity-based costing is simple and intuitively attractive to managers and workers who do not have an accounting background. It provides designers of costing systems new ways to cost products and services, modify behavior, and focus management attention on matters of strategic importance.[1]

■ DEFINING ACTIVITY-BASED COSTING

LEARNING OBJECTIVE 1

Define activity-based costing systems.

Activity-based costing (ABC) is the collection of financial and nonfinancial data about an enterprise's activities for two primary purposes:

- Costing the enterprise's cost objects
- Providing information for effective cost management through activity-based management

[1] Robin Cooper, "Elements of Activity-Based Costing," in *Emerging Practices in Cost Management*, ed. Barry J. Brinker (Boston: Warren Gorham Lamont, 1992), p. D2-21. With permission.

■■EXHIBIT 10–1
General Models of the Traditional Volume-Based Costing System and the Activity-Based Costing System

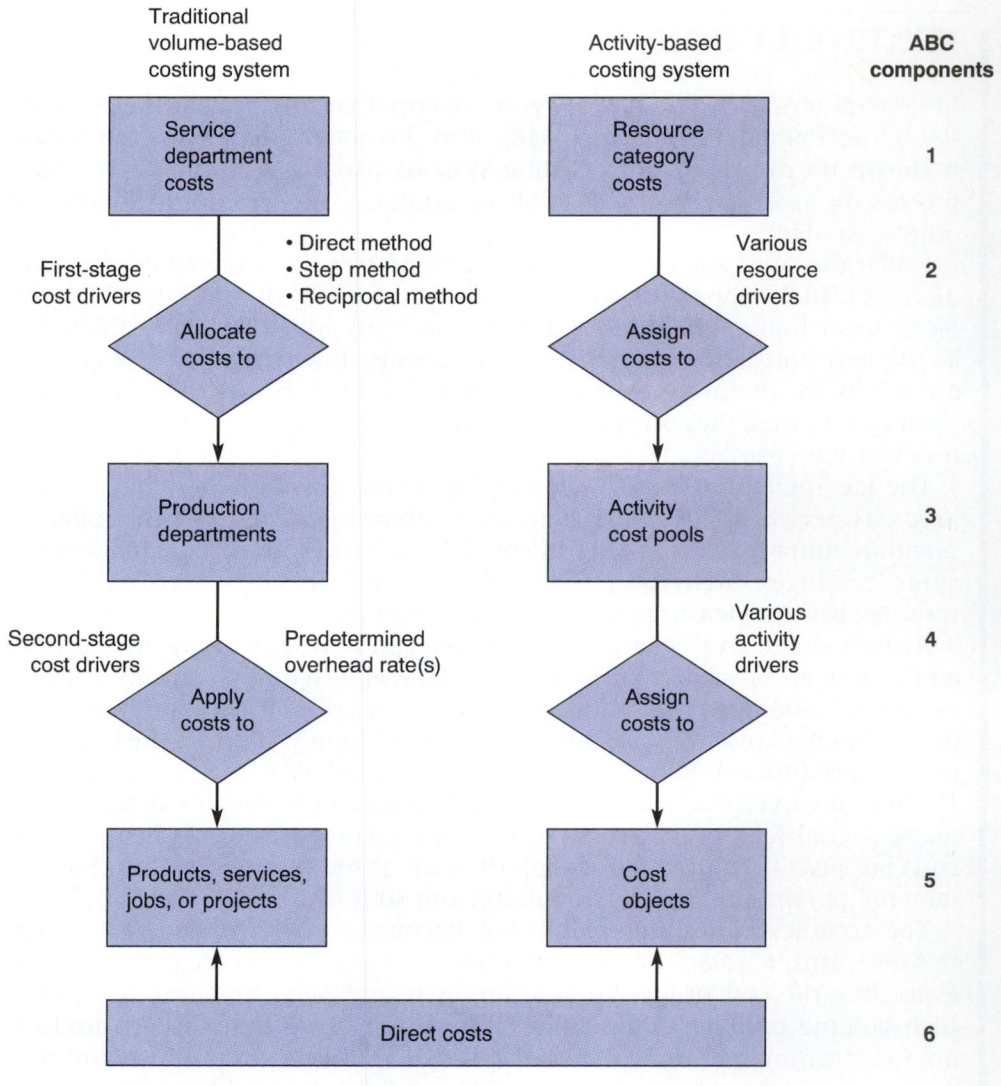

Examining the application of ABC at Eastern Plumas District Hospital.

Exhibit 10–2 shows how ABC works to achieve these two purposes.

Activity analysis is the process of defining and describing activities and their corresponding cost drivers (i.e., resource drivers and activity drivers). Defining activities and cost drivers is the key to building an activity-based costing system. In turn, the ABC system is linked to activity-based management. **Activity-based management (ABM)** uses ABC information to support cost management via continuous improvement or to serve as a guide in completely reengineering activities (i.e., redesigning and rebuilding activities that are operating inefficiently and ineffectively) of the enterprise. Activities and cost drivers are the building blocks of all business processes and operations, so understanding them and their performance is essential to implementing sound cost management practices. Activity-based management is covered in Chapter 11.

Defining the Components of Activity-Based Costing Systems

An activity-based costing system includes six components:

- Resource categories
- First-stage resource drivers
- Activities and activity cost pools

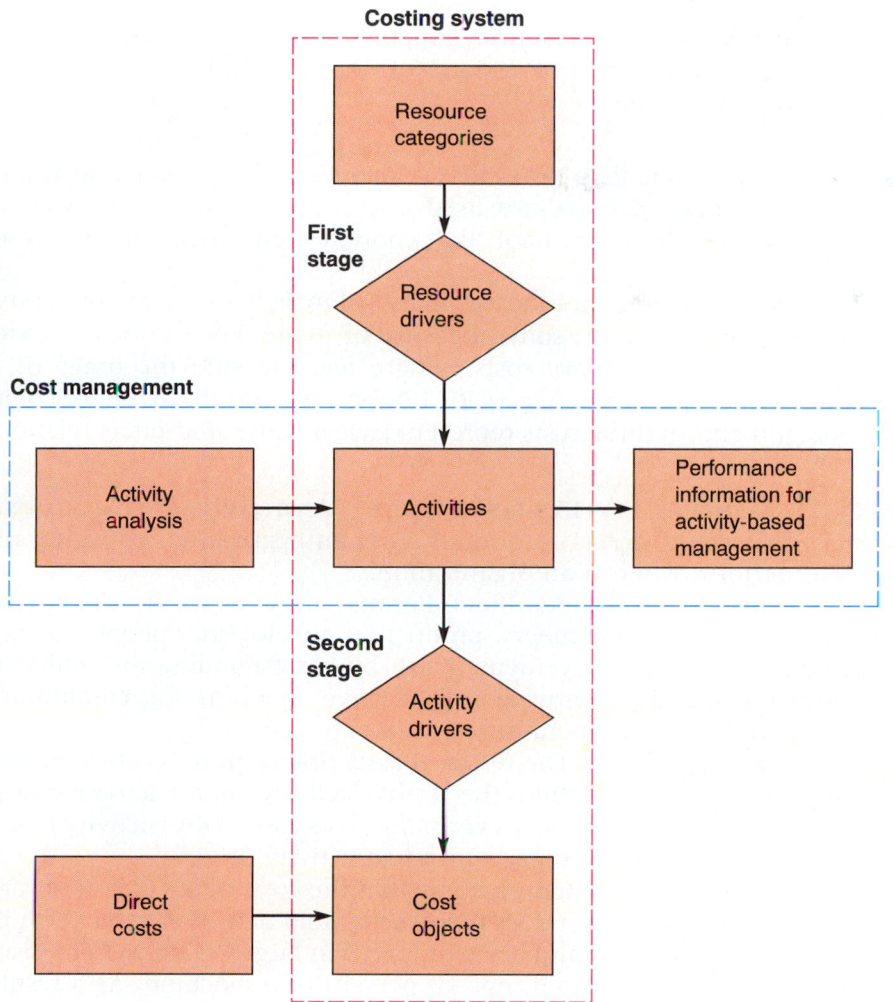

- Second-stage activity drivers
- Cost objects
- Direct cost inputs

RESOURCE CATEGORIES. **Resource categories** represent the sources of costs that support activities. For example, "repairing automobile transmissions" is an activity in a repair shop. Specific mechanics, helpers, tools, utilities, and building space are resources that support this activity.

Typical resources in a manufacturing enterprise include the following:

- Procurement and various material handling and storage resources
- Office space and furniture and fixtures
- Equipment including production machines, transportation equipment, and information technology
- Utilities
- Salaries and benefits
- Buildings
- Accounting
- Engineering
- Insurance, licenses, and taxes

Normally, resources are expressed as cost elements within a chart of accounts or as a list of budgetary items in a budget. When a resource is dedicated to a single activity, assigning costs to the activity to form an activity cost pool is relatively simple. When a resource supports several activities, however, the resource consumption must be assigned among appropriate activities using a first-stage resource driver.

Office space is a resource.

FIRST-STAGE RESOURCE DRIVERS. Activities *drive* the cost of resources. Therefore, **resource drivers** are used to assign resource costs to activities, thereby forming activity cost pools that contain their proper share of resource costs.

The resource driver establishes a relationship between resource costs and activity cost pools based on some measure of usage. For example, headcount measures the usage of salary costs, square feet measure the usage of office occupancy costs, and hours (e.g., CPU hours) measure the usage of computer costs. Assignments of these costs represent a clear cause-and-effect relationship.

ACTIVITIES AND ACTIVITY COST POOLS. An **activity** is what an organization does to convert inputs to outputs. It is an aggregation of highly related tasks that perform work in an organization.

Activities are "natural" identifiers, because they are easily understood by such diverse groups as engineers, production and logistics people, marketers, accountants, and top management. Thus, by corresponding to familiar terms and processes, activities provide an effective medium for communication between accounting and operating personnel.

Activities are costed first. The result of assigning resource costs to an activity is an **activity cost pool.** Often, the terms "activity" and "activity cost pool" are used interchangeably. In any event, the costs assigned to activity cost pools are in turn assigned to cost objects using an activity driver.

Activity-based costing systems assume that the costs of activities are variable, even though this assumption does not exactly hold true in practice. Cost inputs to activities are usually acquired or eliminated in large "chunks." For example, a whole machine is purchased, not 10 percent of a machine. As a result, the costs of these inputs do not vary smoothly according to the activities consumed. The reported product or service costs are therefore linear approximations to what are typically a series of step functions.

SECOND-STAGE ACTIVITY DRIVERS. The costs in activity cost pools are assigned to the cost objects by means of **activity drivers.** The second-stage activity drivers are measures of the consumption of the activity cost pools by cost objects. Like the first-stage resource driver, the second-stage activity driver must capture a cause-and-effect relationship. In this case, the relationship is between the activity cost pools and the cost objects.

COST OBJECTS. **Cost objects** are the point to which activity costs are assigned. A cost object can be almost anything the designer wants it to be. The following are typical cost objects:

- Products
- Services
- Units
- Batches
- Contracts
- Cases
- Jobs
- Projects
- Customers
- Customer groups
- Distribution channels
- Sales territories

Ultimately, activities are performed in order to manufacture products, render services (e.g., contracts, cases, jobs, projects), or support customers.

In some ABC systems, costs are assigned to different types of cost objects at different levels. For example, a *batch* is a higher-level cost object than a single unit of a *product*, where *X* number of *units* make up a batch of the particular product. A *sales territory* is a higher-level cost object than a *customer*. The number of levels of cost assignment varies from one enterprise to the next. Exhibit 10–3, however, generally describes most manufacturing enterprises.

Product-driven activity costs are typically assigned at three levels through the use of activity drivers: the unit-level, batch-level, and product-level. Costs such as direct materials, direct labor, and storage costs are assigned on the basis of a unit of product. Costs of setups are usually assigned in terms of a batch of units of a particular product line. For example, tools and dies are set up to produce a batch of 1,000 units of product A. The product, such as product A, represents a specific product line. When an engineering change is made, it is therefore applicable to the product line.

It makes sense to keep activities of different levels separate because the costs of activities at different levels vary in response to different factors. For example, the cost of the batch-level activity setup varies with the number of batches. By contrast, the cost of a product-level activity such as engineering changes varies with the number of different product lines. Product A, for example, may require many more engineering changes than product B.

The number of levels of cost objects related to customer activities will vary among companies. Typically, there are four levels, such as order-level, customer-level, distribution channel-level, and sales territory-level. In some instances, several cost objects may occur at the same level. For example, a company may have several distribution channels, such as wholesalers, retailers, jobbers, and cooperatives, each of which would be treated as a cost object at the same level.

DIRECT COST INPUTS. **Direct cost inputs** are cost elements that are easily traced to cost objects. For example, a bill of materials and materials requisitions are used to trace direct materials costs to a specific cost object; that is, to a unit of product.

In some situations, especially where direct labor monitors automated processes, maintains equipment, and is salary-based, the only direct cost element is direct materials. At the other extreme, there are instances where three direct cost elements are used as direct cost inputs:

- Direct materials
- Direct labor
- Direct technology (or equipment)

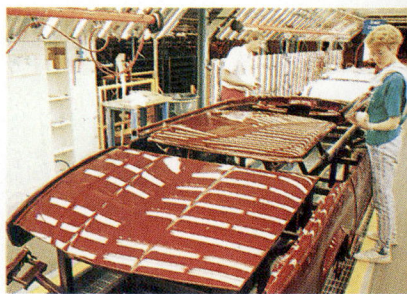
A car is a cost object. The final paint module at Saturn.

■■ EXHIBIT 10–3

Assignment of Costs to Different Levels of Cost Objects

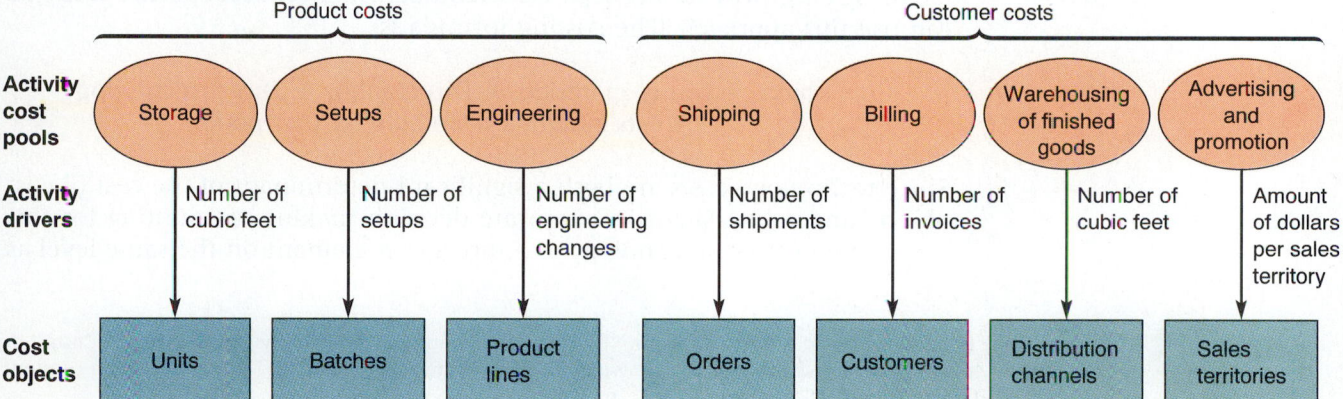

	Product costs			Customer costs			
Activity cost pools	Storage	Setups	Engineering	Shipping	Billing	Warehousing of finished goods	Advertising and promotion
Activity drivers	Number of cubic feet	Number of setups	Number of engineering changes	Number of shipments	Number of invoices	Number of cubic feet	Amount of dollars per sales territory
Cost objects	Units	Batches	Product lines	Orders	Customers	Distribution channels	Sales territories

Therefore, costs can be assigned to cost objects in four ways:

1. All costs are assigned to activity cost pools, and the activity costs are assigned to cost objects via appropriate activity drivers. This approach is applicable to some service organizations. The costing formula is:

    Cost object = Costs assigned from activity cost pools

2. All costs except direct materials costs are assigned to activity cost pools, and the activity costs are assigned to cost objects via appropriate activity drivers. This approach is applicable to manufacturing enterprises in which "direct" labor has become "indirect" and technology costs cannot be traced directly to cost objects. The costing formula is:

    Cost object = Direct materials + Costs assigned from activity cost pools

    In enterprises that are automated, "direct" labor is usually engaged in setups, loading machines, maintenance, troubleshooting, and supervisory activities rather than actually performing work on the product. Moreover, workers frequently work on several products at the same time, making it impossible to trace labor hours intelligently to products.[2]

3. All costs except direct materials and direct labor costs are assigned to activity cost pools, and the activity costs are assigned to cost objects via appropriate activity drivers. This approach is applicable in any organization in which direct materials and direct labor costs are easily traced to cost objects. The costing formula is:

    Cost object = Direct materials + Direct labor
    + Costs assigned from activity cost pools

    This costing approach uses the three cost elements covered in previous chapters:

    ■ Direct materials
    ■ Direct labor
    ■ Overhead

    Although many organizations that use this approach have substantial technology costs, such costs are not easily traced to cost objects. These technology costs are therefore assigned to activity cost pools via resource drivers; then, the activity costs are assigned to cost objects via activity drivers.

4. All costs except direct materials, direct labor, and direct technology (or equipment) are assigned to activity cost pools, and the activity costs are assigned to cost objects via appropriate activity drivers. This approach is applicable to any organization in which direct materials, direct labor, and direct technology costs are easily traced to cost objects. Construction companies and manufacturing enterprises using separate manufacturing cells for specific products can use this approach. The costing formula is:

    Cost object = Direct materials + Direct labor + Direct technology
    + Costs assigned from activity cost pools

Since technology costs are both a significant determinant of the cost of cost objects and a key factor in corporate decision making, accounting for this cost element treats technology as a direct cost element on the same level as

[2] Robin Cooper and Robert S. Kaplan, "How Cost Accounting Systematically Distorts Product Costs," in *Accounting & Management Field Study Perspectives*, ed. William J. Bruns, Jr., and Robert S. Kaplan (Boston: Harvard Business School Press, 1987), p. 215.

direct materials and direct labor. If machinery, equipment, and various pieces of technology that one would find in a highly automated plant or typical construction company can be traced directly to the product, service, job, or project cost object, then "direct technology" should be treated as a separate direct cost element.

A rule of thumb in developing an ABC system is to first identify all costs that can be traced directly to cost objects. Then, all other costs are assigned to activity pools.

▌A Simple Example of How Activity-Based Costing Works

Exhibit 10–4 illustates a simple ABC system that is used to assign financial accounting costs for accounts receivable and accounts payable activity costs to cost objects.

The resource categories in this example include three budgeted items:

- Salaries at $500,000
- Office occupancy at $200,000
- Computers at $300,000

▬▬ EXHIBIT 10–4
An Activity-Based Costing System

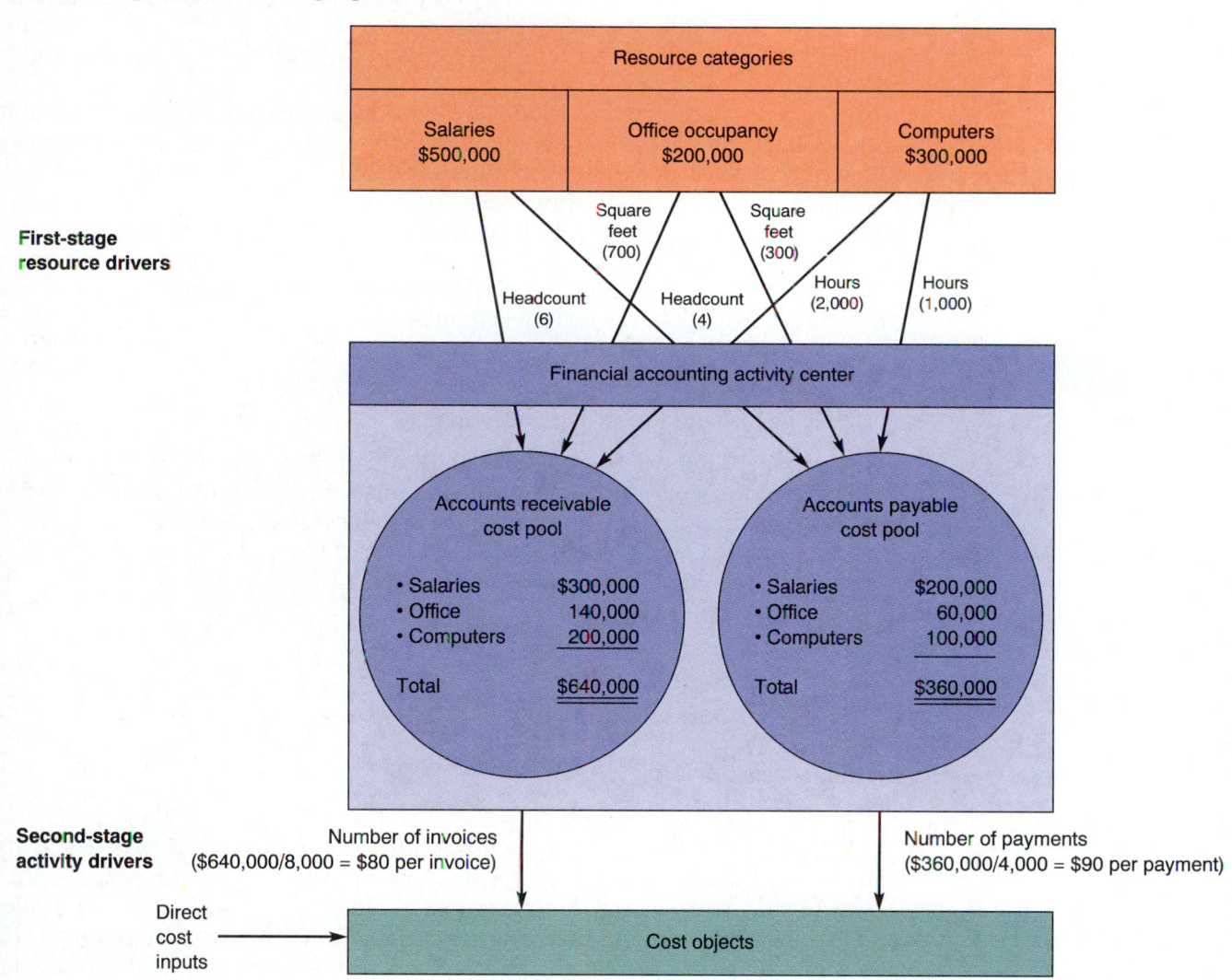

These resource costs are assigned to the two activity cost pools using the following resource drivers:

- Headcount assigns salaries to each activity cost pool on the basis of the number of people who work there.
- Office occupancy costs are assigned to each activity cost pool based on the number of square feet occupied by each activity (i.e., accounts receivable and accounts payable).
- The number of computer hours (e.g., CPU hours) consumed by each activity is used to assign computer costs to each activity cost pool.

The accounts receivable cost pool and the accounts payable cost pool are aggregated into the financial accounting activity center, because they are highly related to it. Other activity cost pools, such as a payroll cost pool, financial reporting cost pool, and so forth, might also be added.

An **activity center** represents an aggregation of related, function-specific activities. The sum of costs in the activity cost pools aggregated in an activity center equals the total costs associated with that activity center. In the example, the total costs assigned to the financial accounting activity center are $1,000,000.

Activity centers are only indirectly involved in the assignment of costs to cost objects. Nevertheless, activity centers do play an important role in the design of most ABC systems. For example, an activity center may correspond to a *responsibility center* where a particular manager is responsible for all the activity cost pools aggregated in that activity center. In other words, an activity center is a manageable set of related activity cost pools. In some instances, an activity center may be a traditional department, such as the financial accounting department. In small companies, the activity cost pools may stand alone and not be aggregated in activity centers.

The second-stage activity drivers are used to assign the accounts receivable cost pool and the accounts payable cost pool to cost objects. The number of invoices processed drives the accounts receivable cost pool and is therefore a reasonable device to assign these costs to cost objects. Likewise, the number of payments serves as an appropriate activity driver to assign the accounts payable cost pool to cost objects.

The direct cost inputs are other costs that can be directly traced to cost objects. Such direct cost elements include the following:

- Direct materials
- Direct labor
- Direct technology (or direct equipment)

The example in Exhibit 10–4 did not have any of these direct cost elements. All costs related to the financial accounting activity were included in the accounts receivable cost pool and the accounts payable cost pool.

▍Additional Factors to Consider When Selecting Cost Drivers

Cost drivers can be:

- Transaction-based
- Time-based
- Dollar-based
- Percentage-based

As a rule of thumb, the appropriate cost driver (i.e., resource driver and activity driver) is one that represents the primary output of the activity. In other words, a direct cause-and-effect relationship exists between changes in the cost driver and costs of the activity. In many instances, a cost driver that captures the *number* of activity transactions rather than the *duration* or *dollar* amount of activity transactions is preferable because it:

- Is readily available
- Is easy to understand, measure, and apply
- Induces beneficial behavior

Substituting cost drivers that capture the *number of transactions generated* by an activity rather than the *duration of the activity* is an important technique for reducing measurement cost. The data required for these transaction-based cost drivers are readily available, because a transaction is generated every time the activity is performed. For example, a materials requisition is required every time materials move from RMI to the factory floor.[3]

Transaction-based cost drivers are not always appropriate, however. For example, if the inspection activity takes varying amounts of time, using "number of inspections" or "number of inspection reports" as an activity driver instead of "actual inspection hours" probably will distort product or service costs. A product or service that requires much inspection time is likely to be undercosted, whereas a product or service that requires little inspection time will be overcosted. How well a given activity driver captures the actual consumption of activity costs by a particular product or service is measured by the *correlation* between the quantities traced to the product or service and the actual quantities the product or service consumed.[4]

The effect that the use of a particular cost driver has on people's behavior must also be considered in selecting cost drivers. As a general rule, people will behave in accordance with how they are being evaluated, as shown in the case on the next page. If the cost driver is used for performance evaluations, then its behavioral effects should be taken into account.

Behavioral effects can be either beneficial or harmful, depending on whether the cost driver motivates people to behave in a way that will help the enterprise achieve its goals or in a way that is undesirable or dysfunctional. For example, a company that wants to reduce the number of unique parts that it processes in order to simplify activities, such as vendor selection, purchasing, inspection, maintenance of the bill of materials, storage, and accounting, may decide to apply the costs of these activities using "number of part numbers" as the cost driver. Then, by evaluating and rewarding product designers according to their ability to design low-cost products, they will be motivated to design products with fewer part numbers.[5]

Care must be exercised, however, when using cost drivers to modify behavior. A particular cost driver may induce too much "beneficial" behavior. For example, if reducing the part numbers causes designers to reduce the functionality and quality demanded by the marketplace, the induced behavior will be harmful.[6]

COMPARING TRADITIONAL VOLUME-BASED COSTING SYSTEMS TO ACTIVITY-BASED COSTING SYSTEMS

Traditionally, overhead costs have been applied according to four volume-related bases:

- Direct labor hours (DLhr)
- Direct labor dollars
- Machine hours (Mhr)
- Materials dollars

LEARNING OBJECTIVE 2

Contrast traditional volume-based costing systems with activity-based costing systems.

---

[3] Cooper, op. cit., p. D2-14.
[4] Ibid.
[5] Ibid., p. D-15.
[6] Ibid.

INSIGHTS & APPLICATIONS

Correcting Harmful Behavior at Purrintin Pet Food Company

Management at Purrintin Pet Food Company was considering building a new 400,000 square-foot warehouse because its existing warehouses were full. The company's storage and distribution costs were allocated based on product value. The use of this costing procedure meant that a 4-cubic-foot bag of dog food was allocated $3.89 in warehousing costs, while a single case of gourmet cat food was allocated $12. This seemingly inexpensive storage cost for the bulky bags of dog food led the manager of dog food to keep excessive inventories of dog food on hand all the time.

By simply changing the assignment of storage and distribution costs to "amount of cubic feet" and "weight of units handled" cost drivers, both behavior and operating policies changed. The dog food product manager learned to manage inventory and no longer ordered in large batches, so the inventory of dog food shrank and the need for a new warehouse evaporated.

As this case shows, arbitrarily spreading storage and distribution costs over products distorts the underlying economics of storage and distribution and can lead to poor decision making and to dysfunctional behavior. On the other hand, reporting costs in accordance with what is causing the costs can lead to good decision making and to beneficial behavior, such as decreasing inventory and reducing storage and distribution costs.[7]

These bases provide a reasonably accurate product cost where overhead is consumed in relation to production volume. For example, employee benefits are related to direct labor, and energy costs are related to machine hours.[8]

The Impact of Diversity and Complexity on Costs

The designer of the costing system, in using these volume-related bases, assumes that all applied costs have the same behavior; that is, the costs increase in direct relationship to the volume of units produced. But many costs do not behave in a volume-related manner. They are driven by diversity and complexity, not by volume. For example, a simple concrete paving project drives costs by volume. The more concrete poured, the greater the costs. But a uniquely designed building with ornate patterns will primarily drive costs by diversity and complexity. Although both the paving project and the one-of-a-kind building project will use concrete, equating the material handling costs of the paving project with those of the building project will be substantially misleading and will generate distorted costs.

The paving project requires limited resources. It needs common forms and equipment but minimal support facilities. In contrast, the building project requires frequent setups, customized forms, and elaborate schemes for moving material.

Assumptions about Overhead Cost Behavior

Many people assume that a large and growing proportion of overhead costs is *fixed*. In a large number of enterprises, the opposite is true. The so-called fixed costs are, in fact, the most variable and most rapidly increasing costs.[9]

Overhead costs vary due to a number of factors. If the enterprise introduces more products, if it needs to expedite more orders, if it has to inspect more

---

[7] Adapted from Michael C. O'Guin and Steven A. Rebischke, "Customer-Driven Costs Using Activity-Based Costing," in *Handbook of Cost Management,* ed. Barry J. Brinker (Boston: Warren Gorham Lamont, 1992), p. B5-10. With permission.

[8] James A. Brimson, *Activity Accounting: An Activity-Based Costing Approach* (New York: John Wiley, 1991), p. 8.

[9] Ibid., p. 225.

INSIGHTS & APPLICATIONS

Cost Accounting at Simplicity and Diversity

Simplicity Company makes one product, turning out 300,000 units per year. Diversity Company produces a number of different products in different batch sizes. For example, product A is produced in 10-unit batches, whereas product B is produced in 1,000-unit batches.

Will Simplicity and Diversity have the same level of overhead costs? If not, which will have the higher overhead costs?

Simplicity does not need a lot of things that Diversity will require, such as setups, material handling, purchasing, engineering, and indirect labor. Simplicity has one setup; Diversity has hundreds. Simplicity's material handling is minimal and simple; Diversity's is extensive and complex. Simplicity has one raw material furnished by one vendor. Therefore, Simplicity doesn't need a purchasing department. Diversity has hundreds of different raw material items. Consequently, one of Diversity's biggest overhead costs is purchasing. Simplicity's product was designed years ago and is easy to make. Consequently, Simplicity doesn't employ engineers and has very little indirect labor. Diversity has a varied product mix of complex products, most of which are difficult to make. The products have an average life cycle of three years. Diversity is, consequently, under pressure to develop innovative products on an ongoing basis. Thus, Diversity employs a large engineering and supervisory staff.

To perform cost accounting at Simplicity, total costs are divided by the number of units produced. The total costs increase by a few percentage points each year due to inflation. The number of units produced each year averages 300,000, plus or minus 5,000 units.

How should cost accounting be conducted at Diversity? Direct materials and direct labor can be traced to each product with a reasonable level of accuracy if sufficient data processing is performed. But what about overhead? Should a volume-based POR be used, or would activity-based cost drivers that apply overhead to products on the basis of each product's consumption of overhead be more accurate? If products A and B (as well as all the other products) are charged with overhead according to a volume-based POR, product B will absorb much more overhead costs than product A because it is a high-volume product with batch sizes of 1,000 compared to batch sizes of 10 for product A. Product A, however, actually requires more setups, material handling, purchasing, engineering, and supervision than does product B because it is much more complex than product B. Product B is also standard, whereas product A offers special customized features that require additional support costs.

If an activity-based costing system is used instead of a volume-based costing system, then the amount of resources being consumed by product A would be assigned to it. Product B would also be costed with a higher degree of accuracy.

components and use more parts, and so forth, it will need larger overhead support to perform these additional activities.

Because many overhead costs are driven by the introduction of new products and the diversity and complexity of production, not by the volume of production, nonproduction volume-related cost drivers are required, such as the number of each of:

- Purchase orders
- Receipts
- Inspections
- Payments
- Setups
- Material movements
- Engineering change orders
- Materials requisitions

ABC authorities, such as Robin Cooper and Robert S. Kaplan, have observed that the most variable and most rapidly increasing costs are often those traditionally classified as fixed, such as equipment and building depreciation, procurement, insurance, supervision and indirect labor, and utilities. This phenomenon occurs in companies that are introducing new products, which in turn will need additional activities such as material handling, setups, inspection, and various other support activities.[10]

---

[10] Robin Cooper, "Cost Classification in Unit-Based and Activity-Based Manufacturing Cost Systems," in *Emerging Practices in Cost Management*, ed. Barry J. Brinker (Boston: Warren Gorham Lamont, 1990), p. 38. With permission.

Product Strategy at Zohr Electronics

Management at Zohr Electronics changed its product mix by introducing low-volume specialty products in its line. Initially, these products did not consume procurement, receiving, engineering, quality control, setup, storage, and other activities. But shortly, as new products were added, the demands for these activities increased substantially.

The introduction of these low-volume specialty products was due in large part to information reported by the division's volume-based product costing system, which used a divisionwide overhead rate based on direct labor hours. This costing system showed that low-volume specialty products cost less to produce than high-volume standard products. The costing system, therefore, reported that low-volume specialty products were among the most profitable products sold by the division.

When Zohr installed a new activity-based costing system, the cost to produce low-volume specialty products was *higher* than the cost to produce high-volume standard products. Using this information, management made the following decisions:

- Dropped certain products
- Increased the price of some low-volume products
- Decreased the price of some high-volume products
- Changed the design of certain complex products to simplify and decrease the demand for an array of activities

How One Product May Be Cross-Subsidizing Another Product

To trace costs to products, the amount of each activity consumed by a product must be determined. For example, a complex product that requires an average of 30 materials requisitions consumes a much greater proportion of the stockroom activity than a simple product, which requires one materials requisition. If processing one materials requisition costs $40, then $1,200 in stockroom activity costs should be charged to the complex product, and $40 should be charged to the simple product.

If product A consumes 70 percent of the purchasing activity and product B consumes 10 percent, then products A and B should be charged with 70 percent and 10 percent of the purchasing costs, respectively. To charge products A and B the same amount of purchasing costs obviously distorts product costs. In such a situation, product B is cross-subsidizing product A. Management may decide to drop product B because it will show a lower profit than it would show if it were assigned the proper amount of purchasing costs. The proper decision may be to eliminate product A instead or to eliminate neither.

Under a traditional volume-based costing system, significant product cost distortions, cross-subsidization, and incorrect management decisions may exist. In general, under a traditional volume-based costing system, low-volume products are undercosted and high-volume products are overcosted. As a result, the risk of making poor decisions increases in proportion to the level of distortion in reported costs.

How the Costing System Influences Decision Making

Exhibit 10–5a shows how an inappropriate overhead application method can distort management's view of the profitability of its product mix. Wysiwyg Computer Products, Inc., produces two different computer circuit boards in a highly automated manufacturing facility. Direct labor costs have typically been in the order of only 5 percent of total product cost. Nevertheless, the company's management accountants continue to use a POR based on direct labor.

Management has become concerned over declining sales in its high-volume circuit board AX. Several competitors have undercut Wysiwyg's price on this product, yet the company's cost data show that it is making only a marginally

■■■■EXHIBIT 10–5
**Wysiwyg Computer
Products, Inc.'s
Overhead Application
Method and Its
Influence on Decision
Making**

(a) Overhead applied based on direct labor cost			(b) Overhead applied based on activities required		
Cost element	Product AX	Product BX	Cost element	Product AX	Product BX
Direct materials	$23.00	$38.00	Direct materials	$23.00	$38.00
Direct labor	$ 7.00	$ 7.00	Direct labor	$ 7.00	$ 7.00
Total overhead at 500% of direct labor	$35.00	$35.00	Setup driver	$10.00	$20.00
			Material handling driver	$14.00	$26.00
SAMC	$65.00	$80.00	SAMC	$54.00	$91.00
Current selling price	$68.00	$90.00	Current selling price	$68.00	$90.00
Gross profit <loss> per unit	$ 3.00	$10.00	Gross profit <loss> per unit	$14.00	<$ 1.00>

Note: SAMC means standard absorptive manufacturing cost.

small profit on sales of circuit board AX. The low-volume circuit board BX appears to be quite profitable, however. Since the company is clearly having difficulty competing on its high-volume product, management has even suggested that circuit board AX be discontinued in favor of the more profitable circuit board BX.

Ada Contrary, a recent graduate of Very Big University's School of Accountancy, has just joined the company. Her curiosity is sparked when she hears a rumor of a major product line being discontinued, and she decides to investigate.

To her surprise, she finds that although direct labor costs are a very small portion of total product costs, Wysiwyg still uses a direct labor overhead application method in costing its products. She knows that an ABC system would be far more appropriate in this highly automated plant and would certainly provide management with a different profitability picture.

Ada does some more research and develops Exhibit 10–5b to present to management. The exhibit shows how the more realistic overhead application provided by the activity-based method can lead to very different pricing and product mix decisions.

Observing the manufacturing process, Ada finds that overhead costs are driven by machine setups and material handling. She elects to use these as the cost drivers in applying overhead between products AX and BX. As the exhibit illustrates, the low-volume nature of product BX requires more frequent machine setups, hence the greater overhead applied to that product based on the setup driver. The process has been streamlined for the high-volume product AX, so it requires fewer setups, and less overhead is applied based on the setup driver.

Product AX makes fewer demands on material handling as well, whereas producing product BX requires many materials requisitions and trips to the storeroom. Therefore, the material handling driver assigns more overhead to product BX than to product AX.

Note that the same amount of total overhead cost ($70) is applied between one unit of circuit board AX and one unit of circuit board BX, regardless of the overhead application method. Under the direct labor overhead application method, however, too much overhead was applied to AX and too little was applied to BX, giving a false impression of the total costs of producing these products.

Management may now decide to reduce circuit board AX's selling price to enable it to compete better. The low-volume circuit board BX is not profitable given the current selling price, so management may decide to raise the price or discontinue the product altogether. By changing the overhead application method used by the company's management accountants, Ms. Contrary saved Wysiwyg from a bad decision and earned herself a substantial salary increase!

In What Kind of Environments Is ABC Appropriate?

If the products in a plant possess similar characteristics, either a volume-based POR or an activity-based cost driver will produce reasonably accurate product costs. In those rare instances where a company produces only one product in a one-department operation, a formal cost accounting system is not even needed. Costs can be assigned to the product simply by dividing total costs by output during the period.

By connecting costs with their causes, ABC enables managers to know, with reasonable accuracy, the consequences of their decisions. The major criticism of ABC in earlier years was the cost of processing data. But as computer costs continue to fall, the most diverse and complex companies can implement and operate an ABC system efficiently on a microcomputer. Moreover, several ABC software packages are available at reasonable cost.

It can be concluded that ABC is especially appropriate in companies where the following are true:

- Competition is high.
- Product mix is diverse in batch sizes, physical sizes, degree of complexity, and raw material characteristics.
- Product life cycles are short, such as three years or less.
- Collection and manipulation of data are performed by an integrated computer-based information system (ICBIS).

As a rule of thumb, companies will find ABC more valuable for developing product or service costs as their products and services become more numerous and diverse and the source of their costs shifts from direct to indirect categories. However, even if product diversity is not a problem, ABC can prove valuable for purposes of *cost management*. Even companies with homogeneous products, or even a single product, can put ABC to good use. The discipline of identifying activities and computing their costs can reveal opportunities either for cutting the cost of performing the activities or for eliminating nonvalue-added activities.

The three strategic goals of ABC systems are summarized in the following schematic:

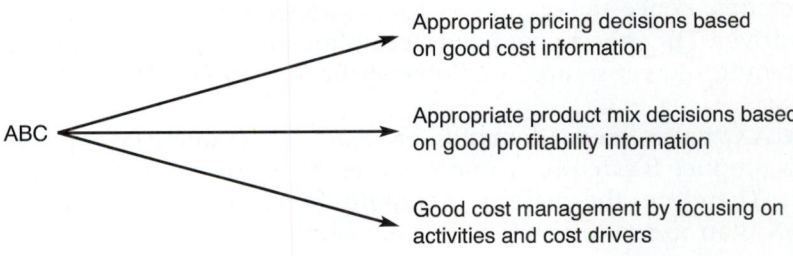

ABC
→ Appropriate pricing decisions based on good cost information
→ Appropriate product mix decisions based on good profitability information
→ Good cost management by focusing on activities and cost drivers

ACTIVITY-BASED COSTING SYSTEM DEVELOPMENT LIFE CYCLE

This section outlines a methodology for developing an activity-based costing system. The methodology is referred to as **ABC systems development life cycle,** which is a structured series of phases followed by the systems project team in developing an ABC system:

- *Phase one.* Plan the system.
- *Phase two.* Analyze and define resource categories.
- *Phase three.* Analyze and define activities.
- *Phase four.* Determine first-stage resource drivers and establish activity cost pools.
- *Phase five.* Determine second-stage activity drivers and assign costs to cost objects.

These phases are shown in the ABC systems development life cycle depicted in Exhibit 10–6. It is referred to as a "life cycle" because the ABC system is dynamic and is subject to continuous improvement and refinement. The ABC systems development life cycle can be used to develop a pilot (or prototype) ABC system or a full-blown enterprisewide system that supplants the present costing system. The ABC systems development life cycle is used in the next sections to develop an ABC system for the Panametric Corporation.

Phase One: Plan the System

Work on developing an ABC system should not start until there is common understanding and agreement throughout the organization. People should

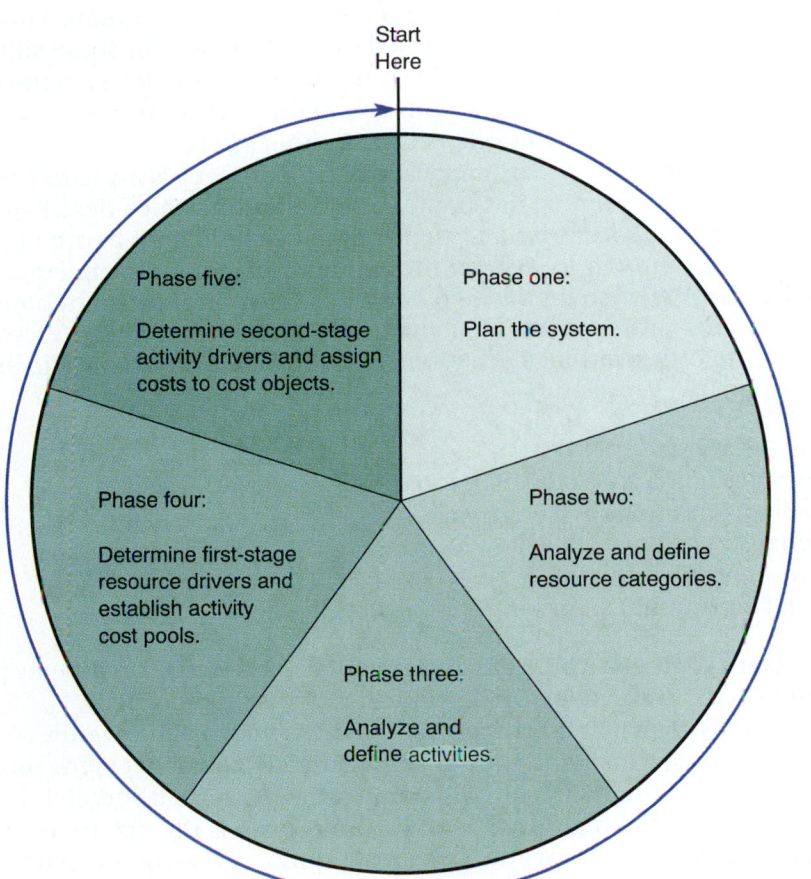

EXHIBIT 10–6
The ABC Systems Development Life Cycle

understand both how an ABC system works and that it has two primary purposes:

- Costing of cost objects
- Providing information for daily operational management, continuous improvement, and, in some instances, business reengineering (Note: Business or activity reengineering is the subject of Chapter 11.)

The following discussion helps provide the common understanding and agreement needed to embark on ABC systems development.

The systems planning phase establishes a broad strategic framework and clear vision of the enterprise and an understanding of how the ABC system will serve the enterprise. An excellent starting point is to hold a number of joint application development sessions that involve a large number of participants throughout the organization.

By fostering active involvement, some of the mistrust and bickering that might otherwise occur between various managers and workers and management accountants is reduced if not eliminated. Ideally, the ABC system will become the workers' and managers' system. They must feel that the ABC system is an integral part of *their* operational control system. Indeed, when these people feel they *own* the system, they are motivated to work with it and strive for its success.

Another reason for involving workers and managers in systems development at Panametric is to enable management accountants to understand in detail what activities are performed and what is required to get the job done. On the other side, workers and managers need to understand what it takes to develop the ABC system and what its purposes are.

In many situations, after an ABC system is installed, users need considerable training to learn how to work with the system. With a participative approach, training requires less time and effort because the people gain more knowledge about the system *while* it is being planned and developed. In some situations, certain workers and managers will become members of the systems project team. They will become *superusers* who are highly skilled in how the system works. These superusers can effectively train other users.

Another key outcome of joint application development is an enterprisewide model, such as that presented in Chapter 3. This model, which describes all the major entities of the enterprise and their relationships, serves as a blueprint of how the organization works, its environment, and its interdependencies.

Normally, the ABC systems development life cycle is performed by a multidisciplinary systems project team that draws its members from different areas throughout the organization. The systems project team at Panametric includes the following:

- Management accountant
- Engineering representative
- Production representative
- Marketing representative
- Logistics representative
- Financial accounting representative

Thus, the management accountant, who generally serves as the systems project leader, can draw on the talent and skills of a diverse work force.

The project team members must work together as partners toward a common end—creating an optimally performing enterprise. Top management support is essential to develop, implement, and operate an ABC system successfully. Serious commitment at the highest level of the enterprise is the key to making the transition to an ABC system work. This is especially true when the ABC system leads to reengineering the business and the way in which people work together. Executives at Panametric strongly support the development of an ABC system, because they believe it will provide reasonably accurate cost information and help them improve operations.

Phase Two: Analyze and Define Resource Categories

In analyzing and defining resource categories, the systems project team may choose to combine certain ledger accounts and budgetary items that are associated with the same or similar resource categories. On the other hand, the team may choose to split certain ledger accounts or budgetary items that are consumed differently by different activities.

The systems project team at Panametric Corporation has divided budgeted items into two resource categories:

- Service resources
- Production resources

The budgeted costs of these resources are presented in Exhibit 10–7.

Phase Three: Analyze and Define Activities

During activity analysis and definition, both service and production activities of an enterprise are identified in order to establish a basis for determining their cost and performance. This process decomposes an organization into elemental activities that are understandable and easy to manage. It is a process of "dividing to conquer."

Activity analysis describes what an enterprise does; that is, how time, effort, and resources are spent and the inputs and outputs of activities. Activities are not necessarily traditional organizational segments, such as departments. In some instances, activities may cross department boundaries. In other instances, a department may contain several activities.

EXHIBIT 10–7
Budgeted Costs of Service and Production Resources

Budget Service and Production Resources For the Year 19X5		
Service resources:		
• Salaries	$ 800,000	
• Benefits	100,000	
• Insurance	20,000	
• Utilities	140,000	
• Depreciation	440,000	$1,500,000
Production resources:		
• Supervision	$ 970,000	
• Benefits	90,000	
• Insurance	60,000	
• Utilities	200,000	
• Depreciation	2,000,000	$3,320,000
Total budgeted overhead resources		$4,820,000

Key management personnel and technical experts are consulted through interviews. Job descriptions are useful, because they are typically written in terms of tasks that make up activities. The interviewing process is usually iterative. Often, the same person has to be interviewed several times to attain the necessary information.

THE ACTIVITY FLOW DIAGRAM.   An **activity flow diagram** describes the activities that are performed in an organization and shows their interdependencies. The symbols used to prepare activity flow diagrams are presented in Exhibit 10–8.

The rectangle represents a source or destination of the initial or final inputs or outputs of the system under analysis. Sources or destinations can be persons, companies, departments, or other systems. They define the boundaries of the system being modeled. Labels of the sources and destinations should be descriptive, such as Vendor, Customer, Finished Goods, and Shop Floor.

To avoid crossing the input and output flow lines, sources and destinations may be duplicated. Normally, sources and destinations should be located on the perimeters of the activity flow diagram. This placement is consistent with their definition as systems boundaries.

Activities, which convert inputs to outputs, are represented by circles. By convention, the name (description) of an activity consists of a verb and an object or object clause, such as Purchasing (or Purchase) Materials, Update Accounts Receivable, or Check Credit.

All activities must have both inputs and outputs. An activity that shows inputs but no outputs is called a "black hole," because the input enters the activity and disappears or nothing takes place. An activity with output but no input is creating something from nothing, which is a "miracle." An activity can have more than one input or output.

Input and output flow is indicated by a line and an arrow. It represents the input and output among sources, destinations, and activities. All input and output flows either initiate an activity or result from an activity. For example, a supervisor on the shop floor (source) issues a materials requisition to the purchase materials activity, which is input that initiates a purchase order output from the purchase materials activity that is sent to a vendor (destination). Each input and output flow line should have a noun or noun clause next to it (usually above the line or to its right or left) describing the input or output that is being transferred. Inputs and outputs can be paper documents, electronic data, materials, and various measurements (e.g., machine hours).

■■■EXHIBIT 10–8
**Activity Flow
Diagram Symbols**

Meaning	Symbol
Source or destination	Source or destination description
Activity that transforms inputs to outputs	Activity description
Input and output flows	Name of input or output flow →

■ EXHIBIT 10–9
Design of Activities Using the Activity Flow Diagram

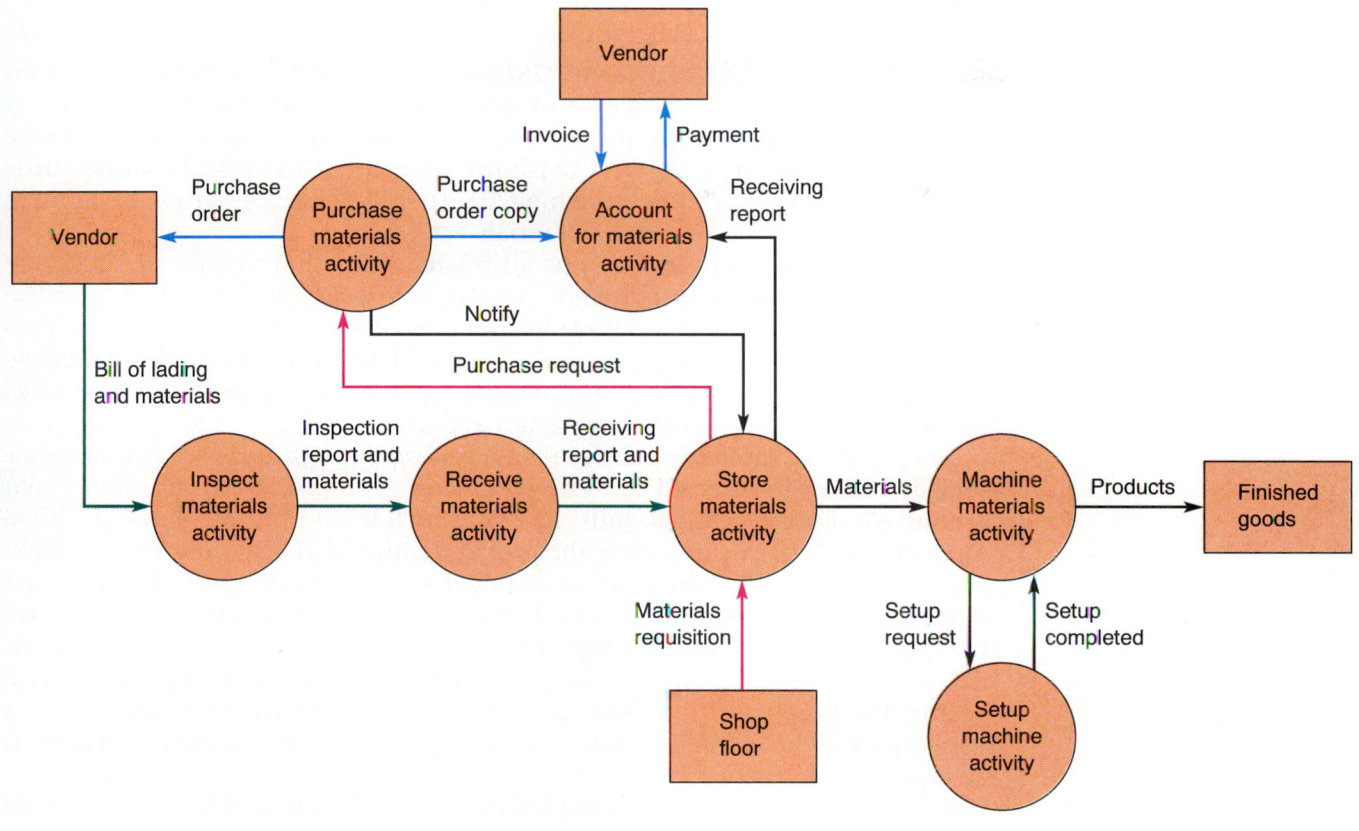

APPLYING THE ACTIVITY FLOW DIAGRAM. Exhibit 10–9 presents an activity flow diagram that models the purchasing, inspecting, receiving, accounting, machining, and setting up activities at Panametric Corporation. The model clearly shows both what activities are being performed and their interdependencies. In many instances, one activity will trigger the performance of another activity.

The initial input to the system is a materials requisition from the shop floor (a source) to the store materials activity. If the materials requested are on hand, they are immediately transferred to the machine materials activity. If they are not on hand, a purchase request is sent to the purchase materials activity, which prepares a purchase order and sends it to the appropriate vendor (a destination). A copy of the purchase order is sent to the accounting activity. The vendor (a source) sends the ordered materials to the inspect materials activity along with a bill of lading. The materials are inspected for quality and specifications. An inspection report and the materials are transmitted to the receive materials activity, which counts the materials, prepares a receiving report, and transmits the report and materials to the store materials activity. If accepted by the store-room personnel (i.e., the store materials activity personnel may reject the materials because of discrepancies), the needed materials are immediately moved to the machine materials activity for processing. Also, a receiving report for the materials is sent to the account for materials activity, which serves as an authorization to pay the vendor's invoice, assuming that no discrepancies exist. From time to time, depending on the product being machined, the machine materials activity requires a setup machine activity. When this need occurs, the machine materials activity prepares a setup request for the setup machine activity, which in turn performs the setup. Upon completion of the machine materials activity, the completed products are transferred to finished goods (a destination). The machine materials activity is responsible for all materials and product movement within Panametric.

AGGREGATING AND DECOMPOSING ACTIVITIES. Activities are composed of **tasks,** which are pieces of work assigned to people or machines. A task may be computational, procedural, or physical. Homogeneous tasks make up a function-specific activity. A **fishbone diagram,** (also called a **cause-and-effect diagram**), illustrated in Exhibit 10–10, can be used as a tool for defining activities, such as the purchase materials activity.

The systems project team groups all related tasks that pertain to and make the activity operational. In Exhibit 10–10, the tasks on the task side of the fishbone diagram represent all the pieces of work necessary to make the purchase materials activity operational. Unrelated tasks, for example, would be verifying quantity and prices and making a payment to a vendor. These tasks are related to the account for materials activity.

The process of combining tasks into a homogeneous group to form a function-specific activity is referred to as **aggregation.** The process of breaking down groups of dissimilar tasks into several function-specific activities is called **decomposition.** In either case, the proper definition of activities requires looking into activities to determine the detailed internal workings of the tasks that make up the activities. Exhibit 10–11 illustrates the aggregation and decomposition processes. Panel (a) shows the aggregation of two previously defined activities into one well-defined, function-specific activity. Checking the invoice against the purchase order and receiving report, and making a payment to a vendor, are actually highly related tasks that make up the account for materials activity.

In panel (b), the previously-defined procure materials activity contains three function-specific activities: purchase materials, inspect materials, and receive materials. All of these activities contain tasks that are related to their specific activities.

Here are some rules of thumb that help in performing aggregation and decomposition:

■ Usually, there should be from two to ten well-defined, function-specific activities per traditional organizational unit or department. In some instances, one small department may equal one activity. In other instances, an activity may

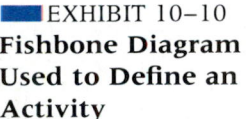
EXHIBIT 10–10
Fishbone Diagram Used to Define an Activity

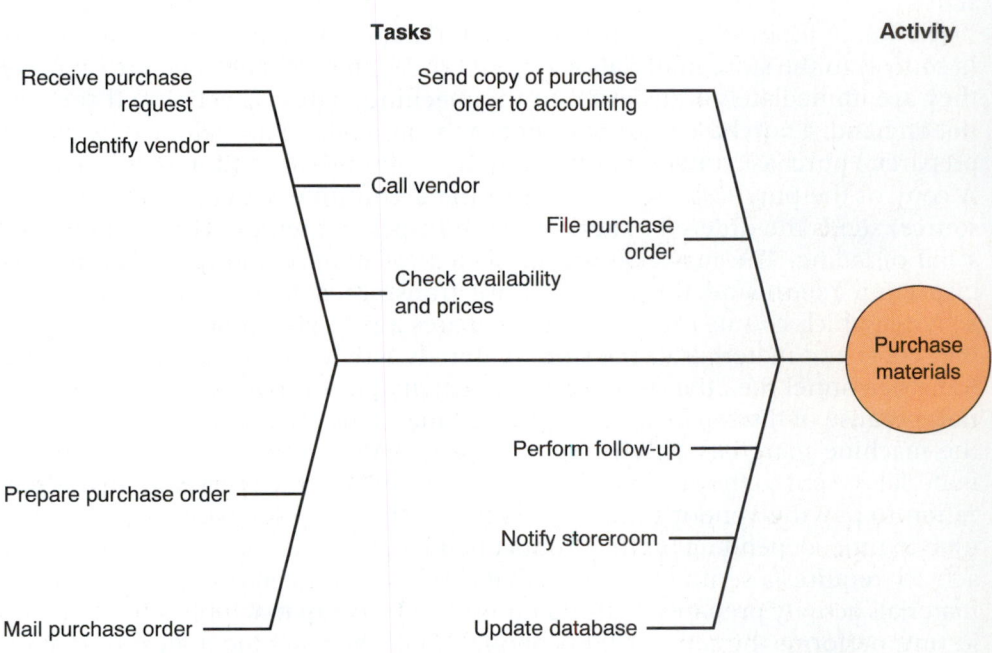

■■■ EXHIBIT 10–11
The Aggregation and Decomposition Processes

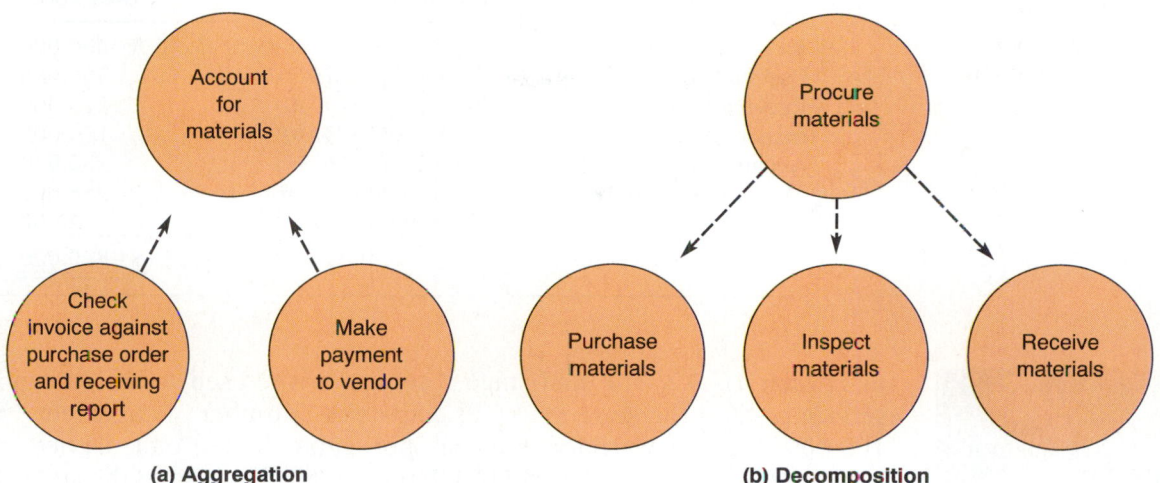

(a) Aggregation   (b) Decomposition

transcend more than one department. If more than ten activities are defined for a typical department (e.g., accounting, procurement, painting, finishing, and milling), then the activities should be reviewed for aggregation. On the other hand, if one activity is defined for one medium- or large-size department, the activity should be reviewed for decomposition.

■ Activities that are the responsibilities of different people should not be aggregated.

■ Generally, an activity should contain no more than five to fifteen well-defined, highly-related tasks.

■ If an activity contains only one task, it has probably been subjected to excessive decomposition.

■ If an activity contains unrelated tasks, it needs to be decomposed.

■ If there is only one input and one output, the activity has been decomposed enough.

■ If there are multiple inputs and outputs, the activity may be a candidate for decomposition. However, a well-defined, function-specific activity may contain two or three inputs and two or three outputs and may not require decomposition.

In addition to interviewing, the systems project team spends a great deal of time observing activities as they are performed. Statistics dealing with time, distance, quantity, and frequency are gathered. For example, an activity dealing with movement of a component may generate the following statistics:

Welding is an activity that consumes resources. Courtesy of Honda of America Manufacturing, Inc.

Time:	15 minutes to move materials from storeroom to machining
Distance:	1,500 feet
Quantity:	One batch of four pallets
Frequency:	Performed 30 times per day, on average

Such statistics can then be used to assist in determining activity costs being consumed.

Phase Four: Determine First-Stage Resource Drivers and Establish Activity Cost Pools

The first-stage resource drivers assign resource costs (defined in phase two) to various activities (defined in phase three) forming activity cost pools, as shown

■EXHIBIT 10–12
Assignment of Resource Category Costs to Activities Forming Activity Cost Pools

Activity	First-Stage Resource Driver	Amount Assigned to Activity Cost Pools
Store materials	(100,000 CF × $6)	$ 600,000
Purchase materials	($900,000 × 10/30)	300,000
Receive materials	($900,000 × 9/30)	270,000
Inspect materials	($900,000 × 5/30)	150,000
Account for materials	($900,000 × 6/30)	180,000
Machine materials	($3,320,000 × .90)	2,988,000
Setup machine	($3,320,000 × .10)	332,000
Total budgeted costs assigned to activity cost pools		$4,820,000

Number of inspections of direct materials is a first-stage resource driver. Courtesy of Honda of America Manufacturing, Inc.

in Exhibit 10–12. The first-stage resource driver used to assign a portion of service costs to the store materials activity is "number of cubic feet," which is 100,000 cubic feet charged at $6 per cubic foot. Total service costs are $1,500,000 less the $600,000 (100,000 CF × $6) charged to the store materials activity. The remaining $900,000 in service costs are assigned to the purchase materials, receive materials, inspect materials, and account for materials activities using "headcount" as the resource driver. The headcount equals 30, with 10 in purchasing, 9 in receiving, 5 in inspecting, and 6 in accounting. Thus, each activity is assigned its fair share of the $900,000 service resource costs.

The $3,320,000 production resource costs are assigned to the machine materials and setup machine activities. Based on a great deal of analysis, the systems project team at Panametric determines that 90 percent of the $3,320,000 ($2,988,000) should be assigned to machine materials and 10 percent ($332,000) to setup machine.

▍Phase Five: Determine Second-Stage Activity Drivers and Assign Costs to Cost Objects

Once the costs of resources consumed by activities have been assigned to the activity cost pools, second-stage activity drivers can be determined and applied. These activity drivers are usually the outputs designated on the activity flow diagram. For example, the primary output of the purchase materials activity is purchase orders. Therefore, the number of purchase orders is the second-stage cost driver for the purchase materials activity cost pool. The costs from this activity cost pool are assigned to products on the basis of how many purchase orders they cause to be processed. For example, a complex product containing hundreds of parts will usually cause more purchase orders to be processed than a simple product containing two or three parts. Thus, the complex product should be charged with the bulk of purchasing costs.

Notice that the purchase materials activity has one input and three outputs, as shown in the activity flow diagram in Exhibit 10–9. The purchase request input is a trigger to activate the purchase materials activity. The three outputs are the purchase orders sent to vendors, the copies of the purchase orders sent to the account for materials activity, and a notification sent to the store materials activity. The cost of the purchase materials activity can be expressed as a cost per purchase request, purchase order, or copy of purchase order. Generally, the best measure, and therefore the best activity driver, is the *primary* output of the activity. In the case of the purchase materials activity, the best activity driver is the purchase order output, because the *primary* reason for performing this activity is to generate purchase orders.

Here are some rules of thumb for determining activity drivers:

■ If an activity has more than one output, the activity should be analyzed further to see if it should be decomposed into more than one activity, each with its own individual output measure. If the activity is indeed function-specific and cannot logically be further decomposed, then the *primary* output should be used as explained earlier.

■ If two or more activities have the same primary output measure, they should be aggregated into one activity.

The result of phase five at Panametric is the completed ABC system design shown in Exhibit 10–13. All of the second-stage activity drivers are designated for each activity cost pool. The direct cost elements, direct materials and direct labor, are also shown. The system is ready to cost products A and B, the two cost objects for Panametric Corporation's ABC system.

In some instances, the systems project team may wish to group several activity cost pools into one activity center as shown in Exhibit 10–14. For example, the activity cost pools of purchase materials, receive materials, inspect materials, and store materials may be included in an activity center called "materials handling." The accounting activity center and account for materials activity cost pool are the same. The machine materials activity cost pool and setup machine activity cost pool may be included in an activity center called "production."

Developing a large number of activity centers leads to a detailed representation of the organization and how it performs its work. But creating separate activity centers for a simple organization or for activity cost pools that are similar or stand on their own may add needless complexity to the ABC system without providing any additional insights into how resources are consumed. Thus, the systems project team should choose activity centers that have a clear meaning according to manageable segments of the organization. Doing so increases the likelihood that managers will use and correctly interpret ABC cost information as they manage activities in the organization.

How activity cost pools are organized within activity centers is irrelevant as

Number of inspections of a finished product is a second-stage activity driver. Courtesy of Honda of America Manufacturing, Inc.

■■■ EXHIBIT 10–13
Activity-Based Costing Model Showing Activity Cost Pools

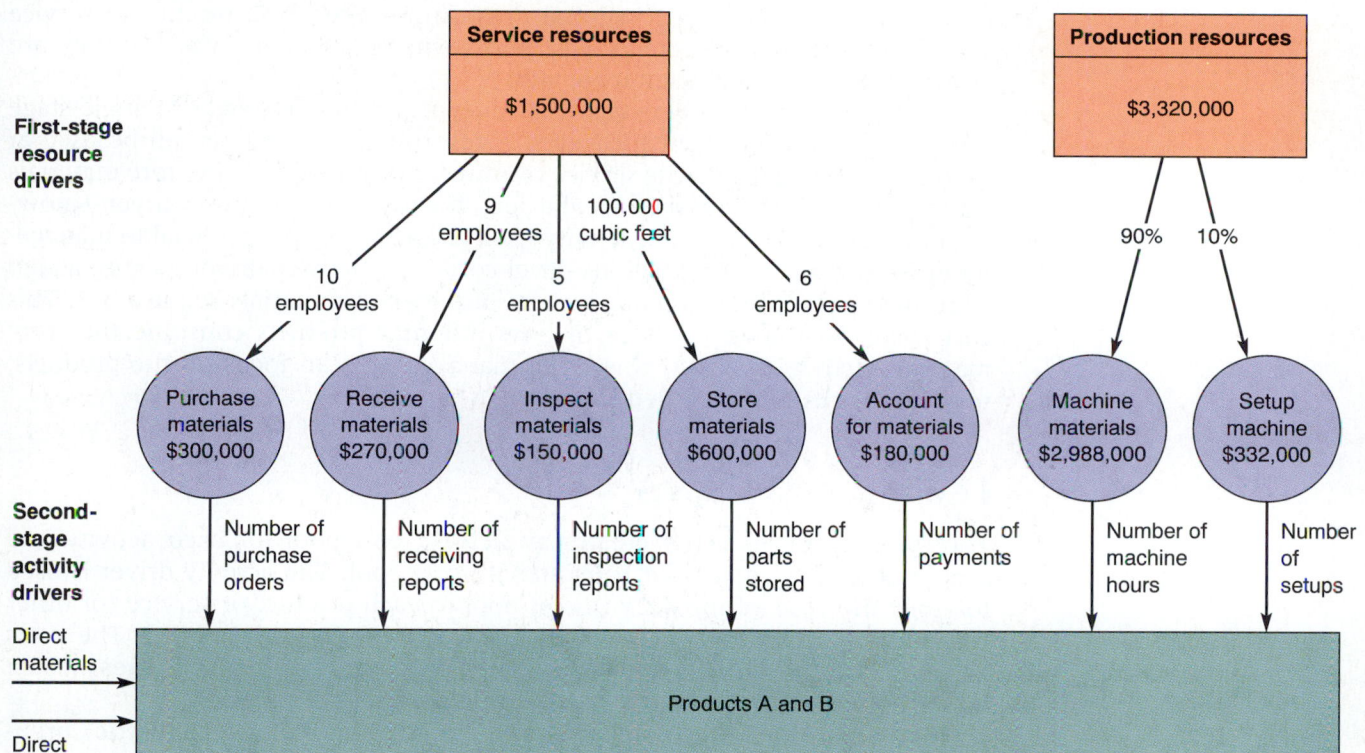

Activity-Based Costing Model Showing Activity Cost Pools Included in Activity Centers

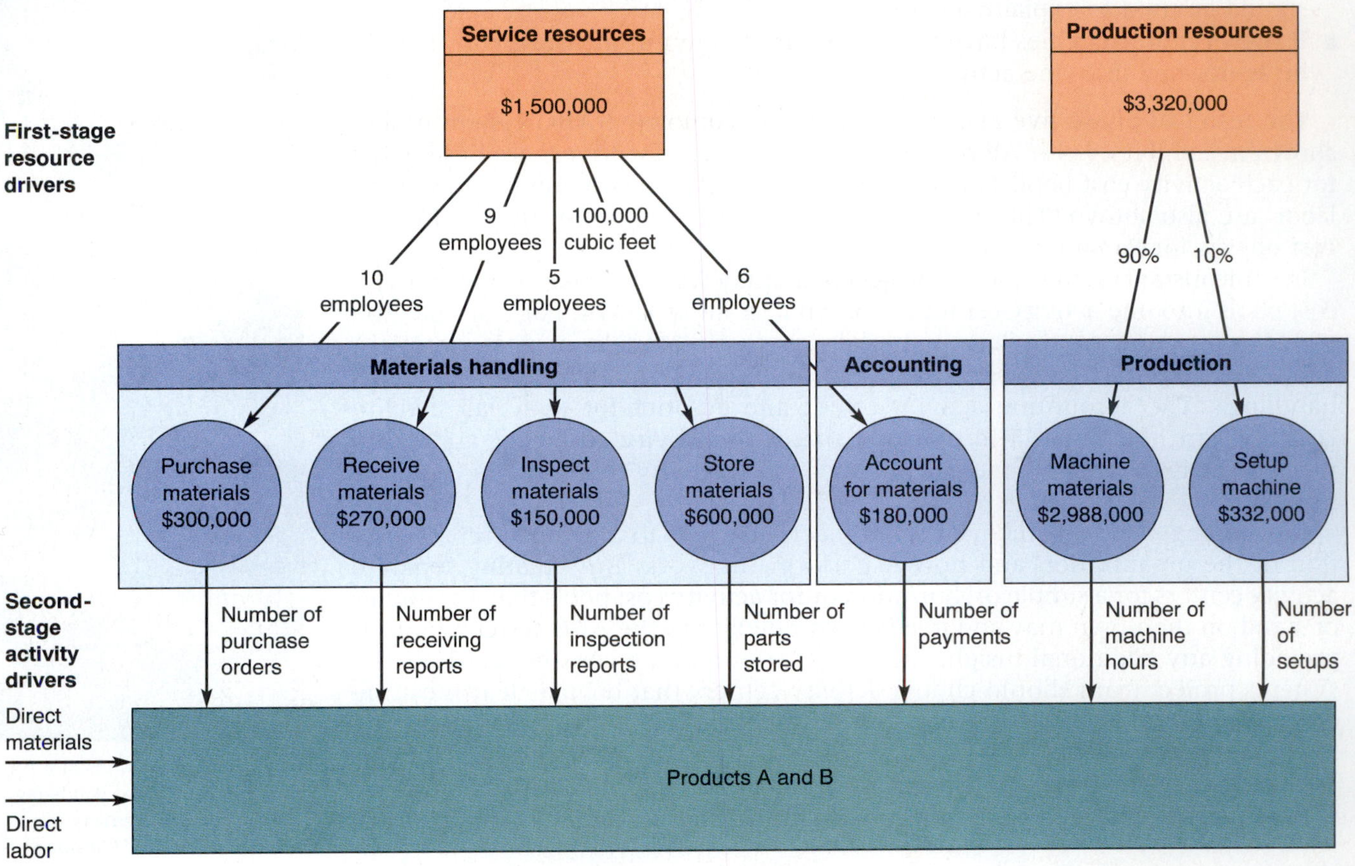

far as *calculations* are concerned and thus cannot affect unit product or service costs. The total cost of activity cost pools will be the same whether they are grouped within activity centers or not.

The advantage of a two-stage cost assignment process over a single-stage procedure is that different measures of resource consumption can be used at each stage. For example, the service resources are assigned to the store materials activity based on the number of cubic feet, the first-stage resource driver. Knowing how many resources the activity itself is consuming is beneficial to management in trying to control activity-level costs. The activity driver used to assign store materials costs to products is the number of materials requisitions. This cost driver is a good measure of how different products consume the store materials activity costs. At this level, management can focus on the products, services, or customers to determine their profitability.

▌Costing Cost Objects

The systems project team creates an activity cost pool for each activity and selects an activity driver for each activity cost pool. The activity driver is used to apply the costs of the activity cost pool to each product or service (or other cost object) according to the amount of activity costs consumed. The costs consumed are assigned to the cost object through a **bill of activities,** which lists activities and associated costs required by the cost object.

The bill of activities for products A and B manufactured by Panametric Corporation is shown in Exhibit 10–15. Production for the period is 50,000 units of

■■■ EXHIBIT 10–15
Bill of Activities for Product-Driven Activities

Bill of Activities, Products A and B
For the Period Ended December 31, 19X5

Activity Cost Pool	Second-Stage Activity Driver Rate	Product A (50,000 units)			Product B (100,000 units)		
		Activity Driver Quantity	Activity Cost	Unit Cost	Activity Driver Quantity	Activity Cost	Unit Cost
Purchase materials	$60 per purchase order	$60 × 4,000	$ 240,000	$ 4.80	$60 × 1,000	$ 60,000	$ 0.60
Receive materials	$90 per receipt	$90 × 2,500	225,000	4.50	$90 × 500	45,000	0.45
Inspect materials	$50 per inspection	$50 × 2,500	125,000	2.50	$50 × 500	25,000	0.25
Store materials	$20 per part stored	$20 × 20,000	400,000	8.00	$20 × 10,000	200,000	2.00
Account for materials	$72 per payment	$72 × 1,500	108,000	2.16	$72 × 1,000	72,000	0.72
Machine materials	$996 per machine hour	$996 × 1,000	996,000	19.92	$996 × 2,000	1,992,000	19.92
Setup machine	$3,320 per setup	$3,320 × 90	298,800	5.98	$3,320 × 10	33,200	0.33
Total activity costs assigned to products			$2,392,800			$2,427,200	
Activity costs per unit				$ 47.86			$24.27
Direct materials costs per unit				60.00			50.00
Direct labor costs per unit				24.00			24.00
Total costs per unit				$131.86			$98.27

product A and 100,000 units of product B. The activity costs consumed by each product are determined by multiplying the activity driver rate times the activity driver quantity generated. For example, product A caused 4,000 purchase orders to be generated during the period. It costs $60 to produce one purchase order. Therefore, product A is charged with $240,000 ($60 × 4,000 purchase orders) of the costs of the purchase materials activity. The cost per unit is $4.80 ($240,000 ÷ 50,000 units). Product B caused only 1,000 purchase orders to be produced, so it is charged with only $60,000 ($60 × 1,000 purchase orders) of the costs of the purchase materials activity. The cost per unit is $0.60 ($60,000 ÷ 100,000 units). The total activity costs assigned to product A and product B are $2,392,800 and $2,427,200, respectively. The activity costs per unit for product A and product B are $47.86 ($2,392,800 ÷ 50,000 units) and $24.27 ($2,427,200 ÷ 100,000 units), respectively. Direct materials and direct labor costs per unit are also included in the bill of activities. This way, the *total* costs per unit for each product are disclosed for management's attention.

The cost per unit for direct materials is determined from the bill of materials displayed in Exhibit 10–16. The actual amount of direct materials used comes from materials requisitions.

At the top of the exhibit is the bill of materials for product A, which is made up of two of part A.1, four of part A.2, and one of part A.3, for a total cost of $60 per unit. Part A.1 is composed of three of component 1.1 and two of component 1.2, for a total cost of $15 per unit. Part A.2 is a stand-alone part. Part A.3 requires one each of components 3.1, 3.2, and 3.3, for a total cost of $10 per unit. At the bottom of the exhibit is the bill of materials for product B, which requires one of part B.1 and one of part B.2, for a total cost of $50 per unit.

As the exhibit shows, product A is more complicated than product B. Because of this added complexity, product A drives the activity cost pools with greater intensity and frequency than does product B.

■ EXHIBIT 10–16
Bill of Materials for Product A and Product B

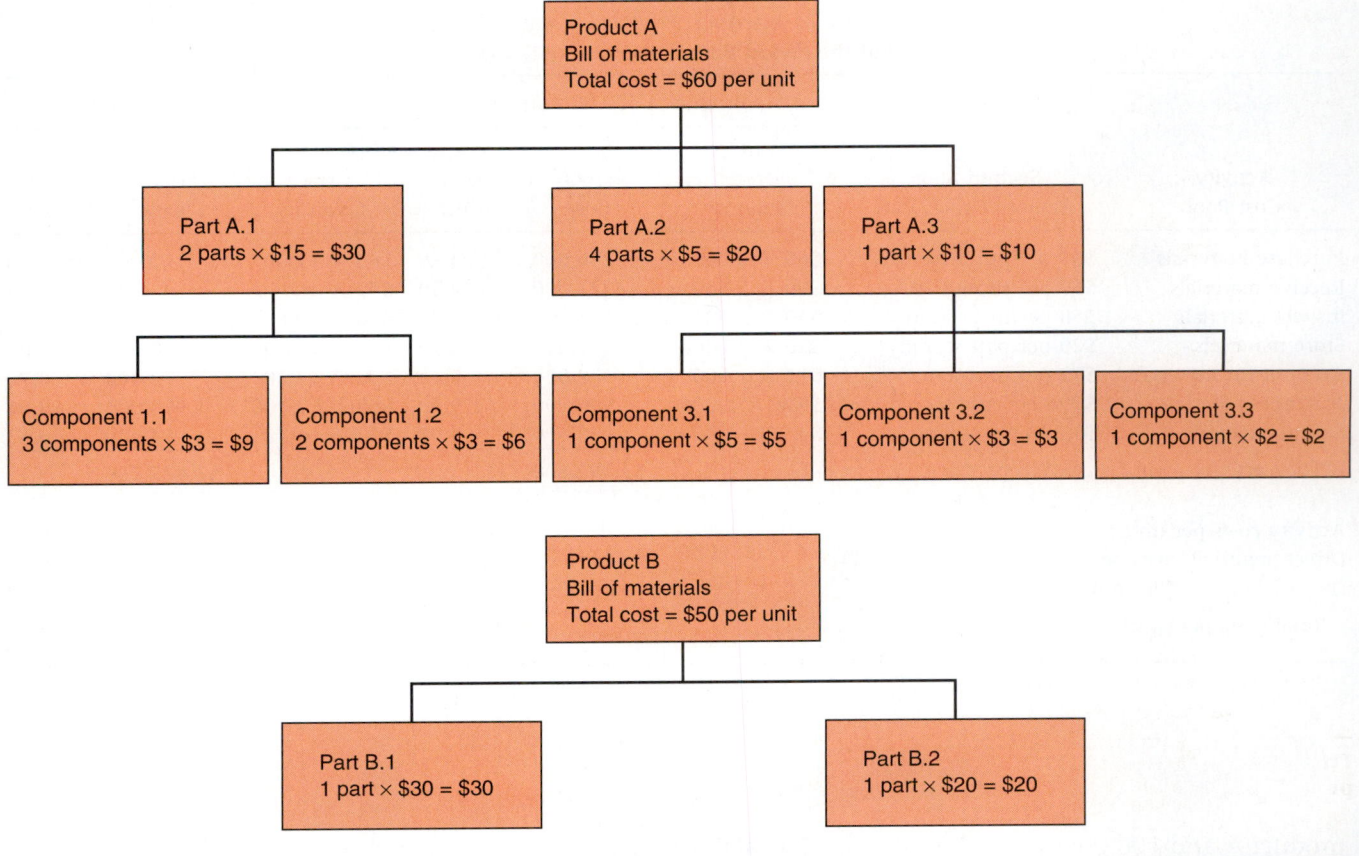

Direct labor costs represent the second direct cost element that is traced directly to the products. These costs are applied to the products based on data collected on time tickets. The cost per unit for direct labor is $24 ($12 × 2 hours) for both products.

An interesting and revealing exercise is to use the data of the Panametric Corporation to calculate the cost per unit of products A and B under four different costing systems:

- Activity-based costing system just presented
- Activity-based costing system using three direct cost elements: direct materials, direct labor, and direct technology
- Traditional volume-based costing system using a plantwide predetermined overhead rate (POR) based on direct labor hours
- Traditional volume-based costing system using two predetermined overhead rates (PORs) based on materials dollars and machine hours

The results are presented in Exhibit 10–17.

The total costs for producing both products are $16,420,000 no matter which costing system is used. The total unit costs, however, present a radically different picture. Under both activity-based costing systems, the total unit costs are the same. However, when direct technology (machine) costs are treated as a direct cost element, one can clearly see that product A is driving most of the activity costs ($27.94 per unit for product A versus $4.35 per unit for product B). But when volume-based costing systems are used, the overhead costs per unit for both products are equal ($32.13 for each) when the POR is based on DLhr or

Activity-based costing:	Product A	Product B
Direct materials	$ 60.00	$50.00
Direct labor ($12 × 2 DLhr)	24.00	24.00
Activity costs	47.86	24.27
Total cost per unit	$131.86	$98.27

EXHIBIT 10–17
Calculation of Unit Costs Using Four Different Costing Systems

Activity-based costing with direct technology as a cost element:	Product A	Product B
Direct materials	$ 60.00	$50.00
Direct labor	24.00	24.00
Direct technology	19.92	19.92
Activity costs	27.94	4.35
Total cost per unit	$131.86	$98.27

Machine (Direct technology):
  A: $2,988,000 × ⅓ = $996,000 ÷ 50,000 units = $19.92 per unit
  B: $2,988,000 × ⅔ = $1,992,000 ÷ 100,000 units = $19.92 per unit

Activities without the machine materials activity:

	Product A	Product B
Purchase materials	$ 240,000	$ 60,000
Receive materials	225,000	45,000
Inspect materials	125,000	25,000
Store materials	400,000	200,000
Account for materials	108,000	72,000
Setup machine	298,800	33,200
Total activity costs	$1,396,800	$435,200

A: $1,396,800 ÷ 50,000 units = $27.94 per unit
B: $435,200 ÷ 100,000 units = $4.35 per unit

Traditional volume-based costing system using a plantwide predetermined overhead rate based on direct labor hours:

	Product A	Product B
Direct materials	$ 60.00	$ 50.00
Direct labor ($12 × 2 DLhr)	24.00	24.00
A: Overhead ($16.067/DLhr × 2 DLhr)	32.13	
B: Overhead ($16.067/DLhr × 2 DLhr)		32.13
Total cost per unit	$116.13	$106.13

Calculation of plantwide predetermined overhead rate based on direct labor hours:

A: Direct labor hours budgeted	100,000
B: Direct labor hours budgeted	200,000
Total direct labor hours budgeted	300,000

Total resources:

Service resources	$1,500,000
Production resources	3,320,000
Total resources budgeted	$4,820,000

$4,820,000 ÷ 300,000 DLhr = $16.067 per DLhr

Traditional volume-based costing system using two predetermined overhead rates based on direct materials dollars and machine hours:

	Product A	Product B
Direct materials	$ 60.00	$ 50.00
Direct labor ($12 × 2 DLhr)	24.00	24.00
A: OH based on materials dollars ($562,500 ÷ 50,000 units)	11.25	
B: OH based on materials dollars ($937,500 ÷ 100,000 units)		9.38
A: OH based on machine hours ($1,106,667 ÷ 50,000 units)	22.13	
B: OH based on machine hours ($2,213,333 ÷ 100,000 units)		22.13
Total cost per unit	$117.38	$105.51

Continued

—Continued
Predetermined overhead rate based on direct materials dollars:
 Service resources:

 A: ($60 × 50,000 units) = $3,000,000 (⅜)
 B: ($50 × 100,000 units) =   5,000,000 (⅝)

  Total direct materials $8,000,000 (⁸⁄₈)

 A: $1,500,000 × ⅜ = $562,500 ÷ 50,000 units = $11.25 per unit
 B: $1,500,000 × ⅝ = $937,500 ÷ 100,000 units = $9.38 per unit

Predetermined overhead rate based on machine hours:
 Production resources:

 A: Machine hours budgeted   1,000 (⅓)
 B: Machine hours budgeted   2,000 (⅔)

  Total machine hours budgeted   3,000 (³⁄₃)

 A: $3,320,000 × ⅓ = $1,106,667 ÷ 50,000 units = $22.13 per unit
 B: $3,320,000 × ⅔ = $2,213,333 ÷ 100,000 units = $22.13 per unit

Note: All numbers are rounded to the nearest penny.

---

near equal ($33.38 for product A and $31.51 for product B) when PORs are based on materials dollars and machine hours.

▌Market-Driven Activity-Based Costing Systems

A market-driven ABC system can be developed along with a product-driven ABC system. Whereas product-driven ABC system costs are assigned to cost objects, such as units, batches of units, and product lines, market-driven ABC system costs are assigned to such cost objects as customers, customer groups, distribution channels, and sales territories. Just as products have varying degrees of complexity and diversity and make different demands on resources and activities, so too do customers, customer groups, distribution channels, and sales territories.

Two different enterprises that produce the same products can incur different market-driven costs, depending on their target customers, distribution strategies, sales territories, and advertising campaigns. The product-driven costs for the two enterprises may be the same, but the market-driven costs will probably be substantially different.

Market-driven activities represent a sizable portion (anywhere from 20 to more than 50 percent) of an enterprise's total costs. Assigning such costs to their sources helps management identify relative profitability of customers, customer groups, distribution channels, and sales territories. These activities may be providing a competitive advantage or disadvantage depending on how resources are deployed to meet the needs of the market.

Exhibit 10–18 shows a general ABC model to cost customers. The resource categories include benefits, depreciation of buildings and a variety of equipment, salaries and commissions, and utilities. These resource costs are assigned to activity cost pools by using such resource drivers as headcount, square feet and cubic feet, hours of equipment usage, and kilowatt hours. Activity cost pools are aggregated into activity centers. Each activity center is managed by a separate person. The second-stage activity drivers assign the costs from the activity cost pools to the customers.

A bill of activities for customer A is presented in Exhibit 10–19. The cost data are assumed for illustrative purposes. A similar bill of activities format can be used for any level of cost object chosen, such as customer groups, distribution channels, or sales territories. In many organizations, it is difficult to assign costs to individual customers. Therefore, customers are usually aggregated into groups, such as distributors and retailers. Each group possesses different charac-

EXHIBIT 10–18
Activity-Based Costing System for Customer-Driven Activities

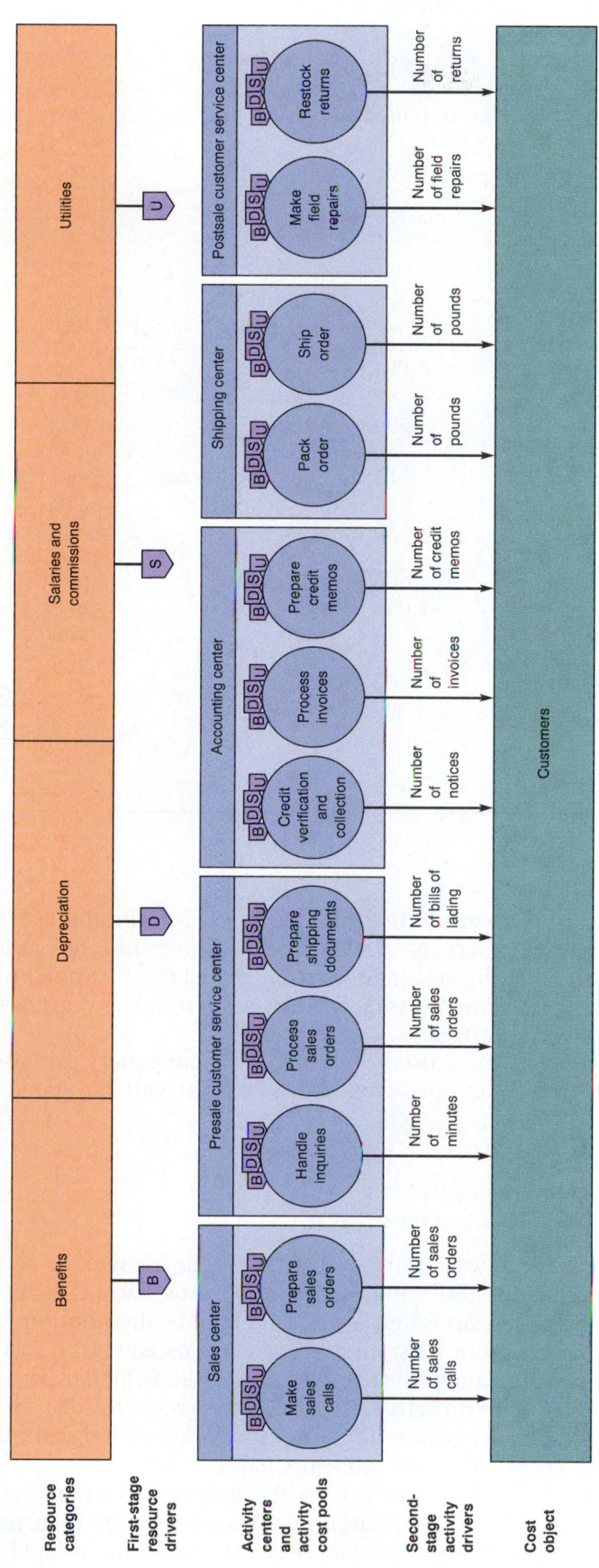

■ EXHIBIT 10–19
Bill of Activities for Market-Driven (Customer) Activities

Bill of Activities
Customer A
For the Period Ended December 31, 19X4

Sales	$200,000
Cost of goods sold*	<140,000>
Gross profit	$ 60,000

Less market-driven activity costs:

Activity Cost Pool	Activity Driver Rate	Activity Driver Quantity	Activity Cost
Make sales calls	$40 per sales call	10 sales calls	$ 400
Prepare sales orders	$30 per sales order	50 sales orders	1,500
Handle inquiries	$10 per minute	100 minutes	1,000
Process sales orders	$80 per sales order	50 sales orders	4,000
Process shipping documents	$40 per shipping document	12 shipping documents	480
Process credit	$60 per notice	2 notices	120
Process invoices	$70 per invoice	50 invoices	3,500
Prepare credit memos	$70 per credit memo	6 credit memos	420
Pack orders	$2 per pound	1,000 pounds	2,000
Ship orders	$3 per pound	1,000 pounds	3,000
Make field repairs	$300 per field repair	3 field repairs	900
Restock returns	$100 per return	6 returns	600

Total market-driven activity costs	< 17,920>
Profit contributed by Customer A	$ 42,080

* Determined from product-driven ABC system.

teristics. Distributors normally buy many units per order and require few shipping destinations. Retailers, on the other hand, purchase few units per order and have many shipping destinations; therefore, they normally create more order processing and shipping transactions. Also, retailers require special packaging and advertising programs.

The same activity drivers used to cost specific customers can also be used to cost customer groups. Other activity drivers that can be added include the following:

- Units per order
- Number of shipping destinations
- Number of special packaging requests

Distribution channel-level activity costs are those incurred to service a particular distribution channel. Although customer groups, such as distributors, retailers, and buying groups, are often also designated as distribution channels, the two are differentiated here. Customer groups are costed on the basis of activities used to meet the demands of customers, as already illustrated. Distribution channels make demands on activities, such as warehousing, distribution centers, trucking, and other transportation modes. In other words, distribution channels involve logistics costs, discussed later in Chapter 13.

Sales territory–level costs are not easily assigned to individual customers, customer groups, or distribution channels. These costs are incurred to develop and maintain a presence in the marketplace. Activities related to the sales territory cost object are advertise and promote, handle product liability claims, handle recalls, set up trade shows, and perform market research.

USING ACTIVITY-BASED COSTING SYSTEMS IN SERVICE ORGANIZATIONS

LEARNING OBJECTIVE 4

Discuss how activity-based costing systems are used in service organizations.

Although differences between manufacturing and service enterprises tend to blur because of manufacturers' increasing emphasis on providing services, service enterprises do have several differentiating characteristics, the primary ones being:

- Little to no inventory
- Output that is often intangible and difficult to define

Despite these differences, service firms are developing costing systems that are very similar to the ABC systems used by manufacturers.

Using ABC Systems in Hospitals

The ABC system for a hospital presented in Exhibit 10–20 recognizes that patients in the same unit need and receive different amounts of nursing care. The diversity in nursing service provided and the amount of money involved are significant. The objective of the ABC system is to measure more accurately how much nursing care each patient requires and to ensure that the patient is charged accordingly.

Each unit's head nurse rates each patient and arrives at a level of "acuteness" on a ten-point scale. Level 10 patients, such as those in cardiac care, need ten times as much nursing care as a level 1 patient. A nursing service charge per day is computed for each level of nursing care activity, and the patient at a particular acuteness level is charged this rate. As a result, each patient's charges reflect more accurately the actual service received. The nursing care activity is driven by acuteness levels. The occupancy and feeding activity is considered a daily cost that is the same for all acuteness levels.[11]

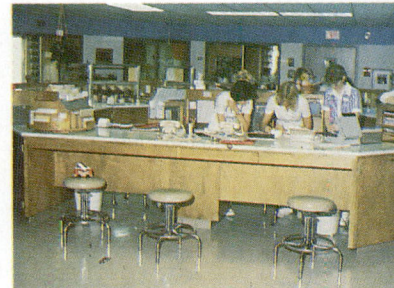

Entering patient cost data. Courtesy of Mayo Foundation.

Using ABC Systems in Railroad Operations

In any given hour, a large freight railroad company operates over one hundred trains, covers thousands of miles, and moves thousands of freight cars. Thousands of shipments are processed every day, each different from the others. To cost this traffic, the railroad company can use a form of ABC, as shown in Exhibit 10–21.

If the freight railroad company were to use a costing system with one all-

---

[11] William Rotch, "Activity-Based Costing in Service Industries," in *Emerging Practices in Cost Management*, ed. Barry J. Brinker (Boston: Warren Gorham Lamont, 1990), p. 60. With permission.

EXHIBIT 10–20

ABC System Used in a Hospital

Resource Categories	Resource Drivers	Activity Cost Pools	Activity Drivers	Cost of Service
■ Nurses ■ Nursing supervision ■ Supplies ■ Facilities ■ Dietary ■ Other overhead	■ Costs related to nursing and acuteness level ■ Costs related to hotel and dietary functions	■ Nursing care ■ Occupancy and feeding	■ Cost per day for each acuteness level ■ Cost per day	■ Nursing service for specified acuteness level ■ Occupancy per day
				Total cost per day

■EXHIBIT 10–21
ABC System Used in a Railroad Company

Resource Categories	Resource Drivers	Activity Cost Pools	Activity Drivers	Cost of Service
■ Maintenance of railroads, yards, and structures ■ Maintenance of equipment and depreciation ■ Transportation support facilities and labor	■ Assignment of resource costs to activity cost pools according to usage	■ Moving freight trains ■ Switching freight trains ■ Handling and depreciation of freight cars ■ Handling freight in and out of freight cars	■ Cost per gross ton mile ■ Cost per yard/train switching minute ■ Cost per freight mile ■ Cost per ton of freight	■ Gross ton miles per shipment × activity driver ■ Yard/train switching minutes per shipment × activity driver ■ Freight car miles per shipment × activity driver ■ Tons of freight per shipment × activity driver
				Total costs of a specific shipment

encompassing activity, that activity would be "moving freight," and the link to service output would be cost per ton mile. But because ton miles of freight are not alike, the railroad company has to relate characteristics of freight shipments to activities and the cost of these activities.

None of the railroad's functional support costs (i.e., costs of the functional divisions of the railroad) relates directly to a shipment. Therefore, the systems project team defines a series of activities and their costs that could be linked to characteristics of shipments. Then they select activity drivers to assign these costs to specific service outputs. For example, each shipment will be on a freight car that will be handled one or more times in one or more switching yards, which represents an activity. The route and train specifications determine how many switching minutes will be needed. The cost of that switching activity carries its fair share of several functional support costs, such as maintenance of track in the yards, maintenance and depreciation of switching equipment, and labor costs in the yards.

The ABC system enables the railroad to derive the actual cost of each shipment by gathering data each day from many locations on movements of trains and shipments. Also, by using the same activity cost information, the railroad can estimate the cost of future shipments, which helps the marketing department identify profitable business.[12] The ABC system necessary to cost railroad services is illustrated in Exhibit 10–22. This ABC system is developed using two-stage cost drivers, similar to the ABC system for product costing in the Panametric Corporation example.

▌ SUMMARY OF LEARNING OBJECTIVES

The major goals of this chapter were to enable you to achieve four learning objectives:

Learning objective 1. Define activity-based costing systems.

Activity-based costing systems measure the cost and performance of resources, activi-

[12] Ibid., pp. 60–61.

■ EXHIBIT 10–22
ABC System for the Railroad Company Developed Using Two-Stage Cost Drivers

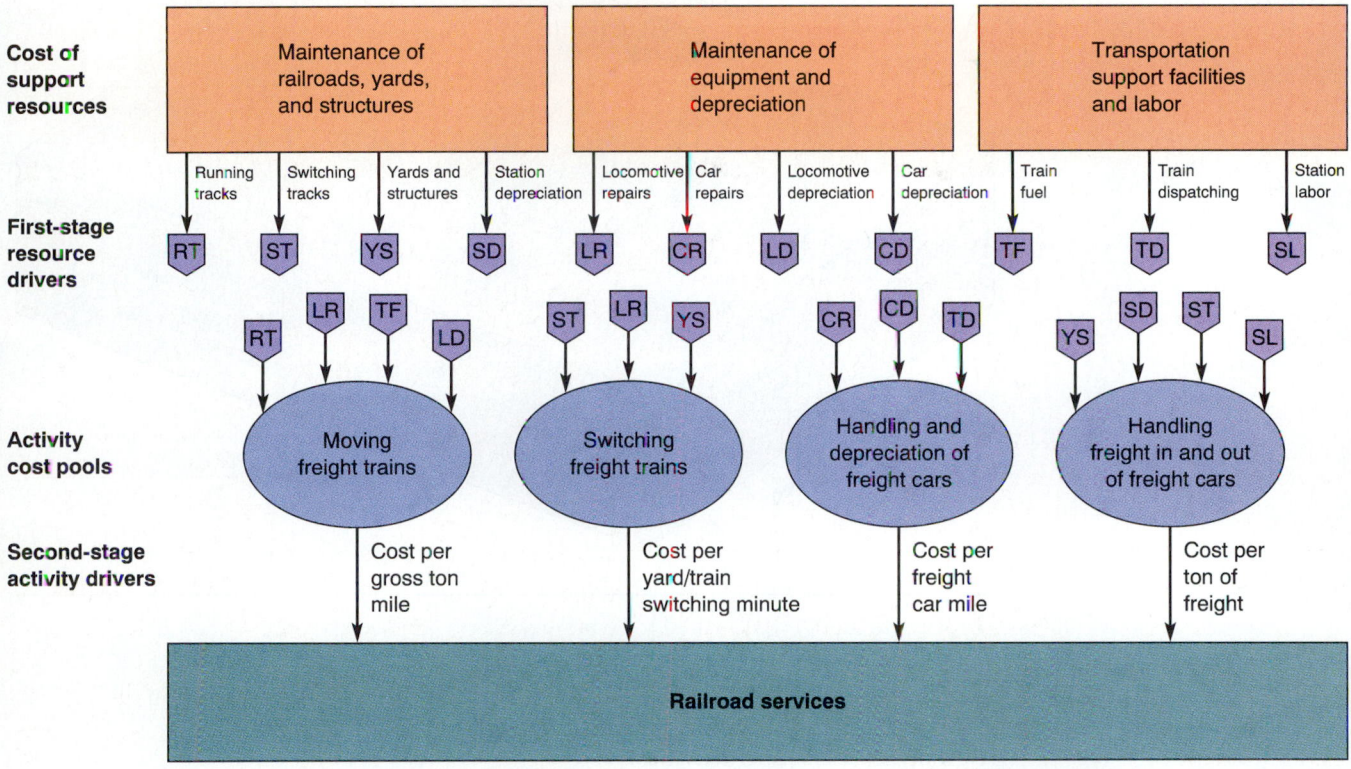

ties, and cost objects. Resource category costs are assigned to activities using resource drivers, thereby forming activity cost pools. Costs from activity cost pools are assigned to cost objects using activity drivers. The key attribute of cost drivers is a cause-and-effect relationship between resources, activities, and cost objects. The relationship is based on the notion that cost objects consume activities and activities consume resources. Both manufacturing and service organizations use ABC systems for cost reporting for a variety of cost objects and for cost management, as shown in Exhibit 10–23. The linkage between cost reporting and cost management indicates that ABC systems are used not just as costing systems but as management tools for the pursuit of excellence.

By understanding where the demands for activities come from, management can focus on eliminating both the demand for the activity and possibly even the activity itself if it does not add value to the enterprise. Cost drivers identify the causes of costs. Thus, management has a tool to address the root causes of costs rather than treating symptoms.

Learning objective 2.   Contrast traditional volume-based costing systems with activity-based costing systems.

Traditional volume-based costing systems focus on *units* of particular products and apply overhead costs on the basis of direct labor hours, direct labor dollars, machine hours, and materials dollars consumed in making the product. By contrast, ABC systems focus on the *activities* performed to produce or service cost objects. Costs are assigned to cost objects based on each cost object's consumption of activities.

Learning objective 3.   Explain how to develop activity-based costing systems.

A multidisciplinary systems project team is chosen to develop the ABC system, which may be a pilot or a full-blown, enterprisewide system. The systems project team follows an engineered, structured methodology called the ABC systems development life cycle, which involves the following phases:

■■EXHIBIT 10–23
Dimensions of ABC Systems

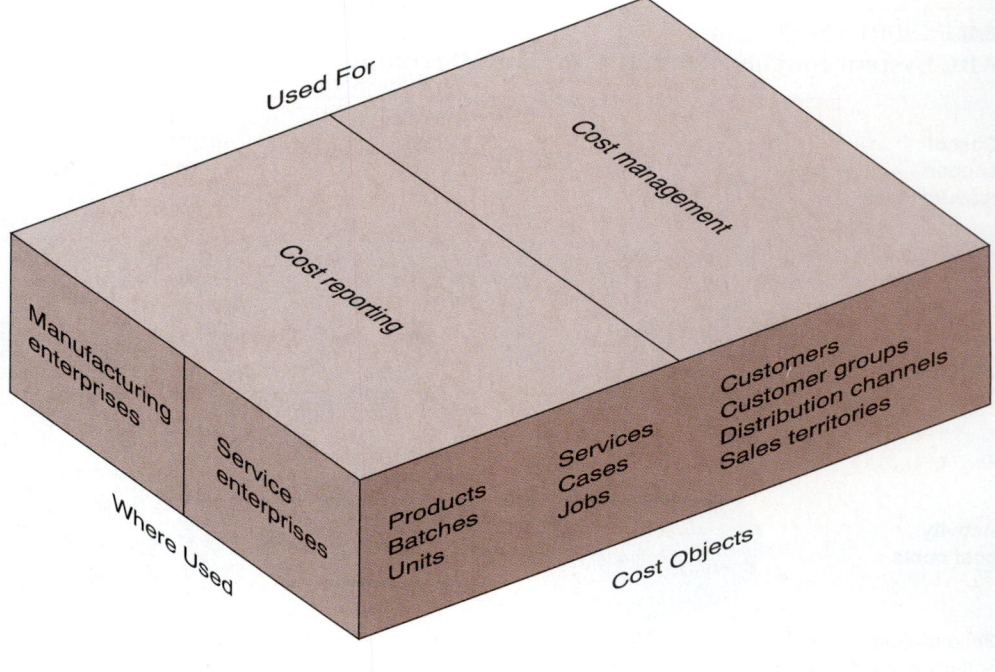

1. Plan the system.
2. Analyze and define resource categories.
3. Analyze and define activities.
4. Determine first-stage resource drivers and establish activity cost pools.
5. Determine second-stage activity drivers and assign costs to cost objects.

The activity flow diagram and the fishbone (cause-and-effect) diagram are two tools used in defining tasks, activities, and activity drivers. The bill of activities provides an excellent method for cost reporting.

Learning objective 4. Discuss how activity-based costing systems are used in service organizations.

Service enterprises have two characteristics that differentiate them from manufacturing enterprises:

■ Little to no inventory
■ Output that is often intangible and difficult to define

Just as manufacturing enterprises can use ABC systems to help them cost products and practice cost management, so too can service organizations. Like manufacturing firms, service organizations include activities that can be analyzed. Also, cost drivers can be selected and used to apply costs to various services in the same manner as they are used to apply costs to products.

▍IMPORTANT TERMS

ABC systems development life cycle   An engineered, structured methodology used by multidisciplinary systems project teams to develop ABC systems.

Activity   A process made up of highly-related tasks that converts inputs to outputs. Activities consume resources to produce outputs.

Activity analysis   The process of defining and describing activities and their corresponding cost drivers.

Activity-based costing (ABC)   A costing methodology that collects financial and operational data about an enterprise's activities for costing cost objects and providing a tool for cost management.

Activity-based management (ABM)   A management approach that uses ABC information to perform continuous improvement, reduce or eliminate nonvalue-added activities, and make strategic decisions.

Activity center   A manageable set of activities or activity cost pools.

Activity cost pool   An activity that has been assigned its portion of resource costs. Costs from activity cost pools are assigned to cost objects using activity drivers.

Activity drivers   Devices that measure the frequency and intensity of the consumption of activity costs by cost objects. They are used to assign activity costs to cost objects.

Activity flow diagram   A modeling tool that describes activities, their interdependencies, and inputs and outputs.

Aggregation   The process of combining tasks into homogeneous groups to form a function-specific activity.

Bill of activities   A compilation of activities and associated costs required by a cost object. If applicable, direct cost inputs are also included. The bill of activities is a cost report used by management.

Cost objects   Anything to which activity costs are assigned.

Decomposition   The process of breaking down groups of dissimilar tasks into several function-specific activities.

Direct cost inputs   Cost elements, such as direct materials, direct labor, and direct technology, that are easily traceable to cost objects.

Fishbone (cause-and-effect) diagram   A modeling tool that defines the tasks that comprise an activity.

Resource categories   Areas that represent the sources of costs that support activities. These are the factors of production that are consumed by activities to produce activity outputs.

Resource drivers   Devices that measure the quantity of resources consumed by activities. They are used to assign portions of resource category costs to activities.

Tasks   The basic work elements of an activity. An aggregation of a set of highly-related tasks makes up a function-specific activity.

DEMONSTRATION PROBLEMS

■ **DEMONSTRATION PROBLEM 1**   *Activity-based costing versus volume-based costing.*

At Milestone Company, product A is a mature product that requires little engineering work. Product B, however, is a relatively new product with some unresolved engineering problems. Following are data related to both products:

	PRODUCT A	PRODUCT B
Production volume	1,000	1,000
Number of engineering changes	2	12
Cost per engineering change	$1,000	$1,000
Direct labor hours per unit	3	2

Required:

a. Using direct labor hours (DLhr) as a base for applying overhead costs, calculate overhead cost per unit and total overhead costs.

b. Using an activity-based costing approach, calculate overhead cost per unit and total overhead costs.

SOLUTION TO DEMONSTRATION PROBLEM 1

a.

	PRODUCT A	PRODUCT B
Overhead applied using DLhr overhead cost per unit:*		
A: $2.80 × 3 DLhr	$8.40	
B: $2.80 × 2 DLhr		$5.60
Total overhead cost:		
A: $8.40 × 1,000 units	$8,400.00	
B: $5.60 × 1,000 units		$5,600.00

* Predetermined overhead rate based on direct labor hours:

Continued

—Continued

Total overhead costs:
   $1,000 per engineering change × 14 engineering changes = $14,000
Total direct labor hours:
   1,000 units × 3 DLhr = 3,000
   1,000 units × 2 DLhr = 2,000   ÷ 5,000 DLhr
   Predetermined overhead rate $2.80 per DLhr

b.

	PRODUCT A	PRODUCT B
Overhead applied using ABC overhead cost per unit:		
A: ($1,000 × 2 engineering changes) ÷ 1,000 units	$2.00	
B: ($1,000 × 12 engineering changes) ÷ 1,000 units		$12.00
Total overhead cost:		
A: $2.00 × 1,000 units	$2,000.00	
B: $12.00 × 1,000 units		$12,000.00

■ **DEMONSTRATION PROBLEM 2**   *Pilot ABC system for determining customer profitability.*

Monarch Equipment Company sells earthmoving equipment to construction companies in the southeastern part of the country. Monarch's manager has been reading about activity-based costing and believes it can be used to help determine customer profitability of Monarch.

The manager wants to start with a pilot ABC system that will include two activities:

■ Process sales orders
■ Perform field repairs (these are repairs that are under warranty by Monarch)

Analyses reveal that the process sales orders activity includes the tasks of enter sales order, verify credit, calculate freight, schedule delivery, and generate invoice. Further analyses indicate that the perform field repairs activity includes dispatch repair team, travel to destination, perform repairs, and return to home base.

Four resource categories, their budgeted costs, and resource drivers are as follows:

RESOURCE CATEGORY	BUDGETED COSTS	RESOURCE DRIVER
Building depreciation	$400,000	Square feet
Equipment depreciation	600,000	Percentage of usage
Utilities	180,000	Cubic feet
Salaries and benefits	800,000	Direct assignment

These budgeted costs are for Monarch's entire operation not just the process sales orders and perform field repairs activities.

Monarch's main building occupies 20,000 square feet, of which 1,000 square feet are devoted to the process sales order activity and 4,000 square feet are allocated to the perform field repairs activity. Five percent of equipment depreciation is charged to the process sales order activity, and 20 percent is charged to the perform field repairs activity. The process sales order activity is charged with $1,600 in utilities based on 8,000 cubic feet at $0.20 per cubic foot. The perform field repairs activity is assigned $6,400 based on 32,000 cubic feet at $0.20 per cubic foot. The process sales orders activity is charged $108,400 in salaries and benefits based on direct assignment. The perform field repairs activity is charged $203,600 based on direct assignment. The process sales orders activity has budgeted 4,000 sales orders; the perform field repairs activity has budgeted 2,000 hours.

Required:
a. Using a fishbone (cause-and-effect) diagram, describe the two activities in terms of their tasks.
b. Develop an ABC design model.
c. Prepare a bill of activities for customer C who made 14 sales orders and consumed 100 hours in field repairs. Customer C purchased $400,000 worth of equipment with cost of goods sold of $260,000.

SOLUTION TO DEMONSTRATION PROBLEM 2

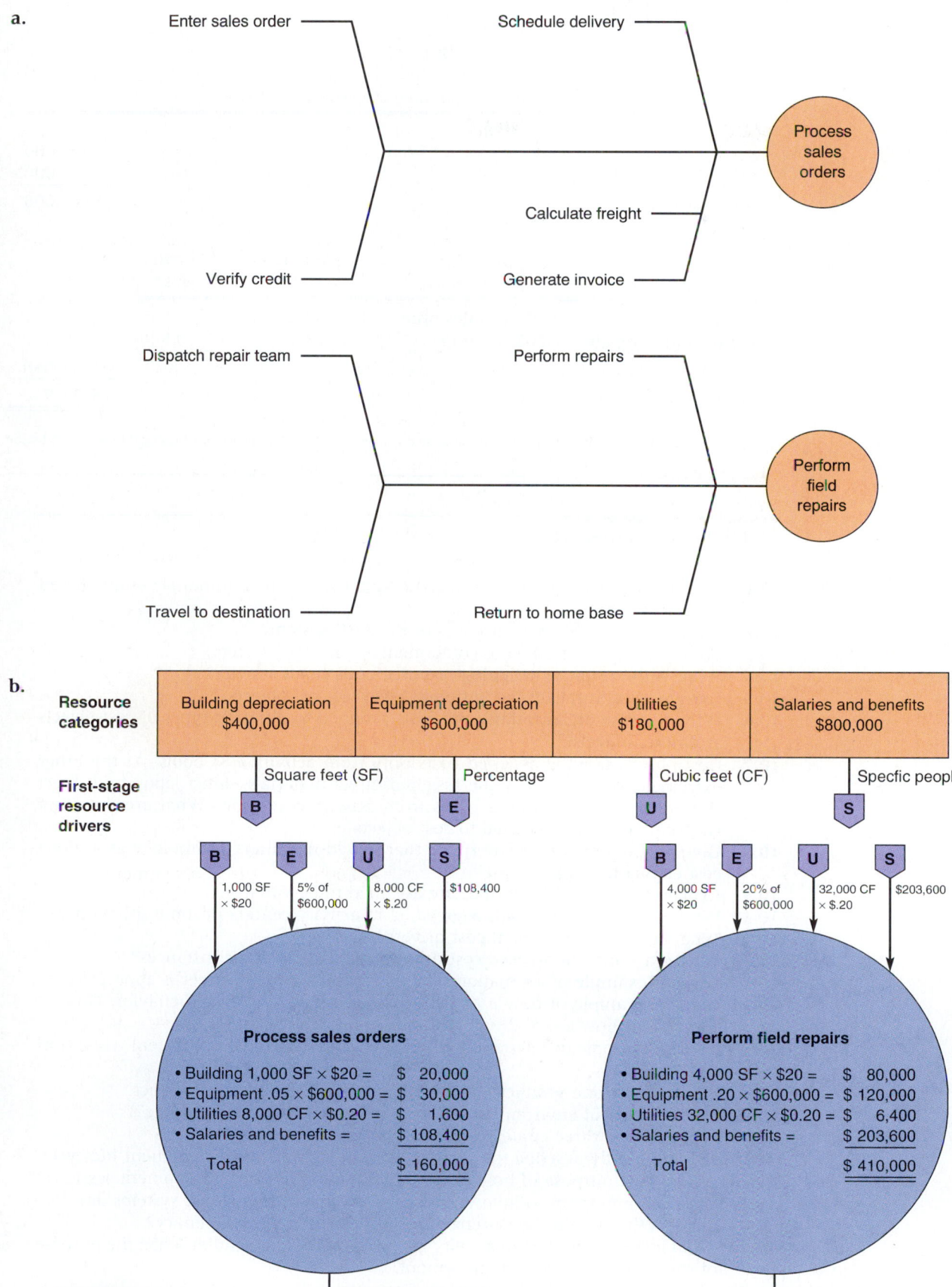

c.

BILL OF ACTIVITIES
CUSTOMER C
FOR PERIOD ENDED DECEMBER 31, 19X4

Sales			$400,000
Cost of goods sold*			<260,000>
Gross profit			$140,000
Less activity costs:			

ACTIVITY COST POOL	ACTIVITY DRIVER RATE	ACTIVITY DRIVER QUANTITY	ACTIVITY COST
Process sales orders	$40 per sales order	14 sales orders	$ 560
Perform field repairs	$205 per hour	100 hours	20,500

Total activity costs	< 21,060>
Profit generated by Customer C	$118,940

* Since Monarch is a distributor, the cost of goods sold is determined by the invoice price charged to Monarch by the original equipment manufacturers.

REVIEW QUESTIONS

10.1 In general terms, differentiate the ABC system from the traditional volume-based costing system.

10.2 What are the two main purposes of the ABC system?

10.3 List and briefly describe the components of an ABC system.

10.4 What is the result of assigning resource costs to an activity?

10.5 Explain what is meant by "different levels of cost objects."

10.6 Why, in some organizations, are costs assigned to different types of cost objects at different levels?

10.7 Cost objects may be assigned costs only from activity cost pools. At the other extreme, cost objects may be assigned direct materials, direct labor, and direct technology costs, as well as costs from activity cost pools. What are the other two ways costs are assigned to cost objects?

10.8 Give an example of an enterprise that would use direct technology as a direct cost element.

10.9 Explain why costs of activities are assumed to be variable.

10.10 Why are activity cost pools aggregated in activity centers in some situations?

10.11 What are the four types of cost drivers?

10.12 Why is a transaction-based cost driver preferable in some instances?

10.13 Give an example of a situation where a time-based cost driver is appropriate.

10.14 Give an example of how a cost driver will induce beneficial behavior. Give an example of how a cost driver will induce harmful behavior.

10.15 Give an example of a situation where a volume-based costing system will distort costs.

10.16 Explain how one product may be cross-subsidizing another product.

10.17 In what kind of environments is activity-based costing appropriate?

10.18 What are the three strategic goals of ABC systems?

10.19 List and briefly describe the phases of the ABC systems development life cycle.

10.20 What is the purpose of holding several joint application development sessions?

10.21 Why is it important to involve workers and managers in ABC systems development? Why should the systems project team be multidisciplinary?

10.22 What is the purpose of an activity flow diagram? Name and describe the purpose of each activity flow diagram symbol.

10.23 What is the purpose of a fishbone (cause-and-effect) diagram?

10.24 What is the purpose of aggregation and decomposition? Summarize the rules of thumb for both processes.

10.25 What constitutes an appropriate activity driver per the activity flow diagram? Summarize the rules of thumb for determining activity drivers.

10.26 What is a bill of activities used for?

10.27 List four market-driven cost objects. If an ABC system cannot cost individual customers, what next-level cost object is used?

10.28 Can ABC systems be used in service organizations? Name two types of service organizations in which ABC systems have been successfully used.

CHAPTER-SPECIFIC PROBLEMS

These problems require responses based directly on concepts and techniques presented in the text.

10.29 *Activity-based costing and volume-based costing contrasted: cost per setup.* Morrison Electronics currently charges setup costs to its products using direct labor hours. Cliff Molson, management accountant, has collected the following data for contrasting the present costing system with an ABC system:

	PRODUCT A	PRODUCT B
Production volume	50	1,000
Cost per setup	$1,000	$1,000
Number of setups	1	2
Batch size	50	500
Total cost of setups	$1,000	$2,000
Direct labor hours per unit	2	2
Total direct labor hours	100	2,000

Required:
Calculate the amount of setup costs per unit using the activity-based approach and the volume-based approach (i.e., direct labor hours).

[Adapted from Peter B. B. Turney]

10.30 *Activity-based costing and volume-based costing contrasted: cost per engineering change.* National Fabricators uses a costing system that charges its engineering change costs to products using direct labor hours as the application base. The following data were collected during activity analysis:

	PRODUCT C	PRODUCT D
Production volume	1,000	500
Cost per engineering change	$1,000	$1,000
Number of engineering changes	2	10
Total cost of engineering changes	$2,000	$10,000
Direct labor hours per unit	3	2

$\times 1,000$ $\times 500$
$\overline{3,000\ Dlh}$ $\overline{1,000}$

Required:
Calculate the engineering change cost per direct labor hour. Then calculate the overhead cost (engineering changes) per unit using the volume-based approach and the activity-based approach.

[Adapted from Peter B. B. Turney]

10.31 *Costing nursing home services.* Shady Pines Nursing Care has established an ABC system as follows:

ACTIVITY COST POOLS	ACTIVITY DRIVER RATE	
Nursing care	Acuteness level 1:	$ 80 per day
	Acuteness level 2:	160 per day
	Acuteness level 3:	240 per day
	Acuteness level 4:	320 per day
	Acuteness level 5:	400 per day
	Acuteness level 6:	480 per day
	Acuteness level 7:	560 per day
	Acuteness level 8:	640 per day
	Acuteness level 9:	720 per day
	Acuteness level 10:	800 per day
Occupancy and feeding		$100 per day

Required:
Calculate the cost per day to care for a person with an acuteness level of 3.

10.32 *Costing a railroad shipment.* Rocky Plateau is a small railroad company that hauls commodities, such as lumber, coal, and ore. The following are data from its ABC system:

ACTIVITY COST POOLS	ACTIVITY DRIVER RATES
Move freight train	$0.60 per gross ton mile
Switch freight train	$100.00 per minute
Handle freight cars	$0.20 per freight car mile
Load and unload	$20.00 per gross ton

Required:
Calculate the cost of a one-ton shipment that will travel 200 miles and require one minute of switching of one freight car.

THINK-TANK PROBLEMS

Although these problems are based on chapter material, reading extra material, reviewing previous chapters, and using creativity may be required to develop workable solutions.

10.33 *Setting up an activity center, activity cost pools, and cost drivers.* The process of designing and implementing an ABC system for support departments usually begins with interviews of the department heads. The interviews yield insights into departmental operations and into the factors that trigger departmental activities. Subsequent analysis traces these activities to specific products.

The following example illustrates the ABC process for an inventory control department responsible for raw materials and purchased components. The annual costs associated with the department (mainly personnel costs) are $500,000.

Q: How many people work for you?
A: Twelve.

Q: What do they do?
A: Six of them spend most of their time handling incoming shipments of purchased parts. They handle everything—from documentation to transferring parts to the WIP stockroom. Three others work in raw materials. After the material clears inspection, they move it into inventory and take care of the paperwork.

Q: What determines the time required to process an incoming shipment? Does it matter if the shipment is large or small?
A: Not for parts. They go directly to the WIP stockroom, and unless the shipment is extremely large, it can be handled in one trip. With raw materials, though, volume can have a big effect on processing time. But there are only a few large raw material shipments. Over the course of a year, the time required to process a part or raw material really depends on the number of times it's received, not on the size of the shipments in which it comes.

Q: What other factors affect your department's work load?
A: Well, there are three people I haven't discussed yet. They disburse raw materials to the shop floor. Again, volume is not really an issue; it's more the number of times materials have to be disbursed.

Q: Do you usually disburse the total amount of material required for a production run all at once, or does it go out in smaller quantities?
A: It varies with the size of the run. On a big run, we can't disburse it all at once—there would be too much raw material on the shop floor. On smaller runs—and I'd say that's 80% of all runs—we'd send it out in a single trip once setup is complete.

In 19X5, this company received 25,000 shipments of purchased parts and

10,000 shipments of raw materials. The factory made 5,000 production runs.

The company manufactures 1,000 units of product A in a year. Product A is a complex product with more than 50 purchased parts and several different types of raw material. During the year, the 1,000 units were assembled in 10 different production runs requiring 200 purchased parts shipments and 50 different raw material shipments.

Product A also consumed 1,000 hours of direct labor out of the factory's total of 400,000 hours.

Required:

a. Draw a large rounded rectangle and label it "Inventory Control Activity Center." Within this rectangle, set up three activity cost pools appropriately titled. Assign the inventory control department's annual costs to the activity cost pools using an appropriate assignment base. Then show three arrows, one from each activity cost pool, pointing to a rectangle called "Product A." Identify an appropriate cost driver for each activity cost pool. Alongside the name of each cost driver, place the cost per transaction of each cost driver.

b. Calculate the inventory control costs for each unit of product A using the ABC model you just designed. Also, using direct labor hours as your base, apply inventory control costs to product A.

c. Calculate the cost difference between the activity-based costing approach and the labor-based costing approach. Explain why the two approaches differ. State which cost figure you have the most faith in and explain why.

[Adapted from Robin Cooper and Robert S. Kaplan]

10.34 *Distinguishing between traditional costing and activity-based costing systems.* Many companies now recognize that their costing systems are inadequate for today's powerful global competition. Managers in companies selling multiple products are making important product decisions based on distorted cost information, as most cost systems designed in the past focused on inventory valuation. To elevate the level of management information, current literature suggests that companies should have as many as three costing systems for (1) inventory valuation, (2) operational control, and (3) activity-based costing, which is also known as individual product cost measurement.

Required:

a. Discuss why the traditional costing system, developed to value inventory, distorts product cost information.

b. Identify the purpose and characteristics of each of the following cost systems:
   1. Inventory valuation.
   2. Operational control.
   3. Activity-based costing.

c. 1. Describe the benefits that management can expect from activity-based costing.
   2. List the steps that a company that uses a traditional costing system would take to implement activity-based costing.

[CMA adapted]

10.35 *Traditional costing system versus activity-based costing system.* The following overhead cost data relate to Huron Industries:

PRODUCT	COSTS RELATED TO DIRECT LABOR	COSTS RELATED TO SETUPS	COSTS RELATED TO PART NUMBER
P1	5 direct labor hours	1 setup	1 part number
P2	50 direct labor hours	3 setups	1 part number
P3	15 direct labor hours	1 setup	1 part number
P4	150 direct labor hours	3 setups	1 part number
	220 direct labor hours	8 setups	4 part numbers
Overhead costs	$5,764	$2,160	$2,000

Total overhead costs $9,924

Required:

a. Calculate the overhead unit costs reported by a traditional costing method using direct labor hours as the base.

b. Calculate the overhead unit costs reported by an ABC system using number of direct labor hours, number of setups, and number of part numbers as cost drivers.

[Adapted from Robin Cooper]

10.36 *Designing an activity-based costing system.* Thortec Industries manufactures different electronic components used in computers. One of these components is a PC board. Its present costing system includes three cost elements:

- Direct materials
- Direct labor
- Overhead

Overhead is applied to products using direct labor dollars. Direct labor represents less than 2 percent of total manufacturing costs. Over 30 minutes of direct labor time per person each day is spent on vouchering labor time directly to individual products.

Sammi Lin, CEO, has become very disenchanted with the present costing system and has hired Teri Alvarez, newly graduated management accountant, to develop a costing system that will produce reasonably accurate cost information.

Teri started by identifying the categories of manufacturing overhead costs. She identified two broad categories: procurement manufacturing overhead and production manufacturing overhead. She analyzed procurement and determined that it was composed of six highly-related activites:

- Parts ordering
- Incoming inspection
- Counting parts
- Documentation
- Movement
- Storage

Teri decided to aggregate these activities into one activity cost pool called "procurement activity cost pool." Further analysis indicated that the number of parts was highly correlated with the procurement activity cost pool. The PC board requires 94 parts, and the procurement overhead is costed at $0.10 per part.

She analyzed the production manufacturing overhead and identified several activities. She grouped the start station activity and the following insertion activities together:

- Axial insertion
- Dip insertion
- Manual insertion
- Backload insertion

Fred Baxter, process engineer, was shocked! He explained, for example, that axial components were much less expensive to insert than dip components. He urged Teri to differentiate between the start station and insertion activities. Upon further analysis, Teri identified the following activities and their drivers:

- Start station and number of raw PC boards (source of raw PC boards is the stockroom) [1 board @ $0.90 each]
- Axial insertions and number of axial insertions [43 @ $0.06 each]
- Dip insertions and number of dip insertions [30 @ $0.17 each]
- Manual insertions and number of manual insertions [13 @ $0.35 each]
- Backload insertions and number of backload insertions [6 @ $0.58 each]

Teri had also aggregated wave solder, test, and defect analysis into one activity. After further analysis, she decomposed these activities as follows:

- Wave solder and number of boards soldered [1 board @ $2.50 each]
- Test and standard time board in test [0.2 hour @ $70.00 per hour]

- Defect analysis and standard time for defect analysis and rework [0.08 hour @ $62.00 per hour]

Required:
a. Explain how direct labor cost should be handled.
b. Develop the final activity flow diagram that models the procurement and production overhead activities.
c. Calculate the cost per PC board for the following:
  - Procurement activities
  - Production activities
d. Comment on how employees at Thortec are likely to view the new costing system.
[Adapted from Debbie Berlant, Reese Browning, and George Foster]

10.37 *Bill of activities and standard costs.* Following are the budgeted data for the Stormor Corporation:

Production Budget
For the Period Ended December 31, 19X5

Budgeted production volume:

Product A	100,000 units
Product B	200,000 units
Total production for the period	300,000 units

Budgeted production costs:

Direct technology:		
Product A	$20,000	
Product B	80,000	$100,000
Activity cost pools:		
Purchasing	$25,000	
Quality control	30,000	
Maintenance	5,000	
Warehousing	75,000	
Expediting	30,000	165,000
Total production costs		$265,000

Direct materials costs are not included in the production budget. Also, because Stormor is highly automated and all labor is handled as indirect labor, a direct labor cost element is not included in the budget.

Direct technology runs at 80 units per hour to produce product A and 40 units per hour to make product B. Product A requires 1,250 hours of machine time per year, and product B requires 5,000 hours. Direct technology costs are assigned to the products on the basis of machine hours.

Activity drivers for Stormor's ABC system follow:

ACTIVITY	ACTIVITY DRIVER	PRODUCT A	PRODUCT B
Purchasing	■ Number of purchase orders per 1,000 units of finished product	10.0	7.5
Quality control	■ Number of hours of quality testing per 1,000 units of finished product	10.0	2.5
Maintenance	■ Number of hours of equipment maintenance per 100 hours of machine time	4.0	1.5
Warehousing	■ Number of units of finished product per pallet	40.0	40.0
Expediting	■ Number of units of finished product	100,000	200,000

Required:
a. Prepare a bill of activities for product A and product B as of December 31,

19X5, assuming that the budgeted amounts are the actual amounts.

b. Following are the actual production data for the period:

	PRODUCT A	PRODUCT B
Production volume	110,000 Units	180,000 Units
Direct technology	$ 30,000	$ 62,000
Purchasing	12,000	14,000
Quality control	21,000	11,000
Maintenance	2,400	2,200
Warehousing	27,000	44,000
Expediting	13,200	18,000
Total actual costs	$105,600	$151,200

Prepare two bills of activities (including direct technology), one for product A and one for product B, showing the standard product costs (i.e., those established by the budget) adjusted to actual costs per unit. The differences between actual and budgeted will be "spending" variances similar to those calculated in Chapter 8.

c. Briefly contrast the traditional standard costing approach covered in Chapter 8 with the ABC approach in terms of variance analysis.

10.38 *Overhead variances adapted to ABC.* A move materials activity cost pool is budgeted with $20,000 for the forthcoming period. Production volume is budgeted at 100,000 units of Doohickeys, the company's only product. The quantity of move materials transactions necessary to support this level of production volume is 10,000. During the period, 102,000 Doohickeys were produced. The actual costs of the move materials activity are $23,100. The number of move materials transactions necessary to produce the 102,000 Doohickeys is 10,500.

Required:
Adapt material covered in Chapter 8 and calculate the spending and efficiency variances for the move materials activity.

10.39 *Costing market-driven activities and determining operating income by sales territory and by product line.* Following is product line information for Teco Corporation:

PRODUCT LINE INFORMATION	PRODUCT LINE A	PRODUCT LINE B	PRODUCT LINE C
Selling price	$10.00	$8.00	$12.00
Unit manufacturing cost	$8.00	$5.00	$11.00
Quantity of units sold and shipped	50,000	40,000	30,000
Average weight of units	3 lb.	4 lb.	6 lb.
Number of sales orders	200	150	100

The market-driven activity information follows:

MARKETING ACTIVITY COST POOLS	ACTIVITY DRIVERS	QUANTITY	MARKETING ACTIVITY COSTS TOTAL	UNIT RATE
Selling	Dollar value of sales	$1,180,000	$59,000	5.0%
Advertising	Quantity of units sold	120,000 units	$36,000	$0.30
Warehousing	Weight shipped	490,000 lb.	$49,000	$0.10
Packing and shipping	Quantity shipped	120,000 units	$30,000	$0.25
Administration	Number of sales orders	450 sales orders	$22,500	$50.00

Sales and orders by sales territories are presented below:

PRODUCT LINE

TRANSACTION BY SALES TERRITORY	TOTAL	A	B	C
Products sold (units):				
East sales territory	70,000	28,000	24,000	18,000
West sales territory	50,000	22,000	16,000	12,000
Totals	120,000	50,000	40,000	30,000
Sales orders:				
East sales territory	290	110	100	80
West sales territory	160	50	80	30
Totals	450	160	180	110

Required:

a. Using a traditional operating income statement format, present operating income by sales territory and operating income by product line. Assume the period ends December 31, 19X5.
b. State what the operating income statements reveal and what management action is warranted.
c. Mention another operating income statement that would reveal information with even greater detail.

10.40 *Determining what really drives costs.* Diamond Industries is a "lights out" fully automated plant with no direct labor. The plant is composed of two activity centers: AC1 and AC2. Diamond makes product A and product B.

Diamond Industries has budgeted 40,000 total machine hours (20,000 to AC1 and 20,000 to AC2) for the forthcoming period. Power is budgeted at $60,000, and setup costs are budgeted at $83,200. The budget calls for 5,000 units of each product to be produced during the period. Each product requires two hours of machine time in AC1 and two hours of machine time in AC2. Machine costs are charged at a rate of $30 per hour in AC1 and $12 per hour in AC2, not counting power and setup costs. AC1 consumes power at $2.25 per machine hour. AC2 consumes power at $0.75 per machine hour.

Setup costs for each product are as follows:

AC1:
  Product A: ($1,000 × 2 setups) = $ 2,000
  Product B: ($1,000 × 50 setups) = 50,000
    Total setup costs of AC1 $52,000

AC2:
  Product A: ($600 × 2 setups) = $ 1,200
  Product B: ($600 × 50 setups) = 30,000
    Total setup costs of AC2 $31,200

The two products require different amounts of setups because product A has a simplified design requiring only two setups in each activity center. Product B has a more complex design requiring different attaching devices. For each run of 100 units of product B, a new attaching device is required, thus causing a new setup. The setup costs per unit are calculated as follows:

AC1:
  Product A: ($2,000 ÷ 5,000 units) = $0.40 per unit
  Product B: ($50,000 ÷ 5,000 units) = $10.00 per unit

AC2:
  Product A: ($1,200 ÷ 5,000 units) = $0.24 per unit
  Product B: ($30,000 ÷ 5,000 units) = $6.00 per unit

Required:

a. Draw an ABC systems model. The first-stage resource drivers are number of machine hours and number of setups. The activity cost pools in each activity center are power, setups, and machine. The activity drivers are number of machine hours and number of units.

b. Using the ABC systems model, calculate the total costs per unit for product A and product B. Assume that 5,000 units of each product were manufactured and sold. Explain why product B's costs per unit are greater than product A's.

c. Combine the setup costs with machine costs, and apply these combined costs and power costs to both products on the basis of machine hours. What are the total costs per unit of each product now? Again, assume that 5,000 units of each product were manufactured and sold.

d. Assume that the sales price is $96 for product A and $100 for product B. Determine the profit (loss) of each product using the costing systems of Requirements (b) and (c). What is management's likely decision if Diamond costs its products in accordance with the costing system of Requirement (b)? Requirement (c)? Which costing system do you recommend? Explain why.

III
Cost Management Systems

Cost management builds on cost accounting, but it is much more than a costing system. Cost management is a set of concepts, methods, and techniques used to provide timely and relevant information to enable managers and workers to evaluate, control, and optimize activities and resources throughout the enterprise.

To be successful, world-class enterprises are stressing the following:

- Activity-based management
- High quality
- Lower inventories while maintaining delivery schedules and customer service
- Target costing and lower life cycle costs
- Increased throughput
- Optimized scarce resources

The management accountant has an opportunity to play a key role in making sure these objectives are achieved. How the management accountant can do this is the subject of the following chapters.

Managing activities is fundamental to the performance of an organization. Chapter 11 builds on Chapter 10 to discuss the role of benchmarking, reengineering, continuous improvement, and performance measurements in activity-based management.

Many companies are beginning to realize the enormous financial losses resulting from poor quality. Consequently, companies in many industries are implementing total quality management (TQM) systems. Chapter 12 examines the costs of quality and shows how various techniques are used to support TQM systems.

Efficient management of the flow of goods from the vendor through production to the customer requires the control of multiple logistics activities. In the face of higher operating costs and increasing pressures from customers for better service, costs of logistics systems must be carefully managed. Chapter 13 presents methods and techniques for managing logistics costs.

The impact of product or service development decisions must be analyzed throughout their life cycles, both from the viewpoint of market strategy and in terms of costs over the life cycles. Chapter 14 analyzes life cycles, target costing, and cost estimating.

The global goal of all for-profit enterprises is to make more profit now and in the future. To achieve this goal, management must reduce, if not eliminate, constraints and increase the system's throughput. Chapter 15 shows how to do this.

Finally, Chapter 16 introduces graphical, simplex, and Karmarkar's methods that are used for allocating scarce resources among competing demands. These methods seek to optimize a linear objective function subject to a set of linear constraints.

11

COST MANAGEMENT THROUGH ACTIVITY-BASED MANAGEMENT

Using computer-generated graphs to evaluate performance.

■ INTRODUCTION

Activity-based costing (ABC) is directly linked to and supportive of activity-based management (ABM), as Exhibit 11–1 (see p. 496) shows. The main purposes of ABC are to:

- Provide costing information on cost objects
- Provide information to enable management to reengineer the business if necessary, and attain continuous improvement

Continuous improvement calls for systematic and small incremental actions. **Reengineering** requires large quantum changes in how the enterprise is currently operating. Companies that contain an inordinate amount of nonvalue-added activities and are no longer competitive are most likely to need reengineering.

As Chapter 10 illustrated, activities are the building blocks of organizations. Activities are what people do everyday. Therefore, if an organization is to change, the change must ultimately be made at the activity level.[1] **Activity-based management (ABM)** is the process of understanding, reengineering, measuring, and making decisions about activities to put the enterprise on the road to continuous improvement and excellence. It turns out that the information collected when developing an ABC system also reveals an organization's activities and how they are performed. Workers and managers can use this knowledge to make their activities faster, higher quality, and more productive. As Exhibit 11–2 (see p. 496) shows, ABM is an ongoing process involving four phases:

- Identify value-added and nonvalue-added activities.
- Reengineer the enterprise.
- Benchmark value-added activities.
- Develop a performance measurement system for continuous improvement.

The ABM process is never completed. It is a constant process of evaluating performance, taking action, and tracking the results. Occasionally, recalibration is needed because of changing business conditions. This recalibration calls for reanalyzing activities, possibly performing additional reengineering, doing new benchmarking, and revising performance measurements. As the management axiom says, "If you don't measure it, it won't improve, and if you don't take the necessary actions, it will get worse." The ABM process helps prevent this from becoming reality. Problems that are ignored never go away by themselves. They grow until they get so big they cannot be ignored. If management wants to manage performance and eliminate cost-consuming activities, management accountants must provide a system to *measure* performance and continue to make sure that the right things are being measured in the right way. Indeed, management accountants must take the lead in measuring and reporting cost management information—both financial and nonfinancial. Helping implement the ABM process will achieve these goals.

The first sections of this chapter describe the four phases of the ABM process. Later sections explain how to prepare specific performance measurements and how to help management *visualize* performance measurements. ■

LEARNING OBJECTIVE 1

Define activity-based management (ABM).

Engineered.   Reengineered.

Ernst & Young is one of several premier consulting firms that assist companies in their reengineering efforts.

---

[1] James A. Brimson and Michael J. Burtha, "Activity Accounting," in *Handbook of Cost Management,* ed. Barry J. Brinker (Boston: Warren Gorham Lamont, 1992), p. C1–5. With permission.

■■■ EXHIBIT 11–1
**Linkage between
Activity-Based
Costing and Activity-
Based Management**

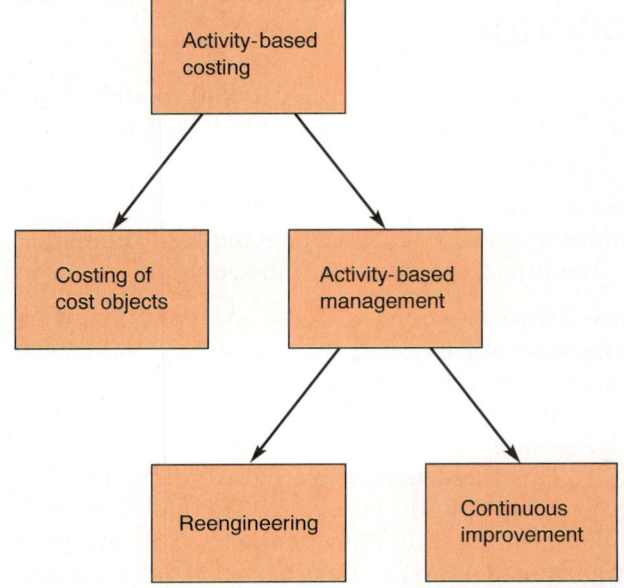

■■■ EXHIBIT 11–2
**The Four Ongoing
Phases of Activity-
Based Management**

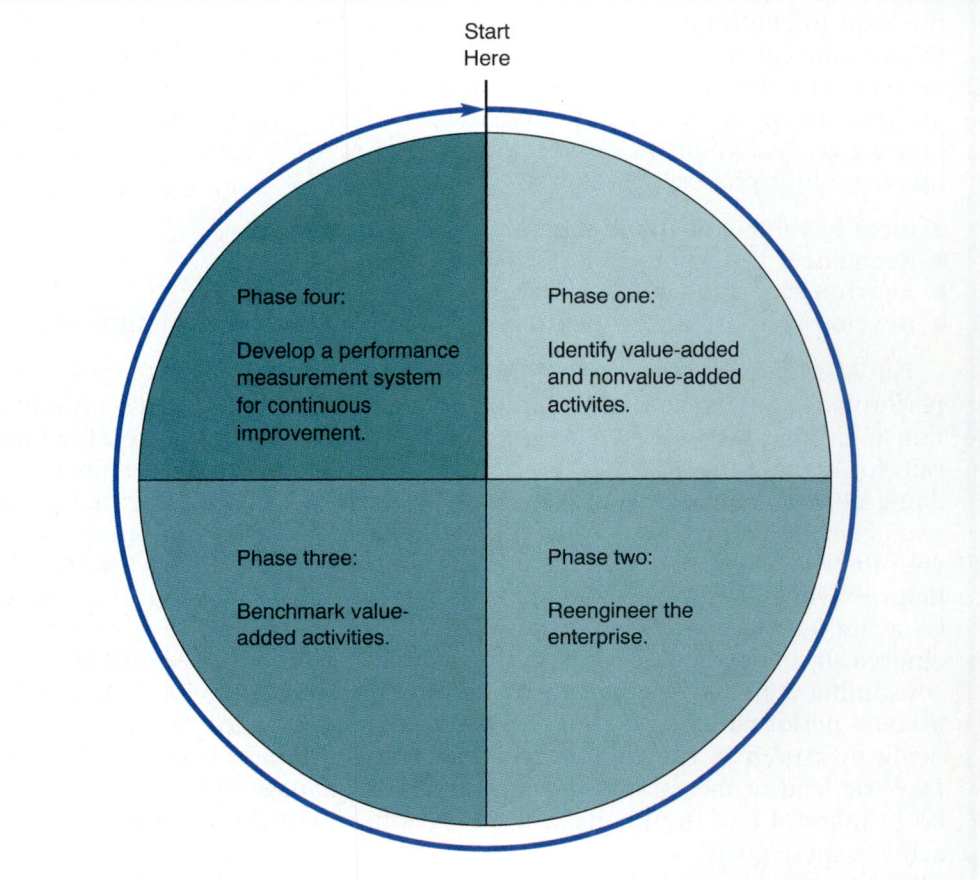

**LEARNING
OBJECTIVE 2**

Describe each phase of
the four-phase ABM
process.

PHASE 1: IDENTIFYING VALUE-ADDED AND NONVALUE-ADDED ACTIVITIES

Value-added activities contribute something that is worthwhile to the enterprise and its customers. Such activities are critical factors that are essential to the enterprise's success.

The Management Accountant as a Business (Re)engineer

QuickPark, Incorporated is a parking lot management company with contracts to oversee garages in several cities across the United States. QuickPark agreed to accept credit cards. Soon after customers complained about how long it took them to exit the garages during the 5–8 PM peak period. Barbara Turner asked her management accountant, Martina Daniels, to investigate the problem.

In addition to recommending a number of logistical changes (e.g., removing concrete barriers to facilitate drivers to switch to faster-moving exit lanes), Daniels designed and implemented a new credit card terminal system that reduced authorization and transaction time by an average of 10 seconds. The projected savings for QuickPark is $500,000 annually.

Several implications for management accountants underlie this case. First, management accountants must be more than merely data gatherers. They must be able to analyze existing activities, identify their weaknesses, and recommend practical improvements, or, in QuickPark's case, completely reengineer the activity. Second, management accountants must take a proactive stance in evaluating emerging technologies for possible customer service and cost savings opportunities. Third, management accountants must be able to uncover causes of problems rather than symptoms.[2]

Types of Value-Added Activities

Value-added activities are of two types. One type adds value to the customer; painting a car or delivering a shipment on time are examples. The second type is essential for the proper functioning of the enterprise. For example, paying employees is not of direct concern to customers, but it does satisfy an organizational need.

Nonvalue-Added Activities

Nonvalue-added activities represent waste; these activities can be reduced or eliminated without decreasing the enterprise's ability to compete and meet customer demands. Armed with a list of nonvalue-added activities, the organization can create teams to find innovative ways to eliminate, reduce, or reengineer those activities. One of the costliest things a company can do is to invest in equipment and people to make nonvalue-added activities more efficient. The goal is to eliminate them altogether or subject them to a major overhaul, not to make them more efficient.

Inspection of incoming raw materials is a nonvalue-added activity that can be eliminated without diminishing the value received by the enterprise or its customers. Customers do not value inspection; they value high quality. If a vendor of raw materials commits to supplying high-quality materials, then inspection is no longer required, and buying testing equipment and hiring more people to inspect the incoming raw materials would waste time and money.

Understanding Activities

Litigating oil spills and other violations is costly. Effort and money should be invested in training activities, which indirectly but effectively reduce litigating activities. Handling accidents and claims is another nonvalue-added activity that can be reduced by implementing strong and effective safety activities, with a target of an injury-free workplace. But simply implementing training and safety activities is not enough. Safety is also improved by *understanding the*

[2] Michael S. Luehlfing, "Driving Out Inefficiency," *Management Accounting*, March 1993, pp. 33–36. Reprinted from *Management Accounting*. Copyright by Institute of Management Accountants, Montvale, N.J.

INSIGHTS & APPLICATIONS

At 3M Cost Management Leadership Is Mandatory

Several years ago, a task force was formed to recommend changes to 3M's traditional accounting operations. The group's mission focused on understanding how management accounting could improve its effectiveness in the age of just-in-time, continuous improvement, activity-based costing, life cycle accounting, optimized operations, and total cost management. Routine analysis of product profitability and cost allocation schemes based on activities continue. Changes in the management accounting system also now include nonfinancial performance measurements that assist management and workers in:

- Improving quality throughout the enterprise
- Reducing production lead time
- Evaluating and streamlining logistics
- Compressing research and development timetables

Management accountants are located in operating units rather than in corporate headquarters offices. This way, operating personnel receive more relevant and timely information, and the accountants are active in day-to-day plant activities. The "cost accounting" specialization of the past has been replaced with a more diversified business exposure and cost management orientation. Activity-based costing and management are used to help manage cost and weed out nonvalue-added activities.[3]

activities. Just because an activity is value-added does not mean that it is being performed efficiently. Workers who take shortcuts, a major cause of accidents, may be pinpointing an inefficient activity, task, or tool.

A pharmaceutical company, for example, makes random surveys of each work cell to ensure that safety activities are being performed precisely. After the survey, a colored sticker is attached to each work cell notice board. A red sticker indicates the work cell has seriously violated safety standards, orange signifies minor violations, and a green sticker indicates complete adherence to all safety activities. A green sticker is highly desired, and the work cells compete vigorously to obtain one.[4]

PHASE 2: REENGINEERING THE ENTERPRISE

From the viewpoint of activities, reengineering is the redesign of how work is done through activities. Because activities are what an organization does, to reengineer the organization, the activities must be reengineered.

Such a radical redesign effort normally takes a minimum of three to five years to complete successfully throughout the organization. That may seem a long time, but remember that existing systems and activities must be torn down and then rebuilt around more efficient and effective activities. A number of major companies including Eastman Kodak, AT&T, Burger King, American Express, Sears, ITT Sheraton Corporation, Chrysler, Xerox, and Caterpillar have gone through or are currently going through major reengineering.

Reengineering Example

The development of an ABC system, described in Chapter 10, reveals the organization *as it is*. The reengineering of the enterprise involves changing the enterprise into *what it should be*.

[3] Adapted from David A. Kunz, "3M Revisited: Evolving for the '90s," *Management Accounting,* October 1992, pp. 37–40. Reprinted from *Management Accounting.* Copyright by Institute of Management Accountants, Montvale, N.J.

[4] Brian H. Maskell, *Performance Measurement for World Class Manufacturing* (Cambridge, Mass.: Productivity Press, 1991), p. 34. With permission.

INSIGHTS & APPLICATIONS

Reengineering: The Redesign of Business Activities

Original Business Activity

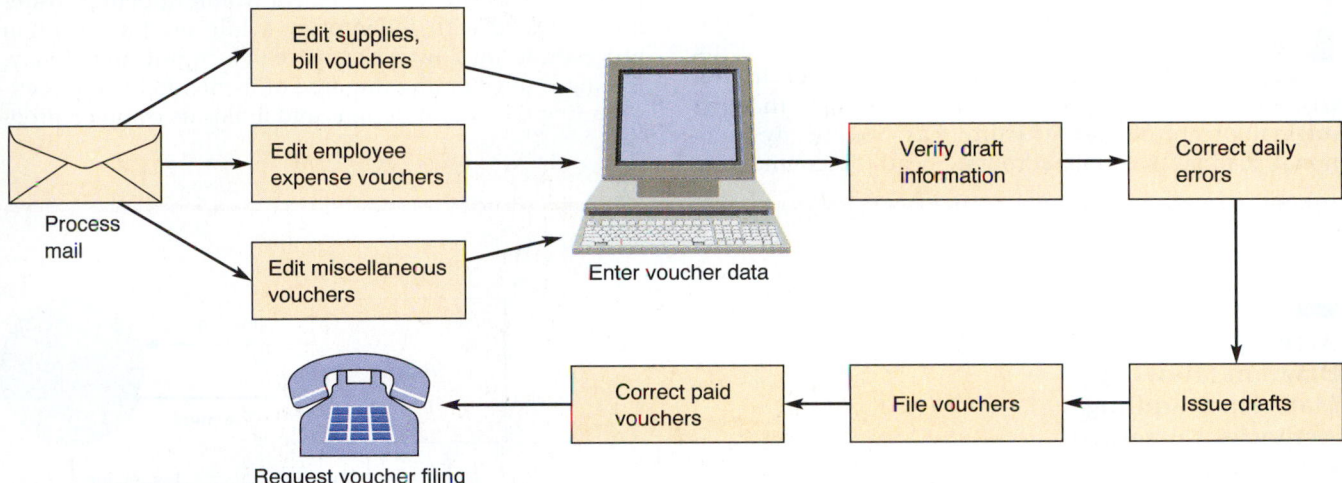

Reengineered Business Activity

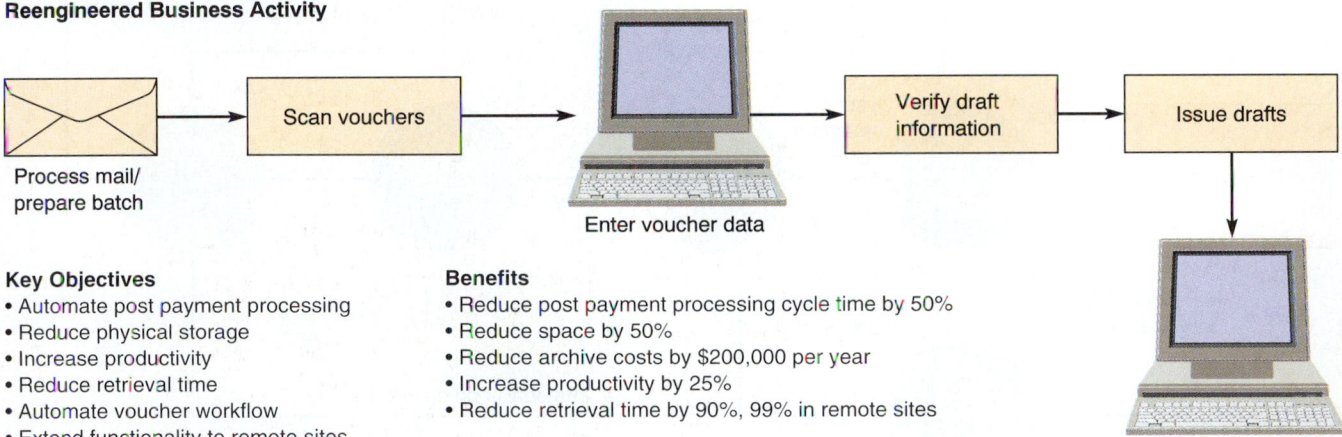

Key Objectives
- Automate post payment processing
- Reduce physical storage
- Increase productivity
- Reduce retrieval time
- Automate voucher workflow
- Extend functionality to remote sites

Adapted from Price Waterhouse.

Benefits
- Reduce post payment processing cycle time by 50%
- Reduce space by 50%
- Reduce archive costs by $200,000 per year
- Increase productivity by 25%
- Reduce retrieval time by 90%, 99% in remote sites

Consider the following procurement, storing, and materials handling activities:

- Schedule production
- Store materials
- Process purchase orders
- Inspect materials
- Pay vendor
- Expedite materials

The activity flow diagram in Exhibit 11–3 (see p. 500) shows these activities. This exhibit represents the organization *as it is*.

INSIGHTS & APPLICATIONS

Boeing's Ultimate Engineering Test

Activities are the focal point of *total* cost management. They must be engineered, benchmarked, and managed to achieve a competitive advantage. Rather than "slash-and-burn" downsizing, companies should concentrate on how efficiently resources are being deployed. After examining themselves, often from a customer perspective, some companies realize that the original organizational structure has become dysfunctional, leading to certain corporate death. Reengineering the organization activity-by-activity creates an enterprise fit to compete in the 90s and beyond.

William Selby, head of parts production at Boeing says, "We saw right away that if we failed to cut costs, we risked a fall in profits, then a decline in our ability to develop new products. It would be the beginning of a death spiral." CEO, Frank Shrontz says that Boeing is going to have to do things differently (reengineer) to survive.

For much of its history, Boeing was insulated from the competitive fires that forged lean companies in steel, paper, autos, and computers. No wonder Boeing's warehouses bulge with inventories, while production often proceeds at the slow, zigzag pace of a crop-duster. Today, Boeing is overcoming the drag of its hierarchy and reengineering the way it designs and builds its complex products.[5]

■■■ EXHIBIT 11–3
Activity Flow Diagram Showing Materials Handling Activities Currently Being Performed

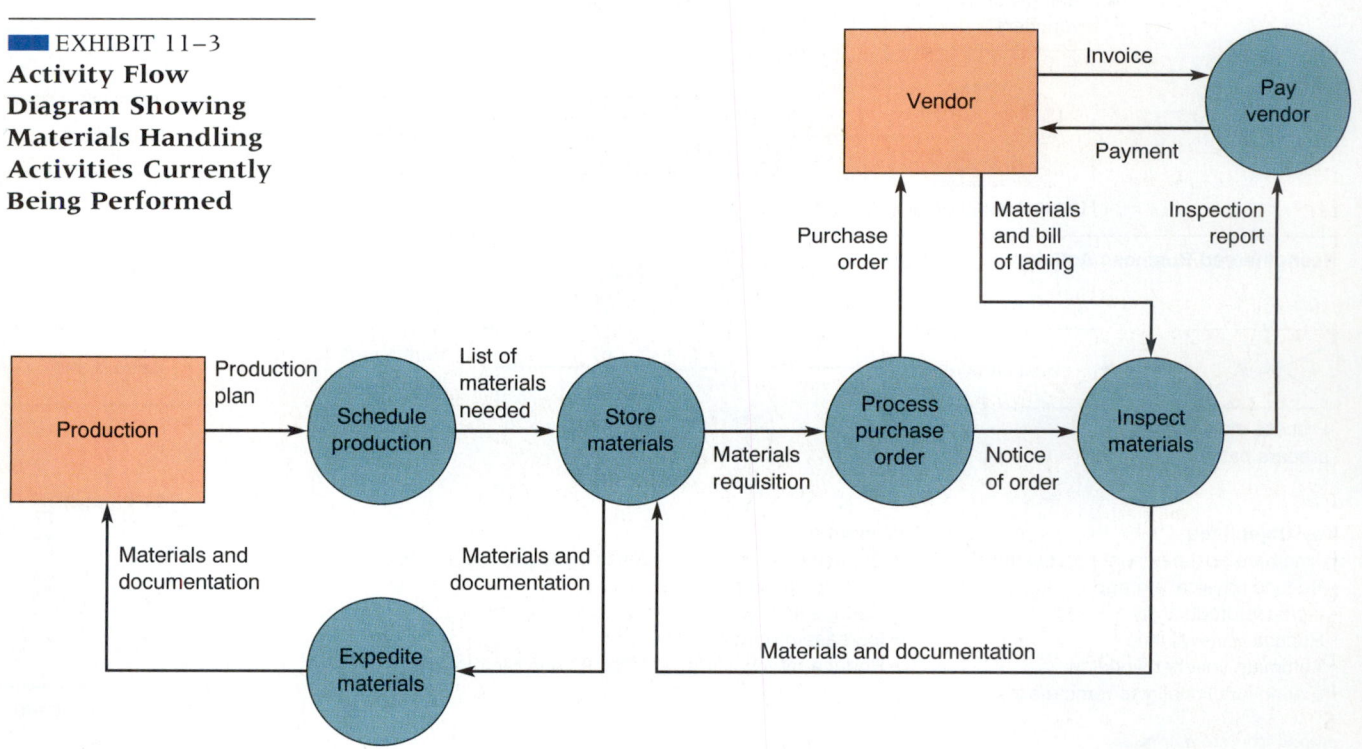

How can this entire materials handling process be reengineered? (The results are presented in Exhibit 11–4.) The production schedule can be sent directly to the vendor who will deliver materials in accordance with the schedule. The vendor is paid weekly (possibly through EDI) on the basis of materials received. Therefore, the new process eliminates all the nonvalue-added activities except schedule production and pay vendor.

The parts can be delivered directly to the plant floor as needed as in a just-in-time system. Once the entire materials handling process has been reengineered, it is no longer necessary to inspect and count parts when they are delivered or to place the parts on the shelf in the storeroom. Eliminating these

[5] Adapted from Shawn Tully, "Can Boeing Reinvent Itself?" *Fortune*, March 8, 1993, pp. 66–73.

■■EXHIBIT 11–4

Activity Flow Diagram Showing Materials Handling Activities after Reengineering

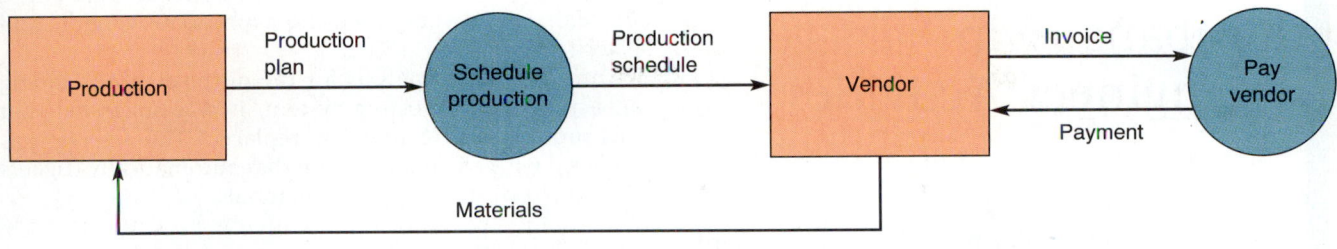

activities reduces overall costs and the cost of products that no longer use these activities.[6]

The results of the reengineering are shown in Exhibit 11–4. This activity flow diagram models the materials handling process as *it should be*. Other methods may also be useful in reengineering activities. For example, installing a kanban system, as described in Chapters 2 and 13, can help eliminate certain nonvalue-added activities as in the case on the next page.

Getting at the Root Cause of Costs

In some instances, nonvalue-added activities, such as moving materials, cannot be totally eliminated. The enterprise may therefore be tempted to try to make this nonvalue-added activity more efficient. The focus, however, should be on the *root cause* of moving materials activity costs and determining what can be changed to reduce these costs. For example, the costs of the moving materials activity are driven not only by the activity driver, such as number of pallets moved, but also by the physical layout of the plant, which is the underlying root cause of the moving materials costs. To reduce the materials moving activity costs, perhaps the physical layout of the plant should be reengineered.

For another example, insertion of components into electronic boards is an activity. To reduce insertion costs, management may be encouraged to replace insertion labor with an automated insertion machine. The acquisition of the machine makes the insertion activity more efficient, but has it increased the company's profitability and competitiveness? Perhaps not, because the company has treated the symptom, which is high insertion cost, rather than the *root cause* of the cost. The root cause of the insertion activity is the state of technology and product design. The current state of technology allows surface mount technology to replace the insertion activity. Rather than increase the efficiency of the insertion activity, an alternative is to invest in surface mount technology. Similarly, the need for the insertion activity might be reduced or eliminated through the redesign of products. In both cases, the company should address the root cause of the need for insertions *before* attempting to improve efficiency. Again, the objective is to correct the source of the cost rather than treat its symptoms.[7]

Keeping It Simple

Simplicity is the watchword of reengineering. Generally, *complexity* is what drives costs; it represents the root cause of costs. Here are just a few complexities that drive costs:

[6] Peter B. B. Turney, "Activity-Based Management," *Management Accounting*, January 1992, p. 24. Reprinted from *Management Accounting*. Copyright by Institute of Management Accountants, Montvale, N.J.
[7] James A. Brimson, *Activity Accounting* (New York: John Wiley, 1991), p. 69.

- Excessive number of vendors
- Excessive number of purchase orders
- Excessive number of accounts payable
- Excessive number of parts
- Excessive number of product engineering changes
- Excessive number of schedule changes
- Excessive number of products
- Excessive number of features, options, and accessories
- Complicated and outdated production activities

Analyzing these complexities enables management to treat the root cause of costs rather than the symptoms. For example, consider the case on the next page.

IBM simplified its ProPrinter as a result of activity analysis. IBM achieved significantly lower product costs by redesigning the ProPrinter with fewer parts, thus reducing the number of vendors and the costs of parts, manufacturing, storage, and handling. For another example of how reducing complexity can lower costs, read the case on page 504.

PHASE 3: BENCHMARKING VALUE-ADDED ACTIVITIES

The "should-be" model prepared during the reengineering phase represents an organization that contains only value-added activities. Just because an activity is value-added, however, doesn't mean that it is performed efficiently and effectively. So, the next phase in the ABM process is **benchmarking,** which involves comparing activities to world-class best practices. Comparisons are made to a similar activity in another company or another part of the organization. The enterprise doing the benchmarking tries to set targets that equal or surpass the best-practices benchmark.

Where Should Benchmarking Be Directed?

Benchmarking should be directed to both world-class competitors and to organizations *outside* the industry. By seeking knowledge from outside the industry, an enterprise may encounter innovations that improve on the accepted industry best practices.[8] For example, Xerox benchmarked L. L. Bean, a premier mail order company, to see how it handled customer orders.

Before performing benchmarking at another site, the company doing the benchmarking should thoroughly understand its own activities. The key activities that appear to be most problematical should define the activities to be benchmarked in the subject companies.

[8] Gregory H. Watson, *The Benchmarking Workbook* (Cambridge, Mass.: Productivity Press, 1992), p. 5. With permission.

INSIGHTS & APPLICATIONS

Trying to Eliminate Nonvalue-Added Cost at Nept Company

Nept Company was in the truck manufacturing business for nearly ten years, but lost its business to stronger, more efficient competitors. Now, Nept has downsized and is making lawn mowers, but the company is finding that it still can't compete.

New management has been brought in to see if it can turn Nept around. Gilland Matthews, the new management accountant, makes a survey of operations. He discusses his findings with Marlo Gleason, the plant manager.

"Why is the product just sitting there?" asks Gilland. "Why does it take three months to get the product through work-in-process when the engineers say it should only take two days to produce it?"

"We're working on it," says Marlo, "by eliminating excessive handling and rework."

"And the way we make motor blocks is a mystery to me. We pour our castings and then turn around and machine off 70 percent of the material! Why do we do that sort of thing? Why do we have all that excess material in the first place?" asks Gilland.

"Yes, I realize Nept's casting equipment and procedures are outdated. We are changing over to new casting and machine technology, which should eliminate most of the scrap."

"I realize that we're all new here and we've got a lot of work to do to eliminate all of Nept's nonvalue-added activities, but I have one more question," says Gilland.

"And what's that?" Marlo asks.

"I just got through reviewing the bill of materials for our Model 12-C mower, and I discovered 60 different screws, bolts, and nuts. I'm not an engineer, but isn't that an example of another nonvalue-added situation?" asks Gilland.

"How so?" asks Marlo.

"Well, I went into assembly yesterday, and I saw a worker there and he was saying, 'Hey, Bill, toss the Phillips screwdriver.' And Bill tosses the Phillips screwdriver. Then, Bill asks somebody else if he has seen the half-inch box wrench, and on and on. I couldn't believe the inefficiencies caused by so many different screws, nuts, and bolts, and workers looking for different tools to assemble them. Can't we make our mowers with a few standardized screws, nuts, and bolts? Or maybe use some plastic snaps instead?" asks Gilland.

"Well, we're in the process of selecting and acquiring automatic wrenches and screwdrivers and devising a method for keeping them organized and handy for the workers," answers Marlo, confidently.

"Apparently I'm not getting my point across," says Gilland, somewhat frustrated. "The point is that having so many different parts is nonvalue-added. Redesigning and standardizing a few parts will increase efficiency of assembly, and you won't need as many tools."

"Well, you'll have to talk to engineering," says Marlo. "The engineers design 'em and we build 'em."

"Maybe what this company needs more than anything is a Department of Common Sense," says Gilland, not hiding his sarcasm.

The fundamental purpose of a site visit is to collect information about the activities the company has selected for benchmarking. Interviewing and observing are the key tools as the company seeks answers to the following questions:

- How do we do it?
- How do the best in the class do it?
- How can we do it as well or better?

Benchmarking is *not* industrial spying. A high code of ethics is necessary in conducting benchmarking studies. For example, when people at Xerox perform benchmarking, they ask that proprietary or confidential information not be divulged to them.

Benchmarking Example

Benchmarking is the key tool for performing continuous improvement or additional reengineering. Once best-practices activities are identified, they become the targets to meet or exceed. Exhibit 11–5 (see p. 504) illustrates a benchmark action plan to surpass a 97 percent on-time delivery benchmark.

One of the most common pitfalls of benchmarking is to simply copy or cherry pick from successful companies. Merely copying activities from other organiza-

INSIGHTS & APPLICATIONS

How Activity-Based Costing Information Reduced Costs at B & D Tool Company

B & D Tool Company makes a wide array of hand tools for the retail trade. The activity-based costing system indicated that the number of parts was a sig-

nificant cost driver. This driver was causing exceptionally high procurement, inspection, receiving, storage, and parts database maintenance costs.

The cost information motivated design engineers to redesign many of the products to use fewer unique parts. In three years, the part count for one division fell from about 5,000 to 800 while the number of vendors fell from over 1,200 to 100. The costs of the activities being consumed by parts count were reduced 70 percent. In addition, quality, functionality, and maintainability of the products improved substantially. Moreover, 15 different products that had been manufactured on separate sequential production lines were redesigned to be manufactured as a family of products in *one* U-shaped production cell.

EXHIBIT 11–5
Benchmark Action Plan

Activity benchmarked:	Shipping
Activity driver:	Number of shipments

Benchmark:

Company:	Thoretic Industries
Dates observed:	03/22
	04/09
	04/17
	05/21
	06/18

Benchmark: 97% on-time delivery

Performance measurement
  to be used to monitor
  continuous improvement: Percent on-time delivery

Milestones	Targets
Short term	90% on-time delivery
Intermediate term	95% on-time delivery
Long term	98% on-time delivery
Breakthrough	100% on-time delivery

---

tions often ignores underlying factors that made the activity successful, such as empowering workers and effective training programs.

Benchmarks Are Not Static

A benchmark does not remain the same over time. Competitive market forces tend to drive benchmark performance trends to ever-higher levels of attainment. Indeed, a benchmark performance does not remain the best practice for long.[9] Therefore, the original target set is actually a *moving* target. Thus, the ABM process is dynamic and must be repeated periodically for vigilant reassessment. Superior performance, or *dantotsu* in Japanese, means "striving to be the best of the best."

[9] Ibid., p. 17.

INSIGHTS & APPLICATIONS

What Is a Management Accountant Doing Here?

Nathan Weaks, management accountant at Automatic Feed Company, reengineered the production scheduling system, but it had never been benchmarked. Mr. Weaks, along with vice president Peter Beck, attended an Association for Manufacturing Technology scheduling conference to benchmark data and determine other scheduling improvements that may be applicable.

At the meeting, the moderator asked what type of managers were represented. There were presidents, vice presidents of manufacturing, production superintendents, and so on. The moderator asked if there were any other types. After a jab from Peter, Nathan said that he was a "treasurer." The group erupted with laughter. One person in the audience quipped, "Why would a bean counter be here?" Nathan replied, "If we could learn to schedule better and obtain one additional inventory turn per year, our company could reduce working capital requirements by $1 million." The laughter ceased and the person who had led the joking said, "Good answer, good answer."

After the conference, Nathan and Peter discussed some areas for improvement. But overall, they were satisfied with their scheduling system's competitiveness.[10]

PHASE 4: DEVELOPING A PERFORMANCE MEASUREMENT SYSTEM FOR CONTINUOUS IMPROVEMENT

Several studies have documented managers' frustration with existing performance measurement systems. Most notable was the survey jointly sponsored by the National Association of Accountants (now Institute of Management Accountants) and Computer Aided Manufacturing–International (CAM-I), in which 60 percent of the 260 financial officers and 64 operating executives surveyed stated that they were dissatisfied with their performance measurement system.[11] Common complaints were that the performance measurements were:

- Too financial
- Irrelevant
- Difficult and complex to understand
- Unclear as to the linkage between activity measures and the enterprise's strategic objectives
- Not customer-driven

Management accountants have long found performance measurements to be valuable tools, but like all tools, they need periodic review to eliminate some, update others, and add new ones to meet changing needs. In the past, some management accounting performance measurements were used to punish. Today, the primary purpose of management accountants' performance measurements is to bring about improvement and make the enterprise successful. A well-designed performance measurement system can be used to encourage day-to-day actions that improve vendor performance, reduce lead times, increase productivity, satisfy customers, and improve quality (total quality management is the subject of Chapter 12).

The only way to improve continuously is to measure continuously the value-added activities and critical success factors of the enterprise. **Performance measurements** ascertain the work done and the results achieved in an activity. They are the devices that determine or calculate the level of execution or

Performance measurement reporting and JIT scheduling.

---

[10] Adapted from Nathan W. Weaks, "The Accountant as Production Scheduler," *Management Accounting*, March 1993, pp. 25–28. Reprinted from *Management Accounting*. Copyright by Institute of Management Accountants, Montvale, N.J.

[11] Robert A. Howell, James D. Brown, Stephen R. Soucy, and Allen H. Seed III, *Management Accounting in the New Manufacturing Environment* (Montvale, N.J.: Institute of Management Accountants, formerly the National Association of Accountants, 1987). With permission.

INSIGHTS & APPLICATIONS

How Are We Doing?

On the sixth day of the month, Carl, the plant manager, walks apprehensively into the controller's office and asks, "Linda, how did the plant do last month?"

"Well, we had an unfavorable purchase price variance of $70,000 and an unfavorable labor efficiency variance of $50,000, but don't worry, the favorable overhead absorption variance of $200,000 more than offset them."

"Wait! Stop! I asked how the plant did last month. I know for a fact that our quality teams improved setup times. I also know that we missed three very important scheduled shipments! I don't want gobbledegook, I want to know how we did!" Carl is now pacing hurriedly around Linda's office, waiting for an explanation.

"Oh," replies Linda, "Sorry, I should have also pointed out that our revised LIFO reserve estimate and an increase in our tax provision due to a new IRS ruling adversely affected us last month. We should be able to counter that this month by adjusting our bad debt reserve."

To this response, Carl simply shrugs his shoulders, turns around to go back to his office, and mumbles something about "bean counters."

If Carl has a difficult time understanding the plant's performance, imagine how well senior management understands the plant's performance. Current manufacturing performance measurement systems are inadequate, but what can be done? Activity-based management helps answer this question.[12]

---

accomplishment. The following performance measurements are stressed in this chapter:

- Vendor performance measurements
- Time-based performance measurements
- Productivity performance measurements
- Customer satisfaction performance measurements

Developing and using a performance measurement system is the key to continuous improvement and cost management.

Building and using a performance measurement system destroys clichés, such as the following:

- "That's the way we've always done it."
- "If it ain't broke, don't fix it."
- "Don't rock the boat. Leave well enough alone."

Such attitudes will not allow companies to achieve success, or even survive, in an increasingly competitive marketplace. For companies that are operating at the margin, such attitudes will prove disastrous. But even efficient and economic enterprises have room for improvement. If these enterprises stand still while their competitors move forward, then they are really moving backward.

Setting Targets

A **target** is a numerical value set by management or customers. Targets can also be derived from benchmarking. For example, assume that during benchmarking an enterprise discovers that the best-practice setup time is 5 minutes. Therefore, the enterprise may establish a target of 10 minutes to be achieved by the end of the quarter, 7 minutes by the following quarter, and 4 minutes by the end of the year. When short-term, intermediate-term, and long-term targets are set, people do not become discouraged trying to meet or exceed targets in the short run. Setting ongoing targets is essential to implementing continuous improvement. Appropriate performance measurements indicate how well the company is meeting or exceeding its targets.

Performance measurements put problems in a proper perspective. Almost

---

[12] Adapted from Mark E. Beishel and K. Richard Smith, "Linking the Shop Floor to the Top Floor," *Management Accounting*, October 1991, p. 25. Reprinted from *Management Accounting*. Copyright by Institute of Management Accountants, Montvale, N.J.

daily, managers hear about many problems, receive voluminous computer printouts, and listen to a host of conflicting complaints. Often, this situation leads to confusion and the setting of wrong priorities. Relevant and consistent performance measurements that show trends help managers cut through the clutter and stay focused on the company's targets instead of emotional issues. Moreover, performance measurements can alert managers to opportunities as well as problems.

Rules for Developing Performance Measurements

The following rules will help develop a viable system of performance measurements:

1. Performance measurements should be supportive of company goals and strategies. They should be traceable to the activities that they measure. They should also be linked to each other for consistency and goal congruency.
2. Performance measurements should be quantifiable. In many instances, ratios serve as appropriate measures. Performance measurements should be appropriate for graphical or other visual display. Many world-class manufacturers display the results of performance measurements throughout the day on boards, charts, or graphs located adjacent to production cells. For an example of how this is done, review the discussion of the visual factory in Chapter 2. Such direct reporting methods can be useful motivators because shop floor personnel are able to monitor their own performance on a continuous basis and the results are displayed for all to see.
3. Performance measurements should be simple, so the person performing or managing the activity can easily and quickly understand the measure. The relationship between performance and the measure of the performance should be readily apparent and easy to explain to other people.
4. Performance measurements should induce beneficial behavior. The people who are being measured must have confidence in the accuracy and relevancy of the measure. Performance measurements should not be influenced directly by factors that are not controllable by the person responsible for the activity being measured. People who are involved and readily accept the performance measurements are likely sources of suggestions for continuous improvement.[13]

    If a firm measures and reports the results of someone's work, that person will be motivated to improve. People concentrate on whatever is measured. Appropriately selected performance measurements give a clear signal to all people in the company about the priorities of the enterprise. But performance measurements themselves must be checked occasionally to see if they are causing dysfunctional behavior. If so, they should be reevaluated and changed.
5. Performance measurements should focus on the positive aspects as well as the problems. As a rule, all performance measures should point out what has been done right, rather than emphasize the negative. For example, it is better to express production efficiency as a yield of good product rather than as a reject rate. It is better to show the orders shipped to customers on time than the number of late shipments. In other words, the shipping activity had a 98 percent on-time delivery performance this week rather than a 2 percent late delivery performance. This practice may be somewhat cosmetic, but it emphasizes that everyone in the organization is concentrating on getting better and better. As in sports, emphasis is on wins rather than losses, hits rather than strikeouts. Athletes, like workers, are motivated by seeing

[13] Jack Bailes, Ilene Kleinsorge, and Larry White, "How Support Services Can Use Process Control," *Management Accounting*, October 1992, p. 47. Reprinted from *Management Accounting*. Copyright by Institute of Management Accountants, Montvale, N.J.

their improvement result in an increase in the performance measurements, (e.g., a graph going upward) rather than in a decrease in errors. Sometimes, however, a graph going downward indicates positive performance, as in time-based performance measures.

6. Performance measurements are intended to foster improvement rather than serve as monitors. Therefore, they should show clearly where improvement has been made and where more improvement is possible, rather than merely monitor people's work.[14] Fast feedback also permits people to understand their work and to resolve problems quickly when they arise. Measurement that is too infrequent may not disclose undesirable variation in performance.

   There will always be areas for improvement, and new problems will occur as products and production change. Continuous improvement is a never-ending journey. When certain targets are reached, it is time to look at changing activities that can take performance to a new plateau.

7. Too many performance measurements can confuse people and actually obscure rather than enlighten. The number of performance measurements that can be used effectively is governed by the law of diminishing marginal utility. Just as the nth glass of water will drown a thirsty person, the nth performance measurement will consume more time and incur more cost than it is worth. Exhibit 11–6 shows this relationship.[15] After the optimum point is reached, adding more performance measurements will result in a dramatic decline in their effectiveness.

❚ Linking Performance Measurements throughout the Enterprise

At the activity level, nonfinancial performance measurements are normally more important than financial performance measurements, because activity operating performance translates into financial performance.[16] Management's

[14] Maskell, op. cit., p. 37.
[15] Richard S. Sloma, *How to Measure Managerial Performance* (New York: Macmillan, 1980), p. 11.
[16] Allen H. Seed III, *Adapting Management Accounting Practice to an Advanced Manufacturing Environment* (Montvale, N.J.: Institute of Management Accountants, formerly the National Association of Accountants, 1988), p. 72. With permission.

■■■ EXHIBIT 11–6
The Law of Diminishing Marginal Utility as It Relates to the Number of Performance Measurements

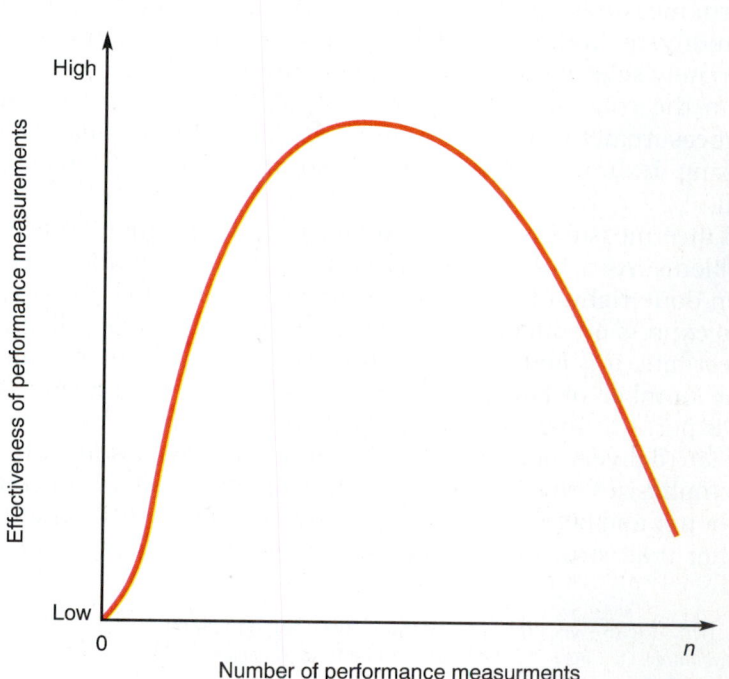

INSIGHTS & APPLICATIONS

Toyota's Idea of Continuous Improvement

Doing everything the same old way is sure to produce the same old results, and nothing is more wasteful than doing with great efficiency that which is totally unnecessary. To remain competitive, managers and workers must continually improve the performance of value-added activities from the executive suite to the shop floor. No enterprise can rest on its past success or performance.

Improvement is not a one-shot task that can be completed in a few months. Improvement to activities, products, and services must be continuous and ongoing. Objective performance measurements help managers and workers understand how well they are improving. Indeed, if performance is to be improved, it must be measured. A sound performance measurement system makes performance *visible* and provides *feedback* that helps everyone do a better job.

Toyota's managers and workers are committed to the concept of continuous improvement or *kaizen*. One consultant calls Toyota's continuous improvement strategy "rapid inch-up." It's another way of saying, "Take enough tiny, fast steps and pretty soon you outdistance the competition." Toyota considers continuous improvement as a dynamic process where workers and managers constantly seek perfection by removing constraints and nonvalue-added activities.

Toyota has long recognized that continuous improvement, in concert with total quality management, JIT systems, target costing, and life cycle costing, has contributed substantially to the production of high-quality, low-cost products. Clearly, such a strategy works for Toyota because it is a top company in quality, productivity, and efficiency. Nevertheless, it keeps getting better. Toyota's viewpoint is "Our current success is the best reason to *change* things." This proactive stance replaces the cliche, "If it ain't broke, don't fix it" with, "If it ain't broke, you haven't looked hard enough."

At Toyota, cost information is used to *manage activities*. Linking cost management with continuous improvement enables managers and workers to focus on activities. Performance measurements assist Toyota in decreasing lead times and increasing quality, productivity, and customer satisfaction. This focusing on activities represents a major paradigm shift from the cost-cutting mind-set of many other organizations.

---

goals are both financial and nonfinancial, however, so performance measurements that reflect both of these goals need to be developed. Traditional financial performance measurements concentrate on the following:

- Sales and market share
- Return on investment (ROI) or return on assets (ROA)
- Net income
- Earnings per share

Many people, especially investors, boards of directors, and executives appear to be hypnotized by these short-term financial measures. Most executives are rewarded largely according to how well they improve these measures, even though most agree that this practice does not contribute to the company's long-term health.

Return on investment (ROI), specifically return on net assets or equity, is affected because increases in automation increase costs in the short term and increase the proportion of investment in machinery and equipment to total investment.[17] Consequently, investments in automation tend to reduce returns in the short term. Old plants with fully depreciated assets show a higher accounting return than new plants with state-of-the-art technology. Thus, the more automated a plant becomes, the less relevant financial accounting performance measurements become.

Using financial performance measurements to improve performance is like concentrating on the scoreboard in a football game. Although the scoreboard tells the coaches whether they are winning or losing, it doesn't provide them with much guidance as to which plays should be called. What the coaches need is information that ultimately affects the score, such as which running plays are most successful, how well the quarterback is passing, how well the defense is stopping the opponent's attack, and so on. In business terms, managers need

[17] Ibid., p. 86.

INSIGHTS & APPLICATIONS

Linking Performance Measurements

Measuring individual activities with overall gross measures is similar to measuring a baseball player on his team's overall performance. It isn't fair to say that a player is no good because his team has a losing record. It is fair, however, to measure that player on RBIs, batting average, or on-base percentage because he can influence those measures directly. In the manufacturing process, it is unfair to measure a foreman on cost of production as a percentage of sales because he cannot control sales price, sales volume, or many elements of cost. It is fair, however, to measure that foreman on machine uptime and setup time, which he can control and influence directly and which eventually will contribute to cost as a percentage of sales. As a baseball player's RBIs will contribute to a team's wins, the foreman's reduced setup times will contribute to improved plant performance *and* financial measures, such as return on assets and earnings per share.[18]

performance measurements of the activities and prior outcomes that *lead* to superior financial *results*.[19]

Financial performance measurements often lead management to employ cost-cutting throughout the organization. Cost-cutting across the board is the conventional way to "manage costs," but it results in reducing or eliminating both nonvalue-added *and* value-added activities. Such efforts work in the short run but usually fail in the long run, because they strip both "fat and muscle" from the organization.

Effective use of nonfinancial performance measurements leads to a reduced dependence on conventional financial reports as the only performance criteria that matter. Most people in an organization do not manage nor are they directly responsible for "dollars." They manage activities and cost drivers that consume dollars. Therefore, focusing on activities that advance the competitiveness of the organization will lead to improved financial performance and ultimately improve profitability and enhance the value of the firm to shareholders.

A variety of performance measurements should be used. Whether nonfinancial or financial, they should be linked together to obtain a complete picture. No single performance measurement is perfect or all-encompassing, but a combination can be used to indicate trends and relationships.

Decision making at all levels in the organization should be synchronized with the company's goals and strategy. Decision making without regard to goals and strategy can be very costly and counterproductive. Therefore, the company should develop a performance measurement system that communicates goals and strategy throughout the organization. For example, achieving shorter production lead times without improving customer satisfaction will not lead to organizational congruency.

Exhibit 11-7 presents an example of performance measurements linked at each organizational level. The chief executive officer's measure of return on assets is supported by or linked to the three performance measurements associated with the vice president of manufacturing: inventory turnover, output per equipment dollar, and output per square foot of plant. The performance measurements associated with the plant manager are production lead time, work-in-process inventory hours, and vendor lead time. These performance measurements are supportive of the vice president's inventory turnover performance measurement. At the foreman level, the performance measurements linked to production lead time are machine uptime and setup time.

[18] Adapted from Beishel and Smith, op. cit., p. 26.
[19] Robert G. Eccles and Philip J. Pyburn, "Creating a Comprehensive System to Measure Performance," *Management Accounting,* October 1992, p. 41. Reprinted from *Management Accounting.* Copyright by Institute of Management Accountants, Montvale, N.J.

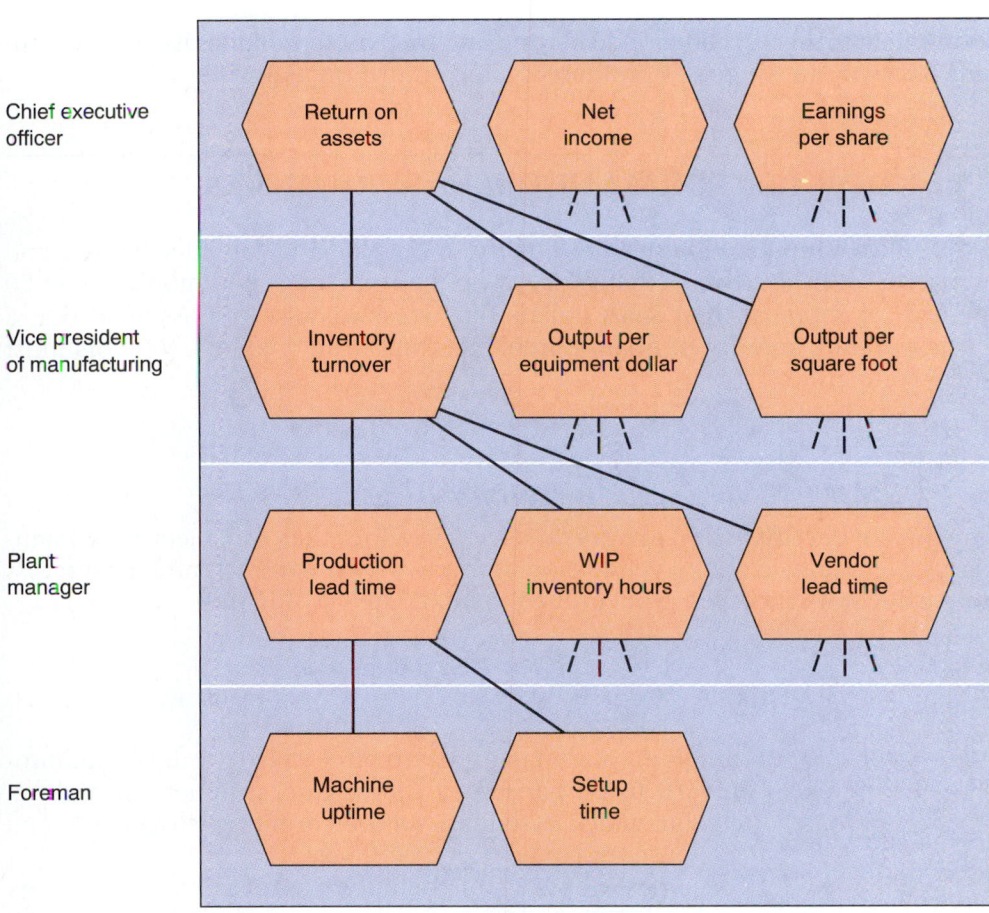

Example of Linking Financial and Nonfinancial Performance Measurements at All Levels in the Organization

Linking performance measurements at each level of the organization ensures congruency and constancy of purpose throughout. Workers and managers at each level can control their measures, and they understand clearly how they support the performance measurements above them. They also know where to look to correct problems that are causing poor performance.[20]

Notice that the performance measurements at the chief executive officer's level are financial. At the vice president's level, they are financial *and* nonfinancial. At both the plant manager's and the foreman's level, they are nonfinancial (or physical).

Activities performed in any enterprise ultimately affect the company's financial health. Shareholders, investment analysts, competitors, and customers measure companies primarily in financial terms. Although overemphasized in the past, financial measures are very much a reality and provide good aggregate measures of an enterprise's overall financial health. By linking nonfinancial physical measures to financial measures, management accountants are not subordinating physical measures to short-term profits, they are supporting the financial health of the enterprise with sound decisions regarding the company's activities. The point is that decisions made about activities *do* impact financial results and therefore the two should be linked.[21]

The performance measurements for managers and workers in the plant should reveal whether the activities are leading to simpler, faster, and better production. The financial performance measurements at the top are checks on the success of reengineering and continuous improvement of activities. For

[20] Ibid.
[21] Ibid., pp. 27–28.

example, reduced production lead time and increased productivity will eventually show up in improved profitability and return on assets.

VENDOR PERFORMANCE MEASUREMENTS

Poor-quality inputs will limit the quality of outputs and the effectiveness and efficiency of production activities. Because manufacturers commonly spend 50 percent or more of their sales dollars on raw materials, it is assumed that a corresponding amount of quality problems come from vendors. Vendors must meet standards of:

- Quality
- Price
- Delivery time

A **vendor certification program** selects vendors that can meet these standards. Generally, certified vendors are given five-year contracts and have access to production schedules. Noncertified vendors are classified as:

- Acceptable
- Probationary
- Unacceptable

With a certification program, manufacturers are often able to reduce the number of vendors to only 10 to 20 percent of the original number and reduce, if not eliminate, nonvalue-added activities, such as ordering, inspecting, and counting.

Certified vendors become extensions of the enterprise. For example, Xerox reduced its vendors from 5,000 to 400, trained them, included them in the design of products, provided specifications, and informed them of Xerox's production schedules. As a result, product costs decreased 10 percent per year and rejects decreased by 93 percent. Indeed, it is a lot easier and less costly to deal with 400 vendors than with 5,000.

Vendor Financial Performance Measurement

A **vendor financial performance measurement,** presented in Exhibit 11–8, discloses unnecessary costs caused by a vendor's nonconformance with specifications for quality and delivery schedules. Vendor nonconformance means that the buying company has to perform nonvalue-added activities that would otherwise be unnecessary, such as those listed on page 513 and in the exhibit.

EXHIBIT 11–8
Vendor Financial Performance Measurement

Nonvalue-Added Activity	Labor Hours per Occurrence	Cost at $60 per Labor Hour
■ Inspection rejection	0.4	$ 24
■ Paperwork rejection	0.2	12
■ Rework at company	5.0	300
■ Materials received too early	4.0	240
■ Materials received too late	8.0	480
■ Excess materials	1.0	60
■ Short materials	4.0	240
Totals	22.6	$ 1,356
Total cost of purchased raw materials:		$33,900

$$\text{Vendor performance index (VPI)} = \frac{\$33,900 + \$1,356}{\$33,900}$$

$$= \underline{1.04}$$

- Inspection rejection
- Paperwork rejection
- Rework at company
- Material received too early
- Material received too late
- Excess material
- Short material

The management accountant assigns labor hours per nonvalue-added activity. For example, inspection rejection may take 0.4 labor hours while rework, if done at the company, may require 5.0 labor hours. Then, it's just a matter of multiplying the labor hours by the total cost per labor hour, which is $60. The results of each delivery are entered in the vendor's record stored in the database. A vendor financial performance measurement record can be set up in the database for each vendor and data compiled over a 6- or 12-month period to derive a valid performance profile. Such profiles enable management to make vendor decisions; that is, eventually to select certified vendors.

The **vendor performance index (VPI)** is calculated by:

$$\text{VPI} = \frac{\text{Cost of purchased raw materials} + \text{Cost of nonvalue-added activities}}{\text{Cost of purchased raw materials}}$$

If the vendor does not cause nonvalue-added activities, then the VPI will equal one. Anything above one is an indication of some form of vendor nonconformance. A VPI of 1.02 to 1.04 may place a vendor on acceptable or probationary status. A VPI greater than 1.04 may be sufficient to eliminate a vendor from doing business with the company. A VPI close to one over a period of time is sufficient for a vendor to achieve certification status.

The VPI can also be used as a bid multiplier for determining the "true" cost of purchasing from a particular vendor. To illustrate, consider the following bid for a part Y:

	VENDOR A	VENDOR B
Bid price for part Y:	$100	$110
× VPI	1.4	1.0
Total cost per part Y:	$140	$110

Based solely on the bid price, Vendor A is the low-cost vendor. After considering past quality and performance as measured by the VPI, Vendor B provides the better overall value.

In high-velocity manufacturing environments, the VPI may be computed daily or weekly. The VPI is also used to compare vendors with similar complexities of supply and material. In time, the absolute best vendors in each area will emerge as potential certified vendors. Other vendors will fall into one of three categories:

- Acceptable (these vendors are working toward certified status)
- Probationary (these vendors are on the boundary of what is acceptable)
- Unacceptable (the company will not do business with these vendors)

Vendor Nonfinancial Performance Measurement

A **vendor nonfinancial performance measurement** is presented in Exhibit 11–9. It rates the following performance measures on the basis of points:

- Quality
- Price
- On-time delivery
- Bonus

■ EXHIBIT 11–9
Vendor Nonfinancial Performance Measurement

Goal:	100+ points for certification
Acceptable:	95–99 points
Probationary:	90–94 points
Unacceptable:	<90 points

Performance measurements:

Quality:		40 points
Zero rejections	= 40 points	
One rejection	= 30 points	
Two rejections	= 20 points	
Three rejections	= 0 points	
More than three rejections	= −40 points	

Price:		20 points
Better price than similar vendors	= 20 points	
Competitive price with similar vendors	= 10 points	
Higher price than similar vendors	= 0 points	

On-time delivery:		40 points
100% on time	= 40 points	
Each percentage point <100%	= −2 points	

Bonus rating:		20 points
Superior performance	= 20 points	
Exceeds goals	= 10 points	
Acceptable	= 0 points	
Needs Improvement	= −10 points	
Unacceptable	= −20 points	

Certified vendor certificate at Bently Nevada Corporation.

To meet the criteria for selection as a certified vendor, a vendor must provide zero- or near zero-defect material at a competitive price at the right time and be willing to improve continually. Although price is a financial measurement, it is not emphasized in the nonfinancial performance measurement in a dollars and cents fashion. In fact, "shopping for the best price" is deemphasized. For example, it is possible for a vendor to have a *higher* price than competing vendors and still reach certified vendor status, because the vendor excels in other performance measures. In a large number of situations, using price as the main selection criterion can be the costliest way to select vendors. What world-class managers want are a few vendors whom they can rely on for quality, on-time delivery, and general performance (e.g., cooperative attitude and willingness to try new technology such as EDI). As long as their prices are "in the ballpark," they will remain certified vendors, and their relationship with the buying company will be a long and profitable one.

Vendors are audited weekly or monthly during the selection process. The goal is for each vendor to receive 100 or 100-plus points. A score between 95 and 99 points is acceptable but indicates a need for improvement. A score between 90 and 94 points puts a vendor on probation and indicates corrective action is needed before the vendor will be taken off probation. A score of less than 90 points means that the vendor's performance is unacceptable, and the vendor is eliminated as a vendor for the company. Usually, it takes anywhere from 6 to 12 months to build a reliable vendor performance score that can be used to certify a vendor. For many companies, having certified vendors is imperative because they are trying to become certified vendors of other enterprises. A vendor cannot become a certified vendor unless it also has certified vendors. Moreover, the vendor has to show continuous improvement if it is to continue to get the enterprise's business. For example, Intel, a vendor to PC manufacturers, has honed its vendor base down to an average of 1.6 vendors per part purchased. Intel's goal is one certified vendor per part.

Performance Measurement That Focuses on Quality

The **vendor quality performance measurement** focuses on the vendor's ability to deliver raw materials of consistently high quality. This performance is calculated as follows:

$$\text{Acceptance percentage} = \frac{\text{Number of parts accepted}}{\text{Number of parts delivered}}$$

A vendor who supplies 1,000 parts with 100 rejects would have a 90 percent acceptance percentage, calculated as follows:

$$\text{Acceptance percentage} = \frac{900 \text{ parts accepted}}{1,000 \text{ parts delivered}}$$
$$= \underline{90\% \text{ parts accepted}}$$

The buying company may set a target of 99.9 percent acceptance percentage, which is one rejected part per 1,000 parts ordered. In this case, an acceptance percentage of 90 percent is far from the company's quality target.

Performance Measurement That Focuses on On-Time Deliveries

The **vendor on-time delivery performance measurement** discloses the vendor's ability to deliver raw materials just-in-time, not too early and not too late. On-time deliveries are important, because early deliveries build up raw materials inventory and late deliveries disrupt production and cause wasteful expediting activities. Exhibit 11–10 gives an example of a bar graph used to track vendor delivery performance. As shown in the exhibit, Eksi is the only vendor that has a chance of becoming a certified vendor. In some companies that want just-in-time delivery, even Eksi would not qualify as a certified vendor, because the "delivery window" is usually measured in hours or minutes.

Performance Measurements That Focus on Vendor Simplicity

The **vendor simplicity performance measurement** calculates two values:

- The number of vendors per product
- The number of purchase orders per product

Vendors	Number of deliveries	Delivery performance for the week ending May 7
Adams	20	
Brown	24	
Chen	17	
Eksi	32	
Zerga	18	

-10 -8 -6 -4 -2 0 2 4 6 8 10

← Number of days early —|— Number of days late →

EXHIBIT 11–10

A Bar Graph Used to Track Vendor Delivery Performance

By reducing the complexity of activities and implementing a certified vendor program, a company can reduce the number of vendors and purchase orders, thereby streamlining vendor relations and reducing costs of vendor-driven activities.

As stated before, complexity is the main culprit that drives costs. Complex products require more vendors, and more vendors drive purchasing and materials handling activities, and so on. Therefore, to see how well the company is doing in simplifying vendor-driven activities, the following performance measurement is recommended:

$$\frac{\text{Number of vendors}}{\text{per product}} = \frac{\text{Number of vendors}}{\text{Number of products}}$$

$$= \frac{1,000}{10}$$

$$= \underline{\underline{100 \text{ vendors per product}}}$$

To measure how the number of vendors is driving the purchasing activity, the following performance measurement is recommended:

$$\frac{\text{Number of purchase orders}}{\text{per product}} = \frac{\text{Number of purchase orders}}{\text{Number of products}}$$

$$= \frac{6,000}{10}$$

$$= \underline{\underline{600 \text{ purchase orders per product}}}$$

Elimination of unprofitable products and the simplification of the remaining products will substantially reduce the number of parts required. A vendor certification program will reduce the number of vendors. And, the need for fewer parts and fewer vendors will, in turn, reduce, if not eliminate, the purchasing activity.

TIME-BASED PERFORMANCE MEASUREMENTS

The use of **time-based performance measurements** means that time is recognized as the equivalent of money, productivity, quality, and resources. Time is manageable and a source of competitive advantage throughout every activity in the organization. The longer an activity takes to perform, the greater the resources it requires. Also, the longer the activity takes, the more likely that work will have to be redone to correct mistakes or defects. Conversely, the shorter the elapsed time, the quicker the activity's response to changes in customer demand.

Lead Time

Lead time is the time between the beginning of a process or activity and the appearance of its results. Reducing lead times increases speed, and speed is the watchword of world-class manufacturers. Speed in world-class manufacturing falls into the following categories:

- Speed of design engineering in getting new products from the design stage to the production stage
- Speed of vendors in getting raw materials to the production process
- Speed of converting raw materials to finished products
- Speed of delivering finished products to customers

Notice the dominant role played by speed in the following definition of a world-class manufacturer of printed circuit boards:

- A facility with a capacity to assemble more than 300 printed circuit boards per eight-hour shift
- A lead time of less than 30 minutes per board from raw materials to ship time
- A setup time of less than 30 minutes for changing the type of board being assembled

The overall performance of an enterprise can be judged by its lead times.

Lead Time Efficiency Ratio

The **lead time efficiency (LTE) ratio performance measurement,** introduced in Chapter 2, indicates the level of value-added and nonvalue-added activities in a process. A lead time is associated with every activity in an organization. The activity lead time efficiency ratio can be a:

- Design engineering lead time efficiency ratio
- Vendor delivery lead time efficiency ratio
- Production lead time efficiency ratio
- Customer delivery lead time efficiency ratio

LTE ratios should be applied throughout the organization—on the plant floor as well as in administrative offices.

Management's concern is that a large portion of costs are driven by a large number of nonvalue-added activities, as shown in the production LTE ratio presented in Exhibit 11–11. The **production lead time** is the interval between the acquisition of raw materials and first stage of production and the time that the finished products come off the production line.

Traditional batch manufacturers have an LTE ratio of 10 percent or less. If the production LTE ratio is 10 percent, that means that 90 percent of the production activities are creating no value. The challenge for cost management

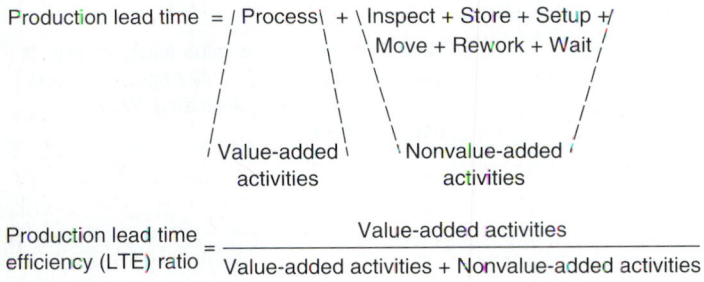

$$\frac{\text{Production lead time}}{\text{efficiency (LTE) ratio}} = \frac{\text{Value-added activities}}{\text{Value-added activities} + \text{Nonvalue-added activities}}$$

Production lead time map:

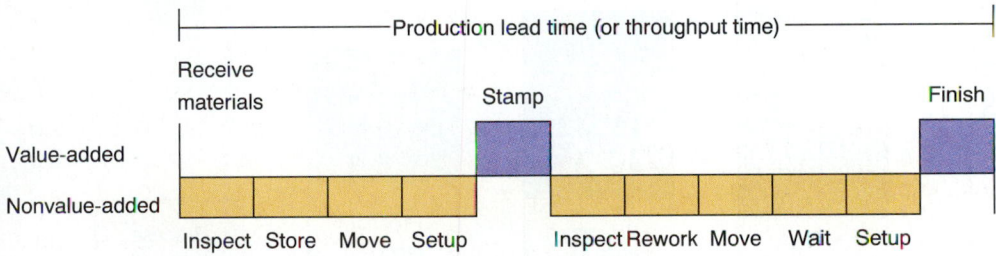

EXHIBIT 11–11
Production Lead Time Efficiency (LTE) Ratio Containing Value-Added and Nonvalue-Added Activities

Note: From the time raw materials are received until the product is completed, nine nonvalue-added activities are performed compared to two value-added activities. The cost management opportunity is to eliminate as many nonvalue-added activities as possible and reengineer the rest, such as redesigning setup procedures and installing production cells to reduce excessive material movement.

is to reduce the 90 percent. In some administrative functions, it is not unusual to see an LTE ratio of 1 percent or less.[22] World-class manufacturers enjoy production LTE ratios of 40 percent or more, some as high as 70 to 80 percent. An LTE ratio of 80 percent means that only 20 percent of the production process includes nonvalue-added activities.

A perfect plant operation achieves a production LTE ratio of one, or 100 percent, as shown in Exhibit 11–12. Such a ratio will probably never be achieved, but by implementing the concepts of reengineering and continuous improvement, an enterprise can strive to bring nonvalue-added activities down to as low a level as possible, as indicated by the graph in Exhibit 11–12. To achieve production LTE ratios of one, the following conditions must exist:

- On-time delivery of high-quality raw materials
- Lot sizes equal to one
- Zero setup time
- Zero time between operations
- Zero defects
- Zero machine downtime

These conditions assume perfectly synchronized operations throughout the production process.

What Are the Results of Improving the LTE Ratio?

Reducing lead times and eliminating nonvalue-added activities improve everything. In Chapter 2, production activities were portrayed as pipelines. At one end, the company pays its vendors for raw materials entering the pipeline. At the other end, the company's customers pay for products delivered. The goal

---

[22] Robert D. McIlhattan, "The Impact of JIT on the Financial Executive: How Cost Management Can Support the JIT Philosophy," in *Cost Accounting for the 90s: Responding to Technological Change* (Montvale, N.J.: Institute of Management Accountants, formerly the National Association of Accountants, 1988), p. 248. With permission.

■■■ EXHIBIT 11–12
Production Lead Time Efficiency (LTE) Ratio of a Perfect Operation

$$\text{Production lead time efficiency (LTE) ratio} = \frac{\text{Process time}}{\text{Process time} + 0} = 1$$

Conditions for achieving an LTE ratio of 1:
- Lot size = 1
- Setup time = 0
- Time between operations = 0
- Defects = 0
- Machine downtime = 0

Note: Process time, a value-added activity, is the only time expended. All nonvalue-added activities have been eliminated. When this occurs, the ratio = 1.

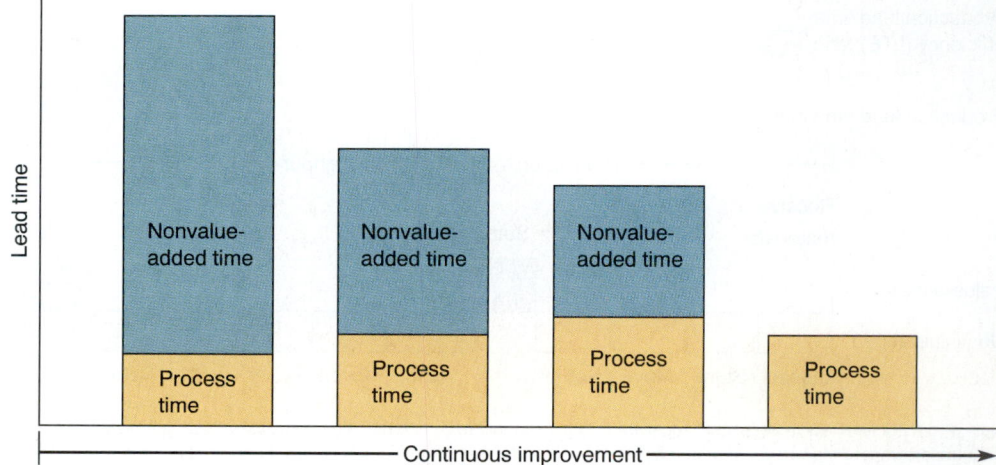

of the company is to reduce the time between payment on one end and receipt on the other. To accomplish this, the company needs to reduce, if not eliminate, nonvalue-added activities. Nonvalue-added activities in the production pipeline (or the administrative, marketing, and distribution pipelines) are like cholesterol in the arteries of a person. They cause problems and increase costs.

Improving the production LTE ratio produces the following positive results:

- Increased cash flow
- Increased profit
- Improved customer service
- Better quality
- Lower inventories
- Less spoilage, scrap, and rework
- Smaller lot sizes
- Faster responsiveness to changes in the marketplace

Contribution Margin Velocity Ratio

The **contribution margin velocity ratio performance measurement** is based on the observation that profitability is a function of both the absolute profitability of a product and the production lead time; it is formulated as follows:

$$\frac{\text{Contribution margin}}{\text{velocity ratio}} = \frac{\text{Product contribution margin}}{\text{Production lead time}}$$

To illustrate the contribution margin velocity ratio, consider two products:

PRODUCT	CONTRIBUTION MARGIN	PRODUCTION LEAD TIME (DAYS)
A	$55	5
B	42	3

Conventional cost accounting determines that product A is more profitable than product B, which is correct in absolute terms. But when the contribution margin velocity ratio is computed for each product, the following results occur:

$$\begin{aligned}\frac{\text{Product A's contribution}}{\text{margin velocity ratio}} &= \frac{\text{Product A's contribution margin}}{\text{Product A's production lead time}}\\[6pt] &= \frac{\$55}{5\text{ days}}\\[6pt] &= \$11 \text{ contribution margin}\\ &\quad\text{ per production day}\end{aligned}$$

$$\begin{aligned}\frac{\text{Product B's contribution}}{\text{margin velocity ratio}} &= \frac{\text{Product B's contribution margin}}{\text{Product B's production lead time}}\\[6pt] &= \frac{\$42}{3\text{ days}}\\[6pt] &= \$14 \text{ contribution margin}\\ &\quad\text{ per production day}\end{aligned}$$

The contribution margin velocity for product A is $11 per production day while it is $14 per production day for product B. Assuming sufficient demand for product B and holding other factors constant, the company would be more profitable selling product B than product A.

❙ The Delivery Production Ratio

The **delivery production (D:P) ratio performance measurement** compares delivery lead time to production lead time. The **delivery lead time (D)** is the lead time required by customers to receive the product or service. The production lead time (P) is the lead time necessary to acquire raw materials and convert them into finished goods ready for shipment to customers.

Assume that the value of D is greater than P, such as:

$$\text{Delivery:Production ratio} = \frac{\text{Production lead time (P)}}{\text{Delivery lead time (D)}}$$

$$= \frac{5 \text{ days}}{10 \text{ days}}$$

$$= \underline{0.50 \text{ times as long to}}$$
$$\underline{\text{produce as to deliver}}$$

In this case, the product can be made to order. The manufacturer, therefore, has a great deal of flexibility to change product mix and customize products.

The following D:P ratio shows that this product takes considerably longer to produce than to deliver:

$$\text{Delivery:Production ratio} = \frac{\text{Production lead time (P)}}{\text{Delivery lead time (D)}}$$

$$= \frac{40 \text{ days}}{10 \text{ days}}$$

$$= \underline{4.00 \text{ times as long to}}$$
$$\underline{\text{produce as to deliver}}$$

In this case, the value of D is less than P, which means the product must be made to stock to anticipate and meet customer demand. If a product is made to stock, a substantial amount of finished goods inventory must be stocked to meet the required customer service level. In this example, it takes four times as long to make the product as it does to deliver the finished product to customers. The manufacturer not only has to spend money on holding and storing finished goods inventory, but must also prepare accurate sales forecasts. Also, the manufacturer cannot offer customized products because there is not enough time to make them. The company has restricted its ability to be flexible and responsive to customers' needs.

Generally, world-class manufacturers' objective is to reduce the D:P ratio continuously until it is less than one. However, producing products much faster than they are delivered will also build up inventory even though this situation gives the manufacturer a great deal of production flexibility. If a manufacturer wants to achieve a continuous flow and synchronized operation, as described in Chapter 2, then a D:P ratio of one is ideal:

$$\text{Delivery:Production ratio} = \frac{\text{Production lead time (P)}}{\text{Delivery lead time (D)}}$$

$$= \frac{5 \text{ days}}{5 \text{ days}}$$

$$= \underline{1.00 \text{ times as long to}}$$
$$\underline{\text{produce as to deliver}}$$

In this way, production is synchronized with delivery, and vice versa. Such a situation means zero inventories and the elimination of all costs related to holding inventory.

INSIGHTS & APPLICATIONS

Reducing Inventories through Shorter Lead Times

"We're beginning to see the critical nature of shorter lead times in the marketplace," stated Keith Buchell, newly hired management accountant.

"How's that?" asked Marshall Evans, inventory manager.

"Lead time is a very powerful weapon. Some of our competitors are gaining additional market share simply because they deliver faster. I don't mean ten percent faster. I mean 50 to 70 percent faster. And they're getting top prices for their ability to perform this way."

"What does all this have to do with inventories?" asked Marshall.

"Well, work-in-process inventory is the same thing as lead time," Keith responded.

"You've lost me," said Marshall, puzzled.

"Look, if we have three months of work-in-process, it's going to take us an average of three months to get everything through the plant. And finished goods inventories should be proportional to production lead times," said Keith.

"I still don't understand," Marshall responded.

"We ship from stock. OK, if it takes us an average of three months to get something through the plant, we're going to need about three and a half or four months of finished goods inventory. But if we can cut our lead time to one week, then we only need one and a half or two weeks of finished goods inventory. Plus, we can probably serve our customers better, and cash flow will increase."

"I see," said Marshall. "If we reduce lead times, we can reduce inventories. If we can reduce inventories, we can drive costs down. We can probably also increase quality. All of this will make us more competitive."

"Right," Keith responded, "and don't forget, improved productivity and increased customer service and satisfaction."

Setup Time

Setup time is the amount of time needed to change production facilities for a different product or service. Setup time is closely linked to a number of other activities, and the faster the setup time, the better these activities will be performed.

The reduction of setup time permits lot sizes to be decreased, thus shrinking work-in-process inventories. Reduced lot sizes, in turn, will enable production lead times to be reduced. Reduced production lead times will give the enterprise more flexibility and allow it to be more responsive to its customers. Reduced production lead times and delivery lead times (i.e., the D : P ratio) will reduce or eliminate the need for finished goods inventories.[23]

Indeed, decreasing setup time is a key element of continuous improvement, as Exhibit 11–13 illustrates. For example, a plant scheduled 40 machine setups for one week at 15 minutes standard time per setup. The actual time for the first setup was 27 minutes, 12 minutes over the standard. By recognizing the unfavorable time variance when it first occurred, corrective action could be taken immediately to eliminate the 12-minute variance. At this point, a supervisor recommended engineering and procedural changes, which, over a 12-month period, reduced the actual setup time to less than 10 minutes, 5 minutes below the original standard setup time of 15 minutes.

The **setup time performance measurement** indicates how efficiently the production facilities are made ready to make another product or provide a service. Clearly, the goal of production management is to reduce the amount of setup time. One way to compute a setup time ratio follows:

$$\text{Setup time} = \frac{\text{Total setup time during the week}}{\text{Number of setups}}$$

$$= \frac{600 \text{ minutes}}{60 \text{ setups}}$$

$$= \underline{\underline{10 \text{ minutes per setup}}}$$

[23] Maskell, op. cit., pp. 145–147.

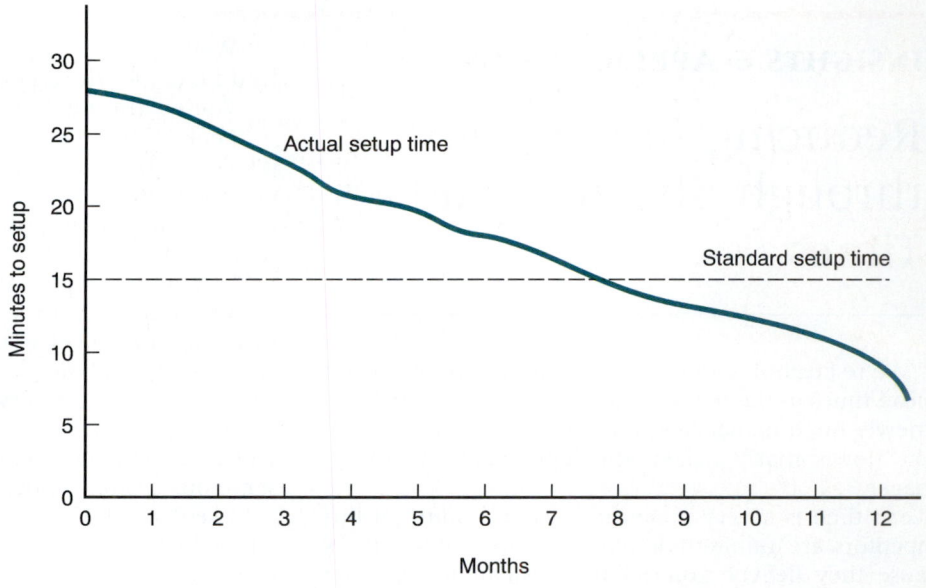

EXHIBIT 11–13
Graph Showing Improvement in Setup Time

Machine Uptime

World-class manufacturing assumes a very high degree of reliability in production and does not tolerate machine failures or downtime. When the production process is ready, it is assumed that the machines will be ready to produce and be in good working order. Therefore, the **machine uptime performance measurement** determines the percentage of time the machine is ready for production when needed. Encapsulated in this one performance measurement are several factors such as the following:

- Reliability
- Mean time to repair (Ideally, repairs shouldn't be needed, but if they are, the mean time to repair should be measured in seconds or minutes.)
- Effectiveness of preventive maintenance programs
- Effectiveness of training programs (Better training should produce machine operators who know how to operate machines properly and care for them.)

Just-in-time manufacturing does not necessarily use machines 100 percent of the time, because the philosophy is that an idle machine is preferable to a machine making product that is not needed immediately. But when a machine or cell *is* required to manufacture product, it must be able to go into action immediately. The following performance measurement indicates the percentage of time the machine is up and ready to process:

$$
\text{Machine uptime} = 1 - \frac{\text{Number of hours machine not ready for production}}{\text{Number of hours machine needed for production}}
$$

$$
= 1 - \frac{2\ \text{hours}}{100\ \text{hours}}
$$

$$
= 1 - .02
$$

$$
= 98\%\ \text{of the time the machine is up and ready to process when needed}
$$

This performance measurement indicates that the machine is ready to process when needed 98 percent of the time. To some, this figure may represent a high degree of machine uptime, but to world-class manufacturers, 98 percent machine uptime may be intolerable, because they expect 100 percent machine uptime. This stringent target is the reason world-class manufacturers install comprehensive preventive maintenance programs. Production personnel are trained to perform basic daily and weekly preventive maintenance tasks, and emphasis is placed on the quality of product made by each machine. Care is taken to make sure that *all* machines are in peak condition *all* the time.

PRODUCTIVITY PERFORMANCE MEASUREMENTS

Although time-based performance measurements provide indirect measures of productivity, the following performance measurements can be used to measure productivity directly:

- Work force productivity performance measurement
- Direct materials yield performance measurement
- Activity productivity performance measurement

Productivity performance measurements ascertain the amount of outputs produced by inputs. Therefore, productivity is normally measured using ratios, such as the following:

$$\text{Productivity} = \frac{\text{Outputs produced}}{\text{Inputs consumed}}$$

A successful enterprise must continue to improve its output of products and services in relation to the inputs of direct labor, direct materials, and activities.

Work Force Productivity

The **work force productivity performance measurement** indicates the number of units produced per direct labor hour. It is calculated as follows:

$$
\begin{aligned}
\text{Work force productivity} &= \frac{\text{Units produced during the day}}{\text{Direct labor hours consumed during the day}} \\
&= \frac{150,000 \text{ units produced}}{3,000 \text{ direct labor hours consumed}} \\
&= 50 \text{ units produced per direct labor hour}
\end{aligned}
$$

A decrease in the denominator with a corresponding increase in the numerator would mean that the work force is becoming more productive.

Direct Materials Yield

The **direct materials yield performance measurement** indicates how efficiently raw materials are being converted into finished products. Its ratio is computed as follows:

$$
\begin{aligned}
\text{Direct materials yield} &= \frac{\text{Number of finished units produced during the day}}{\text{Number of direct materials input during the day}} \\
&= \frac{50,000 \text{ finished units}}{200,000 \text{ direct materials parts}} \\
&= 25\% \text{ direct materials yield}
\end{aligned}
$$

An increase in the denominator without a corresponding increase in the numerator would indicate waste, excessive scrap, or defects.

Activity Productivity

The **activity productivity performance measurement** indicates how efficiently an activity is being performed. The productivity of any activity can be measured by dividing the activity's output volume by the input required by that activity during the same period. For example, assume that the machining activity required 5,000 machine hours to produce 150,000 units during the day. The machining activity's productivity is measured as follows:

$$\text{Machining activity} = \frac{\text{Units produced during the day}}{\text{Machine hours consumed during the day}}$$
$$= \frac{150,000 \text{ units produced}}{5,000 \text{ machine hours consumed}}$$
$$= 30 \text{ units produced per machine hour}$$

CUSTOMER SATISFACTION PERFORMANCE MEASUREMENTS

Customer satisfaction performance measurements determine how well the company is meeting the needs, wants, and expectations of customers. Such performance measurements are subject to change, because the marketplace is dynamic. To a great extent, customers define many of the enterprise's activities. Indeed, without customers there would be no business. Successful businesses know what the customer demands and figure out the best ways to meet those demands.

World-class enterprises view customer satisfaction as the primary reason for being in business. The aim is to be close to the customer and understand fully, on a continuing basis, what it takes to keep the customer satisfied. Most of the performance measurements covered to this point support customer satisfaction either directly or indirectly. For example, high-quality raw materials delivered by the vendor to the manufacturer on time will help to ensure that high-quality finished goods will be produced in a timely manner. Shorter setup times and production lead times reduce customer delivery lead times and enable the manufacturer to be more flexible and responsive to customer needs.

Before customer satisfaction performance measurements are developed, what the customer needs and wants should be established. This information is usually generated from a **customer survey,** such as the one presented in Exhibit 11–14. This initial customer survey will point out areas of strength and weakness and will enable the enterprise to change or better manage its activities to achieve customer satisfaction.

Assuming that items 1 and 3 in the customer survey are rated as very important (e.g., 9 or 10) by the company's customers, then the following performance measurements should be established:

- On-time delivery performance measurement
- Percentage of complete order filling

On-Time Delivery

The **on-time delivery performance measurement** determines if the finished product or service is being delivered at the time specified by the customer. One way to calculate on-time delivery performance is:

CUSTOMER SURVEY

Customer: Metatrax Corporation

Date: 10/18/94

1. You rate the ability of your vendor to make on-time deliveries as:

    Not   Very
    Important   1 2 3 4 5 6 7 8 9 10   Important

2. You rate the ability of your vendor to handle emergency orders as:

    Not   Very
    Important   1 2 3 4 5 6 7 8 9 10   Important

3. You rate the ability of your vendor to fill each order completely without any backorders as:

    Not   Very
    Important   1 2 3 4 5 6 7 8 9 10   Important

4. Please list additional needs and wants:

    _____

    _____

    _____

■ EXHIBIT 11–14
Customer Survey to Determine Needs and Wants of Customers

$$\text{On-time delivery} = \frac{\text{Number of units delivered to customers during the week}}{\text{Number of units committed to customers for the week}}$$

$$= \frac{9,800 \text{ units delivered}}{10,000 \text{ units committed}}$$

$$= 98\% \text{ on-time delivery}$$

Clearly, the objective is to deliver to customers what was promised when it was promised.

Performance measurements, especially those measuring customer satisfaction, are not just for manufacturers. Service companies can also monitor their performance and achieve their goals and strategies with a performance measurement system. For example, airlines regularly compute on-time arrival performance and customer complaint ratios. In fact, delivering the product or service to the customer on time is the culmination of a series of activities being done effectively and efficiently throughout the organization whether it's a manufacturer or a service enterprise.

On-time delivery performance measurements can also be established to measure internal activities. For example, an activity, such as finishing, is a downstream activity of machining. The finishing activity is viewed as a "customer" of the machining activity, and the machining activity is a "vendor" of the finishing activity. In many world-class companies, having "vendors" and "customers" *internal* to the company means that, to the ABM system, customer satisfaction is essential throughout the enterprise. The ABM idea is "We've got to satisfy each other before we can satisfy our ultimate customer."

▌Complete Order Filling

The **complete order filling performance measurement** determines how many orders are completely filled over some time period. If all items are available in the quantities ordered by customers all the time, then the percentage of complete order filling is 100 percent. Normally, this is not the case and some items will have to be backordered (i.e., an order to be filled when stock is renewed). The percentage of complete order filling is calculated as follows:

$$\text{Complete order filling percentage} = 1 - \frac{\text{Number of backorders}}{\text{Number of orders}}$$
$$= 1 - \frac{50 \text{ backorders}}{1,000 \text{ orders}}$$
$$= 1 - .05$$
$$= 95\% \text{ orders completely filled}$$

▌Customer Satisfaction Is an Ongoing Process

It should be stressed that the initial customer survey is not enough. Both customer surveys *and* performance measurements must be an ongoing process. Customers' wants and needs may change, which, in turn, may change the performance measurements. Ongoing customer surveys often use a **snake chart,** which captures the dynamics of the marketplace by showing what customers think is important and how they rate the company in those areas. The snake chart, as shown in Exhibit 11–15, lists six attributes for customers to weigh. The "importance" curve indicates the level of importance the customers give to the listed attributes. The "rating" curve shows how well the customers rate the company on those attributes. In the exhibit, the company excels only in the attributes "complete order fills" and "emergency orders." To achieve total customer satisfaction, the company needs to improve its performance in the other four attributes.

The information supplied by the snake chart is powerful and readily compre-

▌EXHIBIT 11–15
Snake Chart Showing Attribute Weighting by Customers

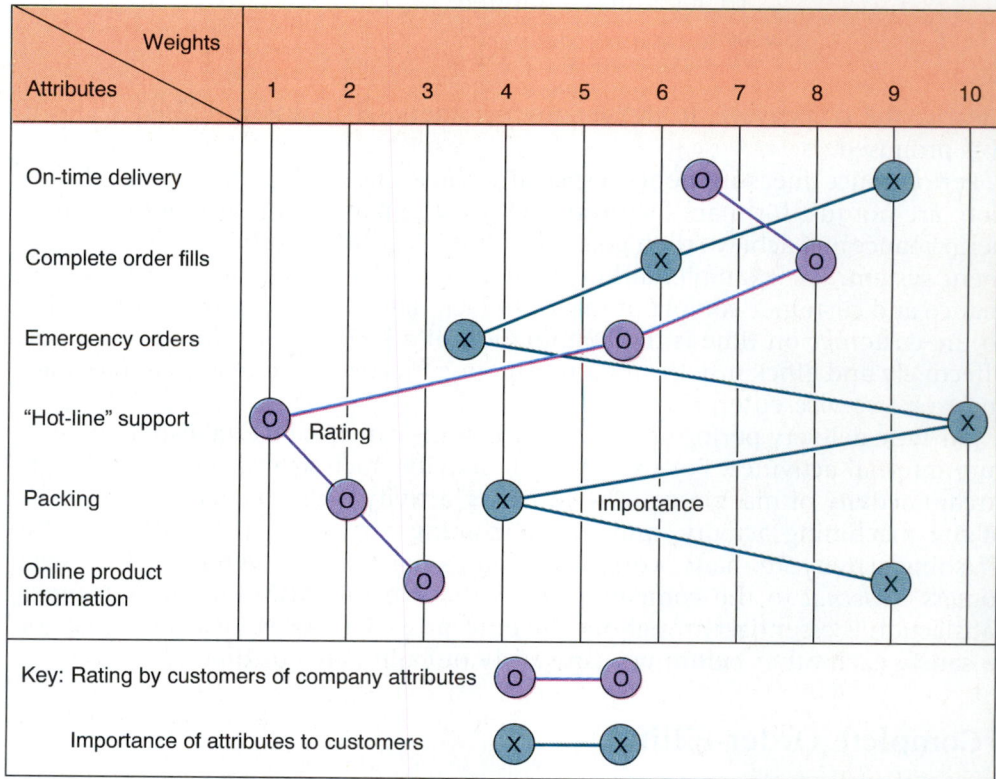

hensible. Its results may often prove surprising. Most marketing managers often *assume* that they have a clear understanding of what customers consider important, but the information disclosed by a snake chart can prove their assumptions are wrong. In any event, an ongoing customer survey process and continuing adjustments to activities and their measurements will eventually result in the two "snakes" being very close to each other, if not completely overlaid.[24]

▌Sales Activity

The final measure of how well the company is achieving total customer satisfaction is the sales activity. Two excellent performance measurements can be used to measure this activity:

- Sales growth performance measurement
- Budgeted sales variance performance measurement

SALES GROWTH. The **sales growth performance measurement** calculates the percentage rate of growth from the last period to the current period. It is computed as follows:

$$\text{Sales growth} = \frac{(\text{Sales this period} - \text{Sales last period})}{\text{Sales last period}} \times 100\%$$

$$= \frac{(\$11{,}000{,}000 - \$10{,}000{,}000)}{\$10{,}000{,}000} \times 100\%$$

$$= \underline{\underline{10\% \text{ sales growth}}}$$

In this case, the performance measurement shows a 10 percent sales growth.

BUDGETED SALES VARIANCE. The **budgeted sales variance performance measurement** compares budgeted sales with actual sales and indicates a variance in percentage terms. If the variance is negative, actual sales are less than budgeted sales. If the variance is positive, actual sales are greater than budgeted sales. The budgeted sales variance performance measurement is calculated as follows:

$$\text{Budgeted sales variance} = \frac{(\text{Actual sales} - \text{Budgeted sales})}{\text{Budgeted sales}} \times 100\%$$

$$= \frac{\$9{,}500{,}000 - \$10{,}000{,}000}{\$10{,}000{,}000} \times 100\%$$

$$= \underline{\underline{-5\% \text{ budgeted sales variance}}}$$

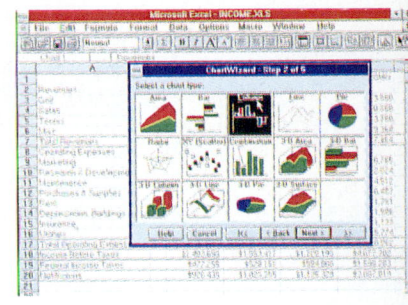

Preparing computer-based graphs. With permission from Microsoft.

▌HELPING MANAGEMENT AND WORKERS VISUALIZE PERFORMANCE INFORMATION

Graphs are devices that present information in image form so it can be visualized and quickly comprehended. Graphs make relationships between numbers visible by turning numerical quantities into various shapes. Graphs pack a large amount of information into a small area. They tend to show the "big picture" or gestalt. Presenting output in image form reinforces the clichés that "a picture

LEARNING OBJECTIVE 4

Explain why care should be taken in developing performance measurements that users can readily visualize, comprehend, and apply.

[24] Ibid., p. 229.

John W. Schmitthenner III, controller at Soladyne Division of Rogers Corporation, uses graphic illustrations to show what direction manufacturing is heading. Courtesy of Rogers Corporation.

is worth a thousand computer printouts" and "seeing the problem is solving the problem." With graphs the viewer can often *see* the *unseen*. Four of the best tools for generating graphs are spreadsheets and graphics software, computer-aided systems and software engineering (CASE) tools, database management systems (DBMS), and fourth-generation languages (4GLs).

The goal of a graph is to convey a clear vision and understanding of the underlying data. To achieve this, the data region of the graph should be emphasized and not be filled with extraneous items. The following guidelines will help achieve this:

- Don't clutter the data region.
- Don't overdo the number of tick marks or grid lines.
- Don't let reference lines interfere with the data.
- Avoid notes, keys, markers, and labels in the data region.
- Use scale breaks only when necessary.
- Don't always insist on including zero magnitudes.[25]

Exhibit 11–16a is an example of an unclear and misleading graph that does not follow these guidelines. The information the graph is trying to convey is lost. Exhibit 11–16b shows the same data with a graphical presentation that does follow the guidelines. Here, the information is clear and readily comprehensible.

Graphs can be divided into categories based on the kind of information they convey.[26] The following categories are particularly well suited for displaying output from a performance measurement system:

- Scattergraphs
- Line graphs
- Control charts
- Bar graphs
- Sectographs
- Picturegraphs

Scattergraphs

Scattergraphs (also called **scatterplots** or **scatter diagrams**) clearly reveal trends of the underlying data. Compare the four *x, y* columns of data in Exhibit 11–17 (see p. 530) to the scattergraphs. Notice how difficult it is to gain insight or detect a trend from the columns of data, whereas the scattergraphs clearly indicate the behavior and trends.[27]

Line Graphs

Line graphs show fluctuations over time by means of a rising and falling line that indicates highs, lows, rapid movement, or stability. Relatively thin lines should be used so that points of reference are not obscured. Using contrasting color for emphasis is more effective than bold lines. Care must be taken to adjust the size of the grid in a line graph after the points of reference are plotted to ensure maximum visibility of the information. Too many grid lines, however, obstruct the view. Too few lines make information difficult to read.[28] In addition, the grid lines should be much lighter than the data lines so that the user's attention is focused on the data lines.

[25] From *The Elements of Graphing Data* by W.S. Cleveland. Copyright © 1985 by Bell Telephone Laboratories, Inc. Reprinted by permission of Brooks/Cole Publishing Company, Pacific Grove, CA 93950; pp. 100–101.
[26] Hilary Goodall and Susan Smith Reilly, *Writing for the Computer Screen* (New York: Praeger Publishers, 1988), p. 103.
[27] F. J. Anscombe, "Graphs in Statistical Analysis," *American Statistician*, February 1973, pp. 17–21.
[28] Ibid., p. 104.

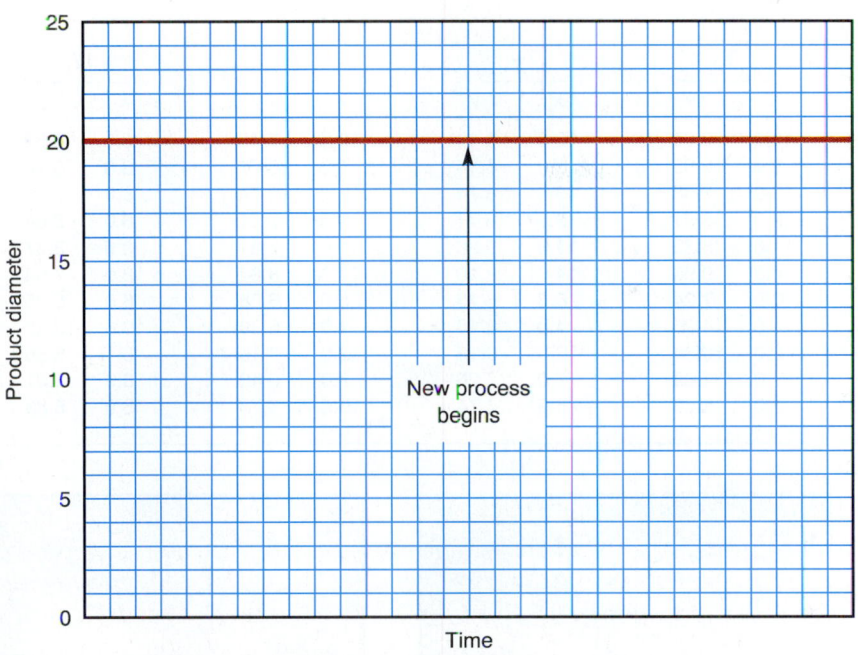

(a) A poorly constructed graphical display

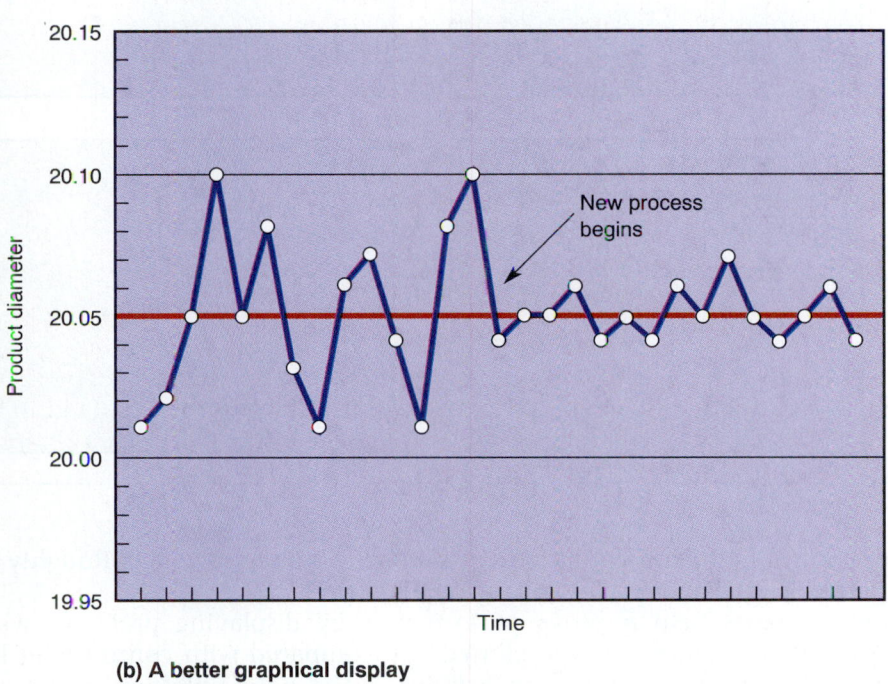

(b) A better graphical display

■EXHIBIT 11–16
**Two Graphical
Displays**

Exhibit 11–18 (see p. 531) shows unit sales of products A and B at Starling Company for the fiscal year 1993. Notice how the grid makes it easier to read the lines at various points on the graph.

Control Charts

Every activity has variation. The more fine-tuned the activity, the less variation there is from the average. The less activity variation, the less waste. A **control chart** is simply a picture of the activity and its variation. It includes upper and

■■■EXHIBIT 11–17
Data Trends and Behavior Revealed in Scattergraphs

I		II		III		IV	
x	y	x	y	x	y	x	y
10.0	8.04	10.0	9.14	10.0	7.46	8.0	6.58
8.0	6.95	8.0	8.14	8.0	6.77	8.0	5.76
13.0	7.58	13.0	8.74	13.0	12.74	8.0	7.71
9.0	8.81	9.0	8.77	9.0	7.11	8.0	8.84
11.0	8.33	11.0	9.26	11.0	7.81	8.0	8.47
14.0	9.96	14.0	8.10	14.0	8.84	8.0	7.04
6.0	7.24	6.0	6.13	6.0	6.08	8.0	5.25
4.0	4.26	4.0	3.10	4.0	5.39	19.0	12.50
12.0	10.84	12.0	9.13	12.0	8.15	8.0	5.56
7.0	4.82	7.0	7.26	7.0	6.42	8.0	7.91
5.0	5.68	5.0	4.74	5.0	5.73	8.0	6.89

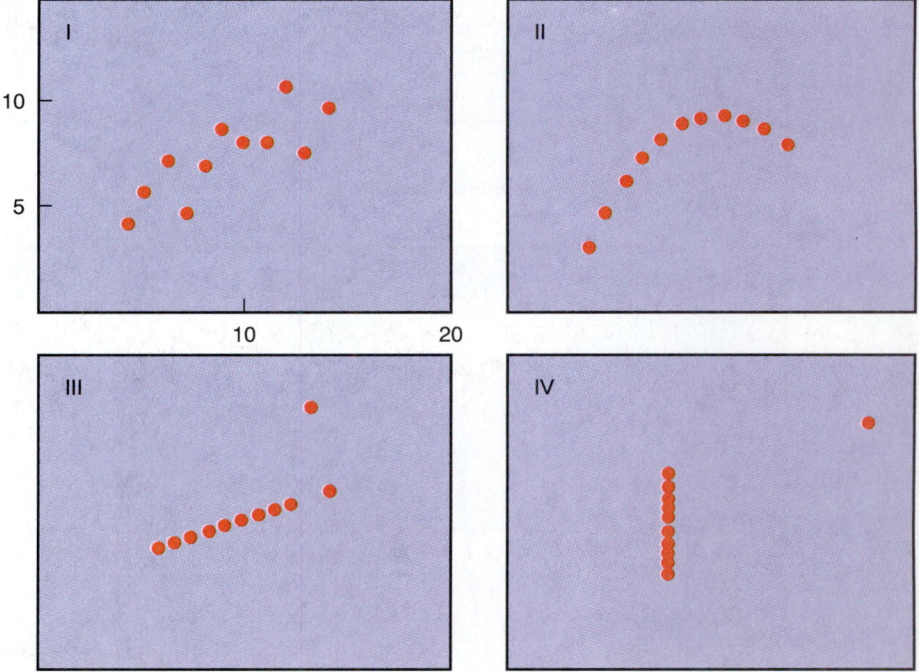

lower control limits drawn on either side of the activity average. Roughly half the points will be above average and half below.[29]

Control charts help improve performance by displaying problems within activities. Performance data are plotted and compared with control limit lines to determine the true state of an activity. If the points plotted on the chart begin to cross or actually cross the control limit lines, it is vital to find out what the problem is, determine its cause, and fix it as rapidly as possible. Corrective action should solve the problem *and* offer ways to prevent it from recurring in the future.

Exhibit 11–19 (see p. 532) presents an example of a control chart. It shows the pack and fill line activity of Morning Flakes for a cereal company. The activity fills material into a package that is labeled to hold 16 ounces of product. The control chart shows results of weight measurements of packages sampled from the line.

Two important pieces of information are readily apparent. First, the average amount of weight in each package is 17.5 ounces. Second, the filling and packing activity is drifting out of control. The weight $(\overline{X})$ is averaging the amount due

[29] Mary Walton, *The Deming Management Method* (New York: Perigee Books published by The Putnam Publishing Group, 1986), p. 114.

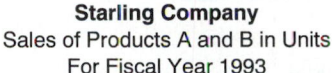

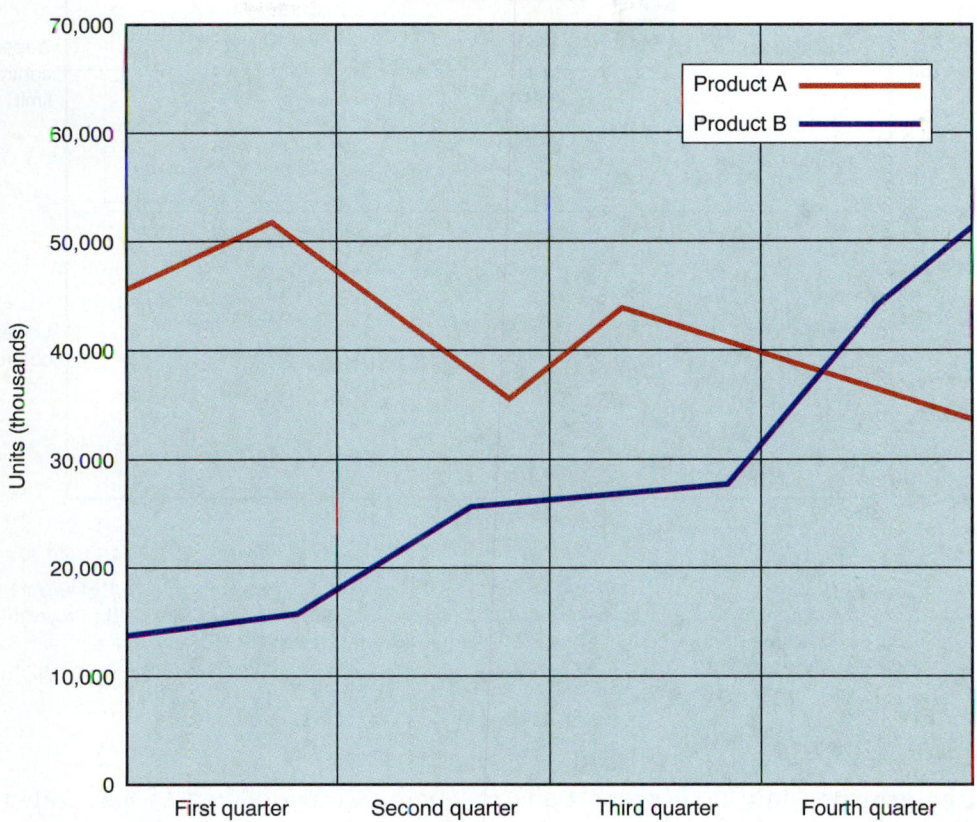

Starling Company
Sales of Products A and B in Units
For Fiscal Year 1993

Note: The lines represent a pattern of weekly sales.

to the variation in packing material from the pack heads. The variation forces the average pack well above the lower specification limit. The lower specification limit must be protected, because labeling requires that each package contain at least 16 ounces of product. The regulatory cost of underpacking is high. Therefore, variation translates directly into higher average material weight. The higher the variation, the greater the waste. Thus, the decision, based on the information displayed in the control chart, should be to change or clean the pack heads on the machines more often to improve pack head performance and decrease variation.

Lower variation translates directly into a decrease in average packing amount and direct cost savings.[30] Controlling variation also helps prevent the activity from drifting out of control. If the control chart does indicate that the activity is drifting out of control, then the pack heads may have to be replaced. A point need not be outside the limits to indicate action. Abrupt shifts or distinct trends within limits are signals for investigation.

Control charts should not be used in isolation but should be integrated with total quality management (TQM), the subject of the next chapter. By using control charts, an enterprise can identify activities that can be improved and thereby stop defects *before* they occur. For example, preventive actions involve machine maintenance and operator training. The more management understands the activity, the more proactive measures can be applied to prevent problems from occurring.

[30] James M. Reeve, "The Impact of Variation on Operating System Performance," in *Performance Measurement in Manufacturing and Service Organizations,* ed. by Peter B. B. Turney (San Diego, Calif.: Proceedings of the Third Annual Management Accounting Symposium, 1989), pp. 83–84.

■ EXHIBIT 11–19
Control Chart of Pack Fill Weight

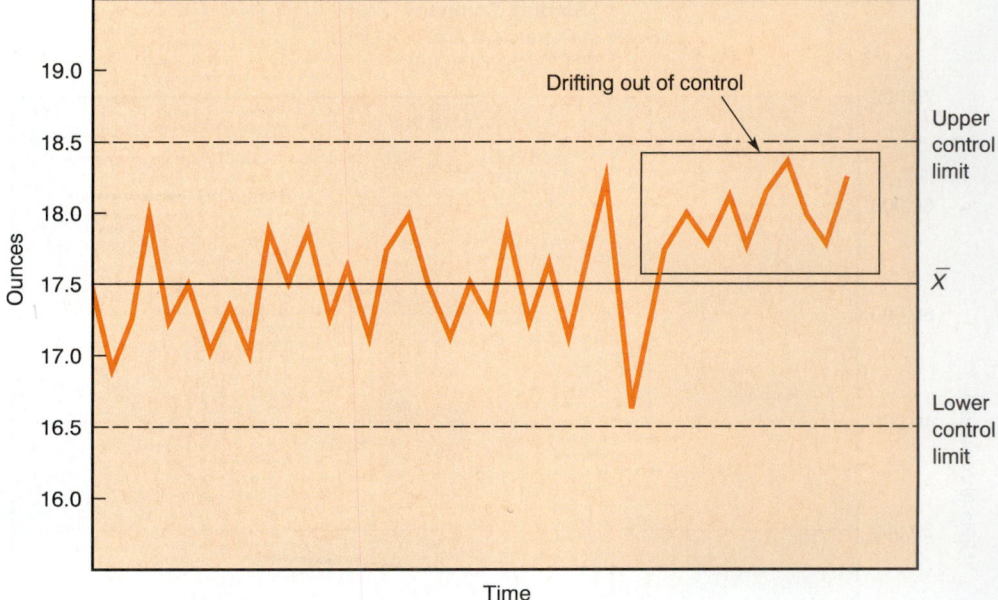

Source: James M. Reeve, "The Impact of Variation on Operating System Performance," in *Performance Excellence in Manufacturing and Service Organizations,* ed. Peter B. B. Turney (San Diego, Calif.: Proceedings of the Third Annual Management Accounting Symposium, March 1989), p. 83.

Using bar graphs to evaluate performance at Nevada Bell.

Bar Graphs

Bar graphs show how proportions or quantities are related to each other. There are two types of bar graphs:

■ Horizontal bar graphs
■ Vertical bar graphs

Each type indicates amounts by placing bars on a grid. The length or height of the bars represents an amount determined by the grid's scale.

Unlike line graphs, bar graphs emphasize totals at specific points rather than fluctuations of data over time. Bar graphs should be used only when the number of amounts to be compared is relatively small. If too many comparisons are made, the bars will be too thin to have much visual impact.[31] In some designs, bars can be differentiated by filling them with contrasting textures and colors.

HORIZONTAL BAR GRAPHS. A **horizontal bar graph** compares different items during the same time frame. For example, the horizontal bar graph in Exhibit 11–20 discloses the amount of idle time for four machines during January 1994.

VERTICAL BAR GRAPHS. A **vertical bar graph** measures the same item at different periods of time. For example, the graph in Exhibit 11–21 (see p. 534) shows changes in minutes required per setup over five consecutive quarters. The company is clearly achieving continuous improvement over time. Furthermore, in the first quarter of 19X5, the company reached its breakthrough target of 15 minutes per setup, which is much better than both the industry average and the benchmark.

[31] Goodall and Reilly, op. cit., p. 105.

INSIGHTS & APPLICATIONS

Tailoring Reports to User Needs

The two owners of a small company were presented with a forecast of working capital every week. One of the owners was very enthusiastic about the information and felt that it was invaluable for short-term planning. The other owner kept complaining that the working capital forecast was useless because "it had too much detail, and the individual numbers in the forecast did not seem to tie into each other." It appeared that the second owner had a difficult time absorbing written material. In order to give him a better understanding of the information in the forecast, a bar graph was inserted. The graph gave a quick overview of the details in the report. It allowed the second owner to grasp the numbers in the report, and it helped everyone to identify important trends.

The moral of this story is that people absorb and understand information in different ways. As managers, we all have been involved with training subordinates, but how much thought goes into training the boss? Whether you know it or not, you actually are teaching things to your boss all the time. Whenever you present information— for example, explaining relationships among data that you compiled and analyzed in an effort to show how the company is performing— you and your boss are in the roles of teacher and learner, respectively.[32]

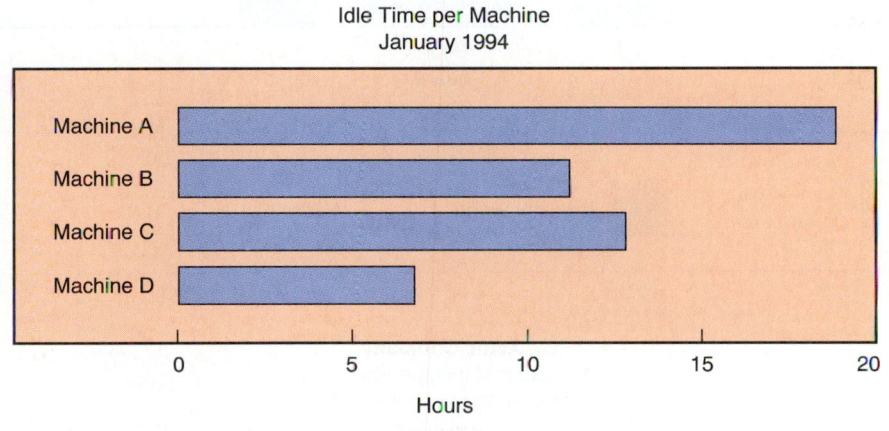

Idle Time per Machine
January 1994

■ EXHIBIT 11–20
Horizontal Bar Graph

Sectographs

Sectographs show how total amounts are divided up. Two popular sectographs are the:

■ Pie chart
■ Layer graph

PIE CHARTS.   In its simplest form, a **pie chart** is a circle that has been segmented into two or more pieces, like slices of a pie—hence the name. Each "slice of the pie" or triangular wedge represents a certain percentage of the whole, and the size of each wedge is proportional to its contribution to the whole. Since the proportional amount is immediately apparent, the visual impact is strong and memorable. The pie chart in Exhibit 11–22 (see p. 534) shows the income statement items for Acme Company.

Pie charts can be combined with bar graphs to display additional information. For example, in Exhibit 11–23 (see p. 535), the pie chart shows percentages of production costs, and the bar graph discloses the breakdown of manufacturing overhead costs.

Pie charts help managers and workers **visualize** an activity's performance.

[32] William Blais, "Training Your Boss," *Management Accounting*, September 1991, p. 47. Reprinted from *Management Accounting*. Copyright by Institute of Management Accountants, Montvale, N.J.

EXHIBIT 11–21
Vertical Bar Graph

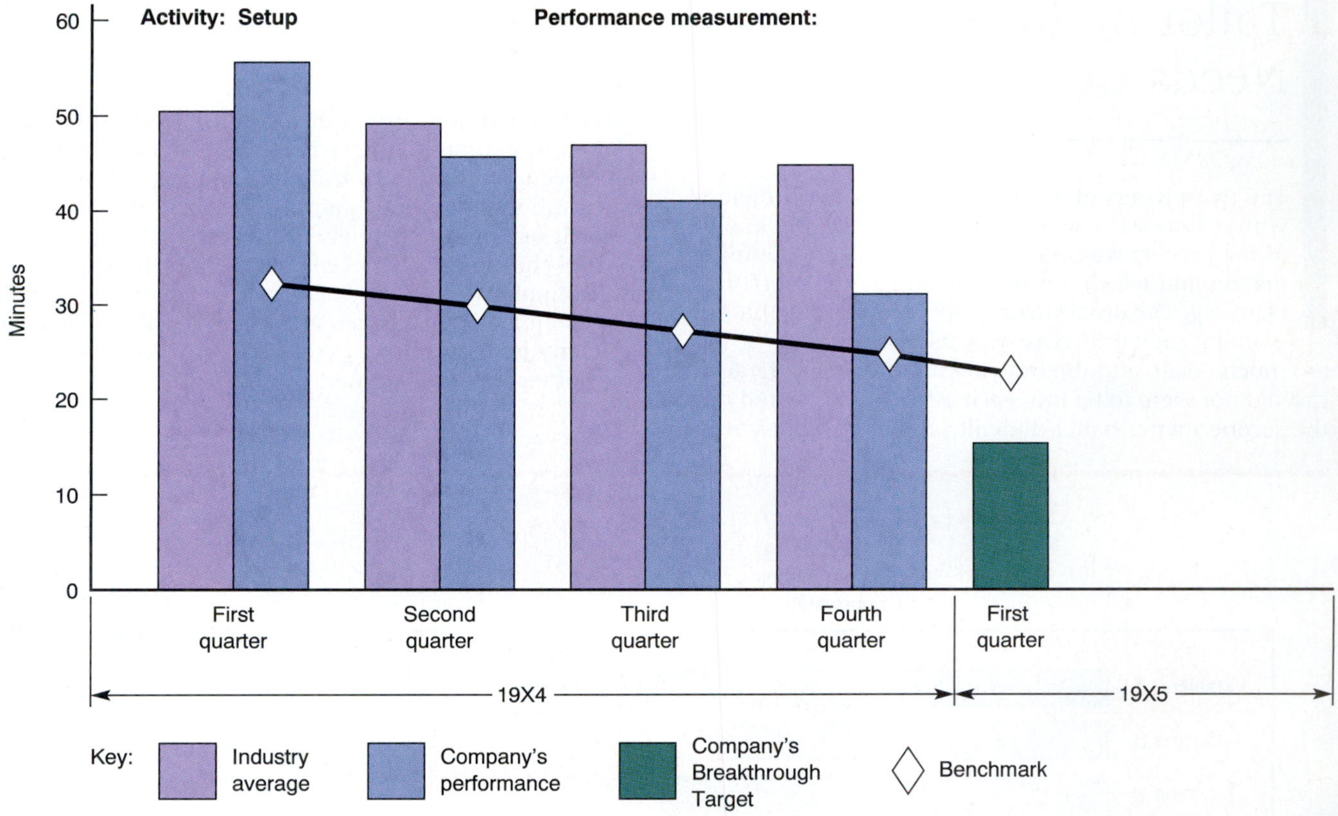

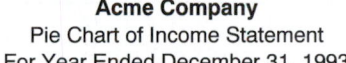

Activity: Setup
Performance measurement:
Minutes
60
50
40
30
20
10
0
First quarter
Second quarter
Third quarter
Fourth quarter
First quarter
19X4
19X5
Key:
Industry average
Company's performance
Company's Breakthrough Target
Benchmark

EXHIBIT 11–22
Pie Chart

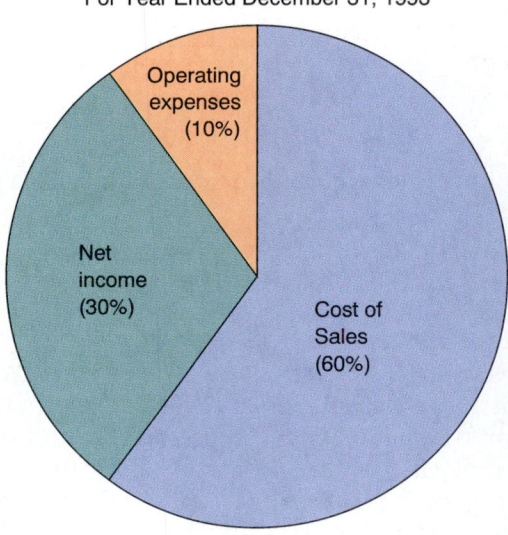

Acme Company
Pie Chart of Income Statement
For Year Ended December 31, 1993
Operating expenses (10%)
Net income (30%)
Cost of Sales (60%)

When pie charts are used to display output from performance measurements, these guidelines should be followed:

- Use fewer than ten wedges to provide adequate differentiation and to avoid "confusion."

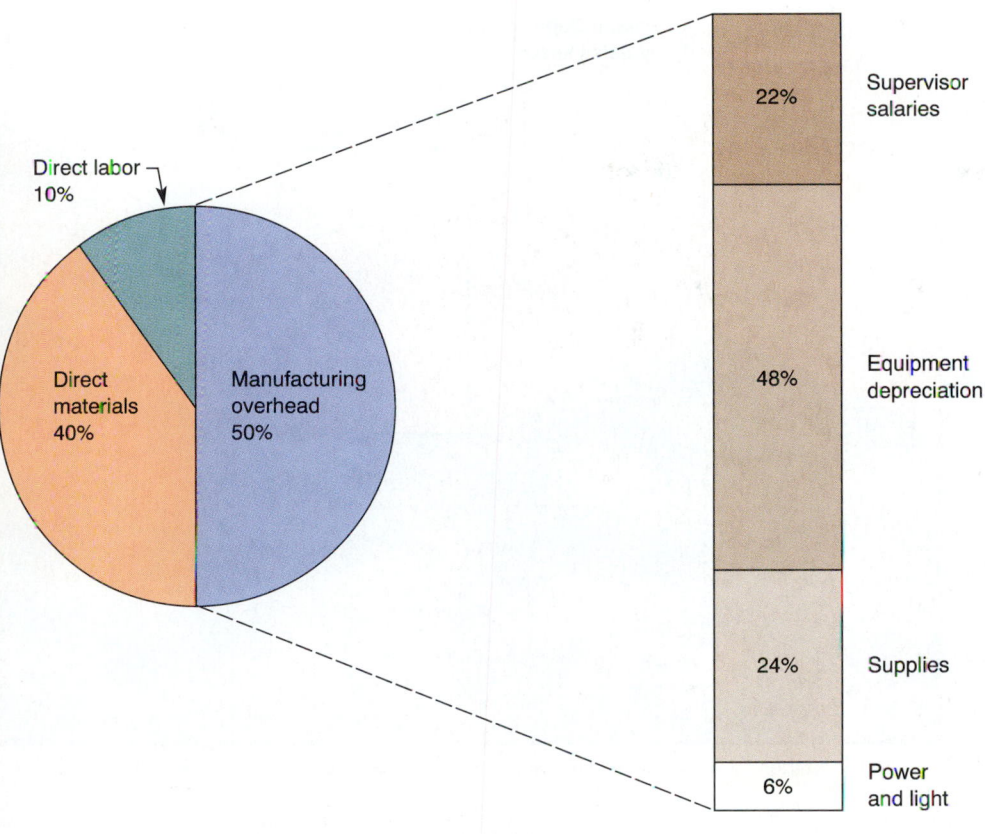

- ■ Identify each wedge with labels and numbers.
- ■ Use contrasting colors or textures to intensify comparisons.
- ■ Explode wedges slightly from the remainder of the pie for emphasis and clarity.

LAYER GRAPHS.   A **layer graph** is created like a line graph, but the areas between the lines represent quantities and add up to a total amount. Each layer is differentiated by using a different color or texture. The layer graph in Exhibit 11–24 (see p. 536) shows sales by salesperson over four quarters at Palace Department Store.

▌Picturegraphs

Picturegraphs are similar to bar charts except that columns of little signs or icons are used in place of bars. Each picture represents a certain quantity of the item illustrated. The picturegraph in Exhibit 11–25 (see p. 536) shows the number of pickup trucks sold over a four-year period in Suffolk County.

Picturegraphs do indeed catch the user's eye, but they are best used to convey a general impression of quantities rather than precise information. In preparing picturegraphs, the following design guidelines should be used:

- ■ Use familiar pictures or symbols. Unfamiliar pictures or symbols must be learned.
- ■ Design pictures and symbols that convey their intended meaning precisely.
- ■ Design for efficiency. In some instances, a picturegraph may consume more display space than text or numbers.
- ■ Choose symbols that are visually distinguishable from other symbols. Users' ability to discriminate alphabetic or alphanumeric information is much more powerful than their ability to discriminate among a large number of symbols.

EXHIBIT 11–24
Layer Graph

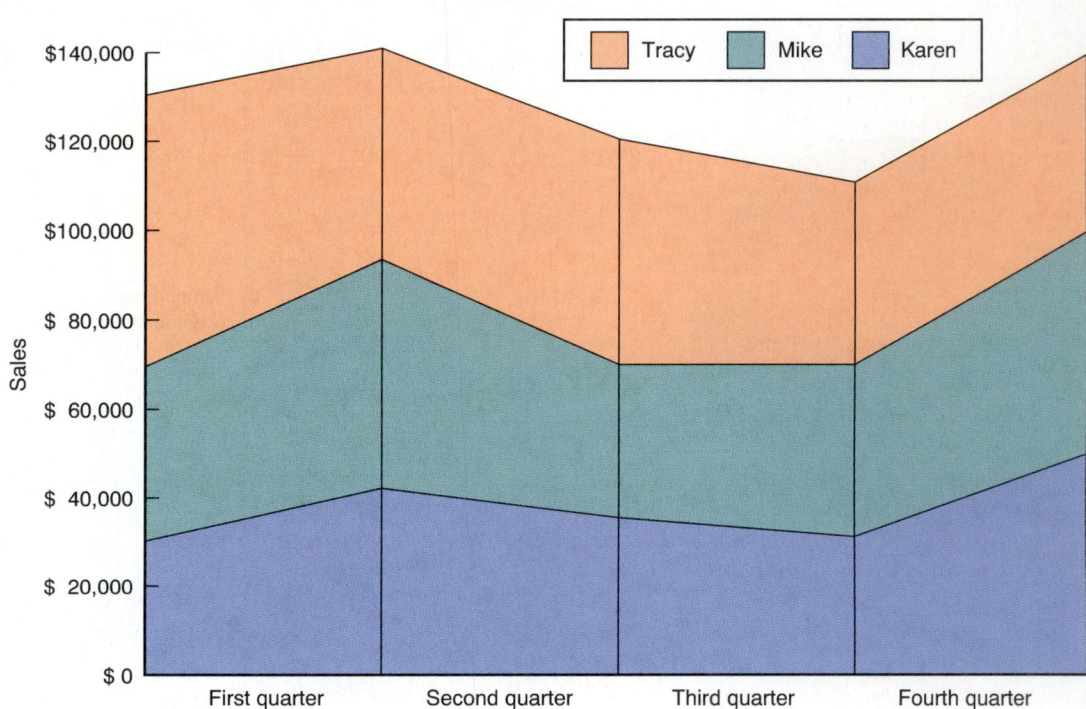

Palace Department Store
Sales by Salesperson for Four Quarters

EXHIBIT 11–25
Picturegraph

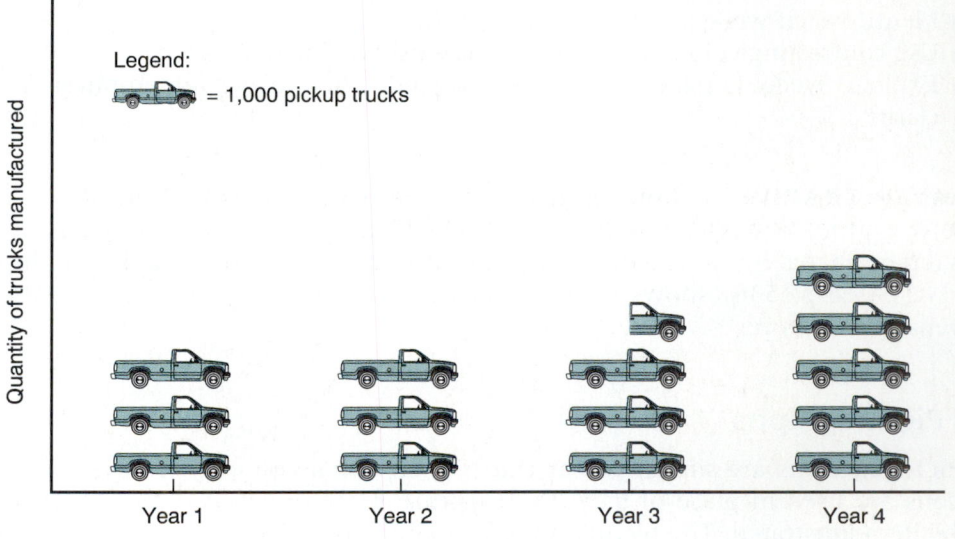

SUMMARY OF LEARNING OBJECTIVES

The major goals of this chapter were to enable you to achieve four learning objectives:

Learning objective 1. Define activity-based management (ABM).

Whereas the activity-based costing (ABC) system is developed to cost objects, activity-based management (ABM) uses information from the ABC system, benchmarking, and performance measurements to reengineer and improve the organization to achieve excellence.

ABM is an ongoing process involving four phases:

Phase 1. Identify value-added and nonvalue-added activities.
Phase 2. Reengineer the enterprise.
Phase 3. Benchmark value-added activities.
Phase 4. Develop a performance measurement system for continuous improvement.

Learning objective 2.   Describe each phase of the four-phase ABM process.

The first phase of the ABM process is directed toward identifying and thoroughly understanding both value-added and nonvalue-added activities. The information for this phase comes from work performed during the development of the ABC system and additional activity analysis.

The second phase entails determining the root causes of costs and reengineering activities. Reengineering can involve any aspect of the enterprise, such as redesigning products or services, restructuring the plant layout, and overhauling or eliminating activities. The reengineering effort moves the enterprise from *what it is* to *what it should be* in order to compete effectively.

Once nonvalue-added activities are eliminated or reengineered, the third phase is implemented, which involves benchmarking the best practices of world-class companies. Benchmarking results will give the enterprise worthwhile targets to meet or exceed.

Targets without measures, however, are destinations without roadmaps. Therefore, to make sure that the enterprise stays on the continuous improvement track and meets or exceeds its targets, the fourth phase is devoted to building a performance measurement system. Performance measurements indicate to managers and workers how well they are doing compared to targets or other criteria established during benchmarking.

The following rules will help in developing performance measurements:

1. Link them for coordination and consistency throughout the organization.
2. Quantify them and display them so they are easily comprehended by users.
3. Make them simple and easy to understand.
4. Select performance measurements that induce beneficial behavior.
5. Make the performance measurements show positives rather than negatives.
6. Use performance measurements that show improvement, trends, and relationships.
7. Use an optimum number of key performance measurements that signify the enterprise's critical success factors.

Learning objective 3.   Summarize vendor, time-based, productivity, and customer satisfaction performance measurements.

Management accountants are not expected to use *all* of the performance measurements summarized in Exhibit 11–26, nor would it necessarily be appropriate for them to do so. However, out of all the performance measurements that could be derived, the ones in this chapter measure most of the critical success factors of most enterprises. (Quality is also a critical success factor, but it is covered in Chapter 12.)

None of these performance measurements measure profitability, return on investment or assets, or earnings per share, but they will help improve these critical financial factors. These performance measurements are simple and easy to understand. They show change and degree of change over time, and that is what is important in performing activity-based management.

Learning objective 4.   Explain why care should be taken in developing performance measurements that users can readily visualize, comprehend, and apply.

Not only is the *substance* of performance measurements important to users, but the *form* in which they are presented is also critical. To assist users in tapping the full potential of performance measurements, the output should be easily accessible, visual, and simple.

Producing reams of computer printouts containing columns of numbers is a good example of a nonvalue-added activity, because such printouts usually wind up in the incinerator without ever being read by anyone. This problem of too much data and not enough information can be solved with graphs, such as the following:

■ Scattergraphs
■ Line graphs

■EXHIBIT 11–26
Summary of Performance Measurements

Performance Area	Specific Performance Measurements	Target
Vendor performance	Vendor financial performance measurement	Elimination of nonvalue-added costs
	Vendor performance index (VPI)	An index of one
	Vendor nonfinancial performance measurement	100-plus points for vendor certification
	Vendor quality performance measurement	100 percent parts accepted
	Vendor on-time delivery performance measurement	Zero late and early deliveries
	Vendor simplicity performance measurement	Minimum number of vendors and purchase orders
Time-based performance	Lead time efficiency (LTE) ratio performance measurement	A ratio that equals one
	Contribution margin velocity ratio performance measurement	Maximize contribution margin of products in terms of production lead time
	Delivery production (D : P) ratio performance measurement	A ratio of one or less
	Setup time performance measurement	Reduction in setup time (zero setup time is ideal)
	Machine uptime performance measurement	100 percent machine uptime
Productivity performance	Work force productivity performance measurement	Increase number of units produced and decrease number of direct labor hours consumed
	Direct materials yield performance measurement	Increase number of units produced and decrease number of direct materials consumed
	Activity productivity performance measurement	Increase number of outputs produced and decrease number of inputs consumed

Note: An initial customer survey should be conducted to determine customer needs, wants, and expectations. Ongoing customer surveys should be conducted and snake charts should be prepared to determine the enterprise's alignment with changing customer needs, wants, and expectations.

Customer satisfaction performance	On-time delivery performance measurement	100 percent on-time delivery if important to customers
	Complete order filling performance measurement	100 percent of orders completely filled if important to customers
	Sales growth performance measurement	Continuing sales growth
	Budgeted sales variance performance measurement	Positive budgeted sales variance

- Control charts
- Bar graphs
- Sectographs
- Picturegraphs

The following summary guidelines will help in selecting the proper graph for the data:

- If comparing correlative data, select a scattergraph.
- If a long series or several series of data are to be displayed over time, use a line graph.
- If variations in a process are to be presented, choose a control chart.
- If different items are to be compared during the same time frame, use a horizontal bar graph.
- If the same item is to be compared at different time periods, use a vertical bar graph.
- If parts of a whole are to be compared, prepare a pie chart.
- If the sizes of total amounts are to be compared over time, use a layer graph.
- If data are to be captured in the form of pictures or symbols, select a picturegraph.
- If using both numbers and graphs will help the user understand the performance measurement better, design the output to combine them in one presentation.

IMPORTANT TERMS

Activity-based management (ABM)   An ongoing process of understanding, reengineering, measuring, and making decisions about activities to put the enterprise on the road to continuous improvement and excellence.

Activity productivity performance measurement   Indicates how efficiently an activity is being performed.

Bar graphs   Blocklike graphs used to compare quantities.

Benchmarking   The process of comparing activities to world-class best practices.

Budgeted sales variance performance measurement   Compares budgeted sales with actual sales and indicates a variance in percentage terms.

Complete order filling performance measurement   Determines the percentage of the orders completely filled over some period of time.

Continuous improvement   The systematic and small incremental actions that enable an enterprise to achieve excellence.

Contribution margin velocity ratio performance measurement   Determines the amount of contribution margin a product generates per unit of production lead time.

Control chart   A graph that shows variation in an activity over time.

Customer satisfaction performance measurements   Determine how well the company is meeting needs, wants, and expectations of customers.

Customer survey   A questionnaire that helps determine the needs, wants, and expectations of customers.

Delivery lead time   Represents the time required by customers to receive the product or service.

Delivery production (D : P) ratio performance measurement   Compares delivery lead time to production lead time.

Direct materials yield performance measurement   Indicates how efficiently raw materials are being converted into finished products.

Graphs   Devices that present information in image form so it can be quickly comprehended. A diagram or chart displayed as a series of one or more points, lines, line segments, curves, or areas that represent one variable in comparison with one or more other variables.

Horizontal bar graph   A bar graph that compares different items during the same time frame.

Layer graph   A line graph in which the areas between the lines represent quantities, which add up to a total amount.

Lead time   The time between the beginning of a process or activity and the appearance of its results.

Lead time efficiency (LTE) ratio performance measurement   A key lead time performance measurement that indicates the level of value-added and nonvalue-added activities in a particular process or operation.

Line graphs   Graphs used to compare fluctuations in several items over time.

Machine uptime performance measurement   Determines the percentage of time the machine is ready for production when needed.

Nonvalue-added activities   Activities that represent waste. They can be reduced or eliminated without decreasing the enterprise's ability to compete and meet customer demands.

On-time delivery performance measurement   Determines if the finished product or service is being delivered at the time specified by the customer.

Performance measurements   Devices used to ascertain the effort expended or work done to execute or accomplish output of an activity.

Picturegraph   A graph made up of columns of pictures or symbols, each of which represents a certain quantity of the item illustrated.

Pie chart   A circle that has been segmented into portions, each of which represents a certain percentage of the whole.

Production lead time   The interval between the acquisition of raw materials and the first stage of production and the time that the finished products come off the production line.

Productivity performance measurements   Ascertain the amount of outputs produced by the inputs consumed.

Reengineering   The process of making substantial changes in how an enterprise currently operates. It involves the redesign of how work is done through activities.

Sales growth performance measurement   Calculates the percentage rate of growth from the last period to the current period.

Scattergraphs (scatterplots or scatter diagrams)   Plots of observations relative to the *x*- and *y*-axes.

Sectographs   Graphs that show how total amounts are divided. Two popular sectographs are pie charts and layer graphs.

Setup time   The amount of time needed to change production facilities for a different product or service.

Setup time performance measurement   Indicates how efficiently the production facilities are made ready to make another product or provide a service.

Snake chart   Shows variances between what customers (or others) deem important and what is currently being done.

Target   A numerical value set by management or customers. It is a goal or objective to meet or exceed that is often established during benchmarking.

Time-based performance measurements   Recognize time as the equivalent of money, productivity, quality, and resources.

Value-added activities   Actions or functions that contribute something worthwhile to the enterprise and its customers. They are essential to the enterprise's success.

Vendor certification program   A process that selects vendors on their ability to meet certain performance measurements. Certified vendors are the buying company's preferred vendors; they establish a long-term, trusting relationship with the buying company.

Vendor financial performance measurement   Discloses unnecessary costs caused by the vendor's nonconformance with specifications for quality and delivery schedules.

Vendor nonfinancial performance measurement   Weights the vendor on quality, price, on-time delivery, and general performance.

Vendor on-time delivery performance measurement   Discloses the vendor's ability to deliver raw materials just-in-time, not too early and not too late.

Vendor performance index (VPI)   Calculated by adding the cost of purchased raw materials to the cost of nonvalue-added activities and dividing the total by the cost of purchased raw materials. An index of one means the vendor has eliminated all nonvalue-added activities.

Vendor quality performance measurement   A measure that focuses on the vendor's ability to deliver raw materials of consistently high quality.

Vendor simplicity performance measurement   Calculates the number of vendors and number of purchase orders per product.

Vertical bar graph   A bar graph that measures the same item at different periods of time.

Work force productivity performance measurement   Indicates the cost per unit of product produced by the work force.

DEMONSTRATION PROBLEMS

■ DEMONSTRATION PROBLEM 1   *Linking performance measurements for over-all organizational performance.*

For constancy of purpose and strategic and goal congruency, performance measurements must be linked in a balanced and coordinated effort. Following are typical statements of goals that are congruent from the senior level to the plant floor:

- Chief executive officer: "We must provide value to our shareholders."
- Vice president of manufacturing: "To achieve success, we must satisfy our customers."
- Plant manager: "To be responsive to customers and flexible in meeting their needs, we must excel in certain activities."
- Plant supervisors and workers: "To be faster, stronger, and better, we must excel in certain activities."

Required:

Make a table with these statements of goals as the left-hand column. In the right-hand column, insert the performance measurements you believe will provide the appropriate feedback to enable the managers and workers at each level to achieve the goals. Also comment on how frequently each level should receive performance feedback.

SOLUTION TO DEMONSTRATION PROBLEM 1

GOALS	PERFORMANCE MEASUREMENTS
Chief executive officer: "We must provide value to our shareholders."	■ Net income ■ Sales and market share ■ Return on investment (ROI) ■ Return on assets (ROA) ■ Earnings per share
Vice president of manufacturing: "To achieve success, we must satisfy our customers."	■ On-time delivery ■ Sales growth ■ Budgeted sales variance
Plant manager: "To be responsive to customers and flexible in meeting their needs, we must excel in certain activities."	■ Lead time efficiency (LTE) ratio ■ Contribution margin velocity ratio ■ Complete order filling ■ Delivery production (D : P) ratio
Plant supervisors and workers: "To be faster, stronger, and better, we must excel in certain activities."	■ Work force productivity ■ Direct materials yield ■ Activity productivity ■ Setup time ■ Machine uptime

Although the performance measurements listed here are directed to organizational levels, in most companies, all levels have access to the performance measurement system. For example, the supervisors and workers on the plant floor can receive feedback on net income, on-time delivery, or lead time efficiency. Also, different managers, supervisors, or workers across levels are given equal access. For example, the vice president of marketing is given performance feedback on return on assets, on-time delivery, delivery production (D : P), and so forth.

Because the decisions made at the senior level are more strategic and long range, performance measurements are usually reported on a monthly or quarterly basis. At the tactical level (e.g., the plant manager), feedback may occur daily or weekly. At the plant-floor level where the activities are actually performed, the feedback is, in many instances, in real-time. Supervisors and workers use the performance measurement output to control or adjust tasks and activities as they are being carried out.

■ DEMONSTRATION PROBLEM 2   *The real costs of purchasing.*

"To achieve world-class status, we must build and maintain long-term partnerships with a small group of vendors that offer the best *overall* value," says Malcolm Ridgeway, management accountant at Evian Company.

"Nortec supplies us with circuit boards at $20 per board," says Melisa Alexander, purchasing agent. "That's cheaper than we can get them from other vendors."

"That's true," says Malcolm, "but I've been doing some analysis and I'm surprised to find that the price of raw materials represents only a fraction of the cost of doing business with vendors."

"How's that?" asks Melisa.

Required:

Despite the attraction of a low price, Nortec causes Evian to perform a number of nonvalue-added activities due to poor quality and vendor performance. Show how much it's really costing Evian to continue doing business with Nortec, assuming the total nonvalue-added costs are $96. Use any cost figure that you consider appropriate for each nonvalue-added activity caused by Nortec. Assume that Evian can purchase circuit boards from Bates Corporation for $80 per board. Bates's vendor performance index (VPI) is 1.1. Calculate Bates's total cost per board.

SOLUTION TO DEMONSTRATION PROBLEM 2

Purchase price per board		$20.00
Average nonvalue-added costs per board:		
■ Inspecting and testing	$14.00	
■ Paperwork	6.00	
■ Reworking	16.00	
■ Materials received too early	14.00	
■ Materials received too late	14.00	
■ Excess materials	12.00	
■ Short materials	12.00	
■ Warehousing and handling	8.00	
Total average nonvalue-added costs per board		$96.00

$$\text{Nortec's vendor performance index (VPI)} = \frac{\$20 + \$96}{\$20}$$

$$= \underline{5.8}$$

	Nortec	Bates
Purchase price per board	$ 20	$ 80
× VPI	5.8	1.1
Total cost per board	$116	$ 88

■ **DEMONSTRATION PROBLEM 3** *Using nonfinancial and financial performance measurements.*

Financial performance measurements used at the plant level may create barriers to achieving profitability and return on investment. For example, to achieve improved production efficiency, an organization might be tempted to manufacture excess inventories to avoid potential unfavorable production volume variances reported by traditional standard costing systems. To obtain lower raw materials cost and eliminate unfavorable purchase price variances, an organization may select vendors based only on price.

Required:

Name a nonfinancial performance measurement that would encourage management to produce only the amount of product that is needed and a financial performance measurement that would encourage management to select vendors based on overall performance.

SOLUTION TO DEMONSTRATION PROBLEM 3

The delivery production (D : P) ratio performance measurement encourages management to achieve a ratio of one or less. A ratio of one means that production is in balance with delivery, which means there is no buildup of excess inventories. The vendor performance index (VPI) evaluates vendors according to price plus costs of nonvalue-added activities that they cause. A ratio of one means that the vendor is in total conformance with the buying company's needs and therefore does not require any nonvalue-added activities to be performed.

REVIEW QUESTIONS

11.1 What are the two main purposes of activity-based costing?

11.2 Name the four phases involved in activity-based management and briefly describe how they work.

11.3 Why is the activity-based management process never considered complete?

11.4 Value-added activities are of two types. Describe these activities.

11.5 Explain the difference between value-added and nonvalue-added activities.

11.6 Describe five complexities that drive costs.

11.7 Describe what is meant by reengineering the enterprise. Give some examples.

11.8 Explain what benchmarking is and how it is accomplished. Name and discuss a common pitfall of benchmarking.

11.9 During benchmarking, what is the fundamental purpose of a site visit?

11.10 Explain why the original benchmark performance target is actually a moving target.

11.11 Name the four types of performance measurements. Discuss four of the seven rules you should follow when developing performance measurements. What benefits are gained through developing and using a performance measurement system?

11.12 Describe two typical traditional financial performance measurements. What are the primary drawbacks of using financial performance measurements?

11.13 Discuss how focusing on and improving nonfinancial performance measurements ultimately leads to improved financial performance.

11.14 How should performance measures change as you move down the organization chart? How are they linked? What checks do they provide?

11.15 Describe how a vendor certification program works and what costs a company can reduce by implementing such a program.

11.16 Name the four vendor nonfinancial performance measurements used in selecting certified vendors. What score must be achieved to become a certified vendor?

11.17 Time is manageable and a source of competitive advantage. Describe the negative impacts of taking longer to perform an activity. Describe the advantages to the firm of performing the same activity in a shorter time frame.

11.18 Reducing lead times increases speed. Name the four categories that speed falls into in world-class manufacturing.

11.19 Name four conditions that must exist to achieve production LTE ratios of one. Identify four positive results achieved by improving the production LTE ratio.

11.20 If a manufacturer wants to achieve a continuous flow and synchronized operation, what D : P ratio would be ideal and why?

11.21 What machine uptime percentage do world-class manufacturers demand and how do they achieve this percentage?

11.22 Name the three types of productivity performance measurements and briefly indicate what they measure.

11.23 Name two types of customer satisfaction performance measurements and briefly indicate what they measure.

11.24 Explain what is meant by the ABM idea that "We've got to satisfy each other before we can satisfy our ultimate customer."

11.25 When a snake chart is used to measure customer satisfaction, what will the two curves on the chart represent? What ultimate goal should be achieved?

11.26 Describe the benefits of using graphs to present performance data.

11.27 Name the various graph styles and state the purpose of each.

CHAPTER-SPECIFIC PROBLEMS

These problems require responses based directly on concepts and techniques presented in the text.

11.28 *Identifying value-added and nonvalue-added activities.* The following are some typical activities for a small tool manufacturer:

_____	Inspecting raw materials
_____	Storing raw materials
_____	Casting tool
_____	Stacking casting
_____	Grinding and polishing tool
_____	Inspecting finished tool
_____	Storing finished tool
_____	Shipping tool

Required:
Insert the type of activity [value-added or nonvalue-added] in the space next to each activity.

11.29 *Calculating vendor financial performance measurements.* Richie Company produces toy train sets for major department stores. Richie uses two vendors to supply the sectional track pieces for its packaged sets. Following are the historical nonvalue-added activities required by Richie for each vendor:

	LABOR HOURS PER STANDARD SHIPMENT SIZE	
	VENDOR A	**VENDOR B**
Inspection rejection	1.5	0.1
Paperwork rejection	5.0	0.5
Rework at company	15.5	1.0
Materials received early	3.0	1.0
Materials received late	20.0	8.0
Excess materials	8.5	1.0
Short materials	13.5	2.5

Required:
If the Richie labor hour cost is $45 for each of these activities, calculate the total nonvalue-added activity cost for each vendor. Then calculate the vendor performance index for each vendor, assuming the cost of purchased raw materials is $60,000 for each standard shipment size.

11.30 *Distinguishing between value-added and nonvalue-added activities.* Identify which of the following are value-added and nonvalue-added activities by placing an X under the appropriate column:

ACTIVITY	VALUE-ADDED	NONVALUE-ADDED
Review of invoices	_____	_____
Engineering parts	_____	_____
Cleanup of excess materials	_____	_____
Dealing with customer complaints	_____	_____
Product delivery	_____	_____
Materials movement	_____	_____
Materials assembly	_____	_____
Inspection of incoming product deliveries	_____	_____
Quality control by all employees	_____	_____
Quality control department	_____	_____
Purchase order preparation	_____	_____
Tracking machine setup time	_____	_____
Storage of raw materials	_____	_____
Using graphs to illustrate performance	_____	_____
Product rework	_____	_____

11.31 *Graphing sales information to show quarterly sales contribution by product.* Ted Andrews, purchasing director, has just handed you the following information and requested that you provide him with a graph of it for his presentation to the board of directors.

1994 SALES

	FIRST QUARTER	SECOND QUARTER	THIRD QUARTER	FOURTH QUARTER
CDs	$ 87,971	$ 98,589	$108,769	$ 73,175
Tapes (audio)	109,870	117,413	127,791	132,418
Tapes (video)	41,147	52,149	57,129	50,111

Required:
Graph the sales information and explain why you selected that particular graph.

11.32 *Graphing information using a control chart.* Bill, the bottling supervisor, tells you that he believes the new bottling line is underfilling the bottles and that he is concerned about the possibility of fines. You ask Bill what makes him believe that the bottles are being underfilled. He replies, "It's just a gut feeling." You tell him to go with his gut feeling; however, you also ask him to provide you with sample data before and after the increase, to confirm that the increase was necessary. The company is producing 12-ounce bottles of liquid soap and has set the minimum and maximum acceptable fill levels at 12.5 and 13.0 ounces, respectively.

TIME	SAMPLE NUMBER	NET WEIGHT (OUNCES)	
1:01	1	12.50	
1:03	2	11.95	
1:05	3	12.15	
1:07	4	12.27	
1:09	5	11.90	←Before
1:11	6	12.50	←After
1:13	7	12.70	
1:15	8	12.95	
1:17	9	12.50	
1:19	10	13.05	
1:21	11	12.75	
1:23	12	12.80	
1:25	13	12.50	
1:27	14	12.45	
1:29	15	13.00	

Required:
Make a control chart and establish whether increasing the fill was indeed necessary.

11.33 *Preparing a performance measurement graph.* The following performance information was obtained during a six-month period for a critical machine in a factory:

MONTH	HOURS OF MACHINE DOWNTIME	HOURS MACHINE NEEDED
April	15.5	105.0
May	12.0	120.0
June	8.0	110.5
July	6.5	105.0
August	9.5	110.0
September	5.0	120.0

Required:
Calculate and graph the machine uptime performance measurement. Discuss what the graph shows. Make any assumptions necessary.

11.34 *Graphing cost of energy use information using various types of graphs.* You are trying to impress upon management the importance of purchasing more energy-efficient vehicles as older models are retired. Senior management does not believe that gasoline fuel costs are that significant. They plan to spend the "fuel efficiency" budget on new heating equipment. Jane Kirkland, CEO, however, requests that you present your findings to her by September 20. You receive the following summary of fuel expenditures:

19X5 ENERGY COSTS

Electricity	$1,579,732
Natural gas	2,510,818
Gasoline	4,372,951
Propane	500,141
Coal	1,150,021

Required:
Graph the above information using the following formats:

a. Pie chart.
b. Dual (pie and bar) chart.
c. Bar chart.
d. Line chart.

11.35 Calculating the vendor performance index. The delivery performances of companies A, B, and C are as follows:

NONVALUE-ADDED ACTIVITY	LABOR HOURS PER OCCURRENCE		
	COMPANY A	COMPANY B	COMPANY C
Inspection rejection	1.3	0.5	0.9
Paperwork rejection	0.2	0.1	0.3
Rework at company	0.2	1.4	1.1
Materials received early	7.0	2.0	3.0
Materials received late	2.8	5.6	1.4
Excess materials	4.0	0.2	0.6
Short materials	0.5	3.7	0.6
Total	16.0	13.5	7.9
Cost of raw materials delivered	$14,000	$12,000	$16,400

Required:
a. Calculate the VPI for each company using a cost of $50 per labor hour.
b. Determine which of the companies should be eliminated as vendors based on the calculated VPI.

11.36 Calculating the vendor quality performance measurement. Infinity Company has gathered the following delivery data for one of its vendors. Infinity wishes to determine if its vendor was able to consistently remain within its target vendor quality performance acceptance percentage of 97%.

	NUMBER OF PARTS	
SHIPMENT	ORDERED/DELIVERED	REJECTED
1	1,200	23
2	800	12
3	1,500	30
4	1,300	34
5	900	32

Required:
a. Calculate the acceptance percentage for each shipment.
b. What trend is indicated?

11.37 Calculating the complete order filling performance measurement. The Triad Company is evaluating how effective its vendors are at completely filling orders when they are placed. The company currently has three vendors that supply part #621357928. Their order filling performances, for the past year follow:

	VENDOR 1	VENDOR 2	VENDOR 3
Number of orders	34	51	86
Number of orders filled completely	29	43	75
Number of backorders	5	8	11

Required:
a. Calculate the complete order filling percentage for each vendor.
a. Determine which vendor has the highest percentage of orders filled completely.

11.38 *Determine what performance measurements to use.* Management just assigned you to report on customer satisfaction and provided the following data:

Total number of deliveries	582
Number of on-time deliveries	513
Number of vendor complaints	5
Number of complete deliveries	504
Number of customer complaints	17

Required:
Select and apply two performance measurements that are applicable to this problem.

11.39 *Calculating the production lead time efficiency (LTE) ratio.* The Rithe Company has compiled the following data on the total time required to produce and store its product:

Production line 1	30 minutes
Production line 2	50 minutes
Quality control inspection	25 minutes
Product movement to storage location	60 minutes
Storing the product in inventory	45 minutes

Required:
a. Determine which of the company's activities are value-added and which are nonvalue-added.
b. Calculate the company's production lead time efficiency ratio.
c. Would the calculated ratio be acceptable in a world-class manufacturing environment? Explain your answer.

11.40 *Calculating the contribution margin velocity ratio.* The Jester Company is analyzing its product mix to determine which of its three products is the most profitable. It has compiled the following data on each of its products:

PRODUCT	ANNUAL SALES	VARIABLE COSTS	FIXED COSTS	PRODUCTION LEAD TIME (DAYS)
A	$ 63,856	$12,776	$31,117	7
B	81,937	28,665	40,923	4
C	120,542	50,125	65,718	6

Required:
Calculate the contribution margin velocity ratio to determine which product produces the highest profits.

11.41 *Calculating the most profitable product.* Karob Kandies produces two kinds of candies: Critter Crunchers and Darb's Drops. Karob Kandies collected the following data on both products:

	CONTRIBUTION MARGIN	PRODUCTION LEAD TIME
Critter Crunchers	$1.50	5.0 minutes
Darb's Drops	1.00	2.5 minutes

Required:
Identify which product is more profitable to produce.

11.42 *Calculating the setup time performance measurement.* Prior to beginning production on each of its seven products, the Robotron Company experiences some downtime in setting up its production line. Over a week's period, the following data were collected:

PRODUCT	NUMBER OF SETUPS	SETUP TIME (MINUTES)	PRODUCTION TIME (MINUTES)
1	5	50	100
2	7	105	210
3	9	108	225
4	12	120	360
5	8	144	320
6	4	80	180
7	6	78	150

Required:
a. Calculate the setup time ratio for each of the products.
b. Identify which product(s) provide(s) the shorter setup time.
c. In general, what benefits are provided by shorter setup times?

11.43 *Graphing a snake chart.* The Eatery Stop has just finished compiling the results of its two-week-long customer satisfaction survey for its new upscale dinner menu items. Its customers provided the following ratings on a scale of 1 to 10, 10 being the best:

	IMPORTANCE TO CUSTOMER	CATEGORY RATING
Quick service	8	6
Accurate service	10	4
Friendly service	8	9
Server knowledge	5	7
Dinners were served hot	7	7
Dinners were tasty	9	6
Dinners were attractive	3	7
Dinners were priced right	8	6

Required:
a. Graph the survey results using a snake chart.
b. Given the differences between the expected service and the delivered service, what are the key areas that the company should focus on to achieve total customer satisfaction?

THINK-TANK PROBLEMS

Although these problems are based on chapter material, reading extra material, reviewing previous chapters, and using creativity may be required to develop workable solutions.

11.44 *Determining value-added and nonvalue-added activities.* In your present or past position, list ten value-added and ten nonvalue-added activities that were a part of your job responsibilities.

11.45 *Reengineering activities.* Cook & Cook Books has a primary operation of receiving and warehousing books from publishers and packing and shipping book requests from bookstores, schools, and libraries. For library requests, a security strip has to be glued into the binding, a due-date card sleeve attached inside, and a clear plastic cover applied to each book prior to shipping. Based on the advice of various business consultants over the years, Cook & Cook has dedicated full-time workers to this process and maintains a storehouse stock of books ready for library shipments. A certain percentage of each new book from each vendor is sent through this library process. Although the per book costs of the library process have decreased significantly, management is increasingly concerned over rising storage costs and the unresponsiveness of the process to library customer demands, among other things.

Required:
As a world-class manufacturing consultant, you are called in to evaluate the library book process. Make any assumptions you deem necessary.
a. Draw an activity flow diagram for the library book process as it is described above.
b. Reengineer the process to world-class standards.
c. Discuss the performance measurements you might use for your reengineered process.
d. What concerns could management have with the existing process? How does your reengineered process address these concerns?

11.46 *Determining manufacturing complexities.* ElectroKing, a large manufacturer of home electric appliances, has been in business for more than 50 years. Although it started by making only electric toasters, ElectroKing now produces over 30 different product classes from microwave ovens to blenders and can openers. Out of respect for its loyal repeat customers, ElectroKing corporate philosophy has been to never discontinue any product. As each new product was introduced over the years, it was considered a new and separate entity; thus, an entire new suite of vendors, parts, and assembly lines were used. To combat the increasing competition from overseas manufacturers, ElectroKing has increased the customization (i.e., options) available for each product, while trying to maintain a constant price.

Required:
List the complexities of this operation that are driving costs. Describe an action management might take to reduce each. Make any assumptions necessary.

11.47 *Calculating the machine uptime percentage.* The foreman over the production line at the Production Time Company has noticed that a certain machine has been experiencing an inordinate amount of downtime. Upon further observation, the foreman noted the machine is not always in working condition when needed and also usually breaks down at least once during production. The foreman has gathered the following data on the machine's performance over a one-week period:

DAY	NUMBER OF HOURS SCHEDULED FOR PRODUCTION	NUMBER OF HOURS MACHINE IS NEEDED FOR PRODUCTION	NUMBER OF HOURS MACHINE WAS NOT READY FOR PRODUCTION
Sun	16	9.50	0.25
Mon	24	16.25	2.75
Tue	24	12.50	1.50
Wed	24	14.00	2.00
Thu	24	13.75	3.75
Fri	24	19.25	2.50
Sat	16	10.75	0.75

Required:
a. Calculate the machine uptime percentage.
b. Would this percentage be acceptable to a world-class manufacturer?
c. According to a benchmarking study of comparable machines, the industry's best uptime for this type of machine ranges from 95 to 98 percent when needed in production. Describe what alternative courses of action the foreman should consider to bring the machine's performance more in line with the industry's best?

11.48 *Determining causes of customer service performance measurements.* Warren Wendellson, sales director of Ardco, Inc., is to present this quarter's sales results to senior management in one hour. He has just received this quarter's customer service performance measurement results from the accounting office, which are as follows:

- Sales growth performance measurement = 8% growth over the previous quarter.
- Budgeted sales variance performance measurement = −3% budgeted sales variance.

Wendellson will be in big trouble if he cannot explain the causes for the variations.

Required:
a. List ten possible causes of the sales increase and the variance between actual and budgeted sales.
b. List ten additional pieces of information that could be of value to Wendellson.

11.49 *Customer satisfaction performance measurement.* As a recently hired management accountant for SlimCo, a large manufacturer of random access memory (RAM) boards supplied to PC clone manufacturers, you have been given the task of evaluating customer satisfaction with SlimCo's performance in relation to how the company can achieve world-class manufacturing (WCM) status. Your search of previous work turned up just informal feelings from the sales staff about how well SlimCo does.

Required:
Design a customer performance measurement program that can assist SlimCo's progress toward achieving WCM status. As part of the program, determine which performance measurements would be useful, explain how they would relate to WCM customer service factors, and design the customer survey form.

12

COST MANAGEMENT THROUGH A TOTAL QUALITY MANAGEMENT SYSTEM

Total quality management is necessary for computer chip manufacturers.

LEARNING OBJECTIVES

After studying this chapter, you should be able to:

1. Discuss total quality management (TQM).

2. Define costs of quality and explain their relationship and trade-offs. In addition, differentiate the costs-of-quality minimization approach from the zero-defects approach.

3. Describe Pareto charts and cause-and-effect diagrams, and discuss how they are used in solving quality problems.

4. Define control charts, and explain how they are used in a TQM system to control processes and activities.

■ INTRODUCTION

With an activity-based management (ABM) system, as described in the previous chapter, many of the nonvalue-added activities have been eliminated. This situation provides a solid foundation on which total quality management (TQM) can thrive. As enterprises strive to become world-class producers of products and services, management accountants need to expand their roles by becoming involved in measuring and evaluating the quality of products and services and the activities that produce them.

Increasingly, battles for competitive superiority and profitability are being won by achieving superior quality. Whether from manufacturing or service organizations, customers demand high-quality products and services. These organizations already have or are installing TQM systems, which focus on designing and building quality in rather than trying to inspect and rework it in. With this new way of managing quality, organizations are discovering positive results. Rather than costs increasing as quality is improved, they actually decrease and other problems are also solved or diminished.

By discussing the meaning and measurement of quality and costs of quality, reporting costs of quality, and presenting problem-solving and process control tools, this chapter provides a guide to initiating and maintaining a TQM system, whether in manufacturing enterprises or service firms. ■

▌TOTAL QUALITY MANAGEMENT

Total quality management (TQM) is an integrated system that anticipates, meets, and exceeds customers' needs, wants, and expectations. Some authorities say that TQM is a never-ending journey and a race without a finish line.

The dimensions of TQM are depicted in Exhibit 12–1. Notice that quality and continuous improvement are increasing while costs of quality and lead times are decreasing. Notice also that the central thrust of a TQM system is total commitment throughout the enterprise and its stakeholders (e.g., vendors and distributors).

Quality and total commitment are discussed in the following subsections. Costs of quality will then be examined in a subsequent major section. Throughput, also called cycle time and lead time, will be discussed in Chapter 15. Continuous improvement has been and will continue to be emphasized throughout this book.

■ EXHIBIT 12–1
Dimensions of TQM

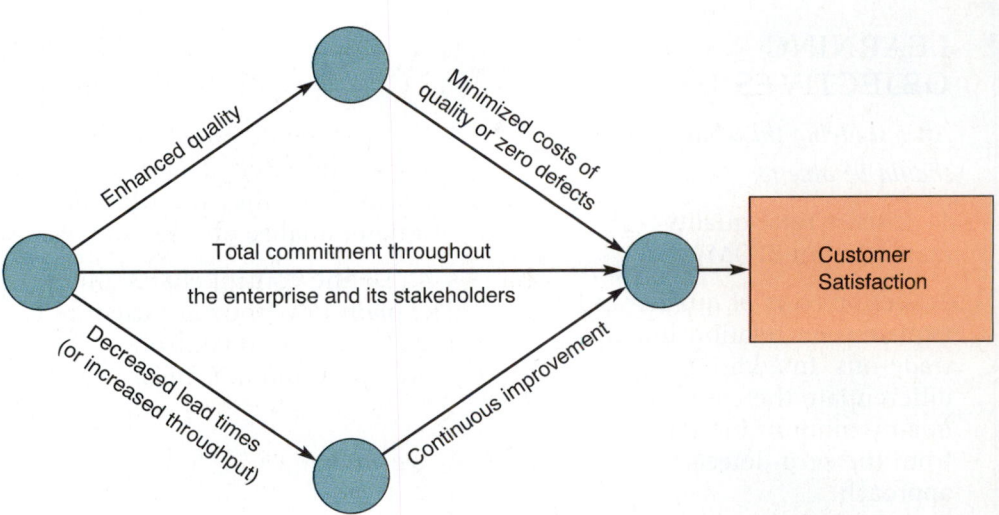

INSIGHTS & APPLICATIONS

Be Sure You Know What Customer Satisfaction Is

Quality is defined by the customer. A technically perfect product or a particular service that does not meet customer expectations will fail, regardless of its "quality," as perceived by workers and managers. The challenge to any company is to determine what customers want and whether they are satisfied with the company, its people, its products, and its services. Otherwise, a well-intentioned TQM system will fail. Obtaining customer feedback is therefore the key to determining customer expectations and setting the foundation for a successful TQM system.

An insurance company thought its customers wanted to see their checks from claims *sooner*. Not so, it turned out. What customers wanted more than reduced cycle time was assurance of the date they would see their money. That little piece of information resulted in big savings. It would have been very expensive to reduce the cycle time for payments of claims, and the company would have been investing in something that was not of great value to its customers.[1]

What Is Quality?

A wide array of definitions of quality are available. Philip B. Crosby, a quality expert, asserts that quality is "conformance to requirements." Another expert in the field, J. M. Juran, defines quality as "fitness for use." Armand V. Feigenbaum, a quality pioneer, states that quality is "what the customer says it is." The International Organization for Standardization (ISO) offers the following: "Quality is the total features and characteristics of a product or service that provide its ability to satisfy stated or implied needs."

Although all these definitions are acceptable, this book will use the following definition: **Quality** is customer satisfaction in which both **internal customers** (people within the enterprise) and **external customers** (ultimate consumers) are considered. Indeed, the goal of TQM is *customer satisfaction.*

Although there is no unambiguous, comprehensive definition of quality that will satisfy everyone, many of its basic attributes are commonly accepted. These attributes include the following:

- Form
- Fit
- Performance
- Features
- Reliability
- Conformance
- Durability
- Serviceability
- Aesthetics
- Consistency

Checking quality at Adolph Coors Company.

Exhibit 12–2 compares the views of traditional management and world-class management on quality. One of the striking differences related to cost management is that quality can be improved while decreasing costs! Traditional wisdom was that improving quality would increase costs. In fact, some people contend that TQM should be called *total cost management*, because substantial cost savings are possible by improving quality.

The emphasis of TQM is to *design* and *build* quality in rather than trying to *inspect* and *repair* quality in. Emphasizing the designing and building in of quality focuses on the *causes* of superior quality. Devoting efforts to inspecting and repairing activities focuses incorrectly on fixing the "symptoms" instead of the "causes" of poor quality. Companies are moving away from the traditional

[1] Adapted from Nancy A. Karabatsos, "The State of Quality: What the Numbers Say," *Training* March 1991, p. 39. Reprinted with permission from the March 1991 issue of TRAINING magazine, Lakewood Publications, Minneapolis, MN. All rights reserved.

■EXHIBIT 12–2
Differing Views on Quality

Traditional Management View	World-Class Management View
■ Improving quality drives up time and costs. ■ Defects and failures of less than 10% are acceptable (95% good units is great). ■ Quality should be inspected and reworked in. ■ Quantity of output is as important as quality.	■ Improving quality reduces time and costs. ■ The goal is zero defects and failures (only 99.9997 to 100% good units will do). ■ Quality should be designed and built in. ■ Without quality, quantity is irrelevant.

■EXHIBIT 12–3
Differences between Products and Services

Products	Services
■ The customer owns an object. ■ The goal of producing products is to reduce variability and make products uniform. ■ A product can be placed in inventory; a sample can be sent in advance for the customer to review. ■ If improperly produced, the product can be pulled off the line or recalled.	■ The customer owns a memory. The experience cannot be sold or passed on to a third party. ■ The goal of service is uniqueness; each customer and each contact are "special." ■ A service happens in a moment. It cannot be stockpiled. ■ If a service is improperly performed, apologies and reparations are the only means of recourse.

Inspecting stamped panels at Honda of America Manufacturing, Inc.

Vehicle quality department testing at Honda of America Manufacturing, Inc.

"inspect-it-in" and even "fix-it-in" approaches to quality toward a newer and broader-based "create-it-in" or "design-it-in" approach.[2]

TQM is typically associated with manufacturing, but quality applies to services as well as to products, although in somewhat different ways. Exhibit 12–3 lists some of the more critical differences.[3]

Many service companies, such as Federal Express and a host of other enterprises, are also employing TQM. Although the quality of service received in hotels, restaurants, and hospitals can be a matter of subjective judgment, it can be monitored and improved. Hotel guests, for example, can be asked if the service met their expectations. A service organization should have a procedure in place to record and deal with customer complaints. It should also hold regular quality review meetings to enable management to discuss and improve the methods of delivering service in order to correct problem areas.

What Is Total Commitment?

Total commitment is the mobilization of *all* managers and the empowerment of workers and stakeholders to engage themselves into linked value-added activities for the purpose of achieving the greatest customer satisfaction at the lowest cost. Quality is everyone's business, and each person is called on to seek perfection. Quality must, indeed, become a way of life.

[2] Tracy E. Benson, "Industry Treats Root Causes," *Industry Week*, June 1, 1992, p. 28.
[3] Ron Zemke, "The Emerging Art of Service Management," *Training*, January 1992, p. 38.

INSIGHTS & APPLICATIONS

Making Organizations Lean and Mean

If you see a successful runner, you will notice that he or she has no excess fat. Top-flight runners are lean. So, if you want to be a top-flight runner, do you simply go on a crash diet? If you believe that, then you will believe that your company can become a tough competitor by laying off people.

If your competitor can assemble an automobile with 28 hours of labor while you require 40, can you become competitive by laying off 30 percent of the people? It comes from making the right products and from delivering the right services. The important key to these three areas is quality . . . total quality . . . quality in everything you do. Total quality provides the lean route to competitiveness.[4]

Andon (the visual factory) and the five S's, discussed in Chapter 2, can serve as the bedrock for total commitment to quality and the way of life. The five S's can be summarized as follows:

- *Seiri.* Organization and sorting out unneeded items
- *Seiton.* Orderliness and arranging efficiently
- *Shitsuke.* Discipline
- *Seiso.* Cleanliness
- *Seiketsu.* Standardization

If *everyone* in an organization practices *andon* and the five S's, the result can be a new outlook throughout the organization and the elimination of defects in products and services and the activities that produce them. Such an approach produces lasting benefits by exposing numerous flaws that contribute to defects and failures.

Seiso, for example, is not just cleaning. It fosters *cooperation* among people to do a simple task such as housekeeping. *Seiso* also uses cleaning to discover and expose the malfunctions, abnormalities, and minor flaws that warn of impending failures and defects. People therefore come to realize the importance of precautionary, preventive action.[5]

TQM is an integrating force, because it involves *everyone* at all levels of the enterprise and links their activities. But TQM doesn't stop there. It also creates a tight linkage with vendors and external customers. This totally integrated system of quality, from inputs through production to outputs, is the essence of TQM and thus requires total commitment.

Some authorities estimate that more than 40 percent of downstream problems are caused by poor design. Hence, design should be linked with production. Since quality of raw materials can impact the quality of the product, companies should work very closely with their vendors to ensure that only high-quality materials enter production. The production process also lends itself to the improvement of quality. Rearranging the physical layout of the shop floor so that it uses U-shaped production cells and the management techniques covered in Chapter 2 is conducive to high-quality products.

Customer satisfaction requires more than individual effort. It requires teams of people empowered to achieve customer satisfaction. It takes consistent and strong commitment from top management to implement TQM. It also takes customized training and a commitment to ensure that what is learned is transferred to the workplace.

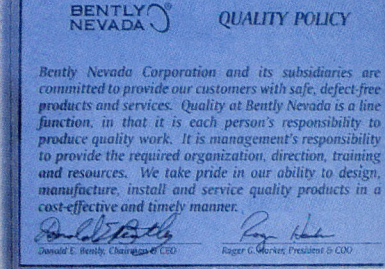

Total commitment to quality at Bently Nevada Corporation.

---

[4] Myron Tribus, ''Lean on Quality,'' *National Productivity Review,* Spring 1992, p. 277. Reprinted with permission from NATIONAL PRODUCTIVITY REVIEW, V11N2, Spring 1992, Copyright 1992 by Executive Enterprises, Inc., 22 West 21st Street, New York, NY 10010-6990. 212-645-7880. ALL RIGHTS RESERVED.

[5] Seiji Tsuchiya, *Quality Maintenance: Zero Defects through Equipment Management* (Cambridge, Mass.: Productivity Press, 1991), pp. 34–36. With permission.

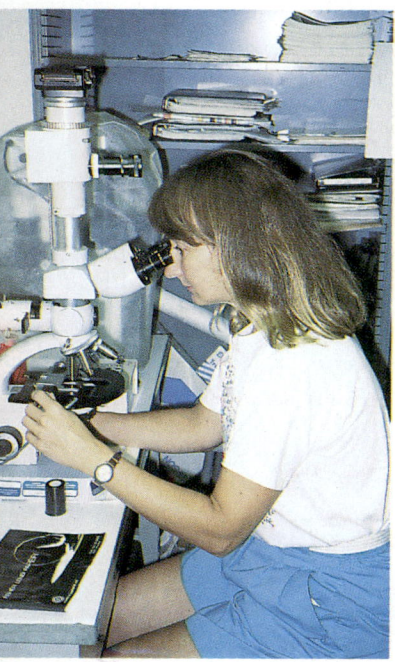

Quality is a never-ending process.

ISO 9000 Compliance and Certification

ISO 9000 is a series of five international quality standards developed by the International Organization for Standardization (ISO) in Geneva, Switzerland. The five standards are as follows:

- The ISO 9000 standard provides some basic definitions and serves as a guide to using the other standards in the series.
- The ISO 9001 standard ensures conformance to requirements during design and development, production, installation, and servicing of products. Enterprises covered under this standard are engineering, construction, and manufacturing companies.
- The ISO 9002 standard specifies a model for quality assurance when only production and installation conformance is required. This standard is particularly relevant to process industries where specific requirements for products are stated in terms of an established design or specification. Chemicals, food, and pharmaceutical companies generally seek certification under this standard.
- The ISO 9003 standard requires only conformance in final inspection and testing. This standard concerns small shops, equipment distributors that inspect and test the products they supply, and divisions within an organization such as laboratories.
- The ISO 9004 standard contains guidance on technical, administrative, and human factors affecting the quality of products and services. This standard provides for developing and implementing a TQM system.[6]

Companies not meeting these mandatory standards may be forced to submit their activities to audits and their products for expensive testing, or more importantly, they may be forbidden to sell them in European and other countries. As is the case with quality in general, ISO 9000 certification is an ongoing process. Once the initial certification is achieved, companies must submit to surveillance or maintenance audit visits twice a year to ensure that there is no degradation of the TQM system.

Many believe that ISO standards are relevant only to companies that export, yet a number of companies that do business only in the United States are seeking ISO certification. They find this beneficial for several reasons. For one thing, a buying company that is ISO-certified will expect its vendors and distributors also to be ISO-certified. A number of American companies, such as AT&T and DuPont, are requiring their suppliers to include ISO compliance in their contracts.[7] Furthermore, when a supplier is ISO-certified, buyers will not feel the need to audit. As a result, both the buying and the selling companies will save time and money. Finally, given the unrelenting drive toward TQM and increasing competition, organizations that embrace ISO standards see them as a better way to manage costs and run a business.

ISO can be summed up in four simple steps:

- Document what you do.
- Do what you said you would do.
- Control nonconformance.
- Control variability.[8]

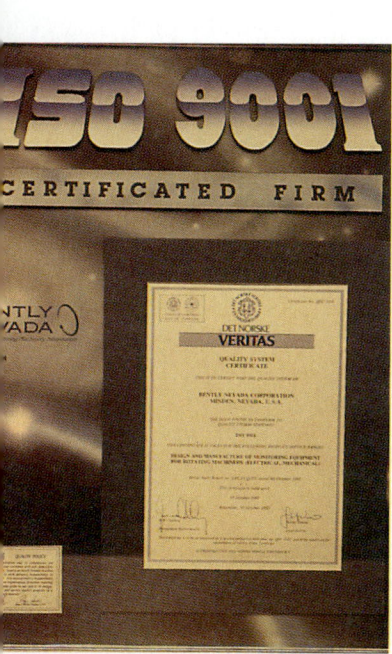

ISO certification at Bently Nevada Corporation.

---

[6] John D. Flister and Joseph J. Jozaitis, "PPG's Journey to ISO 9000," *Management Accounting*, July 1992, pp. 33–34. Reprinted from *Management Accounting*. Copyright by Institute of Management Accountants, Montvale, N.J.

[7] A. Faye Borthick and Harold P. Roth, "Will Europeans Buy Your Company's Products?" *Management Accounting*, July 1992, p. 28. Reprinted from *Management Accounting*. Copyright by Institute of Management Accountants, Montvale, N.J.

[8] Flister and Jozaitis, op. cit., p. 33.

INSIGHTS & APPLICATIONS

IBM's AS/400 Unit Gains ISO 9000 Approval

There is little question that quality and continuous improvement are strategies that are here to stay. Many companies worldwide are using ISO standards as the basis for a companywide TQM system and continuous improvement program. ISO 9000 establishes minimum quality management guidelines against which companies are measured in order to compete for contracts under ISO 9000.

The IBM AS/400 development and manufacturing unit has been recognized by the International Organization for Standardization (ISO) for meeting the ISO 9000 standards for quality. IBM expects the certification to help the firm gain contracts with worldwide government agencies.

TQM systems help companies expand market share. As worldwide competition heats up, ISO 9000 certification will be required for not only marketing products and services internationally, but locally as well.

ISO certification has become a symbol of companies around the world that provide superior quality.

THE COSTS OF QUALITY

Costs of quality consist of prevention, appraisal, internal failure, and external failure costs. Some authorities view prevention as a ''good'' cost and the others as ''bad'' costs. The objective is to minimize and eliminate the ''bad'' costs of quality and manage the ''good'' costs to an appropriate level.[9]

Costs of quality can be substantial. But, in most companies, they are buried in cost of goods manufactured and sold, salaries, travel expenses, insurance, technical services, and so forth. They remain unknown and therefore unmanaged. For many enterprises, one of the greatest opportunities for effective cost management and profit improvement lies in managing costs of quality. The conventional method for reporting, evaluating, and managing costs of quality is to identify all costs of quality under the four major categories mentioned before:

- Prevention costs
- Appraisal costs
- Internal failure costs
- External failure costs

> **LEARNING OBJECTIVE 2**
>
> Define costs of quality and explain their relationship and trade-offs. In addition, differentiate the costs-of-quality minimization approach from the zero-defects approach.

Prevention Costs

Prevention costs are those costs incurred to prevent poor-quality products or services from being produced in the first place. These costs are for the following:

- Doing the job right the first time, every time, through reengineering and continuous improvement efforts
- Improving quality of raw materials through technical support provided by vendors
- Improving knowledge and skills of managers and workers through customized training programs

When quality of design, quality of raw materials, and quality of the production process increase, so do product quality and productivity.

---

[9] Stephen M. Hronec and Steven K. Hunt, ''Quality and Cost Management,'' in *Handbook of Cost Management*, ed. Barry J. Brinker (Boston: Warren Gorham Lamont, 1992), p. A1-25. With permission.

INSIGHTS & APPLICATIONS

Being Penny-Wise and Pound-Foolish

Quality will always cost, but the return on an expenditure for quality always exceeds the money and effort that is expended. Prevention costs are usually the smallest cost that produces the largest returns. The purpose of prevention costs is to improve quality by preventing defects from occurring. Expenditures in this category ensure that "things are done right the first time, every time."

Jerry Tubbs, line manager of Electrograph Products board-dipping operation determines that his equipment is out of specification and will likely be turning out sub-par quality circuit boards. He requests permission from Lesli Reynolds, department manager, to shut down the operation for one day to make some repairs and reset equipment. Permission is denied.

Two weeks later, piles of defective circuit boards line the aisles in the downline departments. Bottlenecks appear throughout the plant as boards are reworked.

Minimizing costs in the board-dipping operation did not minimize costs overall. In fact, it caused costs to rise sharply.[10]

Quality through prevention can be achieved at low cost. All other costs of quality are corrective, the most expensive means of achieving quality. Some would say that correction never achieves quality anyway, it only reworks something that should have never occurred.

Appraisal Costs

Appraisal costs are incurred to identify nonconformities before a product or service reaches another activity and is delivered to the ultimate customer. Appraisal costs include the following:

- Inspection and testing of incoming materials as well as work-in-process
- Supervision
- Quality audits

Inspection is a dominant activity that drives up appraisal costs. The effectiveness of inspection can be measured as follows:

$$\text{Inspection} = \frac{\text{Amount of spoilage or number of defects at inspection}}{\text{Number of units completed in the process}}$$

The desirable result of this performance measurement is a decreasing ratio, as indicated in the following computations:

Period 1:

$$\text{Inspection} = \frac{100 \text{ defective units}}{1,000 \text{ units produced}}$$
$$= \underline{10\% \text{ defects}}$$

Period 2:

$$\text{Inspection} = \frac{50 \text{ defective units}}{1,000 \text{ units produced}}$$
$$= \underline{5\% \text{ defects}}$$

Instead of trying to arrive at the ideal combination of inputs, most organiza-

---

[10] Alfred J. Nanni, Jeffrey G. Miller, and Thomas E. Vollmann, "What Shall We Account For?" *Management Accounting*, January 1988, p. 42. Reprinted from *Management Accounting*. Copyright by Institute of Management Accountants, Montvale, N.J.

tions focus on the completed product by inspecting the problem out. Discovering defects or errors after the job has been done is typical. Inspection keeps most problems away from customers, but it does little to keep costs down or improve the activities that created the defects or errors in the first place. Inspecting problems out takes time and money; it also fails to get to the source of the problem.

Before jumping to the conclusion that all inspection is necessarily bad, one must differentiate between final inspection and process inspection. **Final inspection** is performed to remove unacceptable products or services before they are delivered to the external customer. **Process inspection** is conducted to monitor a process or activity to ensure that it does not produce unacceptable products or services. Process inspection is more preventive because it identifies problems in the process or activity before they get out of control. This identification is achieved by using control charts, which are discussed in detail later in this chapter.

No two products are exactly alike in shape, finish, or dimension. They may seem identical by almost every test, but they are nevertheless different in some respect, causing variability. This variability is monitored by inspecting sample products from the process. As long as the quality attributes being measured are within certain control limits, the process is said to be in control and producing acceptable products. If the monitoring begins to show an out-of-control condition, corrective action is taken immediately to prevent the process from producing a large number of defective products. If process inspection is effective, there should be no need for final inspection.

Internal Failure Costs

Internal failure costs are those costs incurred when products or services fail to meet quality standards, and the defects are identified *after* the products or services are produced but corrected *before* they are delivered to the external customer. Armand V. Feigenbaum says that many companies have a "hidden plant," which is a work force equal to as much as 40 percent of capacity that exists simply to undo mistakes. These internal failure costs entail:

- Rework
- Scrap
- Repair
- Downtime
- Retesting

One performance measurement that helps measure the effectiveness of controlling internal failure costs is calculated as follows:

$$\text{Internal failure causing rework} = \frac{\text{Number of reworked units}}{\text{Number of finished units}}$$

The desirable result of this performance measurement is a decreasing ratio, as shown in the following computations:

Period 1:

$$\text{Internal failure causing rework} = \frac{900 \text{ units reworked}}{3,000 \text{ finished units}}$$
$$= \underline{\underline{30\% \text{ rework}}}$$

Period 2:

$$\text{Internal failure causing rework} = \frac{600 \text{ units reworked}}{3,000 \text{ finished units}}$$
$$= \underline{\underline{20\% \text{ rework}}}$$

▍External Failure Costs

External failure costs are those costs incurred because poor-quality products or services are delivered to external customers. Nonconformities are identified *after* the product or service reaches the ultimate customer. External failure costs are associated with the following:

- Sales returns and allowances
- Recalls
- Warranty repairs
- Replacements
- Product liability insurance
- Handling customer complaints
- Lost sales
- Lost customers

Three performance measurements that help measure the impact of external failure costs are as follows:

$$\text{Sales returns and allowances} = \frac{\text{Dollar value of products returned}}{\text{Total sales dollars}}$$

$$\text{Warranty repairs} = \frac{\text{Cost of warranty repairs}}{\text{Total sales dollars}}$$

$$\text{Replacements} = \frac{\text{Number of replacements}}{\text{Number of units in the field}}$$

The desirable result of these performance measurements is a decreasing ratio, as shown in the following computations:

Period 1:
$$\text{Sales returns and allowances} = \frac{\$10,000 \text{ in sales returns and allowances}}{\$100,000 \text{ sales}}$$
$$= \underline{\underline{10\% \text{ returned}}}$$

Period 2:
$$\text{Sales returns and allowances} = \frac{\$6,000 \text{ in sales returns and allowances}}{\$120,000 \text{ sales}}$$
$$= \underline{\underline{5\% \text{ returned}}}$$

Period 1:
$$\text{Warranty repairs} = \frac{\$5,000 \text{ in warranty repairs}}{\$100,000 \text{ sales}}$$
$$= \underline{\underline{5\% \text{ warranty repairs}}}$$

Period 2:
$$\text{Warranty repairs} = \frac{\$2,400 \text{ in warranty repairs}}{\$120,000 \text{ sales}}$$
$$= \underline{\underline{2\% \text{ warranty repairs}}}$$

Period 1:
$$\text{Replacements} = \frac{400 \text{ replacements}}{4,000 \text{ units in the field}}$$
$$= \underline{\underline{10\% \text{ replacements}}}$$

Period 2:

$$\text{Replacements} = \frac{250 \text{ replacements}}{5,000 \text{ units in the field}}$$
$$= \underline{\underline{5\% \text{ replacements}}}$$

▌ Summary Analysis of Costs of Quality

Prevention and appraisal costs are *voluntary*; that is, these costs *do not* have to be incurred. Internal failure and external failure costs are *involuntary,* because they are costs that the company is forced to pay. The only way to decrease, if not eliminate, these failure costs is by increasing prevention and appraisal costs. TQM is prevention-based. Advocates of TQM try to eliminate not only failure costs but also appraisal costs (usually not process inspection costs).

Prevention and appraisal costs are sometimes called costs of *conformance* (i.e., adherence to quality standards). **Costs of conformance** include all costs incurred in an effort to ensure that products or services meet customer requirements. Internal failure and external failure costs are sometimes referred to as costs of *nonconformance*. **Costs of nonconformance** involve all costs incurred before or during use because of rejections, corrective alterations, refusals of products or services, claims, returns, replacements, and reimbursements. The *costs of quality* equal the sum of conformance and nonconformance costs.

The examples of prevention, appraisal, internal failure, and external failure costs in this chapter are only a guide. Management accountants will have to decide which specific costs most accurately and completely measure costs of quality in their own organizations.

▌ Relationship and Trade-offs between Costs of Quality

Total costs of quality can exceed 60 percent of sales revenue![11] A large number of enterprises are therefore working hard to reduce costs of quality, especially appraisal, internal failure, and external failure costs. The majority of quality experts believe that costs of quality could be reduced below 5 percent of sales revenue by installing a TQM system.

Focusing and spending money on prevention will significantly reduce overall costs of quality. Thus, the cost management rule that pertains to costs of quality is: *Invest in prevention to minimize appraisal, internal failure, and external failure costs.* A small investment in prevention will normally result in a huge savings in other costs of quality.

Exhibit 12–4 (see p. 562) illustrates a hypothetical relationship between costs of quality and the time at which a nonconformity is detected. Clearly, the later a nonconformity is identified in the production process, the greater the cost of correcting it. Moreover, if the nonconforming product or service is identified by the ultimate customer rather than by the producer's appraisal activities, the costs increase dramatically.[12]

Exhibit 12–5 (see p. 562) also demonstrates that prevention and appraisal costs are preferable to failure costs. As companies perform reengineering and practice continuous improvement, the shift will be more and more to prevention with a downward shift in total costs of quality.

Total costs are high when the percentage of conformance to quality standards is low. When percentage of conformance is low, most of the costs incurred are failure costs. Total costs of quality decrease as companies shift their quality expenditures from failure costs to prevention and appraisal costs. This shift is

---

[11] Michael R. Ostrenga, "Return on Investment through the Cost of Quality," in *Emerging Practices in Cost Management,* ed. Barry J. Brinker (Boston: Warren Gorham Lamont, 1992), p. 14-1. With permission.
[12] Wayne J. Morse and Kay M. Poston, "Accounting for Quality Costs in CIM," in *Emerging Practices in Cost Management,* ed. Barry J. Brinker (Boston: Warren Gorham Lamont, 1992), p. 13-3. With permission.

■ EXHIBIT 12–4

Relationship between Costs of Quality and the Time a Nonconformity Is Detected

Source: Wayne J. Morse and Kay M. Poston, "Accounting for Quality Costs in CIM," in *Emerging Practices in Cost Management,* ed. Barry J. Brinker (Boston: Warren Gorham Lamont, 1992), p. I3-3. With permission.

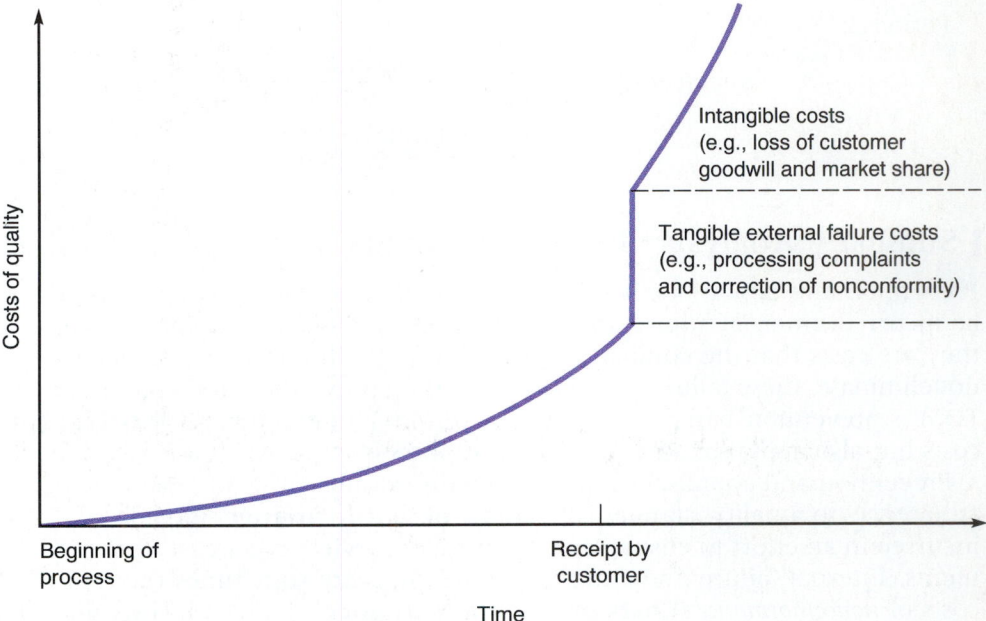

■ EXHIBIT 12–5

Relationship and Trade-offs between Costs of Quality and Conformance to Quality Standards

Source: Wayne J. Morse and Kay M. Poston, "Accounting for Quality Costs in CIM," in *Emerging Practices in Cost Management,* ed. Barry J. Brinker (Boston: Warren Gorham Lamont, 1992), p. I3-4. With permission.

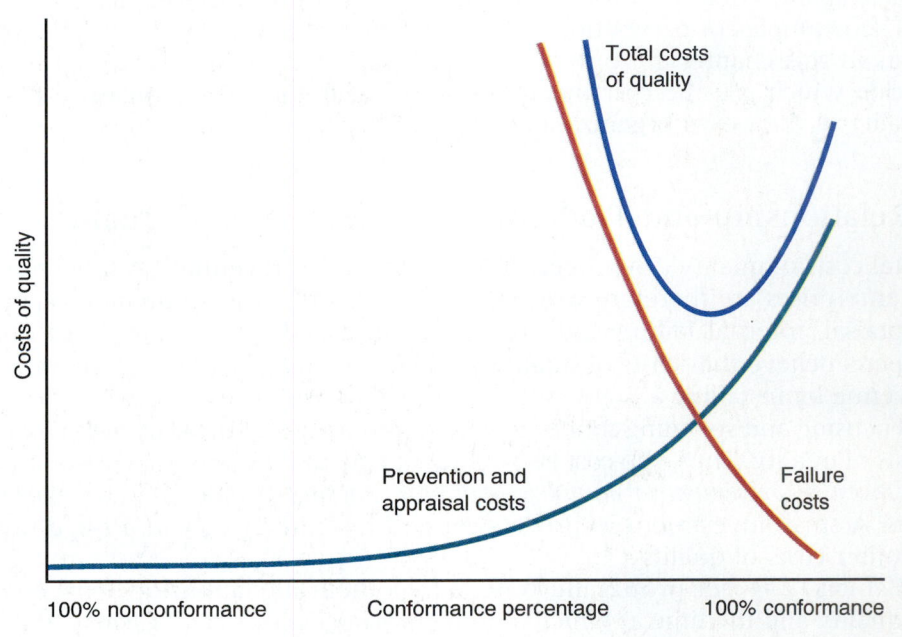

accompanied by a corresponding improvement in quality, and the decrease in failure costs continues until 100 percent conformance is *almost* achieved. At this point, management cannot realize further cost reductions through additional prevention and appraisal expenditures. The focus must then shift to additional reengineering and technological breakthroughs that can shift the prevention and appraisal cost curve down and to the right.

Exhibit 12–6 illustrates how different costs of quality are related and the trade-offs that exist among them. Assume that the maximum number of defects is 5 percent and that a minimum expenditure for prevention is $100. In this case, total costs of quality are minimized at $235, with $160 being spent on prevention and $55 on appraisal. With these quality expenditures, a total defective unit rate of 1.25 percent is expected, which then leads to failure costs of

Prevention Costs	Appraisal Costs	Percentage Defective	Internal Failure Costs	External Failure Costs	Costs of Lost Sales	Total Costs of Quality
$100	$100	5.00%	$50.00	$15.00	$15.00	$280
120	80	3.50	35.00	10.50	10.50	256
140	65	2.25	22.50	6.75	6.75	241
160	55	1.25	12.50	3.75	3.75	235
180	50	.50	5.00	1.50	1.50	238
200	45	0.00	0.00	0.00	0.00	245

■ EXHIBIT 12–6
Minimizing Total Costs of Quality

$16.25 and costs of lost sales of $3.75.[13] Costs of lost sales (and lost customers) may be included in the costs of external failure instead of being shown separately.

▌Reporting Costs of Quality

The performance measurements described earlier are effective for supervisors and workers. To gain top management's attention, the management accountant should prepare quantitative reports on the company's total costs of quality. When the company's quality problems are expressed in financial terms, top management will be more motivated to take action to improve quality.[14]

A form such as the report in Exhibit 12–7 can be used to collect costs of quality. If actual costs are not available, then estimates should be made. Any estimates should be verified by those most directly involved with the cost activities to ensure they are approximately accurate. The report in the exhibit represents the management accountant's first costs-of-quality report to management at Erecto.

The costs-of-quality report should include ratios of costs of quality to sales revenue because they reveal the relative burden of quality costs incurred by the firm. When these ratios are compared to the competition, they can help diagnose quality problems. For example, the ratio of external failure costs to sales revenue is a good gauge of the current level of customer dissatisfaction. A ratio that is high in comparison to that of the company's competitors suggests that customers have suffered unduly from product or service failures. This should signal to management the need for more expenditures on prevention and appraisal. On the other hand, an extremely low ratio may be signaling excessive prevention and appraisal costs.[15]

The purpose of a costs-of-quality report is to make management aware of the magnitude of the costs and to provide a baseline for gauging and tracking the impact of TQM efforts. The report in Exhibit 12–7 shows that Erecto has been spending relatively few dollars on prevention and appraisal. As a result, the company's costs of nonconformance—that is, internal failure and external failure costs—were 55 percent of sales revenue. Erecto's management was astonished to learn that the costs of nonconformance were so high and wanted to know what could be done to reduce them. The answer was to invest in

[13] Adapted from James T. Godfrey and William R. Pasewark, "Controlling Quality Costs," in *World-Class Manufacturing*, ed. Lamont F. Steedle (Montvale, N.J.: Institute of Management Accountants, formerly the National Association of Accountants, 1990), p. 72. With permission.
[14] Morse and Poston, op. cit., p. 13-7.
[15] Thomas P. Edmonds, Bor-Yi Tsay, and Wen-Wei Lin, "Analyzing Quality Costs," in *World-Class Accounting for World-Class Manufacturing*, ed. Lamont F. Steedle (Montvale, N.J.: Institute of Management Accountants, formerly the National Association of Accountants, 1990), p. 83.

INSIGHTS & APPLICATIONS

The Costs of Quality Trade-offs

A viable TQM system can become the ultimate marketing tool. Many customers consider quality more important than price. Today, many enterprises define quality in terms of customer satisfaction or meeting customer needs. This new paradigm includes the cost of lost sales due to external failure as a key measurement. Including the cost of lost sales motivates managers and workers to focus on what is important to an enterprise's success.

Tom Varian of Organizational Dynamics, Incorporated says, "We talk about something called the '1–10–100 Rule,' which states that on a straight ratio, if your people prevent a defect or service failure, that might cost you $1. If your inspection mechanism catches the failure before it reaches the customer, that costs you perhaps $10. But if the defective product or service is delivered to the customer and leads to dissatisfaction, the cost of that failure is $100, because not only have you lost that customer's business, chances are the customer will tell others about the dissatisfying experience. And that's going to cost you real dollars that you would have earned otherwise."[16]

[16] Adapted from Karabatsos, op. cit., p. 39.

■ EXHIBIT 12–7
Costs-of-Quality Report before Prevention Efforts

ERECTO PRODUCTS
Costs-of-Quality Report
Period: 01/01/94 to 12/31/94

Costs-of-Quality Category	A = Actual E = Estimate			Percentage of Sales (Sales = $4,000,000)
Prevention costs:				
■ Quality training	A	$ 5,000		
■ Improvement and reengineering	E	5,000		
■ Technical support for vendors	A	10,000		
■ Preventive maintenance	A	10,000	$ 30,000	0.75%
Appraisal costs:				
■ Inspection and testing of incoming materials	A	$ 40,000		
■ Inspection and testing of work-in-process	A	60,000		
■ Supervision	A	50,000		
■ Quality audits	A	50,000	200,000	5.00
Internal failure costs:				
■ Rework	A	$100,000		
■ Scrap	A	200,000		
■ Repairs	A	100,000		
■ Downtime	E	50,000		
■ Retesting	A	50,000	500,000	12.50
External failure costs:				
■ Returns	A	$200,000		
■ Recalls	A	500,000		
■ Warranty repairs	A	100,000		
■ Replacements	A	250,000		
■ Product liability insurance	A	50,000		
■ Handling customer complaints	A	100,000		
■ Lost sales	E	200,000		
■ Lost customers	E	300,000	1,700,000	42.50
Total costs of quality			$2,430,000	60.75%

INSIGHTS & APPLICATIONS

Measuring the Cost of Lost Customers

Some authorities believe that customer retention has a more powerful effect on profits than market share and many other variables that are traditionally associated with competitive advantage. As customer retention goes up, marketing costs go down. Additionally, loyal customers, in their role as "salespersons," frequently bring in new customers.

Can the costs of lost customers be measured? "Think again," says John Goodman, president of a quality research firm. "They can be measured. Each time a customer has a problem, it creates about a 20 percent impact on loyalty. If 1,000 of your customers have a quality problem, you can say with some certainty that at least 200 of those customers are at risk of being lost. If you know how much each customer is worth (profit), you can multiply this amount by 200 to give the costs of lost customers."[17]

prevention. As prevention costs increase, other costs of quality will decrease. Furthermore, as long as the decrease in failure and appraisal costs is greater than the corresponding increase in prevention costs, the company should continue pursuing and implementing additional preventive measures to further reduce the total costs of quality. Theoretically, if prevention efforts are totally successful, there will be no need to incur appraisal, internal failure, and external failure costs.

After the first costs-of-quality report, Erecto's management made enterprisewide efforts to install preventive measures, with the results shown in Exhibit 12–8. The initial preventive efforts took one year and involved vendors and transportation companies that serve Erecto, but as management realized, prevention is a process that requires ongoing efforts. Understandably, prevention costs rose to 8 percent of sales, but why did appraisal costs also rise? Appraisal costs will normally rise at the beginning of quality efforts as the firm ensures that quality is actually being achieved. At some point, possibly two or three years later, appraisal costs (especially final inspection costs) should decrease as work is done "right the first time, every time."

Why are internal failure and external failure costs still excessive? These nonconformance costs will not disappear immediately. That will take time. Indeed, the total costs of quality at Erecto are still too high. Many authorities, including Philip B. Crosby, an internationally known expert on quality, believe that the total costs of quality should be no more than 2.5 percent of sales. Clearly, Erecto has a long way to go before it achieves this goal. With a continuing focus on prevention, Erecto will be able to reduce appraisal, internal failure, and external failure costs substantially. Over time, even prevention costs such as reengineering and technical support costs for vendors and transportation companies can be reduced, because these earlier costs should not have to be repeated (e.g., certified vendors do not need continuing technical support).

The intent of costs-of-quality reporting is to provide reasonably accurate cost information. The primary purpose is to advise management whether its TQM system is heading in the right direction and actually reducing the total costs of quality. An important consideration for management accountants is to avoid disagreements over minor cost elements.

The Ripple Effect on Costs of Quality

Ripple charts show the impact of defects or failures throughout a series of activities. For example, as Exhibit 12–9 shows, "returns" cause a ripple effect among a number of activities. The total costs of returns (returned goods) in the costs-of-quality report in Exhibit 12–8 were $80,000. The ripple chart shows

[17] Adapted from Karabatsos, op. cit., p. 33.

■■■ EXHIBIT 12–8
Costs-of-Quality Report after Prevention Efforts

ERECTO PRODUCTS
Costs-of-Quality Report
Period: 01/01/95 to 12/31/95

Costs-of-Quality Category	A = Actual E = Estimate		Percentage of Sales (Sales = $5,000,000)
Prevention costs:			
■ Quality training	A	$90,000	
■ Improvement and reengineering	E	80,000	
■ Technical support for vendors	A	90,000	
■ Technical support for transporters	A	60,000	
■ Preventive maintenance	A	80,000	$ 400,000	8.00%
Appraisal costs:			
■ Inspection and testing of incoming materials	A	$60,000	
■ Inspection and testing of work-in-process	A	80,000	
■ Supervision	A	80,000	
■ Quality audits	A	80,000	300,000	6.00
Internal failure costs:			
■ Rework	A	$50,000	
■ Scrap	A	40,000	
■ Repairs	A	50,000	
■ Downtime	E	40,000	
■ Retesting	A	20,000	200,000	4.00
External failure costs:			
■ Returns	A	$80,000	
■ Recalls	A	90,000	
■ Warranty repairs	A	90,000	
■ Replacements	A	80,000	
■ Product liability insurance	A	40,000	
■ Handling customer complaints	A	60,000	
■ Lost sales	E	80,000	
■ Lost customers	E	80,000	600,000	12.00
Total costs of quality			$1,500,000	30.00%

the costs incurred by Erecto to process these returned goods. Other costs that may not be so evident and easy to obtain are costs of replanning production and excess inventory when a large number of goods are returned.[18] Again, such costs should be estimated, but presenting too much detail and too many intangible cost elements should be avoided—that is a sure way to lose the interest of managers and workers.

Managers are always interested in trends. Exhibit 12–10 illustrates a bar chart that shows trends in costs of quality. **Band graphs,** illustrated in Exhibit 12–11 (see p. 568), are visualization techniques in which internal composition and proportions are expressed by the length of a band. Drawing several parallel band graphs makes it easy to compare quantities and proportions and thus to see the trend in costs of quality and the change in profit. Ripple charts and band graphs are additional tools that management accountants can use to make their cost analysis and reporting more effective.

---

[18] The idea for a ripple chart is adapted from Richard K. Youde, "Cost-of-Quality Reporting: How We See It," *Management Accounting*, January 1992, p. 36. Reprinted from *Management Accounting*. Copyright by Institute of Management Accountants, Montvale, N.J.

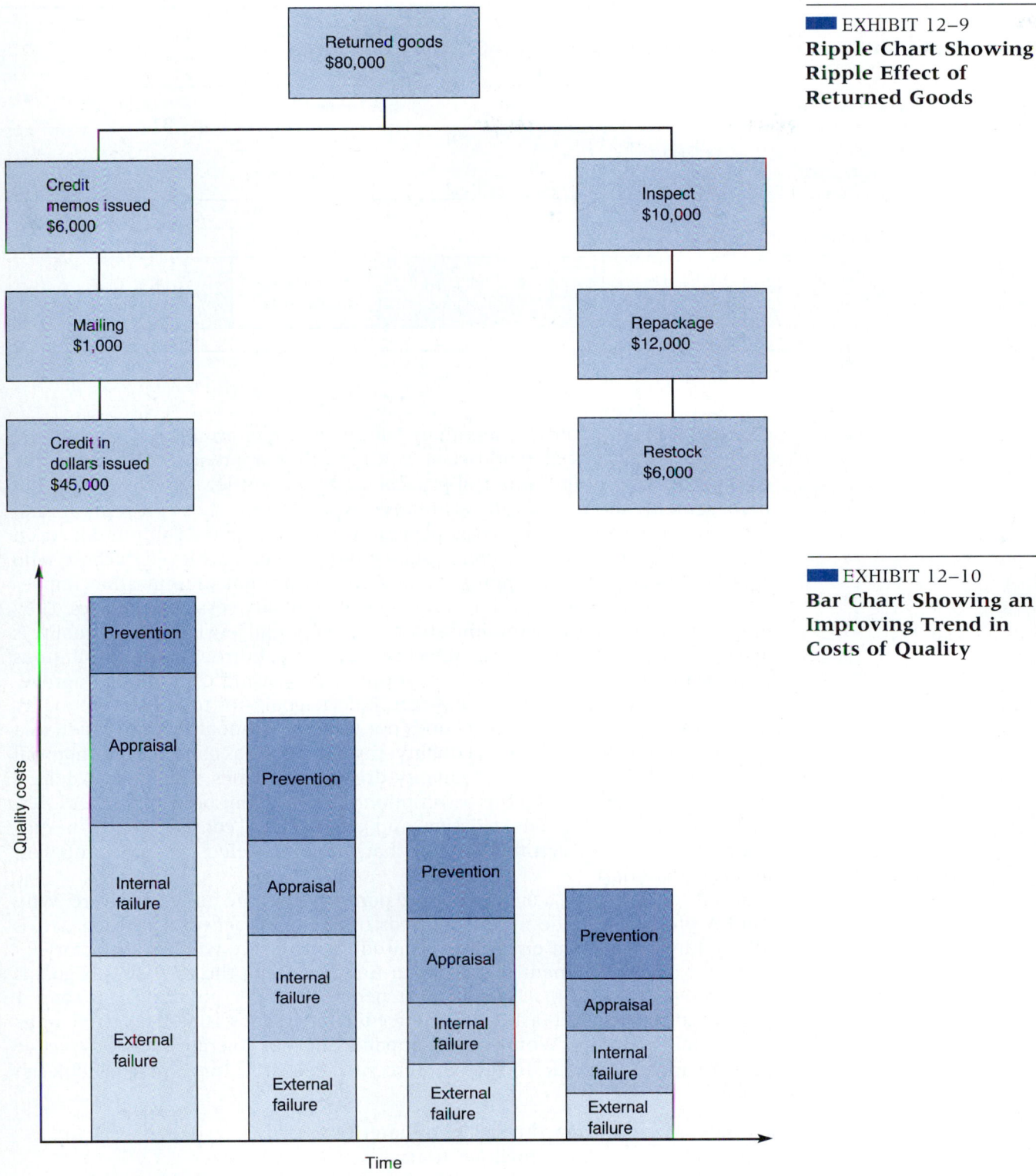

■ EXHIBIT 12–9
**Ripple Chart Showing
Ripple Effect of
Returned Goods**

■ EXHIBIT 12–10
**Bar Chart Showing an
Improving Trend in
Costs of Quality**

Pursuing Zero Defects

Zero defects is a quality standard that calls for products and services to be produced and delivered according to customer requirements. The basis of zero defects is doing it right the first time, every time, and eliminating *all* nonconformities.

The ultimate aim of the zero-defects approach is the elimination of *all* failure costs. Quality experts who emphasize zero defects as the target say that *minimiz-*

■■■ EXHIBIT 12–11
Band Graphs Showing an Improving Trend in Costs of Quality and Profit

Before installation of a TQM system | Costs of quality

| Direct materials costs | Direct labor costs | Overhead costs | Prevention costs | Appraisal and failure costs | Profit |

After installation of a TQM system

| Direct materials costs | Direct labor costs | Overhead costs | Prevention costs | Appraisal and failure costs | Profit |

ing total costs of quality at less than 100 percent conformance undercuts the spirit and objectives of world-class attitudes. This approach differs from the costs-of-quality minimization approach presented earlier, which argues that management should curtail voluntary expenditures (i.e., prevention and appraisal costs) when total costs of quality per unit reach a minimum, even though 100 percent quality conformance has not been achieved.[19] Those who support the zero-defects approach disagree, saying that minimization implies the existence of a single specific optimal level of quality cost expenditures. They emphasize that achieving minimization and an optimal level of costs of quality is actually a *moving target* because of technological breakthroughs and continuous improvement. The focus, therefore, should be on using continuous improvement and prevention to achieve a zero-defects goal, not total costs-of-quality minimization. IBM, for example, does not use costs-of-quality information as a source of motivation to improve quality. Instead, IBM has chosen a nonfinancial target, which is zero defects.[20] Quality-driven companies assume that defects do not exist. They back up this assumption with stringent preventive measures, including top-notch product design and engineering, consistent high-performance activities, and certified vendors that guarantee defect-free parts, supplies, and raw materials.

A zero-defects approach does not use percentage as the unit of measure. Why not? A product is made up of hundreds of parts and activities. If each part is affected by a 1 percent error rate, no product or service will be satisfactory.

A unit of measurement that helps in understanding the zero-defects goal is *parts per million (PPM)*. Usually, most people consider anything less than 1 percent to be small, but a 1 percent defective rate means 10,000 defective units in one million units. World-class companies do not tolerate such a defective rate! In more dramatic terms, 99 percent defect-free (or 1 percent defects) means:

■ 30,000 babies dropped per day in maternity wards
■ 20,000 lost articles of mail per hour
■ Unsafe drinking water almost 15 minutes each day
■ 5,000 incorrect surgical operations per week
■ Two short or long landings at most major airports each day
■ 200,000 incorrect drug prescriptions each year
■ No electricity for over 7 hours each month[21]

---

[19] Godfrey and Pasewark, op. cit., p. 72.
[20] Lawrence P. Carr and Thomas Tyson, "Planning Quality Cost Expenditures," *Management Accounting*, October 1992, p. 55. Reprinted from *Management Accounting*. Copyright by Institute of Management Accountants, Montvale, N.J.
[21] Richard K. Elmer, "Increasing Customer Satisfaction Through Six Sigma," *Take the Next Step in TQM, Implement Zero Defects Management* (Norwalk, Conn.: Productivity Institute, 1992), p. 131. With permission.

One hundred PPM defective is still a large amount in quality-conscious companies, yet it represents only 0.01 percent defective, which *is* quite small but not to people who pursue zero defects. The advantage of the PPM unit of measurement, therefore, is that it transforms seemingly small numbers into large numbers. For example, the 0.01 percent measurement may induce passivity, whereas a 100 PPM defective measurement can create pressure for action.[23] In fact, many companies (e.g., Digital Equipment Company) are achieving around 3 PPM defects, which is 0.0003 percent defects or 99.9997 percent defect-free. A long-term goal at DEC, and at a number of other companies, is around *2 parts per billion (PPB)* defective, which is 99.9999998 percent defect-free.

TOOLS USED TO SOLVE QUALITY PROBLEMS

LEARNING OBJECTIVE 3

Describe Pareto charts and cause-and-effect diagrams, and discuss how they are used in solving quality problems.

Two popular tools used to solve quality problems in activities and processes are:

- Pareto charts
- Cause-and-effect diagrams

These tools help discover quality problems and their root causes. Without such tools, problem solving is often just guesswork, sometimes very expensive guesswork. Based on such analysis, significant changes are made to improve substantially or reengineer processes or activities. Once the proper changes are made, control charts, the subject of the next major section, are used to ensure processes and activities stay in control and continuous improvement is practiced.

Total quality management systems must be supported by an enterprisewide effort. Therefore, problem-solving tools are generally used by teams of people in a joint effort to identify and correct quality problems.

Pareto Charts

The **Pareto chart** is a vertical bar graph that can be used to rank quality problems, such as defects, rework, claims, failures, scrap, spoilage, complaints,

---

[22] Adapted from "Quality Leadership," *Productivity* (Norwalk, Conn.: Productivity Institute, 1992), pp. 1–2. With permission.
[23] Michel Périgord, *Achieving Total Quality Management: A Program for Action* (Cambridge, Mass.: Productivity Press, 1987), p. 110. With permission.

or accidents. The Pareto chart is a good tool to use when the company is making an initial analysis of its activities and does not yet have a TQM system in place. It organizes and portrays data in a way that helps people understand the present performance of activities and processes.

The "Pareto principle," credited to Italian economist Vilfredo Pareto, promotes the so-called 80/20 rule. Pareto discovered that 80 percent of the wealth in his country was concentrated in 20 percent of the population. This principle has been applied to the analysis of a number of things; for example, 20 percent of the inventory items generate 80 percent of the revenue. In the case of quality, the Pareto principle states that 20 percent of the nonconformities generate 80 percent of the quality problems.

The 80/20 rule does not always hold exactly, but a Pareto chart is a way to display the magnitude of quality problems. It separates "the vital few problems from the trivial many."[24] The vital quality problems typically provide the most promising targets for reengineering and improvement efforts.

PRE-IMPROVEMENT AND POST-IMPROVEMENT PARETO CHARTS. Exhibit 12–12 shows pre-improvement and post-improvement Pareto charts depicting the quality problems of an activity that makes bicycle frames. This activity was investigated from July 1 through July 30. The total number (*n*) of defects was 109. The number of defects in each quality problem category was plotted. The worst problems (i.e., the longest bars on the Pareto chart) were "unprocessed" and "deformed." These problems were selected immediately for

[24] Gerald Smith, *Statistical Process Control and Quality Improvement* (New York: Macmillan, 1991), p. 277.

■■■ EXHIBIT 12–12
Pre- and Post-Improvement Pareto Charts

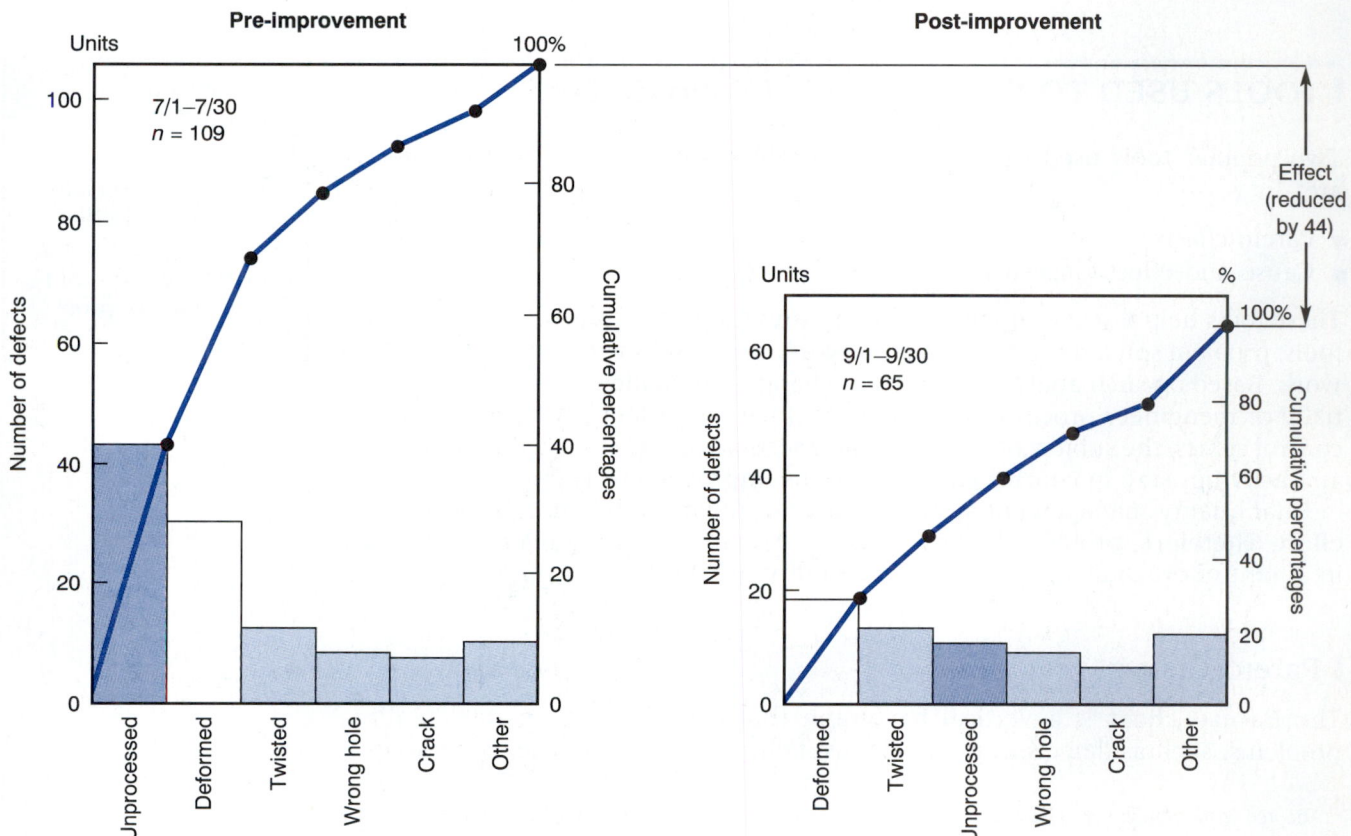

Source: Kazuo Ozeki and Tetsuichi Asaka, *Handbook of Quality Tools: The Japanese Approach* (Cambridge, Mass.: Productivity Press, 1988), p. 145. With permission.

further study and corrective action. Points were also plotted for the cumulative total in each bar and connected with a line to create a graph that shows the relative incremental addition of each category to the total.

After quality improvement actions were taken, data were collected on the same activity from September 1 through September 30. The plots of these data are shown in the post-improvement Pareto chart. Shading is used to keep track of the categories, which are in a different order in the post-improvement Pareto chart. The dramatic improvement is evident.

USING PARETO CHARTS TO SHOW MONETARY LOSSES.   In some instances, the monetary loss can be a better measure of the severity of a quality problem than the number of nonconformities. Exhibit 12–13 presents two Pareto charts: one shows the number of defects ($n = 245$), and the other shows the monetary losses from the defects. Although both charts show the same categories of defects, they are in a different order of significance. The category "breaks," for example, results in the largest monetary loss even though it does not account for the largest number of defects.

▌Cause-and-Effect Diagrams

The Pareto chart is an excellent tool for identifying quality problems and determining their frequency. The next critical step is to ferret out the *root causes*

▬▬EXHIBIT 12–13
Number of Defects Compared to Monetary Losses

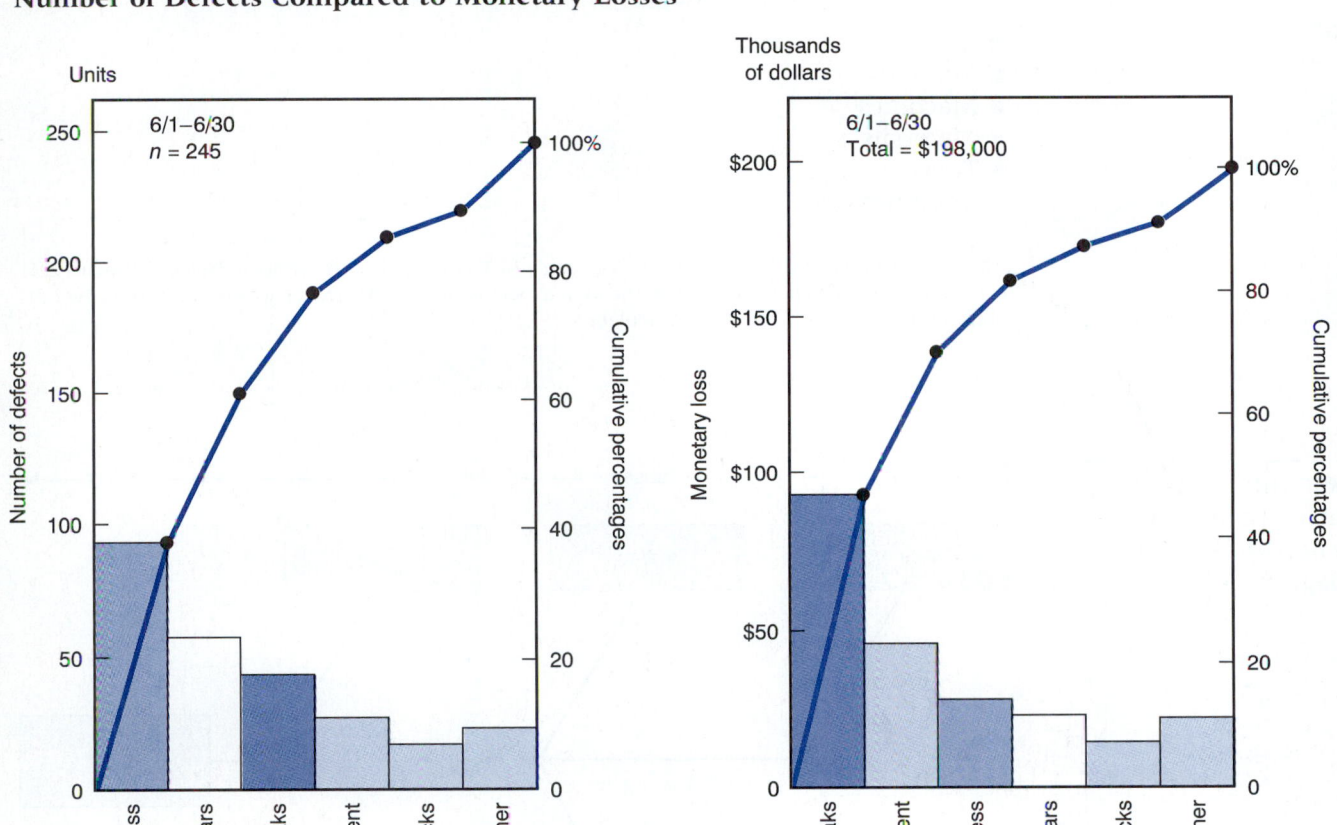

Source: Kazuo Ozeki and Tetsuichi Asaka, *Handbook of Quality Tools: The Japanese Approach* (Cambridge, Mass.: Productivity Press, 1988), p. 146. With permission.

INSIGHTS & APPLICATIONS

Finding the Root Causes of Quality Problems

One of the tasks in a loan department of a bank is to prepare documents for signature by the buyer and seller, and to file them with the Registrar of Deeds. Mortgage and escrow-payment amounts are frequently typed incorrectly by the typing pool. Rather than going back to the source of the problem, loan officers simply toss out the forms with the incorrect numbers on them and have their own secretaries retype them correctly. What happens? Errors continue to show up and unit cost per loan package increases significantly.

If quality and productivity are important to this bank, what should it do? Hiring people to inspect all of the work coming out of the typing pool is not the answer. A better solution is to go back and follow documents through the entire process to find out why the payment amounts are incorrect. Maybe some of the loan officers are providing the wrong information. Maybe the errors are due simply to haste and carelessness in the document-preparation area. The bank must find the cause of the problem and fix it, not just nurse the symptoms.[25]

of quality problems. Here the **cause-and-effect diagram** is a useful tool. It is sometimes called a **fishbone diagram** because of its shape or an **Ishikawa diagram** after the late Professor Kaoru Ishikawa of Japan. In Chapter 10, a modified cause-and-effect diagram was used to show tasks that make up an activity. In this chapter, it is used as its developer intended; that is, to dig for the root causes of tough quality problems.

The basic shape of the cause-and-effect diagram is shown in Exhibit 12–14. Worst-case quality problems identified by the Pareto chart become the spine of the cause-and-effect diagram. Generally, the following "ribs," or main cause categories, are used initially:

- Operators
- Methods
- Machines
- Materials
- Tools
- Environment

[25] Adapted from Ronald W. Butterfield, "Deming's 14 Points Applied to Service," *Training,* March 1991, p. 52. Reprinted with permission from the March 1991 issue of TRAINING magazine. Lakewood Publications. Minneapolis, MN. All rights reserved.

EXHIBIT 12–14
Basic Shape of the Cause-and-Effect Diagram

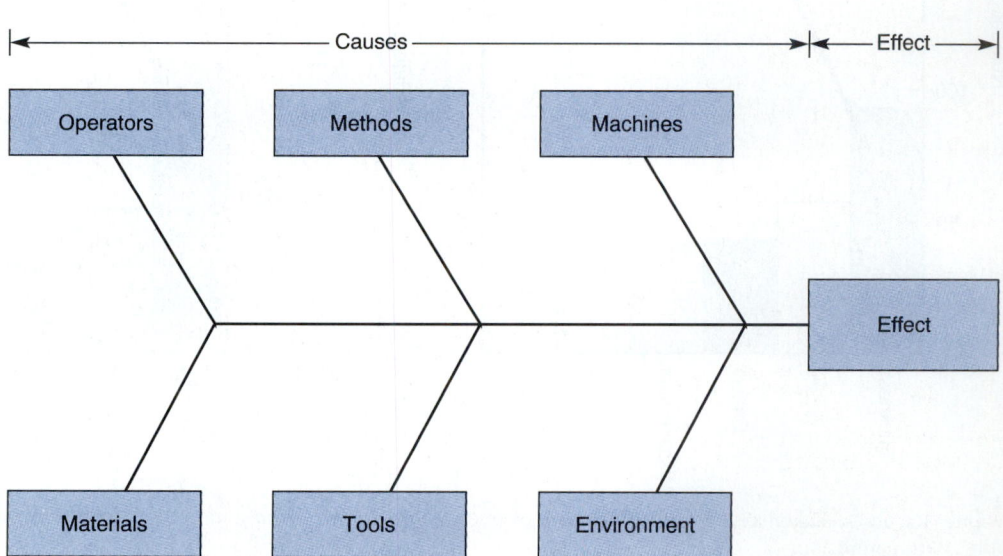

INSIGHTS & APPLICATIONS

Using a Fishbone Diagram to Streamline the Admitting Activity

A fishbone diagram of the admitting activity in a large hospital revealed that new patients had to fill out no less than seven different forms before being admitted to the hospital. A close look at those forms revealed that there were no less than three separate admitting forms—one for men, one for women, and one for children.

A senior staffer recalled that there used to be just one such form, but that it had been divided into separate forms to fulfill requirements of a study project long since completed. A single questionnaire was developed, and in that simple change in the admitting activity the hospital was able to cut ten minutes off the lead time for admitting patients.[26]

Other main cause categories specific to a particular quality problem may be added if the investigating team decides they are relevant. For example, "measurement" and "information" may be added as main cause categories. Some authorities use what they call the 4M's as main cause categories:

- Men
- Methods
- Money
- Machines

In any event, these four categories are the minimum number that should be used.

To help the investigating team organize their thinking, a cause-and-effect diagram without the "bones" and "small bones" (i.e., one containing only main cause categories) may be displayed on a large piece of paper taped to the wall of a meeting room, or a blackboard or whiteboard may be used instead. In some cases, each member is asked to write down what he or she believes to be the root causes on a deck of 50 or so index cards. Then, these cards are attached to the "bones" that connect to the appropriate "rib" or main cause category. "Small bones" can be connected to bigger bones to indicate causes of causes. As the investigation progresses, subdivisions and attachments continue until the root causes are found. Once the root causes are determined, corrective action can be taken.

How can the main cause categories cause quality problems? *Operators* may not perform properly due to negative attitudes or poor training. *Methods* may be outdated and counterproductive. *Machines* may be inadequate for the work performed or poorly maintained. *Materials* may be faulty. *Tools* may be broken or worn. The *environment* may be too hot, cold, dirty, noisy, humid, or dark and therefore negatively influence the process.

Exhibit 12–15 (see p. 574) shows a cause-and-effect diagram devised by a company that has already used Pareto chart analysis to determine that poor adhesion is one of its major quality problems. Now, the cause-and-effect diagram is used to determine the causes of the adhesion problem. At the beginning of the investigation, "Poor adhesion" was written in the effect box. Then the six main cause categories were inserted and their ribs attached to the spine. Members of the investigation team were given index cards to record what they thought were the causes of poor adhesion. These causes were inserted on the cause-and-effect diagram as shown in the exhibit.

The resulting cause-and-effect diagram was checked to make sure that no cause had been left out. The investigating team also went back into the work-

[26] Adapted from Carson Reed, "The Big Q," *Colorado Business Magazine,* March 1991, pp. 50–51. With permission.

■■■EXHIBIT 12–15

Cause-and-Effect Diagram Used to Determine the Causes of Poor Adhesion

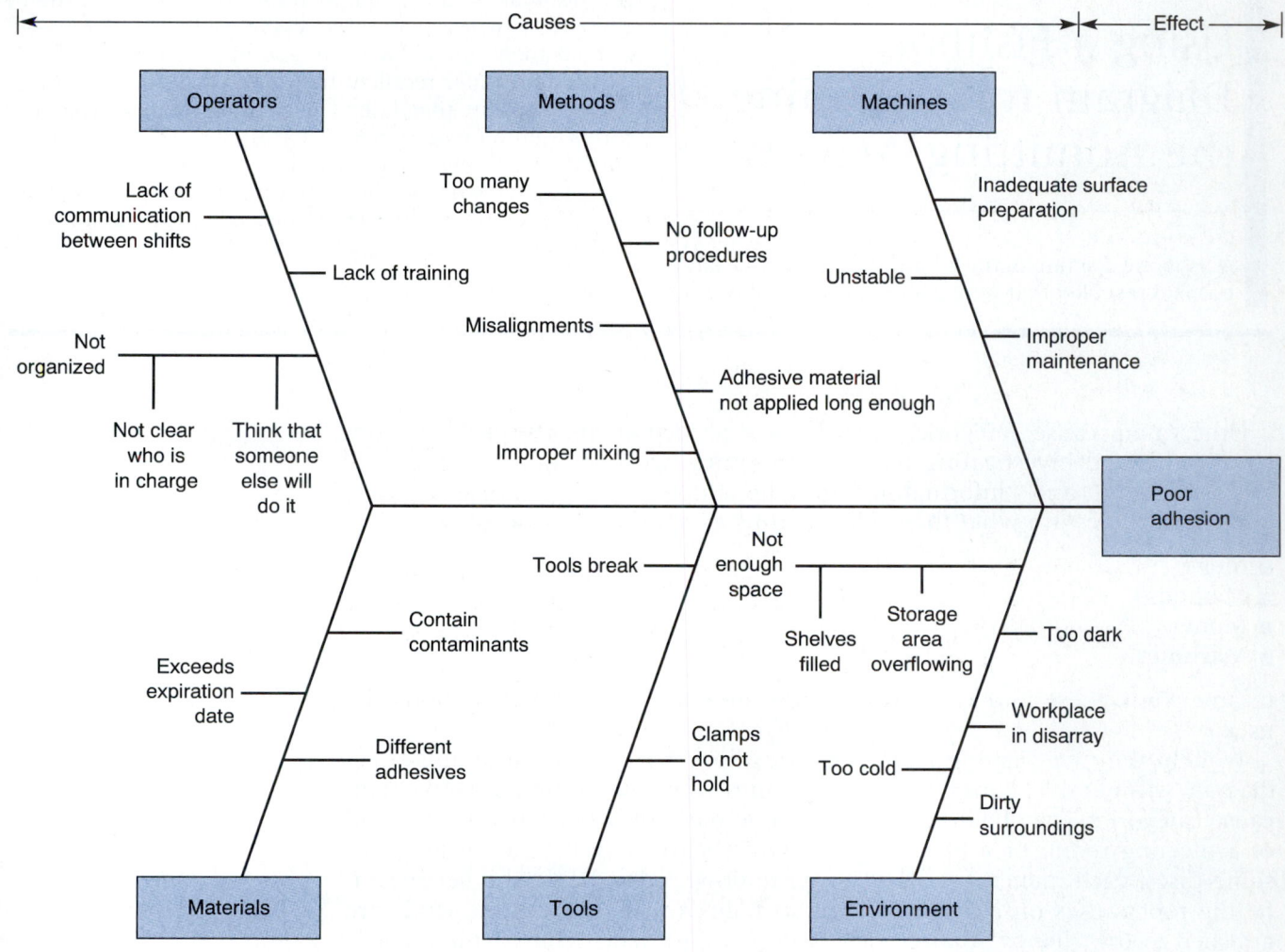

place to discuss the causes with all participants. A consensus was reached, and the cause-and-effect diagram became the basis for correcting the adhesion problem.

TOOLS USED TO KEEP ACTIVITIES AND PROCESSES IN CONTROL

Pareto charts and cause-and-effect diagrams are used to improve or reengineer activities and processes. Presented in this section are **control charts** first introduced in Chapter 11, which are statistical devices used mainly to control processes or activities *after* they have been substantially improved or reengineered and most, if not all, of the quality problems have been corrected. Control charts are also used to analyze and evaluate the process, thus stressing the idea of continuous improvement.

The Statistical Basis for Control Charts

Every process or activity no matter how well it is engineered involves some variation. The study of the behavior of this variation in important quality characteristics is the main objective of control charts. Control charts show the amount and nature of variation by time, indicate statistical control or lack of it, and enable significant changes or patterns in the process or activity to be detected. As Exhibit 12–16 shows, to construct a control chart for X, the vertical scale is calibrated in units of X, and the horizontal scale is marked with respect to time or some other basis for ordering X; then, horizontal lines are drawn through the estimated mean of X and through an extreme value on the upper and lower tail of the normal distribution of X. When 50 percent of the observations of an activity or process are above the average or center line but not outside the upper control limit (UCL) and 50 percent of the observations are below the average or center line but not outside the lower control limit (LCL), the process or activity is considered in control or operating normally.

Any activity or process, no matter how precise, is subject at any given moment to a very large number of random disturbances, all of them so small as to be individually inconsequential. But, together, these random disturbances make the activity's or process's output vary slightly from the average, with the result that no two outputs are exactly alike. Thus, variations on either side of the center line are equally likely. This variability that is always present in a process or activity is the result of **random causes.** The only way to eliminate or reduce a particular set of random causes is to change the process or activity, such as by automating a manual activity.

In addition to the random causes, which are always present, there may be other more obvious sources of variability that cause the process or activity to deviate further from its average. These are **assignable causes,** which result in relatively large variations; these special causes are due to differences in the following:

- Operators
- Machines
- Methods
- Materials
- Tools
- Environment

When variations conform to a statistical pattern that might reasonably be produced by random causes, the assumption is that no special assignable causes are present. The conditions that produced these variations are, accordingly, said to be under control. On the other hand, when the variations in the data do not conform to a pattern that might reasonably be produced by random causes,

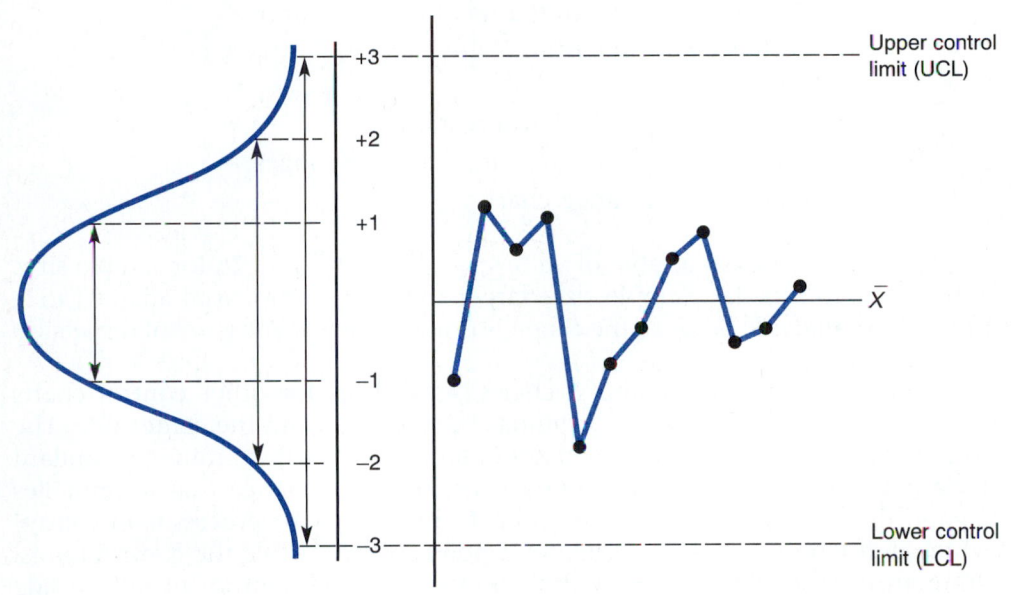

EXHIBIT 12–16
Statistical Basis for Control Charts

Source: Steven M. Hronec and Steven K. Hunt, "Quality and Cost Management," in *Handbook of Cost Management*, ed. Barry J. Brinker (Boston: Warren Gorham Lamont, 1992), p. A1-21. With permission.

one may conclude that one or more assignable causes are at work. In this case, the conditions producing the variations are said to be out of control.

Kinds of Control Charts

A successful process or activity is one that can consistently operate within the required limits of variation. Two kinds of control charts are used to portray this variation:

- **Control charts for variables** describe quality quantitatively in terms of dimension, pressure, voltage, temperature, weight, or other quantifiable characteristics.
- **Control charts for attributes** use qualitative terms, such as "good" or "bad" and "acceptable" or "unacceptable," to describe attributes such as finish and color.

Control charts for both types of data are available for analytical visualization of the data distribution for the quality characteristics being studied.

Control Charts for Variables

The following are the most commonly used control charts for variables:

- $\bar{X}$ chart
- R chart

The $\bar{X}$ **chart** (pronounced ex bar chart) helps control the average of the process or activity. An R **chart** helps control the general variability of the process or activity. Together, the $\bar{X}$ chart and R chart provide reasonably good quality control of the activity's output.

For variables control chart work, the following terminology is generally used:

$$k = \text{Number of groups or sample groups}$$
$$n = \text{Number of observations in each group, the sample size}$$
$$N = \text{Total number of observations } (kn)$$
$$\bar{X} = \text{Arithmetic mean of the } n \text{ observations in each sample group}$$
$$\bar{\bar{X}} = \text{Arithmetic mean of all } N \text{ observations}$$
$$R = \text{Range in any sample (largest value minus smallest value)}$$
$$\bar{R} = \text{Arithmetic mean of the ranges in } k \text{ samples}$$
$$A_2, I_2 = \text{Factors for calculating limits for the } \bar{X} \text{ chart}$$
$$A_2\bar{R} = \text{Distance of limits from } \bar{X} \text{ line}$$
$$\bar{\bar{X}} \pm A_2\bar{R} = \text{Limits for the } \bar{X} \text{ chart}$$
$$\bar{\bar{X}} \pm I_2\bar{R} = \text{Limits for individual observations}$$
$$D_3, D_4 = \text{Conversion factors used in charts for ranges}$$
$$D_3\bar{R}, D_4\bar{R} = \text{Limits for the range chart}$$

Exhibit 12–17 contains a table of values for A_2, I_2, D_3, and D_4 for sample sizes from $n = 2$ to $n = 10$. Sample sizes larger than 10 are not well adapted to $\bar{X}$ and R chart analysis, because the range is not an efficient measure of dispersion in larger sample sizes.

The control limits for $\bar{X}$ and R charts, as well as for other control charts described in this chapter, are ± 3 standard deviations from the center line. The normal curve reveals that 99.7 percent of all the values lie within ± 3 standard deviations (or sigmas) of the center. Therefore, the chance that a point lies beyond the control limits is 0.3 percent. If the activity or process is in control or stable, it would be rare, indeed, for a point to fall outside the control limits, although it is possible. Points that are in an abnormal pattern or fall outside

Number of Observations in Sample (n)	(Limits = $\bar{\bar{X}} \pm A_2 \bar{R}$)			(Limits = $D_3 \bar{R}, D_4 \bar{R}$)	
	d_2	$A_2 = \dfrac{3}{d_2 \sqrt{n}}$	$I_2 = A_2 \sqrt{n}$	D_3	D_4
2	1.128	1.881	2.66	–0–	3.268
3	1.693	1.023	1.77	–0–	2.574
4	2.059	0.729	1.46	–0–	2.282
5	2.326	0.577	1.29	–0–	2.114
6	2.534	0.483	1.18	–0–	2.004
7	2.704	0.419	1.11	0.076	1.924
8	2.847	0.373	1.05	0.136	1.864
9	2.970	0.337	1.01	0.184	1.816
10	3.078	0.308	0.97	0.223	1.777

■■■EXHIBIT 12–17
Factors for $\bar{X}$ Chart and R Chart When n Is Less Than or Equal to 10

the control limits signal an unstable, out-of-control activity. The activity or process can be made stable by identifying and eliminating the causes of the abnormality and taking action to prevent recurrence.

In essence, the two charts reveal the presence of variability both *between* sample groups ($\bar{X}$ chart) and *within* sample groups (R chart). Together, they "spread a net from which it is difficult for an assignable cause to escape."[27]

Constructing and Analyzing $\bar{X}$ and R Charts

The activity for which $\bar{X}$ and R charts will be constructed and analyzed, as an example, is a grinding process that produces guide rollers. The variable being measured is the external diameter (in millimeters) of the guide roller. Five observations ($n = 5$) of the external diameter of the roller are made every hour and are entered in the data sheet in Exhibit 12–18. The five observations from the population of rollers produced during the same hour represent a group. Thirty sample groups ($k = 30$) are gathered during the period from July 16 through July 20. The 150 data points entered in the data sheet are used to construct $\bar{X}$ and R charts and analyze the state of the grinding activity.

Observations are taken from activities or processes in much the same way as a patient's temperature or blood samples are taken at regular intervals to evaluate the state of the patient's health. If results are satisfactory or normal, no action is needed. If results fall outside certain limits, emergency action is called for.

The general rule for sampling an activity or process using the $\bar{X}$ and R charts is "little and often." The reason for sampling *often* (e.g., every hour) is to enable early detection of a process that is approaching or going out of limit, so that timely corrections can be made and less out-of-limit rework will be required. The sample size should be sufficient to disclose the quality conditions of the activity, but no larger. If a sample of 5 tells all that is needed, a sample of 20 tells all that is needed four times over. A sample of 5 every hour is better than 20 every four hours, because if the process goes out of limit, the results will catch it, on average, in one-fourth the time.

Sample sizes of 4 and 5 are the most popular. Most people find it easier to divide by 5 in calculating averages, though sometimes 4 is preferred. Samples of 4 are advisable if measurements are made in quarters of an inch. Samples of 5 are typically used if measurements are in decimals. Occasionally, sample sizes of 2, 3, or 6 to 10 are used.

Generally, it is wise to use more than 20 groups before calculating $\bar{\bar{X}}$ and

[27] William B. Rice, *Control Charts in Factory Management* (New York: John Wiley, 1947), p. 45.

■ EXHIBIT 12–18
$\bar{X}$ Chart and R Chart Data Sheet

Data from Kazuo Ozeki and Tetsuichi Asaka, *Handbook of Quality Tools: The Japanese Approach* (Cambridge, Mass.: Productivity Press, 1988), p. 207.

19X4 Date	Group Number	Measured Values					Sum ΣX	Mean Value $\bar{X}$	Range R
		X_1	X_2	X_3	X_4	X_5			
7/16	1	27	24	28	27	26	132	26.4	4
	2	25	26	29	28	23	131	26.2	6
	3	23	27	25	24	27	126	25.2	4
	4	26	25	28	25	27	131	26.2	3
	5	25	29	25	26	24	129	25.8	5
	6	22	23	29	24	23	121	24.2	7
7/17	7	28	27	25	26	26	132	26.4	3
	8	24	27	27	26	24	128	25.6	3
	9	24	27	26	24	23	124	24.8	4
	10	26	26	25	27	25	129	25.8	2
	11	25	30	23	28	27	133	26.6	7
	12	23	28	25	24	22	122	24.4	6
7/18	13	25	26	23	26	24	124	24.8	3
	14	25	27	23	26	27	128	25.6	4
	15	24	24	25	25	23	121	24.2	2
	16	24	27	23	28	27	129	25.8	5
	17	28	29	25	26	24	132	26.4	5
	18	26	28	27	25	28	134	26.8	3
7/19	19	30	26	30	28	32	146	(29.2)	6
	20	26	29	27	27	28	137	27.4	3
	21	28	26	24	25	25	128	25.6	4
	22	25	27	24	26	27	129	25.8	3
	23	27	29	26	25	23	130	26.0	6
	24	25	24	28	26	21	124	24.8	7
7/20	25	26	25	26	27	25	129	25.8	2
	26	23	24	27	24	28	126	25.2	5
	27	25	26	30	20	27	128	25.6	(10)
	28	23	27	24	28	22	124	24.8	6
	29	27	23	24	25	24	123	24.6	4
	30	25	25	26	24	28	128	25.6	4

$\bar{p}$ control chart $A_2\bar{R} = 2.61$	R control chart	Total	771.6	136
UCL $= \bar{\bar{X}} + A_2\bar{R} = 28.33$	UCL $= D_4\bar{R} = 9.58$	$\bar{\bar{X}} = 25.72$		$\bar{R} = 4.53$
LCL $= \bar{\bar{X}} - A_2\bar{R} = 23.11$	LCL $= D_3\bar{R} =$ ——			

n	A_2	D_4	D_3
4	0.729	2.28	—
5	0.577	2.11	—

A_2 for samples of 5 (Exhibit 12–17) = 0.577
D_3 for samples of 5 (Exhibit 12–17) = 0
D_4 for samples of 5 (Exhibit 12–17) = 2.114
$A_2\bar{R} = 0.577 \times 4.53 = 2.61$
$\bar{X}$ upper control limit (UCL) $= \bar{\bar{X}} + A_2\bar{R} = 25.72 + 2.61 = 28.33$
$\bar{X}$ lower control limit (LCL) $= \bar{\bar{X}} - A_2\bar{R} = 25.72 - 2.61 = 23.11$
R upper control limit (UCL) $= D_4\bar{R} = 2.114 \times 4.53 = 9.58$
R lower control limit (LCL) = Ignore

limit lines. Most people use at least 30 groups and sometimes as many as 50 in calculating $\bar{\bar{X}} \pm A_2\bar{R}$, $D_3\bar{R}$, and $D_4\bar{R}$ for guiding future production.

Values on a control chart should represent groups of observations that are as homogeneous as possible. In other words, the groups should be such that if assignable causes are present, they will show up in differences between groups rather than in differences between the observations in a group. A natural group, for example, would be the output of a given shift. Another example of a natural group would be the output of individual machines in an activity. If one machine is properly maintained while the other is not, grouping observations from both machines would obviously produce erroneous results. The well-maintained machine would be producing good output while the poorly-maintained machine would be producing bad output.

Using graph paper, an $\bar{X}$ scale is drawn on the upper part of the vertical axis and an R scale on the lower part of that axis, as illustrated in Exhibit 12–19. Then, a group number scale is drawn along the horizontal axis. From the data sheet containing samples, the values of $\bar{X}$ and R are plotted, and the points are connected to create a line graph. The $\bar{\bar{X}}$, $\bar{R}$, upper control limit (UCL), and lower control limit (LCL) values calculated at the bottom of the data sheet in Exhibit 12–18 are used to draw the appropriate lines. The control charts are now ready for analysis.

Is the grinding activity stable? Group Number 19 exceeds the UCL in the $\bar{X}$ chart. Group Number 27 exceeds the UCL in the R chart. These results indicate that the grinding activity is not stable. When a point falls outside the control limits, lack of control is indicated, and it will pay to look for the cause. A

■■■EXHIBIT 12–19
$\bar{X}$ and R Control Charts

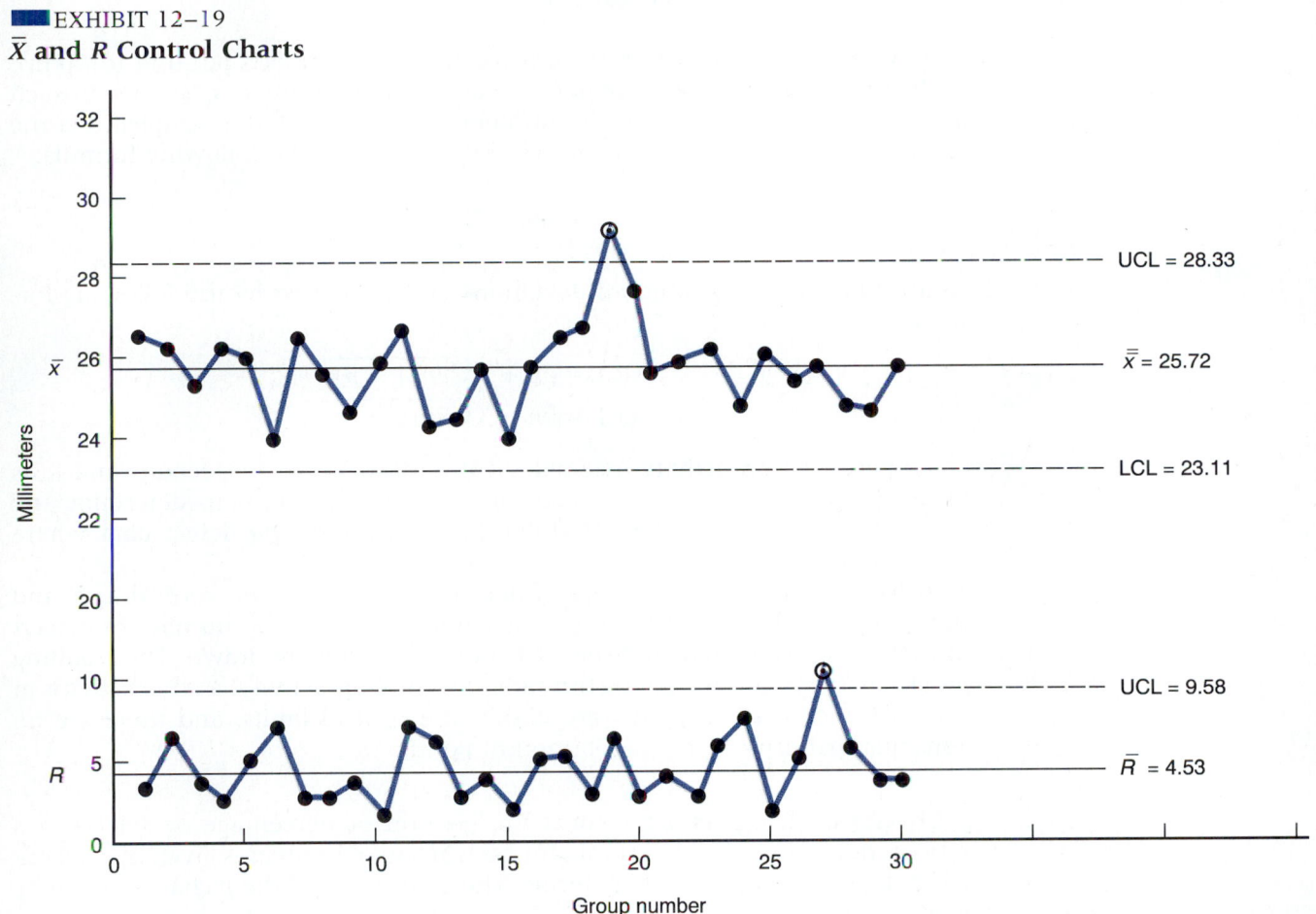

Source: Kazuo Ozeki and Tetsuichi Asaka, *Handbook of Quality Tools: The Japanese Approach* (Cambridge, Mass.: Productivity Press, 1988), p. 210. With permission.

successful process or activity is one that can consistently operate within the required limits of variation.

Control Charts for Attributes

Inspection by variables, as required for $\bar{X}$ and R charts, is not applicable in some activities. For example:

- Many qualities, such as appearance, color, and taste, cannot be checked as variables.
- Some processes call for 100 percent inspection of a combination of attributes on a "pass" or "fail" basis (e.g., food products, motors, or electronic components). Under such circumstances, the best procedure may be to record the number of tests performed and the number of failures (defects), and classify the product as either good or bad. For analyzing and controlling quality on this basis, the following control charts for attributes are used:
  - *pn* charts
  - *p* charts

The following terminology is used for these charts:

k = Number of groups or sample groups
n = Number of observations (items or units) in each group, the sample size
N = Total number of observations (kn)
p = Number of defects per observation
$\bar{p}$ = Arithmetic mean of the number of defects per observation
pn = Number of defects per group

pn **CHARTS.** The *pn* **chart** records the number of defects per unit (or item), such as for a radio unit where defects may exist at a number of points. In such a case, it is natural to count the number of defects per unit sampled. On the *pn* chart, the center line is $\bar{p}n$, which is calculated by the following formula:

$$\bar{p}n = \frac{\Sigma\, pn}{k}$$

Control limits, at ± 3 standard deviations, are calculated by the following formulas:

$$UCL = \bar{p}n + 3\sqrt{\bar{p}n(1 - \bar{p})}$$
$$LCL = \bar{p}n - 3\sqrt{\bar{p}n(1 - \bar{p})}$$

Suppose that an activity assembles 150 radios. Visual inspections and tests by diagnostic equipment are made on each of the radios to determine the number of defects produced. Exhibit 12–20 discloses *pn* defect data where $N = 150$ and $k = 30$.

In Exhibit 12–21, the number of defects is shown on the vertical axis, and the group numbers are shown on the horizontal axis. The number of defects in each group is plotted, and the UCL and center line are drawn. The resulting *pn* chart shows the results of the radio assembling activity. Is this activity in control? Yes, it is. All points are within the control limits, and there are no abnormal patterns in the distribution of points.

p **CHARTS.** The *p* **chart** records the fraction or percentage of defects in a process or activity. The defect rate for each group of samples is given by p where p is a defect rate in percentage terms. The center line of the p chart is given by $\bar{p}$, also in percentage terms.

Sometimes it is not possible to maintain a constant sample size, as is required with *pn* charts. Samples from lots of varying sizes or tests of incoming parts

◼◼◼EXHIBIT 12–20
pn **Chart Data Sheet**

Group Number	Number of Defects, *pn*	Group Number	Number of Defects, *pn*	Group Number	Number of Defects, *pn*	Group Number	Number of Defects, *pn*	Group Number	Number of Defects, *pn*	Group Number	Number of Defects, *pn*
1	1	6	2	11	1	16	6	21	3	26	3
2	3	7	4	12	1	17	4	22	1	27	3
3	1	8	3	13	2	18	3	23	1	28	2
4	0	9	1	14	5	19	1	24	2	29	3
5	2	10	2	15	3	20	2	25	4	30	1
										$\Sigma\, pn$	70
										$\overline{pn}$	2.33

$$\overline{pn} = \frac{\Sigma\, pn}{k}$$
$$= \frac{70}{30}$$
$$= \underline{\underline{2.33}}$$

$$\overline{p} = \frac{\Sigma\, pn}{(N \times k)}$$
$$= \frac{70}{(150 \times 30)}$$
$$= \underline{\underline{0.0156}}$$

$$UCL = 2.33 + 3\sqrt{\overline{pn}(1 - \overline{p})}$$
$$= 2.33 + 3\sqrt{2.33(1 - 0.0156)}$$
$$= 2.33 + 4.54$$
$$= \underline{\underline{6.87}}$$

$$LCL = 2.33 - 4.54$$
$$= \underline{\underline{-2.21}} \quad (\text{Ignore})$$

Data from Kazuo Ozeki and Tetsuichi Asaka, *Handbook of Quality Tools: The Japanese Approach* (Cambridge, Mass.: Productivity Press, 1988), p. 219. With permission.

◼◼◼EXHIBIT 12–21
pn **Chart**

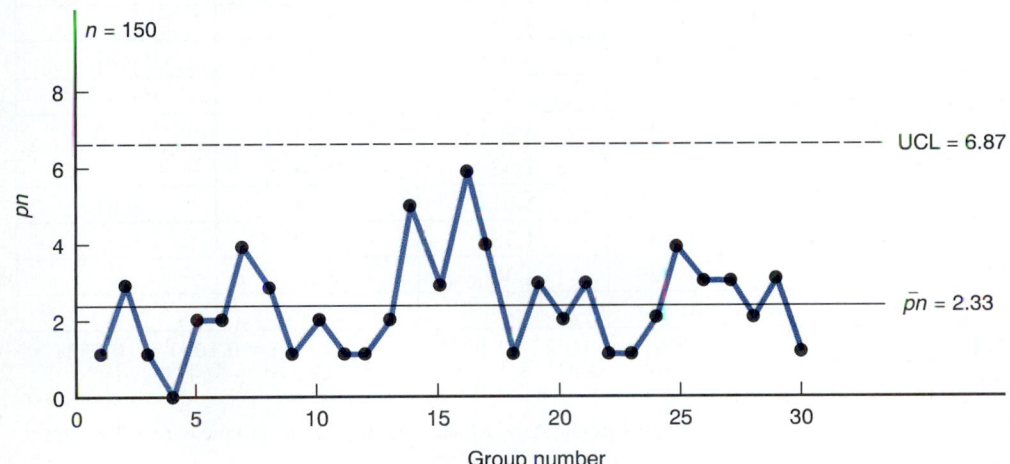

from vendors often result in samples varying considerably in size. Because chance sampling fluctuations decrease as sample size increases, new control limits must be calculated for each point on the chart if the sample size is not constant. Although p charts can be used with sample sizes that are constant, they are also useful in situations where the sample size varies, as in the example given here.

Assume an activity makes frames for railway cars. Random units are taken from each day's process and visually inspected for abrasions, cracks, and warps. The frames are considered "acceptable" or "defective." Exhibit 12–22 shows the sample data collected from July 2 through July 14. Notice that the sample size varies considerably between groups of samples.

Because sample size n is different in each group, each group must have its own individual control limit values at ± 3 standard deviations. To determine them, each individual value of n must be converted into a factor A for each group, using the formula:

$$A = \frac{3}{\sqrt{n}}$$

■EXHIBIT 12–22
p Chart Data Sheet

19X4 Date	Lot Number	Group Number	Sample Size, n	Number of Defects, pn	Defect Rate (%), p	$A = \dfrac{3}{\sqrt{n}}$	$A \times \sqrt{\overline{p}(1-\overline{p})}$ (%)	UCL (%) $\overline{p} + A\sqrt{\overline{p}(1-\overline{p})}$	LCL (%) $\overline{p} - A\sqrt{\overline{p}(1-\overline{p})}$
7/2	5	1	526	3	0.6	0.131	1.32	2.34	—
	6	2	483	6	1.2	0.137	1.37	2.40	—
7/3	7	3	602	5	0.8	0.122	1.23	2.25	—
	8	4	479	2	0.4	0.137	1.38	2.40	—
7/4	9	5	531	9	1.7	0.130	1.31	2.33	—
	10	6	527	4	0.8	0.131	1.31	2.34	—
7/5	11	7	206	8	(3.9)	0.209	2.10	3.13	—
	12	8	395	6	1.5	0.151	1.52	2.54	—
	13	9	610	4	0.7	0.121	1.22	2.24	—
7/6	14	10	608	2	0.3	0.122	1.22	2.25	—
	15	11	586	10	1.7	0.124	1.25	2.27	—
7/9	16	12	212	3	1.4	0.206	2.07	3.10	—
	17	13	231	6	2.6	0.197	1.99	3.01	—
	18	14	571	2	0.4	0.126	1.26	2.29	—
7/10	19	15	550	4	0.7	0.128	1.29	2.31	—
	20	16	382	2	0.5	0.153	1.54	2.57	—
	21	17	415	6	1.4	0.147	1.48	2.50	—
7/11	22	18	906	11	1.2	0.100	1.00	2.03	0.02
	23	19	249	7	2.8	0.190	1.91	2.94	—
7/12	24	20	611	4	0.7	0.121	1.22	2.24	—
	25	21	524	5	1.0	0.131	1.32	2.34	—
7/13	26	22	887	7	0.8	0.101	1.01	2.04	0.01
	27	23	479	6	1.3	0.137	1.38	2.40	—
7/14	28	24	538	3	0.6	0.129	1.30	2.32	—
	29	25	603	5	0.8	0.122	1.23	2.25	—
Total			12,711 (Σn)	130 (Σpn)	$\overline{p} = \Sigma pn / \Sigma n = 0.0102 = 1.02\%$		$\sqrt{\overline{p}(1-\overline{p})} = 0.1005 = 10.05\%$		

Data from Kazuo Ozeki and Tetsuichi Asaka, *Handbook of Quality Tools: The Japanese Approach* (Cambridge, Mass.: Productivity Press, 1988), p. 222. With permission.

The values of A are then used in the following equations, and the resulting limits are drawn above each group:

$$UCL = \bar{p} + A\sqrt{\bar{p}(1 - \bar{p})}$$
$$LCL = \bar{p} - A\sqrt{\bar{p}(1 - \bar{p})}$$

The calculations and interpretation of the chart are easier when the sample size is kept constant. When constant sample times are used and the sample size varies, a single set of control limits can be used as long as the individual sample sizes do not differ too much. If any individual samples or groups of samples differ in size by 25 percent or less of the average sample size, $\bar{n}$ (where $\bar{n} = \Sigma n \div k$), a simplified method can be used to calculate the control limits, using the value of n:

$$UCL = \bar{p} + 3\sqrt{\frac{\bar{p}(1 - \bar{p})}{n}}$$
$$LCL = \bar{p} - 3\sqrt{\frac{\bar{p}(1 - \bar{p})}{n}}$$

Because the values of n in the example (206 to 906) vary more than 25 percent of $\bar{n}$, the simplified method of calculating the control limits cannot be used. In this case, interpreting the chart is trickier because it is more difficult to relate the point pattern to fluctuating control limits.

Exhibit 12–23 presents the resulting p chart. The defect rate p is calibrated on the vertical axis and the group numbers on the horizontal axis. Lines representing the control limits are drawn. Then the defect rate points for each group are plotted. Because the control limits vary for each group, numerical values are not written next to the control limits as was done in other control charts where sample sizes were constant.

Does this p chart represent a stable, in-control process? No, because a point exceeds the UCL in Group Number 7.

Additional Rules of Thumb on Sampling

The following rules of thumb will usually result in a satisfactory job of sampling:

- If the product comes in trays, tubs, or bins, at least a few items should be taken from *every* container.
- Items should be taken from the top, middle, and bottom of each container.
- If the product comes from a continuous process, samples should be taken at intervals, such as shifts or runs.

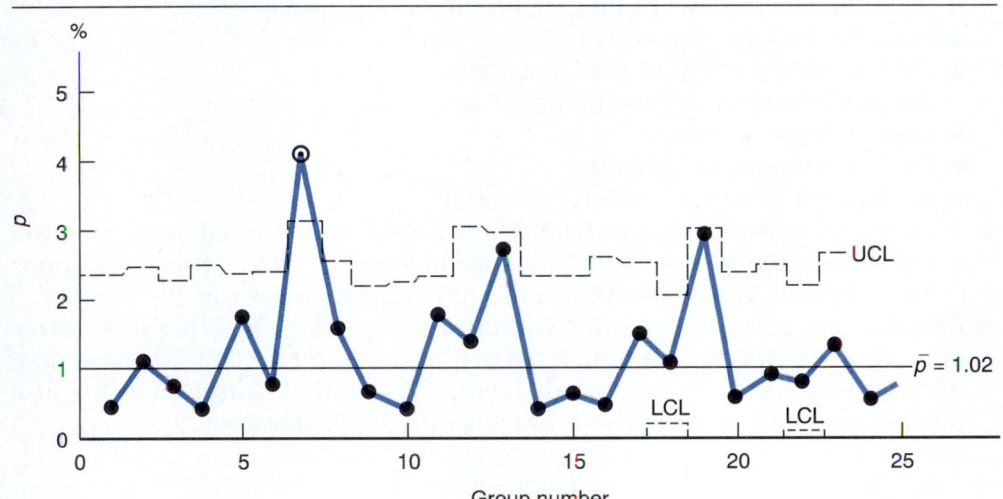

EXHIBIT 12–23
p **Chart**

Source: Kazuo Ozeki and Tetsuichi Asaka, *Handbook of Quality Tools: The Japanese Approach* (Cambridge, Mass.: Productivity Press, 1988), p. 223. With permission.

■ The items should be selected randomly.
■ Inspection, whether visual, gauging, or testing, should always be performed the same way.
■ Visual inspection should have definite objective standards of finish, appearance, color, design, and so forth.
■ All testing instruments should be properly checked and calibrated before inspection begins.

How to Interpret Control Charts

A process or activity is stable when it meets the following criteria:

■ No points are outside the control limits. (A point *on* the control limit is considered *outside* the limit.)
■ There are no abnormal patterns in the distribution of points.

The points on a control chart should follow a completely random pattern if a process or activity is in statistical control. Random distribution should follow the normal frequency distribution.

Points outside the control limits are easy to spot. Spotting abnormal patterns in the distribution is a little more difficult. The following are the kinds of abnormal patterns (see Exhibit 12–24) that may occur:

■ **Shifts.** These patterns occur when the activity finds a new point of central tendency. A continuous sequence of six or seven points on one side of the center line indicates that the activity or process has shifted. Shifts indicate improvements as well as problems in a process. A shift up on the *R* chart, for example, signals trouble because product variation has increased. A shift down on the *R* chart signals process improvement. The potential causes of shifts include:
  ■ Poor maintenance of machines and tools (shift up)
  ■ Careless or poorly trained operators (shift up)
  ■ Change in material, with poor material causing a shift up and better material causing a shift down
  ■ Clamps and fixtures not holding the work in place (shift up)
  ■ Better operators and general improvement in the process or activity causing a shift down
■ **Runs.** A run occurs when 7 successive points, 10 of 11 points, or 12 of 14 points fall on the same side. If the run is upward, the potential causes are:
  ■ Operator fatigue
  ■ Machine and tool wear
  ■ Gauge wear
  ■ Loosening clamps or fixtures that hold work in place
  ■ Machine due for adjustment
  ■ Gradual introduction of poor material
  the run is downward, the potential causes are:
  ■ General improvements
  ■ Better maintenance program
  ■ Gradual introduction of better material
■ **Trends.** These patterns occur when there is a steady rise or fall in the position of the points. The rule of thumb for a trend is six or more consecutive points rising or falling. The causes of trends are the same as for runs.
■ **Erratic.** This pattern occurs if two out of three consecutive points or three or more out of seven points are approaching a control limit or are more than two-thirds of the distance from the center line to the control limit. Because the control limit lines are the average value of ±3 standard deviations (±3

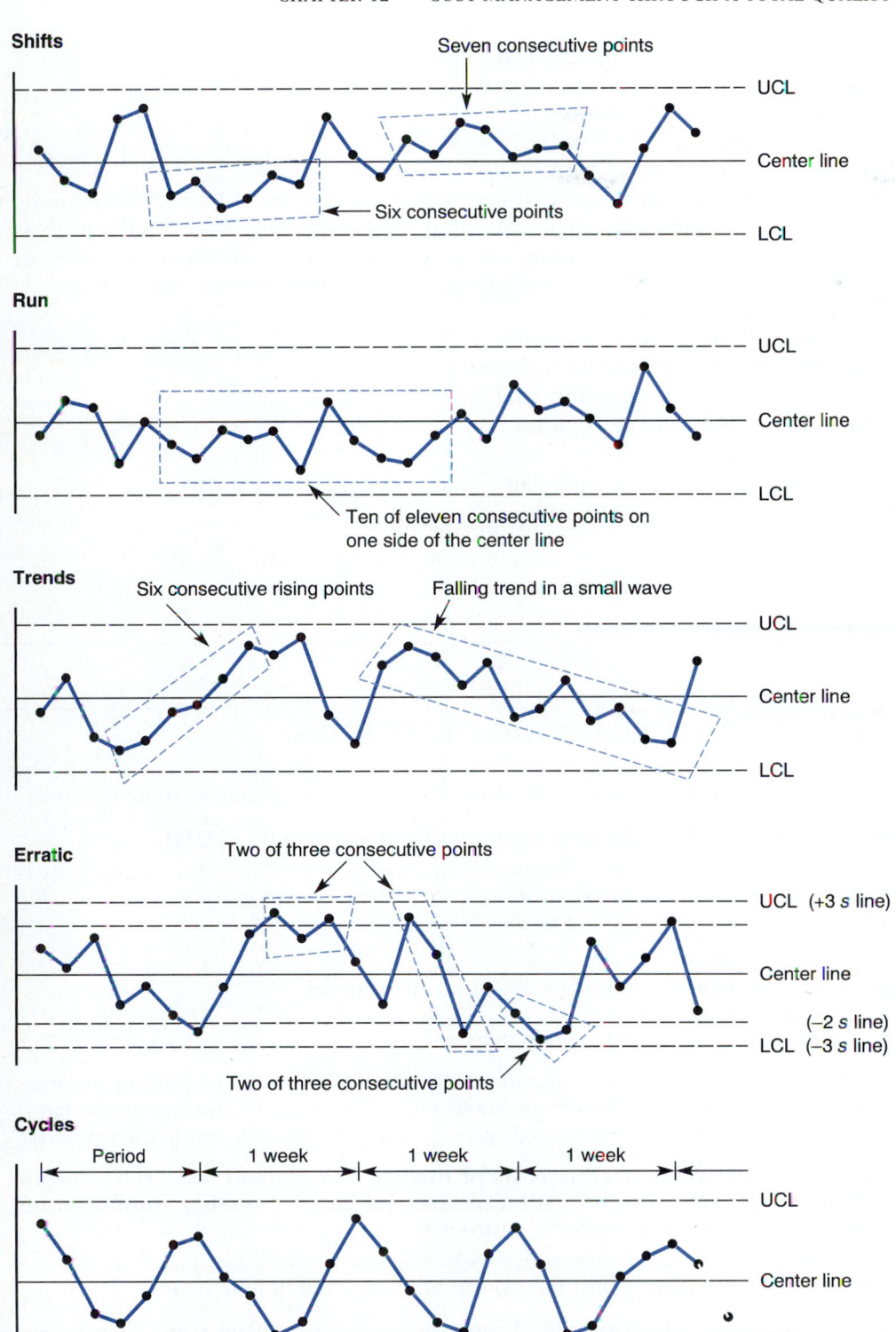

s), the two-thirds line is the value of ±2 standard deviations (±2 *s*). This line is sometimes referred to as the *warning line.*

A steep, zigzag pattern approaching the UCL and then the LCL and back again is an erratic pattern. These frequent ups and downs indicate instability in the process or activity. Potential causes for an erratic pattern include:

- Overadjustments
- Mixture of materials of different quality from upstream activities or suppliers

- Frequent breakdowns and start-ups
- Loose clamps and fixtures that hold work in place
- Poor sampling procedures
- Faulty gauges
- Inconsistent inspection standards
- **Cycles.** These patterns occur when the points move up and down in a periodic waveform. Cycles signal that something is systematically affecting the process or activity. The key to finding causes of cycles is to investigate causes that would change the activity *periodically*. Likely causes of cycle patterns are:
  - Power fluctuations
  - Varying speeds on conveyor belts
  - Temperature and seasonal changes
  - Operator fatigue and shift changes
  - Measurement gauge rotation
  - Maintenance schedules
  - Different vendors of materials
  - Change in sampling methods

SUMMARY OF LEARNING OBJECTIVES

The major goals of this chapter were to enable you to achieve four learning objectives:

Learning objective 1.   Discuss total quality management (TQM).

In the quest for competitive superiority, quality is the key. To ensure that quality is achieved, a TQM system needs to be installed. Such a system integrates the following dimensions to achieve customer satisfaction:

- Enhanced quality
- Continuous improvement in all activities and processes
- Decreased throughput
- Minimized costs of quality or zero defects

A TQM system requires total commitment from everyone throughout the organization as well as from the organization's stakeholders. A TQM system is not a program that is started and stopped, and then started again. It is an ongoing process that never ends.

Learning objective 2.   Define costs of quality and explain their relationship and trade-offs. In addition, differentiate the costs-of-quality minimization approach from the zero-defects approach.

The costs of quality refer to resources spent to assure consistent customer satisfaction. The total costs of quality reflect the expenditures incurred in four areas:

- Prevention costs, which include all expenditures made to avoid errors, defects, failures, dissatisfactions, or any other nonconformities
- Appraisal costs, which include the costs of inspecting, testing, checking, and so forth to assure that nonconformities do not reach internal and external customers
- Internal failure costs are incurred to correct nonconformities *before* they reach external customers
- External failure costs are incurred to correct nonconformities *after* they have been discovered by external customers

Summary formulas for these costs are as follows:

$$\text{Costs of conformance} = \text{Prevention costs} + \text{Appraisal costs}$$
$$\text{Costs of nonconformance} = \text{Internal failure costs} + \text{External failure costs}$$
$$\text{Costs of quality} = \text{Costs of conformance} + \text{Costs of nonconformance}$$

A TQM system is primarily prevention-based, which means that expenditures should be devoted to preventive measures. As more and more preventive measures are installed, the costs for appraisal, internal failure, and external failure will decrease substantially. The idea behind TQM is that it costs much less to prevent quality problems than to correct them. This is why high quality is much less expensive than low quality. Although it is probably impossible to reduce the costs of quality to zero, many authorities contend that it can be reduced to around 2.5 percent of sales. This figure is considerably less than the costs of quality in some companies, which are estimated to be as much as 60 percent of sales.

With the costs-of-quality minimization approach, prevention and some appraisal costs (especially for process inspection) are increased while failure costs are decreased. Total costs of quality continue to decrease until near-perfect quality is achieved. At this point, management cannot realize total costs-of-quality reductions through additional expenditures for prevention and appraisal. The focus then shifts to technological and reengineering breakthroughs to decrease the total costs of quality further.

The aim of the zero-defects approach is to eliminate *all* nonconformities. The focus is on the parts per million (PPM) performance measurement rather than on percentages and cost figures. The ultimate aim of both approaches, however, is the same: To decrease costs of quality while achieving total customer satisfaction, increasing profitability, and attaining competitive superiority.

Learning objective 3.   Describe Pareto charts and cause-and-effect diagrams, and discuss how they are used in solving quality problems.

The Pareto chart is a vertical bar graph that can be used to show the relative frequency of nonconformities, such as defects, errors, failures, and the like. A Pareto chart presents data in descending order, from the largest category to the smallest. Points are plotted for the cumulative total in each bar and are connected with a line to create a graph that shows the relative incremental addition of each category to the total.

Preparing a Pareto chart reveals key quality problems. These key problems are then targeted for improvement efforts. Pre-improvement and post-improvement charts are prepared to determine the effectiveness of the improvement efforts in both financial and nonfinancial terms.

The cause-and-effect diagram derives its name from its use. It is also called an Ishikawa diagram in honor of its developer, Professor Ishikawa, or a fishbone diagram because of its shape. By any name, it is an extremely effective tool for discovering root causes of quality problems. The spine of the "fish" connects to its "head," which represents the problem. The ribs connected to the spine represent main cause categories. Bones attached to ribs represent specific causes. Small bones attached to the bones represent causes of causes. In a meeting, the investigation team develops causes and attaches them at the appropriate places on the diagram in full view of all members. After a great deal of discussion and analysis, a final cause-and-effect diagram reveals root causes of the quality problem.

Learning objective 4.   Define control charts, and explain how they are used in a TQM system to control processes and activities.

There are two basic types of control charts:

- Variables
- Attributes

Both types of control charts are graphic aids for monitoring the status of any process or activity subject to random variations. They consist of three horizontal lines plotted on a horizontal time scale. The center line represents the average or mean value for the process or activity being controlled. The other two lines are the upper control limit (UCL) and the lower control limit (LCL). The processes or activities are measured periodically, and the values are plotted on the control chart. If the value falls within the control limits, no action is taken. If the value falls outside the control limits or plotted points show abnormal patterns, the activity is considered unstable or out of control, and an investigation is made for possible corrective action.

Two of the most widely used control charts for variables are the X chart and R chart, often called the average and range chart, respectively. Both charts are drawn on the same sheet of paper or screen. The X chart tracks the sample group mean. The R chart tracks the sample group range.

Small sample groups, usually four or five items per group, of consecutive items are taken. The dimension, weight, or some other variable of interest is measured, and the measurements are recorded on a data sheet for each sample. The mean and range for each sample group are calculated, recorded, and charted.

Control charts for attributes use pass/fail information for charting. An item passes inspection when it conforms to specifications or requirements, such as appearance, taste, color, and so forth. A nonconforming item fails inspection.

Two of the most commonly used control charts for attributes are *pn* and *p* charts. The *pn* chart tracks the number of nonconforming items in each sample group. It is easier to use than a *p* chart because the percentage of defective items does not have to be calculated. It has one restriction, however. All the sample groups have to be the same size.

The *p* chart tracks the percentage of nonconforming items in each sample group. The sample sizes are large, usually 100 or more, and the sample sizes may vary on a single chart.

"In control" conditions on control charts should exhibit the following characteristics:

- Most of the points are near the center line.
- A few points are near the control limits.
- Only an occasional rare point occurs on or beyond the control limits.
- The points occur in a random manner with no shifts, runs, trends, cycles, or other erratic behavior.

IMPORTANT TERMS

Appraisal costs   Expenditures made to identify nonconformities before a product or service reaches another activity or is delivered to the ultimate customer.

Assignable causes   Special causes that are not an inherent part of the process or activity. Examples include machine maintenance not being performed when scheduled, operators not following prescribed methods, and measurement tools not being read correctly.

Band graphs   Visualization techniques that clearly show not only the trend in costs of quality but also the change in profit. They express their internal composition and proportions by the length of a band.

Cause-and-effect diagram (fishbone diagram, Ishikawa diagram)   A tool for generating and sorting ideas about the causes of variation in a process or activity and for identifying the most likely root causes of quality problems.

Control charts   Statistical devices to identify variation in a process or activity. All processes or activities are subject to random variation despite careful planning, reengineering, and continuous improvement. The aim is to reduce variation to an acceptable level.

Control charts for attributes   Describe in qualitative terms such attributes as finish, color, or other qualitative characteristics that can be classified as "good" or "bad" or "acceptable" or "unacceptable."

Control charts for variables   Describe quality quantitatively in terms of dimension, pressure, voltage, temperature, weight, or other quantifiable characteristics.

Costs of conformance   Expenditures incurred in an effort to ensure that products or services meet customer requirements. These expenditures are for prevention and appraisal.

Costs of nonconformance   Expenditures incurred before or during use because of rejections, corrective alterations, refusals of products or services, claims, returns, replacements, and reimbursements.

Costs of quality   Consist of prevention, appraisal, internal failure, and external failure costs.

Cycles   Patterns that occur when the points move up and down in a periodic waveform.

Erratic   A pattern that occurs if two out of three consecutive points or three or more out of seven points are approaching a control limit or are more than two-thirds of the distance from the center line to the control limit.

External customers   Those who are impacted by the product or service but are not members of the company that produces the product or service, except when an internal customer becomes an external customer (e.g., when a worker for a car manufacturer buys a car from the same manufacturer).

External failure costs Expenditures incurred because poor-quality products or services are delivered to external customers.

Final inspection Activity performed to remove unacceptable products or services before they are delivered to the external customer.

Internal customers Those who are impacted by the product or service and are also members of the company that produces the product or service.

Internal failure costs Expenditures associated with products or services that fail to meet quality standards and are identified and corrected *before* being delivered to the external customer.

***p* chart** A statistical device that records the fraction or percentage of defects in a process or activity.

***pn* chart** A statistical device that records the number of defects per group.

Pareto chart Bar chart, named after the Italian economist Vilfredo Pareto, that categorizes quality problems into the "vital few and the trivial many." Each bar represents a problem category, and its height represents the frequency of occurrence.

Prevention costs Expenditures made to prevent poor-quality products or services from being produced in the first place.

Process inspection Activity performed to monitor a process or activity to ensure that it does not produce unacceptable products or services.

Quality All the characteristics and attributes required to satisfy both internal and external customers.

***R* chart** A statistical device that shows variations in the range in values of sample groups. It helps control the general variability of the process or activity. The *R* chart shows the presence of variability *within* sample groups.

Random causes Common causes that are an inherent part of the process or activity. The variation from the process is what is expected in its usual operation.

Ripple charts Hierarchical graphs that show the impact of defects or failures and other nonconformities throughout a series of activities or processes.

Runs Patterns that occur when 7 or more successive points, 10 of 11 points, or 12 of 14 points fall on the same side of the center line.

Shifts Patterns that occur when an activity finds a new point of central tendency.

Total commitment The mobilization of all managers and the empowerment of workers and stakeholders to engage themselves into linked value-added activities for the purpose of achieving the greatest customer satisfaction at the lowest cost.

Total quality management (TQM) An integrated system that anticipates, meets, and exceeds customers' needs, wants, and expectations. It is the totality of ways for achieving superior quality.

Trends Patterns that occur when there is a steady rise or fall in the position of points.

$\bar{X}$ chart A statistical device used in determining the limits of variation that can be expected in the averages of small sample groups taken from a process or activity. It helps control the average of the process or activity. The $\bar{X}$ chart shows the presence of variability *between* sample groups.

Zero defects A quality standard that calls for products and services to be produced and delivered according to customer requirements. The basis of zero defects is doing it right the first time, and eliminating *all* nonconformities.

DEMONSTRATION PROBLEMS

■ **DEMONSTRATION PROBLEM 1** *Classifying and reporting costs of quality.*

At the beginning of the year, Tricore Company installed a TQM system. By the end of the year, various managers were reporting good results. For example, the production manager stated that scrap and rework had both decreased. The owner of the company was pleased to hear of the success, but wanted a report of the financial impact of the quality improvements. To prepare this report, the following financial data were collected for actual and projected costs for 19X5. Actual and projected sales for 19X5 were $10 million.

TYPES OF COSTS	ACTUAL	PROJECTED
Scrap	$200,000	$300,000
Rework	300,000	500,000
Design	100,000	60,000
Training	100,000	40,000
Incoming inspection	200,000	100,000
Process inspection	100,000	150,000
Final inspection	200,000	100,000
Warranty repairs	100,000	300,000
Recalls	200,000	800,000

Required:

a. Prepare a costs-of-quality report and classify the costs as prevention, appraisal, internal failure, and external failure. If the actual costs are less than the projected costs, show the amount of variance and designate it as F (favorable); if the actual costs are more than the projected costs, show the amount of the variance and designate it as U (unfavorable). Also, calculate the costs of quality as a percentage of sales for both the total actual and projected costs.

b. If prevention costs are "good" costs, explain why an *increase* is designated as unfavorable (U) rather than favorable (F). Also, discuss why a *decrease* in process inspection costs, usually considered a "good" cost, is designated as favorable (F).

c. Assume that all other costs, both actual and projected, were $5 million. Show sales, other costs, costs of quality, and profit using band graphs.

SOLUTION TO DEMONSTRATION PROBLEM 1

a.

Tricore Company
Costs-of-Quality Report
For the Year Ended 19X5

Cost Category	Projected Costs	Actual Costs	Variance
Prevention costs:			
Design	$ 60,000	$ 100,000	<$ 40,000> U
Training	40,000	100,000	< 60,000> U
Total prevention	$ 100,000	$ 200,000	<$100,000> U
Appraisal costs:			
Incoming inspection	$ 100,000	$ 200,000	<$100,000> U
Process inspection	150,000	100,000	50,000 F
Final inspection	100,000	200,000	< 100,000> U
Total appraisal	$ 350,000	$ 500,000	<$150,000> U
Internal failure costs:			
Scrap	$ 300,000	$ 200,000	$100,000 F
Rework	500,000	300,000	200,000 F
Total internal failure	$ 800,000	$ 500,000	$300,000 F
External failure costs:			
Warranty repairs	$ 300,000	$ 100,000	$200,000 F
Recalls	800,000	200,000	600,000 F
Total external failure	$1,100,000	$ 300,000	$800,000 F
Total costs of quality	$2,350,000	$1,500,000	$850,000 F
Percentage of sales	23.50%	15.00%	8.50% F

b. Management had projected (or budgeted) the prevention costs to be $100,000. *Any* expenditure over what management had planned for during the period is considered unfavorable. Other analysis may indicate that the extra $100,000 spent on prevention was money well spent, but such an analysis is beyond the scope of the costs-of-quality report. Costs for process inspection are considered "good" costs to make sure that processes and activities are operating as intended. But the actual costs for process inspection were $100,000, $50,000 less than projected. Is this $50,000 variance favorable? From the viewpoint of the costs-of-quality report, comparing actual costs to projected or budgeted costs, the answer is yes. But from a TQM perspective, it could be that if $50,000 to $100,000 more had been spent on process inspection, the costs of $200,000 for final inspection as well as a good proportion of internal failure and external failure costs could have been reduced. Much more analysis will have to be done before such decisions can be made. The purpose of the costs-of-quality report is to track such costs over time. Management decides how much and what kind of expenditures will be made for quality. However, the costs-of-quality report shows that a $250,000 increase in prevention and inspection, or 2.50% of sales, has apparently decreased internal failure and external failure costs by 11.00% of sales, not including intangible costs, such as lost customer goodwill.

c.

Actual

Sales $10,000,000	Other costs $5,000,000	Quality costs $1,500,000	Profit $3,500,000

Costs of quality

Projected

Sales $10,000,000	Other costs $5,000,000	Quality costs $2,350,000	Profit $2,650,000

■ **DEMONSTRATION PROBLEM 2** *Prepare a cause-and-effect diagram.*

Acme Distributors is a large mail order company that is suffering from poor order processing performance. Over 30 percent of its customer orders are lost, late, or not processed correctly. The main cause categories are:

■ People
■ Methods
■ Machines
■ Materials
■ Environment

Required:

Develop a cause-and-effect diagram that shows the possible causes of why Acme is suffering from poor order processing performance. Make any assumptions you deem necessary.

SOLUTION TO DEMONSTRATION PROBLEM 2

Cause-and-Effect diagram of why Acme is suffering from poor order processing performance: (see p. 592)

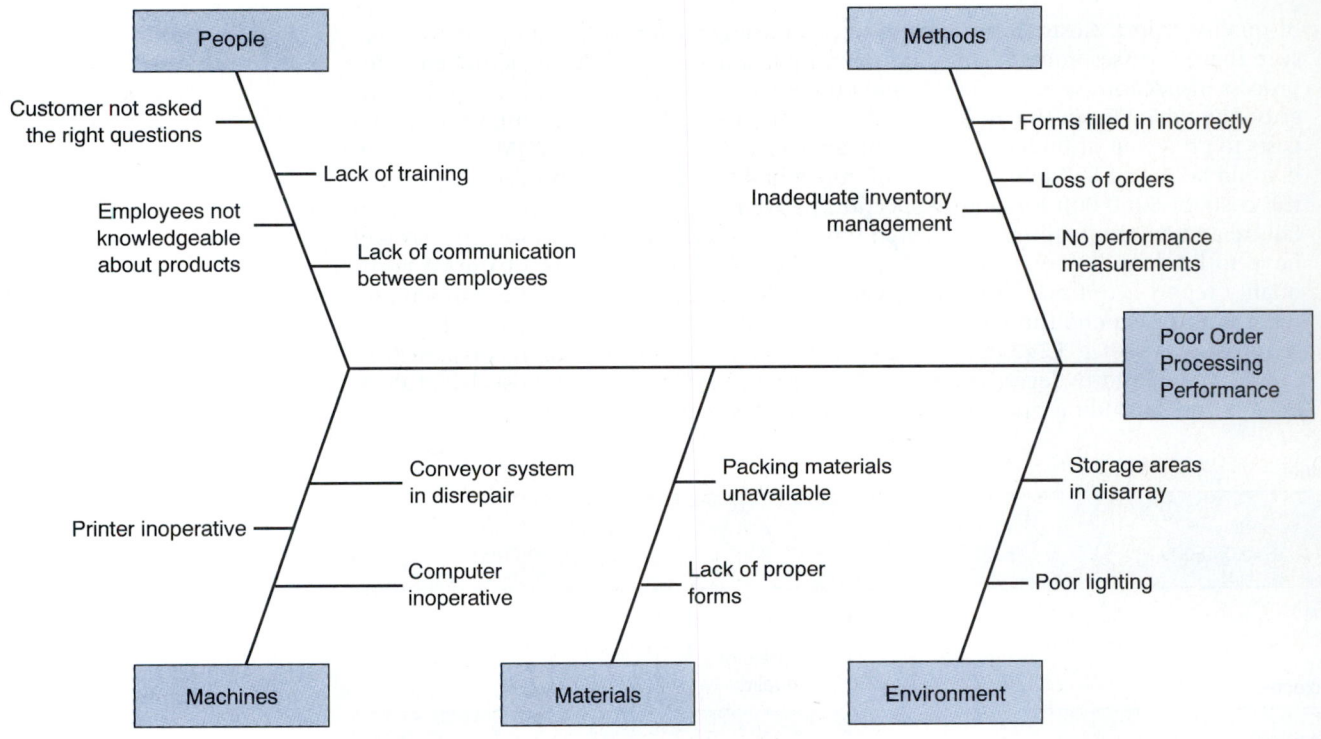

■ **DEMONSTRATION PROBLEM 3** *Preparing a Pareto chart.*

At Metalcraft, Inc., a molding activity stamps a metal fixture into a particular shape. The fixture is then covered with an adhesive and placed in a mold into which rubber is injected. A study was conducted to investigate the number of defects. The period of investigation was from June 1 through June 30. The following data were collected:

DEFECTIVE ITEMS	NUMBER OF DEFECTS
Bad rubber	91
Poor adhesion	128
Cracks	9
Voids	36
Impurities	15
Cuts	23
Other	12

Required:
Prepare a Pareto chart to reveal the results of the investigation.

SOLUTION TO DEMONSTRATION PROBLEM 3

NUMBER	DEFECTIVE ITEMS	NUMBER OF DEFECTS	CUMULATIVE NUMBER
1	Poor adhesion	128	128
2	Bad rubber	91	128 + 91 = 219
3	Voids	36	219 + 36 = 255
4	Cuts	23	255 + 23 = 278
5	Impurities	15	278 + 15 = 293
6	Cracks	9	293 + 9 = 302
7	Other	12	302 + 12 = 314
	Total	314	314

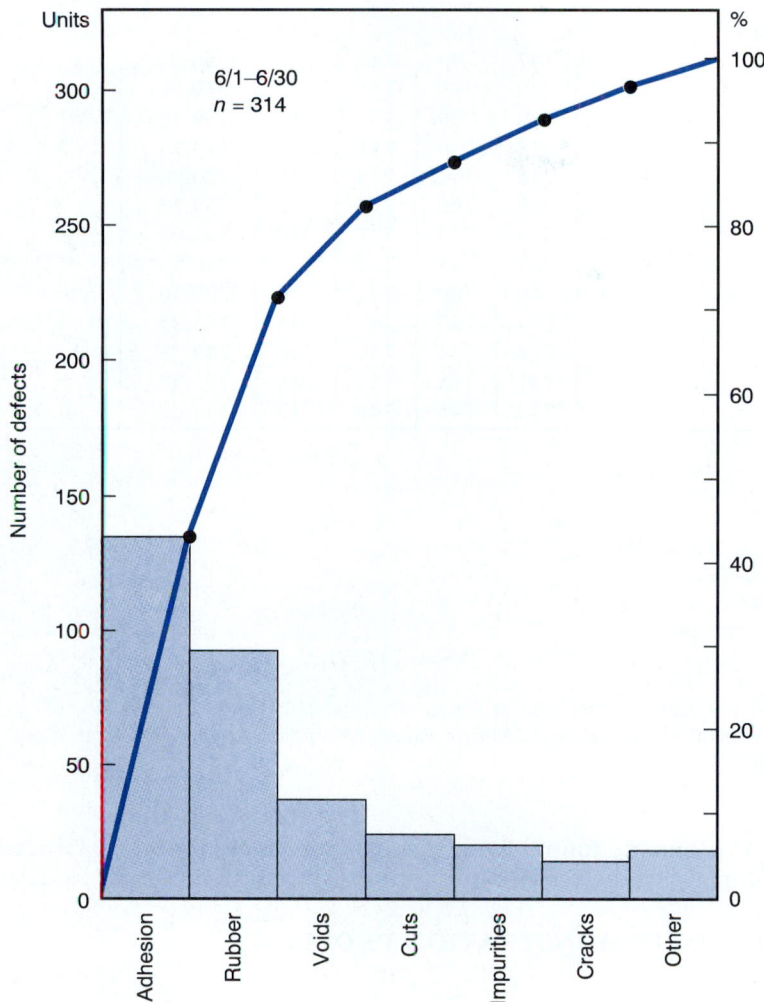

Source: Kazuo Ozeki and Tetsuichi Asaka, *Handbook of Quality Tools: The Japanese Approach* (Cambridge, Mass.: Productivity Press, 1988), p. 143.

■ **DEMONSTRATION PROBLEM 4**   *Calculating $\overline{\overline{X}}$, $\overline{R}$, and control limits.*

Four successive doorknobs from a machining process are measured with a micrometer about every half-hour during two shifts' of production. The measurements are recorded in the following data sheet:

Data Sheet for Doorknobs (in 1/1,000 Inch)

Time	Sample Number	Measurements in Each Sample				Average, $\overline{X}$	Range, R
		a	*b*	*c*	*d*		
Apr. 23							
8:00 A.M.	1	735	745	739	738	739.25	10
8:35	2	742	736	739	737	738.50	6
9:05	3	739	741	739	744	740.75	5
9:25	4	740	736	737	739	738.00	4
10:00	5	738	744	738	742	740.50	6
10:30	6	740	744	739	745	742.00	6
10:55	7	742	739	740	742	740.75	3
11:35	8	741	742	743	736	740.50	7
12:00	9	742	742	736	737	739.25	6
1:00 P.M.	10	746	746	746	745	745.75*	1
1:35	11	749	746	748	744	746.75*	5
2:00	12	745	744	748	746	745.75*	4

Continued

—Continued

2:30	13	747	745	746	746	746.00*	2
3:05	14	739	740	741	738	739.50	3
3:30	15	740	739	739	740	739.50	1
3:45	16	742	739	741	737	739.75	5
4:30	17	740	744	738	738	740.00	6
5:00	18	740	740	735	742	739.25	7
5:30	19	745	742	737	740	741.00	8
6:00	20	739	741	742	740	740.50	3
6:30	21	740	740	742	736	739.50	6
6:55	22	744	745	741	743	743.25	4
7:30	23	748	743	744	736	742.75	12*
8:00	24	741	745	742	746	743.50	5
8:35	25	743	745	746	742	744.00	4
					Totals	18,536.25	129

$\bar{\bar{X}} = 741.45$
$\bar{R} = 5.16$
A_2 for samples of 4 = 0.729
D_3 for samples of 4 = 0
D_4 for samples of 4 = 2.282
$A_2\bar{R} = 0.729 \times 5.16 = 3.76$
$\bar{X}$ limits = $\bar{\bar{X}} \pm A_2\bar{R} = 741.45 \pm 3.76 = 745.21, 737.69$
R limits = $D_3\bar{R} = 0 \times 5.16 = 0$
$\qquad\qquad D_4\bar{R} = 2.282 \times 5.16 = 11.78$
Data from William B. Rice, *Control Charts in Factory Management* (New York: John Wiley, 1947), p. 49

Required:
Calculate $\bar{\bar{X}}$, $\bar{R}$, and the control limits. Are any points out of control? If so, which ones? State what might be the cause of such out-of-control conditions.

SOLUTION TO DEMONSTRATION PROBLEM 4

$$\bar{\bar{X}} = \frac{\Sigma \bar{X}}{k}$$

$$= \frac{18,536.25}{25}$$

$$= \underline{741.45}$$

$$\bar{R} = \frac{\Sigma R}{k}$$

$$= \frac{129}{25}$$

$$= \underline{5.16}$$

A_2 for samples of 4 = 0.729
D_3 for samples of 4 = 0
D_4 for samples of 4 = 2.282
$$A_2\bar{R} = 0.729 \times 5.16$$
$$= \underline{\underline{3.76}}$$

$\bar{X}$ limits:

$$\text{UCL} = \bar{\bar{X}} + A_2\bar{R}$$
$$= 741.45 + 3.76$$
$$= \underline{745.21}$$

$$\text{LCL} = \bar{\bar{X}} + A_2\bar{R}$$
$$= 741.45 - 3.76$$
$$= \underline{737.69}$$

R limits:

$$UCL = D_4 \times \bar{R}$$
$$= 2.282 \times 5.16$$
$$= \underline{\underline{11.78}}$$

$$LCL = D_3 \times \bar{R}$$
$$= 0 \times 5.16$$
$$= \underline{\underline{0}}$$

If plotted on an $\bar{X}$ chart, points Sample Number 10, 11, 12, and 13 would exceed the UCL of 745.21, and would therefore be out of control. On an *R* chart, point Sample Number 23 would exceed the UCL of 11.78.

The cause of the four out-of-control sample averages should be investigated. Possible causes include:

■ Different inspector
■ Improper machine settings

■ **DEMONSTRATION PROBLEM 5**   *Calculating $\bar{p}$ and control limits.*
Assume the following sample data:

Group number:	1	2	3	4	5	6	7	8	9	10
Sample size:	100	110	100	100	110	110	80	100	90	100
Number of defects:	10	12	8	9	11	12	8	10	11	9
Percentage defective:	10.0	10.9	8.0	9.0	10.0	10.9	10.0	10.0	12.2	9.0

Required:
Calculate $\bar{p}$ and determine the UCL and LCL at ±3 standard deviations (or sigmas). What does $\bar{p}$ represent? Explain why points falling outside the LCL should be investigated.

SOLUTION TO DEMONSTRATION PROBLEM 5

$$\bar{p} = \frac{\Sigma\, pn}{\Sigma\, n}$$
$$= \frac{100}{1,000}$$
$$= \underline{\underline{10\%}}$$

$\bar{p}$ represents the center line of the *p* chart.

$$UCL = \bar{p} + 3\sqrt{\frac{\bar{p}(1 - \bar{p})}{n}}$$
$$= 10 + 3\sqrt{\frac{10(100 - 10)}{100}}$$
$$= 10 + (3 \times 3)$$
$$= \underline{\underline{19\%}}$$

$$LCL = \bar{p} - 3\sqrt{\frac{\bar{p}(1 - \bar{p})}{n}}$$
$$= 10 - 3\sqrt{\frac{10(100 - 10)}{100}}$$
$$= 10 - (3 \times 3)$$
$$= \underline{\underline{1\%}}$$

Clearly, if an activity suddenly makes more defects than is normal, points exceeding the UCL will show this and investigation is warranted. But why should anyone be concerned if the activity makes fewer defects than is normal? Points falling below the LCL will indicate this situation. Unless the activity has been improved or reengineered, the causes may be due to a change in how the items are inspected and tested. For example, a new inspector may be inexperienced and therefore fail to find defects.

▎ REVIEW QUESTIONS

12.1 What is the goal of TQM? At what point does a company complete its TQM effort?

12.2 List five attributes of quality.

12.3 TQM designs and builds quality in. How does traditional management try to attain quality? Name some other major differences in the way quality is viewed by traditional and world-class management.

12.4 Which individuals in an organization are involved in the TQM "total commitment" and why?

12.5 What percentage of downstream problems are caused by poor design? What steps can be taken to remedy poor design?

12.6 What "key elements" are necessary to achieve customer satisfaction?

12.7 Describe the ISO 9000 compliance and certification process and its purpose. What are the four required steps?

12.8 Rate the following costs associated with quality, with 1 being the lowest cost and 4 being the highest cost, and explain your reasoning:

_____ Prevention costs

_____ Appraisal costs

_____ Internal failure costs

_____ External failure costs

12.9 Name five types of costs associated with internal failure as well as five types of external failure costs.

12.10 Describe the typical formula used for internal failure performance measurements. Is improvement indicated by an increase or a decrease in this ratio?

12.11 Name three types of performance measurements that can be used to measure external failure.

12.12 Describe the costs of nonconformance.

12.13 What is the cost management rule regarding costs of quality?

12.14 Discuss the effect on the total costs of quality, as well as on quality itself, as companies shift their quality expenditures from failure costs to prevention and appraisal costs.

12.15 What is the "1–10–100 rule"?

12.16 Up to what point should prevention costs continue to be implemented?

12.17 During the first several years of TQM, do appraisal costs tend to increase or decrease? Explain.

12.18 What is the purpose of using ripple charts?

12.19 Discuss the objective of a zero-defects quality standard. What argument can be made against this approach?

12.20 Name the advantage of using parts per million as a defect measurement method.

12.21 Describe a Pareto chart, explain when it is most useful, and indicate what costs-of-quality information can be graphed. Discuss the "Pareto principle" and explain how it relates to Pareto chart analysis.

12.22 Discuss the primary purpose of using a fishbone diagram.

12.23 When would a company use control charts? Briefly describe their purpose and their key graphical features.

12.24 Discuss the difference between "random causes" and "assignable causes." Name the six assignable causes.

12.25 The most common control charts used for variables are the $\bar{X}$ chart and the R chart. Describe how they are used and what they measure.

12.26 Describe the two common control charts used for attributes and explain how they differ.

12.27 Name five of the seven rules of thumb on sampling.

12.28 Name and briefly describe the five abnormal patterns of points in a distribution. Give at least three potential causes for each type of abnormal pattern.

CHAPTER-SPECIFIC PROBLEMS

These problems require responses based directly on concepts and techniques presented in the text.

12.29 *Classifying costs of quality.* Classify the following costs of quality by inserting an X under the appropriate category:

	PREVENTION	APPRAISAL	INTERNAL FAILURE	EXTERNAL FAILURE
1. Final inspection				
2. Warranty repairs				
3. Goods returned				
4. Quality training				
5. Settlement of product liability suit				
6. Field service personnel				
7. Packaging inspection				
8. Complaint department				
9. Rework units from work-in-process				
10. Replacement of defective product				
11. Lost sales				
12. Scrap				
13. Recalls				
14. Downtime caused by defects				
15. Incoming inspection				
16. Maintenance of test equipment				
17. Calibration of test gauges				
18. Design engineering				
19. Quality improvement projects				
20. Reinspection of rework				

12.30 *Preparing a pie chart and bar chart showing percentage of costs of quality.* Costs of quality are 30% of sales. Costs of quality categories are as follows:

- Prevention: 10%
- Appraisal: 20%
- Internal failure: 30%
- External failure: 40%

Required:
Prepare a pie chart that shows the proportion of costs of quality to sales. Separate the costs-of-quality pie segment from the pie chart and draw a bar chart showing the proportion of cost categories to this segment.

12.31 *Improving quality and profitability.* The Mastercraft Company reported the following sales, other costs, and costs of quality for the past three years:

YEAR	SALES	OTHER COSTS	COSTS OF QUALITY
1	$10,000,000	30%	40%
2	12,000,000	32	30
3	15,000,000	34	10

Required:
a. Draw three band graphs depicting the preceding data.
b. Assume that the quality standard is 2.5% of sales. Also assume that sales will be $20,000,000 and other costs are estimated to be 30% of sales for year 4. Draw a band graph that reveals this data. Calculate the dollar amount of other costs, costs of quality, and profit.

12.32 *Preparing a ripple chart.* Rework is a major internal failure cost. Rework costs for Associated Fabricators were $200,000. The rework impacted several other areas with total expenditures of $200,000 as follows:

- Technician wages: $40,000
- Materials handling: $20,000
- Downtime caused by rework: $60,000
- Reinspection of rework: $30,000
- Repackaging: $15,000
- Extra raw materials for rework: $20,000
- Extra overtime wages: $15,000

Required:
Prepare a ripple chart that reflects these costs of rework.

12.33 *Preparing a costs-of-quality report.* The Halstrom Company incurred the following costs of quality:

	19X4	19X5
Warranty repairs	$200,000	$ 50,000
Product recalls	500,000	100,000
Rework	300,000	50,000
Testing	100,000	200,000
Calibration	50,000	100,000
Training	50,000	200,000
Product design	100,000	200,000
Product liability	100,000	50,000
Retesting	200,000	100,000

Required:
Prepare a costs-of-quality report that classifies each of the above costs under the proper costs-of-quality category. Indicate whether the costs are increasing or decreasing and by how much.

12.34 *Decreasing the total costs of quality.* Management of the Lormis Company believes that its overall costs of quality could be further reduced by increasing expenditures in certain key costs-of-quality categories. Management has identified the following costs of quality:

COSTS OF QUALITY	EXPENDITURES
Rework	$ 5,000
Supervision	15,000
Recalls	12,000
Scrap	8,000
Training	14,000
Inspection of work-in-process	20,000
Reengineering efforts	8,000
Repair	10,000
Replacements	10,000
Downtime	9,000
Retesting	4,000
Product liability insurance	11,000
Quality audits	6,000
Continuous improvement	1,000
Warranty repairs	13,000
Testing of incoming materials	8,000

Required:
a. Classify these costs into the four costs-of-quality categories.
b. Determine the total dollars being spent on each costs-of-quality category.
c. Based upon the company's current expenditures by costs-of-quality category, on which cost category should the company concentrate its efforts in order to decrease its overall costs of quality and thereby improve its profitability?

12.35 *Calculating costs-of-quality ratios.* As a management accountant for a start-up electrical household fan manufacturer, you have just been assigned the task of analyzing the company's first two years of operating data. The following operating results were provided to you:

	PERIOD A	PERIOD B
Total sales dollars	$100,000	$110,000
Units produced	10,000	11,000
Defective units	1,429	1,402
Number of reworked units	1,225	1,101
Dollar value of sales returns and allowances	$37,500	$38,600
Number of warranty repairs	98	102
Dollar value of warranty repairs	$980	$1,020
Number of replacements	156	248
Number of units in the field	10,000	21,000

Required:
a. Determine the effectiveness of inspection by calculating the inspection ratio.
b. Measure the effectiveness of controlling internal failure by calculating the internal failure causing rework ratio.
c. Measure the impact of external failure by calculating the following ratios:
   1. Sales returns and allowances.
   2. Warranty repairs.
   3. Replacements.
d. Based upon your ratio analysis, where has the company improved the most?

12.36 *Preparing a trend report.* The management accountant at Proactive Company has calculated and tracked costs of quality as a percentage of sales for the past four years (19X1 was the first year the company implemented a TQM system). This information is presented below:

YEAR	PREVENTION	APPRAISAL	INTERNAL FAILURE	EXTERNAL FAILURE
19X1	2%	6%	10%	20%
19X2	3	7	7	12
19X3	4	7	4	7
19X4	5	3	2	1

Required:
Prepare a bar graph that reveals the trend of these data. Discuss what the graph has to say about the success of the TQM system.

12.37 *Preparing a bar chart showing costs-of-quality trends as a percentage of sales.* The Starbrite Company has had a TQM system in place for three years. The costs of quality as a percentage of sales for these years follow:

	YEAR 1	YEAR 2	YEAR 3
Prevention costs	0.50%	10.00%	2.00%
Appraisal costs	1.00	5.00	3.00
Internal failure costs	15.00	10.00	5.00
External failure costs	30.00	15.00	10.00

Required:
Prepare a bar chart showing the costs-of-quality trends as a percentage of sales.

12.38 *Minimizing costs of quality.* The Progresso Company is planning on implementing a TQM system. Cost projections and defective rates are as follows:

PREVENTION COSTS	APPRAISAL COSTS	PERCENTAGE DEFECTIVE	INTERNAL FAILURE COSTS	EXTERNAL FAILURE COSTS
$ 50,000	$ 60,000	20.00%	$500,000	$800,000
150,000	200,000	15.00	300,000	400,000
200,000	250,000	10.00	250,000	300,000
220,000	200,000	7.00	180,000	150,000
260,000	180,000	4.00	100,000	120,000
280,000	140,000	1.00	80,000	100,000
300,000	100,000	0.001	20,000	30,000
400,000	30,000	0.0001	18,000	15,000

Required:
Determine the combination of costs that minimizes total costs of quality.

12.39 *Preparing Pareto charts to show number of defects and monetary losses.* The Dockman Pants Factory's production from June 1 through June 30 resulted in 245 nonconforming pants. An analysis of the nonconforming pants revealed the following defects:

DEFECT	NUMBER OF PANTS	MONETARY LOSS
Loose threads	95	$ 87,000
Hemming wrong	55	42,000
Material flaw	40	24,000
Tear	20	18,000
Buttonholes	20	10,000
Other	15	17,000
Totals	245	$198,000

The nonconforming pants were discounted according to defect and sold to Cutrate Stores and the monetary losses recorded.

Required:
Prepare a Pareto chart showing the number and types of defects. Prepare a Pareto chart showing the monetary losses by types of defects. In both charts, shade the loose threads bar, crosshatch the hemming wrong bar, and hatch the material flaw bar. The other bars should be clear; that is, no shading or hatching should be used.

12.40 *Preparing a Pareto chart for customer complaints.* The Rusty Bowl Restaurant recorded 260 complaints during a one-week period as follows:

TYPE OF COMPLAINT	NUMBER OF COMPLAINTS
Cold food	105
Salad not fresh	94
Lack of cleanliness	25
Food tastes bad	13
Poor service	10
Food too greasy	9
Flimsy utensils	2
Not courteous	2

Required:
Prepare a Pareto chart for the preceding data.

12.41 *Preparing pre-improvement and post-improvement Pareto charts.* The grinding process in Ingersoll Company was producing various defects. A quality investigation team discovered a total of 81 cases containing the following number and type of defects:

Defect A = 40
Defect B = 10
Defect C = 8
Defect D = 7
Defect E = 6
Defect F = 4
Other   = 6

A number of improvements were installed in the grinding process to reduce these defects. One month later, the quality investigation team again took a sample from the grinding process and discovered a total of 44 cases containing the following number and type of defects:

Defect A = 8
Defect B = 9
Defect C = 7
Defect D = 7
Defect E = 3
Defect F = 5
Other   = 5

Required:
Prepare a pre-improvement Pareto chart and a post-improvement Pareto chart. Shade defect A in both charts.

12.42 *Preparing a cause-and-effect diagram.* The main cause categories of late shipments at the Flying Dragon Distribution Company are people, information, equipment, and procedures. The underlying causes follow:

■ Incomplete data on form
■ Lack of performance measures
■ Too many authorizations
■ No follow-up
■ Forklift unavailable
■ Trucks unavailable
■ Printer failure
■ Forms unavailable
■ Lack of communication between shifts
■ Lack of training
■ Failure to collect correct and sufficient data from customers

Required:
Prepare a cause-and-effect diagram for the preceding information.

12.43 *Preparing an Ishikawa diagram.* You are the owner of a dairy operation. Milk production is dropping when it should be increasing. You are about to contact the agricultural extension agent when your college-educated daughter expounds on the benefits of analyzing the situation using an Ishikawa diagram.

You and your daughter identify the following items as possible reasons for the decrease in milk production:

■ Clogged milking equipment
■ Cows sold and not replaced
■ Decline in quality of breeding stock
■ Failure to completely milk cows
■ Failure to impregnate cows at appropriate time
■ Inaccurate milk measurement by milk cooperative
■ Inaccurate milk production gauges
■ Inadequately trained milker
■ Lack of feed grain
■ Milk theft
■ Poor-quality feed
■ Stray voltage from milking equipment

Required:
Prepare an Ishikawa diagram based upon the preceding information.

12.44 *Preparing a cause-and-effect diagram.* A molding process makes motor blocks. The worst defect is cracks in the motor block. An investigation team is trying to determine the causes of such cracks. The team uses the 4M method for main cause categories. The team discovered the following root causes:

- Molding equipment worn
- Poor maintenance
- Molded blocks allowed to cool too quickly
- Too much pressure applied
- Material contains contaminants
- Quality of material fluctuates
- Operators' poor physical condition because they are tired and nervous
- Inadequate training

Required:
Prepare a cause-and-effect diagram based on the preceding information.

12.45 *Analyzing sample data with $\overline{X}$ and R charts.* Data for 20 samples of five are shown below. These measurements represent deviations from specified nominal net weight grams of a medicated cream packaged in glass jars.

	2	1	3	0	3	3	1	1	2	2
	1	0	0	0	2	0	1	0	0	1
	0	-2	-1	-2	1	0	0	0	0	0
	-1	-3	-2	-2	0	0	0	0	-1	-1
	-2	-3	-3	-3	-1	-1	-1	-1	-1	-3
Total	0	-7	-3	-7	5	2	1	0	0	-1

	1	3	2	2	2	1	2	5	1	4
	0	1	2	1	-1	1	1	2	1	1
	0	1	1	0	-2	0	-1	2	-1	0
	-1	1	1	-1	-2	-1	-1	1	-1	0
	-1	-1	1	-2	-3	-2	-3	-1	-2	0
Total	-1	5	7	0	-6	-1	-2	9	-2	5

Source: Harrison M. Wadsworth, Jr., Kenneth S. Stephens, and A. Blanton Godfrey, *Modern Methods for Quality Control and Improvement* (New York: John Wiley, 1986), p. 145.

Required:
Calculate $\overline{X}$ and R for the data. Then calculate $\overline{\overline{X}}$ and $\overline{R}$ and theri UCL and LCL. Plot the data on the $\overline{X}$ and R control charts and state whether the packaging activity is in control. Explain why.

12.46 *Calculation of $\overline{\overline{X}}$, $\overline{R}$, and control limits.* In a packaging process, the weight of each package must be controlled as accurately as possible. From this process, an inspector takes a sample from each batch made. Over ten successive batches, the inspector obtained the following results ($\overline{X}$ values have been rounded):

BATCH NUMBER	MEASURED VALUE X_1	X_2	X_3	X_4	X_5	AVERAGE, $\overline{X}$	RANGE, R
1	177	176	177	178	175	176.6	3
2	178	179	176	180	177	178.0	4
3	174	177	177	176	175	175.8	3
4	175	178	180	172	176	176.2	8
5	175	175	174	173	174	174.2	2
6	177	178	176	178	175	176.8	3
7	170	175	178	177	173	174.6	8
8	172	177	177	176	177	175.8	5
9	181	174	174	175	176	176.0	7
10	174	175	175	175	173	174.4	2

Required:
Calculate $\bar{\bar{X}}$, $\bar{R}$, and control limits at 1.96 and 3.00 standard deviations from $\bar{X}$. A_2 for a sample size of 5 at 1.96 standard deviations is 0.38. What could the control limits set at 1.96 (or two) standard deviations be used for?

12.47 *Calculating UCL and LCL for $\bar{X}$ and R and commenting on the number of sample groups.* Five sample groups taken from a milling process resulted in the following data:

SAMPLE GROUP	MEAN	RANGE
1	40.0/4 = 10.0	10.2 − 9.8 = 0.4
2	40.0/4 = 10.0	10.4 − 9.8 = 0.6
3	39.6/4 = 9.9	10.1 − 9.7 = 0.4
4	40.0/4 = 10.0	10.5 − 9.9 = 0.6
5	40.4/4 = 10.1	10.3 − 9.7 = 0.6

Required:
a. Calculate the UCL and LCL for $\bar{X}$ and R. Is the milling process in control?
b. Comment on the number of sample groups. Should there be more or less?

12.48 *Calculating and discussing UCL and LCL for R.* Twenty-five samples of $n = 10$ observations have been taken from a finishing activity. The average sample range was 0.02 centimeter.

Required:
a. Determine upper and lower control limits for sample ranges.
b. What are R charts used for? Discuss the meaning of your solution in Requirement (a).

12.49 *Revising $\bar{p}n$ and control limits after assignable causes are eliminated.* A continuous production process in a foundry makes truck frames. A random sample of 50 frames is taken from each day's output and inspected for cracks, abrasions, and nonconformities. The results of 28 days of past operations are as follows:

DATE	NUMBER OF DEFECTS, *pn*	DATE	NUMBER OF DEFECTS, *pn*
April 27	1	May 11	2
28	2	12	1
29	1	13	1
30	2	14	1
May 1	2	15	2
2	8	16	2
3	7	17	2
4	8	18	3
5	10	19	1
6	8	20	1
7	2	21	2
8	3	22	3
9	3	23	1
10	3	24	2

Required:
Calculate $\bar{p}n$ and the control limits for the preceding data. What days represent out-of-control conditions? Should $\bar{p}n$ and the control limits be revised? Explain why or why not.

12.50 *Spotting abnormalities and out-of-control conditions.* The following graph illustrates a distribution of points on a control chart:

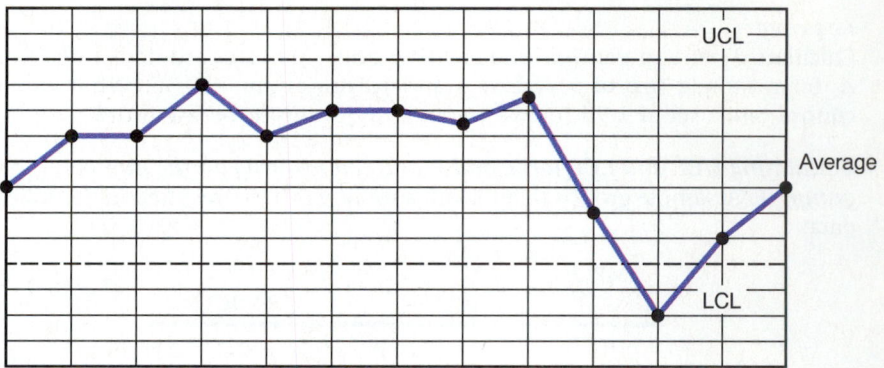

Required:

Circle the points that are out of control. Explain why you circled these points.

THINK-TANK PROBLEMS

Although these problems are based on chapter material, reading extra material, reviewing previous chapters, and using creativity may be required to develop workable solutions.

12.51 *Costs-of-quality analysis.* The chief executive officer (CEO) of Ukiah Company believes that the firm can improve its profitability substantially by implementing a TQM system. Before committing the company to a TQM system, however, the CEO wants a preliminary estimate of the total costs of quality currently being incurred. The following information is available from the past year:

1. Sales revenue: $10,000,000; profit: $1,000,000
2. During the year, 2,000 units already sold and under warranty had to be repaired. Warranty repair costs average $100 per unit.
3. Nine inspectors are employed to perform final inspection. Each earns an annual salary of $30,000.
4. The company installed a quality training program that it requires its employees to take. The estimated annual cost of the program is $100,000.
5. Six employees handle customer complaints. Each earns an annual salary of $40,000.
6. A customer canceled an order that would have increased profits by $300,000. The customer's reason for cancellation was poor product quality.
7. Each year, approximately 10,000 units are rejected in final inspection. It costs $50 per unit to rework these units.
8. The company gave sales allowances totaling $500,000 due to substandard products being returned by customers.
9. Total scrap is $600,000, of which 80% is quality related.
10. Product liability insurance premium is $100,000 per year.
11. Depreciation for testing equipment is $400,000 per year.
12. Retesting for reworked items runs approximately $200,000 annually.
13. Process inspection runs $300,000 annually.

Required:

a. Prepare a costs-of-quality report, classifying costs by category.
b. Calculate the ratio of quality costs to sales for each category.
c. Prepare a pie chart for the costs of quality. Discuss the distribution of the costs of quality among the four categories. Are they properly distributed? Explain.
d. Discuss how the company can improve its quality and at the same time reduce total costs of quality.
e. By how much will profits increase if quality costs are reduced to 2.5% of sales?

12.52 *Preparing a pie chart and bar chart to show percentage of costs of quality.* Costs of quality for Prime Company are 20% of sales. Costs of quality include the following:

- External failure costs, which are about 25 to 30% of costs of quality
- Internal failure costs, which are about 30 to 35% of costs of quality
- Appraisal costs, which are about 20 to 25% of costs of quality
- Prevention costs, which are about 5 to 10% of costs of quality

Required:

Draw a pie chart showing by a separated segment the costs of quality of 20%. Then draw a vertical bar chart showing the proportion of each category of cost contained within the separated pie chart segment. Discuss how Prime Company could improve its distribution of costs of quality.

12.53 *Preparing a fishbone diagram.* You are an entrepreneur who owns and manages a convenience store in Florida. Recently, your operation has been experiencing significant inventory variations, such as shortages in inventory and overages in related inventory items. This problem directly affects the profitability of your operation and your success in implementing just-in-time delivery.

Required:

Develop a fishbone diagram that shows the possible causes of the operation's inventory variation. Draw upon your professional business experience in solving this significant problem.

12.54 *Quality performance and ethical behavior.* Zelac Manufacturing gives bonuses and trips to famous vacation spots in January to its plant managers who are able to incur less costs of quality than were budgeted. Travis Scarborough is plant manager of a plant in North Dakota. He decided to take the following actions during the last quarter of the year to beat the budgeted amounts and create a favorable production volume variance:

- Inspectors for final inspection will be transferred to a quality training program. The removal of inspectors will result in less rework and downtime. By increasing the quantity of products, the plant will incur less internal failure costs and also improve its production volume variance. Moreover, by transferring the inspectors to a quality training program, the budgeted level for prevention costs can be met.
- Travis also intends to delay all replacements and warranty repairs until the beginning of next year. This decision will increase customer dissatisfaction substantially, but Travis will try to get back in the good graces of customers next year when he reinstates the policy of promptly dealing with dissatisfied customers. In the meantime, his actions will enable him to incur internal failure costs substantially less than what was budgeted.

Required:

a. Assess Travis's ethical behavior. Is he justified in taking the actions described in the problem?
b. You are a CMA and the chief management accountant at Zelac. What will you do if Travis takes the preceding actions? Refer to the ethical code for management accountants in Chapter 1.
c. Provide a better way of measuring plant manager's quality performance than budgeting costs of quality for the managers to meet or beat. Also, comment on how a production volume variance may induce plant managers to produce low-quality products.

13 COST MANAGEMENT FOR LOGISTICS

Some parts are received from other suppliers at Deere & Company.

LEARNING OBJECTIVES

After studying this chapter, you should be able to:

1. Discuss how an electronic data interchange (EDI) system can support logistics and reduce costs.

2. Define procurement, and explain how procurement costs can be reduced.

3. Describe the transportation activity, and examine how productivity of this activity can be increased.

4. Explain how to manage inventory costs.

5. Describe the warehousing activity, and explore ways to manage warehouse costs.

■ INTRODUCTION

Just as management accountants, production people, and engineering personnel join forces in developing methods of costing products and services and managing production costs, so must management accountants and logistics personnel work together to manage logistics costs. The potential payoff of effective cost management for logistics is substantial, because logistics costs account for 20 to more than 50 percent of total costs in most companies. Often, logistics costs exceed production costs.

   Logistics systems consist of the integration of procurement, transportation, inventory management, and warehouse activities to provide the most cost-effective means of meeting internal and external customer requirements. **Logistics costs** are expenditures incurred for planning, implementing, controlling, and operating all logistics activities.[1] This chapter is intended to assist management accountants in improving identification, measurement, and management of logistics costs. ■

■ USING ELECTRONIC DATA INTERCHANGE IN THE LOGISTICS SYSTEM

LEARNING OBJECTIVE 1

Discuss how an electronic data interchange (EDI) system can support logistics and reduce costs.

Electronic data interchange (EDI) was described in Chapter 3 as a set of standards and information technology that enable purchase orders, invoices, and payments, to be transferred *electronically* between participating companies. Many companies and industries are moving toward implementation of EDI technology. Besides interconnecting companies with suppliers, customers, and common carriers, EDI systems are used by commercial banks to handle electronic financial transactions (e.g., paying suppliers and common carriers and collecting from customers).

■ Improving Performance and Gaining Cost Savings with EDI

A customer order triggers the logistics system. The ability to capture all pertinent data immediately and ensure their timely flow to all users has direct impact on the effectiveness and efficiency of the entire logistics system. Mishandled customer orders and slow or erratic flows of information can lead to lost customers and excessive procurement, transportation, inventory, and warehousing costs, as well as disruptions in the production process. EDI provides the foundation for the logistics system and offers significant potential for improving logistics performance and increasing profits.

EDI in action at Saturn.

   Significant cost savings can be realized with a fully integrated EDI system compared to nonelectronic communications. For example, Service Merchandise, Inc., a major catalog discount retailer, has been able to cut the cost of a single purchase order transaction from $50 to $15 using EDI.[2] This cost savings is due to:

- Reduced errors
- Reduced paperwork
- Increased order processing speed, which decreases costs throughout the logistics system

---

[1] Statements on Management Accounting (Statement Number 4-P), *Practices and Techniques: Cost Management for Logistics* (Montvale, N.J.: The Institute of Management Accountants, 1992), p. 23. With permission.
[2] E. Wainright Martin, Daniel W. DeHayes, Jeffrey A. Hoffer, and William C. Perkins, *Managing Information Technology: What Managers Need to Know* (New York: Macmillan, 1991), p. 221.

INSIGHTS & APPLICATIONS

Not Just Bean Counters Anymore

Management accountants represent how companies convert activities into dollars, and, hopefully, profits.

Management accountants should, therefore, be walking the shop floor, talking to marketing, advertising, and logistics managers to find out what these departments need and then fulfilling those needs. Terry Zinsli, a management accountant and management team player at Coors' Shenandoah Brewery reports on logistics and customer service in addition to other activities throughout the enterprise. Zinsli's advice to management accountants is to look for opportunities. Learn everything about the *internal* customer in order to be a resource and business adviser.[3]

Designing an EDI System

The management accountant at Moparts, Inc., has proposed an EDI system to replace the company's present paper-based logistics systems. A commercial bank will be connected to the EDI technology to serve as a financial clearinghouse. The new EDI system design is illustrated in Exhibit 13–1.

Key Elements of the EDI System

Chapter 3 described the EDI system from the viewpoint of computers and telecommunications. The EDI system also requires other key elements to make it workable for an organization, including the following:

- Bar codes
- Customer order model

[3] Adapted from Susan Jayson, "Playing on the Management Team," *Management Accounting,* March 1993, p. 24. Reprinted from *Management Accounting.* Copyright by Institute of Management Accountants, Montvale, N.J.

■ EXHIBIT 13–1
EDI System Design at Moparts, Inc.

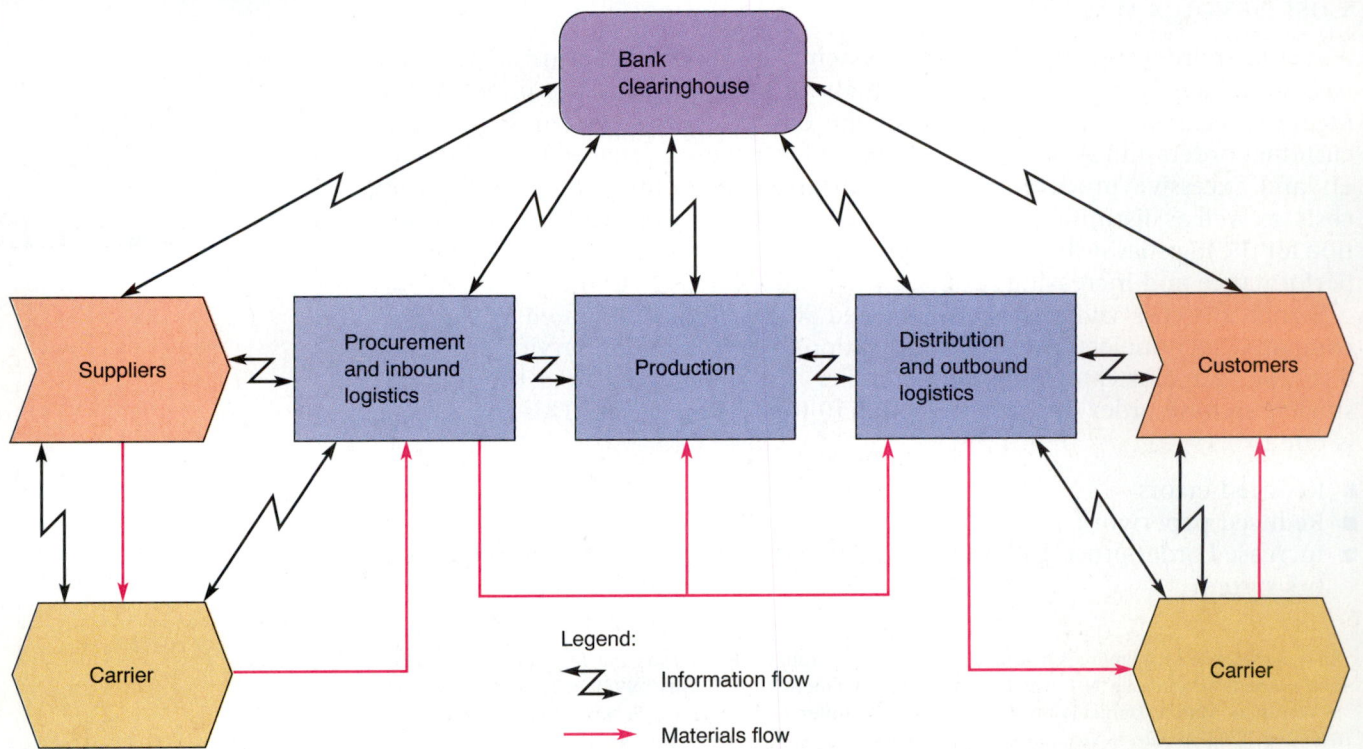

INSIGHTS & APPLICATIONS

Ford Is Building Tighter Links with Suppliers through EDI

Ford is using electronic data interchange (EDI) to forge tighter links with its suppliers, trim the firm's operating expenses, increase worker productivity, and reduce inventory levels at plants. EDI is helping Ford not only reduce its costs but its suppliers are cutting costs as well.

"We've really come to rely on the system," says Ginny Cooper, materials coordinator for Cold Heading Company, a Detroit supplier of fasteners to Ford. "The system gives us instantaneous updated information so we can check how closely our production systems are running with Ford's."

"Basically, this is a win-win situation," says Joseph Phelan, manager of supplier communications at Ford. "Our livelihoods depend on customer satisfaction, and by making our suppliers more integrated members of the Ford team, we can respond faster to customer needs and, ultimately, provide higher quality products."[4]

- Picking and packing lists
- Portable terminals
- Flash reports
- Inventory control models

BAR CODES.   All items in inventories use bar codes for identification and for product movement on computerized conveyor belts. As an item moves along the conveyor belt, it is scanned automatically, identified, and routed to the correct spur of the conveyor where it will be unloaded for production, loaded for shipment, or placed in a warehouse. All pertinent data relating to the item and its movement are also fed into the EDI system for producing various management reports, such as the order activity report in Exhibit 13–2.

CUSTOMER ORDER MODEL.   To make an EDI system functional, a number of software modules must be utilized. *Structured English* or *pseudocode* is used in designing these software modules. For example, Exhibit 13–3 illustrates a module of the customer order model designed in structured English. Other modules that check credit, process backorders, and so forth are designed in a similar

---

[4] Joanne Cummings, "Another Bright Idea," *Network World*, November 25, 1992, pp. 31–37. Copyright November 25, 1992 by Network World, Inc., Framingham, MA 01701. Reprinted from *Network World*.

■■ EXHIBIT 13–2
Daily Order Activity Report

				ORDER ACTIVITY REPORT				
Date DD/MM/YY								
Purchase Order Number	Customer ID Number	Item Number	Date Ordered	Quantity Ordered	Date Shipped	Quantity Shipped	Quantity Backordered	Quantity Canceled
XXXXXX	XXXXXX	XXXXXX	DD/MM/YY	XXXXXXX	DD/MM/YY	XXXXX	XXXXX.XX	XXXXX.XX
XXXXXX	XXXXXX	XXXXXX	DD/MM/YY	XXXXXXX	DD/MM/YY	XXXXX	XXXXX.XX	XXXXX.XX

Control totals
  Shipped Quantity Total   XXXXXXXX.XX
  Backordered Quantity Total   XXXXXXXX.XX
  Canceled Quantity Total   XXXXXXXX.XX

EXHIBIT 13-3
Structured English Used to Specify Customer Order Model

```
ORDER ENTRY:
  FOR each customer PURCH_ORDER
    GET CUSTOMER record
    IF CUST_NUMBER is valid
      SET INVOICE_HEADER record
      ENTER CUST_NAME, CUST_ADDR,
        DATE_ORDER, and PO_NUMBER
        in INVOICE_RECORD
      WRITE INVOICE_HEADER record
      GET DISCOUNT from table
    ELSE
      DISPLAY "Invalid Customer Number"
      QUIT ORDER_ENTRY
    ENDIF
    FOR each line item
      COPY ITEM_NUMBER and QTY_ORDERED
        on INVOICE_RECORD
      GET ITEM_PRICE from price table
      SET ITEM_SUBTOTAL to ITEM_PRICE
        × QTY_ORDERED × (100% − DISCOUNT)
      SET INVOICE_TOTAL to sum
        of ITEM_SUBTOTAL
      WRITE INVOICE_RECORD
    ENDFOR
    PREPARE BILL_OF_LADING
  ENDFOR
EXIT ORDER_ENTRY.
```

Orders from across the country stream through McKesson's data center.

manner. Once the design has been approved, it is *automatically* programmed in a computer language (e.g., COBOL or C) and integrated into the system using computer-aided software engineering (CASE) tools, such as Andersen's Foundation suite of CASE tools, Ernst & Young's Navigator Systems Series CASE tools, and Price Waterhouse's Arrae CASE tools. All the integrated software modules that drive the customer order model automatically perform procedures necessary to service a customer order and run the EDI system.

AUTOMATICALLY GENERATING PICKING AND PACKING LISTS. All customer orders automatically generate a picking and packing list, such as the list in Exhibit 13-4. The picking and packing list tells pickers in the warehouse which items have been ordered and must be picked, where they can be picked, and the most efficient sequence in which they should be picked. Bar codes are automatically prepared and attached to the picking and packing list.

Pickers retrieve ordered products, affix the proper shipping bar codes, and send the products down a conveyor belt in trays to a laser scanner. The laser scanner reads the bar codes, determines which order an item belongs to, and tips its tray down the appropriate packing chute.

At the bottom of the chute, packers, who also have a copy of the picking and packing list, assemble orders and pack them in boxes for shipping. Packers affix a second bar code to the outside of each box, and a second laser scanner ensures that each box is routed to the appropriate loading dock for shipment via a specific common carrier or company truck. At this point, the central EDI computer takes over and begins to prepare EDI data, such as bills of lading, shipment notices, and invoices. Also, all pertinent records in the database are updated automatically.

USING PORTABLE TERMINALS. Inventory counting and verification are

MM/DD/YY

SHIPMENT PICKING AND PACKING LIST

Customer Number

Assigned Picker

Loading Dock Assigned

Picking Sequence	Product Number	Warehouse Number	Aisle Number	Shelf Number
⋮	⋮	⋮	⋮	⋮
Total				

Weight   Packing Instructions

Carrier

Special Instructions

---

handled by computer terminals hung from workers' belts. A laser-wand attachment is used to read the product identification bar code of every item in inventory. These data are then transmitted to the central EDI computer for update of the inventory database.

Every salesperson in the field has a laptop computer, which also has access to the EDI system. These laptops are used for electronic mail and paging as well as for facilitating a sale to a customer. The salesperson, sitting in a customer's office, can access a variety of models ranging from engineering specifications and design aids to economic analyses. Upon making a sale, the salesperson immediately transmits the sales data to the system to begin customer order processing.

USING FLASH REPORTS. Flash reports are generated automatically by the EDI system and displayed on terminal screens at strategic points throughout the company. Examples of flash reports include receiving orders, shipping orders, and rejected customer orders. Generally, flash reports require immediate action by some designated worker or manager. For example, warehouse workers receive a flash report notifying them what products will arrive, when, and by which carrier.

INVENTORY CONTROL MODELS. Inventory control models, like the customer order model, must be integrated into the EDI system. Inventory control deals with *when* to order or produce items and *how much* to order or produce. The when-to-order-or-produce question is answered by reorder points programmed into the system. The system monitors the depletion of inventory and automatically initiates an order to replenish the inventory when the reorder point is reached or exceeded. The how-much-to-order-or-produce question is usually answered by a mathematical model. These inventory control models, referred

Replenishing store shelves is a simpler, quicker task for drug retailers using McKesson's ordering equipment.

to as economic order quantity (EOQ) or economic batch quantity (EBQ) models, are described later in this chapter.

Other methods of controlling inventory are just-in-time (JIT) coupled with a kanban system, as described in Chapter 2. Material requirements planning (MRP) and manufacturing resource planning (MRP II) are software packages that can also be incorporated into EDI systems to aid inventory management, as described in Chapter 3.

<table>
<tr><td>

LEARNING OBJECTIVE 2

Define procurement, and explain how procurement costs can be reduced.

</td></tr>
</table>

MANAGING PROCUREMENT COSTS

Procurement includes the purchasing function and verification of inbound raw materials or products at the receiving dock. This logistics activity has the following goals:

- Select and evaluate suppliers (covered in Chapter 11)
- Provide an uninterrupted flow of materials and services to operate the enterprise
- Minimize inventory costs
- Acquire materials and services at the lowest cost and at the quality that best meets the company's needs
- Operate the procurement activity at the lowest possible cost
- Ensure that the correct product is received in the correct quantity and with acceptable quality

Managing the Procurement Activity

In addition to careful evaluation and selection of suppliers, the procurement activity itself should be managed properly. Following are selected performance measurements that will help accomplish this:

$$\text{Purchase orders per buyer} = \frac{\text{Number of purchase orders per week}}{\text{Number of buyers}}$$

$$= \frac{400 \text{ purchase orders}}{20 \text{ buyers}}$$

$$= 20 \text{ purchase orders per buyer per week}$$

$$\text{Administrative cost per purchase order} = \frac{\text{Administrative cost per week}}{\text{Number of purchase orders per week}}$$

$$= \frac{\$8,000 \text{ administrative costs}}{400 \text{ purchase orders}}$$

$$= \$20 \text{ per purchase order}$$

$$\text{Service to production} = \frac{\text{Number of complaints from production per week}}{\text{Number of orders released to production per week}}$$

$$= \frac{4 \text{ complaints from production}}{100 \text{ orders released to production}}$$

$$= 4\% \text{ of orders released to production received complaints}$$

The Relationship of Just-in-Time to Procurement

The most effective approach to managing the costs of the procurement activity is to reduce the need for this activity. JIT procurement achieves this goal by developing long-term relationships with a *few* certified suppliers.

The characteristics of the JIT procurement activity are interrelated. They are grouped in Exhibit 13–5 under three general categories: suppliers, quantities, and quality.

WHAT ARE THE BUYER BENEFITS OF JIT PROCUREMENT?   Exhibit 13–6 summarizes the benefits of JIT procurement to the buyer. All the benefits result in substantial cost savings for the buying company.

WHAT ARE THE SUPPLIER BENEFITS OF JIT PROCUREMENT?   Exhibit 13–7 summarizes the certified supplier benefits of JIT procurement. The certified supplier or vendor receives a long-term purchase agreement from the buyer. This provides the supplier with the opportunity to reduce nonvalue-added activities, reduce capacity and resources, retain a trained labor force, reduce inventories, and implement JIT procurement systems with its own suppliers.[5]

[5] James R. Stock and Douglas M. Lambert, *Strategic Logistics Management*, 2d ed. (Homewood, Ill.: Irwin, 1989), p. 487. With permission.

Suppliers:
- Few and certified
- Long-term contracts
- Nearby
- Minimal paperwork
- Suppliers extend JIT procurement to their suppliers

Quantities:
- Steady amount
- Frequent deliveries in small lots

Quality:
- Close relationship among buyers, suppliers, and quality assurance people
- High reliability
- Ease of use

EXHIBIT 13–5
Characteristics of JIT Procurement

Material costs:
- Reduced inventory carrying costs
- Reduced transportation costs because of nearby suppliers
- Reduced prices because of long-term agreements and cost savings

Administrative costs:
- Overall reduction of procurement activities
- Less paperwork
- Less labor
- Less supervision
- Less contract negotiation

Design costs:
- Fast response to engineering changes
- Participation of supplier in design innovations, functional analysis, target costing, and quality specifications

Productivity:
- Reduced scrap and rework
- Reduced inspection
- Reduced production delays

EXHIBIT 13–6
Buyer Benefits of JIT Procurement

Materials costs:
■ Reduced finished and work-in-process inventory carrying costs
■ Reduced purchased inventories if JIT is used with the company's own suppliers

Administrative costs:
■ Increased control of finished goods inventory because outgoing shipments are steady and predictable
■ Less paperwork
■ Less labor
■ Less supervision
■ Reduced long-term risk of doing business

Design costs:
■ Participates with buying company's new product development teams
■ Ability to plan ahead for design changes

Productivity:
■ Ability to predict resource and capacity needs
■ Assists in the retention of a trained labor force

LEARNING OBJECTIVE 3

Describe the transportation activity, and examine how productivity of this activity can be increased.

MANAGING TRANSPORTATION COSTS

Transportation involves the movement of products (raw materials, parts, supplies, subassemblies, work-in-process, finished goods) from point-of-origin to point-of-consumption. Transportation creates place utility by delivering the product to where it is needed. Transportation also provides time utility according to how quickly the product is moved; that is, how long the time-in-transit is.[6]

Transportation can account for 50 percent or more of the cost of basic raw materials, such as iron ore, coal, and cement. Transportation costs for such items as computers or jewelry may be less than 1 percent.

Any one or more of five transportation modes—motor, rail, air, water, or pipeline—may be selected. In addition, modal combinations are available, such as rail-motor (piggybacking), motor-air, and so forth.

Costing the Transportation Activity

Costs for private carriage, such as a fleet of trucks, provide a good example of costing the transportation activity. Transportation costs are normally assigned to one or more of the following cost objects:

■ Loads
■ Shipments
■ Products

Vehicle loading docks at Saturn.

ASSIGNING TRANSPORTATION COSTS TO THE LOAD. The cost drivers used are hours, loads, and miles. Exhibit 13–8 shows how these costs are assigned, using one load from Memphis to Dallas as an example. The truck did not carry a load on its return trip to Memphis, its home terminal, so this is referred to as "empty backhaul miles."

Certain time-related costs are assigned according to hours of use. For example, in Exhibit 13–8, drivers are paid on an hourly basis, so driver wages and fringe benefits are assigned using hours. Depreciation is time-dependent in that depreciation expense is usually computed as a fixed charge per month regardless of business activity. The total hours should be used to assign depreciation and terminal facilities expense.

[6] Ibid., p. 173.

Load: Mixed
   Origin: Memphis   Destination: Dallas
   Loaded Miles: 500   Empty Miles: 500   Load Ratio: 50%
   Driving Hours: 16   Unloading Hours: 2   Loading Hours: 2

Assignment of costs by hours:

■ Driver wages and fringe benefits ($10 × 20 hours)	$200
■ Tractor depreciation ($5 × 20 hours)	100
■ Trailer depreciation ($2 × 20 hours)	40
■ Terminal facilities ($8 × 20 hours)	160
Costs by hours	$500

Assignment of costs by load:

■ Dispatching ($20 × 1 load)	$ 20
■ Administration ($100 × 1 load)	100
■ Other operating costs ($40 × 1 load)	40
Costs by load	$160

Assignment of costs by miles:

■ Fuel and oil ($0.30 × 1,000 miles)	$300
■ Tractor maintenance ($0.10 × 1,000 miles)	100
■ Trailer maintenance ($0.02 × 1,000 miles)	20
■ Tires and tubes ($0.08 × 1,000 miles)	80
■ Insurance ($0.04 × 1,000 miles)	40
■ Accidents ($0.02 × 1,000 miles)	20
Costs by miles	$560
Total transportation costs for the load	$1,220

Certain costs are best assigned on a fixed charge per load. Dispatching costs are often assigned on a per-load basis. To avoid seasonal fluctuations, dispatching costs can be calculated by dividing a 12-month total of this cost element by the total number of loads handled during that period. Administration and other operating costs (e.g., labor for preparing paperwork for each load) are also assigned on a per-load basis.

Certain costs are a function of miles operated. For such costs, both loaded and empty miles are used. The per-mile charge is determined by using averages. For example, the trailer maintenance cost per mile is calculated by determining the cost of maintaining trailers over a 12-month period and dividing by the miles operated.

ASSIGNING LOAD COSTS TO SHIPMENTS.   The second stage of costing the transportation activity involves assigning costs to specific shipments. A load may be composed of one or more shipments. For example, one load may contain shipment 1 for customer A, shipment 2 for customer B, and shipment 3 for customer C, or all three shipments may be consigned to customer A. In some instances, one load may represent one shipment. In this case, the total transportation costs for the load are the same as the total transportation costs for the shipment.

The most commonly used basis for assigning load costs to shipments is cwt-miles. Cwt stands for hundredweight. Cwt-miles for each shipment on the load are calculated by multiplying the shipment weight in cwt by the miles traveled. For example, assume that a truck leaves the terminal facilities with three shipments of four different products, weighing a total of 50,000 pounds (500 cwt). The truck makes two intermediate stops before reaching the final delivery point, a distance of 500 miles, and returns empty to the point of origin. Further, assume that it is management's policy to assign empty backhaul miles to the original outbound load.[7] The total cost of the load, as previously calculated, is $1,220. The assignment of miles, weight, and costs to each shipment is illustrated in Exhibit 13–9.

ASSIGNING LOAD COSTS TO PRODUCTS. Assigning load costs to products is similar to assigning load costs to shipments. In both cases, the costs of transporting the load are assigned on the basis of cwt-miles, as illustrated in Exhibit 13–10. The major difference is that the assignment of costs to products requires determining the total cwt-miles by product, calculated in panel (a) of Exhibit 13–10. Once cwt-miles by product are calculated, the load costs are assigned to each product based on the percentage of total cwt-miles, as summarized in panel (b).[8]

---

[7] Managers and dispatchers devote a great deal of effort to reducing the number of empty backhaul miles. A load (one shipment) that travels 1,000 miles from origin to destination is a value-added activity. To return the truck empty to its origin is a costly nonvalue-added activity. Consequently, effort is devoted to finding a return load to eliminate empty backhaul miles.

[8] Stock and Lambert, op. cit., pp. 86–88.

■■ EXHIBIT 13–9
Assigning Load Costs to Each Shipment

Shipment Number	Miles: Origin to Destination	Weight (in cwt) per Shipment	Shipment Cwt-Miles	Percentage of Total Cwt-Miles	Assigning Shipment Costs
1	100	100	10,000	5.6%	$ 67.78
2	300	150	45,000	25.0%	305.00
3	500	250	125,000	69.4%	847.22
Totals		500	180,000	100.0%	$1,220.00

■■ EXHIBIT 13–10
Assigning Load Costs to Products

(a) Distribution of weight and miles by product

Shipment Number	Product Code	Product Weight (in cwt) by Shipment	Miles	Cwt-Miles
1	A	40	100	4,000
	C	60	100	6,000
2	A	50	300	15,000
	B	40	300	12,000
	C	60	300	18,000
3	A	80	500	40,000
	B	60	500	30,000
	C	40	500	20,000
	D	70	500	35,000
Totals		500		180,000

(b) Product cost assignment

Product Code	Product Weight (in cwt)	Cwt-Miles	Percentage of Total Cwt-Miles	Cost Assigned to Products
A	170	59,000	32.8%	$ 400.16
B	100	42,000	23.3%	284.26
C	160	44,000	24.4%	297.68
D	70	35,000	19.5%	237.90
Totals	500	180,000	100.0%	$1,220.00

Reporting Transportation Costs

The preceding costing methods can provide cost information by load, by shipment, and by product. Modifications can be made to provide cost information by customer, by sales region, by plant, and so forth. Also, cost-per-mile reports can be prepared, similar to the one presented in Exhibit 13–11.

Monthly (or weekly) driver cost analysis reports, as illustrated in Exhibit 13–12, are also appropriate for transportation cost management. Such reports provide detailed operating cost information by driver and are used by management for driver performance analysis. Although Jones drove 12,000 miles for the month, which is high performance, the cost for fuel and oil, at $0.60 per mile, was exorbitant. The 1.9 miles per gallon of fuel reflect this exorbitant cost. Management should examine such unusual performance costs immediately.

Using Individual Performance Measurements for Reporting Transportation Costs

Transportation activity improvements are vital to the success of the logistics system. Following are some of the more popular performance measurements that indicate the effectiveness and efficiency of the transportation activity:

$$\text{Customer complaints} = \frac{\text{Number of customer complaints per week}}{\text{Number of shipments per week}}$$

$$= \frac{5 \text{ customer complaints}}{100 \text{ shipments}}$$

$$= 5\% \text{ of the shipments had customer complaints}$$

$$\text{Damage claims} = \frac{\text{Number of damage claims per week}}{\text{Number of shipments per week}}$$

$$= \frac{2 \text{ damage claims}}{100 \text{ shipments}}$$

$$= 2\% \text{ of the shipments had damage claims}$$

■■■ EXHIBIT 13–11
Transportation Cost-per-Mile Report

Origin	Destination	Loads	Weight (in Pounds)	Total Miles Operated	Total Loaded Miles Operated	Load Ratio	Total Variable Costs	Cost per Mile
Memphis	El Paso	4	200,000	8,000	6,400	80%	$8,400	$1.05
Cleveland	Chicago	5	220,000	2,000	1,000	50%	$2,600	$1.30

■■■ EXHIBIT 13–12
Monthly Driver Cost Analysis Report

Driver Name	Total Miles Operated	Tractor Cost per Mile	Trailer Cost per Mile	Wages and Benefits per Mile	Fuel and Oil Costs per Mile	Miles per Gallon of Fuel
Brown	10,000	$0.20	$0.05	$0.35	$0.24	5.3
Jones	12,000	0.21	0.06	0.33	0.60	1.9

$$\text{Late delivery} = \frac{\text{Number of late deliveries per week}}{\text{Number of shipments per week}}$$

$$= \frac{10 \text{ late deliveries}}{100 \text{ shipments}}$$

$$= \underline{\underline{10\% \text{ of the shipments were late}}}$$

$$\text{Cost per ton-mile} = \frac{\text{Total transportation costs per week}}{(\text{Total miles} \times \text{Total tons shipped}) \text{ per week}}$$

$$= \frac{\$400,000 \text{ transportation costs}}{20,000 \text{ miles} \times 500 \text{ tons}}$$

$$= \underline{\underline{\$0.04 \text{ per ton-mile}}}$$

$$\text{Cost of fuel per mile for Truck X} = \frac{\text{Total cost of fuel for Truck X per week}}{\text{Total miles for Truck X per week}}$$

$$= \frac{\$650 \text{ cost of fuel Truck X}}{2,500 \text{ miles Truck X}}$$

$$= \underline{\underline{\$0.26 \text{ cost of fuel per mile}}}$$

$$\text{Miles per gallon of fuel for Truck X} = \frac{\text{Total miles for Truck X per week}}{\text{Gallons of fuel used by Truck X per week}}$$

$$= \frac{2,500 \text{ miles Truck X}}{500 \text{ gallons Truck X}}$$

$$= \underline{\underline{5 \text{ miles per gallon}}}$$

$$\text{Percentage of loaded miles for Truck X} = \frac{\text{Loaded miles per week}}{\text{Loaded miles per week} + \text{Empty backhaul miles per week}}$$

$$= \frac{2,000 \text{ loaded miles per week}}{2,000 \text{ loaded miles per week} + 500 \text{ empty backhaul miles per week}}$$

$$= \underline{\underline{80\% \text{ loaded miles}}}$$

> **LEARNING OBJECTIVE 4**
>
> Explain how to manage inventory costs.

MANAGING INVENTORY COSTS

Inventory represents the largest single investment in assets for most distributors, retailers, wholesalers, and some manufacturers. Managing inventory costs revolves around two decisions:

- *How much* to order or produce
- *When* to order or produce

The availability of the right item at the right time at the right place is necessary for satisfying customers and operating the production process. Too much inventory, however, can reduce profitability and impinge on management's ability to implement an effective and efficient logistics system. Proper inventory management requires an optimum balance between understocking and overstocking. The following are three popular approaches to inventory management:

- Economic order quantity (EOQ) model, reorder point, and safety stock approach
- Material requirements planning (MRP) approach
- Just-in-time (JIT) approach

Why Do Enterprises Need Inventories?

As a general statement, the function of inventory is to meet demands of customers and production and to ensure a smooth, efficient operation. Only under the following ideal conditions would inventories not be needed:

- Market and production demand is known with certainty.
- Raw materials are delivered just in time.
- There are zero setup and lead times.
- Interruptions do not occur in transportation or production.
- Quantity discounts on unit costs are not available.
- Procurement costs are insignificant.[9]

Many companies generally do not experience these conditions. Thus, a large number of enterprises need to carry some level of inventory.

What Are Inventory Costs?

While inventories help balance supply and demand and protect the business from uncertainties, they also incur costs. The following groups of inventory costs should be managed:

PROCUREMENT COSTS. **Procurement costs** include costs incurred for placing purchase orders with suppliers, receiving inventory, preparing work orders for ordering a production lot, and setting up production systems. When inventory is purchased, costs are incurred for preparing requisitions and purchase orders, receiving and inspecting shipments, placing materials in storage, and processing invoices. When production orders are generated, costs are incurred for paperwork activities, materials handling, and production setups. Of course, with the implementation of certified vendor programs, JIT, and EDI, most of these costs can be eliminated.

INVENTORY CARRYING COSTS.   **Inventory carrying costs,** the costs associated with the quantity of inventory stored, include a number of different cost components and generally represent one of the highest costs of the logistics system. These costs are usually estimated as a percentage of the cost of inventory and can be categorized into the following groups:

- *Capital costs*. Money invested in inventory is usually a major cost component. Carrying inventory ties up money that could be used for other types of investments. Therefore, the company's opportunity cost of capital, which is the rate of return that could be realized from some other investment, should be used to reflect the true capital costs.
- *Inventory service costs*. These costs include ad valorem (personal property) taxes and fire and theft insurance, an expense of carrying inventory. Taxes vary depending on the state in which inventories are held and, in general, directly with inventory levels. Insurance rates are not strictly proportional to inventory levels, since insurance is usually purchased to cover a certain value

[9] Charles D. Mecimore and James K. Weeks, *Techniques in Inventory Management and Control* (Montvale, N.J.: Institute of Management Accountants, formerly the National Association of Accountants, 1987), p. 9. With permission.

of product for a specified time period. Insurance rates also depend on the construction of the warehouse, its age, security measures, and fire prevention equipment.

■ *Storage space costs.* Storing inventory results in warehousing costs. Also, work-in-process inventory takes up valuable floor space and acts as a bottleneck that interrupts a smooth synchronized manufacturing process.

■ *Inventory risk costs.* These costs include the following:
  ■ Obsolescence
  ■ Damage
  ■ Shrinkage
  ■ Relocation of inventory

The cost of obsolescence is the cost of each unit that must be disposed of at a loss because it can no longer be sold at regular price. This cost is the difference between the original cost of the unit and its disposal value. Damaged inventory cost is also the difference between the original cost of the unit and its disposal value. Shrinkage involves theft of inventory. It also results from poor record keeping or shipping wrong products or quantities to customers. Relocation costs are incurred when inventory is shipped from one warehouse location to another to avoid obsolescence.

STOCKOUT COSTS. Stockout costs arise when an inventory item is demanded but is not readily available to the customer or the production process. When finished goods are unavailable to deliver to a customer, sales are lost or backorder costs are incurred. If sales are lost, the stockout costs equal the forgone contribution margin plus a loss in goodwill. If the stockout is backordered, costs are incurred to prepare and process related paperwork and possibly to pay high freight premiums. When materials needed for production are not in stock, costs of interruption, such as machine downtime and idle capacity, occur.[10]

Inventory management at Interstate Drug Distribution Company.

In general, the correct level of inventory is the level that will minimize the total of these three cost categories. Such minimization is difficult to achieve, however, because some of these costs are in direct conflict with one another. For example, high levels of inventory increase carrying costs but decrease stockout costs. Purchasing raw materials more often will increase procurement costs but decrease carrying costs. The minimization cost problem therefore has two dimensions: how much to order or produce during a production run and how often to order. The how-much-to-order decision involves a trade-off between procurement costs and carrying costs. The when-to-order decision involves a trade-off between carrying costs and stockout costs.

Calculating the Economic Order Quantity for a Merchandising Firm

There are many different methods of determining how much inventory merchandising firms (e.g., distributors, wholesalers, and retailers) should order. The best-known model used in this area is the classic **economic order quantity (EOQ) model,** which reveals how much to procure when a reorder point is reached. The goal of the EOQ model is to minimize the opposing costs of procuring and carrying inventory, as shown graphically in Exhibit 13–13. The EOQ model assumes no stockout costs will be incurred because demand is assumed to be known and constant throughout the year.

The EOQ model is particularly applicable for **independent demand** items, which are free from influence of other items. For example, the demand for snow skis does not depend on the demand for refrigerators. Independent demand

[10] Ibid., p. 12.

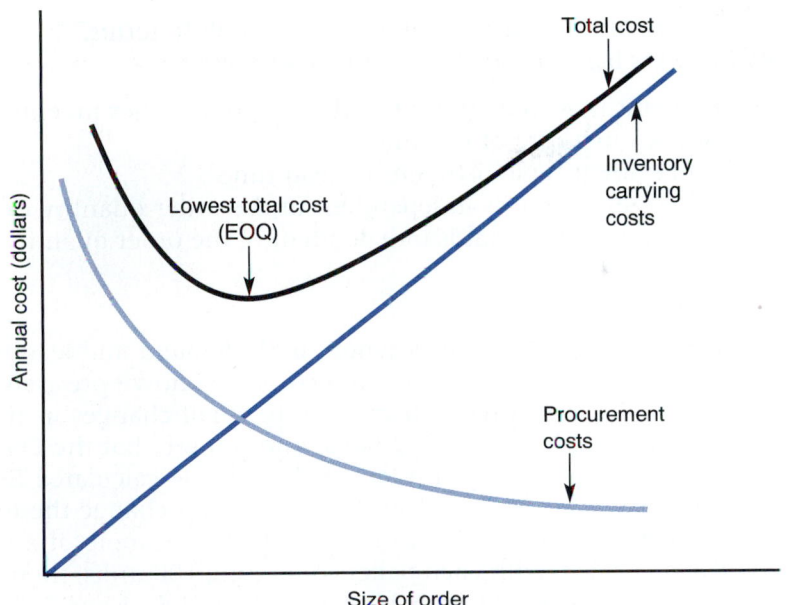

■■■■EXHIBIT 13–13
**Cost Trade-offs
Required to
Determine the Most
Economical Quantity
to Procure**

is fairly stable, once allowances are made for seasonal variation. Generally, independent demand items are carried on a continual basis.

The EOQ in units can be calculated using the following formula:

$$EOQ = \sqrt{\frac{2DP}{CV}}$$

where:

D = Annual demand in units
P = Cost of procuring one order
C = Annual inventory carrying costs (as a percentage of product cost)
V = Average cost or value of one unit of inventory

The EOQ formula states that the economic order quantity varies directly with demand and procurement costs and varies inversely with carrying costs. Due to the square rooting, a quadrupling of demand results only in a doubling of the EOQ.

Assume the following data: The annual demand (D) for product X is 2,400 units, and the cost of procuring (P) one order is $10. Further assume that annual carrying costs (C) are 20 percent of product cost, and the average cost or value (V) of one unit of product X is $1.50. These data are substituted in the EOQ formula as follows:

$$EOQ = \sqrt{\frac{2(2,400)(\$10)}{(.20)(\$1.50)}}$$

$$= \sqrt{160,000}$$

= 400 units per order, which requires
   six purchase orders per year to
   meet annual demand of 2,400 units

If the annual carrying costs per unit are known, the formula becomes:

$$EOQ = \sqrt{\frac{2DP}{C}}$$

where C is the annual carrying costs per unit in absolute terms.

The EOQ model is based on the following assumptions:

- Only one product is involved, and it is independent of other inventory items
- A constant and known rate of demand
- A constant and known replenishment or lead time
- A stable purchase price that is independent of the order quantity or time
- A stable transportation cost that is independent of the order quantity or time
- A constant unit carrying cost
- No stockouts occur

One, however, rarely finds a situation where both demand and lead time are constant, both are known with certainty, and costs are known precisely. Fortunately, the EOQ model is relatively insensitive to small changes in the input data. Referring to the graph in Exhibit 13–13, one can see that the EOQ curve is relatively flat around the solution point. Although the calculated EOQ was 400 units, an EOQ variation of, say, 100 units might not change the total cost significantly. Knowing this relationship is helpful. For example, if a shipping container holds five pallets, with each pallet containing 100 units, then increasing the order to 500 units would probably be the logical decision.[11]

Adjusting the Economic Order Quantity for Volume Discounts

By ordering quantities larger than the minimum, sales quantity price discounts and transportation volume rate discounts may be available. To illustrate, refer to the EOQ calculated for product X, which was 400 units. No sales quantity price discount was available. Now assume the availability of the following sales quantity price discounts:

ORDER SIZE (UNITS)	SALES QUANTITY DISCOUNT
2,400	10%
1,200	8
800	6
600	4
480	2
400	2

With sales quantity price discounts, the purchase price of inventory is not constant but is affected by the change in prices due to the varying discount percentages. The objective, therefore, is to identify an EOQ that minimizes not only the sum of procurement and carrying costs, but also the purchase price of inventory.

Exhibit 13–14 shows the effect of sales quantity price discounts. Notice that the order quantity that minimizes total cost (1,200 units per order) differs from the EOQ computed earlier (400 units per order) when no sales quantity price discount was available. The procurement of 400 units per order would require six orders per year. This option is not as attractive as making two orders per year at 1,200 units per order. A similar analysis can be made to take advantage of transportation volume rate discounts.

Calculating the Economic Order Quantity for a Manufacturing Firm

The preceding EOQ formula is equally appropriate for calculating the optimum size of a production order or production run, sometimes called an economic

[11] Stock and Lambert, op. cit., p. 407.

◾◾◾**EXHIBIT 13–14**
Cost Trade-offs to Determine the Most Economic Order Quantity with Sales Quantity Price Discounts Included

	Number of Orders Annually					
	1 order	2 orders	3 orders	4 orders	5 orders	6 orders
List price per unit	$1.50	$1.50	$1.50	$1.50	$1.50	$1.50
Quantity discount	10%	8%	6%	4%	2%	2%
Discount price per unit	$1.35	$1.38	$1.41	$1.44	$1.47	$1.47
Size of order in units	2,400	1,200	800	600	480	400
Average inventory in units	1,200	600	400	300	240	200
Cost of average inventory	$1,620.00	$828.00	$564.00	$432.00	$352.80	$294.00
Cost of total inventory (a)*	$3,240.00	$3,312.00	$3,384.00	$3,456.00	$3,528.00	$3,528.00
Carrying cost (20% of average) (b)	324.00	165.60	112.80	86.40	70.56	58.80
Cost to order (c)	10.00	20.00	30.00	40.00	50.00	60.00
Total cost per year: (a) + (b) + (c)	$3,574.00	$3,497.60	$3,526.80	$3,582.40	$3,648.56	$3,646.80

*Cost of total inventory = Discount price per unit × Total units ordered annually.

batch quantity (EBQ) or economic production run (EPR). For production, V is the variable manufacturing cost per unit, and P represents an estimate of the setup cost. To illustrate, assume that stock item XYZ-8 is manufactured rather than purchased. The pertinent input data are:

$$D = 12,000 \text{ units}$$
$$P = \$200$$
$$C = 30\%$$
$$V = \$4 \text{ per unit}$$

The optimum size of a production run is calculated as follows:

$$EBQ = \sqrt{\frac{2(12,000)(\$200)}{(.30)(\$4)}}$$

$$= \sqrt{4,000,000}$$

= 2,000 units per production order, which requires six production runs per year to meet annual demand of 12,000 units

▌Managing Inventory under Uncertainty

Rarely are lead times and demand known with certainty. Consequently, management has the option of either maintaining additional inventory in the form of safety stock or incurring stockout costs. **Safety stock** is an amount of inventory held in excess of **cycle stock** (one-half of the EOQ) because of uncertainty in demand and lead time. This situation leads to an additional cost trade-off; that is, inventory carrying costs versus stockout costs. Two methods are used for managing inventory under conditions of uncertainty:

■ Fixed quantity, variable period method
■ Variable quantity, fixed period method[12]

[12] Mecimore and Weeks, op. cit., pp. 14–15.

FIXED QUANTITY, VARIABLE PERIOD METHOD. Under the fixed quantity, variable period method, illustrated in Exhibit 13–15, the order size is a fixed quantity that is placed at variable time intervals (the quantity may be determined by the EOQ formula). Inventory is monitored continuously, and when on-hand inventory falls to a reorder point, a fixed quantity is ordered.

The **reorder point** is a predetermined minimum level required to satisfy demand during the order cycle, which is five days in the example. The **order cycle** includes all of the time that elapses from the placement of the order until the product is received and ready for sale or usage. Order cycle is also referred to as **lead time** or **replenishment cycle.**

VARIABLE QUANTITY, FIXED PERIOD METHOD. Under the variable quantity, fixed period method, illustrated in Exhibit 13–16, the order size is a variable quantity that is placed at fixed time intervals. Inventory is reviewed periodically, and orders are placed to bring the inventory up to some predetermined level.

While the two methods are mutually exclusive, it is possible to use one method with one group of inventory items and the other method with other groups or classes of inventory items. In general, the fixed quantity, variable period method is well suited for situations where items are ordered infrequently in large quantities compared to usage, such as with low-value items. This method works well when controlled by a computer system that monitors usage and automatically generates an order when the reorder point is reached.

The variable quantity, fixed period method is well suited for situations where groups of items are ordered for replenishment relatively frequently from one source and the inventory items are high-value items that require tight control through periodic physical checks. In this situation, more human intervention is necessary.[13]

[13] Ibid.

■EXHIBIT 13–15

Fixed Quantity, Variable Period Inventory Model with an Order Cycle of Five Days

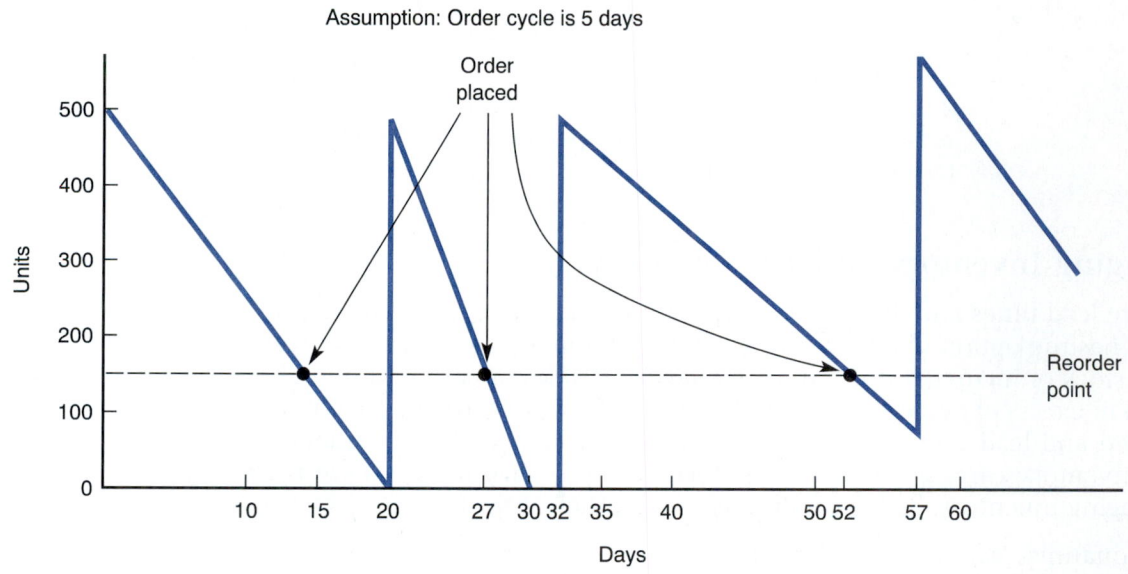

Source: James R. Stock and Douglas M. Lambert, *Strategic Logistics Management,* 2d ed. (Homewood, Ill.: Irwin, 1987), p. 411. With permission.

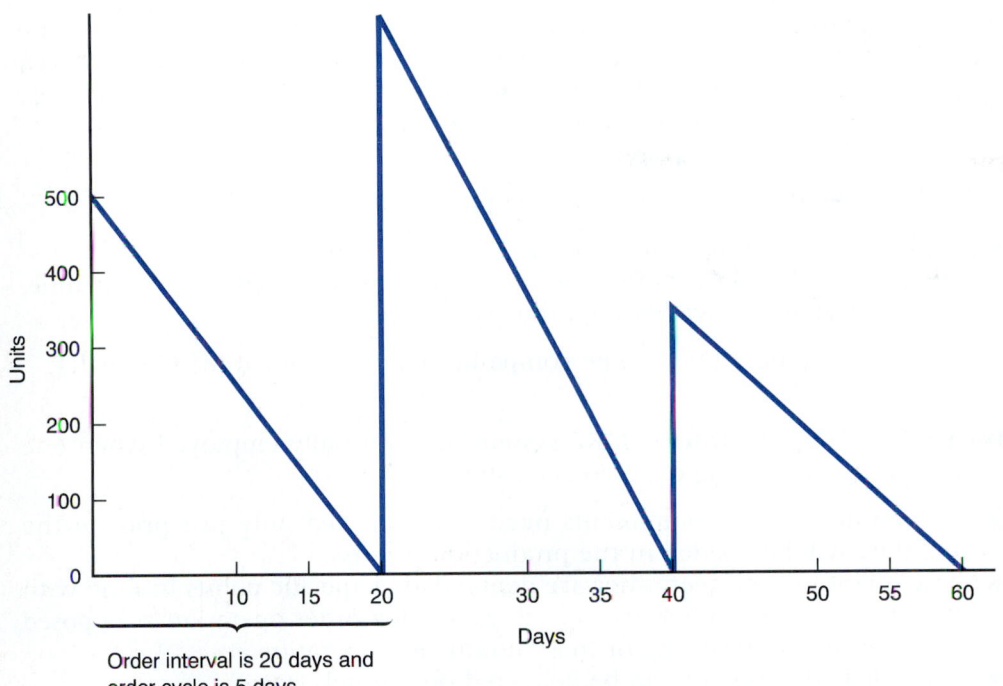

Source: James R. Stock and Douglas M. Lambert, *Strategic Logistics Management,* 2d ed. (Homewood, Ill.: Irwin, 1987), p. 411.

Material Requirements Planning

As described in Chapter 3, material requirements planning (MRP) is a computer-based inventory management system that focuses first on the amount and timing of finished products demanded and then computes the demand for raw materials, parts, and subassemblies at each preceding stage of production and from the vendor. Once management makes a forecast of demand for the final product, the quantities required for all components that make up that finished product can be computed based on **dependent demand.** All these components are *dependent* on the finished product. For example, an automaker's demand for four tires and a transmission depends on the production of autos. Conversely, the demand for a car is independent in the sense that a car is not a component of another product. Whereas the EOQ model focuses on inventory management under conditions of *independent* demand, MRP focuses on inventory management under conditions of *dependent* demand.

DEPENDENT DEMAND AND TIME-PHASED PROCUREMENT.   The essential concepts of MRP are dependent demand and **time-phased procurement** (a planned amount to be ordered in each time period). Dependent demand is based on the master production schedule, which initiates and drives procurement and manufacturing activities. Once the raw materials, parts, and subassemblies necessary to support a specific production schedule are identified, MRP provides a time-phased logic to manage their timely arrival (rather than using the reorder point described earlier in the discussion of the EOQ model).

The logic behind dependent demand is that safety stocks are not needed to support a time-phased procurement program such as MRP. The basic notion of time phasing is that raw materials, parts, and subassemblies need not be carried in inventory as long as they are available when needed. Since this assumption is not always realistic, some MRP systems do allow for small safety stocks. To gain some level of safety stocks, a common practice is to build *safety time* into the material requirements plan. For example, a part may be ordered one week earlier than necessary to ensure timely arrival. Another popular approach is to increase the quantity of components by some arbitrary percentage (e.g., 5 percent) to serve as a safety stock, or cushion.

OBJECTIVES OF MRP.   MRP has two primary objectives:

■ Eliminate or minimize safety stocks
■ Deliver raw materials, parts, and subassemblies at exactly the right time, place, and quantity needed (i.e., the JIT concept)

Because of these objectives, some companies have combined MRP with JIT.

WHEN TO EMPLOY MRP.   MRP systems are normally employed when one or more of the following conditions exist:

■ Demand-dependent components need to be stocked only just prior to the time they will be needed in the production process.
■ Large quantities of inventories are demanded at specific points in time with little or no usage at other times, such as in a job order operation as opposed to a continuous processing or mass-production operation.
■ All needed components can be delivered on a timely basis.

Effective employment of the MRP system requires knowledge of the following:

■ What to produce, how much, and when, as spelled out in the master production schedule
■ Quantity and type of raw materials, parts, and subassemblies needed to make the finished product, as specified in the bill of materials (BOM)
■ The amount of inventory in stock, as recorded in the inventory records file
■ What items are on order, as listed in purchase orders outstanding
■ How long it takes to get various components, as indicated by lead times compiled in the inventory records file

AN MRP EXAMPLE.   A simplified version of a master production schedule is shown in Exhibit 13–17. It shows planned output for finished product A. The schedule indicates that 100 units of product A will be needed for shipment to customers at the *start* of week 8. The master production schedule is based on what is *needed*, not what is *possible*.

The bill of materials (BOM) contains a listing of all the raw materials, parts, and subassemblies that are needed to produce one unit of product A, as illustrated in Exhibit 13–18. The quantity of each component that goes into the production of product A is included in parentheses. It can be readily seen that product A is composed of three B's and two C's. In addition, each B consists of three D's and two E's. Similarly, each C requires one E and two F's. Each F is made up of one G and two D's.

When the items are needed must be determined next. This task requires knowing the lead times, which, in turn, indicate when procuring or making the items must begin to meet the production of product A eight weeks from

■EXHIBIT 13–17
**Master Production
Schedule for Product A**

	Week number							
Product A	1	2	3	4	5	6	7	8
Quantity								100

■■■EXHIBIT 13–18
Bill of Materials (BOM) for Product A

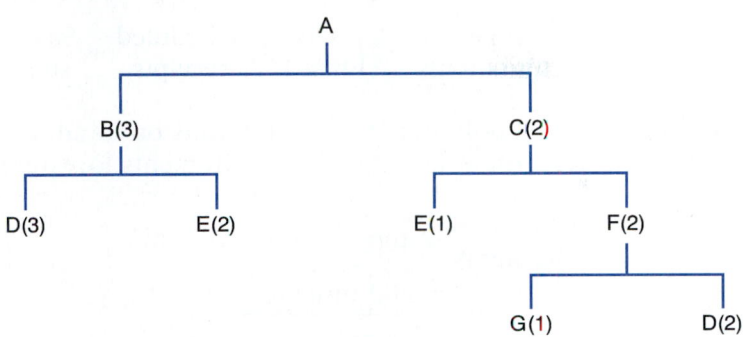

■■■EXHIBIT 13–19
Time-Phased Requirements for Raw Materials, Parts, and Subassemblies to Make Product A

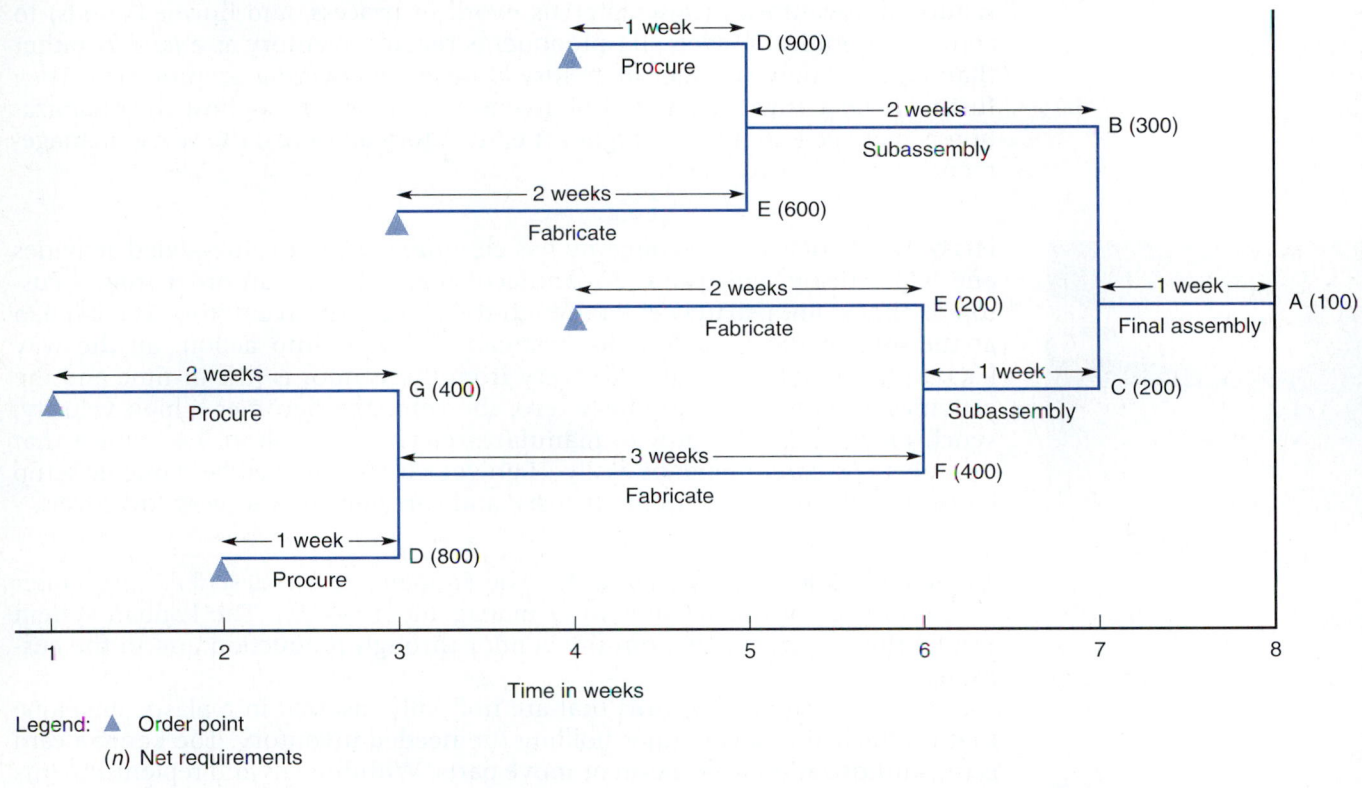

now. When the bill of materials is turned on its side and lead times are included, as illustrated in Exhibit 13–19, a time-phased product structure is created.

The time-phased requirements can be readily seen in the exhibit. For example, raw material G must be ordered at the start of week 1, D at the start of week 2 and week 4. Fabrication of E and F must begin at the start of week 3, and so forth.

The quantities that were previously generated from the BOM are for *gross requirements*. They did not take into account any inventory that is currently on hand or due to be received. The quantities of raw materials, parts, and subassemblies that must be acquired to meet the demand generated by the master production schedule are the *net requirements*. Net requirements are calculated by subtracting from gross requirements, the sum of inventory on hand

and any scheduled receipts, and then adding in safety stock, if applicable, as shown by the following formula:

$$\text{Net requirements} = \text{Gross requirements} - \left(\text{On hand} + \text{Scheduled receipts} + \text{Safety stock}\right)$$

In the preceding example, only item G has 100 units on hand. None of the other items are on hand or on order. The net requirements for G are:

$$\text{Net requirements} = 400 - (100 + 0 + 0)$$
$$= \underline{\underline{300 \text{ units of G}}}$$

Just-in-Time

As discussed in Chapter 2, the objective of JIT, a demand-pull approach, is to reduce all inventories (raw materials, work-in-process, and finished goods) to zero or insignificant levels. JIT proponents regard inventory as a *liability* rather than an *asset*; they consider inventory a means of covering up problems. They further believe that the amount of inventory is a measure of how the organization is managed; that is, the higher the inventory amounts, the worse management's performance.

JIT in action at Saturn.

HOW JIT WORKS.   If a company has eliminated its nonvalue-added activities and is practicing synchronized manufacturing, it can fill an order from a customer almost immediately even though there are zero inventories. The kanban at the end of the process pulls upstream activities into action, all the way back to the supplier. Because delivery from the vendor is just-in-time and the activities, such as setup, are near zero, the company becomes a high-velocity, synchronized manufacturer (a manufacturer with very short lead times) that can meet customer demands easily. High velocity is achieved by reducing setup costs, quality costs, procurement costs, and carrying costs to very low levels.

JIT AND ITS KANBAN SYSTEM.   The kanban system, described in Chapter 2, is the heart of the JIT inventory management system. The kanban system PULLS the raw materials from the vendor through production and to the customer.

A kanban system uses cards that are normally inserted in a plastic envelope that is attached to a container holding the needed inventory. The kanban card is the authorization to work on or move parts. Withdrawals and replenishments occur all the way up and down the line from finished goods to vendors. The kanban system uses three cards:

- Withdrawal kanban
- Production kanban
- Vendor kanban

A **withdrawal kanban** specifies the quantity that a subsequent activity should withdraw from the preceding activity. A **production kanban** states the quantity that the preceding activity should produce. A **vendor kanban** specifies how many raw materials the supplier should deliver. Also stated on the vendor kanban card are the time and place of delivery.

A JIT EXAMPLE.   Exhibit 13–20 presents examples of the three types of kanbans for Power Motors. Exhibit 13–21 shows the flow and linkage throughout the kanban system at Power Motors. Because JIT is a demand-pull system,

INSIGHTS & APPLICATIONS

JIT versus Traditional Manufacturing

Time is a strategic resource. Fast-response manufacturing has therefore become an important competitive tool. With JIT manufacturing, most suppliers are clustered around automakers' assembly plants, making timely delivery cheaper and more reliable. Some traditional U.S. assembly plants and suppliers are scattered around the country. Some parts take weeks to be shipped, which increases both the amount of inventory in transit and the supplies needed to guard against interrupted production. Some authorities estimate that with the traditional way of ordering and delivering inventory, at any time more than half of the company's inventory is on trucks and trains.

Withdrawal kanban

Activity: Customer ordering Product Number: 176A Product Name:	Preceding Activity: Assembly
Number of Containers: Container Capacity:	Subsequent Activity: Ship to Bigelow Co.

Production kanban for assembly

Activity: Assembly Product Number: 176A Product Name:	Preceding Activity: Staging
Number of Containers: Container Capacity:	Subsequent Activity: Customer ordering

Production kanban for staging

Activity: Staging Product Number: 176A Product Name:	Preceding Activity: Suppliers
Number of Containers: Container Capacity:	Subsequent Activity: Assembly

Vendor kanban for supplier of housings

Part Number: Part Name: Housing Number of Containers: Container Capacity:	Buying Company: Power Motors
Time to Deliver: Name of Supplier:	Receiving Location: Staging

Vendor kanban for supplier of armatures

Part Number: Part Name: Armature Number of Containers: Container Capacity:	Buying Company: Power Motors
Time to Deliver: Name of Supplier:	Receiving Location: Staging

EXHIBIT 13–20
Kanbans for Power Motors' Inventory Management and Production System

EXHIBIT 13–21
Flow and Linkage of a Kanban System

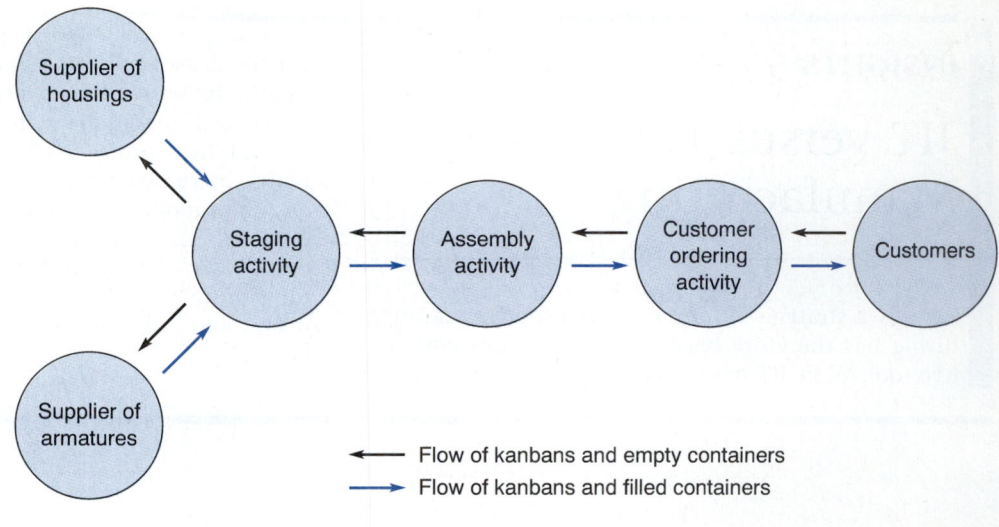

←——— Flow of kanbans and empty containers
———→ Flow of kanbans and filled containers

the only thing that will start the production process is a customer order. The Bigelow Company sends an order for ten electric motors to the customer ordering activity of Power Motors. When the order is received, customer ordering prepares a withdrawal kanban and keeps it there for reference and control. Customer ordering also prepares a production kanban and attaches it to two empty containers that are transported to the assembly activity. This kanban signals the assembly activity to begin production. To do so, a production kanban must be prepared for the staging activity. This production kanban is attached to the two empty containers and moved to staging. Next, the staging activity prepares two vendor kanbans for delivery of ten housings and ten armatures that will be staged and assembled to make the ten electric motors ordered by Bigelow. When the parts are delivered to staging at 8:00 A.M., this first activity begins. When the first container is completed with five electric motors, the production kanban is attached to it, and it is moved to the assembly activity. When the assembly activity is completed, the container and the attached production kanban are moved to the ordering activity where the electric motors are made ready for shipment to Bigelow as soon as the second container arrives with the other five motors.

The use of kanbans ensures that a subsequent activity withdraws (or pulls) the product from the preceding activity in the required quantity at the necessary time. The kanban system, including the kanban containers and cards, controls the preceding activity by permitting it to produce only the quantities withdrawn by the subsequent activity. This way, inventories are kept at a minimum and the parts arrive just-in-time to be used.

A simple kanban system can be found in any restaurant. The customer places an order with a waiter who, in turn, gives the order to the kitchen. The meal is prepared and transferred to the waiter who checks it and gives it to the customer who ordered it. The only difference between this system and Power Motors' kanban system is that the waiter does not transfer a container to the kitchen. Also, suppliers for the restaurant usually deliver daily rather than at several intervals during the day.

It should be pointed out that although the goals of JIT are laudable, not all enterprises can fully implement these goals. For example, a cabinet manufacturer in Missouri cannot achieve JIT delivery from a lumber supplier located in Oregon. More than likely, the deliveries will be weekly or monthly with the size of the truckload being the most economical size to order at one time.

On the other hand, JIT is the *only* way some companies can operate. For example, a fish market, because of the perishability of its product, must operate according to JIT principles.

Measuring Inventory Management Effectiveness and Efficiency

No matter which inventory management approach is used (i.e., EOQ, reorder point, and safety stock; MRP; or JIT), almost every enterprise, at one time or another, is faced with the problems of surplus, short, incorrect, and obsolete inventory and inadequate attention to high-value items. Whatever the reasons for such conditions, the management accountant must provide information that will help management take corrective action to manage inventory more effectively and efficiently. Two methods can be used to provide such information:

- Contribution-by-value analysis
- Turnover ratios

USING THE CONTRIBUTION-BY-VALUE ANALYSIS METHOD.   One of the simplest and most effective ways to manage inventories efficiently is the **contribution-by-value analysis method** (also called the **ABC analysis method**), which is based on Pareto's principle, as presented in Chapter 12. This law states that in most situations a relatively small percentage of certain objects contributes a relatively high percentage of output.

For example, review the contribution-by-value analysis report in Exhibit 13–22. This report reveals that A items account for 20 percent of the products in inventory but contribute 80 percent of sales. The B items account for 30 percent of the products and add an additional 15 percent of sales. The C items account for 50 percent of the products but add only 5 percent of sales. The Pareto chart in Exhibit 13–23 presents a visual interpretation of the information in the contribution-by-value analysis report.

EXHIBIT 13–22

Contribution-by-Value Analysis Report Showing the Relative Contributions of Products A, B, and C

Product Item	Product Count	Cumulative Percentage of Total Product Items	Annual Dollar Sales	Cumulative Dollar Sales	Cumulative Percentage of Total Contribution	Product Classification
A600	1	5.0%	$600,000	$ 600,000	30.0%	A
Z412C	2	10.0	400,000	1,000,000	50.0	A
B784	3	15.0	300,000	1,300,000	65.0	A
Q445	4	20.0	300,000	1,600,000	80.0	A
B797	5	25.0	90,000	1,690,000	84.5	B
C984Q	6	30.0	60,000	1,750,000	87.5	B
C776A	7	35.0	50,000	1,800,000	90.0	B
A444O	8	40.0	40,000	1,840,000	92.0	B
M121	9	45.0	30,000	1,870,000	93.5	B
M14R	10	50.0	30,000	1,900,000	95.0	B
D122	11	55.0	15,000	1,915,000	95.8	C
D127C	12	60.0	14,000	1,929,000	96.5	C
E951	13	65.0	12,000	1,941,000	97.1	C
E962	14	70.0	12,000	1,953,000	97.7	C
R4805	15	75.0	11,000	1,964,000	98.2	C
RS77	16	80.0	10,000	1,974,000	98.7	C
RS201	17	85.0	9,000	1,983,000	99.2	C
T12R	18	90.0	8,000	1,991,000	99.6	C
T17C	19	95.0	7,000	1,998,000	99.9	C
S776	20	100.0	2,000	2,000,000	100.0	C

EXHIBIT 13–23

Pareto Chart Showing the Relative Contributions of Products A, B, and C

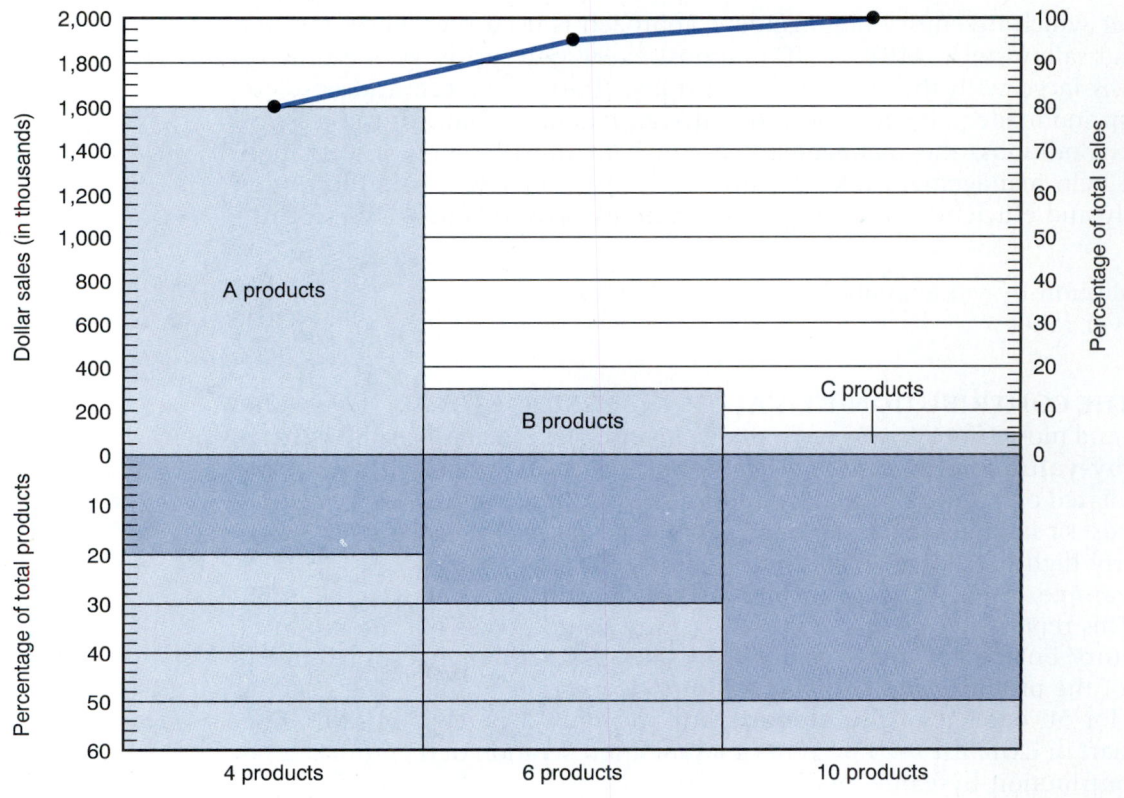

For the A items, management should provide sufficient safety stocks and high levels of service. B items should receive less attention and probably lower or zero safety stocks. As for the C items, management may actually consider eliminating some of the products from inventory because their contribution to sales revenue is minimal.

USING TURNOVER RATIOS. Ratios are one of the most common methods for measuring inventory management effectiveness and efficiency. The following are typical turnover ratios:

$$\text{Raw materials} = \frac{\text{Cost of raw materials used}}{\text{Average raw materials inventory}}$$

$$\text{Work-in-process} = \frac{\text{Cost of goods manufactured}}{\text{Average work-in-process inventory}}$$

$$\text{Finished goods} = \frac{\text{Cost of goods sold}}{\text{Average finished goods inventory}}$$

The data for these turnover ratios are derived from financial accounting data. Thus, they are influenced by the financial accounting procedures used for measuring periodic income. For example, a writedown of inventory will usually be charged against cost of goods sold so that the writedown, which may be an indicator of inventory *inefficiency*, will actually *increase* inventory turnover. Also, the various inventory costing procedures (e.g., FIFO, LIFO) make interpretation of inventory turnovers very complex. For example, how does one interpret the turnover ratio of the current cost of goods sold to the average inventory costed by the LIFO inventory costing procedure when LIFO inventory may be costed at prices that occurred many years ago? Moreover, there is a problem of aggregating data. For instance, a moderately rapid turnover ratio for the inventory may obscure the fact that half of the inventory is turning very slowly and the other half very rapidly.[14]

Calculating turnover ratios on a unit basis helps minimize the preceding problems and makes the ratios more meaningful. For an individual product, the inventory turnover is the ratio of the number of units sold or issued to the average number of units on hand, such as:

$$\frac{\text{Product X}}{\text{Turnover Ratio}} = \frac{\text{Number of units of product X sold during the month}}{\text{Average number of units of product X on hand during the month}}$$

Assume 1,200 units of product X were sold during March. At the beginning of March, 500 units were on hand, and at the end of March, 300 units were on hand, giving an average number of units on hand during March of 400 [(500 + 300) ÷ 2]. Thus, the turnover ratio of product X is 3, calculated as follows:

$$\frac{\text{Product X}}{\text{Turnover Ratio}} = \frac{1,200 \text{ units of product X}}{400 \text{ average units on hand}}$$
$$= \underline{3 \text{ turns during March}}$$

Turnover ratios should be used only as indicators. Using them as a sole measure of inventory management effectiveness and efficiency can backfire. For example, the traditional assumption is that the higher the turnover, the better. A better goal may be to carry zero inventory. In a JIT environment, this is the goal. In other environments that depend on some amount of inventory on hand, a zero-inventory policy would cause problems, such as stockouts and excessive procurement costs. Any meaningful application of turnover ratios must, therefore, implicitly assume that high turnovers are only desirable to the extent that they are compatible with effective and efficient operations. Inventory turnovers are worth improving only if there is no substantial increase in procurement costs or significant loss of sales resulting from excessive stockouts. Turnover ratios are only useful if they can be related in some way to inventory management costs and the optimum decisions of *how much* and *when* to order.[15]

MANAGING WAREHOUSING COSTS

Warehousing is the link between the producer and the customer. It is the activity in the logistics system that stores products (raw materials, parts, supplies, subassemblies, work-in-process, finished goods) at and between the point-of-origin and point-of-consumption.

What Are the Reasons for Warehousing?

In general, the warehousing of inventories is necessary for the following reasons:

- To achieve transportation economies
- To achieve production economies
- To maintain a source of supply

> **LEARNING OBJECTIVE 5**
>
> Describe the warehousing activity, and explore ways to manage warehouse costs.

[14] Mecimore and Weeks, op. cit., pp. 108–109.
[15] Ibid., p. 110.

■ To meet changing market conditions (e.g., seasonality and demand fluctuations)
■ To achieve a desired level of customer service[16]

Costing and Budgeting Warehousing Activities

Warehousing is a major activity in many logistics systems. The warehousing activity itself consists of specific activities, such as receiving; storing; order picking, packing, and staging; and shipping.

A management accounting system should produce a variety of performance measurements to help managers examine warehousing productivity. For instance, financial performance measurements include the following:

Deere & Company's online computerized inventory control system calculates the most efficient path for parts pickers to follow.

$$\text{Receiving and storage cost per unit} = \frac{\text{Total receiving and storage costs per week}}{\text{Average number of units stored per week}}$$
$$= \frac{\$2,400 \text{ receiving and storage costs}}{8,000 \text{ units stored}}$$
$$= \underline{\$0.30 \text{ per unit}}$$

$$\text{Picking costs per unit} = \frac{\text{Total picking costs per week}}{\text{Number of units picked per week}}$$
$$= \frac{\$1,200 \text{ picking costs}}{6,000 \text{ units picked}}$$
$$= \underline{\$0.20 \text{ per unit}}$$

$$\text{Packing costs per unit} = \frac{\text{Total packing costs per week}}{\text{Number of units packed per week}}$$
$$= \frac{\$6,000 \text{ packing costs}}{6,000 \text{ units packed}}$$
$$= \underline{\$1.00 \text{ per unit}}$$

$$\text{Staging costs per shipment} = \frac{\text{Total staging costs per week}}{\text{Number of shipments staged per week}}$$
$$= \frac{\$80,000 \text{ staging costs}}{4,000 \text{ shipments staged}}$$
$$= \underline{\$20.00 \text{ per shipment}}$$

$$\text{Loading costs per shipment} = \frac{\text{Total loading costs per week}}{\text{Number of loads per week}}$$
$$= \frac{\$200,000 \text{ loading costs}}{2,000 \text{ loads}}$$
$$= \underline{\$100 \text{ per load}}$$

Demurrage costs (i.e., the costs for detaining a transportation vehicle) are also important. Increasing demurrage costs indicate poor dock scheduling for inbound and outbound shipments. Performance measurements for inbound and outbound shipments can be calculated in the following manner:

---

[16] Stock and Lambert, op. cit., p. 271.

$$\text{Inbound demurrage costs per load} = \frac{\text{Total inbound demurrage costs per week}}{\text{Number of loads received during the week}}$$

$$= \frac{\$20,000 \text{ inbound demurrage costs}}{100 \text{ inbound loads}}$$

$$= \underline{\$200 \text{ per inbound load}}$$

$$\text{Outbound demurrage costs per load} = \frac{\text{Total outbound demurrage costs per week}}{\text{Number of loads shipped during the week}}$$

$$= \frac{\$30,000 \text{ outbound demurrage costs}}{200 \text{ outbound loads}}$$

$$= \underline{\$150 \text{ per outbound load}}$$

Parts are retrieved automatically in less than 80 seconds at Deere & Company.

Can the Procurement and Warehouse Activities Be Eliminated?

Clearly, procurement and warehouse activities add costs incrementally to products. By applying JIT and EDI techniques, these activities can be reduced or eliminated, as illustrated in Exhibit 13–24. (see p. 636)

By using JIT and EDI techniques, the procurement activity can be eliminated, along with the $1.00 per pallet cost. Direct delivery of raw materials to production eliminates the warehouse activities cost of $3.00 per pallet and the materials handling cost of $1.00 per pallet. Similarly, transportation to the finished goods warehouse, finished goods warehouse activities, interfacility transportation, distribution center warehouse activities, and order processing activities, which incur a combined cost of $10.00 per pallet, can be eliminated with JIT and EDI. In fact, JIT and EDI techniques help reduce overall costs by $15.00 per pallet ($19.00 − $4.00).

Not all companies can take full advantage of JIT and EDI techniques, however, especially those that experience marked seasonality in production or sales patterns. In fact, some companies such as food processors must stockpile raw materials and run production full-time during a two- or three-month period immediately after the crop is harvested. After the products are packed, food processing companies must store the products in warehouses throughout the year until they are sold.

Similarly, the seasonal requirements for toys and clothing usually cannot be supplied by current production capacity. Therefore, many companies use warehousing to store products in advance of heavy selling seasons in order to facilitate smooth production throughout the year.

SUMMARY OF LEARNING OBJECTIVES

The major goals of this chapter were to enable you to achieve five learning objectives:

Learning objective 1.   Discuss how an electronic data interchange (EDI) system can support logistics and reduce costs.

An EDI system embedded in the integrated computer-based information system (ICBIS) acts as a nerve center for the logistics system. Information from the ICBIS helps to coordinate all the logistics activities. Implementing EDI into the ICBIS provides the potential to increase logistics productivity and thereby reduce total costs.

A high-quality, fast information flow facilitates the integration of all logistics activities. Conversely, a poor flow of information, which can allow lost orders, bottlenecks, and

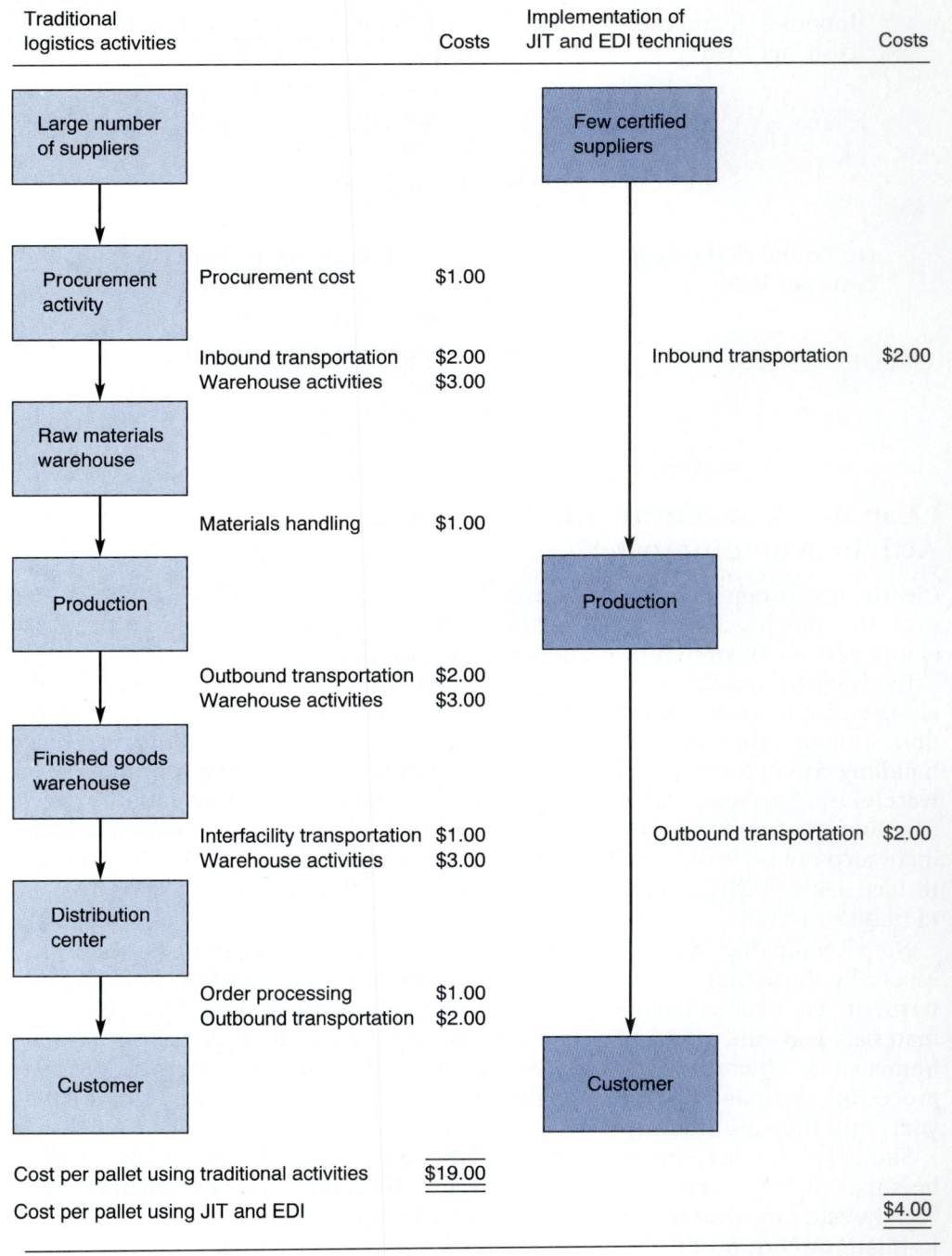

■ EXHIBIT 13–24
Comparing Costs of Traditional Logistics Activities with Implementation of JIT and EDI Techniques

errors to go undetected, can create confusion and inefficiencies within the logistics system.

The cost associated with achieving a rapid flow of error-free information is more than offset by cost savings realized throughout the logistics system. For example, assume that servicing a customer requires four days for order transmittal and processing, two days for warehouse processing, and one day for air freight transportation. An investment in an EDI system could reduce transmittal and processing time to one day. With the five extra days gained from this efficiency, the company can choose a less expensive transportation mode or improve customer service, thus differentiating itself from its competitors.

Learning objective 2. Define procurement, and explain how procurement costs can be reduced.

Procurement costs are incurred to get the right product to the right place at the right price and at the right time. Because procurement costs represent a substantial cost of doing business, this activity's performance should be measured. Implementing JIT techniques can help reduce procurement costs. Traditionally, the buying company has assumed the role of monitoring the quality of purchased materials, inspecting and counting materials for quality and quantity, and returning poor-quality materials to the supplier for rework and adjustments. The ultimate goal of the buying company is to be able to certify suppliers as sources of high-quality materials and thus eliminate all the preceding nonvalue-added activities associated with procurement.

Learning objective 3.   Describe the transportation activity, and examine how productivity of this activity can be increased.

Transportation, together with warehousing, adds time and place utility to products. The five basic modes of transportation—motor, rail, air, water, and pipeline—provide movement of products between where they are produced and where they are consumed. Each mode has different cost and service characteristics.

Typically, transportation costs are assigned to loads, shipments, and products for costing purposes. Also, a variety of performance reports and measurements help management increase transportation productivity.

Learning objective 4.   Explain how to manage inventory costs.

The objective of managing inventory costs is to maintain the lowest possible inventory consistent with customer service and production goals. This objective revolves around two decisions:

- How much to order or produce
- When to order or produce

Three inventory management approaches help deal with these decisions:

- EOQ, reorder point, and safety stock
- MRP
- JIT

Inventory costs include:

- Procurement (or setup) costs
- Carrying costs
- Stockout costs

The EOQ model minimizes the total of carrying costs and procurement (or setup) costs.

Managing inventory under uncertainty entails minimizing the trade-off between carrying costs and stockout costs. Two methods are used to do this:

- Fixed quantity, variable period method
- Variable quantity, fixed period method

The MRP and JIT approaches to inventory management seek to overcome assumptions regarding stable usage and independent demand that are required for EOQ calculations. Whereas EOQ calculations result in a uniform order quantity that may be ordered in a fixed or variable time interval, the order sizes generated by MRP and JIT are more flexible to accommodate irregular usage.

MRP and JIT approaches are used primarily by manufacturers that make products that are dependent on other components. For example, the production of a leaf blower requires a motor and various parts that must be procured or made. All of this inventory—that is, the leaf blower (the finished product) and its various components (raw materials, parts, and subassemblies)—is not made or ordered *until needed.* Thus, the MRP and JIT approaches are based on demand-pull and just-in-time concepts that minimize or eliminate *all* inventories.

For MRP and JIT to work, all activities of the logistics system must be fully integrated and efficient. A weak link in the logistics chain can spell disaster for either inventory management approach. For example, transportation becomes an even more critical activity under MRP and JIT. Although warehousing is reduced under MRP and JIT, a relatively small facility may be needed to consolidate and stage raw materials for input to production and output finished goods for shipping to external customers.

Two key methods are used to measure inventory management effectiveness and efficiency:

- Contribution-by-value analysis method
- Turnover ratios

Learning objective 5.   Describe the warehousing activity, and explore ways to manage warehouse costs.

The purpose of warehousing is to provide place and time utility for inventory management. The relative importance of warehousing, however, varies among companies.

A number of performance measurements should be prepared to help manage specific warehousing activities effectively and efficiently. In companies where JIT and EDI techniques are implemented, procurement and warehousing activities can be reduced, if not eliminated, thus reducing a substantial amount of logistics costs while increasing the effectiveness and efficiency of the logistics system.

IMPORTANT TERMS

Contribution-by-value analysis method (ABC analysis method)   A method based on Pareto's principle, which states that a relatively small percentage of certain objects contributes a relatively high percentage of output.

Cycle stock   An amount of inventory equal to half the economic order quantity.

Dependent demand   A situation where the demand for raw materials, parts, and subassemblies is derived from plans to make certain finished products.

Economic order quantity (EOQ) model   A formula for minimizing inventory carrying and procurement costs. The EOQ model can also be used to calculate the optimum size of a production order.

Independent demand   A situation where inventory items are not connected or related to each other.

Inventory carrying costs   Expenditures incurred for holding inventory.

Logistics costs   Expenditures incurred for planning, implementing, controlling, and operating all logistics activities.

Logistics systems   Represent the integration of procurement, transportation, inventory management, and warehouse activities to provide the most cost-effective means of meeting internal and external customer requirements.

Order cycle (lead time or replenishment cycle)   Includes all the elapsed time from placement of an order until the product is received and ready for sale or usage.

Procurement   A logistics activity that includes purchasing and receiving verification of inbound raw materials or products.

Procurement costs   Expenditures incurred either for placing purchase orders with suppliers and receiving inventory or for preparing work orders for ordering a production lot and setting up for production.

Production kanban   States the quantity that the preceding activity should produce.

Reorder point   A predetermined minimum level required to satisfy demand during the order cycle.

Safety stock   An amount held to protect against demand and order cycle (lead time) variabilities.

Stockout costs   Expenditures incurred for not having inventory available when needed.

Time-phased procurement   A planned amount of raw materials, parts, and subassemblies to be ordered or fabricated in each time period.

Transportation   A logistics activity that involves movement of materials and products from origin to destination.

Vendor kanban   Specifies how many raw materials the supplier should deliver.

Warehousing   Serves as a link between the producer and the customer. Specific activities include receiving; storage; order picking, packing, marking, and staging; and shipping.

Withdrawal kanban   Specifies the quantity that a subsequent activity should withdraw from the preceding activity.

DEMONSTRATION PROBLEMS

- **DEMONSTRATION PROBLEM 1**   *Preparing driver productivity and fuel reports.*

Bob Matthews and Butch Smith are truck drivers for Cleveland Express. Data related to their performance during June 19X4 follow:

Driver	Total Miles Operated	Total Loaded Miles Operated	Total Fuel Costs	Gallons of Fuel Consumed
Matthews	10,000	7,300	$2,500	2,000
Smith	12,000	7,800	4,500	3,000

Required:

a. Prepare a driver productivity report for the month. The total standard miles that a driver is supposed to operate per month is 9,500 miles. The standard load ratio is 80%.

b. Prepare a driver fuel report for the month. The standard miles per gallon (MPG) is 4.9; the standard cost per gallon is $1.30.

SOLUTION TO DEMONSTRATION PROBLEM 1

a.

CLEVELAND EXPRESS
DRIVER PRODUCTIVITY REPORT
FOR THE MONTH OF JUNE 19X4

MILES OPERATED

Driver	Total Actual Miles Operated	Total Standard Miles per Month	Total Miles Operated Variance
Matthews	10,000	9,500	500
Smith	12,000	9,500	2,500

LOAD RATIO

Driver	Total Actual Miles Operated	Total Loaded Miles Operated	Actual Load Ratio	Standard Load Ratio	Load Ratio Variance
Matthews	10,000	7,300	73%	80%	< 7%>
Smith	12,000	7,800	65%	80%	<15%>

b.

CLEVELAND EXPRESS
DRIVER FUEL REPORT
FOR THE MONTH OF JUNE 19X4

Driver	Gallons Consumed	Actual MPG	Standard MPG	MPG Variance	Actual Cost per Gallon	Standard Cost per Gallon	Cost Variance
Matthews	2,000	5.0	4.9	0.1	$1.25	$1.30	$0.05
Smith	3,000	4.0	4.9	<0.9>	$1.50	$1.30	<$0.20>

■ **DEMONSTRATION PROBLEM 2** *Determining the EOQ and order cycle for a distributor.*

Big-O, a local distributor for a national tire company, expects to sell approximately 10,000 low-ride tires of a certain size next year. Annual carrying costs are $10 per tire, and procurement costs are $80 per order. The distributor operates 300 days a year.

Required:

a. Determine the EOQ.

b. How many times a year should the store reorder?

c. Determine the length of an order cycle.

SOLUTION TO DEMONSTRATION PROBLEM 2

a.

$$EOQ = \sqrt{\frac{2DP}{C}}$$

$$= \sqrt{\frac{2(10,000)\$80}{\$10}}$$

$$= \underline{\underline{400 \text{ tires}}}$$

b. Number of orders per year:

$$\frac{D}{EOQ} = \frac{10,000 \text{ tires}}{400 \text{ tires}}$$

$$= \underline{\underline{25 \text{ orders per year}}}$$

c. Length of order cycle:

$$\frac{EOQ}{D} = \frac{400 \text{ tires}}{10,000 \text{ tires}}$$

$$= \underline{\underline{4\% \text{ of the distributor's year}}}$$

or

$$4\% \times 300 \text{ days} = \underline{\underline{12\text{-day order cycle (or lead time)}}}$$

Thus, on the average, it must take 12 workdays from the placement of the order until the tires are received and ready for sale with an EOQ of 400 tires and a demand of 10,000 tires.

■ **DEMONSTRATION PROBLEM 3**   *Calculating an EOQ in which carrying costs are stated as a percentage of the purchase price of an item rather than as a dollar amount per unit.*

The Master's Voice TV Company plans to purchase 5,000 picture tubes a year at $150 each. Procurement costs are $30, and annual carrying costs are 20% of the purchase price.

Required:
a. Calculate the EOQ.
b. Calculate the total annual cost of procuring and carrying the picture tubes.

SOLUTION TO DEMONSTRATION PROBLEM 3.

a.
$$EOQ = \sqrt{\frac{2DP}{CV}}$$

$$= \sqrt{\frac{2(5,000)\$30}{.20(\$150)}}$$

$$= \underline{\underline{100 \text{ picture tubes}}}$$

b. Total annual costs = Procurement costs + Carrying costs
$$= (D/EOQ) \times P + (EOQ/2) \times CV$$
$$= (5,000/100) \times \$30 + (100/2) \times .20(\$150)$$
$$= \$1,500 + \$1,500$$
$$= \underline{\underline{\$3,000}}$$

Notice that the procurement and carrying costs are equal at the EOQ, which is at the optimum point (or minimum total cost point).

■ **DEMONSTRATION PROBLEM 4**   *Calculating the reorder point.*

The invoice printing operation at Sierra Power Company uses three boxes of printer paper per day. It takes the supplier five days to deliver an order of printer paper.

Required:
Determine at what point Sierra should place its order.

SOLUTION TO DEMONSTRATION PROBLEM 4

$$
\begin{aligned}
\text{Usage} &= 3 \text{ boxes per day} \\
\text{Lead time} &= 5 \text{ days} \\
\text{Reorder point} &= \text{Usage} \times \text{Lead time} \\
&= 3 \text{ boxes per day} \times 5 \text{ days} \\
&= \underline{\underline{15 \text{ boxes}}}
\end{aligned}
$$

Therefore, Sierra should reorder when 15 boxes are left in inventory.

■ **DEMONSTRATION PROBLEM 5**   *Calculating an EBQ for a manufacturer.*
Storite makes plastic filing cabinets for floppy disks. The management accountant has collected the following data:

Setup cost	$500 per batch
Carrying cost	$20 per unit per year
Expected annual demand	5,000 units

Required:
Compute the EBQ and explain what it means.

SOLUTION TO DEMONSTRATION PROBLEM 5

$$
\begin{aligned}
\text{EBQ} &= \sqrt{\frac{2(5,000)\$500}{\$20}} \\
&= \underline{\underline{500 \text{ units per batch}}}
\end{aligned}
$$

The optimal decision is to produce 500 units at a time, which means that there will be 10 production runs (or batches) per year (5,000 units annual demand ÷ 500 units produced per run). The EBQ means that carrying costs equal setup costs as indicated below:

$$
\begin{aligned}
\text{Carrying costs} &= (500/2) \times \$20 &= \$\ 5,000 \\
\text{Setup costs} &= (5,000/500) \times \$500 &= \underline{\ \ 5,000} \\
\text{Total costs} &= &\underline{\underline{\$10,000}}
\end{aligned}
$$

■ **DEMONSTRATION PROBLEM 6**   *Calculating the EOQ, safety stock, and reorder point.*
Humdinger Trucks purchases motors from Birmingham Diesel. The plant manager is trying to determine the lot size that should be ordered so as to minimize the sum of carrying and setup costs. She also wants to avoid stockouts, since any stockout would shut down the assembly line. To help her make her decision, you have supplied the following data:

- Annual demand for motors: 20,000
- Unit carrying cost: $100
- Setup cost: $900
- Average demand for motors: 65 per day
- Maximum demand for motors: 70 per day
- Lead time: 5 days

Required:
Calculate the EOQ, safety stock, and reorder point for the plant manager.

SOLUTION TO DEMONSTRATION PROBLEM 6

$$
\begin{aligned}
\text{EOQ} &= \sqrt{\frac{2(20,000)\$900}{100}} \\
&= \underline{\underline{600 \text{ motors per run}}}
\end{aligned}
$$

Safety stock:

Maximum usage	70 motors
Average usage	65 motors
Difference	5 motors
Lead time	× 5 days
Safety stock	25 motors

$$\text{Reorder point} = (\text{Average usage} \times \text{Lead time}) + \text{Safety stock}$$
$$= (65 \times 5) + 25$$
$$= 350 \text{ motors remaining in inventory}$$

■ **DEMONSTRATION PROBLEM 7**   *Making an ABC analysis.*

The following data represent annual sales at the Chic Boutique

ITEM	ANNUAL DEMAND	SALES PRICE	ANNUAL DOLLAR SALES
1	200	$ 50	$ 10,000
2	3,000	100	300,000
3	1,000	70	70,000
4	200	80	16,000
5	2,000	200	400,000
6	500	50	25,000
7	1,000	50	50,000
8	400	60	24,000
9	800	100	80,000
10	500	50	25,000

Required:

Using a bar graph, classify the inventory items as A, B, or C based on annual dollar sales value.

SOLUTION TO DEMONSTRATION PROBLEM 7

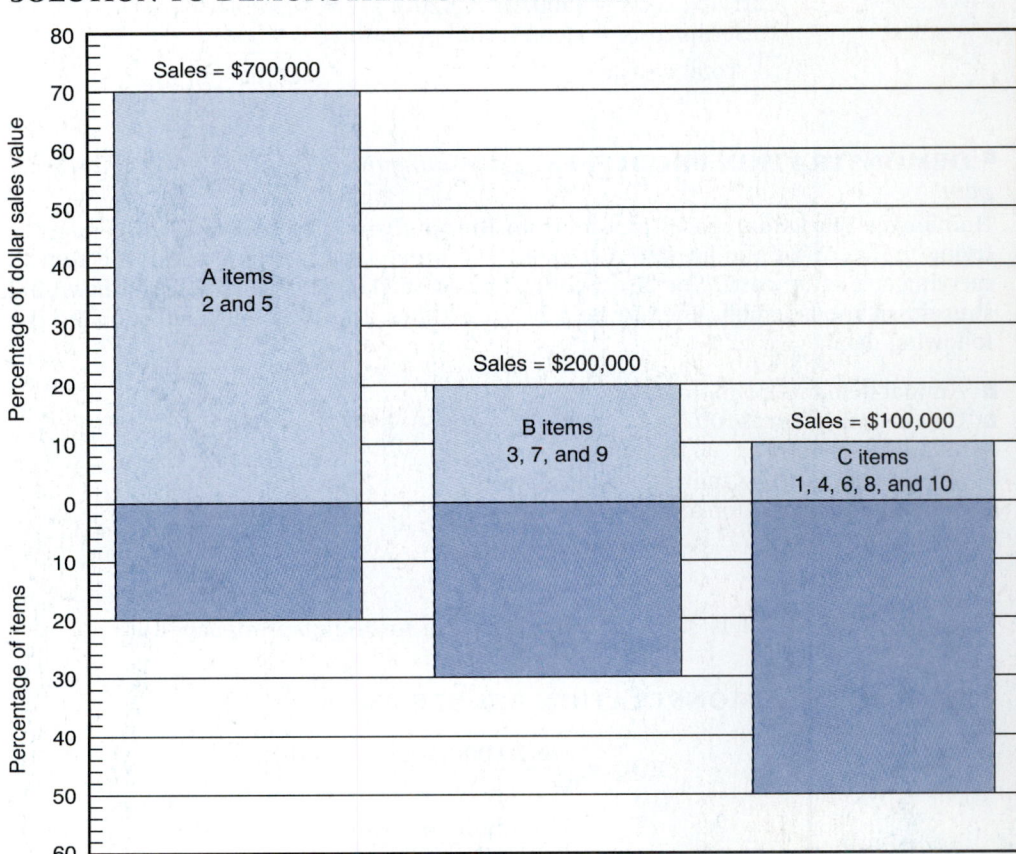

REVIEW QUESTIONS

13.1 The management of inventory costs revolves around two decision criteria. Name them.

13.2 Ignoring safety stock, which of the following is a valid computation of the reorder point?

    a. The economic order quantity.
    b. The economic order quantity multiplied by the anticipated demand during the lead time.
    c. The anticipated demand during the lead time.
    d. The square root of the anticipated demand during the lead time.

13.3 What is the difference between the EOQ model for merchandising firms and the EOQ model for manufacturing firms?

13.4 What are the main reasons that an organization has inventory?

13.5 What are the assumptions of the EOQ model?

13.6 A decrease in carrying costs will:

    a. Increase the safety stock required.
    b. Decrease the economic order quantity.
    c. Have no effect on the economic order quantity.
    d. Increase the economic order quantity.
    e. Decrease the number of orders issued per year.

13.7 Safety stocks are used to compensate for:

    a. Variability in inventory demand rates and lead time.
    b. Variability in inventory prices and lead times.
    c. Variability in inventory demand rates and prices.
    d. Inventory obsolescence and sales returns.
    e. Variability in customer needs and inventory pricing.

13.8 A company would use the EOQ model to:

    a. Minimize the unit purchase price of inventory.
    b. Minimize the number of orders placed during the year.
    c. Minimize the cost of placing orders.
    d. Minimize the combined costs of placing orders and carrying inventory.
    e. Minimize the required amount of safety stock.

13.9 The inventory management model that follows Pareto's principle is the:

    a. Economic order quantity (EOQ) model.
    b. Material requirements planning (MRP) model.
    c. ABC analysis model.
    d. Just-in-time (JIT) model.
    e. Lead time model.

13.10 When the level of safety stock is increased:

    a. Lead time will increase.
    b. Lead time will decrease.
    c. The frequency of stockouts will decrease.
    d. Carrying costs will decrease.
    e. Procurement costs will decrease.

13.11 Describe how EDI enhances the logistics system.

13.12 Discuss the types of information bar codes provide in an EDI system.

13.13 Identify four goals of the procurement function.

13.14 Name two characteristics of JIT procurement in relation to supply, quantity, and quality considerations.

13.15 Which of the following is *not* a benefit of JIT procurement to the supplier?

    a. Reduced nonvalue-added activities.
    b. Increased ability to predict resource and capacity needs.
    c. Increased inventories.

d. Reduced labor force.

e. Increased control over outbound shipments.

13.16 What are the three cost drivers of transportation costs?

13.17 Name the three cost objects to which transportation costs are normally assigned.

13.18 Name the three popular approaches to inventory management.

13.19 The simple economic production run model will only apply to situations in which the production rate:

a. Equals the demand rate.

b. Is less than the demand rate.

c. Is greater than the demand rate.

d. Exceeds the supply rate.

e. For the period covered equals the projected sales for the period.

13.20 Which one of the following items is *not* included in the annual carrying costs of inventory?

a. Cost of capital.

b. Insurance on inventory.

c. Annual warehouse depreciation.

d. Taxes on inventory.

e. Inventory breakage on stored inventory.

13.21 Contrast independent and dependent demand. Give an example of each.

13.22 When is it appropriate to employ MRP?

13.23 Which one of the following is *not* a benefit of JIT inventory management?

a. Increased cash discounts on purchases.

b. A reduction in the number of suppliers.

c. A reduction in procurement costs.

d. Less checking on quality and quantity of delivered raw materials.

e. A reduction in the total value of inventories on hand.

13.24 If one optimizes the inventory turnover ratio for a particular item, which costs will not increase?

a. Total reorder costs.

b. Stockout costs.

c. Unit reorder costs.

d. Carrying costs.

e. Procurement costs.

13.25 Which condition would justify accepting a low inventory turnover ratio from the viewpoint of inventory management?

a. High obsolescence costs.

b. High carrying costs.

c. High stockout costs.

d. Short lead times.

e. Low procurement costs.

13.26 Name four types of stockout costs.

13.27 What are the two primary objectives of MRP?

13.28 What condition(s) should exist before MRP is used?

13.29 The kanban system uses three cards. Name them and describe the information they contain.

13.30 What is the primary benefit of using a kanban system?

13.31 What are the main reasons that an organization uses warehousing?

CHAPTER-SPECIFIC PROBLEMS

These problems require responses based directly on concepts and techniques presented in the text.

13.32 *Calculating performance measures to help manage procurement costs.* Magna Distributors processed 8,000 purchase orders last year using ten purchasing agents. This year Magna processed 10,000 purchase orders employing eight purchasing agents. Administrative costs were $480,000 last year; this year, they are $460,000. Last year, 900 production orders were released, and there were 18 complaints associated with these orders. This year, 1,200 production orders were released, and there were 48 complaints associated with these orders.

Required:
Calculate performance measures for the preceding situation, and discuss what the results may be indicating to management.

13.33 *Determining characteristics of JIT procurement.* Following is a random list of characteristics that may or may not be applicable to JIT procurement:

_____ Large number of suppliers.
_____ Short-term contracts.
_____ Certified suppliers.
_____ Suppliers scattered throughout the country.
_____ Frequent deliveries in small quantities.
_____ High quality of incoming materials.
_____ Excessive amount of record keeping.
_____ Close relationship with suppliers.
_____ Price is the primary criterion used to select suppliers.

Required:
Insert a T for true or an F for false in the spaces provided.

13.34 *Determining certified supplier benefits of JIT procurement.* Following is a random list of items that may or may not be applicable to a certified JIT supplier:

_____ More paperwork.
_____ Reduced long-term risk of doing business.
_____ Reduced ability to predict resource and capacity needs.
_____ Does not participate with buying company's new product development team.
_____ Less supervision.
_____ Increased control of finished goods.
_____ Reduced work-in-process and finished goods carrying costs.
_____ More labor.
_____ Increased ability to plan ahead for design changes.
_____ Increased ability to retain a trained labor force.

Required:
Insert a T for true or an F for false in the spaces provided.

13.35 *Assigning load costs to shipments.* The Top Speed Trucking Company's management accountant is conducting an analysis of the company's transportation costs. He has collected the following data for one day:

SHIPMENT NUMBER	MILES: ORIGIN TO DESTINATION	WEIGHT (IN CWT) PER SHIPMENT
2289	200	15,000
2291	350	11,000
2292	150	8,000
2293	225	13,000
2294	275	12,000

Total load costs = $8,700

Required:
a. Calculate the cwt-miles per shipment.
b. Calculate the percentage of total cwt-miles.
c. Assign the shipment costs.

(Note: Do not consider "empty backhaul miles.")

13.36 *Calculating performance measurements for the transportation activity.* The Transport-It-All Company has gathered the following information, which it plans to use in evaluating the efficiency and effectiveness of its transportation activity over the past fiscal year:

Number of shipments	667,000
Total miles shipped	500,000
Total tons shipped	470
Number of customer complaints	51,000
Number of damage claims	28,000
Number of late deliveries	121,000
Total transportation costs	$8,000,000

Required:
Calculate the following performance measurements for the procurement activity:
a. Customer complaints.
b. Damage claims.
c. Late deliveries.
d. Cost per ton-mile.

13.37 *Classifying inventory costs.* Following are a variety of costs:

_____   Purchase order forms.
_____   Telephone call to a vendor.
_____   Purchasing agent's salary.
_____   Wages of receiving personnel.
_____   Parts awaiting use.
_____   Profit lost due to inventory nonavailability.
_____   Preparing and issuing checks to suppliers.
_____   Production setups.
_____   Money invested in inventory.
_____   Ad valorem taxes.
_____   Insurance premiums for inventory on hand.
_____   Security measures.
_____   Freight for relocating inventory.
_____   Postage for purchase orders.
_____   Property taxes on warehouses.
_____   Disposal of inventory at a price less than its cost.
_____   Wages for inventory record keeping.
_____   Shipping charges for rush orders.
_____   Losses due to theft.
_____   Costs of handling backorders.

Required:
Indicate whether each of the preceding costs would be considered a cost of ordering (O); that is, a procurement or setup cost; a cost of carrying (C); or a cost of stockout (S).

13.38 *Calculating the reorder point.* The Cartex Company uses a part to which the following data are applicable:

■ Annual usage in units	20,000
■ Working days per year	250
■ Safety stock in units	800
■ Lead time in working days	30

Units of the part will be required evenly throughout the year.

Required:
Calculate the reorder point.

13.39 *Determining the reorder point.* Ritenice Pen Company uses an average of 400 ink inserts per day, and lead time averages five days. Because both usage rate and lead times are variable, Ritenice carries a safety stock of 500 ink inserts to reduce the chance of a stockout.

Required:
Determine the reorder point.

13.40 *Calculating the EOQ.* The Family Clothing Store sells three main products: pants, dresses, and shoes. The following data are available on each product:

| | PROCUREMENT | CARRYING | |
PRODUCT	COST	COST	DEMAND
Pants	$4.00	$2.00	1,000
Dresses	6.00	5.00	1,500
Shoes	3.00	1.50	800

Required:
Calculate the EOQ for each product.

13.41 *Determining annual carrying cost per unit.* Hector Motors, Inc., is a single-product company. Various annual costs relating to its product follow:

Cost per unit:
- Freight-in on purchases $0.20
- Storage   0.12
- Insurance   0.10

Total per year:
- Interest that could have been earned
  on alternate investment funds $800
- Units required   10,000

Required:
Determine the annual carrying cost per unit.

[CMA adapted]

13.42 *Analyzing an EOQ diagram.* The accompanying diagram represents the EOQ model:

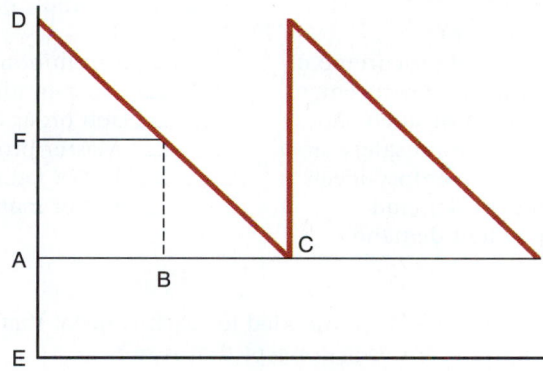

Required:
a. Which line segment represents the reorder lead time?
b. Which line segment identifies the quantity of safety stock maintained?
c. Which line segment represents the length of time to consume the total quantity of materials ordered?

[CMA adapted]

13.43 *Determining material requirements in an MRP system.* Following is a bill of materials (BOM) for product A:

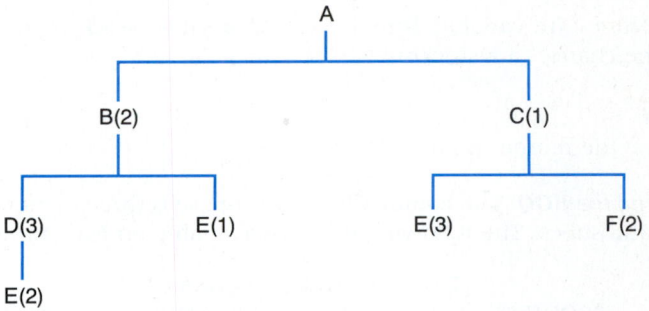

Required:

a. Determine the gross material requirements for B, C, D, E, and F to make one unit of product A.

b. Determine the gross material requirements to produce 100 units of product A.

c. Assume that D has 100 on hand and E has 300 on hand, 200 scheduled to be received (i.e., on order), and 100 in safety stock. Calculate the net material requirements for D and E. None of the other components have any inventory on hand, on order, or in safety stock.

13.44 *Cost savings resulting from increasing the turnover rate.* Markquic Company's budgeted sales and budgeted cost of sales for the coming year are $144,000,000 and $90,000,000, respectively. Short-term interest rates are expected to average 10%.

Required:

If Markquic can increase inventory turnover from its present level of 9 times per year to a level of 12 times per year, what cost savings would be expected in the coming year?

[CMA adapted]

13.45 *Identifying concepts associated with MRP.* Following are various concepts that may or may not be associated with MRP:

_____ Lead time	_____ Steady demand
_____ Safety time	_____ Sporadic demand
_____ Reorder point	_____ JIT
_____ Time-phased procurement	_____ Continuous manufacturing
_____ Constant-rate procurement	_____ Mass-production operation
_____ Elimination of safety stock	_____ Job order operation
_____ Minimization of safety stock	_____ Master production schedule
_____ Constant inventory levels	_____ Bill of lading
_____ Dependent demand	_____ Bill of materials
_____ Independent demand	

Required:

Insert a T for true in the spaces provided for each concept that is associated with MRP and an F for false for each concept that is not.

13.46 *Calculating turnover ratios.* The management accountant at Z-Bender Company has gathered the following data on Z-Bender's inventories to assist him in evaluating the effectiveness and efficiency with which its inventories are being managed:

Number of units sold of product Z	14,700
Cost of goods sold	$70,300
Cost of goods manufactured	$44,000
Cost of raw materials used	$27,500
Average number of units on hand of product Z	4,900
Average finished goods inventory	$21,300
Average work-in-process inventory	$11,000
Average raw materials inventory	$6,000

Required:
Calculate the turnover ratios for:
a. Raw materials.
b. Work-in-process.
c. Finished goods.
d. Product Z.

13.47 *Calculating financial performance measurements to determine warehousing productivity.* The management accounting system at Triostep Company has accumulated the following warehousing-related information in its database for the prior month:

Receiving and storage costs	$6,400
Picking costs	$10,500
Packing costs	$19,500
Staging costs	$494,000
Loading costs	$1,580,000
Inbound demurrage costs	$890,000
Outbound demurrage costs	$1,670,000
Average number of units stored	32,000
Average number of units picked and packed	30,000
Average number of shipments staged	13,000
Average number of loads loaded and shipped	10,000
Average number of loads received	12,900

Required:
Calculate the following financial performance measurements:
a. Receiving and storage costs per unit.
b. Picking costs per unit.
c. Packing costs per unit.
d. Staging costs per shipment.
e. Loading costs per shipment.
f. Outbound demurrage costs per load.

THINK-TANK PROBLEMS

Although these problems are based on chapter material, reading extra material, reviewing previous chapters, and using creativity may be required to develop workable solutions.

13.48 *Determining the impact of transportation volume rate discount.* O'Leary Wholesalers has collected the following data on its product A:

Annual sales volume	5,400 units
Cost per unit	$6
Holding cost	20% per year
Ordering cost per order	$40

Required:
a. Calculate the EOQ using the above data.
b. Assume that the most desirable transportation rate is achieved when a quantity of 900 units is ordered as compared to the EOQ-recommended order calculated in Requirement (a). Also assume that the transportation rate for the EOQ is $1.80 per unit, but if the order is 900, the rate drops to $1.45 per unit. Explain the impact of this transportation volume rate discount. Taking into consideration the potential transportation savings by purchasing in 900-unit lot sizes, determine the cheapest way to order product A.

13.49 *Calculating expected usage.* Compurite Computer Company began producing laptop computers last year. At that time the company forecasted the need for 10,000 integrated circuits annually. During the first year, the company placed orders when the inventory dropped to 600 units so that it would have enough to produce laptops continuously during a three-week lead time. Unfortunately, the company ran out of this component on several occasions, and costly production delays resulted. Careful study of last year's experience resulted in the following expectations for the coming year:

WEEKLY USAGE	PROBABILITY OF USAGE	LEAD TIME	PROBABILITY OF LEAD TIME
280	.2	3 weeks	.1
180	.8	2 weeks	.9
	1.0		1.0

The study also suggested that the usage during a given week was statistically independent of usage during any other week and usage was also statistically independent of lead time.

Required:
a. Calculate the expected usage during a regular production week.
b. Calculate the expected usage during lead time.
c. If the company reorders integrated circuits when the inventory has dropped to a level of 700 units, what is the probability that it will run out of this component before the order is received?

[CMA adapted]

13.50 *Determining procurement and carrying costs.* Toyland is a wholesale distributor of toys. The company leases space in a public warehouse and is charged according to square feet occupied. Toyland has decided to employ the EOQ formula to determine the optimum number of cases of toys to order.

The company placed 2,400 orders last year. Data for the high-activity month, low-activity month, and the year for the procurement and warehouse operations are as follows:

	HIGH-ACTIVITY MONTH (160 ORDERS)	LOW-ACTIVITY MONTH (100 ORDERS)	ANNUAL COSTS
Purchasing:			
Manager	$ 1,600	$1,600	$ 23,400
Clerks	1,750	1,250	18,000
Supplies	400	260	3,500
Warehouse:			
Supervisor	1,550	1,550	18,600
Receiving clerks	2,200	1,700	20,500
Shipping clerks	2,800	2,500	31,200
Totals	$10,300	$8,860	$115,200

The annual charges for the warehouse totaled $12,750 last year. In addition, the annual insurance and property taxes on the toys stored in the warehouse amounted to $1,500 and $2,250, respectively. The average monthly inventory last year was $75,000.

Long-term capital investments are expected to earn 12% after income taxes. Toyland is subject to an effective income tax of 40%.

Required:
a. Determine the variable cost of placing an order that would be used in the EOQ formula.
b. Determine the annual carrying cost, stated as a percentage, that would be used in the EOQ formula.

[CMA adapted]

13.51 *Computing EOQ and safety stock.* Clyde Peterson, general manager for Adam Desk Company, is exasperated because the company exhausted its finished goods inventory of Style 103–Modern Desk twice during the previous month. This led to customer complaints and disrupted the normal flow of operations.

"We ought to be able to plan better," declared Peterson. "Our annual sales demand is 18,000 units for this model or an average of 75 desks per day based upon our 240-day work year. Unfortunately, the sales pattern is not this uniform. Our daily demand on that model varies considerably. If we do not have the units on hand when a customer places an order, 35% of the time we lose the sale, 40% of the time we pay an extra charge of $24 per unit to expedite shipping when the unit becomes available, and 25% of the time the customer will accept a backorder at no out-of-pocket cost to us.

"When we run out of units, we cannot convert immediately because we would disrupt the production of our other products and cause cost increases. The setup process for this model results in the destruction of 12 finished desks, leaving no salvageable materials. Once we get the line up, we can produce 200 units per day. I would prefer to have several planned runs of a uniform quantity rather than the short unplanned runs often required to meet unfilled customer orders."

The management accountant has suggested that the company adopt an EOQ model to determine optimum production runs and then establish a safety stock to guard against stockouts. The cost data for the Modern Desk, which sells for $110, are readily available from the management accounting records. The manufacturing costs are as follows:

Direct materials	$30
Direct labor (2 DLhr @ $7)	14
Manufacturing overhead:	
Variable (2 DLhr @ $3)	6
Fixed (2 DLhr @ $5)	10
Total manufacturing cost	$60

The management accountant estimates that the company's carrying costs are 19.2% of the incremental out-of-pocket manufacturing costs. This percentage can be broken down into a 10.8% variable rate and an 8.4% fixed rate.

The EOQ formula referred to by the management accountant is as follows:

$$EOQ = \sqrt{\frac{2DC}{K}}$$

where

D = Annual demand in units
C = Cost of placing an order
K = Annual unit cost of carrying inventory

Required:
a. Adam Desk Company can solve part of its production scheduling problems by adapting the EOQ model to determine the optimum production run.
  1. Explain what costs the company would be attempting to balance when it adapts the EOQ model to production runs.
  2. Calculate the optimum quantity that Adam Desk Company should manufacture in each production run of Style 103–Modern Desk.
  3. Calculate the number of production runs of Modern Desks that Adam Desk Company would schedule during the year based upon the optimum quantity calculated in Requirement (a)2.
b. Adam Desk Company should establish a safety stock level to guard against stockouts.
  1. Explain what factors affect the designated size of the safety stock for any inventory item.
  2. Calculate the minimum safety stock level that Adam Desk Company could afford to maintain for the Style 103–Modern Desk and not be worse off than if it were unable to fill orders equal to an average day's demand.
[CMA adapted]

13.52 ***Discussing the implementation of JIT.*** Over the past several years, many companies have decided to implement a JIT production system. They have met with varying degrees of success because implementation of JIT is dependent on many factors such as management commitment to and employee acceptance of the process. In addition, a company must be willing to change the way it thinks about its employees, suppliers, and customers if it is going to be successful in using JIT procedures.

Required:
a. In general, describe several actions that a company can take to facilitate an organizational change.
b. To ensure the success of a JIT production system, describe the relationship a company must establish with its:
   1. Suppliers.
   2. Customers.
   3. Employees.
c. The success of a JIT production system requires changes in management skills and behavior.
   1. Describe at least two changes in management skills and behavior that will be required to ensure a successful transition to a JIT production system.
   2. Identify several steps a company can take to achieve the changes described in Requirement (c)1.

[CMA adapted]

13.53 *Analyzing procurement costs.* The Premier Cuisine Restaurant Company owns and operates seven different restaurants in the San Francisco Bay area. The purchasing function is centralized in the downtown San Francisco home office. The company also has one centralized warehouse. The warehouse manager recently voiced concern to management regarding the broad types of glassware being carried in inventory, many of which contained specialized logos and many of which are no longer being used in the restaurants. He also expressed concern that he continues to receive orders for specialized glassware from each restaurant, thus, further building up the diverse glassware inventory as well as keeping unit costs high. Management asked that the warehouse manager provide them with a breakdown of the number of different types of glassware currently in stock by major glassware type. The following data were provided to management:

TYPE OF GLASSWARE	NUMBER OF DIFFERENT PLAIN GLASS ITEMS	STOCK ITEMS OF GLASS WITH LOGOS
Long-stem wine	5	2
Short-stem wine	5	3
Dessert wine	4	1
Champagne	2	0
Cognac	3	2
Margarita	3	0
Tall	4	3
Medium	5	4
Short	4	3
Shot	3	9
Glass mug	6	2
Dessert bowl	6	0

When management reviewed these data with purchasing, it was also found that this glassware had been ordered from a total of 13 vendors.

Required:
a. Identify the primary weaknesses or diseconomies with the company's current procurement function.
b. Discuss how JIT could help alleviate the ailments of the current procurement function.
c. Discuss what additional benefits the company could derive from installing JIT in its procurement activity.
d. Besides JIT, discuss how the procurement function could be further streamlined and costs reduced through application of the manufacturing concept of reducing the number of parts and using standard parts whenever possible.

13.54 *Making an ABC (contribution-by-value) analysis.* Quality Auto Parts makes 10 different replacement parts for the automotive industry. Following are the items, their annual demand, unit price, and annual dollar sales volume.

ITEM	ANNUAL VOLUME (UNITS)	UNIT PRICE	ANNUAL DOLLAR SALES VOLUME
521	600	$ 15.00	$ 9,000
471	1,000	18.00	18,000
492	500	160.00	80,000
555	1,000	1.00	1,000
876	400	40.00	16,000
721	1,600	20.00	32,000
475	1,000	1.20	1,200
135	200	5.00	1,000
317	600	3.00	1,800
556	1,000	95.00	95,000

Required:
a. Prepare a contribution-by-value analysis report.
b. Draw a Pareto chart that depicts the analysis.
c. Discuss policies that may be based on ABC analysis.

13.55 *Determining the impact of inventory turns on inventory carrying costs.* Average inventory at one turn is $900,000. The carrying costs are 30% of the average inventory.

Required:
a. Prepare a schedule showing the impact of inventory turns on carrying costs. Set up a column in your schedule titled "Inventory Turns." Under this column include 10 turns, starting with one turn.
b. Discuss the results of your schedule.

14

COST MANAGEMENT THROUGH LIFE CYCLE ANALYSIS AND TARGET COSTING

Team approach at JI Case.

LEARNING OBJECTIVES

After studying this chapter, you should be able to:

1. Define market life and cost life cycles, and describe how they are used in analyzing and managing costs over the entire life cycle of a product or service.

2. Explain how functional analysis is used to achieve target costs.

3. Describe how activity-based costing and activity-based management are used to meet target costs.

4. Discuss how parametric cost estimating methods may be used in estimating costs.

■ INTRODUCTION

A major trend occurring at many firms is the early and continuing involvement with new products or services by teams comprised of engineers, management accountants, marketing professionals, and logistics personnel. Their involvement ensures that new products and services are launched in a timely manner and that costs are minimized and profits maximized throughout the products' or services' life cycle.

Management accountants need to focus on every stage of the product cost life cycle, not just the production stage. Management accountants must be involved with the design of new products, assisting design engineers and others with cost estimates and target costs. They should also understand the activity value chain and help determine how costs can be reduced throughout this chain.

This chapter presents a framework for estimating and managing costs and assessing the consequences of decisions made at different stages of the life cycle of a product or service. A key objective is to establish target costs throughout the life cycle of new products or services *before* they enter production. Two methods used to set target costs are functional analysis and activity-based costing systems. The parametric cost estimating method is helpful in estimating costs of new products or services. ▬▬▬

▌LIFE CYCLE ANALYSIS

Understanding and analyzing both the product market life and cost life cycles are necessary for effective cost management. Analyzing the consequences of cost-reducing decisions over the life of a product or service can significantly increase a company's profits. Making the correct early decisions in market life and cost life cycles can dramatically affect later stages.

LEARNING OBJECTIVE 1

Define market life and cost life cycles, and describe how they are used in analyzing and managing costs over the entire life cycle of a product or service.

▌The Market Life Cycle

A product or service has a **market life cycle,** which includes five stages:

- *Pre-introductory stage* in which the product concept is developed and all activities necessary to produce, market, distribute, and service the product are poised for implementation.
- *Introduction stage* in which the product is launched into the market.
- *Growth stage,* which is typified by consumer acceptance.
- *Maturity stage,* which is characterized by market saturation, strong brand loyalty, and stabilized sales volume and profits.
- *Decline stage,* which is the final stage of the market life cycle. It is marked by a continued decline in sales and eventual abandonment of the product or service.

At one time, the average market life cycle was about 15 years. Today, it can be less than three years. For example, new computer products are introduced at very frequent intervals. When market life cycles were 10 to 15 years or more, management accountants could report costs on an after-the-fact basis because there was sufficient time to make adjustments and improve productivity and profitability. With a market life cycle anywhere from one to three years, however, many factors that influence product or service profitability will be incurred *prior* to entering production. In today's competitive world, management's goal

INSIGHTS & APPLICATIONS

Product Development at Pharmaceutical Companies

New product development performance is a major factor in winning the race to market, positioning products successfully against competitors, and minimizing development resource requirements. Pharmaceutical companies have an opportunity to establish a stronger competitive position and superior financial returns by significantly improving product development performance.

High pharmaceutical profit margins make delays in the product launch (i.e., from development to production and marketing) extremely costly. For example, a six-month delay can result in lost contributions of $40 million or more. Consequently, the reduction in profit potential that losing the race would entail considerably outweighs the incremental development resources required to meet target launch dates.[1]

---

is to get new products to market *on time* at or less than the *target cost*. After-the-fact cost reporting is thus of little value in managing costs.[2]

Analyzing the Cost Life Cycle

The product **cost life cycle** presented in Exhibit 14–1 provides a total cost life cycle profile. It includes cost curves starting with product development, then production, and on into logistics and service support until the product or service market life cycle ends. These life cycle cost curves are particularly important to management accountants and others who are trying to achieve target costs and make their companies more competitive.

Traditionally, management accountants have not been concerned with costs in the development stage of a new product or service, nor with logistics, marketing, and service costs. Their primary concern was with production costs. The best time, however, to manage these costs is during development *before* the product or service goes into production. Many authorities observe that 80 to 90 percent of the life cycle costs of a new product or service are committed during development, as shown in Exhibit 14–2.[3] Focusing on costs *after* the product or service enters production results in only 10 to 20 percent of costs being manageable.[4] Thus, the key to managing these life cycle costs is to focus attention on the development phase.[5] Decisions made during this phase will impact the enterprise's resources far into the future. As some authorities point out, one dollar spent on activities that occur prior to production, such as market research and product or service design based on target costing, can save from $8 to $10 in production, marketing and sales, logistics, and service costs.[6]

---

[1] Adapted from Charles Beever and Mary Jo Veverka, *A Winning Approach to New Product Development* (New York: Booz, Allen & Hamilton, 1988). With permission.

[2] James A. Brimson, "CAM-I Cost Management Systems Project," in *Cost Accounting, Robotics, and the New Manufacturing Environment*, ed. Robert Capettini and Donald K. Clancy (Sarasota, Fla.: American Accounting Association, 1988), p. 5.8.

[3] Collie Berliner and James A. Brimson, *Cost Management for Today's Advanced Manufacturing* (Boston: Harvard Business School Press, 1988), pp. 156–157.

[4] James R. Anderson, "Unit Manufacturing Cost Tracking Systems at Xerox," in *Cost Accounting for the 90s: Responding to Technological Change* (Montvale, N.J.: Institute of Management Accountants, formerly the National Assocation of Accountants, 1988), p. 187. With permission.

[5] Michael D. Shields and S. Mark Young, "Managing Product Life Cycle Costs: An Organizational Model," in *Emerging Practices in Cost Management*, ed. Barry J. Brinker (Boston: Warren Gorham Lamont, 1992), p. G3-1. With permission.

[6] Richard L. Engwall, "Cost Management Systems for Defense Contractors," in *Cost Accounting for the 90s: Responding to Technological Changes* (Montvale, N.J.: Institute of Management Accountants, formerly the National Association of Accountants, 1988), pp. 205–225. With permission.

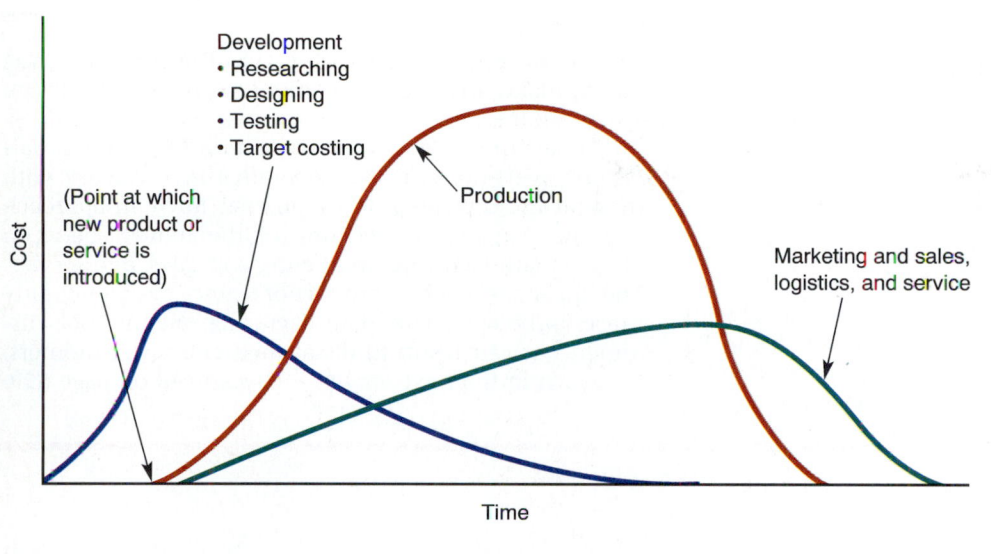

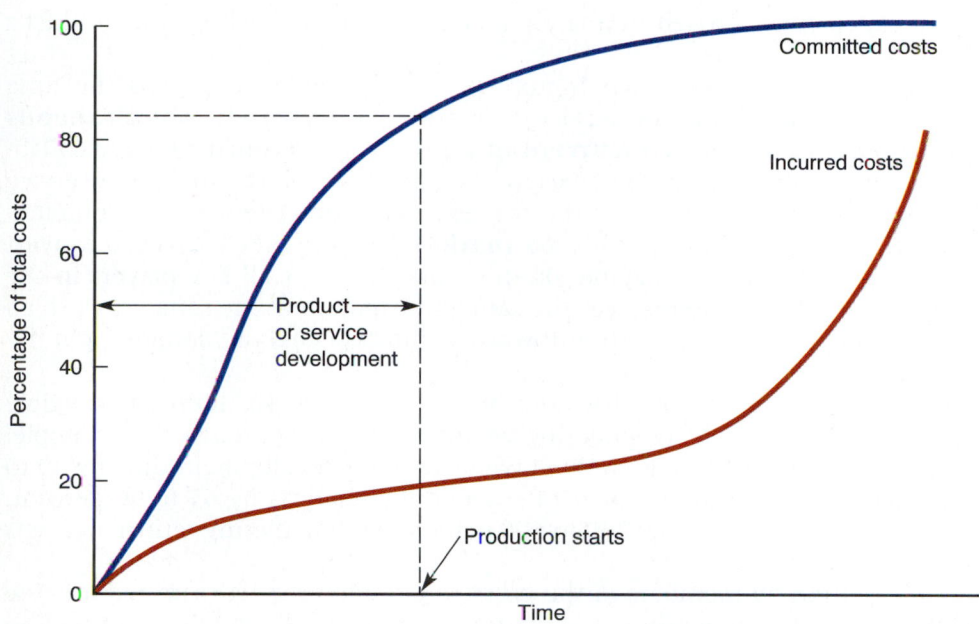

▌ Linear Approach versus Simultaneous Engineering

The **linear approach** is a sequential, uncoordinated design process in which each functional area of the enterprise focuses on its own needs and priorities. It is an "over-the-wall" approach to bringing a new product or service to market. The phrase "over-the-wall" refers to a department's (e.g., engineering) interest in completing its objectives while giving little consideration to how the work it produces impacts the work of other departments (e.g., production, logistics, marketing).[7] In essence, a department completes its assigned work and then throws the work over-the-wall to the next department involved in the project. The over-the-wall process is symptomatic of linear project management in which departments do not work collaboratively. The result is a failure to satisfy all the functional needs of the company (i.e., marketing's need for a product with consumer appeal, service department's desire for a product that is easy to service, finance's goal to use the least expensive parts, and manufacturing's need to have a simple manufacturing process with few parts to assemble). By

Simultaneous engineering team.

[7] Peter Drucker, "The Coming of the New Organization," *Harvard Business Review,* January-February 1988, pp. 45–53.

INSIGHTS & APPLICATIONS

Throwing the New Car Design over the Wall

At Clunker Motors, the engineers designed a car with an engine that required many different holes to be drilled and tapped at multiple angles. A simpler engine with fewer parts would have been less expensive to produce and easier to service. But manufacturing had to make the engine according to engineering design specifications.

Clunker's vehicles are designed in a linear (or serial) fashion with little or no cooperative involvement with those at the next step of the process. Such an approach does not support a "meeting of the minds" between design, manufacturing, marketing and sales, and service. The linear approach to product or service design not only causes problems with manufacturing, an internal customer, but can result in dissatisfied external customers, as shown in the next *Insights & Applications* on page 659.

failing to design quality in and consider downstream life costs, this uncoordinated, expedient approach ultimately increases costs throughout the product's life cycle.[8]

The over-the-wall approach is not only costly, but it lengthens the time it takes to get a product or service to market. Alternatively, **simultaneous engineering** (also called **concurrent engineering**) is a concurrent and collaborative design process, which strives to integrate and balance product or service development, from initiation of the concept to customer feedback. Simultaneous engineering reduces the **time-to-market** (i.e., the time it takes to convert a product idea into a marketable product) and involves all key players in the product team. Everyone receives the same information at the same time, so all team members can work together toward a common goal of "doing it right the first time."

According to the National Institute for Defense Analysis, there are tangible benefits to simultaneous engineering versus the linear approach. For example, simultaneous engineering is credited with reducing development time by 30 to 70 percent, reducing the number of engineering changes by 65 to 90 percent, improving overall quality by 200 to 600 percent, and increasing return on assets by 20 to 120 percent.

Collaboration by members of the cross-functional product team reduces the myopic focus by integrating the various people and activities required to develop, manufacture, market, distribute, and service high-quality, innovative products quickly and successfully. A key performance measurement of a product team is time-to-market, which is a measure of the team's effectiveness at converting ideas into marketable and profitable products.

Some typical improvements from simultaneous engineering include the following:

- Reducing number of parts
- Reducing nonvalue-added activities
- Improving quality
- Increasing manufacturability
- Increasing flexibility

As can be readily seen, all these improvements are in concert with world-class manufacturing.

Chapter 12 emphasized how preventive measures can eliminate downstream costs of quality, especially final inspection, internal failure, and external failure costs. This prevention-based philosophy is important because the earlier in the product development process that prevention techniques (e.g., modular design, prototype testing, designing for manufacturability) can be applied, the lower

[8] Shields and Young, op. cit., p. G3-3.

Throwing the New Car to the Customer

Scott Farley is manager of mechanics at Wilson Motors, a local car dealer that sells Clunker cars. Winnie Gorham, an owner of a Clunker, drives her new car into Wilson Motors' shop, gets out of the car, and approaches Scott.

"Hi Scott," says Winnie.

"Good morning, Winnie," Scott responds. "What can I do for you?"

"The engine in my new Clunker is acting up. Maybe it needs a tune-up, or new spark plugs. Can I have it done by noon?"

"Maybe by noon day after tomorrow," Scott laughs.

"You've got to be kidding," Winnie says, somewhat frustrated.

"No, I'm not kidding," says Scott, now frowning. "To do a simple tune-up, we have to dismount the engine so we can reach two spark plugs that we otherwise can't get to. The engine is poorly designed and difficult to service."

"And what's all this going to cost me?" Winnie asks.

"Assuming it's a regular tune-up, it'll cost you $250," Scott replies.

"What?" Winnie exclaims. "I can't believe a simple tune-up will cost $250."

"It's the labor cost, Winnie," Scott explains. "A mechanic has to dismount the engine and move it away from the chassis to replace two of the spark plugs and make other adjustments. Maybe Clunker Motors will redesign the engine next time for easier service."

"There won't be a next time for me," says Winnie. "I'll not buy another Clunker, ever!"

"I can't say that I blame you," Scott responds.

---

the final inspection, internal failure, and external failure costs that will be incurred. Simultaneous engineering teams design quality in *before* the production stage begins. Some traditional companies, using the linear design approach, try to achieve quality *during* production, an inopportune time to be thinking about quality.

Using Quality Function Deployment

Quality function deployment (QFD) is a method that assures quality *while* the product or service is still in the development stage.[9] The key focus of QFD is on determining customer requirements and then developing the product or service to meet or exceed those requirements. QFD reduces the need to redesign and make modifications after the product or service is launched into the marketplace. One of the major ideas presented in Chapter 12 was "designing quality in"; QFD is the method that supports this idea.

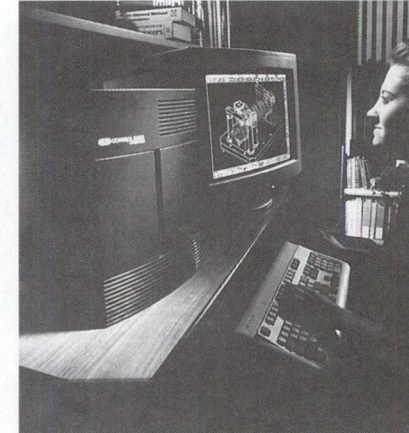

Designing quality in.

Most of the time, customer requirements are determined from ideas, complaints, characteristics, issues, and so forth expressed by customers. The development team is therefore faced with a great deal of verbal, qualitative data gathered from customer surveys and other market research methods. QFD helps the team organize and prioritize these data.

With the data structured, the development team not only understands what the customers say they want but, possibly, what the customers want but are not expressing. These unexpressed wishes lead to what has been called "exciting quality" and "customer delight." The development team has to design in "expected quality," or no one will buy the product or use the service. But today many companies are trying to look beyond expected quality to design in exciting quality. An example in the manufacturing sector was the addition of cup holders in cars. Ten or fifteen years ago, few cars except Japanese cars had cup holders.

---

[9] For a full treatment of QFD, see James L. Bossert, *Quality Function Deployment: A Practitioner's Approach* (Milwaukee, Wis.: ASQC Quality Press, 1991); R. John Aalbregtse, "Target Costing," in *Handbook of Cost Management*, ed. Barry J. Brinker (Boston: Warren Gorham Lamont, 1992); and Yoji Akao, ed., *Quality Function Deployment: Integrating Customer Requirements into Product Design* (Cambridge, Mass.: Productivity Press, 1990).

INSIGHTS & APPLICATIONS

Simultaneous Engineering at Boeing

Boeing aims to shrink the time needed to manufacture a plane from more than a year to just six months by 1998. Its traditional method for designing aircraft was a three-phase process with each phase being completed in sequence. Worse, the three groups have little contact until their initial designs are completed. As a result, tooling specialists often receive blueprints for parts that either can't be manufactured or are too expensive to produce. In such cases they send blueprints back for revision. The process forces each group to turn out reams of corrections, consuming millions of hours a year.

Boeing hopes to capture huge savings by enabling groups to design new aircraft simultaneously rather than in sequence. When the group decides to alter the design of a major part, it has the authority to make the changes itself, rather than waiting months for approvals from higher-ups.

Reengineering efforts, just-in-time inventory management, and simultaneous engineering are innovations that are expected to give Boeing the billions in savings that it needs. Says Grace Robertson, program director, "We expect a substantial reduction in design, development, and manufacturing costs."[10]

Customers did not look for this feature in a car, but they were pleased when they got it. Later, the cup holder, once a customer delight, became a customer requirement.[11] In the merchandising sector, Nordstrom Department Stores, located in the western United States, offers not only expected service, but a delightful and satisfying shopping experience. In Nordstrom's case, this kind of quality didn't just happen, it was *designed in*.

As also seen in the Pacioli Bookstore case on page 662, QFD is not just for manufacturing companies. Unlike a product, a service is not a measurable material object because it is often intangible and immediate. Nevertheless, the service industry (e.g., hospitals, retailers, hotels, restaurants) is finding it necessary to use QFD in developing a quality design for its services. QFD makes it possible to clarify, plan, and design a service to be offered and to conduct total quality management (TQM) throughout the service's life cycle.

Matching Capacity with Demand

Product or service cost life cycles can also be reduced by optimally matching production capability with product or service demand. This capacity matching is illustrated in Exhibit 14–3. The capacity line represents a step function because capacity is acquired in whole increments; that is, one cannot purchase part of a machine.

A company that is planning to introduce a new product or service is willing to invest in excess capacity because it anticipates growth in demand during the growth stage. With all else constant, this capacity ensures that the product or service is delivered to customers without delay.

As soon as the product or service moves through the growth and maturity stages, decisions to add capacity are weighed carefully because excess capacity is very costly. If the company is introducing a new product or service or revitalizing the present one, then a proper level of capacity must be acquired to meet a new growth stage.

---

[10] Adapted from Shawn Tully, "Can Boeing Reinvent Itself?" *Fortune*, March 8, 1993, pp. 66–73. © 1993 Time Inc. All rights reserved.
[11] Bossert, op cit., pp. 18–19.

INSIGHTS & APPLICATIONS

Bashing Silos But Not Quality

Chrysler's enterprisewide study led to its platform team concept (i.e., the simultaneous engineering team approach) composed of design engineers, manu-facturing personnel, management accountants, and vendors. With this new approach, departmental "silos" have gone the way of the K car. No longer is a product tossed over-the-wall from vertical department to vertical department.

Once the company decides it will build a new car "platform" of certain dimensions, functions, cost, and price, the platform team works to see that these parameters are met. The Viper was the first car produced under the new working arrangement. It was designed and built under the target cost in three and a half years instead of the normal five.

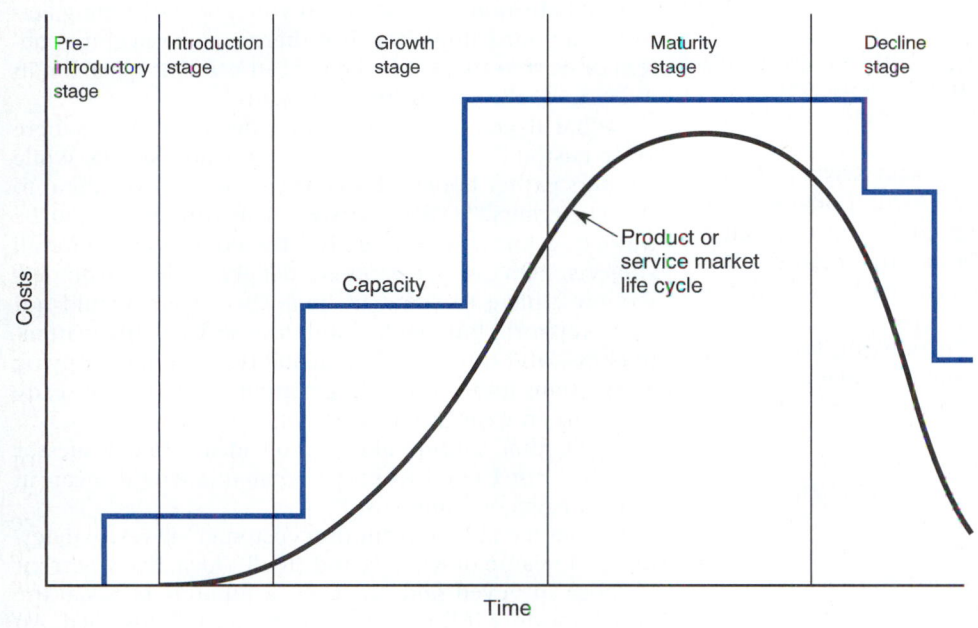

■ EXHIBIT 14–3
Resource Capacity Matched with Product or Service Demand

SETTING TARGET COSTS WITH FUNCTIONAL ANALYSIS

LEARNING
OBJECTIVE 2

Explain how functional analysis is used to achieve target costs.

A goal of management is to produce products or services that meet consumer needs and price and quality expectations over the product's or service's entire life cycle. For the product or service to be profitable, it must be designed within the established target cost. One method used to achieve the target cost is functional analysis.

What Is Target Costing and How Is It Used as a Cost Management Method?

Target costing is a cost management method for reducing the overall cost of a product or service over its entire life cycle by employing better specification and design procedures at the lowest possible cost. Target costing is not a method for day-to-day cost management. Rather, it is a cost planning method that focuses on controlling design specifications, production techniques, and logistics. Target costing contributes to the goal of delivering a competitive product or service to the marketplace. Target cost is computed as follows:

INSIGHTS & APPLICATIONS

Using QFD to Design the Bookstore for Professor Pacioli

Professor Marvin Pacioli has just retired. He plans to open a bookstore to supplement his rather meager retirement income. Before embarking on this entrepreneurial venture, he calls one of his previous students, Kristy Paton, for assistance. Following are parts of their conversation.

"Before I launch my bookstore, I want to make sure that I've covered all bases and don't spend money on things that are not important to my customers," said Professor Pacioli.

"I couldn't agree with you more," said Kristy. "In fact, we are currently studying quality function deployment, or QFD, which helps people design quality into a product or service *before* it is introduced to the market. This method is certainly in line with your wish to do things right the first time."

"I think this is exactly what I'm looking for to help me design my bookstore from a quality viewpoint before opening it. Would you mind helping me apply the QFD method?" said Professor Pacioli.

"Not at all," said Kristy. "As a matter of fact, Tom Hardaway, Heidi Franz, and myself are looking for a project to do as part of the course requirement. Tom is an industrial engineering major and Heidi is a marketing major. I'll be the management accountant. We'll form a simultaneous engineering team."

"That sounds great," said Professor Pacioli excitedly. "When can we get started?"

"Let me coordinate with the team members. Then, I'll call you next Monday and we'll set up a definite schedule," said Kristy.

After meeting with Professor Pacioli, Kristy's team performed a marketing survey to determine customer requirements and customer ratings. The team used the planning and design matrix shown in Exhibit 14–4. After conducting a session with Professor Pacioli and benchmarking the competition—the university bookstore—the matrix was completed.

"You know, this QFD method has really opened my eyes," said Professor Pacioli. "However, I wish that we had done this three weeks earlier."

"Why is that?" Tom asked.

"Well, I have already signed a lease that will give me the space for a reading room, and now I discover that customers don't want that facility. That means I'll be spending about one-third more for rent than required. This is very unfortunate. I should have been more careful. I didn't practice what I preached; that is, doing it right the first time. Now, I'm committed to a 10-year lease with about 1,500 square feet of space that I don't need."

"All is not lost," said Heidi. "While using QFD, the team is supposed to look for exciting quality or customer delight. I believe we've done a thorough job in analyzing what customer requirements are and relating them to the design parameters for your bookstore. If you invest in these design parameters, you will be providing quality that the customer expects. And you'll be performing better than your competitor. But there is that nagging problem of wasted space. Maybe we can use that space for an exciting quality or customer delight."

"What if you used the extra space as a place where your customers can sit, relax, and enjoy snacks while runners gather books, charge them, and deliver them to the customers?" asked Kristy. "The runners would be trained to know how to gather the books quickly for all subjects. On the customer delight side, customers wouldn't have to stand in line. This design would not only support, but go beyond fast service, high attentiveness, and quick book availability. Customers buying a few items and not needing runners would have ready access to an express checkout lane."

"Well, that sounds like a good idea," said Professor Pacioli. "But I need to know what this would mean in terms of revenue and cost."

The team conducted another customer survey to determine the value of Kristy's and Heidi's idea. Sixty percent of those surveyed said that they would buy books at the new bookstore if this design parameter was installed. An expected value for revenue was calculated, resulting in additional revenue of $5,000 per month. Expenses including the $900 rent for the extra space amounted to $4,300 per month. Therefore, the expected profit is $700 per month.

"I am really pleased with the work you people have done," said Professor Pacioli. "I now have a clear vision of how I'm going to design quality into the bookstore before it is opened. To celebrate, you all are invited to my house Saturday for lasagna. I make a great lasagna! Then, after we eat, I'll show you a video of *The History of Double Entry Bookkeeping*!"

$$\text{Target cost} = \text{Target price} - \text{Target profit}$$

A product's or service's sales price is heavily influenced by prevailing market forces. Individual companies are rarely able to sell a product or service for a price higher than the market price unless they are able to differentiate their product or service from the competition. A company can differentiate its product or service in several ways:

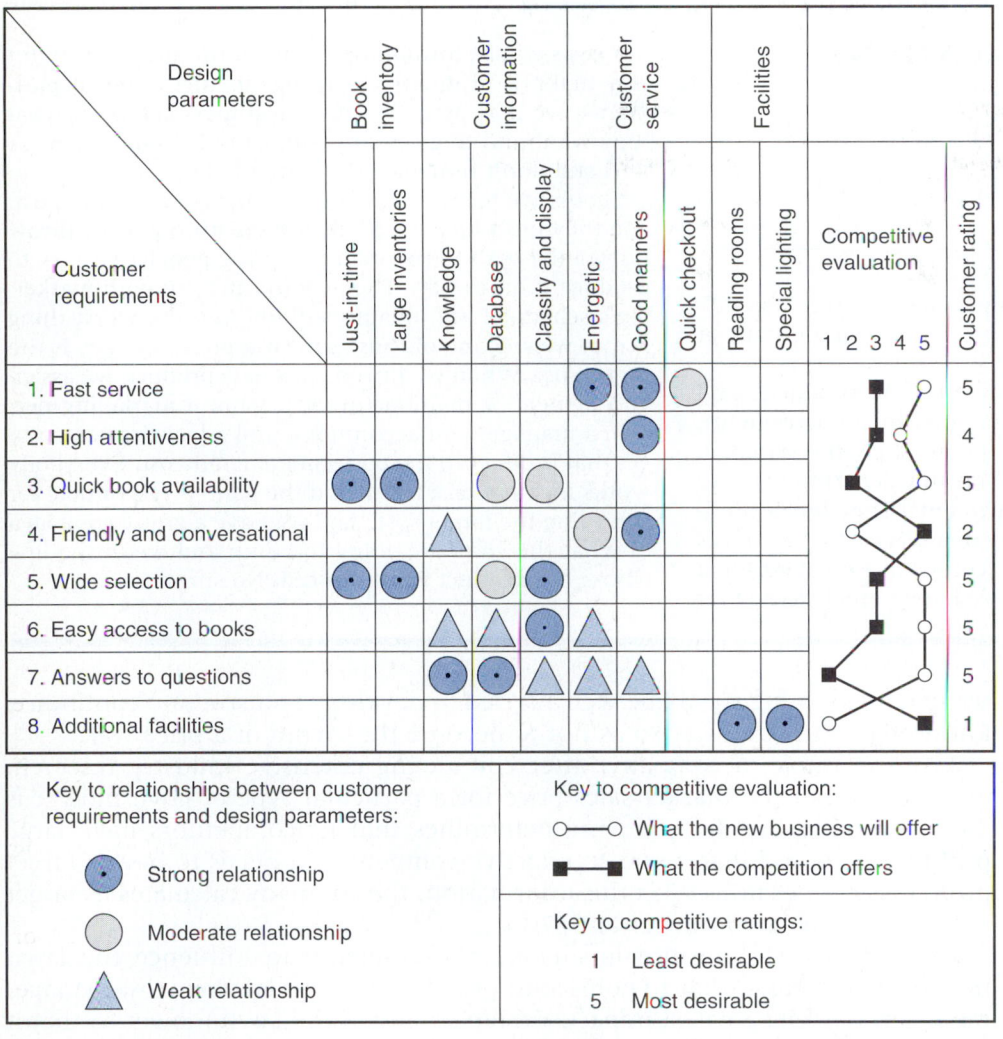

Planning and Design Matrix for New Bookstore

■ Product enhancements, such as eliminating product defects and uncovering additional uses for the product

■ Ancillary product enhancements, such as making product packaging more appealing and improving customer service

■ Additional product development, such as providing features not previously available[12]

If a company chooses not to differentiate its product or service (i.e., decides to compete on price), it must offer the product at a target price equal to or less than the market price in order to obtain its target profit. To compete on price, a company must thoroughly understand the pricing strategy of its competitors. If, for example, a competitor is using a price skimming strategy, which provides the opportunity for large marginal profits, a target costing strategy must take into account the possibility of a price war, which the low-cost producer most likely will win. On the other hand, if the competition is using a market penetration pricing strategy, which provides limited marginal profit, a target costing strategy may prove to be more effective because the competitors' low profit margins will allow little room for price reductions. In either case, any company

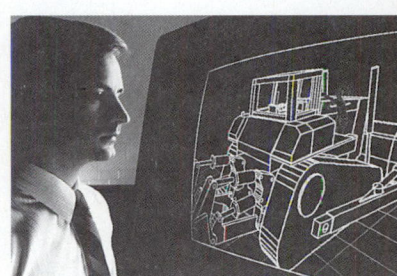

Functional analysis at Caterpillar, Inc.

[12] Chester R. Wasson, *Dynamic Competitive Strategy & Product Life Cycles* (St. Charles, Ill.: Challenge Books, 1974), p. 174.

INSIGHTS & APPLICATIONS

Target Costing at Masterson Industries

"What is this target costing I keep hearing about?" said Robert Cooper, a long-time cost accountant at Masterson Industries.

"The focus is on the total cost of the product," said Edna Mallory, newly hired management accountant.

"I don't understand your point," Robert responded.

"In the past, we've focused on our departments. But customers don't buy our departments. They buy a product that performs a certain way or a service that achieves a goal. Customers will pay a certain price range for a particular product or service. We have to make sure that our costs will be low enough to meet this price constraint and make a profit. By focusing on measuring departments, we may actually cause customers *not* to get what they want and to go to our competitors," said Edna.

"I still don't understand," stated Robert.

"Look, we measure the engineering department's cost, and they introduce the product prematurely. They throw it over-the-wall to the manufacturing people who try to produce it on the fly. They try to catch up with marketing's schedule, and quality suffers. And the worst thing is that we sell one of those son-of-a-guns. The key is the target cost. When we introduce a new product, we assign an engineer, a manufacturing person, a marketing person, a management accountant, and a logistics person to get that product to the customer at a fair cost. Everybody works together as a team, and the team is responsible for achieving the target cost. And we have a pretty good idea of what the costs are going to be up and down the line before the product is introduced. No surprises."

using target costing would be well advised to develop extensive and continuing knowledge of its industry so as not to become the victim of a price war.

As an example, a company, after conducting extensive industry research, determines that the market sales price for a particular type of lawn mower is $500. Additionally, the company determines that its competitors have large profit margins and that, to be an effective competitor, it needs to have a target profit of $230 per unit. With this information, the company calculates its target cost for its new lawn mower at $270.

This target cost information enables the company to influence the lawn mower design costs prior to going into production—this is when cost management can have its greatest impact. Designers design the lawn mower so that it can be produced at the target cost of $270. This approach is sometimes referred to as "design to cost." A target cost is attainable, but only with considerable effort and analysis.[13]

▌ Are Target Costs the Same as Standard Costs?

Target costs are conceptually different from standard costs. Standard costs are predetermined from internal analysis of the production process; that is, standard costs are production-driven. Target costs come from external sources, primarily the analysis of markets and competitors; that is, target costs are market-driven. Moreover, target costs are established for all activities of the product life cycle, as shown in Exhibit 14–5.

During the introduction and growth stages of a product life cycle, standard costing techniques are often used inappropriately. During these two stages of the product life cycle, standard costing techniques are ineffective as a cost management tool because they provide after-the-fact cost information during a production phase that is changing rapidly as production is ramped up to meet market demand. Target costing, on the other hand, is a more valuable cost management tool during these stages because it provides proactive, before-the-fact information, rather than reactive, after-the-fact information.

Additionally, target costs are dynamic. They are often revised in the pre-introductory stage and several times again during the introduction and growth

[13] Michiharu Sakurai, "Target Costing and How to Use It," in *Emerging Practices in Cost Management*, ed. Barry J. Brinker (Boston: Warren Gorham Lamont, 1990), p. 255. With permission.

Clipper Lawn Mower		
Estimated market life cycle:	4 years	
Estimated sales:	100,000 units	
Target sales price:	$500	
	Per Unit	**Total**
Development target cost	$ 10	$ 1,000,000
Production target cost	200	20,000,000
Marketing target cost	20	2,000,000
Logistics target cost	30	3,000,000
Service target cost	10	1,000,000
Total unit target cost	$270	
Total life cycle target cost		$27,000,000

■■■ EXHIBIT 14–5
Target Costs for a New Lawn Mower

stages of the product life cycle. As a result, the target cost for a product or service changes several times over its entire life cycle. In fact, world-class manufacturers expect the target cost to decrease over the product's or service's life cycle as a result of continuous improvement.

What Is Functional Analysis and How Is It Used in Conjunction with Target Costing?

A **function** is an action or feature of a product or service. **Functional analysis** is a cost management technique that focuses on the various functions and design costs of a product or service. "Functional analysis contributes to cost management by assisting in the identification of cost reduction possibilities by eliminating or modifying functions of the product or service. Alternatively, functional analysis can, on occasion, lead the designer to add new functions to the product or service if the target profit is greater than the target cost generated by the additional functions."[14] It is important to remember that the objective of cost management is to generate a greater return on assets, not merely to reduce costs. In addition to providing a focus for cost management, functional analysis provides a way to discover how more (or less) investment in products or services may lead to increased profits.[15]

For example, a large range of new materials or new parts may be considered, functions may be modified, or two or more functions may be combined into one function. When functions are eliminated or combined, certain direct labor and overhead costs may no longer be required. The elimination of a function (or the combining of functions) may also eliminate the need for a machine and labor to operate the machine, thus decreasing direct labor, depreciation, insurance, maintenance, and utility costs.

Functional analysis can be applied to both products and services throughout their life cycles. It is particularly useful during the pre-introductory stage of a new product or service, however, because costs can normally be affected much more easily during this phase than after investment is made and production starts.

[14] Takeo Yoshikawa, John Innes, and Falconer Mitchell, "Cost Management through Functional Analysis," in *Emerging Practices in Cost Management*, ed. Barry J. Brinker (Boston: Warren Gorham Lamont, 1990), p. 243. With permission.
[15] Ibid., p. 248.

INSIGHTS & APPLICATIONS

Achieving the Target

As the deadline approached to unveil a demonstration model, Ethel Watson, the product design team's management accountant, discovered that the cost of the P-270 was only 35 percent lower than its predecessors. "I was the bean counter," she says, "and there were too many beans. I felt responsible, but I couldn't believe Harold Faig (project team manager) would hold us back for 5 percent. Now, I know better."

Faig's response to the news was: "Unacceptable. If we don't make the 40 percent target cost, we won't do it." The team returned to work and squeezed an additional 5 percent out of the machine in time to beat the deadline.

When P-270, renamed Vista, hit the market, there was an agonizing lull. "Then suddenly, *whoosh*," says Bill Reinhart, one of the team members. Milacron won't release exact numbers, but in Vista's first full year of production, the company sold 2.5 times as many of the machines as it had in the best year of Vista's predecessor.[16]

With functional analysis, costs are allocated to functional areas of the product or service under analysis. Production or service prototypes are assigned costs, based on their functions, to evaluate the product's or service's potential profitability.[17]

USING A SIMULTANEOUS ENGINEERING APPROACH.   Generally, functional analysis is a team activity involving five areas of expertise:

- Engineering and design
- Management accounting
- Production
- Marketing
- Logistics

The goal of the functional analysis team is to perform functional cost analysis and propose alternative designs of the product or service for optimal cost management. At Toyota, the team meetings are chaired by the senior vice president in charge of accounting or finance.[18]

In some situations, several competing teams will be organized to tackle the same product or service. These teams will all have the same goals, such as:

- Maintain the quality of the product, but reduce the cost by 30 percent
- Add two new specific functions to the product without increasing its cost or reducing its quality[19]

DEVELOPING A FUNCTIONAL FAMILY TREE.   A **functional family tree** is the logical diagram of each *function* of the product or service, not each *part* of the product or service. A general model of a functional family tree is presented in Exhibit 14–6.

The functions (i.e., actions and features) help determine the success of a product or service in the market. For example, Exhibit 14–7 shows the functional family tree for a propelling ballpoint pen. Each function is defined in terms of a verb and a noun. The primary function of a propelling ballpoint pen

---

[16] Adapted from Peter Nulty, "The Soul of an Old Machine," *Fortune*, May 21, 1990, p. 19. © 1993 Time Inc. All rights reserved.

[17] Masayasu Tanaka, "Cost Planning and Control Systems in the Design Phase of a New Product," in *Japanese Management Accounting*, ed. Yasuhiro Monden and Michiharu Sakurai (Cambridge, Mass.: Productivity Press, 1989), p. 53. With permission.

[18] Takao Tanaka, "Target Costing of Toyota," *Journal of Cost Management*, Spring 1993, p. 7.

[19] Takeo Yoshikawa, John Innes, and Falconer Mitchell, "Japanese Cost Management Practices," in *Handbook of Cost Management*, ed. Barry J. Brinker (Boston: Warren Gorham Lamont, 1992), p. F3-14. With permission.

■■■ EXHIBIT 14–6
General Model of a Functional Family Tree

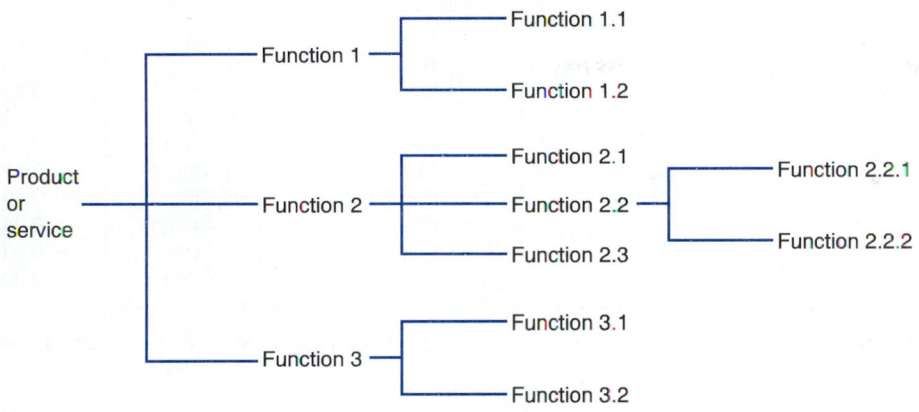

■■■ EXHIBIT 14–7
Propelling Ballpoint Pen Functional Family Tree

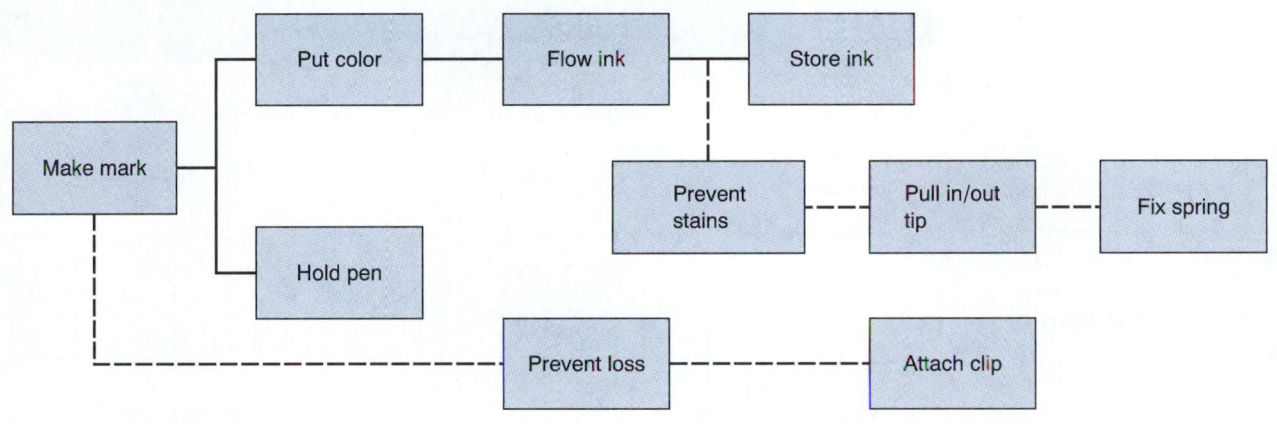

is to "make mark." To perform this primary function, subfunctions, such as "put color" and "hold pen," are needed.[20]

To assign a target cost to the new product or service, the management accountant, as a member of the team, must perform the following steps:

1. Define and classify functions.
2. Evaluate the importance of functions.
3. Assign target costs to each function.

If target costs are not being met, the designers must make design changes. As stated before, this iterative process is based on the concept of "design to cost," the main principle of cost management at the product's or service's design phase.

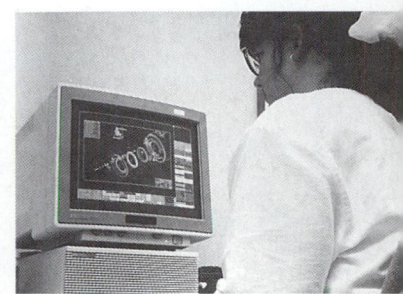

UniMac's Andrea Oberlander, assistant system administrator, calls up exploded part on HP's ME10 CAD package. Courtesy of Creative Communications Services.

DEVELOPING A PARTS-FUNCTIONS-COST MATRIX.   Exhibit 14–8 is the parts-functions-cost matrix, which shows the links among the parts and functions of the propelling ballpoint pen, together with their associated costs. These costs will become the focus of assessing the pen's potential success.[21]

Exhibit 14–9 is an alternative functional family tree of the original propelling

---

[20] Takeo Yoshikawa, John Innes, and Falconer Mitchell, "Cost Management Through Functional Analysis," in *Emerging Practices in Cost Management*, ed. Barry J. Brinker (Boston: Warren Gorham Lamont, 1992), p. O2-2. With permission.

[21] Ibid., p. O2-3.

| Part Number | Name of Parts | Function | | Cost |
		Transitive Verb	Noun	
1	Tip	Flow	Ink	$0.80
2	Barrel	Hold	Pen	1.20
3	Cartridge	Store	Ink	0.30
4	Top	Store	Ink	0.20
5	Ink	Put	Color	0.15
6	Cap	Pull in/out	Tip	0.12
7	Spring	Pull in/out	Tip	0.10
8	Stopper	Fix	Spring	0.08
9	Clip	Prevent	Loss	0.13
10	Screw	Attach	Clip	0.02
				$3.10

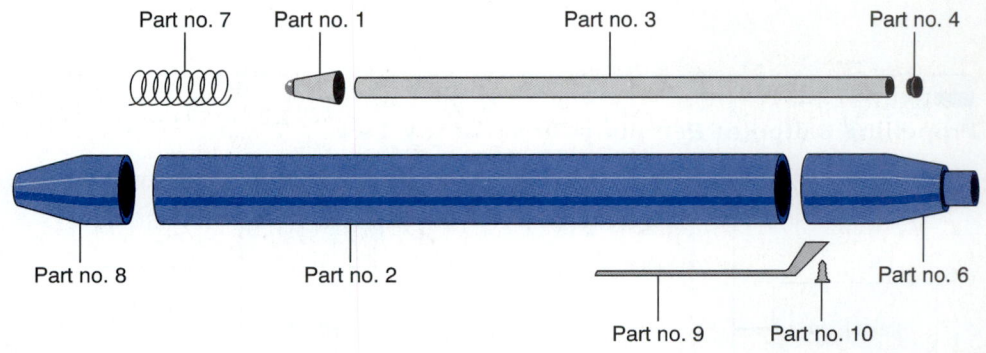

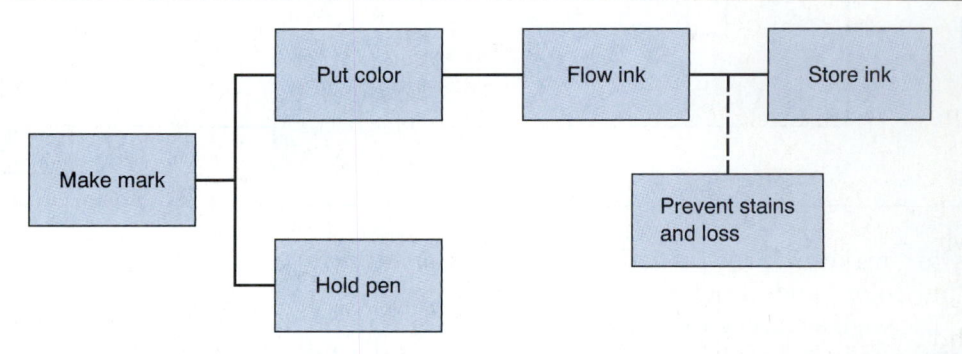

ballpoint pen design. Here, the two functions of preventing stains and pre-venting loss are integrated. Exhibit 14–10 shows the parts-functions-cost matrix for this new design. The number of parts required in the first design falls from ten to only six. The result is a cost reduction of over one-third (from $3.10 to only $2.00).[22]

If management's target cost is in the $2.00 range, then the propelling ballpoint pen design will be scrapped, and the disposable ballpoint pen design will become a strong candidate for a new product produced and sold by the company. Additional functional analysis, however, may result in another design alternative, which will give the ballpoint pen new functions, such as "erase ink." This alternative design will probably increase costs, but it may also permit a larger incremental increase in the sales price of the ballpoint pen, resulting in higher profit margins. In any case, after the selected alternative design is implemented, the management accountant will review the results to verify the accuracy of the parts-functions-cost matrix data.

[22] Ibid., p. O2-4.

Part Number	Name of Parts	Function		Cost
		Transitive Verb	Noun	
1	Tip	Flow	Ink	$0.50
2	Barrel	Hold	Pen	1.00
3	Cartridge	Store	Ink	0.20
4	Top	Store	Ink	0.10
5	Ink	Put	Color	0.12
6	Cap	Prevent	Stain/loss	0.08
				$2.00

■■■EXHIBIT 14–10
Parts-Functions-Cost Matrix for the Disposable Ballpoint Pen

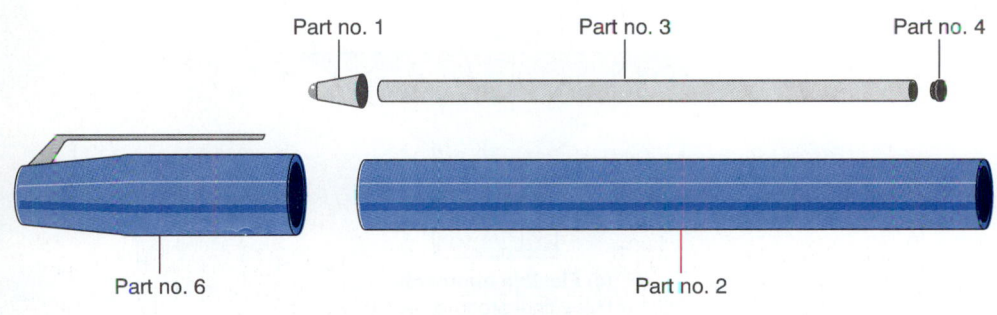

Increasing Flexibility through Functional Analysis

Reducing the number of different parts is a major goal of target costing. The greater the number of different parts required to make the product, the greater its complexity. Complexity drives up costs. Moreover, if complexity is high, flexibility will be low.

Products should be designed not only with as few parts as possible, but also with as many standard parts as possible. Unique parts, even though they may be few in number, will drive up costs and reduce flexibility. Standard parts are readily available (probably from certified vendors) and can be obtained with short lead times, at less cost, and in smaller quantities.[23]

One General Electric location provided its designers with an incentive to reduce part numbers in their products. As a result, 1,000 parts were eliminated in two months. This reduction in part numbers led to the elimination of 39,000 shop orders per year and 125,000 fewer parts being ordered, made, or stocked.[24]

The "mushroom concept," discussed in Chapter 2, substantially increases a manufacturer's flexibility, because a large variety of finished products are obtained from a small number of parts and subassemblies. The manufacturer differentiates its products toward the end of the production process, as shown in Exhibit 14–11c. The closer to the end of the production process the manufacturer can differentiate its products, the more flexible it will be in meeting the needs of its customers. Unlike the other two approaches in the exhibit, the mushroom approach gives customers a wide choice, provides flexibility of production mix, and has the added advantage of making it easier and quicker to introduce new products or make product enhancements.[25]

Solid modeling is making inroads at UniMac. Here, Andrea Oberlander, assistant system administrator, and James Tate, design engineer, explore possibilities on HP's ME30 design package. Courtesy of Creative Communications Services.

[23] Brian H. Maskell, *Performance Measurement for World Class Manufacturing* (Cambridge, Mass.: Productivity Press, 1991), p. 178. With permission.

[24] Hal Mather, *Competitive Manufacturing* (Englewood Cliffs, N.J.: Prentice-Hall, 1988).

[25] Ibid., pp. 186–187.

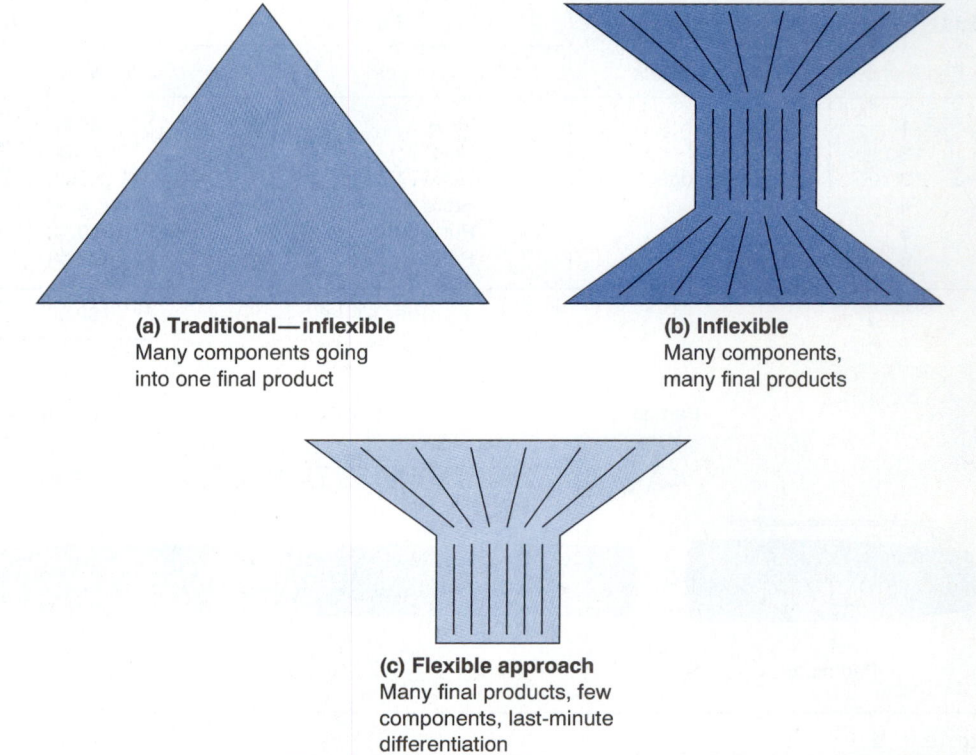

■■EXHIBIT 14–11
Product Design Approaches

Source: Brian H. Maskell, *Performance Measurement for World Class Manufacturing* (Cambridge, Mass.: Productivity Press, 1991), p. 187. With permission.

(a) Traditional—inflexible
Many components going into one final product

(b) Inflexible
Many components, many final products

(c) Flexible approach
Many final products, few components, last-minute differentiation

---

LEARNING OBJECTIVE 3

Describe how activity-based costing and activity-based management are used to meet target costs.

▌SETTING TARGET COSTS WITH ACTIVITY-BASED COSTING AND MANAGEMENT SYSTEMS

Whereas functional analysis helps achieve a target cost for a product or service according to functions provided to customers, using activity-based costing (ABC) systems to set a target cost involves focusing on activities and their cost drivers used to produce a product or provide a service. A powerful way to go about setting a target cost is to use functional analysis and ABC in combination.

▌Cost Management during Design

According to Pete Dybsand, senior finance manager at Boeing, cost is a focal point for the design teams. "We provide the cost-driver information to the teams, so engineering will know what area to simplify or eliminate," says Dybsand.[26]

Product costs can be reduced by using designs that decrease the demand for high-cost activities. Activity-based costing enables design engineers to understand the impact of different designs on product costs and manufacturing flexibility. Creating designs that enable products to be produced easier and faster will reduce product costs and the need for activity resources.

▌Understanding the Activity Value Chain

An **activity value chain** is used to develop and support an enterprise's production and delivery of products and services throughout their life cycles.[27] An

---

[26] Adopted from Esther L. Hayman, "A Meeting of the Minds at Boeing," *Management Accounting,* April 1993, pp. 30–32. Reprinted from *Management Accounting.* Copyright by Institute of Management Accountants, Montvale, N.J.

[27] Adapted from Michael E. Porter, *Competitive Advantage: Creating and Sustaining Superior Performance* (New York: Free Press, 1985).

■■■EXHIBIT 14–12
A Company's Activity Value Chain

Research and development	Inbound logistics	Production	Outbound logistics	Marketing and sales	Service
• Researching	• Issuing purchase orders	• Setting up	• Materials handling	• Advertising	• Field repairs
• Performing simultaneous engineering	• Receiving	• Cutting	• Storing	• Customer calls	• Recalls
• Conducting quality function deployment (QFD)	• Inspecting	• Drilling	• Packaging	• Traveling	• Customer inquiries
• Prototyping and testing	• Storing	• Lathing	• Shipping	• Processing sales orders	
• Target costing	• Materials handling	• Painting and buffing	• Preparing shipping documents	• Analysis of customer problems	
		• Engineering	• Installing		

example of this value chain is shown in Exhibit 14–12. The activities linked together represent strategic-level activities found in almost any enterprise. The items listed under each strategic-level activity are a sampling of specific activities performed to support the strategic-level activities. Management's aim is to develop an activity value chain that includes specific activities that add value to products and services throughout their life cycle. Virtually all of a company's activities exist to support the production, delivery, and servicing of products and services throughout their life cycles.

▌Analyzing and Managing the Activities

Analyzing and managing activities within the activity value chain can result in effective cost management. For example, just-in-time (JIT) and certified vendors can reduce inbound logistics costs. Computer-integrated manufacturing (CIM) and JIT can reduce production costs. Electronic data interchange (EDI) and JIT can reduce outbound logistics, marketing, and sales costs. Total quality management and modular design can reduce service costs. The analysis of the activity value chain should involve individuals from all activities, to ensure that the concerns of activities impacted by the product are given adequate consideration.

Analyzing and managing activities can reduce costs in four ways:[28]

■ *Activity reduction.* Reduce the time or effort required to perform the activity. For example, simultaneous engineering reduces time-to-market.
■ *Activity elimination.* Eliminate the activity entirely. For example, installing EDI and JIT can eliminate the need to prepare purchase orders and checks for invoice payments.
■ *Activity selection.* Select the low-cost alternative from a set of design alternatives. For example, design A can be produced with 14 parts whereas design B requires 60 parts. The designs are equal in quality, functionality, and consumer acceptance, but design A will reduce inventory, production, and service costs. For another example, activity 1 inserts a part through a hole in a circuit board. Activity 2 attaches a part to the circuit board using surface-mount equipment. The two alternatives require different equipment, setups, and

[28] Peter B. B. Turney, "How Activity-Based Costing Helps Reduce Costs," in *Emerging Practices in Cost Management,* ed. Barry J. Brinker (Boston: Warren Gorham Lamont, 1992), p. D5-3. With permission.

other resources and entail different costs. These differences should influence the designer's decision.

■ *Activity sharing.* Make changes that permit activities to be shared with other products to yield economies of scale. For example, the drilling machine that drills holes in components for other products is used to drill holes for components of the new product.

The phrase "managing the activities" is not an idle exercise in semantics. Managing activities is at the crux of activity-based costing and activity-based management, as pointed out in Chapters 10 and 11. To focus on cost reduction alone, however, may result in wrong decisions being made. For example, a manager may focus on reducing setup costs by spreading them over as many units as possible. But, producing a large batch of units may generate output in excess of current demand and thus add to storage and materials handling costs. So, by focusing on reducing setup costs per unit of product, management has actually done nothing to reduce setup activity costs. In fact, management has increased the cost of storage and materials handling. Had the focus instead been on analyzing and managing setup, storage, and materials handling activities, all three activities could have been streamlined, reducing the resources they consume.

A painting and buffing activity provides another example. The painting process requires buffing to remove blemishes in the product's finish. But the need to buff the paint can be eliminated if the cause of the poor finish is identified and corrected.[29]

Eliminating Nonvalue-Added Costs and Reducing Value-Added Costs

Exhibit 14–13 illustrates the type of information that can be obtained through an activity-based costing (ABC) system. In this example, one of the strategic-level activities is customer service, which includes several specific activities in the enterprise's activity value chain, with an aggregate activity cost of $107,000. Almost 85 percent of this total is for value-added costs, while the remaining 15 percent is for nonvalue-added costs. The exhibit also shows that the target cost team, through an in-depth analysis of each specific activity, has identified an opportunity to reduce costs by $37,000, or 35 percent of the total, while providing the same, or a better level of customer service. The other activities are analyzed in the same manner with similar cost reductions. The results are a target cost of $775,000 and an improvement margin of $324,000 ($1,099,000 original cost − $775,000 target cost). The ABC system can be used to establish target cost savings opportunities and then determine the best means of realizing these opportunities for improvement.[30]

Understanding the Value Chain of Vendors and Customers

Besides analyzing and managing the company's activity value chain, the target cost team must also understand the value chain of its vendors and customers. By understanding stakeholder value chains, it is sometimes possible to make changes that benefit all parties. For example, a large bakery was purchasing millions of eggs from vendors. A major activity the vendors performed was packaging and shipping eggs so they wouldn't break during transit. A major activity of the bakery was breaking eggs and disposing of shells. Both activities were wasteful to the parties performing them.

UniMac's engineering coordinator Michael Murphy enlists HP's ME10 CAD package to design a laundry plan. Courtesy of Creative Communications Services.

[29] Ibid., p. D5-1.

[30] Lawrence S. Maisel and Eileen Morrissey, "Using Activity-Based Costing to Improve Performance," in *Handbook of Cost Management*, ed. Barry J. Brinker (Boston: Warren Gorham Lamont, 1992), pp. B4-18 to B4-20. With permission.

■■EXHIBIT 14–13
Value-Added Cost Analysis and Target Cost Information through Activity-Based Costing

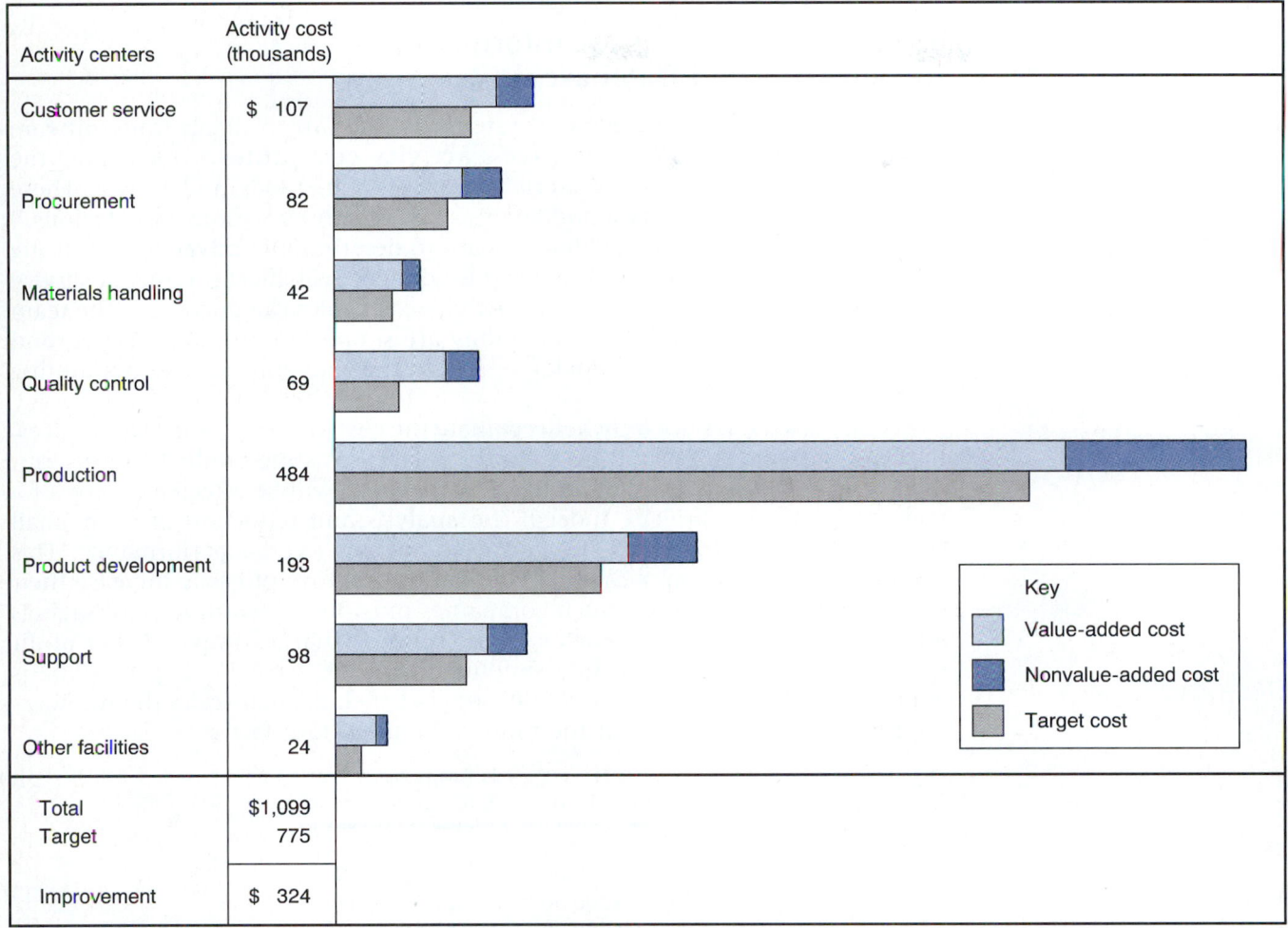

Activity centers	Activity cost (thousands)
Customer service	$ 107
Procurement	82
Materials handling	42
Quality control	69
Production	484
Product development	193
Support	98
Other facilities	24
Total	$1,099
Target	775
Improvement	$ 324

Key
Value-added cost
Nonvalue-added cost
Target cost

Source: Lawrence S. Maisel and Eileen Morrissey, "Using Activity-Based Costing to Improve Performance," in *Handbook of Cost Management,* ed. Barry J. Brinker (Boston: Warren Gorham Lamont, 1992), p. B4-19. With permission.

Analysis of the activities resulted in changes. The egg vendors broke the eggs and shipped the yolks and whites in tank trucks and sold the shells. The bakery received eggs ready for immediate production. Value was added and waste was reduced, a win-win situation.

Another way logistics costs can be reduced is to introduce interchangeable components as late in the activity value chain as possible; that is, application of the mushroom concept. For example, a manufacturer of telephones designed the product so that costly internal mechanisms could be fabricated and shipped *without* covers. The covers available included a wide variety of styles and colors. Specific covers were shipped separately and stocked by the retailers to meet the tastes of local customers.

Products can be designed to reduce costs throughout the activity value chain. Products requiring fewer parts reduce inbound logistics costs. Products that are simple in design and easier to assemble increase manufacturability and reduce production costs. Products that are compact, lightweight, and easy to package and handle reduce outbound logistics costs. Products that are simple in design require less special training for marketing professionals. Moreover, less complex products are generally more appealing to customers. A product with quality designed and built in will reduce external failure costs, thereby reducing the need for service activities.

Maintaining ABC Cost Information in Computerized Databases

A variety of database management systems (DBMS) are available from software vendors to store, maintain, and access **activity cost tables,** which show the cost effects of using different materials, production methods, and designs. These cost tables permit easy access and analysis of costs under various assumptions.[31] Such tables enable the development team to determine in advance how using different activities and product and service designs will affect product or service costs. Cost information generated by activity cost tables can encourage the team to redesign products and services so they are simpler to produce, deliver, and use. Activity cost tables are supplementary to the conventional cost accounting system.

Activity cost tables not only help estimate the cost of new products or services, they also provide a basis for lowering the costs of existing products or services. These tables show the cost of all the activities that will be affected by any of a wide range of cost drivers. Indeed, the analysis and reduction of even small costs can have a dramatic effect on a company's overall performance. This situation is especially applicable to companies that cannot easily increase their sales volume or sales price. Such companies must look inward for cost savings and productivity increases. For example, suppose that a company's net profit per sales dollar is 2 percent. In a simplified manner, a cost savings of $0.02 is equivalent to an increase of $1.00 in sales. At such a small scale, the numbers seem rather insignificant, but the ratio is the important factor:[32]

A Cost Savings of	Is Equivalent to a Sales Increase of
$0.02	$1.00
$2.00	$100.00
$200.00	$10,000.00
$2,000.00	$100,000.00
$20,000.00	$1,000,000.00

Indeed, when one realizes that a cost savings of $20,000 is equivalent to a sales increase of $1,000,000, the value of activity cost tables becomes apparent.

Exhibit 14–14 illustrates the general structure of activity cost tables. This example involves production activities, specifically the drilling activity. But the same structure can be used for inbound logistics, outbound logistics, other production activities, marketing and sales, and service activities.

Assume that 500,000 components for a new product will require that a hole be drilled. The hole must be one-half inch in diameter, but its depth has not been determined. Exhibit 14–15 shows activity cost tables for three hole depths: three inches, five inches, and seven inches, each one-half inch in diameter. Each activity cost table also contains three types of material: plastic, steel, and aluminum.

The highest cost for the drilling activity is $16,000,000 (500,000 components × $32), based on the use of a steel component with a seven-inch hole depth. The lowest cost for the drilling activity is $7,000,000 (500,000 components × $14), based on a plastic component and a three-inch hole depth. If the design engineer can adjust the design of the product so that a plastic compo-

---

[31] Takeo Yoshikawa, John Innes, and Falconer Mitchell, "Cost Tables: A Foundation of Japanese Cost Management," in *Emerging Practices in Cost Management,* ed. Barry J. Brinker (Boston: Warren Gorham Lamont, 1990), p. 262. With permission.

[32] Bernard J. LaLonde, John R. Grabner, and James F. Robeson, "Integrated Distribution Systems: A Management Perspective," *International Journal of Physical Distribution Management,* October 1970, p. 46.

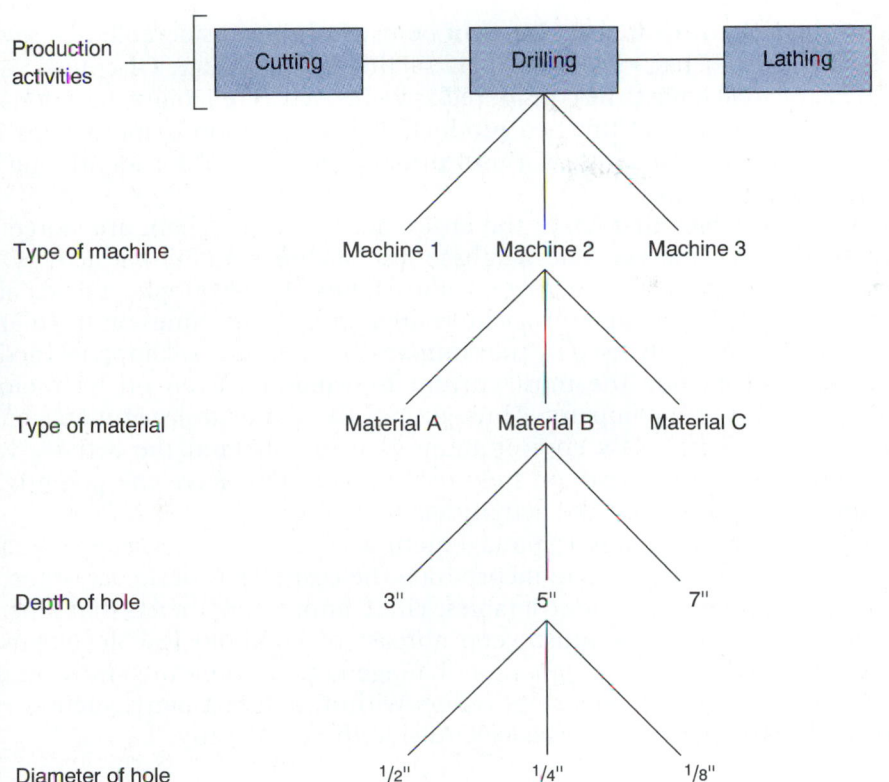

Production activities — Cutting — Drilling — Lathing

Type of machine — Machine 1   Machine 2   Machine 3

Type of material — Material A   Material B   Material C

Depth of hole — 3"   5"   7"

Diameter of hole — 1/2"   1/4"   1/8"

■■EXHIBIT 14–14
The General Structure of Cost Tables

Source: Takeo Yoshikawa, John Innes, and Falconer Mitchell, "Cost Tables: A Foundation of Japanese Cost Management," in *Emerging Practices in Cost Management,* ed. Barry J. Brinker (Boston: Warren Gorham Lamont, 1990), p. 264. With permission.

Activity: Drilling Depth of hole: 3"		Machine: Vulcan Power Drill Diameter of hole: 1/2"		
Type of material	Direct Materials	Direct Labor	Overhead	Total
Plastic	$ 6	$ 3	$ 5	$14
Steel	8	5	8	21
Aluminum	10	4	6	20

Activity: Drilling Depth of hole: 5"		Machine: Vulcan Power Drill Diameter of hole: 1/2"		
Type of material	Direct Materials	Direct Labor	Overhead	Total
Plastic	$ 8	$ 4	$ 6	$18
Steel	11	6	9	26
Aluminum	13	5	7	25

Activity: Drilling Depth of hole: 7"		Machine: Vulcan Power Drill Diameter of hole: 1/2"		
Type of material	Direct Materials	Direct Labor	Overhead	Total
Plastic	$ 9	$ 5	$ 7	$21
Steel	13	8	11	32
Aluminum	15	6	9	30

■■EXHIBIT 14–15
Drilling Activity Cost Tables

nent with a hole three inches deep can be used, then considerable cost savings can be realized in just one small part of the new product. Of course, other design factors will have to be considered as well, such as reliability, functionality, and serviceability of the finished product. This illustration demonstrates how activity cost tables can serve as a useful management tool for identifying cost reduction opportunities.

Activity cost tables that cover the entire activity value chain are stored and maintained in a database. The database also includes additional activity cost tables not used in current activity value chains. For example, the database includes information on all known alternative drilling machines on the market, even those not currently used by the company. In this way, a company's activity cost tables will include the most current information, even on technologies not employed by the company. Thus, one of the major tasks of management accountants in world-class environments is to understand the activity value chain and to stay up-to-date on new technologies that have the potential for reducing costs throughout the activity value chain.

A primary goal of Japanese management accountants is to keep cost tables as up-to-date as possible and to incorporate the cost effects of the latest technological developments into the cost tables. This commitment means that Japanese management accountants must keep abreast of technological developments outside their own company. Japanese management accountants draw on their own experience, the experience of others within their company, such as engineers, and the expertise of specialists outside their company.

LEARNING OBJECTIVE 4

Discuss how parametric cost estimating methods may be used in estimating costs.

ANOTHER COST MANAGEMENT TOOL: PARAMETRIC COST ESTIMATING

Some form of cost estimating is needed during the early, conceptual design stages. **Parametric cost estimating** provides a set of methods that are used to help satisfy this need.

Parametric Cost Estimating: An Overview

A simple example of parametric cost estimating is the use of a parameter such as *dollars per square foot* in the construction industry, as discussed in Chapter 5. The cost of building a new home can be approximated by multiplying the number of square feet by a typical value of this parameter. An architect might be able to provide such an estimate for a client on the day of their first meeting, whereas a detailed estimate would not be possible until blueprints are finalized.

Parametric cost estimating is prevalent in the aerospace industry and in shipbuilding. A first cut estimate for the development cost of a prototype airplane or manned spacecraft would probably be based on its weight. Hence, a parameter with units such as *thousands of dollars per kilogram* would be appropriate in this case.[33]

Construction, mining, power plants, computers, and electronics also have characteristically long product development lead times; parametric cost estimating has, therefore, gained widespread application in these industries as well. In fact, many businesses can benefit from parametric cost estimating methods. But, perhaps more importantly, such methods provide increased visibility for planning and control activities at the inception of a project.[34]

---

[33] D. M. Ashford and P. Q. Collins, ''The Prospects for European Aerospace Transporters Part I: The Derivation of a First Order Parametric Method for Estimating the Development Cost of Aerospace Transporters,'' *The Aeronautical Journal*, 1989, pp. 1–10.

[34] Paul F. Gallagher, *Parametric Estimating for Executive and Estimators* (New York: Van Nostrand Reinhold, 1982).

Developing a Database to Provide Historical Data for Applicable Parameters

The success of parametric cost estimating methods hinges on whether applicable parameters and comparable values from previous projects are available to be used in estimating new projects.[35] These data are usually stored in tabular form, either on paper or within a computerized database management system. Advances in computer technology have greatly improved the accuracy and acceptance of parametric cost estimates.

The data necessary for a parametric database can be obtained from a number of sources both within and outside the organization. Costs are certainly included, but so too are the project characteristics that have been found to drive those costs. Such characteristics can include weight, volume, capacity, number of circuits or voltages, horsepower, speed, service ceiling, seating capacity, thrust, or any other parameter that shows a high degree of correlation with cost.[36]

Parametric Cost Estimating Methods

Parametric cost estimating methods are becoming more sophisticated and widespread. Three methods are used to develop good parametric cost estimating models:

- The activities focus
- The work elements focus
- The standards focus

FOCUSING ON ACTIVITIES.   The **activities focus method** concentrates on the most identifiable or most influential activities of a project. Exhibit 14–16 shows three **cost estimating relationships (CERs)** derived from historical information for a particular kind of project. Of the three, activity 3 has the best CER. Activity 1 is not quite as good, because the cost varies little with large differences in activity 1 values. Most often, the historical CER data will fall within a narrow band, or a "sleeve" of experience, as shown in Exhibit 14–17. The straight line of the CER represents a valid estimating relationship, but due to the concept of the learning curve, the lower boundary may be a more realistic estimate. Thus, some degree of professional judgment must be used when evaluating CERs. In this case, the CERs are similar to the cause-and-effect relationships discussed in Chapter 10.

FOCUSING ON WORK ELEMENTS.   The **work elements focus method** is best suited for estimating unusual programs or projects in cooperation with engineers and managers. It involves using a Gantt chart (see Chapter 24) to determine each work element's length in the overall project's life cycle. Typically, the manager or foreman responsible for each work element develops work element cost estimates based on CER data for materials, labor, and equipment required to complete similar work elements during previous projects. Finally, the work element estimates are summed to generate time period and project costs.

FOCUSING ON STANDARDS.   The **standards focus method** is commonly used in promoting estimating consistency between different cost estimators working on the same (or different) projects. The approach can either focus on

Darwin Gilmore, (left), electrical design engineer and administrative assistant to the executive vice president, and Harold Hern, director of engineering, review copy of drawing printed from HP's ME10 CAD package. Courtesy of Creative Communications Services.

Bengt-Ake Bruce, (left), executive vice president, goes over a UniMac technical manual with Gary Cowen, the Florida company's president. Illustrations were prepared with HP's ME30 solid modeling package. Courtesy of Creative Communications Services.

[35] Ibid., p. 8.
[36] Ibid., p. 9.

■EXHIBIT 14–16
Three Project CERs Using Activities as Independent Variables

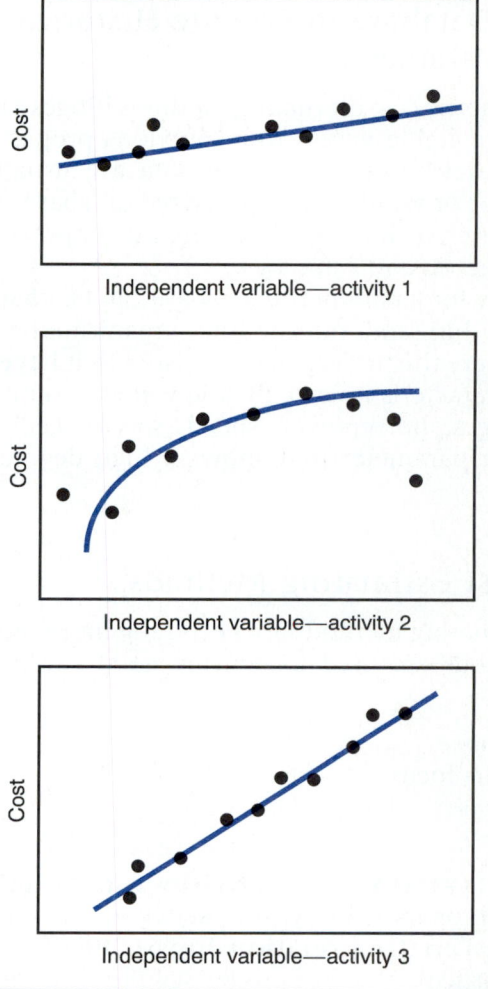

Independent variable—activity 1

Independent variable—activity 2

Independent variable—activity 3

■EXHIBIT 14–17
A Generic Linear CER with Upper and Lower Boundaries

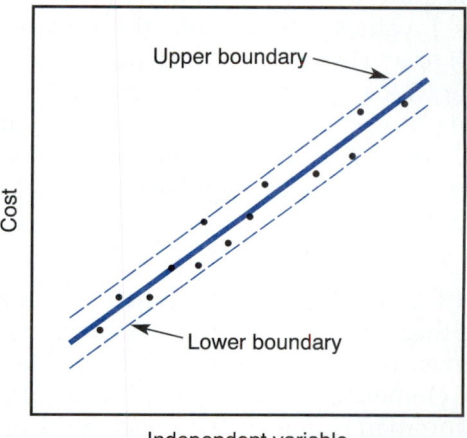

standard work elements or standard modular subassemblies. If standard work elements are used, a project needs to be broken down into a work element structure at the appropriate level of detail. The cost estimator then uses standard costs or hourly standards to derive an estimated cost. If standard modular subassemblies are used, the design is broken down into an analogous set of subassemblies. The cost estimator would use time standards (often referred to as standard hours), obtained through time and motion studies, to derive an estimated cost.

INSIGHTS & APPLICATIONS

A Work Elements Focus Method Estimating Example

A comprehensive and well-defined organization of work items is essential to the preparation of an estimate for any project. A contractor and management accountant need a method to identify work elements contained in the project's written specifications.

A builder is considering constructing a customized house and has used a work breakdown structure (WBS), as illustrated in Chapter 5, to specify each work element. Appropriate managers and foremen have estimated completion times for each work element needed to construct the house, as shown in the Gantt chart in Exhibit 14–18. Examination based on similar work elements performed in the past resulted in the estimated costs shown in Exhibit 14–19. Totaling up the values gives the complete estimate of $100,000 for the first month, $250,000 for the second month, and $50,000 for the third and final month.

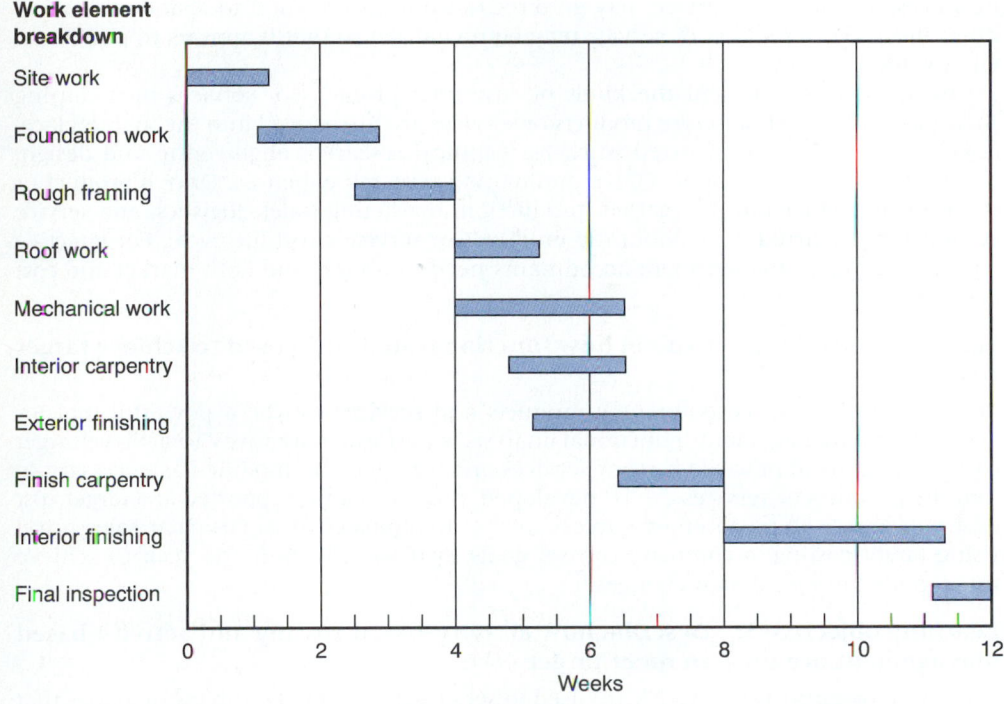

EXHIBIT 14–18
Gantt Chart Showing Estimated Start and Completion Times for Work Elements of a Customized House

EXHIBIT 14–19
Work Elements Focus Example Cost Estimates

Manager	Work Elements	Material and Equipment Costs	Labor Costs	Total Estimated Cost
Jones	Site work	$ 2,000	$ 3,000	$ 5,000
Jones	Foundation	10,000	25,000	35,000
Smith	Rough framing	30,000	30,000	60,000
Caston	Roof work	20,000	15,000	35,000
Abrams	Mechanical work	20,000	50,000	70,000
Carey	Interior carpentry	10,000	50,000	60,000
Harris	Finish carpentry	35,000	15,000	50,000
Jones	Exterior finishing	12,000	23,000	35,000
Harris	Interior finishing	16,000	32,000	48,000
Ogden	Final inspection	–0–	2,000	2,000

Time standards can be maintained as parametric relationships; that is, the standard hours required to produce a gear might be represented by an equation having variables of diameter and number of teeth. The standards approach has the ability to generate quick, yet reliable estimates.

SUMMARY OF LEARNING OBJECTIVES

The major goals of this chapter were to enable you to achieve four learning objectives:

Learning objective 1.   Define market life and cost life cycles, and describe how they are used in analyzing and managing costs over the entire life cycle of a product or service.

The market life cycle of a product or service generally includes these stages: preintroductory, introduction, growth, maturity, and decline to abandonment. In some instances, a product or service may go directly from introduction to abandonment. In other instances, a product or service may be revitalized so that it appears to possess an endless life.

Cost life cycles represent the kinds of costs that products or services incur during their market life cycles. Before products or services are introduced into the marketplace, development costs are incurred, such as technical research, engineering and design, quality function deployment (QFD), and market research expenses. Once a product or service is introduced to the market, production, marketing, sales, logistics, and service costs will be incurred throughout the product's or service's cost life cycle. For effective cost management, management accountants need to understand both market and cost life cycles.

Learning objective 2.   Explain how functional analysis is used to achieve target costs.

The setting of target costs for new products and services can be a powerful tool for effective cost management. Functional analysis is performed as a way to achieve target costs. Functions of new products or services are analyzed and modified as necessary so that the products or services can be developed, produced, and supported at a target cost that will enable them to enjoy success in the marketplace at a particular sales price. Using target costing, a company can set goals for cost reduction and seek to achieve those goals through design changes.

Learning objective 3.   Describe how activity-based costing and activity-based management are used to meet target costs.

Activity-based costing systems are used to set target costs by identifying activities that are performed by companies throughout their activity value chain. With ABM, each activity is systematically analyzed so that nonvalue-added activities can be eliminated and value-added activities can be strengthened and performed in the most efficient way possible, all in an effort to meet target costs.

Learning objective 4.   Discuss how parametric cost estimating methods may be used in estimating costs.

One of the most difficult tasks in management accounting is estimating costs of new products or projects. The parametric cost estimating methods provide a structured, engineered way to come to grips with this difficult and important task. Methods used in parametric cost estimating include the following:

- Focusing on the most identifiable or the most influential activities in new products or projects
- Focusing on work elements, especially when products or projects are unusual or customized
- Focusing on standard work elements or standard subassemblies of fairly common products or projects

IMPORTANT TERMS

Activities focus method   A parametric cost estimating method that estimates the total cost of a project, product, or service by focusing on the most identifiable or influential activities.

Activity cost tables   Tables generally stored in a database management system (DBMS) that contain cost data for a wide variety of activities throughout the activity value chain.

Activity value chain   A linkage of strategic activities, including research and development, inbound logistics, production, outbound logistics, marketing and sales, and service. Each strategic activity is composed of specific activities and tasks. The aim of the activity value chain is to bring value to products and services throughout their life cycle.

Cost estimating relationships (CERs)   The relationship of cost to some other variable or variables.

Cost life cycle   A combination of curves that shows the behavior and magnitude of development, production, marketing, logistics, and service costs of products and services over their market life cycles.

Function   An action or feature of a product or service.

Functional analysis   A cost management technique that focuses on and evaluates the various functions of a product or service design. It is used to achieve a target cost.

Functional family tree   A logical diagram of each function of a product or service.

Linear approach   A sequential, uncoordinated, over-the-wall process of designing new products or services.

Market life cycle   A concept that illustrates the limited life of a product or service. It uses a curve to profile the duration of a product or service from the time it is conceived until it is abandoned by the firm and its customers. Generally, a market life cycle includes several stages: pre-introductory, introduction, growth, maturity, and decline and abandonment. In some instances, a product or service may get a new lease on life through revitalization efforts or suffer early abandonment due to changes in the marketplace.

Parametric cost estimating   A set of methods that attempt to estimate the cost to produce and bring to market a product or service or to build a project or complete a job.

Quality function deployment (QFD)   A method to assure that quality is designed into a new product or service while it is in the development stage.

Simultaneous engineering (concurrent engineering)   A concurrent and collaborative design process in which all players work together toward a common product or service development goal.

Standards focus method   A parametric cost estimating method that uses standards as parameters for estimating costs of a project, product, or service.

Target costing   A cost management tool for optimizing the overall cost of a product or service over its entire cost life cycle. Target costing determines what the cost of a product or service should be, based on the selling price of the product or service less a target profit.

Time-to-market   The time it takes to convert an idea into a marketable product or service.

Work elements focus method   A parametric cost estimating method that estimates the cost of a project, product, or service by concentrating on the length of time and cost of individual work elements.

DEMONSTRATION PROBLEMS

■ DEMONSTRATION PROBLEM 1   *Performing life cycle analysis.*

The management accountant at the Fillmore Company has collected the following data in preparation for a life cycle analysis of one of its products, a forklift truck:

Item	This Year	Change over Last Year	Average Annual Change over the Last Four Years
Annual sales	$40,000,000	+1.0%	+18.2%
Unit sales price	$2,100	+1.9	+ 6.4
Unit profit	$400	−0.6	+ 2.6
Total profit	$5,800,000	+1.2	+26.7

Required:
Determine what stage the forklift is in.

SOLUTION TO DEMONSTRATION PROBLEM 1
Sales are stabilizing, having grown only 1% over the past year. Average annual growth was much higher during prior years, at 18.2%. Unit sales price growth has slowed, and unit profit margins are beginning to shrink. Total profit is also beginning to level off. All these signs suggest the *early maturity stage.*

■ DEMONSTRATION PROBLEM 2   *Functional analysis.*
The latest development at KeepSake Enterprises is a personal diary book. The product will have a classical design with a lock and a flowered cover.

Required:
Draw a functional family tree for KeepSake's personal diary.

SOLUTION TO DEMONSTRATION PROBLEM 2

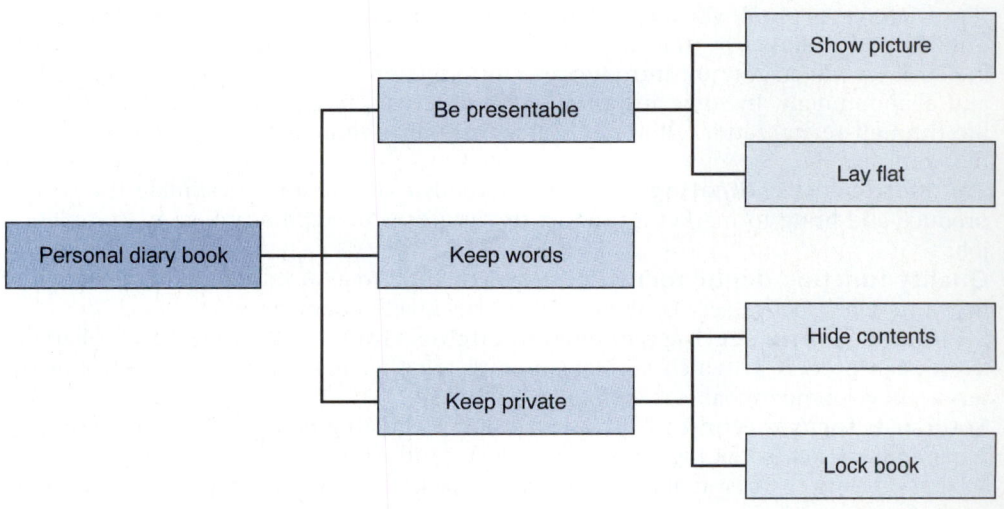

■ DEMONSTRATION PROBLEM 3   *Target cost.*
Tour De Frame Manufacturing Company is considering the development of a new cross-training bicycle. Extensive industry research has determined that a market sales price of no more than $600 would be feasible. Since the competition has relatively small profit margins, the profit margin for this product would only need to be $150.

Required:
With the understanding that the service, logistics, and marketing activities of the product life cycle will be relatively small compared to the other activities, develop a target cost table for each product life cycle activity for this cross-training bicycle. Use your best guess estimate of such costs.

SOLUTION TO DEMONSTRATION PROBLEM 3

■ Product: Cross-training bicycle
■ Target price: $600
■ Target profit: $150

Development target cost	$150
Production target cost	200
Marketing target cost	50
Logistics target cost	30
Service target cost	20
Total unit target costs	$450

■ DEMONSTRATION PROBLEM 4   *Normalized CER.*

HotMax Conditioner Company is considering building a new heating unit rated at 4,000 BTUs. Research into past heater development, both inside and outside HotMax, resulted in the following information:

MODEL	SIZE (BTU)	DATE	DEVELOPMENT COST
30A	1,050	1990	$ 52,250
35A	1,500	1991	68,000
B3D	1,360	1991	58,950
C2A	2,550	1990	120,950
106	3,000	1992	143,300
108	3,200	1992	166,700
3AD	2,820	1993	145,000

Required:

Develop a CER, normalized to 1993, assuming 5% inflation, to determine an estimate of development costs for HotMax's new heating unit. Comment on the confidence of this estimate.

SOLUTION TO DEMONSTRATION PROBLEM 4

To normalize the data, we calculate the 1993 value of the development costs based on an increase of 5% each year. Thus:

MODEL	SIZE (BTU)	DATE	DEVELOPMENT COST	ADJUSTED COST (1993)
30A	1,050	1990	$ 52,250	$ 60,486
35A	1,500	1991	68,000	74,970
B3D	1,360	1991	58,950	64,992
C2A	2,550	1990	120,950	140,015
106	3,000	1992	143,300	150,465
108	3,200	1992	166,700	175,035
3AD	2,820	1993	145,000	145,000

Plotting the BTUs versus the adjusted costs, we have:

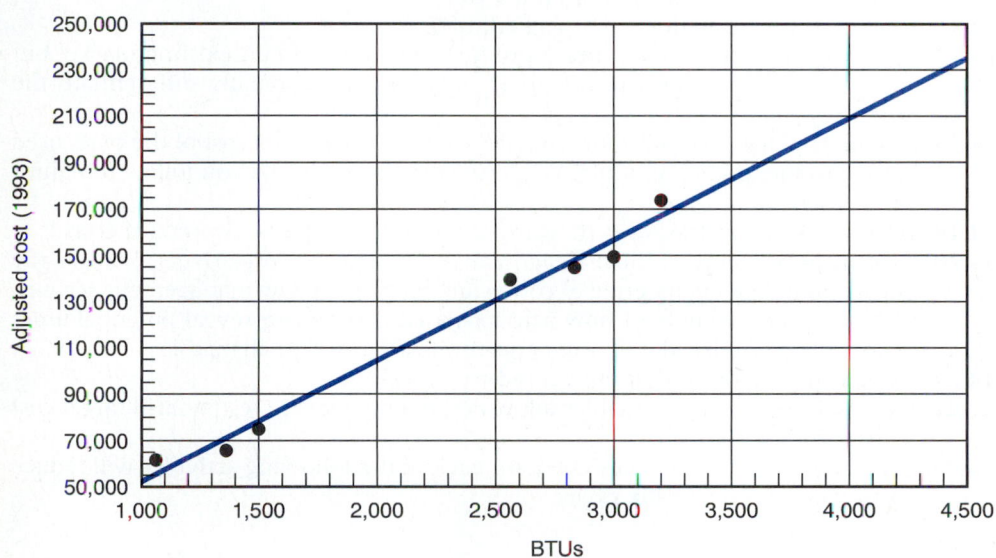

To estimate the development costs for the new 4,000-BTU model, we read off the CER at $210,000. This CER looks good, with very little variation off the trend line. However, we are using part of the trend beyond the largest data point (at 3,200 BTUs); thus, there is the risk that the trend will be different past 3,200.

REVIEW QUESTIONS

14.1   What are the stages of the product or service life cycle?

14.2   A sign on the way to an abandoned mine reads: "Choose your ruts carefully; you will be in them for the next 15 miles." How does this sign apply to life cycle analysis, especially committed costs?

14.3   "A manufacturer with little understanding of the differences between life cycle stages might assume that the best way to maximize profits is always to maximize revenues and minimize costs. However, maximizing revenues and minimizing costs at every stage of a product's life cycle does not necessarily lead to maximum profits over the entire life of a product." Discuss this statement.

14.4   How much of the costs of a product or service are committed during the development stage?

14.5   "Decisions made from a life cycle perspective lead to better long-term results than decisions made without such a perspective." Comment on this statement.

14.6   Explain the difference between linear and simultaneous engineering.

14.7   What are some of the documented benefits of simultaneous engineering?

14.8   What is the "over-the-wall" approach?

14.9   How does simultaneous engineering differ from the "over-the-wall" approach?

14.10   What is the purpose of quality function deployment (QFD)? Give an example.

14.11   A product's sales (in millions) are as follows. What stage of the product life cycle is this product in as of the second quarter, 19X5?

	19X4	19X5
First quarter	$ 1.5	$21.0
Second quarter	2.5	3.0
Third quarter	6.0	
Fourth quarter	15.0	

14.12   Once a target cost is established for a product, will that cost remain stable? Explain why or why not.

14.13   In some cases, target costing uses market price to set target costs and profits in the development of products and services. Yet, competing on price can be fraught with dangers. Explain the dangers of competing on market price.

14.14   Explain how target costing can reduce costs over the entire life cycle of a product or service.

14.15   What is a product's functional family tree?

14.16   What are three functions of a pocketknife?

14.17   If a company wants to produce a product to compete in an existing market but does not want to compete on price, how can the company differentiate the product?

14.18   As a management accountant, you are asked to review the cost of the parts used in the production of a product. What two principles should you follow to reduce parts costs?

14.19   What are some of the ways reducing the number of parts can reduce costs?

14.20   Explain how a new product design can affect activity cost drivers. Explain the impact on design engineering of cost estimates prepared by management accountants. Give an example of how activity-based costing can reveal potential areas of cost reduction by identifying opportunities for design changes.

14.21   Explain how activity sharing can reduce costs.

14.22   Explain how activity cost tables allow design engineers to test what-if target cost scenarios.

14.23   Give an example of how designing for each of the following activities will reduce costs over a product's life cycle:

a. Production.

    b. Marketing.

    c. Logistics.

    d. Service.

14.24 Why would one want to know what product life cycle stage a product is in when setting up production facilities?

14.25 "By the time products reach the maturity stage, decisions to add capacity should be weighed very carefully because excess capacity is costly and disadvantageous to companies that compete primarily on price." Discuss this comment.

14.26 "A company can reduce product costs by successfully matching its capacity to the demand for its product." Discuss this comment.

14.27 Expain how the "mushroom concept" can increase flexibility and decrease the cost of a product over its entire life cycle.

14.28 For what purposes are activity cost tables used?

14.29 Chocolate Importers delivers bulk chocolate to Sweety-Pie Candy Company in 10-pound, wrapped, molded bars of chocolate. Sweety-Pie unpacks, unwraps, and melts the solid bars of chocolate for raw materials input in the candy-making process. Discuss how Chocolate Importers and Sweety-Pie can revise their activities to reduce costs for both companies.

14.30 "Failure to adopt an activity value chain perspective can lead companies to make costly errors. On the other hand, beneficial linkages throughout the enterprise, including with suppliers and customers, can be achieved if management accountants understand the activity value chain." Discuss this statement.

14.31 "Designing a product to reduce postpurchase costs of the customer can be a major weapon in capturing competitive advantage." Comment on this statement.

14.32 Assume that you are a manufacturer of heavy, bulky containers that you supply to two large manufacturers. Discuss how you would develop a linkage to your two major customers that would, in turn, reduce costs for all parties.

14.33 In the late 1980s, Sealtite Envelope Company lost profits and went bankrupt because it was caught unawares by a significant change from sheet-fed machines to roll-fed machines. With sheet-fed machines, an envelope company buys large rolls of paper 40–60 inches wide, which are cut into sheets, cut into blanks in die-cutting machines, and finally fed by hand into folding-and-gluing machines. With roll-fed machines, the envelope company buys narrow rolls of paper 5–11 inches wide, which are converted directly into envelopes in one combined operation. Discuss how a database containing activity cost tables about the new roll-fed technology might have prevented Sealtite from going bankrupt.

14.34 When setting up a parametric database, what should one look for when selecting a cost parameter?

CHAPTER-SPECIFIC PROBLEMS

These problems require responses based directly on concepts and techniques presented in the text.

14.35 *Analyzing the market life cycle and its relationship to the cost life cycle.* Different types of costs are incurred at different stages of the product or service market life cycle.

Required:

Insert the market life cycle stage or stages at which the maximum level of the following costs will occur:

TYPE OF COST	MARKET LIFE CYCLE
Development	_____
Production	_____
Marketing	_____
Sales	_____
Logistics	_____
Service	_____

14.36 *Determining the life cycle stages.* The Marlin Company makes and sells two fishing tackle products, Deepsea and Angler. Tommy Hogan, management accountant, is conducting a life cycle analysis to identify the current stage of each product in its life cycle. The profiles for the two products are as follows:

PRODUCT	ITEM	THIS YEAR'S PERFORMANCE	CHANGE OVER LAST YEAR	AVERAGE ANNUAL CHANGE OVER THE LAST THREE YEARS
Deepsea	Annual sales	$ 5,200,000	− 2.9%	+ 1.1%
	Unit sales price	450	+ 0.1	+ 0.6
	Unit profit	60	− 2.8	− 0.7
	Total profit	780,000	− 8.1	+ 0.3
Angler	Annual sales	10,300,000	+80.9	+41.5
	Unit sales price	160	+10.6	+ 9.4
	Unit profit	80	+14.7	+19.2
	Total profit	6,800,000	+87.3	+41.5

Required:
Determine which stage of its life cycle each product is in and explain your answer.

14.37 *Matching market characteristics with life cycle stages.* Following is a list of various activities and market characteristics:

ACTIVITIES AND MARKET CHARACTERISTICS	LIFE CYCLE STAGE
A new product concept	_____
Entrance of competitors	_____
Shrinking sales	_____
Stable sales	_____
Strong brand loyalty	_____
Product dropped	_____
Rapid sales increases	_____
Rapid ramp up of production	_____
Product design	_____
Market research	_____
Build prototype	_____
Test prototype	_____
Initiate production	_____

Required:
Insert the appropriate life cycle stage—pre-introductory, introduction, growth, maturity, or decline and abandonment—in the space provided after each activity or characteristic.

14.38 *Preparing and costing a bill of materials (BOM).* AlarmSys Company produces an alarm system for use in automobiles. These systems are offered as original equipment by most automakers.

The alarm system consists of four modules. The alert module is composed of a siren and a headlight-flashing driver. The control module consists of a keypad, a valet override switch, and two remote controls. The brain module is composed of a CPU chip and 16 memory chips on one circuit board. Finally, the sensor module includes six door switches, three tip switches, and a motion detector. The cost for one unit of each component is as follows:

COMPONENT	COST (EACH)
Siren	$15.00
Headlight driver	4.00
Keypad	5.00
Valet switch	1.00
Remote control	6.00
CPU chip	6.00
Memory chip	2.00
Circuit board	3.00
Door switch	0.50
Tip switch	0.75
Motion detector	9.00

Required:

Construct a bill of materials (BOM) for the car alarm system. In your BOM diagram, show how the product is broken down into modules and further into components. Then calculate the total cost of the product.

14.39 *Analyzing and managing activities.* Management at Jones and Company is trying to reduce costs in an effort to improve overall profitability. Tom, the new management accountant, suggests that they analyze the corporate activities and search for cost reduction opportunities among those activities.

Required:

Explain how Jones and Company can reduce costs by analyzing activities.

14.40 *Determining the cost impact of using different parts.* Jacob and Son produces housings for three computer manufacturers. To produce these housings, the company uses the following parts:

PART	COST	ASSEMBLY TIME IN MINUTES
T51	$ 1.00	1
A19	1.50	1
A97	2.00	1
R78	0.50	2
S71	0.75	1
S53	0.50	1
S32	0.75	1
V15	1.00	3
V18	5.00	6
V92	2.00	1
P8	2.75	3
P3	4.25	1
	$22.00	22 minutes

The parts purchasing, storage, and auditing charges are $0.05 per part. The hourly wage costs average $15.00 per hour. Management accountant, Dee Kendrix, must determine whether she should recommend to management that parts A97, S53, and P8 be replaced by part A3 and parts V15 and P3 be replaced by part T15. The costs and assembly times associated with parts A3 and T15 are $5.00 at 6 minutes and $5.25 at 5 minutes, respectively.

Required:

Determine what Dee should recommend to management about parts A3 and T15.

14.41 *Estimating the bid price of a house.* As a custom home builder, you have determined that the cost of the type of houses you build can be estimated with a high degree of accuracy using the following parameters, plus the cost of the land:

Cost per square foot of house	$69.75
Cost per square foot of glass	4.50

Required:

Given that a potential customer wants a 1,650-square-foot house with the equivalent of 20% of the floor space in windows and glass doors and that the cost of the land on which the house will be built is $38,250, calculate the bid price. You expect to make a 32% profit based on the total estimated cost, including the land.

14.42 *Determining cost estimating relationships (CERs).* Biltmore is a major custom housing construction contractor. Susan Liggett, owner, has asked you, the management accountant, to determine the best CER for use in the early, conceptual design phase of each of Biltmore's future projects. Information from last year's Biltmore work is summarized as follows:

HOUSE NUMBER	FINAL TOTAL COST	INTERIOR (SQUARE FEET)	NUMBER OF ROOMS	LOT (SQUARE FEET)
1	$110,000	2,500	9	35,000
2	65,000	1,300	6	19,500
3	96,000	2,200	6	25,500
4	160,000	4,200	10	25,000
5	132,000	3,500	10	20,000
6	67,000	1,500	7	19,000
7	112,000	2,700	9	22,000
8	89,000	2,000	9	23,500
9	81,000	1,900	8	26,000
10	139,000	3,500	9	24,500

Required:
Determine which cost estimating relationship (CER) should be used in the future. Briefly comment on how comfortable Susan should be with this decision.

14.43 *Parts-functions-cost matrix.* OpenAll manufactures small kitchen tools and appliances. Its latest potential product is a hand-crank can opener. The can opener is designed to be hand-held, open cans, and hold the lid. Following are the major parts of the product:

PART	COST	PART NUMBER
Upper handle	$0.26	631
Lower handle	0.24	632
Handle grips	0.13	630
Cutting wheel	0.31	11
Gear assembly	0.18	33
Magnet	0.08	940
Magnet arm	0.11	941

Required:
Develop a parts-functions-cost matrix for this product.

14.44 *Normalization of database.* A major manufacturer of electric generators is developing a cost database from historical data, both internal and external to the company. The following information was obtained from various sources:

	INTERNAL				EXTERNAL		
MODEL	HORSEPOWER	DATE	COST	MODEL	HORSEPOWER	DATE	COST
110	10	1976	$114	A-32	11	1985	$188
113	13	1978	128	A-43	22	1987	272
220	20	1982	200	D-103	15	1981	180
215	15	1983	195	D-104	17	1988	259
330	30	1990	360	D-106	23	1992	347
335	35	1993	434	Q-A5	30	1989	352
				A-A3	28	1988	322

Required:
Develop a parts-functions-cost matrix for this product.

14.45 *Parametric cost estimating approaches.* The following are different project estimating situations:

_____	A large construction project with three different cost estimators.
_____	A long duration project comprising six different departments.
_____	A bridge construction of unique design.
_____	An airport runway construction project where historical runway length CER information is known.

_____ A new computer system composed of off-the-shelf modularized subassemblies.

Required:

In the space provided, insert the type of basic approach (i.e., work elements focus, activities focus, standards focus) that is most appropriate for each situation.

THINK-TANK PROBLEMS

Although these problems are based on chapter material, reading extra material, reviewing previous chapters, and using creativity may be required to develop workable solutions.

14.46 **_Deciding what to do in the pre-introductory stage._** When Iowa Beef Processors was being formed, its strategy was to be the low-cost producer of beef. Following are two alternatives facing Iowa Beef Processors during its pre-introductory (or formative) stage:

ALTERNATIVE 1	ALTERNATIVE 2
■ Automate	■ Use manual methods
■ Ship cattle to rail centers and then to plants	■ Build plants next to large feedlots
■ Cleave carcasses into various pieces and box the pieces at the plant	■ Ship whole carcasses

Required:

Choose the alternative that you believe would generate the most cost savings for Iowa Beef Processors. Explain your choice.

14.47 **_Identifying nonvalue-added activities._** Exhibit 14–12 presents an activity value chain and a list of activity cost drivers.

Required:

Making any assumptions you deem necessary:

a. Explain which activities are nonvalue-added and which are value-added.
b. Give an example of how a company can reduce total costs by developing beneficial linkages in the activity value chain and thereby reduce, if not eliminate, nonvalue-added activities.

14.48 **_Analyzing a comparative activity value chain._** The following are the activity value chains and costs of two competing airlines:

ACTIVITY VALUE CHAIN	PEOPLE MOVER COST PER 10,000 SEAT-MILES	AIR BUS COST PER 10,000 SEAT-MILES
Advertising	$ 1,200	$ 1,800
Ticketing offices	2,600	3,200
Ticket counter	2,300	2,900
Gate operations	3,700	4,100
Baggage facilities	3,100	4,000
Fleets	5,600	7,200
Aircraft operations	15,000	20,000
On-board service	2,000	6,500
	$35,500	$49,700

Required:

a. Study the comparative activity value chains and recommend how Air Bus may be able to close the $14,200 cost gap between it and People Mover.
b. Discuss how a comparative activity value chain analysis can help a company (e.g., Air Bus) manage costs.

14.49 *Choosing between two options.* Fredrik Manufacturing produces valves for waste treatment plants. The market for these valves is saturated. Ron Fredrik, CEO, is trying to decide how to allocate $100,000 in available budget—the funds have been requested by both the sales manager for market expansion activities and by the finance manager for use in reducing costs. The sales manager assures Ron that he can increase sales by $5,500,000 while the finance manager assures him that she can reduce the cost of goods sold by 3.5%. The cost of goods sold is $160 per unit, and the sales price is $200 per unit. Last year, Fredrik Manufacturing had sales of $50,000,000.

Required:
Determine which of the two options provides the greater increase in profit.

14.50 *Functional analysis.* Northwestern Electric Company manufactures electronic communication products. One of their most popular products is Model 1010, a combination phone, FAX, and answering machine. Due to increased competition from foreign manufacturers, the profit margin on Model 1010 is dropping and nearing zero.

Required:
Perform a functional analysis to determine the possibility of eliminating or modifying a function of Model 1010 for cost reduction. Make any assumptions necessary.

14.51 *Parametric cost estimating.* You are the new management accountant at FitRite Model Company, a manufacturer of plastic airplane and car models. FitRite's organization includes design, production, and marketing departments. A new model of the latest stealth airplane is being considered, which will be part of FitRite's High-Tech Aircraft line.

Required:
As the management accountant, you have been instructed to lead a cost estimating team for this model concept. Describe the cost estimating technique you will use to ensure proper cost management for the new product. Also, what approaches would you use to ensure that quality is designed in and that time-to-market is reduced?

14.52 *Linear versus simultaneous engineering.* PerfectPerk Appliance Company has determined that a new drip coffee maker might be profitable if developed within the year. The product would be a new venture for PerfectPerk, as it has only developed percolator coffee makers in the past.

Required:
For this product, comment on the potential problems and benefits of the traditional linear, simultaneous engineering, and quality function deployment (QFD) approaches in ultimately satisfying marketing, service, finance, and manufacturing department needs. Make any assumptions you deem necessary.

15

THE THEORY OF CONSTRAINTS: EMPHASIZING THROUGHPUT

LEARNING OBJECTIVES

After studying this chapter, you should be able to:

1. State the global goal of a for-profit enterprise.

2. Explain the differences between a cost world orientation and a throughput world orientation, and compare the two orientations with regard to how well they support continuous improvement.

3. Describe each phase of the focusing process defined by the theory of constraints (TOC).

4. Discuss how the theory of constraints can be applied in manufacturing firms, and how it can be integrated with existing just-in-time and total quality management systems.

Increasing throughput means more profitable operations.

Computers are involved at all points in the manufacturing process to keep the flow of tractor production going at the most efficient pace at Deere & Company.

■ INTRODUCTION

Chapter 2 introduced the concepts and elements of world-class manufacturing (WCM) as they relate to American manufacturing enterprises. It was made clear American enterprises have, in effect, been playing a game of "catch-up" with firms in other industrialized nations in implementing WCM techniques. Manufacturing firms in nations, such as Germany and Japan, are years ahead of their American counterparts in embracing total quality management (TQM), just-in-time (JIT), and continuous improvement. But, have the Japanese and the Germans simply adopted these new manufacturing methods only to sit back and reap the rewards while the United States catches up? Certainly not. The philosophy of continuous improvement demands that WCM techniques evolve over time, forever pushing manufacturing and service enterprises to higher levels of excellence. The question thus arises: Where is this WCM revolution taking the world's best manufacturing firms today, now that JIT and TQM are becoming old news? The answer will change forever the way management accountants view their work.

Continuous improvement implies change, and lots of it. Many of these changes and decisions will be small and incremental. Other changes will be larger, possibly even revolutionary, and may involve total reengineering of the enterprise. In all cases, management accountants are intensely concerned with developing and maintaining the measurements that enable managers and workers to judge the impact of **local** changes and decisions on the organization as a whole. But how can managers and workers be certain that these changes are benefiting the enterprise, that they really do represent continuous improvement, and that they are not just the result of manipulating numbers and words?[1] The only way to judge the changes is to ask whether they contribute to the **global** goal of the enterprise, a seemingly trivial question, but one that is often overlooked or overshadowed by a multitude of local performance measures.

A for-profit enterprise has only one global goal. Is the global goal of Ford Motor Company to produce cars as efficiently as it can? Is the global goal of General Dynamics to gain bargaining power in Washington for its board of directors? Is the global goal of Procter & Gamble to capture more market share? The answer is a resounding no in all three cases! All of these companies share the same global goal: *to make more profit now and in the future.*[2] To be effective, all the performance measurements a company uses must show the correlation between its actions and its progress toward this single global goal.

▋ THE COST WORLD ORIENTATION VERSUS THE THROUGHPUT WORLD ORIENTATION

Traditionally, management accountants have lived in a cost world. Most managers are reviewed, rated, and granted raises based on their ability to control and reduce costs.[3] With the advent of JIT, inventories became a new focal point. Since JIT philosophy views inventory as a liability rather than an asset, over the last decade, U.S. manufacturers have scrambled to eliminate as much inven-

---

[1] Eliyahu M. Goldratt and Jeff Cox, *The Goal: A Process of Ongoing Improvement* (Great Barrington, Mass.: North River Press, 1986), p. 33. With permission.
[2] Ibid., p. 58.
[3] John W. Covington, "Moving from the Cost World to the Throughput World," *The Theory of Constraints Managing in the Throughput World* (New York: Institute for International Research, 1992), p. 4.

INSIGHTS & APPLICATIONS

Local Objectives versus the Global Goal

The theory of constraints emphasizes over and over again that local (e.g., departments, manufacturing cells) optima do not necessarily add up to an optimum total system. The theory also warns that when evaluating local performance in terms of a plan (e.g., production plan, budget), the quality of the plan itself should be judged in terms of throughput, inventory, and operating expense.

How many times has your company worked so hard to win a bid and once it was won, it turned out to be a disaster? How many times have you seen a foreman forced to break setups, go to overtime, in order to expedite some pieces, just to find them two weeks later gathering dust in a warehouse? How many times have you almost climbed the walls to meet tolerances that shouldn't have been there in the first place? Our experience shows that over 90 percent of the problems that industrial organizations are struggling with, on a day to day basis, belong to that category wherein we try to satisfy local objectives that do not match, at all, the global goal.[4]

---

tory as possible. But, should enterprises be focusing on *just* cost or *just* inventory? Probably not. When more than one significant performance measurement (such as cost *and* inventory) exists, it is the relationships between the measurements that should be considered, not the measurements themselves.[5] Following are a few such relationships:

$$\text{Net profit} = \text{Throughput} - \text{Operating expense}$$
$$\text{Return on inventory} = \text{Net profit} \div \text{Inventory}$$
$$\text{Productivity} = \text{Throughput} \div \text{Operating expense}$$
$$\text{Inventory turnover} = \text{Throughput} \div \text{Inventory}$$

By having a few relationships such as these in place, enterprises establish a base line by which to determine continuous improvement. After all, not every change is an improvement, but certainly every improvement is a change.[6]

Throughput is defined as the rate at which the system generates profit through sales and equals sales less raw materials costs (raw materials are direct materials). Throughput is often referred to as **contribution** or **contribution margin** by theory of constraints (TOC) authorities. In any case, it is the money that is available for paying *all* the bills after the company has paid for raw materials. **Inventory** is the money the enterprise has invested in things it intends to sell and includes plant, property, equipment, and inventories valued only at raw materials costs. **Operating expense** is the money spent to convert inventory into throughput. It includes all salaries (direct labor is not differentiated from administrative salaries), utilities, supplies, advertising, insurance, taxes, and so forth. The aim of management is to increase throughput while decreasing inventory and operating expense.

How often does an enterprise begin an improvement project, reap some quick initial gains, but then find the rate of improvement slowing drastically as the project seems to run out of steam?[7] This common scenario might be represented by curve A in Exhibit 15–1. Does this constitute the desired continuous improvement? Of course not. Instead, enterprises seek to achieve continual operating improvement, as depicted by curve B. To achieve this ongoing improvement, however, management accountants will have to change the way in which they prioritize throughput, operating expense, and inventory.

The Saturn Manufacturing complex is designed for throughput.

Caterpillar emphasizes throughput.

[4] Ibid., p. 47.

[5] Ibid., p. 2.

[6] Eliyahu M. Goldratt, *What Is This Thing Called Theory of Constraints and How Should It Be Implemented?* (Great Barrington, Mass.: North River Press, 1990), p. 10.

[7] Covington, op. cit., p. 2.

■ EXHIBIT 15–1
Short-Term Improvement Graph

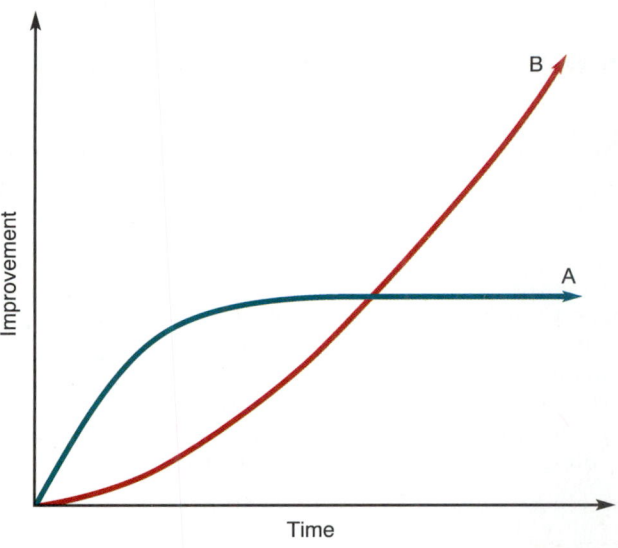

Priorities of the Cost World Orientation

A traditional **cost world orientation** prioritizes the aforementioned three elements as follows:

1. Operating expense
2. Throughput
3. Inventory

In other words, management's primary focus is always on the allocation of costs to various products and the control and reduction of those costs. But, can this cost world orientation ever support the continuous improvement of curve B? Consider the following relationship:

$$\text{Net profit} = \text{Throughput} - \text{Operating expense}$$

If the global goal of enterprises is to make more profit now and in the future, then net profit is an appropriate performance measurement. Assume that through some incredible feat of cost management, operating expense is reduced to zero, not overnight, but slowly and steadily over some time period. Despite the heroic effort, this is not the continuous improvement of curve B, because the improvement process is doomed to fizzle out as costs approach zero.

Priorities of the Throughput World Orientation

From JIT delivery of raw materials to shipment to customers, Saturn emphasizes throughput.

The solution to the problem is simple: Make throughput the *first* priority. Why? In the net profit relationship, either operating expense must be reduced or throughput must be increased to achieve the global goal of more profit now and in the future. But, as just stated, operating expense is limited by zero, whereas throughput is essentially unbounded. Therefore, the only order of priority that will support the ongoing improvement illustrated by curve B is the **throughput world orientation:**

1. Throughput
2. Inventory
3. Operating expense

In the throughput world, throughput gets first priority and inventory moves into second place. The objective is to simultaneously increase throughput while reducing inventory and operating expense.

INSIGHTS & APPLICATIONS

Best in the Industry

Launching a schedule in a company in which entrenched constraints and conflicts exist is launching chaos. The basic element of an integrated computer-based information system (ICBIS) is a scheduling system (e.g., MRP's master production schedule or JIT's kanban system). Such a system should be implemented where constraints can be identified and eliminated and major conflicts can be resolved. In this case, a realistic schedule can help maximize throughput. More-over, the only inventory present at any time should be that which guarantees the throughput.

The accounting department at Automatic Feed Company created a *production* scheduling system that is considered to be the best in the industry. Meeting customer delivery requirements and simultaneously providing team members with an even work flow is the scheduling challenge.

Annual sales have more than doubled and the new scheduling system has been an important tool in identifying bottlenecks (constraints) to company growth. For example, last November, orders were received that increased annual sales an additional 60 percent. The scheduling system identified how to handle this increase by selectively adding 25 percent to the work force in bottleneck areas.[8]

The throughput of an enterprise is closely linked to the market. To meet market demands, production lead time, delivery lead time, and work-in-process inventories must be reduced. Such reductions give enterprises the flexibility to deal effectively with shortened product market life cycles. Focusing on throughput enables companies to be streamlined and flexible and implement synchronous activities, as explained in Chapter 2.

Now that the world's best manufacturing and service firms are shifting to a throughput world focus, where do management accountants turn their attention? To answer this question, management accountants must first understand the limitations to improvement in the **throughput chain.** These limiting factors, called **constraints,** are the activities, rules, or policies that prevent an enterprise from achieving or exceeding its global goal. Throughput cannot occur at a rate faster than the slowest activity or person in the system.

The formal process of identifying and then taking steps to remove constraints that have global impact is known as the **theory of constraints (TOC).**[9] Thus, the TOC is a process of continuous improvement to clear the throughput chain of all constraints. A company that is not employing the TOC and eliminating constraints in the throughput chain is probably working on what Dr. Eliyahu M. Goldratt calls a "choopchik." To illustrate, Dr. Goldratt describes a plant manager who devotes considerable effort to reducing the setup time on a particular machine from four hours to 15 minutes. Is this a worthwhile achievement? Not necessarily. If the setup reduction does not affect the plant's primary constraint, then it will not increase throughput, and if it does not increase throughput, it will not increase the enterprise's net profit or its responsiveness to market demands.[10]

Any activity or process of an enterprise, not just the manufacturing process, can be studied with the TOC. For example, a design and drafting function of an enterprise can be considered an activity where the "product" is a set of blueprints "sold" to the manufacturing department. The activity, as outlined in Exhibit 15–2, has a number of tasks that can be studied for constraints. For example, if "drafting" is the constraint, the company may consider the purchase of a computer-aided design (CAD) system to eliminate this constraint.

Though the TOC can be applied to nonmanufacturing activities, it has traditionally been used in manufacturing. The mechanics of this latest evolution in world-class manufacturing are addressed next.

---

[8] Adapted from Nathan W. Weaks, "The Accountant as Production Scheduler," *Management Accounting,* March 1993, pp. 25–28. Reprinted from *Management Accounting.* Copyright by Institute of Management Accountants, Montvale, N.J.

[9] Goldratt, op. cit., p. 4.

[10] John H. Sheridan, "Throughput with a Capital 'T,'" *Industry Week,* March 4, 1991.

**Nonmanufacturing
Designing and
Drafting Activity
Example**

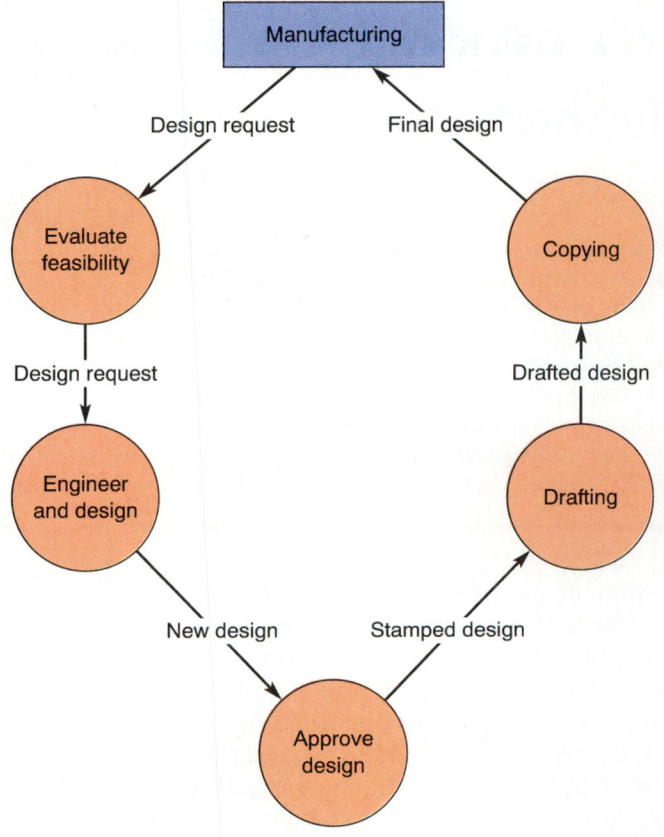

<hr>

LEARNING
OBJECTIVE 3

Describe each phase of
the focusing process
defined by the theory
of constraints (TOC).

WHAT ARE THE ELEMENTS OF CONSTRAINTS MANAGEMENT?

The performance of any system or business is limited by its constraints. Intuitively, a system's constraints can be defined as anything that prevents the system from achieving or exceeding its global goal. In reality, enterprises have very few *real* constraints, yet any such system must have at least one constraint.[11]

The improvement process that the TOC uses to manage these constraints to sort out the important few from the trivial many, is known as **focusing.** Embedded in this process are techniques for stimulating employee involvement; determining root causes of problems; and generating simple, workable solutions to these problems.

Focusing

The process of focusing can be described from two different perspectives:

1. The perspective of the system to be improved where the system's own terminology is used
2. The perspective of the improvement process itself where the improvement process's terminology is used

TOC authorities generally agree that both descriptions are very helpful, and only when both are considered together does a nondistorted picture emerge.[12] To illustrate these techniques, the SimpleCo Manufacturing example is used.

[11] Goldratt, op. cit., p. 4.
[12] Ibid., p. 7.

INSIGHTS & APPLICATIONS

SimpleCo Manufacturing

SimpleCo is a manufacturer of two products, which are assembled from three types of raw materials on three primary production lines, as illustrated in Exhibit 15–3. For simplicity, it is assumed there are no WIP inventories, no wait times for raw materials, and no setup times; in addition, workers do not take breaks and are not absent. In essence, it is a "perfect" manufacturing environment. As shown, the process involves seven activities performed by four workers [W1, W2, W3, and W4] for the times indicated.

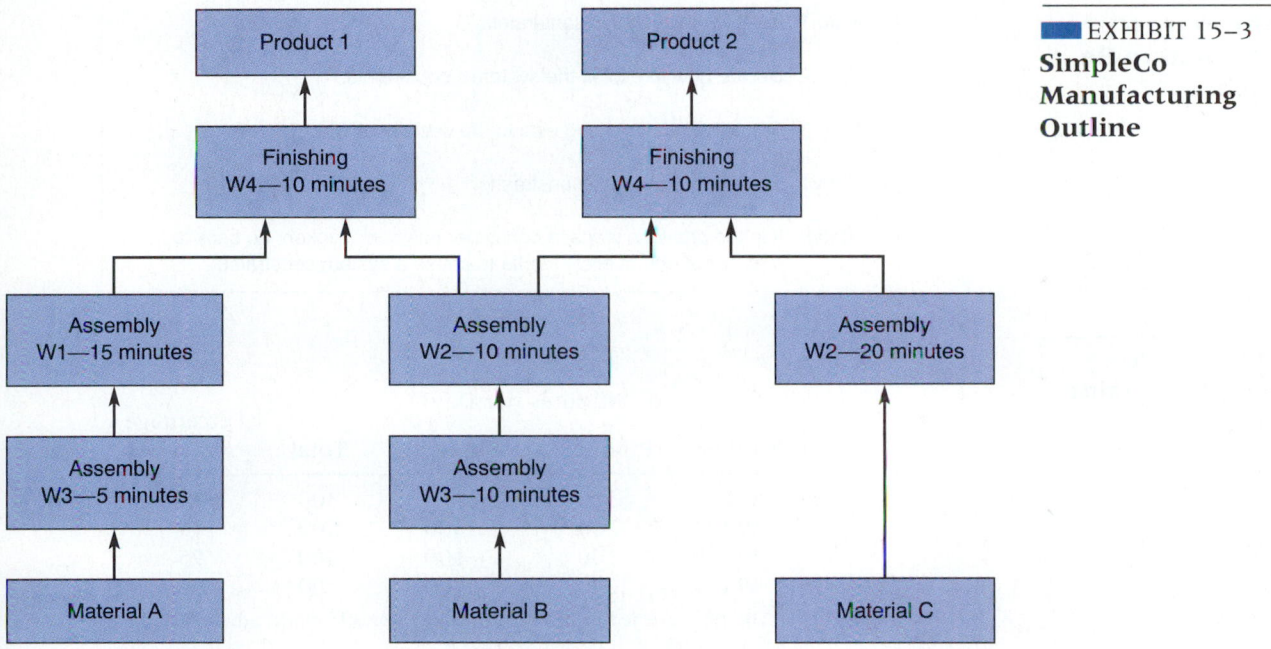

EXHIBIT 15–3
SimpleCo Manufacturing Outline

FOCUSING WITH SYSTEM TERMINOLOGY.   The steps in the focusing process, using the terminology of the system to be improved, are presented next. Exhibit 15–4 summarizes these five steps.[13]

Step 1.   Identify the system's constraints.

In a manufacturing operation, step 1 might involve such tasks as determining the number of machine setups that can be performed in a day, gathering statistics on the frequency of machine breakdowns, or calculating the process load for an assembly line. Once the system constraints have been identified, they should be prioritized according to their impact on the enterprise's global goal.[14] This may not sound very revolutionary, but most managers never get beyond the local performance measurements particular to their work groups or departments.

Identifying the constraints means that the few items that are in short supply have been determined. These are the items that limit the global goal of the enterprise.[15] Now the focus can be on core problems, as trivialities are deemphasized.

[13] Ibid., p. 5.
[14] Ibid., p. 5.
[15] Ibid., p. 5.

INSIGHTS & APPLICATIONS

Identifying SimpleCo Constraints

Assume the market demand for products 1 and 2 is 20 units and 10 units per day, respectively. The total time needed by all the workers each day to produce the demand is shown in Exhibit 15–5. In a typical workday, 420 minutes are available for production by each of the four workers. Therefore, since worker W2 would have to work the most, and for more time than is available, W2 is the constraint in this manufacturing example.

■ EXHIBIT 15–4

The Focusing Process from the Perspective of the System to Be Improved

Using the terminology of the system to be improved, the focusing process is:
Step 1   Identify the system's constraints.
Step 2   Decide how to exploit the system's constraints.
Step 3   Subordinate everything else to the decision in step 2.
Step 4   Elevate the system's constraints.
Step 5   If in the previous steps, a constraint has been broken, go back to step 1, but do not allow inertia to cause a system constraint.

■ EXHIBIT 15–5

SimpleCo Constraint Evaluation

	Minutes per Day*			
Worker	Product 1	Product 2	Total	Percentage Available
W1	300	—	300	71%
W2	200	300	500	119
W3	300	100	400	95
W4	200	100	300	71

* The time needed to produce the full domestic market demand of each product.

Step 2. Decide how to exploit the system's constraints.

Step 2 involves simply looking at the requirements of the operation and determining how each constraint identified in step 1 must be managed to satisfy those requirements. In a manufacturing operation, the system's constraints might be exploited by developing a predetermined production schedule that runs a certain piece of equipment (identified as a constraint in step 1) at 100 percent. Decisions regarding the mix of products to be produced by a particular machine may also be important. Regardless of the type of enterprise, however, step 2's purpose is always to utilize or capitalize on the constraints to generate the greatest amount of revenue possible.

Step 3. Subordinate everything else to the decision in Step 2.

But, how should the vast majority of a system's activities that are not constraints be managed? It is important to remember that the overall performance of the system is dictated by the constraints.

Everything consumed by the constraints is supplied by the **nonconstraints.**[16] For example, on an assembly line, machine B requires raw materials produced by machine A, plus the direct labor of one operator. The processing speed of

[16] Ibid., p. 5.

INSIGHTS & APPLICATIONS

Exploiting SimpleCo's Constraint

Given the simplifying assumptions about SimpleCo's manufacturing environment, management's only means of exploiting the constraint is to determine the best product mix. Assuming products 1 and 2 can each be sold for $100 and that raw material costs for A, B, and C are $30, $20, and $10, respectively, management calculated the throughput contribution of worker W2 for each product, as shown in Exhibit 15–6. The calculation indicated that product 1 should be produced to meet domestic market demand. Any extra time worker W2 has per day should be used to produce product 2.

Under the traditional approach, also shown in Exhibit 15–6, product 2 would be the priority, with excess capacity devoted to product 1. What is the impact of these decisions on the goal of making more profit? Assuming total daily operating expenses of $1,400, exploiting the constraint results in a product mix of 20 of product 1 and 7 of product 2, for a daily net profit of $90. By following the traditional approach, a product mix of 12 of product 1 and 10 of product 2 with a loss of $100 would result! These calculations are shown in Exhibit 15–7.

TOC Approach

	Product 1	Product 2
Selling price (SP)	$100	$100
Raw material costs (RM)	$50	$30
Contribution (C = SP − RM)	$50	$70
Constraint time (W2 time per product)	10 minutes	30 minutes
Dollars per constraint minute	$5.00	$2.33

Product 1 is preferable.

Traditional Approach

	Product 1	Product 2
Selling price (SP)	$100	$100
Raw material costs (RM)	$50	$30
Contribution (C = SP − RM)	$50	$70
Direct labor time per product	50 minutes	50 minutes
Dollars per direct labor minute	$1.00	$1.40

Product 2 is preferable.

Notes: Under TOC, throughput per unit, or C in the above equation, is a form of contribution margin per unit (see Chapter 18) that deducts only the cost of raw materials per unit from the sales price per unit. Throughput per unit can easily be modified to the more common form of contribution margin per unit by also deducting other variable costs, such as direct labor.

EXHIBIT 15–6
SimpleCo Throughput Analysis

machine B is such that it is a constraint. Machine A is capable of producing material twice as fast as needed by machine B, and machine A's operator has spare time, so both machine A and its operator are nonconstraints.

Is there any point in managing a nonconstraint such as machine A to supply more to machine B than it can consume? The enterprise would not sell any more. It would only build up work-in-process inventory between the two machines. Of course, the cost world orientation says that inventory is bad because of its carrying cost. The throughput world orientation says that the impact of inventory on quality and lead times seriously jeopardizes the enterprise's ability to make more profit now and in the future.[17] If the enterprise

[17] Covington, op. cit., p. 4.

INSIGHTS & APPLICATIONS

Subordinating to SimpleCo's Constraint

The production manager, ever aware of the efficiency percentage ratios of her workers, noticed that workers 1 and 4 had significantly lower ratings than the other workers. Using traditional management concepts, she prepared a bonus pay system (for top management's review) to motivate each worker to be more efficient.

Management realized, however, that since worker W2 is the constraint, increasing the efficiencies of the other workers would neither change the net profit of SimpleCo nor reduce operating expense. Therefore, they decided to focus not on the efficiency of each worker, but on the ability of each worker to provide output at worker W2's capacity.

■ EXHIBIT 15-7
SimpleCo Net Profit Analysis

		TOC Approach		Traditional Approach
Sales revenue:				
Product 1	20 × $100	$2,000	12 × $100	$1,200
Product 2	7 × $100	$ 700	10 × $100	$1,000
Raw material costs:				
Product 1	20 × <$50>	<$1,000>	12 × <$50>	<$ 600>
Product 2	7 × <$30>	<$ 210>	10 × <$30>	<$ 300>
Throughput		$1,490		$1,300
Operating expense		<$1,400>		<$1,400>
Net profit <loss>		$ 90		<$ 100>

Product Mix Calculation*

TOC approach: Maximize product 1
    Product 1:
        20 @ 10 minutes each (W2) ⇒ 200 minutes ⇒ 220 minutes remaining
    Product 2:
        220 minutes @ 30 minutes each (W2) ⇒ 7 products

Therefore, 20/7 mix. That is, 20 units of product 1 and 7 units of product 2 daily.

Traditional approach: Maximize product 2
    Product 2:
        10 @ 30 minutes each (W2) ⇒ 300 minutes ⇒ 120 minutes remaining
    Product 1:
        120 minutes @ 10 minutes each (W2) ⇒ 12 products

Therefore, 12/10 mix. That is, 12 units of product 1 and 10 units of product 2 daily.

* Since management has already determined that worker W2 is the constraint, each product mix approach will attempt to maximize worker W2's time.

releases material into the plant according to the needs of the constraints, allowing sufficient time for the material to arrive, then the nonconstraints will nearly manage themselves.

Step 4. Elevate the system's constraints.

Once the enterprise understands how to manage its constraints and nonconstraints, it does not stop there—not if continuous improvement is the strategy! The company can still do a great deal about its constraints. After ensuring that existing constraints are used in the best possible way, the next step is to reduce their limitations on the system's performance; that is, to **elevate** the constraints.

INSIGHTS & APPLICATIONS

Elevating SimpleCo's Constraint

The sales manager, thinking that net profit might increase if SimpleCo could sell more products, went overseas. As a result of the trip, the manager found a market for both products at a selling price of $71 per item. The overseas market would not affect the current domestic market. Unfortunately, analysis of the information presented in Exhibit 15–8 showed that selling either of the products overseas would result in less net profit per item than SimpleCo can realize in the local market, since the overseas dollars per constraint values were less than the underdeveloped domestic product 2 dollars per constraint of $2.33.

After evaluating options to relieve the constraint of worker W2, management decided to add another W2 worker [W2b] for $100 per day, increasing the total daily operating cost to $1,500 to fulfill the domestic market demand. The constraint was elevated, and management increased net profit to $200, as shown in Exhibit 15–9.

■ **EXHIBIT 15–8**
SimpleCo Overseas Market Analysis

TOC Approach	Product 1 (Overseas)	Product 2 (Overseas)
Selling price (SP)	$71	$71
Raw material costs (RM)	$50	$30
Contribution (C = SP − RM)	$21	$41
Constraint time (W2 time per product)	10 minutes	30 minutes
Dollars per constraint minute	$2.10	$1.37
Neither product is preferable.		
Market demand	10	10

■ **EXHIBIT 15–9**
SimpleCo Net Profit Analysis

Sales revenue:			
Product 1	20 × $100	$2,000	
Product 2	10 × $100	$1,000	
Raw material costs:			
Product 1	20 × <$50>	<$1,000>	
Product 2	10 × <$30>	<$ 300>	
Throughput		$1,700	
Operating expense		<$1,500>	
Net profit <loss>		$ 200	

The processing speed of a machine or worker is a constraint. How can this constraint be elevated? One possible way is to replace the machine or worker with a faster one. Other possibilities include upgrading the machine by retrofitting a component part, giving the worker additional training, or changing the design of the product to eliminate the need for the type of processing the machine or worker performs. A constraint is not always a machine or worker. It can be a policy or a rule. Whatever the constraint, there must be a way of reducing its limiting impact.

Step 5. If, in the previous steps, a constraint has been broken, go back to step 1.

If a constraint is elevated and the enterprise continues to elevate it, sooner or later it will cease to be a constraint. The constraint is broken. For example, machine A is twice as fast as machine B, the constraint. Machine B is upgraded so its speed is tripled. Is machine B still a constraint? No, the constraint is broken! Now machine A is the bottleneck in the process. The previous constraint

Some constraints can be broken with technology.

INSIGHTS & APPLICATIONS

Reevaluating SimpleCo

After the addition of worker W2b, management realized that the domestic market demand had become the new constraint since all workers now had "idle" time. They remembered the sales manager's analysis and considered using the overseas market to sell more products to eliminate worker idle time. Since product 1 had the higher dollar per constraint value, they tentatively decided to sell this product overseas. After reevaluating the workers' time for meeting the domestic market they determined that worker W3 would limit the excess production, as shown in Exhibit 15–10, so only one extra product 1 could be produced each day for overseas sales. The new net profit was calculated to be $221, as shown in Exhibit 15–11, a slight increase over the domestic market net profit.

■■EXHIBIT 15–10
**New SimpleCo
Constraint Evaluation**

Minutes per Day*

Worker	Product 1 (20 units)	Product 2 (10 units)	Total	Excess Time
W1	300	—	300	120
W2	200	300	500	340
W3	300	100	400	20
W4	200	100	300	120

20 minutes (W3) @ 15 minutes each (product 1) ⇒ one extra product 1

* The time needed to produce the full domestic market demand of each product.

■■EXHIBIT 15–11
**New SimpleCo Net
Profit Analysis**

Sales revenue:
Product 1	20 × $100	$2,000
Product 2	10 × $100	$1,000
Product 1 (overseas)	1 × $71	$ 71

Raw material costs:
Product 1	20 × <$50>	<$1,000>
Product 2	10 × <$30>	<$ 300>
Product 1 (overseas)	1 × <$50>	<$ 50>
Throughput		$1,721
Operating expense		<$1,500>
Net profit <loss>		$ 221

is no longer limiting the system, but has been replaced by a new constraint. Now the management accountant must return to step 1 and cycle through the focusing process again.

This step requires a warning of sorts. In many enterprises, many rules and policies seem to be created to deal with current constraints. Sometimes these rules are formally declared and enforced; other times they become intuitive. In most cases, the rules or policies were very appropriate at the time they were instituted. A problem occurs, however, when a constraint is broken and nobody bothers to go back and review the applicable rules and policies. The system ends up wallowing in a sea of **policy constraints,** or **inertia.** The original reasons have long since gone, but the policies remain.

INSIGHTS & APPLICATIONS

Breaking SimpleCo Inertia

After agreeing to go into the overseas market with one product 1 per day, management realized the decision, although profitable, was steeped in the inertia of policies and mindsets from the W2 constraint days. Realizing that in a constraint-driven process, changing the constraint changes everything, SimpleCo decided to reevaluate the constraint and product mix for the total domestic and overseas market. As Exhibit 15–12 shows, worker W3 is the new constraint since W3 would be the most overworked. W3 would now be overworked by 155 percent (650 demand time ÷ 420 available time). Exhibit 15–13 displays the new product mix calculations in relation to the new constraint W3.

The result was shocking—SimpleCo should maximize product 2, both domestically and overseas, before partially meeting the domestic demand for product 1! By relieving its W2 constraint, SimpleCo dramatically changed its focus from product 1 to product 2. The resulting net profit calculation is given in Exhibit 15–14. By reevaluating the entire operation and determining a new product mix, SimpleCo was able to increase net profit as shown in Exhibit 15–15.

■■ EXHIBIT 15–12
New SimpleCo Constraint Evaluation

Minutes per Day*

Worker	Product 1 (20)	Product 2 (10)	Product 1 (Overseas) (10)	Product 2 (Overseas) (10)	Total Work Time Demanded	Available Work Time	Percentage Overworked
W1	300	—	150	—	450	420	107
W2	200	300	100	300	900	840	107
W3	300	100	150	100	650	420	155
W4	200	100	100	100	500	420	119

Thus, W3 is the new constraint.

* The time needed to produce the full market demand of each product.

■■ EXHIBIT 15–13
New SimpleCo Constraint Analysis and Product Mix

	Product 1	Product 2	Product 1 (Overseas)	Product 2 (Overseas)
Selling price (SP)	$100	$100	$71	$71
Raw material costs (RM)	$50	$30	$50	$30
Contribution (C = SP − RM)	$50	$70	$21	$41
Constraint time (W3 minutes per product)	15 minutes	10 minutes	15 minutes	10 minutes
Dollars per constraint minute	$3.33	$7.00	$1.40	$4.10
Market demand	20	10	10	10

Product mix calculation:

Product 2	10 @ 10 min. ⇒	100 minutes
Product 2 (overseas)	10 @ 10 min. ⇒	100 minutes
Product 1	14 @ 15 min. ⇒	210 minutes
Total		410 minutes (10 minutes unusable)

Sales revenue:		
Product 2	10 × $100	$1,000
Product 2 (overseas)	10 × $71	$ 710
Product 1	14 × $100	$1,400
Raw material costs:		
Product 2	10 × <$30>	<$ 300>
Product 2 (overseas)	10 × <$30>	<$ 300>
Product 1	14 × <$50>	<$ 700>
Throughput		$1,810
Operating expense		<$1,500>
Net profit <loss>		$ 310

Scenario		Daily Net Profit
Traditional	W2 constraint	<$100>
TOC	W2 constraint	$ 90
TOC	Market constraint	$200
Wrong product mix	W3 constraint	$221
TOC	W3 constraint	$310

With this warning, step 5 becomes: If, in the previous steps, a constraint has been broken, go back to step 1, but do not allow inertia to cause a system constraint.[18] Too few of the constraints in organizations today are real. The vast majority are nothing but devastating policy constraints.

FOCUSING WITH IMPROVEMENT PROCESS TERMINOLOGY. As noted earlier, the focusing process can also be conducted using the terminology of the improvement process itself. This process involves three steps, summarized in Exhibit 15–16.[19] By being aware of both descriptions of focusing, an enterprise will obtain a clear view of its constraints and thereby avoid misapplying its efforts.

Step 1. Decide what to change.

Managers tend to concentrate on what they feel they have some control over or knowledge of. Therefore, most of their activity is directed at taking the corrective actions that they already know how to take. As a consequence, managers tend to drift from one small problem to another, putting out fires and filling up their days with trivialities, rather than pinpointing and solving the core problems that need to be addressed.

The TOC attempts to transform management from an informal art into a science. In the hard sciences such as physics, chemistry, and biology, the method of proof used most extensively is called the effect-cause-effect method,[20] which is discussed in more detail later. For now, the **effect-cause-effect method** strives to explain the existence of as many natural effects as possible by postulating a minimum number of assumptions. Managers can use the effect-cause-effect method to pinpoint core problems in enterprises. Only through this method will root causes be revealed, not just symptoms.

Step 2. Decide what to change to.

Complicated solutions to problems rarely, if ever, work. This idea is somewhat

[18] Goldratt, op. cit., p. 6.
[19] Ibid., p. 7.
[20] Ibid., p. 22.

Using the terminology of the improvement process itself, the focusing process is:
Step 1   Decide what to change: • Pinpoint the core problems! • Use the effect-cause-effect method. Step 2   Decide what to change to: • Construct simple, practical solutions! • Use the evaporating clouds method. Step 3   Decide how to cause the change: • Induce the appropriate people to invent solutions! • Use the Socratic method.

EXHIBIT 15–16
The Focusing Process from the Perspective of the Improvement Process Itself

hard to swallow in today's world, where people are fascinated by sophistication, technology, and contrived complexity. Yet, nothing is as sophisticated as a simple solution, because such a solution requires a great deal of thought about the root causes of the problem. If a solution is complicated, it is probably just treating the symptoms.

More will be said about finding simple solutions later. Dr. Eliyahu M. Goldratt and others have developed a technique known as the **evaporating clouds method,** which aims at eliminating the problem by eliminating the element of compromise and generating a solution that makes the problem's root cause disappear.[21]

Step 3. Decide how to cause the change.

Whereas steps 1 and 2 may be considered technical decisions, step 3 is definitely a psychological one. Fortunately, people are well equipped to make this decision because the very act of surviving the politics of an organization gives them a good intuitive understanding of the psychological processes involved. This understanding is important because the main thrust of this step is overcoming the organization's psychological resistance to change.

As mentioned earlier in this chapter, not every change is an improvement, but every improvement is most definitely a change. Something cannot be improved unless it is changed. The difficulty is that any change will be perceived as a threat to the security of someone in the organization, which will naturally lead to emotional resistance to the change. This resistance can only be overcome by creating a stronger emotion in favor of the change.

This stronger emotion is "ownership of the idea." When people devise a solution to a problem themselves, they take ownership of it. Suddenly their own resistance to change is overcome by their desire to advance the idea that they own. One of the most effective methods of encouraging the appropriate people to invent solutions is the Socratic method.[22]

Simply put, the **Socratic method** never gives an individual the correct answer or tells the individual what should be done. Instead, a series of precise, pointed questions are asked that lead the individual to deduce the answers for himself or herself. If the right people are induced in this way to invent solutions to the organization's problems, emotional resistance to change can be reduced or eliminated. Thus, these three methods—effect-cause-effect, evaporating clouds, and Socratic—are the keys to this aspect of the focusing process. A detailed discussion of each of these methods follows.

---

[21] Ibid., p. 37.
[22] Robert E. Fox, "The Constraint Theory," *The Theory of Constraints Managing in the Throughput World* (New York: Institute for International Research, 1992), p. 51.

The Effect-Cause-Effect Method

The problems perceived in enterprises are more often than not just symptoms of some hidden, but central difficulty. These central core problems are what must be pinpointed if the enterprise is to achieve the focusing step of "decide what to change." If management is regarded as an art, the enterprise will probably never move forward, but if management is treated as a science, a whole host of scientific tools become available. One of these tools, the effect-cause-effect method of scientific proof, is the means by which the TOC identifies core problems in a sea of symptoms.

Most sciences have evolved through three distinct stages.[23] During the first stage, **classification,** scientists become familiar with the subject. Initially, they gather information. Then, as the quantity of information becomes overwhelming, they arrange it using some systematic classification strategy, maybe introducing some exception rules to account for pieces that do not quite fit.

As part of the classification efforts, information is summarized using statistics, tables, and graphs. This task invariably leads to the second evolutionary stage of a science, **correlation,** where patterns and common trends among the various graphs and tables are identified. The primary difficulty with such correlations is that the reason why they exist may not be understood.

Most correlations are extremely helpful, but not understanding their underlying cause and effect can be detrimental. In the late 1970s, surveys found that Japanese companies carried substantially less inventory than their American competitors. It was also apparent that the overall performance of the Japanese companies was superior. The obvious correlation "inventory is a liability" was broadcast from sea to shining sea, and most manufacturing firms engaged in a concerted effort to pare inventories down to near-zero.[24] Although this effort was, in general, effective in improving performance, drastic reductions in raw materials inventory actually penalized these firms by straining vendor relations and making the firms less responsive to their markets.

The third evolutionary stage for a science is **effect-cause-effect,** a departure from the classification and correlation stages. Here scientists are less concerned with having a vast number of correlations; one observed effect is enough. Now the scientists speculate about a plausible cause for this effect. They hypothesize, using some educated guessing and knowing full well that the hypothesis may be wrong. The scientists then think carefully about what other effects would be observed if the hypothetical cause does, in fact, exist.

If these other effects are observed, perhaps after years of experimentation, the hypothesis is validated into theory; if the effects are never observed, the hypothesis is scrapped or modified, and the process begins all over again. Ultimately, by utilizing the entire process of constructing the effect-cause-effect logic, management accountants have a very powerful method for persuading others. More importantly, they have revealed the fundamental causes of the enterprise's problems, such as outdated policies, so that a simple solution can now be developed and applied.

The Evaporating Clouds Method

Root causes of problems do not just pop up. They have usually existed within organizations for many months or even years. People generally are aware of all the usual "accepted" solutions, but the persistence of the problem indicates that all these perceived solutions are insufficient.[25] Usually, these accepted solutions, which do not work, are compromises designed to threaten the security of as few people as possible.

---

[23] Goldratt, op. cit., p. 23.
[24] Ibid., p. 30.
[25] Ibid., p. 36.

INSIGHTS & APPLICATIONS

A Historical Effect-Cause-Effect Example

In the second century A.D., Claudius Ptolomaeus Ptolemy, after observing the effects and relations between the earth, sun, moon, and stars, hypothesized that the earth was the center of the universe and that all celestial bodies rotated around it. Unfortunately, the modifications necessary to make Ptolemy's theory match subsequent years of celestial observations also made the theory cumbersome and inelegant. In the sixteenth century A.D., Nicolaus Copernicus published his sun-centered theory, which effectively replaced Ptolemy's earth-centered one. Further experiments and observations have only slightly modified the Copernican theory, and thus the cosmos can be explained by relatively simple means.

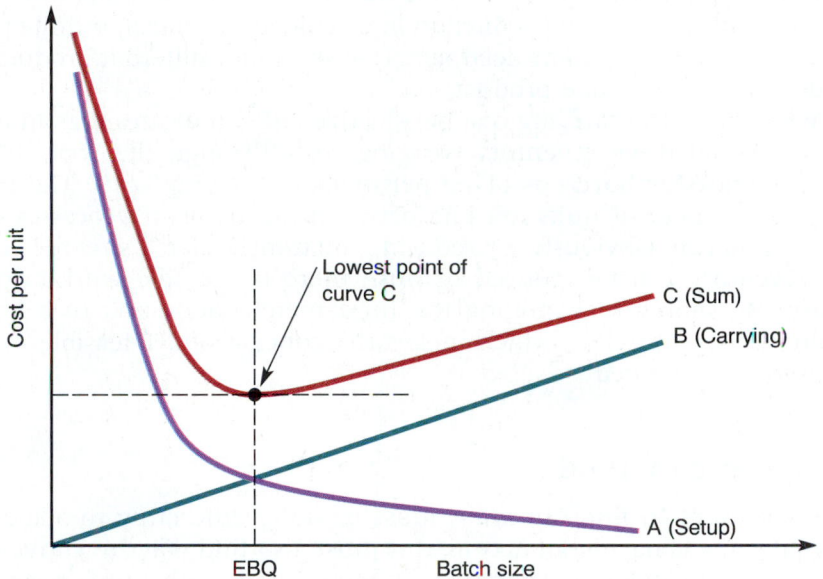

**EXHIBIT 15–17
Graphical Representation of the Economic Batch Quantity (EBQ) Calculation**

To avoid this stagnation, people must be induced to invent simple solutions that bypass the avenue of compromise. They should reexamine the foundations of systems and create an environment where the core problem cannot exist. This is the evaporating clouds method, probably best illustrated by an example.

In a manufacturing operation, production managers are concerned with the determination of batch sizes. This batch size, or **economic batch quantity (EBQ),** is the number of units of product to be run on a machine or assembly line given one setup of the equipment. The EBQ problem can be stated as follows: Find the batch size that will result in the minimum cost per unit. Batch size will impact cost per unit through setup cost and carrying cost. The EBQ is a compromise between these two costs.

Exhibit 15–17 shows three cost curves.[26] As curve A shows, increasing the batch size reduces the cost per unit because the setup cost is divided among more units. Obviously, the lowest unit cost from a setup perspective is achieved when the batch size is infinite. But, as curve B shows, when the batch size is increased, the time the batch is held also increases, thus increasing the carrying cost of inventory. The lowest unit cost from an inventory perspective is achieved when the batch size is 1.

Therefore, finding a solution to the EBQ problem is restricted by the question: What compromise between setup cost and carrying cost should be made? The

[26] Ibid., p. 44.

answer is shown by curve C, which is simply the sum of curves A and B. The lowest point of curve C is the EBQ, a compromise that represents the lowest-cost batch size.

But, is this really the optimal solution for achieving the global goal, or are management accountants unnecessarily plagued by preconceived notions and restrictive accounting conventions? The originators of JIT chose to abandon the EBQ altogether because they felt EBQ invalidly assumes that there is only one batch size and only one definition of a batch. Instead, JIT recognizes two batch sizes: process batch and transfer batch. The widespread acceptance of the EBQ model was a constraint on manufacturing enterprises for years because of an accounting convention!

How, exactly, does JIT overcome the limitations of the EBQ model? First, setup costs should be considered. As stated before, the more units in a production run, the lower the unit cost because the cost of one setup is spread over more units. The best scenario, from a setup cost perspective, is an infinitely large number of units in the production run. JIT calls this number of units the **process batch.** A dedicated production line achieves this ideal, infinite process batch, because the equipment need never be set up for different products. The line is dedicated to just one product.

But, what about the carrying cost perspective? EBQ indicates that an infinite batch size would drive inventory carrying costs through the roof. JIT now defines the **transfer batch** as being pertinent to carrying costs. The transfer batch is the number of units left idle between machines or processes during the production run. Obviously, by reducing the transfer batch size, the carrying cost of inventory can be reduced because there is less idle work-in-process inventory. By simply reexamining the fundamental definition of a batch, a constraint can be elevated, which makes the concept of JIT feasible. A cloud has therefore evaporated!

The Socratic Method

It is not sufficient to find out what must be done differently to achieve the global goal. The management accountant must also find ways to convey what all people must do and enlist their support rather than combat their resistance.[27] The process by which the TOC attempts to achieve this is called the Socratic method.

In most organizations, change is induced through fear and insecurity. Managers try to overcome the immediate insecurity resulting from change by provoking the long-term insecurity of what will happen if change is not brought about. Unfortunately, when fire is used to fight fire in this way, somebody always gets burned. If continuous improvement is to exist in this type of enterprise, an environment of constant insecurity will prevail.[28] Is this really what is desired?

The 2,500-year-old Socratic method provides a different way of inducing change. Everybody has the ability to invent, if skillfully induced. And once people invent something for themselves, they actually take ownership. In an enterprise, people can be induced to invent solutions to problems using their own common sense. Because the invention is their own, they will see it as a product of their own thinking and will therefore not feel threatened by it. In fact, they will be eager to implement it.

Of course, the enterprise wants everyone to rally behind the same solution to a particular problem, or chaos will result. Such a thought process can be achieved by asking a series of very precise, pointed questions, but without giving the answers. Supplying people with the answers denies them the opportunity of

Improved throughput starts with the ready acquisition of quality raw materials.

[27] Ibid., p. 20.
[28] Ibid., p. 14.

finding those same answers for themselves.[29] In contrast, people led down a logical path by a knowledgeable mentor who only asks questions will feel an overwhelming sense of pride when they ultimately figure out the answers for themselves. This sense of pride will remain even if they realize that others, such as the mentor, have invented the same solution before.

HOW IS THE THEORY OF CONSTRAINTS BEST APPLIED?

LEARNING OBJECTIVE 4

Discuss how the theory of constraints can be applied in manufacturing firms and how it can be integrated with existing just-in-time and total quality management systems.

Up to this point, the discussion has concentrated on what the TOC is. Now the focus shifts to how the TOC is applied in an enterprise.

Reaching a Consensus

With many internal improvement projects, such as the implementation of a new information system, it is sufficient to begin with a **pilot project.** Pilot projects initially implement changes in just one division, department, or work group. Then, once the bugs have been worked out and the pilot proves itself a success, the remainder of the organization comes on board, and the improvement project is implemented enterprisewide.

In implementing the TOC, however, it is necessary to reach a consensus among all activities in the enterprise prior to starting any significant improvement efforts.[30] The reason for this is simple. In the throughput world, all parts of the organization as well as external entities such as vendors and customers are considered part of an interdependent throughput chain. If throughput is improved in one pilot department by the elevation of some constraint, other departments may immediately become constraints.

Since only the pilot department is practicing the TOC, other departments do not elevate their constraints, and the pilot department will be forced to operate at less than its new full capacity. Ultimately, pressure to reduce operating expense will become focused on the pilot department, and the resulting layoffs will punish the very people who improved. Clearly, this result will not provide much of an incentive for the remainder of the organization.

Reaching Synergism: JIT, TQM, and TOC

By now one might be wondering, "does the TOC make the JIT and TQM elements of world-class manufacturing obsolete?" Are these three concepts contradictory or complementary? Certainly, JIT, TQM, and TOC all share the same global goal: to increase the ability of the company to make more profit now and in the future.[31] In this sense, JIT, TQM, and TOC are, indeed, complementary concepts. At the same time, the three concepts also interact so that each actually enhances the others as part of a single, ongoing, uniform implementation procedure.[32]

If JIT seems unlikely to enhance TQM or TOC, that is probably because JIT was once narrowly defined as the "zero-inventory" method. Yet, JIT is much more. JIT attacks the long setup times and large WIP inventories that are a bane to protecting future throughput. Thus, JIT's focus is really on increasing throughput—the highest-priority element in the throughput world orientation.

---

[29] Ibid., p. 18.
[30] Ibid., p. 97.
[31] Goldratt, op. cit., p. 111.
[32] James T. Mackey, ed., *Cases from Management Accounting Practice*, vol. 8 (Montvale, N.J.: Institute of Management Accountants, 1992).

Similarly, TQM's interactive role might seem unclear if TQM is narrowly defined as "a means of improving customer service and product quality." Yet, TQM attacks the variability and the disruptive effects of poor-quality products that are a bane to protecting current throughput. Thus, like JIT, TQM's focus is really on increasing throughput—the highest-priority element in the throughput world orientation.

Finally, if it is unclear how the TOC might enhance JIT or TQM, that is probably because the TOC has been seen by some as nothing but a crusade against local performance measurements and traditional cost accounting principles. Of course, this chapter has shown the TOC to be much more. The TOC attacks the concept that the best total system throughput will be achieved by individually maximizing local (workcenter) throughputs. Obviously, the TOC's focus is on increasing throughput—the highest-priority element in the throughput world orientation.

Dr. Goldratt sums up the synergy of JIT, TQM, and TOC best:

It is about time to realize that JIT's primary focus is not the reduction of inventory on the shop floor. It is not just a mechanical kanban technique. It is definitely a new overall management philosophy.

It is about time to realize that TQM's primary focus is not the quality of the products. It is not just a mechanical statistical process control technique. It is definitely a new overall management philosophy.

It is about time to realize that TOC's primary focus is not bottlenecks on the shop floor. It is not just a mechanical optimized production technique. It is definitely a new overall management philosophy.[33]

Viewed simply as methods for enhancing the local performance measurements of the cost oriented world, these three management philosophies could easily be regarded as separate. But, in the context of the throughput oriented world, where an entire enterprise single-mindedly pursues the global goal of making more profit now and in the future, the three management philosophies are, in fact, one and the same. The three only differ "in the tools, procedures, and systems they offer management to adjust to the entirely different world"—the throughput world.[34]

SUMMARY OF LEARNING OBJECTIVES

The major goals of this chapter were to enable you to achieve four learning objectives:

Learning objective 1. State the global goal of a for-profit enterprise.

Although many for-profit businesses state such "goals" as producing the highest-quality products, giving the best customer service, or increasing market share by 50 percent, these are really just strategies for achieving the real global goal. All for-profit enterprises have the single global goal of making more profit, both now and in the future.

Learning objective 2. Explain the differences between a cost world orientation and a throughput world orientation, and compare the two orientations with regard to how well they support continuous improvement.

The cost world orientation and the throughput world orientation differ primarily in the way management prioritizes the elements of operating expense, inventory, and throughput. In the cost world, managers are primarily concerned with operating expense and concentrate on reducing costs by improving a whole host of local perfor-

---

[33] Eliyahu M. Goldratt, *The Haystack Syndrome: Sifting Information out of the Data Ocean* (Great Barrington, Mass.: North River Press, 1990), pp. 8–9. With permission.

[34] Eliyahu M. Goldratt, "The Paradigm Shift," *The Theory of Constraints Journal*, vol. 1, no. 6 (New Haven, Conn.: Avraham Y. Goldratt Institute, 1987), p. 14.

mance measurements. Throughput and inventory management are their second and third priorities, respectively.

In the throughput world, managers realize that the vast majority of local performance measurements are, at best, irrelevant to the enterprise's global goal. Improving throughput becomes their primary focus. Inventory management is their second priority, while operating expense is a distant third.

Only the throughput world orientation can support continuous improvement. This is because improvement should be measured only by the enterprise's global goal of making more profit now and in the future. Operating expense can be reduced, but improvement in this area is limited because expenses cannot be reduced below zero. There are no such limits on throughput; it can increase indefinitely. If throughput is emphasized rather than operating expense, profits have no bounds.

Learning objective 3.   Describe each phase of the focusing process defined by the theory of constraints (TOC).

Using the terminology of the system to be improved, the focusing process consists of the following steps:

Step 1. Identify the system's constraints.   Constraints are those bottlenecks, inhibitors, and limiting factors that prevent an enterprise from reaching or exceeding its global goal. Once constraints have been identified, they should be prioritized according to their impact on performance.

Step 2. Decide how to exploit the system's constraints.   This step answers the question: ''How can the enterprise's current limiting factors be used to maximize throughput?'' On a manufacturing floor, this might involve running a particular machine at 100 percent capacity.

Step 3. Subordinate everything else to the decision in step 2.   The constraints are all that matter. Everything consumed by the constraints is supplied by the nonconstraints. There is no point in managing the nonconstraints to produce more than the constraints can use because throughput will not increase.

Step 4. Elevate the system's constraints.   If throughput is to be increased, the limiting effects of the constraints must be removed. Any action that improves the performance of a constraint will improve throughput.

Step 5. If, in the previous steps, a constraint has been broken, go back to step 1, but do not allow inertia to cause a system constraint.   After a certain amount of improvement, a constraint will be elevated to the point that it no longer limits the enterprise. One or more previous nonconstraints will now take its place in limiting the throughput chain. At this point, the focusing process should be performed again to identify and elevate these new constraints.

Using the terminology of the improvement process itself, the focusing process consists of the following steps:

Step 1. Decide what to change.   The root causes of problems facing an enterprise must be identified. It is not sufficient simply to identify symptoms. The TOC provides a formal, scientific approach to identifying root causes through the use of the effect-cause-effect method.

Step 2. Decide what to change to.   Simple, practical solutions to the enterprise's core problems must be found. Complicated solutions do not work. They are difficult to implement and typically treat only the symptoms, not the root causes. The evaporating clouds method can be used to create an environment where a core problem can no longer exist. This method of problem solving is superior to the typical compromise approach because the problem is completely removed.

Step 3. Decide how to cause the change.   Once a solution has been devised, the appropriate people in the organization must be motivated to implement it. The chief roadblock to implementation is the organization's psychological resistance to change. This psychological force can be overcome if people are allowed to invent solutions themselves; they take ownership of their invention and are motivated to implement it. The Socratic method can be used to induce all the people in the organization to arrive at the same solution found in step 2.

Learning objective 4.   Discuss how the theory of constraints can be applied in manufacturing firms and how it can be integrated with existing just-in-time and total quality management systems.

Although many improvements can be implemented using a pilot project, the TOC should be implemented enterprisewide and simultaneously. To achieve this, the enterprise must obtain a consensus among the managers of all activities prior to beginning TOC implementation.

A throughput-oriented production management and scheduling system can help in implementing the TOC enterprisewide by providing all activities with information from an integrated computer-based information system (ICBIS). The TOC is fully compatible with JIT and TQM. Any implementation effort should seek to build a synergy among these three management philosophies, so that each enhances the others as they work together in a concerted effort to achieve the enterprise's global goal.

IMPORTANT TERMS

Classification The first evolutionary stage of a science. During this stage, information about the subject is gathered and grouped according to some organizational scheme. Summary statistics describing the information may also be produced.

Constraints Any activities, rules, or policies that prevent the enterprise from achieving or exceeding its global goal.

Correlation The second evolutionary stage of a science. During this stage, conclusions are drawn about the statistics provided by the classification stage. These conclusions are based solely on the observed information that has been gathered; they do not attempt to explain the correlations.

Cost world orientation A management philosophy based on traditional cost accounting principles. Managers subscribing to this philosophy make the control and reduction of operating expense their first priority.

Economic batch quantity (EBQ) The number of units of product to be run on a machine or assembly line that results in the minimum cost per unit.

Effect-cause-effect method The third evolutionary stage of a science. During this stage, scientists make an educated guess at an underlying explanation for an observed effect or problem. Then experiments are conducted in the hope of observing other, unrelated effects that would have to exist if the hypothesis were true. If the effects are observed, the hypothesis becomes theory.

Elevate The process of improving the performance of a constraint in order to reduce or eliminate its effect on the overall performance of a business enterprise.

Evaporating clouds method A method of problem solving used to remove a fundamental, core problem. Most problem solving begins by accepting the existence of the problem as a given and then takes a compromise approach to limit the problem's symptoms. In contrast, evaporating clouds method actually causes the problem to disappear. It achieves this by changing the problem's environment so that the problem can no longer exist.

Focusing The formal, scientific process used by the theory of constraints to identify core problems, invent simple solutions to those problems, and induce people in an organization to implement those solutions.

Inertia A tendency of some workers and managers to maintain the status quo. It is a disinclination to act often governed by the cliché, "If it ain't broke, don't fix it."

Inventory The money the enterprise has invested in things it intends to sell and includes inventories valued only at raw material costs and property, plant, and equipment.

Global Pertains to the entire business enterprise as a whole. The global goal of an enterprise, for example, is to make more profit now and in the future.

Local Pertains to some small portion of a business enterprise, such as a division, department, or work group. A local performance measurement, for instance, might be machine utilization as a percentage of capacity.

Nonconstraints Those activities of a system that do not, at this time, limit the overall throughput of the system. Nonconstraints supply the constraints.

Operating expense The money spent to convert inventory into throughput.

Pilot project A method for implementing an improvement project that begins with one small area of a business organization, such as a department. Once the project has proved itself in the pilot area, it is implemented in the remainder of the business organization. This method is not recommended when implementing the theory of constraints.

Policy constraints   Not real, physical constraints, but rather a set of rules or policies that limit what may be done and thus impose constraints on the performance of an enterprise. Most policy constraints were probably valid at one time, but the need for them has gone while the policy lives on.

Process batch   In a just-in-time system, the size of a production run given one setup of the equipment.

Socratic method   A method of inducing people in an organization to implement changes aimed at improving the organization's performance. Individuals invent solutions, thereby taking ownership of them, in response to a series of precise, pointed questions.

Theory of constraints (TOC)   The formal, scientific approach to identifying and elevating limiting constraints in an enterprise. The TOC embraces a throughput world orientation, the effect-cause-effect method of proof, the evaporating clouds problem-solving method, and the Socratic method.

Throughput (contribution or **contribution margin)**   The rate at which the system generates profit through sales. It is equal to sales less raw material costs. A measure of manufacturing productivity that corresponds to sales. Since sales, the receipt of money for goods and services, drive the throughput chain, throughput is a good measure of overall productivity of the enterprise and its stakeholders.

Throughput chain   The entire, interdependent sequence of activities that produces a product from raw materials and then sells the product, earning profit for the business enterprises involved. The throughput chain extends beyond the physical boundaries of any one enterprise and has links to vendors and customers.

Throughput world orientation   A management philosophy that recognizes that continuous improvement can only be achieved by making the enhancement of throughput the organization's first priority. This enhancement is achieved by elevating constraints along the throughput chain.

Transfer batch   In a just-in-time system, the number of units of work-in-process moved from one work cell or machine to another work cell or machine at any one time.

DEMONSTRATION PROBLEMS

■ DEMONSTRATION PROBLEM 1   *Net profit calculation: Traditional approach versus theory of constraints approach.*

Matador Equipment Company sells lawn mowers in the western part of the country. Matador offers four models: 110, 120, 210, and 220, with the primary differences being engine size and cutting width. Total operating expense for Matador is $30,500 per month. Following are monthly data related to each product:

ITEM	MODEL 110	MODEL 120	MODEL 210	MODEL 220
Market demand (units)	140	150	100	135
Selling price (per unit)	$125	$170	$150	$200
Raw material costs (per unit)	$55	$80	$65	$90
Direct labor (hours per unit)	1.45	1.50	1.55	1.70
Worker A (hours per unit)	0.50	0.50	–0–	–0–
Worker B (hours per unit)	–0–	–0–	0.60	0.60
Worker C (hours per unit)	0.65	–0–	0.65	–0–
Worker D (hours per unit)	–0–	0.60	–0–	0.65
Worker E (hours per unit)	0.30	0.40	0.30	0.45

Required:

a. Use the traditional approach to calculate net profits.

b. Assuming each worker can work only 175 hours per month, calculate the net profits using the TOC approach.

SOLUTION TO DEMONSTRATION PROBLEM 1

a. Total sales:

Model 110: 140 × $125 = $17,500
Model 120: 150 × $170 = 25,500
Model 210: 100 × $150 = 15,000
Model 220: 135 × $200 = 27,000
$85,000

Total raw material costs:

Model 110: 140 × $55 = $ 7,700
Model 120: 150 × $80 = 12,000
Model 210: 100 × $65 =   6,500
Model 220: 135 × $90 = 12,150
$38,350

Net profit = [$85,000 − ($38,350 + $30,500)] = $16,150

b. Constraint calculation:

HOURS REQUIRED PER MONTH TO PRODUCE MARKET DEMAND

WORKER	MODEL 110	MODEL 120	MODEL 210	MODEL 220	TOTAL
A	70	75	–0–	–0–	145
B	–0–	–0–	60	81	141
C	91	–0–	65	–0–	156
D	–0–	90	–0–	87.75	177.75
E	42	60	30	60.75	192.75

Worker E is the constraint.

ITEM	MODEL 110	MODEL 120	MODEL 210	MODEL 220
Sales price (SP)	$125	$170	$150	$200
Raw material costs (RM)	$55	$80	$65	$90
Contribution (C = SP − RM)	$70	$90	$85	$110
Constraint hours	0.30	0.40	0.30	0.45
Dollars per constraint hour	$233.33	$225.00	$283.33	$244.44

Therefore, Matador needs to maximize 210, then 220, then 110, and finally 120.

PRODUCT	NUMBER OF UNITS	CONSTRAINT HOURS	TOTAL HOURS	REMAINING HOURS
Model 210	100	0.30	30	145
Model 220	135	0.45	60.75	84.25
Model 110	140	0.30	42	42.25
Model 120	105	0.40	42	0.25 (unusable)

Note: 105 is used because that is all that can be produced with the 42.25 hours remaining (42.25 ÷ 0.40 = 105.6 or 105).

Thus,

PRODUCT	NUMBER OF UNITS	CONTRIBUTION	TOTAL
Model 210	100	$ 85	$ 8,500
Model 220	135	110	14,850
Model 110	140	70	9,800
Model 120	105	90	9,450
		Total sales	$42,600
		Operating expense	<$30,500>
		Net profit	$12,100

■ **DEMONSTRATION PROBLEM 2**   *Elevating constraints.*

As detailed in Demonstration Problem 1, Matador Equipment Company has a constraint with worker E that prevents the company from producing enough model 120s to meet market demand. Management is considering two options to eliminate the constraint: Option 1 is to add an additional part-time worker E for 100 hours a month at an additional operating expense of $2,000 per month. Option 2 is to implement a change of worker duties that would result in an overall increase in direct labor time for each product as follows:

HOURS PER UNIT

	MODEL 110	MODEL 120	MODEL 210	MODEL 220
Direct labor	1.50	1.60	1.60	1.75
Worker A	0.60	0.55	–0–	–0–
Worker B	–0–	–0–	0.70	0.70
Worker C	0.65	–0–	0.65	–0–
Worker D	–0–	0.65	–0–	0.65
Worker E	0.25	0.40	0.25	0.40

Required:
Should management agree to increase the direct labor times for each product? In each option, what would be the new constraint?

SOLUTION TO DEMONSTRATION PROBLEM 2

Option 1. Constraint calculation:

HOURS REQUIRED PER MONTH TO PRODUCE MARKET DEMAND

WORKER	MODEL 110	MODEL 120	MODEL 210	MODEL 220	TOTAL	PERCENTAGE AVAILABLE[a]
A	70	75	–0–	–0–	145	83
B	–0–	–0–	60	81	141	81
C	91	–0–	65	–0–	156	89
D	–0–	90	–0–	87.75	177.75	102
E	42	60	30	60.75	192.75	70

[a] The percentage available for workers A, B, C, and D is based on the standard 175 hours per month. For worker E, the percentage available is based on 275 hours (175 standard hours plus 100 part-time hours).

Worker D is now the constraint.

ITEM	MODEL 110	MODEL 120	MODEL 210	MODEL 220
Sales price (SP)	$125	$170	$150	$200
Raw material costs (RM)	$55	$80	$65	$90
Contribution (C = SP − RM)	$70	$90	$85	$110
Constraint hours	–0–	0.60	–0–	0.65
Dollars per constraint hour	∞	$150.00	∞	$169.23

Therefore, the company can produce the market demand for models 110 and 210. For these models, the market is the constraint. Then the company needs to maximize model 220, then model 120.

PRODUCT	NUMBER OF UNITS	CONSTRAINT HOURS	TOTAL HOURS	REMAINING HOURS
Model 110	140	–0–	–0–	175
Model 210	100	–0–	–0–	175
Model 220	135	0.65	87.75	87.25
Model 120	145	0.60	87.00	0.25 (unusable)

Thus,

PRODUCT	NUMBER OF UNITS	CONTRIBUTION	TOTAL
Model 110	140	$70	$ 9,800
Model 210	100	85	8,500
Model 220	135	110	14,850
Model 120	145	90	13,050
		Total sales	$46,200
		Operating expense	<$32,500>
		Net profit	$13,700

Difference in net profit = ($13,700 after elevating E constraint − $12,100 before elevating E constraint)
= $1,600

Option 2. Constraint calculation:

HOURS REQUIRED PER MONTH TO PRODUCE MARKET DEMAND

WORKER	MODEL 110	MODEL 120	MODEL 210	MODEL 220	TOTAL	PERCENTAGE AVAILABLE
A	84	82.50	–0–	–0–	166.50	95
B	–0–	–0–	70	94.5	164.50	94
C	91	–0–	65	–0–	156	89
D	–0–	97.50	–0–	87.75	185.25	106
E	35	60	25	54	174	99

Worker D is now the constraint.

Since the constraint is the same as Option 1, the product totals would be calculated similarly. Thus, the net profit would be:

PRODUCT	NUMBER OF UNITS	CONTRIBUTION	TOTAL
Model 110	140	$ 70	$ 9,800
Model 210	100	85	8,500
Model 220	135	110	14,850
Model 120	134	90	$12,060
		Total sales	$45,210
		Operating expense	<$30,500>
		Net profit	$14,710

Difference in net profit = ($14,710 after an overall increase in direct labor time − $12,100 before elevating constraints)
= $2,610

As Option 2 creates the larger net profit, it should be implemented even though it increases the direct labor hours for each product.

REVIEW QUESTIONS

15.1 What kind of performance measurements offer the best way to evaluate the performance of an enterprise?

    a. Local.
    b. Global.
    c. Throughput.
    d. Elevated.

15.2 What are the two different ways the process of focusing can be described?

15.3 Effective performance measurements must show the correlation between actions and what global goal?

15.4 Which of the following quantities is limited by zero?

    a. Throughput.
    b. Net profit.
    c. Operating expense.
    d. Productivity.

15.5 Name and describe the management orientation that supports continuous improvement.

15.6 List and describe the steps of the focusing process from the perspective of the system to be improved.

15.7 List and describe the steps of the focusing process from the perspective of the improvement process itself.

15.8 Which of the following lists reflects the way the cost world orientation prioritizes operating expense, inventory, and throughput?

    a. Operating expense, throughput, inventory.
    b. Throughput, inventory, operating expense.
    c. Sales, inventory, cost.
    d. Inventory, operating expense, throughput.

15.9 Describe the concept of a constraint and its effect on the throughput chain.

15.10 When a constraint has been broken during the focusing process, what undesirable effect might become a new system constraint?

15.11 Name and describe the three evolutionary steps of a science.

15.12 Which of the following terms would not pertain to the method of evaporating clouds?

    a. Simple solutions.
    b. Reexamining organizational foundations.
    c. Core problems.
    d. Compromise.

15.13 Describe how the Socratic method motivates people to change.

15.14 Which of the following is the primary reason for an organization's psychological resistance to change?

    a. Threatened security.
    b. Fear of failure.
    c. "Ownership" of an idea.
    d. Lack of improvement.

15.15 Describe the condition that is necessary before any significant implementation of the theory of constraints can begin.

15.16 Describe how the theory of constraints should be implemented when JIT and TQM systems already exist in an organization.

❙ CHAPTER-SPECIFIC PROBLEMS

These problems require responses based directly on concepts and techniques presented in the text.

15.17 ***Applying the five steps of focusing to your daily life.*** The five steps of focusing can be applied to your daily life. Let's assume you find yourself constantly running out of time. There are simply not enough hours in a day for school, work, and family life.

    Required:
    Apply the five focusing steps to your own personal "throughput chain." If, for example, commuting to and from school and work is limiting the time you have for other activities, you might identify your long commute as a constraint. One possible way to elevate this constraint is to move closer to your workplace or school. Identify at least three other constraints and elevate them.

15.18 ***Prioritizing in the cost orientation world and the throughput orientation world.*** Following are groups of accounting quantities, relationships, or performance measurements:

GROUP I	GROUP II
Work-in-process inventory	Raw materials inventory
Machine downtime	Insurance premiums
Utilities expense	Worker productivity

GROUP III	GROUP IV
Labor costs	Buffers or kanbans
Transfer batch size	Machine setup costs
Sales forecasts	Product pricing

Required:

a. You are an old-school "cost world" manager who is dubious about the new-fangled ways. Prioritize the items within each group according to the attention you will give them in the daily operation of your manufacturing plant.

b. Your feet are planted firmly in the "throughput world." Prioritize the items within each group according to the attention you will give them in the daily operation of your manufacturing plant.

15.19 *Classifying items by cost and throughput world orientations.* Rick and Ralph, managers at Table Rockers, Inc., have responsibility for separate production lines that manufacture the company's single product, the table rocker, which is used by small shipping companies to provide a steady table top for ship restaurants. Rick manages by cost, while Ralph manages by throughput.

Required:

Determine which of the following items would be valued by Rick's management orientation. By Ralph's management orientation.

Machine capacity	Ineffective distribution
Energy expenditures	Maintenance contract fee
Auditing expenses	Painting charge
Unreliable suppliers	Poor machine maintenance
Labor costs	Supplies outlay
Restricted amount of raw materials	

15.20 *Identifying the constraint.* Nome & Fitz, Inc., produces specialty pencils for sale to its market in Japan. Three processes are used to produce the pencils: drilling, inserting, and packaging. Each of these processes is performed at a separate station.

Required:

a. Draw a diagram to show the entire process.

b. Given the following information, identify the constraint:
- The drilling function (D) can drill 20,000 pencils per hour.
- The inserting function (I) can insert 2,500 pencils per seven-minute period.
- The packaging function (P) can pack 9,000 pencils per half-hour.

c. What options can management take to elevate the constraint?

15.21 *Determining the impact of elevating local constraints.* Fred Andrews, manager of manufacturing at Kendrix & Son, has just taken a class in the theory of constraints. Fred's department fits into the throughput chain in the following manner:

Fred's department

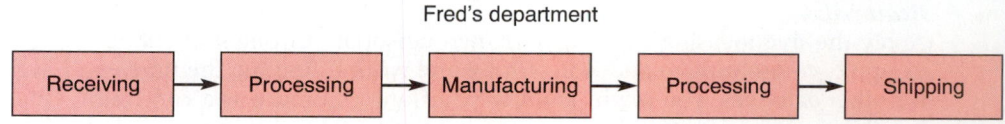

Receiving → Processing → Manufacturing → Processing → Shipping

Fred identifies constraints in his department and implements corrective actions to elevate the constraints. He is the only department manager who is attempting this, however.

Required:

Explain the likely outcome of Fred's actions and how you would have attempted to improve throughput at Kendrix & Son.

15.22 ***Making a product mix decision.*** Sanatos Company makes and sells three products: A, B, and C. The following data relate to these products:

	A	B	C
Demand in units	110	100	90
Selling price per unit	$90	$110	$95
Raw material costs per unit	$40	$50	$50
Constraint C2 minutes per unit	10	15	5

Required:

a. Calculate the contribution per constraint minute for each product.
b. Determine the product mix. The total number of minutes available is 2,450 per day.

15.23 ***Identifying constraints.*** AmeriRug will begin to produce and sell one-size-fits-all wigs in two colors: blonde and brown. The brown wig is projected to be the better seller with sales of 100 wigs per week, whereas the blonde wigs will only have sales of 50 per week. AmeriRug determined, via benchmarking, that the following five factory workers will perform as follows: Al, the hair sorter, spends 15 minutes per blonde wig and only 10 minutes per brown wig; Betty, who glues the hair to the cap, spends 10 minutes per blonde wig and 20 minutes per brown wig; Charles, who trims and styles, takes 5 minutes and 15 minutes for each blonde and brown wig, respectively; Diana wraps and packs each blonde wig in 25 minutes, and Ed wraps and packs each brown wig in 20 minutes.

Required:

Determine the constraint for this wig factory if each worker can only work 2,100 minutes per week.

15.24 ***Calculating product mix.*** TillAll is a large manufacturer of three types of farm implements: plows, tills, and knives. The following table shows pertinent information for each product:

	PLOWS	TILLS	KNIVES
Sales price	$250	$200	$150
Raw material costs	$100	$100	$75
Worker A time (minutes)	–0–	30	30
Worker B time (minutes)	20	10	5
Worker C time (minutes)	20	–0–	5

Required:

Assuming that the operating expense is $1.25 per worker minute, calculate the profit margin for each product (profit margin is defined as Sales − [Raw material costs + Operating expense]), and determine the product mix based on this traditional approach. Then, assuming worker B is the constraint, determine the product mix based on the TOC approach. Compare the two results and comment.

15.25 ***Importance of throughput.*** A manufacturer is considering implementing JIT, TQM, and/or TOC. The company anticipates that JIT will reduce inventory by 4% per year, TQM will reduce operating expense 5% per year, and TOC will increase throughput by 3% per year. Current operating expense is $1,000,000 per year, inventory is $500,000, and throughput is $2,000,000 per year.

Required:

a. Plot the net profit and return on inventory for the next 20 years for the three changes. What do the results say about the world-class orientation of prioritizing throughput?
b. Assume that all three changes are implemented together. Plot the net profit

and return on inventory for the next 20 years. Do the three changes work together or against each other?

15.26 *Calculating the product mix priority by the traditional approach and the TOC approach.* Nichols Company produces and sells products A, B, and C. Following are data pertaining to these products:

	A	B	C
Selling price	$9.00	$9.50	$4.40
Materials	$3.00	$2.20	$1.00
Labor	$1.50	$2.10	$.90
Overhead	$2.10	$2.90	$1.50
Constraint time	.40	.45	.20

Required:
a. Calculate the optimum product mix priority using the traditional approach.
b. Calculate the optimum product mix priority using the TOC approach.

Note: The optimum mix priority means the product produced first, the one produced second, and the one produced third. For example, the optimum mix may be to produce product B, then product C, and finally product A. Thus, the optimum mix would be:

PRODUCT	PRIORITY
B	1
C	2
A	3

THINK-TANK PROBLEMS

Although these problems are based on chapter material, reading extra material, reviewing previous chapters, and using creativity may be required to develop workable solutions.

15.27 *Discussing the change in direct labor costs.* Ninety years ago, overhead in a manufacturing operation was probably about 10% of direct labor costs. Today, due in large part to increasing automation, overhead may be as much as five or ten times the direct labor cost. Explain how this transformation has resulted in labor being essentially a fixed cost in most manufacturing enterprises today.

15.28 *Determining a monthly production schedule.* Bakker Industries sells three products (products 611, 613, and 615), which it manufactures in a factory consisting of four departments (Departments 1 through 4). Both labor and machine time are applied to the products in each of the four departments. The machine processing and labor skills required in each department are such that neither machines nor labor can be switched from one department to another.

Bakker's management is planning its production schedule for the next several months. There are labor shortages in the community. Some of the machines will be out of service for extensive overhauling. Available machine and labor time by department for each of the next six months are as follows:

	MONTHLY CAPACITY AVAILABILITY (BY DEPARTMENT)			
	1	2	3	4
Normal machine capacity in machine hours	3,500	3,500	3,000	3,500
Capacity of machines being repaired in machine hours	<500>	<400>	<300>	<200>
Available machine capacity in machine hours	3,000	3,100	2,700	3,300
Labor capacity in direct labor hours	4,000	4,500	3,500	3,000
Available labor in direct labor hours	3,700	4,500	2,750	2,600

LABOR AND MACHINE
SPECIFICATIONS PER UNIT OF PRODUCT

PRODUCT	LABOR AND MACHINE TIME	DEPARTMENT 1	DEPARTMENT 2	DEPARTMENT 3	DEPARTMENT 4
611	Direct labor hours	2	3	3	1
	Machine hours	2	1	2	2
613	Direct labor hours	1	2	—	2
	Machine hours	1	1	—	2
615	Direct labor hours	2	2	1	1
	Machine hours	2	2	1	1

The Sales Department's forecast of product demand over the next six months is as follows:

PRODUCT	MONTHLY SALES VOLUME
611	500 units
613	400 units
615	1,000 units

Bakker's inventory levels will not be increased or decreased during the next six months. The unit price and cost data valid for the next six months follow:

PRODUCT

	611	613	615
Unit costs:			
Direct materials	$ 7	$ 13	$ 17
Direct labor			
Department 1	12	6	12
Department 2	21	14	14
Department 3	24	—	16
Department 4	9	18	9
Variable overhead	27	20	25
Fixed overhead	15	10	32
Variable selling	3	2	4
Unit selling price	$196	$123	$167

Required:
a. Determine if the monthly sales demand for the three products can be met by Bakker Industries' factory. Use the monthly requirement by department for machine hours and direct labor hours for the production of products 611, 613, and 615 in your calculations.
b. What monthly production schedule should Bakker Industries select in order to maximize its dollar profits? Support the schedule with appropriate calculations, and present a schedule of the contribution to profit that would be generated by the production schedule selected.

[CMA adapted]

15.29 *Subordinating nonconstraints.* A recent TOC analysis of a local manufacturer identified the heat treating activity as the constraint for a production line. The line also includes the cold stamping and the forming activities before heat treating, and the painting and the packing activities after.

Required:
Traditional performance measurements focused on individual activity efficiency, and workers have been diligent in attempting to maximize their measurement. In light of the TOC approach, where every activity is subordinate to the constraint, what performance measurements would you select for the upstream and downstream activities?

15.30 *Using the evaporating clouds method.* At Electrico, management determined that its global goal should be to maximize profit and shareholder value. The method it selected to achieve this goal was to reduce the expenditures of a few large nonprofit-generating departments. The major portion of the expenditure reduction occurred in the Lines department. The budget reduction significantly reduced line maintenance and tree trimming, transformer replacements, and upgrading of utility line posts.

As a result of this decision, management markedly reduced budgeted expenses. At the same time, however, the strategy increased the expenditures for emergency and unplanned outages. This reduced profits and shareholder value as well as significantly increasing the number of customer complaints.

Required:

Use the evaporating clouds method to develop a better solution to maximizing profits and shareholder value at Electrico. (Remember, try to keep your solution[s] as simple as possible.)

15.31 **Using the Socratic method.** John D. Ere, a line supervisor of the light manufacturing processes, has been with the company for 20 years. He is dedicated to the company, but tends to want things always to be done his way. Jean Yuss, supervisor of the heavy manufacturing activities, is a hard worker and very intelligent. She will implement anything you request, but does not take the initiative to go farther than your specific instructions.

Required:

Discuss how the Socratic method can help you, as a new supervisor of John and Jean, to implement the continuous improvement mentality of JIT, TQM, and TOC that your traditional manufacturing company desperately needs.

15.32 **Achieving synergism.** JIT, TQM, and TOC are supposed to work toward the same objective, which is to increase profits now and in the future. Together, they interact and actually enhance the performance of each element.

Required:

a. Explain the individual goal for the following:
   1. JIT.
   2. TQM.
   3. TOC.
b. Discuss the overall goal of JIT, TQM, and TOC.

15.33 **Using the Socratic method.** Mabel, recently promoted to department manager, is having a problem with employee theft as her employees test her management ability and the system. Mabel comes to you, her mentor, for help in solving this employee problem. You decide that this is a good opportunity to build her managerial skills and confidence by employing the Socratic method. Based on your experience, you recognize that the solution to the problem is to prohibit employees from bringing bags, newspapers, and the like into the cash handling and inventory areas.

Required:

Further develop the following scenario using the Socratic method to guide Mabel in identifying the above solution.

Mabel: Do you have a moment? I've got a situation I need some help with.
You: Sure, Mabel, come on in.
Mabel: Well, I've been noticing a lot of cash and inventory variances. I'm pretty sure these variances are being caused by employee theft.
You: Yes, and . . .
Mabel: Well, I was wondering what you would suggest to stop this.

15.34 **Charging a manager for bottlenecks.** "Dollar days of inventory" treats inventory as a loan from the bank. The WIP inventory passing through Department A stays in the department five days, and the department is charged for this loan.

Required:

a. Assume that the average value of WIP inventory in Department A is $20,000.

Calculate the amount of "dollar days of inventory" that should be charged to Department A's manager.

b. If the WIP inventory sitting in Department A is caused by a bottleneck (constraint) in the department, discuss the likely behavior of Department A's manager when she is charged with dollar days of inventory.

c. Comment on how the dollar days of inventory measurement may induce desirable behavior for other managers in an organization, such as the marketing and purchasing manager.

d. Discuss why throughput focuses on products *sold* rather than products *produced*.

16 LINEAR PROGRAMMING: THE GRAPHICAL AND SIMPLEX METHODS

Cray Research Supercomputers are needed to run sophisticated LP models.

LEARNING OBJECTIVES

After studying this chapter, you should be able to:

1. Explain linear programming and its components and assumptions.

2. Describe the graphical method, and apply it in solving both maximization and minimization linear programming problems.

3. Describe the simplex method, and use it in solving both maximization and minimization linear programming problems.

4. Discuss Karmarkar's method of solving linear programming problems.

■ INTRODUCTION

Linear programming (LP) is an application of matrix algebra used to solve a broad class of problems that can be represented by a system of linear equations. A **linear equation** is an algebraic equation whose variable quantity or quantities are in the first power only and whose graph is a straight line. LP problems are characterized by an objective function that is to be maximized or minimized, subject to a number of constraints. Both the objective function and the constraints must be formulated in terms of a linear equality or inequality. Typically, the objective function will be to maximize profits (e.g., contribution margin) or to minimize costs (e.g., variable costs). The following assumptions must be satisfied to justify the use of linear programming:

- *Linearity.* All functions, such as costs, prices, and technological requirements, must be linear in nature.
- *Certainty.* All parameters are assumed to be known with certainty.
- *Nonnegativity.* Negative values of decision variables are unacceptable.

Two approaches are commonly used to solve LP problems:

- Graphical method
- Simplex method

The **graphical method** is limited to LP problems involving two decision variables and a limited number of constraints due to the difficulty of graphing and evaluating more than two decision variables. This restriction severely limits the use of the graphical method for real-world problems. The graphical method is presented first here, however, because it is simple and easy to understand.

The computer-based **simplex method** is much more powerful than the graphical method and provides the optimal solution to LP problems containing thousands of decision variables and constraints. It uses an iterative algorithm to solve for the optimal solution. Moreover, the simplex method provides information on slack variables (unused resources) and shadow prices (opportunity costs) that is useful in performing sensitivity analysis. ■

■ CONSTRUCTING LINEAR PROGRAMMING PROBLEMS AND SOLVING THEM GRAPHICALLY

We will use the following Bridgeway Company case to introduce the graphical method and illustrate how it solves LP maximization problems. Bridgeway Company manufactures a printer and keyboard. The contribution margins of the printer and keyboard are $30 and $20, respectively. Two types of skilled labor are required to manufacture these products: soldering and assembling. A printer requires 2 hours of soldering and 1 hour of assembling. A keyboard requires 1 hour of soldering and 1 hour of assembling. Bridgeway has 1,000 soldering hours and 800 assembling hours available per week. There are no constraints on the supply of raw materials. Demand for keyboards is unlimited, but at most 350 printers are sold each week. Bridgeway wishes to maximize its weekly total contribution margin.

■ Constructing the Linear Programming Problem for Maximization of the Objective Function

Constructing the LP problem requires four steps:

Step 1. Define the decision variables.

Step 2. Define the objective function.
Step 3. Determine the constraints.
Step 4. Declare sign restrictions.

Agribusiness cost management requires an optimized balance of constraints.

STEP 1: DEFINE THE DECISION VARIABLES. In any LP problem, the **decision variables** should completely describe the decisions to be made. Bridgeway must decide how many printers and keyboards should be manufactured each week. With this in mind, the decision variables are defined as follows:

$$X = \text{Number of printers to produce weekly}$$
$$Y = \text{Number of keyboards to produce weekly}$$

STEP 2: DEFINE THE OBJECTIVE FUNCTION. The **objective function** represents the goal that management is trying to achieve. The goal in Bridgeway's case is to maximize (max) total contribution margin. For each printer that is sold, $30 in contribution margin will be realized. For each keyboard that is sold, $20 in contribution margin will be realized. Thus, the total contribution margin for Bridgeway can be expressed by the following objective function equation:

$$\max Z = \$30X + \$20Y$$

where the variable Z denotes the objective function value of any LP problem. In the Bridgeway case, Z equals the total contribution margin that will be realized when an optimal mix of products X (printer) and Y (keyboard) is manufactured and sold.

STEP 3: DETERMINE THE CONSTRAINTS. A **constraint** is simply some limitation under which the enterprise must operate, such as limited production time or raw materials. In Bridgeway's case, the objective function grows larger as X and Y increase. In other words, if Bridgeway were free to choose any values for X and Y, the company could make an arbitrarily large contribution margin by choosing X and Y to be very large. The values of X and Y, however, are restricted by the following three constraints:

- *Constraint 1.* Each week, no more than 1,000 hours of soldering time may be used. Thus, constraint 1 may be expressed by:

$$2X + Y \leq 1{,}000$$

because it takes 2 hours of soldering to produce one printer and 1 hour of soldering to produce one keyboard. The inequality sign means that the total soldering time for both products X and Y cannot exceed the 1,000 soldering hours available, but could be less than the available hours.
- *Constraint 2.* Each week, no more than 800 hours of assembling time may be used. Thus, constraint 2 may be expressed by:

$$X + Y \leq 800$$

- *Constraint 3.* Because of limited demand, at most 350 printers should be produced each week. This constraint can be expressed as follows:

$$X \leq 350$$

STEP 4: DECLARE SIGN RESTRICTIONS. To complete the formulation of an LP problem, the following question must be answered for each decision

Choose production levels for printers (X) and keyboards (Y) that:

$$\max Z = \$30X + \$20Y \quad \text{(objective function)}$$

and satisfy the following:

$2X + Y \leq 1,000$	(soldering time constraint)
$X + Y \leq 800$	(assembling time constraint)
$X \leq 350$	(demand constraint for printers)
$X \geq 0$	(sign restriction)
$Y \geq 0$	(sign restriction)

■■■EXHIBIT 16–1
Summary of the Linear Programming Problem for Bridgeway Company

variable: Can the decision variable assume only nonnegative values, or is it allowed to assume both positive and negative values? In most LP problems, positive values are assumed. For example, in the Bridgeway case, production cannot be less than zero units. Therefore, the sign restrictions are:

$$X \geq 0$$
$$Y \geq 0$$

These four steps and the formulation of the LP problem for Bridgeway are summarized in Exhibit 16–1. This LP problem provides the necessary data to develop a graphical solution.

Graphical Solution to the Maximization Linear Programming Problem

The following are two of the most basic concepts associated with LP:

- Feasible region
- Optimal solution

The graphical solution involves two steps:

Step 1. Graphically determine the feasible region.
Step 2. Search for the optimal solution.

STEP 1: GRAPHICALLY DETERMINE THE FEASIBLE REGION.   The **feasible region** represents the set of all feasible solutions to an LP problem. In the Bridgeway case, the feasible region is the set of all points (X, Y) satisfying all of the following constraints:

$$2X + Y \leq 1,000$$
$$X + Y \leq 800$$
$$X \leq 350$$
$$X \geq 0$$
$$Y \geq 0$$

For a point (X, Y) to be in the feasible region, (X, Y) must satisfy all the above inequalities. A graph containing these constraint equations is shown in Exhibit 16–2. Note that the only points satisfying the nonnegativity constraints are the points in the first quadrant of the X, Y plane. This is indicated by the arrows pointing to the right from the y-axis and upward from the x-axis. Thus, any point that is outside the first quadrant cannot be in the feasible region.

In plotting equation $2X + Y \leq 1,000$ on the graph, the following questions are asked: How much of product X could be produced if all resources were

Feasible Region for the Bridgeway Problem

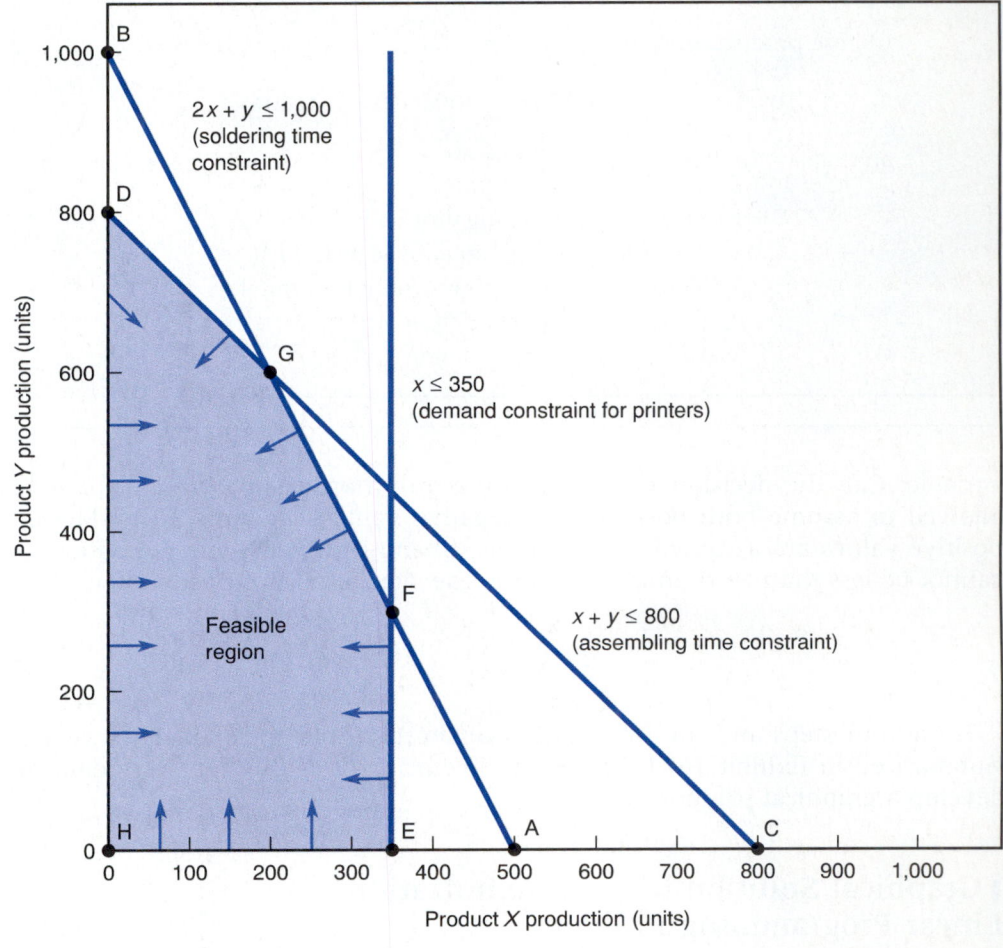

allocated to it? In this equation, a total of 1,000 hours of soldering time is available. If all 1,000 hours are allocated to product X, 500 printers can be produced each week. On the other hand, how much of product Y could be produced if all resources were allocated to it? If all 1,000 soldering hours are allocated to produce Y, then 1,000 keyboards can be produced each week. Thus, the line on the graph expressing the soldering time constraint equation extends from the 500-unit point A on the x-axis to the 1,000-unit point B on the y-axis.

The equation associated with the assembling capacity constraint has been plotted on the graph in a similar manner. If 800 assembling hours are allocated to product X, then 800 printers can be produced. If, on the other hand, 800 assembling hours are allocated to product Y, then 800 keyboards can be produced. This analysis results in line CD.

Since equation $X \leq 350$ concerns only product X, the line expressing the equation on the graph does not touch the y-axis at all. It extends from the 350-unit point E on the x-axis and runs parallel to the y-axis, thereby signifying that regardless of the number of units of X produced, no more than 350 units of X can ever be sold.

Exhibit 16–2 shows that the set of points in the quadrant that satisfies all constraints is bounded by the five-sided polygon HDGFE. Any point on this polygon or in its interior is in the feasible region. Any other point fails to satisfy at least one of the inequalities and thus falls outside the feasible region.

STEP 2: SEARCH FOR THE OPTIMAL SOLUTION. Having identified the feasible region for the Bridgeway case, we now search for the **optimal solu-**

tion, which will be the point in the feasible region that maximizes the objective function. In Bridgeway's case, this is:

$$\max Z = \$30X + \$20Y$$

To find the optimal solution, we graph lines so that all points on a particular line have the same Z-value. In a maximization problem, such lines are called **isoprofit lines;** in a minimization problem, they are called **isocost lines.** The parallel lines are created by assigning various values to Z in the objective function to provide either higher profits or lower costs.

A graph showing the isoprofit lines for Bridgeway Company appears in Exhibit 16–3. The isoprofit lines are broken to differentiate them from the lines that form the feasible region. To draw an isoprofit line, any Z-value is chosen, then the x- and y-intercepts are calculated. For example, a contribution margin value of $6,000 gives a line with intercepts at 200 printers and 300 keyboards:

$$\$6,000 = \$30X + \$20(0) \qquad \$6,000 = \$30(0) + \$20Y$$
$$X = 200 \qquad\qquad Y = 300$$

Since all isoprofit lines are of the form $\$30X + \$20Y$ = contribution margin, they all have the same slope. Consequently, once an isoprofit line is drawn, all other isoprofit lines can be found by moving parallel to the initial line. Another isoprofit line is found by selecting a contribution margin of $9,000, which gives a line having intercepts at 300 printers and 450 keyboards:

$$\$9,000 = \$30X + \$20(0) \qquad \$9,000 = \$30(0) + \$20Y$$
$$X = 300 \qquad\qquad Y = 450$$

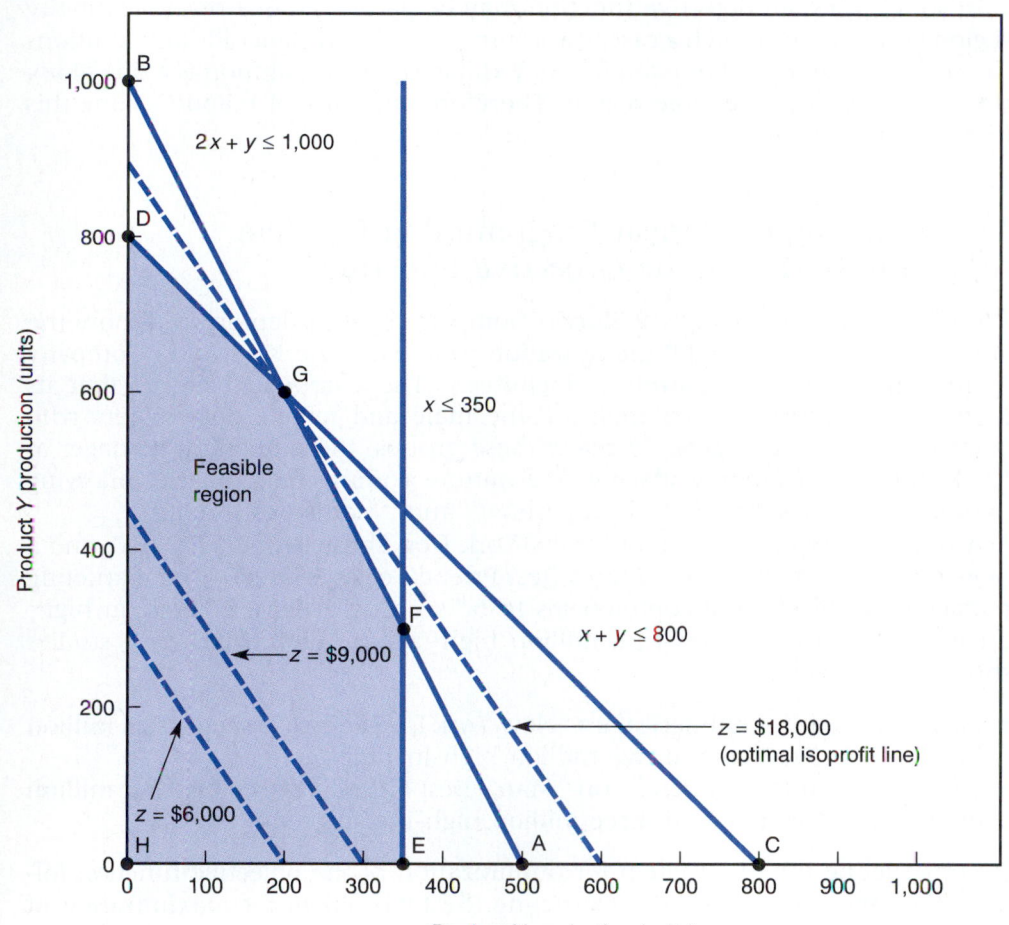

■■■EXHIBIT 16–3
Graph Showing the Optimal Solution of the Bridgeway Problem

Isoprofit lines move in a northeast direction; that is, upward and to the right. After a while, the isoprofit lines will no longer intersect the feasible region. The isoprofit line intersecting the last vertex of the feasible region defines the largest Z-value of any point in the feasible region and indicates the optimal solution to the LP problem. In Exhibit 16–3, the isoprofit line passing through point G is the last isoprofit line to intersect the feasible region. Thus, point G is the point in the feasible region with the largest Z-value and is therefore the optimal solution to the Bridgeway problem. Note that point G is located at the intersection of lines $2X + Y = 1,000$ and $X + Y = 800$. Solving these two equations simultaneously results in:

$$X = 200$$
$$Y = 600$$

The optimal value of Z (i.e., the total contribution margin) may be found by substituting these values of X and Y into the objective function. Thus, the optimal value of Z is:

$$\max Z = \$30(200) + \$20(600)$$
$$= \underline{\underline{\$18,000}}$$

The five corners of the feasible region, designated by HDGFE, will yield different product mixes between X and Y. The calculations are presented in Exhibit 16–4, starting at the origin and going clockwise around the feasible region. These calculations also show that the optimal production mix is 200 printers and 600 keyboards. Any other production mix will result in a lower total contribution margin.

In some cases, an objective function may be parallel to one of the feasibility region boundaries. In such a case, the optimal solution will include any solutions that lie on the border. For example, in Exhibit 16–5 the solution is a line along the boundary of the feasible region. Therefore, any mix of E and C along this line will be optimal.

Constructing the Linear Programming Problem for Minimization of the Objective Function

We will use the following K9 Kondo Company case to demonstrate how the graphical method solves LP minimization problems. The K9 Kondo Company manufactures climate-controlled doghouses. The company believes that its high-volume customers are high-income male and female dog owners who want to pamper their pets. To reach these groups, the marketing manager at K9 Kondo is considering placing one-minute commercials on the following national TV shows: "New York Dog Show" and "Man's Best Friend."

A one-minute commercial on "New York Dog Show" costs $200,000, and a one-minute commercial on "Man's Best Friend" costs $50,000. The marketing manager would like the commercials to be seen by at least 60 million high-income women and at least 36 million high-income men. Marketing studies show the following:

■ Each one-minute commercial on "New York Dog Show" is seen by six million high-income women and two million high-income men.
■ Each one-minute commercial on "Man's Best Friend" is seen by three million high-income women and three million high-income men.

Constructing the LP problem for minimization of the objective function follows the same steps used in constructing the LP problem for maximization of the objective function:

Corner of the Feasible Region	Units Produced	
	X	Y
H	–0–	–0–
D	–0–	800
G	200	600
F	350	300
E	350	–0–

	X	Y	Total Contribution Margin
H:	$30(0)	+ $20(0) =	$ –0–
D:	$30(0)	+ $20(800) =	$16,000
G:	$30(200)	+ $20(600) =	$18,000*
F:	$30(350)	+ $20(300) =	$16,500
E:	$30(350)	+ $20(0) =	$10,500

* Optimal solution.

EXHIBIT 16–4
Z-Value for Each Corner in the Feasible Region

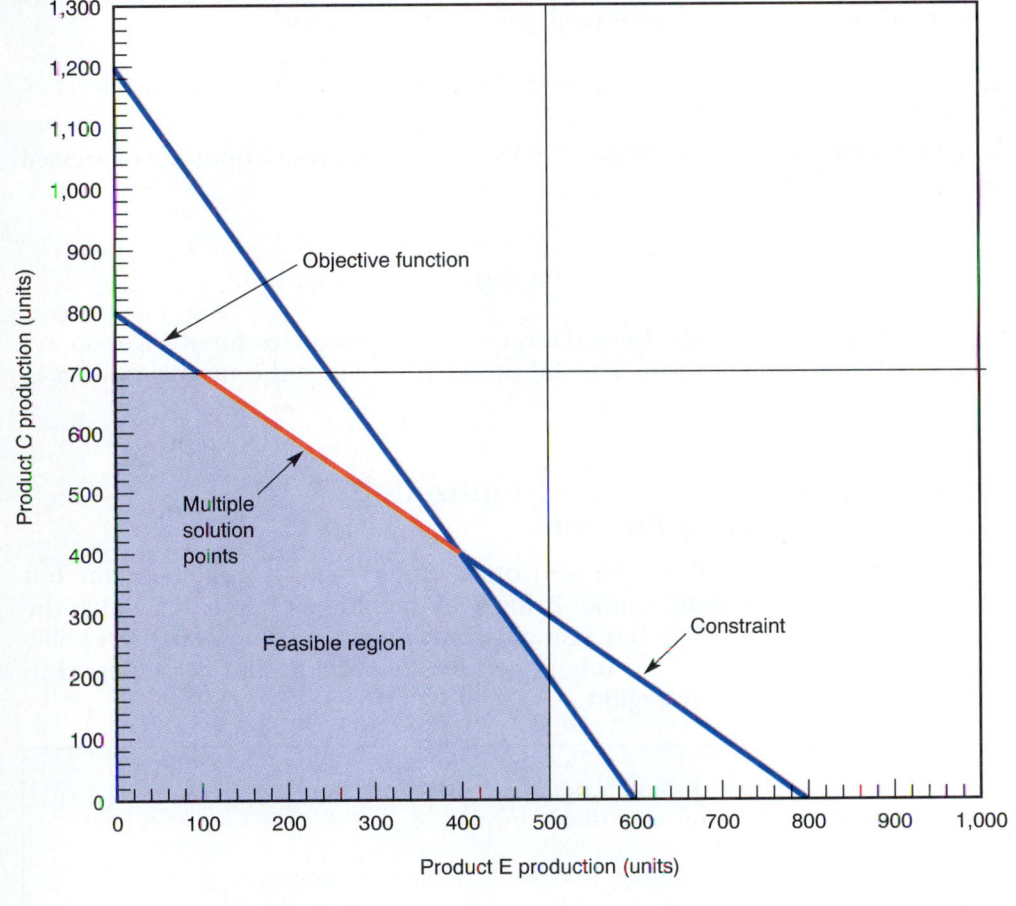

EXHIBIT 16–5
Multiple Optimal Solutions Graphic Example

Step 1. Define the decision variables.
Step 2. Define the objective function.
Step 3. Determine the constraints.
Step 4. Declare sign restrictions.

STEP 1: DEFINE THE DECISION VARIABLES. The marketing manager at K9 Kondo must decide how many "New York Dog Show" and "Man's Best

Friend" one-minute commercials to purchase. Therefore, the decision variables are:

X = Number of one-minute "New York Dog Show" commercials purchased

Y = Number of one-minute "Man's Best Friend" commercials purchased

STEP 2: DEFINE THE OBJECTIVE FUNCTION. The marketing manager is trying to minimize total advertising cost. Thus, the objective function (in thousands of dollars) is:

$$\min Z = \$200X + \$50Y$$

STEP 3: DETERMINE THE CONSTRAINTS. The values of X and Y are restricted by the following constraints:

■ *Constraint 1.* The commercials must reach at least 60 million high-income women. Thus, constraint 1 may be expressed by:

$$6X + 3Y \geq 60$$

■ *Constraint 2.* The commercials must reach at least 36 million high-income men. Thus, constraint 2 may be expressed by:

$$2X + 3Y \geq 36$$

STEP 4: DECLARE SIGN RESTRICTIONS. The sign restrictions are expressed by:

$$X \geq 0$$
$$Y \geq 0$$

These four steps and the formulation of the LP problem for K9 Kondo are summarized in Exhibit 16–6. This LP problem provides the necessary data to develop a graphical solution.

▌Graphical Solution to the Minimization Linear Programming Problem

Like the Bridgeway problem, the K9 Kondo problem has a feasible region, but K9 Kondo's feasible region, unlike Bridgeway's, contains points for which the value of at least one variable can assume arbitrarily large values. Such a feasible region is sometimes called an unbounded feasible region, but it is referred to here as simply the feasible region.

■EXHIBIT 16–6

Summary of the Linear Programming Problem for K9 Kondo Company

Choose number of commercials on "New York Dog Show" (X) and "Man's Best Friend" (Y) that:

$$\min Z = \$200X + \$50Y \quad \text{(objective function)}$$

and satisfy the following:

$$6X + 3Y \geq 60 \quad \text{(high-income women constraint)}$$
$$2X + 3Y \geq 36 \quad \text{(high-income men constraint)}$$
$$X \geq 0 \quad \text{(sign restriction)}$$
$$Y \geq 0 \quad \text{(sign restriction)}$$

The graphical solution includes two steps:

Step 1. Graphically determine the feasible region.
Step 2. Search for the optimal solution.

STEP 1: GRAPHICALLY DETERMINE THE FEASIBLE REGION.   The feasible region for K9 Kondo's advertising campaign is shown in Exhibit 16–7. Note that $6X + 3Y \geq 60$ is satisfied by points on or above the line AB and that $2X + 3Y \geq 36$ is satisfied by the points on or above the line CD. The only points satisfying all of the constraints are in the shaded region bounded by the *x*-axis, CEB, and the *y*-axis. This is the feasible region.

Line AB, which represents the plot of constraint $6X + 3Y \geq 60$, is determined by first plotting the end points of the line $6X + 3Y = 60$. Setting first Y and then X equal to 0, we have:

$$6X = 60 \qquad 3Y = 60$$
$$X = 10 \qquad Y = 20$$

Therefore, end point A is $X = 10$ and $Y = 0$, and end point B is $X = 0$ and $Y = 20$.

Next, the constraint $2X + 3Y \geq 36$ is plotted by first plotting the end points of the line $2X + 3Y = 36$. Again, setting first Y and then X equal to 0, we have:

$$2X = 36 \qquad 3Y = 36$$
$$X = 18 \qquad Y = 12$$

Manufacturing is subject to a number of constraints. Courtesy Honda of America Manufacturing, Inc.

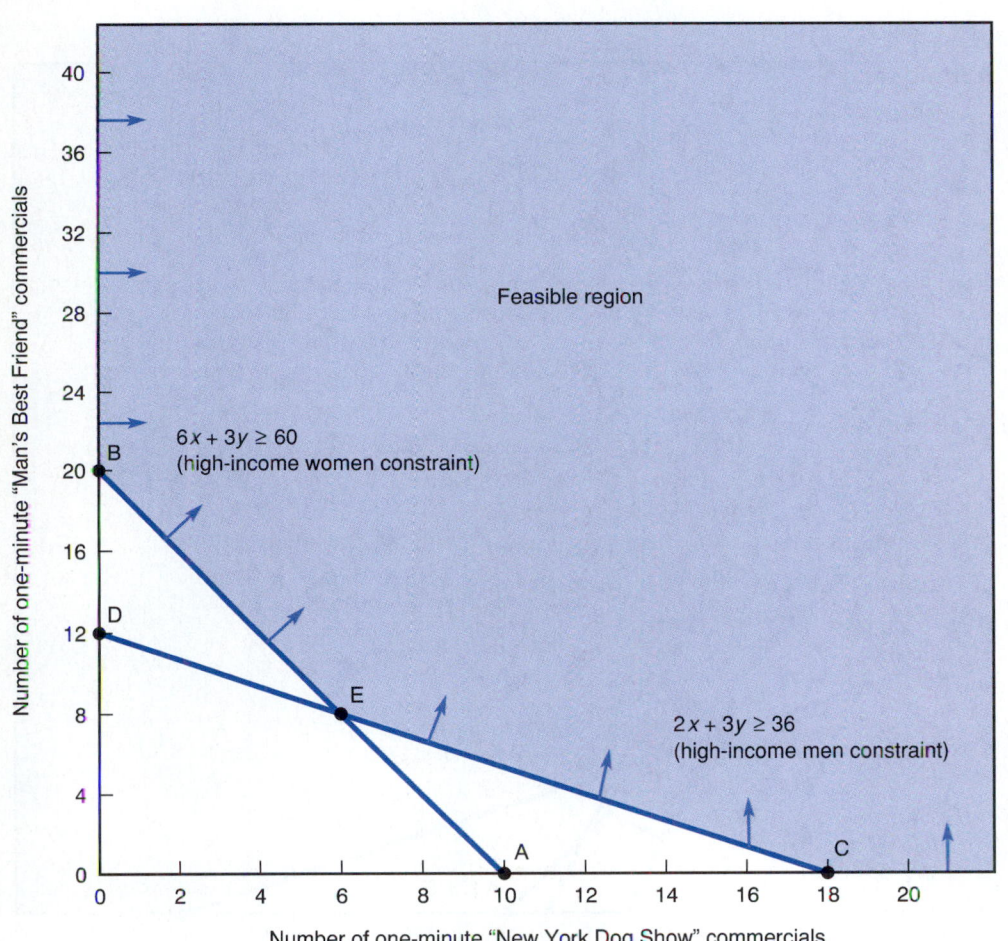

EXHIBIT 16–7
Feasible Region for the K9 Kondo Problem

Therefore, end point C is $X = 18$ and $Y = 0$, and end point D is $X = 0$ and $Y = 12$.

STEP 2: SEARCH FOR THE OPTIMAL SOLUTION. Note that instead of isoprofit lines these are isocost lines. The objective function is

$$\min Z = \$200X + \$50Y$$

and the marketing manager's goal is to minimize total advertising costs. Consequently, feasible values for X and Y that minimize Z must be chosen. Thus, the optimal solution to the K9 Kondo LP problem is the point in the feasible region with the *smallest Z*-value.

Consider an arbitrary cost of $1,800,000. That is, $Z = \$1,800$ and the isocost line is

$$\$1,800 = \$200X + \$50Y$$

as shown in Exhibit 16–8. Another parallel isocost line $1,400 = \$200X + \$50Y$ is also shown in Exhibit 16–8. Thus, the direction of minimum cost (i.e., decreasing Z) is toward the southwest; that is, downward and to the left. At a cost of $800,000 ($Z = \$800$), the isocost line is beyond the feasible region and therefore does not represent a feasible solution. The optimum isocost line is the one that intersects point B, because this is the farthest southwest point in the feasible region. Thus, point B is the optimal solution to the K9 Kondo problem. Or stating it another way, point B has the smallest Z-value of any point in the feasible region.

EXHIBIT 16–8
Graph Showing The Optimal Solution for the K9 Kondo Problem

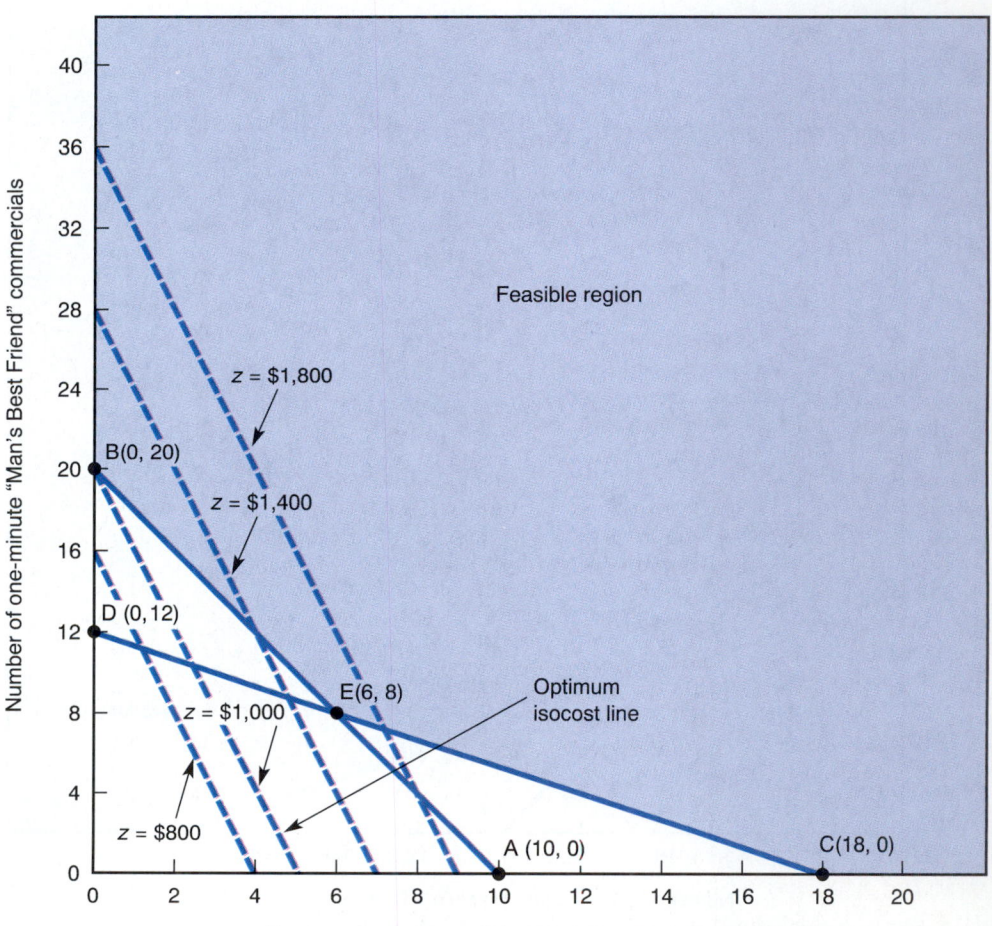

Notice that the set of feasible solutions has three corner points B, E, and C. By inspection, we see that:

$$B = (0, 20)$$
$$C = (18, 0)$$

Notice that point E is at the intersection of lines $6X + 3Y = 60$ and $2X + 3Y = 36$. Point E is obtained by finding the simultaneous solution to these two equations:

$$
\begin{array}{rcr}
6X + 3Y &=& 60 \\
-2X - 3Y &=& -36 \\
\hline
4X &=& 24 \\
X &=& 6
\end{array}
$$

Substituting $X = 6$ into $2X + 3Y = 36$ yields:

$$
\begin{array}{rcl}
2(6) + 3Y &=& 36 \\
3Y &=& 24 \\
Y &=& 8
\end{array}
$$

Thus, point E = $(X = 6, Y = 8)$.

Now, the corner points of BEC are tested. The three corners will yield different mixes of one-minute commercials on "New York Dog Show," represented by X, and on "Man's Best Friend," represented by Y. The calculations are presented in Exhibit 16–9. The optimal advertising plan is to purchase 20 one-minute commercials on "Man's Best Friend" and zero one-minute commercials on "New York Dog Show." The total optimal advertising cost is $1,000,000.

EXHIBIT 16–9
Z-Value for Each Corner in the Feasible Region

Corner of the Feasible Region	One-Minute Commercials Purchased	
	X	Y
B	–0–	20
E	6	8
C	18	–0–

	X	Y	Total Advertising Cost
B:	$200(0)	+ $50(20)	= $1,000,000*
E:	$200(6)	+ $50(8)	= $1,600,000
C:	$200(18)	+ $50(0)	= $3,600,000

* Optimal solution.

USING THE SIMPLEX METHOD TO SOLVE MAXIMIZATION PROBLEMS

LEARNING OBJECTIVE 3

Describe the simplex method, and use it in solving both maximization and minimization linear programming problems.

Solving LP problems graphically is only practical when there are two decision variables. Moreover, the graphical method becomes cumbersome when there are many constraints. Real-world LP problems typically have thousands of corner points.

Oil companies use linear pro-gramming to allocate resources.

The reigning champ for handling such problems is the *simplex method,* devised in 1947 by George B. Dantzig of Stanford University.[1] The simplex method provides an iterative algorithm that systematically locates feasible corner points that will improve the objective function value until the optimal solution is reached. Regardless of the number of decision variables and constraints, the simplex algorithm applies the key characteristic of any LP problem: An optimal solution always occurs at a corner point of the feasible region. The simplex algorithm finds corner-point solutions, tests them for optimality, and stops once an optimal solution is found.

Before discussing the simplex steps required to maximize an objective function, a few concepts from linear algebra must be introduced.[2] These concepts are relatively basic and can be explored further in any introductory linear algebra text.

Scalars, Matrices, and Vectors

The numbers used in daily life are called **scalars.** Scalars are simply single numbers, or variables used to identify single numbers. A number such as 8 is a scalar.

People who have used a spreadsheet such as Lotus 1-2-3 or who have done any computer programming already have a good understanding of the concept of a **matrix.** A matrix is a rectangular array of numbers having m rows and n columns; it is typically contained in brackets. For instance, one can refer to the 2×4 matrix $[A]$ and identify the individual numbers with a subscripted lower-case a, such as a_{ij}. In the following matrix, the subscripts i and j identify the row and column, respectively, of each matrix entry:

$$[A] = \begin{bmatrix} a_{11} & a_{12} & a_{13} & a_{14} \\ a_{21} & a_{22} & a_{23} & a_{24} \end{bmatrix}$$

A **vector** is a type of matrix having either an m dimension of 1 (row vector) or an n dimension of 1 (column vector). Here, a column vector **[b]** and a row vector **[c]** are shown below:

$$[\mathbf{b}] = \begin{bmatrix} b_1 \\ b_2 \\ b_3 \\ b_4 \end{bmatrix} \qquad [\mathbf{c}] = \begin{bmatrix} c_1 & c_2 & c_3 & c_4 \end{bmatrix}$$

Arithmetic Operations with Matrices and Vectors

Solving an LP problem by the simplex method requires three linear algebra operations: multiplying a vector by a matrix (which results in a vector), multiplying a vector by a vector (which results in a scalar), and subtracting a vector from a vector (which results in a vector).

To multiply a row vector by a matrix, the vector must have the same number of columns as the matrix has rows; otherwise, the operation is impossible. The following illustration shows how this multiplication is performed:

---

[1] William G. Wild, Jr., and Otis Port, ''The Startling Discovery Bell Labs Kept in the Shadows,'' *Business Week,* September 21, 1987, p. 69.

[2] Stewart Venit and Wayne Bishop, *Elementary Linear Algebra* (Boston: PWS Publishers, 1985).

$$[\mathbf{c}] \times [A] = [c_1 \quad c_2 \quad c_3] \begin{bmatrix} a_{11} & a_{12} & a_{13} & a_{14} \\ a_{21} & a_{22} & a_{23} & a_{24} \\ a_{31} & a_{32} & a_{33} & a_{34} \end{bmatrix}$$

$$= [(c_1 a_{11} + c_2 a_{21} + c_3 a_{31}) \quad (c_1 a_{12} + c_2 a_{22} + c_3 a_{32})$$
$$(c_1 a_{13} + c_2 a_{23} + c_3 a_{33}) \quad (c_1 a_{14} + c_2 a_{24} + c_3 a_{34})]$$

The entries in each column of the matrix are multiplied by the entries in the vector, then summed to produce the entries in the resulting row vector.

The next illustration demonstrates how a row vector may be multiplied by a column vector. The result is a scalar. This operation is just a special case of the preceding operation, as vectors are just special types of matrices. Again, the number of columns in the row vector is equal to the number of rows in the column vector:

$$[\mathbf{c}] \times [\mathbf{b}] = [c_1 \quad c_2 \quad c_3] \begin{bmatrix} b_1 \\ b_2 \\ b_3 \end{bmatrix}$$

$$= c_1 b_1 + c_2 b_2 + c_3 b_3$$

Finally, to subtract a row vector from a row vector, the first entry of the second vector is subtracted from the first entry of the first vector, which yields the first entry of the resulting row vector. The second entries of the vectors are then subtracted, yielding the second entry of the result, and so on until all entries have been subtracted:

$$[\mathbf{c}] - [\mathbf{d}] = [c_1 \quad c_2 \quad c_3] - [d_1 \quad d_2 \quad d_3]$$
$$= [(c_1 - d_1) \quad (c_2 - d_2) \quad (c_3 - d_3)]$$

Additionally, matrices are added and subtracted in a similar manner.

Row-Reduced Matrix Form

The number of nonzero rows in a matrix is known as its **rank.** A matrix column containing a single one (1) in any position, with the remaining column entries being zeros, is known as an **elementary column.** A matrix is said to be in **row-reduced form** if the number of elementary columns is equal to the rank of the matrix. The following matrices $[B]$, $[C]$, and $[D]$ serve as examples:

$$[B] = \begin{bmatrix} 1 & 3 & 1 & 0 \\ -1 & 2 & 0 & 1 \\ 0 & 0 & 0 & 0 \end{bmatrix} \quad [C] = \begin{bmatrix} 2 & 0 & 3 & 0 \\ 1 & 1 & 2 & 0 \\ 3 & 0 & 4 & 1 \end{bmatrix} \quad [D] = \begin{bmatrix} 2 & 0 & 0 & 2 & 1 \\ 1 & 1 & 0 & 1 & 0 \\ -1 & 0 & 1 & 4 & 0 \end{bmatrix}$$

Which of these are row-reduced matrices? $[B]$ is a row-reduced matrix, because its rank is 2 (only the top two rows are nonzero) and it has two elementary columns (3 and 4). $[D]$ is also row-reduced, since its rank is 3 and columns 2, 3, and 5 are elementary. However, $[C]$ is not row-reduced, since its rank is 3 but only columns 2 and 4 are elementary. One more elementary column is needed.

How might matrix $[C]$ be put into row-reduced form? That is, how can one more elementary column be created? Since each row of a matrix represents the coefficients of an equation, all the numbers in any row of a matrix can be multiplied by an appropriate constant without disrupting the meaning of the matrix. Thus, a particular value can be changed to a 1. Also, since the matrix represents a system of simultaneous linear equations, rows can legally be added or subtracted from each other. Consequently, the other values can be changed to zeros in the column where the 1 is. Multiplying the first row of matrix $[C]$ by 0.5 gives:

$$[C] = \begin{bmatrix} 1 & 0 & 1.5 & 0 \\ 1 & 1 & 2 & 0 \\ 3 & 0 & 4 & 1 \end{bmatrix}$$

which produces a 1 in the first position of row 1.

Next, row 1 is subtracted from row 2 to obtain:

$$[C] = \begin{bmatrix} 1 & 0 & 1.5 & 0 \\ 0 & 1 & 0.5 & 0 \\ 3 & 0 & 4 & 1 \end{bmatrix}$$

Finally, row 1 is subtracted from row 3 three times to get:

$$[C] = \begin{bmatrix} 1 & 0 & 1.5 & 0 \\ 0 & 1 & 0.5 & 0 \\ 0 & 0 & -0.5 & 1 \end{bmatrix}$$

which produces the needed zeros in the first column. Matrix $[C]$ is now in row-reduced form.

Pivoting a Matrix

The key to iteration in the simplex algorithm is a matrix procedure called **pivoting.** This is merely the row-reduction technique just presented; the goal is to obtain a one (1) in a particular position in the matrix, with all other column entries becoming zero. Once the pivot entry is chosen (which is a location in the matrix), the row and column containing the pivot entry are called the pivot row and pivot column, respectively. All the values in the pivot row are then divided by the value in the pivot entry position to obtain a one (1) in the pivot entry position. Then, the pivot row is used to obtain zeros in the rest of the pivot column by subtracting the pivot row the required number of times from the other rows. The matrix has now been "pivoted about" the pivot entry.

A Simplex Maximization Example

The simplex algorithm can be used to solve LP problems in which the goal is to maximize the objective function. The following example is necessarily simple to illustrate the mechanics of the algorithm; it could easily be solved graphically. The method is the same for more complex problems.[3] The simplex solution of a minimization LP problem is described in a later section.

The AeroTech machine shop has time available on three machines, and the shop's owner wishes to schedule production of two types of fastening pins. The owner's objective is to maximize the profit resulting from the proposed production run.

[3] Dakota Ulrich Greenwald, *Linear Programming: An Explanation of the Simplex Algorithm* (New York: Ronald Press, 1957).

Lathe A is used for rough turn of the pin stock and has 50 hours of time available. Lathe B is used to finish turn the fastening pins and has 36 hours available. The third machine, grinder G, is used to finish grind each pin, thereby completing the production process. The grinder has 81 hours available. Manufacturing times for pin lots, in hours, are summarized as follows:

MACHINE
LOT TIMES

	A	B	G
Pin Type 1	10	6	4.5
Pin Type 2	5	6	18.0

AeroTech's profit on these pins is \$9 per lot for Type 1 and \$7 per lot for Type 2.

Before the simplex algorithm can be applied, the LP problem must be set up using the four steps introduced in the graphical method section.

STEP 1: DEFINE THE DECISION VARIABLES.   In this example, the production mix of Types 1 and 2 must be "programmed" for maximum profitability. Hence, the unknown number of lots of each pin type can be represented as follows:

$$X_1 = \text{Number of lots of pin Type 1}$$
$$X_2 = \text{Number of lots of pin Type 2}$$

STEP 2: DEFINE THE OBJECTIVE FUNCTION.   The machine shop owner's goal can be expressed by the following objective function equation:

$$\max Z = \$9X_1 + \$7X_2$$

This equation has one term for the profit generated by producing pin Type 1 and another term for the profit generated by producing pin Type 2. Together, they equal AeroTech's profit, Z, which is to be maximized.

STEP 3: DETERMINE THE CONSTRAINTS.   This simplified example is limited only by the machine times available for the production of fastening pins. Using these times, along with the lot manufacturing times for each pin type, the following constraints can be formulated:

$$10X_1 + 5X_2 \leq 50 \quad \text{(lathe A)}$$
$$6X_1 + 6X_2 \leq 36 \quad \text{(lathe B)}$$
$$4.5X_1 + 18X_2 \leq 81 \quad \text{(grinder G)}$$

STEP 4: DECLARE SIGN RESTRICTIONS.   Of course, the machine shop cannot produce a negative number of fastening pins of either type. Therefore:

$$X_1 \geq 0$$
$$X_2 \geq 0$$

Exhibit 16–10 summarizes the complete LP problem for AeroTech machine shop. So far, the procedure has been the same as for the graphical method described at the beginning of this chapter. Now, six additional steps, known as the *simplex algorithm,* are performed to arrive at an optimal solution.

STEP 5: CONVERT THE LP TO STANDARD MATRIX FORM.   Before solving a problem using the simplex algorithm, the objective function and constraints

■■■ EXHIBIT 16–10
**Summary of the
Linear Programming
Problem for AeroTech
Machine Shop**

Choose production levels for Type 1 pins (X_1) and Type 2 pins (X_2) that:

$$\max Z = \$9X_1 + \$7X_2 \text{ (objective function)}$$

and satisfy the following:

$$10X_1 + 5X_2 \leq 50 \quad \text{(lathe A time constraint)}$$
$$6X_1 + 6X_2 \leq 36 \quad \text{(lathe B time constraint)}$$
$$4.5X_1 + 18X_2 \leq 81 \quad \text{(grinder G time constraint)}$$
$$X_1 \geq 0 \quad \text{(sign restriction)}$$
$$X_2 \geq 0 \quad \text{(sign restriction)}$$

must be placed in standard matrix notation, and inequalities must be removed through the use of **slack variables.** To eliminate the inequalities present in the three time constraints of Exhibit 16–10, the slack variables X_3, X_4, and X_5 are introduced. They replace each inequality with an equals sign.

$$10X_1 + 5X_2 + X_3 \qquad\qquad = 50 \quad \text{(lathe A)}$$
$$6X_1 + 6X_2 \qquad + X_4 \qquad = 36 \quad \text{(lathe B)}$$
$$4.5X_1 + 18X_2 \qquad\qquad + X_5 = 81 \quad \text{(grinder G)}$$

The physical meaning of the slack variables in the AeroTech problem is the remaining spare machine time given a particular solution for X_1 and X_2. Ideally, given an optimum solution, X_3, X_4, and X_5 would all be zero, but this is seldom the case. For our purposes here, however, the slack variables merely provide a convenient way of converting inequalities to equalities.

This standard matrix notation for an LP objective function is:

$$\max Z = [c][x]$$

where [c] contains the coefficients in the objective function (all slack variable coefficients are zero). The objective function must satisfy:

$$[A][x] = [b]$$
$$[x] \geq 0$$
$$[b] \geq 0$$

where [x] is the variable vector, [A] is the matrix of constraint coefficients for the variables, and [b] is the right-hand side vector from the constraint equation.

To complete step 5, the AeroTech LP problem is presented in its standard matrix form:

$$\max Z = [c][x]$$

$$= [\$9 \quad \$7 \quad \$0 \quad \$0 \quad \$0] \begin{bmatrix} X_1 \\ X_2 \\ X_3 \\ X_4 \\ X_5 \end{bmatrix}$$

and satisfy:

$$[A][\mathbf{x}] = [\mathbf{b}]$$

$$\begin{bmatrix} 10 & 5 & 1 & 0 & 0 \\ 6 & 6 & 0 & 1 & 0 \\ 4.5 & 18 & 0 & 0 & 1 \end{bmatrix} \begin{bmatrix} X_1 \\ X_2 \\ X_3 \\ X_4 \\ X_5 \end{bmatrix} = \begin{bmatrix} 50 \\ 36 \\ 81 \end{bmatrix}$$

One should make certain that the original objective function and constraints from these matrices can be recreated. Also, notice that matrix $[A]$ is row-reduced, a necessary condition of the standard form for the simplex method.

STEP 6: PREPARE THE FIRST TABLEAU.   The following matrix, called a **tableau,** is associated with the solution:

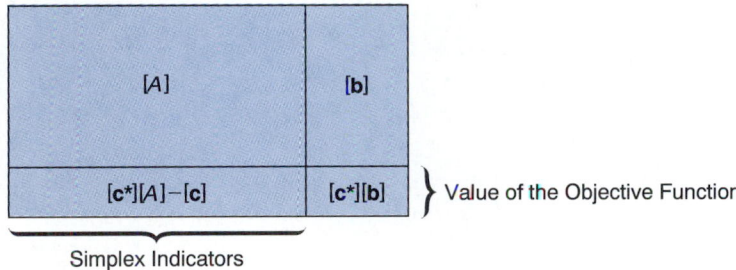

The matrix $[A]$ and the vectors $[\mathbf{b}]$ and $[\mathbf{c}]$ were defined in step 5. The vector $[\mathbf{c^*}]$ is a subset of $[\mathbf{c}]$ containing the coefficients of the variables that are currently defined by elementary columns in matrix $[A]$. For the initial tableau, the initial slack variables' coefficients are in $[\mathbf{c^*}]$. This will become clearer as the simplex tableau of Exhibit 16–11 is filled in.

Two columns have been added to the left-hand side of the tableau in the exhibit. The leftmost column simply indicates which decision variables are currently elementary. Across the table from each of these variables, one finds the value of 1 in an elementary column in $[A]$. The same variable appears at the top of that elementary column.

The next column from the left contains the values of $[\mathbf{c^*}]$. In this first tableau, the variables in the leftmost column are just the slack variables. In $[\mathbf{c}]$, the slack variables all have coefficients of zero, so in this first tableau, the subset vector $[\mathbf{c^*}]$ is:

$$[\mathbf{c^*}] = [0 \quad 0 \quad 0]$$

The operations $[\mathbf{c^*}][A] - [\mathbf{c}]$ and $[\mathbf{c^*}][\mathbf{b}]$ can now be carried out, as shown in the exhibit, and the rest of the tableau completed. The portion of the tableau corresponding to $[\mathbf{c^*}][\mathbf{b}]$ contains the value of the objective function (the profit, or Z, in this case) for the current solution.

The portion of the tableau corresponding to $[\mathbf{c^*}][A] - [\mathbf{c}]$ contains the *simplex indicators* for the current solution. Simplex indicators show in each column how much Z will decrease per unit increase of the variable. These indicator numbers are vital for the next four steps of the simplex algorithm.

STEP 7: CHECK TO SEE IF THE CURRENT SOLUTION IS MAXIMAL.   If no simplex indicator is negative, the solution is maximal, and the algorithm

■ EXHIBIT 16–11

Preparation of the First Simplex Tableau for the AeroTech Problem

[c*]		X_1	X_2	X_3	X_4	X_5	[b]
X_3	0	10	5	1	0	0	50
X_4	0	6	6	0	1	0	36
X_5	0	4.5	18	0	0	1	81

$$[\mathbf{c}] = [9\ 7\ 0\ 0\ 0] \quad [\mathbf{c^*}] = [0\ 0\ 0]$$

$$[\mathbf{c^*}][A] - [\mathbf{c}] = \begin{bmatrix} 0 & 0 & 0 \end{bmatrix} \begin{bmatrix} 10 & 5 & 1 & 0 & 0 \\ 6 & 6 & 0 & 1 & 0 \\ 4.5 & 18 & 0 & 0 & 1 \end{bmatrix} - \begin{bmatrix} 9 & 7 & 0 & 0 & 0 \end{bmatrix}$$

$$= \begin{bmatrix} 0 & 0 & 0 & 0 & 0 \end{bmatrix} - \begin{bmatrix} 9 & 7 & 0 & 0 & 0 \end{bmatrix}$$

$$= \begin{bmatrix} -9 & -7 & 0 & 0 & 0 \end{bmatrix}$$

$$[\mathbf{c^*}][\mathbf{b}] = \begin{bmatrix} 0 & 0 & 0 \end{bmatrix} \begin{bmatrix} 50 \\ 36 \\ 81 \end{bmatrix} = 0$$

Pivot entry

	[c*]	X_1	X_2	X_3	X_4	X_5	[b]	Quotients — Minimum quotient (pivot row)
X_3	0	(10)	5	1	0	0	50	50/10 = 5
X_4	0	6	6	0	1	0	36	36/6 = 6
X_5	0	4.5	18	0	0	1	81	81/4.5 = 18
		−9	−7	0	0	0	0	

Pivot column

terminates. The values of the decision variables and the objective function can be read directly from the table. The optimization is complete.

STEP 8: CHECK TO SEE IF NO MAXIMAL SOLUTION EXISTS. If some simplex indicators are negative, and no entry in that column is positive, there is no maximal solution, and the algorithm terminates. Either there is an inconsistency in the constraints of the LP problem, or the feasible region is unbounded. In either case, the LP problem cannot be optimized as formulated.

STEP 9: CREATE A NEW TABLEAU TO FIND A BETTER SOLUTION. Another tableau will be created that proceeds from the basic solution of the first tableau to another solution that might satisfy steps 7 or 8. This iteration is performed by pivoting matrices in the current tableau and reevaluating the simplex indicators.

STEP 10: REPEAT STEP 9 UNTIL EITHER STEP 7 OR STEP 8 IS SATISFIED.
The simplex algorithm is iterative. Recalling the graphical approach to optimizing an LP problem, the simplex algorithm simply proceeds around the perimeter of the feasible region, stopping at corner points along the way to test for optimality. A new tableau is associated with each corner point.

To continue with the AeroTech problem, the bottom of Exhibit 16–11 should be revisited. Two of the simplex indicators are negative; therefore, step 7 is not satisfied. There is at least one positive value in the columns above these negative indicators, so step 8 is not satisfied. Therefore, we must proceed to step 9 and generate a new tableau.

To create the new tableau, an entry in the current tableau is selected about which to pivot. First, the most negative simplex indicator having a positive value above it in [A] is selected (−9 in the exhibit). In essence, the greatest negative value indicates which variable will increase Z by the greatest rate. The column above this indicator is the pivot column.

Second, for each *positive* entry in the pivot column in [A], the entry in **[b]** on that row is divided by the entry in the pivot column of [A], and the resulting quotient is noted (three such quotients are shown in the exhibit, one for each row of [A]). Each of these quotients is the largest value the pivot column variable can be without exceeding the constraint of that row.

Finally, the smallest of these quotients is determined. It indicates the largest value of the pivot column variable that is assured of not violating any constraints. The row corresponding to this quotient is the pivot row. The pivot entry is at the intersection of the pivot row and the pivot column (the circled 10 is the pivot entry in the exhibit).

Exhibit 16–12 shows the second tableau for AeroTech. Since **[c*]** is not needed beyond the first tableau, the leftmost columns are omitted. To create this second tableau, the entire first tableau is transformed by the pivoting process described earlier. This pivoting also affects the entire last row of the tableau, and the right-hand column. All values in the pivot row are divided by the pivot entry, which leaves a 1 in the pivot position. Then, multiples of the resulting pivot row are subtracted from the tableau's other rows to leave zeros in the pivot column.

Once again, the second tableau does not satisfy steps 7 and 8, so a third tableau must be generated, starting with the selection of a pivot entry. The only negative simplex indicator in the exhibit is −2.5, so that column becomes the pivot column. Recomputing the three quotients and finding their minimum results in the second row being chosen as the pivot row. The pivot entry (3) is circled.

Exhibit 16–13 shows the third tableau produced by pivoting the second tableau around its pivot entry. Note that in the third tableau, none of the simplex indicators are negative, satisfying step 7 of the algorithm. Therefore, this tableau represents an optimal solution to the AeroTech problem, and no further iterations are necessary.

The solution values in the tableau in Exhibit 16–13 are read as follows. First, the objective function (Z) value from the lower right corner of the tableau is read, in this case, 50. AeroTech can expect to make a profit of $50 from the optimal production run. But what is this optimal production run? How many fastening pins of Types 1 and 2 should be produced? This question is answered in the rightmost **[b]** column of the tableau.

■ EXHIBIT 16–12
The Second Simplex Tableau for the AeroTech Problem

X_1	X_2	X_3	X_4	X_5	[b]
1	0.5	0.1	0	0	5
0	3	−0.6	1	0	6
0	15.75	−0.45	0	1	58.5
0	−2.5	0.9	0	0	45

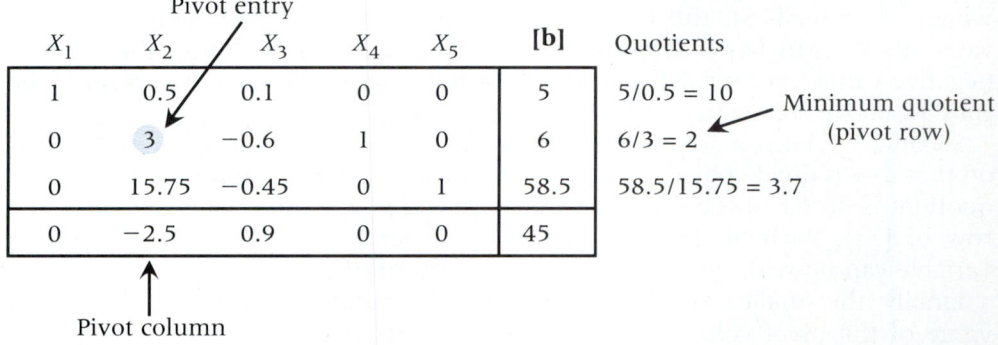

Pivot entry

X_1	X_2	X_3	X_4	X_5	[b]	Quotients
1	0.5	0.1	0	0	5	5/0.5 = 10
0	3	−0.6	1	0	6	6/3 = 2
0	15.75	−0.45	0	1	58.5	58.5/15.75 = 3.7
0	−2.5	0.9	0	0	45	

Minimum quotient (pivot row)

Pivot column

First, find the elementary columns in [A] of the third tableau. Then, note the decision variables to which these columns correspond and the row on which each column's 1 is located. For instance, the first column of the tableau is elementary and corresponds to the variable X_1. This column has a 1 in the first row. It is now possible to read across this row to the far right. The value of 4 appears in the first row of **[b]**, meaning that four lots of pin Type 1 should be produced.

Similarly, the value of 2 appears in the second row of **[b]**, meaning that two lots of pin Type 2 should be produced. The value of 27 in row three of **[b]** means that 27 hours of unused (slack) time remain on grinder G because the third elementary column corresponds to X_5. Having completed the LP problem, AeroTech's owner can now run the machines to this optimal schedule.

▌ Sensitivity Analysis

When an optimal solution is reached, management would often like to know how the optimal values would react to a change in the initial formulation of the LP problem, but it is not practical to rework the entire problem for each possible change. Fortunately, the information can be obtained directly through an analytical approach called **sensitivity analysis** (also referred to as **postoptimality analysis**). Sensitivity analysis basically looks at the question of "what if" a variable is different from that originally estimated. The widespread use of computers has made sensitivity analysis a common extension of linear program-

X_1	X_2	X_3	X_4	X_5	[b]
1	0	0.2	−0.167	0	4
0	1	−0.2	0.33	0	2
0	0	2.7	−5.2	1	27
0	0	0.4	0.833	0	50

■■■ EXHIBIT 16–13
The Third and Final Simplex Tableau for the AeroTech Problem

No simplex indicator is negative. Maximal.

X_1	X_2	X_3	X_4	X_5	[b]	
1	0	0.2	−0.167	0	4	⟵ Solution for X_1 (4 lots)
0	1	−0.2	0.33	0	2	⟵ Solution for X_2 (2 lots)
0	0	2.7	−5.2	1	27	⟵ Solution for X_5 (27 hours)
0	0	0.4	0.833	0	50	

Optimal solution   Profit ($50)

ming. Most linear programming computer packages include the results of sensitivity analysis as a part of the normal printout.

Shadow Prices

A **shadow price** represents the change in the objective function that would result from the addition or reduction of one unit of a resource, such as machine time or labor time. Shadow pricing, a form of sensitivity analysis, shows how sensitive the optimal value of the objective function would be to adding or reducing resources. For example, is it worthwhile to pay workers an overtime rate? If the increase in overtime pay is $1,000 and results in an increase of $800 in the optimal objective function, the addition of overtime work is not worthwhile.

The shadow price "value" of adding one additional unit of a resource can be readily determined by examining the last row of the final tableau. Each value is the shadow price for that variable. For example, as shown in Exhibit 16–13, the shadow price of slack variable X_3 is 0.4. Since slack variable X_3 is directly associated with constraint 1, this means that a one-hour increase in Lathe A's time would result in an increase in Z of $0.40.

USING THE SIMPLEX METHOD TO SOLVE MINIMIZATION PROBLEMS

In the preceding discussion of maximization problems using the simplex algorithm, the constraints were of the following form:

$$[E][\mathbf{x}] \leq [\mathbf{b}]$$
$$[\mathbf{x}] \geq 0$$
$$[\mathbf{b}] \geq 0$$

where $[E]$ contains the constraint coefficients for the variables, not including slack variables.

The first simplex tableau could be formed around the subset vector $[\mathbf{c^*}] = 0$, which relates to starting at the origin in a graphical plot of the feasible region.[4] Most maximization problems will fit this form nicely, but the majority of minimization problems will not contain the origin as a feasible point. They often have constraints of the following form:

$$[E][\mathbf{x}] \geq [\mathbf{b}]$$

A quick review of Exhibit 16–2 (a maximization problem) shows that the origin (0, 0) is a corner point of the feasible region, but in Exhibit 16–7 (a minimization problem) the origin is outside the feasible region. Thus, such a simplex minimization problem cannot be started from the origin because it is not a feasible point.

To overcome this difficulty, a modification of simplex called the two-phase procedure is employed. The first phase of this procedure uses *subtracted* slack variables plus additional artificial variables to find a corner point of the feasible region and to produce a tableau based on that point. The second phase then drops the artificial variables and uses the feasible point to optimize the LP problem similar to the way described for the LP maximization problem.

An additional concern with all minimization problems is the evaluation of the simplex indicators. Whereas negative indicators were sought in the maximization problem for AeroTech machine shop, positive indicators are looked for in a minimization problem. The maximum simplex indicator in a minimization problem indicates the variable that will reduce Z at the greatest rate. The pivot column will contain a positive indicator, but the pivot row will be determined exactly as before.

A Simplex Minimization Example

Consider the following LP problem, which was solved graphically as the K9 Kondo Company problem earlier in this chapter:

$$\min Z = \$200X + \$50Y$$

subject to the following:

$$6X + 3Y \geq 60$$
$$2X + 3Y \geq 36$$
$$X \geq 0$$
$$Y \geq 0$$

Phase One of the Two-Phase Procedure

First, the problem is converted to standard matrix form by subtracting the slack variables J and K from the constraints. Then, the artificial variables M and N are added to produce the following equality constraints:

---

[4] Frederick Arthur Ficken, *The Simplex Method of Linear Programming* (New York: Holt, Rinehart and Winston, 1961).

$$\begin{bmatrix} 6 & 3 & -1 & 0 & 1 & 0 \\ 2 & 3 & 0 & -1 & 0 & 1 \end{bmatrix} \begin{bmatrix} X \\ Y \\ J \\ K \\ M \\ N \end{bmatrix} = \begin{bmatrix} 60 \\ 36 \end{bmatrix}$$

For phase one, a "rigged" objective function is used, which contains only the artificial variables. The use of these artificial variables and the rigged objective function may seem strange and, for the purposes here, will have to be taken on faith. In matrix form, the rigged objective function is:

$$\min Z = [\mathbf{a}][\mathbf{x}]$$

$$= [0 \quad 0 \quad 0 \quad 0 \quad 1 \quad 1] \begin{bmatrix} X \\ Y \\ J \\ K \\ M \\ N \end{bmatrix}$$

The first tableau is at the top of Exhibit 16–14. The vector [**a***] contains the coefficients of the artificial variables from the rigged objective function since the artificial variables are defined by the elementary columns in matrix [A]. The simplex indicators are then computed, and the value of the objective function is determined as shown.

Because this is a minimization problem, the highest value positive simplex indicator is selected to determine the pivot column; in this case, 8 is chosen. As before, the quotients for this tableau are computed, and the minimum quotient is chosen as the pivot row. Again, the minimum quotient value indicates the largest value the pivot column variable can be without violating any of the constraints. The pivot entry, in this case 6, is circled.

Pivoting twice yields the tableau at the bottom of Exhibit 16–14. Because there are now no positive simplex indicators, phase one is completed. The value of the objective function in the lower right corner of the tableau gives valuable information. In the tableau, this value is zero, indicating that there is a solution to the problem if one wishes to proceed with phase two. If the value were nonzero, no solution to the LP problem would exist, and the process would not be continued.

Phase Two of the Two-Phase Procedure

Phase one found a corner point in the feasible region that permits the simplex method to optimize the minimization LP problem. Exhibit 16–15 shows the first tableau of phase two. The columns of [A] corresponding to the artificial variables M and N are simply deleted and the rows are reordered, if necessary, so the 1's of the elementary columns are in the same order as the objective function coefficients. The original objective function is, of course, restored to read in matrix form, as shown on page 749.

■■■EXHIBIT 16–14

Tableau Associated with Phase One of the Two-Phase Simplex Minimization Problem

Artificial Slack Variables

	[a*]	X	Y	J	K	M	N	[b]
M	1	6	3	−1	0	1	0	60
N	1	2	3	0	−1	0	1	36

$[a] = [\,0\ 0\ 0\ 0\ 1\ 1\,]$ $[a*] = [\,1\ 1\,]$

$$[a*][A] - [a] = \begin{bmatrix} 1 & 1 \end{bmatrix} \begin{bmatrix} 6 & 3 & -1 & 0 & 1 & 0 \\ 2 & 3 & 0 & -1 & 0 & 1 \end{bmatrix} - \begin{bmatrix} 0 & 0 & 0 & 0 & 1 & 1 \end{bmatrix}$$

$$= \begin{bmatrix} 8 & 6 & -1 & -1 & 1 & 1 \end{bmatrix} - \begin{bmatrix} 0 & 0 & 0 & 0 & 1 & 1 \end{bmatrix}$$

$$= \begin{bmatrix} 8 & 6 & -1 & -1 & 0 & 0 \end{bmatrix}$$

$$[a*][b] = \begin{bmatrix} 1 & 1 \end{bmatrix} \begin{bmatrix} 60 \\ 36 \end{bmatrix} = 96$$

Pivot entry

	[a*]	X	Y	J	K	M	N	[b]	Quotients
M	1	6	3	−1	0	1	0	60	60/6 = 10 ← Minimum quotient (pivot row)
N	1	2	3	0	−1	0	1	36	36/2 = 18
		8	6	−1	−1	0	0	96	

Pivot column

Pivot entry

X	Y	J	K	M	N	[b]	Quotients
1	0.5	−0.167	0	0.167	0	10	10/0.5 = 20
0	2	0.333	−1	−0.333	1	16	16/2 = 8 ← Minimum quotient (pivot row)
0	2	0.333	−1	−1.333	0	16	

Pivot column

X	Y	J	K	M	N	[b]
1	0	−0.25	0.25	0.25	−0.25	6
0	1	0.167	−0.5	−0.167	0.5	8
0	0	0	0	−1	−1	0

Value is zero, therefore a solution to the LP exists.

End of phase one

■■■■EXHIBIT 16–15
**Creation of the First
Tableau in Phase Two
of the Simplex
Minimization Problem**

[c*]	X	Y	J	K	M	N	[b]
X	200	1	0	−0.25	0.25	0.25	−0.25	6
Y	50	0	1	0.167	−0.5	−0.167	0.5	8

$[c] = [200\ 50\ 0\ 0]$ $[c*] = [200\ 50]$

$$[c*][A] - [c] = \begin{bmatrix} 200 & 50 \end{bmatrix} \begin{bmatrix} 1 & 0 & -0.25 & 0.25 \\ 0 & 1 & 0.167 & -0.5 \end{bmatrix} - \begin{bmatrix} 200 & 50 & 0 & 0 \end{bmatrix}$$

$$= \begin{bmatrix} 200 & 50 & -41.65 & 25 \end{bmatrix} - \begin{bmatrix} 200 & 50 & 0 & 0 \end{bmatrix}$$

$$= \begin{bmatrix} 0 & 0 & -41.65 & 25 \end{bmatrix}$$

$$[c*][b] = \begin{bmatrix} 200 & 50 \end{bmatrix} \begin{bmatrix} 6 \\ 8 \end{bmatrix} = 1,600$$

Pivot entry

[c*]	X	Y	J	K	[b]
X	200	1	0	−0.25	(0.25)	6
Y	50	0	1	0.167	−0.5	8
		0	0	−41.67	25	1,600

Pivot column

$$\min Z = [c][x]$$

$$= [200\ \ 50\ \ 0\ \ 0] \begin{bmatrix} X \\ Y \\ J \\ K \end{bmatrix}$$

Noting that the elementary columns in $[A]$ correspond to the variables X and Y, the subset vector $[c*]$ can be determined and the simplex indicators recalculated as shown in the exhibit. This leaves the complete first tableau of phase two shown at the bottom. Note that the leftmost Z columns have been eliminated from the tableau including the $[a*]$ column. Also, note that no row ordering was necessary since the 1's of the elementary column were in the same order as the objective function coefficients.

There is one positive simplex indicator in the tableau, which is 25. In the $[A]$ column above this indicator, there is only one positive value, 0.25, which automatically becomes the pivot value. In this case, it is not necessary to compute quotients to determine the pivot row because there is only one positive

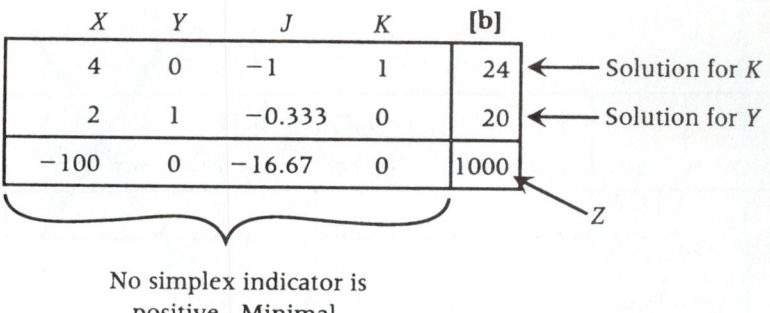

	X	Y	J	K	**[b]**
	4	0	−1	1	24	← Solution for K
	2	1	−0.333	0	20	← Solution for Y
	−100	0	−16.67	0	1000	← Z

No simplex indicator is positive. Minimal.

Use the second constraint

$2X + 3Y + 0J - 1K = 36$

to obtain a solution for X:

$2X + 3(20) + 0 - 1(24) = 36$

$X = 0$

pivot column value to choose from. Exhibit 16–16 shows the second tableau obtained by pivoting the first.

All simplex indicators are nonpositive so the solution is now minimized and the simplex algorithm terminates. The location of the elementary columns in this tableau should be studied. The number 24 in **[b]** is the optimal value of the slack variable K. The number 20 in **[b]** is the optimal value of the decision variable Y. The tableau provides no value for the decision variable X, so its optimal value is zero. Finally, the value of the objective function is 1,000 (or $1,000,000). Note that the simplex solution is the same as that found graphically earlier in the chapter for the K9 Kondo Company problem.

THE LINDO COMPUTER PACKAGE

If the use of linear programming in industry has been restricted, it has been because of two difficulties: (1) the cost of collecting the necessary input data and (2) the cost of solving large LP problems.[5] The first of these roadblocks is being removed as many firms develop integrated information and database systems. Since the solution of LP problems is purely mechanical, these problems are best assigned to the computer. Therefore, rapid reductions in the cost of computer hardware are removing the second roadblock.

Of course, computers require software to solve problems. Probably the most common linear programming software package in use today is LINDO, an acronym for *Linear INteractive Discrete Optimizer*. LINDO is most at home running on a mainframe or minicomputer, such as Digital's VAX, where it applies the simplex algorithm to solve LP problems having up to 5,000 rows and 15,000 variables. LINDO/PC is a microcomputer-based version of the package with somewhat reduced capabilities. In addition to linear programming, the packages are capable of optimizing integer and quadratic equations as part of more advanced models.

LINDO is started in a default mode called VERBOSE. This mode assumes the

---

[5] Linus Schrage, *Linear, Integer, and Quadratic Programming with LINDO* (Palo Alto, Calif.: Scientific Press, 1984).

user has a small problem and simply wants to enter the problem, solve it, print the entire solution, and optimally look at the RANGE report. For large problems where one would never want the entire solution report printed, but would browse through the solution, LINDO may be switched to a mode called TERSE.[6]

Novice LINDO users may find the following commands useful:

COMMAND	USE
MAX	Start input of a maximization problem
MIN	Start input of a minimization problem
END	End problem input
GO	Solve the current problem
LOOK	Print portions of the current problem
ALTER	Alter an element of the current problem

The LINDO command prompt is a colon (:), and a question mark (?) indicates that LINDO is waiting for further input. The following example illustrates the use of these prompts.

Assume the following simple LP problem:

$$\max Z = 2X + 3Y \quad \text{(objective function)}$$

and satisfy:

$$4X + 3Y \leq 10$$
$$3X + 5Y \leq 12$$

The following LINDO input is valid for describing this model:

```
MAX 2X+3Y
ST
4X+3Y≤10
3X+5Y≤12
```

where the acronym ST means "subject to the following constraints." As can be seen in Exhibit 16–17, expressions involving "greater than or equal to" or "less than or equal to" operators are entered using just the "greater than" ($>$) or "less than" symbol ($<$), respectively. LINDO assumes the equals sign in such cases, a feature that can be overridden if the user does, in fact, intend a strict inequality.

Exhibit 16–17 illustrates a LINDO screen display, showing user input and program responses. As can be seen, LINDO is a command-oriented rather than a menu-oriented package. A wide range of commands is available, any of which can be executed at any time without wading through numerous menus. This format allows the package to function easily for the novice who is solving a simple problem such as the one above, yet allows LINDO to have many advanced features that might appeal to a mathematician. Such features enable a wide range of users to benefit from LINDO's capabilities.

SOLVING LINEAR PROGRAMMING PROBLEMS WITH KARMARKAR'S METHOD

LEARNING OBJECTIVE 4

Discuss Karmarkar's method of solving linear programming problems.

Prior to 1984, most scientists and mathematicians thought that the simplex method was as far as they could go. A number of relatively easy-to-use decision support packages based on the simplex method have been available for years. Even when LP problems are not terribly complex, however, solving them can

---

[6] Linus Schrage, *User's Manual: Linear, Integer, and Quadratic Programming with LINDO*, 2d ed. (Palo Alto, Calif.: Scientific Press, 1985).

■ EXHIBIT 16–17
A Typical LINDO Terminal Session Showing Prompts, User Input of a Maximization Problem, and Output

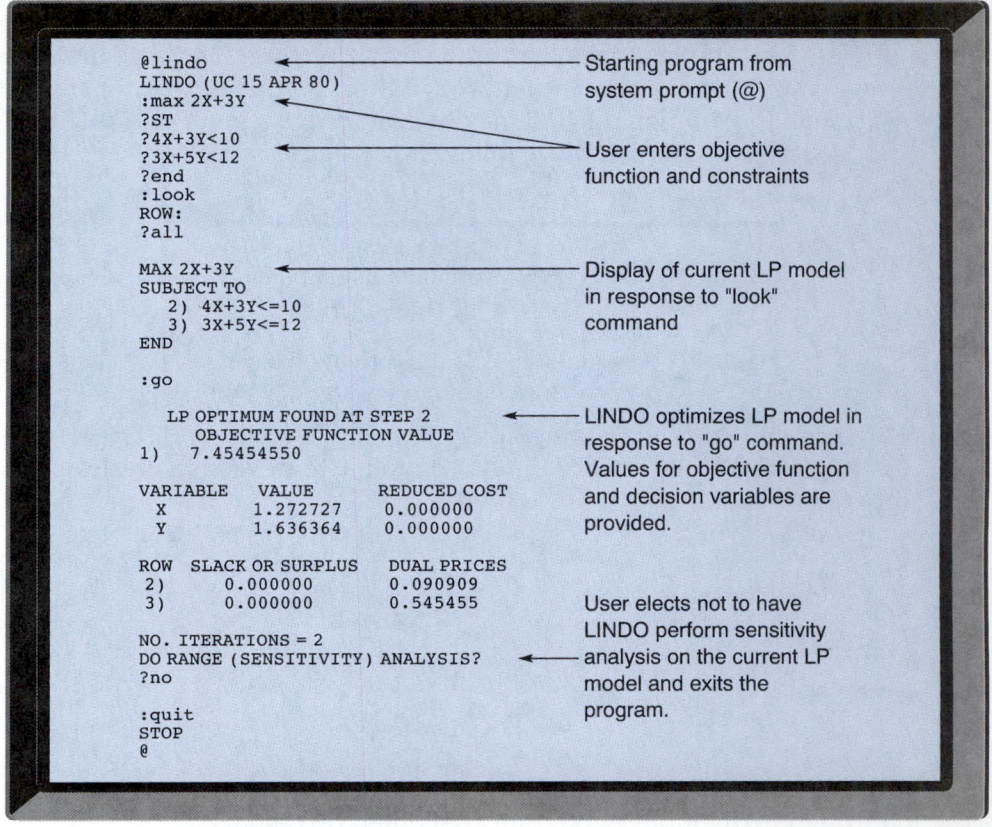

```
@lindo                              ← Starting program from
LINDO (UC 15 APR 80)                  system prompt (@)
:max 2X+3Y
?ST
?4X+3Y<10                            ← User enters objective
?3X+5Y<12                             function and constraints
?end
:look
ROW:
?all

MAX 2X+3Y                            ← Display of current LP model
SUBJECT TO                            in response to "look"
    2) 4X+3Y<=10                      command
    3) 3X+5Y<=12
END

:go

     LP OPTIMUM FOUND AT STEP 2     ← LINDO optimizes LP model in
        OBJECTIVE FUNCTION VALUE      response to "go" command.
1)  7.45454550                        Values for objective function
                                      and decision variables are
VARIABLE    VALUE      REDUCED COST   provided.
   X      1.272727     0.000000
   Y      1.636364     0.000000

ROW  SLACK OR SURPLUS   DUAL PRICES
 2)      0.000000        0.090909     User elects not to have
 3)      0.000000        0.545455     LINDO perform sensitivity
                                      analysis on the current LP
NO. ITERATIONS = 2                  ← model and exits the
DO RANGE (SENSITIVITY) ANALYSIS?      program.
?no

:quit
STOP
@
```

chew up so much computer time that the answer is useless before it is found.

In November 1984, a 28-year-old mathematician named Narendra Karmarkar publicly announced that he had discovered a quick way to solve problems so hideously complicated that they often defy even the most powerful supercomputers. Fittingly, Bell Laboratories, Karmarkar's employer, was the home of the first transistors, the devices that made computerization possible in the first place. Karmarkar's discovery is loaded with significance.

Testing has shown that **Karmarkar's method** is many times faster than the classic simplex method. An implementation of Karmarkar's method outperformed one implementation of the simplex method by a factor of over 50 on medium-scale problems of 5,000 variables.[7] AT&T (Bell Labs' parent) sold the first software product based on Karmarkar's method to the Air Force's Military Airlift Command (MAC).

On a typical day, thousands of Air Force planes ferry cargo and passengers among airfields scattered around the world. Determining how to fly various routes, deciding which aircraft should be used, and scheduling pilots and ground personnel are the primary functions of the MAC. Getting all the pieces to play together is a classic challenge in linear programming. In fact, the MAC's LP problem contains upward of 150,000 variables and 12,000 constraints. If a computer could wring out just a couple of percentage points of added efficiency, it would be worth millions of dollars. Karmarkar's method has enabled the MAC to do just that. Now, Delta Airlines uses Karmarkar's method to develop a monthly schedule for 7,000 pilots and more than 400 aircraft, with significant cost savings.

Some major airlines use Karmarkar's method.

---

[7] Andrew A. Rockett and John C. Stevenson, ''Karmarkar's Algorithm,'' *Byte*, September 1987, p. 146.

Improving on the Simplex Method

How does Karmarkar's method work? A common analogy compares an LP problem to a geodesic dome. In the graphical problems of this chapter, two-dimensional feasible regions were plotted on the x and y axes. The simplex examples had two variables and therefore had two-dimensional feasible regions. Since the addition of each new variable adds another dimension to the feasible region, LP problems with three variables are difficult, and problems with four or more variables are impossible to visualize graphically. Therefore, it helps to think of the feasible region of an LP problem as a geodesic dome in multiple dimensions.

Each of the dome's corners is a possible solution. The task is to find which one holds the best solution. With the simplex method, the program "lands" on one corner and inspects it. Then it scouts the adjacent corners to see if there is a better answer; if so, it heads off in that direction. The procedure is repeated at every corner until the program finds itself boxed in by worse solutions.

Karmarkar's method employs a radically different tactic. It starts from a point within the multidimensional feasible region and finds the optimal solution by taking a shortcut that avoids the tedious surface route. From this interior point, the region is "projected" to reconfigure its shape. Then, the method determines in which direction the solution lies. Finally, the problem structure is allowed to return to its original shape, and the program jumps toward the solution, pausing at intervals to repeat the exercise and home in on the answer.[8]

New Solutions to Old Problems

Karmarkar's method applies to a variety of commercial problems.[9] An airline trying to coordinate scheduling efficiently is one example. An energy producer managing the movement of oil among ships, storage tanks, and refineries is another. Yet another example is the classic LP problem of locating distribution centers geographically for a manufacturing firm. In truth, answering most of what are termed "what-if" questions involves simulation, backed up by linear programming.

Perhaps the greatest benefits will be in the use of simulation for everyday operations.[10] Problems that used to take hours of expensive time on the corporate mainframe can now be performed in minutes, or possibly even performed on a desktop microcomputer in a short time. These benefits can only be a boon to productivity and cost management.

SUMMARY OF LEARNING OBJECTIVES

The major goals of this chapter were to enable you to achieve four learning objectives:

Learning objective 1.   Explain linear programming and its components and assumptions.

Linear programming consists of a sequence of steps that lead to an optimal solution to a class of problems dealing with the allocation of scarce resources. There are three popular linear programming methods:

[8] Wild and Port, op. cit., p. 70.
[9] "Birth of a Method," *Computer Decisions*, February 12, 1985, p. 48.
[10] Jack W. Farrell, "The Karmarkar Maneuver," *Traffic Management*, February 1985, p. 85.

- Graphical method
- Simplex method
- Karmarkar's method

All LP problems are composed of four components:

- Objective function
- Decision variables
- Constraints
- Feasible region

The objective function deals with two types of objectives:

- *Maximization* of such things as profits, revenue, or productivity
- *Minimization* of such things as cost, time, or scrap

Decision variables are simply choices available to management in terms of the amount of input or output. Constraints are limitations that restrict alternatives available to management. Together, the constraints define the set of all feasible combinations of decision variables, which is called the *feasible region*. LP methods (graphical, simplex, or Karmarkar) systematically search the feasible region for the combination of decision variables that will yield an optimal solution in terms of the objective function.

To use linear programming effectively, certain assumptions must be satisfied:

- *Linearity.* All functions, such as costs, prices, and technological requirements, must be linear in nature.
- *Certainty.* All parameters are assumed to be known with certainty.
- *Nonnegativity.* Negative values of decision variables are unacceptable.

Learning objective 2.   Describe the graphical method, and apply it in solving both maximization and minimization linear programming problems.

The graphical method is used to find optimal solutions for two-variable LP problems. This method involves plotting the constraints on a graph and identifying the feasible region.

The optimal solution for a maximization problem is found by moving the objective function, which is an isoprofit line, away from the origin until it intersects the extreme corner point of the feasible region, which is a polygon. The optimal solution occurs where the isoprofit line intersects the extreme corner point, or where the isoprofit line overlays one of the boundaries.

Graphical minimization problems are similar to maximization problems except for two differences. One is that the constraints are usually of the "greater than or equal to" kind rather than "less than or equal to." This difference causes the feasible region to be outside the polygon instead of inside. The other difference is that the objective is to *minimize* something, such as cost. The optimum corner point is found by moving the objective function, which is an isocost line, toward the origin rather than away from it.

Learning objective 3.   Describe the simplex method, and use it in solving both maximization and minimization linear programming problems.

Most real-world LP problems have more than two variables and are therefore too complex for the graphical method. The simplex method is a general-purpose algorithm that is widely used to solve multivariable and multiconstraint LP problems.

With the simplex method, a series of iterations is conducted until an optimal solution is found. Often, the iterations and computations can become overwhelming and thus call for the use of computer software packages, such as LINDO. Still, some familiarity with manual calculations is useful in understanding how the simplex algorithm works.

Learning objective 4.   Discuss Karmarkar's method of solving linear programming problems.

The most significant change in linear programming solution methods is Karmarkar's method. This relatively new method often takes considerably less computer time to solve very large LP problems.

The simplex method's algorithm discovers a solution by moving from one adjacent corner point to the next, following the *outside* edges of the feasible region. Alternatively, Karmarkar's method takes a shortcut by following a path of points on the *inside* of the feasible region. Although the simplex method will likely continue to be used for many LP problems, software that supports Karmarkar's method is already being used by a number of companies as well as federal government agencies.

IMPORTANT TERMS

Constraint   A limit to the degree to which an objective can be pursued.

Decision variables   Represent choices available to decision makers in terms of amounts of either inputs or outputs.

Elementary column   A matrix column containing a single one (1) in any position, with the remaining column entries being zeros.

Feasible region   A feasible solution space that contains the set of all possible combinations of decision variables.

Graphical method   An approach to optimally solving LP problems involving two decision variables and a limited number of constraints.

Isocost lines   A set of parallel lines that represent the objective function of an LP problem. They indicate constant amounts of cost at various solution values. They are used to solve an LP minimization problem graphically.

Isoprofit lines   A set of parallel lines that represent the objective function of an LP problem. They indicate constant amounts of profit at various solution values. They are used to solve an LP maximization problem graphically.

Karmarkar's method   An approach to optimally solving large-scale LP problems efficiently. It starts from a point within the multidimensional feasible region and finds the optimal solution by taking a shortcut that avoids the tedious surface route of the simplex method.

Linear equation   An algebraic equation whose variable quantity or quantities are in the first power only and whose graph is a straight line.

Linear programming (LP)   An application of matrix algebra used to solve a broad class of problems that can be represented by a system of linear equations. It is used to determine the best allocation of multiple scarce resources to achieve an optimal solution.

Matrix   A rectangular array of numbers having m rows and n columns; it is typically contained in brackets.

Objective function   The linear mathematical equation that states the objective of an LP problem. The major objective of a typical enterprise is to maximize profits or minimize costs.

Optimal solution   The solution to an LP problem that provides the best answer to the objective function.

Pivoting   The key iterating process of the simplex algorithm.

Rank   The number of nonzero rows in a matrix.

Row-reduced form   A matrix in which the number of elementary columns is equal to the rank of the matrix.

Scalars   Single numbers or variables used to identify single numbers. It is a quantity that has magnitude but no direction in space.

Sensitivity analysis (postoptimality analysis)   An analysis that projects how much a solution might change, given changes in the variables.

Shadow price   The value of one additional unit of a resource in the form of one more hour of machine time or labor time or other scarce resource in linear programming.

Simplex method   An approach to optimally solving multivariable, multiconstraint LP problems. The simplex method applies an algorithm iteratively to locate feasible corner points in a systematic fashion until it arrives at the best solution (i.e., the highest profit or lowest cost).

Slack variables   Represent the amount of each resource that will not be used if the solution is implemented. Under the simplex method, constraints (inequalities) are converted to equations (equalities) by adding slack variables. Slack variables are always nonnegative.

Tableau   A table or matrix of the coefficients used in the problem equations. It represents a solution of the simplex algorithm in tabular form. By inspecting the bottom row of each tableau in a series of tableaus, one can immediately tell if it represents the optimal solution. Each tableau corresponds to a corner point of the feasible region. The initial tableau corresponds to the origin. Subsequent tableaus are developed by shifting to an adjacent corner point in the direction that yields an optimal solution.

Vector   A type of matrix having either an *m* dimension of 1 (row vector) or an *n* dimension of 1 (column vector).

DEMONSTRATION PROBLEMS

■**DEMONSTRATION PROBLEM 1**   *Developing a linear programming problem.*
The Marlowe Company manufactures and sells two products, *A* and *B*. Demand for the two products has grown to such a level that Marlowe can no longer meet the demand with its present resources. The company can work a total of 800,000 direct labor hours (DLhr) annually using three shifts. A total of 250,000 hours of machine time is available annually. The unit sales price for product *A* is $49.90. The unit sales price for product *B* is $84.50. The company plans to use linear programming to determine a master production schedule that maximizes its contribution margin. Overhead is assigned on a machine hour (Mhr) basis. The unit production requirements and unit cost data follow:

	PRODUCT *A*		PRODUCT *B*	
Raw materials		$ 4		$ 8
Direct labor	1 DLhr @ $6	6	2 DLhr @ $6	12
Variable overhead	0.5 Mhr @ $16	8	2 Mhr @ $8	16
Fixed overhead	1.5 Mhr @ $10	15	3 Mhr @ $10	30

Required:
a. Develop the objective function that will maximize Marlowe's contribution margin (*CM*).
b. Develop the constraint function for the direct labor.
c. Develop the constraint function for the machine capacity.

SOLUTION TO DEMONSTRATION PROBLEM 1
a. The objective function that will maximize Marlowe's total contribution margin (*CM*):

$$\max CM = 31.90A + 48.50B$$

The total variable unit cost of product *A* is $18 ($4 raw materials + $6 direct labor + $8 variable overhead). The *CM* is $31.90 ($49.90 unit sales price − $18 variable cost). Similarly, the total variable unit cost of product *B* is $36 ($8 raw materials + $12 direct labor + $16 variable overhead), and the *CM* is $48.50 ($84.50 unit sales price − $36 variable cost). Thus, the objective function should maximize the total *CM* from both products.
b. The constraint function for the direct labor is:

$$A + 2B \leq 800,000$$

Because 800,000 direct labor hours are available, the function must be equal to or less than 800,000. Every unit of product *A* requires 1 hour of direct labor, and every unit of product *B* requires 2 direct labor hours.
c. The constraint function for the machine capacity is:

$$0.5A + 2B \leq 250,000$$

Because 250,000 hours of machine time are available, the function must be equal to or less than 250,000 machine hours. Every unit of product *A* requires 0.5 hours, and every unit of product *B* requires 2 hours.

■**DEMONSTRATION PROBLEM 2**   *Using the graphical method to solve a maximization LP problem.*
Office Designs manufactures and sells two kinds of desktop pen and pencil sets. The Executive (*E*) is a high-quality set, while the Clerical (*C*) is of somewhat lower quality. The contribution margin (*CM*) is $8 for each Executive set sold and $2 for each Clerical set sold. Each Executive set requires twice as much manufacturing time as is required

for a Clerical set. If only Clerical sets are made, the company has the capacity to manufacture 1,200 sets daily. Enough pen and pencil components are available to make 800 sets daily of Executive and Clerical combined. Executive requires a special marble pedestal, of which only 500 per day are available. Clerical requires a metal pedestal, of which 700 per day are available. The company can sell all the Executive and Clerical sets that it produces.

Required:
a. Formulate the problem.
b. Use the graphical method to find the optimal solution.
c. Management wants to know what the optimal solution will be if the number of available marble pedestals is reduced to 400. Prepare a graph showing this postoptimal solution.

SOLUTION TO DEMONSTRATION PROBLEM 2
a. The objective function maximizes the total contribution margin (CM), where the CM is \$8 for each Executive (E) set and \$2 for each Clerical (C) set. Therefore, the objective function for Office Designs is:

$$\max CM = 8E + 2C$$

Certain constraints exist. First, only enough manufacturing time is available to produce 1,200 sets of C, if only C is made. It takes twice as much manufacturing time to produce E. The company does not have to use all its manufacturing capacity. The first constraint is stated as:

$$2E + C \le 1{,}200$$

Second, enough pen and pencil components are available to produce 800 desktop sets of any combination daily. This constraint is stated as:

$$E + C \le 800$$

Third, the pedestals for each set are also limited in supply. Only 500 marble pedestals are available daily to make E, and only 700 metal pedestals are available daily for C. Mathematically, these two constraints become:

$$E \le 500$$
$$C \le 700$$

Finally, although it's common sense, for mathematical completeness, the following nonnegativity constraints are necessary:

$$E \ge 0$$
$$C \ge 0$$

Putting all the preceding material together, the LP problem is formulated as:

$$\max CM = 8E + 2C$$

where

$$2E + C \le 1{,}200$$
$$E + C \le 800$$
$$E \le 500$$
$$C \le 700$$
$$E \ge 0$$
$$C \ge 0$$

b. Because there are only two variables, this LP problem lends itself to the graphical method. The constraints are graphed first because they will determine what solutions to the problem are possible. The feasible solution boundaries are obtained by graphing the inequalities as if they were equalities and then noting where the solution must lie relative to the equation. For example, the first constraint, $2E + C \leq 1,200$ is graphed as $2E + C = 1,200$. If $C = 0$, $2E = 1,200$, and $E = 600$. If $E = 0$, $C = 1,200$. Thus, the end points that are used to draw the $2E + C \leq 1,200$ constraint line are $E = 600$ and $C = 1,200$. This constraint line as well as all the others are shown in the following graph. When all constraints are simultaneously enforced, the shaded area results. This area is the feasible region. It represents the set of all feasible solutions to Office Designs' LP problem.

The CM equation can now be graphed. To do this, various levels of CM may be assumed; for example, \$2,400 and \$3,200. As the CM level is increased, the isoprofit lines (the dashed lines in the graph) will shift away from the origin. As the graph makes clear, the maximum CM level will occur at a corner point of the feasible region. This will always be the case. It is possible, however, that the maximum isoprofit line could be parallel to a constraint line. In such a case, both corners of the constraint as well as all the points on the constraint line would represent optimum solutions. Normally, a unique optimum occurs at a single point (vertex), as is the case with Office Designs.

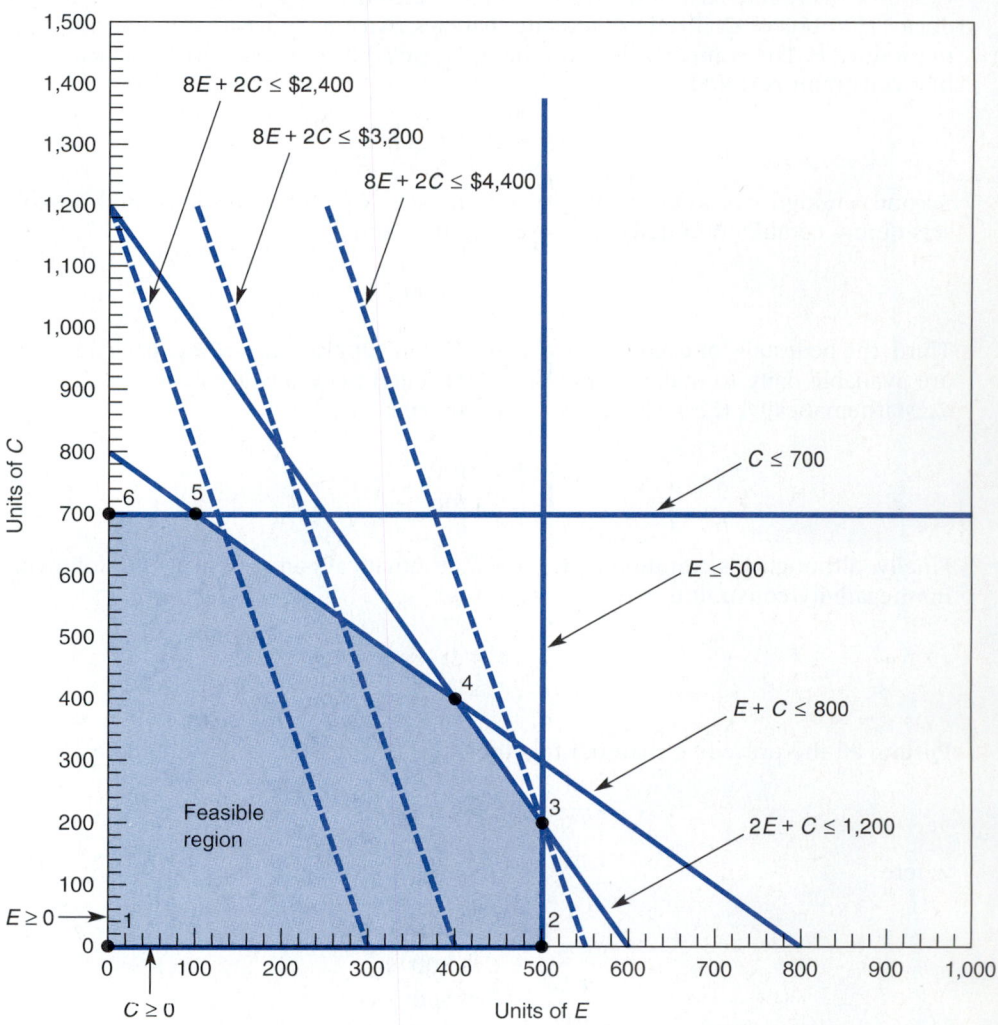

Graphical Solution to Office Designs' LP Problem

To confirm the preceding discussion, the optimal solution is determined by evaluating all corner points of the feasible region, as numbered in the graph. This evaluation is presented as follows:

CORNER POINT	E, C COORDINATES	$CM = 8E + 2C$
1	0, 0	$8(0) + $2(0) = $ –0–
2	500, 0	$8(500) + $2(0) = $4,000
3	500, 200	$8(500) + $2(200) = $4,400
4	400, 400	$8(400) + $2(400) = $4,000
5	100, 700	$8(100) + $2(700) = $2,200
6	0, 700	$8(0) + $2(700) = $1,400

The total CM is maximized at $4,400, with 500 Executive and 200 Clerical desktop pen and pencil sets being produced. This maximum profit is represented by the isoprofit line that intersects corner point 3.

c. Once the optimal solution is reached, it is important to know how the solution will change based on a change in the initial formulation. This is achieved by employing sensitivity or postoptimality analysis. In the case of Office Designs, management wants to know what the optimal solution will be if the number of marble pedestals is reduced to 400. Such a change causes the original constraint line $E \leq 500$ to shift leftward, reducing the feasible region, as shown in the following graph. The revised optimal solution occurs at corner point 4, where 400 sets of E and 400 sets of C are the optimum number of sets to produce. The total CM at this corner point is $8(400) + $2(400) = $4,000. The total CM is less than could be made before, but it is still the best possible solution when the supply of marble pedestals is reduced to 400.

Graphical Solution to Office Designs' LP Problem When the Supply of Marble Pedestals Is Reduced to 400

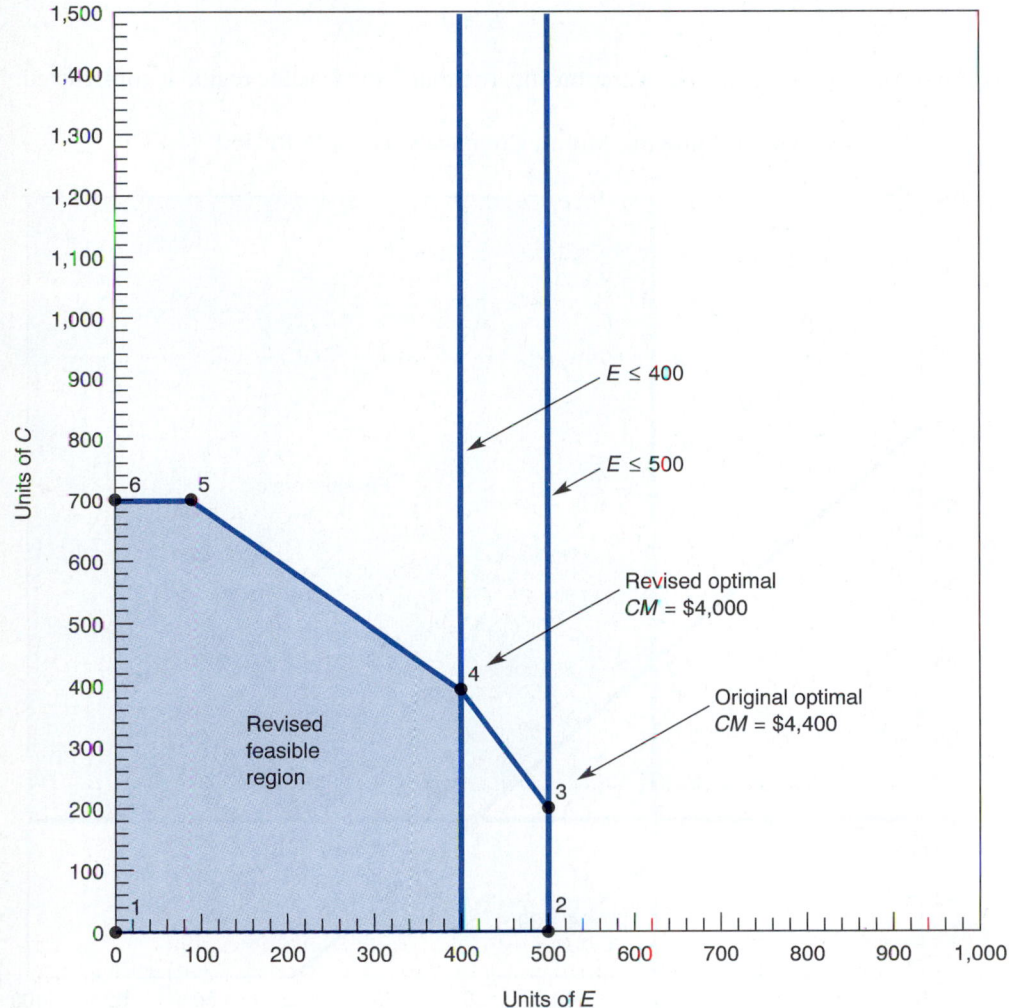

■ **DEMONSTRATION PROBLEM 3** *Using the graphical method to solve a minimization LP problem.*

Moran Chemicals produces two types of chemicals:

- ■ Insecticide *A*
- ■ Herbicide *B*

Chemical *A* costs Moran $3,000 per ton; *B* costs $3,500 per ton. Moran's production superintendent has specified that at least 30 tons of *A* and at least 20 tons of *B* must be produced during the next month. Moreover, the superintendent observes that an existing inventory of a highly perishable raw material needed in both chemicals must be used within 30 days. In order to prevent the loss of this expensive raw material, Moran must produce a total of at least 70 tons of chemicals next month.

Required:
a. Formulate the LP problem
b. Solve the LP problem graphically.

SOLUTION TO DEMONSTRATION PROBLEM 3
a. Total cost $(TC) = 3{,}000A + 3{,}500B$

where

$$A \geq 30$$
$$B \geq 20$$
$$A + B \geq 70$$
$$A \geq 0$$
$$B \geq 0$$

b. To solve Moran's LP problem graphically, the following feasible region is constructed.

Graph Showing Moran Chemicals' Feasible Region

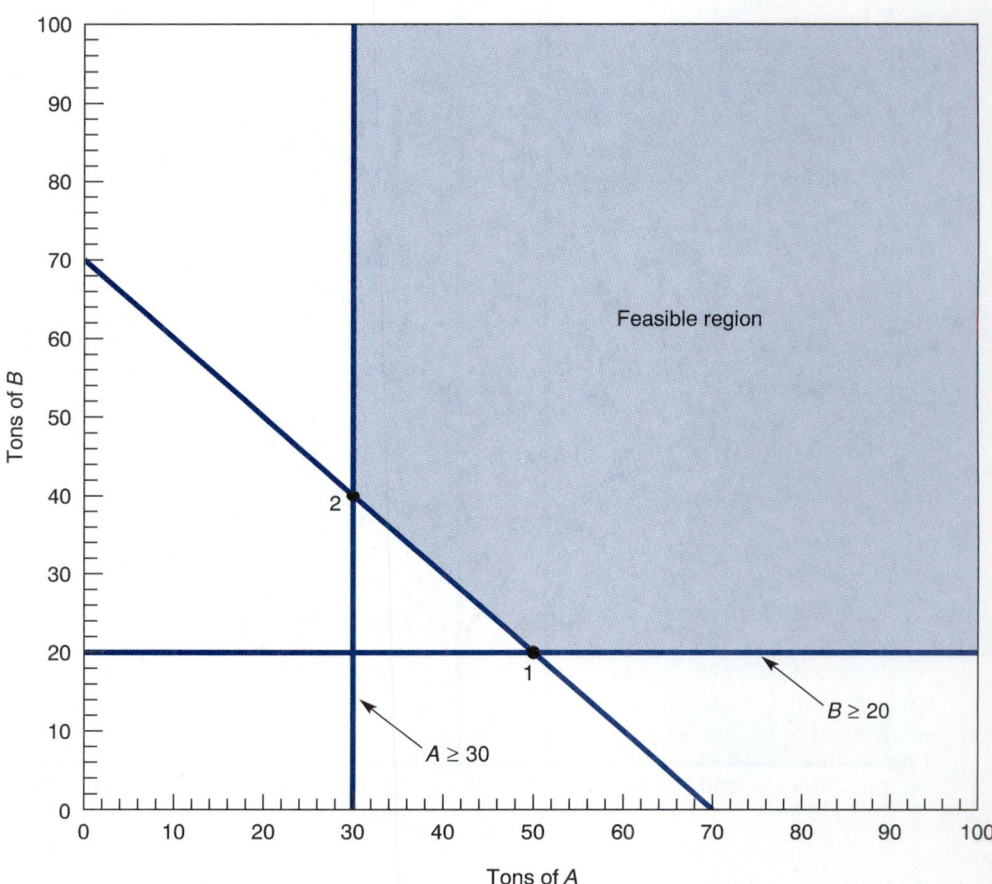

The minimization LP problem is unbounded on the right side and on the top. As long as it is bounded inward, corner points can be determined. The optimal solution will always occur at one of the corner points, or along one of the boundary lines. In the case of Moran's LP problem, there are only two corner points, 1 and 2. At point 1, $A = 50$ and $B = 20$. At point 2, $A = 30$ and $B = 40$. The optimal solution is found at the point yielding the lowest total cost:

$$TC \text{ at point } 1 = 3{,}000A + 3{,}500B$$
$$= 3{,}000(50) + 3{,}500(20)$$
$$= 150{,}000 + 70{,}000$$
$$= \underline{\underline{\$220{,}000}}$$

$$TC \text{ at point } 2 = 3{,}000A + 3{,}500B$$
$$= 3{,}000(30) + 3{,}500(40)$$
$$= 90{,}000 + 140{,}000$$
$$= \underline{\underline{\$230{,}000}}$$

The lowest cost to Moran is at point 1. Thus, Moran should produce 50 tons of A and 20 tons of B.

■**DEMONSTRATION PROBLEM 4**   *Using the simplex method to solve a maximization LP problem.*

Rock Fellow Oil Refinery refines crude oil into gasoline and diesel. Crude oil inputs to the refinery can be a maximum of 100 million barrels per quarter, and the maximum energy usage per quarter is 42 million BTUs. Historical statistics show that the maximum uptime for the refinery is 75 days per quarter. The diesel process uses 2 million BTUs, which is twice as much energy as the gasoline process, and a diesel batch process takes only 3 days compared to 4 days for a gasoline batch. Each diesel and gasoline batch uses 4 million barrels and 10 million barrels, respectively. Each gasoline batch nets $50,000 and each diesel batch nets $60,000.

Required:
a. Formulate this maximization problem.
b. Use the simplex method to find the optimal solution.

SOLUTION TO DEMONSTRATION PROBLEM 4
a. The objective function maximizes the total net contribution (NC) where the net is $60,000 for each diesel ($D$) batch and $50,000 for each gasoline (G) batch. Therefore, the objective function for Rock Fellow is:

$$\max NC = 60D + 50G$$

Three stated constraints exist. First, only 100 million barrels of crude oil can be input to the refinery. Since D uses 4 million barrels per batch and G uses 10 million barrels per batch, the first constraint can be stated as:

$$4D + 10G \leq 100$$

Second, energy consumption is limited to 42 million BTUs. It takes twice as much energy to produce D as G. Thus, the constraint is:

$$2D + G \leq 42$$

Third, crude oil can be refined only 75 days per quarter. Each D batch takes 3 days, and each G batch takes 4 days. Mathematically, this constraint is:

$$3D + 4G \leq 75$$

Putting all this together, the LP problem is formulated as:

$$\max NC = 60D + 50G$$

where

$$4D + 10G \leq 100$$
$$2D + G \leq 42$$
$$3D + 4G \leq 75$$

b. Setting up the first tableau, with the formulated problem from above, we have:

D	G	X_1	X_2	X_3	**[b]**
4	10	1	0	0	100
2	1	0	1	0	42
3	4	0	0	1	75
−60	−50	0	0	0	0

where the bottom row is obtained by:

$$[\mathbf{c^*}][A] - [\mathbf{c}]$$

or

$$[0 \quad 0 \quad 0] \begin{bmatrix} 4 & 10 & 1 & 0 & 0 \\ 2 & 1 & 0 & 1 & 0 \\ 3 & 4 & 0 & 0 & 1 \end{bmatrix} - [60 \quad 50 \quad 0 \quad 0 \quad 0]$$

The bottom right corner is calculated as:

$$[\mathbf{c^*}][\mathbf{b}]$$

and since $[\mathbf{c^*}]$ is all zeros, the resulting scalar is 0.

Now, since the bottom row has negative values, we need to find the pivot entry. Choosing the first column (D) as the pivot column since its simplex indicator is the most negative, we calculate the quotients (b/D) to determine the pivot row, as follows:

D	G	X_1	X_2	X_3	**[b]**	b/D
4	10	1	0	0	100	100/4 = 25
2	1	0	1	0	42	42/2 = 21 ← Pivot row
3	4	0	0	1	75	75/3 = 25
−60	−50	0	0	0	0	

Pivot column

Thus, the pivot value is the 2.

Pivoting around the 2, we generate the second tableau:

D	G	X_1	X_2	X_3	**[b]**
0	8	1	−2	0	16
1	0.5	0	0.5	0	21
0	2.5	0	−1.5	1	12
0	−20	0	30	0	1,260

Note that as a result of the pivot, all values in the pivot column (D) are now 0, except for the 1 where the pivot value was.

Since the last row still has negative values, another pivot value must be determined, as shown:

D	G	X_1	X_2	X_3	**[b]**	b/D
0	8	1	−2	0	16	$16/8 = 2$ ← Pivot row
1	0.5	0	0.5	0	21	$21/0.5 = 42$
0	2.5	0	−1.5	1	12	$12/2.5 = 4.8$
0	−20	0	30	0	1,260	

Pivot column

Thus, the pivot value is the 8.

Pivoting around the 8, we generate the third tableau:

D	G	X_1	X_2	X_3	**[b]**
0	1	0.125	−0.25	0	2
1	0	−0.0625	0.625	0	20
0	0	−0.3125	−0.875	1	7
0	0	2.5	25	0	1,300

Note that as a result of the pivot, all values in the pivot column (G) are now 0, except for the 1 where the pivot value was. Also, note that the first pivot column (D) did not change.

Since there are no negative values in the last row, we have converged to a solution. The value in the bottom right corner is the maximum. In this case, the maximum net is $1,300,000. (Recall that the objective function used thousands of dollars.)

What is the product mix? We look to the D column for the lone value of 1, then look at the value in the rightmost column of that row—in this case, 20. This means that Rock Fellow should make 20 batches of diesel (D). Doing the same for G, we see a value of 2—thus, Rock Fellow should make only 2 batches of gasoline (G).

In summary, the optimal solution is:

- $1,300,000 net per quarter
- 20 diesel batches per quarter
- 2 gasoline batches per quarter

■ **DEMONSTRATION PROBLEM 5**   *Using the simplex method to solve a minimization LP problem.*

Given the following minimization problem:

$$\min Z = 21X + 18Y$$

subject to:

$$5X + 10Y \geq 100$$
$$2X + Y \geq 20$$

Required:

Use the simplex method to find the optimal solution.

SOLUTION TO DEMONSTRATION PROBLEM 5

PHASE 1:

First, the tableau is generated by subtracting the slack variables and then adding artificial variables:

X	Y	S_1	S_2	A_1	A_2	**[b]**
5	10	−1	0	1	0	100
2	1	0	−1	0	1	20
7	11	−1	−1	0	0	120

The bottom row is calculated as follows:

$$[a*][A] - [a]$$

where **[a]** is a vector of length [A] with only 1s for each of the artificial columns and **[a*]** has only 1s for the number of artificial columns of [A]. Thus, we have:

$$[1 \quad 1] \begin{bmatrix} 5 & 10 & -1 & 0 & 1 & 0 \\ 2 & 1 & 0 & -1 & 0 & 1 \end{bmatrix} - [0 \quad 0 \quad 0 \quad 0 \quad 1 \quad 1]$$

which is essentially a summation of all the columns except the artificial columns. For the bottom right, the following is used:

$$[a*][b]$$

which results in 120, again just the summation of the values of **[b].**

Now we pivot until all positive values are eliminated along the bottom row (except for the far right "optimization" value). If the far right value is not zero, a solution does not exist, and we would stop. The pivoting process for our problem is as follows: After the first pivot:

X	Y	S_1	S_2	A_1	A_2	**[b]**
0.5	1	−0.1	0	0.1	0	10
1.5	0	0.1	−1	−0.1	1	10
1.5	0	0.1	−1	−1.1	0	10

After the second pivot:

X	Y	S_1	S_2	A_1	A_2	**[b]**
0	1	−0.133	0.333	0.133	−0.33	6.67
1	0	0.067	−0.667	−0.067	0.67	6.67
0	0	0	0	−1	−1	0

Now that the bottom row is nonpositive and the bottom right value is zero, a solution is assured, and we can proceed to phase 2.

PHASE 2:

Now a new first tableau is constructed, using the nonartificial values in the last phase 1 tableau and sorting the rows. The bottom row is calculated from scratch with now familiar maximization equations:

$$[c*][A] - [c]$$

or

$$[21 \quad 18] \begin{bmatrix} 1 & 0 & 0.067 & -0.667 \\ 0 & 1 & -0.133 & 0.33 \end{bmatrix} - [21 \quad 18 \quad 0 \quad 0]$$

The bottom right corner is calculated as:

$$[c*][b]$$

or

$$[21 \quad 18] \begin{bmatrix} 6.67 \\ 6.67 \end{bmatrix}$$

The resulting first tableau is thus:

X	Y	S_1	S_2	**[b]**
1	0	0.067	−0.667	6.67
0	1	−0.133	0.33	6.67
0	0	−1.0	−8	260

If the bottom row contained any positive values, it would be necessary to pivot until all the values in the bottom row (excluding the bottom right value) were nonpositive, but that is not the case here.

Since all the bottom row values are nonpositive, the values are optimized. This tableau is read in the same way as the maximization case—the bottom right value is the minimized Z-value; the X column reveals a single value in the first row; the Y column has a single value in the second row.

In summary, the optimum solution is:

$$Z = 260$$

when

$$X = 6.67$$
$$Y = 6.67$$

■ DEMONSTRATION PROBLEM 6   *Using linear programming for sensitivity analysis.*

Fugi Disk Company cannot meet the demand for its preformatted 3½-inch floppy disks. Fugi markets two types of disks: HD (high density) for newer computers and DD (double density) for older ones. Fugi can realize a profit of $0.32 for each DD disk and $0.30 for each HD disk. Unfortunately, Fugi is limited to 2,500 plastic DD disk cases and 400 disk boxes each day due to manufacturing limitations. Each box holds either 10 HD or 10 DD disks. The supply of box and disk labels is unlimited. The bulk formatting machine operates 420 minutes per day and can format two disks at a time; it has auto-feed and auto-eject mechanisms and can format an HD disk in 18 seconds and a DD disk in 15 seconds, including the loading and ejection times.

Required:
Use sensitivity analysis to find the optimal solution.

SOLUTION TO DEMONSTRATION PROBLEM 6

Formulating the linear programming problem, the objective function is:

$$0.30H + 0.32D = \text{Maximize profit}$$

The constraints are:

$$1.00D \leq 2,500 \text{ (disk cases)}$$
$$0.30H + 0.25D \leq 840 \text{ (minutes)}$$
$$0.10H + 0.10D \leq 400 \text{ (boxes)}$$

Using a linear programming computer program to calculate the solution, we input the objective function and constraints as (see next page):

Linear Programming

Data Screen

Number of constraints (2-99) 3
maximize

Number of variables (2-99) 2

Fugi Disk Company

Options-> NO step Cmputr PrtOFF

	x1	x2		RHS
maximize	0.30	0.32		
const 1	0.00	1.00	<	2500.00
const 2	0.30	0.25	<	840.00
const 3	0.10	0.10	<	400.00

The output screens show:

Linear Programming

Solution

Number of constraints (2-99) 3
maximize

Number of variables (2-99) 2

Fugi Disk Company

Options-> NO step Cmputr PrtOFF

	x1	x2		RHS	Shadow
maximize	0.30	0.32			
const 1	0.00	1.00	<	2500.00	0.07
const 2	0.30	0.25	<	840.00	1.00
const 3	0.10	0.10	<	400.00	0.00
Values ->	716.67	2500.0		$1,015.00	

Linear Programming

Solution

Number of constraints (2-99) 3   Number of variables (2-99) 2

maximize

Fugi Disk Company

Solutions value = 1015

	Shadow Prices	Slack or Surplus	Original RHS	Lower Limit	Upper Limit
const 1	0.070000	0.00	2500.00	0.00	5000.00
const 2	1.00	0.00	840.00	625.00	1680.00
const 3	0.00	78.3333	400.00	321.6667	800.00

Evaluating these output screens, Fugi management found that the optimal solution would be 2,500 DD disks and 716 HD disks (rounded down to whole disks). After examining the shadow prices, the floor supervisor suggested adding 2.25 hours to the operation of the formatting machine by shuffling schedules and assigning some overtime. The extra cost would be $200 per day.

When the total format machine minutes were changed from 840 to 1,110 and the computer program was rerun, the following output screens resulted:

Linear Programming

Solution

Number of constraints (2-99) 3   Number of variables (2-99) 2

maximize

Fugi Disk Company

Options-> NO step Cmputr PrtOFF

	x1	x2		RHS	
maximize	0.30	0.32			Shadow
const 1	0.00	1.00	<	2500.00	0.02000
const 2	0.30	0.25	<	1110.00	0.00
const 3	0.10	0.10	<	400.00	3.00
values ->	1500.0	2500.0		$1,250.00	

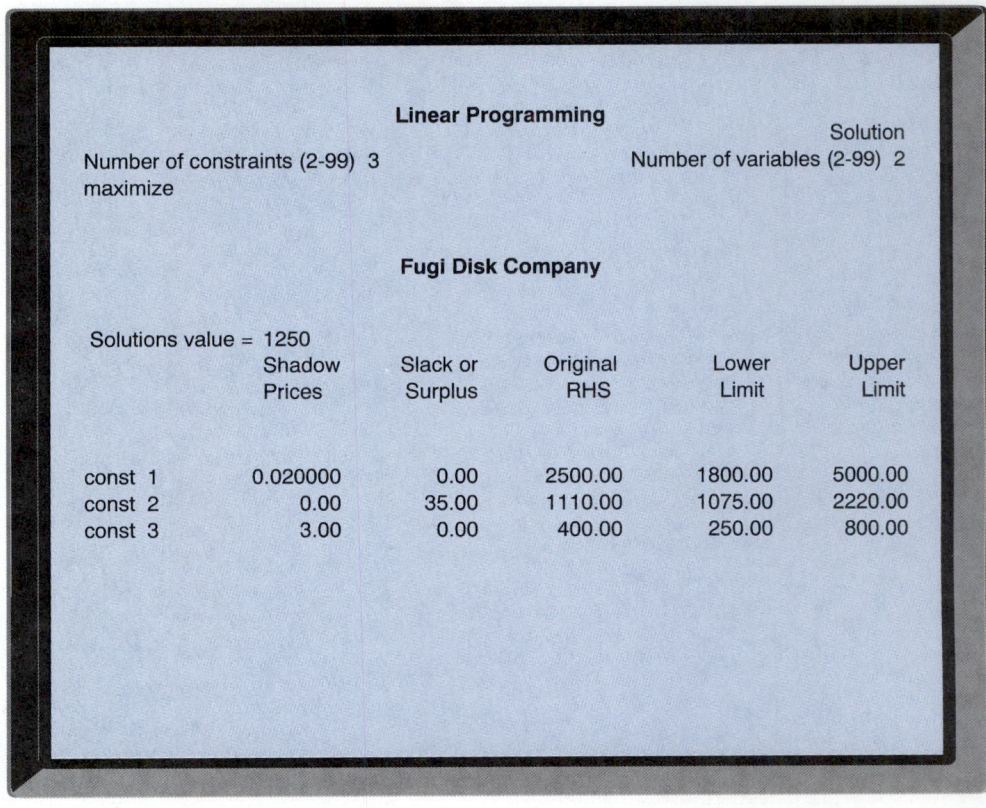

Since the new profit of $1,250 per day is greater than the old profit plus the extra cost ($200), it would be advantageous for Fugi to implement the increase in formatting machine hours.

REVIEW QUESTIONS

16.1   What does the feasible region represent?

16.2   Give two reasons why the graphical method is only practical for small LP problems.

16.3   What does moving an objective function line toward the origin represent? Moving the line away from the origin?

16.4   Which values are used to construct the objective function and the constraints?

    a. LINDO parameters.
    b. Decision variables.
    c. Pricing policy.
    d. Sensitivity constraints.
    e. Shadow prices.

16.5   Which of the following do almost all practical applications of linear programming require?

    a. Graphs.
    b. Matrices.
    c. Objective functions.
    d. Computers.
    e. Market surveys.

16.6   What are the four steps for constructing an LP problem?

16.7   Which of the following procedures is employed to solve simplex linear programming problems?

a. Shadow prices.
b. Graphs.
c. Integral calculus.
d. Expected value.
e. Matrix algebra.

16.8 In linear programming, shadow prices measure the:

a. Cost of the optimum solution.
b. Contribution margins hidden from production.
c. Addition or reduction of one unit of each of the resources.
d. Contribution of a product.
e. Volume price discounts.

16.9 In linear programming, the increase in profit when one more unit of a limited resource is made available is indicated by:

a. The feasible region.
b. The objective function.
c. Nonnegativity constraints.
d. Shadow prices.
e. Incremental decision variables.

16.10 Which points do the simplex method "land on"?

16.11 What steps are required in solving a maximization problem using the simplex method?

16.12 What is the purpose of the first phase in using the simplex method for a minimization problem?

16.13 What is the primary difference between the simplex method and Karmarkar's method?

CHAPTER-SPECIFIC PROBLEMS

These problems require responses based directly on concepts and techniques presented in the text.

16.14 *Graphical solution to LP minimization problem.* Given the following LP problem:

$$\min Z = 33X + 10Y$$

subject to:

$$X + Y \geq 15$$
$$X \geq 2$$
$$3X + Y \geq 33$$
$$X + 2Y \geq 18$$

Required:
Use the graphical method to find the optimal solution.

16.15 *Graphical solution to LP maximization problem.* Given the following LP problem:

$$\max Z = 3X + 2Y$$

subject to:

$$5X + Y \leq 100$$
$$X + 2Y \leq 50$$
$$Y \leq 15$$

Required:
Use the graphical method to find the optimal solution.

16.16 *Determining the objective function and constraint.* The Teaque Company makes three products: A, B, and C. Management wants to maximize profits on these products. The contribution margin for each product follows:

PRODUCT	CONTRIBUTION MARGIN
A	$3
B	8
C	6

The production requirements and departmental capacities, by departments, are as follows:

DEPARTMENT	PRODUCTION REQUIREMENTS BY PRODUCT (HOURS) A	B	C
Assembling	2	4	2
Painting	1	2	3
Finishing	2	3	1

DEPARTMENT	DEPARTMENTAL CAPACITY (TOTAL HOURS)
Assembling	40,000
Painting	27,000
Finishing	42,000

Required:

a. Determine the objective function formula.
b. Specify the constraint for the Finishing Department.

16.17 *Developing the objective function, constraint function, and nonnegativity constraints.* The Galloway Company manufactures and sells shirts and dresses in its two-department factory. Galloway uses linear programming to determine its optimum product mix. Data related to the two products follow:

	SHIRTS	DRESSES
Selling price per unit	$25	$40
Cost data per unit:		
Variable manufacturing cost	8	10
Variable selling cost	3	5
Fixed manufacturing cost	4	8
Fixed selling cost	1	2

MACHINE HOUR DATA

	CUTTING	FINISHING
Shirts	10 minutes	15 minutes
Dresses	6 minutes	30 minutes
Monthly capacity	1,000 hours	2,000 hours

Required:

a. Develop the objective function that will maximize the contribution margin.
b. Develop the monthly machine hour constraints.
c. Develop the monthly nonnegativity constraints.

16.18 *Graphical solution to LP problem.* Neil and Neil book publishers are getting ready to print covers for their latest mass-market novel. (The current trend is to produce different covers for the same book, ideally to generate interest in the book and increase sales.) For this book, the publisher has decided to use predominantly green and predominantly blue covers. Based on a marketing department request, at least 144 covers need to be produced each day, 32 of which should be blue.

Due to idiosyncrasies of the color printing process, blue covers take 2 minutes and green covers take 4.5 minutes each to print. Daily deliveries of raw blue pigment are at least 90 ounces due to vendor contracts. All other raw pigments (e.g., yellow pigment) are not a constraint. Blue covers use one ounce each whereas green covers use half an ounce each of the raw blue pigment. Raw materials costs are predicted to be $0.10 for each green cover and $0.17 for each blue cover. Efficiency goals require the printing press to be run at least 420 minutes each day.

Required:
Use the graphical method to find the optimal solution.

16.19 *Graphical solution to LP problem.* SpatulaCity Industries has only two products, Thick and Thin spatulas. The company nets $200 on a batch of Thin spatulas and $300 on each Thick spatula batch. SpatulaCity has only 100 tons of plastic available each day, with Thick spatula batches using 4 tons each and Thin spatula batches using 2 tons each. The finishing process takes 2 hours and 3 hours for each Thick and Thin batch, respectively, with a finishing process daily capacity of 90 hours. A contract with a large department store requires SpatulaCity to make at least 3 Thick batches per day.

Required:
a. Use the graphical method to find the feasible region.
b. Can 25 batches of Thin spatulas be optimally made each day?

16.20 *Developing the objective function and constraints.* The Harrington Corporation manufactures and sells three products: anchor bolts (A), bearings (B), and casters (C). There are 150 direct labor hours available. Machine hour capacity allows 100 anchor bolts only; 50 bearings only; 40 casters only; or any combination of the three that does not exceed the capacity. Data associated with the products follow:

PRODUCT	SELLING PRICE	VARIABLE COST PER UNIT	FIXED COST PER UNIT	DIRECT LABOR HOURS PER UNIT
A	$4.00	$1.00	$2.00	2
B	3.50	0.50	2.00	2
C	6.00	2.00	3.00	3

Required:
a. Develop the objective function to maximize the total contribution margin from Harrington's three products.
b. Develop the direct labor hour constraint.
c. Develop the machine hour constraint.

[CMA adapted]

16.21 *Simplex solution to LP maximization problem.* Given the following LP problem:

$$\max Z = 15X + 13Y$$

subject to:

$$X + Y \leq 9$$
$$X \leq 3$$
$$Y \leq 8$$

Required:
Use the simplex method to find the optimal solution.

16.22 *Simplex solution to LP minimization problem.* Given the following LP problem:

$$\min Z = 12X + 5Y$$

subject to:

$$X + Y \geq 25$$
$$X + 3.5Y \geq 30$$
$$6X + 5Y \geq 50$$

Required:
Use the simplex method to find the optimal solution.

16.23 *Simplex solution to LP problem.* Bear Chemical Company is planning to introduce two types of pain reliever products. The first, an aspirin and decongestant combination, will be marketed as a cold pill. The second will be just a plain aspirin pill. Due to spoilage of material, only 100 kilograms of raw decongestant can be used each week. Every 100 batches of cold pills require a half kilogram of decongestant and one-quarter kilogram of raw aspirin compound. Every 100 batches of plain pills use only one-third kilogram of raw aspirin compound. Bear can only use 540 kilograms of raw aspirin compound each week due to purchase contract requirements. Marketing has determined that no more than 300 batches of plain pills need to be manufactured each week. The pill press machine takes 10 minutes to make each cold pill batch and 9 minutes to make each plain pill batch.

Required:
Use the simplex method to find the optimal solution to maximize the use of the pill press machine.

16.24 *Simplex solution to LP problem.* A large food manufacturer is attempting to minimize the cost of the raisins that are included in one of its cereal products. It has a choice between two types of raisins—Best Quality and Good Quality. Best Quality raisins cost $0.023 and Good Quality raisins cost $0.010 each. Advertising claims of "2 scoops" in each box create the necessity to have at least 500 raisins in each box. Customer taste tests have proven that at least 250 of the raisins in each box have to be Best Quality to meet quality requirements. Due to damage during the mixing and packaging processes and the fact that the Best Quality raisins are more fragile, tests have shown that the Good Quality raisins are more visually appealing in the box. Therefore, marketing requires a minimum of 100 Good Quality raisins in each box.

Required:
Use the simplex method to find the optimal solution.

| THINK-TANK PROBLEMS

Although these problems are based on chapter material, reading extra material, reviewing previous chapters, and using creativity may be required to develop workable solutions.

16.25 *Comprehensive linear programming problem using the graphical method.* Home Cooking Company offers monthly service plans providing prepared meals that are delivered to the customers' homes and that need only be heated in a microwave or conventional oven. The target market for these meal plans includes double-income families with no children and retired couples in the upper-income brackets.

Home Cooking offers two monthly plans—Premier Cuisine and Haute Cuisine. The Premier Cuisine plan provides frozen meals that are delivered twice each month: this plan generates a profit of $120 for each monthly plan sold. The Haute Cuisine plan provides freshly prepared meals delivered on a daily basis and generates a profit of $90 for each monthly plan sold. Home Cooking's reputation provides the company with a market that will purchase all the meals that can be prepared.

All meals go through food preparation and cooking steps in the company's kitchens. After these steps, the Premier Cuisine meals are flash frozen. The time requirements per monthly meal plan and hours available per month are as follows:

	PREPARATION	COOKING	FREEZING
Hours required:			
Premier Cuisine	2	2	1
Haute Cuisine	1	3	0
Hours available	60	120	45

For planning purposes, Home Cooking uses linear programming to determine the most profitable number of Premier Cuisine and Haute Cuisine monthly meal plans to produce.

Required:
a. Using the notations P = Premier Cuisine and H = Haute Cuisine, state the objective function and the constraints that Home Cooking should use to maximize profits generated by the monthly meal plans.
b. Graph the constraints on Home Cooking's meal preparation process. Be sure to clearly label your graph.
c. By using the graph prepared in Requirement (b) or by making the necessary calculations, determine the optimal solution to Home Cooking's objective function in terms of the number of:
   1. Premier Cuisine meal plans to produce.
   2. Haute Cuisine meal plans to produce.
d. Calculate the optimal value of Home Cooking's objective function.
e. If the constraint on preparation time could be eliminated, determine the revised optimal solution in terms of the:
   1. Number of Premier Cuisine meal plans to produce.
   2. Number of Haute Cuisine meal plans to produce.
   3. Resulting profit.

[CMA adapted]

16.26 *Determing the objective function, constraints, and assumptions of an LP problem.*
The Tripro Company produces and sells three products, hereafter referred to as products A, B, and C. The company is currently changing its short-range planning approach in an attempt to incorporate some of the newer planning techniques. The controller and some of his staff have been conferring with a consultant on the feasibility of using a linear programming model for determining the optimum product mix.

Information for short-range planning has been developed in the same format as in prior years. This information includes expected sales prices and expected direct labor and material costs for each product. In addition, variable and fixed overhead costs were assumed to be the same for each product because approximately equal quantities of the products were produced and sold.

PRICE AND COST INFORMATION (PER UNIT)

	A	B	C
Selling price	$25.00	$30.00	$40.00
Direct labor	7.50	10.00	12.50
Direct materials	9.00	6.00	10.50
Variable overhead	6.00	6.00	6.00
Fixed overhead	6.00	6.00	6.00

All three products use the same type of direct material, which costs $1.50 per pound of material. Direct labor is paid at the rate of $5.00 per direct labor hour. There are 2,000 direct labor hours and 20,000 pounds of direct materials available each month.

Required:
a. Formulate and label the linear programming objective function and constraint functions necessary to maximize Tripro's contribution margin. Use Q_A, Q_B, and Q_C to represent units of the three products.
b. What underlying assumptions must be satisfied to justify the use of linear programming?
c. The controller, upon reviewing the data presented and the linear programming

functions developed, performed further analysis of overhead costs. He used a multiple linear regression model to analyze the overhead cost behavior. The regression model incorporated observations from the past 48 months of total overhead cost and the direct labor hours for each product. The following equation was the result:

$$Y = \$5,000 + 2X_A + 4X_B + 3X_C$$

where:

Y = Monthly total overhead in dollars
X_A = Monthly direct labor hours for product A
X_B = Monthly direct labor hours for product B
X_C = Monthly direct labor hours for product C

The total regression has been determined to be statistically significant as has each of the individual regression coefficients. Reformulate the objective function for Tripro Company using the results of this analysis.

[CMA adapted]

16.27 *Determining product mix and shadow price.* The Frey Company manufactures and sells two products—a toddler bike and a toy highchair. Linear programming is employed to determine the best production and sales mix of bikes and chairs. This approach also allows Frey to speculate on economic changes. For example, management is often interested in knowing how variations in selling prices, resource costs, resource availabilities, and marketing strategies would affect the company's performance.

The demand for bikes and chairs is relatively constant throughout the year. The following economic data pertain to the two products:

	BIKE (B)	CHAIR (C)
Selling price per unit	$12	$10
Variable cost per unit	8	7
Contribution margin per unit	$ 4	$ 3
Raw materials required:		
Wood	1 board foot	2 board feet
Plastic	2 pounds	1 pound
Direct labor required	2 hours	2 hours

Estimates of the resource quantities available in a nonvacation month during the year are as follows:

Wood   10,000 board feet
Plastic   10,000 pounds
Direct labor   12,000 hours

The graphic formulation of the constraints of the linear programming model that Frey Company has developed for nonvacation months accompanies the problem. The algebraic formulation of the model for the nonvacation months is as follows:

Objective function: max $Z = 4B + 3C$

The constraints are:

$$B + 2C \le 10,000 \text{ board feet}$$
$$2B + C \le 10,000 \text{ pounds}$$
$$2B + 2C \le 12,000 \text{ direct labor hours}$$
$$B, C \ge 0$$

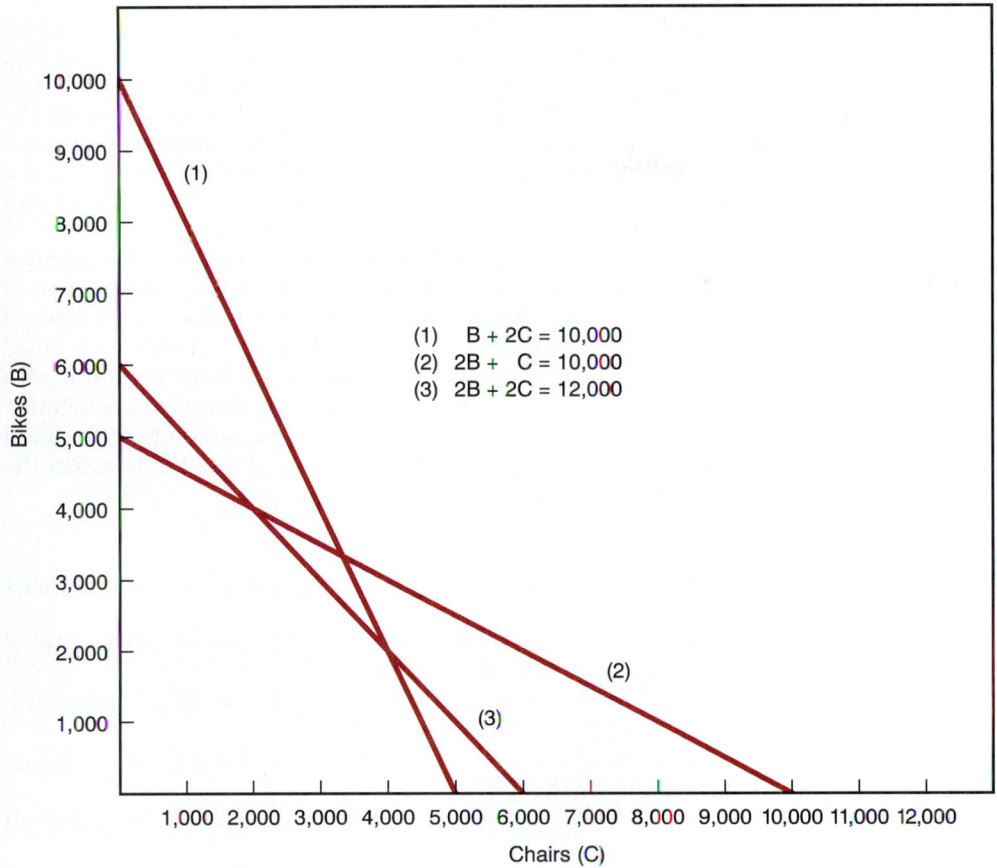

The results from the linear programming model indicate that Frey Company can maximize its contribution margin (and thus profits) for a nonvacation month by producing and selling 4,000 toddler bikes and 2,000 toy highchairs. This sales mix will yield a total contribution margin of $22,000 for a nonvacation month.

Required:
a. During the months of June, July, and August, the total direct labor hours available are reduced from 12,000 to 10,000 hours per month due to vacations.
   1. What would be the best product mix and maximum total contribution margin when only 10,000 direct labor hours are available during a month?
   2. The "shadow price" of a resource is defined as the marginal contribution of a resource or the rate at which profit would increase (decrease) if the amount of the resource were increased (decreased). Based on your solution to Requirement (a)1, what is the shadow price on direct labor hours in the original model for a vacation month?
b. Competition in the toy market is very strong. Consequently, the prices of the two products tend to fluctuate. Can analysis of data from the linear programming model provide information to management that will indicate when price changes to meet market conditions will alter the optimum product mix? Explain your answer.

[CMA adapted]

16.28 *Identifying and discussing the application of linear programming.* The firm of Miller, Lombardi, and York was recently formed by the merger of two companies providing accounting services. York's business was providing personal financial planning, while Miller and Lombardi conducted audits of small governmental units and provided tax planning and preparation for several commercial firms. The combined firm has leased new offices and acquired several microcomputers that are used by the professional staff in each area of service. In the short run, however, the firm does not have the financial resources to acquire computers for all of the professional staff.

The expertise of the professional staff can be divided into three distinct areas that match the services provided by the firm, i.e., tax preparation and planning, insurance and investments, and auditing. Since the merger, however, the new firm has had to turn away business in all three areas of service. One of the problems is that although the total number of staff seems adequate, the staff members are not completely interchangeable. Limited financial resources do not permit hiring any new staff in the near future, and, therefore, the supply of staff is restricted in each area.

Rich Oliva has been assigned the responsibility of allocating staff and computers to the various engagements. The management has given Oliva the objective of maximizing revenues in a manner consistent with maintaining a high level of professional service in each of the areas of service. Management's time is billed at $100 per hour, and the staff's time is billed at $70 per hour for those with experience, and $50 per hour for the inexperienced staff. Pam Wren, a member of the staff, recently completed a course in quantitative methods at the local university. She suggested to Oliva that he use linear programming to assign the appropriate staff and computers to the various engagements.

Required:
a. Identify and discuss the assumptions underlying the linear programming model.
b. Explain the reasons why linear programming would be appropriate for Miller, Lombardi, and York in making staff assignments.
c. Identify and discuss the data that would be needed to develop a linear programming model for Miller, Lombardi, and York.
d. Discuss objectives, other than revenue maximization, that Rich Oliva should consider before making staff allocations.

[CMA adapted]

16.29 *Graphical solution to LP minimization problem.* Modern Air is planning to add jet service to Chattanooga. Before purchasing the plane, Modern needs to determine the seat split between first and coach class. Modern's marketing department has already stated that the new plane should have at least 8 first-class seats. Modern's flight attendants have stated that to maintain adequate customer service, there should be, on average, one attendant for each 20 first-class seats or 50 coach seats. Modern's cabin designers have found that the average first-class seat takes the equivalent cabin space of one and one-half coach seats. Modern's marketing department also found that the average first-class passenger is on a short business trip with a combined person and luggage weight of 210 pounds. On the other hand, the average coach-class passenger is on an extended trip with a combined person and luggage weight of 230 pounds.

Required:
a. Modern is considering purchasing a model G-535, which is designed to lift 50,000 pounds of passenger (people + baggage) weight, can accommodate four attendants, and has the equivalent cabin room for 210 coach-class seats. With this plane, Modern's cost accountants have calculated a contribution of $110 for each first-class passenger and, due to severe competition from other airlines, only $50 for each coach passenger. What should be the cabin seat split?
b. Modern is also considering the purchase of a model G-535e—the efficiency version of the model G-535. With the G-535e, due to lower jet fuel costs, the contribution for each passenger would increase by 10%. Part of the decrease in operating costs is due to the passenger weight capacity being reduced by 10,000 pounds. What should the cabin seat split be for the model G-535e?
c. Based on the results from Requirements (a) and (b), briefly comment on the following:
1. What is the importance of each constraint?
2. Should Modern Air consider a smaller cabin size (and thus less expensive) jet?

16.30 *Simplex solution to LP maximization problem.* Matador Equipment Company sells lawn mowers in the western part of the country. They offer four models:

110, 120, 210, 220, with the primary differences being engine size and cutting width. Following are monthly data related to each product. Each worker can work only 175 hours per month.

ITEM	MODEL 110	MODEL 120	MODEL 210	MODEL 220
Market limit (units)	140	150	100	135
Selling price (per unit)	$125	$170	$150	$200
Materials cost (per unit)	$55	$80	$65	$90
Direct labor (hours per unit)	1.45	1.55	1.55	1.70
Worker A (hours per unit)	0.50	0.50	–0–	–0–
Worker B (hours per unit)	–0–	–0–	0.60	0.60
Worker C (hours per unit)	0.65	–0–	0.65	–0–
Worker D (hours per unit)	–0–	0.65	–0–	0.65
Worker E (hours per unit)	0.30	0.40	0.30	0.45

Required:
Use the simplex method to answer the following:
a. What is the product mix?
b. What is the constraint?
c. What is the total contribution? (Contribution is defined as selling price minus materials cost.)

16.31 *Simplex solution to LP minimization problem.* Molly Brewer is the transportation coordinator for Midvale public schools. Midvale is a growing city and has just recently added its second high school. Molly is in the process of deciding how much the added transportation facilities will cost. She has been asked to determine the most efficient student split from a transportation perspective, which will be an important deciding factor in the school board's decision. The city has been divided into six sections, with the mileage relationship as follows:

FROM SECTOR	A	B	C	D	E	F
A	0	2	4	2	3	5
B	2	0	2	3	2	3
C	4	2	0	5	3	2
D	2	3	5	0	2	4
E	3	2	3	2	0	2
F	5	3	2	4	2	0

MILES TO SECTOR

The schools are in sectors B and E, and because of federal regulations, each has to have at least 100 bused students. Students within a school sector will go to that school on local buses. The minimum number of students in each sector that would take a school bus is as follows:

SECTOR	STUDENTS
A	30
B	45
C	64
D	21
E	25
F	61

Required:
Set up the LP problem and calculate the initial tableau.

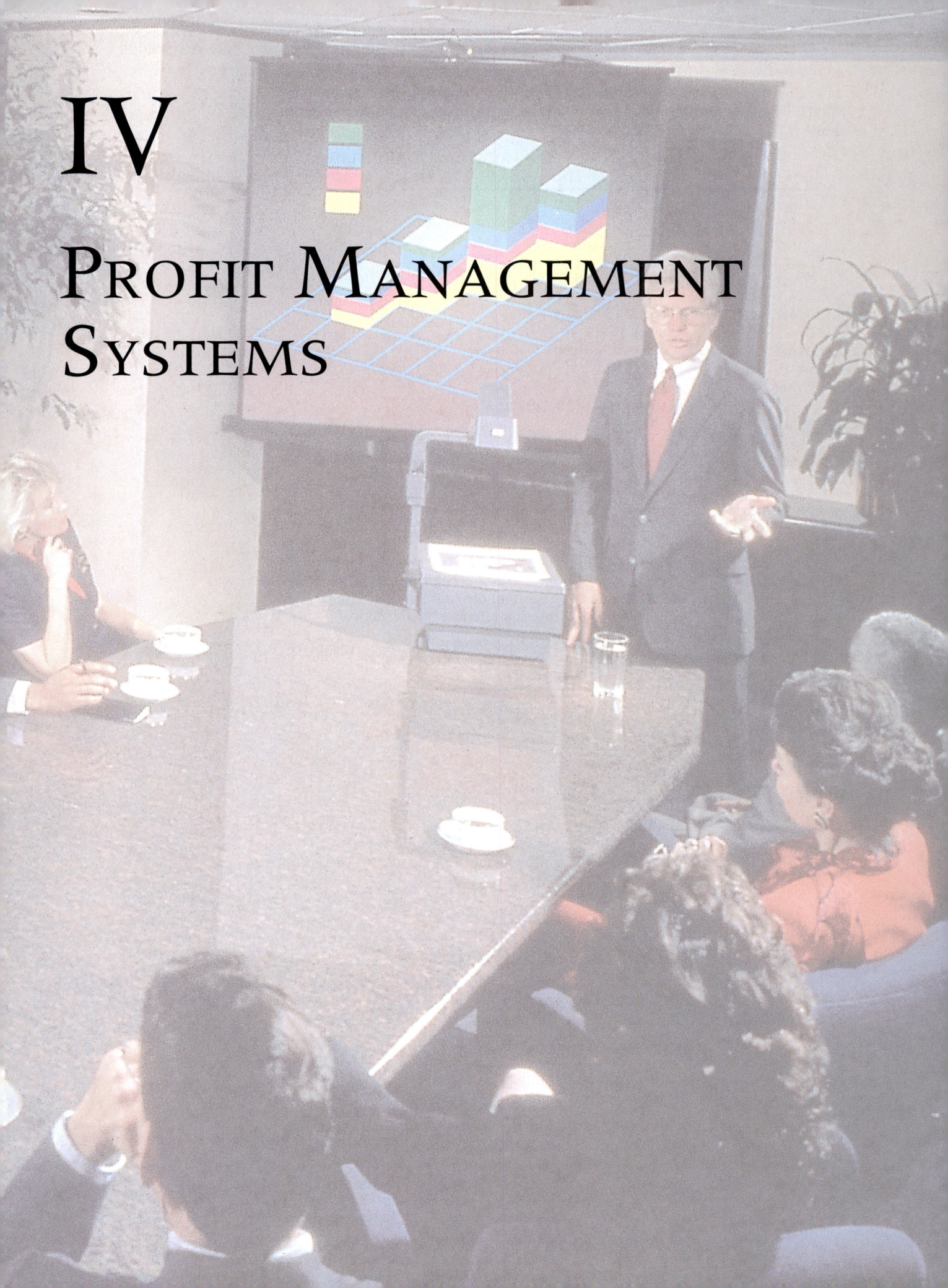

IV

PROFIT MANAGEMENT SYSTEMS

■ The modern management accountant is concerned with more than designing high-quality cost accounting and cost management systems. Many management accounting activities are concerned with planning, controlling, and evaluating profit centers. Cost management is just one aspect of profit management. From this perspective, cost management systems are a subset of the overall management accounting system. Part IV presents five chapters dealing with the three decision-making functions of profit center managers.

Within the planning function, Chapter 17 introduces the need for strategic planning and provides a methodology for developing a strategic plan. This is the basis for the master budget. This process is presented in detail, showing how to prepare each of the supporting schedules leading to the pro forma statements. The schedules and pro formas are linked together within a demonstration problem spreadsheet program.

Once the master budget is completed, it can undergo a number of revisions. Chapter 18 provides a model for efficiently calculating the effects of alternative profit plans. This model is called CVP analysis, and it begins with the development of a profit equation. Incremental CVP analysis, sensitivity analysis, and financial planning software programs are also covered.

Incremental CVP analysis is an important profit management tool that is used in identifying the relevant costs of the alternatives profit center managers consider during their monitoring and controlling function. Chapter 19 applies incremental CVP analysis to specific profit management decisions.

Chapter 20 uses the profit equation to construct a segmented contribution margin–based income statement format. This type of income statement allows management to analyze and evaluate the profit contribution of different types of profit center segments within an enterprise, as well as the contribution of their managers.

Finally, Chapter 21 addresses one of the thorniest topics in profit management for large, decentralized, and/or multinational enterprises. Transfer pricing involves the planning, control, and evaluation decisions concerning the transfer and/or sale of products between segments within the enterprise. Uniquely, this chapter applies the relevant costs approach to solving this problem. Chapter 21 also provides an interesting application of incremental CVP analysis that links together the material presented in the previous chapters. The chapter then explains how management accounting systems design is related to various reward systems used for profit center management. ▬

17 STRATEGIC PLANNING AND THE MASTER BUDGET

Budgeting is a team effort.

LEARNING OBJECTIVES

After studying this chapter, you should be able to:

1. Discuss strategic planning and list its component steps.

2. Define the budgets that make up the master budgeting process.

3. Prepare the operating budgets for a manufacturing enterprise.

4. Explain how operating budgets are used in merchandising and service firms.

5. Describe how operating budgets are used to facilitate planning, controlling operations, and evaluating performance.

■ INTRODUCTION

The master budget is a vital tool that management accountants can use to assist enterprise members in planning, controlling, and evaluating activities. Before any budget is prepared, however, an enterprise should develop a strategic plan.

Once an enterprise has developed a strategic plan, the next step is to translate this plan into short-term and long-term budgets for implementation. The master budget contains both the short-term operating budgets and the long-term capital budget. The master budget translates and summarizes the financial results of the strategies chosen for the upcoming year. The strategies (plans) an enterprise chooses are directed toward accomplishing its goals. In this way, the budgets provide a tight, goal-congruent, rational linkage with the strategic plan.[1] ▬

▌STRATEGIC PLANNING

Strategic planning is defined by the Institute of Management Accountants as a systematic and formalized process for purposefully directing and controlling future operations toward desired objectives for periods extending beyond one year. The strategic planning process begins with a mission statement (see p. 782), which sets out the enterprise's purposes. These should include both the business purposes and the social (responsibility) purposes to employees, the community, and the environment. Bently Nevada Corporation's mission statement is the first of six steps in the strategic planning process, shown in Exhibit 17–1.

Step 1:	Define the enterprise's mission and prepare a formal mission statement.
Step 2:	Establish objectives that, if achieved, should accomplish the mission.
Step 3:	Define operating goals for the master budget period.
Step 4:	Analyze the external and internal environments.
Step 5:	Determine strategies (actions) to capitalize on external opportunities and internal strengths and to overcome external threats and internal weaknesses.
Step 6:	Measure results against the strategies planned.

■EXHIBIT 17–1
Steps in the Strategic Planning Process

▌Defining Objectives and Goals

Objectives are long-run statements of what the enterprise wants to accomplish. They serve as criteria for assessing long-run effectiveness. Objectives should be linked to the mission, so that if they are realized, organizational survival should result. Goals are measurable translations of objectives. They are bound by a time period, usually the master budget time frame (the budget horizon). Progress toward goal achievement is measured by the management accounting system and other information systems (manufacturing and marketing LANs, for example).[2] Objectives and goals are often found in the Management Letter included in annual statements and in the Articles of Incorporation.

Among the objectives IMAX (see p. 783) includes in its mission statement are the following:

---

[1] Goal congruence and rational decision making were first discussed in Chapter 7.

[2] Different management and organizational design texts define goals and objectives differently. Semantics are not important here. What is important is the concept of rationally linking the mission statement through goals and objectives to the operational plans for the budget horizon. An excellent discussion can be found in Chapter 2 of J. L. Gibson, J. M. Ivancevich, and J. H. Donnelly, Jr., *Organizations: Behavior, Structure and Processes*, 6th ed. (Dallas, Tex.: BPI, 1988).

In day-to-day business activities, as well as in long-term planning, strategic decisions must be made. It is vital that a framework for decision making be established that accurately reflects corporate priorities and promotes consistency. At Bently Nevada we have the following priorities:

Safety
We continuously strive to create a safer workplace for our employees and to produce products that function at peak performance and safety levels. We will only design and market systems that reliably and effectively monitor the behavior of your machinery. Safety also applies to the environment. Bently Nevada is concerned about ecology and is taking every step possible to ensure protection of the environment.

Quality
We define quality as "conformance to customer requirements." Second only to safety, our highest priority is to consistently provide high quality products and services. Above all, we have a deep commitment to continually improve the way we assist our customers. We've worked hard over the past 35 years to achieve our reputation as the top vendor in our industry and we are proud of it!

Timeliness
Fast, reliable deliveries and prompt replies to inquiries are essential to our mutual success. Although timeliness is of the utmost importance, we will never jeopardize safety or quality to meet deadlines.

Cost
We will continue to provide products of increasingly better value through improved technology and better manufacturing methods. This process of continuous improvement allows us to pass along savings to you. Our commitment to you is to provide the best value in the industry.

Courtesy of Bently Nevada Corporation

- Create a world-class manufacturing environment
- Obtain a 10 percent market share in the next five years

For the upcoming year, IMAX has established four goals:

- To provide customer service and flexibility, IMAX has a three-day cycle time policy for custom configurations and a two-day shipping time policy on standard configurations.
- To maintain high quality and low inventories of materials, IMAX is developing relationships with a few high-quality suppliers.
- To promote a team concept, cross-training programs, just-in-time (JIT) cells, and quality circles have been made integral parts of the management plan.
- To work toward its 10 percent market share objective, IMAX has set a sales goal of 3,200 Highstepper Pentiums™ for the upcoming year.

Considering External and Internal Critical Factors

Strategic planning attempts to develop a combination of strategies to maximize the enterprise's performance while considering all critical factors, both external and internal.

External critical factors include the following:

- Customers
- Vendors
- Shareholders
- Government
- Competitors
- Product or service life cycles

Internal critical factors include the following:

Many factors must be considered during the budgeting process.

- Employees
- Activity-based management (ABM)

INSIGHTS & APPLICATIONS

IMAX Computers and the Highstepper Pentium™

Managing a new venture is often a greater challenge than managing an established business. To meet this challenge, it is critical that the start-up company implement a comprehensive budgeting process.

IMAX Computers, a small start-up company, offers a new line of personal computers known as Highstepper Pentium™. Competition in the microcomputer industry is intense, and the technology can change rapidly. Flexibility, quality, and customer service are key success criteria. IMAX management believes their market niche is in the west coastal United States. In the short run, to establish itself, IMAX is concentrating its marketing efforts in this region. In the long run, national and international sales will be important for growth. Consequently, the Highstepper Pentium™ is advertised in national trade publications and at trade conventions.

- Total quality management (TQM)
- Logistics
- Target costing, new product development, and life cycle analysis
- Throughput analysis
- Constraint optimization

These, and other, critical environmental factors can be organized into the organization's internal strengths and weaknesses, and its external opportunities and threats (SWOT). SWOT takes into account the interactions between the organization and its environment with respect to what the organization does or plans to do (its objectives and goals). Management should understand:

- What the organization can do well
- What it cannot do very well
- Where it is vulnerable
- What countermeasures are appropriate against these vulnerabilities
- Where the opportunities are
- How to take advantage of those opportunities

By using SWOT as a guidepost, alternate courses of action can be evaluated to determine how well the enterprise overcomes its weaknesses and threats, and capitalizes on its strengths and opportunities in attempting to achieve its goals and objectives.

The internal environment revolves around the corporate culture. Culture is composed of generally accepted rules of behavior passed from generation to generation of employees. Five basic elements influence corporate culture:

- The internal environment created by management
- Its values
- Its heroes
- Rites and rituals (regular social activities)
- The informal communication (cultural) network

The external environment can be characterized in six dimensions:

- The firm's competition
- Its legal and political environment
- Economic conditions
- External social and cultural values and customs
- Technological environment within the industry
- International business and cultural environments[3]

[3] L. E. Boone and D. L. Kurtz, *Management*, 3d ed. (New York: Random House, 1987), pp. 52–54. We thank Professor Tom Wright of the Managerial Sciences Department at the University of Nevada for these references and his insights.

INSIGHTS & APPLICATIONS

Monsanto's Introduction of Cycle-Safe

Monsanto's efforts to introduce Cycle-Safe illustrate the impact of a firm's external environment and the difficulty in predicting management's future environment.

Although Monsanto went to great lengths to ensure the safety of Cycle-Safe and received a favorable response to the new product, management did not anticipate the FDA ban. Two dimensions of the external environment—legal and social-cultural—impacted on Monsanto. The company believed that the FDA ban was largely the result of the intense environmental concerns that permeated society at the time.

Monsanto took a proactive stance to the FDA ban of Cycle-Safe. First it initiated legal action . . . [then] Monsanto refiled Cycle-Safe with the FDA and finally received its approval.[4]

Analyzing and predicting the external environment, even in the short run of the master budget horizon, can be at best risky and at worst uncertain:[5]

IMAX, in considering its sales goal and its goals for the world-class manufacturing objective, identified a number of external opportunities and threats:

- Many customer orders are for standard configurations. Therefore, many Highstepper Pentiums™ can be manufactured in a continuous (process) flow. While this can smooth production operations, a three-day finished goods inventory will have to be maintained because of the inherent variability in sales and because IMAX, as a start-up company, is unable to forecast short-term demand accurately.

- Although a few high-quality suppliers are available in the Silicon Valley area of northern California, establishing frequent deliveries (i.e., daily) for a JIT supply situation is not likely in the short run. A 10-day lead time is required for PC boards.

- IMAX chose to locate in Reno, Nevada, because of the area's distribution channels to the primary West Coast market and its low business and property taxes. Also, IMAX management feels it can establish a good relationship with the local government, and obtain favorable tax status by building a factory there.

- Through the local banking community and the Small Business Development Center at the University of Nevada, Reno, IMAX can apply for an SBA loan and develop long-run relationships for creating an EDI system.

- The new national government appears ready to support a proposed amendment to the Americans with Disabilities Act that will provide funding for small businesses with active policies for employing the handicapped.

IMAX management also has identified certain internal strengths and weaknesses that can impact its goal achievement:

- Production and administration facilities can be designed to facilitate efficient operations by handicapped employees. Many of the production processes are amenable to wheelchair-bound employees. Since IMAX is a new company, the plant and administration facilities can be designed for easy access and travel by handicapped employees. For example, fairly cheap land allows for single-story construction. When purchasing office equipment, two-drawer

---

[4] Ibid.

[5] An uncertain environment is one in which the possible outcomes are not known. A risky environment has known outcomes to which probabilities of happening can be attached. Forecasting in risky environments can benefit from the use of expected value and probability statistical analyses.

file cabinets (instead of four-drawer) should be selected to allow easy access by handicapped personnel.

- Employees are willing to learn and are motivated to produce high-quality computers. They are also able to design the technology platforms needed to become a world-class manufacturer. These include the ICBIS's LANs and an EDI system for suppliers and some customers.
- The owners have insufficient funds for capital improvements and working capital. This problem can be partly mitigated by the availability of SBA loan guarantees and possibly funds from special federal programs (noted above).
- To help overcome the funding problems, employees are willing to participate in a futures option in a stock purchase program if and when IMAX publicly offers stock (part of the five-year plan).

Setting Strategies

A strategy is a method or action to achieve a goal. For example, installation of new production facilities to make turbochargers for diesel engines represents a new program for an enterprise. Locating the facilities near a truck manufacturer and becoming the manufacturer's major JIT supplier represents a strategy. With a clear mission, it is easier to perform sales forecasting and coordinate resources so activities and departments can work together for a common purpose. All people throughout the organization know what business they are in, what their purposes are, how they plan to conduct business, who their customers are, and what will be required to get the job done right the first time.

To ensure goal congruence and rational linkages in the strategic plan, environmental SWOTs should be matched with goals that they can affect. Strategies (and tactics, or specific plans of action) should be matched with specific environmental factors. Matching strategies and environmental factors promotes a proactive (rather than reactive) stance as management attempts to influence the enterprise's environmental dimensions.

Measuring Results

Each action should have a desired result that can be specified in a measurable way. The financial outcomes desired can then be compared against actual results. Profit variances are calculated to measure these differences just as cost variances are used to compare standard and actual costs.[6]

Variance analysis should not be restricted to budget-to-actual comparisons for the master budget period, however. Long-range trend comparisons illustrating the changes in budgets, standards, and variances should also be presented, possibly with the use of spreadsheet graphics, to facilitate continuous improvement. The effectiveness criteria developed by the firm should reflect where it is in its life cycle. Short-run criteria emphasize production and sales effectiveness, efficiency, and customer satisfaction. Both sets of stakeholders, external customers and employees, should be considered. Measures of product quality, on-time delivery, and service are important external customer criteria. Measures of employee turnover, absenteeism, attitudes, and learning are important "internal customer" criteria. Long-run criteria measure the changes in short-term results over time and additionally include overall organizational changes in flexibility and adaptivity.[7]

---

[6] Using profit variances in evaluating a profit center manager's performance follows the same logic as using cost variances in evaluating cost center managers. Profit center performance evaluation is presented in Chapter 20. Cost center performance evaluation was covered in Chapters 8 and 9.

[7] Gibson, et al., op. cit., p. 11.

THE MASTER BUDGET

The **master budget** is a quantitative expression of a plan of action usually for the forthcoming fiscal year. It is a comprehensive set of all operating budgets and includes budgeted financial statements as well as a capital budget. The master budget model is illustrated in Exhibit 17–2.

Strategic Planning Compared with Budgeting

Strategic planning is different from preparing annual budgets, although the two are interrelated. One chief difference is the time period involved. Budgeting

EXHIBIT 17–2
The Master Budget Model

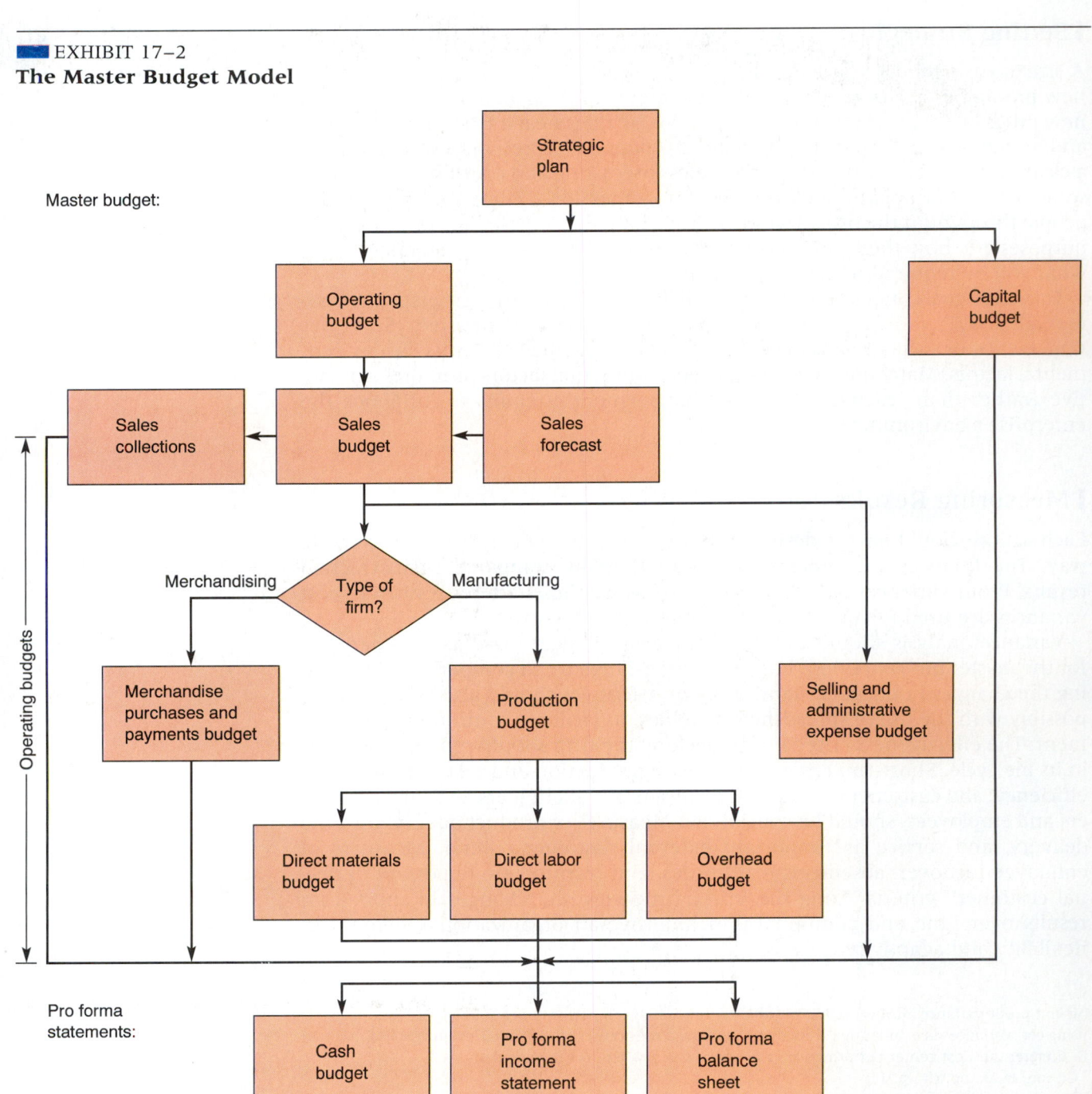

primarily involves one year, whereas strategic planning ultimately covers a period that can be three years, ten years, or more, depending on the firm's mission and objectives. The strategic plan is long range; the annual budget is short range. They are interrelated because the master budget is a tool used to achieve one or more of the actions outlined in the strategic plan.

Another difference is that the strategic plan contains relatively little financial data, whereas the master budget is financially based. The main parts of a strategic plan are narrative; for example: "To increase the quality of our products and decrease costs of quality, *a total quality management (TQM) system should be implemented.*" The objective is in normal type and the goal is italicized. Other examples follow the same pattern:

- "To increase aftertax return to shareholders from 12 to 18 percent during the next five years, *we need to increase sales from $50 million to $90 million during this period by decreasing time-to-market of new products by 20 percent.*"
- "To increase our market share from 16 to 20 percent within the next four years, *we must decrease our delivery time by 30 percent.*"
- "To reduce production costs by 20 percent within two years, *we must eliminate nonvalue-added activities and reengineer value-added activities.*"

Role of Management Accountants in Strategic Planning and Budgeting

To a great extent, the reasons for strategic planning and budgeting are to enable management to reengineer and continuously improve the organization, ensuring its success. During strategic planning, management accountants should review the mission, objectives, goals, and strategies looking for conflicts. For example, an enterprise might be reducing raw materials costs by substituting cheaper materials, while at the same time attempting to eliminate internal and external failure costs. These may be in conflict unless the cheaper raw materials meet quality standards. If this is indeed the case, then both can be achieved. On the other hand, if a trade-off is necessary, the people involved should be made aware which one has the greater priority.

Management accountants can also assist managers in determining how they should change the current situation to improve performance.[8] In simple terms, the enterprise must know where it is before it can determine where it wants to be.

Further, management accountants can provide reports comparing actual to budget. They can also develop a broad range of performance measurements. Both financial and nonfinancial information serve as a backdrop for strategic planning and budgeting; for example, product or service costs, activity analysis (e.g., determination of nonvalue-added activities), costs of quality, logistics costs, target costs, life cycle analysis, throughput, and constraint analysis can all be used.

Consequently, modern management accountants perform many roles in the strategic planning and master budgeting process. They serve as organizers, overseers, facilitators, and even "number crunchers."[9] As already noted, a link should exist between strategic planning and the master budget. The principal people who "audit" this link are management accountants. The manner in which the budgeting process is performed and the frequency of budget revisions can promote this linkage.

---

[8] Review Chapter 2 on world-class concepts, Chapter 3 on enterprisewide modeling, and Chapter 7 on setting standard costs.

[9] For example, modern management accountants create computer programs that prepare the budgets. Although management accountants are responsible for preparing budgets, they are not responsible for creating the raw data needed. This would be inconsistent with participative budgeting, as well as with the competency and objectivity standards of ethical conduct.

Zero-Based Budgeting

Many traditional enterprises prepare annual budgets using last year's budget and actual results as a starting point. The upcoming year's budget often simply adjusts the previous year's budget by changing prices without *necessarily* questioning the validity or appropriateness of last year's expenditures with respect to the organization's strategic plan. One of the main pitfalls with this approach is that the budgeting process may not give adequate consideration to continuous improvement. Implicitly, projected expenditures are justified because the activities creating them were accepted as legitimate *last year*. Another serious pitfall, especially prevalent with governmental operations in adverse economic environments, is the attitude of "spend it or lose it." If any efficiencies have resulted in cost savings, the surplus funds are spent at the end of the fiscal year on nonbudgeted items. This frantic spending occurs because the responsibility center managers fear that their budgets will be cut if they do not spend all the funds budgeted in the previous year.

Zero-based budgeting presents an alternative approach to the incremental budgeting process just described. Under zero-based budgeting, each activity, department, or division is periodically rolled back to a zero budget and evaluated critically. Then, each responsibility center manager has to justify every activity and its costs as a condition of the responsibility center's continuation or elimination. Some businesses and government agencies apply zero-based budgeting during strategic planning, activity-based management (ABM), and reengineering initiatives, as discussed in Chapter 11.

Zero-based budgeting can be used as a tool for allocating funds for the annual master budget. Traditionally, incremental budgets worked on the assumption that *all* activities were worthy of receiving budget increases to cover increasing costs. The question, therefore, was not whether to continue the activity, but rather how much the current level of funding should be increased. In contrast, zero-based budgeting questions each activity in the current budget and determines whether it should be supported as is, reengineered, or eliminated, consistent with the objectives and goals in the strategic plan.

Continuous Budgeting

The **budget horizon** is the length of time the master budget covers. Master budgets normally span the fiscal year of an enterprise. To achieve effective decision making and cost management, annual operating budgets are usually broken down into shorter time periods, such as quarters, months, or weeks. A frequent variation of the fiscal-year operating budget is the **continuous budget** in which a 12-month forecast is always available by adding a month or a quarter in the future and dropping the month or quarter just ended. This rolling budget process reflects the dynamics of the enterprise and forces managers to rethink operations constantly no matter what time of the year it is.

Integrated computer-based information systems (ICBISs) with comprehensive databases are especially useful in supporting continuous budgeting. By using simulation models, forecasting techniques, and electronic spreadsheets, managers can determine the impact of various operating alternatives on the master budget and generate the results almost instantaneously. For example, if the cost of raw materials has changed significantly or a competitor is setting lower prices that have to be met, computer programs can quickly produce revised operating budget alternatives that reflect the new raw materials costs and management's new pricing decisions. Management then selects the operating budget that appears to be most feasible for the forthcoming period. Management also may want to analyze the effect of adding or dropping a product line. Computer programs can update current budgeted data, answer what-if questions, and generate a new master budget showing the effects of alternative proposals.

The Master Budget Components

LEARNING OBJECTIVE 2

Define the budgets that make up the master budgeting process.

An **operating budget** (the major subject of this chapter) is the first part of the master budget, representing expected results of operations. For manufacturing firms, it contains the sales, production, direct materials, direct labor, manufacturing overhead, and selling and administrative expense budgets. In merchandising firms, the budgets for manufacturing costs are replaced with budgets for merchandise purchases and payments, as shown in Exhibit 17–2. Service enterprises have only sales and expense budgets.

The operating budget serves many roles in strategic planning, master budgeting, and responsibility accounting:

- An operating budget is a *planning* tool because it is a written plan for the future operations of an enterprise congruent with the strategic planning objectives.
- An operating budget is a *control* tool because it helps manage sales, costs, and profits by setting guidelines. People are less inclined to spend money for things that are not needed if they know all expenditures will be compared with specific line items in the budget.
- An operating budget is a *performance evaluation* tool because budgets can reveal the progress, or lack of progress, of managers. A budget, therefore, is just as likely to enhance a manager's career as it is to be detrimental to a manager's career.
- Moreover, managers can also use budgets as *self-evaluation* tools.
- An operating budget can be a *motivational* tool, especially when managers and workers take part in preparing the budget. If, on the other hand, the budget is forced on them, the budget will probably be viewed as a threat.
- An operating budget is a means of *communication and coordination*. A budget conveys the objectives the enterprise is trying to achieve.

The **capital budget** focuses on planned capital outlays for property, plant, and equipment. It is a listing of all approved long-term expenditures planned to improve an enterprise's operating capacity and efficiency. The capital budgeting methodology is covered in Chapters 22 through 24.

The master budget culminates in estimated financial statements, referred to as **pro forma statements.** These statements include the following:

- Cash budget
- Budgeted income statement
- Budgeted balance sheet

STEPS IN PREPARING THE OPERATING BUDGETS

LEARNING OBJECTIVE 3

Prepare the operating budgets for a manufacturing enterprise.

Preparing the operating budgets involves the following eight steps:

1. Make a sales forecast.
2. Prepare the sales budget.
3. Develop the production budget.
4. Prepare the direct materials purchases budget.
5. Prepare the direct labor budget.
6. Prepare the manufacturing overhead budget.
7. Prepare the selling and administrative expenses budget.
8. Prepare budgeted financial statements.

These steps are addressed in the following sections.

What will sales be?

Step 1: Make the Sales Forecast

The **sales forecast** is a projection of the number of products to be sold within the budget horizon. It is the basis of the sales budget, which, in turn, is the basis for all of the other operating budgets. Consequently, the accuracy of the sales forecast directly affects the reliability of the master budget.

Sales forecasts can be classified in many ways. Among the most common are sales by products, by product lines, by distribution channels, by class of customer, and by territories. The following methods are normally used to forecast sales:

- Estimate method
- Statistical method

THE ESTIMATE METHOD. The estimate method is essentially subjective and assumes that the forecaster's knowledge and experience are sufficient to develop reliable forecasts. Generally, one of the following processes is used to develop the sales forecast:

- *Top-down*. A small group of strategic-level managers determines the sales forecast generally with aid from their staff. Often, this approach results in a sales goal being communicated to lower-level managers. In enterprises with highly centralized decision making and well-defined lines of authority, an autocratic approach sometimes results, based on top management's belief in a Theory X level of motivation in employees. While this approach may be adequate in very stable organizations and external environments, it may not be effective in other situations. More importantly, an autocratic process does not assure that employees will accept the budget as legitimate. Consequently, they may not be motivated to attempt to achieve it. Instead, employees may fight the budget, claiming that it places unrealistic demands upon them. Dysfunctional behavior may also result even if top management uses a consultative approach to budgeting. In this approach, top management consults with operations personnel, but the final forecast and budgets are set at the top without formal employee agreement.

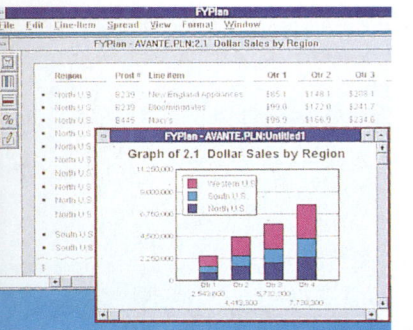

FYPlan's flexible reporting and graphing capabilities allow users to view data any way they choose.

- *Bottom-up*. The key feature of this approach is that multiple levels of managers and salespersons are involved in the forecasting process. As an example, many companies require that individual sales representatives estimate sales for their sales areas. These estimates are then combined to obtain a total sales figure. In contrast to the autocratic and consultative approaches, this approach relies on participative budgeting. Often, many iterations of sales forecasts, operating budgets, and pro forma statements are conducted before the final agreement of operations personnel is obtained. This approach is based on a Theory Y belief in motivation. Operating personnel are motivated to prepare realistic budgets and accept them as valid benchmarks for performance evaluation. There is also some evidence that line management and shop floor personnel will set and achieve more ideal standards than top management would set. The bottom-up approach is particularly effective in unstable external environments requiring decentralized operations.

THE STATISTICAL METHOD. In contrast to the estimate method, the statistical method uses objective data, such as financial, operating, and economic data, as a basis for forecasts. Historical financial and operating data are generated by management accountants and stored on computer databases. Economic data are obtained from government publications, trade journals, consultants, and various research companies. External data, such as housing starts, regulatory effects, automobile production, weather forecasts, oil prices, projected interest rates, projected inflation rate, and projected GNP, are also used. Both the internal and external data are fed into various sophisticated statistical and econometric models to generate sales forecasts.

Then, the forecasts are presented to the budget committee for approval. Three versions may be considered:

- Best case
- Worst case
- Most likely case

A best case budget is prepared with the assumption that everything will work out as planned. A worst case budget predicts just the opposite and includes the necessary corrective actions that would be performed if the anticipated problems occur. For example, management may establish a line-of-credit just in case additional funds are needed. A most likely case budget includes normal disruptions, constraints, and estimation errors.

The budget committee decides which sales forecast is most reasonable and supportive of the strategic plan. In addition, a budget committee may sometimes make specific recommendations for increasing sales, quality improvement, faster delivery, efficient order processing, advertising campaigns, and the like.

Returning to the IMAX case, top management chose a participative budgeting approach to setting the sales forecast. IMAX's sales staff, armed with a simple questionnaire, surveyed their customers to determine how many Highstepper Pentiums™ they planned to buy and how much they would be willing to pay. IMAX's entire budget is based on the sales forecast—the number of Highstepper Pentiums™ that it will sell and the price they will be sold for. Sales forecasting is the main "gear" that drives all the other "budget gears," and it is the most uncertain part of IMAX's budgeting process. It must be supported by a combination of facts, market surveys, detailed analysis, and assumptions. The data from these surveys were given to IMAX's management accountant, Hal Segiguchi, who entered the data into a spreadsheet program. The program produces the sales budget discussed next.

Step 2: Prepare the Sales Budget

Once a sales forecast is made, a sales budget is prepared. The **sales budget** is the expected sales in units and dollars and includes a schedule of cash collections from sales. It serves as a basis for preparing the other budgets. Clearly, the sales level affects the production and purchasing levels, the operating expense levels, as well as cash flow.

The sales budget should be supportive of the strategic plan. For example, management must be careful about deviating from long-term pricing strategies to meet short-term sales projections.

Hal Segiguchi used one of the Highstepper Pentiums™ to run the spreadsheet program, which generated different results based on several sets of assumptions about pricing and promotion. The spreadsheet program includes an "add-in" program for statistical forecasting and sensitivity analysis.[10] The results were sent to the budget committee for review. The forecast and pricing they selected were returned to Hal, who prepared the sales budget. To keep the procedures and calculations to a manageable level, only the budgets for the second quarter of 1995 are presented in the exhibits that follow.

Exhibit 17–3 presents the sales forecast, which is based on a stable sales price of $2,000 per computer. The sales staff, based on their survey results, believe 20 percent of IMAX's customers will pay in cash. Cash sales for each month in the second quarter of 1995 comprise the first set of four "sources of cash from sales" included in the Collections of Sales schedule.

---

[10] The Lotus® add-in @RISK is demonstrated in D. F. Togo, "A Spreadsheet Approach to Stochastic Financial Modeling," *Journal of Accounting Education,* Fall, 1992, pp. 321–327.

■ EXHIBIT 17–3
IMAX's Sales Budget

SALES FORECAST:	Feb.	March	April	May	June	July	Aug.
Sales (units)	350	250	200	230	270	300	220
× sales price	$2,000	$2,000	$2,000	$2,000	$2,000	$2,000	$2,000
Sales revenues	$700,000	$500,000	$400,000	$460,000	$540,000	$600,000	$440,000

COLLECTIONS OF SALES: Amounts Collected

Month	Sales	Formula	April	May	June
This month–cash*					
April	$400,000 × 20%		$80,000		
May	$460,000 × 20%			$92,000	
June	$540,000 × 20%				$108,000
This month–credit**					
April	$400,000 × 80% × 50% × 98%		156,800		
May	$460,000 × 80% × 50% × 98%			180,320	
June	$540,000 × 80% × 50% × 98%				211,680
From last month's credit sales					
March	$500,000 × 80% × 35%		140,000		
April	$400,000 × 80% × 35%			112,000	
May	$460,000 × 80% × 35%				128,800
From 2 months ago–credit sales					
February	$700,000 × 80% × 14%		78,400		
March	$500,000 × 80% × 14%			56,000	
April	$400,000 × 80% × 14%				44,800
Total cash collected from sales in 2nd quarter:			$455,200	$440,320	$493,280

*Cash sales = 20% of each month's total sales.
**Credit sales collection pattern = 50% collected in month of sale (less 2% discount), 35% in next month, 14% two months after sales, and 1% bad debts.

MANUAL CALCULATIONS PROCEDURES:

1. *Find information on when sales are collected.*
   (Cash versus Credit Sales, and Credit Collection Pattern)
2. *Setup schedule format.*
   (3 columns + 1 column for each month included in the budget period. There will be 1 group of rows for each source of cash. For this example, there are 4 sources of cash deposited into the bank each month. Within each group of rows, there will be 1 row for each month in the budget period.)
3. *Write in given information.*
   (In column 1, write down the month that belongs on each row; in column 2, write in the sales for that month; and then, in column 3, write in the multiplication chains [the collection formula].)
4. *Turn on your calculator and complete each month's column.*
   (The last three columns in the "Amounts Collected" section.)

The sales staff has two choices for credit sales: extending in-house credit or accepting national credit cards. When in-house credit is offered, a **credit collection pattern** is used to show how much of a month's credit sales are projected to be collected in that month and in subsequent months. The following pattern is used in Exhibit 17–3:

■ Fifty percent of a month's credit sales will be collected within that month.

- Thirty-five percent of a month's credit sales will be collected in the subsequent month (a "one-month lag").
- Fourteen percent of a month's credit sales will be collected two months in the future (a two-month lag on collections).
- One percent of a month's credit sales are projected to be uncollectible.
- To collect credit sales within the month of sale, IMAX will have to offer a 2 percent credit sales discount. This can be justified by the cost savings from not having to send out monthly statements to credit customers paying from the invoices.

The sales manager and staff decided against accepting national credit cards because they would charge a 3 percent fee, maintaining the separate bank accounts required by each card would involve extra costs, and IMAX could be backcharged for sales rejected by the credit card companies. The credit card companies' experience in backcharges is greater than the 1 percent of in-house credit sales projected to be uncollectible.

Exhibit 17–3's schedule for Collections of Sales includes four sources of cash deposits into IMAX's bank account within any given month. The first section of the exhibit includes the cash sales for that month. The second section represents deposits from credit sales made during the month. The third section, and the third type of cash deposits made in a month, comes from collections of credit sales made in the previous month. The fourth section includes deposits from collections of credit sales made two months ago.

The "Formula" column of the schedule shows the multiplication chains that represent the credit collection pattern. The first set of percentages (20 and 80 percent) are the portion of a month's sales that are cash versus credit. The second set of percentages (50, 35, and 14 percent, respectively) are the percentages of a month's credit sales collected in subsequent months. The third set of percentages in the chain represents the net amounts collected within the month of sale adjusted for the 2 percent credit sales discount.[11] Procedures for setting up this section of the sales budget manually, and verifying the amounts, are presented at the bottom of Exhibit 17–3.

Step 3: Develop the Production Budget

The **production budget** presents the production quota for the budget period, adjusted for planned changes in finished goods inventory levels. The production budget is used in conjunction with raw materials inventory plans to prepare the direct materials purchases budget. It is also used to prepare the direct labor budget and manufacturing overhead budgets.

Although the sales budget is usually developed before the production budget, there should be continuous communication between production and marketing to ensure that production requirements are somewhat uniform throughout the year and capacity is not exceeded. With a stable production policy, manufacturing resources will be better utilized. Moreover, careful planning of production, inventory levels, labor needs, and other resource requirements can result in significant savings.

Exhibit 17–4 presents IMAX's production budget. According to this budget, sufficient units have to be available to meet sales needs and provide for the desired ending inventory. Because of the production cycle time for the Highstepper Pentium™ and inherent uncertainty in daily sales, three days of FGI is desired.[12] Consequently, each month's *beginning* FGI should be 10 percent (3 of 30 days in a month) of the month's projected sales. This is equivalent to having a desired *ending* FGI equal to 10 percent of next month's sales forecast.

---

[11] If a 2 percent discount is offered, then only 98 percent of the amount charged will be collected.
[12] This was an external threat included in the environmental analysis section of the strategic plan.

■ EXHIBIT 17–4
IMAX's Production Budget

	April	May	June	July
Sales (in units)	200	230	270	300
Plus desired ending FGI	23	27	30	
Units needed	223	257	300	
Less beginning FGI	<20>	<23>	<27>	
Production quota	203	234	273	

Note: Ending FGI = 10% of next month's sales forecast.

How much direct materials will be needed?

Step 4: Prepare the Direct Materials Purchases Budget

The **direct materials purchases budget** presents the expected usage of direct materials in production and facilitates planning of purchases. It also assists managers in reducing ordering and carrying costs, whether the inventory management approach is economic order quantity (EOQ) and safety stock, material requirements planning (MRP), or just-in-time (JIT).

A direct material's required quantity is a function of its standard quantity and the production quota. The engineering staff and production personnel, through developing a bill of materials and standard cost card, know how many direct materials (the standard quantity) are required to produce a finished computer. The direct materials standard price is normally estimated by the purchasing manager. In addition, the purchasing manager plans direct material inventory levels, purchases, and the cost of these purchases.

Sufficient direct materials must be available to meet production needs and provide the desired ending direct materials inventory for each month in the budget period. Thus, part of the direct materials requirement will normally exist in the form of beginning direct materials inventory. The remainder will be purchased from suppliers. A 10-day supply of PC boards is needed for production of the Highstepper Pentium™ (a 10-day supply is one-third of a month). Since IMAX is unable to negotiate JIT deliveries, one-third of the projected PC boards needed in a month should be in that month's beginning direct materials inventory. Or, equivalently, a month's ending direct materials inventory should be one-third of the next month's projected PC boards needed.

The direct materials purchases budget is normally accompanied by a computation of expected cash disbursements for direct materials purchases. This schedule is necessary for developing the cash budget. Disbursements for direct materials consist of payments for some of the prior month's purchases and some of the current month's purchases. Because PC board shipments are received every 10 days, two-thirds of a month's purchases are paid within that month, and the last one-third of the month's purchases are paid in the next month.[13] The direct materials purchases budget for PC boards is illustrated in Exhibit 17–5, which includes only the budget for PC boards. Each direct material included on the standard cost card has its own purchases and payments budget. Obviously, the use of a computer program is advantageous. This program can be part of the MRP II program in the production LAN or a component of the standard cost program in the management accounting LAN; alternatively, it can reside in a centralized database in an ICBIS, accessed by each LAN as needed. The standard cost card is presented on page 801 in Exhibit 17–10.

---

[13] The shipments received on the 1st and 10th of the month are paid on the 10th and 20th of the month, respectively, in order to capture the purchase discount included in the standard price calculation. The shipment received on the 20th of the month can be paid on the 1st of the next month and still take the purchase discount.

■**EXHIBIT 17–5**
IMAX's Direct Materials Purchases Budget for PC Boards

		March	April	May	June	July
Production quota		245	203	234	273	292
× standard quantity of PC boards		5	5	5	5	5
PC boards needed for current production		1,225	1,015	1,170	1,365	1,460
Plus ending inventory	1/3	338	390	455	487	
Less beginning inventory	1/3	<408>	<338>	<390>	<455>	
PC boards to purchase		1,155	1,067	1,235	1,397	
× standard price		$100	$100	$100	$100	
Total purchase cost		$115,500	$106,700	$123,500	$139,700	
ACCOUNTS PAYABLE PAYMENT SCHEDULE:						
To pay this month	2/3		$71,133	$82,333	$93,133	
Owed from last month	1/3		38,500	35,567	41,167	$46,567
Cash outflow for accounts payable payments			$109,633	$117,900	$134,300	

Notes:
1. The production quotas for March and July were based on sales from Exhibit 17–3.
2. Ending PC boards inventory = one-third of next month's needs.
3. Supplier payment terms require payment of two-thirds of a month's purchases within the month in order to obtain the purchase discount included in the standard price.

Step 5: Prepare the Direct Labor Budget

The production quota is also used as a basis for the **direct labor budget.** This budget contains the direct labor hours to schedule each month, the direct labor cost, and a schedule of cash flows for the payment of labor-related costs.

The method used to convert production quota to direct labor hours varies from one company to another. Some companies have comprehensive standard cost records and sufficient experience to estimate standard direct labor hours fairly accurately. On the other hand, if the product is new, an industrial engineer may set up time and motion studies and learning curve analyses to develop reliable labor standard quantities.

After meeting with the cell workers, IMAX's industrial engineer determined that 20 direct labor hours will be required to complete one Highstepper Pentium™. The standard direct labor rate includes the wage rates budgeted and the projected payroll taxes and fringe benefits. Standard labor hours are based on practical standards, with allowances for inspection time within each task.[14] The resulting direct labor budget is shown in Exhibit 17–6.

How much direct labor will be needed?

Step 6: Prepare the Manufacturing Overhead Budget

The **manufacturing overhead budget** contains the expected cost of all indirect manufacturing elements necessary to meet the production budget. The manufacturing overhead budget summarizes the overhead costs of all the different responsibility centers. Like different direct materials, each responsibility center should have a separate overhead budget. Therefore, overhead cost equations are needed for each overhead resource, activity, service center, and pro-

---

[14] Issues dealing with motivation and responsibility accounting in budgeting standard costs are discussed in Chapter 7.

■■■EXHIBIT 17–6
IMAX's Direct Labor Budget

		March	April	May	June	July
Production quota		245	203	234	273	
× standard quantity		20	20	20	20	
Direct labor hours to schedule		4,900	4,060	4,680	5,460	
× standard price		$15	$15	$15	$15	
Total direct labor cost		$73,500	$60,900	$70,200	$81,900	
WAGES PAYABLE PAYMENT SCHEDULE:						
To pay this month	75%		$45,675	$52,650	$61,425	
Owed from last month	25%		18,375	15,225	17,550	$20,475
Cash outflow for wages payable payments			$64,050	$67,875	$78,975	

Note: Workers are paid weekly so the last week's labor cost is paid in the first week of the next month.

duction department. As all overhead flows into the production departments' overhead accounts and predetermined overhead rates (PORs) within the production budgeting process, the PORs include all the different indirect and support activities. This allows the management accountant to prepare a summary budget for all overhead costs using the departmental PORs. To further simplify the concept, assume IMAX uses just one plantwide variable overhead (VOH) POR and fixed overhead (FOH) POR.

Exhibit 17–7 presents the summary overhead budget for IMAX. The VOH POR of $10 per direct labor hour captures all the VOH items within the factory. The budgeted fixed overhead of $40,000 per month includes $25,000 per month in building and equipment depreciation. Note that this is subtracted from the budgeted overhead because it is not a cash cost. Also note that in the Payment Schedule, all overhead costs are paid on a one-month lag. In other words, all overhead costs incurred in a month are paid in the next month.

A word of caution is in order. Many fixed overhead costs are not incurred uniformly throughout the year. For example, property taxes and insurance may only be paid semiannually or annually. In these situations, the fixed overhead costs should be budgeted in amounts representative of when actual payments are expected to be made. This further highlights the necessity of having separate budgets for individual overhead activities. The IMAX illustration in Exhibit 17–7 is oversimplified.

How much manufacturing overhead will be needed?

Step 7: Prepare the Selling and Administrative Expenses Budget

The **selling and administrative expenses budget** includes planned expenditures for nonmanufacturing activities. Like the costs in the manufacturing overhead budget, selling and administrative expenses can be divided into variable and fixed components.

To develop this budget, IMAX managers in charge of marketing and administration analyzed the amount of resources they needed to meet the sales budget. The results of this analysis are presented in Exhibit 17–8. This summary budget uses the same format as the summary overhead budget. Like the overhead budgets, selling and administrative budgets should be individually prepared by each responsibility center manager.

A word of caution is in order when budgeting variable selling and administra-

▮▮▮EXHIBIT 17–7
IMAX's Manufacturing Overhead Budget

	March	April	May	June	July
Production quota	245	203	234	273	
× direct labor standard quantity	20	20	20	20	
Direct labor hours to schedule	4,900	4,060	4,680	5,460	
× VOH POR	$10	$10	$10	$10	
Total VOH cost	$49,000	$40,600	$46,800	$54,600	
Total FOH cost	40,000	40,000	40,000	40,000	
Less noncash FOH items: Depreciation	<25,000>	<25,000>	<25,000>	<25,000>	
Total cash-related FOH costs	$15,000	$15,000	$15,000	$15,000	
Total budgeted cash overhead	$64,000	$55,600	$61,800	$69,600	

MANUFACTURING OVERHEAD PAYMENT
SCHEDULE:

		March	April	May	June	July
To pay this month	0%		$ –0–	$ –0–	$ –0–	
Owed from last month	100%		64,000	55,600	61,800	$69,600
Cash outflow for overhead payments			$64,000	$55,600	$61,800	

Notes:
1. Noncash items are subtracted from FOH because only cash-paid costs should appear on the cash budget.
2. All overhead costs are paid on a one-month lag.

▮▮▮EXHIBIT 17–8
IMAX's Selling and Administrative Expenses Budget

	March	April	May	June	July
Sales revenues (Exhibit 17–3)	$500,000	$400,000	$460,000	$540,000	
× variable selling expenses	5%	5%	5%	5%	
Total variable selling expenses	25,000	20,000	23,000	27,000	
Total fixed selling expenses	20,000	25,000	20,000	20,000	
Total fixed administrative expenses	130,000	120,000	125,000	150,000	
Less noncash expenses: Depreciation	<5,000>	<5,000>	<5,000>	<5,000>	
Total cash-related fixed S & A expenses	$145,000	$140,000	$140,000	$165,000	
Total cash S & A expenses budgeted	$170,000	$160,000	$163,000	$192,000	

SELLING AND ADMINISTRATIVE
EXPENSES PAYMENT SCHEDULE:

		March	April	May	June	July
To pay this month	0%		$ –0–	$ –0–	$ –0–	
Owed from last month	100%		170,000	160,000	163,000	$192,000
Cash outflow S & A expenses payments			$170,000	$160,000	$163,000	

Notes:
1. Noncash items are subtracted from fixed administrative expenses because only cash-paid costs
   should appear on the cash budget.
2. All selling and administrative expenses are paid on a one-month lag.

tive expenses. Some expenses vary with sales *revenues*, such as the 5 percent sales commission used in the IMAX case, other expenses, though, such as shipping costs, vary with sales *volume*. Consequently, the budget may contain two variable selling expense lines. Consistent with activity-based costing, some administrative expenses may vary with the activities performed. For example, some order processing and accounts receivable costs will vary with the number of shipments and/or sales orders processed.

Step 8: Prepare Budgeted Financial Statements

The foregoing budgets produce the necessary data to prepare IMAX's pro forma (budgeted) financial statements. These statements include the following:

- The **cash budget** discloses the expected cash inflows and outflows for the budget period. The cash budget is interrelated to all the other budgets and is the starting point for the preparation of the pro formas.
- The sales budget, standard cost card, and selling and administrative expenses budget provide the data necessary to prepare the **pro forma income statement.** Additional data on other income, other expenses, and income taxes are also gathered from other sources and included.
- The **pro forma balance sheet** shows the projected financial position of the enterprise at the end of the budget period. Many of the amounts needed are created in the process of preparing the operating budgets. As these amounts are identified, they can be "posted" to the pro forma balance sheet. Detailed instructions for preparing the pro formas are presented next.

THE CASH BUDGET.   Exhibit 17–9 presents IMAX's cash budget for the second quarter, 1995. It pulls together much of the data generated in the preceding steps. Hal Segiguchi's spreadsheet program copied the monthly totals from the operating budgets into this report. He then input into the Data Section of the program amounts for nonoperational cash flows obtained from general ledger personnel and the Finance Department.

Prior to Hal's new spreadsheet program and Highstepper Pentium,™ he had to prepare the budgets manually. Obviously, this was a time-consuming and complex process. Hal followed these steps in manually preparing IMAX's budgets:

Step 1. *Get a big table.* In the middle of the table, Hal placed a sheet of four-column accounting working paper for the cash budget. On each side of this paper, Hal placed a sheet of working paper for the pro forma income statement and balance sheet. His strategy was to develop the operating budgets as needed to provide the amounts for the cash budget. As soon as amounts needed for the income statement and balance sheet were created on an operating budget, they were "posted" to the pro formas. In this way, the cash budget served as the focal point for his manual process. Additionally, this process allowed Hal to prepare the pro formas simultaneously with the operating budgets.

Step 2. *Begin the cash budget.* Hal then began with the cash budget's first entry. If this entry needed a supporting schedule, he would prepare it, post the amounts to the cash budget and pro formas, and then place the schedule next to the pro formas on the table. Hal set up the cash budget format by dividing it into three sections:

- The "Cash from Operations" section reports on the cash flows from operations for each month in the budget horizon. IMAX's management used the Cash from Operations subtotal as a measure of cash "profitability" resulting from the production and sales of the Highstepper Pentium™. This subtotal answers the question, "Do each month's *operations* generate a positive cash flow?"
- The second section lists nonoperational sources and uses of cash. The subtotal "Monthly Cash Flow" is used by IMAX management as a measure of the month's cash profitability. This subtotal answers the question, "Does the *month as a whole* generate a positive cash flow?" Hal obtained the information for this section from the capital budget

▆ EXHIBIT 17–9

IMAX's Cash Budget for the Second Quarter

CASH BUDGET
SECOND QUARTER, 1995

	April	May	June	Totals
OPERATIONAL CASH INFLOWS:				
From product sales (Exhibit 17–3)	$455,200	$440,320	$493,280	$1,388,800
OPERATIONAL CASH OUTFLOWS:				
Direct materials (Exhibit 17–5)	$109,633	$117,900	$134,300	361,833
Direct labor (Exhibit 17–6)	64,050	67,875	78,975	210,900
Manufacturing overhead (Exhibit 17–7)	64,000	55,600	61,800	181,400
Selling & Admin. expenses (Exhibit 17–8)	170,000	160,000	163,000	493,000
Income taxes (Exhibit 17–11)	<450>	3,844	4,536	7,930
TOTAL OPERATIONAL CASH OUTFLOWS	<$407,233>	<$405,219>	<$442,611>	<$1,255,063>
CASH FROM OPERATIONS	$47,967	$35,101	$50,669	$133,737
NONOPERATIONAL SOURCES & USES:				
Notes receivable collections	7,000	–0–	7,000	14,000
Equipment purchases	<5,000>	<10,000>	<10,000>	<25,000>
Notes payable payments	<40,000>	<40,000>	<40,000>	<120,000>
TOTAL NONOPERATIONAL CASH FLOWS	<$38,000>	<$50,000>	<$43,000>	<$131,000>
MONTHLY CASH FLOW	$9,967	<$14,899>	$7,669	$2,737
Beginning cash balance	20,000	24,917	20,000	20,000
CASH SURPLUS/<DEFICIT>	$29,967	$10,018	$27,669	$22,737
FINANCING:				
Beginning line-of-credit balance	$5,000	$–0–	$9,982	$5,000
Interest	<50>	–0–	<100>	<150>
Borrowings	–0–	9,982	–0–	9,982
Repayments	<5,000>	–0–	<7,569>	<12,569>
Ending line-of-credit balance	–0–	9,982	2,413	2,413
ENDING CASH BALANCE	$24,917	$20,000	$20,000	$20,000

and general ledger personnel in the Accounting Department. Sources are positive amounts as they will be deposited into IMAX's bank account. Uses are payments and, thus, are shown as negative amounts.

▪ The last section "Financing" addresses the need for short-term financing. In some months, all businesses have surplus cash left over. In other months, there may not be sufficient deposits to cover the anticipated payments. In these months, a company needs a **line-of-credit** with its bank. A line-of-credit is analogous to an individual having overdraft protection. The bank temporarily deposits funds into IMAX's account to cover a projected deficit. This is a short-term, usually unsecured, loan. When a surplus balance is projected, the bank withdraws the surplus to pay the interest on the loan and then to pay off the principal balance. In this way, IMAX's bank is a stakeholder in the company. IMAX's bank requires that a cash budget, with a financing section, be updated quarterly and provided to the bank as a condition of maintaining the line-of-credit.

The Financing section really begins with the calculation of the monthly bank account balance (the "Cash Surplus/〈Deficit〉" subtotal). This is the sum of the Monthly Cash Flow subtotal plus the beginning cash balance for that month. On April 1, IMAX projects a $20,000 beginning cash balance, which is its minimum required balance according to the line-of-credit agreement with the bank. Whenever IMAX projects a balance less than $20,000, the bank will deposit enough money to bring the balance up to this amount. Whenever IMAX projects an ending balance greater than $20,000, the bank will use the surplus to repay the line-of-credit balance.

On April 1, IMAX expects to owe a $5,000 balance on its line-of-credit. For April, the bank will charge 1 percent simple interest and deduct this amount ($50) from the bank account. Therefore, the monthly interest charge is shown as a negative amount in the cash budget because it will be withdrawn from IMAX's bank account. In April, IMAX projects an ending bank account balance of $29,967 before line-of-credit financing (i.e., the "Cash Surplus/<Deficit>"). It is in a position to pay back the entire balance on its line-of-credit. First, $50 will be deducted from the bank account for interest expense, then $5,000 for principal. This leaves a projected ending line-of-credit balance of zero and an ending bank account balance of $24,917.

The ending cash balance for April becomes the beginning cash balance for May. Once this is known, Hal can calculate May's cash surplus or deficit and determine whether any line-of-credit financing is needed. Because May's cash surplus is only projected to be $10,018, IMAX will need to borrow $9,982 on its line-of-credit so it can maintain its minimum required cash balance of $20,000.

In June, IMAX projects a cash surplus of $27,669. The bank will first use $100 of the surplus to pay one month's interest and then use the balance ($7,569) to partially repay the line-of-credit principal. At the end of June, IMAX will still owe $2,413 on its line-of-credit.

Considering the second quarter in total, IMAX operations will generate a positive cash flow of $133,737. Including nonoperational cash flows, the second quarter as a whole will generate a positive cash flow of only $2,737, however. The $2,737 will be used to pay $150 in line-of-credit interest and $2,587 of the beginning line-of-credit balance.

To prepare the "Totals" column in the cash budget, most lines can simply be added across. The beginning cash balance line should not be added across into the Totals column, though. The Totals column represents the entire second quarter—April 1, 1995, through June 30, 1995. Consequently, the beginning cash balance should be the beginning balance on April 1; that is, the $20,000. The cash surplus or deficit in the Totals column is then the sum of the quarter's cash flow plus the April 1st beginning balance.

Similarly, the beginning line-of-credit balance on April 1 is the beginning balance in the Totals column. The ending line-of-credit balance in the June column (the June 30th balance) becomes the ending balance for the quarter (which also ends on June 30th). The ending June cash balance is the ending cash balance for the second quarter. The cash surplus minus interest, plus borrowings, and minus repayments should sum to the ending cash balance for each month and for the quarter in the Totals column.

Step 3. *Prepare supporting schedules and operating budgets as needed.* The first line of the cash budget is cash deposits from the sales of Highstepper Pentiums™. This information comes from Exhibit 17–3. Each line in the first section of the cash budget requires a supporting schedule (operating budget). As each operating budget is prepared, amounts needed for the pro formas are posted to them, as discussed in the next step.

Step 4. *Complete the cash budget and pro formas.* After individual amounts are posted to the cash budget, income statement, and balance sheet, the income statement is completed. The income tax liability is posted to the cash budget, and it is completed as described in step 2 above. Finally, the balance sheet is completed. Specific steps in posting amounts to the pro formas are discussed next.

THE PRO FORMA INCOME STATEMENT.   Prior to completing the income statement, Hal Segiguchi obtained the standard cost card for the Highstepper Pentium™ from the MRP II LAN. It is presented in Exhibit 17–10. The pro forma income statement is shown in Exhibit 17–11. The sales budget (Exhibit 17–3) and the standard cost card (Exhibit 17–10) provide the information to project Gross Profit for each month.[15] Exhibit 17–8 provides the information on selling and administrative expenses. Note that the expenses are used and not the cash totals for each month. Expenses include depreciation even though it is not included in the cash outflows for the cash budget. Income taxes are projected to be 20 percent of pretax operating income less line-of-credit interest.

THE PRO FORMA BALANCE SHEET.   The pro forma balance sheet is presented in Exhibit 17–12. Most of the amounts are posted to it as the operating budgets are prepared. Some amounts require special calculations not reflected on the operating budgets. For example, the accounts receivable balance can be computed upon completion of the sales budget, as shown in note 1 to the balance sheet. The current portion of the notes receivable represents three more

---

[15] Bad debts are 1 percent of gross revenues. Sales discounts are the month's gross revenues × 80% credit sales × 50% collected within the month × 2% discount taken on these payments. COGS is the standard absorptive manufacturing cost × the monthly sales forecast (volume).

■ EXHIBIT 17–10
Data and Standard Cost Card for IMAX's Highstepper Pentium™

DATA SECTION: STANDARD COSTS

Manufacturing Inputs	Price	Output Quantity	Loss %
PC boards	$100.00	5.00	0.00%
Direct labor	$15.00	16.00	20.00%
Variable overhead	$10.00 per DLhr		
Fixed overhead	$7.50 per DLhr		
Normal production volume (in units)	3,200 per year		

SOLUTION SECTION: STANDARD COST CARD & MANUFACTURING COST EQUATION

IMAX COMPUTERS
Highstepper Pentium™
STANDARD COST CARD

MANUFACTURING INPUTS	STANDARD PRICES	STANDARD QUANTITIES	STANDARD COSTS
PC boards	$100.00 each	5 boards/computer	$500/computer
Direct labor	$15.00/DLhr	20 DLhr/computer	$300/computer
Variable overhead	$10.00/DLhr	20 DLhr/computer	$200/computer
Fixed overhead	$7.50/DLhr	20 DLhr/computer	$150/computer
STANDARD ABSORPTIVE MANUFACTURING COST			$1,150/computer

Monthly computer production costs = $40,000 per month + $1,000/computer

Note: The 20 DLhr standard quantity is 16 DLhr ÷ (1 − 20%). The $1,000 per computer is the sum of the variable standard costs. Refer to Chapter 7.

■ EXHIBIT 17–11
IMAX's Pro Forma Income Statement

IMAX COMPUTERS
Pro Forma Income Statement
Second Quarter, 1995

	April	May	June	Totals
Sales revenues (Exhibit 17–3)	$400,000	$460,000	$540,000	$1,400,000
Less sales discounts	<3,200>	<3,680>	<4,320>	<11,200>
Less bad debts	<4,000>	<4,600>	<5,400>	<14,000>
Net sales	$392,800	$451,720	$530,280	$1,374,800
Less cost of goods sold (Exhibit 17–10)	<230,000>	<264,500>	<310,500>	<805,000>
Gross profit	$162,800	$187,220	$219,780	$569,800
Less selling and administrative expenses (Exhibit 17–8):				
Variable selling expenses	20,000	23,000	27,000	70,000
Fixed selling expenses	25,000	20,000	20,000	65,000
Fixed administrative expenses	120,000	125,000	150,000	395,000
Total selling & admin. expenses	<165,000>	<168,000>	<197,000>	<$530,000>
Net pretax operating income	<$2,200>	$19,220	$22,780	$39,800
Less line-of-credit interest (Exhibit 17–9)	<50>	–0–	<100>	<150>
Less income taxes −20%	450	<3,844>	<4,536>	<7,930>
Net operating income	<$1,800>	$15,376	$18,144	$31,720

Note: COGS is calculated by multiplying the standard absorptive manufacturing cost by the monthly sales forecast.

bimonthly collections in 1995 (in August, October, and December according to the cash budget).

The beginning property, plant, and equipment account balance ($2,500,000) comes from the projected March 30th balance, as does the accumulated depreciation balance ($450,000). The current liability balances come directly from the operating budgets referenced in the "Exhibit" column. As Hal Segiguchi calculated each amount, he noted his calculations below the balance sheet. Based on his past experiences with the budget committee, he knew he would need to explain where these amounts came from. The notes provide him with the necessary "audit trail."

LEARNING OBJECTIVE 4
—
Explain how operating budgets are used in merchandising and service firms.

Master Budgeting Differences in Nonmanufacturing Enterprises

The foregoing budgeting steps can also be used in preparing the operating budget in merchandising and service firms. The operating budgets are much simpler in nonmanufacturing enterprises because these firms do not make products.

In a merchandising organization, a **merchandise purchases budget** replaces the production budget and its associated direct materials, direct labor, and manufacturing overhead budgets as illustrated in Exhibit 17–2. A merchandise purchases budget is a statement showing the cost of merchandise to be purchased to meet estimated sales and ending merchandise inventory needs. A typical budget is illustrated in Exhibit 17–13.

Note the similarities between this budget and the direct materials budget in

▬■ EXHIBIT 17–12
IMAX's Pro Forma Balance Sheet

IMAX COMPUTERS
Pro Forma Balance Sheet
June 30, 1995

ASSETS:	Exhibit	Balance	Totals
Current:			
Cash	17–9	$20,000	
Accounts receivable	note 1	263,200	
Notes receivable	note 2	21,000	
Raw materials inventory	17–5	48,700	
Work-in-process inventory	none	–0–	
Finished goods inventory	17–4	34,500	$387,400
Noncurrent:			
Notes receivable	note 3	$84,000	
Property, plant, & equipment	note 4	2,525,000	
Less accumulated depreciation	note 4	<540,000>	2,069,000
TOTAL ASSETS			$2,456,400
LIABILITIES:			
Current:			
Accounts payable	17–5	$46,567	
Wages payable	17–6	20,475	
Overhead payable	17–7	69,600	
Selling & Admin. expenses payable	17–8	192,000	
Line-of-credit payable	17–9	2,413	
Notes payable	note 5	240,000	$571,055
Noncurrent:			
Notes payable	note 6		1,600,000
TOTAL LIABILITIES			$2,171,055
OWNERS' EQUITY:			
Beginning balance	note 7	$253,625	
Plus second quarter net income	17–11	31,720	285,345
TOTAL LIABILITIES AND OWNERS' EQUITY			$2,456,400

Notes:
1. Accounts receivable (Exhibit 17–3): May revenues × 80% × 14%; June revenues × 80% × (35% + 14%).
2. Notes receivable-current (Exhibit 17–9): $7,000 is collected every other month.
3. Notes receivable-long run: two years remaining after 1995 at $7,000 every other month.
4. Property, plant & equipment: purchased $25,000 (Exhibit 17–9); depreciation of $75,000 (Exhibit 17–7 FOH) plus $15,000 (Exhibit 17–8 S & A Expenses).
5. Notes payable-current: $40,000 per month from Exhibit 17–9.
6. Notes payable-long term: 40 months remaining after 1995 at $40,000 per month (Exhibit 17–9).
7. Owners' equity: there is no drawing account as owners are paid salaries included in S & A expenses.

Exhibit 17–5. The only difference is that instead of calculating the number of computers to manufacture as the basis for direct material purchases, in this budget, sales revenues are used to project merchandise purchases. Assume that IMAX purchases Highstepper Pentiums™ and Cost of Goods Sold equals 60 percent of sales revenues.[16] Sales revenues are calculated using retail sales prices. Merchandise is purchased at cost, however, not at retail sales price. Thus, revenues first have to be converted into their corresponding cost of the computers

Many students prepare budgets for books, lab fees, and other expenses.

---

[16] A 60 percent COGS ratio results in a 40 percent Gross Profit ratio.

■ EXHIBIT 17–13
IMAX'S Merchandise Purchases Budget

Item:	Formula:	March	April	May	June	July
Sales		$500,000	$400,000	$460,000	$540,000	$600,000
COGS	60.00%	$300,000	$240,000	$276,000	$324,000	$360,000
+Ending inventory (10-day supply)	1/3	80,000	92,000	108,000	120,000	
<Beginning inventory>	1/3	<100,000>	<80,000>	<92,000>	<108,000>	
GROSS PURCHASES		$280,000	$252,000	$292,000	$336,000	
NET PURCHASES	98.00%	$274,400	$246,960	$286,160	$329,280	
ACCOUNTS PAYABLE PAYMENT SCHEDULE:						
To pay this month (1st two monthly shipments)	2/3		$164,640	$190,773	$219,520	
Owed from last month	1/3		91,467	82,320	95,387	$109,760
Cash outflow for accounts payable payments			$256,107	$273,093	$314,907	

MANUAL CALCULATIONS PROCEDURES:

1. *Write down sales revenues.*
   (Double underline so revenues are not added into gross purchases totals.)
2. *Convert revenues into cost of goods sold.*
   (Sales are purchased at cost, not at retail sales prices. Use COGS ratio.)
3. *Calculate beginning and ending FGI requirements.*
   (Use COGS, not revenues, in calculating beginning and ending FGI.)
4. *Adjust gross purchases to net purchases.*
   (Always take purchase discounts.)
5. *"Flow out" net purchases into the months they are really paid.*
   (Just as was done in Exhibit 17–5 for direct materials purchases.)

sold. The beginning and ending merchandise inventories also have to be calculated at cost, using projected COGS in the second line of the budget.

The 10-day ending merchandise inventory requirement represents one-third of the next month's COGS (sales at cost), using a 30-day month. The 10-day requirement is due to IMAX only being able to receive shipments every 10 days. Purchase discount terms of 2%/10, N30[17] mean that the first two shipments received in a month (two-thirds of the month's purchases) will have to be paid for within that month if the purchase discount is to be taken. Therefore, two-thirds of a month's purchases are paid within the month, and one-third can be paid in the first week of the next month (still taking the discount on the third shipment). The five-step procedure at the bottom of the exhibit explains how to verify these amounts manually.

An operating budget for a service firm is prepared in the same manner as for a merchandising firm, except it does not include a purchases budget for merchandise inventory. But a purchases budget for supplies is often prepared in the same format as the merchandise purchases budget. Both in merchandising and service enterprises, a "direct labor" budget is usually prepared for sales personnel (merchandising) or for those providing professional services directly to customers (e.g., lawyers' time, engineers' time, CPAs' time, and so forth).

[17] If purchases are paid within 10 days, a 2 percent discount can be taken. If they are not paid within the 10-day discount period, then the entire amount is due within 30 days.

MASTER BUDGETING AND RESPONSIBILITY ACCOUNTING

The management accountant serves two responsibility accounting roles in the strategic planning and master budgeting process. First is the functional role discussed earlier. The management accountant serves as a facilitator and coordinator in the budgeting process. Especially in the absence of ICBISs, purchasing needs to know what production is planning. Production obviously needs to know what sales and marketing personnel are planning. Conversely, sales and marketing need to know whether production bottlenecks will be created and whether supplies and materials will be available when needed.

Hal Segiguchi, within his functional role, also serves as an auditor, making sure the process runs effectively and efficiently, producing the desired results. Historically, he was also the "number cruncher," actually preparing the budgets when they were done manually. Now he uses his spreadsheet program and the new Highstepper Pentium™.

The operating budgets represent what is planned. Periodic reports also should be produced comparing actual results against the budget to determine how well plans are being met (management-by-exception). Detailed reports should be given to managers who are responsible for the items they have budgeted. These reports often include sales and cost variances. Summary reports are distributed to higher levels of management. These often include summary income statement and balance sheet comparisons against the pro formas.[18]

Behavioral Role in the Planning Process

In addition to fulfilling the functional role, the management accountant must be aware of the many behavioral implications of the planning process. In this behavioral role, the management accountant needs to "see the big picture": how the planning, operational control, and performance evaluation processes are linked together to motivate people properly in an enterprise.

During the process of creating the master budget, the management accountant should be aware of a phenomenon called "budgetary slack," which often occurs when budgets are used for control and performance evaluation. **Budgetary slack** describes a tendency of managers to underestimate revenues and overestimate expenditures in order to build in allowances for unexpected declines in revenue and/or unforeseen expenses. Some allowances may be desirable, especially in manufacturing firms with long product cycle times. For example, it is not uncommon for construction firms to allow up to a 20 percent allowance for contingencies in the budget for a subdivision or a shopping center.

However, to be on the safe side and make themselves look good as the year progresses, operating managers may further underestimate sales (or production) and overestimate costs. This "padding of the budget" increases the likelihood that the managers will be able to achieve the budget with less effort.[19]

Allowing budgetary slack creates problems because of the interaction among budget elements. If sales are understated, problems can arise in production and logistics. Budgetary slack can cause an inefficient allocation of scarce resources. It hides waste and decreases the objectivity of performance evaluations.

One approach that top management can use to reduce budgetary slack is to establish a reward system that rewards operating managers who set high revenue and production estimates and low cost estimates (ideal standards) and then achieve them. Another approach is to use zero-based budgeting.

---

[18] Performance evaluation of profit center managers is covered in Chapter 20.

[19] This can lead to setting manufacturing cost standards that are too loose, as discussed in Chapter 7.

Most importantly, operations management and shop floor personnel need to internalize their budgets. Top management must convey the perception that the operating budgets belong to the managers who create them. This is difficult because the master budgeting process is iterative. Often, once the master budget is prepared, it undergoes a number of revisions before agreement is reached on a final plan. Operations managers need to understand how all the pieces fit together and why changes from the original budgets they submitted may be needed for the enterprise to accomplish its goals and objectives.

Behavioral Role in Operational Control

If operations personnel perceive the process as autocratic, they may regard the master budget as something imposed by top management. Efforts to achieve imposed budgets may result in dysfunctional behaviors. For example, excessive pressure to meet imposed production quotas, while maintaining ideal standards, may cause product quality to decline. This is contrary to IMAX's world-class manufacturing long-range objective.

In daily control of profit center operations, desires of various managers to achieve their individual responsibility center budgets may create conflicts within the profit center. Consider sales and marketing's desire to achieve its sales budget. Price concessions may be made to certain customers for special orders. These rush orders interrupt normal production scheduling and may cause costs to be higher than standard. Production personnel may resist processing these orders if they are held responsible for the resulting production volume variance and various cost variances.

One way to overcome this suboptimizing behavior is to develop a cost variance reporting system that identifies the sources and causes of cost variances by tracing them back to the people really responsible for them. A visual factory and an ICBIS are useful components of a profit and cost management system. If rush orders are a significant component of the sales budget, then this may signal the need for capital budgeting plans to reengineer the plant into a JIT process or a mushroom process that will allow for greater flexibility.[20]

Behavioral Role in Performance Evaluation

The master budgeting process also creates behavioral implications for performance evaluation. In addition to providing real-time information on variances for daily operations control, budget variance reports must be linked to performance evaluation and rewards. Employees may reject the budget as irrelevant if they are not provided feedback about variances or held accountable for budget deviations. They have to believe that the master budgeting process is important, not only for the firm's survival but also for each individual's survival. The budget, and performance evaluation against it, must also lead to rewards the employees consider valuable.

If the budgeting process is to be effective in motivating goal-congruent actions:

- There must be a strategic plan defining the enterprise's mission, its objectives, and goals for the budget horizon.
- The goals must be linked to objectives in a rational way, and objectives must lead to accomplishing the firm's mission.
- The master budget must be linked to the goals in a manner that operations personnel can understand and accept.
- The operating budgets must be used in performance evaluation.
- Performance evaluation must lead to rewards accepted as valid by those being held responsible for budget achievement.

[20] These ideas were considered in Chapters 8, 2, and 3, respectively.

SUMMARY OF LEARNING OBJECTIVES

The major goals of this chapter were to enable you to achieve five learning objectives:

Learning objective 1.   Discuss strategic planning and list its component steps.

Strategic planning is a systematic process for defining the mission, long-run objectives, and short-term goals of an enterprise. The mission statement defines the firm's purpose. Objectives are long-run statements of what the firm wants to accomplish. Goals are short-run translations of objectives, bounded by time and are measurable. Goals become the basis for the master budget. The master budget, in turn, is used to plan operations for the budget period, to monitor and control daily operations, and to evaluate performance. Budgets provide the benchmarks for control and performance evaluation.

Exhibit 17–1 lists six steps in the strategic planning process. In the first three steps, the enterprise's mission, objectives, and goals are defined. Step 4 involves an analysis of the enterprise's environment. The environment is decomposed into internal strengths and weaknesses and external opportunities and threats (SWOT). In step 5, strategies are set to capitalize on strengths and opportunities, and overcome weaknesses and threats. Finally, in step 6, results are compared against budget in a real-time mode for operational control and in formal variance reports for performance evaluation.

Learning objective 2.   Define the budgets that make up the master budgeting process.

The master budget is comprised of a capital budget and operating budgets. The capital budget translates into financial terms the plans for property, plant, and equipment acquisitions, market expansion, new product development, and other plans of a long-run nature. The operating budgets focus on short-run operations. The master budgeting process is summarized in Exhibit 17–2.

Operating budgets begin with the sales budget (Exhibit 17–3). This includes the sales forecast in units and revenues and a schedule of cash collections of sales. The sales budget is the basis for the remaining operating budgets. In manufacturing firms, a production budget (Exhibit 17–4) is prepared next detailing the production quota for the budget horizon. This leads to budgets for direct materials purchases, direct labor, and manufacturing overhead (Exhibits 17–5, 6, and 7). In merchandising firms, a merchandise purchases budget (Exhibit 17–13) is prepared instead of the production budgets. The basic purpose of these budgets is to schedule the acquisition and payment for these resources. The last operating budget is the selling and administrative expenses budget (Exhibit 17–8). While preparing the operating budgets, the pro forma statements are also created. The pro forma statements include the cash budget, budgeted income statement, and budgeted balance sheet (Exhibits 17–9, 11, and 12).

Learning objective 3.   Prepare the operating budgets for a manufacturing enterprise.

As summarized above, both manufacturing and nonmanufacturing firms prepare a sales budget, selling and administrative expense budget, and the three pro forma statements. A manufacturing firm also prepares operating budgets for production activities. A merchandising firm prepares a merchandise purchases budget. These budgets are illustrated again in this chapter's demonstration problems.

Learning objective 4.   Explain how operating budgets are used in merchandising and service firms.

As in manufacturing firms, the sales budget is the focal point for the operating budgets in merchandising and service firms. In merchandising firms, sales create the need for merchandise purchases. Service firms often prepare separate budgets for the supplies needed to provide their services.

Budgeting labor is equally important in manufacturing, merchandising, and service firms. In merchandising firms, "direct labor" can be thought of as the sales and service personnel necessary to satisfy customer needs. In a service firm, direct labor can be thought of as those who actually provide the service to a firm's customers.

All three types of enterprises incur selling and administrative expenses. In service firms, "selling" expenses may be thought of as those expenses directly traceable to individual services and customers.

Learning objective 5. Describe how operating budgets are used to facilitate planning, controlling operations, and evaluating performance.

As was first discussed in Chapters 7 and 8, the management accountant has two roles in responsibility accounting. Within the functional role, the management accountant serves as a facilitator in the master budgeting process. Communication and coordination are important in providing operations personnel with a sense of the "big picture." This is necessary because the original budgets will have to be revised if they, in aggregate, will not lead to the firm's goals. Coordination is also important in the daily scheduling and control of operations. The management accountant also has a functional responsibility to develop budget variance reports for performance evaluation.

In the behavioral role, the management accountant is involved in assuring that employees are properly motivated to budget, control operations, and evaluate and reward performance. Operations personnel need to participate in, and internalize, their budgets. They must believe that they, not top management, are responsible for preparing and achieving the budget. If operating personnel accept the budget as legitimate, they are likely to be better motivated to coordinate and control operations to achieve it. Finally, if the operating budgets are accepted as legitimate, they should be used as benchmarks for performance evaluation. The motivational linkages end with performance evaluations leading to acceptable rewards.

▌IMPORTANT TERMS

Budget horizon   The time period covered by the master budget. In many firms this is a year, budgeted by month or by quarter.

Budgetary slack   Excess costs (or lower sales) purposefully built into a budget to provide protection against unforeseen events. It is often called "padding the budget."

Capital budget   A listing of all approved long-term expenditures for property, plant, and equipment necessary to meet the strategic plan of the enterprise.

Cash budget   A period-by-period (monthly or quarterly) statement of expected cash flows from operations, nonoperational activities, and line-of-credit financing.

Continuous budget   An evolving, dynamic budget in which a 12-month forecast is always available by adding a month or a quarter in the future and dropping the month or quarter just ended.

Credit collection pattern   A listing of the percentage of a month's (or quarter's) sales that will be collected in that month and in subsequent months. These percentages are used to determine the projected cash deposits from the collection of sales within the sales budget.

Direct labor budget   A statement used by manufacturing firms that shows the labor hours to budget, labor cost, and when these costs will be paid. It is based on the production quota.

Direct materials purchases budget   A statement used by manufacturing firms that shows how much and when direct materials should be purchased, and when they will be paid. It is also based on the production quota.

Line-of-credit   This is an overdraft protection agreement between a firm and its bank. Usually, it is an unsecured short-term loan automatically deposited into the firm's bank account to cover checks the firm has written. Repayments also are usually automatically withdrawn by the bank if a surplus cash balance exists at the end of a month.

Manufacturing overhead budget   A statement that summarizes all expected manufacturing costs other than direct material and direct labor costs as well as expected cash payments for those costs.

Master budget   A series of interrelated budgets that quantify management's expectations about revenues, expenses, cash flow, net income, and financial position. The operating budgets, the capital budget, and the pro forma statements are the three major components of the master budget.

Merchandise purchases budget   A statement prepared by merchandising firms that shows the cost of merchandise to be purchased to satisfy estimated sales demand and ending inventory needs. It also shows the scheduled payments for merchandise purchases. A similar budget can be prepared for a service firm's purchases of supplies.

Operating budget A component of the master budget that represents expected results of operations of a manufacturing, merchandising, or service organization. In a manufacturing firm, operating budgets include a production budget, direct materials purchases, direct labor, and overhead expenditures. Merchandising firms prepare a merchandise purchases budget. All types of firms prepare selling and administrative expenses budgets as part of the operating budget.

Production budget A statement specifying the number of units of a product to be manufactured within the budget horizon to meet sales demand and provide the desired ending finished goods inventory.

Pro forma balance sheet An estimate of the enterprise's financial position at the end of the budget period.

Pro forma income statement A statement showing estimated revenues and expenses from income-producing activities for the budget period.

Pro forma statements Budgeted cash flow, income, and balance sheet statements.

Sales budget An estimate of sales in units and dollars expected during the budget period as well as an estimate of cash receipts.

Sales forecast A component of the sales budget that shows how many products or services are planned by period within the budget horizon.

Selling and administrative expenses budget A budget that shows nonmanufacturing expenses planned during a budget period.

Strategic planning The process of defining the mission, objectives, and goals of an enterprise. It also includes an analysis of the firm's internal and external environments, its strategies, and an evaluation of actual results compared against the master budget.

Zero-based budgeting A budgeting process that requires each responsibility center to justify all of its planned activities and budgeted costs, as though the budget were being developed for the first time.

DEMONSTRATION PROBLEMS

■ DEMONSTRATION PROBLEM 1 *Operating budgets for the first quarter of 1995.*
John Williams, one of the project engineers at IMAX, has suggested that IMAX purchase FAX-modem cards to install in Highstepper Pentiums™. He proposes a "spin-off" company that he will run. John wishes to borrow $5,000 from IMAX to set up the company. He can pay back IMAX $250 per month. In support of his suggestion, John has prepared the following information.

DATA SECTION:

ITEMS:	NOVEMBER	DECEMBER	JANUARY	FEBRUARY	MARCH	APRIL
Sales (units)	25	40	10	20	30	25
Sales price	$100	$100	$100	$100	$100	$100

NOTE: Cash sales:	40% of total sales for any month
Credit sales collected:	60% in the month of sale;
	30% the next month;
	8% in the following month;
	2% uncollectable.
Credit sales discount:	1% if bills paid within month of sale.

MERCHANDISE PURCHASES:
Gross profit ratio:	50%
Ending finished goods inventory:	50% of next month's sales
Purchase discount:	2%/15,N30 (assume a 30-day month)

OPERATING EXPENSES:
Selling expenses: Variable		2% of gross sales each month	
Selling expenses: Fixed	$1,000	$1,000	$1,000
Administrative expenses	200	200	200
Income taxes	100	200	300
Depreciation included in selling expenses	500	500	500

Continued

—Continued

	January	February	March
OTHER CASH FLOW ITEMS:			
Loan from IMAX	$5,000		
Equipment purchases		$5,000	
Notes payable payments	$250	$250	$250
LINE-OF-CREDIT FINANCING:			
Beginning cash balance	$–0–		
Minimum cash balance	$1,000		
Beginning line-of-credit balance	–0–		
Line-of-credit interest rate	12% per year		

Required:
John has asked your help in completing the following:

a. A sales budget.
b. A merchandise purchases budget.
c. A cash budget for the first quarter of 1995.

SOLUTION TO DEMONSTRATION PROBLEM 1

a. John Williams' sales budget:

SALES FORECAST:	November	December	January	February	March
Sales (units)	25	40	10	20	30
× sales price	$ 100	$ 100	$ 100	$ 100	$ 100
Sales revenues	$2,500	$4,000	$1,000	$2,000	$3,000

COLLECTIONS OF SALES: Amounts Collected

Month	Sales	Formula	January	February	March
This month–cash					
January	$1,000 × 40%		$400		
February	$2,000 × 40%			$800	
March	$3,000 × 40%				$1,200
This month–credit					
January	$1,000 × 60% × 60% × 99%		356		
February	$2,000 × 60% × 60% × 99%			713	
March	$3,000 × 60% × 60% × 99%				1,069
From last month's credit sales					
December	$4,000 × 60% × 30%		720		
January	$1,000 × 60% × 30%			180	
February	$2,000 × 60% × 30%				360
From 2 months ago–credit sales					
November	$2,500 × 60% × 8%		120		
December	$4,000 × 60% × 8%			192	
January	$1,000 × 60% × 8%				48
Total cash collected from sales in 1st quarter:			$1,596	$1,885	$2,677

b. John Williams' merchandise purchases budget:

Item:	Formula:	December	January	February	March	April
Sales		$4,000	$1,000	$2,000	$3,000	$2,500
COGS	50%	$2,000	$500	$1,000	$1,500	$1,250
+Ending inventory (15 days supply)	50%	250	500	750	625	
<Beginning inventory>	50%	<1,000>	<250>	<500>	<750>	

Continued

—Continued

	Formula:	December	January	February	March
GROSS PURCHASES		$1,250	$750	$1,250	$1,375
NET PURCHASES	98%	$1,225	$735	$1,225	$1,348

ACCOUNTS PAYABLE PAYMENT SCHEDULE:

To pay this month (see note below)	50%		$368	$612	$674
Owed from last month	50%		612	368	613	$674
Cash outflows for accounts payable payments			$980	$980	$1,287

Note: Purchase discount terms are 2%/15, N30. This means that half of a month's purchases must be paid within the month, but half can wait until the next month to be paid, with all purchase discounts being taken. The $368 in February was rounded up because the $612 was rounded down resulting in the correct cash outflow of $980.

c. John Williams' cash budget:

**CASH BUDGET
FIRST QUARTER, 1995**

	January	February	March	Totals
OPERATIONAL CASH INFLOWS:				
From product sales (solution part a)	$1,596	$1,885	$2,677	$6,158
OPERATIONAL CASH OUTFLOWS:				
Merchandise purchases (solution part b)	$980	$980	$1,287	3,247
Selling expenses: Variable	20	40	60	120
Selling expenses: Fixed	500	500	500	1,500
Administrative expenses	200	200	200	600
Taxes	100	200	300	600
TOTAL OPERATIONAL CASH OUTFLOWS	<$1,800>	<$1,920>	<$2,347>	<$6,067>
CASH FROM OPERATIONS	<$204>	<$35>	$330	$91
NONOPERATIONAL SOURCES & USES:				
Loan from IMAX	5,000	–0–	–0–	5,000
Equipment purchases	–0–	<5,000>	–0–	<5,000>
Notes payable payments	<250>	<250>	<250>	<750>
TOTAL NONOPERATIONAL CASH FLOWS	$4,750	<$5,250>	<$250>	<$750>
MONTHLY CASH FLOW	$4,546	<$5,285>	$80	<$659>
Beginning cash balance	–0–	4,546	1,000	$–0–
CASH SURPLUS/<DEFICIT>	$4,546	<$739>	$1,080	<$659>
FINANCING:				
Beginning line-of-credit balance	$–0–	$–0–	$1,739	$–0–
Interest	–0–	–0–	<17>	<17>
Borrowings	–0–	1,739	–0–	1,739
Repayments	–0–	–0–	<63>	<63>
Ending line-of-credit balance	–0–	1,739	1,676	1,676
ENDING CASH BALANCE	$4,546	$1,000	$1,000	$1,000

REVIEW QUESTIONS

17.1 What is the relationship between the strategic plan and the master budget?

17.2 How does a strategic plan differ from a master budget?

17.3 Define an objective. How does it differ from a goal?

17.4 What is SWOT? How does a SWOT analysis benefit the strategic plan?

17.5 What are strategies? How do they relate to the master budget?

17.6 What are the three components of a master budget?

17.7 List four functional roles for the management accountant in the strategic planning and master budgeting process.

17.8 How does zero-based budgeting differ from traditional, incremental budgeting approaches?

17.9 How is the budget horizon affected by continuous budgeting?

17.10 List the different budgets included within the operating budget.

17.11 Describe the different roles the operating budget serves in strategic planning, master budgeting, and responsibility accounting.

17.12 How does a capital budget differ from an operating budget?

17.13 What are the three pro forma financial statements prepared as part of the master budget?

17.14 What is the relationship between a sales forecast and a sales budget?

17.15 Contrast the two methods for preparing a sales forecast.

17.16 What is the difference between the top-down and bottom-up approaches to estimating sales?

17.17 Describe three types of statistical sales forecasts. Why are all three needed?

17.18 What is a credit collection pattern and how can it be represented as a simple multiplication chain?

17.19 If a company budgets both cash and credit sales and expects up to a two-month lag in collections of credit sales, how many sources of cash deposits are there within a month? Explain.

17.20 Why are the credit sales for months preceding the budget horizon needed when preparing the sales budget? How many preceding months' sales are required?

17.21 When preparing the production budget, the sales forecast for the month following the budget horizon is needed. Why?

17.22 When preparing the direct materials purchases budget, why are the month preceding and the month following the budget horizon needed?

17.23 Why is it necessary to have many overhead budgets instead of just one summary budget?

17.24 Why is depreciation subtracted in the fixed overhead budget?

17.25 Not all variable selling and administrative expenses vary with sales volume. Give an example of a type of selling and administrative expense that can vary with other factors than sales volume.

17.26 What are the three sections of the cash budget? What is the purpose of each section?

17.27 Why is a line-of-credit important?

17.28 Which lines of the cash budget do not add across into the Totals column?

17.29 How does the cash selling and administrative expenses totals from that budget need to be modified for use in the pro forma income statement?

17.30 When is a merchandise purchases budget used instead of the production operating budgets?

17.31 How does the COGS ratio differ from the Gross Profit ratio?

17.32 Why do revenues have to be converted into COGS as the first step in preparing the merchandise purchases budget?

17.33 What two responsibility accounting roles does the management accountant serve in the master budgeting process?

17.34 How can budgetary slack influence the master budget?

17.35 Do you think more or less slack will be included in the master budget if the process is perceived as an autocratic one?

CHAPTER-SPECIFIC PROBLEMS

These problems require responses based directly on concepts and techniques presented in the text.

17.36 *Multiple-choice questions.*

1. All of the following are characteristics of the strategic planning process *except:*

   a. Emphasis on the long run.
   b. Analysis and review of departmental budgets.

c. Analysis of consumer demand and demographics.
d. Analysis of competitive forces and technology.

2. A budget is:

a. A quantitative expression of a plan.
b. A control and performance evaluation tool.
c. A communication, coordination, and motivational tool.
d. All of the above.

3. Currently, Pulte Company uses the operational budget only as a planning tool. Management has decided that it should also be used for control purposes. To implement this change, the management accountant must:

a. Perform zero-base budgeting.
b. Organize a budget committee.
c. Revise the financial accounting system.
d. Provide timely reports to managers indicating variances between actual and budgeted values.

4. A budget system referred to as "continuous budgeting":

a. Consolidates the direct materials purchase budgets into a blanket purchase order for continuous delivery of raw materials.
b. Drops the current month or quarter and adds a future month or quarter as the current month or quarter is completed.
c. Ranks activities from a zero base to high priority on a continuum.
d. Represents a process performed in preparing a flexible budget.

5. From top management's viewpoint, the use of budgetary slack:

a. Increases the likelihood of inefficient resource allocation.
b. Increases the ability to identify potential budget weaknesses.
c. Increases the ability to identify potential budget strengths.
d. Enables management to perform continuous budgeting.

6. The budgeting process should motivate operating managers to work toward company objectives. Which of the following is *least* likely to motivate operating managers?

a. Setting budget targets at challenging, but attainable levels.
b. Participating in the budgeting process.
c. Holding operating managers accountable for activities they control.
d. Having senior management set budget levels.

7. In developing a comprehensive operating budget, which of the following should be performed first?

a. Develop a production resource budget.
b. Develop a sales budget.
c. Determine the selling and administrative expenses budget.
d. Prepare a budgeted balance sheet.

17.37 *Preparing the production budget.* Masstore Company's sales budget shows the following estimates for the year ending December 31, 1995:

QUARTER	UNITS
First	60,000
Second	50,000
Third	40,000
Fourth	80,000
Total	230,000

January 1996 sales are forecast to be 70,000 units. The quantity of finished goods inventory at the end of each quarter is equal to 30% of the next quarter's budgeted sales in units.

Required:

Determine the units to be produced during each quarter.

17.38 ***Comprehensive profit plan.*** The Palms Manufacturing Company makes two basic products known as Cee and Dee. Data that have been assembled by the managers follow:

	CEE	DEE
Requirements for finished unit:		
Product information:		
Raw material 1	10 pounds	8 pounds
Raw material 2		4 pounds
Raw material 3	2 units	1 unit
Direct labor	5 hours	8 hours
Product information:		
Sales price	$100	$150
Sales units	12,000	9,000
Estimated beginning inventory	400	150
Desired ending inventory	300	200

RAW MATERIALS

	1	2	3
Cost	$2.00 per pound	$2.50 per pound	$0.50 per unit
Estimated beginning inventory	3,000	1,500	1,000
Desired ending inventory	4,000	1,000	1,500

The direct labor wage rate is $4 per hour. Overhead is applied on the basis of direct labor hours. The tax rate is 40%.

The budgeted sales level is divided into quarters. Palms estimated that 20% of the annual sales will be in the first quarter, 30% in the second, and 25% in the third and fourth quarters. The beginning inventory of finished products has the same cost per unit as the ending inventory. The work-in-process inventory is negligible.

PALMS MANUFACTURING COMPANY
SALES FORECASTS BY PRODUCTS
19X1

	CEE		DEE		
	UNITS	DOLLARS	UNITS	DOLLARS	TOTAL DOLLARS
First quarter	2,400	$ 240,000	1,800	$ 270,000	$ 510,000
Second quarter	3,600	360,000	2,700	405,000	765,000
Third quarter	3,000	300,000	2,250	337,500	637,500
Fourth quarter	3,000	300,000	2,250	337,500	637,500
Total	12,000	$1,200,000	9,000	$1,350,000	$2,550,000

FACTORY OVERHEAD INFORMATION

Indirect materials	$ 10,000
Miscellaneous supplies and tools	5,000
Indirect labor	40,000
Supervision	20,000
Payroll taxes and fringe benefits	75,000
Maintenance costs—fixed	20,000
Maintenance costs—variable	10,000

Depreciation	70,000
Heat, light, and power—fixed	8,710
Heat, light, and power—variable	5,090
Total	$263,800

SELLING AND ADMINISTRATIVE EXPENSE INFORMATION

Advertising	$ 60,000
Sales salaries	200,000
Travel and entertainment	60,000
Depreciation—warehouse	5,000
Office salaries	20,000
Executive salaries	250,000
Supplies	4,000
Depreciation—office	6,000
Total	$605,000

Required:
Prepare the following:
a. Production budget.
b. Direct materials purchase budget.
c. Direct labor budget.
d. Factory overhead budget.
e. Cost of goods sold budget, with schedule of ending inventory.
f. Selling and administrative expense budget.
g. Budgeted income statement.

[CMA adapted]

17.39 *Determining units of material to be purchased.* Reid Company is budgeting sales of 100,000 units of product R for the month of September. Production of one unit of product R requires two units of material A and three units of material B. Actual inventory units at September 1 and budgeted inventory units at September 30 are as follows:

	ACTUAL	BUDGETED
Product R	20,000	10,000
Material A	25,000	18,000
Material B	22,000	24,000

Required:
Determine how many units of material B Reid is planning to purchase during September.

[AICPA adapted]

17.40 *Budgeting cash.* Information pertaining to Noskey Corporation's sales revenue follows:

	NOVEMBER 1994 (ACTUAL)	DECEMBER 1994 (BUDGET)	JANUARY 1995 (BUDGET)
Cash sales	$ 80,000	$100,000	$ 60,000
Credit sales	240,000	360,000	180,000
Total sales	$320,000	$460,000	$240,000

Management estimates that 5% of credit sales are uncollectible. Of the credit sales that are collectible, 60% are collected in the month of sale and the remainder in the month following the sale. Purchases of inventory are equal to next month's sales, and the gross profit margin is 30%. All purchases of inventory are on account; 25% are paid in the month of purchase, and the remainder are paid in the month following the purchase.

Required:
a. Calculate the budgeted cash collections in December 1994 from November 1994 credit sales.
b. Calculate budgeted total cash receipts in January 1995.
c. Calculate budgeted total cash payments in December 1994 for inventory purchases.

[CMA adapted]

17.41 *Budgeting for a retailer.* D. Tomlinson Retail seeks your assistance in developing cash and other budget information for May, June, and July. At April 30, the company had cash of $5,500, accounts receivable of $437,000, inventories of $309,400, and accounts payable of $133,055. The budget is to be based on the following assumptions:

■ *Sales.* Each month's sales are billed on the last day of the month. Customers are allowed a 3% discount if payment is made within 10 days after the billing date. Receivables are booked gross. 60% of the billings are collected within the discount period, 25% are collected by the end of the month, 9% are collected by the end of the second month, and 6% prove uncollectible.

■ *Purchases.* 54% of all purchases of material and selling, general, and administrative expenses are paid in the month purchased and the remainder in the following month. Each month's units of ending inventory are equal to 130% of the next month's units of sales. The cost of each unit of inventory is $20. Selling, general, and administrative expenses, of which $2,000 is depreciation, are equal to 15% of the current month's sales.

Actual and projected sales are as follows:

	DOLLARS	UNITS
March	$354,000	11,800
April	363,000	12,100
May	357,000	11,900
June	342,000	11,400
July	360,000	12,000
August	366,000	12,200

Required:
a. Determine the budgeted purchases for May and June.
b. Determine the budgeted cash disbursements during June.
c. Determine the budgeted cash collections during May.
d. Determine the budgeted number of units of inventory to be purchased during July.

[AICPA adapted]

17.42 *Budgeting for a retailer.* The Russon Corporation is a retailer whose sales are all made on credit. Sales are billed twice monthly, on the 10th of the month for the last half of the prior month's sales, and on the 20th of the month for the first half of the current month's sales. The terms of all sales are 2/10, net/30. Based upon past experience, accounts receivable are collected as follows:

Within the discount period	80%
On the 30th day	18%
Uncollectible	2%

Russon's average markup on its products is 20% of the sales price. All sales and purchases occur uniformly throughout the month.

The sales value of shipments for May and the forecasts for the next four months follow:

	REVENUES
May (actual)	$500,000
June	600,000
July	700,000
August	700,000
September	400,000

Russon purchases merchandise for resale to meet the current month's sales demand and to maintain a desired monthly ending inventory of 25% of the next month's sales. All purchases are on credit with terms of net/30. Russon pays for 50% of a month's purchases in the month of purchase and 50% in the month following the purchase.

Required:

a. Determine how much cash will be collected in September from sales made in August.
b. Calculate the budgeted dollar value of inventory on August 31.
c. Determine how much cash will be collected from accounts receivable collections during July.
d. Determine how much merchandise should be purchased during June.
e. Determine the amount that should be budgeted in August for the payment of merchandise.

[CMA adapted]

THINK-TANK PROBLEMS

Although these problems are based on chapter material, reading extra material, reviewing previous chapters, and using creativity may be required to develop workable solutions.

17.43 ***Analyzing the behavioral impact of strategic planning.*** Sovera Enterprises, an expanding conglomerate, was founded 35 years ago by Emil Sovera. The company's policy has been to acquire businesses that show significant profit potential; if a business fails to attain projected profits, it is usually sold. Currently, the company consists of eight businesses acquired throughout the years; three of these businesses are described here.

LaBue Videodiscs produces a line of videodisc players. The sale of videodisc players has not met expectations, but LaBue's management believes that the company will succeed in being the first to develop a moderately priced videodisc recorder/player. Market research predicts that the first company to develop this product will be a star.

Ulysses Travel Agencies also showed potential, and the travel industry is growing. However, Ulysses's market share has declined for the last two years even though Sovera has contributed a lot of money to Ulysses's operations. The travel agencies located in the midwestern and eastern sections of the country have been the biggest drain on resources.

Reddy Self-Storage was one of the first self-storage companies to open. For the last three years, Reddy has maintained a large market share while growth in the self-storage market has slowed considerably.

Ron Ebert, chairman of Sovera, prepared the agenda for the company's annual planning meeting where the present businesses were evaluated and strategies for future acquisitions were formulated. The following statements of strategy for each of the subsidiary companies discussed were formulated on the basis of the master plan:

- *LaBue Videodiscs.* Sovera's discretionary resources are to be employed to support the growth of this business. The future officers of Sovera are to be developed here.
- *Ulysses Travel Agencies.* An orderly disposal of the least profitable locations is the initial objective. Once the disposals are complete, an acceptable profit and growth strategy for the remaining locations will be formulated.
- *Reddy Self-Storage.* The strategy for this company is to maintain efficient operations and maximize the generation of cash for use in the further development of Sovera's other businesses.

These strategy statements were part of the strategic plan presented to Sovera's board of directors. The directors' only debate was whether Sovera should sell the entire Ulysses organization rather than parts of it. However, the board approved all three statements as presented and circulated them to managers throughout the three units as the corporation's "new marching orders."

Required:

a. Identify corporate policies and practices needed for strategic planning to be effective.

b. Identify at least four general characteristics that differentiate the three businesses described above, and explain how these characteristics influenced the formation of a different strategy for each business.

c. Discuss the likely effects of the three strategy statements on the behavior of top management and middle management of each of the three businesses.

[CMA adapted]

17.44 *Explaining budgetary slack and zero-based budgeting.* Bob Bingham is the controller of Atlantis Laboratories, a manufacturer and distributor of generic prescription pharmaceuticals. He is currently in the process of preparing the annual budget and reviewing the current business plan. The business unit managers of Atlantis prepare and assemble the detailed operating budgets with technical assistance from the corporate accounting staff. The final budgets are then presented by the business unit managers to the corporate executive committee for approval. The corporate accounting staff reviews the budgets for adherence to corporate accounting policies, but no detailed review for reasonableness of the line items within the budget is done.

Bingham is aware that the upcoming year for Atlantis may be a difficult one due to the expiration of a major patent and the loss of a licensing agreement for another product line. He also knows that during the budgeting process, "budgetary slack" is created in varying degrees throughout the organization. Bingham believes this slack has a negative effect on the overall business objectives of Atlantis Laboratories and should be eliminated where possible.

Required:

a. Define budgetary slack.

b. Explain the advantages and disadvantages of budgetary slack from the point of view of each of the following:

1. The business unit manager who must achieve the budget.
2. Corporate management.

c. Bob Bingham is considering implementing zero-based budgeting at Atlantis Laboratories.

1. Define zero-based budgeting.
2. Describe how zero-based budgeting could be advantageous to Atlantis Laboratories in controlling budgetary slack.
3. Discuss the disadvantages Atlantis Laboratories might encounter from using zero-based budgeting.

[CMA adapted]

17.45 *Preparing a direct materials purchases budget.* The Press Company manufactures and sells industrial components. The Whitmore Plant is responsible for producing AD-5 and FX-3. Plastic, brass, and aluminum are used in the production of these two products.

Press Company has adopted a 13-period reporting cycle in all of its plants for budgeting purposes. Each period is four weeks long and has 20 working days. The projected inventory levels for AD-5 and FX-3 at the end of the current (seventh) period and the projected sales for these two products for the next three four-week periods follow:

| | PROJECTED INVENTORY LEVEL (IN UNITS) | PROJECTED SALES (IN UNITS) | | |
	END OF SEVENTH PERIOD	EIGHTH PERIOD	NINTH PERIOD	TENTH PERIOD
AD-5	3,000	7,500	8,750	9,500
FX-3	2,800	7,000	4,500	4,000

Past experience has shown that adequate inventory levels for AD-5 and FX-3 can be maintained if 40% of the next period's projected sales are on hand at the end of a reporting period. Based on this experience and the projected sales, the

Whitmore Plant has budgeted production of 8,000 AD-5 and 6,000 FX-3 in the eighth period. Production is assumed to be uniform for both products within each four-week period.

The raw material specifications for AD-5 and FX-3 are as follows:

	AD-5	FX-3
Plastic	2.0 lb.	1.0 lb.
Brass	0.5 lb.	—
Aluminum	—	1.5 lb.

Sales of AD-5 and FX-3 do not vary significantly from month to month. Consequently, the safety stock incorporated into the reorder point for each of the raw materials is adequate to compensate for variations in the sales of the finished products.

Raw material orders are placed the day the quantity on hand falls below the reorder point. Whitmore Plant's suppliers are very dependable so the given lead times are reliable. The outstanding orders for plastic and aluminum are due to arrive on the tenth and fourth working days of the eighth period, respectively. Payments for all raw material orders are remitted in the month of delivery. Purchase data and raw materials inventory status are as follows:

	PURCHASE PRICE PER POUND	STANDARD PURCHASE LOT (IN POUNDS)	REORDER POINT (IN POUNDS)	PROJECTED INVENTORY STATUS AT THE END OF THE SEVENTH PERIOD (IN POUNDS) ON HAND	ON ORDER	LEAD TIME IN WORKING DAYS
Plastic	$0.40	15,000	12,000	16,000	15,000	10
Brass	0.95	5,000	7,500	9,000	—	30
Aluminum	0.55	10,000	10,000	14,000	10,000	20

Required:
Whitmore Plant is required to submit a report to corporate headquarters of Press Company summarizing the projected raw material activities before each period commences. The data for the eighth period report are being assembled. Determine the following items for plastic, brass, and aluminum for inclusion in the eighth-period report:
a. Projected quantities (in pounds) of each raw material to be issued to production.
b. Projected quantities (in pounds) of each raw material ordered and the date (in terms of working days) the order is to be placed.
c. The projected inventory balance (in pounds) of each raw material at the end of the period.
d. The payments for purchases of each raw material.

[CMA adapted]

17.46 *Preparing a budgeted statement of financial position.* The Breckenridge Institute is a not-for-profit foundation that undertakes scientific research on a contract basis. The institute regularly does research for federal, state, and local governments as well as for business firms.

The objectives of the institute, as established by the board of trustees, are to operate a financially sound, not-for-profit organization and to provide quality research at reasonable costs for the government and business community. The board is also committed to operate with a minimum amount of debt.

Pursuant to these objectives, management has tried to develop the capability of serving its clients without using outside consultants or subcontracting work to other laboratories. Consequently, the institute has gained an excellent reputation for its research capabilities and for the economical manner in which it is operated.

Following are the Statement of Financial Position for the institute at April 30, 19X6; the Statement of Operations showing the actual results for the year ended April 30, 19X6; and the budgeted amount for the coming year ending April 30, 19X7; and the Statement of Cash Receipts and Disbursements presenting actual results and budgeted figures for the years ending April 30, 19X6 and 19X7, respectively:

BRECKENRIDGE INSTITUTE
STATEMENT OF FINANCIAL POSITION (000 OMITTED)
APRIL 30, 19X6

ASSETS				EQUITIES			
Current assets:				Current liabilities:			
Cash			$ 110	Accounts payable			$ 120
Marketable securities			80	Accrued payroll, payroll taxes, and			
Accounts receivable:				benefits			46
Government contracts		$230		Due to outside consultants			20
Private contracts	$150			Interest payable			16
Less allowance for				Current portion of long-term debt			60
uncollectibles	10	140	370	Total current liabilities			262
Materials and supplies			64	Long-term debt			240
Prepaid insurance			6	Total liabilities			502
Total current assets			630	Original capital		$1,000	
Plant and equipment (net of				Accumulated excess of revenues over			
depreciation)			1,200	expenditures		328	1,328
Total assets			$1,830	Total equities			$1,830

STATEMENT OF OPERATIONS (000 OMITTED)			CASH RECEIPTS AND DISBURSEMENTS (000 OMITTED)		
	ACTUAL RESULTS FOR THE YEAR ENDED 4/30/X6	BUDGET FOR THE YEAR ENDED 4/30/X7		ACTUAL RESULTS FOR THE YEAR ENDED 4/30/X6	BUDGET FOR THE YEAR ENDED 4/30/X7
Revenues from operations:			Receipts:		
Federal government	$1,500	$1,650	Contracts:		
State and local gov-			Federal, state and		
ernment	224	250	local governments	$1,700	$1,820
Private (less provi-			Private	1,200	1,300
sion for bad debts				2,900	3,120
of $19 and $25)	1,216	1,335	Interest	4	2
Interest	4	2	Sales of marketable		
Total revenues	2,944	3,237	securities	—	50
Operating expenses:			Total receipts	2,904	3,172
Personnel:			Disbursements:		
Salaries	1,390	1,300	Salaries and wages	1,560	1,510
Wages	175	200	Employee benefits	260	300
Employee benefits			Consultant fees	15	230
and payroll taxes	273	300	Employee training		
Consultants	35	250	programs	20	35
Employee training	20	35	Materials and supplies	540	575
Materials and supplies	548	600	Utilities	55	65
Utilities	60	60	Insurance	20	22
Insurance	20	20	Other expenses	117	123
Depreciation	160	165	Interest	18	16
Other expenses	117	123	Retirement of debt	60	60
Interest charges	16	14	Purchases of capital		
Total operating			equipment	80	315
expenses	2,814	3,067	Total disbursements	2,745	3,251
Excess of revenues			Increase <decrease>		
over expenses	$ 130	$ 170	in cash	$ 159	$ <79>

During the construction of the budget, the following additional information was developed:

1. Purchases of materials and supplies were budgeted at $610,000.
2. Write-offs of specific accounts receivable are estimated as follows:
   a. $8,000 of the accounts receivable balance at April 30, 19X6.
   b. Uncollectible accounts of $12,000 from fiscal 19X7 sales to be written off in fiscal 19X7.

3. The unusually large budgeted expenditure for capital equipment is part of a three-year program begun in 19X6 to enable the institute to enter new areas of scientific research. Similar amounts will be spent in the next two years for additional equipment. Increased revenues from the new capabilities will not be significant until 19X9.
4. The increased level of consultant fees is expected to continue until the capital expansion program is complete.

Required:

a. In addition to the two budgeted statements already prepared for the coming fiscal year, prepare a budgeted statement of financial position as of April 30, 19X7, for presentation to the board of trustees.
b. Prepare a report that identifies the financial difficulties the institute's management will face in the next several years in fulfilling the objectives established by the board of trustees.

[CMA adapted]

17.47 *Preparing a projected income statement.* The Metropolitan News, a daily newspaper, services a community of 100,000. The paper has a circulation of 40,000, with 32,000 copies delivered directly to subscribers. The rate schedule for the paper is as follows:

	DAILY	SUNDAY
Single issue price	$0.15	$0.30
Weekly subscription		$1.00
(includes daily and Sunday)		

The paper has experienced profitable operations as can be seen from the Income Statement for the year ended September 30, 19X4 (numbers are in thousands):

Revenue:		
Newspaper sales	$2,200	
Advertising sales	1,800	$4,000
Costs and expenses:		
Personnel costs:		
Commissions:		
Carriers	$ 292	
Sales	73	
Advertising	48	
Salaries:		
Administration	250	
Advertising	100	
Equipment operators	500	
Newsroom	400	
Employee benefits	195	1,858
Newsprint		834
Other supplies		417
Repairs		25
Depreciation		180
Property taxes		120
Building rental		80
Automobile leases		10
Other		90
Total costs and expenses		3,614
Income before income taxes		386
Income taxes		154
Net income		$ 232

The Sunday edition usually has twice as many pages as the daily editions. Direct edition variable costs for 19X3–X4 are shown in the following schedule:

| | COST PER ISSUE | |
	DAILY	SUNDAY
Paper	$0.050	$0.100
Other supplies	0.025	0.050
Carrier and sales commissions	0.025	0.025
	$0.100	$0.175

The company has scheduled the following changes in operations for the next year and anticipates some increased costs:

1. The building lease expired on September 30, 19X4, and has been renewed with a change in the rental fee provisions from a straight fee to a fixed fee of $60,000 plus 1% of newspaper sales.
2. The Advertising Department will eliminate the payment of a 4% advertising commission on contracts sold by its employees. An average of two-thirds of the advertising has been sold on a contract basis in the past. The salaries of the four employees who solicited advertising will be raised from $7,500 each to $14,000 each.
3. Automobiles will no longer be leased. Employees whose jobs require automobiles will use their own and be reimbursed at $0.15 per mile. The leased cars were driven 80,000 miles in 19X3–X4, and it is estimated that the employees will drive some 84,000 miles next year on company business.
4. Cost increases estimated for next year:
   - Newsprint, $0.01 per daily issue and $0.02 for the Sunday paper
   - Salaries:
     Equipment operators, 8%
     Other employees, 6%
   - Employee benefits (from 15% of personnel costs excluding carrier and sales commissions to 20%), 5%
5. Circulation increases of 5% in newsstand and home delivery are anticipated.
6. Advertising revenue is estimated at $1,890,000 with $1,260,000 from employee-solicited contracts.

Required:
a. Prepare a projected income statement for Metropolitan News for the 19X4–X5 fiscal year using a format that shows the total variable costs and total fixed costs for the newspaper (round calculations to the nearest thousand dollars).
b. The management of Metropolitan News is contemplating one additional proposal for the 19X4–X5 fiscal year—raising the rates for the newspaper to the following amounts:

	DAILY	SUNDAY
Single issue price	$0.20	$0.40
Weekly subscription (includes daily and Sunday)		$1.25

The company estimates that the newspaper's circulation would decline to 90% of the currently anticipated 19X4–X5 level for both newsstand and home delivery sales if this change is initiated. Calculate the effect on the projected 19X4–X5 income if this proposed rate increase is implemented.

[CMA adapted]

 17.48 *Preparing budgets and comparing actual with budgeted costs.* The Melcher Company produces farm equipment at several plants. The business is seasonal and cyclical in nature. The company has attempted to use budgeting for planning and controlling activities, but the variable nature of the business has caused some company officials to be skeptical about the usefulness of budgeting to the company. The accountant for the Adrian Plant has been using a system she calls "flexible budgeting" to help plant management control operations.

The company president asks the management accountant to explain what the term means, how she applies the system at the Adrian Plant, and how it can be applied to the company as a whole. The accountant presents the following data as part of her explanation:

ACTUAL DATA FOR
JANUARY 19X3

Hours worked	8,400
Units produced	3,800
Costs incurred:	
Material (24,000 lb.)	$36,000
Direct labor	25,200
Indirect labor	6,000
Indirect materials	600
Repairs	1,800
Depreciation	3,250
Supervision	3,000
Total	$75,850

BUDGET DATA FOR 19X3

Normal monthly capacity of the plant in direct labor hours			10,000 hours
Material costs	6 lb.	@ $1.50	$9.00/unit
Labor costs	2 hours	@ $3.00	$6.00/unit

OVERHEAD ESTIMATE
AT NORMAL MONTHLY CAPACITY

Variable (controllable):	
Indirect labor	$6,650
Indirect materials	600
Repairs	750
Total variable	8,000
Fixed (noncontrollable):	
Depreciation	3,250
Supervision	3,000
Total fixed	6,250
Total fixed and variable	$14,250
Planned units for January 19X3	4,000
Planned units for February 19X3	6,000

Required:
a. Prepare a budget for January.
b. Prepare a report for January comparing actual and budgeted costs for the actual activity for the month.
c. Can flexible budgeting be applied to the nonmanufacturing activities of the company? Explain your answer.

[CMA adapted]

17.49 *Employing flexible budgeting.* The University of Boyne offers an extensive continuing education program in many cities throughout the state. For the convenience of its faculty and administrative staff and also to save costs, the university operates a motor pool. The motor pool operated with 20 vehicles until February of this year when an additional automobile was acquired, increasing the total to 21 vehicles. The motor pool furnishes gasoline, oil, and other supplies for the cars and hires one mechanic who does routine maintenance and minor repairs. Major repairs are done at a nearby commercial garage. A supervisor manages the operations.

Each year the supervisor prepares an operating budget for the motor pool. The budget informs university management of the funds needed to operate the pool.

Depreciation on the automobiles is recorded in the budget in order to determine the cost per mile.

The following schedule presents the annual budget approved by the university. The actual costs for March are compared to one-twelfth of the annual budget.

UNIVERSITY MOTOR POOL
BUDGET REPORT
FOR MARCH 19X6

	ANNUAL BUDGET	ONE-MONTH BUDGET	MARCH ACTUAL	OVER* UNDER
Gasoline	$24,000	$2,000	$2,800	$800*
Oil, minor repairs, parts, and supplies	3,600	300	380	80*
Outside repairs	2,700	225	50	175
Insurance	6,000	500	525	25*
Salaries and benefits	30,000	2,500	2,500	—
Depreciation	26,400	2,200	2,310	110*
	$92,700	$7,725	$8,565	$840*
Total miles	600,000	50,000	63,000	
Cost per mile	$0.1545	$0.1545	$0.1360	
Number of automobiles	20	20	21	

The annual budget was constructed based on the following assumptions:

- 20 automobiles in the pool.
- 30,000 miles per year per automobile.
- 15 miles per gallon per automobile.
- $0.60 per gallon for gas.
- $0.006 per mile for oil, minor repairs, parts, and supplies.
- $135 per automobile in outside repairs.

The supervisor is unhappy with the monthly report comparing budget and actual costs for March. He claims it presents his performance for March unfairly. His previous employer used flexible budgeting to compare actual costs to budgeted amounts.

Required:
a. Employing flexible budgeting techniques, prepare a report that shows budgeted amounts, actual costs, and monthly variation for March.
b. Explain briefly the basis of your budget figure for outside repairs.

[CMA adapted]

17.50 *Forecasting cash position and managing cash.* The Barker Corporation manufactures and distributes wooden baseball bats. The bats are manufactured in Georgia at its only plant. This is a seasonal business with a large portion of its sales occurring in late winter and early spring. The production schedule for the last quarter of the year is heavy in order to build up inventory to meet expected sales volume.

The company experiences a temporary cash strain during this heavy production period. Payroll costs rise during the last quarter because overtime is scheduled to meet the increased production needs. Collections from customers are low because the fall season produces only modest sales. This year the company's concern is intensified because prices are increasing during the current inflationary period. In addition, the Sales Department forecasts sales of fewer than one million bats for the first time in three years. This decrease in sales appears to be caused by the popularity of aluminum bats.

The cash account builds up during the first and second quarters as sales exceed production. The excess cash is invested in U.S. Treasury bills and other commercial paper. During the last half of the year, the temporary investments are liquidated to meet the cash needs. In the early years of the company, short-term borrowing was used to supplement the funds released by selling investments, but this has not been necessary in recent years. Because costs are higher this year, the treasurer asks for a forecast for December to judge if the $40,000 in temporary investments will be adequate to carry the company through the month with a minimum balance of $10,000. Should this amount ($40,000) be insufficient, she wants to begin negotiations for a short-term loan.

The unit sales volume for the past two months and the estimate for the next four months are as follows:

October (actual)	70,000	January (estimated)	90,000
November (actual)	50,000	February (estimated)	90,000
December (estimated)	50,000	March (estimated)	120,000

The bats are sold for $3 each. All sales are made on account. Half of the accounts are collected in the month of the sale, 40% are collected in the month following the sale, and the remaining 10% in the second month following the sale. Customers who pay in the month of the sale receive a 2% cash discount.

The production schedule for the six-month period beginning with October reflects the company's policy of maintaining a stable year-round work force by scheduling overtime to meet the following production schedules:

October (actual)	90,000	January (estimated)	90,000
November (actual)	90,000	February (estimated)	100,000
December (estimated)	90,000	March (estimated)	100,000

The bats are made from wooden blocks that cost $6 each. Ten bats can be produced from each block. The blocks are acquired one year in advance so they can be properly aged. Barker pays the supplier one-twelfth of the cost of this material each month until the obligation is retired. The monthly payment is $60,000.

The plant is normally scheduled for a 40-hour, five-day work week. During the busy production season, however, the work week may be increased to six 10-hour days. Workers can produce 7.5 bats per hour. Normal monthly output is 75,000 bats. Factory employees are paid $4 per hour (up $0.50 from last year) for regular time and time and one-half for overtime.

Other manufacturing costs include variable overhead of $0.30 per unit and annual fixed overhead of $280,000. Depreciation charges totaling $40,000 are included among the fixed overhead. Selling expenses include variable costs of $0.20 per unit and annual fixed costs of $60,000. Fixed administrative costs are $120,000 annually. All fixed costs are incurred uniformly throughout the year.

The controller has accumulated the following additional information:

1. The balances of selected accounts as of November 30, 19X4, are as follows:

Cash	$ 12,000
Marketable securities	
(cost and market are the same)	40,000
Accounts receivable	96,000
Prepaid expenses	4,800
Accounts payable	
(arising from raw material purchases)	300,000
Accrued vacation pay	9,500
Equipment note payable	102,000
Accrued income taxes payable	50,000

2. Interest to be received from the company's temporary investments is estimated at $500 for December.
3. Prepaid expenses of $3,600 will expire during December, and the balance of the prepaid account is estimated at $4,200 for the end of December.
4. Barker purchased new machinery in 19X4 as part of a plant modernization program. The machinery was financed by a 24-month note of $144,000. The terms call for equal principal payments over the next 24 months with interest paid at the rate of 1% per month on the unpaid balance at the first of the month. The first payment was made on May 1, 19X4.
5. Old equipment, which has a book value of $8,000, is to be sold during December for $7,500.
6. Each month the company accrues $1,700 for vacation pay by charging Vaca-

tion Pay Expense and crediting Accrued Vacation Pay. The plant closes for two weeks in June when all plant employees take a vacation.

7. Quarterly dividends of $0.20 per share will be paid on December 15 to stockholders of record. Barker Corporation has authorized 10,000 shares. The company has issued 7,500 shares, and 500 of these are classified as treasury stock.

8. The quarterly income taxes payment of $50,000 is due on December 15, 19X4.

Required:

a. Prepare a schedule that forecasts the cash position at December 31, 19X4. What action, if any, will be required to maintain a $10,000 cash balance?

b. Without prejudice to your answer in Requirement (a), assume Barker regularly needs to arrange short-term loans during the November-to-February period. What changes might Barker consider in its methods of doing business to reduce or eliminate the need for short-term borrowing?

[CMA adapted]

17.51 *Preparing a revised operating budget.* The Mason Agency, a division of General Service Industries, offers consulting services to clients for a fee. The corporate management at General Service is pleased with the performance of the Mason Agency for the first nine months of the current year and has recommended that the division manager of the Mason Agency, Richard Howell, submit a revised forecast for the remaining quarter, as the division has exceeded the annual plan year-to-date by 20% of operating income. An unexpected increase in billed hour volume over the original plan is the main reason for this gain in income. The original operating budget for the first three quarters for the Mason Agency follows:

The Mason Agency
1994–1995 Operating Budget

	First Quarter	Second Quarter	Third Quarter	Total Nine Months
Revenue				
Consulting fees				
Management consulting	$315,000	$315,000	$315,000	$ 945,000
EDP consulting	421,875	421,875	421,875	1,265,625
Total consulting fees	$736,875	$736,875	$736,875	$2,210,625
Other revenue	10,000	10,000	10,000	30,000
Total revenue	$746,875	$746,875	$746,875	$2,240,625
Expenses				
Consultant salary expense	$386,750	$386,750	$386,750	$1,160,250
Travel and related expense	45,625	45,625	45,625	136,875
General and administrative expense	100,000	100,000	100,000	300,000
Depreciation expense	40,000	40,000	40,000	120,000
Corporate allocation	50,000	50,000	50,000	150,000
Total expenses	$622,375	$622,375	$622,375	$1,867,125
Operating income	$124,500	$124,500	$124,500	$373,500

When comparing the actuals for the first three quarters to the original plan, Howell analyzed the variances and will reflect the following information in his revised forecast for the fourth quarter:

- The division currently has 25 consultants on staff, 10 for management consulting and 15 for EDP consulting, and has hired three additional management consultants to start work at the beginning of the fourth quarter in order to meet the increased client demand.
- The hourly billing rate for consulting revenues is market acceptable and will remain at $90 per hour for each management consultant and $75 per hour for each EDP consultant. However, due to the favorable increase in billing hour volume when compared to plan, the hours for each consultant will be increased by 50 hours per quarter. There is no learning curve for billable consulting hours for new employees.
- The budgeted annual salaries and actual annual salaries, paid monthly, are the same at $50,000 for a management consultant and 8% less for an EDP consultant. Corporate management has approved a merit increase of 10% at the beginning of the fourth quarter for all 25 existing consultants, while the new consultants will be compensated at the planned rate.
- The planned salary expense includes a provision for employee fringe benefits amounting to 30% of the annual salaries; however, the improvement of some corporatewide employee programs will increase the fringe benefit allocation to 40%.
- The original plan assumes a fixed hourly rate for travel and other related expenses for each billing hour of consulting. These are expenses that are not reimbursed by the client, and the previously determined hourly rate has proven to be adequate to cover these costs.
- Other revenues are derived from temporary rentals and interest income and remain unchanged for the fourth quarter.
- General and administrative expenses have been favorable at 7% below the plan; this 7% savings on fourth quarter expenses will be reflected in the revised plan.
- Depreciation for office equipment and microcomputers will stay constant at the projected straight-line rate.
- Due to the favorable experience for the first three quarters and the division's increased ability to absorb costs, the corporate management at General Service Industries has increased the corporate expense allocation by 50%.

Required:
a. Prepare a revised operating budget for the fourth quarter for the Mason Agency that Richard Howell will present to General Service Industries. Be sure to furnish supporting calculations for all revised revenue and expense amounts.
b. Discuss the reasons why an organization would prepare a revised forecast.
[CMA adapted]

17.52 *Preparing a flexible budget.* Pearsons, a successful regional chain of moderately priced restaurants, each with a carryout delicatessen department, is planning to expand to a nationwide operation. As the chain gets larger and covers more territory, managerial control and reporting techniques become more important.

The company's management believes that a budget program for the entire company as well as for each restaurant-deli unit is needed. The budget presented below has been prepared for the typical unit in the chain. Once a new unit is in operation, it is expected to perform in accordance with the budget.

All units are of approximately the same size with a similar amount of space devoted to the carryout delicatessen. The facilities and the equipment used are uniform in all units. The unit operators are expected to implement the advertising program recommended by the corporation. The corporation charges a franchise fee, which is a percentage of gross sales, for the use of the company name, the building and facilities design, and the advertising advice.

The unit in Akron, Ohio, was selected to test the budget program. Its performance for the year ended December 31, 19X5, compared to the typical budget, is presented next:

PEARSONS RESTAURANT-DELI
AKRON, OHIO
NET INCOME FOR THE YEAR ENDED
DECEMBER 31, 19X5

ACTUAL RESULTS

	DELICATESSEN	RESTAURANT	TOTAL	BUDGET	OVER <UNDER> BUDGET
Gross sales	$1,200	$2,000	$3,200	$3,500	<$300>
Purchases	780	800	1,580	1,600	< 20>
Hourly wages	60	700	760	925	<165>
Franchise fee	36	60	96	105	< 9>
Advertising	100	200	300	300	—
Utilities	76	100	176	195	< 19>
Depreciation	50	75	125	125	—
Lease expense	30	50	80	80	—
Salaries	30	50	80	80	—
Total	1,162	2,035	3,197	3,410	<213>
Net income before income taxes	$ 38	< $35>	$ 3	$ 90	<$ 87>

Required:

a. Prepare a schedule that compares a flexible budget for the deli line of the Akron restaurant-deli to its actual performance.

b. Would a complete report, comparing a flexible budget to the performance of each of the two operations, make the problems of the Akron operation easier to identify? Explain, using an example from the problem and your answer to Requirement (a).

c. Should a flexible budget comparison to actual performance become part of the regular reporting system for the following?
   1. The annual review.
   2. A monthly review.
   Explain your answer.

[CMA adapted]

17.53 *Developing a cash budget.* The Triple-F Health Club (Family, Fitness, and Fun) is a nonprofit family-oriented health club. The club's board of directors is developing plans to acquire more equipment and expand the club facilities. The board plans to purchase about $25,000 of new equipment each year and wants to establish a fund to purchase the adjoining property in four or five years. The adjoining property has a market value of about $300,000.

The club manager, Jane Crowe, is concerned that the board has unrealistic goals in light of the club's recent financial performance. She has sought the help of a club member with an accounting background to assist her in preparing a report to the board supporting her concerns.

The club member reviewed the club's records, including the cash basis income statement presented next:

TRIPLE-F HEALTH CLUB
STATEMENT OF INCOME (CASH BASIS)
FOR YEARS ENDED OCTOBER 31
(000 OMITTED)

	1995	1994
Cash revenues:		
Annual membership fees	$355.0	$300.0
Lesson and class fees	234.0	180.0
Miscellaneous	2.0	1.5
Total cash received	591.0	481.5
Cash expenses:		

Continued

—Continued

	1995	1994
Manager's salary and benefits	36.0	36.0
Regular employees' wages and benefits	190.0	190.0
Lesson and class employees' wages and benefits	195.0	150.0
Towels and supplies	16.0	15.5
Utilities (heat and light)	22.0	15.0
Mortgage interest	35.1	37.8
Miscellaneous	2.0	1.5
Total cash expenses	496.1	445.8
Cash income	$ 94.9	$ 35.7

- Other financial information as of October 31, 1995:
  - Cash in checking account, $7,000
  - Petty cash, $300
  - Outstanding mortgage balance, $390,000
  - Accounts payable arising from invoices for supplies and utilities that are unpaid as of October 31, 1995, $2,500
- No unpaid bills existed on October 31, 1994.
- The club purchased $25,000 worth of exercise equipment during the current fiscal year. Cash of $10,000 was paid on delivery, and the balance was due on October 1 but has not been paid as of October 31, 1995.
- The club began operations in 1989 in rental quarters. In October 1991, it purchased its current property (land and building) for $600,000, paying $120,000 down and agreeing to pay $30,000 plus 9% interest annually on November 1 until the balance was paid off.
- Membership rose 3% during 1995. The club has experienced approximately this same annual rate since it opened.
- Membership fees were increased by 15% in 1995. The board has tentative plans to increase the fees by 10% in 1996.
- Lesson and class fees have not been increased for three years. The board policy is to encourage classes and lessons by keeping the fees low. The members have taken advantage of this policy, and the number of classes and lessons has increased significantly each year. The club expects the percentage growth experienced in 1995 to be repeated in 1996.
- Miscellaneous revenues are expected to grow at the same percentage as experienced in 1995.
- Operating expenses are expected to increase. Hourly wage rates and the manager's salary will need to be increased 15% because no increases were granted in 1995. Towels and supplies, utilities, and miscellaneous expenses are expected to increase 25%.

Required:
a. Construct a cash budget for 1996 for the Triple-F Health Club.
b. Identify any operating problem(s) that this budget discloses for the Triple-F Health Club. Explain your answer.
c. Is Jane Crowe's concern that the board's goals are unrealistic justified? Explain your answer.

[CMA adapted]

17.54 *Profit planning for small businesses.* Small businesses are usually the first organizations to feel the effects of a recessionary economy and are generally the last to recover. Two major reasons for small business financial difficulties are managerial inexperience and inadequate financing or financial management.

Small business managers frequently have problems in planning and controlling profits, including revenue generation and cost reduction activities. These important financial methods are especially critical during a recessionary period. The financial problems of small businesses are further compounded when there are poor accounting records and inexperience in the management of money.

Required:
a. Profit planning is critical for the planning and controlling of profits of a small

business. Identify key features that need to be considered when developing a profit plan.

b. The management accountant can help assure that good accounting records exist in an organization. Discuss the key features that form the basis for a good accounting system that will support management decisions.

c. Explain how the management accountant can assist an organization in adopting measures to assure appropriate money management.

[CMA adapted]

17.55 *Preparing a revised budgeted cash receipts and disbursements statement.* The Pantex Corporation has gone through a period of rapid expansion to reach its present size of seven divisions. The expansion program has placed strains on its cash resources. Therefore, the need for better cash planning at the corporate level has become very important.

At the present time, each division is responsible for the collection of receivables and the disbursements for all operating expenses and approved capital projects. The corporation does exercise control over division activities and has attempted to coordinate the cash needs of the divisions and the corporation. However, it has not yet developed effective division cash reports from which it can determine the needs and availability of cash in the next budgetary year. As a result of inadequate information, the corporation permitted some divisions to make expenditures for goods and services that need not have been made or that could have been postponed until a later time, while other divisions had to delay expenditures that should have had a greater priority.

The 19X8 cash receipts and disbursements plan prepared by the Tapon Division for submission to the corporate office is as follows:

TAPON DIVISION
BUDGETED CASH RECEIPTS AND DISBURSEMENTS
FOR THE YEAR ENDED DECEMBER 31, 19X8
(000 OMITTED)

Receipts:	
Collections on accounts	$9,320
Miscellaneous	36
	9,356
Disbursements:	
Production:	
Raw materials	2,240
Labor and fringe benefits	2,076
Overhead	2,100
Sales:	
Commissions	395
Travel and entertainment	600
Other	200
Administrative:	
Accounting	80
Personnel	110
General management	350
Capital expenditures	1,240
	9,391
Excess of receipts over <under> disbursements	<$35>

The following additional information was used by the Tapon Division to develop the cash receipts and disbursements budget:

■ *Receipts.* Miscellaneous receipts are estimated proceeds from the sales of unneeded equipment.

■ *Sales.* Travel and entertainment represents the costs required to produce the sales volume projected for the year. The other sales costs consist of $50,000 for training new sales personnel, $25,000 for attendance by sales personnel at association meetings (not sales shows), and $125,000 for sales management salaries.

■ *Administration.* The personnel costs include $50,000 for salary and department operating costs, $20,000 for training new personnel, and $40,000 for management training courses for current employees. The general management costs include $310,000 in salaries and office costs for the division management plus $10,000 for officials' travel to Pantex Corporation meetings and $30,000 for industry and association conferences.

- *Capital expenditures.* Planned expenditures for capital items during 19X8 are as follows:

CAPITAL PROGRAMS APPROVED BY THE CORPORATION

Items ordered in 19X8 for delivery in 19X8	$300,000
Items to be ordered in 19X8 for delivery in 19X8	$700,000
New programs to be submitted to corporation during 19X8	$240,000

Required:

Present a revised budgeted cash receipts and disbursements statement for the Tapon Division. Design the format of the revised statement so that it includes adequate detail to improve the corporation's ability to judge the urgency of the cash needs. Such a statement would be submitted by all divisions to provide the basis for overall corporation cash planning.

[CMA adapted]

17.56 ***Preparing a pro forma schedule of cash receipts and disbursements.*** CrossMan Corporation, a rapidly expanding crossbow distributor to retail outlets, is in the process of formulating plans for 1994. Joan Caldwell, director of marketing, has completed her 1994 forecast and is confident that sales estimates will be met or exceeded. The following sales figures show the growth expected and will provide the planning basis for other corporate departments:

MONTH	FORECASTED SALES	MONTH	FORECASTED SALES
January	$1,800,000	July	$3,000,000
February	2,000,000	August	3,000,000
March	1,800,000	September	3,200,000
April	2,200,000	October	3,200,000
May	2,500,000	November	3,000,000
June	2,800,000	December	3,400,000

George Brownell, assistant controller, has been given the responsibility for formulating the cash flow projection, a critical element during a period of rapid expansion. The following information will be used in preparing the cash analysis:

- CrossMan has experienced an excellent record in accounts receivable collection and expects this trend to continue. Sixty percent of billings are collected in the month after the sale and 40% in the second month after the sale. Uncollectible accounts are nominal and will not be considered in the analysis.
- The purchase of the crossbows is CrossMan's largest expenditure; the cost of these items equals 50% of sales. Sixty percent of the crossbows are received one month prior to sale, and 40% are received during the month of sale.
- Prior experience shows that 80% of accounts payable are paid by CrossMan one month after receipt of the purchased crossbows, and the remaining 20% are paid the second month after receipt.
- Hourly wages, including fringe benefits, are a factor of sales volume and are equal to 20% of the current month's sales. These wages are paid in the month incurred.
- General and administrative expenses are projected to be $2,640,000 for 1994. The composition of the expenses is given below. All of these expenses are incurred uniformly throughout the year except the property taxes. Property taxes are paid in four equal installments in the last month of each quarter.

Salaries	$ 480,000
Promotion	660,000
Property taxes	240,000
Insurance	360,000
Utilities	300,000
Depreciation	600,000
Total	$2,640,000

■ CrossMan makes income tax payments in the first month of each quarter based on the income for the prior quarter. CrossMan's income tax rate is 40%. CrossMan's net income for the first quarter of 1994 is projected to be $612,000.

■ CrossMan has a corporate policy of maintaining an end-of-month cash balance of $100,000. Cash is invested or borrowed monthly, as necessary, to maintain this balance.

■ CrossMan uses a calendar year reporting period.

Required:

a. Prepare a Pro Forma Schedule of Cash Receipts and Disbursements for Cross-Man Corporation, by month, for the second quarter of 1994. Be sure that all receipts, disbursements, and borrowing/investing amounts are presented on a monthly basis. Ignore the interest expense and/or interest income associated with the borrowing/investing activities.

b. Discuss why cash budgeting is particularly important for a rapidly expanding company such as CrossMan Corporation.

[CMA adapted]

17.57 *Ethics in budgeting.* Norton Company, a manufacturer of infant furniture and carriages, is in the initial stages of preparing the annual budget for 1995. Scott Ford has recently joined Norton's accounting staff and is interested in learning as much as possible about the company's budgeting process. During a recent lunch with Marge Atkins, sales manager, and Pete Granger, production manager, Ford initiated the following conversation:

Ford: "Since I'm new around here and am going to be involved with the preparation of the annual budget, I'd be interested to learn how the two of you estimate sales and production numbers."

Atkins: "We start out very methodically by looking at recent history, discussing what we know about current accounts, potential customers, and the general state of consumer spending. Then, we add that usual dose of intuition to come up with the best forecast we can."

Granger: "I usually take the sales projections as the basis for my projections. Of course, we have to make an estimate of what this year's closing inventories will be, and that sometimes is difficult."

Ford: "Why does that present a problem? There must have been an estimate of closing inventories in the budget for the current year."

Granger: "Those numbers aren't always reliable since Marge makes some adjustments to the sales numbers before passing them on to me."

Ford: "What kind of adjustments?"

Atkins: "Well, we don't want to fall short of the sales projections so we generally give ourselves a little breathing room by lowering the initial sales projection anywhere from 5–10%."

Granger: "So, you can see why this year's budget is not a very reliable starting point. We always have to adjust the projected production rates as the year progresses and, of course, this changes the ending inventory estimates. By the way, we make similar adjustments to expenses by adding at least 10% to the estimates; I think everyone around here does the same thing."

Required:

a. Marge Atkins and Pete Granger have described the use of budgetary slack.
   1. Explain why Atkins and Granger behave in this manner, and describe the benefits they expect to realize from the use of budgetary slack.
   2. Explain how the use of budgetary slack can adversely affect Atkins and Granger.

b. As a management accountant, Scott Ford believes that the behavior described by Marge Atkins and Pete Granger may be unethical and that he may have an obligation not to support this behavior. By citing the specific standards of competence, confidentiality, integrity, and/or objectivity from *Standards of Ethical Conduct for Management Accountants,* explain why the use of budgetary slack may be unethical.

[CMA adapted]

18 ANALYZING COST-VOLUME-PROFIT RELATIONSHIPS

Running CVP simulations. Courtesy of Novell, Inc.

LEARNING OBJECTIVES

After studying this chapter, you should be able to:

1. Build a profit equation for an enterprise or product line.

2. Use cost-volume-profit (CVP) analysis to analyze different profit-making alternatives.

3. Apply CVP formulas to situations involving sales mixes and income taxes.

4. Describe how computer programs can assist in CVP analysis.

■ INTRODUCTION

Cost-volume-profit (CVP) analysis involves the study of the interrelationships among the following elements:

- Per-unit variable costs
- Total fixed costs
- Volume or level of activity
- Prices of products
- Mix of products sold

The goal of CVP analysis is to create an equation that can be used to predict a firm's profit. This **profit equation** can also be used to predict the change in profits, or in any element in the equation, for different alternatives a profit center manager may wish to consider. Expressing the relationships among sales prices, sales volume, variable costs, and fixed costs within an equation creates a powerful tool for the master budgeting process and for operational control decisions profit center managers make.

Strategic planning and master budgeting do not end when a cash budget and pro forma statements are created. The process is iterative in that once the results of the strategic plan are translated into a master budget, it may be revised many times before a final master budget is set. Throughout the process, the budget committee (or upper management) will consider many potential changes. In these committee meetings, the management accountant does not have the time to input changes and recreate a new master budget. Rather, management wants to know the answers to such questions as the following:

- If we increase sales volume by cutting sales prices, will profits increase or decrease, and by how much?
- If variable or fixed costs can be changed, what effect will the change have on projected profits?
- If we undertake an advertising campaign that can increase sales volume, how will projected profits change?

To answer these questions, the management accountant must be able to calculate quickly and accurately what happens to projected profits for each alternative being considered. The profit equation and CVP analysis provide such a tool.

Profit center managers can use this same tool to help them analyze various opportunities during the course of day-to-day and month-to-month operations. From this perspective, CVP analysis is a bridging concept between profit center planning decisions and operational control decisions. It is useful in both decision-making functions.

This chapter introduces CVP analysis. Chapter 19 then applies this technique to specific types of operational control decisions. Next, Chapter 20 shows how the profit equation is used to develop an income statement format useful in the third decision-making function, profit center performance evaluation. Finally, CVP analysis is used in Chapter 21 to solve an increasingly perplexing problem faced by profit center managers in decentralized and multinational enterprises (i.e., transfer pricing).

LEARNING OBJECTIVE 1

Build a profit equation for an enterprise or product line.

■ COST-VOLUME-PROFIT BASICS

The best way to understand cost-volume-profit (CVP) analysis is to apply it. But before the profit equation is developed, the assumptions behind CVP analysis should be understood. These are the same basic assumptions used in building cost equations, first introduced in Chapter 7.

What Are the Basic CVP Assumptions?

Three assumptions are usually made when developing CVP relationships and profit equations, and when subjecting data to CVP analysis:

1. The behavior of both revenues and costs is linear throughout the relevant range. Linearity means that revenues and costs can be graphed as straight lines. For this to happen, sales prices must remain constant per unit, and all costs must be divisible into variable and fixed elements.[1]
2. Inventory quantities remain unchanged during the year. The number of units in beginning WIP and FGI equals the number of units in these ending inventories.
3. The sales mix is constant. The sales mix is the combination of products that make up total sales.

These assumptions simplify CVP relationships, and when the assumptions are valid, CVP analysis is very accurate in predicting profits. Normally, however, business operations do not match the assumptions exactly. In such cases, the resulting analysis is an approximation, but is still quite helpful in decision making.

Building the Profit Equation

The profit equation begins with the manufacturing cost equation. The Quick-Button case on the next page demonstrates how it is developed.

Both of the variable costs are manufacturing costs. The fixed manufacturing costs include the automated button-making machine and the work area costs for making buttons. Carrie developed the following manufacturing cost equation:

$$\text{Annual manufacturing costs for Quick-Button} = \$400 \text{ per year} + \$1.50 \text{ per button}$$

There are no variable selling and administrative costs, but there are fixed costs for the display kit (a selling expense) and the liability insurance (an administrative expense). Adding these costs to the manufacturing costs yields a total cost equation:

$$\text{Total annual costs for Quick-Button} = \$1,000 \text{ per year} + \$1.50 \text{ per button}$$

Revenues minus costs equals profit. By including the projected revenues in this equation, a profit equation can be developed. Revenues equal sales price multiplied by sales volume. Notice that no particular value is used for sales volume. As in the cost equation, volume is the independent variable.

$$\text{Revenues} - \text{Total costs} = \text{Profit}$$

($2.00 per button × Sales volume)
− [$1,000 per year + ($1.50 per button × Sales volume)] = Profit

Reorganizing the equation:

$$(\text{Revenues} - \text{Variable costs}) - \text{Fixed costs} = \text{Profit}$$

[($2.00 per button × Sales volume)
− ($1.50 per button × Sales volume)] − $1,000 per year = Profit

---

[1] In creating a cost equation to predict total manufacturing costs in Chapter 7, the same linearity assumption was used. Linearity means that over the relevant range, variable costs are constant per unit and fixed costs are constant in total.

INSIGHTS & APPLICATIONS

Applying CVP Analysis at Quick-Button

Carrie Copolla is planning to start a business called Quick-Button. She will make and sell 2½-inch plastic-coated, pin-back buttons. She plans to contract with schools, churches, political candidates, service organizations, and booster clubs to provide for their button needs.

With an automated button-making machine, Carrie can prepare a button with a selected preprinted design in less than 30 seconds. She will have access to over 3,000 colorful, popular preprinted designs that are attached to the front of the button and covered with plastic. The button requires a button set, which is composed of a metal front, pin-back, and plastic cover.

Based on a great deal of research, Carrie has prepared a schedule of estimated price and costs for her business plan:

QUICK-BUTTON
ESTIMATED PRICE AND COSTS FOR 1995

Sales price per button		$2.00
Variable costs per button:		
Preprinted design	$ .50	
Button set	1.00	$1.50
Fixed costs:		
Automated button-making machine		$ 300
Display kit		400
Liability insurance		200
Work area		100
Total fixed costs		$1,000

Revenues minus *total* variable costs equals **contribution margin**. Contribution margin is the total dollars available after covering variable costs that can be used to pay for fixed costs and to provide a target profit. Contribution margin is most useful, though, when it is expressed on a per-unit basis:

[(Sales price − Variable costs per unit) × Volume] − Fixed Costs = Profit
[($2.00 per button − $1.50 per button) × Volume] − $1,000 per year = Profit

This version of the profit equation is very useful in analyzing profit-making decisions. Sales price minus variable costs per unit equals **contribution margin per unit (CMU)**.[2] CMU can be thought of as the incremental profit from one product available to pay for the fixed costs and to provide a profit. For Quick-Button, Carrie calculates a CMU of $0.50 ($2.00 sales price − $1.50 variable costs per unit). From a profit management point of view, a button is worth $0.50. Every time one more button is sold, Carrie will receive another $0.50. This $0.50 can be used to help pay for the fixed costs. If the fixed costs have been covered already, then this $0.50 becomes extra profit. Substituting CMU into the profit equation:

(CMU × Volume) − Fixed costs = Profit
($0.50 per button × Volume) − $1,000 per year = Profit

Should Carrie go into the button-making business? To make this decision, Carrie needs to answer a number of questions, for example:

■ How many buttons must be sold to cover fixed costs?

[2] Traditionally, management accountants have called CMU "marginal income." This term causes some confusion, because marginal income is also used in economics, and the accountant's definition of marginal income is not precisely the same as the economist's. In economics, marginal income is marginal revenue minus marginal cost, where marginal cost is an absorption cost and includes a per-unit profit amount. For the management accountant, a better term to use might be incremental or differential profit.

- What sales volume is necessary to realize a target profit?
- For any projected sales volume, is there much risk of not covering the fixed costs?

Break-even Analysis

To answer the first equation, the **break-even point (BEP)** must be calculated. This is the sales volume at which Quick-Button earns zero profit. BEP will give Carrie a benchmark to consider for her business. BEP is a key measurement in CVP analysis and can be computed by two methods:

- The equation approach
- The contribution margin approach

THE EQUATION APPROACH.   The **equation approach** uses the profit equation:

$$(\$0.50 \text{ per button} \times \text{Volume}) - \$1,000 \text{ per year} = \text{Profit}$$

At the BEP, the profit goal is zero:

$$(\$0.50 \text{ per button} \times \text{Volume}) - \$1,000 \text{ per year} = \$0$$

Solving for volume (BEP):

$$\text{BEP} = \$1,000 \text{ per year} \div \$0.50 \text{ per button}$$
$$= \underline{2,000 \text{ buttons per year}}$$

What is the break-even point on a finished product?

In instances where the percentage relationship between variable costs and sales is known, but not the per-unit relationship, the following variation of the profit equation, using a **contribution margin ratio (CM ratio),** is appropriate. The CM ratio is created by dividing CMU by sales price or dividing the contribution margin by revenues.

$$(\text{CM ratio} \times \text{Revenues}) - \text{Fixed costs} = \text{Profit}$$

In an attempt to better understand this version of the profit equation, Carrie rotated it 90 degrees, creating a **contribution margin–based income statement.** She then created a spreadsheet program to perform CVP analysis. It is illustrated in Exhibit 18–1. Her contribution margin–based income statement format organizes costs by behavior (variable versus fixed costs) and calculates the contribution margin as a subtotal.[3] She also added per-unit and percentage columns to the income statement format.

In creating this income statement format, Carrie did not calculate fixed costs on a per-unit or percentage basis. Fixed costs are constant in total, but change with volume when expressed as a per-unit or percentage amount.[4]

In the percentage column, Carrie calculated both variable costs and contribution margin as a percentage of sales. This can be done using either the total amounts or the per-unit amounts. Dividing variable costs by sales creates a **variable cost ratio,** while dividing CMU by sales price, or contribution margin by revenues, yields the CM ratio.

---

[3] A traditional income statement format, used in financial reporting, organizes costs by function, not by behavior. Costs are grouped into product costs versus expenses with a subtotal created for gross profit.
[4] Fixed costs vary inversely with volume. Thus, every time Carrie changes her sales forecast, the fixed costs per unit will change. Thus, the profit, if expressed on a per-unit basis, will also change with volume, making it as unstable as fixed cost per unit.

■■■ EXHIBIT 18–1
Quick-Button's CVP Program

DATA SECTION:

Sales price	$2.00
Variable costs	$1.50
Volume	2,000
Fixed costs	$1,000

SOLUTION SECTION:

QUICK-BUTTON
PRO FORMA INCOME STATEMENT
FOR 1995

	PER UNIT	PERCENTAGE	TOTALS @ 2,000
Sales revenues	$2.00	100%	$4,000
Less variable costs	<$1.50>	<75%>	<$3,000>
Contribution margin	$0.50	25%	$1,000
Less fixed costs			<$1,000>
NET INCOME			$0

PROFIT EQUATION:

NET INCOME = [(SALES PRICE − VARIABLE COSTS) × VOLUME] − FIXED COSTS
  [($2.00   − $1.50   ) × VOLUME] − $1,000

BREAK-EVEN REVENUES:

  BER = (FIXED COSTS + TARGET PROFIT) / CM RATIO
  BER = $4,000 per year

BREAK-EVEN VOLUME:

  BEP = (FIXED COSTS + TARGET PROFIT) / CMU
  BEP = 2,000 units per year

The CM ratio is most useful when dealing with multiple products, whereas CMU is most useful when analyzing individual product lines. For example, consider a large discount retailer such as Wal-Mart, Inc. In any store, there are literally thousands of products, and customers may purchase any number of products at any one time. Attempting to calculate a CMU for each product would be inefficient. A better way to analyze CVP relationships is to look at averages, expressed as percentages. Using the Quick-Button illustration in Exhibit 18–1, for every *dollar* of sales, on average, $0.25 (25% of revenues) will be available to contribute to paying the fixed costs and generating the profit goal. Substituting the CM ratio and fixed costs into the profit equation, Carrie calculated break-even *revenues* (*BER*) as:

(CM ratio × Revenues) − Fixed costs = Profit
(25% × Revenues) − $1,000 per year = $0

To calculate BER:

BER = $1,000 per year ÷ 25%
  = $4,000 per year

Notice that in Exhibit 18–1. Carrie used the BEP as her sales volume to verify the accuracy of the above calculations. Once the BEP is known, Carrie could also have calculated BER by multiplying BEP by sales price (2,000 buttons × $2.00 per button = $4,000).

THE CONTRIBUTION MARGIN APPROACH. The **contribution margin approach** to CVP analysis uses the profit equation in its factored form:

$$\text{Target sales volume} = (\text{Fixed costs} + \text{Profit}) \div \text{CMU}$$

To calculate BEP:

$$
\begin{aligned}
\text{BEP} &= (\$1,000 + \$0) \div \$0.50 \text{ per button} \\
&= \underline{2,000 \text{ buttons per year}}
\end{aligned}
$$

Many retailers use CVP analysis for pricing decisions.

Carrie found this version of the profit equation easiest to explain to nonaccountants and the quickest way to perform CVP analysis. Simply interpreted, how many half-dollars are needed to cover $1,000? Obviously, 2,000 fifty-cent pieces are required to generate $1,000. Since each button contributes 50 cents, this is equivalent to asking how many buttons must be sold to generate $1,000 (the amount needed to just cover the fixed costs with nothing left over for profit).

Solving for sales *revenues*:

$$\text{Target sales revenues} = (\text{Fixed costs} + \text{Profit}) \div \text{CM ratio}$$

To calculate BER:

$$
\begin{aligned}
\text{BER} &= (\$1,000 \text{ per year} + \$0) \div 25\% \\
&= \underline{\$4,000 \text{ per year}}
\end{aligned}
$$

The CVP Chart

The CVP chart is a graphic presentation of the profit equation. Many decision makers prefer graphics instead of numbers because they can "see" a "picture" of the business. Moreover, a chart enables them to understand the relationship of cost, volume, and profit over a range of activity. Quick-Button's CVP chart is displayed in Exhibit 18–2. Carrie considered her relevant range to include sales volumes from zero to 5,000 buttons per year.

Sales volume is plotted on the horizontal axis and dollars on the vertical axis. The loss and profit areas are designated with arrows. To the left of the BEP, Carrie will suffer a loss because total costs are greater than revenues. To the right of the BEP, she will earn a profit because revenues are greater than total costs. In plotting the total costs line, she also included the fixed costs line to differentiate between total fixed and variable costs.

INCREMENTAL CVP ANALYSIS

The contribution margin approach, using the factored form of the profit equation, lends itself to incremental analysis. This type of CVP analysis often addresses "what-if" questions. For example, what if sales volume can be increased by 400 buttons? How much will profits *increase*? Or, what if Carrie sets a profit goal greater than zero (the BEP)? How many *more* buttons must

LEARNING OBJECTIVE 2

Use cost-volume-profit (CVP) analysis to analyze different profit-making alternatives.

■ EXHIBIT 18–2
Quick-Button's CVP Chart

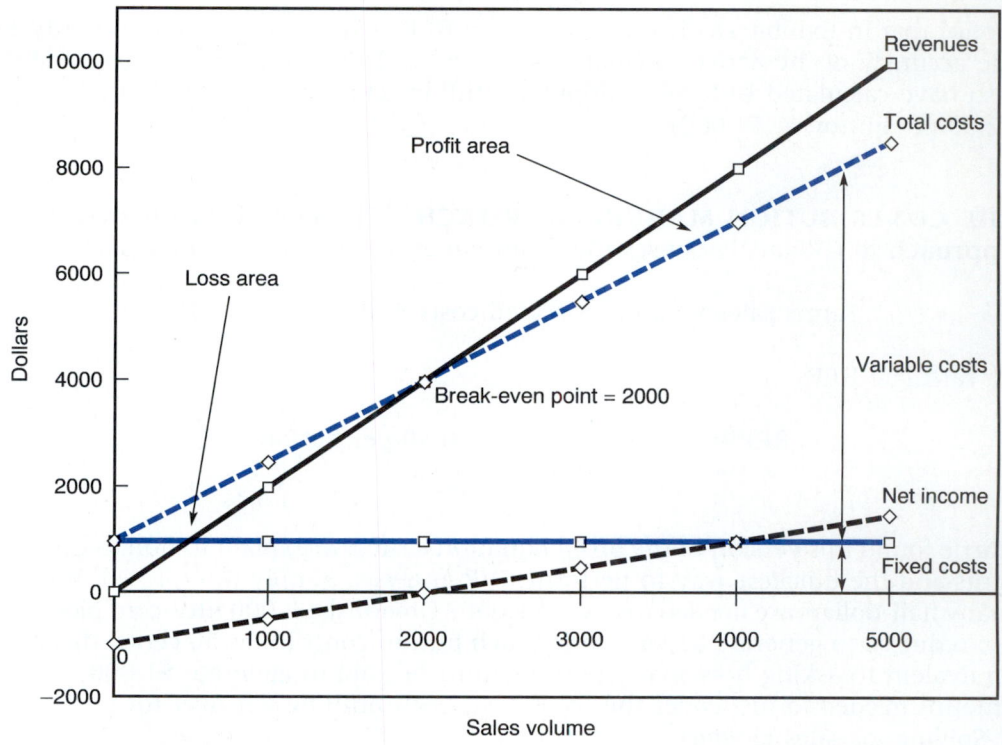

she sell to obtain this target profit? This latter question is the second of the three questions Carrie is considering with respect to Quick-Button.

Incremental CVP analysis at Bently Nevada Corporation.

CVP Rules

Before demonstrating how CVP analysis is done incrementally, some mathematical relationships must be understood. These are called "CVP rules."

1. A dollar change in contribution margin creates the same dollar change in profit (within the relevant range).
2. A unit change in volume multiplied by CMU equals the change in contribution margin.
3. A percentage change in volume multiplied by contribution margin equals the change in contribution margin.
4. A dollar change in revenues multiplied by the CM ratio equals the change in contribution margin. (*Caution*: This relationship is only true if the change in revenues is caused by a change in volume, not by a change in sales price.)
5. A dollar change in fixed costs creates the opposite change in profit (as fixed costs go up, profit goes down).
6. If there is a change in sales price or variable costs per unit (the elements of CMU), calculate the change in CMU first. Then multiply it by volume to obtain the change in contribution margin.
7. If there are simultaneous changes in one or both elements of CMU and in sales volume, calculate the new contribution margin and compare it to the old contribution margin to obtain the change in contribution margin.

These rules are summarized and demonstrated in Exhibit 18–3.

"What-If" Analysis

"What-if" questions are asked in master budgeting meetings as well as during day-to-day operations of the profit center manager. Using the factored form

The purpose of these rules is to provide an efficient means of calculating the change in profit associated with an alternative course of action being considered by profit center managers. Rule 1 relates the change in profit to the change in contribution margin. If the change in contribution margin is known, then the change in profit is also known. Rules 2 through 7 are concerned with calculating the change in contribution margin. Each rule is illustrated using the Quick-Button data in Exhibit 18–1.

Rule	Description
1	$\$\Delta$CM = $\$\Delta$Profit

If CM increased by $200, profit will increase by $200.

2	ΔVolume $\times$ CMU = $\$\Delta$CM

If 400 more buttons can be sold, each generating another 50 cents in CMU, CM will increase by $200.

3	%ΔVolume $\times$ CM = $\$\Delta$CM

If volume increases by 20% (400 buttons), CM will increase by $200 (20% of the $1,000 CM).

4	$\$\Delta$Revenues $\times$ CM ratio = $\$\Delta$CM

If revenues increase by $800, contribution margin will increase by $200 (25% of revenues). *Caution:* This relationship is only true if the change in revenues is caused by a change in volume, not by a change in sales price. See rule 6 for calculating the effect of a change in sales price.

5	+$\$\Delta$Fixed costs = $-\$\Delta$Profit

If fixed costs go up $100, profit will go down $100.

6	ΔSales price or variable costs per unit: calculate ΔCMU and multiply by volume to obtain the ΔCM.

If sales price increases by 15 cents and variable costs per unit increase by 10 cents, CMU will increase by 5 cents, and CM will increase by $100 ($.05 $\times$ 2,000 buttons).

7	ΔCMU and ΔVolume: calculate new CMU, new CM, and then compare new CM to old CM in order to obtain the ΔCM.

If CMU increases 10 cents to $0.60 per button, but volume decreases to 1,500 buttons, the new CM = $900 ($0.60 $\times$ 1,500 buttons), which is a decrease in CM of $100 from the original amount in Exhibit 18–1.

Legend

Δ	change	CM	contribution margin
$	dollars	CMU	contribution margin per unit
%	percentage		

(the contribution margin approach) of the profit equation and thinking incrementally will allow modern management accountants to answer these questions immediately without returning to their desks for more calculations. Profit center managers are not likely to be pleased when a management accountant says, "I'll have to get back to you later on that." They need quick and accurate answers *within the meeting*. To illustrate, consider the following scenario based on the Quick-Button example found on the next page:

Wouldn't it have been better if Carrie had responded, "Let's see. If sales volume increases 300 buttons with a CMU of 50 cents each, then contribution margin will increase $150. This will cover the incremental advertising costs of

Obtaining a Bank Loan for Quick-Button

Carrie Copolla decided she should make and sell quick-buttons. Since she does not have sufficient capital to start up her business, she set up an appointment with her banker, hoping to obtain a short-term, unsecured line-of-credit until Quick-Button starts to make sufficient profits and cash flows to cover her costs.

Her banker, John Enterest, reviewed her master budget, in particular, her cash budget for the upcoming year.

He was concerned that the sales forecast will not be sufficient for her to repay a loan. So, they began considering various alternatives to increase sales.

"Well, Carrie, what if you bought and distributed some advertising brochures promoting your buttons? If an expenditure of $100 could increase sales volume by 300 buttons, would this generate any extra profits?"

Carrie responded, "Gee, I don't know. I'll work up the numbers, but it will take me a while."

John was a little perturbed. "O.K., but I can't make a loan decision until I know the answer. It looks like we will have to schedule another meeting to go over your figures. I'm going on vacation next week, so we'll have to set up a meeting again in three weeks or so, depending on my work load when I return."

$100 and leave an extra $50 in profits." If Carrie had been proficient in incremental CVP analysis, the meeting could have continued without having to be rescheduled sometime in the future!

WHAT IF I CAN INCREASE SALES VOLUME?   At her meeting with John Enterest, Carrie forecast a sales volume of 2,400 buttons, as shown in Exhibit 18–4. She now knows this is 400 buttons above her BEP. Because of her inability to answer John's question, Carrie realized the need to become more competent in incremental CVP analysis for solving what-if questions. While John was on vacation, Carrie separated his question into two parts: (1) What is the effect on profits if sales volume increases by 300 buttons? and (2) What is the effect on profits from spending $100 on advertising?

$$\Delta\text{Target sales volume} = \Delta(\text{Fixed costs} + \text{Profit}) \div \text{CMU}$$
$$+300 \text{ buttons} = \Delta(0 + \text{Profit}) \div \$0.50$$

Solving for the change in profit:

$$\Delta\text{Profit} = +300 \text{ buttons} \times \$0.50$$
$$= \underline{\underline{+\$150}}$$

Alternatively, Carrie can use CVP rule 2:

$$\Delta\text{Volume} \times \text{CMU} = \$\Delta\text{CM}$$
$$+300 \text{ buttons} \times \$0.50 \text{ per button} = \underline{\underline{+\$150}}$$

If 300 more buttons can be sold, each generating another 50 cents in CMU, then contribution margin will increase by $150. Applying rule 1, a change in contribution margin will yield the same change in profit. This is true only over the relevant range in which total fixed costs do not change if volume changes. Carrie can also solve for the change in profits by using the profit equation approach. The equation, though taking longer to solve, will always work.

$$(\text{CMU} \times \text{Volume}) - \text{Fixed costs} = \text{Profit}$$
$$(\$0.50 \text{ per button} \times 2,700 \text{ buttons}) - \$1,000 \text{ per year} = \underline{\underline{\$350}}$$

Carrie's original base case projection (2,400 buttons per year in Exhibit 18–4) showed a profit of $200. Thus, profit will increase $150 to $350.

DATA SECTION:

Sales price	$2.00
Variable costs	$1.50
Volume	2,400
Fixed costs	$1,000

SOLUTION SECTION:

QUICK-BUTTON
PRO FORMA INCOME STATEMENT
FOR 1995

	PER UNIT	PERCENTAGE	TOTALS @ 2,400
Sales revenues	$2.00	100%	$4,800
Less variable costs	<$1.50>	<75%>	<$3,600>
Contribution margin	$0.50	25%	$1,200
Less fixed costs			<$1,000>
NET INCOME			$200

PROFIT EQUATION:

NET INCOME = [(SALES PRICE − VARIABLE COSTS) × VOLUME] − FIXED COSTS
$$[(\quad \$2.00 \quad - \quad \$1.50 \quad) \times \text{VOLUME}] - \quad \$1,000$$

BREAK-EVEN REVENUES:

BER = (FIXED COSTS + TARGET PROFIT) / CM RATIO
BER = $4,000 per year

BREAK-EVEN VOLUME:

BEP = (FIXED COSTS + TARGET PROFIT) / CMU
BEP = 2,000 units per year

To finish this example, the increase in contribution margin results from an increase in fixed costs (the $100 expenditure for advertising). CVP rule 5 states that a change in fixed costs causes the opposite change in profit. In other words, if fixed costs go up $100, then profit goes down $100. Subtracting the change in fixed costs from the change in contribution margin produces the net $50 increase in profit.

WHAT IF I SET A TARGET PROFIT GOAL?   Originally, Carrie also wanted to know, "What sales volume is necessary to realize a target profit?" Assume Carrie sets a profit goal of $200 for 1995. As Exhibit 18–4 shows, she will have to sell 2,400 buttons. She can solve for this incrementally:

$$\Delta \text{Target sales volume} = \Delta(\text{Fixed costs} + \text{Profit}) \div \text{CMU}$$
$$= (0 + \$200) \div \$0.50 \text{ per button}$$
$$= +400 \text{ buttons}$$

Carrie will have to sell 400 buttons above the BEP (2,000 buttons). But what if she wants *another* $300 in profits? If Carrie wants $300 more in profits, *regardless of the level of profits she already has,* she will have to sell another 600 buttons.

In this illustration, Carrie set an absolute dollar amount of profit. Conceptually, this is just another fixed cost—the payment to the owner. But, what if she stated her profit goal as a percentage of sales revenues? For example, Carrie sets a profit goal of 5 percent of sales. Exhibit 18–5 shows the sales revenues necessary to achieve a 5 percent profit. The projected profit of $250 is 5 percent of the $5,000 sales revenues.

In this situation, conceptually speaking, a profit goal stated as a percentage of revenues is just another variable cost. Therefore, profit will not be in the numerator of the profit equation because it is not an absolute amount (a fixed cost). Instead, it will now be in the denominator:

$$\text{Target sales revenues} = \text{Fixed costs} \div (\text{CM ratio} - \text{Profit percentage})$$
$$= \$1,000 \div (25\% - 5\%)$$
$$= \underline{\underline{\$5,000 \text{ per year}}}$$

Many different types of what-if questions can be asked:

- What if a special order is possible? What is the lowest sales price Carrie can bid?
- What if a firm has an opportunity to buy a part instead of making it? Will buying increase profits?
- What if a part can be sold instead of processed further into a final product? Will selling it now increase profits?
- What if a firm does not have enough materials or labor to make all the different types of products it usually sells? Which products should be made?

These kinds of profit management questions are considered in the next chapter. Incremental CVP analysis provides a powerful tool for the management accountant to use in efficiently answering such questions.

Margin of Safety

The third question Carrie originally considered involves the risk of not covering fixed costs (i.e., not breaking even). Measuring this risk involves the calculation of the **margin of safety.** This is the difference between the sales forecast and the break-even point and can be expressed by the following equation:

$$\text{Margin of safety} = \frac{\text{Sales forecast} - \text{BEP}}{\text{Sales forecast}}$$
$$= \frac{2,400 \text{ buttons} - 2,000 \text{ buttons}}{2,400 \text{ buttons}}$$
$$= \underline{\underline{16\%}}^{5}$$

Quick-Button's sales can decrease by 400 buttons, or 16 percent of the sales forecast, before Carrie suffers a loss. If actual sales are below the forecast by more than 16 percent, then Carrie will not break even. These computations can be a useful guide. If the marketing and cost data that Carrie has collected are fairly accurate, then she and John Enterest can consider this a high margin of safety, which indicates low risk. They do not expect that her sales forecast will be off by more than 16 percent. If, on the other hand, her margin of

---

[5] 400 buttons ÷ 2,400 buttons = 16.67%. This should be rounded down, not up. Using the same logic, (conservatism), if the BEP includes a fraction of a unit, it should always be rounded up.

DATA SECTION:

Sales price	$2.00
Variable costs	$1.50
Volume	2,500
Fixed costs	$1,000

SOLUTION SECTION:

QUICK BUTTON
PRO FORMA INCOME STATEMENT
FOR 1995

	PER UNIT	PERCENTAGE	TOTALS @ 2,500
Sales revenues	$2.00	100%	$5,000
Less variable costs	<$1.50>	<75%>	<$3,750>
Contribution margin	$0.50	25%	$1,250
Less fixed costs			<$1,000>
NET INCOME			$250

PROFIT EQUATION:

NET INCOME = [(SALES PRICE − VARIABLE COSTS) × VOLUME] − FIXED COSTS
　　　　　　[(　$2.00　−　$1.50　) × VOLUME] −　$1,000

BREAK-EVEN REVENUES:

BER = (FIXED COSTS + TARGET PROFIT) / CM RATIO

BER = $4,000 per year

BREAK-EVEN VOLUME:

BEP = (FIXED COSTS + TARGET PROFIT) / CMU

BEP = 2,000 units per year

safety was 5 percent, then even a small decline in sales would result in a loss. Consequently, a low margin of safety indicates a high risk of not breaking even.

MULTIPLE PRODUCTS AND INCOME TAX CONSIDERATIONS

LEARNING
OBJECTIVE 3
—
Apply CVP formulas to situations involving sales mixes and income taxes.

The Quick-Button case involved just one product, but many enterprises sell multiple products. Furthermore, all profit-making enterprises are subject to income taxes. These extensions to CVP analysis are considered next.

Sales Mix

Sales mix is the relative distribution of sales among the various products sold by a business. Suppose that Tommy Telford is preparing a business plan to launch his venture, New-Wave Designs. He plans to make and market designer caps and T-shirts. Tommy has prepared a projected sales mix for the first fiscal year as follows:

PRODUCT	ESTIMATED UNIT SALES	SALES MIX
Caps	15,600	60%
T-shirts	10,400	40%
	26,000	100%

The sales mix for caps and T-shirts can be expressed as relative percentages (as here) or as the ratio of 60 percent to 40 percent (60:40). If this sales mix remains constant over the budget horizon, both the BEP and the sales necessary to achieve a target profit can be calculated using the CVP and break-even equations presented earlier in this chapter.

To illustrate the calculation of the BEP for New-Wave Designs, assume that fixed costs are $24,000. In addition, assume that the unit sales price and variable costs are as follows:

PRODUCT	UNIT SALES PRICE	UNIT VARIABLE COST
Caps	$2.00	$1.40
T-shirts	$5.00	$3.50

In computing the BEP, each product is considered as a component of an overall New-Wave product called the "package."[6] To calculate the BEP, a weighted-average sales price, variable cost per package, and CMU are needed:

Weighted-average package sales price:
$$(\$2.00 \times .60) + (\$5.00 \times .40) = \quad \$3.20$$
Less weighted-average package variable cost:
$$(\$1.40 \times .60) + (\$3.50 \times .40) = \quad <\$2.24>$$
$$\text{Weighted-average CMU} = \quad \$0.96$$

The package's variable cost ratio is 70 percent of sales ($2.24 ÷ $3.20), and the CM ratio is 30 percent ($0.96 ÷ $3.20). The overall BEP is computed using the profit equation in its factored format:

BEP = Fixed costs of $24,000 ÷ CMU of $0.96 per package
  = 25,000 packages

Because the sales mix is 60 percent for caps and 40 percent for T-shirts, the BEP is 15,000 caps (25,000 packages × .60) and 10,000 T-shirts (25,000 packages × .40). The foregoing analysis is summarized in the following contribution margin income statement:

NEW-WAVE DESIGNS
CONTRIBUTION MARGIN INCOME STATEMENT
FOR YEAR ENDED DECEMBER 31, 1995

	CAPS	T-SHIRTS	TOTAL
Sales:			
15,000 units × $2.00	$30,000		$30,000
10,000 units × $5.00		$50,000	50,000
Total sales	$30,000	$50,000	$80,000

Continued

---

[6] The shirt and hat are considered to be packaged together as a "composite" product, like shampoo with conditioner, toothpaste with a toothbrush, or a "special value-pak meal" at a fast-food restaurant. While each of these products can be sold individually, they can also be sold together.

—Continued

	CAPS	T-SHIRTS	TOTAL
Less variable costs:			
15,000 units × $1.40	21,000		21,000
10,000 units × $3.50		35,000	35,000
Total variable costs	<$21,000>	<$35,000>	<$56,000>
Contribution margin	$9,000	$15,000	$24,000
Less fixed costs			< 24,000>
Profit			$ –0–

If Tommy wants to earn a target profit of $20,400:

$$\text{Target sales volume} = (\text{Fixed costs} + \text{Profit}) \div \text{CMU}$$
$$= (\$24,000 + \$20,400) \div \$0.96$$
$$= 46,250 \text{ packages}$$

The sales quota for caps is 27,750 (60 percent of 46,250), and for T-shirts it is 18,500 (40 percent of 46,250). This can also be solved incrementally. The profit goal changes from zero (BEP) to $20,400:

$$\Delta\text{Target sales volume} = \Delta(\text{Fixed costs} + \text{Profit}) \div \text{CMU}$$
$$= (\$0 + \$20,400) \div \$0.96 \text{ per package}$$
$$= +21,250 \text{ packages}$$

Sales volume of caps will have to increase 12,750 (60 percent of 21,250) from the BEP of 15,000 caps to 27,750 caps. Sales volume of T-shirts will have to increase 8,500 (40 percent of 21,250) from its BEP of 10,000 to 18,500 T-shirts.

Income Tax Considerations

If Tommy realizes a profit of $20,400, he will have to pay income taxes and self-employment taxes. Assume these two taxes amount to 40 percent:

$$\text{Aftertax profit} = \text{Pretax profit} - \text{Taxes}$$
$$= \$20,400 - (\$20,400 \times 40\%)$$
$$= \$12,240$$

This profit amount is not acceptable to Tommy because he wants $20,400 after taxes. The aftertax profit is 60 percent (1 − Tax rate) of the pretax profit. Solving for the pretax profit needed:

$$\text{Pretax profit} = \text{Aftertax profit} \div (1 - \text{Tax rate})$$

Substituting this into the profit equation:

$$\text{Target sales volume} = \frac{\text{Fixed costs} + \dfrac{\text{Aftertax profit}}{(1 - \text{Tax rate})}}{\text{CMU}}$$

$$\text{Target sales volume} = \frac{\$24,000 + \dfrac{\$20,400}{(1 - 40\%)}}{\$0.96 \text{ per package}}$$

$$= 60,417 \text{ packages per year}[7]$$

---

[7] Target sales volume = 60,416.67 packages. This should always be rounded up, not down. Selling 60,416 packages will not quite produce the target profit.

What if Tommy's target profit is not an absolute dollar amount, but rather is 5 percent of sales revenues after taxes?

$$\text{Target sales revenues} = \text{Fixed costs} \div \left[\text{CM ratio} - \frac{\text{Profit percentage}}{(1 - \text{Tax rate})} \right]$$

$$= \$24,000 \div \left[30\% - \frac{5\%}{(1 - 40\%)} \right]$$

$$= \underline{\$110,770 \text{ per year (rounded up)}}$$

SENSITIVITY ANALYSIS AND FINANCIAL PLANNING SOFTWARE

In addition to the preceding analysis, modern profit management also involves **sensitivity analysis,** which shows how the profit equation responds to changes in the CVP parameters. Sensitivity analysis is a helpful tool for showing the results of different assumptions about the CVP elements. It involves examining the impact of reasonable changes in "base case" assumptions. For example, management accountants might make calculations using several different estimates of variable costs, fixed costs, and sales prices. The effect of these changing parameters on the break-even point can then be studied relative to a most likely scenario.

Essentially, sensitivity analysis is an approach for dealing with uncertain data and other decision risks. Decisions always involve inputs, such as assumptions, estimates, and simplifications, all of which are prone to errors of varying degrees.[8] Sensitivity analysis can be used to:

- Identify those variables that are most/least sensitive to changes in assumptions.
- Make better profit decisions.
- Decide which data estimates should be refined.
- Focus managerial attention on the most critical elements of a scenario.[9]

This analysis may consider only a few variables, or it may systematically consider all. It may analyze only one variable at a time (known as relative sensitivity), multiple variables, or scenarios of plausible sets of changes. These sensitivities may then be presented through words, tables, or graphs.

Rapid advances in desktop computer technology have removed the barrier of burdensome calculations from sensitivity analysis. Data points are easily obtained through multiple runs of a simple spreadsheet model. Hard-copy output can then be automatically generated to summarize the results. This output usually takes the form of a line graph, bar chart, or break-even graph (CVP chart), all with varying axes and notations.

A sensitivity analysis can be done using any measure, for example, injuries per year, net sales revenue, internal rate of return, present worth, or profit. No matter what form the output takes, it will always show how the chosen measure varies as decision parameters are changed within reasonable limits.

LANs help facilitate sensitivity analysis. Courtesy of Novell, Inc.

[8] Joseph A. Russo, *Sensitivity Analysis: An Introduction for Managers* (New York: Center for Applied Research, Lubin School of Business, Pace University, 1990), p. 1.

[9] Ted G. Eschenbach and Lisa S. McKeague, "Exposition on Using Graphs for Sensitivity Analysis," *The Engineering Economist*, Summer 1989, pp. 315–333.

Using Graphical Sensitivities with CVP Analysis

The Quick-Button case can be used to illustrate sensitivity analysis. Based on new sales and cost data and incremental CVP analyses that Carrie Copolla performed for various alternatives, she now estimates the following:

- Sales price per button: $1.30
- Variable cost per button: $0.52
- Fixed costs (one year): $1,560

This will be the base case for her sensitivity analysis. The break-even point is still 2,000 buttons annually.

Carrie has also determined what she considers to be limits of reasonable change for her price and cost data. To be competitive, she feels her button sales price can vary plus or minus 19 percent from her $1.30 estimate. Her variable cost estimate could change by as much as 15 percent. Finally, fixed costs could be 10 percent less than estimated, but they could be as much as 30 percent higher. Carrie uses this information with her profit equation to create a micro-computer spreadsheet program generating three tables.

Exhibit 18–6 holds variable cost and fixed costs at their base case values while varying sales price over the 19 percent range. The table also shows the percentage change from the base case for each sales price. The goal of her three tables is to calculate the break-even point under each condition, as shown in the last column.

Exhibit 18–7 holds sales price and fixed costs at their base case values while changing the variable cost per unit. Similarly, Exhibit 18–8 varies only the fixed costs over its range.

The percentage change from the base case, and the BEP from the three spreadsheet tables are plotted in Exhibit 18–9. Each of the three plots represents the relative sensitivity of the BEP to a particular parameter. The plots intersect

---

EXHIBIT 18–6

Spreadsheet Analysis of Sales Price Sensitivity for Quick-Button

Sensitivity of BEP to Sales Price					
Sales price	$1.30	+/- 19%			
Variable cost	$0.52				
Fixed cost	$1,560				
BEP	2,000				
Percentage change from base	New sales price	New CMU	New BEP	Change in BEP	%change in BEP
-19%	$1.05	$0.53	2,944	944	47%
-15%	1.11	0.59	2,645	645	32%
-12%	1.14	0.62	2,517	517	26%
-8%	1.20	0.68	2,295	295	15%
-4%	1.25	0.73	2,137	137	7%
0%	1.30	0.78	2,000	0	0%
4%	1.35	0.83	1,880	(120)	-6%
8%	1.40	0.88	1,773	(227)	-11%
12%	1.46	0.94	1,660	(340)	-17%
15%	1.50	0.98	1,592	(408)	-20%
19%	1.55	1.03	1,515	(485)	-24%

EXHIBIT 18–7

Spreadsheet Analysis of Variable Cost Sensitivity for Quick-Button

Sensitivity of BEP to Variable Cost					
Sales price	$1.30				
Variable cost	$0.52	+/- 15%			
Fixed cost	$1,560				
BEP	2,000				
Percentage change from base	**New variable cost per unit**	**New CMU**	**New BEP**	**Change in BEP**	**%change in BEP**
-15%	$0.44	$0.86	1,814	(186)	-9%
-12%	0.46	0.84	1,858	(142)	-7%
-8%	0.48	0.82	1,903	(97)	-5%
-4%	0.50	0.80	1,950	(50)	-3%
0%	0.52	0.78	2,000	0	0%
4%	0.54	0.76	2,053	53	3%
8%	0.56	0.74	2,109	109	5%
12%	0.58	0.72	2,167	167	8%
15%	0.60	0.70	2,229	229	11%

EXHIBIT 18–8

Spreadsheet Analysis of Fixed Cost Sensitivity for Quick-Button

Sensitivity of BEP to Fixed Cost					
Sales price	$1.30				
Variable cost	$0.52				
Fixed cost	$1,560	+30%/-10%			
BEP	2,000				
Percentage change from base	**New fixed cost**	**CMU**	**New BEP**	**Change in BEP**	**%change in BEP**
-10%	$1,404	$0.78	1,800	(200)	-10%
-6%	1,466	0.78	1,880	(120)	-6%
-2%	1,529	0.78	1,961	(39)	-2%
0%	1,560	0.78	2,000	0	0%
4%	1,622	0.78	2,080	80	4%
8%	1,685	0.78	2,161	161	8%
12%	1,747	0.78	2,240	240	12%
16%	1,810	0.78	2,321	321	16%
20%	1,872	0.78	2,400	400	20%
24%	1,934	0.78	2,480	480	24%
28%	1,997	0.78	2,561	561	28%
30%	2,028	0.78	2,600	600	30%

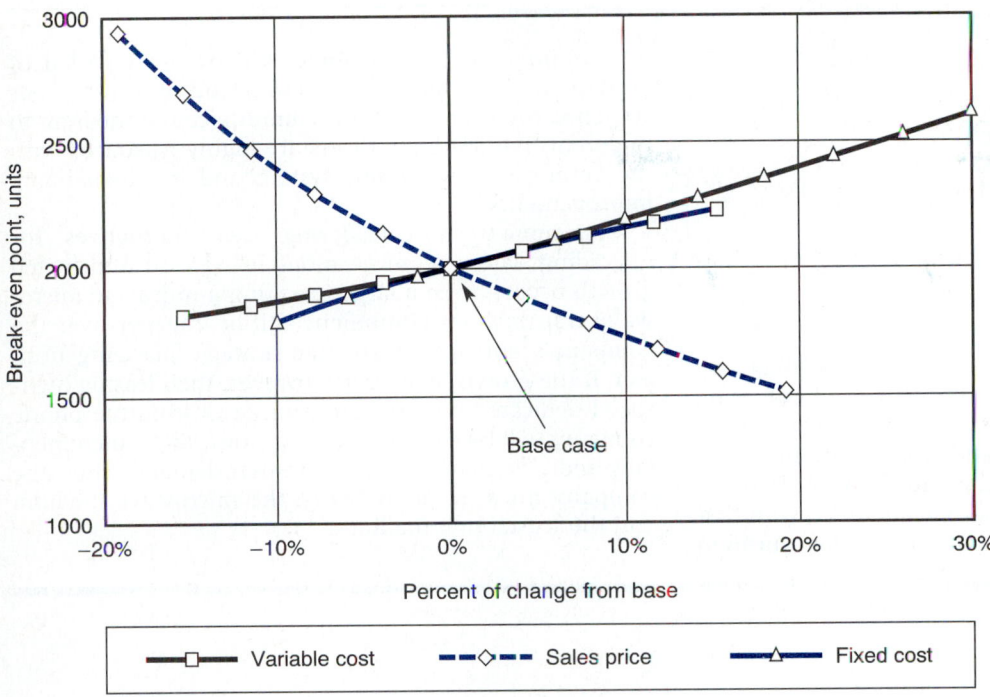

Combined Relative Sensitivity Graph for Quick-Button

at the base case. From this graph, Carrie can see that the break-even point, in units sold, for her Quick-Button business is most sensitive to the price she charges for her buttons since that curve has the greatest slope. Therefore, if she wants to decrease the number of units needed to break even, the most effective way to do so is to raise her price. Decreasing either variable or fixed costs is not nearly as effective since these trend lines are flatter.[10]

A more typical planning and forecasting situation will very likely involve a great many more inputs than just price and costs. In such cases, sensitivity analysis can assist profit managers in making the most effective use of planning resources by allocating them to researching the most critical of the inputs.

Using Graphical Sensitivity Analysis for Decision Making

Sensitivity analysis provides knowledge to managers to help them explore how certain changes may affect a decision. In the accompanying NPV Corporation case (see p. 852), sensitivity analysis gives management a chance to experiment with different assumptions before making a final decision.

Besides the uncertainty in the demand's growth rate, other base case assumptions can be challenged. For example, the problem horizon (study period) and the discount rate are somewhat arbitrary selections, and the initial cost of microwave installations is often higher than expected. Top management insists that the effects of these uncertainties on the present value of the project be analyzed before a decision is made. The chief variables to be analyzed and their limits of reasonable change are as follows:

■ *Microwave*. Initial cost (−40%, +100%), operating costs (−40%, +60%), capacity (−10%, +20%), and life (−40%, +100%).
■ *Leased lines*. Cost per line, including amortization of company-supplied interfaces (−20%, +20%), and growth rate of line rates (−80%, +300%).
■ *General*. Demand's growth rate (−100%, +50%) and discount rate (−50%, +70%).

[10] Raising the sales price is a positive change from the base case and is represented by moving to the right along the horizontal axis. As the sales price increases, the BEP decreases. Decreasing variable or fixed costs (moving to the left from the base case on these lines) also reduces the BEP. As the percentage change from the base case increases (moving along the horizontal axis), the sales price line, having the greatest slope, yields the largest change in the BEP (the vertical axis).

INSIGHTS & APPLICATIONS

Upgrading Data Communications at NPV Corporation

NPV Corporation, a regional commercial lending firm with its home office in Phoenix, has been operating a single branch office in Tucson for the last eight years.

About one hundred miles and two mountain ranges separate these offices. Since the Tucson branch office opened, its information system has been linked with that of the home office by low-speed data communication over ordinary telephone lines. An extended period of growth in the company's Tucson lending activity has stretched the capacity of this communication medium to the point that lending officers are highly frustrated with the response time of the system and are demanding improvements.

Management is considering two alternatives for upgrading data communications at NPV. If anticipated growth occurs, then a large investment in private microwave transmission equipment will be cheaper over the company's anticipated 20-year strategic planning horizon. If the growth is slower, however, then leasing high-speed dedicated data transmission lines from the phone company will be cheaper, because lines can be incrementally added to match increases in user demand. Thus, the company must decide between the microwave medium and the leased line medium.

The relative sensitivity of the alternatives' present worth (PW) to each variable is shown in Exhibit 18–10. Note that the vertical axis represents the difference in present worth (PW) between the two alternatives, and the horizontal line at zero is a line of indifference. Above this line, microwave is preferred. Below this line, the leased lines is preferred. Management has already determined a single most likely scenario for the project, and this is taken as the base case. In the exhibit, the base case clearly favors the microwave alternative because it occurs above the line of indifference.

EXHIBIT 18–10
Preferred Relative Sensitivity Graph for NPV Corporation

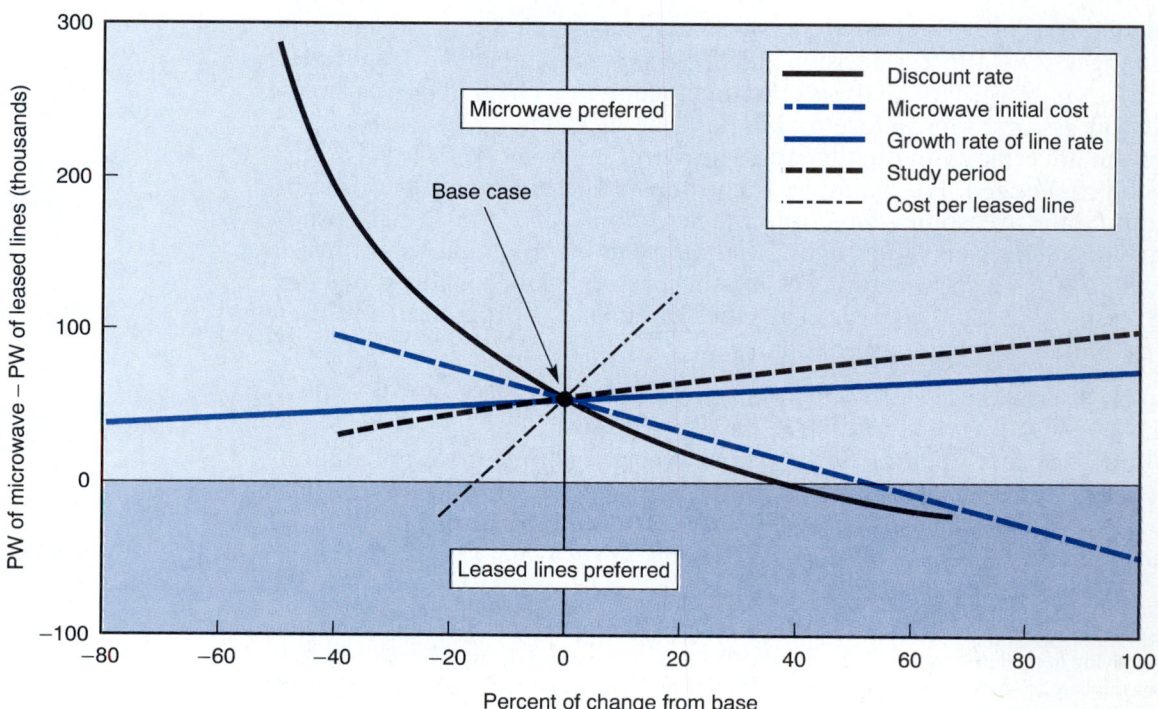

It's important to realize that the natural units for the analyzed variables may be different from each other. For instance, the discount rate is in percent, while the microwave initial cost is in dollars, and the demand's growth rate is in megabits per second per year. For this reason, to readily compare the graphs a common metric must be identified. In Exhibit 18–10, this is the percentage change from the base case, which is shown as the horizontal axis. Of course, lines representing the variables all intersect at the base case point.

Financial Planning Software

Although spreadsheet programs can perform many types of profit planning analyses, financial planning software is often more efficient. It also provides many more sophisticated calculations than can be done with a spreadsheet program, as shown in the Amherst Company case on page 854.

BUILDING A WHAT-IF SCREEN.   With these data, a what-if screen produced by a microcomputer financial planning software program[11] can be set up to reveal the results of changing conditions. The initial what-if screen and its results are displayed in Exhibit 18–11. At the bottom of the screen are the equations and data used by the program to generate the values at the top of the screen. This initial screen becomes the base case. When a variable receives a new definition (i.e., is changed), this definition replaces the one in the base case. The base case, however, is still stored in memory and can be recalled at any time.

Suppose that management wants to see the results if dollar sales grow by 15 percent rather than 25 percent per period, while variable costs remain the same as in the base case. All the management accountant has to do is change the

[11] Paul Gray, *Guide to IFPS/Personal®: The Interactive Financial Planning System for Personal Computers* (New York: McGraw-Hill, 1988).

EXHIBIT 18–11
**Initial What-if Screen
(in Thousands)**

	1	2	3	4	5
Sales	100.00	125.00	156.25	195.31	244.14
Variable Costs	75.00	100.00	125.00	150.00	175.00
Contribution Margin	25.00	25.00	31.25	45.31	69.14
Contribution Margin (CM) Ratio	0.25	0.20	0.20	0.23	0.28

Sales = 100, Previous Sales * 1.25
Variable Costs = 75, 100, 125, 150, 175
Contribution Margin = Sales − Variable Costs
Contribution Margin (CM) Ratio = Contribution Margin / Sales

INSIGHTS & APPLICATIONS

Amherst Company's Master Budgeting

Assume that management at Amherst Company wants to project CVP data for five periods. Marketing has estimated that dollar sales for the first period will be $100,000 and will increase by 25 percent each period. Cost accounting projects the variable costs at $75,000 for the first period, $100,000 for the second period, $125,000 for the third period, $150,000 for the fourth period, and $175,000 for the fifth period.

The management accountant has just installed IFPS/Personal®, an interactive financial planning system for PCs. What-if and goal-seek are two features of IFPS/Personal® that allow managers to ask questions and receive an answer in real-time. The what-if feature permits managers to change the definition of one or more variables temporarily to see what the change implies. The base case remains in memory and can be recalled whenever the management accountant needs it.

The goal-seek feature enables the management accountant to determine the value a particular variable has to have to achieve a desired level of performance. Managers can specify their goal either as:

■ Performance at a single point in time
■ Performance over the entire time horizon

multiplier to 1.15 instead of 1.25. The results are computed instantly and displayed on the screen as presented in Exhibit 18–12.

The management accountant can also change several variables, not just one, when creating a what-if screen. For example, the management accountant may want to determine the effect of simultaneous changes in both dollar sales and variable costs:

$$\text{Sales} = 100, \text{Previous} \times 1.12$$
$$\text{Variable costs} = 70, \text{Previous} + 20$$

The program will immediately compute new values based on these new variables.

In many what-if analyses, the management accountant may want to change a variable in one or more periods from its value in the base case. The what-if feature can be used for all periods, as in the preceding examples, or for selected periods. To illustrate, if management expects no change in dollar sales for two periods but wants to give new values thereafter:

$$\text{Sales} = \text{Prior 2}, \text{Previous} \times 1.20$$

The user can also update the base case if new assumptions lead to better results than the initial base case assumptions. In other words, the user has created a new base case against which other what-if cases are to be judged. If desired, the user can keep the initial base case and save the new base case under another name. In this way, both the initial and the updated models are available for use.

USING THE GOAL-SEEK FEATURE. Another powerful feature of this software is goal-seek. Through goal-seek, the program calculates the value a particular variable has to have to achieve a desired level of performance. For example, the management accountant might type the goal as:

$$\text{Goal: Contribution margin} = 25, \text{Previous} + 20$$

This goal states that the contribution margin is to start at $25,000 and to increase by $20,000 each period.

Once the goal is established, the program asks for the variable to be adjusted:

$$\text{Adjust: Variable costs}$$

The program then solves the model and displays the results as shown in Exhibit 18–13.

■■■EXHIBIT 18–12
Second What-if Screen (in Thousands)

	1	2	3	4	5
Sales	100.00	115.00	132.25	152.09	174.90
Variable Costs	75.00	100.00	125.00	150.00	175.00
Contribution Margin	25.00	15.00	7.25	2.09	−0.10
Contribution Margin (CM) Ratio	0.25	0.13	0.05	0.01	−0.00

Sales = 100, Previous Sales * 1.15
Variable Costs = 75, 100, 125, 150, 175
Contribution Margin = Sales − Variable Costs
Contribution Margin (CM) Ratio = Contribution Margin / Sales

■■■EXHIBIT 18–13
Goal-Seek Screen (in Thousands)

	1	2	3	4	5
Sales	100.00	125.00	156.25	195.31	244.14
Variable Costs	75.00	80.00	91.25	110.31	139.14
Contribution Margin	25.00	45.00	65.00	85.00	105.00
Contribution Margin (CM) Ratio	0.25	0.36	0.42	0.44	0.43

Sales = 100, Previous Sales * 1.25
Variable Costs = 75, 100, 125, 150, 175
Contribution Margin = Sales − Variable Costs
Contribution Margin (CM) Ratio = Contribution Margin / Sales

Goal-seek:
    Goal: Contribution Margin = 25, Previous + 20
    Adjust: Variable Costs

The modern management accountant provides valuable and real-time CVP analyses during profit planning meetings. Courtesy of Bently Nevada Corporation.

The results of the goal-seek screen indicate that variable costs must be reduced to the amounts shown for each period if the company is to realize a contribution margin increase of $20,000 in each period beginning with a contribution margin of $25,000 in period 1.

Goal-seek can also be used in just one period, say, period 4. For example, the user might specify:

> Goal: Contribution margin [4] = 60
> Adjust: Sales [4]

In the base case (Exhibit 18–11), sales of $195,310 in period 4 produce a contribution margin of $45,310. If management can control variable costs at $150,000 and increase sales to $210,000, then the company will achieve a contribution margin of $60,000.[12]

ANALYZING TARGET PROFITS. Assume that the Amherst Company is planning to expand its operations and is considering three alternatives with target profits set at $100,000, $150,000, and $200,000, respectively. To round out the scenario, the management accountant estimates fixed costs at $200,000, $300,000, and $400,000, respectively, for the three alternative expansion plans. The contribution margin (CM) ratio can range from .40 to .60 for each alternative.

Management wants to know the dollar sales level that the enterprise must generate to earn the target profits. The program accesses the fixed costs, target profit, and CM ratio at each level, inputs them in the profit equation, and computes the 27 sales revenues shown on the CVP analysis screen in Exhibit 18–14.

Managers can input new values for target profits, fixed costs, and CM ratios to see the effect of changing these variables and to gain a clearer perspective

---

[12] This screen is not displayed here, but the target sales can be manually verified.

■■EXHIBIT 18–14
CVP Analysis Screen (in Thousands)

Sales required to generate target profits of:

Fixed costs	CM ratio	100	150	200
200	.40	750	875	1000
	.50	600	700	800
	.60	500	583	667
300	.40	1000	1125	1250
	.50	800	900	1000
	.60	667	750	833
400	.40	1250	1375	1500
	.50	1000	1100	1200
	.60	833	917	1000

by viewing a wide range of cost, volume, and profit patterns. The objective of such analyses is to enhance management's decision-making acumen. The use of spreadsheet programs and financial planning software can contribute to improving profit management, resulting in a high-quality profit management accounting system.

SUMMARY OF LEARNING OBJECTIVES

The major goals of this chapter were to enable you to achieve four learning objectives:

Learning objective 1.   Build a profit equation for an enterprise or product line.

The profit equation provides a means of expressing the relationships among variable and fixed costs, sales volume, and their effects on profit. Within a specified relevant range, a linear equation is usually created. It is assumed that sales price and variable costs are constant per unit, fixed costs are constant in total, beginning and ending inventory levels do not change, and sales mix is constant when dealing with multiple products.

The profit equation, especially in its factored form, allows the management accountant to quickly and accurately calculate the profit for any level of sales volume within the relevant range. It also promotes incremental analysis by measuring the change in any variable within the equation, given target values for the other variables. The profit equation and its most useful factored forms are summarized in Exhibit 18–15.

■■EXHIBIT 18–15
The Profit Equation

$$(\text{CMU} \times \text{Volume}) - \text{Fixed costs} = \text{Profit}$$

Solved for:

	Target Sales Volume	Target Sales Revenues
Profit goal is a fixed amount:		
Pretax profit goal:	$\dfrac{(\text{Fixed costs} + \text{Profit})}{\text{CMU}}$	$\dfrac{(\text{Fixed costs} + \text{Profit})}{\text{CM ratio}}$
Aftertax profit goal:	$\dfrac{\text{Fixed costs} + \dfrac{\text{Aftertax profit}}{(1 - \text{Tax rate})}}{\text{CMU}}$	$\dfrac{\text{Fixed costs} + \dfrac{\text{Aftertax profit}}{(1 - \text{Tax rate})}}{\text{CM ratio}}$
Zero-profit goal (break-even):	$\dfrac{\text{Fixed costs}}{\text{CMU}}$	$\dfrac{\text{Fixed costs}}{\text{CM ratio}}$
Profit goal is a variable amount:		
Pretax profit goal:	$\dfrac{\text{Fixed costs}}{\text{CMU} - \text{Profit per unit}}$	$\dfrac{\text{Fixed costs}}{\text{CM ratio} - \text{Profit percentage}}$
Aftertax profit goal:	$\dfrac{\text{Fixed costs}}{\text{CMU} - \dfrac{\text{Profit per unit}}{(1 - \text{Tax rate})}}$	$\dfrac{\text{Fixed costs}}{\text{CM ratio} - \dfrac{\text{Profit percentage}}{(1 - \text{Tax rate})}}$

Incremental analyses:

$$\Delta\text{Target sales volume} = \Delta(\text{Fixed costs} + \text{Profit}) \div \text{CMU}$$
$$\Delta\text{Target sales revenues} = \Delta(\text{Fixed costs} + \text{Profit}) \div \text{CM ratio}$$

(See also Exhibit 18–3 for CVP rules.)

Learning objective 2. Use cost-volume-profit (CVP) analysis to analyze different profit-making alternatives.

The break-even point (BEP) is a critical measurement in CVP analysis. It is at this point that total costs equal total sales and the profit is zero. CVP and break-even analysis can be performed by using the equation approach or the contribution margin approach. Regardless of the method used, the results will be the same.

The equation approach is based on the profit equation:

$$(\text{CMU} \times \text{Volume}) - \text{Fixed costs} = \text{Profit}$$

The contribution margin approach is based on the contribution margin, which is sales revenues less variable costs. The contribution margin is most useful when stated as contribution margin per unit (CMU) or as a contribution margin (CM) ratio. The contribution margin approach uses the profit equation in one of its factored forms (see Exhibit 18–15).

The following data apply to Pizza King:

■ Unit sales price: $10
■ Unit variable cost: $6
■ Fixed costs: $2,000

To calculate the BEP:

$$\text{BEP} = \frac{\text{Fixed costs}}{\text{CMU}} = \frac{\$2,000}{\$4} = \underline{\underline{500 \text{ pizzas}}}$$

A contribution margin–based income statement proves this computation:

Sales ($10 × 500)	$5,000
<Variable costs ($6 × 500)>	<3,000>
Contribution margin	$2,000
<Fixed costs>	<2,000>
Profit	$ –0–

CMU is the amount that each pizza contributes to covering fixed costs and to profit. If CMU is $4 per unit, each pizza sold will provide $4 to cover fixed costs and contribute to profit. If Pizza King sells 600 pizzas, the first 500 will cover the $2,000 in fixed costs ($4 × 500 pizzas), and the last 100 pizzas will contribute $400 to profit ($4 × 100 pizzas).

The CM ratio is computed as follows:

$$\text{CM ratio} = \frac{\text{CMU}}{\text{Sales price}} = \frac{\$4}{\$10} = \underline{\underline{40\%}}$$

Using the CM ratio, the break-even revenue (BER) is computed as follows:

$$\text{BER} = \frac{\$2,000}{.40}$$
$$= \underline{\underline{\$5,000}}$$

If the target profit for Pizza King is $800, then the sales revenue necessary to achieve this target profit is computed as follows:

$$\text{Revenue goal} = \frac{\$2,000 + \$800}{.40}$$
$$= \underline{\underline{\$7,000}}$$

The sales volume necessary to meet the target profit of $800 is 700 pizzas ($7,000 ÷ $10 sales price per pizza). This can also be computed as follows:

$$\text{Sales quota} = \frac{\$2,000 + \$800}{\$4}$$
$$= 700 \text{ pizzas}$$

Working incrementally, the additional sales volume and revenues needed to generate an additional $800 in profit can be calculated as:

$$\Delta\text{Target sales volume} = \Delta(\text{Fixed costs} + \text{Profit}) \div \text{CMU}$$
$$= +\$800 \div \$4 \text{ per pizza}$$
$$= +200 \text{ pizzas (above BEP)}$$

$$\Delta\text{Target sales revenues} = \Delta(\text{Fixed costs} + \text{Profit}) \div \text{CM ratio}$$
$$= +\$800 \div 40\%$$
$$= +\$2,000 \text{ (above BER)}$$

The margin of safety is the excess of budgeted sales over break-even sales. As a percentage, the margin of safety is computed as follows:

$$\text{Margin of safety (\%)} = \frac{\text{Budgeted sales} - \text{Break-even sales}}{\text{Budgeted sales}}$$
$$= \frac{700 \text{ pizzas} - 500 \text{ pizzas}}{700 \text{ pizzas}}$$
$$= 28\% \text{ (rounded down)}$$

Managers use the margin of safety to evaluate budgeted operations for the forthcoming period or to determine the degree of risk in launching a new business venture. A high margin of safety serves as a cushion and means low risk. A low margin of safety means high risk.

Learning objective 3.   Apply CVP formulas to situations involving sales mixes and income taxes.

Sales mix, also termed product mix, is the relative distribution of sales among multiple products. Assume that Sierra Sid sells two products, A and B.

	PRODUCT A	PRODUCT B
Sales price	$20	$15
Variable costs	<10>	<6>
Contribution margin	$10	$ 9

The sales mix is 25 percent product A and 75 percent product B. Product C, which is the overall product, is composed of products A and B. Total fixed costs are $7,400. How many units of each must Sierra Sid sell to break even? The following calculations are used to answer this question:

$$\text{Weighted-average sales price} = (\$20.00 \times .25) + (\$15.00 \times .75)$$
$$= \$16.25 \text{ per product C}$$

$$\text{Weighted-average variable costs} = (\$10.00 \times .25) + (\$6.00 \times .75)$$
$$= \$7.00 \text{ per product C}$$

$$\text{Product C BEP} = \frac{\text{Fixed costs}}{\text{CMU}}$$
$$= \frac{\$7,400}{\$16.25 - \$7.00}$$
$$= 800 \text{ units of product C}$$

$$\text{Product A BEP} = 800 \text{ units} \times .25$$
$$= 200 \text{ units of product A}$$

$$\text{Product B BEP} = 800 \text{ units} \times .75$$
$$= \underline{\underline{600 \text{ units of product B}}}$$

Proof of the preceding calculations is illustrated in the following contribution margin income statement:

SIERRA SID
CONTRIBUTION MARGIN INCOME STATEMENT
FOR YEAR ENDED DECEMBER 31, 1995

	PRODUCT A	PRODUCT B	TOTALS
Sales:			
200 units × $20	$4,000		$ 4,000
600 units × $15		$9,000	9,000
Total sales	$4,000	$9,000	$13,000
Less variable costs:			
200 units × $10	$2,000		$ 2,000
600 units × $6		$3,600	3,600
Total variable costs	<$2,000>	<$3,600>	<$ 5,600>
Contribution margin	$2,000	$5,400	$ 7,400
Less fixed costs			< 7,400>
Profit			$ –0–

Assume Sierra Sid sets an after-tax profit goal of $15,000 and anticipates an income tax rate of 20 percent. How many total products (Product C) will have to be sold to obtain this target profit?

$$\text{Sales quota} = \frac{\text{Fixed costs} + \dfrac{\text{Aftertax profit}}{(1 - \text{Tax rate})}}{\text{CMU}}$$
$$= \frac{\$7,400 + [\$15,000 \div (1 - 20\%)]}{\$9.25}$$
$$= \underline{\underline{2,828 \text{ total products (rounded up)}}}$$

Learning objective 4.   Describe how computer programs can assist in CVP analysis.

Electronic spreadsheets and various financial planning software packages provide an efficient way for management accountants and managers to work directly with the computer, taking advantage of its computational speed and its ability to store massive amounts of data. These software packages provide a simple, natural way of communicating with the computer. Moreover, most of these packages are interactive; they permit the user to sit at the workstation or PC and receive instant feedback. Thus, the user can easily create new CVP models, ask what-if questions, and obtain answers quickly and at a low cost. The results are less drudgery for management accountants and increased quality of decision making in profit management.

IMPORTANT TERMS

Break-even point (BEP)   The sales volume at which revenues equal total costs, and there is zero profit.
Contribution margin   Sales revenues minus variable costs. It is the amount that contributes toward covering fixed costs and then toward profits.
Contribution margin approach   A method of CVP analysis that focuses on the contribution margin, using the profit equation in one of its factored forms.
Contribution margin–based income statement   An income statement format in which total variable costs are subtracted from sales revenues, creating the contribution margin subtotal, from which fixed costs are then subtracted to yield net income. It

differs from a traditional financial accounting format in that costs are organized by behavior rather than by function.

Contribution margin per unit (CMU)   Sales price minus variable costs per unit. It is the incremental money available from selling one more product that is used to cover fixed costs and contribute to profits.

Contribution margin ratio (CM ratio)   The contribution margin per unit expressed as a percentage of the selling price.

Cost-volume-profit (CVP) analysis   The determination and study of the relationships among cost, volume or level of activity, and profit. CVP analysis involves the creation and use of the profit equation.

Equation approach   A CVP analysis method that uses the profit equation in its unfactored format: (CMU × Volume) − Fixed costs = Profit.

Margin of safety   The sales volume in excess of the break-even point. It is usually expressed as a percentage of the sales forecast and is used as a measure of break-even riskiness.

Profit equation   Usually, a linear equation used to summarize CVP relationships. It is: (CMU × Volume) − Fixed costs = Profit.

Sales mix   The relative combination in which an organization's products are sold. Sales mix is calculated by expressing the sales of each product as a percentage of total sales.

Sensitivity analysis   A type of profit management analysis, usually using software programs, that measures the riskiness of the amounts used in the profit equation. It shows how profit and volume change as other amounts change by certain percentages or absolute amounts.

Variable cost ratio   The percentage relationship between variable costs and sales revenues.

DEMONSTRATION PROBLEMS

■ DEMONSTRATION PROBLEM 1   *Break-even calculations.*

Quickround manufactures golf carts. The following data pertain to this product:

Unit sales price	$800
Unit variable costs	$300
Total fixed costs	$100,000

Required:
a. Compute the BEP and BER using the equation approach.
b. Compute the BEP and BER using the contribution margin approach.
c. The expected (or budgeted) sales for the next period are 300 golf carts. Compute the margin of safety.

SOLUTION TO DEMONSTRATION PROBLEM 1

a.
$$(\text{CMU} \times \text{Volume}) - \text{Fixed costs} = \text{Profit}$$
$$(\$500 \text{ per cart} \times \text{Volume}) - \$100,000 = \$0$$
$$\text{BEP} = \underline{\underline{200 \text{ golf carts}}}$$

BER can be calculated by multiplying BEP by the sales price:

$$\text{BER} = 200 \text{ golf carts} \times \$800 \text{ per cart}$$
$$= \underline{\underline{\$160,000}}$$

b. The contribution margin approach simply uses the profit equation in one of its factored forms. To calculate how many units must be sold to break even, total fixed cost is divided by CMU:

$$\text{BEP} = \frac{\text{Fixed costs}}{\text{CMU}}$$

$$= \frac{\$100,000}{\$800 - \$300}$$

$$= \frac{\$100,000}{\$500}$$

$$= \underline{200 \text{ golf carts}}$$

$$\text{BER} = \frac{\text{Fixed costs}}{\text{CM ratio}}$$

$$= \frac{\$100,000}{(\$800 - \$300) \div \$800}$$

$$= \frac{\$100,000}{0.625}$$

$$= \underline{\$160,000}$$

c.

$$\text{Margin of safety} = \frac{\text{Sales forecast} - \text{BEP}}{\text{Sales forecast}}$$

$$= (300 \text{ carts} - 200 \text{ carts}) \div 300 \text{ carts}$$

$$= \underline{33.33\%}$$

■ **DEMONSTRATION PROBLEM 2** *Sales mix.*

Landscape Products is a two-product company making square-pointed shovels and yard rakes. The following budget is developed for the next period:

	SHOVEL	RAKE	TOTALS
Sales in units	18,200	7,800	26,000
Sales revenues @ $20 and $14	$364,000	$109,200	$473,200
<Variable costs> @ $12 and $9	<218,400>	<70,200>	<288,600>
Contribution margin @ $8 and $5	$145,600	$ 39,000	$184,600
Fixed costs			<106,500>
Net income			$ 78,100

Note: Total sales in units are made up of 70% shovels and 30% rakes.

Required:
Compute the BEP for both products.

SOLUTION TO DEMONSTRATION PROBLEM 2

The weighted-average CMU is computed as follows:

Weighted-average sales price = ($20 × .70) + ($14 × .30) = $18.20
Weighted-average variable costs = ($12 × .70) + ($9 × .30) = $11.10
Weighted-average CMU = $18.20 − $11.10 　　　 = $ 7.10

$$\text{BEP} = \frac{\text{Fixed costs of } \$106,500}{\$7.10}$$

$$= \underline{15,000 \text{ units}}$$

BEP (shovels) = 15,000 units × .70
= 10,500 shovels

BEP (rakes) = 15,000 units × .30
= 4,500 rakes

Assuming that the sales mix will not change, Landscape must sell 10,500 shovels and 4,500 rakes next period to break even.

■ **DEMONSTRATION PROBLEM 3**   *Break-even calculation considering income taxes.*

Gladstone Company's projected data are as follows:

Sales ($100 × 2,000 units)		$200,000
Variable costs ($60 × 2,000 units)	$120,000	
Fixed costs	60,000	<180,000>
Net income before taxes		$ 20,000
Income taxes (40%)		<8,000>
Net income after taxes		$ 12,000

Required:
How many units will Gladstone have to sell to earn $30,000 in net income after taxes?

SOLUTION TO DEMONSTRATION PROBLEM 3

$$\text{Unit sales} = \frac{\text{Fixed costs} + [\text{Target profit} \div (1 - \text{Tax rate})]}{\text{CMU}}$$

$$= \frac{\$60,000 + [\$30,000 \div (1 - .40)]}{\$40}$$

$$= 2,750 \text{ units}$$

Sales ($100 × 2,750 units)		$275,000
Variable costs ($60 × 2,750 units)	$165,000	
Fixed costs	60,000	<225,000>
Net income before taxes		$ 50,000
Income taxes (40%)		<20,000>
Net income after taxes		$ 30,000

REVIEW QUESTIONS

18.1   List and briefly define the elements involved in cost-volume-profit (CVP) analysis.

18.2   What are the two goals (purposes) of a profit equation?

18.3   Why is the master budgeting process iterative?

18.4   What is the role of CVP analysis in the master budgeting process?

18.5   How can CVP analysis help profit center managers in their operational control role?

18.6   What are the three basic CVP assumptions?

18.7   Which assumptions also apply to cost equations?

18.8   What is the relationship between a cost equation and a profit equation?

18.9   How are sales revenues and sales prices related?

18.10   What is the independent variable in the profit equation? Why is it the same as in the manufacturing cost equation?

18.11   Define contribution margin and contribution margin per unit. How are they related?

18.12   Write out the profit equation used in the equation approach to CVP analysis.

18.13   Define the break-even point.

18.14   Describe and distinguish between the equation approach and the contribution margin approach.

18.15   How can the profit equation be written as a function of revenues?

18.16   What is the format for the contribution margin–based income statement? How does it differ from the traditional format used in financial reporting?

18.17   Why are fixed costs and profit included only in the totals column and not expressed on a per-unit basis?

18.18   What is the purpose of expressing contribution margin on a per-unit and a percentage basis?

18.19 Compare and contrast the variable cost ratio and the contribution margin ratio.

18.20 How is the CM ratio useful in multiple product CVP analysis?

18.21 Intepret how CMU and fixed costs are related in break-even analysis.

18.22 What is a CVP chart?

18.23 How is incremental CVP analysis useful in profit management decisions?

18.24 Using the data in Exhibit 18–1, make up simple numeric examples to illustrate each of the CVP rules for incremental analysis.

18.25 Describe "what-if" analysis.

18.26 Why can a profit goal, stated as an absolute dollar amount, be considered as just another fixed cost of the business?

18.27 How does the profit equation change if the profit goal is stated as a variable amount?

18.28 Define, illustrate, and interpret the margin of safety.

18.29 Define sales mix.

18.30 How is aftertax profit related to pretax profit, and how is the profit equation modified to account for an aftertax target profit?

18.31 Define sensitivity analysis.

18.32 What is goal-seek analysis?

18.33 Explain how financial planning software can be useful in CVP analysis.

CHAPTER-SPECIFIC PROBLEMS

These problems require responses based directly on concepts and techniques presented in the text.

18.34 **Break-even analysis.** The estimates made for Glaxot Company, a one-product company, are as follows:

GLAXOT COMPANY
PROJECTED ABSORPTION COSTING INCOME STATEMENT
FOR THE YEAR ENDED DECEMBER 31, 1995

Sales revenue ($100 per unit × 100 units)			$10,000
Manufacturing cost of goods sold:			
Direct materials	$1,400		
Direct labor	1,500		
Variable overhead	1,000		
Fixed overhead	500		<4,400>
Gross margin			$ 5,600
Selling expenses:			
Variable	$ 600		
Fixed	1,000	$1,600	
Administrative expenses:			
Variable	500		
Fixed	1,000	1,500	
Total selling and administrative expenses			<3,100>
Net income before income taxes			$ 2,500

Required:
a. How many units of the product must Glaxot sell to break even?
b. What would be the net income before income taxes if projected unit sales increased by 25%?
c. What would dollar sales be at the BEP if fixed overhead increased by $1,700?
[AICPA adapted]

18.35 **Multiple choice, income taxes.** The following statement of income for Davann Company represents the operating results for the fiscal year just ended. Davann had sales of 1,800 tons during the current year. The manufacturing capacity of Davann's facilities is 3,000 tons.

DAVANN COMPANY
VARIABLE COSTING INCOME STATEMENT
FOR THE YEAR ENDED DECEMBER 31, 1995

Sales		$900,000
Variable costs:		
Manufacturing	$315,000	
Selling costs	180,000	
Total variable costs		<$495,000>
Contribution margin		$405,000
Fixed costs:		
Manufacturing	$ 90,000	
Selling	112,500	
Administration	45,000	
Total fixed costs		<$247,500>
Income before income taxes		$157,500
Income taxes (40%)		<63,000>
Net income after income taxes		$ 94,500

Required:
Choose the best answer. Each item is independent of every other item.

a. The break-even volume in tons for 1995 is (1) 420 tons, (2) 1,100 tons, (3) 495 tons, (4) 550 tons, (5) some other amount.

b. If the sales volume is estimated to be 2,100 tons in the next year, and if prices and costs stay at the same levels and amounts next year, Davann can expect aftertax net income of (1) $135,000, (2) $110,250, (3) $283,500, (4) $184,500, (5) some other amount.

c. Davann plans to market its product in a new territory. Davann estimates that an advertising and promotion program costing $61,500 annually would need to be undertaken for the next two or three years. In addition, a $25 per ton sales commission over and above the current commission would be required for the sales force in the new territory. How many tons would have to be sold in the new territory to maintain Davann's current aftertax income of $94,500? (1) 307.5 tons, (2) 1,095.0 tons, (3) 273.333 tons, (4) 1,545.0 tons, (5) some other amount.

d. Davann is considering replacing a highly labor-intensive process with an automatic machine. This would result in an increase of $58,500 annually in manufacturing fixed costs. The variable manufacturing costs would decrease $25 per ton. The new break-even volume in tons would be (1) 990 tons, (2) 1,224 tons, (3) 1,854 tons, (4) 612 tons, (5) some other amount.

e. Ignore the facts presented in Requirement (d) and now assume that Davann estimates that the per-ton selling price would decline 10% next year. Variable costs would increase $40 per ton, and the fixed costs would not change. What sales volume in dollars would be required to earn an aftertax net income of $94,500 next year? (1) $1,140,000, (2) $825,000, (3) $1,500,000, (4) $1,350,000, (5) some other amount.

[CMA adapted]

18.36 CVP analysis. The Stillson Company makes a single product. It sold 40,000 units last year with the following results:

Sales		$700,000
Variable costs	$400,000	
Fixed costs	150,000	<550,000>
Net income before taxes		$150,000
Income taxes (40%)		<60,000>
Net income after income taxes		$ 90,000

Stillson plans to improve its product by replacing a component that has a cost of $3 per unit with a new and better component costing $5 per unit in the coming year. A new machine will also be needed to increase plant capacity. The machine will cost $20,000 with a useful life of 5 years and no salvage value. The company uses straight-line depreciation on all plant assets.

Required:
a. What was Stillson's BEP in unit sales last year?
b. How many units would Stillson have had to sell in the last year to earn $180,000 in net income after income taxes?
c. If Stillson holds the sales price constant and makes the component change, how many units must be sold in the coming year to break even?
d. If Stillson holds the sales price constant and makes the suggested changes, how many units will the company have to sell to make the same net income as it made after income taxes last year?
e. If Stillson wishes to maintain the same CM ratio, what selling price per unit must it charge next year to cover the increased component costs?

18.37 *CVP analysis.* Printrite is a retailer for print modules. The projected aftertax net income for the current year is $600,000 based on a sales volume of 400,000 print modules. Printrite has been selling the print modules at $32 each. The variable costs consist of the $20 per unit purchase price charged by the vendor and a handling cost of $4 per module. Printrite's annual fixed costs are $2,200,000. Printrite's income tax rate is 40%. Management expects that the unit purchase price of the print modules will increase 30%.

Required:
a. What is Printrite's BEP for the current year in unit sales?
b. What would be the aftertax income for the current year with an increase of 10% in sales volume?
c. What will the dollar sales have to be in the coming year to maintain the same aftertax net income as projected for the current year if unit selling price remains at $32?
d. In order to cover a 30% increase in the print module's purchase price for the coming year and still maintain the current CM ratio, what must the selling price be for the coming year?

18.38 *Break-even analysis for a two-product company.* Tranco manufactures two products, Gizmo and Widget. The following are projections for the coming year:

| | GIZMOS | | WIDGETS | | |
	UNITS	AMOUNT	UNITS	AMOUNT	TOTALS
Sales	10,000	$10,000	7,500	$10,000	$20,000
Costs:					
Variable		6,000		3,000	9,000
Fixed		2,000		5,600	7,600
		<$ 8,000>		<$ 8,600>	<$16,600>
Net income before taxes		$ 2,000		$ 1,400	$ 3,400

Required:
a. What is the BEP for Gizmos, assuming the facilities are not used jointly?
b. What is the BER for Widgets, assuming the facilities are not used jointly?
c. What is the composite CMU, assuming that consumers purchase composite units of four Gizmos and three Widgets?
d. If consumers purchase composite units of four Gizmos and three Widgets, what is the BEP?
e. If a composite unit is defined as one Gizmo and one Widget, what is the composite CM ratio?
f. If Gizmos and Widgets become one-to-one complements and there is no change in Tranco's cost function, what is the BER?

18.39 *Margin of safety in dollar sales.* The Stackrite Company makes printer attachments. The company budgets a margin of safety of 20% for 19X4. Fixed costs are budgeted at $240,000 annually. Variable costs are $6 per attachment. The sales price per attachment is $12.

Required:
Compute the margin of safety in dollar sales.

THINK-TANK PROBLEMS

Although these problems are based on chapter material, reading extra material, reviewing previous chapters, and using creativity may be required to develop workable solutions.

18.40 *Break-even analysis.* All-Day Candy Company is a wholesale distributor of candy. The company services grocery, convenience, and drug stores in a large metropolitan area. All-Day has achieved small but steady growth in sales over the past few years while candy prices have been increasing. The company is formulating its plans for the coming fiscal year. Following are the data used to project the current year's aftertax net income of $110,400.

Average selling price	$4.00 per box
Average variable costs:	
Cost of candy	$2.00 per box
Selling expenses	0.40 per box
Total	$2.40 per box
Annual fixed costs:	
Selling	$ 160,000
Administrative	280,000
Total	$ 440,000
Expected annual sales volume (390,000 boxes)	$1,560,000
Tax rate	40%

Manufacturers of candy have announced that they will increase prices of their products an average of 15% in the coming year due to increases in raw materials (sugar, cocoa, peanuts, and so on) and labor costs. All-Day Candy Company expects that all other costs will remain at the same rates or levels as the current year.

Required:
a. What is All-Day Candy Company's BEP in boxes of candy for the current year?
b. What selling price per box must All-Day Candy Company charge to cover the 15% increase in the cost of candy and still maintain the current CM ratio?
c. What volume of sales in dollars must the All-Day Candy Company achieve in the coming year to maintain the same net income after taxes as projected for the current year if the selling price of candy remains at $4 per box and the cost of candy increases 15%?

[AICPA adapted]

18.41 *Change in sales mix and income taxes.* Hewtex Electronics manufactures two products—tape recorders and electronic calculators—and sells them nationally to wholesalers and retailers. The Hewtex management is very pleased with the company's performance for the current fiscal year. Projected sales through December 31,19X7, indicate that 70,000 tape recorders and 140,000 electronic calculators will be sold this year. The projected earnings statement follows:

HEWTEX ELECTRONICS
PROJECTED EARNINGS STATEMENT
FOR THE YEAR ENDED DECEMBER 31, 19X7

| | TAPE RECORDERS | | ELECTRONIC CALCULATORS | | |
	TOTAL AMOUNT (000 OMITTED)	PER UNIT	TOTAL AMOUNT (000 OMITTED)	PER UNIT	TOTAL (000 OMITTED)
Sales	$1,050	$15.00	$3,150	$22.50	$4,200.00
Production costs:					
Direct materials	280	4.00	630	4.50	910.00
Direct labor	140	2.00	420	3.00	560.00
Variable overhead	140	2.00	280	2.00	420.00
Fixed overhead	70	1.00	210	1.50	280.00
Total production costs	<630>	<9.00>	<1,540>	<11.00>	<2,170.00>
Gross margin	$ 420	$ 6.00	$1,610	$11.50	$2,030.00
Fixed selling and administrative					<1,040.00>
Net income before income taxes					$ 990.00
Income taxes (55%)					<544.50>
Net income					$ 445.50

It shows that Hewtex will exceed its earnings goal of 9% on sales after income taxes.

The tape recorder business has been fairly stable the last few years, and the company does not intend to change the tape recorder price. Competition among manufacturers of electronic calculators has been increasing, however. Hewtex's calculators have been very popular with consumers. In order to sustain this interest in their calculators and to meet the price reductions expected from competitors, management has decided to reduce the wholesale price of its calculator from $22.50 to $20.00 per unit effective January 1, 19X8. At the same time, the company plans to spend an additional $57,000 on advertising during fiscal year 19X8. As a consequence of these actions, management estimates that 80% of its total revenue will be derived from calculator sales compared to 75% in 19X7. As in prior years, the sales mix is assumed to be the same at all volume levels.

The total fixed overhead costs will not change in 19X8, nor will the variable overhead cost rates (applied on a direct labor hour base). However, the cost of materials and direct labor is expected to change. The cost of solid-state electronic components will be cheaper in 19X8. Hewtex estimates that material costs will drop 10% for the tape recorders and 20% for the calculators in 19X8. Direct labor costs for both products will increase 10% in the coming year, however.

Required:
a. How many tape recorder and electronic calculator units did Hewtex Electronics have to sell in 19X7 to break even?
b. What volume of sales is required if Hewtex Electronics is to earn a profit in 19X8 equal to 9% on sales after income taxes?
c. How many tape recorder and electronic calculator units will Hewtex have to sell in 19X8 to break even?

[CMA adapted]

18.42 *CVP relationships and income taxes.* R. A. Ro and Company, maker of quality handmade pipes, has experienced a steady growth in sales for the past five years. However, increased competition has led Mr. Ro, the president, to believe that an aggressive advertising campaign will be necessary next year to maintain the company's present growth.

To prepare for next year's advertising campaign, the company's accountant has prepared and presented Mr. Ro with the following data for the current year, 19X7:

COST SCHEDULE

Variable costs:	
Direct materials	$ 3.25/pipe
Direct labor	8.00/pipe
Variable overhead	2.50/pipe
Total variable costs	$13.75/pipe
Fixed costs:	
Manufacturing	$ 25,000
Selling	40,000
Administrative	70,000
Total fixed costs	$135,000
Selling price, per pipe	$25
Expected sales, 19X7 (20,000 units)	$500,000
Tax rate	40%

Mr. Ro has set the sales target for 19X8 at a level of $550,000 (or 22,000 pipes).

Required:
a. What is the projected aftertax net income for 19X7?
b. What is the BEP in units for 19X7?
c. Mr. Ro believes an additional selling expense of $11,250 for advertising in 19X8, with all other costs remaining constant, will be necessary to attain the sales target. What will be the aftertax net income for 19X8 if the additional $11,250 is spent?
d. What will be the BEP in dollar sales for 19X8 if the additional $11,250 is spent for advertising?
e. If the additional $11,250 is spent for advertising in 19X8, what is the required sales level in dollar sales to equal 19X7's aftertax net income?
f. At a sales level of 22,000 units, what is the maximum amount that can be spent on advertising if an aftertax net income of $60,000 is desired?

[CMA adapted]

18.43 *Break-even analysis with step fixed costs.* Sierra Hospital operates a general hospital that rents space and beds to separate departments such as pediatrics, maternity, and surgery. Sierra Hospital charges each separate department for common services to its patients, such as meals and laundry, and for administrative services, such as billing and collections. Space and bed rentals are fixed for the year.

For the year ended June 30, 19X7, the Pediatrics Department at Sierra Hospital charged its patients an average of $65 per day, had a capacity of 60 beds, operated 24 hours per day for 365 days, and had total revenue of $1,138,800.

Expenses charged by the hospital to the Pediatrics Department for the year were as follows:

BASIS FOR ALLOCATION

	PATIENT-DAYS	BED CAPACITY
Dietary	$ 42,952	
Janitorial		$ 12,800
Laundry	28,000	
Laboratory	47,800	
Pharmacy	33,800	
Repairs and maintenance	5,200	7,140
General administrative services		131,760
Rent		275,320
Billings and collections	87,000	
Other	18,048	25,980
	$262,800	$453,000

The only personnel directly employed by the Pediatrics Department are supervising nurses, nurses, and aides. The hospital has minimum personnel requirements based on total annual patient-days. Hospital requirements, beginning at the minimum expected level of operation, follow:

ANNUAL PATIENT-DAYS	AIDES	NURSES	SUPERVISING NURSES
10,000–14,000	21	11	4
14,001–17,000	22	12	4
17,001–23,725	22	13	4
23,726–25,550	25	14	5
25,551–27,375	26	14	5
27,376–29,200	29	16	6

These staffing levels represent full-time equivalents, and it should be assumed that the Pediatrics Department always employs only the minimum number of required full-time equivalent personnel.

Annual salaries for each class of employee are as follows: supervising nurses, $18,000; nurses, $13,000; and aides, $5,000. Salary expense for the year ended June 30, 19X7, was $72,000, $169,000, and $110,000 for supervising nurses, nurses, and aides, respectively.

Required:
a. Compute the following:
   1. The number of patient-days in the Pediatrics Department for the year ended June 30, 19X7. (Each day a patient is in the hospital is known as a "patient-day.")
   2. The variable cost per patient-day for the year ended June 30, 19X7.
   3. The total fixed costs, including both allocated fixed costs and personnel costs, in the Pediatrics Department for each level of operations shown above (i.e., total fixed costs at the 10,000–14,000 patient-day level of operation, total fixed costs at the 14,001–17,000 patient-day level of operation, and so forth).
b. Using the data computed in Requirement (a) and using any other data as needed, compute the *minimum* number of patient-days required for the Pediatrics Department to break even. You may assume that variable and fixed cost behavior and revenue per patient-day will remain unchanged in the future.
c. Determine the minimum number of patient-days required for the Pediatrics Department to earn an annual profit of $80,000.

[AICPA adapted]

18.44 *Break-even analysis and target profits.* Starling Company is a small but growing manufacturer of telecommunications equipment. The company has no sales force of its own; instead, it relies completely on independent sales agents to market its products. These agents are paid a commission of 15% of selling price for all items sold.

Li Kim, Starling's controller, has just prepared the company's budgeted income statement for next year. The statement follows:

STARLING COMPANY
BUDGETED INCOME STATEMENT
FOR THE YEAR ENDED DECEMBER 31,19X6

Sales		$16,000,000
Manufacturing costs:		
Variable	$7,200,000	
Fixed overhead	2,340,000	<9,540,000>
Gross margin		6,460,000
Selling and administrative costs:		
Commissions to agents	2,400,000	
Fixed marketing costs	120,000*	
Fixed administrative costs	1,800,000	<4,320,000>
Net operating income		2,140,000

Continued

—Continued

Less fixed interest cost	<540,000>
Income before income taxes	1,600,000
Less income taxes (30%)	<480,000>
Net income	$ 1,120,000

* Primarily depreciation on storage facilities.

As Li handed the statement to Tom Remski, Starling's president, she commented, "I went ahead and used the agents' 15% commission rate in completing these statements, but we've just learned that they refuse to handle our products next year unless we increase the commission rate to 20%."

"That's the last straw," replied Tom angrily, "Those agents have been demanding more and more, and this time they've gone too far. How can they possibly defend a 20% commission rate?"

"They claim that after paying for advertising, travel, and the other costs of promotion, there's nothing left over for profit," replied Li.

"I say it's just plain robbery," retorted Tom. "And I also say it's time we dumped those people and got our own sales force. Can you get your people to work up some cost figures for us to look at?"

"We've already worked them up," said Li. "Several companies we know about pay a 7.5% commission to their own salespeople, along with a small salary. Of course, we would have to handle all promotion costs, too. We figure our fixed costs would increase by $2,400,000 per year, but that would be more than offset by the $3,200,000 (20% × $16,000,000) that we would avoid on agents' commissions."

The breakdown of the $2,400,000 cost figure follows:

Salaries:	
Sales manager	$ 100,000
Salespersons	600,000
Travel and entertainment	400,000
Advertising	1,300,000
Total	$2,400,000

"Super," replied Tom. "And I note that the $2,400,000 is just what we're paying the agents under the old 15% commission rate."

"It's even better than that," explained Li. "We can actually save $75,000 a year, because that's what we're having to pay the auditing firm now to check out the agents' reports. So our overall administrative costs would be less."

"Pull all of these numbers together and we'll show them to the executive committee tomorrow," said Tom. "With the approval of the committee, we can move on the matter immediately."

Required:

a. Compute Starling Company's BEP in sales dollars for 19X6, assuming:
   1. That the agents' commission rate remains unchanged at 15%.
   2. That the agents' commission rate is increased to 20%.
   3. That the company employs its own sales force.
b. Assume that Starling Company decides to continue selling through agents and pays the 20% commission rate. Determine the volume of sales that would be required to generate the same net income as in the budgeted income statement for 19X6.
c. Determine the volume of sales at which net income would be equal regardless of whether Starling Company sells through agents (at a 20% commission rate) or employs its own sales force.
d. Based on the data in Requirements (a) through (c), make a recommendation as to whether the company should continue to use sales agents (at a 20% commission rate) or employ its own sales force. Give reasons for your answer.

[CMA adapted]

18.45 *Break-even analysis and target profits.* RayLok, Inc., has invented a secret process to measure light intensity and manufactures a variety of products related to this process. Each product is independent of the others and is treated as a separate profit-loss division. Product (division) managers have a great deal of freedom to manage their divisions as they think best. Failure to produce target division profit is dealt with severely, but rewards for exceeding one's profit objective are lavish.

The DimLok Division sells an add-on automotive accessory that automatically dims a vehicle's headlights by sensing a certain intensity of light coming from a specific direction. DimLok has had a new manager in each of the three previous years because the predecessor manager failed to reach RayLok's target profit. Don Barnes has just been promoted to manager and is studying ways to meet the current target profit for DimLok.

The two profit targets for DimLok for the coming year are $800,000 plus an additional profit of $20 for each DimLok unit sold. Other constraints on division operations follow:

■ Production cannot exceed sales since RayLok's corporate advertising program stresses completely new product models each year, even though the "newness" of the models may be only cosmetic.
■ The DimLok selling price may not vary above the current selling price of $200 per unit but may vary as much as 10% below $200.
■ A division manager may elect to expand fixed production or selling facilities; however, the target objective that is related to fixed costs is increased by 20% of the cost of such expansion. Furthermore, a manager may not expand fixed facilities by more than 30% of existing fixed cost levels without approval from the board of directors.

Barnes is now examining data gathered by his staff to determine if DimLok can achieve its target profits of $800,000 *and* $20 per unit. A summary of these reports shows the following:

■ Last year's sales were 40,000 units at $200 per unit.
■ The present capacity of DimLok's manufacturing facility is 40,000 units per year, but capacity can be increased to 80,000 units per year by an increase in annual fixed costs of $1,000,000.
■ Present variable costs amount to $80 per unit, but if commitments are made for more than 60,000 units, DimLok's vendors are willing to offer raw material discounts amounting to $20 per unit, beginning with unit number 60,001.
■ Sales can be increased up to 100,000 units per year by committing large blocks of product to institutional buyers at a discounted unit price of $180. However, this discount would apply only to sales in excess of 40,000 units per year.

Barnes believes that these projections are reliable, and he is now trying to determine what DimLok must do to meet the profit objectives assigned by RayLok's board of directors.

Required:
a. Calculate the dollar value of DimLok's present annual fixed costs.
b. Determine the number of units that DimLok must sell in order to achieve both profit objectives. Be sure to consider all constraints in determining your answer.
c. Without prejudice to your answer in Requirement (b), assume Don Barnes decides to sell 40,000 units at $200 per unit and 24,000 units at $180 per unit. Prepare a pro forma (i.e., forecasted) income statement for DimLok showing whether or not Don Barnes's decision will achieve DimLok's profit objectives.

[CMA adapted]

18.46 *Break-even analysis and optimal production plan.* The PTO Division of the Galva Manufacturing Company produces power take-off units for the farm equipment business. The PTO Division, headquartered in Peoria, has a newly renovated, automated plant in Peoria and an older, less automated plant in Moline. Both plants produce the same power take-off units for farm tractors that are sold to most domestic and foreign tractor manufacturers.

The PTO Division expects to produce and sell 192,000 power take-off units during the coming year. The division production manager has the following data available regarding the unit costs, unit prices, and production capacities for the two plants:

	PEORIA		MOLINE
Selling price		$150.00	$150.00
Variable manufacturing cost	$72.00		$88.00
Fixed manufacturing cost	30.00		15.00
Commission (5%)	7.50		7.50
General and administrative expense	25.50		21.00
Total unit cost		<135.00>	<131.50>
Unit profit		$ 15.00	$ 18.50
Production rate per day		400 units	320 units

- All fixed costs are based on a normal year of 240 working days. When the number of working days exceeds 240, variable manufacturing costs increase by $3 per unit in Peoria and $8 per unit in Moline. Capacity for each plant is 300 working days.
- Galva Manufacturing charges each of its plants a per-unit fee for administrative services such as payroll, general accounting, and purchasing, as Galva considers these services to be a function of the work performed at the plants. For each of the plants at Peoria and Moline, the fee is $6.50 and represents the variable portion of general and administrative expense.

Wishing to maximize the higher unit profit at Moline, PTO's production manager has decided to manufacture 96,000 units at each plant. This production plan results in Moline operating at capacity and Peoria operating at its normal volume. Galva's corporate controller is not happy with this plan as he does not believe it represents optimal usage of PTO's plants.

Required:
a. Determine the annual break-even units for each of PTO's plants.
b. Calculate the operating income that would result from the division production manager's plan to produce 96,000 units at each plant.
c. Determine the optimal production plan to produce the 192,000 units at PTO's plants in Peoria and Moline, and calculate the resulting operating income for the PTO Division. Be sure to support the plan with appropriate calculations.

[CMA adapted]

18.47 *Segmented contribution and CVP analysis.* Kalifo Company manufactures a line of electric garden tools that are sold in general hardware stores. The company's controller, Sylvia Harlow, has just received the sales forecast for the coming year for Kalifo's three products: weeders, hedge clippers, and leaf blowers. Kalifo has experienced considerable variations in sales volumes and variable costs over the past two years, and Harlow believes the forecast should be carefully evaluated from a CVP viewpoint. The preliminary budget information for 19X8 is presented as follows:

	WEEDERS	HEDGE CLIPPERS	LEAF BLOWERS
Unit sales	50,000	50,000	100,000
Unit selling price	$28	$36	$48
Variable manufacturing cost per unit	$13	$12	$25
Variable selling cost per unit	$5	$4	$6

For 19X8, Kalifo's fixed factory overhead is budgeted at $2,000,000, and the company's fixed selling and administrative expenses are forecasted to be $600,000. Kalifo has an effective tax rate of 40%.

Required:
a. Determine Kalifo Company's budgeted net income for 19X8.
b. Assuming the sales mix remains as budgeted, determine how many units of each product Kalifo Company must sell in order to break even in 19X8.
c. Determine the total dollar sales Kalifo Company must sell in 19X8 in order to earn an aftertax net income of $450,000.
d. After preparing the original estimates, Kalifo Company determined that its variable manufacturing cost of leaf blowers would increase 20% and the

variable selling cost of hedge clippers could be expected to increase $1 per unit. However, Kalifo has decided not to change the selling price of either product. In addition, Kalifo has learned that its leaf blower has been perceived as the best value on the market, and it can expect to sell three times as many leaf blowers as any other product. Under these circumstances, determine how many units of each product Kalifo Company would have to sell in order to break even in 19X8.

e. Explain the limitations of CVP analysis that Sylvia Harlow should consider when evaluating Kalifo Company's 19X8 budget.

[CMA adapted]

19 MAKING SHORT-RUN PROFIT MANAGEMENT DECISIONS

Consensus decision making.

LEARNING OBJECTIVES

After studying this chapter, you should be able to:

1. Identify the relevant profit elements for short-run profit management decision making.

2. Use incremental CVP analysis in special-order decisions, and discuss the qualitative and legal factors associated with setting prices.

3. Analyze scarce-resource situations.

4. Perform incremental CVP analysis for the make-or-buy decision, and discuss the qualitative factors applicable to such decisions.

5. Apply incremental CVP analysis to the sell-or-process-further decision.

6. Describe how incremental CVP analysis is used for decision making under conditions of uncertainty and risk.

■ INTRODUCTION

Profit center managers are continually faced with the problem of choosing among alternative courses of action. This chapter considers typical questions addressed by these managers, such as the following:

■ What price should management set for special orders?
■ What if an insufficient amount of a component, used in multiple products, is available? Which products should continue to be produced, and which should be temporarily stopped?
■ Should the enterprise make a component used in the manufacture of a product or should it buy the component from an outside supplier?
■ Should the organization sell a product at some intermediate stage or should it process the product further?
■ How can the differential profits of various alternatives be calculated if outcomes are uncertain or probabilistic?

How successful the enterprise will be depends largely on whether it finds the right answers to decision problems like these. Relevant information about costs and revenues helps produce the right answers. In profit management information systems design, relevance and incremental CVP analysis are key factors. This chapter illustrates the use of these techniques in the following:

■ The special-order decision
■ The scarce-resource decision
■ The make-or-buy decision
■ The sell-or-process-further decision
■ Profitability analysis of uncertain and probabilistic outcomes

This chapter focuses primarily on short-run operational decisions. **Short-run decisions** are tactical, operating decisions that usually do not require significant and permanent resource commitments and involve a period of a year or less. In other words, short-run decisions involve only revenues, variable costs, and avoidable fixed costs. A second characteristic of short-run decisions is that they usually can be changed or reversed very quickly if more advantageous opportunities become available.

Generally, **long-run decisions** (sometimes referred to as strategic or capital project investment decisions) require large outlays of money, which increase fixed costs substantially. Net cash flow over several years and income tax considerations are important decision criteria for long-run decisions (covered in Part V of this text). One of the major differences between short-run and long-run decisions is that for long-run decisions, the future net cash flows must be discounted to the present using an appropriate discount factor. For short-run decision making, the discount factor is ignored. In other words, unlike long-run decisions, short-run decisions do not include the time value of money.

Decision making, both short run and long run, is usually thought of as a rational process. Rationality implies that the decision maker seeks to optimize outcomes. A rational decision-making process includes the following steps:

1. Identify and define the problem or need.
2. Analyze the problem or need, and define the desired objective to achieve.
3. Identify and develop alternatives.
4. Analyze and determine the consequences of each alternative.
5. Choose the best alternative.
6. Implement the alternative.
7. Review and evaluate the decision, and report on its progress.

This rational decision-making process is often performed under conditions of uncertainty and risk. Later, this chapter presents decision-making criteria

A team approach to short-run decision making.

for resolving decisions under these conditions. The roles of the management accounting system and the management accountant are to provide both the financial and nonfinancial information needed, facilitate and coordinate the gathering and use of information, and assure that proper decision-making techniques are employed. __

IDENTIFYING RELEVANT PROFIT ELEMENTS

LEARNING OBJECTIVE 1

Identify the relevant profit elements for short-run profit management decision making.

Before any decision is made, the **profit elements** (sales volume, sales price, variable costs, contribution margin, and fixed costs) that are relevant to that decision must be identified. In order for profit elements to be **relevant,** they must possess two characteristics:

■ They must occur in the *future*.
■ They must be *different* for each alternative ("differential items").

A Sunk Cost Is Not a Relevant Cost

A **sunk cost** is a cost incurred in the *past*. Past decisions cannot be changed. Only *new* decisions can be made in the future. Consequently, costs already incurred because of a past decision should not affect a new decision. These costs cannot be refunded and the decision undone. Because the past cannot be changed, sunk costs cannot be changed; therefore, they are irrelevant to decisions involving future actions and alternatives.

For example, Snowski Company has 1,000 pairs of defective downhill racing skis. They have a standard absorptive manufacturing cost of $80 per pair. Since the skis already have been manufactured and the production costs spent, the $80 is irrelevant to a future decision about what to do with them. The skis cannot be "unmade" and the money "unspent."

Relevant Profit Elements Occur in the Future

John Kali, an ex-Olympic downhill medalist and new manager of the Snowski product line, is considering what to do with the defects. If the skis are remachined at a (future) cost of $10 per set, they can be sold for $70 per pair. Alternatively, the defective skis can be sold now (as is) for $55 per pair. Which alternative is more desirable, and what are the relevant costs and revenues? John Kali's incremental CVP analysis comparing the two alternatives is presented in Exhibit 19–1. Snowski should remachine the defective skis, realizing a $5,000 increase in net profit, rather than sell the defective skis now.[1]

Analyzing Differential and Incremental Cost and Revenue

In addition to pertaining to the future, a relevant item must differ among the alternatives being considered. All costs and revenues that remain the same regardless of the decision should be removed from the analysis so attention can be focused on **incremental cost and revenue** and **differential cost and revenue** that influence the decision's outcome and the choice between alternatives. Incremental cost and revenue are profit elements unique to an alternative being considered. Differential cost and revenue are those profit elements that differ between alternatives. For example, in Exhibit 19–1, the sales price of $70 per pair and the additional manufacturing costs of $10 per pair for the rework

---

[1] All profit calculations are pretax. See Chapter 18 for converting pretax profits to aftertax profits.

■ EXHIBIT 19–1
Snowski's Differential CVP Analysis

ΔSales price:		
Remachined	$70	
Sold now	<55>	+$ 15
Less Δvariable costs		<+10>
ΔContribution margin per pair (CMU)		+$ 5
× Volume		× 1,000 pairs of skis
ΔContribution margin and pretax profit		+$5,000

Note: Δ = "the change in."

option are incremental profit elements associated with that alternative. When comparing this alternative to the option of selling the defective skis now, the difference in sales price of $15 and the incremental variable costs of $10 are differential elements relevant to the choice between the two alternatives.[2]

The alternatives are analyzed by calculating the incremental and differential costs, cost savings, and revenues for each alternative and selecting the one offering the greatest economic and qualitative advantages. The Silver State Mining example will illustrate the irrelevance of future costs that do not differ between alternatives and the relevance of future costs that do differ. Silver State Mining is considering the purchase of a new labor-saving machine. The present cost structure without the machine and the expected cost structure with the machine are as follows:

	PRESENT COSTS	EXPECTED COSTS WITH THE NEW MACHINE
Tons of ore produced	100,000	100,000
Sales price per ton	$1,000	$1,000
Direct labor cost per ton	$300	$280
Variable overhead per ton	$200	$200
Fixed overhead, other	$1,200,000	$1,200,000
Fixed overhead, new machine	–0–	$600,000

The new machine promises a cost savings of $20 per ton in direct labor costs, but will increase fixed costs by $600,000 per period. Revenues, all other costs, and the total number of tons produced, will remain the same. Therefore, the only relevant costs are the per-unit labor costs and the fixed costs associated with the new machine:

Savings in direct labor costs (100,000 tons at a cost savings of $20 per ton)	$2,000,000
Less increase in fixed costs	<600,000>
Net cost savings expected with the new machine	$1,400,000

This example focuses attention on the differential variable and fixed costs. It is one thing to define whether a cost is variable or fixed, but it is something else to determine how costs are related to decisions. At times, profit center managers are too quick to classify fixed costs as sunk. Fixed costs that have occurred in the past *are* sunk and are irrelevant to the decision, but other fixed costs—those that will occur in the future and are different between alternatives—are relevant. The $600,000 in fixed overhead (FOH) for the new machine

[2] Differential and incremental cost and revenue are the same when only one future alternative is compared with the status quo. For example, if the only alternative being considered is to sell the defective skis now for $55, then the decision is between throwing them away and selling them as defects. Throwing away defects is the current policy and, therefore, the status quo. The incremental revenue (the $55 sales price) is the only differential element between this alternative and maintaining the status quo. Incremental and differential cost and revenue are not the same when multiple future alternatives are considered, as demonstrated in Exhibit 19–2.

will occur in the future if it is purchased and will not occur if the machine is not purchased. Thus, the $600,000 is both a future and a differential cost. Therefore, it is relevant to the analysis. The $1,200,000 in other FOH, though it will occur in the future, is not relevant because it is not different between the two alternatives. For a profit element to be relevant, it must be *both* a future and a differential item.

The management accountant must also consider the relevant range in incremental CVP analysis.[3] In periods of rapid sales growth, certain fixed costs behave as step costs; that is, if sales grow fast enough, fixed costs can change in total beyond the relevant range for the profit equation. Supervisory salaries, administrative and marketing costs, and rents are fixed costs that can increase quickly. Simply identifying these costs as fixed and not allowing for potential increases can lead to wrong decisions.

▍Opportunity Costs and Benefits

An **opportunity cost** is the differential benefit from another more profitable alternative that is given up when a less profitable alternative is chosen. Although opportunity costs are not recorded in the accounting system's general ledger, all decisions involving alternative courses of action entail such costs. Considering opportunity costs forces managers to recognize the potential profits foregone by not choosing a more profitable alternative. Opportunity costs and benefits also provide a means of ranking alternatives in terms of their opportunities to generate extra profits.

Continuing the Snowski example from Exhibit 19–1, if the defective skis are sold now, John Kali is giving up the opportunity to make another $5,000 in profits from remachining them. The decision to sell the skis now has a $5,000 opportunity cost. However, John has identified another alternative. He considers Snowski to be a world-class manufacturer and believes these defects should not have happened. Normally, these skis sell for $100 per pair. Selling them now or remachining them so they can be sold at a discounted price may hurt the company's quality image with its customers. Thus, neither of the original two alternatives may be a good idea. John's new alternative is to rework the skis to their normal quality at a cost of $50 per pair and then sell them at their normal sales price of $100. The three alternatives are compared in Exhibit 19–2a.

Which alternative should John choose? If profit is the only criterion, alternative 2 (remachining) generates $5 per pair ($5,000 in total for the 1,000 skis) more in incremental profit than alternative 3 (selling now as is), and $10 per pair more than alternative 1 (rework). Therefore, alternative 3 (the second best alternative) has an opportunity cost of $5 per pair. Choosing this alternative means giving up the opportunity to have *another* $5 per pair profit, which is available if alternative 2 is chosen.

Similarly, by choosing alternative 1, John Kali will give up the opportunity to have another $10 per pair profit, which he can have by choosing alternative 2 instead. So, alternative 1 has a $10 per pair opportunity cost.

What about the most profitable alternative (alternative 2)? It cannot (by definition) have an opportunity cost because there is no better alternative that has been identified, at least in terms of profit. In fact, alternative 2 creates an opportunity to realize $5 per pair in additional profits over the next best alternative (alternative 3). Modifying the microeconomic idea of opportunity cost to aid profit management decision making, alternative 2 has an **opportunity benefit** of $5 per pair. Only the alternative with the greatest incremental profit has an opportunity benefit. All less profitable alternatives have an opportunity cost. The opportunity benefit of the best alternative is the differential profit between it and the second best alternative. The formulas for calculating opportunity costs and benefits are shown in Exhibit 19–2b.

---

[3] The relevant range was first discussed in Chapter 7 and again in Chapter 18.

■■■EXHIBIT 19–2
Snowski's Opportunity Costs and Benefits

a.

Alternatives:	ΔSales price	−	ΔVariable costs	=	ΔProfit	Opportunity Benefit	<Cost>
1: Rework	$100	−	$50	=	+$50 per pair		<$10> per pair
2: Remachine	$70	−	$10	=	+$60 per pair	$5 per pair	
3: Sell now	$55	−	$0	=	+$55 per pair		<$5> per pair

b.

Opportunity benefit: The incremental profit of the best alternative less the incremental profit of the second best alternative.
Opportunity cost: The incremental profit of this alternative less the incremental profit of the best alternative.
Note: The best alternative is defined as the alternative with the greatest incremental profit.

John Kali did not choose alternative 2, though. Snowski is a world-class manufacturer, and selling inferior-quality skis (defects, whether remachined or not) is not congruent with its product quality goal. Snowski's customers consider its skis to be the best, not cheap seconds. John chose alternative 1, even though it has an opportunity cost of $10 per pair ($10,000 in total).

John discussed his choice with his boss, arguing that the marginal utility of maintaining a high-quality image is greater than the marginal utility for the differential profits of $10,000 that could be realized by choosing alternative 2 instead of alternative 1. His boss was impressed with how John quantified and measured the concept of marginal utility. Though the boss's marginal utility for another $10,000 was greater than her marginal utility for maintaining a quality image, she respected John's decision.

LEARNING OBJECTIVE 2

▬▬

Use incremental CVP analysis in special-order decisions, and discuss the qualitative and legal factors associated with setting prices.

▮THE SPECIAL-ORDER PRICING DECISION

One of the primary responsibilities of a profit center manager is the setting of sales prices. There are three types of price-setting decisions:

- Normal pricing for the sales forecast volume
- Special sales order pricing
- Pricing of products sold between profit centers within the same enterprise

The first two types of pricing decisions are considered next. The third, called transfer pricing, is reserved for Chapter 21.

The long-run pricing of products and services for the general marketplace is a complex process. Cost is only one factor to be considered. Other factors that are often more important include competitors' prices and customers' desires. Costs, however, play an important and direct role in pricing special orders.

Sometimes a company receives an order for a standard product but is asked to quote a special, onetime only price. To get this business, a company often finds itself engaged in competitive bidding that it otherwise would not do. A **special-order decision** then involves the sale of normal or customized products at a discounted or special price. Most management accountants believe that such problems can be efficiently solved by the contribution margin approach to CVP analysis.

Special-Order Decision When Idle Capacity Exists

If idle capacity[4] exists, the lowest price that can be quoted for a special order must cover its incremental costs. In this case, the order will yield zero profit. The minimum price, then, is a break-even price for the special order. Normal fixed costs are not relevant to pricing special orders when sufficient idle capacity exists to fill the order, because the fixed costs will be incurred whether the order is accepted or not. When there are no differential fixed costs associated with a special order, the sales price only has to recover the variable costs. In other words, the minimum acceptable sales price, or the break-even price on the order, is the price that creates a zero contribution margin per unit (CMU). Any additional revenue in excess of the variable costs will increase profits. This increase is equal to the CMU multiplied by the sales volume involved in the special order.

In considering a special order that will allow a company to make use of current idle capacity, the relevant costs are direct materials, direct labor, variable overhead, and any incremental selling or administrative expenses. Depreciation, as well as other fixed costs, are irrelevant because these costs will be incurred whether the company takes the special order or not. In the Storagetek case on the next page, review how management sets the price on magnetic tape drives.

In negotiating a price for the special order, Storagetek should set the minimum selling price so that it is equal to the incremental costs associated with the special order:

Direct materials	$10
Direct labor	4
Variable overhead	2
Distribution cost	1
Incremental cost per unit	$17

In considering overhead, only VOH is included in the incremental costs because FOH will be incurred regardless of whether the order is accepted. The minimum sales price of $17 yields a zero CMU. At this price, Storagetek just breaks even on the order.

What if Storagetek wants to increase its operating income by $40,000 from this special order? The $40,000 averages $2 per tape drive unit ($40,000 ÷ 20,000 units). Thus, the sales order must generate a $2 CMU, and a sales price of $19 should be charged. The minimum (break-even) price of $17 just covers variable costs, generating zero CMU and profit. With a profit goal of $40,000, an increase in selling price of $2 per unit is necessary. Therefore, the minimum price of $17 plus $2 will give a selling price that covers all variable costs and contributes $2 per unit to operating profit. This can be calculated by using the profit equation in its factored form and solving for volume:

$$\Delta \text{Target sales volume} = \frac{\Delta(\text{Fixed costs} + \text{Profit})}{\Delta \text{CMU}}$$

$$20,000 \text{ units} = \frac{+\$40,000}{\Delta \text{CMU}}$$

$$\Delta \text{CMU} = +\$2 \text{ per unit}$$

Special-Order Decision When Not Enough Surplus Capacity Exists

In some cases, a firm may not have enough capacity to manufacture the special order and still continue normal production levels. The Metalcraft case on page 883 illustrates this situation.

---

[4] Idle capacity means that the enterprise is not producing at its maximum, full capacity level. It has some surplus capacity available that can be used to make more products if there is a demand for them.

INSIGHTS & APPLICATIONS

Storagetek's Pricing of a Special Order When Idle Capacity Exists

Storagetek, a manufacturer of computer auxiliary storage devices, received a special order for 20,000 magnetic tape drive units from the public school system in its community. As part of its long-range strategic perspective, Storagetek views the community as an important stakeholder. Realizing the financial condition of the school district, management wants to make a concession in its normal sales price.

Storagetek normally sells its magnetic tape drive units for $40 each. Incremental distribution costs for this order will be $1 per unit. Storagetek has sufficient existing capacity to manufacture the additional units.

Storagetek's standard absorptive manufacturing cost, based on a production quota of 300,000 units, is as follows:

Direct materials	$10
Direct labor	4
Variable overhead	2
Fixed overhead	3
	$19

Should the special order from Oxnard be accepted? The following calculations show that Metalcraft does not have the necessary plant capacity in the third quarter to produce the special order for 20,000 toolboxes from Oxnard:

Monthly plant capacity	80,000	Mhr
Estimated monthly capacity use (based on production quota: 80,000 Mhr × .80)	<64,000>	Mhr
Excess capacity per month	16,000	Mhr
Period for special order (third quarter)	× 3	months
Total excess capacity available	48,000	Mhr

The machine hours required to produce this special order (volume × standard machine hours) are calculated as follows:

$$\text{Required Mhr} = 20,000 \text{ toolboxes} \times 3 \text{ Mhr per toolbox}$$
$$= 60,000 \text{ Mhr}$$

The Oxnard order for 20,000 toolboxes will require 60,000 machine hours, but only 48,000 machine hours are available in the third quarter. To accept this order, Metalcraft will have to give up making regular toolboxes for normal sales so that the extra machine hours required for the Oxnard order are available. What if Metalcraft diverts 12,000 machine hours of regular production to produce the special order? In this case, 4,000 toolboxes of normal production and sales will have to be sacrificed (12,000 machine hours needed ÷ 3 standard machine hours per toolbox). From an economic viewpoint, is this a proper decision? As Exhibit 19–3 shows, a $30,000 opportunity cost is associated with this special order.

Even if this special order would produce an opportunity benefit, appropriate profit management requires consideration of other factors before accepting the order. Giving up normal sales, even though only in the short run, raises the potential for customer ill will. In other words, normal customers may purchase from a competitor of Metalcraft. The loss of normal customers is more serious in situations where products have a short customer use life and resales to the same customers (repeat business) are important. For example, a dairy products

INSIGHTS & APPLICATIONS

Metalcraft's Special-Order Decision When Not Enough Capacity Exists

Metalcraft manufactures a toolbox for do-it-yourself mechanics. Metalcraft has received a special-order inquiry for 20,000 toolboxes from Oxnard Corporation, a large chain of hardware stores based in Europe. The toolboxes are to be manufactured during the third quarter. The toolboxes will be marketed under Oxnard's own label. Oxnard has offered Metalcraft $60 per toolbox for the 20,000 toolboxes to be delivered by October 1.

The selling price and standard cost card for regular toolboxes are as follows:

Regular sales price per toolbox $95.00

Standard costs per toolbox:

Direct materials	$25.00
Direct labor	
($6.00 × 5 labor hours)	30.00
Variable overhead	
($1.50 × 3 machine hours)	4.50
Fixed overhead	
($2.50 × 3 machine hours)	7.50
Standard absorptive manufacturing cost	$67.00

In addition, Metalcraft normally incurs $10.50 per toolbox in variable selling expenses. No incremental selling or administrative expenses are expected with this special order, though.

Oxnard has specified the use of plastic instead of metal for certain components of the toolbox. Because of these different specifications, direct materials will cost $22 instead of $25 per toolbox. Management has estimated that the remaining costs, labor time and machine time, will be the same.

Metalcraft's production capacity is limited to the total machine hours available, which is 80,000 machine hours per month. Management estimates that the plant will be operating at 80 percent of full capacity during the third quarter.

■ EXHIBIT 19–3
Metalcraft's Special Order When Insufficient Capacity Exists to Fill It

Contribution margin from special order:			
Sales price		$60.00	
Less incremental variable costs:			
Direct materials	$22.00		
Direct labor ($6.00 × 5 labor hours)	30.00		
Variable overhead ($1.50 × 3 machine hours)	4.50	<56.50>	
CMU		$ 3.50	
Total contribution margin ($3.50 × 20,000 toolboxes)			$ 70,000
Opportunity cost because of lost regular sales:			
Regular sales price		$95.00	
Less variable costs:			
Direct materials	$25.00		
Direct labor	30.00		
Variable overhead	4.50		
Selling expenses	10.50	<70.00>	
Normal CMU		$25.00	
Total opportunity cost ($25.00 × 4,000 regular toolboxes)			<100,000>
Net opportunity benefit/<opportunity cost> of accepting special order			**<$ 30,000>**
Incremental CVP analysis:			
Special-order CMU			$ 3.50
× ΔVolume			× 20,000
ΔContribution margin on special order			$ 70,000
Less CM lost from normal sales ($25 × 4,000 toolboxes)			< 100,000>
Net Δcontribution margin and net ΔProfit			**<$ 30,000>**

company will sell milk, butter, and cheese to the same customers over and over again.

If these customers purchase from a competitor because a special order has cut off the normal supply, then future sales may also be lost. If the company loses market share permanently, fixed costs per unit will increase, and management may be tempted to raise normal sales prices to compensate for the reduced volume. This price increase may drive more customers to the competition, which, in turn, may prompt management to continue to raise prices as volume drops and fixed costs per unit increase. Thus, a vicious circle is created that could, in the long run, drive the firm out of business.

Consider the effect on Metalcraft's competition. As customers flee to Metalcraft's competitors, the competitors's volume increases. Consequently, they can reduce sales prices (because their fixed costs per unit will go down) while maintaining the same total contribution margin. As their prices drop, more customers may leave Metalcraft for the competition's products. In the long run, the result may be a further decline in the competitors' prices. Even more customers may leave Metalcraft, accelerating the loss of its market share and eventual exit from the business.

While this scenario is extreme, it illustrates the need to consider customer satisfaction (a characteristic of a world-class manufacturer) and the possible effects on long-run sales from accepting a special order when insufficient surplus capacity exists.

Special-Order Decisions when Differential Fixed Costs are Incurred

Special orders can require special equipment, special product (or packaging) design work, special shipping, and other unique activities that will create an incremental fixed cost for the special order. In such cases, these fixed costs are relevant to the special-order decision. The Magic Keyboard case on the next page illustrates this situation.

This analysis is presented in Exhibit 19–4. The Worldwide order should be rejected because it is unprofitable in the short run with the present price and

---

■ EXHIBIT 19–4
Magic Keyboard's Special Order Containing Differential Fixed Costs

Contribution margin from special order:			
Price offered per keyboard		$82	
Less incremental variable costs per keyboard:			
Direct materials	$35		
Direct labor ($8 × 4 hours)	32		
Variable overhead ($2 × 5 machine hours)	10	<77>	
Contribution margin per keyboard (CMU)		$ 5	
Total contribution margin ($5 × 8,000 keyboards)			$ 40,000
Less differential fixed costs of order:			
Setup costs	$20,000		
Special machine	30,000		<50,000>
Net loss of accepting special order			**<$10,000>**
Incremental CVP analysis:			
Special-order CMU			$5
× ΔVolume			× 8,000
ΔContribution margin on special order			$40,000
Less Δfixed costs			<50,000>
Net Δprofit			**<$10,000>**

INSIGHTS & APPLICATIONS

Magic Keyboard's Special-Order Decision When Differential Fixed Costs Are Incurred

Magic Keyboard makes keyboards for personal computers. It has received a special-order inquiry from Worldwide Corporation, a manufacturer of personal computers to be marketed in China. The order calls for 8,000 keyboards containing Chinese characters. The standard absorptive manufacturing cost for this keyboard is as follows:

Direct materials	$ 35
Direct labor	
($8 × 4 labor hours)	32
Variable overhead	
($2 × 5 machine hours)	10
Normal fixed overhead	
($6 × 5 machine hours)	30
Standard absorptive manufacturing cost	$107

In addition, Magic Keyboard will incur $20,000 in special setup costs and will have to purchase a $30,000 special machine to manufacture the keys containing Chinese characters. This machine will be discarded once the special order is completed. Should Magic Keyboard accept an offer of $82 per keyboard from Worldwide?

---

cost structure. But what sales volume or price will make this order acceptable? First, consider the break-even volume (BEP) necessary for this order:

$$BEP = \text{Fixed costs} \div CMU$$
$$= \$50,000 \div \$5$$
$$= \underline{10,000 \text{ keyboards}}$$

The BEP is the indifference volume for this order. If exactly 10,000 keyboards are ordered, there will be zero profit on the special order. More than 10,000 keyboards will generate an incremental contribution margin and profit of $5 per keyboard (the CMU). If less than 10,000 keyboards are ordered, this order will be unprofitable at a rate of $5 per keyboard below the BEP. In this example, the order is for only 8,000 keyboards. This creates a loss of $10,000 (2,000 units below BEP × $5 per unit).

What is the minimum acceptable sales price for this special order? This question is also conceptualized as a BEP question:[5]

$$BEP = \text{Fixed costs} \div CMU$$
$$8,000 \text{ keyboards} = \$50,000 \div CMU$$
$$CMU = \underline{\$6.25 \text{ per keyboard}}$$

CMU will have to increase by $1.25 over the original CMU of $5.00 projected in Exhibit 19–4. If variable costs cannot be reduced, then the sales price will have to be increased from $82.00 per keyboard to $83.25. In the absence of overriding qualitative factors, the order should be rejected if volume or sales price cannot be renegotiated to the minimum amounts calculated.

In the Snowski case earlier, John Kali chose a suboptimal profit alternative because of his desire to maintain Snowski's product quality image. Are there any qualitative factors in the Magic Keyboard case that might have a greater marginal utility to management than the marginal utility of the Worldwide order's opportunity cost? One factor may be the desire to enter this new foreign market on a long-run basis. Selling initially at a loss to gain permanent entry

---

[5] In this situation, the BEP is given, and the equation is solved for the CMU.

into this market may be justified within Magic Keyboard's market penetration strategy.

The Full Cost Approach versus the Contribution Margin Approach to Pricing

The preceding analyses are suitable for price setting in the short run, but the contribution margin approach (using incremental CVP analysis) may be inappropriate for long-run pricing decisions. An enterprise must recover not only its normal variable costs, but also its normal fixed costs if it intends to remain in business.

A general cost-based price-setting model can be illustrated as follows:

Variable costs per unit	$xxx (floor)	⎫
+ Fixed costs per unit	xxx	⎬ Pricing
+ Desired profit per unit	xxx	⎬ range
Target sales price	xxx (ceiling)	⎭

The full cost approach to price setting is based on absorption costing. The target sales price, if set at the ceiling, includes all variable costs, an allocation of fixed costs including marketing and administrative costs, and the desired profit. The major drawback to this approach is that fixed costs and profit are expressed on a per-unit basis. If volume changes, fixed costs per unit change inversely. Therefore, this model is only appropriate in short-term decisions when the volume is known (a fixed amount).

The contribution margin approach to price setting, starting with the floor price, provides the price setter with flexibility for setting prices within the pricing range. The main criticism leveled against the contribution margin approach is that it is not appropriate for setting normal sales prices (for the sales projection used in the master budget). Absorption costs are required in setting normal sales prices so that all costs can be recovered through sales prices, and the firm's profit goal realized.

The general model presents a range for setting sales prices that is bounded by a floor and a ceiling price. The floor price reminds the price setter that a special sales order can be priced as low as its variable cost per unit. This is the contribution margin approach to pricing. The ceiling price reminds the price setter that in order to cover fixed costs and realize the master budget profit goal, the normal sales price must be set for the products included in the master budget's sales forecast. The normal price is based on an absorptive (full) cost including a target profit. Thus, the ceiling represents the price management must set on regular sales to achieve its profit goal.

Under what conditions can the price setter move toward the floor and set a price based on variable costs alone? Appropriate conditions include the following:

■ A company receives a special order that does not affect the attainment of normal sales volume, and fixed costs truly will not change.
■ A company with idle capacity receives a special order that does not affect the attainment of normal sales volume, as in the Storagetek case.
■ A company faced with stiff competition and tough competitive bidding situations may be willing to forego profits in the short run in order to capture market share (penetration pricing) for long-run benefit.
■ Without the order, the lack of work will necessitate shutting down part of production, thus causing the company to incur increased unemployment insurance, training costs if the skilled employees do not return after the layoff, and huge start-up costs after returning from a lengthy shutdown.

Using the contribution margin approach for short-run decision making generates more meaningful information for management such as the relationship of the variable and fixed costs to volume and profit, as described in Chapter 18. This approach permits management to determine the impact that volume changes, resulting from price adjustments, will have on net profit.

One area where the full cost approach to price setting is frequently used, however, is in government contracts. Here, the full cost includes administrative costs along with an allowable profit margin. Similarly, most utility commissions use the full cost approach in setting rates. Many utility companies are publicly owned and must provide an adequate return to their stockholders in order to generate future expansion capital. Finally, companies use the full cost approach (at least as a starting point) when considering long-term pricing of new products.

Considering Qualitative and Legal Factors When Setting Prices

Management must also consider certain qualitative and legal factors when setting prices. What will be the impact on regular customers if they find out that other customers, some of whom may be their competitors, received special prices? Will they take their business elsewhere? How will competitors react? Will special pricing spark a price war?[6]

What about legal ramifications? When setting prices, management must take care to abide by certain legislation such as the *Robinson-Patman Act*, which forbids quoting different prices to competing customers unless the difference in price can be traced directly to differences in manufacturing, selling, or distribution costs. The prices used in enforcing the act are based on full costs. Thus, a price difference cannot be justified by omitting the fixed overhead for special orders in cases where excess capacity exists. Most price differences are justified on the basis of marketing and transportation cost variations rather than on FOH costs.

Also, pricing is subject to antidumping laws in many foreign markets. These laws are designed to protect a domestic manufacturer in its home market in instances where it is in direct competition with a foreign supplier. Therefore, the price setter has to charge a "fair" price for goods being shipped abroad.

In addition to making decisions about sales prices and special orders, profit center managers are responsible for different types of production decisions involving the following:

- Scarce resources
- Making or buying components
- Selling or further processing of components

Each of these decisions will be considered in turn.

THE SCARCE-RESOURCE DECISION

LEARNING OBJECTIVE 3

Analyze scarce-resource situations.

The **scarce-resource decision** involves choosing which product to produce when there is a shortage of a component part used in more than one product. Management at QuickCalc, Inc., faces such a decision (see p. 888).

QCI should produce the product that has the highest contribution margin per unit of the scarce resource. As Exhibit 19–5 shows, the company should produce desktop calculators. For every chip used in producing desktop calculators, QCI will realize $5 in contribution margin. In the short run, this will be the most productive use of this scarce resource.

Maximizing short-run profit should not be the only decision criterion, though. QCI should consider whether any customers will be lost if either of

---

[6] In many industries, it may be difficult to keep a special price a secret. In the Metalcraft and Magic Keyboard cases, however, the orders involved foreign markets. If the two firms are otherwise only in domestic markets, these foreign customers may not compete with current customers.

INSIGHTS & APPLICATIONS

QuickCalc's Supply Problems

QuickCalc, Inc. (QCI), manufactures hand-held calculators, desktop calculators, and word processors (intelligent typewriters). Each product uses a different number of standard computer chips for microprocessing.

QCI's JIT suppler is Entil. The Entil plant, located in Iowa, was recently damaged by a tornado, and QCI will not receive enough chips during the next month to support production of all three product lines.

QCI management is considering which product line to continue producing in the short run and which products to suspend temporarily. The following information is available within the management accounting LAN:

	HAND-HELD CALCULATORS	DESKTOP CALCULATORS	WORD PROCESSORS
Chips' standard quantities	4 chips	3 chips	6 chips
Products' CMUs	$10 per unit	$15 per unit	$24 per unit

■ EXHIBIT 19–5
QuickCalc's Scarce-Resource Decision

	Hand-held Calculators	Desktop Calculators	Word Processors
Products' CMUs	$10 per unit	$15 per unit	$24 per unit
÷ Chip's standard quantities	÷ 4 chips per unit	÷ 3 chips per unit	÷ 6 chips per unit
Contribution margin per unit of the scarce resource (per chip)	$2.50 per chip	$5.00 per chip	$4.00 per chip

the other products is not available. This analysis also assumes that the products are heterogeneous in that the sales of one product line do not affect the sales of the other product lines. QCI management may also wish to consider the possibility of future supply shortages.

This last concern may involve the analyses presented in the next two sections. Continuing supply problems and/or internal and external failure costs for a component may lead management to consider making it instead of buying it.

LEARNING OBJECTIVE 4

Perform incremental CVP analysis for the make-or-buy decision, and discuss the qualitative factors applicable to such decisions.

▍THE MAKE-OR-BUY DECISION

The decision of whether to make a fabricated part or component internally, or to purchase it from an external supplier, is called a **make-or-buy decision.** For example, a division of General Motors may make headlights for its automobiles, or it may buy the headlights from one or more external suppliers.

As with all decisions, management must deal with both qualitative and quantitative factors. Qualitative factors relate to the:

- Quality of the component
- Reliability of the supplier
- Technical capability of the supplier
- Financial strength and reputation of the supplier
- Ability of the supplier to maintain confidential information that may otherwise be revealed to competitors by the supplier

INSIGHTS & APPLICATIONS

Nextyme's Make-or-Buy Decision

For the past five years, Nextyme has produced hard drives for its personal computers. Because material costs have steadily increased, Nextyme's management is reviewing the decision to continue to make the hard drives and has identified the following facts:

1. Nextyme's equipment used to manufacture hard drives has a book value of $500,000.
2. A $75,000 unsecured note is still outstanding on the equipment used to manufacture hard drives.
3. The space now used by the hard drives production department could be used by an assembly depart-

ment. Expanded assembly production will generate an additional $250,000 contribution margin annually.
4. Otherwise, the current facility will have to be expanded at a cost of $250,000.
5. Fifty employees who work in Nextyme's hard drives production department will be terminated and given eight weeks' severance pay if hard drives are purchased.
6. Cegate, a reputable manufacturer, produces hard drives of equal quality by a new efficient process.
7. Hard drives can be purchased from Cegate for $87.50 per unit.
8. Cegate is willing to sign a long-term contract and agree to JIT delivery.
9. Cegate has a large supply of a special chip that is in short supply. This chip is critical in the production of hard drives.
10. Nextyme is planning on entering the educational market.

■ Impact on the morale of the enterprise's employees if the labor force is reduced
■ Type of contract entered into with the supplier, such as length of time and number of units

Quantitative factors relate to the:

■ Incremental production costs for each unit
■ Unit cost of purchasing from the supplier
■ Availability of production capacity to manufacture the components
■ Opportunity costs and benefits from using facilities for production rather than for other purposes

Companies must determine whether to make or buy various parts.

The above Nextyme case highlights both qualitative and quantitative factors relative to a make-or-buy decision. The relevant quantitative and qualitative factors are marked by an X in the following table:

Facts	Quantitative Factors	Qualitative Factors
1. Book value	—	—
2. Unsecured note	—	—
3. Opportunity cost	X	—
4. Expansion cost	X	—
5. Employee terminations	X	X
6. Supplier's reputation	—	X
7. Price per unit	X	—
8. Sales contract and JIT delivery	—	X
9. Availability of chip	—	X
10. Market strategy	—	—

Because of the factors involved in terminating employees, Nextyme's management should consider retraining them so that they can be used in the new expanded assembly production. If this decision is made, then the severance pay will not be paid. The employees' salaries or wages will not be a differential cost because they will be paid under both alternatives. However, the retraining costs do become a relevant cost.

▌The Make-or-Buy Decision When No Significant Resource Commitment Is Involved

In this section, no significant change in asset or capital commitment is associated with the decision of whether to manufacture the part or purchase it from an outside supplier. To illustrate the quantitative side of the make-or-buy decision, Wanderer management (see p. 891) is trying to decide whether to continue making 10,000 cooling units or buy them from Thermo, an outside supplier. Thermo can supply all the units needed and meet Wanderer's quality specifications.

The relevant cost of "making" the unit compared with the cost of "buying it" is shown in Exhibit 19–6. All the variable costs are relevant because they are also avoidable costs. The FOH standard cost ($20) multiplied by the production quota (10,000 cooling units) equals the budgeted FOH of $200,000 per year. If 70 percent is unavoidable ($140,000), then only 30 percent ($60,000) is avoidable and, therefore, relevant. If exactly 10,000 cooling units are made, then the average opportunity benefit from continuing production (versus buying the units from Thermo) is $10 per unit ($100,000 difference if bought ÷ 10,000 cooling units).

The analysis shown in Exhibit 19–6 can be done using just the differential amounts between the two alternatives, which are shown in the last (rightmost) column. Modern management accountants, confident in their abilities, will use the differential analysis at profit planning meetings to provide quick answers to such "what-if" questions. If profit managers want a hard-copy analysis or computer screen display, the management accountant should consider designing the three-column format in Exhibit 19–6. It may prove to be more understandable to the managers.

The 10,000 cooling units expected to be needed may not be the actual quantity needed next year. Seldom will the production quota and actual output be the same. At what volume will Wanderer be indifferent between making and buying the units?

$$BEP = \text{Fixed costs} \div CMU$$
$$= \$60,000 \div \$16$$
$$= \underline{3,750 \text{ cooling units}}$$

If only 3,750 cooling units are actually needed, there will be no differential effect on profits from making them or buying them. The 3,750-volume level is the indifference volume between the two alternatives. If less than 3,750 units are actually needed, then buying the units is the more profitable alternative. If more than 3,750 units are needed, however, then making them is the more profitable alternative. Every time one more part is made (instead of purchased), Wanderer saves another $16. If another 6,250 units (10,000-unit production

---

◼ EXHIBIT 19–6
Wanderer's Make-or-Buy Decision

	Make	Buy	Difference If Bought
Incremental variable costs ($90 + $40 + $10)	$140	$156	$16
× Volume	× 10,000	× 10,000	× 10,000
ΔTotal variable costs	$1,400,000	$1,560,000	$160,000
ΔContribution margin	<$1,400,000>	<$1,560,000>	<$160,000>
Less Δfixed costs		<−60,000>	<−60,000>
ΔProfit	<$1,400,000>	<$1,500,000>	<$100,000>

INSIGHTS & APPLICATIONS

Wanderer's Make-or-Buy Decision

Wanderer, Inc., makes recreational vehicles. For its yearly production, Wanderer needs 10,000 cooling units that it currently makes in-house. The following quantitative information is available:

Standard absorptive manufacturing cost to make one cooling unit:

Direct materials	$ 90
Direct labor	40
Applied variable overhead	10
Applied fixed overhead	20
	$160

Wanderer can buy the cooling units from Thermo (a maker of similar cooling units) for a price of $156 per unit. Seventy percent of the applied fixed overhead will continue regardless of which decision is made. What should Wanderer do?

---

quota less 3,750 to "break even") are needed, the company will save $16 on each, and differential profits will increase by $100,000 (the difference shown in Exhibit 19–6).

The 6,250 units expected to be needed above the indifference volume is a margin of safety of 62.5 percent. In other words, demand for cooling units would have to drop more than 62.5 percent before the decision to continue making cooling units becomes unprofitable.[7]

If the facilities now being used to produce the cooling units would otherwise be idle, Wanderer should continue to produce its own cooling units. But suppose the new-product design group presents a proposal for a portable cooling unit for summertime campers who want to maintain the comforts of home. This new product, called KoolPac, will generate an annual contribution margin of $300,000 and can be manufactured in the production department currently used to make cooling units. The analysis is presented in Exhibit 19–7. Now, continuing production of cooling units involves an opportunity cost. The original differential profits of $100,000 (Exhibit 19–6) are more than offset by the additional $300,000 in profits generated by Koolpac. If Koolpac can generate $300,000 in incremental profits, Wanderer will be $200,000 better off from buying the cooling units and making KoolPac products.

---

[7] Margin of safety calculations were presented in Chapter 17.

	Make	Buy	Difference If Bought
Incremental variable costs			
($90 + $40 + $10)	$140	$156	$16
× Volume	× 10,000	× 10,000	× 10,000
ΔTotal variable costs	$1,400,000	$1,560,000	$160,000
ΔContribution margin:			
From the change in variable costs	<$1,400,000>	<$1,560,000>	<$160,000>
From KoolPac sales		300,000	300,000
Net Δcontribution margin	<1,400,000>	<1,260,000>	140,000
Less Δfixed costs		<−60,000>	<−60,000>
ΔProfit	<$1,400,000>	<$1,200,000>	$200,000

EXHIBIT 19–7
Wanderer's Make-or-Buy Decision with an Alternative Use for Its Facilities

The Make-or-Buy Decision When a Significant Resource Commitment Is Involved

If the make-or-buy decision calls for investment in facilities necessary to make the part, extensive capital budgeting analysis is required. Such long-run asset commitments involve projecting cash flows and discounting them to their present value and then comparing the net present value of the make alternative with those of other available projects. Also, tax consequences of the investment in the productive facilities have to be evaluated. These situations entail a long-run investment decision analysis that is not considered in this chapter. Such decisions are covered in Part V.

Make-or-Buy Decisions for Services

Make-or-buy decisions also are made for services, sometimes referred to as outsourcing. **Outsourcing** occurs when an organization decides to acquire a service from an external supplier rather than performing that service internally. For example, an enterprise may turn over its information systems hardware, software, and personnel to an outside vendor, which then supplies the information system as a service to the enterprise for a fee. The advantage of outsourcing is that it allows a vendor that specializes in a service to provide that service while the enterprise concentrates on its core business, focusing on what it does best. As an executive of Kodak said, ''We're in the photographic, pharmaceutical, and chemical businesses, not information system services. Therefore, we have outsourced all of these services.''

Another form of outsourcing is **privatization,** in which a service provided by local, state, or federal government agencies is changed from public to private control. Notwithstanding the political factors, the decision to privatize is similar to a make-or-buy decision.

<table>
<tr><td>

LEARNING OBJECTIVE 5

Apply incremental CVP analysis to the sell-or-process-further decision.

</td><td>

THE SELL-OR-PROCESS-FURTHER DECISION

The **sell-or-process-further** decision involves choosing whether to sell a marketable product at some intermediate stage or to process it further into a different (''final'') product. As a general rule, it will always be more profitable to continue processing so long as the incremental revenue from the sale of the final product exceeds the incremental processing costs to make it.

For example, should Wham-O (see p. 893) sell Quik-Gro or process it further into Quik-Kleen? Exhibit 19–8 presents this decision within a decision-tree format. The decision tree contains two types of nodes:

</td></tr>
</table>

- The square node represents a decision or action point. This is the action chosen by the decision maker.
- The circle or oval node represents an event. In this case, events are incremental revenues.

The net advantage (opportunity benefit) of processing Quik-Gro further into Quik-Kleen is $5,000 per batch. The initial production costs incurred to produce Quik-Gro (direct materials and conversion costs) are irrelevant in deciding whether to process Quik-Gro further. These initial costs are incurred regardless of whether Quik-Kleen is produced and, therefore, are not differential costs.

In many industries with vertically integrated enterprises, such as oil and gas, the selling or further processing of joint products often becomes a short-run operational decision. Product mixes need to be adjusted in response to changing market demands, competition, and volatility in raw material prices. Finding the most profitable mix given the current circumstances involves the sell-or-process-further analysis. For example, should raw crude oil be sold from the oil

INSIGHTS & APPLICATIONS

Wham-O's Decision to Sell or Process Further

Among its many products, Wham-O produces a potash and ammonium compound, called Quik-Gro, in 10,000-gallon batches from a raw material that costs $1 per gallon. Total conversion costs (direct labor costs plus applied overhead costs) are $4,000. This compound can be sold as a fertilizer ingredient to a large agribusiness distributor for $3 per gallon.

Alternatively, Wham-O can process Quik-Gro further into an industrial cleaner, called Quik-Kleen, which can be sold for $6 per gallon. Quik-Kleen production requires additional conversion costs of $7,000 per 10,000-gallon batch. Also, 30 percent of the gallons of Quik-Gro will evaporate during processing.

fields or processed further in the refining plant? If refined, should motor oil, gasoline, fuel oil, kerosene, or lubricants be made?

In deciding to process a joint product further, all costs previously incurred become sunk costs and are irrelevant.[8] These joint product costs are incurred prior to the stage at which processing can stop and the product can be sold. That is, joint product costs are irrelevant in decisions about what to do with a product from the split-off point forward. Relevant items are the future, differential costs that will be incurred and the future, differential revenue that will be generated as a result of subsequent processing into final products. It will always be profitable to continue processing a joint product after the split-off point so long as the incremental revenue from the processing exceeds the incremental processing costs. This is demonstrated in the UNR Ranch case and Exhibit 19–9.

The first decision point is at "Time 0." The decision alternatives are to sell the pig for $100 or process it further into quarters. The students, with the help

---

[8] Chapter 6 introduced joint products and presented methods for allocating joint production costs incurred prior to the split-off point. Because joint processing costs are sunk and are not relevant to the decision about what to do with the joint products, joint production cost allocations to the products are not necessary and are also irrelevant to the decision.

■■ EXHIBIT 19–8
Wham-O's Sell-or-Process-Further Decision

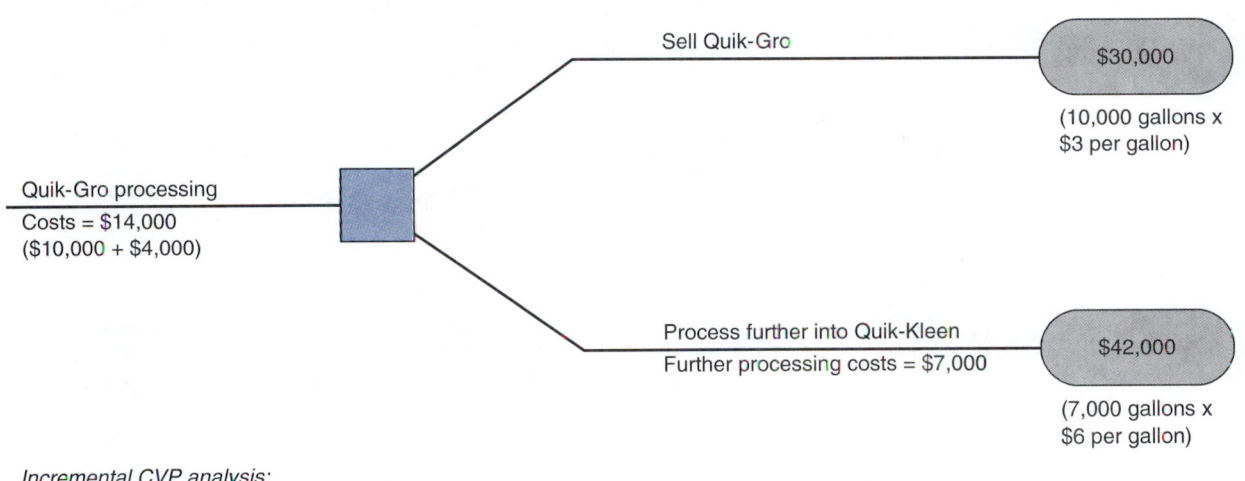

Incremental CVP analysis:

ΔRevenues from further processing	+$12,000
Less: ΔIncremental costs from further processing	<7,000>
ΔProfit from further processing	+$ 5,000

INSIGHTS & APPLICATIONS

UNR Ranch Pig Production

The School of Agriculture at the University of Nevada, Reno (UNR) owns many farms and ranches. Among them is the Pig Farm. UNR's Agricultural Experimental Station provides high-grade feed, and students raise high-quality pigs.

At the end of the spring semester, the students are faced with a decision about what to do with the pigs they raised. Raising a piglet costs $75. The pigs can be sold to a local meat-processing plant for $100 each or processed further.

Further processing first results in the pig being slaughtered and quartered. Joint processing costs to this split-off point are $200. The quarters can be sold to local casinos for use in their restaurants or processed further into ham, pork chops, sausage, and other end products. The current market prices for pig quarters and final products, along with the costs for processing each quarter further into its final products, are presented in Exhibit 19–9.

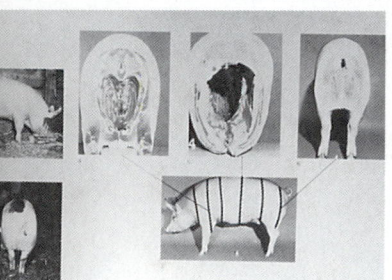

Meat processing plants make sell-or-process-further decisions.

of a management accounting major, decided to process further based on the following analysis:

ΔRevenues from further processing ($325 − $100)	+$225
Less Δincremental costs from further processing	<200>
ΔProfit from further processing	+$ 25

The costs of raising the piglet, incurred prior to the decision point (Time 0), are irrelevant as they have already been incurred and are sunk.

The second decision faced by the students is whether to sell the quarters at the split-off point (Time 1) or further process each quarter into its final products. They performed the same incremental CVP analysis for each quarter:

QUARTER 1:

ΔRevenues from further processing ($300 − $100)	+$200
Less Δincremental costs from further processing	<100>
ΔProfit from further processing	+$100

QUARTER 2:

ΔRevenues from further processing ($400 − $100)	+$300
Less Δincremental costs from further processing	<150>
ΔProfit from further processing	+$150

QUARTER 3:

ΔRevenues from further processing ($150 − $75)	+$75
Less Δincremental costs from further processing	<75>
ΔProfit from further processing	$–0–

QUARTER 4:

ΔRevenues from further processing ($100 − $50)	+$50
Less Δincremental costs from further processing	<80>
ΔProfit from further processing	<$30>

Processing quarter 4 has an opportunity cost, so the students decided to sell that quarter of the pig instead of processing it further. They did decide to process the first two quarters further, realizing differential profits of $250 ($100 + $150). Since it was close to summer break and they had a lot of other school work to do, they decided to sell quarter 3 rather than processing

EXHIBIT 19–9
UNR Pig Farm's Joint Processing Decision

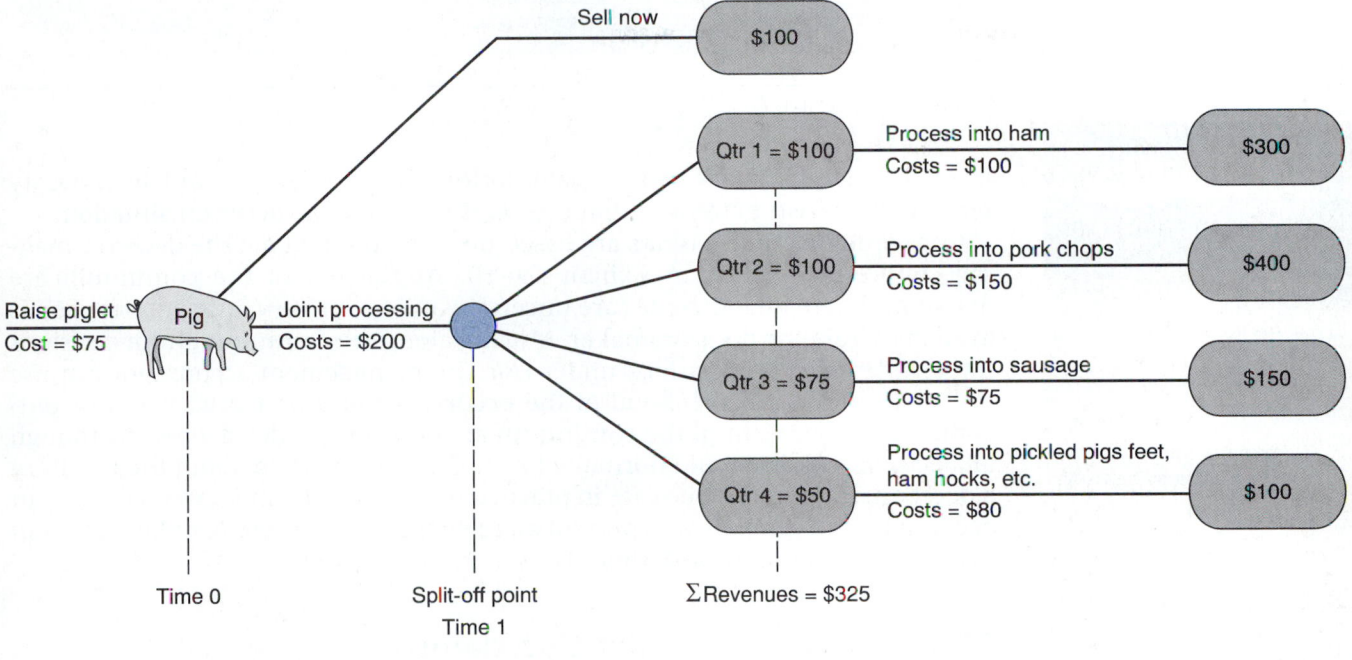

it into sausage. There is no opportunity cost or benefit from processing this quarter further.

However, the agriculture class in the previous fall semester decided to process quarter 3 further. Students are paid an hourly wage to work at the Pig Farm. It was close to Christmas, and they wanted the extra money (instead of the extra time off) from producing sausage. In situations that have no differential profit, profit managers may want to leave the further processing decision to their workers. At certain times, the workers may want the extra work and wages. At other times, they may prefer the time off.

DECISION MAKING UNDER CONDITIONS OF UNCERTAINTY AND RISK

Most decision models are formulated and solved assuming the availability of *perfect* information. This situation is generally referred to as **decision making under certainty.** For example, if the sales price per unit is forecast at $10 and variable cost is budgeted at $4, then the contribution margin is $6—no more, no less. The availability of *uncertain* information about decision alternatives leads to two other categories of decision-making situations:

- Decisions under risk
- Decisions under uncertainty

Decision making under risk involves situations in which information can be expressed in terms of probabilities. Under risk conditions, management recognizes that the budgeted CMU, sales volume, and similar data are not known with certainty. Rather, they are random variables that can be represented in terms of probability distributions, even though their exact values are unknown.

Decision making under uncertainty involves situations in which no probabilities can be determined because outcomes and events are not known. Thus,

LEARNING OBJECTIVE 6

Describe how incremental CVP analysis is used for decision making under conditions of uncertainty and risk.

■■■ EXHIBIT 19–10
The Decision-Making Continuum

Decisions Under Uncertainty	Decisions Under Risk	Decisions Under Certainty
Little or no information	Information based on probabilities	Perfect information

Deciding to build a thermal power plant may be risky.

from the standpoint of the available information, certainty and uncertainty represent the two extreme situations, and risk is the in-between situation.

Consequently, all decisions are based on some point along the decision-making continuum shown in Exhibit 19–10. At the left of the continuum are decisions where the outcomes are uncertain and no, or very little, information is available to aid the decision maker. Moving along the continuum from decisions under *uncertainty* to decisions under *risk*, the management accountant can use probabilities for the likelihood of the occurrence of a particular event or outcome. At the far right of the continuum are decisions under *certainty*. Although all decision makers would normally like to be totally certain about the results of a decision, this is rarely the case in practice. The role of the modern management accountant is to prepare and present all relevant information including different events that may occur and their associated probabilities.

Decision Making under Uncertainty

Bobbi's Boutique (see p. 897) demonstrates some of the uncertainties commonly faced by new entrepreneurs. The payoff table (or matrix) for Bobbi's swimsuit decision is shown in Exhibit 19–11. In a payoff table, the actions are listed on the left as rows, and the events (sales volumes) are listed at the top as columns. The payoffs (incremental contribution margins) for each action-event outcome are listed in the matrix cells; one payoff is associated with each action-event pair.

If the number of swimsuits that will be sold during the season (the event in this case) could be known with certainty before the order is placed, Bobbi would have an easy time making the decision. For example, if the demand will be 150, then she would merely look down column V_2 in the payoff table and choose the action that yields the highest payoff (which is $2,100 for A_3) and order 300 swimsuits. In real-world situations, however, profit center managers will not know with certainty which events will occur. Choosing the optimal decision in the face of uncertainty is the essence of the decision maker's problem. Some common criteria for choosing the "best" course of action follow.

MAXIMIN CRITERION. The maximin criterion maximizes the minimum profit of the various alternatives. This decision-making strategy entails "picking the best of the worst." In other words, choose the action that has the highest incremental contribution margin (CM) associated with its worst outcome. The action of ordering 100 swimsuits (A_1) provides the "maximum minimum" (maximin) payoff of $700 ($A_2$'s minimum payoff is $0 and A_3's minimum payoff is $600). The maximin criterion is an ultraconservative criterion because it hedges against the worst thing that can happen.[9]

MAXIMAX CRITERION. The maximax criterion maximizes the maximum profit. Where maximin is overly pessimistic, maximax is superoptimistic. Maximax chooses the action that produces the "best of the best." Using this criterion, Bobbi would purchase 300 swimsuits in order to take advantage of the price

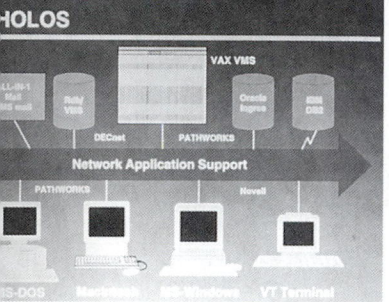

Computers assist executives in decision-making. Courtesy of Holistic Systems, Inc.

[9] If the payoff table contained costs (or losses) instead of profits, the maximin criterion would have to be reversed to minimax; that is, minimize the maximum cost.

INSIGHTS & APPLICATIONS

Bobbi's Boutique

Bobbi Ayarbe, the owner of Bobbi's Boutique, must decide how many women's swimsuits of a certain style to order for the summer season. This particular style must be ordered in batches of 100. If the order is for 100, the cost is $50 per swimsuit. If the order is for 200, the cost is $45 per swimsuit. If the order is for 300 or more, the cost is $38 per swimsuit. During the summer season, the selling price is $60. Any swimsuits left unsold at the end of the season can be sold for $30 in an "end-of-season clearance sale."

Bobbi, new to the business and unsure about her customers' demand for this style of swimsuit, cannot estimate sales volume or even establish a probability distribution of potential sales. So, based on her judgment, Bobbi picked sales volume of 100, 150, and 200.

Clearly, she cannot sell more swimsuits than she orders. Often, customers buying swimsuits also purchase related products, such as hats, matching beach shoes, and the like. If Bobbi orders less than is demanded, she projects she will lose $3 in contribution margin from the sales of these related products for each swimsuit a customer wants to buy but cannot because it is out of stock.

■■ EXHIBIT 19–11
Payoff Table for Bobbi's Boutique

	EVENTS (SALES VOLUMES)		
ACTIONS	V_1 100	V_2 150	V_3 200
A_1: ORDER 100 SWIMSUITS	$1,000	$ 850	$ 700
A_2: ORDER 200 SWIMSUITS	–0–	1,500	3,000
A_3: ORDER 300 SWIMSUITS	600	2,100	3,600

CMU calculations:

Normal sales:
   A_1 = $10 per suit ($60 sales price − $50 purchase price) if 100 ordered
   A_2 = $15 per suit ($60 − $45 purchase price) if 200 ordered
   A_3 = $22 per suit ($60 − $38 purchase price) if 300 ordered

Year-end sales:
   A_1 = no year-end sales since only 100 suits ordered
   A_2 = <$15> per suit ($30 sales price − $45 purchase price) if 200 ordered
   A_3 = <$8> per suit ($30 − $38 purchase price) if 300 ordered

Cell value calculations:

		ΔCM
A_1V_1:	CMU = $10, volume = 100	$1,000
A_1V_2:	($10 × 100 suits) − ($3 CMU lost × 50 suits excess demand)	850
A_1V_3:	($10 × 100 suits) − ($3 CMU lost × 100 suits excess demand)	700
A_2V_1:	($15 × 100 suits) + (<$15> × 100 sold at year-end)	–0–
A_2V_2:	($15 × 150 suits) + (<$15> × 50 sold at year-end)	1,500
A_2V_3:	($15 × 200 suits)	3,000
A_3V_1:	($22 × 100 suits) + (<$8> × 200 sold at year-end)	600
A_3V_2:	($22 × 150 suits) + (<$8> × 150 sold at year-end)	2,100
A_3V_3:	($22 × 200 suits) + (<$8> × 100 sold at year-end)	3,600

---

discount, sell 200 during the summer season, and sell 100 at year-end, thus realizing a maximum profit of $3,600.

The maximax criterion may be used by enterprises that can absorb the worst outcomes or by enterprises that need to "go for broke" to survive. This criterion is a high-risk strategy, as the recommended course is to choose the action that can yield the best outcome regardless of the other potential outcomes.

MINIMAX REGRET CRITERION.   The minimax regret criterion focuses on the opportunity cost ("regret") that might result from choosing a particular course of action. Regret is measured for a specific outcome as the difference between the best possible payoff and the actual payoff for each event. Using the minimax regret criterion, the decision maker selects the action that minimizes the maximum loss (or regret) or maximizes the minimum payoff.

An enterprise that is struggling to survive may employ this decision criterion in order to reduce the chance of failure. The minimax regret criterion may also be used as a hedging strategy when minimizing losses is more important than maximizing profits. Minimax regret is a risk-averse decision criterion.

To use the minimax regret decision rule, the payoff table is converted to a regret table, as illustrated in Exhibit 19–12. Each entry in the payoff table is subtracted from the largest entry in its column. The result is the opportunity cost of that outcome. It is entered into the corresponding cell of the regret table. To illustrate this for cell V_1A_3 of the regret table:

Largest entry in column V_1 of the payoff table	$1,000
Less cell V_1A_3 value from the payoff table	<600>
Regret Table value for cell V_1A_3	$400

The largest entry in a column will have zero regret. The action yielding the highest incremental contribution margin for each volume (event) is the most profitable alternative for that event. Thus, it has an opportunity benefit rather than an opportunity cost.

If Bobbi Ayarbe orders 100 swimsuits and the demand is 200, then her regret is $2,900 because she could have made $2,900 more by ordering 300 swimsuits had she known beforehand that demand would actually be 200 swimsuits. If, however, she had ordered 100 swimsuits and demand is 100 swimsuits, her regret is zero.

The optimum action is to order 300 swimsuits, which minimizes her maximum regret. This is shown in the table entitled "Maximum Regrets for Each Action" in Exhibit 19–12.

■■EXHIBIT 19–12
Minimax Calculations for Bobbi's Boutique

PAYOFF TABLE

		EVENTS	
ACTIONS	V_1 100	V_2 150	V_3 200
A₁: ORDER 100 SWIMSUITS	$1,000	$ 850	$ 700
A₂: ORDER 200 SWIMSUITS	–0–	1,500	3,000
A₃: ORDER 300 SWIMSUITS	600	2,100	3,600

REGRET TABLE

		EVENTS	
ACTIONS	V_1 100	V_2 150	V_3 200
A₁: ORDER 100 SWIMSUITS	—	$1,250	$2,900
A₂: ORDER 200 SWIMSUITS	$1,000	600	600
A₃: ORDER 300 SWIMSUITS	400	—	—

MAXIMUM REGRETS FOR EACH ACTION

ACTIONS	MAXIMUM REGRET
A₁: ORDER 100 SWIMSUITS	$2,900
A₂: ORDER 200 SWIMSUITS	1,000
A₃: ORDER 300 SWIMSUITS	400

Decision Making under Risk

When probabilities for various demand levels can be estimated, managers move into that portion of the decision-making continuum designated as decision making under risk. The probabilities are used to calculate the expected value of each action. The expected value of an action is the weighted average of the payoffs for that action, where the weights are the probabilities of the various mutually exclusive events that can occur.

EXPECTED VALUE CRITERION.   The expected value criterion involves the following steps:

- Assigning a probability to each event with the probabilities summing to one
- Calculating the expected value of each action by multiplying each incremental contribution margin by its corresponding probability and summing the results
- Choosing the action whose expected value is the largest

To illustrate the calculations, assume Bobbi assigns the following probability distribution to the events based on past data, experience, and judgment:

Event	Probability
V_1: demand = 100	0.5
V_2: demand = 150	0.3
V_3: demand = 200	0.2
	1.0

Bobbi's expected values (profits) for each action are shown in Exhibit 19–13.

Action A_1: Order 100 Swimsuits

Event	Probability	Profit	Weighted Profit
V_1: demand = 100	0.5	$1,000	$500
V_2: demand = 150	0.3	850	255
V_3: demand = 200	0.2	700	140
	1.0		$895

Expected profit = $895

Action A_2: Order 200 Swimsuits

Event	Probability	Profit	Weighted Profit
V_1: demand = 100	0.5	$ –0–	$ –0–
V_2: demand = 150	0.3	1,500	450
V_3: demand = 200	0.2	3,000	600
	1.0		$1,050

Expected profit = $1,050

Action A_3: Order 300 Swimsuits

Event	Probability	Profit	Weighted Profit
V_1: demand = 100	0.5	$ 600	$300
V_2: demand = 150	0.3	2,100	630
V_3: demand = 200	0.2	3,600	720
	1.0		$1,650

Expected profit = $1,650

EXHIBIT 19–13
Bobbi's Boutique Expected Profits

Using the expected value criterion, she should order 300 swimsuits with an expected incremental contribution margin and profit of $1,650.

DECISION-TREE ANALYSIS.   The preceding examples presented decision criteria for evaluating single-stage alternatives. No future decisions depended on the decision taken now. This section considers a multistage decision process in which dependent decisions are made in tandem. The decision tree is a graphical tool that facilitates a multistage decision process. Each event in the decision process is shown by a separate branch of the decision tree. This graphical approach often helps to clarify a complicated decision problem. The decision tree helps profit center managers examine all possible outcomes and facilitates an orderly, rational process.

The decision tree, which is normally drawn from left to right, shows actions, events, and their resulting payoffs (in the final branches of the decision tree). The value (outcome) of each branch is multiplied by its probability of occurrence to determine the expected payoff of that particular branch's outcome.

The decision tree shown in Exhibit 19–14 summarizes Telstar's alternatives presented in the *Insights & Applications* on page 901. Telstar management assumes that VSAT sales will be either high or low. Starting with node 1, a decision point, management must decide whether to build a large factory or a small factory. Node 2 is an event with two branches representing the high- and low-sales outcomes. Node 3 is also an event with two branches representing high and low sales.

Telstar management will consider possible future expansion of the small factory only if sales over the first two year turns out to be high. This is the reason node 4 represents a decision point with its two branches; that is, the "expansion" and "no expansion" decisions. Again, nodes 5 and 6 are events with the branches emanating from each representing high and low sales. The numbers at the end of the terminal branches represent the corresponding profits.

EXHIBIT 19–14
Decision Tree for Telstar's Factory Capital Project

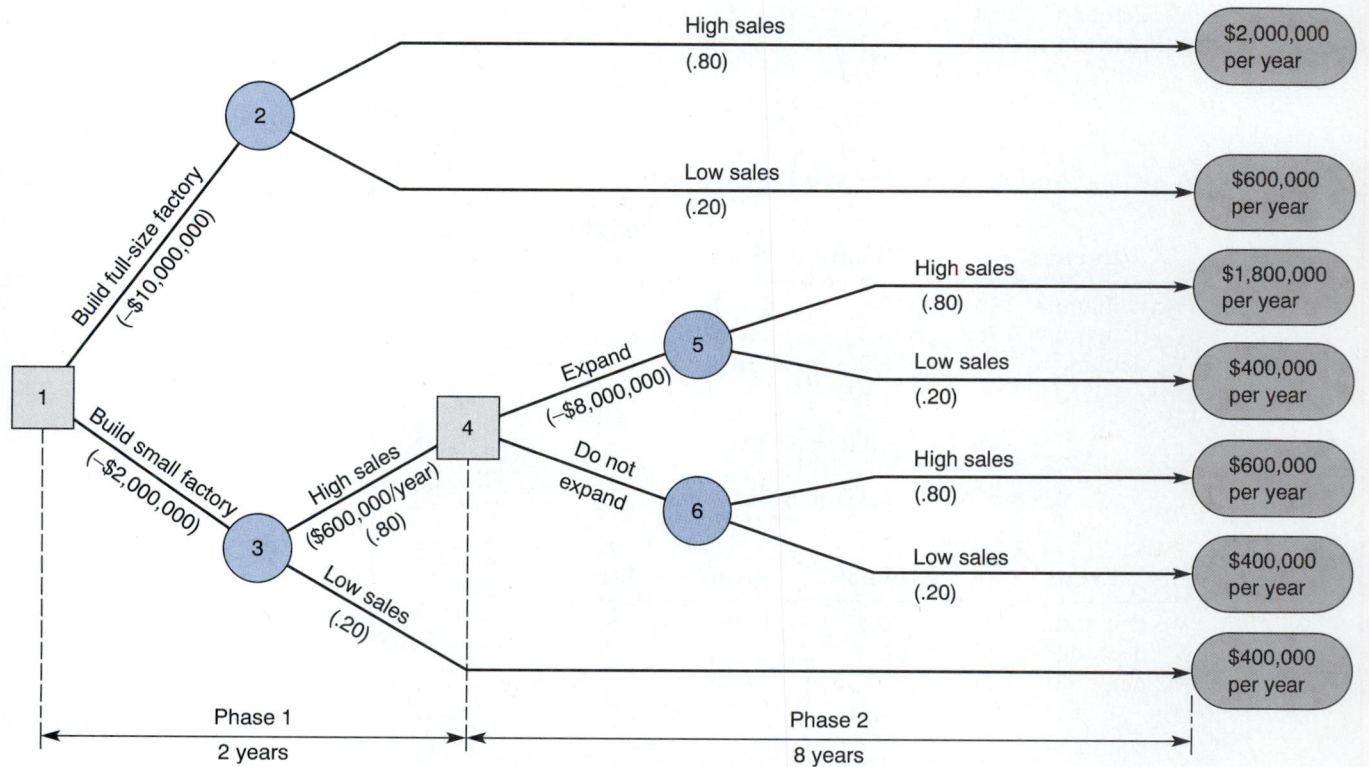

INSIGHTS & APPLICATIONS

Telstar's Capital Project Alternatives

Telstar is planning on making very small aperture terminals (VSATs) for telecommunication applications. The company has the option of building a full-size factory, or a small factory now and then deciding two years from now whether it should be expanded.

The multiphase decision problem arises because if Telstar decides to construct a small factory now, another decision must be made in two years regarding expansion. The decision therefore involves two phases:

Phase 1. A decision must be made now regarding the size of the factory.

Phase 2. A decision must be made two years from now regarding expansion, assuming that Telstar decides to construct a small factory now.

Telstar, as part of its strategic planning process, is interested in studying the capital project decision over a 10-year period. A market survey indicates that the probabili-ties of high and low sales over the next 10 years are .80 and .20, respectively. The immediate construction of a full-size factory will cost $10 million and a small factory will cost $2 million. The expansion of the small factory two years from now is expected to cost $8 million. Alternatives and estimates of their associated annual profits are as follows:

- A full-size factory and high sales will generate profits of $2,000,000 annually. If demand is low, profits will be $600,000 annually.
- If a small factory is built now, Telstar will consider expansion only if sales for the first two years are high.
- An expanded small factory with high sales will provide profits of $1,800,000 annually. If demand is low, profits will be $400,000 annually.
- A small factory with no expansion and high sales will yield a profit of $600,000 for each of the 10 years.
- A small factory with no expansion and high sales in the first two years followed by low sales will generate a profit of $400,000 in each of the remaining eight years.
- The market survey indicates that if sales are low for the first two years, with a small factory they will remain low for the remaining eight years, producing a profit of $400,000 annually.

The alternatives are evaluated using the expected value criterion. The decision analysis process is performed by **backward induction,** which starts with the payoffs at the far right side of the decision tree and works backward to a decision point. Moving backward to an event node from which the different branches emanate, the expected value of that particular node can be determined. Continuing to work backward through the decision tree, the expected value of making a specific decision is next determined. Therefore, the calculations start at the end of phase 2 and move backward to phase 1. For the last eight years, the two alternatives at node 4 are calculated as follows:

- Expected profit with expansion (node 5)
  = {[($1,800,000 × .80) + ($400,000 × .20)] × 8 years} − $8,000,000
  = $4,160,000

- Expected profit with no expansion (node 6)
  = [($600,000 × .80) + ($400,000 × .20)] × 8 years
  = $4,480,000

Consequently, at node 4, the decision calls for no expansion and the expected profit is $4,480,000. This is shown in Exhibit 19–15. A double line is drawn through the "expand" branch (leading to node 5) to indicate it has an opportunity cost and, thus, is not the preferred alternative.

The phase 1 calculations corresponding to node 1 are as follows:

- Expected profit with full-size factory (node 2)
  = {[($2,000,000 × .80) + ($600,000 × .20)] × 10 years} − $10,000,000
  = $7,200,000

■ EXHIBIT 19–15
Decision Tree for Telstar's Plant Expansion Project with Expected Values

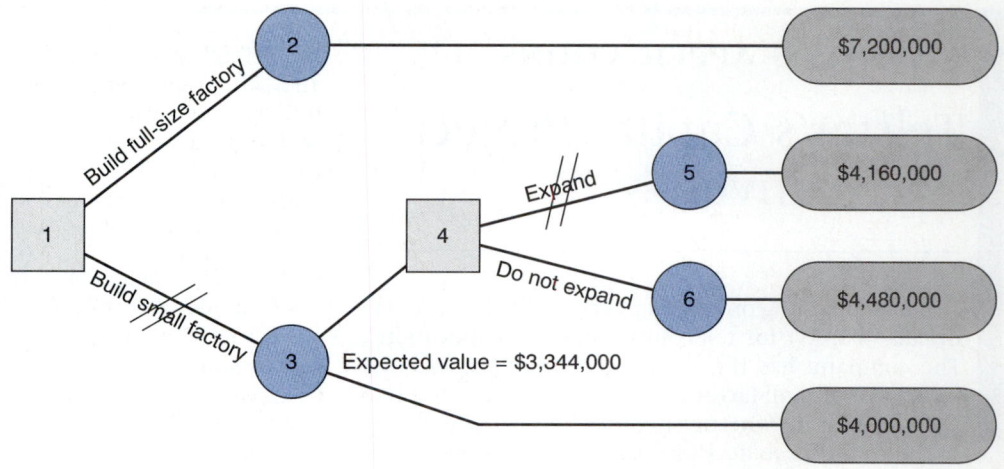

■ Expected profit with small factory (node 3)
= {[$4,480,000 + ($600,000 per year × 2 years)] × .80}
+ [($400,000 per year × 10 years) × .20] − $2,000,000
= $3,344,000

Thus, the optimal decision at node 1 is to build a full-size factory now. Its expected opportunity benefit is $3,856,000 ($7,200,000 − $3,344,000).

SUMMARY OF LEARNING OBJECTIVES

The major goals of this chapter were to enable you to achieve six learning objectives:

Learning objective 1.   Identify the relevant profit elements for short-run profit management decision making.

All revenue and cost information is relevant for profit management decision making except sunk costs, and revenues and costs that will not differ among alternatives. A machine can manufacture product A, which will provide revenue of $200,000, or it can be used to manufacture product B, which will provide revenue of $275,000. The differential, and thus relevant, revenue is $75,000. An opportunity benefit results if the machine is used to produce product B, and an opportunity cost results if product A is made.

On the cost side, if the standard direct labor cost to make 10,000 products without a new machine is $150, but is $10 with the new machine, the differential (relevant) cost is $1,400,000 [($150 − $10) × 10,000 products]. This is then compared to the machine's cost to determine its opportunity cost or benefit. If future fixed costs are $500,000 with or without the machine, then the $500,000 is irrelevant.

Although they do not represent actual dollar outlays, opportunity costs do represent economic benefits that are foregone as a result of pursuing some course of action. Therefore, they are relevant in decision making. Care must be exercised not to overlook these costs as they should be part of the quantitative analysis.

For a student, the cost of studying on Saturday night may be the sacrifice of not going to a social event. The student hopes that the opportunity benefits from studying will have a greater marginal utility than going to the social event.

Learning objective 2.   Use incremental CVP analysis in special-order decisions, and discuss the qualitative and legal factors associated with setting prices.

In determining whether to accept additional sales at a special price, management must consider productive capacity and the difference in revenue and cost caused by the new business. If the enterprise is operating at full capacity, the additional production may increase both fixed and variable manufacturing costs, or it may require giving up some normal sales. But if the current production volume is below full capacity, additional business may be undertaken without increasing fixed manufacturing costs. Therefore, with surplus capacity available, variable costs are usually the only costs to consider in deciding whether to accept or reject an order at a special price below the regular price.

In other situations, a special order may require incremental fixed costs to be incurred. If so, these fixed costs are relevant. When normal sales have to be given up because sufficient surplus capacity is not available, then the contribution margin lost on the sales given up also becomes relevant to the special-order decision.

Assume that a bicycle manufacturer is operating at 60 percent capacity. The standard absorptive manufacturing cost of the bicycle is $80, composed of $55 in variable costs and a standard FOH cost of $25. The regular price in the domestic market is $150. The manufacturer receives an offer from an exporter for 10,000 bicycles at a special price of $75. If the manufacturer accepts the offer, it will still be operating below full capacity. Pricing policies in the domestic market will not be affected, and no pricing laws, such as the *Robinson-Patman Act,* will be broken. Should the manufacturer accept the offer? Yes, because each bicycle will generate an incremental CMU of $20 ($75 special sales price less $55 in incremental variable production costs). Of course, if the order involves special shipping costs, these are also relevant.

One of the dangers of pricing an item below its regular price is that regular customers may take their business elsewhere. Also, various countries have passed antidumping laws, which impose duties on imported products found to have been sold in a particular country at less than fair market value. If the special price of $75 per bicycle will be viewed as an unfair price subject to antidumping penalties, the company should consider these penalties as well.

Learning objective 3.   Analyze scarce-resource situations.

Scarce-resource situations arise when an enterprise does not have enough of a certain direct material, class of labor, or direct technology to produce the expected volume of multiple products using that resource. In these situations, if only one product is to be produced until the shortage is over, it should be the product that yields the highest contribution margin per unit of the scarce resource. This is calculated by dividing each product's CMU by the standard quantity of the scarce resource it uses.

This analysis is only valid, though, when sales of one product do not affect sales of the other products, and only one product is to be produced during the shortage. Qualitative factors should also be considered in this decision. Will some normal business be lost if the other products are temporarily discontinued? Is this shortage expected to be a temporary or permanent problem? Is the industry so competitive that if the company loses business to competitors, they will be able to lower their sales prices and thus attract even more business away from this company?

Learning objective 4.   Perform incremental CVP analysis for the make-or-buy decision, and discuss the qualitative factors applicable to such decisions.

The decision of whether to produce a component of the company's final product internally or to buy the part from a supplier is called the make-or-buy decision. In a make-or-buy decision, management considers only the costs relevant to the decision. If the total relevant costs of production are less than the cost of buying the part, it should be produced in-house.

To illustrate, a company has been purchasing a part for $4, but the company has excess capacity and feels it can produce 60,000 parts per period at the following costs:

Direct materials	$1.50
Direct labor	1.00
Variable overhead	0.90
	$3.40

Fixed costs are expected to increase by $10,000 per year if the part is made. The company, however, has an opportunity to let a small fabricator use these idle facilities for annual rent of $30,000. Should the company make or buy the part?

ΔCMU if made ($4.00 − $3.40)	+$ 0.60
× Volume	× 60,000
ΔContribution margin	+$36,000
Less Δfixed overhead	<10,000>
Opportunity cost of renting idle facilities	<30,000>
ΔProfit if made	<$ 4,000>

Based on this quantitative analysis, a $4,000 opportunity cost is associated with making the part. The future, extra FOH is relevant because it is different under the two alternatives. Also, the company would lose the annual rent of $30,000 if it chooses to make the part. Therefore, the $30,000 is treated as an opportunity cost of making the part.

As with all decisions, the company should consider qualitative factors, such as the following when considering a make-or-buy decision:

- Quality of the component
- Reliability of suppliers
- Technical capability of suppliers
- Financial strength and reputation of suppliers
- Confidentiality of sensitive information
- Impact on employees if the enterprise turns to outside suppliers

In this case, the company may choose to make the part because the extra $4,000 cost is not as important as the increased control it will have over part quality and availability if it makes the part. In other words, better control over quality and delivery from making the part is more important (has a greater marginal utility) than the $4,000 differential cost involved.

Learning objective 5.   Apply incremental CVP analysis to the sell-or-process-further decision.

In some manufacturing firms, a product can be sold at a certain point in the process (e.g., at its split-off point), or it can be processed further into a final product and sold. If the increase in revenue generated from processing is more than the additional processing costs, then further processing is advisable.

A slaughterhouse can sell 40,000 raw hams per year at an average price of $20 per ham at the point where hogs are butchered and sold to meat distributors, or the slaughterhouse can cure, cut, and package the hams and sell them for an average price of $38 per ham. The additional processing costs are $480,000. Should the hams be processed further?

ΔRevenues if processed further [($38 − $20) × 40,000 hams]	$720,000
ΔIncremental processing costs	<480,000>
ΔProfits from further processing	$240,000

There is a $240,000 advantage (opportunity benefit) to processing the raw hams further.

Learning objective 6.   Describe how incremental CVP analysis is used for decision making under conditions of uncertainty and risk.

Decision making can be thought of as taking place along a continuum and can be categorized into three types depending on the information available:

- Decision making under uncertainty
- Decision making under risk
- Decision making under certainty

A number of criteria for making decisions under uncertainty exist based on the assumption that no probability distributions are available. It is usually assumed that payoffs (or outcomes) can be calculated for each of the alternatives. The following criteria are used under such conditions:

- Maximin criterion
- Maximax criterion
- Minimax regret criterion

In decision making under risk, outcomes can be expressed probabilistically. The expected values of outcomes can be calculated and expressed within decision trees to provide a graphic picture of single-stage and multistage decision problems. Many decision-making situations can use the expected value criterion with good results. Moreover, this criterion is analytically simple, which makes it particularly appealing to decision makers.

IMPORTANT TERMS

Backward induction   A form of decision-tree analysis, which works backward from the end branches of the tree diagram to the first decision fork and carries forward only the best action, each step of the way, while eliminating all inferior ones.

Decision making under certainty   A situation in which the decision maker has perfect information.

Decision making under risk   A situation in which the degree of knowledge about outcomes is expressed in terms of probabilities.

Decision making under uncertainty   A situation in which probabilities of outcomes are unknown or cannot be determined.

Differential cost and revenue   The costs and revenues that are different between alternatives. Differential elements occurring in the future are relevant to profit management decisions.

Incremental cost and revenue   The additional costs incurred and revenue generated because of a particular alternative. Incremental elements that differ between alternatives are relevant to profit management decisions.

Long-run decisions   Decisions that affect asset investments and the long-run profitability of an enterprise.

Make-or-buy decision   A decision that compares the cost of producing a component or providing a service internally with the cost of purchasing the component or service from an external supplier.

Opportunity benefit   The differential profit of the best (most profitable) alternative over the second best alternative.

Opportunity cost   A potential benefit that is foregone because one course of action is chosen over another. It is the difference between the incremental profit of that alternative and the incremental profit of the best alternative.

Outsourcing   When an organization decides to acquire a service from an external supplier rather than performing that service in-house.

Privatization   To turn over public properties and services to private enterprise.

Profit elements   The items that effect profit, which are composed of sales volume, sales price, variable costs, contribution margin, and fixed costs.

Relevant   A term used to describe those costs and revenues that are pertinent to the decision-making process. Relevant profit elements occur in the future and differ between alternatives.

Scarce-resource decision   A decision to produce one product while temporarily suspending the production of other products because of a shortage in a resource used in manufacturing those products.

Sell-or-process-further decision   A decision that involves choosing whether to sell a marketable product at some intermediate stage or process it further into a different form to be sold at a later stage.

Short-run decisions   Operational decisions that involve selecting an action that will have an impact on the enterprise over a relatively short time period. These decisions are usually fairly routine and do not require significant and permanent resource commitments.

Special-order decision   A situation in which management is considering accepting a onetime sales order at a price below its normal sales price.

Sunk cost   A cost already incurred. Because it has already happened, it cannot be changed. Sunk costs are irrelevant in calculating the differential profitability of future alternatives.

DEMONSTRATION PROBLEMS

■ DEMONSTRATION PROBLEM 1 *Determining relevant qualitative and quantitative factors.*

Magna Company produces motors that fit into its main product line of landscaping equipment. Because material costs have steadily increased, management is reviewing the decision to continue making these motors. The management accountant has identified the following facts:

1. The equipment used to produce the motors has a book value of $400,000.
2. The space now occupied by the motor manufacturing department could be used for storage, thereby eliminating the current need to rent storage space.
3. Management is planning on opening a market in Kansas.
4. Comparable motors can be purchased from an outside supplier for $100.
5. The outside supplier will sign a long-term contract and a nondisclosure agreement.
6. The people who work in the motor manufacturing department would be discharged and given four weeks' severance pay.
7. A $100,000 promissory note is still outstanding on the equipment used in producing the motors.

Required:
Indicate by number the relevant qualitative and quantitative factors.

SOLUTION TO DEMONSTRATION PROBLEM 1

RELEVANT QUALITATIVE FACTORS	RELEVANT QUANTITATIVE FACTORS
—	2
4	4
5	—
6	6

■ DEMONSTRATION PROBLEM 2 *Make-or-buy decision under risk.*

Paxton Company needs a special part for the coming year. The equipment needed to make the part can be rented for $130,000 for one year. Alternatively, Paxton can buy the parts from another company and avoid the rental cost. Because the demand may be high with a probability of 0.7 or low with a probability of 0.3 and contribution margins vary, the management accountant prepared the following decision tree:

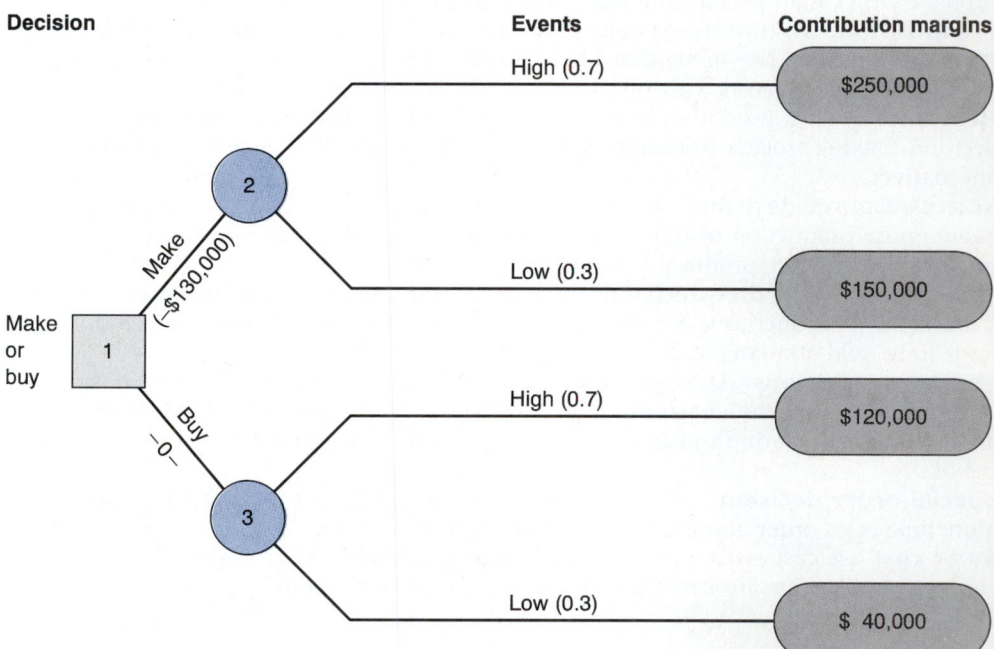

Required:
Calculate the expected value of the decision at node 1.

SOLUTION TO DEMONSTRATION PROBLEM 2

Expected value of making the parts (node 2)
        = ($250,000 × .7) + ($150,000 × .3) − $130,000
        = $90,000

Expected value of buying the parts (node 3)
        = ($120,000 × .7) + ($40,000 × .3)
        = $96,000

The largest expected value (contribution margin) is achieved if the parts are bought from the outside supplier.

■ **DEMONSTRATION PROBLEM 3**   *Sell-or-process-further decision.*
Viking Processors makes three products from a single direct material input. Cost and revenue data are as follows:

	PRODUCT		
	A	B	C
Sales value at the split-off point	$150,000	$120,000	$ 80,000
Sales value after further processing	230,000	160,000	100,000
Allocated joint costs	100,000	90,000	40,000
Costs of further processing	60,000	50,000	10,000

Required:
Determine which products should be sold at the split-off point and which should be processed further.

SOLUTION TO DEMONSTRATION PROBLEM 3
Analysis of the sell-or-process-further decision:

	PRODUCT		
	A	B	C
Sales value after further processing	$230,000	$160,000	$100,000
Less sales value at the split-off point	<150,000>	<120,000>	<80,000>
Incremental revenue from further processing	$ 80,000	$ 40,000	$ 20,000
Less cost of further processing	<60,000>	<50,000>	<10,000>
Incremental profit ⟨loss⟩ from further processing	$ 20,000	<$ 10,000>	$ 10,000

This analysis shows that products A and C should both be processed further. Product B should be sold at the split-off point. Allocated joint costs are irrelevant because they are sunk.

■ **DEMONSTRATION PROBLEM 4**   *Special-order decision.*
Parker Company sells its product at a price of $30 per unit. Parker's standard absorptive manufacturing cost based on a capacity of 200,000 units is as follows:

Direct materials	$ 6
Direct labor	4
Overhead (60% is fixed)	10
Cost per unit	$20

Parker received a special order for 20,000 units from a foreign distributor. The only differential selling costs that would be incurred on this order would be $3 per unit for shipping. Parker has sufficient existing capacity to manufacture the additional units.

Required:
a. Determine the minimum selling price that Parker should set for the special order.

b. Determine the selling price that should be set if Parker's targeted profit on the special order is $100,000.

SOLUTION TO DEMONSTRATION PROBLEM 4

a. The minimum selling price should be equal to the incremental costs associated with the special order. The incremental costs are as follows:

Direct materials	$ 6
Direct labor	4
Variable overhead (40% of $10)	4
Shipping cost	3
Incremental costs per unit	$17

Thus, the minimum selling price is $17. Of the total overhead, only VOH is considered an incremental cost because the fixed overhead will be incurred regardless of whether the order is taken.

b. A target profit of $100,000 calls for an increase in the selling price of $5 ($100,000 ÷ 20,000 units). Therefore, the selling price required to achieve the target profit of $100,000 is $22 ($17 + $5).

■ **DEMONSTRATION PROBLEM 5**   *Decision making under uncertainty.*
Margo Reed is the marketing manager for a large manufacturer of sporting equipment. She has proposed to top management that the company open some specialty stores in one of three cities: Los Angeles, San Diego, or San Francisco. Although she has some previous experience in the specialty store business, the popularity of these stores is difficult to predict. She nevertheless categorizes the popularity into high, medium, and low and constructs the following payoff table:

	EVENTS		
ACTIONS	HIGH DEMAND	MEDIUM DEMAND	LOW DEMAND
LOS ANGELES	$10	$ 6	$4
SAN DIEGO	14	10	6
SAN FRANCISCO	20	12	5

Profits (i.e., payoffs) are in millions of dollars. Under conditions of uncertainty, Margo cannot predict anything about which volumes (demands) will most likely occur. She can, however, use various criteria for choosing the "best" course of action.

Required:
a. Using the maximin criterion, determine the city in which the specialty stores should be located.
b. Using the maximax criterion, determine the city in which the specialty stores should be located.
c. Construct a regret table using the minimax regret criterion.

SOLUTION TO DEMONSTRATION PROBLEM 5
a. Management will choose to open specialty stores in the city that will have the largest profitability under the worst state of nature (outcome). From Margo's payoff table, it is clear San Diego would be chosen because it has a minimum profit of $6 million for its worst case event (low demand). The worst outcome for Los Angeles is $4 million, and for San Francisco, $5 million.
b. In this superoptimistic scenario, management is adventuresome and attracted to large gains. San Francisco is chosen, with a $20 million profit, because this is the maximum profit across all demand levels.
c. Regret table:

	EVENTS		
ACTIONS	HIGH DEMAND	MEDIUM DEMAND	LOW DEMAND
LOS ANGELES	$10	$6	$2
SAN DIEGO	6	2	—
SAN FRANCISCO	—	—	1

Each column's regret figures are calculated by subtracting each payoff in a column from the highest payoff in that column. In other words, the opportunity costs of each action within each event (demand level) are the cells' values. Maximum regrets are as follows:

ACTION	MAXIMUM REGRETS
Los Angeles	$10
San Diego	6
San Francisco	1

Choosing San Francisco minimizes the maximum regret. This decision strategy is appropriate when management wants to minimize the opportunity cost of the worst event happening for each city.

■ **DEMONSTRATION PROBLEM 6**   *Decision making under risk.*
Management at Corvair Aircraft Dealers is considering stocking heavy utility helicopters on consignment. They will order one or two helicopters for this season's inventory, but no more or less. There is a $100,000 cost for carrying each excess helicopter and a $400,000 contribution margin for each helicopter sold. Following are the probabilities of the season's demand:

PROBABILITY	DEMAND
0.1	0
0.5	1
0.4	2
1.0	

Required:
a. Build a payoff table.
b. Construct a decision tree, and through backward induction, calculate the appropriate decision.

SOLUTION TO DEMONSTRATION PROBLEM 6

a.

Event / Action	Demand		
	0	1	2
Order 1 helicopter	<$100,000>	$400,000	$400,000
Order 2 helicopters	<$200,000>	$300,000	$800,000

b.

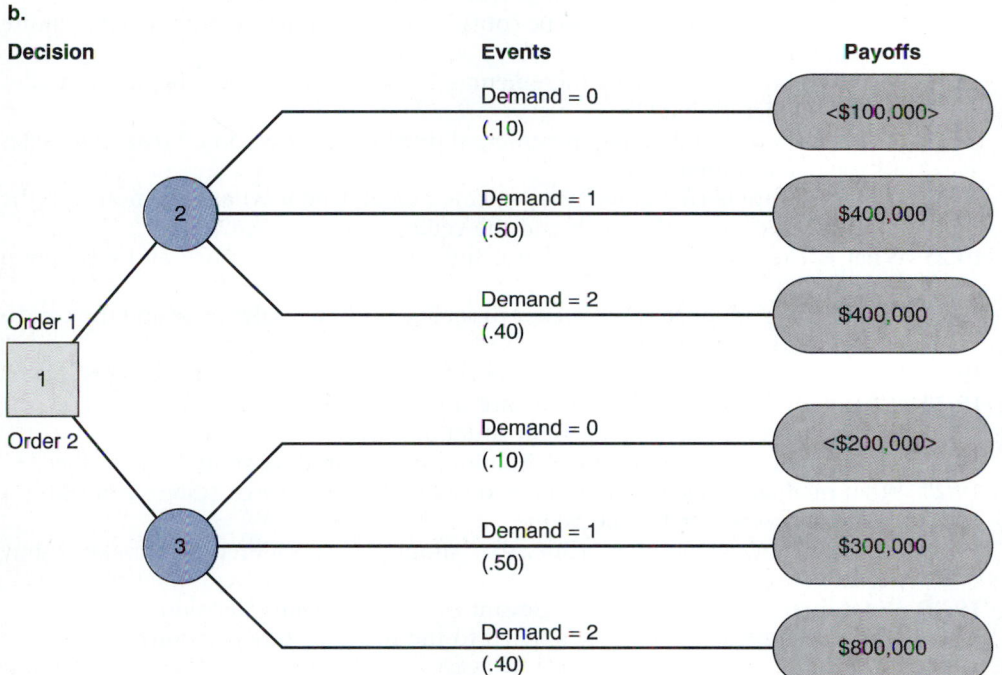

Expected value of ordering 1 helicopter:
$$= (<\$100,\!000> \times .10) + (\$400,\!000 \times .50) + (\$400,\!000 \times .40)$$
$$= \underline{\underline{\$350,\!000}}$$

Expected value of ordering 2 helicopters:
$$= (<\$200,\!000> \times .10) + (\$300,\!000 \times .50) + (\$800,\!000 \times .40)$$
$$= \underline{\underline{\$450,\!000}}$$

Thus, the optimal decision at node 1 is to order two helicopters, with an expected value of $450,000.

REVIEW QUESTIONS

19.1 List and briefly describe four profit management decision-making situations.

19.2 Distinguish between strategic long-run decisions and routine short-run decisions.

19.3 List the steps in a rational decision-making process.

19.4 What are the five profit elements and when are they relevant to short-run profit management decision making?

19.5 Describe the two characteristics of relevant profit elements.

19.6 Why are sunk costs irrelevant to short-run operational decisions?

19.7 Distinguish between incremental and differential profit elements. Under what conditions will they be the same? When will they be different?

19.8 Why is the relevant range an important factor in operational profit management decisions?

19.9 What is meant by the term opportunity cost? Give an example of an opportunity cost in decision making.

19.10 Define opportunity benefit. Under what circumstances will an alternative have an opportunity benefit instead of an opportunity cost?

19.11 What are the formulas for calculating an opportunity cost and an opportunity benefit?

19.12 What is the relationship between opportunity cost and marginal utility?

19.13 List three types of sales price-setting decisions.

19.14 How does a special-order situation differ from a normal sales price setting decision for the sales used in the master budget?

19.15 What is the minimum sales price for a special order that incurs no incremental fixed costs when adequate surplus capacity exists to fill the order?

19.16 Explain the relevance of plant capacity when a special-order decision is being considered.

19.17 What qualitative factors should be considered when a special order would require normal sales to be given up?

19.18 For special orders involving incremental fixed costs, how can a break-even sales volume be determined?

19.19 For special orders involving incremental fixed costs, how can a break-even sales price be determined?

19.20 Develop a simple cost-based price-setting model. Under what conditions can the floor price be used? When should the ceiling price be used?

19.21 What is the relationship between a full cost–based sales price and absorption costing?

19.22 What is the relationship between a variable cost–based sales price and the contribution margin approach?

19.23 Under which five conditions is an absorptive cost–based sales price appropriate?

19.24 What qualitative and legal factors are involved in setting prices?

19.25 Explain a scarce-resource decision situation.

19.26 In a temporary scarce-resource situation, which product should be produced?

19.27 What qualitative factors should be considered in the scarce-resource decision?

19.28 Illustrate a make-or-buy decision.

19.29 Are there any qualitative factors that should be considered in a make-or-buy decision?

19.30 What quantitative factors are relevant in a make-or-buy decision?

19.31 How can margin of safety be applied to the make-or-buy decision?

19.32 Explain how opportunity costs enter into the make-or-buy decision.

19.33 Explain why outsourcing and privatization involve make-or-buy decisions.

19.34 Characterize the sell-or-process-further decision.

19.35 "It will always be profitable to continue processing a joint product after the split-off point so long as the incremental revenue from such processing exceeds the incremental costs." Do you agree? Explain.

19.36 Distinguish between decision making under conditions of certainty, uncertainty, and risk.

19.37 What is the key difference between decision making under uncertainty and decision making under risk?

19.38 What is a payoff table? Can it be used for decision making under uncertainty and decision making under risk?

19.39 Explain why the maximin criterion is appropriate for a risk-averse decision maker.

19.40 Explain why the maximax criterion is appropriate for a risk-seeking, superoptimistic decision maker.

19.41 Explain how the minimax regret criterion is used in decision making.

19.42 How is expected value calculated and used in decision making under risky situations?

19.43 What is the nature of decision trees and how do they aid decision making?

CHAPTER-SPECIFIC PROBLEMS

These problems require responses based on concepts and techniques presented in the text.

19.44 *Multiple-choice questions.*

1. In a make-or-buy decision:

   a. Only variable costs are relevant.
   b. Fixed costs that can be avoided in the future are relevant.
   c. Fixed costs that will continue regardless of the decision are relevant.
   d. Only conversion costs are relevant.

2. In a make-or-buy decision, which of the following qualitative factors is usually considered?

   a. Special technology.
   b. Reliability of delivery.
   c. Special skills and materials requirements.
   d. Quality control.
   e. All of the above.

3. Which of the following qualitative factors favor the buy choice in a make-or-buy decision?

   a. Maintaining a long-run relationship with suppliers.
   b. Quality control.
   c. Use of idle capacity.
   d. All of the above.

4. In considering a special order that will enable a company to make use of presently idle capacity, which of the following costs would be irrelevant?

   a. Direct materials.
   b. Depreciation.
   c. Direct labor.
   d. Variable overhead.

5. From a long-run perspective, the major pitfall in the contribution margin approach to pricing is:

   a. Its failure to recognize depreciation expense.
   b. Its failure to recognize fixed costs.
   c. Its inability to control administrative costs.
   d. Its inability to control waste.

6. Expected value in decision making is:

a. A standard deviation using the probabilities as weights.
b. An arithmetic mean using the probabilities as weights.
c. The square root of the squared deviations.
d. The standard deviation divided by the coefficient of determination.

19.45 *Make-or-buy decision.* Marvel Company needs 10,000 units of a part to be used in the production of one of its products. If Marvel buys the part from Sterling Company instead of making it, Marvel could not use the released facilities in another manufacturing activity. Sixty percent of the fixed overhead applied will continue regardless of Marvel's decision. The following information is available:

Cost to Marvel to make the part:

Direct materials	$25
Direct labor	6
Variable overhead	14
Fixed overhead	15
	$60
Cost to buy the part	$56

Required:
a. Calculate Marvel's total relevant costs to make the part.
b. Determine which alternative is more attractive to Marvel and by what amount.

19.46 *Make-or-buy decision to maximize net benefits.* Stewart Industries has been producing two bearings, components B12 and B18, for use in production. Data regarding these two components follow:

	B12	B18
Machine hours required per unit	2.5	3.0
Standard cost per unit:		
Direct materials	$ 2.25	$ 3.75
Direct labor	4.00	4.50
Manufacturing overhead		
Variable*	2.00	2.25
Fixed**	3.75	4.50
	$12.00	$15.00

* Variable manufacturing overhead is applied on the basis of direct labor hours.
** Fixed manufacturing overhead is applied on the basis of machine hours.

Stewart's annual requirement for these components is 8,000 units of B12 and 11,000 units of B18. Recently, Stewart's management decided to devote additional machine time to other product lines, with the result that only 41,000 machine hours per year can be dedicated to the production of the bearings. An outside company has offered to sell Stewart the annual supply of the bearings at prices of $11.25 per unit for B12 and $13.50 per unit for B18. Stewart wants to schedule the otherwise idle 41,000 machine hours to produce bearings so that the company can minimize its costs (maximize its net benefits).

Required:
a. What is the net benefit (loss) per machine hour that would result if Stewart Industries accepts the supplier's offer of $13.50 per unit for component B18?
b. Determine the combination of purchasing and manufacturing that will maximize benefits.

[CMA adapted]

19.47 *Profit from processing further.* Ashwood Company manufactures three main products, F, G, and W, from a joint process. Joint costs are allocated on the basis of relative sales value at split-off. Additional information for June production activity follows:

	F	G	W	TOTAL
Units produced	50,000	40,000	10,000	100,000
Joint costs	?	?	?	$450,000
Sales value at split-off	$420,000	$270,000	$60,000	$750,000
Additional costs if processed further	$88,000	$30,000	$12,000	$130,000
Sales value if processed further	$538,000	$320,000	$78,000	$936,000

Required:
What is the opportunity cost or benefit from further processing of each product?

[AICPA adapted]

19.48 *Profit from processing further.* Warfield Corporation manufactures products C, D, and E from a joint process. Joint costs are allocated on the basis of relative sales value at split-off. Additional information follows:

	C	D	E	TOTAL
Units produced	6,000	4,000	2,000	12,000
Joint costs	$72,000	?	?	$120,000
Sales value at split-off	?	?	$30,000	$200,000
Additional costs if processed further	$14,000	$10,000	$6,000	$30,000
Sales value if processed further	$140,000	$60,000	$40,000	$240,000

Required:
a. What is the opportunity cost or benefit from further processing of each product?
b. Should product D be processed further and then sold?

[AICPA adapted]

19.49 *Sell-or-process-further decision.* The Yerrington Company has 1,000 obsolete water coolers at a manufacturing cost of $30,000. If the coolers are refurbished for $6,000, they could be sold for $10,000. If the coolers are scrapped, they could be sold for $2,000.

Required:
Determine which alternative is more attractive and indicate the total relevant costs for that alternative.

19.50 *Sell-or-process-further decision.* Yardley Corporation uses a joint process to produce products A, B, and C. Each product may be sold at its split-off point or processed further. Additional processing costs are entirely variable and are traceable to the respective products. Joint production costs were $50,000 and are allocated by Yardley using the relative sales value at the split-off point. Additional information follows:

PRODUCT	UNITS PRODUCED	SALES VALUE AT SPLIT-OFF	IF PROCESSED FURTHER SALES VALUE	IF PROCESSED FURTHER ADDITIONAL COSTS
A	20,000	$ 45,000	$60,000	$20,000
B	15,000	75,000	98,000	20,000
C	15,000	30,000	62,000	18,000

Required:
To maximize profits, which products should Yardley process further?

[AICPA adapted]

19.51 *Sell-or-process-further decision.* Watkins Company produces three products, X, Y, and Z, from a particular joint process. Each product may be sold at the point of split-off or processed further. Additional processing requires no special facilities, and production costs of further processing are entirely variable and traceable to the products involved. Last year all three products were processed beyond split-off. Joint production costs for the year were $60,000. Sales values and costs needed to evaluate Watkins' production policy follow:

		SALES	IF PROCESSED FURTHER	
PRODUCT	UNITS PRODUCED	VALUE AT SPLIT-OFF	SALES VALUE	ADDITIONAL COSTS
X	6,000	$25,000	$42,000	$9,000
Y	4,000	41,000	45,000	7,000
Z	2,000	24,000	32,000	8,000

Joint costs are allocated to the products in proportion to the relative physical volume of output.

Required:
a. For units of Z, what is the unit production cost most relevant to the sell-or-process-further decision?
b. To maximize profits, which products should Watkins process further?

[AICPA adapted]

19.52 *Special-order decision.* Baxter Company manufactures soccer balls. The estimated income statement for the year before any special order is as follows:

	AMOUNT	PER UNIT
Sales	$8,000,000	$20.00
Cost of goods sold	<6,800,000>	<17.00>
Gross profit	1,200,000	3.00
Administrative and selling	<320,000>	<0.80>
Operating income	$ 880,000	$ 2.20

Fixed costs included in the estimated income statement are $2,400,000 in cost of goods sold and $120,000 in administrative and selling expenses. Baxter received a special order for 60,000 soccer balls at $15 each. There will be no additional administrative and selling expenses if Baxter accepts. Baxter has sufficient capacity to manufacture 60,000 additional soccer balls.

Required:
Calculate the unit relevant cost of the special order and state whether Baxter should accept it.

19.53 *Decision making under uncertainty.* Following is a payoff table of an investor:

EVENTS

STATES OF NATURE

ACTIONS	WAR	PEACE	DEPRESSION
Defense stocks	20	1	−6
Junk bonds	9	8	0
High-grade bonds	4	4	4

Only three investment strategies are considered: defense stocks, junk bonds, and high-grade bonds. Also, only three states of nature are considered: war, peace, and depression. Ignore all impacts of capital gains, taxes, and so on, and assume that the investor has determined her rate of return (in percent) for each of the nine action-event combinations as shown in the payoff table. Also, assume probabilities cannot be determined.

Required:
a. Calculate the optimal action using the maximin criterion.
b. Calculate the optimal action using the maximax criterion.
c. Calculate the optimal action using the minimax regret criterion.

19.54 *Expected value criterion for introducing a new product and selecting a machine.* A company is considering three alternative machines to produce a new product. The cost structures (unit variable costs plus avoidable fixed costs) for the three machines are shown below. The selling price is unaffected by the machine used.

Single-purpose machine $0.60 + $20,000
Semiautomatic machine $0.40 + $50,000
Automatic machine $0.20 + $120,000

The demand for units of the new product is described by the following probability distribution:

DEMAND	PROBABILITY
200,000	0.4
300,000	0.3
400,000	0.2
500,000	0.1

Required:
a. Calculate expected demand. Calculate the expected costs of using the semiautomatic machine.
b. Based on expected demand calculated in Requirement (a), which machine should be selected?

[CMA adapted]

19.55 *Expected value criterion.* Your client wants your advice on which of two alternatives he should choose. One alternative is to sell an investment now for $10,000. Another alternative is to hold the investment three days, after which he can sell it for a certain selling price based on the following probabilities:

SELLING PRICE	PROBABILITY
$ 5,000	0.4
8,000	0.2
12,000	0.3
30,000	0.1

Required:
Using probability theory, which of the following is the most reasonable statement?
a. Hold the investment three days because the expected value of holding exceeds the current selling price.
b. Hold the investment three days because of the chance of getting $30,000 for it.
c. Sell the investment now because the current selling price exceeds the expected value of holding.
d. Sell the investment now because there is a 60% chance that the selling price will fall in three days.

[AICPA adapted]

19.56 *Expected profit.* The Tyson Company is considering hiring several new employees to handle an overload from a new contract. If the new people are not hired, there will be delays in contract work. The following payoff matrix has been prepared for analyzing whether new people are needed:

	HIRE NEW PEOPLE	DO NOT HIRE NEW PEOPLE
Retain new customers	$100,000	$75,000
Lose new customers	25,000	50,000

Based on past experience, the company expects to retain 75% of the new customers with no new hires.

Required:
Calculate the expected profit for the "no hire" decision.

[CMA adapted]

19.57 *Expected value analysis used in the make-or-buy decision.* The Unimat Company manufactures a unique thermostat that yields dramatic cost savings from effective climatic control of large buildings. The efficiency of the thermostat is dependent upon the quality of a specialized thermocoupler. These thermocouplers are purchased from Cosmic Company for $15 each.

Since early 1993, an average of 10% of the thermocouplers purchased from Cosmic have not met Unimat's quality requirements. The number of unusable thermocouplers has ranged from 5% to 25% of the total number purchased and has resulted in failures to meet production schedules. In addition, Unimat has incurred additional costs to replace the defective units because the rejection rate of the units is within the range agreed upon in the contract.

Unimat is considering a proposal to manufacture the thermocouplers. The company has the facilities and equipment to produce the components. The Engineering Department has designed a manufacturing system that will produce the thermocouplers with a defective rate of 4% of the number of units produced. The following schedule presents the engineer's estimates of the probabilities that different levels of variable manufacturing cost per thermocoupler will be incurred under this system. The variable manufacturing cost per unit includes a cost adjustment for the defective units at the 4% rate. Additional annual fixed costs incurred by Unimat if it manufactures the thermocoupler will amount to $32,500.

ESTIMATED VARIABLE MANUFACTURING COST PER GOOD THERMOCOUPLER UNIT	PROBABILITY OF OCCURRENCE
$10	0.1
12	0.3
14	0.4
16	0.2
	1.0

Unimat Company will need 18,000 thermocouplers to meet its annual demand requirements.

Required:
Prepare an expected value analysis to determine whether Unimat Company should manufacture the thermocouplers.

[CMA adapted]

19.58 *Scarce resources.* Jumpin Jack Clothing manufactures three different lines of children's clothing. Bell-bottom jump suits (product 1), western cut jumpers (product 2), and suspender jeans (product 3) all require the use of a special sewing machine. Information about the three products follows:

	PRODUCT		
	1	2	3
Sewing machine standard hours	5	4	2
Contribution margin per unit	$10	$12	$8

Not enough sewing machine hours are available to fill demand for all three product lines.

Required:
Assuming only one product line will be produced, which one should it be? Are there any assumptions about your analysis that management should be aware of?

19.59 *Scarce resources.* Custom Manufacturing runs a job shop. It has orders for three custom jobs, each requiring very specialized labor. Only one employee has the skills to do this type of work. The following information is available about the three jobs:

PRODUCT

	1	2	3
Standard direct labor hours	10	8	5
Contribution margin per unit	$10	$12	$8

Required:

Assuming only one job can be accepted because of the limited amount of specialized labor time available, which job is the most profitable?

19.60 *Scarce resources.* St. Mary's hospital performs three different types of blood tests for a certain disease. Each of these tests requires the use of a highly specialized molecular separation machine. The lab is considering performing only one of the tests and discontinuing the other two, because only one machine is currently available. The following information has been obtained from the accounting LAN:

TEST

	1	2	3
Machine time required (hours)	1.50	2.00	0.75
Contribution margin per test	$15	$20	$9

Required:

Which test should be performed, and which tests should be dropped? What ethical factors would you want the lab to consider in making this decision?

THINK-TANK PROBLEMS

Although these problems are based on chapter material, reading extra material, reviewing previous chapters, and using creativity may be required to develop workable solutions.

19.61 *Make-or-buy decision.* When you completed your audit of the Scoopa Company, management asked for your assistance in deciding whether to continue manufacturing a part or to buy it from an outside supplier. The part, which is named Faktron, is a component used in some of the finished products of the company.

From your audit working papers and from further investigation, you develop the following data as being typical of the company's operations:

■ The annual requirement for Faktrons is 5,000 units. The lowest quotation from a supplier was $8 per unit.

■ Faktrons have been manufactured in the Precision Machinery Department. If Faktrons are purchased from an outside supplier, certain machinery will be sold and would realize its book value.

■ Following are the total costs of the Precision Machinery Department during the year under audit when 5,000 Faktrons were made:

Direct materials	$67,500
Direct labor	50,000
Indirect labor	20,000
Light and heat	5,500
Power	3,000
Depreciation	10,000
Property taxes and insurance	8,000
Payroll taxes and other benefits	9,800
Other	5,000

■ The following Precision Machinery Department costs apply to the manufacture of Faktrons: direct materials, $17,500; direct labor, $28,000; indirect labor, $6,000; power, $300; other $500. The sale of the equipment used for Faktrons would reduce the following costs by the amounts indicated: depreciation, $2,000; property taxes and insurance, $1,000.

■ The following additional Precision Machinery Department costs would be incurred if Faktrons were purchased from an outside supplier: freight, $0.50 per unit; indirect labor for receiving, materials handling, inspection, $5,000. The cost of the purchased Faktrons would be considered a Precision Machinery Department cost.

Required:
a. Prepare a schedule comparing the total costs of the Precision Machinery Department (1) when Faktrons are made and (2) when Faktrons are bought from an outsider supplier.
b. Discuss the considerations in addition to the cost factors that you would bring to the attention of managers in assisting them in deciding whether to make or buy Faktrons. Include in your discussion the considerations that might be applied to the evaluation of the outside supplier.

[AICPA adapted]

19.62 ***Make-or-buy decision.*** Leland Manufacturing uses 10 units of part number KJ37 each month in the production of radar equipment. The unit cost to manufacture one unit of KJ37 is as follows:

Direct materials	$ 1,000
Materials handling (20% of direct materials cost)	200
Direct labor	8,000
Overhead (150% of direct labor)	12,000
Total manufacturing cost	$21,200

Materials handling represents the direct variable costs of the Receiving Department that are applied to direct materials and purchased components on the basis of their cost. This is a separate charge in addition to manufacturing overhead. Leland's annual manufacturing overhead budget is one-third variable and two-thirds fixed. Scott Supply, one of Leland's reliable vendors, has offered to supply part KJ37 at a unit price of $15,000.

Required:
a. If Leland purchases the KJ37 units from Scott, the capacity Leland used to manufacture these parts would remain idle. What would be the opportunity cost of KJ37 should Leland decide to purchase the parts from Scott?
b. Assume Leland is able to rent all idle capacity for $25,000 per month. If Leland decides to purchase the 10 units from Scott, what would be Leland's opportunity cost for KJ37?
c. Assume that Leland does not wish to commit to a rental agreement but would use idle capacity to manufacture another product that would contribute $52,000 per month. If Leland elects to manufacture KJ37 in order to maintain quality control, what would be Leland's opportunity cost?

[CMA adapted]

19.63 ***Make-or-buy decision.*** Sarbec Company needs a total of 125 tons of sheet steel, 50 tons of 2-inch width and 75 tons of 4-inch width, for a customer's job. Sarbec can purchase the sheet steel in these widths directly from Jensteel Corporation, a steel manufacturer, or it can purchase sheet steel from Jensteel that is 24 inches wide and have it slit into the desired widths by Precut, Inc. Both vendors are local and have previously supplied materials to Sarbec.

Precut specializes in slitting sheet steel that is provided by a customer into any desired width. When negotiating a contract, Precut tells its customers that there is a scrap loss in the slitting operation, but that this loss has never exceeded 2.5% of input tons. Precut recommends that if a customer has a specific tonnage requirement, it should supply an adequate amount of steel to yield the desired quantity. Precut's charges for steel slitting are based on good output, not input handled.

The 24-inch wide sheet steel is a regular stock item of Jensteel and can be shipped to Precut within five days after receipt of Sarbec's purchase order. If Jensteel is to do the slitting, shipment to Sarbec would be scheduled for 15 days after receipt of Sarbec's purchase order. Precut has quoted delivery at 10 days after receipt of the sheet steel. In prior dealings, Sarbec has found both Jensteel and Precut to be reliable vendors with high-quality products.

Sarbec has received the following price quotations from Jensteel and Precut:

JENSTEEL CORPORATION RATES

SIZE	GAUGE	QUANTITY	COST PER TON
2 inch	14	50 tons	$210
4 inch	14	75 tons	200
24 inch	14	125 tons	180

PRECUT, INC., STEEL SLITTING RATES

SIZE	GAUGE	QUANTITY	PRICE PER TON OF OUTPUT
2 inch	14	50 tons	$18
4 inch	14	75 tons	15

FREIGHT AND HANDLING CHARGES

DESTINATION	COST PER TON
Jensteel to Sarbec	$10.00
Jensteel to Precut	5.00
Precut to Sarbec	7.50

In addition, Precut has informed Sarbec that if it purchases 100 output tons of each width, the per-ton slitting rates would be reduced 12%. Sarbec knows that the same customer will be placing a new order in the near future for the same material and estimates it would have to store the additional tonnage for an average of two months at a carrying cost of $1.50 per month for each ton. There would be no change in Jensteel's prices for additional tons delivered to Precut.

Required:
a. Prepare an analysis that will show whether Sarbec Company should:
   1. Purchase the required slit steel directly from Jensteel Corporation.
   2. Purchase the 24-inch wide sheet steel from Jensteel and have it slit by Precut into 50 output tons 2 inches wide and 75 output tons 4 inches wide.
   3. Take advantage of Precut's reduced slitting rates by purchasing 100 output tons of each width.
b. Without prejudice to your answer to Requirement (a), present three qualitative arguments why Sarbec Company may favor the purchase of the slit steel directly from Jensteel Corporation.

[CMA adapted]

19.64 Sell-or-process-further decision. Gossett Chemical Company uses comprehensive annual profit planning procedures to evaluate pricing policies, finalize production decisions, and estimate unit costs for its various products. One particular product group involves two joint products and two by-products. This product group is analyzed separately each year to establish appropriate production and marketing policies.

The two joint products—ALCHEM-X and CHEM-P—emerge at the end of processing in Department 20. Both chemicals can be sold at this split-off point— ALCHEM-X for $2.50 per unit, and CHEM-P for $3.00 per unit. By-product BY-D20 also emerges at the split-off point in Department 20 and is salable without further processing for $0.50 per unit. Unit costs of preparing this by-product for market are $0.03 for freight and $0.12 for packaging.

CHEM-P is sold without further processing, but ALCHEM-X is transferred to Department 22 for additional processing into a refined chemical labeled as ALCHEM-XF. No additional raw materials are added in Department 22.

ALCHEM-XF is sold for $5.00 per unit. By-product BY-D22 is created by the additional processing in Department 22, and it can be sold for $0.70 per unit. Unit marketing costs for BY-D22 are $0.05 for freight and $0.15 for packaging.

Gossett Chemical Company accounts for by-product production by crediting the net realizable value of by-products produced to production costs of the main products. The relative sales value method is used to allocate net joint production costs for inventory valuation purposes.

A portion of the 19X5 profit plan established in September 19X4 is presented next:

	UNITS OF PRODUCTION	
	CHEM-P	ALCHEM-XF
Estimated sales	400,000	210,000
Planned inventory change	−8,000	−6,000
Required production	392,000	204,000
Minimum production based upon joint output ratio	392,000	210,000
By-product output		
BY-D20 90,000		
BY-D22 60,000		

	COSTS	
BUDGETED PRODUCTION COSTS	DEPARTMENT 20	DEPARTMENT 22
Raw material	$160,000	—
Costs transferred from 20*	—	$225,000
Hourly direct labor	170,000	120,000
Variable overhead	180,000	140,800
Fixed overhead	247,500	188,000
	$757,500	$673,800

	CHEM-P	ALCHEM-XF
Budgeted marketing costs	$196,000	$105,000

* The cost transferred to Department 22 is calculated as follows:

Sales value of output:			
ALCHEM-X (210,000 × $2.50)		$ 525,000	31%
CHEM-P (392,000 × $3.00)		1,176,000	69%
		$1,701,000	100%
Department 20 costs		$ 757,500	
Less BY-D20 (90,000 × $0.35)		<31,500>	
Net costs:		$ 726,000	
ALCHEM-X	31%	$ 225,000	or $1.07 per unit
CHEM-P	69%	501,000	or $1.28 per unit
Allocated net costs	100%	$ 726,000	

Shortly after this budget was compiled, the company learned that a chemical that would compete with ALCHEM-XF was to be introduced. The Marketing Department estimated that a permanent price reduction to $3.50 a unit would be required for ALCHEM-XF to be sold in present quantities. Gossett must now reevaluate the decision to process ALCHEM-X further.

The market for ALCHEM-X will not be affected by the introduction of this new chemical. Consequently, the quantities of ALCHEM-X that are usually processed into ALCHEM-XF can be sold at the regular price of $2.50 per unit. The costs for marketing ALCHEM-X are estimated to be $105,000. If the further processing is terminated, Department 22 will be dismantled, and all costs will be eliminated except equipment depreciation, $18,400; supervisory salaries, $21,200; and general overhead, $35,200.

Required:
a. Should Gossett sell ALCHEM-X at the split-off point or continue to process it further in Department 22? Prepare a schedule of relevant costs and revenues to support your answer.
b. During discussions of the possible dropping of ALCHEM-XF, one person noted that the manufacturing margin for ALCHEM-X would be 57.2% [(2.50 − 1.07)/2.50] and 57.3% for CHEM-P. The normal markup for products sold in the market with ALCHEM-X is 72%. For the CHEM-P portion of the line, the markup is 47%. He argues that the company's unit costs must be incorrect because the margins differ from the typical rates. Briefly explain why Gossett's rates for the two products are almost identical when "normal" rates are not.
[CMA adapted]

19.65 Special-order decision. Anchor Company manufactures several different styles of jewelry cases. Management estimates that during the third quarter of 19X6 the company will be operating at 80% of normal capacity. Because Anchor desires a higher utilization of plant capacity, the company will consider a special order.

Anchor has received special-order inquiries from two companies. The first order is from JCP, Inc., which would like to market a jewelry case similar to one of Anchor's cases. The JCP jewelry case would be marketed under JCP's own label. JCP, Inc., has offered Anchor $5.75 per jewelry case for 2,000 cases to be shipped by October 1, 19X6. The cost data for the Anchor jewelry case, which would be similar to the specifications of the JCP special order, are as follows:

Regular selling price per unit	$9.00
Costs per unit:	
Raw materials	$2.50
Direct labor 0.5 hours @ $6.00	3.00
Overhead 0.25 machine hours @ $4.00	1.00
Total costs	$6.50

According to the specifications provided by JCP, Inc., the special-order case requires less expensive raw materials. Consequently, the raw materials will cost only $2.25 per case. Management has estimated that the remaining costs, labor time, and machine time will be the same as for the Anchor jewelry case.

The second special order was submitted by the Krage Company for 7,500 jewelry cases at $7.50 per case. Like the JCP cases, these jewelry cases would be marketed under the Krage label and have to be shipped by October 1, 19X6. However, the Krage jewelry case is different from any jewelry case in the Anchor line. The estimated per-unit costs of this case are as follows:

Raw materials	$3.25
Direct labor 0.5 hours @ $6.00	3.00
Overhead 0.5 machine hours @ $4.00	2.00
Total costs	$8.25

In addition, Anchor will incur $1,500 in additional setup costs and will have to purchase a $2,500 special device to manufacture these cases; this device will be discarded once the special order is completed.

The Anchor manufacturing capabilities are limited to the total machine hours available. The plant capacity under normal operations is 90,000 machine hours per year or 7,500 machine hours per month. The budgeted fixed overhead for 19X6 amounts to $216,000. All manufacturing overhead costs are applied to production on the basis of machine hours at $4.00 per hour.

Anchor will have the entire third quarter to work on the special orders. Management does not expect any repeat sales to be generated from either special order. Company practice precludes Anchor from subcontracting any portion of an order when special orders are not expected to generate repeat sales.

Required:

Should Anchor Company accept either special order? Justify your answer and show your calculations.

[CMA adapted]

19.66 *Emphasizing the contribution margin approach in price setting for a special order.* E. Berg and Sons build custom-made pleasure boats that range in price from $10,000 to $250,000. For the past 30 years, Mr. Berg, Sr., has determined the selling price of each boat by estimating the cost of material, labor, and a prorated portion of overhead and adding 20% to these estimated costs.

For example, a recent price quotation was determined as follows:

Direct materials	$ 5,000
Direct labor	8,000
Overhead	2,000
	15,000
Plus 20%	3,000
Selling price	$18,000

The overhead figure was determined by estimating total overhead costs for the year and allocating them at 25% of direct labor.

If a customer rejected the price and business was slack, Mr. Berg, Sr., would often be willing to reduce his markup to as little at 5% over estimated costs. Thus, average markup for the year is estimated at 15%.

Mr. Ed Berg, Jr., has just completed a course on pricing and believes the firm could use some of the techniques discussed in the course. The course emphasized the contribution margin approach to pricing, and Mr. Berg, Jr., feels such an approach would be helpful in determining the selling prices of their boats.

Total overhead, which includes selling and administrative expenses for the year, has been estimated at $150,000, of which $90,000 is fixed and the remainder is variable in direct proportion to direct labor.

Required:
a. Assume the customer in the example rejected the $18,000 quotation and also rejected a $15,750 quotation (5% markup) during a slack period. The customer countered with a $15,000 offer.
   1. What is the difference in net income for the year between accepting or rejecting the customer's offer?
   2. What is the minimum selling price Mr. Berg, Jr., could have quoted without reducing or increasing net income?
b. What advantages does the contribution margin approach to pricing have over the approach used by Mr. Berg, Sr.?
c. What pitfalls, if any, are there to contribution margin pricing?

[CMA adapted]

19.67 *Special-order decision.* George Jackson operates a small machine shop. He manufactures one standard product available from many other similar businesses, and he also manufactures products to customer order. His accountant prepared the following annual income statement:

	CUSTOM SALES	STANDARD SALES	TOTAL
Sales	$50,000	$25,000	$75,000
Material	$10,000	$ 8,000	$18,000
Labor	20,000	9,000	29,000
Depreciation	6,300	3,600	9,900
Power	700	400	1,100
Rent	6,000	1,000	7,000
Heat and light	600	100	700
Other	400	900	1,300
	<$44,000>	<$23,000>	<$67,000>
	$ 6,000	$ 2,000	$ 8,000

The depreciation charges are for machines used in the respective product lines. The power charge is apportioned on the estimate of power consumed. The rent is for the building space, which has been leased for 10 years at $7,000 per year. The rent and heat and light are apportioned to the product lines based on the amount of floor space occupied. All other costs are current expenses identified with the product line incurring them.

A valued custom parts customer has asked Jackson to manufacture 5,000 special units for him. Jackson is working at capacity and would have to give up some other business to take this order. He cannot renege on custom orders already agreed to, but he could reduce the output of his standard product by about one-half for one year while producing the specially requested custom part. The customer is willing to pay $7.00 for each part. The material cost will be about $2.00 per unit, and the labor will be $3.60 per unit. Jackson will have to spend $2,000 for a special device that will be discarded when the job is done.

Required:
a. What is the incremental cost of the 5,000-unit order?
b. What are the total fixed costs of the order?
c. What is the full cost of the special order?
d. What is the opportunity cost of taking the order?
e. What would be the cash advantage (disadvantage) if Jackson accepts the order?

[CMA adapted]

19.68 *Selection of the least-cost alternative.* Video Recreation, Inc. (VRI), is a supplier of video games and video equipment such as large-screen televisions and video-cassette recorders. The company has recently concluded a major contract with Sunview Hotels to supply games for the hotel video lounges. Under this contract, a total of 4,000 games will be delivered to Sunview Hotels throughout the western United States, and all of the games will have a warranty period of one year for both parts and labor. The number of service calls required to repair these games during the first year after installation is estimated as follows:

NUMBER OF SERVICE CALLS	PROBABILITY
400	0.1
700	0.3
900	0.4
1,200	0.2

VRI's Customer Service Department has developed three alternatives for providing the warranty service to Sunview:

■ *Plan 1.* VRI would contract with local firms to perform the repair services. It is estimated that six such vendors would be needed to cover the appropriate areas and that each of these vendors would charge an annual fee of $15,000 to have personnel available and to stock the appropriate parts. In addition to the annual fee, VRI would be billed $250 for each service call and would be billed for parts used at cost plus a 10% surcharge.

■ *Plan 2.* VRI would allow the management of each hotel to arrange for repair service when needed and then would reimburse the hotel for the expenses incurred. It is estimated that 60% of the service calls would be for hotels located in urban areas where the charge for a service call would average $450. At the remaining hotels, the charge would be $350. In addition to these service charges, parts would be billed at cost.

■ *Plan 3.* VRI would hire its own personnel to perform repair services and to do preventive maintenance. Nine employees, located in the appropriate geographical areas, would be required to fulfill these responsibilities, and their average salary would be $24,000 annually. The fringe benefit expense for these employees would amount to 35% of their wages. Each employee would be scheduled to make an average of 200 preventive maintenance calls during the year; each of these calls would require $15 worth of parts. Because of this preventive maintenance, it is estimated that the expected number of hotel calls for repair service would decline 30%, and the cost of parts required for each repair service call would be reduced by 20%.

VRI's Accounting Department has reviewed the historical data on repair costs for equipment installations similar to those proposed for Sunview Hotels and found that the cost of parts required for each repair occurred in the following proportions:

PARTS COST PER REPAIR	PROPORTION
$30	15%
40	15
60	45
90	25

Required:

VRI wishes to select the least-cost alternative to fulfill its warranty obligations to Sunview Hotels. Recommend which of the three plans VRI should adopt. Support your recommendation with appropriate calculations and analysis.

[CMA adapted]

19.69 *Payoff and expected value.* The Wentworth Company manufactures modular furniture for the home and uses a monthly variance system to control costs of the manufacturing departments. Edward Collins is the supervisor of the Assembly Department and is reviewing the monthly variance analysis for November:

Standard cost of production materials	$275,000
Materials price variance	–0–
Materials quantity variance, unfavorable	19,000
	$294,000

Collins has gathered the following information to assist him in deciding whether or not to investigate the unfavorable materials quantity variance:

Estimated cost to investigate the variance	$ 4,000
Estimated probability that the Assembly Department is operating properly	90%
If the Assembly Department is operating improperly:	
Estimated cost to make the necessary changes	$ 8,000
Estimated present value of future unfavorable variances that would be saved by making the necessary changes	$40,000

Required:

a. Recommend whether or not Wentworth Company should investigate the unfavorable materials quantity variance. Support your recommendation by:
1. Preparing a payoff table for use in making the decision.
2. Computing the expected value of the cost of each possible action.
b. Edward Collins is uncertain about the probability estimate of 90% for proper operation of the Assembly Department. Determine the probability estimate of the Assembly Department operating properly that would cause Collins to be indifferent between the two possible actions.

[CMA adapted]

19.70 *Payoff table and the decision process.* Jackston, Inc., manufactures and distributes a line of Christmas toys. The company has neglected to keep its dollhouse line current. As a result, sales have decreased to approximately 10,000 units per year from a previous high of 50,000 units. The dollhouse has been redesigned recently and is considered by company officials to be comparable to its competitors' models. The company plans to redesign the dollhouse each year in order to compete effectively. Joan Blocke, the sales manager, is not sure how many units can be sold next year, but she is willing to place probabilities on her estimates. Blocke's estimates of the number of units that can be sold during the next year and the related probabilities are as follows:

ESTIMATED SALES IN UNITS	PROBABILITY
20,000	0.1
30,000	0.4
40,000	0.3
50,000	0.2

The units would be sold for $20 each.

The inability to estimate the sales more precisely is a problem for Jackston. The number of units of this product is small enough to schedule the entire year's sales in one production run. If the demand is greater than the number of units manufactured, then sales will be lost. If demand is below supply, the extra units cannot be carried over to the next season and would be given away to various charitable organizations. The production and distribution cost estimates follow:

UNITS MANUFACTURED

	20,000	30,000	40,000	50,000
Variable costs	$180,000	$270,000	$360,000	$450,000
Fixed costs	140,000	140,000	160,000	160,000
Total costs	$320,000	$410,000	$520,000	$610,000

The company intends to analyze the data to facilitate making a decision as to the proper size of the production run.

Required:
a. Prepare a payoff table for the different sizes of production runs required to meet the four sales estimates prepared by Joan Blocke for Jackston, Inc. If Jackston, relied solely on the expected monetary value approach to make decisions, what size of production run would be selected?
b. Identify the basic steps that are taken in any decision process. Explain each step by reference to the situation presented in the problem and your answer for Requirement (a).

[CMA adapted]

19.71 *Introduction of a new product using the contribution margin approach based on most likely outcomes and expected value.* Sofak Company is a manufacturer of precision sensing equipment. Jerry Adams, one of Sofak's project engineers, has developed a prototype of an automatic testing kit that could continually evaluate water quality and chemical content in hot tubs. Adams believes that this kit will permit domestic tub owners to control water quality better at substantially reduced costs and with less time invested. The management of Sofak is convinced that the kit will have strong market acceptance. Furthermore, this new equipment uses the same technology that Sofak employs in manufacturing some of its other equipment. Therefore, Sofak can use existing facilities to produce the product.

Adams is ready to proceed with developing cost and profit plans for the testing kit. He asked the Marketing Department to develop a suggested selling price and estimate the sales volume. The Marketing Department contracted with Statico, a marketing research company, to develop price and volume estimates.

Based on an analysis of the market, Statico considered unit prices between $80 and $120. Within this price range, it recommended a price of $100 per kit. The frequency distribution of the unit sales volume that Sofak could expect at this selling price is as follows:

ESTIMATED UNIT SALES
VOLUME AT $100

ANNUAL UNIT SALES VOLUME	PROBABILITY
50,000	0.25
60,000	0.45
70,000	0.20
80,000	0.10

Sofak's Profit Planning Department accumulated cost data that Adams had requested. The new product will require direct materials costing $25 per unit and will require two hours of direct labor time to manufacture. Sofak is currently in contract negotiations with its union, making any projections of labor costs difficult. The current direct labor cost is $8 per direct labor hour (DLhr). Representatives of management who are negotiating with the union have estimated the following possible settlements and related probabilities:

DIRECT LABOR COST PER HOUR	PROBABILITY OF SETTLEMENT AMOUNTS
$8.50	0.30
$8.80	0.50
$9.00	0.20

Sofak applies manufacturing overhead to its products using a plantwide rate of $15 per DLhr. This rate was based on a planned activity level of 900,000 DLhr that represents 75% of practical capacity. The budgeted manufacturing overhead costs for the current fiscal year are as follows:

SOFAK COMPANY
SCHEDULE OF BUDGETED MANUFACTURING
OVERHEAD COSTS
FOR THE FISCAL YEAR ENDED NOVEMBER 30, 19X6

	BUDGETED ANNUAL COST	COST PER DLhr
Variable:		
Supplies	$ 360,000	$ 0.40
Materials handling	315,000	0.35
Heat, light, power	1,125,000	1.25
Fixed:		
Supervisory salaries	1,440,000	1.60
Depreciation, building	4,410,000	4.90
Depreciation, equipment	3,420,000	3.80
Property taxes on factory	1,620,000	1.80
Insurance	810,000	0.90
Total budgeted costs	$13,500,000	$15.00

The introduction of the new product will require some changes in the manufacturing plant. Although the plant is below capacity and current facilities can be used, a new production line requiring a supervisor would be opened. The annual cost of the supervisor would be $28,000. In addition, one piece of equipment that Sofak does not own would have to be obtained under an operating lease at an annual cost of $150,000.

Sofak has already paid Statico $132,000 for the marketing study that was mentioned previously. Statico has agreed to conduct the promotion and distribution of the new product for a fee of $6 per unit once Sofak introduces it.

Required:

Determine the annual pretax advantage (disadvantage) that Sofak Company could expect from the introduction of the new product by using:

a. A deterministic approach based on the most likely outcomes.
b. An expected value approach.

[CMA adapted]

19.72 *Introduction of a new product and decision-tree analysis.* Brandon Appliance Corporation, a predominant producer of microwave ovens, is considering the introduction of a new product—a microwave oven that will defrost, cook, brown, and broil food as well as sense when the food is done.

Brandon must decide on a course of action for implementing this new product line. An initial decision must be made whether or not to (1) market the product at all, (2) introduce the product in a marketing test, or (3) nationally distribute the product from the onset. If a marketing test is conducted, Brandon must then decide whether it wishes to abandon the product line or make it available for national distribution.

The Finance Department has provided some cost information and probability estimates relating to this decision. The preliminary costs for research and development have already been incurred and are considered irrelevant to the marketing decision. A success nationally will increase profits by $5,000,000, and a failure will reduce them by $1,000,000, while abandoning the product will not affect profits. The test market analysis will cost Brandon an additional $100,000.

If a market test is not performed, the probability of success in a national campaign is estimated to be 45%. If the market test is performed, the probability of a favorable test result is 60%. With favorable test results, the probability for national success is estimated to be 80%. However, if the test results are unfavorable, the national success probability is only 10%.

Required:
Determine the course of action Brandon Appliance Corporation should follow for the introduction of its new product line by:
a. Constructing a decision-tree diagram that analyzes all the alternatives presented above.
b. Performing backward induction to determine the optimal course of action using the new change in profits as the payoff.

[CMA adapted]

19.73 *Choosing the best product model.* Steven Company has been producing component parts and assemblies for use in the manufacture of microcomputers and microcomputer peripheral equipment since 1992. The company plans to introduce a magnetic tape cartridge backup unit for IBM-compatible microcomputers in the near future.

Steven's Research and Development (R&D) and Market Research Departments have been working on this project for an extended period, and the combined development costs incurred to date amount to $1,500,000. R&D produced several alternative designs for the backup units. Three of the designs were approved for development into prototypes, and from these only one will be manufactured and sold. Market Research has determined that the appropriate selling price would be $400 per unit, regardless of the model selected.

The estimated demand schedule for three different market situations is shown. These three demand levels are the only ones the company considers feasible, and other demand levels are not expected to occur. Steven can meet all demand levels because its fixed plant currently is below full capacity.

	UNIT SALES	PROBABILITY OF OCCURRENCE
Light demand	20,000	0.25
Moderate demand	80,000	0.60
Heavy demand	120,000	0.15

Steven's accounting and engineering staffs have worked together to develop manufacturing cost estimates for each of the three model designs. Costs for the three models follow. Manufacturing overhead, 40% of which is variable, is applied to Steven's products using a plantwide application rate of 250% of direct labor dollars.

	MODEL A	MODEL B	MODEL C
Unit costs:			
Direct materials	$150	$100	$114
Direct labor	40	50	48
Manufacturing overhead	100	125	120
Total unit costs	$290	$275	$282
Other costs:			
Tooling and advertising	$3,000,000	$4,500,000	$4,100,000
Incurred development costs	1,500,000	1,500,000	1,500,000

Steven has decided to employ an expected value model in its analysis to reach a decision as to which of the three prototypes it will manufacture and sell.

Required:

a. Develop a payoff table to determine the expected monetary value for each of the three models Steven Company could manufacture. Based on your analysis, identify the prototype model Steven should manufacture and sell.

b. Steven Company's costs for a backup unit design that was not developed into a prototype were estimated as follows:

Unit costs:	
Direct materials	$130
Direct labor	46
Manufacturing overhead	115
Total unit costs	$291

Other costs:	
Tooling and advertising	$4,000,000
Incurred development costs	1,500,000

If this design had been developed by Steven into a viable model, it would have sold for $400 and had the same expected demand as the other models. Steven's management eliminated this model from consideration because it was considered an inadmissable act, i.e., the calculation of its payoff would have been irrelevant. Explain why the model design was considered an inadmissable act, thus making the calculation of its payoff irrelevant.

c. Steven Company could have employed a decision-tree model in this situation. Explain how the decision-tree model could have been employed in making this decision (no calculations are required).

[CMA adapted]

19.74 *Decision-tree analysis.* Global Credit Corporation (GCC) provides retail and banking institutions throughout the United States and Canada with credit histories of individuals who are seeking various types of financing such as home mortgages, car loans, and retail store credit cards. GCC has branch offices in most major cities in order to provide rapid service to its customers. GCC employs a database system, and the database is maintained at the home office in Kansas City for security purposes. Each branch office is equipped with computer terminals that provide direct access to the database for information retrieval. However, all data entry is completed in Kansas City.

GCC employs a staff of approximately 500 data-entry clerks at the home office. The company hires inexperienced personnel and provides a training course immediately upon hiring. Hiring inexperienced personnel allows GCC to realize an average savings of $3,000 per new employee. Glen Webster, director of human resources, has just completed a review of the employment records of the data-entry clerks and has discovered that only 50% of the trainees complete the training course satisfactorily and continue their employment with GCC. The remaining 50% are found lacking in aptitude for the job and are dismissed. While Webster is aware that the turnover rate for this type of position is typically high, this particular problem indicates a failure in the selection process.

Because the full training course for each data-entry clerk costs GCC $600 and the retention rate is so poor, Webster is considering using a battery of tests to assist in determining which individuals should be hired and trained. The testing program would cost $200 per applicant to administer. Webster estimates that 75% of the applicants would score at or above the minimum cutoff, i.e., achieve an acceptable score. Those applicants who achieve an acceptable score and are hired would be given an abbreviated training course at a cost of $300. Those applicants who would be hired despite scoring below the cutoff point would still be given the full training course so there would be no savings in training costs.

After the results of the testing program are known, the Human Resource Department would consider other employee attributes before making a decision. As a result of this additional screening, Webster estimates that 90% of the high-scoring applicants would be hired and sent to the abbreviated training course, and 10% of the low-scoring applicants would be hired and sent to the full training course. The remaining applicants would not be hired.

To assist in his decision regarding the testing program, Webster has assigned probabilities to satisfactory and unsatisfactory training course completion under varying conditions. These probabilities are presented as follows:

TRAINING COURSE COMPLETION

TESTING/NONTESTING	SATISFACTORY	UNSATISFACTORY
Test acceptable	.7	.3
Test not acceptable	.2	.8
No test	.5	.5

Required:
a. Glen Webster has decided to use decision-tree analysis to determine whether or not GCC should initiate a testing program for the applicants for the data entry positions.
   1. Explain why decision-tree analysis can be employed in this situation.
   2. Discuss the disadvantages associated with decision-tree analysis.
b. Formulate the decision-tree framework for analyzing whether GCC should initiate a testing program or continue with its current employment practices.
c. Using the backward induction method, determine whether GCC should select the testing program. Support your decision with appropriate calculations.

[CMA adapted]

19.75 *Steps in a rational decision-making process.* During the early 1990s, ProSoft Corporation developed and marketed business applications software for mini-computers, achieving a significant market share and a secure position in the industry. After maturing at this level of success, the company's mission became less clear. Further software development for minicomputers was seen as costly with little value to the company, as the market for major business applications was saturated and the minor applications had limited markets.

In order to maintain ProSoft's market share, management decided to enter the growing personal computer field. While major programming would be required to make the company's existing software compatible with personal computers (PCs), management viewed the commitment of all personnel to this project as critical to the continued growth of ProSoft. The emphasis was to be placed on product development, with minimal effort directed toward market analysis.

After weeks of executive strategy sessions regarding product specifications, management imposed the task deadlines and set the date for the introduction of its first PC product, an accounting package for general ledger, accounts payable, and accounts receivable applications. Three months prior to the introduction date, ProSoft began an advertising and dealer promotion campaign announcing the new product and setting the introduction date. Several technical problems arose during development, but the staff believed that a few time-saving measures would enable them to complete the package in time to meet the announced date. Management felt considerable pressure to meet this date as ProSoft had previously missed an announced date and suffered the consequences.

Two weeks before the announced date, ProSoft's marketing personnel learned that an updated version of the PC operating software that ProSoft's new package was designed to interact with was to be released shortly. The marketing staff knew that features could quickly be added to ProSoft's new product to take advantage of the new features in the operating software; however, there would not be time to field test the program changes. The technical personnel warned the marketing staff of the dangers of releasing a product without proper field testing, but these warnings were not heeded. Management, with encouragement from the marketing staff, made the decision to incorporate the features necessary to take advantage of the new operating software and introduce the product on the scheduled date.

Not long after ProSoft made the first shipments of its new software, customers began to complain about processing problems in the accounts payable and accounts receivable modules. Very quickly, it was determined that portions of ProSoft's new package were not compatible with the updated operating software. To correct the problem, the company had to rewrite the software and manuals and replace all existing product. The technical personnel were not dedicated to the development of the next PC product, and this problem fragmented their efforts. The revised product was not available for three months, causing a loss of sales. The financial impact of the $1.7 million error on the company with annual profits of $1.1 million was devastating.

Required:

a. Identify the steps in the general decision-making process.

b. Using the steps identified in Requirement (a), describe the weaknesses in ProSoft's decision-making process.

c. Recommend changes to correct the weaknesses identified in Requirement (b).

[CMA adapted]

19.76 *Rational decision-making process.* Sally Hamm, business manager of the Parkside School District, is preparing for the upcoming meeting of the District School Board. In addition to presenting reports on the routine operations of the district, Hamm will be expected to make recommendations on two special agenda items. The first item addresses the number of high school classroom teachers for the upcoming school year; the second involves the inclusion of computer courses in the adult education program. Both of these items have budget implications that must be addressed. Hamm is responsible for developing the district's budget under the direction of, and within the guidelines, established by the School Board. Once the board approves the budget, it is voted on by the citizens in the school district, i.e., the citizens accept or reject the district's budget.

Hamm must determine the number of teachers that will be needed to teach grades 10, 11, and 12 at Parkside Regional High School next year. The salary line is always the largest single item in the school budget and will be the subject of intense discussion before it is voted on by the citizens. To aid in making her recommendation, Hamm has the following information available: the current high school enrollment, the current ninth grade enrollment, historical data on students transferring in and out of the district, and statistics on the number of students that can be expected to drop out of Parkside Regional High School. The Parkside School District has always maintained a teacher-student ratio that is at or above the state average.

The administrators at Parkside Regional High School have proposed that the computer facilities at the high school be utilized in the evenings to conduct adult education courses to gain increased benefits from the investment in these facilities. Hamm has been given little information about this program although she has been told that additional materials would be required (e.g., additional software and training manual) which could be expensive. There is little formal information available about local interest in a program of this nature, and Hamm is not sure that the program will generate enough revenue to defray the costs. Based on Hamm's recommendation, a decision about this program will be reached at the upcoming meeting.

Required:

a. Identify the steps in the general decision-making process under rational and objective conditions.

b. Citing examples from the situation given above, differentiate between decision making under conditions of risk and decision making under conditions of uncertainty.

[CMA adapted]

20 SEGMENTING THE ENTERPRISE FOR PROFIT PERFORMANCE EVALUATION

Goal congruency across segments requires open communications.

LEARNING OBJECTIVES

After studying this chapter, you should be able to:

1. Examine responsibility centers and state their purpose.

2. Relate responsibility centers and responsibility accounting system design to profit performance evaluation.

3. Segment the profit center's income statement for segment and manager performance evaluation.

4. Identify the relevant profit elements for the add-or-drop decision, and describe how product life cycle analysis and the growth/share matrix are used.

5. Calculate profit performance measures for investment center managers.

6. Discuss Kyocera's amoeba system and new organizational structures in American firms.

■ INTRODUCTION

An enterprise should continuously strive to develop the organizational structure that most effectively and efficiently uses its resources. As enterprises grow and activities become more complex, some division of responsibility is necessary.

In large organizations, one person or a small group simply will not have enough time or sufficient information to make all the decisions. Thus, many medium to large enterprises divide their organizational structure into responsibility centers and place managers in charge of these centers. Then, a **responsibility accounting system** measures the performance of these managers against their budgets. Responsibility accounting, when properly used in performance evaluation and coupled with an accepted reward system, holds managers accountable for their actions; that is, the activities they manage and the financial factors they control.

To run their responsibility centers effectively and efficiently, managers need information detailing the results of their decisions. To operate successfully, a responsibility accounting system must provide complete and timely feedback that reports on responsibility center performance, either favorable or unfavorable. ■━━

LEARNING OBJECTIVE 1

━

Examine responsibility centers and state their purpose.

❙ RESPONSIBILITY CENTERS

A **responsibility center (RC)** is a segment of the organization in which a manager is held accountable for a specified set of activities and financial factors, including investment, revenue, and cost decisions. A general model of an RC appears in Exhibit 20–1. Responsibility centers may be created in various ways, but generally the enterprise first divides responsibility by activities; for example:

- Activities related to business functions
- Activities related to products or services
- Activities related to geographic regions

The responsibility accounting system then reports on each RC's financial performance.

❙ Activities Related to Business Functions

A large number of enterprises divide responsibilities by activities related to business functions. Typical business functions include:

- Finance
- Engineering
- Production
- Marketing
- Logistics

Panel (a) of Exhibit 20–2 presents an organization chart for such an organization, and panel (b) provides a specific example for the business functions of an oil company.

Each manager is responsible for a number of activities related to a particular business function. The chief executive officer (CEO) is responsible for long-range strategic planning and coordinating the activities of all managers. For example, the development of a new product requires coordination among all managers, as described in Chapter 14.

Lower-level RCs can also be designated. For example, the manager of logistics may assign a set of responsibilities to a manager of transportation, a manager

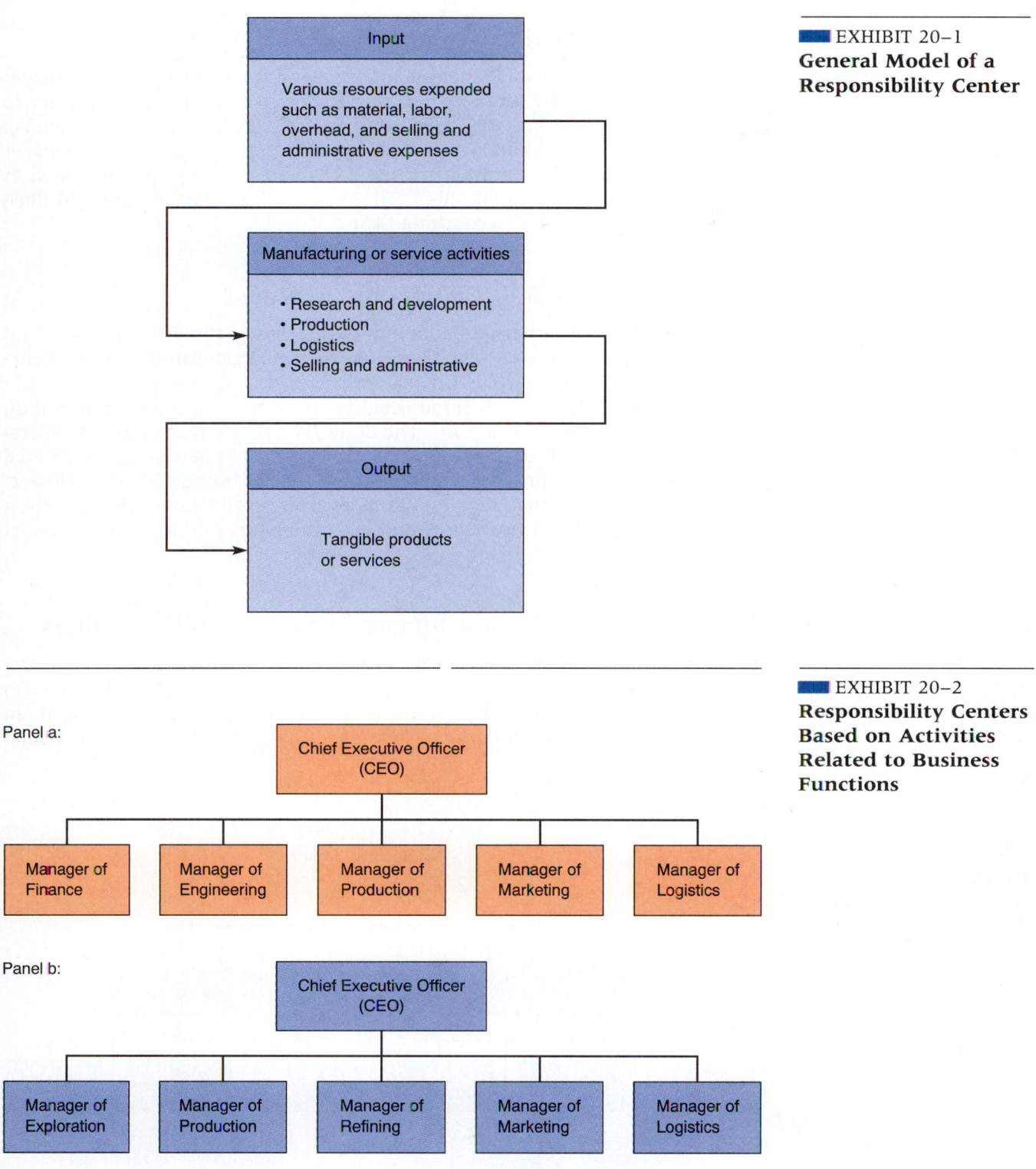

■■■ EXHIBIT 20–1
General Model of a Responsibility Center

■■■ EXHIBIT 20–2
Responsibility Centers Based on Activities Related to Business Functions

of warehousing, and so forth. The manager of transportation is responsible for delivering inbound, interfacility, and outbound shipments. The transportation manager is accountable for the delivery of the proper products, on schedule, to the correct destination, and at reasonable cost. At a higher level, the manager of logistics is responsible for coordinating all logistics activities, including transportation.

Activities Related to Product Lines or Services

Some organizations set up RCs based on product lines or services. The manager of each product line or service is responsible for all the activities necessary to develop, produce, market, and deliver that product line or service. For example, a manufacturer of trucks and earth-moving equipment would put one manager in charge of trucks and another in charge of the earth-moving equipment, as shown in panel (a) of Exhibit 20–3. The organization chart in panel (b) illustrates the RCs of a public accounting firm.

Activities Related to Geographic Regions

If an organization is dispersed nationally or internationally, RCs may be set up according to geographic regions. For example, an organization may be structured as shown in Exhibit 20–4.

In this exhibit, the CEO is responsible for the activities of the organization as a whole, which is his or her RC. The domestic operations and foreign operations are RCs with a chief operating officer (COO) at their helms. Each divisional RC is headed by a vice president. Divisions, in turn, are broken down into lower-level RCs, such as product lines, and then by business function. Alternatively, a division can be broken down into business functions without using product lines as separate RCs.

Advantages and Disadvantages of Responsibility Centers

In organizations that are divided into RCs, decision-making authority is widely diffused among a number of managers. Managers at levels below top management have authority to make certain major decisions without clearing them first through central headquarters. Creating autonomous RCs is a fundamental

▬ EXHIBIT 20–3
Responsibility Centers Based on Activities Related to Product Lines and Services Rendered

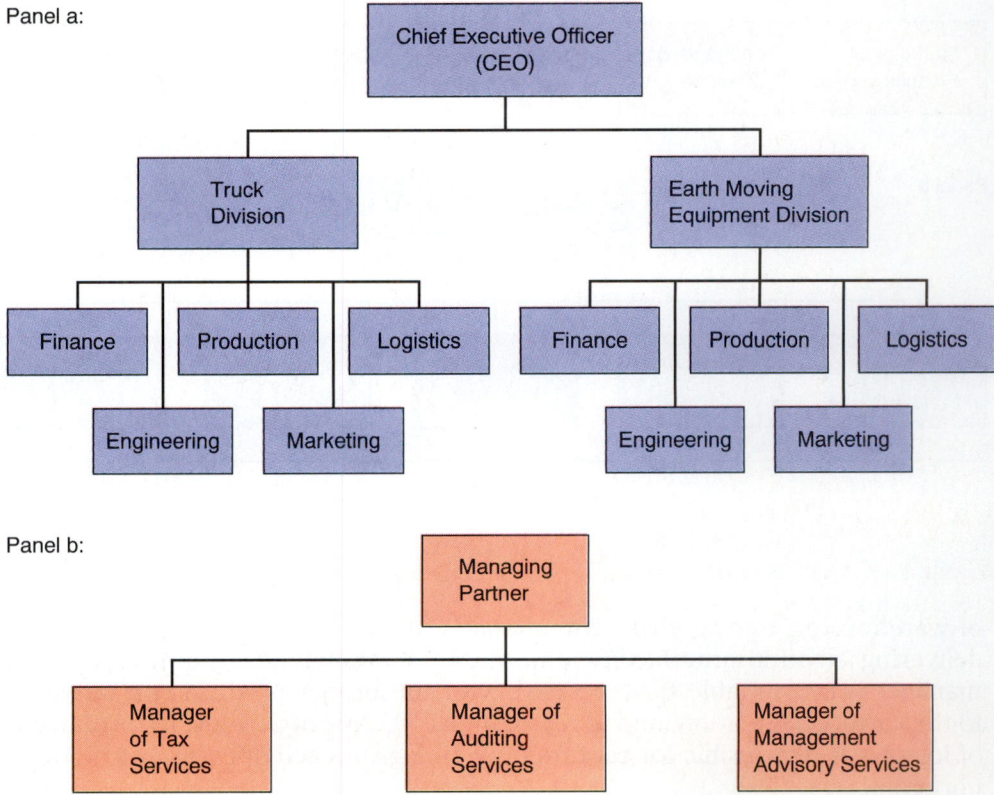

■■■EXHIBIT 20–4
Responsibility Centers Based on Activities Related to Geographic Regions

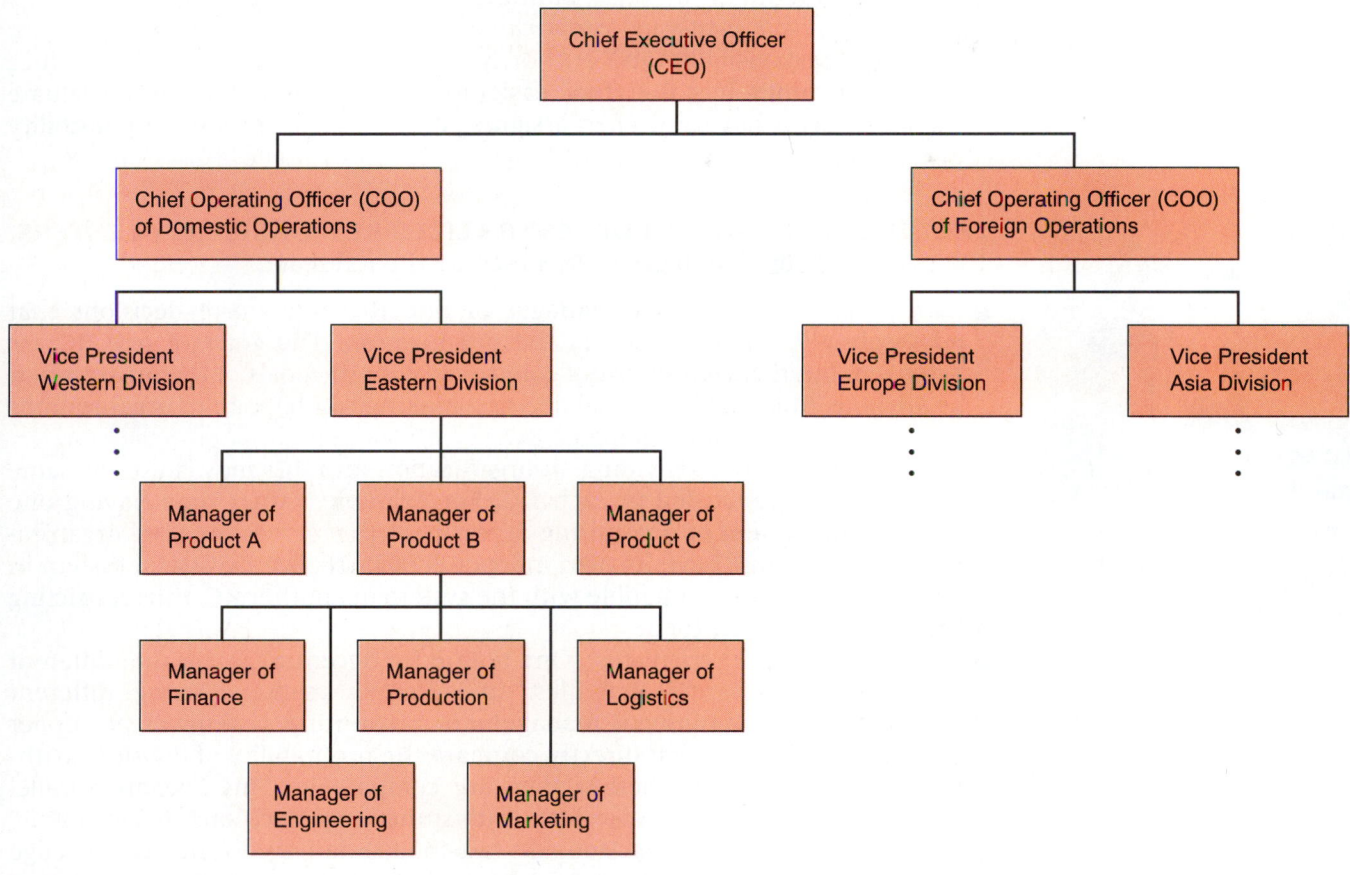

tactic in decentralization. Such an arrangement offers both advantages and disadvantages.

THE ADVANTAGES OF DECENTRALIZED RESPONSIBILITY CENTERS.
The purported advantages of decentralizing an organization into autonomous RCs include the following:

■ *Focused decision making.* Some enterprises have grown so large that neither top management nor one person can cope efficiently with the volume, breadth, and diversity of the decisions that must be made. Managers of smaller segments possess a better understanding of how the segment operates and what its needs are. Thus, their attention is focused exclusively on the RC to which they are assigned.
■ *Closer to the action.* Because RC managers are closer to the activities and financial factors that they manage, they are on "top of things" and can make more informed decisions.
■ *Timely decision making.* Because RC managers do not have to go through a chain of command to gain approval from top management, they can respond immediately to situations.
■ *Training ground for managers.* Responsibility center managers learn by doing. As they prove their ability to manage smaller segments, they are promoted and given more responsibility.
■ *Engenders motivation.* Being given the responsibility and authority to make their own decisions increases RC managers' incentives to strive for successful outcomes.

■ *Enhances strategic planning.* Because top management is relieved of short-term planning and day-to-day decisions, they can devote more of their time and efforts to long-range strategic planning for the entire enterprise.

■ *Easier to evaluate managers' performance.* Responsibility center managers are given the responsibility and authority to make decisions that will produce certain outcomes. It is, therefore, easier to evaluate them than it is to evaluate managers who have not been assigned well-defined areas of responsibility and authority.

THE DISADVANTAGES OF DECENTRALIZED RESPONSIBILITY CENTERS. The purported disadvantages of RCs include the following:

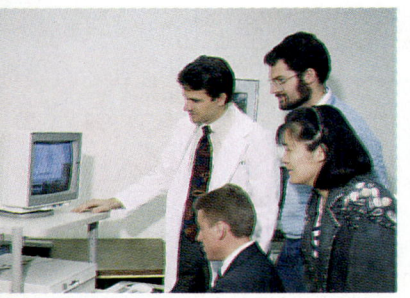

Management accountants and physicians evaluating responsibility centers at Washoe Medical Center.

■ *Lack of goal congruency.* A manager of one RC may make decisions that adversely affect another RC in the organization. The goals of one RC are achieved, but the decision is not congruent with the goals of the organization as a whole. Such dysfunctional decision making can happen in organizations that have highly interdependent RCs.

■ *Duplication of activities.* Dividing an organization into RCs may cause the same activity to be duplicated in each RC. For example, rather than having one information system or accounting department that serves the total organization, each RC may have its own independent LAN. Even worse, a system in one RC may not be compatible with the system in another RC, thus restricting interaction between them.

■ *Difficulty to compare performance.* One reason for decentralizing is that different RCs perform different activities, in different markets, using different resources. Many traditional management accounting systems create upper management reports that directly compare the profitability of divisions without proper regard to whether they are comparable. This "deadly parallel evaluation strategy" can also lead to dysfunctional decisions. For example, would the manager of a McDonald's fast-food restaurant located on the edge of a small town want to be compared against a restaurant located next to a high school or college campus, especially if the managers have no control over the location of their restaurants? If bonuses and profit sharing are based solely on the revenues or profits generated, then the first manager will not compare favorably to the second, even though the first may be doing a better job.

The Role of the Information System in Decentralization

Decentralization requires trade-offs such as the need for LANs to support localized, timely decision making versus centralized information systems to minimize duplication of information processing activities. One of the most serious conflicts from decentralization is the potential sacrifice of goal congruence due to autonomous decision making with RCs. Thus, maximizing employee empowerment and goal congruence become primary goals. So that RCs and their local area networks (LANs) can function cooperatively, an integrated computer-based information system (ICBIS) is needed to link them together. To have decentralized RCs without an ICBIS can actually inhibit effective and efficient local decision making.

A centralized information system is needed to provide divisional information to corporate headquarters. Centralized information about corporate and other RC activities is also needed by RC managers. The ICBIS is more than just a mainframe system with dumb terminals, though. It is an effective combination of microcomputer-based LANs, linked to wide area networks (WANs) (possibly using minicomputers) and to the corporate headquarter's mainframe.

A modern trend in computer architecture design to support decentralization is downsizing (or "rightsizing") of the ICBIS. This involves moving away from centralized mainframe systems to client/server networked microcomputers.

INSIGHTS & APPLICATIONS

Downsizing at Blockbuster Video

The interoperable cooperative ICBIS makes optimum use of all resources, assigning the right application to the appropriate level of computer power. Permitting local workstations to prepare transactions and update the database without the use of a mainframe is cost-effective systems design in many companies. More-over, the PC (or workstation) provides a much friendlier user interface. Interoperable computer architectures enable applications to be distributed enterprisewide in an optimal fashion. Such an enterprisewide ICBIS strategy emphasizes decentralized, but cooperative management among all segments of the enterprise.

One of Blockbuster's policies is that a movie rented at one store can be returned to any other store. With over 150 outlets, the mainframe video tracking system had to be run every night. Sara Bond, information systems director, downsized the system into a 150-node network of PCs linked through a minicomputer server. Block-buster has reported maintenance and support costs savings of approximately $3.2 million annually. Manage-ment also claims that productivity has increased from the more accurate and timely tracking of video rentals.

Proponents of client/server systems offer many benefits of these system architectures:

- Increased user performance at less cost
- User-friendly interfaces such as graphical displays, no matter where the users are accessing the system (e.g., from another's office, at home, on the RC's shopfloor, or while traveling)
- The ability to distribute centralized information throughout the enterprise so users have real-time access to needed information
- Increased decision-making flexibility at the local levels (where the work is being done)

For example, Eastman Kodak Company's new client/server ICBIS has resulted in a cooperative decision-making synergism, improving morale and strengthen-ing communications while achieving large cost savings. The above Blockbuster Video case exemplifies the trend in downsizing and the distribution of computer resources to end users.

For many applications, the mainframe is still the only workable technology platform. The question is not whether a mainframe or LAN-based architecture is applicable. Rather, it is the dividing line between which applications should be run on a mainframe versus a smaller computer. This dividing line involves the following considerations:

- *The size of the application.* Some applications require gigabytes of online storage while pulling together data from numerous locations. LANs are not powerful enough to support many large-scale applications.
- *The kind of application planned for the system.* Some applications use millions of records with complex reporting modules. Micro- and minicomputers may not possess fast enough processing speeds to handle such large databases.
- *The number of end users.* When the number of users enters the hundreds, then a mainframe system is probably necessary.

Decentralization requires *interoperable architectures* based on global enter-prisewide systems supporting local end user decision making. Such an ICBIS design mirrors the organizational design. A key design tenet is assigning the right applications to the appropriate level and location of computer hardware. For example, mainframes process transactions that have already been edited, validated, and formatted by microcomputers, thereby updating the corporate

INSIGHTS & APPLICATIONS

Interoperability at Simco Manufacturing

Simco, a large steel fabricator, has grown, as many multinationals have, by acquiring smaller companies and setting them up as profit centers. Each RC had its own information system, leading to hardware, software, and data redundancies, as well as incompatible and sometimes conflicting information.

James Kirby, Simco's CIO, designed an interoperable

ICBIS with a centralized corporate database with online, real-time (OLRT) end-user access. After about six months of operation, Simco's RC managers favorably evaluated it pointing out that it allowed them access to different kinds of applications and information regardless of their location.

The RC managers wanted and got an information system that allowed them to be able to run an application on whatever machine they happened to be at. This linkage provided interconnectivity of all nodes on the network and portability of applications to any node. With the previous system, Simco's LANs focused on isolated divisional needs rather than strategic interoperability with other segments of the company.

database. LAN workstations provide a more friendly user interface for data input and queries, as demonstrated in the above Simco case.

HIERARCHICAL SEGMENTATION FOR PROFIT PERFORMANCE EVALUATION

Regardless of how RCs are created, the responsibility accounting system must measure the RC manager's success in achieving his or her master budget goals. Not all managers will have responsibility for the same financial factors, though. There are three financial factors:

- Cost
- Profit
- Investment

Some managers will control only costs. Others will control both cost and revenue to produce a profit. A few will be in charge of all three financial factors. A manager of an activity, such as transportation, will normally have responsibility only for certain costs. A product line manager may be assigned responsibility for that line's costs *and* revenues. A manager of a geographic division usually will be assigned responsibility for cost, revenue, and investment.

The Cost Center

A cost center is any RC where the manager can exert influence over cost but has little, if any, authority to influence revenues or investments in fixed assets. A production department and a maintenance department are good examples of a cost center. A cost center can produce a product or render a service.

Management accountants traditionally have used standard costs and cost variances to evaluate the performance of cost centers. An example of a detailed cost variance report for July's activities in producing Tigerade at Nulife Sports Drink, Inc., was presented in Exhibit 8–12. This case will also be used to develop the responsibility accounting reports for the product line (profit center) manager.

In addition to traditional cost variance reports, the responsibility accounting system should supply cost center managers with nonfinancial information needed for continuous improvement. Traditionally, many accountants and

Emergency trauma centers are usually set up as cost centers at hospitals.

managers believed that the cost center manager was responsible only for monetary inputs (i.e., costs) and that the management accounting system only needed to relate these inputs to outputs. In today's competitive world, this approach is insufficient. An array of performance measurements are available to the management accountant to measure costs and report on how well these costs are being employed (i.e., performance measurements related to activities). A review of Part III, and especially Chapter 11, may be helpful at this point.

In general, the decision to use standard costs and cost variances is made considering the needs of both responsibility accounting and product costing. Traditional responsibility accounting systems using standard costs and flexible budgets have relied on the measurement and analysis of variances as the primary mechanism for performance evaluation.

This sole reliance on cost variance analysis for performance evaluation, especially the emphasis on labor-based measurements, has been the object of growing criticism from both academics and practitioners, however. By measuring and rewarding direct labor efficiency, other important criteria, such as competitive priorities of customer service, quality, lead time reduction, and on-time delivery are often minimized or ignored. Workers attempt to "play the system" by:

- Processing production orders with easily achievable standards ahead of those orders needed to meet delivery schedules
- Overloading the most efficient machines in spite of the availability of less efficient machines that would permit delivery schedules to be met
- Producing excess quantities to spread setup time and absorb fixed overhead
- Overlooking quality problems in order to achieve favorable efficiency variances

As responsibility accounting systems evolve, a variety of financial and nonfinancial performance measurements will be used, as presented in previous chapters. Moreover, standards or targets will be established for groups of interrelated RCs, where quality, lead time, cost, and customer objectives require that those centers behave as a team. Performance credit will be given to all RCs within the group when products are completed through the last RC.

The Profit Center

A profit center is any RC where the manager has the authority and responsibility to make decisions that will affect the costs *and* revenues of that center. The profit center manager, however, has little, if any, decision-making power concerning investments in fixed assets.

Clearly, the profit center manager needs information regarding costs and revenues. Proper performance evaluation compares the master budget and flexible budget against actual costs and revenues, reporting profit variances. **Segmented income statements** are output from the management accounting LAN for this purpose. Using the contribution margin format, "mini income statements" (segmented income statements) can be created for each RC. These mini income statements and their profit variance reports will be illustrated in the next major section of this chapter.

Universities set up profit centers such as the Athletic Department.

The Investment Center

An **investment center** is any RC where the manager has the authority and responsibility to make decisions that will affect the costs, revenues, and investments of that center. Thus, there is an expected return on investment on the assets deployed in the center. The investment center approach is usually applied to autonomous business units (i.e., divisions) and is rarely used in measuring the performance of internal service activities, such as logistics.

Investment centers usually represent major segments of an organization.

Profit analysis provides an appraisal of costs and revenues only. In an investment center, a third dimension should be evaluated: the amount of capital employed. How effective are the assets being used to generate revenue? Does the return on sales justify the investment? If not, what steps can be taken to correct the unfavorable performance?

To help investment center managers answer these questions and gauge their progress toward meeting their financial goals, management accountants use several financial performance measurements. Two of the most popular measurements are:

■ Return on investment (ROI)
■ Residual income (RI)

These will also be illustrated later in the chapter.

Levels of Reporting in Responsibility Accounting

In decentralized organizations, the structure of the RCs may be similar to that of Magna Corporation shown in Exhibit 20–5. At the highest level are the investment centers. At the company level are the profit centers. The lowest levels are the cost centers.

Another objective of responsibility accounting is to tailor performance reports to their appropriate levels. Part of Mallard Company's organization chart is illustrated in Exhibit 20–6. Only the bold-bordered blocks in the example will

■■EXHIBIT 20–5
Investment, Profit, and Cost Centers of Magna Corporation

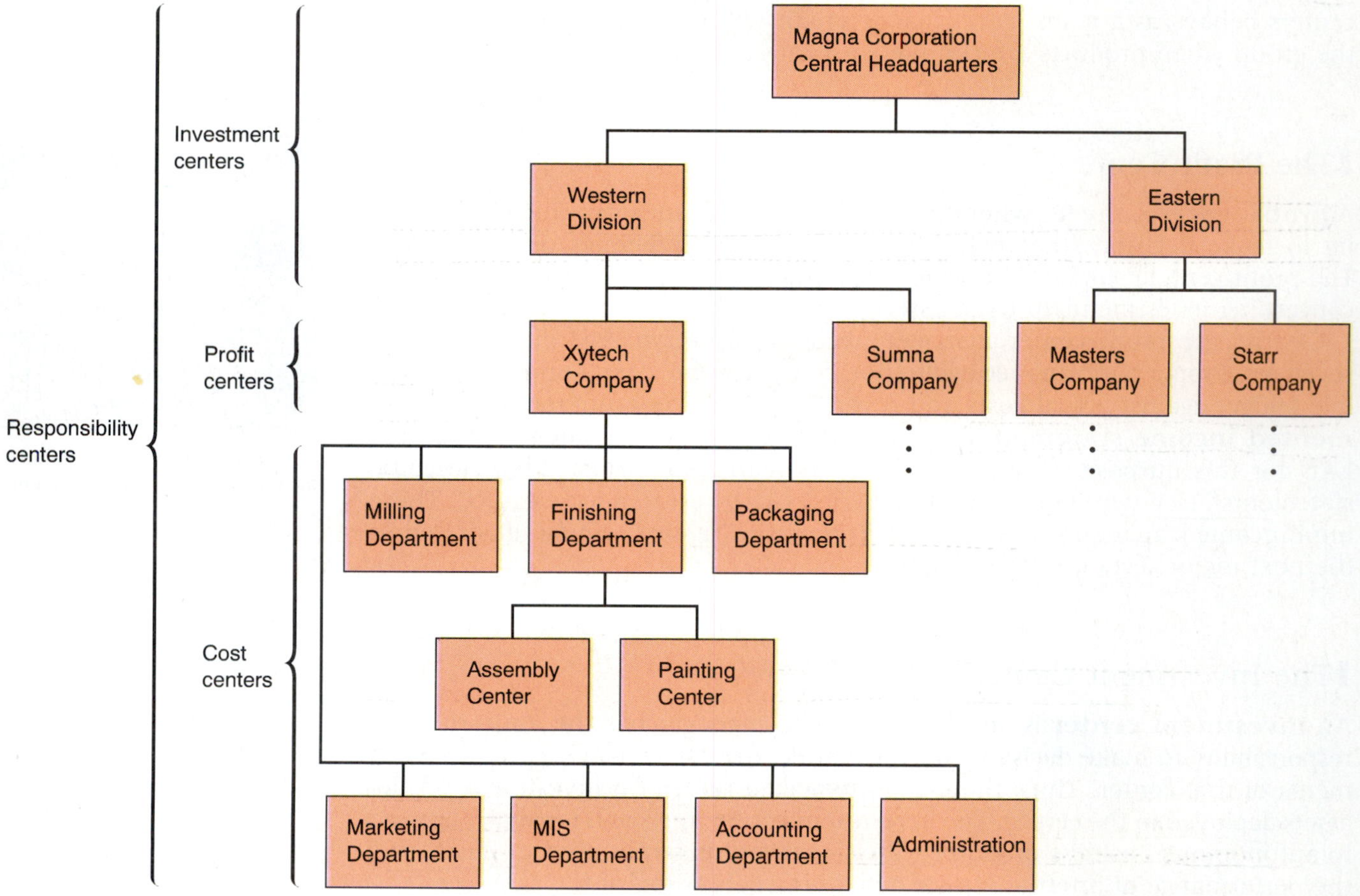

Responsibility centers

Investment centers
- Magna Corporation Central Headquarters
- Western Division
- Eastern Division

Profit centers
- Xytech Company
- Sumna Company
- Masters Company
- Starr Company

Cost centers
- Milling Department
- Finishing Department
- Packaging Department
- Assembly Center
- Painting Center
- Marketing Department
- MIS Department
- Accounting Department
- Administration

■■ EXHIBIT 20–6
Responsibility Centers of Mallard Company

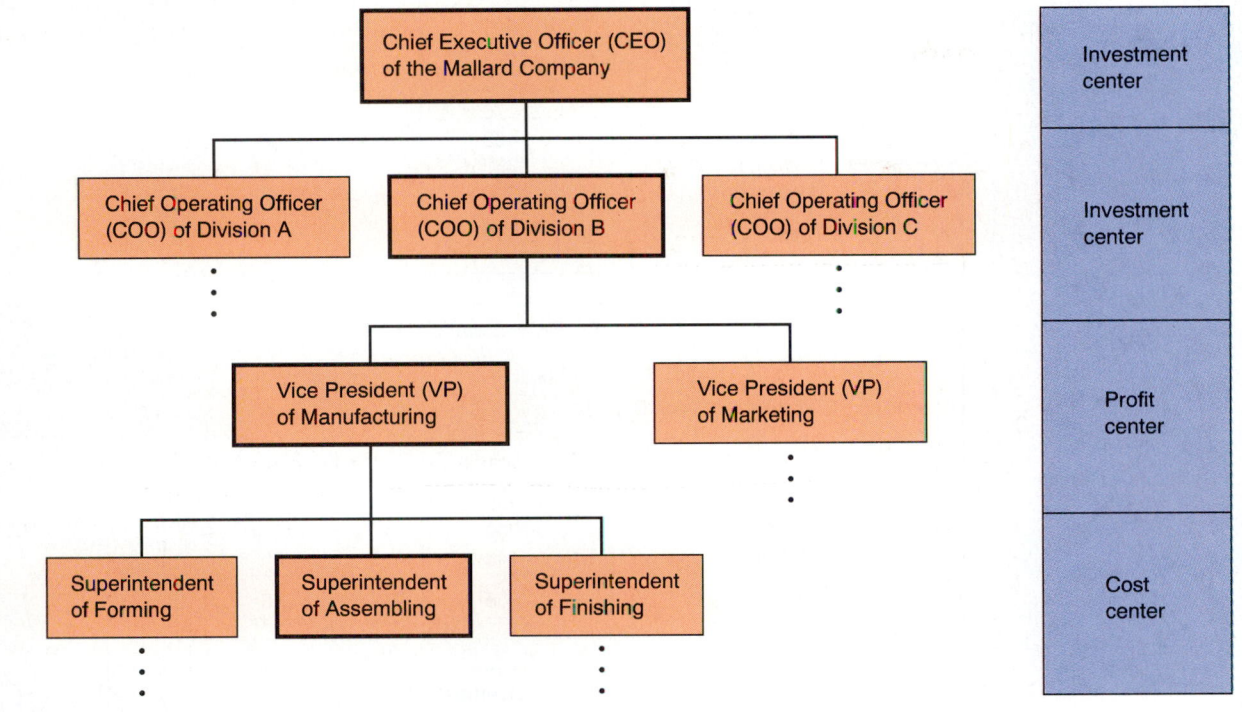

be used for illustrative purposes. Exhibit 20–7 illustrates the overhead reports for each RC and the relationship of each report to the next higher echelon of responsibility. Starting with report A at the bottom of Exhibit 20–7, the Assembling Department superintendent receives a detailed report that discloses the costs of the overhead items within his RC and the amount under or over the budget.

Report B provides the vice president of manufacturing with performance figures for her RC, including the Forming, Assembling, and Finishing Departments within manufacturing. Report C provides the chief operating officer (COO) of Division B with performance figures for this division and summary figures for the manufacturing and marketing departments within Division B. Report D provides the CEO at company headquarters with summary figures for the three divisions that comprise the Mallard Company. Variances from budget can be traced downward through the organization as needed to show where management can control costs.

▌The Importance of Controllability in Responsibility Accounting

No matter what RC level is being evaluated, responsibility accounting is effective only when the RC manager being evaluated has internalized a sense of ownership, autonomy, and controllability. In order to ensure this, activities and financial factors deemed to be uncontrollable for a particular manager should be excluded when evaluating this person's performance. However, it is important to recognize that costs that are not controllable at a certain level are controllable elsewhere in the enterprise. For example, while the head of a department may have influence over the amount of space her area consumes, it is unlikely that she will have control over her own salary and benefits.

■■EXHIBIT 20–7
**Levels of Reporting
for Selected
Responsibility Centers
of Mallard Company**

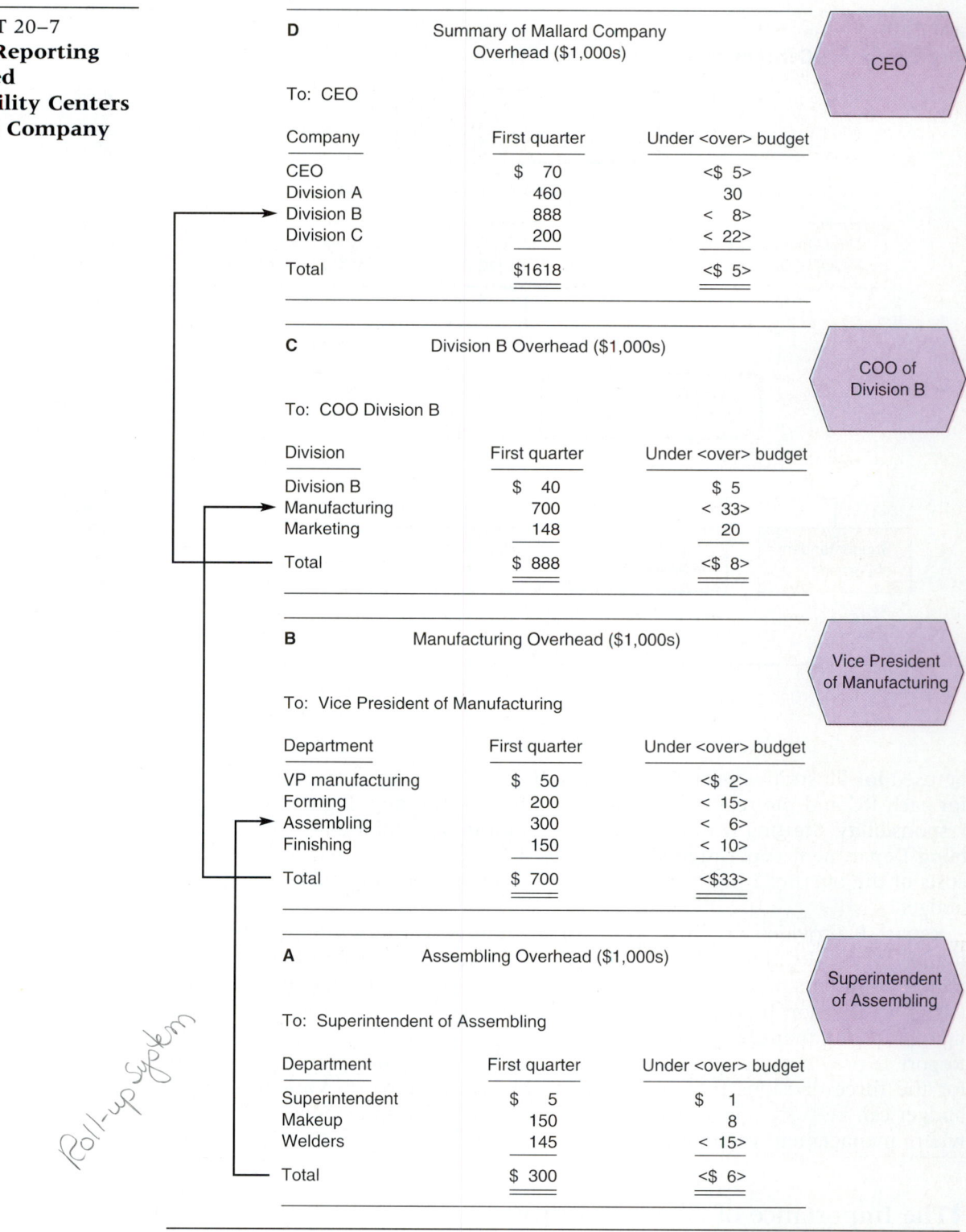

D — Summary of Mallard Company Overhead ($1,000s)

To: CEO

Company	First quarter	Under <over> budget
CEO	$ 70	<$ 5>
Division A	460	30
Division B	888	< 8>
Division C	200	< 22>
Total	$1618	<$ 5>

CEO

C — Division B Overhead ($1,000s)

To: COO Division B

Division	First quarter	Under <over> budget
Division B	$ 40	$ 5
Manufacturing	700	< 33>
Marketing	148	20
Total	$ 888	<$ 8>

COO of Division B

B — Manufacturing Overhead ($1,000s)

To: Vice President of Manufacturing

Department	First quarter	Under <over> budget
VP manufacturing	$ 50	<$ 2>
Forming	200	< 15>
Assembling	300	< 6>
Finishing	150	< 10>
Total	$ 700	<$33>

Vice President of Manufacturing

A — Assembling Overhead ($1,000s)

To: Superintendent of Assembling

Department	First quarter	Under <over> budget
Superintendent	$ 5	$ 1
Makeup	150	8
Welders	145	< 15>
Total	$ 300	<$ 6>

Superintendent of Assembling

Roll-up system

In a responsibility accounting system, attention is directed toward managers and how much money they are spending to perform their activities. Successful operation of a responsibility accounting system therefore rests on two assumptions:

■ Spending is subject to control.
■ Responsibility for spending can be directly traced to a specific manager.

In practice, these assumptions contain some degree of subjectivity. As part of the strategic planning and master budgeting process, there must be consensus and agreement about who is responsible for budgeting and controlling each of the enterprise's activities. Explicit recognition of the responsibility assumptions is a prerequisite for a high-quality responsibility accounting system.

Indeed, the ability to control spending is not an absolute, but rather a matter of degree driven by:

- Level of authority
- Time

This does not mean that some spending is clearly controllable and other spending is definitely uncontrollable, but that all spending is controllable at some level of authority at some point in time. The manager of a production department may not control the expenditures for machines or the insurance for the machines in her department, but her manufacturing superintendent may. In summary, if a manager's decision can substantially influence the amount of spending, then the spending is assumed to be controllable by that manager.

Some companies report all profit center costs within segmented income statements and profit variance reports, even though some of the costs are not directly controllable by the managers. This approach is a violation of effective responsibility accounting, and creates ethical concerns in the areas of competency, integrity, and objectivity.

The rationale behind reporting uncontrollable costs is that it makes managers aware of the *total* costs of their activities. For example, even though an enterprise may be highly decentralized, some support services may be centralized at corporate headquarters. Often, ICBIS and accounting services, human resources departments, and some advertising activities are performed for the divisions. By allocating the costs of these corporate services to the divisions, using service department allocation techniques (Chapter 9) and activity-based costing techniques (Chapter 10), the divisional managers will be more aware of the costs and, consequently, so upper management believes, will not use these services wastefully or abuse them.

The modern management accountant must be very careful in allocating common corporate costs to the divisions. Not only do divisional managers seldom have control over the costs of these services, but if actual costs are allocated to the divisions, the corporate service center managers will have little incentive to control these costs. As Chapter 9 illustrated, traditional actual cost allocation systems, designed primarily for financial accounting purposes, can destroy the legitimacy of the responsibility accounting system.

Divisional managers may only have control over how much of a service they use. Consistent with the techniques described in Chapter 9, then, service department costs should be allocated using a budgeted rate for the variable costs and budgeted lump-sum allocations for the fixed costs. This will allow proper variance reporting in accordance with the controllability axiom. If a policy decision is made to include noncontrollable costs, such costs should be categorized separately in responsibility reports to emphasize that they are not considered controllable at that level.

Is There One Prescribed Way to Create Responsibility Centers?

Organization structures are too varied to permit generalization, as is readily apparent from the preceding description of the different ways to create RCs. Enterprises differ so widely in their goals, operations, philosophies, and personnel that no single form of organization structure and RCs will work for all of them. All RCs, however, require the following:

- Clear-cut lines of responsibility must be drawn.
- Responsibility must be coupled with commensurate authority.

Fuzzy lines of responsibility will bring only bickering and buck-passing. But giving RC managers responsibility for something they have no authority to control is even worse. Thus, to make the RC idea work, managers must be given clear responsibilities and sufficient authority to meet those responsibilities.

LEARNING OBJECTIVE 3

Segment the profit center's income statement for segment and manager performance evaluation.

SEGMENTED INCOME STATEMENTS AND PROFIT CENTER PERFORMANCE EVALUATION

In evaluating a profit center's financial performance, the management accounting system has two basic goals:

- To report on the profitability of the segment
- To report on the performance of the segment manager

First, this section will present two formats for the segmented income statement. Then, reporting for each of the two goals will be examined. Finally, the usefulness of segmented income statements in the decision to continue or drop a product line will be addressed.

Functional Form and Contribution Margin–Based Income Statements

For financial reporting, the income statement organizes costs by their functions (product costs versus operating expenses). This format also employs absorption costing in that fixed overhead is absorbed into the product cost. When segmenting an income statement, using the absorption costing principle, indirect costs (common fixed costs across all profit centers) are allocated to (absorbed by) the profit centers, as presented in the Nulife case on the next page.

As Exhibit 20–8 shows, Nulife has been allocated $30,000 in common corporate costs.[1] Of this amount, $18,000 was allocated to Tigerade and $12,000 was allocated to Lions Crunch. The controller explained to Karen that these allocations are for corporate services provided to the profit centers, such as centralized accounting and human resources department costs.

Upon further investigation, Karen discovered that Nulife uses a very common allocation method. These *actual* costs are allocated based on the relative sales revenues of each product. Tigerade, generating $360,000 of Nulife's $600,000 total revenues (which is 60 percent), was allocated 60 percent of the common corporate costs. Lions Crunch generated 40 percent of Nulife's revenues ($240,000 ÷ $600,000) and was allocated 40 percent of the $30,000. This allocation method has been justified by an "ability to bear" philosophy. The more revenues a product creates, the greater its ability to absorb ("bear") the common fixed costs.

Karen is suspicious of this technique, though, when it is used in evaluating product profitability and profit center manager performance. As she explained to J. B., if sales revenues of one product go down, then the allocation of common fixed costs will also go down, making the *product* look more profitable. Allocations to the other products will then increase, making them look worse, even though there may not have been any real change in their profitability.

To illustrate this to J. B., Karen prepared the analysis following Exhibit 20–8. Assume that Tigerade revenues drop $100,000 to $260,000.

---

[1] Allocated corporate costs are the last line item under selling and administrative expenses.

INSIGHTS & APPLICATIONS

Nulife Sport Drink, Inc.

This case is a continuation of the case used in Chapter 8 to illustrate cost variance reporting. Nulife has segmented itself by product line. Tigerade sports drink is one of Nulife's profit centers. The manager of this segment, J. B. Fuller, has just introduced a new related product line, Lions Crunch health bars. Both products are considered to be within this profit center.

In attempting to establish Lions Crunch, Nulife has marketed it in two regions, the East Coast and the West Coast. J. B. Fuller has just received his July income statement, segmented by product line. This is presented in Exhibit 20–8. Obviously, he is concerned about the poor reported performance of Lions Crunch, and he has asked the new management accountant, Karen Rosenau, to analyze it and report back to him.

After consulting with the corporate controller, Karen believes the company is using good absorption costing techniques for financial reporting purposes. However, she also believes that reformatting the income statement based on a contribution margin approach, as illustrated in chapters 18 and 19, can provide more useful information for evaluating the real profitability of Lions Crunch.

	Tigerade	Lions Crunch	Nulife Totals
Revenues	$360,000	$240,000	$600,000
Less cost of goods sold:			
Variable manufacturing costs	225,250	60,000	285,250
Fixed manufacturing costs	12,100	25,000	37,100
Total production costs	<237,350>	<85,000>	<322,350>
Gross profit	$122,650	$155,000	$277,650
Less selling and administrative expenses:			
Variable selling costs	44,750	80,000	124,750
Fixed selling and administrative costs	47,900	65,000	112,900
Allocated corporate costs	18,000	12,000	30,000
Total selling and administrative costs	<110,650>	<157,000>	<267,650>
Net income	$ 12,000	<$ 2,000>	$ 10,000

■ **EXHIBIT 20–8**
Nulife's July Income Statement: Functional Form, Absorption Costing Format

	TIGERADE	LIONS CRUNCH	NULIFE TOTALS
New sales revenues	$260,000	$240,000	$500,000
New relative sales revenue ratios	52%	48%	100%
New allocation of common corporate costs	$15,600	$14,400	$30,000
Change in allocation of common corporate costs	<$2,400>	+$2,400	–0–

Because Tigerade revenues decreased, the allocated common costs went down for Tigerade. In effect, this makes Tigerade appear more profitable than it is. Tigerade's variable cost ratio is 75 percent (($225,250 + $44,750) ÷ $360,000) and its CM ratio is 25 percent. If Tigerade revenues go down by $100,000, then its contribution margin and net income drop $25,000 (CVP rules 4 and 1, respectively, Exhibit 18–3). The decrease in Tigerade profits of $25,000 is partially masked by the $2,400 reduction in allocated common corporate costs.

Meanwhile, there was no real change in the sales, costs, or profits of Lions Crunch. But, because Tigerade revenues went down, Lions Crunch is now allocated another $2,400 in common corporate costs. This makes Lions Crunch's profit performance look worse, when there should be no difference.

With respect to J. B.'s performance evaluation, she argued that the allocated common corporate "overhead" should *not* be included in evaluating a *manager's* performance. J. B. Fuller has no control over the costs of these corporate services, especially the *actual* costs. They should also not be considered in evaluating the *segment's* real profit contribution to covering overall corporate costs and generating profits.

J. B. Fuller was perplexed. He has no control over the costs of the common corporate services, nor is he allowed to outsource these services if he can obtain them cheaper from another supplier, or perform them within his profit center if he can do it cheaper than corporate headquarters. Karen agreed. Both in measuring the real profitability of the products and in evaluating J. B. Fuller's performance, these common fixed costs should not be included. To determine the real profitability of the products, Karen created a worksheet in a spreadsheet program to segment the income statement by product line, using a contribution margin approach that separates the allocated common fixed corporate costs from the direct costs of each product line. This format is displayed in Exhibit 20–9.

The only difference in the product net incomes between the two income statement formats is that allocated common fixed costs are included under the **functional form, absorption costing–based income statement** in Exhibit 20–8, whereas under the contribution margin–based approach the common fixed costs are reported separately just in the totals column. The functional form, absorption costing–based income statement allocates all costs to all product lines. The **contribution margin–based income statement** format organizes costs by behavior and separates the common fixed costs from the direct fixed costs of the segments.

Evaluating Profit Center Profitability

Karen believes that by separating the common fixed costs from the direct fixed costs, a better measure of the true profitability of the product lines results.

EXHIBIT 20–9
Nulife's July Income Statement: Contribution Margin Format

	Tigerade[a]			Lions Crunch			Nulife Totals	
	Per unit[b]	Percent	Totals	Per unit	Percent	Totals	Percent	Totals
Revenues	$40	100%	$360,000	$24	100%	$240,000	100%	$600,000
Less variable costs:								
Variable manufacturing costs	25	63%	225,250	6	25%	60,000	47%	285,250
Variable selling costs	5	12%	44,750	8	33%	80,000	21%	124,750
Total variable costs	<30>	<75%>	<270,000>	<14>	<58%>	<140,000>	<68%>	<410,000>
Contribution margin	$10	25%	$ 90,000	$10	42%	$100,000	32%	$190,000
Less direct fixed costs:								
Fixed manufacturing costs			12,100			25,000		37,100
Fixed selling and								
administrative costs			47,900			65,000		112,900
Total fixed costs			<60,000>			<90,000>		<150,000>
Segment margin			$ 30,000			$ 10,000		$ 40,000
Less common fixed costs								<30,000>
Net income								$ 10,000

Notes:

a. Sales volume for Tigerade = 9,000 cases; sales volume for Lions Crunch = 10,000 cases.

b. The per unit and percent columns are calculated by working backwards from the totals column. For example, the $225,250 total variable manufacturing costs for Tigerade (from Exhibit 8–12) divided by 9,000 cases = $25.0278 per case. Dividing $225,250 by Tigerade revenues of $360,000 = 62.5694% for the percent column. The per unit and percent columns are formatted to the nearest whole dollar and percentage for clarity in presentation.

THE USEFULNESS OF SEGMENT MARGINS.   The "direct" profit generated by each product line is measured in its segment margin. In Exhibit 20–9, J. B. Fuller sees that each product creates positive profits for use in covering the common fixed costs of Nulife and in generating overall corporate profits. In other words, Tigerade contributed $30,000 in direct profits and Lions Crunch contributed another $10,000.

J. B. found this format more useful because it reports each product's contribution margin for use in short-run decisions (illustrated in Chapters 18 and 19), as well as each product's segment margin for use in evaluating the profitability of those segments.

University bookstores are profit centers.

SUBSEGMENTING PRODUCT LINES INTO GEOGRAPHIC TERRITORIES.
J. B. Fuller is also interested in the profitability of the two sales territories where Lions Crunch has been test marketed. So, he asked Karen to use her spreadsheet program to create a Lions Crunch income statement segmented by East Coast and West Coast. Exhibit 20–10 presents her report.

Karen explained to J. B. how she prepared her report. First, the Lions Crunch income statement in Exhibit 20–9 is the same as in the Lions Crunch Totals column of Exhibit 20–10. Lions Crunch direct fixed selling and administrative costs (Exhibit 20–9) were $65,000 in July. Of this amount, $50,000 represented selling expenses directly traceable to each sales territory ($10,000 on the East Coast and $40,000 on the West Coast).

The remaining $15,000 (of the $65,000 total) represented common administrative costs of Lions Crunch. Both regions are serviced by a single manufacturing plant, so its $25,000 in FOH is also common to the territories. Therefore, neither of these amounts is included in the regional segment margins. Instead, these costs are separately reported only in the Totals column for Lions Crunch (Exhibit 20–10). To summarize, of the $90,000 in direct fixed costs of Lions Crunch, $50,000 is directly traceable to each region and $40,000 is common to them.

■■■ EXHIBIT 20–10
Segmented Income Statement for Lions Crunch

	East Coast[a]			West Coast			Lions Crunch	
	Per unit[b]	Percent	Totals	Per unit	Percent	Totals	Percent	Totals
Revenues	$24	100%	$96,000	$24	100%	$144,000	100%	$240,000
Less variable costs:								
Variable manufacturing costs	6	25%	24,000	6	25%	36,000	25%	60,000
Variable selling costs	5	21%	20,000	10	42%	60,000	33%	80,000
Total variable costs	<11>	<46%>	<44,000>	<16>	<67%>	<96,000>	<58%>	<140,000>
Contribution margin	$13	54%	$52,000	$ 8	33%	$ 48,000	42%	$100,000
Less direct fixed selling costs			<10,000>			<40,000>		<50,000>
Segment margin (Direct profit)			$42,000			$ 8,000		$ 50,000
Less common fixed costs:								
Fixed manufacturing costs								25,000
Fixed administrative costs								15,000
Total fixed costs								<40,000>
Net income								$ 10,000

Notes:
a. Sales volume for East Coast = 4,000 cases; sales volume for West Coast = 6,000 cases.
b. See note b in Exhibit 20–9 concerning calculations of per unit and percentage amounts.

J. B. Fuller now has a better picture for evaluating the profitability of each region. While both contributed positively, the East Coast significantly outperformed the West Coast. This was expected, J. B. explained to Karen. Attempting to penetrate the very competitive West Coast was expensive. Variable selling expenses (coupons, higher commissions to retail jobbers) were twice as high as on the East Coast. This caused a lower CMU and CM ratio for the West Coast. Furthermore, fixed advertising costs were four times greater than on the East Coast. One bit of good news, though, was that West Coast sales actually were higher than the East Coast.

Evaluating Profit Center Manager Performance

J. B. Fuller then returned to his analysis of Tigerade and Lions Crunch (Exhibit 20–9). "Well, I guess I should give those two accounting interns you suggested I hire to manage each product line a bonus. It looks like the Tigerade intern should get three times the bonus of the Lions Crunch intern, though."

Karen interrupted with a warning, "The segment margins may not be the best performance measure for evaluating a manager. Some of the direct fixed costs of a segment may not really be *controllable* by the segment manager. For example, if a division provides its segments with administrative services, including accounting, ICBIS, and/or advertising, then these costs should be separated from the direct fixed costs that the segment managers can control."

J. B. responded, "O.K., they had control over their production, distribution, and sales. So these costs should be controllable direct costs of the product lines.[2] But wait a minute, the interns have no control over their own salaries. I control that. So keep the salaries within the calculations of the segment margins, but separate them from the controllable direct fixed costs."

THE USEFULNESS OF CONTROLLABLE SEGMENT MARGINS. Karen modified her spreadsheet program by separating the direct fixed costs of each product line ($60,000 and $90,000 in Exhibit 20–9) into those that were controllable by the managers and those that were not. Her new report is shown in Exhibit 20–11. The fixed selling expenses within each product were separated from the salaries of the accounting interns (that were journalized and posted to individual product line administrative expense accounts within the accounting system). Karen created a new subtotal, **controllable segment margin.** This can be used to evaluate the profit created from the activities under the control of the managers. Controllable segment margin includes only those activities for which the manager has decision-making responsibilities.

J. B. Fuller was impressed. "Based on this report, I think I should only give twice the bonus to the Tigerade intern. His decisions generated $50,000 toward covering common fixed costs and creating profits, while the Lions Crunch intern generated only $25,000 in controllable segment margin."

Again Karen interrupted with a warning. "The segments may not be directly comparable. We have to guard against falling into the "deadly parallel evaluation strategy" without first comparing their performance against their budgets. For example, using the controllable segment margins that *actually resulted* does not take into consideration differences between the two segments that are reflected in their budgets.

"We should not just automatically compare the actual results of each segment, nor should we compare only the *actual* performance of a segment against its previous year. Although this has been a common practice at Nulife, there is no guarantee that this year is comparable to last year. A number of strategic

---

[2] Normally, it is assumed that all variable costs and, thus, contribution margins are controllable by profit center segments.

■■■EXHIBIT 20–11
Nulife's July Income Statement: Controllable Contribution Margin Format

	Tigerade[a]			Lions Crunch			Nulife Totals	
	Per unit[b]	Percent	Totals	Per unit	Percent	Totals	Percent	Totals
Revenues	$40	100%	$360,000	$24	100%	$240,000	100%	$600,000
Less variable costs:								
Variable manufacturing costs	25	63%	225,250	6	25%	60,000	47%	285,250
Variable selling costs	5	12%	44,750	8	33%	80,000	21%	124,750
Total variable costs	<30>	<75%>	<270,000>	<14>	<58%>	<140,000>	<68%>	<410,000>
Contribution margin	$10	25%	$ 90,000	$10	42%	$100,000	32%	$190,000
Less controllable direct fixed costs:								
Fixed manufacturing costs			12,100			25,000		37,100
Fixed selling costs			27,900			50,000		77,900
Total controllable direct fixed costs			<40,000>			<75,000>		<115,000>
Controllable segment margin			$ 50,000			$ 25,000		$ 75,000
Less uncontrollable direct fixed costs:								
Fixed administrative costs			<20,000>			<15,000>		<35,000>
Segment margin			$ 30,000			$ 10,000		$40,000
Less common fixed costs								<30,000>
Net income								$ 10,000

Notes:

a. Sales volume for Tigerade = 9,000 cases; sales volume for Lions Crunch = 10,000 cases.
b. See note b in Exhibit 20–9 concerning calculations of per unit and percentage amounts.

and environmental factors could make the actual results of one year completely different from the actual results of another year.

"For example, remember the manager of our gourmet health food product line at last year's bonus meeting? He argued that this line's profitability had increased substantially over the previous year and that he should receive a substantial bonus. However, the corporate controller pointed out that in the previous year, the manager's actual profits were below that year's master budget. Further, the difference between his actual and budgeted profits last year was even worse than in the previous year!

"While year-to-year comparisons are important in measuring long-run continuous improvement, these comparisons should be between the annual *budgets* of the segment. Annual budget-to-budget comparisons are important for moving toward world-class status. Budget-to-actual comparisons for a particular time period (such as July or the year) are just as important, though, in measuring short-run operating performance." Karen prepared a spreadsheet program to compare July's budgeted and actual performance for each product line manager. Only the Tigerade report is illustrated in Exhibit 20–12.

PROFIT VARIANCE ANALYSIS.   Karen's report includes only those activities that are controllable by the segment manager. In other words, the income statement ends with controllable segment margin. She felt this was important

██ EXHIBIT 20–12
Summary Tigerade Profit Variance Report for July

	MASTER BUDGET (VOLUME = 10,000)		SALES VOLUME VARIANCE	FLEXIBLE BUDGET (VOLUME = 9,000)		ACTUAL PROFIT TOTALS	FLEXIBLE BUDGET VARIANCES
	Per unit	Totals (a)	(b − a)	Per unit	Totals (b)	(c)	(d)*
Revenues	$35	$350,000		$35	$315,000	$360,000	$45,000 F
Less variable costs:							
Variable manufacturing costs	26	260,000		26	234,000	225,250	8,750 F
Variable selling costs	5	50,000		5	45,000	44,750	250 F
Total variable costs	<31>	<310,000>		<31>	<279,000>	<270,000>	9,000 F
Contribution margin	$ 4	$ 40,000	<$4,000> U	$ 4	$36,000	$90,000	$54,000 F
Less controllable direct fixed costs:							
Fixed manufacturing costs		12,000			12,000	12,100	<100> U
Fixed selling costs		28,000			28,000	27,900	100 F
Total controllable direct fixed costs		<40,000>			<40,000>	<40,000>	–0–
Controllable segment margin		$ –0–	<$4,000> U		<$4,000>	$ 50,000	$54,000 F

* d = c − b for revenues, contribution margin, and controllable segment margin; d = b − c for costs.

for proper use of profit variances in performance evaluation. This is an example of one component of a high-quality responsibility accounting system. **Profit variances** are the difference between the master budget pro forma income statement and the actual segmented income statement for Tigerade. Profit variances are comprised of:

- Sales variances
- Cost variances

Sales variances include:

- Sales price variance
- Sales volume variance

Cost variances include:

- Variable and fixed spending variances for selling and administrative expenses
- Variable and fixed spending and usage variances for production costs

Karen also prepared the detailed profit variance report illustrated in Exhibit 20–13. She used both reports together in explaining the difference between budgeted and actual profits in July due to the activities under the control of Tigerade's manager.

First, as she explained to J. B. Fuller, July's pro forma income statement from the master budget cannot be directly compared against the actual income statement. The master budget was based on a sales quota of 10,000 cases of Tigerade. Actual sales were only 9,000 cases. Even if there are no profit variances, a difference will result simply because of the difference in volume. The actual sales revenues, variable costs, contribution margin, and controllable segment margin will be less than the master budget just because 9,000 cases were sold instead of the 10,000 cases used to create the master budget.

So, Karen first compared the master budget against the flexible budget for July. A **flexible budget** is a budget created at the end of the period using the actual volume. The flexible budget then provides the standards to use in evaluating actual results. Both the master budget and the flexible budget are based on the profit equation for Tigerade:

	Spending	Usage	Totals
Sales variances:			
Sales volume variance			<$ 4,000>
Sales price variance			45,000
Total sales variances			$41,000
Selling and administrative expenses variances:			
Variable costs	$ 250		250
Fixed costs	100		100
Total S & A variances	$ 350		$ 350
Production costs variances:			
Direct materials	<4,000>	<$3,000>	<7,000>
Direct labor	8,750	5,000	13,750
Variable overhead	1,250	750	2,000
Fixed overhead	<100>	n/a	<100>
Total production variances	$5,900	$2,750	$ 8,650
Variance totals			$50,000

Note: Favorable variances are positive amounts, unfavorable variances are negative amounts.

Profit Equation

Tigerade monthly
    controllable   = (CMU × Volume) − Controllable direct fixed costs
segment margin

For the master budget sales quota of 10,000 cases of Tigerade:

Tigerade monthly
    controllable   = ($4 per case × 10,000 cases) − $40,000
segment margin

$$= \underline{\underline{\$0}}$$

For the actual sales volume of 9,000 cases, the flexible budget profit is:

Tigerade monthly
    controllable   = ($4 per case × 9,000 cases) − $40,000
segment margin

$$= \underline{\underline{<\$4,000>}}$$

Selling 1,000 cases less than budget means that $4 per case (its CMU) is lost. Thus, contribution margin, controllable segment margin, Tigerade segment margin, and Nulife profits will go down $4,000. This $4,000 difference is captured in the **sales volume variance**. The sales volume variance measures the difference between the master budget contribution margin and the flexible budget contribution margin due to a difference between the sales quota and actual sales volume. The variance formula is:

Sales volume variance = Budgeted contribution margin per unit
            × (Actual sales volume − Sales forecast)
        = $4 per case × (9,000 cases − 10,000 cases)
        = <$4,000> unfavorable

Because the sales volume variance explains the difference between planned and actual profits due to selling a different volume than budgeted, it is shown between the master budget and the flexible budget in Exhibit 20–12. It is also reported as the first sales variance in Exhibit 20–13.

The flexible budget variances (the last column in Exhibit 20–12) are the differences between the flexible budget amounts and the actual results. Actual sales revenues were $45,000 greater than budgeted for this volume (9,000 cases). This is due to the actual sales price being higher than the budgeted sales price. The difference between planned and actual profits due to a difference in budgeted and actual sales prices is captured in the **sales price variance:**

Spend. variance =
Actual − Flex. Budget

Sales price variance = Actual sales volume
$\times$ (Actual sales price − Budgeted sales price)
= 9,000 cases $\times$ ($40 per case − $35 per case)
= $45,000 favorable

In interpreting this variance to J. B. Fuller, Karen explained that if sales price increases $5 per unit, then CMU will increase $5. For 9,000 cases, contribution margin and profits will then increase $45,000 over budget.

After explaining the sales variances, Karen moved to the selling and administrative expenses variances. She calculated spending variances by just subtracting the actual costs from the flexible budget costs. Although the variances were favorable in July, they were insignificant, representing only 0.5 percent of the flexible budget amounts [$350 ÷ ($45,000 + $28,000)]. She then concluded with the production cost variances. These are summarized in the last section of Exhibit 20–13. Their detailed calculations, in total dollars, per unit, and as a percentage of standard, are presented in Exhibit 8–12.

J. B. Fuller had only one more question. "Why wasn't the FOH volume variance reported in either Exhibit 20–12 or 20–13?" This was a little hard for Karen to explain, so she began with the following calculations:

FOH volume variance = FOH standard cost
$\times$ (Actual volume − Budgeted volume)
= $1.20 per case $\times$ (9,000 cases − 10,000 cases)
= <$1,200> unfavorable

Other fixed costs volume variance = Other fixed standard costs
$\times$ (Actual volume − Budgeted volume)
= $2.80 per case $\times$ (9,000 cases − 10,000 cases)
= <$2,800> unfavorable

not sure about this!

From Tigerade's standard cost card (Exhibit 8–11), the sales price needs to be marked up $1.20 (the FOH standard cost) above variable costs to provide sufficient contribution margin to pay for the total FOH. This assumes that 10,000 cases of Tigerade will be sold. Also assuming 10,000 cases of sales volume, the sales price will have to be marked up another $2.80 ($28,000 ÷ 10,000 cases) to cover the other fixed selling and administrative costs. In total, Tigerade's sales price needs to be $4.00 higher than its variable cost. In other words, it has to generate a $4.00 CMU to cover fixed costs and target profit (which was budgeted at zero) if 10,000 cases are sold.

But 10,000 cases were not sold. The lost contribution margin from lower actual sales is captured in the sales volume variance. The $4.00 CMU used in the formula includes $1.20 for FOH and $2.80 for other fixed costs. Therefore, the FOH volume variance is already included in the sales volume variance. This is why Karen reported it as not applicable (n/a) in Exhibit 20–13.

J.B. now understood the need for profit variance analysis when evaluating the managers' performance. Before he could decide on bonuses, he asked Karen to prepare a similar analysis for Lions Crunch.

The Add-or-Drop Decision

The **add-or-drop decision** deals with whether to add, drop, or continue a particular product, line of products, enterprise segment, or service. Both qualitative and quantitative factors must be considered when making such decisions. Ultimately, however, any decision to add or drop a product, product line, department, or territory is going to center on the impact the decision will have on overall enterprise profits.

CONSIDERING QUALITATIVE FACTORS. The decision to add or drop a product, product line, segment, or service is often complicated by various marketing considerations. Many enterprises believe they are obligated to carry a range of sizes, colors, styles, flavors, or related items. These marketing factors can outweigh persuasive quantitative data to the contrary.

Often certain products are sold at a loss (based on full costs) in order to attract customers. For example, a shoe store may sell socks at $1 a pair to attract customers to the store in the hope of selling shoes at regular price. In some enterprises, these "loss leaders" are considered an integral part of marketing strategy. These qualitative issues represent legitimate factors that management accountants must consider.

CONSIDERING QUANTITATIVE FACTORS.   If the question involves dropping a product, service, or segment, then only the fixed costs that can be avoided by dropping the item are subtracted from that item's contribution margin. If the result is positive, then the item should be kept (or added) because this amount increases the profits of the enterprise. The Computerworld case on the next page demonstrates this analysis.

Direct fixed costs are directly traceable to each product line, but they may or may not be avoided if the product line is dropped. All or part of these costs may be sunk costs that will continue even if the product line is dropped. Indeed, this is the situation at Computerworld because a large portion of the direct fixed costs for office supplies is depreciation on display racks and cases. Moreover, managers of the office supplies product line will be kept on the payroll even if the product line is dropped, although some employees who specialize in office supplies will be discharged. In Computerworld's case, the $16,000 in direct fixed costs is composed of the following items (in thousands):

Cost Item	Avoidable	Unavoidable
Depreciation of display racks and cases		$ 7
Salaries of managers		4
Salaries of discharged employees	$5	
Total direct fixed costs	$5	$11

The common fixed costs of $18,000 cannot be avoided by dropping the office supplies product line, because they are composed of store rent and general management salaries that will continue even if office supplies are dropped. The company originally expected that some of the common fixed administrative costs could be avoided, such as reducing the accounting staff, but upon further investigation, this does not appear likely. Therefore, the common fixed costs are unavoidable regardless of the decision with respect to office supplies.

If Computerworld drops the office supplies product line, the company's overall net income will decrease by $25,000 each month. Computerworld will lose

INSIGHTS & APPLICATIONS

Computerworld's Product Line Cost Analysis

Computerworld is a small retail chain that sells personal computers, peripherals such as printers, software packages, and office supplies.

Management of Computerworld is concerned about the loss in the office supplies line as reported on the functional form, absorption costing-based income statement used for financial reporting. Common fixed costs of $18,000 were allocated to it, resulting in a reported loss of $4,000.[3] Several managers have recommended that to improve the company's overall net income, office supplies must be dropped. The management accountant for Computerworld explained that the decision rests on what costs can be avoided to offset the loss in contribution margin if the office supplies product line is dropped. She went on to tell them that both direct fixed costs and common fixed costs must be considered. Data (in thousands of dollars) on these four product lines for the past month are as follows:

	PERSONAL COMPUTERS	PERIPHERALS	SOFTWARE PACKAGES	OFFICE SUPPLIES	TOTALS
Sales	$800	$200	$400	$300	$1,700
Variable costs	<500>	<100>	<250>	<270>	<1,120>
Contribution margin	300	100	150	30	580
Direct fixed costs	<150>	<40>	<70>	<16>	<276>
Segment margin	$150	$ 60	$ 80	$ 14	$ 304

$30,000 in contribution margin and only avoid (save) $5,000 in direct fixed costs.

SUPPLEMENTARY METHODS USED IN THE ADD-OR-DROP DECISION. Two supplementary methods are available that can help in making the add-or-drop decision:

- Product life cycle analysis
- Growth/share matrix

Using Product Life Cycle Analysis

Product life cycle analysis is a useful aid to managers who must determine how to allocate scarce resources to products or product lines in a manner that will maximize enterprise profitability.[4] A graph of sales volume and net profit at various stages of the product life cycle is presented in Exhibit 20–14.

Managers can use the product life cycle graph to monitor product profitability and to drop products when they become unprofitable. In the maturity and decline stages, it is important to determine if other products will contribute more per dollar of cost. At some point during the decline stage, management may decide to hasten the product's decline so that cash can be generated to support products that will sustain the enterprise's profitability in the long run.[5] A good example is Intel's efforts in 1992 to supplant its less profitable 386 microprocessor with the 486 chip, although the 386 was nowhere near the end of its life cycle. In 1993, Intel introduced Pentium,™ a microprocessor that is designed to replace the 486 microprocessor.

[3] Subtracting allocated common fixed costs of $18,000 from the reported segment margin of $14,000 produces the absorption costing–based net loss of <$4,000>.

[4] Douglas M. Lambert, *The Product Abandonment Decision* (Montvale, N.J.: National Association of Accountants; Hamilton, Ontario: Society of Management Accountants of Canada, 1985), p. 9. With permission.

[5] Ibid., p. 10.

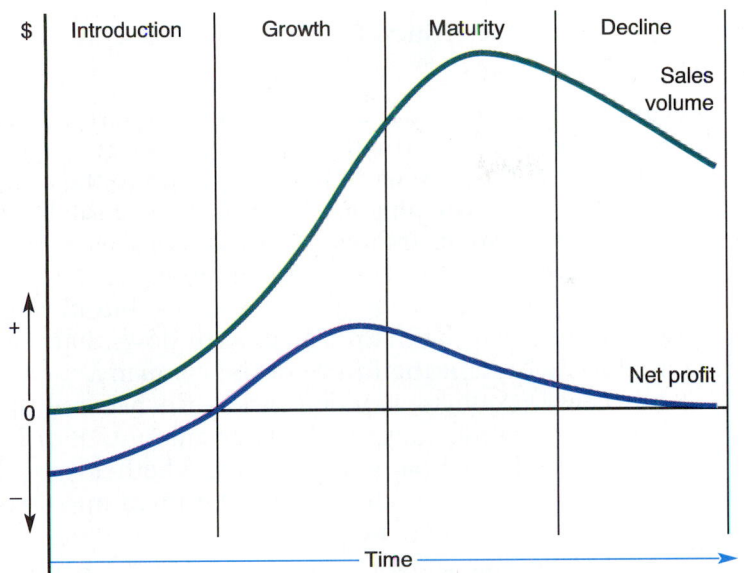

■ EXHIBIT 20–14
Sales Volume and Net Profit at Various Stages of the Product Life Cycle

Using the Growth/Share Matrix

The **growth/share matrix** is based on the following assumptions:

- Cash flow is a measure of business success.
- Cash use is a function of market growth.
- Cash generation is a function of the product's market share. The result is a growth/share matrix like the one illustrated in Exhibit 20–15. Each quadrant describes a different type of product with fundamentally different cash flow

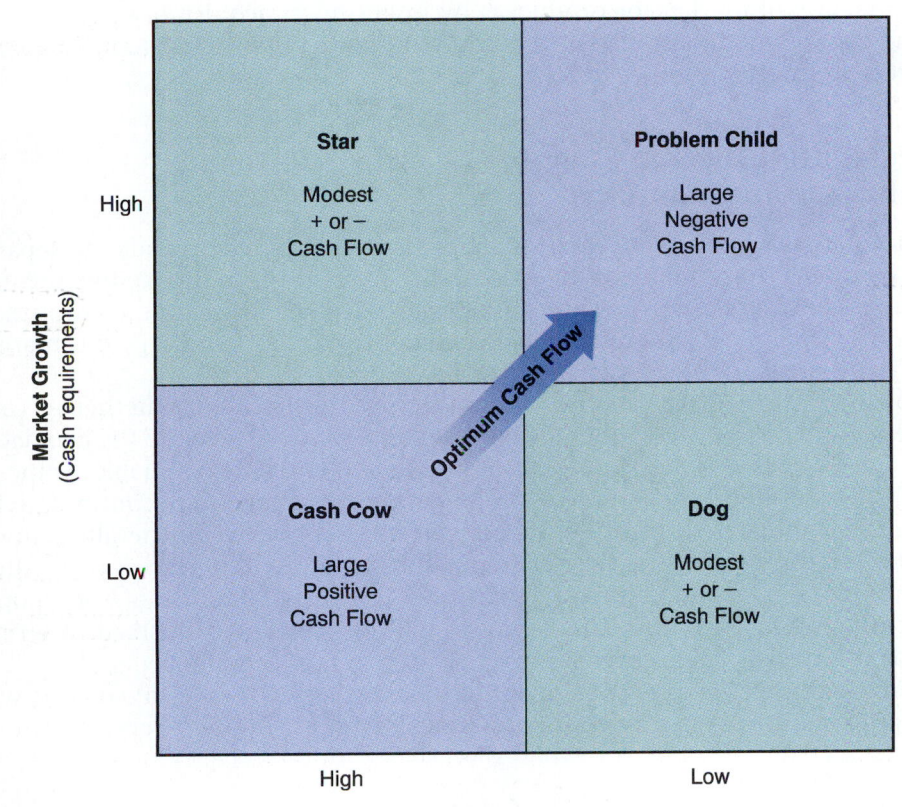

■ EXHIBIT 20–15
Growth/Share Matrix

Source: Michael E. Porter, *Competitive Strategy: Techniques for Analyzing Industries and Competitors* (New York: Free Press, 1980), p. 362. With permission.

positions and specific characteristics. Each type of product requires a specific management strategy:

- *Cash cows.* Because of their high market share, these products generate more cash than is required by the low-growth market in which they operate. These products provide the main source of cash and earnings to the enterprise and can be used to fund other developing products, such as in the Lotus example on the next page. The arrow in Exhibit 20–15 demonstrates how proceeds from cash cows are used to support problem children.
- *Stars.* These products generate a large gross cash flow, but most of the cash is used to support their high growth rate. As growth slows, stars become cash cows. These products represent the future of the company.
- *Problem children.* These products generate little cash because of their low market share. At the same time, they require large amounts of cash to support their high growth rate. The company must decide whether to try to achieve a high market share for these products by turning them into stars and ultimately cash cows or to drop them altogether.
- *Dogs.* These products neither generate nor require much cash. Because of their low market share and low growth, dogs offer little opportunity for future profits. Generally, the most effective decision is to drop these products.[6]

Preparing product profitability reports that show cash flows is one method that is used to validate the positioning of products on the growth/share matrix. The management accountant plays a significant role in this process.

The growth/share matrix can also be expanded to show both the present and future positions of each product as determined by product life cycle analysis and the marketing strategy of the enterprise. For example, Exhibit 20–16 highlights the following strategies for products A through G:

- Aggressively support newly introduced product A to ensure dominance
- Continue present strategies for products B and C to ensure maintenance of market share
- Gain share of market for product D by investing in acquisitions
- Narrow and modify the range of models of product E to focus on one segment
- Drop products F and G[7]

Segmented Income Statements and Performance Evaluation in Summary

In summary, a high-quality profit management system will include the separation of direct from common fixed costs in segmenting profit center income statements. Subtracting the direct fixed costs from a segment's contribution margin creates a new subtotal called "segment margin." The segment margin is a useful measure of segment profitability.

However, the segment margin cannot be used in deciding whether to continue or discontinue the segment. Consideration has to be given to the avoidable costs involved in this decision. Not all direct fixed costs are avoidable. Some of the fixed assets, and the depreciation expense they create, may continue to be used. If so, then these future costs are not different between the alternatives to continue or discontinue the segment. If they are not differential costs, then they are not relevant to this decision.[8] Analogously, if some of the people currently employed within this segment will be reassigned (instead of terminated), then their labor costs are not relevant to this decision.

Consideration should also be given to whether any common fixed costs will change if a segment is dropped. Sometimes corporate support services can be

---

[6] Ibid., pp. 11–12.

[7] George S. Day, "Diagnosing the Product Portfolio," *Journal of Marketing,* April 1977, p. 13. With permission.

[8] Consult Chapter 19 for a discussion of which costs are relevant in profit center decisions.

INSIGHTS & APPLICATIONS

Taking Care of the Cash Cow

Lotus Development Corporation has pumped over $100 million into a groupware product called Notes, which is designed to improve communication among users. Lotus has yet to make much of a return on its Notes investment. Key employees have left, unconvinced that the company's future lies with Notes rather than its cash cow Lotus 1-2-3 spreadsheet. Lotus

1-2-3 generates two-thirds of the company's revenue. Lotus is totally dependent on 1-2-3 profits to fund research and development for other products.

But today, Lotus Notes® is hailed as a breakthrough product that allows people to access, track, share, and organize information throughout the enterprise. But, Lotus Notes® also has many potential rivals, including software vendors of development tools, E-mail, document management systems, and workflow programs.

Lotus managers said the company shifted toward Notes realizing it couldn't maintain growth in a mature, competitive spreadsheet market. The company continues to diversify without abandoning its 1-2-3 spreadsheet. In fact, Lotus has implemented scheduled spreadsheet enhancements to revitalize its famous cash cow product.[9]

---

[9] Marc Ferranti and Beth Freedman, "Lotus Enters 2nd Decade Armed with Communications Strategy," *PC Week*, June 1, 1992, p. 14.

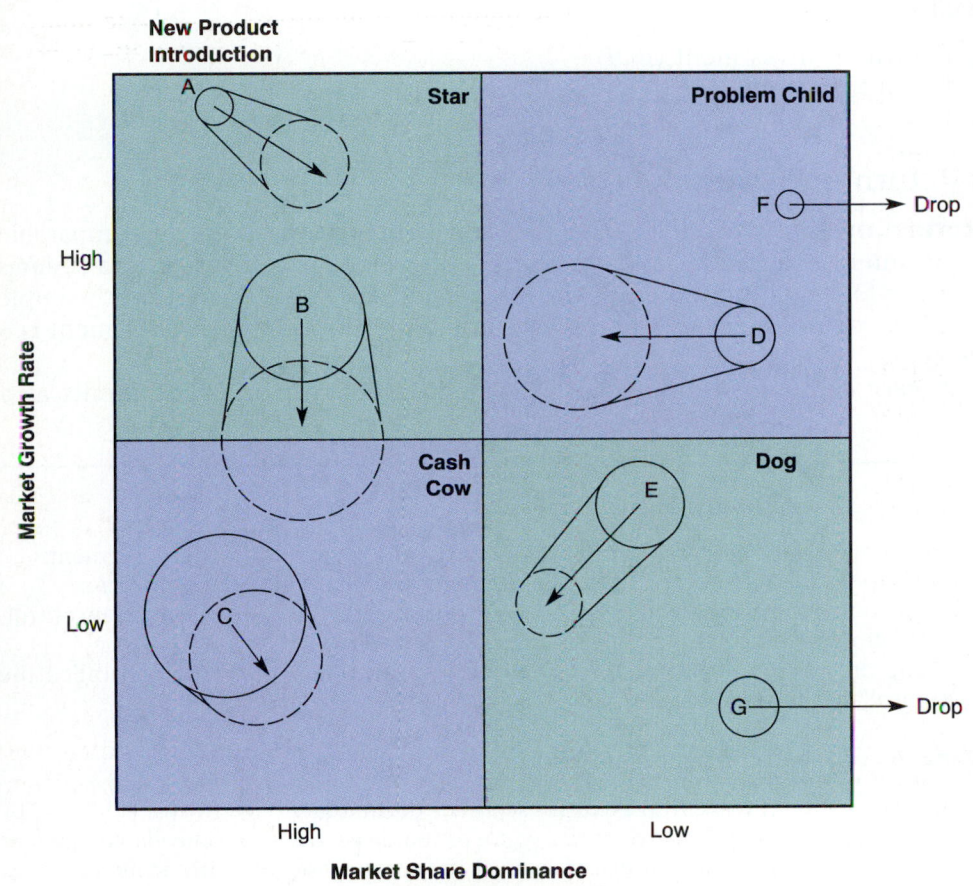

New Product Introduction

Market Growth Rate

High / Low

Star

Problem Child

Cash Cow

Dog

F → Drop

G → Drop

Market Share Dominance
(Share relative to largest competitor)

High / Low

■ EXHIBIT 20–16

Using the Growth/ Share Matrix for Product Decision Making

Source: George S. Day, "Diagnosing the Product Portfolio," *Journal of Marketing*, April 1977, p. 34. With permission.

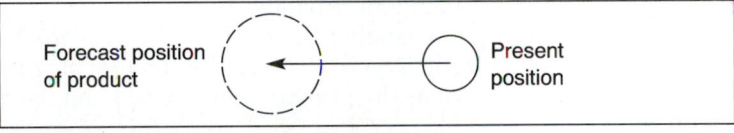

Forecast position of product   Present position

Diameter of circle is proportional to product's contribution to total company sales volume.

downsized if less services are now needed. These cost savings become relevant to this decision. Finally, in making the add-or-drop decision, supplemental analyses such as the product life cycle graph and the growth/share matrix may be helpful.

When evaluating the performance of a segment manager, the direct fixed costs within a segment need to be broken down into those that are controllable and those that are uncontrollable. The subtotal controllable segment margin that results from subtracting only the controllable direct fixed costs from the segment's contribution margin is useful for evaluating the performance of the profit center manager. However, proper performance evaluation requires the comparison of actual results against the master budget. Therefore, profit variances need to be calculated and reported to those responsible for them. Exhibit 20–17 summarizes the steps in preparing and using segmented income statements.

<table>
<tr><td>

LEARNING OBJECTIVE 5

Calculate profit performance measures for investment center managers.

</td><td>

EVALUATING INVESTMENT CENTER PROFITABILITY

Investment center managers are also responsible for profit management. Thus, segmented income statements are the first step in evaluating the profitability of investment centers and their managers. At this level of an enterprise's management hierarchy, however, asset investment responsibilities should be included in the analysis. Two commonly used financial measures of asset profitability are:

- Return on investment (ROI)
- Residual income (RI)

Return on Investment

Return on investment (ROI) (also called **return on assets**) is comparable to an interest rate on a savings account. If one dollar is invested in a savings account for one year and earns six cents in interest, then this account's simple interest rate is 6 percent. The return earned on this one-dollar investment is 6 percent.

A very common technique in reporting profits is to calculate profits as a

</td></tr>
</table>

■ EXHIBIT 20–17
Summary Steps in Segmenting the Income Statement and in Performance Evaluation

To prepare the segmented income statement:

1. Identify the allocation of common fixed costs and remove it from the segment.
2. Using only the direct fixed costs of a segment, calculate its segment margin.
3. Break down the direct fixed costs into controllable direct fixed costs versus uncontrollable direct fixed costs.
4. Using only the controllable direct fixed costs, calculate a new subtotal called the controllable segment margin.

Using the segmented income statement in decision making:

1. Use the segment margin to measure segment profitability.
2. To evaluate the performance of the segment manager, use the controllable segment margin. This should be compared against the master budget, with profit variances reported.
3. When making a decision about adding or dropping segments:
   a. Adjust the segment margin by changing the direct fixed costs to the avoidable direct fixed costs. The result is the segment margin lost by dropping the segment.
   b. Prepare graphical analyses such as the growth/share matrix and the product life cycle graph.

percentage of sales. Many profit center managers relate to sayings such as, "My profit margin last month was 15 percent." In other words, each dollar of sales returned 15 cents in net income. Investment center managers, concerned with asset investments, relate to returns (profits) measured against assets instead of sales revenues. ROI is computed as follows:

$$ROI = \frac{\text{Investment center net income}}{\text{Investment center assets}}$$

For the one-dollar savings account's interest rate calculation:

$$ROI = \$0.06 \text{ per year} \div \$1.00$$
$$= \underline{\underline{6\%}}$$

While ROI is a useful measure of the rate of return on investments, it can provide even more meaningful information if it is decomposed into its two component ratios. **Profit margin** is income divided by sales revenues. It is a short-term measure of operating efficiency, evaluating how much profit is generated from a dollar of sales. **Asset turnover ratio** is revenues divided by assets. It is a longer-term measure of the effectiveness of asset usage. This ratio provides a measure of how effective a dollar investment is in creating sales revenues. When multiplied together, these two ratios yield ROI:

$$ROI = \underbrace{\frac{\text{Investment center net income}}{\text{Investment center sales}}}_{\textit{Profit margin}} \times \underbrace{\frac{\text{Investment center sales}}{\text{Investment center assets}}}_{\textit{Asset turnover}}$$

Notice that the investment center's total sales revenue is the denominator of the first ratio and the numerator of the second. Mathematically, the two ratios can be reduced to ROI. From a performance evaluation perspective, though, each component ratio provides important information. The profit margin focuses on the rate of earnings generated by each sales dollar. Asset turnover focuses on the use of assets and indicates the rate at which sales are being generated for each dollar invested.

This decomposition also focuses attention on how investment center managers can improve their ROI:

- By increasing sales
- By reducing costs
- By reducing assets

For example, Exhibit 20–18 reports the ROIs for the two Magna Corporation investment centers previously illustrated in Exhibit 20–5. Although the Eastern and Western Divisions have the same profit margins, the Eastern Division's asset turnover is larger than the Western Division's (1.25 times compared to 0.80 times). In interpreting these ratios to upper management, the management accountant would explain that each dollar invested in the Eastern Division generates $1.25 in sales revenues and each dollar of sales contributes $0.20 in profits. For the Western Division, each dollar invested generates only $0.80 in sales, although this division also yields $0.20 in profits from each dollar of sales. Obviously, the Eastern Division uses its assets more effectively, resulting in an ROI of 25 percent compared to the Western Division's ROI of 16 percent.

These ratios help focus managerial attention on the areas where ROI can be improved. Should the investment center manager look first to the income statement for operating improvements? An actual profit margin below the master budget profit margin signals this investigation. Should the manager look instead to the balance sheet for areas to improve in asset management? A lower than budget asset turnover ratio signals this course of action. Areas of

■■■ EXHIBIT 20–18
ROIs for Eastern and Western Divisions

$$ROI = Profit\ margin \times Asset\ turnover$$

$$= \frac{Net\ income}{Sales} \times \frac{Sales}{Assets}$$

$$Eastern\ Division\ ROI = \frac{\$100,000}{\$500,000} \times \frac{\$500,000}{\$400,000}$$

$$= 20\% \times 1.25\ times$$

$$= \underline{\underline{25\%}}$$

$$Western\ Division\ ROI = \frac{\$140,000}{\$700,000} \times \frac{\$700,000}{\$875,000}$$

$$= 20\% \times 0.80\ times$$

$$= \underline{\underline{16\%}}$$

investigation are summarized in Exhibit 20–19. To improve profits on sales, the manager might investigate whether the sales prices for products are set too low. Maybe the sales mix contained too many products with low CM ratios. If there are no problems with sales price and mix, the managers should investigate costs and cost variances.

In investigating asset turnover, is actual sales volume less than budgeted? If actual sales volume is not the cause of a low ROI, maybe the investment in assets, both in mix and amount, should be rethought. For example, accounts receivable collections may be improved, lowering the average balance owed the division. Similarly, investments in inventories (RMI, WIP, and FGI) might be reduced as part of a program moving toward JIT production and delivery.

WHAT SHOULD BE INCLUDED IN NET INCOME? In designing a high-quality responsibility accounting system, the management accountant must consider which items to include in the segment's ROI calculations. For example, the net income figure used could be the absorption costing-based segment profit, segment margin, segment margin before taxes and interest, or controllable segment margin. The most appropriate figure for evaluating the performance of the manager would include only the revenues and costs over which he or she has control. For example, taxes would not be included unless the manager is responsible for tax planning. Costs allocated from corporate headquarters would also be omitted.

■■■ EXHIBIT 20–19
Areas to Investigate When ROI is Less Than Budgeted

Profit Margin lower than expected?	Asset Turnover Ratio lower than expected?
■ Sales price variance[a]	■ Sales price variance[a]
■ Sales volume variance[a]	■ Sales volume variance[a]
■ Manufacturing cost variances	■ Inventory turnover ratio
■ Selling and administrative expenses cost variances	■ Accounts receivable turnover ratio
■ CM ratio and sales mix[b]	■ Current (or quick) ratio
	■ Age of fixed assets and depreciation methods used

Notes:

a. Sales variances affect both the denominator of profit margin and the numerator of the asset turnover ratio.

b. For multiple product divisions, a CM ratio below budget may be due to a problem with sales mix.

WHICH ASSETS SHOULD BE INCLUDED IN THE BASE?   Possible alternatives to consider in selecting the base are total assets, total active or employed assets, total assets minus current liabilities, total assets minus total liabilities, fixed assets, or some combination or modification of these. As a general rule, the asset base should include those asset and liability accounts over which the manager has control and responsibility.

For example, if the manager has responsibility for the incurrence and payment of current liabilities and for managing other items that make up working capital, then total assets less current liabilities may provide the most suitable base. A manager who does not have any control over incurrence and payment of creditors would want to exclude all liabilities from the base and use total assets instead. For another example, if a manager has no control over accounts receivable, it should not be included in the asset base.

Consideration should also be given to the purpose of the segment's assets. To illustrate, maybe a building is vacant and is being held for future expansion. Should the building be included in the asset base, the investment center manager might be motivated to sell it to reduce the ROI denominator. No earnings would be lost, and the investment center's ROI would increase. Thus, excluding idle assets from the asset base deters such potentially dysfunctional behavior. Of course, if there are no plans for the idle building, the proper decision might be to sell it.

Another factor to consider is whether the asset base should consist of the beginning balance, ending balance, or an average of the assets for the time period. Use of either the beginning or ending balance may encourage managers to adjust the asset base at year-end. Moreover, this approach does not consider changes in assets during the period due to cyclical or seasonal fluctuations. Consequently, the asset base should represent a monthly or quarterly average. In more stable situations, a simple average may be sufficient (i.e., the asset base at the beginning of the period plus the asset base at the end of the period divided by two).

HOW TO VALUE ASSETS IN THE BASE.   What dollar value should be assigned to assets? Three common choices are:

■ Gross book value
■ Net book value
■ Current value

Gross book value and net book value are popular choices because these figures are easily obtained from the financial accounting database. However, neither gross book value nor net book value is completely satisfactory. The problem arises in comparing investment centers (such as the Eastern and Western Divisions in Exhibit 20–18). If one division is comprised of old assets with a lower gross book value and greater accumulated depreciation, then its ROI will be higher than a newer division with a large investment in assets and little accumulated depreciation. The older division's ROI will also be greater than the newer division's simply because there is less depreciation expense (so the numerator, net income, will be higher) and a lower gross or net investment (so the denominator will be lower).

To partially overcome this problem, current asset costs may be used in calculating ROI. The current value (also called replacement cost) is the amount required to replace the segment's assets. Using current cost is an attractive way to value assets because it represents an enterprise's investment in an investment center at the time the ROI is calculated. Current value is not widely used, however, because it is difficult to determine and is subject to dispute.

IS ROI A VALID PERFORMANCE MEASUREMENT?   There is a need to rethink the way managers use summary financial performance measurements such as ROI to evaluate investment centers. If ROI is used, it should be used in conjunction with other financial and nonfinancial performance measurements. Otherwise, a fixation on improving the elements of one performance measurement while neglecting other activities can hurt the enterprise in both the short run and the long run.

Used alone, ROI can produce distorted information. For example, managers who retain older, mostly depreciated assets report much higher ROIs than managers who invest in new assets. Managers who are evaluated this way may not be inclined to invest in assets that would make the company more competitive.

ROI-based measurements enable executives to generate greater profits from financial activities than from managing their assets better. Although a full explanation of financial activities is beyond the scope of this text, these activities include the following:

- Financial accounting procedures, such as depreciation methods (e.g., straight-line versus declining-balance method) and inventory costing procedures (e.g., LIFO versus FIFO). Choosing a particular method based solely on its effect on net income is "cooking the books." Management accountants can be placed in an ethical dilemma if they are instructed to use particular methods because of an investment center manager's desire to manipulate segment margin.
- Mergers and acquisitions
- Divestitures and spin-offs
- Debt swaps and discounted debt repurchases
- Sale-leaseback arrangements
- Leveraged buyouts

It is difficult to imagine that a focus on creating wealth through the rearrangement of ownership claims, rather than through managing tangible and intangible assets more effectively, will help enterprises survive as world-class competitors. The final and most damaging problem with ROI-based measures is the incentive they give managers to reduce expenditures on intangible investments, such as research and development, quality improvement, human resources, and customer relations. To reduce expenditures in these areas immediately improves ROI, but the long-term effect of such reductions may be disastrous.[10]

Of course, these problems can be avoided if the primary evaluation criteria are not based on comparisons *between divisions* (a deadly parallel evaluation) or on *year-to-year actual profit comparisons* within a segment. Proper performance evaluation should foremost be based on a comparison of *budgeted performance against actual*. One of the most important roles for the modern management accountant is in changing the traditional mentality that emphasizes comparing past and present performance. This mentality has led to the questioning of ROI as a valid performance metric. It has also led to the development of another financial measure, residual income.

Residual Income

Residual income (RI) is the net operating income that an investment center earns above some minimum rate of return on assets. For example, return to Exhibit 20–18 and assume that top management at Magna Corporation uses its average ROI of 15 percent as the minimum rate of return on Eastern and Western Division assets. The residual incomes for both divisions are calculated in Exhibit 20–20. Stated as a formula, residual income is:

---

[10] Robin Cooper and Robert S. Kaplan, *The Design of Cost Management Systems* (Englewood Cliffs, N.J.: Prentice-Hall, 1991), p. 62.

	Eastern Division	Western Division
Net operating income	$100,000	$140,000
Less minimum rate of return:		
$400,000 × 15%	<60,000>	
$875,000 × 15%		<131,250>
Residual income	$ 40,000	$ 8,750

■■■ EXHIBIT 20–20
RIs for Eastern Division and Western Division

RI = Net operating income − (Asset base × Minimum rate of return)

There are a number of choices for the minimum rate of return. Some companies use the weighted-average cost of capital, the overall corporate average ROI, or the incremental borrowing rate (interest rate) for the invested assets. Thus, it is often viewed as an imputed charge for the use of corporate funds for the assets of the segment. The minimum rate of return can also be changed from period to period consistent with market rate fluctuations or to adjust for risk.

The major advantage of RI as a performance measurement is that it gives consideration not only to a minimum rate of return on investment in assets, but also to the absolute size of the earnings generated by each division. Moreover, traditional management accounting theory argues that being measured by RI motivates managers to make profitable investments that would otherwise be rejected by managers evaluated with ROI.

To demonstrate this, suppose the manager of the Eastern Division has an opportunity to make an investment that will produce a ROI of 17 percent. The manager would probably reject the investment because she is already earning a rate of return of 25 percent. Because her performance is being measured by ROI, she will not be motivated to reduce her current rate of return. If Magna Corporation's average ROI is less than 17 percent, then rejecting this 17 percent ROI investment is a lost opportunity that would have benefited the total enterprise.

On the other hand, if the manager's performance is evaluated using RI, she will choose the investment because this will increase her RI.[11] Thus, goal congruency is more likely to be achieved by using RI rather than ROI as an investment center performance measurement. However, this traditional theory is based on some questionable assumptions. As an illustration, consider the information in Exhibit 20–21.

▎Which Measure Better Motivates the Investment Center Manager?

Traditional theory argues that the Eastern Division manager will not wish to undertake this project in 1995 because her 1995 ROI will be lower than her division's 1994 ROI. The corporation wants this project, however, as 1995 corporate average ROI will increase (over 1994). Thus, the use of ROI to evaluate performance motivates the manager to make the opposite decision than corporate headquarters desires.

If the manager is evaluated with RI, she will want the project, congruent with corporate desires. The RI decision rule is to accept projects with a positive RI. Since this project's projected ROI is greater than the corporate average, it yields a positive RI.

[11] This assumes that Magna uses a minimum rate of return less than 17 percent, such as its average ROI of 15 percent in Exhibit 20–20.

■ EXHIBIT 20-21
The Above Average Division's Investment Decision

MAGNA CORPORATION'S EASTERN DIVISION

Eastern Division ROI, 1994	25%
Projected ROI on investment project for 1995	17%
Corporate average ROI, 1994	15%
Investment required in project	$1,000,000
Residual income calculation:	
Income from project ($1,000,000 × 17%)	$170,000
Less minimum required by Magna ($1,000,000 × 15%)	<$150,000>
Residual income [Investment × (Project ROI − Corporate average ROI)]	$ 20,000

Notes:

1. Assume corporate headquarters will only support projects that will increase its overall average ROI. Thus, 15% is used as the "hurdle rate" in RI calculations.
2. A different version of the RI formula when the corporate average ROI is used as the RI hurdle rate is:

Investment center assets × (Investment center ROI − Corporate average ROI)

IMPLICIT ASSUMPTIONS SUPPORTING ROI OVER RI. Underlying this traditional argument are two implicit assumptions. One assumption is that the manager's performance is evaluated by comparing past and present ROIs. According to this assumption, the manager is motivated to reject the project out of fear that accepting it will lead to a lower 1995 ROI, as compared to the 1994 ROI, and thus to a "bad" evaluation.

Although there may be some descriptive validity to the assumption that current performance is compared against past performance, the modern management accountant should caution Magna management against assuming this method is optimal or even correct. Normatively, performance should be evaluated by comparing actual to planned (budgeted) performance. Cost center managers should be evaluated with cost variances, which compare standard costs against actual costs. Profit center managers should be evaluated by comparing pro forma income statements to actual income. Investment center managers should be evaluated by comparing budgeted and actual ROI (or RI).

If this is the best project the Eastern Division manager can find, she will budget a lower ROI for 1995 than the division obtained in 1994. Then, if the project's projected ROI is realized, a positive performance evaluation should result. In this case, the use of ROI or RI will not have any differential effect on the manager's planning decisions. Thus, it cannot be claimed (inferred) that RI is better than ROI *in motivating investment center planning decisions.*

The second assumption is that managers do not "see through" the accounting numbers in identifying an investment's effect on corporate profitability and ROI, and that they will not make investment decisions in the corporation's best interests. In other words, managers at this level are more motivated to improve their segment ROI than to improve the corporation's ROI.

Based upon common sense, this behavior should not be expected. Managers who have reached this level of the organization see through the accounting conventions used to evaluate performance and are highly motivated to make decisions in the best interests of the corporation. Thus, concern that a manager will not accept the 17 percent project if evaluated with ROI, but will accept it if evaluated with RI, has no basis if the manager is highly motivated to make corporate goal-congruent decisions. Again, the claim that RI leads to better planning (capital budgeting) decisions is not supported.

ALTERNATIVE BEHAVIORAL ASSUMPTIONS. Assume investment center managers are highly motivated to make goal-congruent decisions regardless of the accounting numbers used in their performance evaluations. Does it make any difference whether ROI or RI is used? According to one argument, practically attainable standards should be budgeted and used in evaluating cost center managers because these managers are not highly enough motivated to respond to ideal standards. At the investment center manager level, though, ideal standards are more consistent with their high levels of motivation. This argument may lead to the conclusion that ROI is better than RI because it is the tougher standard. For example, returning to Exhibit 20–21, the tougher standard would be to tell the manager to search for projects that beat her ROI rather than projects that generate positive RI.

Assume the organization wants an accounting measure of performance that supports the manager's motivation to search for the best projects possible. RI is not consistent with this goal as it provides a minimum hurdle rate. It is easier for the manager to find an investment project that clears the 15 percent RI hurdle than to search for projects that can improve her existing 25 percent ROI.

Before concluding that ROI is a better evaluation technique than RI, though, consider the situation presented in Exhibit 20–22. In this situation, the Western Division's ROI is less than the corporate average. Here, the tougher standard is RI. ROI is not consistent with the goal of supporting the manager's search for the best project because he could accept this 12 percent project, which would increase his ROI but lower the corporate average.

The corporation's goal in choosing an accounting technique for performance evaluation is to use the method that best supports a manager's search for the most profitable investment projects, whether or not the manager shares this motivation. If the divisional ROI is above the corporate average, then ROI is the tougher (ideal) standard. If, conversely, the divisional ROI is lower than the corporate average, then RI becomes the tougher standard. Thus, neither ROI nor RI is optimal. Choosing the method most consistent with corporate goals requires a comparison of divisional ROI to the corporate average.

Assuming that managers at this level of the organization are highly and intrinsically motivated, the following "warnings" are offered in conclusion:

- While financial measures of performance will always be important, they should not be the sole measures used in evaluating investment center managers. Some of the nonfinancial measures presented in Part III of this text are at least equally important at this level of the organization.
- Investments are long-run decisions. The use of short-run financial measures such as ROI and RI may inappropriately focus attention on the immediate payoffs (effects on first- and second-year profits) rather than long-run continuous improvements. The discounted cash flow and capital budgeting tech-

---

MAGNA CORPORATION'S WESTERN DIVISION

Western Division ROI, 1994	10%
Projected ROI on investment project for 1995	12%
Corporate average ROI, 1994	15%
Investment required in project	$1,000,000
Residual income calculation:	
Income from project ($1,000,000 × 12%)	$120,000
Less minimum required by Magna ($1,000,000 × 15%)	<$150,000>
Residual income [Investment × (Project ROI − Corporate average ROI)]	<$ 30,000>

■ EXHIBIT 20–22
The Below Average Division's Investment Decision

niques described in Part V of this text may be more relevant planning, control, and evaluation measures than ROI and RI.

■ When choosing short-run financial measures, be careful not to choose a method that can *demotivate* the managers. ROI may be a better evaluation metric for divisions with ROIs greater than the corporate average. RI, on the other hand, may be better for divisions with ROIs less than the corporate average.

In their movement toward world-class status, some companies are reengineering their organizations. Along with this, their responsibility accounting systems are measuring financial and nonfinancial activities. The Kyocera Corporation example illustrates one such attempt.

<table>
<tr><td>

LEARNING OBJECTIVE 6

Discuss Kyocera's amoeba system and new organizational structures in American firms.

</td></tr>
</table>

THE AMOEBA SYSTEM: A SPECIFIC KIND OF ORGANIZATIONAL SEGMENTATION

Kyocera Corporation is a Japanese manufacturing company that produces sophisticated ceramic materials, semiconductors, electronic equipment, optical precision instruments, and cameras. One secret of Kyocera's success is its profit management program. Kyocera instills a thorough profit management attitude in every employee. This management system is called the **amoeba system.**[12]

Features of the Amoeba System

Kyocera's smallest units are called "amoebas" because each performs similarly to the simple microorganism. An amoeba is a single cell, flexible in shape, that multiplies by cell division. Kyocera's "amoeba" is similarly flexible regarding work quantities. When it has a large amount of work or many kinds of tasks, it divides into smaller units. It moves from one section of the factory to another, breaking itself down when necessary. If factory work decreases, members of the amoeba join other amoebas or other nonfactory areas such as marketing or engineering.[13]

The Kyocera amoeba is similar to a profit center in that it bears profit responsibility. To increase profits, amoebas use their own discretion when tackling cost reduction problems.[14] Kyocera's amoeba system is a result of pursuing the merits of being small and simple. Generally, the smaller and simpler a unit, the more efficient and effective it is.

An amoeba is usually composed of 3 to 50 members. In the production area, the amoebas are divided according to each process of the production line. In marketing, they are assigned to each section of a particular product according to region.

Kyocera has some 400 amoebas, each controlled by a supervisory division. There are about 50 divisions controlled by a division headquarters. Exhibit 20–23 illustrates Kyocera's organizational structure.

How Amoebas Multiply, Disband, and Form New Units

Amoebas divide and break up in response to changes in the following:

■ Output
■ Worker's added value per hour

---

[12] Kazuki Hamada and Yasuhiro Monden, "Profit Management at Kyocera Corporation: The Amoeba System," in *Japanese Management Accounting: A World Class Approach to Profit Management*, edit. Yasuhiro Monden and Michiharu Sakurai (Cambridge, Mass.: Productivity Press, 1989), pp. 197–198. With permission.
[13] Ibid., p. 198.
[14] Ibid., p. 199.

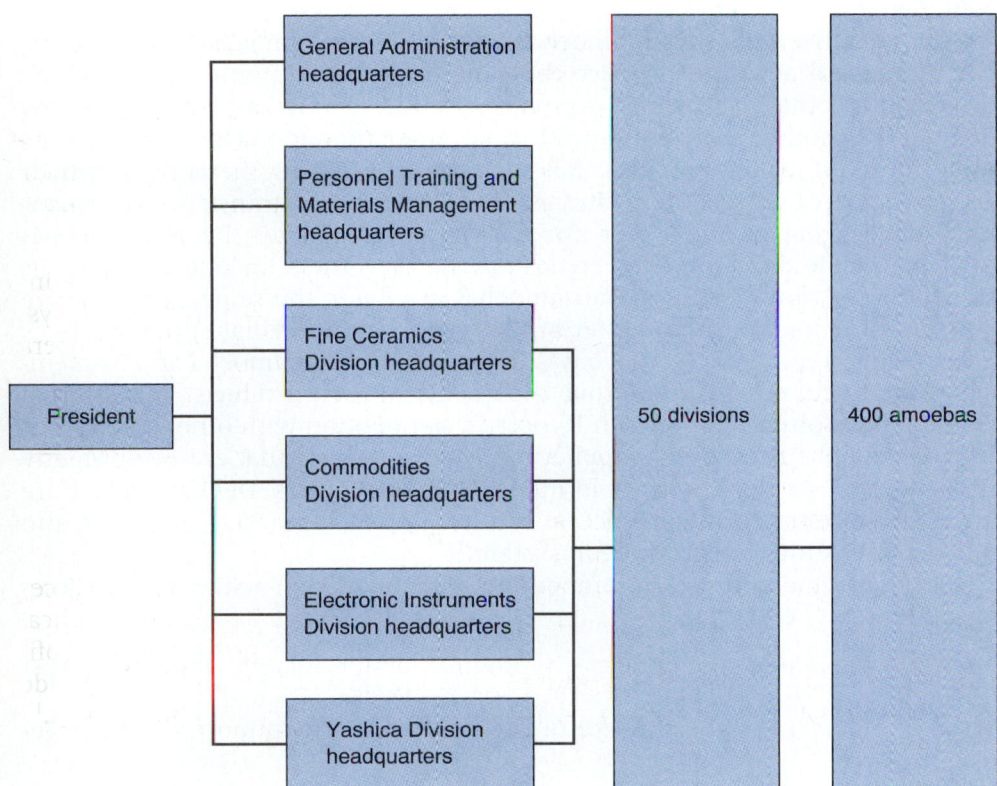

■ EXHIBIT 20–23
Kyocera's Organizational Structure

Source: Kazuki Hamada and Yasuhiro Monden, "Profit Management at Kyocera Corporation: The Amoeba System," in *Japanese Management Accounting: A World Class Approach to Profit Management*, ed. Yasuhiro Monden and Michiharu Sakurai (Cambridge, Mass.: Productivity Press, 1989), p. 200. With permission.

The following examples illustrate how an amoeba responds to typical situations:

■ When output is low and the added value per labor hour is high, the amoeba must multiply. When the amoeba is too big, its mobility decreases, and it no longer has the advantages of being small and simple. The amoeba will then be divided or reduced in scale.

■ When both output and added value per labor hour are high, the amoeba remains as it is.

■ When output is high and the added value per labor hour is low, the amoeba must scale down its members or rearrange its organization. If this is still ineffective, the amoeba must disband.

■ When both output and the added value per labor hour are low, the amoeba would be disbanded. This situation, however, has never happened at Kyocera.[15]

Amoeba division is an everyday occurrence at Kyocera. When needed, a new amoeba is formed instantly. Under these conditions, neither age nor training is essential to become the head of an amoeba. What matters is the individual's ability to handle the job. If judged unsuitable, a head is replaced immediately. Also, the head does not necessarily make a higher wage than other amoeba members.[16]

Transferring Products between Amoebas

At Kyocera, an amoeba adopts an independent profit system, even though it is small in scale. Satisfactory transfer prices (discussed in the next chapter) must be determined because they influence the performance of the amoebas.[17] A

[15] Ibid., pp. 201–202.
[16] Ibid., p. 202.
[17] Ibid., p. 200.

transfer price is what a supply amoeba charges a buying amoeba for its product.

A number of amoebas produce the same or similar intermediate products (i.e., products that can be sold to external customers as is or used as a raw material by another amoeba to produce another product). The amoebas may trade the intermediate products that they produce among themselves at their discretion. Prices charged to the buying amoebas (i.e., the transfer price), quantity, delivery dates, and other conditions are negotiated by the amoebas involved. While one amoeba searches among the others for one to supply its needs most advantageously, other amoebas are doing the same. Amoebas are always on the lookout for a better buyer for their intermediate products.[18]

The competition among amoebas is indeed keen. Each amoeba and its members strive to cut costs and improve the quality of their products. This internal competition is often sharper than Kyocera's competition with other companies. A buyer amoeba rejects any supplier amoeba's products that are even slightly higher in price or slightly lower in quality than it requires. Delivery delays are out of the question. This practice introduces external market conditions into the company's internal production system.[19]

This environment of severe competition and negotiation achieves the following goals:

- Encourages amoeba members to produce better quality and lower cost products
- Makes amoeba members aware of the importance of sound profit management
- Teaches amoeba members about real market conditions

Amoebas are authorized to trade intermediate products with outside companies. When conditions (e.g., price, quality, and delivery) offered by supplying amoebas are unreasonable, the buying amoeba will search for a satisfactory external vendor. This means that amoeba members must be well informed not only about other amoebas' activities, but also about the external markets.[20]

Evaluating Performance of Amoebas

Performance evaluation is viewed as a motivating tool to stimulate competition among the amoebas. It also indicates when to divide or disband an amoeba or form a new one. One important performance measure is added value per labor hour, illustrated in Exhibit 20–24.

The value added per labor hour is $64. This performance measurement is calculated daily, and the results officially announced. The results of the performance evaluations are used to improve future performance. Results are carefully reviewed, and policies for improving performance are discussed and decided.

Downsizing and Outsourcing: An Amoeba System in Disguise

The trend in many American firms is downsizing, which involves moving away from hierarchical, vertically integrated enterprises toward leaner, more flexible organizations that outsource many activities and add temporary employees for specific activities and projects. Firms that do this are often called *modular corporations*. The process of adding temporary employees because of downsizing and outsourcing is similar to forming and disbanding amoebas.

[18] Ibid.
[19] Ibid., p. 201.
[20] Ibid.

The following data apply to Amoeba A:

- Total shipment = $100,000
- Purchasing costs from other amoebas = $8,000
- Purchasing costs from external vendors = $10,000
- Total labor hours = 1,000
- Amount paid to marketing = $12,000
- Amount paid to general administration = $6,000

Step 1. Total output = Total shipment − Purchasing costs from other amoebas
$$= \$100,000 - \$8,000$$
$$= \underline{\underline{\$92,000}}$$

Step 2. Deduction of sales = Total output − (Purchasing costs from external vendors + Marketing costs + General administrative costs)
$$= \$92,000 - (\$10,000 + \$12,000 + \$6,000)$$
$$= \underline{\underline{\$64,000}}$$

Step 3. Added value per labor hour = Deduction of sales ÷ Total labor hours
$$= \$64,000 \div 1,000 \text{ DLhr}$$
$$= \underline{\underline{\$64/\text{DLhr}}}$$

SUMMARY OF LEARNING OBJECTIVES

The major goals of this chapter were to enable you to achieve six learning objectives:

Learning objective 1.   Examine responsibility centers and state their purpose.

Responsibility centers are segments of an organization with a manager in charge of specified activities and certain financial factors. The purpose of RCs is to streamline decision making throughout the total enterprise. The manager is closely in tune with his or her RC and can therefore make more informed decisions. Also, by making decisions locally, time is not wasted waiting for decisions from corporate management. Thus, the creation of independent profit and investment centers often is part of a decentralization strategy.

Profit centers can be created by segmenting an organization along the lines of its business functions, product lines or services, and/or geographic regions. Often the responsibility accounting system will report on each segment in total, with subsidiary reports by subsegments within the responsibility center. For example, a profit center may be created for each major product line, with subsegmentation into individual products and then into regions for each product.

Delegating profit and investment responsibility to segments can create a number of competitive advantages, including more focused and timely decision making, improved managerial training, and increased motivation due in part to profit performance evaluations. The downside to RCs is that dysfunctional decisions may result if segment profitability is the primary measure for performance evaluation, and inappropriate segmentation techniques are used by the management accountant. Also, some services may be duplicated, increasing their total costs to the enterprise. Finally, upper management may be tempted to evaluate managers by comparing their results against each other, even though the characteristics of each segment are different.

The ICBIS plays an important role in minimizing the inherent conflicts between decentralized operations and the need for goal congruence. Many enterprises are downsizing their ICBISs, by developing client/server systems through networking. These interoperable architectures attempt to optimize the mix of applications and hardware to meet the information needs of both corporate headquarters and local end users.

Learning objective 2.   Relate responsibility centers and responsibility accounting system design to profit performance evaluation.

There are three financial factors:

■ Cost
■ Profit
■ Investment

Thus, any RC, whether it is divided by business function, product or service line, or geographic region, can be further defined in terms of the financial factors for which the manager is responsible. A cost center manager is accountable only for costs. A profit center manager is accountable for costs and revenues. An investment center manager is accountable for costs, revenues, and investments.

In measuring financial performance, cost center managers are evaluated in terms of meeting standard costs. Profit center managers are evaluated by means of segmented income statements. Investment center managers are evaluated by return on investment (ROI) and residual income (RI).

Learning objective 3. Segment the profit center's income statement for segment and manager performance evaluation.

In evaluating the profitability of a profit center, a mini income statement should be created for it. Absorption costing techniques are not appropriate for this because they allocate all corporate "overhead" to the segments. Whether a segment continues or is discontinued will usually have no effect on these costs. Thus, they are not relevant to the calculation of the profits generated by the segment, which the enterprise can use to cover its common costs and to generate a profit goal for the overall organization.

A high-quality responsibility accounting system will use a contribution margin approach when preparing the segment's income statement. Fixed costs should be separated into those that are direct fixed costs of the segment and those that are common to the segments (e.g., corporate overhead costs). Only the direct fixed costs should be subtracted from the segment's contribution margin. The resulting profit measure is called the segment margin. It provides a valid measure of the segment's contribution to the corporation.

In evaluating the performance of the segment manager, the direct fixed costs should be subdivided into controllable and uncontrollable. Subtracting the controllable direct fixed costs from the segment's contribution margin yields a controllable segment margin for use in evaluating the manager's performance. The elements making up the controllable segment margin should then be compared against the master budget. Profit variances provide valuable information in assessing whether the manager achieved his or her profit goals.

Learning objective 4. Identify the relevant profit elements for the add-or-drop decision, and describe how product life cycle analysis and the growth/share matrix are used.

Generally, as long as a profit center generates a positive segment margin, it is contributing to covering some of the common fixed costs of the enterprise. For example, a family shoe store sells men's, women's, and children's shoes. The men's shoe department reports the following data:

Sales	$150,000
Less variable costs	<100,000>
Contribution margin	50,000
Less direct fixed costs	<60,000>
Segment margin	<$ 10,000>

Although it might seem that overall profits would increase by $10,000 if men's shoes were dropped, this assumes that the $60,000 in direct fixed costs will disappear if this segment disappears. In other words, the management accountant must ask which of the direct fixed costs are avoidable (will disappear) if the segment is discontinued. Only the avoidable direct fixed costs should be subtracted from the contribution margin in calculating the segment margin lost from discontinuing this product line. In this case, if all of the direct fixed costs, such as the manager's salary, insurance, rent, utilities, display cabinets, and so forth, are not avoidable, the men's department should be continued.

Moreover, typically both quantitative and qualitative factors must be considered. For

INSIGHTS & APPLICATIONS

Beware of Cost Allocations

Chicken Delight, a producer of packaged Chicken Nuggets, purchased a machine to perform the packaging function. The machine, however, came in only one type and size.

Chicken Delight ran the machine about two hours a day, which was enough to package all Chicken Nuggets. The machine stood idle for the other 22 hours. All the depreciation costs of the machine were assigned to Chicken Nuggets, and this product made a substantial profit.

Then, Chicken Delight developed a new product called *Chicken Crispies*, which would not compete with Chicken Nuggets and could be packaged by the same machine. But when the cost accountant allocated part of the machine costs to the new product, it showed a loss. Consequently, management turned Chicken Crispies down, because the company had a policy that, "Any new product must generate a 30 percent profit."

Chicken Delight's total profit would have increased had it produced the new product. Nevertheless, the company rejected it. Such is the danger of cost allocations.

---

example, if the men's shoe department is discontinued, families that previously came to the shoe store for a complete line of shoes may go elsewhere.

The point of the above Chicken Delight example is that many costs are not avoidable, especially indirect costs that need to be allocated in order to be included in a product's cost. The management accountant must identify both the direct costs and the avoidable costs associated with an add-or-drop decision.

Product life cycle analysis helps management determine when a product or product line is ready for discontinuance. The growth/share matrix provides management with a perspective on which products should be supported and which ones should be dropped. Both can provide supplemental nonfinancial information that aids in the add-or-drop decision.

Learning objective 5.   Calculate profit performance measures for investment center managers.

The return on investment (ROI) formula is widely used for evaluating the performance of an investment center because it summarizes, in one amount, many aspects of an investment center manager's responsibilities. ROI is calculated as the product of two ratios:

$$\text{ROI} = \underbrace{\frac{\text{Investment center net income}}{\text{Investment center sales}}}_{\textit{Profit margin}} \times \underbrace{\frac{\text{Investment center sales}}{\text{Investment center assets}}}_{\textit{Asset turnover}}$$

Profit margin provides information about the operational control decisions of the segment. It captures what has happened on the segment's income statement. Asset turnover measures how effectively the segment's assets are being used in generating sales. It relates balance sheet elements under the control of the manager to the sales it created by those assets.

When evaluating an investment center, the management accountant must decide which assets to include in the asset base and how they will be valued. For example, should assets over which the investment center manager has little control be included? Once included, should the assets be valued at gross book value, net book value, or current value? Should idle assets be included? Should liabilities be subtracted? How these questions are answered can affect the behavior of the investment center manager.

As an alternative to ROI, some organizations use residual income (RI) to measure investment center performance. RI is calculated as follows:

$$\text{RI} = \text{Net operating income} - (\text{Asset base} \times \text{Minimum rate of return})$$

Instead of providing a profit measure in terms of a rate (percentage), RI provides an absolute dollar amount above the minimum required by corporate headquarters. Traditionally, it has been argued that RI is better than ROI at motivating an investment center manager to make goal-congruent investment decisions. This argument, though, is based upon some questionable assumptions. Both ROI and RI can be effectively used to motivate investment center managers. At this level of the organization, however, both financial and nonfinancial performance measurements should be considered in properly evaluating managerial performance.

Learning objective 6.   Discuss Kyocera's amoeba system and new organizational structures in American firms.

To make its operations more efficient and effective, Kyocera analyzed the strengths and weaknesses of conventional management systems, such as those using cost and profit RCs, and then developed an amoeba system. Kyocera also developed a performance evaluation method providing added value per labor hour. This performance evaluation method encourages amoebas to compete with one another, thereby reducing total costs of the entire enterprise. The successful application of the amoeba system has helped Kyocera enjoy a reputation as a very profitable company that produces high-quality products. Many American firms are downsizing (sometimes called "rightsizing") and hiring temporary employees. This approach is similar to an amoeba system.

IMPORTANT TERMS

Add-or-drop decision   A decision that deals with whether to add, drop, or continue a particular product, line of products, enterprise segment, or service.

Amoeba system   A responsibility system in which segments of an enterprise are divided into organic, flexible units that have full cost and profit responsibilities.

Asset turnover ratio   Segment sales revenues divided by segment assets. This ratio is one of two that make up ROI. It measures the usage (effectiveness) of segment assets in creating sales revenues.

Contribution margin–based income statement   An income statement format that organizes costs by their behavior rather than by their function. It is used as the basis for segmenting the income statement in evaluating the profit performance of managers and segments.

Controllable segment margin   The subtotal created by subtracting controllable direct fixed costs from contribution margin. It is used to evaluate the profit performance of a segment manager.

Cost center   A responsibility center whose manager has control over the incurrence of costs, but has no control over the generation of revenues or the use of investment funds.

Flexible budget   A budget prepared using the actual sales volume realized by a segment. It is used for comparing the effects of differences between actual sales prices and costs, and budgeted sales prices and costs on the profit goals of the segment.

Functional form, absorption costing–based income statement   The income statement format used in financial reporting. All fixed costs are allocated (absorbed) by the segments and products of the organization.

Growth/share matrix   A graphical presentation of the types of products within a segment in terms of their cash flow–generating capabilities. It is useful in making add-or-drop decisions.

Investment center   A responsibility center whose manager has control over the incurrence of costs, the generation of revenues, and the deployment of investment funds.

Product life cycle analysis   A technique that helps managers determine how to allocate scarce resources to products or product lines in a manner that will maximize enterprise profitability. It is useful in add-or-drop decisions.

Profit center   A responsibility center whose manager has control over the incurrence of costs and the generation of revenues, but has no control over the use of investment funds.

Profit margin   Segment income divided by segment revenues. This ratio measures the operational efficiency of a segment in creating profits and is one of the two ratios comprising ROI.

Profit variances   Profit variances measure the difference between the master budget (pro forma income statement) and the actual profits of a segment. Profit variances include sales variances and cost variances.

Residual income (RI)   A measure of an investment center's earnings in relation to the minimum rate of return required by the corporation. It is the segment margin remaining after providing the overall corporation with sufficient profits to cover its minimum required rate of return.

Responsibility accounting system   Part of the accounting system that measures and reports on the performance of responsibility centers and their managers.

Responsibility center (RC)   A segment of the organization in which a manager is held accountable for a specified set of activities and financial factors.

Return on investment (ROI) (return on assets)   The ratio of earnings produced by an investment center to the investment in that center. It is usually calculated by dividing the center's earnings (net operating income) by its average investment in assets.

Sales price variance   This sales variance measures the difference between budgeted contribution margin and actual contribution margin due to a difference in budgeted and actual sales prices.

Sales volume variance   This sales variance measures the difference between budgeted and actual contribution margins due to a difference in the sales forecast and actual sales volume.

Segment margin   A measure of the profitability of a segment. It is calculated by subtracting the direct fixed costs of a segment from its contribution margin.

Segmented income statement   An income statement that reports the profitability of various segments within an organizational unit. The unit can be segmented by product line, business function, and/or geographic regions.

❚DEMONSTRATION PROBLEMS

■**DEMONSTRATION PROBLEM 1**   *Segmented income statements.*

JB Trucking is a regional freight hauling firm in northern California and Nevada. For performance evaluation purposes the income statement is segmented into delivery areas. One area, Truckee Meadows, serves Reno, Nevada, and Lake Tahoe, California. Information about the January freight deliveries includes:

	RENO	LAKE TAHOE
Number of deliveries	50	40
Delivery revenues	$5,000	$8,000
Direct variable costs per delivery	$50	$75
Controllable direct fixed costs	$500	$1,500
Uncontrollable direct fixed costs	$500	$800
Allocated common fixed costs	$1,900	$3,100

Direct variable costs include fuel, oil, truck depreciation (per mile basis), and load weight fees. Controllable direct fixed costs include drivers' license fees, license plates, and truck registration fees. Uncontrollable direct fixed costs include monthly maintenance performed at JB Trucking's maintenance facility in Reno. The monthly maintenance is required by state law, and JB Trucking management performs this to control quality. The maintenance center is a profit center, as is each delivery area. Lake Tahoe costs are uniformly higher than Reno costs for three reasons:

■ Each delivery run to Tahoe is much longer than within the Reno area. This increases the variable costs of fuel and depreciation.
■ Deliveries to Tahoe require state license fees for both Nevada and California.
■ Because Tahoe runs involve significantly more miles per delivery, maintenance is performed twice a month.

The common fixed costs allocated by the Truckee Meadows regional dispatchers office include dispatching, administration, and marketing (selling loads to customers) costs.

JB Trucking management is concerned about the functional form, absorption costing–based income statement used to report to external stakeholders. Both Reno and Lake Tahoe reported a net loss due to the heavy snowfall during the month. Deliveries also took longer because of the increased tourist traffic between Reno and Lake Tahoe.

Required:

a. Create a segmented income statement using a contribution margin format that can be used to evaluate the performance of each Truckee Meadows's delivery area and the drivers within each area.

b. Explain how common fixed costs are allocated to the segments, and describe the effect of this allocation on segment profitability.

SOLUTION TO DEMONSTRATION PROBLEM 1

a. Following is the segmented income statement for the Truckee Meadows region. This format, often called a *variable costing format* on professional certification exams, identifies the controllable segment margin for driver performance evaluation, as well as the segment margin of each territory for segment evaluation.

	RENO[a] PER UNIT[b]	PERCENT	TOTALS	LAKE TAHOE PER UNIT	PERCENT	TOTALS	TRUCKEE MEADOWS PERCENT	TOTALS
Revenues	$100	100%	$5,000	$200	100%	$8,000	100%	$13,000
Less variable costs	<50>	<50%>	<2,500>	<75>	<37%>	<3,000>	<42%>	<5,500>
Contribution margin	$50	50%	$2,500	$125	63%	$5,000	58%	$7,500
Less controllable direct fixed costs			<500>			<1,500>		<2,000>
Controllable segment margin			$2,000			$3,500		$5,500
Less uncontrollable direct fixed costs			<500>			<800>		<1,300>
Segment margin			$1,500			$2,700		$4,200
Less common fixed costs								<5,000>
Net income								<$800>

Notes:
a. Sales volume for Reno = 50 deliveries; sales volume for Lake Tahoe = 40 deliveries.
b. See Exhibit 20–9 note b for calculations of per unit and percentage amounts.

b. Reno revenues ($5,000 of the $13,000 total for Truckee Meadows) represent 38% of total revenues for Truckee Meadows. Lake Tahoe revenues represent 62% of the total. Using the relative sales revenues to allocate common fixed costs, Reno is allocated $1,900 (38% of the $5,000), and Lake Tahoe is allocated $3,100 (62% of $5,000). Because these allocated amounts are greater than each segment margin by $400, each route shows a net loss of $400 on the income statement used for external financial reporting.

The real profit contributions of Reno and Lake Tahoe are both positive, as indicated by their segment margins of $1,500 and $2,700, respectively. However, the profit they generate for JB Trucking is even greater because the maintenance department is treated as a profit center and, thus, is probably billing maintenance charges at a price higher than its costs.

■DEMONSTRATION PROBLEM 2 *Calculating profit variances.*

Elixir Corporation makes and sells two products, A and B. Following are relevant data for the month of May:

	A	B
Budgeted sales price per unit	$6.00	$10.00
Less variable costs per unit	<3.00>	<7.50>
Budgeted CMU	$3.00	$ 2.50
Budgeted sales in units	300	200
Actual units sold	240	270
Actual sales price per unit	$6.00	$9.50
Actual CMU	$3.00	$2.00

Required:
a. Calculate the sales volume variance.
b. Calculate the sales price variance.

c. Briefly explain to each manager the difference between master budget pro forma income and actual income for May due to sales activities.

SOLUTION TO DEMONSTRATION PROBLEM 2

a. Sales volume variances:

$$\text{Sales volume variance} = \text{Budgeted CMU} \times (\text{Actual volume} - \text{Budgeted volume})$$

■ For product A:

$$= \$3.00 \text{ per unit} \times (240 \text{ units} - 300 \text{ units})$$
$$= <\$180> \text{ unfavorable}$$

■ For product B:

$$= \$2.50 \text{ per unit} \times (270 \text{ units} - 200 \text{ units})$$
$$= \$175 \text{ favorable}$$

b. Sales price variances:

$$\text{Sales price variance} = \text{Actual sales volume} \times (\text{Actual sales price} - \text{Budgeted sales price})$$

■ For product A:

$$= 240 \text{ units} \times (\$6.00 \text{ per unit} - \$6.00 \text{ per unit})$$
$$= \$0$$

■ For product B:

$$= 270 \text{ units} \times (\$9.50 \text{ per unit} - \$10.00 \text{ per unit})$$
$$= <\$135> \text{ unfavorable}$$

c. Actual profits for product A are less than budgeted profits by $180 because the sales forecast was not achieved. For product B, actual profit is greater than its master budget goal by $40. Apparently, the reduction in sales price of 50 cents from budget resulted in an increase in sales volume. The extra contribution margin generated from the additional volume was $40 more than the lost contribution margin due to the reduction in sales price.

■ DEMONSTRATION PROBLEM 3   *ROI and residual income.*

The Institute of Management Accountants has issued *Statements on Management Accounting Number 4D,* "Measuring Entity Performance," to help management accountants deal with the issues associated with measuring entity performance. Managers can use these measures to evaluate their own performance or the performance of subordinates, to identify and correct problems, and to discover opportunities. A number of performance measures are available to assist managers in measuring achievement. To present a more complete picture of performance, it is strongly recommended that several of these performance measures be utilized and that they be combined with nonfinancial measures such as market share, new product development, and human resource utilization. The following commonly-used performance measures are derived from the traditional historical accounting system:

■ Profit margin (percent)
■ Asset turnover
■ Return on the investment in assets
■ Residual income

Required:
For *each* of the performance measures identified above:

a. Describe how the measure is calculated.
b. Describe the information provided by the measure.
c. Explain the limitations of this information.

[CMA adapted]

SOLUTION TO DEMONSTRATION PROBLEM 3

a.
$$\text{Profit margin} = \text{Segment income} \div \text{Segment revenues}$$
$$\text{Asset turnover} = \text{Segment revenues} \div \text{Segment assets}$$
$$\text{Return on investment} = \text{Profit margin} \times \text{Asset turnover}$$
$$\text{Residual income} = \text{Segment income} - (\text{Segment assets} \times \text{Corporate minimum required rate of return})$$

b. Profit margin is a short-run measure of operating efficiency; it measures in percentage terms the profit generated from a dollar of sales. Asset turnover is a measure of asset usage effectiveness. It shows how many dollars of sales are created by a dollar invested in this investment center. ROI is simply an interest rate. It shows what percentage of every dollar invested in the segment is returned to corporate headquarters as segment profit. Instead of measuring the segment's return to the parent company in terms of a percentage of the investment in it, RI provides this information in terms of an absolute dollar value.

c. A number of different amounts can be used in both the numerator and denominator of ROI. For example, the net income figure can be the absorption costing-based segment profit, segment margin, segment margin before taxes and interest, or controllable segment margin. The asset base can include the segment's gross assets, net assets, or some subset of its assets. With respect to RI, the asset base and minimum required rate of return also can be based on a number of different values.

At times, the management accountant may be asked to choose a valuation technique to "cook the books," allowing the investment center manager to look more favorable than might be appropriate. In accordance with the IMA's standards for ethical conduct, the management accountant should resist these temptations and choose the values that most accurately and fairly represent performance.

Many of the limitations concern the potential for dysfunctional decision-making behaviors. Ethically, the management accountant has a responsibility to make sure that if deadly parallel evaluations are used, the investment centers are truly comparable. Many of the problems that can result may be avoided if the management accountant remembers that, first and foremost, proper performance evaluation requires a comparison of budgeted to actual performance. Finally, proper performance evaluation should not overemphasize the importance of financial performance measures. At this level of the organization, many nonfinancial performance measures may be more relevant.

REVIEW QUESTIONS

20.1 What is the role of a responsibility accounting system within the accounting LAN?

20.2 What is the role of a responsibility accounting system within the performance evaluation–reward system of an enterprise?

20.3 Is a responsibility center the same thing as a segment? Explain.

20.4 Describe three ways of segmenting an enterprise by activities.

20.5 What are the advantages of decentralizing an enterprise into autonomous responsibility centers?

20.6 What are the disadvantages of decentralizing an enterprise into autonomous responsibility centers?

20.7 What are the three financial factors used to categorize responsibility centers?

20.8 For each of the three types of financial factors associated with responsibility centers, what should be output from the responsibility accounting system?

20.9 What motivational problems can result from overemphasizing cost variance minimization in performance evaluation?

20.10 What is a segmented income statement?

20.11 Why is controllability an important criterion for a high-quality responsibility accounting system?

20.12 What role does the master budgeting process play in controllability identification?

20.13 What are the pros and cons of allocating common corporate service costs to the enterprise's segments?

20.14 In reporting on profit center financial performance, what are the two goals of the responsibility accounting system?

20.15 What is the difference between a functional form, absorption costing–based income statement and a contribution margin–based income statement?

20.16 What problems are created by using a functional form, absorption costing–based income statement in evaluating performance?

20.17 How can using a contribution margin–based income statement overcome the problems identified in Question 20.16?

20.18 In a responsibility accounting system using a contribution margin–based income statement to evaluate profit center financial performance, costs are classified into which of the following categories?

a. Prime and conversion costs.
b. Direct and indirect costs.
c. Controllable and noncontrollable costs.
d. Variable and fixed costs.

20.19 Explain the most common method of allocating common fixed costs to segments. What problems are created by this method?

20.20 What is the first step in segmenting a profit center's income statement?

20.21 What purpose is served by creating the subtotal "segment margin"?

20.22 The direct fixed costs of the subsegments plus the fixed costs common to the subsegments equals which amount?

20.23 What has to be done to a segmented income statement if it is to be used in evaluating the performance of the profit center manager?

20.24 What is the purpose of creating the subtotal "controllable segment margin"?

20.25 Describe a deadly parallel performance evaluation strategy.

20.26 What type of comparisons should be made in evaluating long-run continuous improvement?

20.27 Why are year-to-year comparisons of actual profits not as relevant as year-to-year budget comparisons?

20.28 What two types of variances are included in profit variances?

20.29 Which two variances are included in sales variances?

20.30 Which variances make up cost variances?

20.31 What is a flexible budget and how is it related to a profit equation?

20.32 What information does a sales volume variance convey?

20.33 What is the informational value of a sales price variance?

20.34 Why wasn't the FOH volume variance included in the profit variance report shown in Exhibit 20–13?

20.35 Explain the add-or-drop decision.

20.36 Should any qualitative factors be considered in the add-or-drop decision?

20.37 What role do avoidable costs play in the add-or-drop decision? Why aren't direct fixed costs always relevant to this decision?

20.38 Explain the relevance of product life cycle analysis in deciding whether to add or drop products.

20.39 Explain the relevance of the growth/share matrix in deciding whether to add or drop products.

20.40 Explain in a simple, intuitively appealing manner what ROI is.

20.41 Which two financial ratios make up ROI?

20.42 What information is conveyed by each of the ratios in ROI?

20.43 Explain the relationship between asset turnover and profit margin in understanding ROI.

20.44 What dysfunctional behaviors might result from an overemphasis on ROI in investment center performance evaluation?

20.45 Which comparisons should be made to properly evaluate performance?

a. Actual results between divisions.
b. Year-to-year actual profit comparisons.
c. Budget-to-actual for the time period.

20.46 How does RI differ from ROI?

20.47 When evaluating an investment decision, can RI be explained using ROI?

20.48 What is the traditional argument against using ROI? What is the traditional argument for using RI?

20.49 What are the two behavioral assumptions supporting the argument for using RI instead of ROI in investment decision making?

20.50 How can the use of ideal standards be justified in choosing an accounting measure of performance for the investment decision?

20.51 For which divisions should ROI be used as a hurdle rate in the investment decision? For which divisions should RI be used?

20.52 What is an amoeba?

20.53 Describe the "value added per labor hour" calculation.

CHAPTER-SPECIFIC PROBLEMS

These problems require responses based directly on concepts and techniques presented in the text.

20.54 *Segmenting the income statement.* This is a continuation of Demonstration Problem 1. The Lake Tahoe segment has two truck drivers. Prepare a segmented income statement with segment margins and controllable segment margins for each driver. The following information may be useful:

	ALBERT	GEORGE
Number of deliveries	25	15
Delivery revenues	$3,875	$4,125
Direct variable costs per delivery	$75	$75
Controllable direct fixed costs	$750	$750
Uncontrollable direct fixed costs	$400	$400
Allocated common fixed costs	$1,598	$1,502

Required:

Evaluate the performance of each truck driver.

20.55 *Segmented income statement.* Stratford Corporation is a diversified company whose products are marketed both domestically and internationally. The company's major product lines are pharmaceutical products, sports equipment, and household appliances. At a recent meeting of Stratford's board of directors, there was a lengthy discussion on ways to improve overall corporate profitability without new acquisitions as the company is already heavily leveraged. The members of the board decided that they required additional financial information about individual corporate operations in order to target areas for improvement.

Dave Murphy, Stratford's controller, has been asked to provide additional data that would assist the board in its investigation. Stratford is not a public company and, therefore, has not prepared complete income statements by segment. Murphy has regularly prepared an income statement by product line through contribution margin. However, Murphy now believes that income statements prepared through operating income along both product lines and geographic areas would provide the directors with the required insight into corporate operations. Murphy has the following data available to him:

	PRODUCT LINE			
	PHARMACEUTICAL	SPORTS	APPLIANCES	TOTAL
Production sales in units	160,000	180,000	160,000	500,000
Average selling price per unit	$8.00	$20.00	$15.00	
Average variable manufacturing cost per unit	$4.00	$9.50	$8.25	
Average variable selling expense per unit	$2.00	$2.50	$2.25	

Continued

—Continued

	PHARMACEUTICAL	SPORTS	APPLIANCES	TOTAL
Fixed factory over-head excluding depreciation				$500,000
Depreciation of plant and equipment				$400,000
Administrative and selling expenses				$1,160,000

Murphy had several discussions with the division managers for each product line and compiled the following information from these meetings:

- The division managers concluded that Murphy should allocate fixed factory overhead on the basis of the ratio of the variable costs expended per product line/or per geographic area to total variable costs.
- Each of the division managers agreed that a reasonable basis for the allocation of depreciation on plant and equipment would be the ratio of units produced per product line/or per geographic area to the total number of units produced.
- There was little agreement on the allocation of administrative and selling expenses so Murphy decided to allocate only those expenses that were directly traceable to the segment being delineated; i.e., manufacturing staff salaries to product lines and sales staff salaries to geographic areas. Murphy used the following data for this allocation:

[Handwritten margin notes: "FOH Var.Cost per prod : n geo ; TotalVC   deprec. = units prod/geo per prod/geo : Total # units   adm + Sell exp :"]

MANUFACTURING STAFF		SALES STAFF	
Pharmaceutical	$120,000	United States	$ 60,000
Sports	140,000	Canada	100,000
Appliances	80,000	Europe	250,000

- The division managers were able to provide reliable sales percentages for their product lines by geographic area:

PERCENTAGE OF UNIT SALES

	UNITED STATES	CANADA	EUROPE
Pharmaceutical	40%	10%	50%
Sports	40	40	20
Appliances	20	20	60

Using this information, Murphy prepared the following product line income statement:

STRATFORD CORPORATION
STATEMENT OF INCOME BY PRODUCT LINES
FOR THE FISCAL YEAR ENDED APRIL 30, 1995

PRODUCT LINES

	PHARMACEUTICAL	SPORTS	APPLIANCES	UNALLOCATED	TOTAL
Sales in units	160,000	180,000	160,000		
Sales	$1,280,000	$3,600,000	$2,400,000	$ —	$7,280,000
Variable manufacturing and selling costs	960,000	2,160,000	1,680,000	—	4,800,000
Contribution margin	$ 320,000	$1,440,000	$ 720,000	—	$2,480,000
Fixed costs:					
Fixed factory overhead	$ 100,000	$ 225,000	$ 175,000	—	$ 500,000
Depreciation	128,000	144,000	128,000	—	400,000
Administrative and selling expense	120,000	140,000	80,000	820,000	1,160,000
Total fixed costs	$ 348,000	$ 509,000	$ 383,000	$ 820,000	$2,060,000
Operating income (loss)	$ <28,000>	$ 931,000	$ 337,000	$<820,000>	$ 420,000

[Handwritten annotations near table: "8.00", "20.00", "15.00", "6", "12", "10.50", "32%"]

Required:

a. Prepare a segmented income statement for Stratford Corporation based on the company's geographic areas of sales. The statement should be in good form and show the operating income for each segment.

b. As a result of the information disclosed by both segmented income statements (by product line and by geographic area), recommend areas where Stratford Corporation should focus its attention in order to improve corporate profitability.

[AICPA adapted]

20.56 *Absorption costing versus contribution margin.* The Maalox Company produces a single product. Data from the company's records for 19X4 operations are as follows:

Projected unit sales		3,800
Units to be produced		4,000
Beginning inventory, finished goods		–0–
Estimated ending inventory, finished goods		200
Selling price per unit		$20
Variable costs per unit:		
Direct materials	$4	
Direct labor	1	
Variable manufacturing overhead	2	
Variable selling and administrative	2	$9
Fixed costs for 19X4:		
Fixed manufacturing overhead	$16,000	
Fixed selling and administrative	$20,000	

Required:

a. Compute the manufacturing cost per unit using the absorption costing method.

b. Prepare an income statement suitable for external financial reporting.

c. Prepare an income statement using the contribution margin approach.

d. Assume that sales remain at 3,800 units as projected, but production equals sales. Prepare two income statements based on this assumption, one prepared using absorption costing and the other using the contribution margin approach.

20.57 *Discussing a performance evaluation system.* Darmen Corporation is one of the major producers of prefabricated houses in the home building industry. The corporation consists of two divisions: (1) Bell Division, which acquires the raw materials to manufacture the basic house components and assembles them into kits, and (2) the Cornish Division, which takes the kits and constructs the homes for final home buyers. The corporation is decentralized, and the management of each division is measured by its income and return on investment.

Bell Division assembles seven separate house kits using raw materials purchased at the prevailing market prices. The seven kits are sold to Cornish for prices ranging from $45,000 to $98,000. The prices are set by Darmen's corporate management using prices paid by Cornish when it buys comparable units from outside sources. The smaller kits with the lower prices have become a larger portion of the units sold because the final house buyer is facing prices that are increasing more rapidly than personal income. The kits are manufactured and assembled in a new plant just purchased by Bell this year. The division had been located in a leased plant for the past four years.

All kits are assembled upon receipt of an order from the Cornish Division. When the kit is completely assembled, it is loaded immediately on a Cornish truck. Thus, Bell Division has no finished goods inventory.

The Bell Division's accounts and reports are prepared on an actual cost basis. There is no budget, and standards have not been developed for any product. A factory overhead rate is calculated at the beginning of each year. The rate is designed to charge all overhead to the product each year. Any under- or over-applied overhead is allocated to the cost of goods sold account and work-in-process inventories.

Bell Division's annual report is presented next. This report forms the basis of the evaluation of the division and its management by corporate management.

BELL DIVISION
PERFORMANCE REPORT
FOR THE YEAR ENDED DECEMBER 31, 1994

	1994	1993	INCREASE OR <DECREASE> FROM 1993 AMOUNT	PERCENT CHANGE
Summary data				
Net income ($000 omitted)	$34,222	$31,573	$2,649	8.4
Return on investment	37%	43%	<6>%	<14.0>
Kits shipped (units)	2,000	2,100	<100>	<4.8>
Production data (in units)				
Kits started	2,400	1,600	800	50.0
Kits shipped	2,000	2,100	<100>	<4.8>
Kits in process at year-end	700	300	400	133.3
Increase <decrease> in kits in process at year-end	400	<500>	—	—
Financial data ($000 omitted)				
Sales	$138,000	$162,800	$<24,800>	<15.2>
Production costs of units sold:				
Raw material	32,000	40,000	<8,000>	<20.0>
Labor	41,700	53,000	<11,300>	<21.3>
Factory overhead	29,000	37,000	<8,000>	<21.6>
Cost of units sold	102,700	130,000	<27,300>	<21.0>
Other costs:				
Corporate charges for personnel services	228	210	18	8.6
Accounting services	425	440	<15>	<3.4>
Financing costs	300	525	<225>	<42.9>
Total other costs	953	1,175	<222>	<18.9>
Adjustments to income:				
Unreimbursed fire loss	—	52	<52>	<100.0>
Raw material losses due to improper storage	125	—	125	—
Total adjustments	125	52	73	140.4
Total deductions	103,778	131,227	<27,449>	<20.9>
Division income	$ 34,222	$ 31,573	$ 2,649	8.4
Division investment	$ 92,000	$ 73,000	$ 19,000	26.0
Return on investment	37%	43%	<6>%	<14.0>

Additional information regarding corporate and division practices is as follows:

- The corporate office does all the personnel and accounting work for each division.
- The corporate personnel costs are allocated on the basis of the number of employees in the division.
- The accounting costs are allocated to the division on the basis of total costs excluding corporate charges
- The division administration costs are included in factory overhead.
- The financing charges include a corporate imputed interest charge on division assets and any divisional lease payments.
- The division investment for the return on investment calculation includes division inventory and plant and equipment at gross book value.

Required:
a. Discuss the value of the annual report presented for the Bell Division in evaluating the division and its management in terms of:
  1. The accounting techniques employed in the measurement of division activities.

2. The manner of presentation.
3. The effectiveness with which it discloses differences and similarities between years.
   b. Present specific recommendations you would make to the management of Darmen Corporation to improve its accounting and financial reporting system.

[CMA adapted]

20.58 *Discussing budgets and responsibility accounting.* The Argon County Hospital is located in the county seat. Argon County is a well-known summer resort area. The county population doubles during the vacation months (May–August), and hospital activity more than doubles during these months. The hospital is organized into several departments. Although it is a relatively small hospital, its pleasant surroundings have attracted a well-trained and competent medical staff.

An administrator was hired a year ago to improve the business activities of the hospital. Among the new ideas he has introduced is responsibility accounting. This program was announced along with quarterly cost reports supplied to department heads. Previously, cost data were presented to department heads infrequently. The following are excerpts from the announcement and the report received by the laundry supervisor:

> The hospital has adopted a "responsibility accounting system." From now on you will receive quarterly reports comparing the costs of operating your department with budgeted costs. The reports will highlight the differences (variations) so you can zero in on the departure from budgeted costs (this is called "management by exception"). Responsibility accounting means you are accountable for keeping the costs in your department within the budget. The variations from the budget will help you identify what costs are out of line, and the size of the variation will indicate which ones are the most important. Your first quarterly report accompanies this announcement.

ARGON COUNTY HOSPITAL
PERFORMANCE REPORT—LAUNDRY DEPARTMENT
JULY-SEPTEMBER 19X3

	BUDGET	ACTUAL	<OVER> UNDER BUDGET	PERCENT <OVER> UNDER BUDGET
Patient-days	9,500	11,900	<2,400>	<25>
Pounds of laundry processed	125,000	156,000	<31,000>	<25>
Costs:				
Laundry labor	$ 9,000	$12,500	$<3,500>	<39>
Supplies	1,100	1,875	<775>	<70>
Water, water heating and softening	1,700	2,500	<800>	<47>
Maintenance	1,400	2,200	<800>	<57>
Supervisor's salary	3,150	3,750	<600>	<19>
Allocated administration costs	4,000	5,000	<1,000>	<25>
Equipment depreciation	1,200	1,250	<50>	<4>
	$21,550	$29,075	$<7,525>	<35>

Administrator's comments: Costs are significantly above budget for the quarter. Particular attention needs to be paid to labor, supplies, and maintenance.

The annual budget for 19X3 was constructed by the new administrator. Quarterly budgets were computed as one-fourth of the annual budget. The administrator compiled the budget from analysis of the prior three years' costs. The analysis showed that all costs increased each year, with more rapid increases between the second and third year. He considered establishing the budget at an average of the prior three years' costs, hoping that the installation of the system would reduce costs to this level. However, in view of the rapidly increasing prices, he finally chose 19X2 costs less 3% for the 19X3 budget. The activity level, measured by patient-days and pounds of laundry processed, was set at the 19X2 volume, which was approximately equal to the volume of each of the past three years.

Required:
a. Comment on the method used to construct the budget.
b. What information should be communicated by variations from budgets?
c. Does the report effectively communicate the level of efficiency of this department? Give reasons for your answer.

[CMA adapted]

20.59 *Discussing responsibility accounting and budgeting.* Family Resorts, Inc., is a holding company for several vacation hotels in the northeast and mid-Atlantic states. The firm originally purchased several old inns, restored the buildings, and upgraded the recreational facilities. Vacationing families have been receptive to the inns because they offer many services for children and allow parents time for themselves. Since the completion of the restorations ten years ago, the company has been profitable.

Family Resorts has just concluded its annual meeting of regional and district managers. This meeting is held each November to review the results of the previous season and to help the managers prepare for the upcoming year. Prior to the meeting, the managers have submitted proposed budgets for their districts or regions, as appropriate. These budgets have been reviewed and consolidated into an annual operating budget for the entire company. The 1995 budget has been presented at the meeting and was accepted by the managers.

To evaluate the performance of its managers, Family Resorts uses responsibility accounting. Therefore, the preparation of the budget is given close attention at headquarters. If major changes need to be made to the budgets submitted by the managers, all affected parties are consulted before the changes are incorporated. Following are two pages from the budget booklet that all managers received at the meeting:

FAMILY RESORTS, INC.
RESPONSIBILITY SUMMARY
($000 OMITTED)

Reporting unit: Family Resorts
Responsible person: President

Mid-Atlantic Region	$605
New England Region	365
Unallocated costs	<160>
Income before taxes	$810

Reporting unit: New England Region
Responsible person: Regional manager

Vermont	$200
New Hampshire	140
Maine	105
Unallocated costs	<80>
Total contribution	$365

Reporting unit: Maine District
Responsible person: District manager

Harbor Inn	$ 80
Camden Country Inn	60
Unallocated costs	<35>
Total contribution	$105

Reporting unit: Harbor Inn
Responsible person: Innkeeper

Revenue	$600
Controllable costs	<455>
Allocated costs	<65>
Total contribution	$ 80

FAMILY RESORTS, INC.
CONDENSED OPERATING BUDGET—MAINE DISTRICT
FOR THE YEAR ENDED DECEMBER 31, 1995
($000 OMITTED)

	REGION				NEW ENGLAND REGION			MAINE DISTRICT INNS		
	FAMILY RESORTS	MID-ATLANTIC	NEW ENGLAND	NOT ALLO-CATED*	VERMONT	NEW HAMPSHIRE	MAINE	NOT ALLO-CATED**	HARBOR	CAMDEN COUNTRY
Net sales	$7,900	$4,200	$3,700		$1,400	$1,200	$1,100		$600	$500
Cost of sales	4,530	2,310	2,220		840	720	660		360	300
Gross margin	$3,370	$1,890	$1,480		$ 560	$ 480	$ 440		$240	$200
Controllable expenses:										
Supervisory expense	$ 240	$ 130	$ 110		$ 35	$ 30	$ 45	$ 10	$ 20	$ 15
Training expense	160	80	80		30	25	25		15	10
Advertising expense	500	280	220	$ 50	55	60	55	15	20	20
Repairs and maintenance	480	225	255		90	85	80		40	40
Total controllable expenses	$1,380	$ 715	$ 665	$ 50	$ 210	$ 200	$ 205	$ 25	$ 95	$ 85
Controllable contribution	$1,990	$1,175	$ 815	$<50>	$ 350	$ 280	$ 235	$<25>	$145	$115
Expenses controlled by others:										
Depreciation	$ 520	$ 300	$ 220	$ 30	$ 70	$ 60	$ 60	$ 10	$ 30	$ 20
Property taxes	200	120	80		$ 30	30	20		10	10
Insurance	300	150	150		50	50	50		25	25
Total expenses controlled by others	$1,020	$ 570	$ 450	$ 30	$ 150	$ 140	$ 130	$ 10	$ 65	$ 55
Total contribution	$ 970	$ 605	$ 365	$<80>	$ 200	$ 140	$ 105	$<35>	$ 80	$ 60
Unallocated costs†	160									
Income before taxes	$ 810									

* Unallocated expenses include a regional advertising campaign and equipment used by the regional manager.
** Unallocated expenses include a portion of the district manager's salary, district promotion costs, and the district manager's car.
† Unallocated costs include taxes on undeveloped real estate, headquarters expense, legal fees, and audit fees.

Required:

a. Responsibility accounting has been used effectively by many companies, both large and small.
   1. Define responsibility accounting.
   2. Discuss the benefits that accrue to a company using responsibility accounting.
   3. Describe the advantages of responsibility accounting for the managers of a firm.

b. Family Resorts, Inc.'s budget was accepted by the regional and district managers. Based on the facts presented, evaluate the budget process employed by Family Resorts by addressing the following:
   1. What features of the budget preparation are likely to result in the managers adopting and supporting the budget process?
   2. What features of the budget presentation shown here are likely to make the budget attractive to managers?
   3. What recommendations, if any, could be made to the budget preparers to improve the budget process? Explain your answer.

[CMA adapted]

20.60 *Explaining the purposes and behavioral aspects of a responsibility accounting system.* Kelly Petroleum Company has a large oil and natural gas project in Oklahoma. The project has been organized into two production centers (Petroleum Production and Natural Gas Production) and one service center (Maintenance). Additional information about the Maintenance Center follows:

Maintenance Center activities and scheduling. Don Pepper, Maintenance Center manager, has organized his maintenance workers into work crews that serve the two production centers. The maintenance crews perform preventive maintenance and repair equipment both in the field and in the central maintenance shop.

Pepper is responsible for scheduling all maintenance work in the field and in the central shop. Preventive maintenance is performed according to a set schedule established by Pepper and approved by the production center managers. Breakdowns are given immediate priority in scheduling so that downtime is minimized. Thus, preventive maintenance occasionally must be postponed, but every attempt is made to reschedule it within three weeks.

Preventive maintenance work is the responsibility of Pepper. However, if a significant problem is discovered during preventive maintenance, the appropriate production center supervisor authorizes and supervises the repair after checking with Pepper.

When a breakdown in the field occurs, the production centers contact Pepper to initiate the repairs. The repair work is supervised by the production center supervisor. Machinery and equipment sometimes need to be replaced while the original equipment is repaired in the central shop. This procedure is followed only when the time to make the repair in the field would result in an extended interruption of operations. Replacement of equipment is recommended by the maintenance work crew supervisor and approved by a production center supervisor.

Routine preventive maintenance and breakdowns of automotive and mobile equipment used in the field are completed in the central shop. All repairs and maintenance activities taking place in the central shop are under the direction of Pepper.

■ *Maintenance Center accounting activities.* Pepper has records identifying the work crews assigned to each job in the field, the number of hours spent on the job, and the parts and supplies used on the job. In addition, records for the central shop (jobs, labor hours, parts and supplies) have been maintained. However, this detailed maintenance information is not incorporated into Kelly's accounting system.

Pepper develops the annual budget for the Maintenance Center by planning the preventive maintenance that will be needed during the year, estimating the number and seriousness of breakdowns, and estimating the shop activities. He then bases the labor, parts, and supply costs on his plans and estimates and develops the budget amounts by line item. Because the timing of the breakdowns is impossible to plan, Pepper divides the annual budget by 12 to derive the monthly budget.

All costs incurred by the work crews in the field and in the central shop are accumulated monthly and then allocated to the two production cost centers based upon the field hours worked in each production center. This method of cost allocation has been used on Pepper's recommendation because he believed that it was easy to implement and understand. Furthermore, he believed that it was impossible to incorporate a better allocation system into the monthly report due to the wide range of salaries paid to maintenance workers and the fast turnover of materials and parts.

The November cost report provided by the Accounting Department is as follows:

OKLAHOMA PROJECT
MAINTENANCE CENTER COST REPORT
FOR THE MONTH OF NOVEMBER 1994
($000 OMITTED)

	BUDGET	ACTUAL	PETROLEUM PRODUCTION	NATURAL GAS PRODUCTION
Shop hours	2,000	1,800	—	—
Field hours	8,000	10,000	6,000	4,000
Labor, electrical	$ 25.0	$ 24.0	$ 14.4	$ 9.6
Labor, mechanical	30.0	35.0	21.0	14.0
Labor, instrumentation	18.0	22.5	13.5	9.0
Labor, automotive	3.5	2.8	1.7	1.1
Labor, heavy equipment	9.6	12.3	7.4	4.9
Labor, equipment operation	28.8	35.4	21.2	14.2

Continued

—Continued

	BUDGET	ACTUAL	PETROLEUM PRODUCTION	NATURAL GAS PRODUCTION
Labor, general	15.4	15.9	9.6	6.3
Parts	60.0	86.2	51.7	34.5
Supplies	15.3	12.2	7.3	4.9
Lubricants and fuels	3.4	3.0	1.8	1.2
Tools	2.5	3.2	1.9	1.3
Accounting and data processing	1.5	1.5	0.9	0.6
Totals	$213.0	$254.0	$152.4	$101.6

■ *Production center managers' concerns.* Both production center managers have been upset with the method of cost allocation. Furthermore, they believe the report is virtually useless as a cost control device. Actual costs always seem to deviate from the monthly budget, and the proportion charged to each production center varies significantly from month to month. Maintenance costs have increased substantially since 1992, and the production managers believe that they have no way to judge whether such an increase is reasonable. The two production managers, Pepper, and representatives of corporate accounting have met to discuss these concerns. They concluded that a responsibility accounting system could be developed to replace the current system. In their opinion, a responsibility accounting system would alleviate the production managers' concerns and accurately reflect the activity of the Maintenance Center.

Required:

a. Explain the purposes of a responsibility accounting system, and discuss how such a system could resolve the concerns of the production center managers of Kelly Petroleum Company.

b. Describe the behavioral advantages generally attributed to responsibility accounting systems that the management of Kelly Petroleum Company should expect if the system is effectively introduced for the Maintenance Center.

c. Describe a report format for the Maintenance Center that would be based on a responsibility accounting system, and explain which, if any, of the Maintenance Center's costs should be charged to the two production centers.

[CMA adapted]

20.61 *Discontinuance decision.* Condensed monthly operating income data for Cosmo, Inc., for November 19X4 is presented below. Additional information regarding Cosmo's operations follows the statement.

	TOTAL	MALL STORE	TOWN STORE
Sales	$200,000	$80,000	$120,000
Less variable costs	<116,000>	<32,000>	<84,000>
Contribution margin	$ 84,000	$48,000	$ 36,000
Less direct fixed costs	<60,000>	<20,000>	<40,000>
Store segment margins	$ 24,000	$28,000	<$ 4,000>
Less common fixed costs	<10,000>	<4,000>	<6,000>
Operating income	$ 14,000	$24,000	<$ 10,000>

■ One-fourth of each store's direct fixed costs would continue through December 31, 19X5, if either store were closed.

■ Cosmo allocates common fixed costs to each store on the basis of sales dollars.

■ Management estimates that closing the Town Store would result in a 10% decrease in Mall Store sales, while closing the Mall Store would not affect Town Store sales.

■ The operating results for November 19X4 are representative of all months.

Required:

a. If Cosmo closed the Town Store, what would be the monthly increase (decrease) in Cosmo's operating income during 19X5?

b. Cosmo is considering a promotional campaign at the Town Store that would not affect the Mall Store. Increasing annual promotional costs at the Town Store by $60,000 would increase Town Store's sales by 10%. What would be the monthly increase (decrease) in Cosmo's operating income during 19X5 if this campaign is undertaken?

c. One-half of Town Store's dollar sales are from items sold at variable cost to attract customers to the store. Cosmo is considering dropping these items, a move that would reduce the Town Store's direct fixed costs by 15% and result in a loss of 20% of the remaining Town Store's sales volume. This change would not affect the Mall Store. If Cosmo dropped the items sold at variable cost, what would be the monthly increase (decrease) in Cosmo's operating income during 19X5?

[CMA adapted]

Relative Market Share

		High	Low
Market Growth	High	Star	Problem Child
	Low	Cash Cow	Dog

20.62 Growth/share matrix. The market growth/share classifications can be depicted in the above manner:

Problem children are products that promise high growth rates but have relatively small market shares, such as new products that are similar to their competitors. Stars are high-growth, high-market share products that tend to mature into cash cows. Cash cows are slow-growing established products that can be "milked" for cash to help the stars and problem children and to introduce new products. The dogs are low-growth, low-market share items that are candidates for elimination. Understanding where a product falls within this market growth/share matrix is important when deciding which products to keep and which ones to drop.

Required:
Discuss the applicability or nonapplicability of using a growth/share matrix in deciding whether to keep or drop products.

20.63 Add-or-drop decision. The Sklar Company carries three products. Sales and cost information for the preceding month for each separate product line and for the company in total follows:

PRODUCTS

	TOTALS	A	B	C
Sales	$310,000	$160,000	$90,000	$60,000
Less variable costs	<112,000>	<50,000>	<30,000>	<32,000>
Contribution margin	$198,000	$110,000	$60,000	$28,000
Less fixed costs:				
Salaries	$ 54,000	$ 30,000	$14,000	$10,000
Depreciation	12,000	5,000	4,000	3,000
Utilities	7,000	4,000	2,000	1,000
Advertising	22,000	10,000	6,000	6,000
Rent	26,000	15,000	7,000	4,000
Insurance	8,000	4,000	2,000	2,000
Administrative	42,000	22,000	12,000	8,000
Total fixed costs	<171,000>	<90,000>	<47,000>	<34,000>
Net income (loss)	$ 27,000	$ 20,000	$13,000	<$ 6,000>

Product C shows a net loss of $6,000 for the month. Management believes that dropping product C would cause profits in the company as a whole to improve. Tim Sandifer, the management accountant, has been asked to analyze the situation and present his findings next Monday.

Tim gathers the following facts:

■ Salaries are paid to employees working directly in each product line area. All of the employees working in the product C area would be discharged if the product line is dropped.

■ Depreciation represents depreciation on fixtures and equipment that were customized for each product line. Their resale value is very small.

■ Utilities represent costs for the entire company. The amount charged to each product line represents an allocation based on square feet of floor space occupied.

■ Rent represents an amount paid for the entire building that houses the company. It is allocated to the product lines on a basis of square feet of floor space occupied. The monthly rent of $26,000 is fixed under a long-term lease agreement.

■ Insurance represents the amount of premium paid within each of the product lines.

■ Administrative costs are allocated to the product lines on the basis of sales dollars. Total administrative costs will not change if product C is dropped.

Required:
a. Identify those costs that are avoidable and those costs that are not avoidable if product C is dropped.
b. Determine how dropping product C will affect the overall profits of the company.
c. Explain to management why they should either retain product C or drop it.

20.64 *Calculating ROI and RI.* Selected data from Calumet Company's accounting records reveal the following:

Sales	$500,000
Average invested capital	$200,000
Net income	$40,000
Imputed interest rate	10%
Capital turnover	3.0

Required:
a. Calculate the return on investment (ROI)
b. Calculate the residual income (RI)

20.65 *Calculating ROI and RI.* Raddington Industries produces tool and die machinery for manufacturers. The company expanded vertically in 19X4 by acquiring one of its suppliers of alloy steel plates, Reigis Steel Company. In order to manage the two separate businesses, the operations of Reigis are reported separately as an investment center.

Raddington monitors its divisions on the basis of both unit contribution and return on average investment (ROI), with investment defined as average operating assets employed. Management bonuses are determined on ROI. All investments in operating assets are expected to earn a minimum return of 11% before income taxes.

Reigis's cost of goods sold is considered to be entirely variable while the division's administrative expenses are not dependent on volume. Selling expenses are a mixed cost with 40% attributed to sales volume. Reigis's ROI has ranged from 11.8% to 14.7% since 19X4. During the fiscal year ended November 30, 19X9, Reigis contemplated a capital acquisition with an estimated ROI of 11.5%; however, division management decided against the investment because it believed that the investment would decrease Reigis's overall ROI.

The 19X9 operating statement for Reigis follows. The division's operating assets employed were $15,750,000 at November 30, 19X9, a 5% increase over the 19X8 year-end balance.

REIGIS STEEL DIVISION
OPERATING STATEMENT
FOR THE YEAR ENDED NOVEMBER 30, 19X9
($000 OMITTED)

Sales revenue		$25,000
Less expenses:		
Cost of goods sold	$16,500	
Administrative expenses	3,955	
Selling expenses	2,700	23,155
Income from operations before income taxes		$ 1,845

Required:
a. Calculate the unit contribution for Reigis Steel Division if 1,484,000 units were produced and sold during the year ended November 30, 19X9.
b. Calculate the following performance measures for 19X9 for the Reigis Steel Division:
   1. Pretax return on average investment in operating assets employed (ROI).
   2. Residual income (RI) calculated on the basis of average operating assets employed.
c. Explain why Reigis management would have been more likely to accept the contemplated capital acquisition if RI rather than ROI had been used as a performance measurement.
d. The Reigis Steel Division is a separate investment center within Raddington Industries. Identify several items that Reigis should control if it is to be evaluated fairly by either the ROI or RI performance measurement.

[CMA adapted]

20.66 *Ethical considerations.* Investment center managers are often subjected to substantial pressures to meet or exceed a target ROI. In some situations, managers are able to achieve the target ROI by "cooking the books."

Required:
a. Define "cooking the books" and list ways that it can be performed.
b. Discuss the ethical ramifications of not adhering to ethical accounting policies and procedures.
c. Discuss the pros and cons of exerting pressures on investment center managers to meet or exceed a target ROI.

20.67 *Calculating ROI and RI and comparing their results.* Lawton Industries has manufactured prefabricated houses for over 20 years. The houses are constructed in sections to be assembled on customers' lots.

Lawton expanded into the precut housing market in 19X0 when it acquired Presser Company, one of its suppliers. In this market, various types of lumber are precut into the appropriate lengths, banded into packages, and shipped to customers' lots for assembly. Lawton decided to maintain Presser's separate identity and, thus, established the Presser Division as an investment center of Lawton.

Lawton uses return on average investment (ROI) as a performance measure with investment defined as operating assets employed. Management bonuses are based in part on ROI. All investments in operating assets are expected to earn a minimum return of 15% before income taxes.

Presser's ROI has ranged from 19.3% to 22.1% since it was acquired in 19X0. Presser had an investment opportunity in 19X5 that had an estimated ROI of 18%. Presser's management decided against the investment because it believed the investment would decrease the division's overall ROI.

The 19X5 operating statement for Presser Division follows. The division's operating assets employed were $12,600,000 at the end of 19X5, a 5% increase over the 19X4 year-end balance.

PRESSER DIVISION
OPERATING STATEMENT
FOR THE YEAR ENDED DECEMBER 31, 19X5
($000 OMITTED)

Sales revenue		$24,000
Cost of goods sold		15,800
Gross profit		$ 8,200
Operating expenses:		
Administrative	$2,140	
Selling	3,600	5,740
Income from operations before income taxes		$ 2,460

Required:
a. Calculate the following performance measures for 19X5 for the Presser Division of Lawton Industries:
   1. Return on average investment in operating assets employed (ROI).
   2. Residual income calculated on the basis of average operating assets employed.
b. Would the management of Presser Division have been more likely to accept the investment opportunity in 19X5 if RI had been used as a performance measure instead of ROI? Explain your answer.
c. The Presser Division is a separate investment center within Lawton Industries. Identify the items Presser must control if it is to be evaluated fairly by either the ROI or RI performance measure.

20.68 *Contribution margin volume variance.* The following information is available for the Mitchelville Products Company for the month of July:

	FLEXIBLE BUDGET	ACTUAL
Units	4,000	3,800
Sales revenue	$60,000	$53,200
Variable manufacturing costs	$16,000	$19,000
Fixed manufacturing costs	$15,000	$16,000
Variable selling and administrative expense	$8,000	$7,600
Fixed selling and administrative expense	$9,000	$10,000

Required:
Calculate the contribution margin volume variance for July.

[CMA adapted]

20.69 *Sales price variance.* Actual and budgeted information about the sales of a product for June are as follows:

	ACTUAL	BUDGET
Units	8,000	10,000
Sales revenue	$92,000	$105,000

Required:
Calculate the sales price variance for June.

▌THINK-TANK PROBLEMS

Although these problems are based on chapter material, reading extra material, reviewing previous chapters, and using creativity may be required to develop workable solutions.

20.70 *Converting from absorption costing to variable costing.* The Daniels Tool & Die Corporation has been in existence for a little over three years; sales have been increasing each year as Daniels builds a reputation. The company manufactures dies to its customers' specifications; as a consequence, it uses a job order cost system. Factory overhead is applied to the jobs based on direct labor hours, utilizing the absorption costing method. Over- or underapplied overhead is treated as an adjustment to cost of goods sold. The company's income statements for the last two years are as follows:

DANIELS TOOL & DIE CORPORATION
19X6–19X7 COMPARATIVE INCOME STATEMENTS

	19X6	19X7
Sales	$840,000	$1,015,000
Cost of goods sold:		
Finished goods, 1/1	25,000	18,000
Cost of goods manufactured	548,000	657,600
Total available	$573,000	$ 675,600
Finished goods, 12/31	18,000	14,000
Cost of goods sold before overhead adjustment	$555,000	$ 661,600
Underapplied factory overhead	36,000	14,400
Cost of goods sold	$591,000	$ 676,000
Gross profit	$249,000	$ 339,000
Selling expenses	82,000	95,000
Administrative expenses	70,000	75,000
Total operating expenses	152,000	170,000
Operating income	$ 97,000	$ 169,000

DANIELS TOOL & DIE CORPORATION
INVENTORY BALANCE

	1/1/X6	12/31/X6	12/31/X7
Raw material	$22,000	$30,000	$10,000
Work-in-process:			
Costs	$40,000	$48,000	$64,000
Direct labor hours	1,335	1,600	2,100
Finished goods:			
Costs	$25,000	$18,000	$14,000
Direct labor hours	1,450	1,050	820

Daniels used the same predetermined overhead rate (POR) in applying overhead to production orders in both 19X6 and 19X7. The rate was based on the following estimates:

Fixed factory overhead	$25,000
Variable factory overhead	$155,000
Direct labor hours	25,000
Direct labor costs	$150,000

In 19X6 and 19X7, actual direct labor hours expended were 20,000 and 23,000, respectively. Raw materials put into production were $292,000 in 19X6 and $370,000 in 19X7. Actual fixed overhead was $37,400 for 19X7 and $42,300 for 19X6, and the planned direct labor rate was the direct labor rate achieved.

For both years, all of the reported administrative costs were fixed, while the variable portion of the reported selling expenses results from a commission of 5% of sales revenue.

Required:

a. For the year ended December 31, 19X7, prepare a revised income statement for Daniels Tool & Die Corporation utilizing the variable costing method. Be sure to include the contribution margin on your statement.

b. Prepare a numerical reconciliation of the difference in operating income between Daniels Tool & Die Corporation's 19X7 income statement prepared on the basis of absorption costing and the revised 19X7 income statement prepared on the basis of variable costing.

c. Describe both the advantages and disadvantages of using variable costing.

[CMA adapted]

20.71 *Reporting operating costs by segments.* The Scent Company sells men's toiletries to retail stores throughout the United States. For planning and control purposes, the Scent Company is organized into 12 geographic regions with two to six territories within each region. One salesperson is assigned to each territory and has exclusive rights to all sales made in that territory. Merchandise is shipped from the manufacturing plant to the 12 regional warehouses, and the sales in each territory are shipped from the regional warehouse. National headquarters allocates a specific amount at the beginning of the year for regional advertising.

The net sales for the Scent Company for the year ended September 20, 19X4, totaled $10 million. Costs incurred by national headquarters for national administration, advertising, and warehousing are summarized as follows:

National administration	$250,000
National advertising	125,000
National warehousing	175,000
	$550,000

The results of operations for the South Atlantic Region for the year ended September 30, 19X4, are as follows:

SCENT COMPANY
STATEMENT OF OPERATIONS
SOUTH ATLANTIC REGION
FOR THE YEAR ENDED SEPTEMBER 30, 19X4

Net sales		$900,000
Costs and expenses:		
Advertising fees	$ 54,700	
Bad debt expense	3,600	
Cost of sales	460,000	
Freight-out	22,600	
Insurance	10,000	
Salaries and employee benefits	81,600	
Sales commissions	36,000	
Supplies	12,000	
Travel and entertainment	14,100	
Wages and employee benefits	36,000	
Warehouse depreciation	8,000	
Warehouse operating costs	15,000	
Total costs and expenses		753,600
Territory contribution		$146,400

The South Atlantic Region consists of two territories—Green and Purple. The salaries and employee benefits consist of the following items:

Regional vice president	$24,000
Regional marketing manager	15,000
Regional warehouse manager	13,400
Sales personnel (one for each territory with each receiving the same base salary)	15,600
Employee benefits (20%)	13,600
	$81,600

The sales personnel receive a base salary plus a 4% commission on all items sold in their territory. Bad debt expense has averaged 0.4% of net sales in the past. Travel and entertainment costs are incurred by sales personnel calling upon their customers. Freight-out is a function of the quantity of goods shipped and the distance shipped. Thirty percent of the insurance is expended for protection of the inventory while it is in the regional warehouse, and the remainder is incurred for the protection of the warehouse. Supplies are used in the warehouse for packing the merchandise that is shipped. Wages relate to the hourly paid employees who fill orders in the warehouse. The warehouse operating costs account contains such costs as heat, light, and maintenance.

The following cost analyses and statistics by territory for the current year are representative of past experience and are representative of expected future operations:

COST ANALYSIS BY TERRITORY

	GREEN	PURPLE	TOTAL
Sales	$300,000	$600,000	$900,000
Cost of sales	$184,000	$276,000	$460,000
Advertising fees	$21,800	$32,900	$54,700
Travel and entertainment	$6,300	$7,800	$14,100
Freight-out	$9,000	$13,600	$22,600
Units sold	150,000	350,000	500,000
Pounds shipped	210,000	390,000	600,000
Sales personnel miles traveled	21,600	38,400	60,000

Required:

a. The top management of Scent Company wants the regional vice presidents to present their operating data in a more meaningful manner. Therefore, management has requested that the regions separate their operating costs into the fixed and variable components of order getting, order filling, and administration. The data are to be presented in the following format:

TERRITORY COSTS

	GREEN	PURPLE	REGIONAL COSTS	TOTAL COSTS
Order getting				
Order filling				
Administration				

Using management's suggested format, prepare a schedule that presents the costs for the region by territory with the costs separated into variable and fixed categories by order getting, order filling, and administrative functions.

b. Suppose the top management of Scent Company is considering splitting the Purple Territory into two separate territories (Red and Blue). From the data that have been presented, identify what data would be relevant to this decision (either for or against), and indicate what other data you would collect to aid top management in its decision.

[CMA adapted]

20.72 *Segment reporting and ethical considerations.* Pittsburgh-Walsh Company (PWC) is a manufacturing company whose product line consists of lighting fixtures and electronic timing devices. The Lighting Fixtures Division assembles units for the upscale and mid-range markets. The Electronic Timing Devices Division manufactures instrument panels that allow electronic systems to be activated and deactivated at scheduled times for both efficiency and safety purposes. Both divisions operate out of the same manufacturing facilities and share production equipment.

PWC's budget for the year ending December 31, 19X0, is as follows:

PITTSBURGH-WALSH COMPANY
BUDGET FOR THE YEAR ENDED DECEMBER 31, 19X0
($000)

| | LIGHTING FIXTURES | | ELECTRONIC TIMING | |
	UPSCALE	MID-RANGE	DEVICES	TOTALS
Sales	$1,440	$770	$800	$3,010
Variable expenses:				
Cost of goods sold	720	439	320	1,479
Selling and administrative	170	60	60	290
Contribution margin	550	271	420	1,241
Fixed overhead expenses	140	80	80	300
Segment margin	410	191	340	941
Common fixed expenses:				
Overhead	48	132	120	300
Selling and administrative	11	31	28	70
Net income (loss)	$ 351	$ 28	$192	$ 571

The budget was prepared on a business segment basis under the following guidelines:

■ Variable expenses are directly assigned to the incurring division.
■ Fixed overhead expenses are directly assigned to the incurring division.
■ Common fixed expenses are allocated to the divisions on the basis of units produced that bear a close relationship to direct labor. Included in common fixed expenses are costs of the corporate staff, legal expenses, taxes, staff marketing, and advertising.
■ The production plan is for 8,000 upscale fixtures, 22,000 mid-range fixtures, and 20,000 electronic timing devices.

PWC established a bonus plan for division managers that requires them to meet the budget's planned net income by product line, with a bonus increment if the division exceeds the planned product line net income by 10% or more.

Shortly before the year began, the CEO, Jack Parkow, suffered a heart attack and retired. After reviewing the 19X0 budget, the new CEO, Joe Kelly, decided to close the lighting fixtures mid-range product line by the end of the first quarter and use the available production capacity to grow the remaining two product lines. The marketing staff advised that electronic timing devices could grow by 40% with increased direct sales support. Increases above that level and increased sales of upscale lighting fixtures would require expanded advertising expenditures to increase consumer awareness of PWC as an electronics and upscale lighting fixture company. Kelly approved the increased sales support and advertising expenditures to achieve the revised plan. Kelly advised the divisions that for bonus purposes the original product line net income objectives must be met, but he did allow the Lighting Fixtures Division to combine the net income objectives for both product lines for bonus purposes.

Prior to the close of the fiscal year, the division controllers were furnished with preliminary actual data for review and adjustment, as appropriate. These preliminary year-end data reflect the revised units of production amounting to 12,000 upscale fixtures, 4,000 mid-range fixtures, and 30,000 electronic timing devices and are as follows:

PITTSBURGH-WALSH COMPANY
PRELIMINARY ACTUALS FOR THE YEAR ENDED DECEMBER 31, 19X0
($000)

| | LIGHTING FIXTURES | | ELECTRONIC TIMING | |
	UPSCALE	MID-RANGE	DEVICES	TOTALS
Sales	$2,160	$140	$1,200	$3,500
Variable expenses:				
Cost of goods sold	1,080	80	480	1,640
Selling and administrative	260	11	96	367
Contribution margin	820	49	624	1,493
Fixed overhead expenses	140	14	80	234
Segment margin	680	35	544	1,259
Common fixed expenses:				
Overheads	78	27	195	300
Selling and administrative	60	20	150	230
Net income (loss)	$ 542	$<12>	$ 199	$ 729

The controller of the Lighting Fixtures Division, anticipating a similar bonus plan for 19X1, is contemplating deferring some revenues into the next year on the pretext that the sales are not yet final, and accruing in the current year expenditures that will be applicable to the first quarter of 19X1. The corporation would meet its annual plan, and the division would exceed the 10% incremental bonus plateau in the year 19X0 despite the deferred revenues and accrued expenses contemplated.

Required:
a. 1. Outline the benefits that an organization realizes from segment reporting.
   2. Evaluate segment reporting on a variable cost basis versus an absorption cost basis.
b. 1. Segment reporting can be developed based on different criteria. What criteria must be present for division management to accept being evaluated on a segment basis?
   2. Why would the management of the Electronics Timing Devices Division be unhappy with the current reporting, and how should the reporting be revised to gain their acceptance?
c. Explain why the adjustments contemplated by the controller of the Lighting Fixtures Division are unethical by citing the specific standard of competence, confidentiality, integrity, and/or objectivity from the *Standards of Ethical Conduct for Management Accountants.*

[CMA adapted]

20.73 *Identifying responsibilities and evaluating performance.* Sarah Johnson was hired on July 1, 1992, as assistant general manager of the Botel Division of Staple, Inc. It was understood that she would be elevated to general manager of the division on January 1, 1994, when the then current general manager retired, and Johnson was duly promoted as planned. In addition to becoming acquainted with the division and the general manager's duties, Johnson was specifically charged with the responsibility for developing the 1993 and 1994 budgets. As general manager in 1994, she was, obviously, responsible for the 1995 budget.

Staple is a multiproduct company that is highly decentralized. Each division is quite autonomous. The corporation staff approves division-prepared operating budgets but seldom makes major changes in them. The corporation staff actively participates in decisions requiring capital investment (for expansion or replacement) and makes the final decisions. The division management is responsible for implementing the capital program. The major method used by Staple to measure division performance is contribution return on division net investment. The budgets that follow were approved by the corporation. Revision of the 1995 budget is not considered necessary even though 1994 actual departed from the approved 1994 budget.

BOTEL DIVISION
($000)

ACCOUNTS	ACTUAL 1992	ACTUAL 1993	ACTUAL 1994	BUDGET 1994	BUDGET 1995
Sales	$1,000	$1,500	$1,800	$2,000	$2,400
Less division variable costs:					
Material and labor	250	375	450	500	600
Repairs	50	75	50	100	120
Supplies	20	30	36	40	48
Less division managed costs:					
Employee training	30	35	25	40	45
Maintenance	50	55	40	60	70
Less division committed costs:					
Depreciation	120	160	160	200	200
Rent	80	100	110	140	140
Total	600	830	871	1,080	1,223
Division net contribution	$ 400	$ 670	$ 929	$ 920	$1,177
Division investment:					
Accounts receivable	100	150	180	200	240
Inventory	200	300	270	400	480
Fixed assets	1,590	2,565	2,800	3,380	4,000
Less accounts and wages payable	<150>	<225>	<350>	<300>	<360>
Net investment	$1,740	$2,790	$2,900	$3,680	$4,360
Contribution return on net investment	23%	24%	32%	25%	27%

Required:
a. Identify Sarah Johnson's responsibilities under the management and measurement program described above.
b. Appraise Sarah Johnson's performance in 1994.
c. Based upon your analysis, what changes would you recommend to the president in the responsibilities assigned to managers or in the measurement methods used to evaluate division management?

[CMA adapted]

20.74 *Explaining unfavorable variance between budgeted and actual contribution margin.* Funtime, Inc., manufactures video game machines. Market saturation and technological innovations have caused pricing pressures that have resulted in declining profits. To stem the slide in profits until new products can be introduced, top management has turned its attention to both manufacturing economies and increased production. To realize these objectives, an incentive program has been developed to reward production managers who contribute to an increase in the number of units produced and effect cost reductions.

The production managers have responded to the pressure of improving manufacturing in several ways that have resulted in increased completed units over normal production levels. The video game machines are put together by the Assembly Group, which requires parts from both the Printed Circuit Boards (PCB) and the Reading Heads (RH) groups. To attain increased production levels, the PCB and RH groups began rejecting parts that previously would have been tested and modified to meet manufacturing standards. Preventive maintenance on machines used in the production of these parts has been postponed with only emergency repair work being performed to keep production lines moving. The Maintenance Department is concerned that there will be serious breakdowns and unsafe operating conditions.

The more aggressive Assembly Group production supervisors have pressured maintenance personnel to attend to their machines at the expense of other groups. This has resulted in machine downtime in the PCB and RH groups, which, when coupled with demand for accelerated parts delivery by the Assembly Group, has led to more frequent parts rejections and increased friction among departments.

Funtime operates under a standard cost system. The standard costs for video game machines are as follows:

STANDARD COST PER UNIT

COST ITEM	QUANTITY	COST	TOTAL
Direct materials:			
Housing unit	1	$20	$ 20
Printed circuit boards	2	15	30
Reading heads	4	10	40
Direct labor:			
Assembly Group	2 hours	8	16
PCB group	1 hour	9	9
RH group	1.5 hours	10	15
Variable overhead	4.5 hours	2	9
Total standard cost per unit			$139

Funtime prepares monthly performance reports based on standard costs. The following is the contribution report for May 19X4, when production and sales both reached 2,200 units:

FUNTIME, INC.
CONTRIBUTION REPORT
FOR THE MONTH OF MAY 19X4

	BUDGET	ACTUAL	VARIANCE	
Units	2,000	2,200	200	F
Revenue	$400,000	$440,000	$40,000	F
Variable costs:				
Direct materials	180,000	220,400	<40,400>	U
Direct labor	80,000	93,460	<13,460>	U
Variable overhead	18,000	18,800	<800>	U
Total variable costs	278,000	332,660	<54,660>	U
Contribution margin	$122,000	$107,340	<$14,660>	U

Funtime's top management was surprised by the unfavorable contribution to overall corporate profits in spite of the increased sales in May. Jack Rath, cost accountant, was assigned to identify and report on the reasons for the unfavorable contribution results as well as the individuals or groups responsible. After review, Rath prepared the following usage report:

FUNTIME, INC.
USAGE REPORT
FOR THE MONTH OF MAY 19X4

COST ITEM	QUANTITY	ACTUAL COST
Direct materials:		
Housing units	2,200 units	$ 44,000
Printed circuit boards	4,700 units	75,200
Reading heads	9,200 units	101,200
Direct labor:		
Assembly	3,900 hours	31,200
Printed circuit boards	2,500 hours	23,760
Reading heads	3,500 hours	38,500
Variable overhead	9,900 hours	18,800
Total variable cost		$332,660

Rath reported that the PCB and RH groups supported the increased production levels but experienced abnormal machine downtime, causing workers to be idle and necessitating the use of overtime to keep up with the accelerated demand for parts. The idle time was charged to direct labor. Rath also reported that the production managers of these two groups resorted to parts rejections, as opposed to testing and modification procedures formerly applied. Rath determined that the Assembly Group met management's objectives by increasing production while using lower than standard hours.

Required:

a. For May 19X4, Funtime's labor rate variance was $5,660 unfavorable, and the labor efficiency variance was $200 favorable. By using these two variances and calculating the following variances, prepare an explanation of the $14,660 unfavorable variance between budgeted and actual contribution margin during May 19X4.
   1. Materials price variance.
   2. Materials quantity (usage) variance.
   3. Variable overhead efficiency variance.
   4. Variable overhead spending variance.
   5. Contribution margin volume variance.
b. 1. Identify and briefly explain the behavioral factors that may promote friction among the production managers and between the production managers and the maintenance manager.
   2. Evaluate Jack Rath's analysis of the unfavorable contribution results in terms of its completeness and its effects on the behavior of the production groups.

[CMA adapted]

20.75 *Evaluating the budget process and return on assets for planning and control.* Clarkson Company is a large multidivision firm with several plants in each division. A comprehensive budgeting system is used for planning operations and measuring performance. The annual budgeting process starts in August, five months prior to the beginning of the fiscal year. At this time, the division managers submit proposed budgets for sales, production and inventory levels, and expenses. Capital expenditure requests also are formalized at this time. The expense budgets include direct labor and all overhead items that are separated into fixed and variable components. Direct materials are budgeted separately in developing the production and inventory schedules.

The expense budgets for each division are developed from its plants' results, as measured by the percentage variation from an adjusted budget in the first six months of the current year and a target expense reduction percentage established by the corporation.

To determine plant percentages, the plant budget for the just completed half-year period is revised to recognize changes in operating procedures and costs outside the control of plant management (e.g., labor wage rate changes, product style changes, and so forth). The difference between this revised budget and the actual expenses is the controllable variance and is expressed as a percentage of the actual expenses. This percentage is added (if unfavorable) to the corporate target expense reduction percentage. A favorable plant variance percentage is subtracted from the corporate target. If a plant had a 2% unfavorable controllable variance and the corporate target reduction was 4%, the plant's budget for the next year should reflect costs approximately 6% below this year's actual costs.

Next year's final budgets for the corporation, the divisions, and the plants are adopted after corporate analysis of the proposed budgets and a careful review with each division manager of the changes made by corporate management. Division profit budgets include allocated corporate costs, and plant profit budgets include allocated division and corporate costs.

Return on assets is used to measure the performance of divisions and plants. The asset base for a division consists of all assets assigned to the division, including its working capital, and an allocated share of corporate assets. For plants, the asset base includes the assets assigned to the plant plus an allocated portion of the division and corporate assets. Recommendations for promotions and salary increases for the executives of the divisions and plants are influenced by how well the actual return on assets compares with the budgeted return on assets.

The plant managers exercise control only over the cost portion of the plant profit budget because the divisions are responsible for sales. Only limited control over the plant assets is exercised at the plant level.

The manager of the Dexter Plant, a major plant in the Huron Division, carefully controls his costs during the first six months so that any improvement appears after the target reduction of expenses is established. He accomplishes this by careful planning and timing of his discretionary expenditures.

During 1994, the property adjacent to the Dexter Plant was purchased by Clarkson Company. This expenditure was not included in the 1994 capital budget. Corporate management decided to divert funds from a project at another plant since the property appeared to be a better long-term investment.

Also during 1994, Clarkson Company experienced depressed sales. In an attempt to achieve budgeted profit, corporate management announced in August that all plants were to cut their annual expenses by 6%. In order to accomplish this expense reduction, the Dexter Plant manager reduced preventive maintenance and postponed needed major repairs. Employees who quit were not replaced unless absolutely necessary. Employee training was postponed whenever possible. The raw materials, supplies, and finished goods inventories were reduced below normal levels.

Required:
a. Evaluate the budget procedure of Clarkson Company with respect to its effectiveness for planning and controlling operations.
b. Is the Clarkson Company's use of return on assets to evaluate the performance of the Dexter Plant appropriate? Explain your answer.
c. Analyze and explain the Dexter Plant manager's behavior during 1994.

[CMA adapted]

20.76 *Evaluating ROA as a single performance measurement.* The Motor Works Division of Roland Industries is located in Fort Wayne, Indiana. A major expansion of the division's only plant was completed in April 19X4. The expansion consisted of an addition to the existing building, additional new equipment, and the replacement of obsolete and fully depreciated equipment that was no longer efficient or cost-effective.

Donald Futak became the manager of the Motor Works Division, effective May 1, 19X4. Futak had a brief meeting with John Poskey, vice president of operations for Roland Industries, when he assumed the division manager position. Poskey told Futak that the company employed return on gross assets (ROA) for measuring performance of divisions and division managers. Futak asked whether any other performance measures were ever used in place of or in conjunction with ROA. Poskey replied, "Roland's top management prefers to use a single performance measure. There is no conflict when there is only one measure. Motor Works should do well this year now that it has expanded and replaced all of that old equipment. You should have no problem exceeding the division's historical rate. I'll check back with you at the end of each quarter to see how you are doing."

Poskey called Futak after the first quarter results were complete because the Motor Works' ROA was considerably below the historical rate for the division. Futak told Poskey at that time that he did not believe that ROA was a valid performance measure for the Motor Works Division. Poskey indicated that he would get back to Futak. Futak did receive perfunctory memorandums after the second and third quarters, but there was no further discussion on the use of ROA. Now Futak has received the following memorandum:

May 24, 19X5

TO: Donald Futak, Manager—Motor Works Division
FROM: John Poskey, Vice President of Operations
SUBJECT: Division Performance

The operating results for the fourth quarter and for our fiscal year ended on April 30 are now complete. Your fourth quarter return on gross assets was only 9%, resulting in a return for the year of slightly under 11%. I recall discussing your low return after the first quarter and reminding you after the second and third quarters that this level of return is not considered adequate for the Motor Works Division.

The return on gross assets at Motor Works has ranged from 15% to 18% for the past five years. An 11% return may be acceptable at some of Roland's other divisions, but not at a proven winner like Motor Works—especially in light of your recently improved facility.

I would like to meet with you at your office on Monday, June 3, to discuss ways to restore Motor Works' return on gross assets to its former level. Please let me know if this date is acceptable to you.

Futak is looking forward to meeting with Poskey. He knows the division's ROA is below the historical rate, but the dollar profits for the year are greater than prior years. He plans to explain to Poskey why he believes return on gross assets is not an appropriate performance measure for the Motor Works Division. He also plans to recommend that ROA be replaced with three measures—dollar profit, receivables turnover, and inventory turnover. These three measures would constitute a set of multiple criteria that would be used to evaluate performance.

Required:
a. On the basis of the relationship between John Poskey and Donald Futak, as well as the memorandum from Poskey, identify apparent weaknesses in the performance evaluation process of Roland Industries. Do not include in your answer any discussion on the use of return on assets (ROA) as a performance measure.
b. From the information presented, identify a possible explanation of why Motor Works Division's ROA declined in the fiscal year ended April 30, 19X5.
c. Identify criteria that should be used in selecting performance measures to evaluate operating managers.
d. If John Poskey does agree to use multiple criteria for evaluating the performance of the Motor Works Division as Donald Futak has suggested, discuss whether the multiple criteria of dollar profit, receivables turnover, and inventory turnover would be appropriate.

[CMA adapted]

20.77 *Eliminating dysfunctional behavior.* Wright Company employs a computer-based data processing system for maintaining all company records. The present system was developed in stages over the past five years and has been fully operational for the last 24 months.

When the system was being designed, all department heads were asked to specify the types of information and reports they would need for planning and controlling operations. The Systems Department attempted to meet the specifications of each department head. Company management specified that certain other reports be prepared for department heads. During the five years of systems development and operations, there have been several changes in the department head positions due to attrition and promotions. The new department heads often requested additional reports according to their specifications. The Systems Department complied with all of these requests. Reports were discontinued only upon request by a department head, and then only if it was not a standard report required by top management. As a result, few reports were in fact discontinued. Consequently, the data processing system was generating a large quantity of reports each reporting period.

Company management became concerned about the quantity of information that was being produced by the system. The Internal Audit Department was asked to evaluate the effectiveness of the reports generated by the system. The audit staff determined early in the study that more information was being generated by the data processing system than could be used effectively. They noted the following reactions to this information overload:

1. Many department heads would not act on certain reports during periods of peak activity. The department head would let these reports accumulate with the hope of catching up during a subsequent lull.
2. Some department heads had so many reports that they either did not act at all upon the information or made incorrect decisions because they misused the information.
3. Frequently, report data would indicate a need for action, but nothing would be done until the department head was reminded by someone who needed the decision. These department heads did not appear to have developed a

priority system for acting on the information produced by the data processing system.

4. Department heads often would develop the information they needed from alternative, independent sources, rather than utilizing the reports generated by the data processing system. This was often easier than trying to search among the reports for the needed data.

Required:

a. Indicate, for each of the observed reactions, whether they are functional or dysfunctional behavioral responses. Explain your answer in each case.

b. Assuming one or more of the responses were dysfunctional, recommend procedures the company could employ to eliminate the dysfunctional behavior and to prevent its recurrence.

[CMA adapted]

21 PRODUCT TRANSFERS WITHIN A COMPANY

Some companies transfer products between segments.

LEARNING OBJECTIVES

After studying this chapter, you will be able to:

1. Distinguish between components made in cost centers and intermediate products made in profit centers.

2. Understand the management accounting system's goals for transfer costing and transfer pricing.

3. Determine how the different cost and price options can affect managerial decision making, planning, cost management, and performance evaluation.

■ INTRODUCTION

A **transfer** simply involves moving a component part of a product from one responsibility center (RC) to another within a company. Most products consist of many component parts. Some of these parts can be sold as products themselves, rather than being used to make a "final" product in a different RC. Thus, there are two types of parts that can be transferred: parts that are not sold to outside customers **(components),** and parts that can be sold to outside customers. In economics, parts that can be sold or transferred are called **intermediate products.**

Cost centers within a factory produce components. In planning, they need to budget standard costs. In control and evaluation, they are accountable for keeping costs within the standards budgeted (i.e., not incurring cost variances). When transferring components, the issue is, "What cost should be used for a component transferred to or from another RC?" For example, if a manager uses components made by other RCs, then she needs to know what they will cost in budgeting her product's cost.

A number of different cost options can be used. Actual cost or standard cost could be chosen. With each of these options, the cost could be based on variable costing or absorption costing. Which of these cost options will best help cost center managers budget, control operations, and evaluate performance?

Some managers may be allowed to sell what they make rather than just transferring it to another RC as an intermediate product. Managers who have sales responsibilities are called profit center managers. Now the management accounting information must help the manager making the intermediate product determine whether to sell it or transfer it. This profit center manager's question is, "Which customer (an outside customer or the next RC) will allow me to make the most profit?"

The management accounting system must also help the manager who needs the intermediate product to decide whether to buy it from the other manager or from an outside supplier. The question this manager wants to answer is, "Which supplier (an outside source or the other RC) will minimize my cost of getting this part?"

The company's upper management also needs information about transfers between profit centers, because of its concern with maximizing the company's overall profit. This information concerns whether the intermediate product was transferred when this transfer should have increased corporate profit. Upper management will also want to know whether the extra profit that should have resulted was actually realized.

LEARNING OBJECTIVE 1

Distinguish between components made in cost centers and intermediate products made in profit centers.

∎ TRANSFERS FROM COST CENTERS

The different types of transfers that a company might make are illustrated in the Yard Equipment Company situation in Exhibit 21–1. Yard Equipment Company is organized into a number of RCs that are called divisions. The Braxton Division makes motors that can be used in different products manufactured by Yard Equipment Company. The Clipper Division makes one of these products, lawn mowers. Other RCs make products such as grass trimmers, edgers, blowers, and so forth.

LEARNING OBJECTIVE 2

Understand the management accounting system's goals for transfer costing and transfer pricing.

∎ Yard Equipment Company's Goals for the Divisions

What are the responsibilities of the Braxton manager? She should produce quality motors on time for the needs of Clipper and the other product divisions.

■■EXHIBIT 21–1
Yard Equipment Company Responsibility Centers

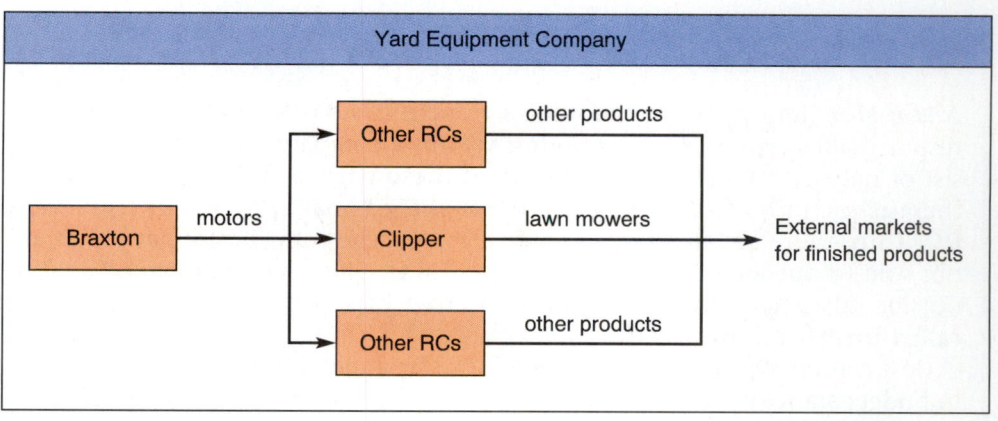

Motors may be transferred internally or sold externally. Courtesy of Outboard Marine Corporation.

She should also budget motor production costs and control costs on a day-to-day basis, avoiding unfavorable cost variances. Yard Equipment Company has formally designed the Braxton Division to be a *cost center,* in which the manager is only responsible for product quality, cost, and quota.

The Clipper manager also needs to budget and control the costs of making lawn mowers. Because each lawn mower needs a motor, he has to budget the cost of a motor along with the other manufacturing cost elements. The Clipper manager has an added responsibility, though. In addition to budgeting and controlling costs, he has to budget sales because the Clipper Division is a *profit center.* The lawn mowers' sales price has to be high enough to cover all the budgeted costs, including motors, as well as yielding the target profit Yard Equipment Company desires.

From Yard Equipment Company's standpoint, the cost used for a transferred motor must motivate the Braxton manager to control her production costs. It must also provide the company with a way to evaluate her cost control performance. Additionally, the transfer cost should allow the Clipper Division manager to budget motor costs for lawn mower production.

Transfer Costing Options

A **transfer cost** is the value used in the accounting system to record *required* transfers from production cost centers. In recommending a transfer cost to the managers involved, the management accountant has to consider three issues.

■ Should the value be based upon the component's sales price or cost?
■ If cost is used, should it be the component's actual or standard cost?
■ If cost is used, should it be calculated by the variable or absorption costing method?

In this situation, Braxton is a *cost center.* It makes motors that are transferred to the other product divisions. Because it is a cost center, Braxton does not sell motors to customers outside the company. All motors are transferred to the other divisions to be used only in Yard Equipment's products.

Exhibit 21–2a presents Braxton's standard costs and actual costs, along with the number of motors budgeted and actually produced in May. In May, Braxton's variable cost variances averaged $10 per motor unfavorable, and there was an unfavorable fixed overhead budget variance of $1,000 (averaging another $10 per motor). If the *actual cost* of $200 per motor is used to transfer motors, Yard Equipment Company's goals may not be realized. The Braxton manager has little incentive to control her costs if she knows that whatever the actual cost ends up being, it will be transferred to the Clipper Division. In other words, all $20 per motor of her cost variances will be "buried" in the cost of the motors transferred and, thus, in the cost of the lawn mowers.

	Standard Costs		Actual Costs	
	Per Unit	Totals	Per Unit	Totals
Variable costs	$100	$10,000	$110	$11,000
Fixed costs	80	8,000	90	9,000
Total costs	$180	$18,000	$200	$20,000
Production volume:	100 motors			

■■■■EXHIBIT 21–2a
Braxton's Budgeted and Actual Data for May

If all the cost variances are included in the transfer cost of the motor, the company will have a harder time evaluating both managers' performance. In this example, the Clipper manager budgeted $180 for a motor (its standard absorptive manufacturing cost), but motors were transferred at the actual cost of $200 each. The result is a $20 per motor unfavorable motor purchase price variance for the Clipper Division.[1] The $2,000 price variance is more than 11 percent over budget ($20 ÷ $180 = 11.11%). A variance this high will probably be investigated by the Clipper manager, who will then "appeal" it to upper management, claiming that the variance is not his responsibility and that he should not be held accountable for it in his performance evaluation. Upper management will then go to the Braxton manager and spend considerably more time trying to resolve this issue and correctly assign responsibility and evaluate performance.

What if all the major components of a lawn mower are made in various divisions and transferred to the Clipper Division? If their *actual costs* are used as the transfer costs, then the cost of the lawn mower will include all the cost variances from all the supplying divisions. To evaluate the performance of each manager, Yard Equipment Company needs to know which variances belong with each component, but because all the variances are hidden in the lawn mower's cost, it will not be easy to identify them and, thus, to evaluate each manager properly.

The Clipper Division manager will also have a harder time trying to budget his costs, as he will not know what cost to use for motors until they are transferred. By then it may be too late to adjust the lawn mower's sales price for the different (higher) motor cost. Customers expect the sales price to be the same from month to month.

The company needs a transfer cost that can isolate cost variances for each division. The management accounting system can provide this information by transferring motors at their *standard absorptive manufacturing cost,* shown in the following T-account of Braxton's cost flows:

WORK-IN-PROCESS INVENTORY: BRAXTON DIVISION

Actual costs are debited to the General Ledger account: $20,000	Costs transferred out to Clipper: ($180 × 100 motors) $18,000
Balance = $2,000	

The $2,000 debit balance remaining in the Braxton Division's WIP general ledger account represents the sum of the May cost variances. The Braxton manager knows she will be responsible for these variances, as she is responsible for this account. Having this responsibility should motivate her to control motor production costs. By isolating the manager's variances within her account, Yard Equipment Company will be better able to evaluate her (and the other managers') performance. Finally, by knowing that motors will be transferred at $180,

[1] From Chapter 8, a direct material spending (price) variance = actual motors purchased multiplied by (standard price − actual price). The difference between standard and actual motor "price" is $20 unfavorable. For 100 motors transferred, this is $2,000.

the Clipper Division manager will be better able to budget the costs of making lawn mowers.

Should the standard variable or absorptive cost be used? In this example, the standard absorptive manufacturing cost of $180 has been used. When building the cost of a lawn mower, all production costs need to be included so that an adequate markup and sales price result. Further, by including the budgeted fixed overhead in the transferred cost of the lawn mower, the $1,000 fixed overhead spending variance remains in the Braxton Division's account, improving performance evaluation and cost management motivation.

When the standard variable costing method is used, the fixed overhead is not included in the per-unit motor cost. All the fixed overhead of the company is journalized to a separate fixed overhead account and ultimately written off to cost of goods sold (at year-end) as a lump-sum amount. Thus, with a variable costing system, it may be more difficult to trace fixed overhead spending and volume variances to the individual RCs where they were caused.

Market Price–Based Transfer Costing

It is *theoretically* possible for Clipper to obtain motors from an external supplier rather than from Braxton. If so, then there is a market price for motors that might serve as a transfer cost. The external market price for motors represents the opportunity cost to Clipper for obtaining motors. If the company discontinued the Braxton Division, then the market price would be the cost Clipper would have to budget for motors when establishing the standard cost of a lawn mower.

While market price may be an opportunity cost for obtaining motors, it is not a real cost. Remember that Clipper must get motors from Braxton, and Braxton must supply motors to Clipper. If market price were used as the transfer cost, then the cost of lawn mowers would be overstated, assuming Braxton's cost of making motors is less than the cost of buying motors from an external supplier. Also, market prices may change, which could make the Clipper Division manager's budgeting more difficult than if he used Braxton's standard cost.

Consider using market price to transfer motors to Clipper. Assume that Clipper can buy motors from an outside source at $250 each. The following T-account illustrates the cost flows for Braxton's general ledger account:

WORK-IN-PROCESS INVENTORY: BRAXTON DIVISION

Actual costs are debited to the General Ledger account: $20,000	Costs transferred out to Clipper: ($250 × 100 motors) $25,000
	Balance = $5,000

How should Yard Equipment Company's management interpret the $5,000 credit balance? If Clipper had bought the motors from an outside source, then Yard Equipment Company would have lost $7,000 in profits ($250 to buy − $180 to make = $70 per motor for 100 motors). In other words, because Braxton made the motors, the company saved $7,000, less, of course, the $2,000 in unfavorable cost variances Braxton had in May. In effect, the transfer resulted in $5,000 of extra profits for Yard Equipment Company.

But did Braxton really make $5,000 in profits for Yard Equipment Company? No. In fact, the cost of lawn mowers is $5,000 less than what is shown in the accounting system.

LAWN MOWER COSTS AS SHOWN ON CLIPPER'S BOOKS:

	PER UNIT	TOTALS
Motors transferred from Braxton	$250	$25,000
Other variable costs of lawn mower	140	14,000
Fixed costs		9,000
Total manufacturing costs		$48,000

YARD EQUIPMENT COMPANY'S REAL COSTS:

	PER UNIT	TOTALS
Motors made by Braxton	$200	$20,000
Clipper's variable costs of lawn mower	140	14,000
Fixed costs		9,000
Total manufacturing costs		$43,000

Using $250 as the cost of motors overstated the real cost of a lawn mower ($200 as shown in Exhibit 21–2a). By using market price, Braxton becomes a *pseudo profit center* in the accounting system. If the accounting system for Yard Equipment Company produces a segmented income statement, then the Braxton Division would show a $5,000 profit, while the Clipper Division would show this $5,000 as an extra cost of lawn mowers. In reality, Braxton's profit is created at Clipper's expense! Braxton really does not sell motors for $250, and this manager has no control over outside prices for motors. Thus, she should not be given credit for this pseudo profit in her performance evaluation.

Using a transfer cost that is greater than the motor's cost is called "marking up" cost to determine a sales price. Adding any amount of markup to the cost of a motor when transferring will result in a reported profit for Braxton within the accounting system. Some companies set their transfer costing policies so that some markup is added to the cost of a motor. Whether this markup creates a transfer cost of $250 or some lesser amount, an unreal profit is reported for the supplying division. What is the purpose of marking up cost since it appears to inhibit performance evaluation and misstates the cost of the motor to the divisions using it?

Two reasons have been given. First, consider the situation faced by a *multinational company*. For example, making motors in Mexico is cheaper than making motors in California due to lower wage rates among other things. If motors are made in Mexico, then the cost of a lawn mower made in California will be lower and the lawn mower's profit higher. Of course, more profit means more income taxes. Assume that California's state income tax rate is higher than Mexico's federal tax rate. If the 100 motors made in May are "sold" from Braxton's Mexico plant to Clipper's California plant for $250 each, then $5,000 of the ultimate profit from lawn mowers will appear to be made (and taxed) in Mexico. This movement of $5,000 in profits to a lower tax region saves taxes for Yard Equipment Company, thus increasing the company's aftertax profit.

Some universities use a marked-up transfer cost for purchases, effectively creating a pseudo profit center.

This is just one example of the importance of transfer costing policies for international companies. There are many other considerations, of course, which are also complex and serious. They are not covered in this book, but are covered in advanced tax and international accounting courses. It is important to note, however, that the accountant has an ethical and social responsibility in choosing a transfer cost (or a transfer price for profit center transfers, discussed in the next section).

The second reason for using cost plus markup for transfer costing is that doing so creates a "profit responsibility" for the Braxton manager. Some accounting theorists argue that if a cost center manager is responsible for profit, then she will be able to "see the big picture" and act in the best interests of the company (i.e., make more goal-congruent decisions). In other words, she will act as if she owned her own company, making and selling motors. An argument can be made against this approach, though. If making a profit results in more goal-congruent decisions, why doesn't the company let the Braxton manager sell motors to real customers for real cash? Redesigning the company so that Braxton is a real profit center creates other problems, however. These are considered in the next section.

TRANSFERS FROM PROFIT CENTERS

Assume Braxton Motors is reorganized from a cost center to a profit center. This means that the Braxton manager now sells motors to outside customers. What are Yard Equipment Company's goals with respect to transfers between Braxton and Clipper? These will vary depending upon whether Braxton is required to transfer to Clipper and Clipper to obtain motors from Braxton, or whether both managers are free to make the transfer decision themselves. Each situation will be considered next. Exhibit 21–2b includes the same cost information as in Exhibit 21–2a, along with new information needed to analyze these profit center situations.

Required Transfers from a Profit Center

If Braxton is required to transfer motors to Clipper, but free to sell motors not needed by Clipper to outside customers, then Braxton is partly a cost center and partly a profit center. To the extent that Braxton must provide all the motors Clipper needs, with the Braxton manager having no choice in the matter, it is a cost center. The Braxton manager is responsible for product quality, delivery to Clipper (and other RCs using motors), and production cost control.

However, Braxton also sells motors to external customers. Thus, it is a real profit center. The goals Yard Equipment Company sets for a profit center include those for a cost center and the additional goal of maximizing profits from motor sales. The accounting system will now have to provide information that supports both of the following:

- The managers' abilities to budget and control costs and assess profit potential of various sales opportunities
- The evaluation of profit and cost performance by Yard Equipment Company's management

In this situation, Braxton is required to transfer motors to Clipper. From Yard Equipment Company's point of view, Braxton's primary responsibility is to supply Clipper. Only secondarily can it sell surplus motors externally. The accounting system will best support the information needs of managers if the management accountant treats this situation as a transfer costing issue. In the last section, three transfer cost options were considered: using a sales price versus the component's cost, using actual versus standard cost, and using absorption versus variable cost. As was true for transfers from cost centers, using standard absorptive manufacturing cost best supports the informational needs of management. This is illustrated in Exhibit 21–3.

Braxton's income statement reports the COGS (production costs) for all 100 motors and then subtracts the standard cost allowed for the 80 motors transferred out. This results in a net COGS for the 20 motors sold. As Exhibit 21–3

Car dealerships set market price-based transfer prices for new car preparation charges to the sales department, effectively transferring some of the new car sales profits to the service department.

■ EXHIBIT 21–2b
Braxton's Budgeted and Actual Data for May

	Standard Costs		Actual Costs	
	Per Unit	Totals	Per Unit	Totals
Variable costs	$100	$10,000	$110	$11,000
Fixed costs	80	8,000	90	9,000
Total costs	$180	$18,000	$200	$20,000
Production volume:	100 motors			
Sales volume:	100 motors (80 transferred to Clipper and 20 sold to outside customers at $300 each)			

■■■ EXHIBIT 21–3
Gross Profit for Braxton Division

	Budgeted		Actual		Variances	
	Per Unit	Totals	Per Unit	Totals	Per Unit	Totals
Sales (20 motors sold)	$300	$ 6,000	$300	$ 6,000	$–0–	$ –0–
<COGS>						
(100 motors produced)						
Variable	100	10,000	110	11,000	<10>	<1,000>
Fixed	80	8,000	90	9,000	<10>	<1,000>
<Transferred> (80 motors)	180	<14,400>	180	<14,400>		
Net COGS (20 motors)	<180>	<3,600>	<280>*	<5,600>*	<100>*	<2,000>*
Gross profit	$120	$ 2,400	$ 20	$ 400	<$100>	<$2,000>

*Note: Production cost variances for all 100 motors averaged $20 per motor unfavorable. This $2,000 in cost variances had to be recovered by the gross profit made on the 20 motors sold externally. The $2,000 = $100 per motor *sold* reducing the actual gross profit per unit from $120 to $20.

shows, Braxton's cost variances remain in Braxton's income statement. They are not "buried" in the cost of the motors transferred to Clipper, which would happen if actual costs were used as the transfer cost.

If motors were transferred at the $300 market price, then a $10,000 gross profit would be reported for Braxton, even though it only had a real gross profit of $400. This is shown in Exhibit 21–4.

The $10,000 gross profit reported for Braxton includes two components. After Braxton covers its cost variances from the "real" gross profits made on motors sold to external customers, $400 of real gross profit remains (see Exhibit 21–3). The second component of the reported gross profit is due to the pseudo profit created by the transfer to Clipper. This equals $9,600 ($300 − $180 production cost = $120 per motor for 80 motors transferred). Reporting $10,000 in gross profits for Braxton may lead Yard Equipment Company's management to believe that the Braxton manager is doing a much better job than she really is.

Recommendation: Unless there is some overriding reason to create pseudo profits in the supplying division, when transfers are required, treat the supplying division as a cost center with respect to the intermediate product transferred. Transferring at standard absorptive manufacturing cost allows the cost variances created by Braxton to remain within that responsibility center. These cost variances are not obscured by pseudo profits that would result from using a market price to record transfers. This helps management evaluate the performance of the managers involved in the transfers. Proper evaluation and rewards should motivate Braxton's manager to control costs. The use of standard cost for trans-

Casinos use transfer prices for complimentary meals offered to special guests.

■■■ EXHIBIT 21–4
Gross Profit with Transfers at Market

	Budgeted		Actual		Variances	
	Per Unit	Totals	Per Unit	Totals	Per Unit	Totals
Sales (100 motors)	$300	$30,000	$300	$30,000	$–0–	$ –0–
<COGS>						
Variable	100	10,000	110	11,000	<10>	<1,000>
Fixed	80	8,000	90	9,000	<10>	<1,000>
COGS	<180>	<18,000>	<200>	<20,000>	<20>	<2,000>
Gross profit	$120	$12,000	$100	$10,000	<$20>	<$2,000>

fer costing should also help Clipper's manager budget lawn mower costs and profits.

▌Optional Transfers from a Profit Center

Transfer costing is the setting of a cost for required transfers. A **transfer price** is an "internal" sales price for optional transfers of intermediate products from a profit center to other RCs. Two of the responsibilities of a profit center manager are to choose customers and set sales prices that will maximize profits. With respect to the transfer decision, this means that the Braxton manager can choose whether or not to "sell" motors to the Clipper manager. This also means that the Clipper manager can choose to "buy" motors from Braxton or other suppliers. Thus, a *joint decision* will be required. Both managers will have to mutually agree to transfer motors.

In the preceding analyses of required transfers, using the standard absorptive manufacturing cost as the transfer cost was recommended. Because this is an absorption cost, the analysis focused on cost of goods sold and gross profit. Gross profit is a subtotal in the functional form, absorption costing-based income statement (from Chapter 20).

As the situations switch to optional transfers from profit centers and transfer pricing, the analysis changes from an absorption costing perspective to variable costing and contribution margin analysis. In the following section, then, the emphasis will change to analyzing a transfer's effect on contribution margin per unit (CMU), contribution margin (CM), and segment margin (SM). This is consistent with the tools developed in Chapters 18, 19, and 20 for analyzing profit decisions and evaluating profit centers.

In fact, the transfer decision is simply a special sales order, make-or-buy, or sell-or-process-further decision (all covered in Chapter 19), depending on which manager's perspective is being considered. The decision to transfer requires incremental CVP analysis (Chapter 18). Performance evaluation uses segmented contribution margin-based income statements for the two divisions (Chapter 20).

The analysis becomes somewhat complex, however, because four different entities, each with its own profit, must be simultaneously considered. The entities involved, and the specific type of profit used for each one in the following discussions, are summarized below:

ENTITY	PROFIT MEASURE USED
The transfer decision itself:	The transfer's differential profit
The selling and buying divisions:	Each division's CMU, CM, and SM
The overall corporation:	Overall corporate profits

When discussing transfer pricing, these different profit terms will be used. To avoid confusion, it is important to remember that there will be a differential profit associated with the choice between transferring or not. This differential profit will affect the CMU, CM, and SM of each division's income statement as well as the overall corporate profits.

A transfer price creates a CMU for each intermediate product transferred from the supplying division. Of course, as noted above, this also creates an extra cost for the division using the intermediate product. This raises a new set of concerns for Yard Equipment Company's management. As examples, consider the following questions:

- How much extra CMU should the accounting system report for Braxton (and extra cost for Clipper) because of a transfer?
- Since a profit to one manager is a cost to the other manager, and they are both rewarded for maximizing their segment margins, how can Yard

Equipment Company minimize the conflict between them over the transfer price?

■ Can a transfer pricing policy be created that will motivate the managers to transfer when doing so will increase overall corporate profits?

■ How will the profit center managers be rewarded for making the right transfer decision?

■ How will the profit center managers know when to transfer (i.e., when a transfer creates a differential profit for Yard Equipment Company)?

■ How will the company know if the predicted profit from a transfer was realized?

Obviously, the management accountant will have to deal with a number of complex and interesting issues when developing a transfer pricing policy for optional transfers between profit centers. These include motivational questions, reward and evaluation issues, reporting formats, and ethical issues. Each will be considered in the following sections.

TRANSFER PRICING POLICIES FOR OPTIONAL PROFIT CENTER TRANSFERS

Fundamentally, a transfer pricing policy has two goals:

■ The accounting system should provide the relevant information the managers need to determine when a transfer will increase overall corporate profits.

■ The accounting system should report on whether the transfer resulted in the anticipated differential profit.

Multinationals like Bently Nevada Corporation analyze transfer options between global profit centers linked by an ICBIS.

Determining an Optional Transfer's Differential Profit

The first goal for the management accounting system is to provide information that will indicate whether a transfer creates a differential profit for Yard Equipment Company. If so, then the two division managers should agree to transfer motors from Braxton to Clipper. The differential profit depends on the opportunity costs of the two managers. The opportunity costs, in turn, depend on the following:

■ Whether Braxton has enough surplus capacity to fill Clipper's order

■ Whether any differential fixed costs will be needed if motors are transferred

■ Whether Clipper can purchase motors from another supplier

The following sections will first consider the situation in which Braxton has enough surplus capacity to make the motors Clipper needs. Then, the situations in which Braxton has no surplus capacity for the Clipper order and only limited surplus capacity are examined. Next, the analysis will be expanded to include differential fixed costs. Finally, situations in which there are no other suppliers for motors will be considered.

The second goal of the management accounting system is to report whether the differential profits were realized. This involves determining a transfer price and reporting any cost variances related to the transfer. The transfer price, in turn, depends upon how the managers will be rewarded for transferring an intermediate product when doing so should increase Yard Equipment Company's overall profits. These issues will be discussed in later sections.

Consider the new relevant information needed to calculate opportunity costs and determine whether a differential profit results in these intermediate product transfer situations. To illustrate, assume that Braxton's production costs are the same as in the previous examples (Exhibit 21–2b). There also are other variable costs (selling and administrative) of $90 per motor when selling to regular (external) customers. If Braxton transfers motors to Clipper, though, it can save $15 per motor of these normal variable selling costs. This savings represents $5 in delivery costs and $10 in packaging costs. It is important to realize that for motors transferred within Yard Equipment Company, the variable costs will probably be different from the variable costs of normal motor sales to regular external customers. The relevant information is summarized in Exhibit 21–5.

SELLING DIVISION WITH SURPLUS CAPACITY SITUATION. In the first optional transfer situation, Braxton is currently selling 100 motors to external customers at $300 each. Braxton has the capacity to produce 150 motors. The Clipper Division manager wants to purchase no more than 50 motors, so Braxton has sufficient surplus capacity to fill the Clipper order without giving up any normal external sales.

The Clipper manager has two alternatives: buy motors from Braxton, or buy from an outside supplier for $275 each. All other things being equal, his decision rule is to buy the cheaper motor. His decision is to "buy internally" (transfer) if the transfer price is less than or equal to the current external purchase price of $275. Obviously, he would accept a transfer price lower than $275 (i.e., $200, $100, or even free; the lower the price, the better from his point of view!). Thus, the $275 external purchase price is a **ceiling transfer price** because it is the maximum price the buying division manager is willing to pay for motors.

Next, consider the Braxton manager. Her decision rule is to at least break even on an internal sale, so as to maintain her current segment margin. When

---

■ EXHIBIT 21–5
Relevant Data for the Transfer Decision

BRAXTON MOTORS DIVISION

Production data:

| Current volume: | 100 motors, all sold to external customers |
| Capacity: | 150 motors could be produced in a month |

	Standard costs		Actual costs	
	Per Unit	Totals	Per Unit	Totals
Cost data:				
Normal variable costs (for external sales):				
Production costs	$100	$10,000	$110	$11,000
Other variable costs	90	9,000	90	9,000
Totals	$190	$19,000	$200	$20,000
Internal variable costs (for transfers):				
Production costs	$100		$110	
Other variable costs	75		75	
Totals	$175		$185	

| Sales price: | Motors sold to outside customers at $300 each |

CLIPPER LAWN MOWER DIVISION

Purchase price for motors from external supplier:	$275 each
Other variable costs of making lawn mowers:	140
Sales price for lawn mowers:	600

Place a paper clip on this page so that you can refer back to these amounts when reading the following sections!

she has enough surplus capacity for the transfer, her two alternatives are to sell to Clipper or not to produce these extra 50 motors at all because there is no other buyer for them. If there were other external customers, she would be selling more motors to them! The transfer price must be high enough to at least cover her "internal variable costs" of transferring, which are budgeted at $175 (Exhibit 21–5).[2]

Therefore, her decision is to sell to Clipper if the transfer price is greater than or equal to $175. However, the Braxton manager will accept a transfer price of $250, or $300, or more—the higher the price, the better from her viewpoint. Thus, she has a minimum acceptable price, but no maximum price. This **floor transfer price** is equal to her budgeted variable cost of $175 to produce and deliver an extra motor to Clipper.

Third, consider the motivations of Yard Equipment Company. Its decision rule (*ceteris paribus*) is to obtain motors at the cheapest cost. The company perceives two alternatives. It can make these extra motors (in the Braxton Division) for $175 or buy them (through the Clipper Division) from an outside source for $275. Obviously, the company wants a transfer, as this will yield a cost savings of $100 per motor.[3] This is illustrated in Exhibit 21–6.

In this situation, Yard Equipment Company saves $100 per motor if Braxton transfers motors to Clipper. How is this $100 cost savings calculated? Looking at the bottom line of Exhibit 21–6, it is the ceiling transfer price minus the floor transfer price. More formally, it is the difference in the opportunity costs of the buying and selling divisions.

Clipper, the buying division, can purchase motors externally for $275 each. If he can buy motors for the same or less from Braxton, then he will want a transfer.[4] Thus, the $275 external purchase price is the buying division manager's opportunity cost. It costs the Braxton manager $175 to produce and deliver a motor to the Clipper Division. She will not want to do this unless the transfer price is at least $175, so that she breaks even on the transfer. Therefore, the selling division manager's opportunity cost is the internal variable cost associated with the transfer.

Thus, there is a **range of transfer prices** acceptable to both managers. This range is bounded by the ceiling and floor prices. If a range exists—in other words, if the ceiling is greater than the floor—then Yard Equipment Company will always realize a differential profit from transferring. If the accounting system provides this information to the managers, then they will know whether or not they should agree to transfer motors. In this situation, the managers should decide to transfer. This is only true, though, if Braxton has sufficient surplus capacity to fill the Clipper order. A modified analysis is needed if Braxton is operating at full capacity.

---

[2] From her perspective, this is just a special-order situation, which was covered in Chapter 19.

[3] From the company's perspective, this is a simple make-or-buy decision as presented in Chapter 19.

[4] He is willing to pay the same price of $275 for transferred motors from Braxton because, even though he won't save any money, he may have greater control over the quality of the motors and they may be more likely to be delivered on time if they are produced within Yard Equipment Company.

Range of transfer prices:	When Braxton has surplus capacity:	
CEILING: (determined by Clipper)	External purchase price:	$275.00
FLOOR: (determined by Braxton)	Internal variable cost:	$175.00
Variable costs saved by transferring: (for Yard Equipment Company)	Ceiling minus floor:	$100.00

■ EXHIBIT 21–6

The Transfer's Differential Profit When the Selling Division has Surplus Capacity

THE SELLING DIVISION AT FULL CAPACITY SITUATION. Consider a different situation in which Braxton is producing at maximum capacity for external sales. Now it is making all the motors it can (150 per month). The calculation of the floor changes because the Braxton manager's alternatives are different from those in the surplus capacity situation. She can continue to sell every motor that can be made to normal external customers, or she can sell to Clipper instead. Again, her decision rule is to at least break even on the internal sale. In this case, break even means maintaining the same contribution margin she now has by selling all 150 motors to normal external customers.

She is currently budgeting for a $110 CMU per motor sold externally ($300 sales price − $190 normal variable costs = $110). Normal variable selling costs of $15 can be saved when selling internally ($90 compared to $75 in Exhibit 21–5). This savings can be passed along to Clipper by reducing the transfer price from the current sales price of $300 to $285. At this price, the CMU per motor on an internal sale will equal the current CMU on these same motors sold externally. As long as the manager can make the same CMU from selling to Clipper as she made from selling the same motors to other customers, she will be willing to transfer. She calculates the floor transfer price as follows:

$$\begin{array}{c} \text{Floor transfer price} \\ \text{when operating at} \\ \text{full capacity} \end{array} = \text{Normal sales price} - \begin{array}{c} \text{Normal variable} \\ \text{costs saved by} \\ \text{transferring} \end{array}$$

To "test" whether this floor price is correct, she can do the following analysis:

	CURRENT EXTERNAL SALES	PROPOSED INTERNAL SALE
Sales price	$300	(Solve for this)
Less variable costs	<190>	<175>
Contribution margin per motor	$110 ⟶	$110

Must have at
least the same CMU

Her minimum transfer price equals the variable costs of a transferred motor ($175) plus the CMU lost from not selling the motor to a normal customer ($110). This leads to another way to calculate the floor price. Let:

$$\begin{aligned} \text{IVC} &= \text{Internal variable cost} \\ \text{CMU} &= \text{Contribution margin per motor lost by not} \\ & \quad \text{selling to a normal customer} \\ \text{DFC} &= \text{Differential fixed cost per motor, if any} \\ & \quad \text{exists, created by a transfer (a fixed cost that} \\ & \quad \text{would not exist with a normal sale)} \\ \text{Floor transfer price} &= \text{IVC} + \text{CMU} + \text{DFC} \end{aligned}$$

Then:

With surplus capacity: $175 = $175 + $0 + $0
At full capacity: $285 = $175 + $110 + $0

When a differential fixed cost exists with a transfer, it should be unitized and added into the formula. This is covered in Exhibit 21–10 later. The benefit of this approach is that it provides one formula that can be used to calculate the floor in almost all situations.[5] Any of the three methods just illustrated can be used to calculate the floor price. Choose the one that is easiest to understand.

---

[5] This formula is from Ralph L. Benke, Jr., and James Don Edwards, *Transfer Pricing: Techniques and Uses* (New York: Institute of Management Accountants, formerly the National Association of Accountants, 1980), p. 111. With permission.

The Clipper manager's decision, however, is not influenced by whether Braxton is operating at full capacity or has enough surplus capacity for the transfer. His decision rule is still not to pay more than the current external purchase price of $275. Thus, the ceiling transfer price remains the same as in the surplus capacity situation.

Will Yard Equipment Company realize a differential profit if motors are transferred, instead of sold externally, when Braxton is at full capacity? As in the surplus capacity situation in Exhibit 21–6, the differential profit to Yard Equipment Company is the ceiling price minus the floor price. Since the ceiling price of $275 is less than the floor price of $285, this difference is negative. In other words, there is an opportunity cost to Yard Equipment Company of $10 per motor if motors are transferred.

One way to reconcile this calculation is by considering upper management's evaluation of this potential transfer. Yard Equipment Company views this as a sell-or-process-further decision. The motors can be sold now to external customers with an expected CMU of $110, or they can be processed further; that is, transferred to Clipper and used in the making of lawn mowers. Processing further (transferring) saves the company $100 in the cost of acquiring the motor ($175 budgeted cost to make and deliver from Braxton versus $275 cost for Clipper to buy externally). However, transferring means that Braxton will not be able to sell the motors to its normal customers. Thus, the $110 CMU from those sales will be lost. The net result to Yard Equipment Company is a $10 per motor loss. It saved $100 in the cost of each motor, but lost $110 per motor by not selling them now.[6] In this case, Yard Equipment Company is better off if no transfer occurs. This is illustrated in Exhibit 21–7.

COMPARING THE SURPLUS AND FULL CAPACITY SITUATIONS. To compare the two selling division situations, Exhibits 21–6 and 21–7 are combined in Exhibit 21–8. This is called the **"Transfer Pricing Matrix."**[7]

In comparing the two situations, it is important to determine the source of the motors to be transferred. When the selling division is operating at full capacity, the floor price is different from when the division has enough surplus capacity for the transfer, because the opportunities of the selling division manager are different.

However, the difference between the ceiling and floor of the transfer price range always determines the transfer's differential profit to the overall corporation. In this example, when Braxton has enough surplus capacity to fill Clipper's order, there is a $100 per motor differential profit to Yard Equipment Company if the transfer takes place. If Braxton is producing at maximum capacity for current external sales, transferring will result in a differential loss of <$10>.

---

[6] This $10 per motor loss is a negative differential CMU for each motor transferred from Yard Equipment Company's perspective. A change in CMU filters down "penny-for-penny" into a change in CM, SM, and overall corporate profits.

[7] This presentation approach is adapted from M. Thomas, "A Matrix Approach to Transfer Pricing," *Journal of Accounting Education*, 1991, pp. 137–147.

Range of transfer prices:	When Braxton has <u>no</u> surplus capacity:	
CEILING: (determined by Clipper)	External purchase price:	$275.00
FLOOR: (determined by Braxton)	External sales price Less variable costs saved:	$300.00 <15.00> $285.00
Transfer's differential contribution margin per motor: (for Yard Equipment Company)	Ceiling minus floor:	<$10.00>

■■■EXHIBIT 21–7
The Transfer's Differential Profit When the Selling Division is at Full Capacity.

■ EXHIBIT 21–8
The Transfer Pricing Matrix

Range of transfer prices:	Transferred product made with selling division surplus capacity: (Exhibit 21-6)	Transferred product taken from normal customer sales: Full capacity situation (Exhibit 21-7)
CEILING: (determined by the "buying" division: Clipper)	External purchase price: $275.00	External purchase price: $275.00
FLOOR: (determined by the "selling" division: Braxton)	Internal variable cost: $175.00	External sales price less variable costs saved by transferring: $285.00
Transfer's differential contribution margin per motor: (for the "company": Yard Equipment)	Ceiling – Floor: $100.00	Ceiling – Floor: <$10.00>

THE LIMITED CAPACITY SITUATION. What happens if Clipper wants more motors than the surplus capacity available in Braxton? For example, assume Clipper wants 75 motors. Referring back to Exhibit 21–5, Braxton only has the surplus capacity to produce 50 motors without giving up some of the 100 motors currently being sold. Thus, if Braxton transfers 75 motors, it will not be able to sell 25 motors to normal customers. This decision is a special-order situation with insufficient surplus capacity. By adding two lines to the bottom of the Transfer Pricing Matrix in Exhibit 21–8, the limited surplus capacity situation can easily be evaluated. The calculation of the transfer's differential profit in this situation is shown in Exhibit 21–9.

In this case, transferring the first 50 motors increases overall corporate profits by $5,000. However, transferring the last 25 motors will cost the company $250 in profits it could have had if it had not transferred them and instead had sold them to regular customers. The net change in overall corporate profits from transferring all 75 motors is the sum of these amounts ($5,000 − $250 = $4,750). Since Yard Equipment Company will be $4,750 better off if a transfer takes place, the managers should decide to transfer. Obviously, if it is possible to purchase only 25 motors from Clipper's external source at a price of $275 each, then 50 motors should be transferred and 25 purchased. In those situations in which it is not possible to purchase smaller quantities at the same price, then the Exhibit 21–9 analysis is appropriate.

TRANSFERS THAT INCUR DIFFERENTIAL FIXED COSTS. So far, the only differential costs from transferring were the variable costs Braxton would have to incur to make and deliver motors to Clipper. But Clipper now wants 20 motors with a special name plate stamped on them. This will require Braxton to purchase a stamping machine for $1,000. The machine cannot be used on regular motors and will have no resale (scrap) value after the order is filled. When a transfer creates differential fixed costs, the Transfer Pricing Matrix can be modified to present the transfer's differential profit for both the surplus and full capacity situations, as shown in Exhibit 21–10.

Note that the calculation format is based upon the contribution margin approach for profit calculations presented in Chapters 18, 19, and 20. Now, assume that the $275 external purchase price includes the special name plate. First, the differential CMU per motor is computed. Then, it is multiplied by sales volume to obtain contribution margin. Finally, fixed costs are subtracted from contribution margin to arrive at net profit. When Braxton has sufficient

Range of transfer prices:	Transferred product made with selling division surplus capacity: (Exhibit 21-6)	Transferred product taken from normal customer sales: Full capacity situation (Exhibit 21-7)
CEILING: (determined by the "buying" division: Clipper)	External purchase price: $275.00	External purchase price: $275.00
FLOOR: (determined by the "selling" division: Braxton)	Internal variable cost: $175.00	External sales price less variable costs saved by transferring: $285.00
Transfer's differential contribution margin per motor: (for the "company": Yard Equipment)	Ceiling − Floor: $100.00	Ceiling − Floor: <$10.00>
Motors transferred from: (multiply by contribution margin per motor)	x 50 motors	x 25 motors
Total contribution margin from surplus or full capacity :	$5,000.00	<$250.00>

■ EXHIBIT 21–9
The Transfer's Differential Profit When There Is Insufficient Capacity Available in the Selling Division

Range of transfer prices:	Transferred product made with selling division surplus capacity: (Exhibit 21-6)	Transferred product taken from normal customer sales: Full capacity situation (Exhibit 21-7)
CEILING: (determined by the "buying" division: Clipper)	External purchase price: $275.00	External purchase price: $275.00
FLOOR: (determined by the "selling" division: Braxton)	Internal variable cost: $175.00	External sales price less variable costs saved by transferring: $285.00
Transfer's differential contribution margin per motor: (for the "company": Yard Equipment)	Ceiling − Floor: $100.00	Ceiling − Floor: <$10.00>
Motors transferred from: (multiply by contribution margin per motor)	x 20 motors	x 20 motors
Contribution margin from surplus or full capacity situation:	$2,000.00	<$200.00>
Less differential fixed costs	<1,000.00>	<1,000.00>
Net profit from transfer: (pre-tax)	$1,000.00	<$1,200.00>

■ EXHIBIT 21–10
The Transfer's Differential Profit with Differential Fixed Costs

surplus capacity to fill the order, Yard Equipment Company will be $1,000 better off if the 20 motors are transferred. When Braxton does not have surplus capacity to fill Clipper's demand, but a transfer occurs anyway, Yard Equipment Company will be $1,200 worse off than if Clipper were to purchase motors externally at $275 each.

Consider the surplus capacity situation column in Exhibit 21–10. What is the minimum number of motors that can be transferred before Yard Equipment Company incurs a loss from transferring? In other words, at what volume will Yard Equipment Company be indifferent between transferring versus buying motors from an external supplier? This is the volume where there is no differential profit; that is, the break-even point. The break-even formula is:

$$\frac{\text{Differential fixed costs of } \$1{,}000}{\text{Contribution margin per motor of } \$100} = 10 \text{ motors}$$

IMPUTING THE CEILING WHEN NO EXTERNAL SUPPLIER EXISTS. The Transfer Pricing Matrix approach also works even when there is no external supplier for the transferred motors. In this case, the ceiling price is imputed using basic cost-volume-profit techniques presented in Chapters 18 and 19.

This example assumes that Clipper has received a special order for lawn mowers from the city's Parks and Recreation Department. These lawn mowers will be used to mow the baseball fields for the Little League teams and the city softball leagues. The city can only afford to pay $400 each for the lawn mowers. Referring back to Exhibit 21–5, the normal lawn mower sales price is $600. The Clipper manager wants to accept this order because he feels a civic obligation and his division currently has enough surplus capacity to produce the lawn mowers without giving up any normal sales.

However, Braxton is the only available source for the motors. Because there are no other suppliers, there is no ceiling price (which was $275) available for the transfer's differential profit analysis. All other information is the same as used in Exhibit 21–5.

As this is a special sales order for Clipper, the lawn mower sales price could go as low as the incremental costs of making and delivering the special-order lawn mowers. Using the Exhibit 21–5 information, the Clipper manager performs the following analysis:

Special-order sales price	$400
Less other variable costs of making lawn mowers in Clipper Division	<140>
CMU per special lawn mower before the cost of a motor from Braxton	$260

From the Clipper manager's viewpoint, motors could cost up to $260 each. If so, then the CMU on this order would be $0, and there would be no differential profit or loss for Clipper from the sale of these mowers to the city. If the price of a motor is less than $260, Clipper will realize a positive CMU. Thus, the Clipper manager can spend up to $260 for a motor (a maximum transfer price), if he is willing to make no profit on the order. The $260 becomes the ceiling transfer price for the Transfer Pricing Matrix. Exhibit 21–11 shows how the ceiling price row is modified to present this situation.

If Braxton has the surplus capacity to produce the motors needed by Clipper for this special order, and the motors are transferred, then Yard Equipment Company is $85 per lawn mower better off. If Braxton does not have any excess capacity available to make motors, then this order would result in a $25 loss per lawn mower to Yard Equipment Company.

CALCULATING A TRANSFER'S DIFFERENTIAL PROFIT: CONCLUDING REMARKS. By using the Transfer Pricing Matrix format presented in Exhibit 21–8, the Braxton and Clipper managers can determine whether to transfer in

Range of transfer prices:	Transferred product made with selling division surplus capacity: (Exhibit 21-6)	Transferred product taken from normal customer sales: Full capacity situation (Exhibit 21-7)
CEILING: (determined by the "buying" division: Clipper)	Imputed: $260.00	Imputed: $260.00
FLOOR: (determined by the "selling" division: Braxton)	Internal variable cost: $175.00	External sales price less variable costs saved by transferring: $285.00
Transfer's differential contribution margin per motor: (for the "company": Yard Equipment)	Ceiling – Floor: $85.00	Ceiling – Floor: <$25.00>

EXHIBIT 21-11
The Transfer's Differential Profit When There is No Other Supplier for the Intermediate Product

any optional transfer situation they may encounter. This format can be used to calculate the transfer's differential profitability in the following situations:

- When Braxton has sufficient surplus capacity for the transfer and when it has no surplus capacity available (Exhibit 21–8)
- When Braxton has only limited capacity (not enough) available (Exhibit 21–9)
- When the transfer creates differential fixed costs (Exhibit 21–10)
- When there is no other supplier of the intermediate product (Exhibit 21–11)

The two profit center managers should agree to transfer whenever Yard Equipment Company will realize an increase in overall corporate profits from transferring. If Yard Equipment Company has created these divisions as real profit centers, however, the two managers must make a joint decision about transferring. Why would the two managers, knowing that they should transfer, not agree to do so? The reason is that, with certain types of reward systems, they may also have to mutually agree on a transfer price, which they may not be able to do. The rest of this chapter considers the role of the transfer price in optional transfer situations between profit centers.

Setting the Transfer Price

To record the transfer within the accounting system, a transfer price is needed. Three questions must be answered:

1. What are the options?
2. What is the effect of each option on the divisional segment margins of Clipper and Braxton?
3. Who should set the transfer price?

TRANSFER PRICE OPTIONS AND THEIR EFFECTS ON DIVISIONAL SEGMENT MARGINS. The transfer price affects the SMs reported by each division, because the transfer price is the sales price for transferred motors in the Braxton Division and the cost of motors in the Clipper Division. If the transfer price increases, Braxton Division's CMU, CM, and SM will go up. At the same time, though, the cost of motors to Clipper Division will also go up, and its CMU, CM, and SM will go down. This can be important to the two managers if they are rewarded for maximizing their individual division SMs. In this situation, the Braxton manager will want the highest transfer price possible, but the

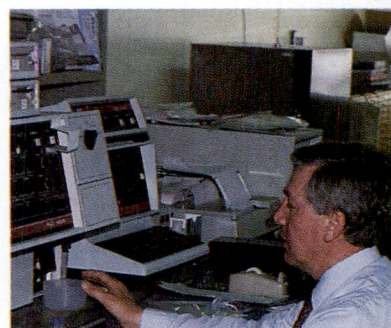

The Flow Cytometry Lab provides analyses for the rest of the university, but a $75 per hour transfer price is charged.

Clipper manager will want the lowest transfer price possible. To illustrate, three transfer prices will be analyzed.

■ *Using the ceiling price.* Refer back to Exhibit 21–8. Consider setting the transfer price at the ceiling of the transfer price range in the first column. This is the external purchase price of a motor ($275). Clipper then can buy a motor externally for $275 or internally for $275. If the cost of a motor is the same, the Clipper manager will be indifferent between buying externally or transferring because he will not save any money from either option.

   If the transfer price is $275, though, the Braxton manager will realize a $100 CMU from transferring. She will sell the motors to Clipper for $275 and incur $175 in variable costs, resulting in the $100 CMU.

■ *Using the floor price.* Now consider setting the transfer price at the floor, which is $175 if Braxton has sufficient surplus capacity for the order or $285 if no surplus capacity is available. In this case, Braxton will not show any change in CMU from transferring. With surplus capacity, both the internal sales price (transfer price) and the variable costs are $175, yielding no contribution margin per motor. With no surplus capacity, whether Braxton sells externally at $300 per motor or internally at $285, the CMU will be the same.

   What happens to Clipper's segment margin, though, if the transfer price is set at the floor? Currently, Clipper can buy motors externally for $275 each. If it can get them from Braxton for $175, it will save $100, and the CMU per lawn mower will go up $100. If the floor price of $285 is used because Braxton has no surplus capacity available, then Clipper will see its CMU go down $10 because the cost of a motor has increased $10 (from $275 to $285).

■ *Using the midpoint of the transfer price range.* In the Surplus Capacity column of Exhibit 21–8, the transfer price range is $175 to $275. The midpoint of this range is halfway between these two endpoints; that is, at $225. In the Full Capacity column, halfway between the two endpoints ($275 and $285) is $280.

   What happens to both divisions' CMUs if the transfer price is set at the midpoint of the range ($225 with surplus capacity, $280 at full capacity)? In the surplus capacity situation, Braxton will realize a differential CMU of $50 per motor ($225 sales price − $175 cost), and Clipper will also realize a $50 differential CMU per lawn mower ($225 motor cost instead of $275).

   In the full capacity situation, each division will report a $5 per motor loss on the transfer. For Clipper, the transfer price will be $280, which is $5 per motor more than the current external purchase price of $275. If the cost of a motor goes up $5, the CMU on a lawn mower goes down $5. For Braxton, the transfer price would be $280, which will only yield a CMU of $105 ($280 − $175). This is $5 less than the current CMU Braxton can make on each of these motors by selling them to normal customers.

What do these examples indicate?

■ If the transfer price is set at the ceiling of the range, all of the transfer's differential profit appears in the selling division's (Braxton's) income statement.
■ If the transfer price is set at the floor, all of the transfer's differential profit appears in the buying division's (Clipper's) income statement.
■ If the transfer price is set at the midpoint of the range, then the divisions share the transfer's differential profit (or loss) equally.
■ Also notice that for each transfer price option, the differential CMUs reported by the two divisions will always sum to the transfer's differential profit.

This leads to two conclusions.

First, the transfer's differential profit for Yard Equipment Company is independent of the transfer price finally set (the transfer price cannot influence the differential profitability to the overall corporation).[8]

This conclusion may seem rather surprising, since a sales price usually determines profit. This is true in two-party sales transactions, but even though a transfer price is the internal sales price for an intermediate product, the transfer situation is a three-party sales transaction. In addition to the buying and selling divisions, the corporation that owns both of them is a stakeholder. Their decision should be based upon whether the transfer creates a differential profit which will increase overall corporate profits. Their joint decision should not be based on how much they may be able to increase their segment margins through the use of a particular transfer price.

Secondly, the transfer price is only a profit-sharing rule between the two transferring divisions.

As with any sales price, a profit results for the seller (Braxton). The profit can be positive or negative. Consider the surplus capacity situation in Exhibit 21–8 again. If the transfer price is set at the floor, Braxton's CMU is zero. If it is set at the ceiling, Braxton's CMU equals the entire differential profit realized from the transfer, which is $100. Setting the transfer price at the midpoint, Braxton's CMU is $50, half of the total.

For Clipper (the "buyer"), the price paid for motors is a cost of making lawn mowers. If the transfer price is set at the ceiling, Clipper's cost for a motor is the same $275 whether the motor is purchased from Braxton (transferred) or purchased from an external supplier. Setting the transfer price at the floor of $175, Clipper saves $100 on the cost of a motor if it is transferred. This savings is all of the transfer's differential profit. If the transfer price is set at the midpoint of the range, Clipper's cost savings on a motor equals $50 (current motor cost of $275 versus the transfer at $225), which is half of the total. The point to remember is that the transfer price affects the CMU, CM, and SM of each division, but it does not affect the differential profit that the corporation realizes from the transfer.

WHO SHOULD SET THE TRANSFER PRICE?   This depends upon how Yard Equipment Company rewards the two managers for making the right decision. Four reward policies are possible, only one of which does not depend upon the transfer's differential profit:

- *Reward system not based on the transfer's differential profit.* With this reward system, Yard Equipment Company either does not specially reward the managers for making the correct decision, or it gives them a set amount (a bonus) that is not based on the differential profits created by the transfer. The logic behind not specially rewarding the managers is that they should make good decisions because doing so is part of their job. Managers should not receive a special reward for just doing their jobs.

  Yard Equipment management may decide, however, that each manager should get a bonus of $1,000 (or some other amount). The managers will not care how much of the transfer's differential profit appears in their income statements because it will not affect their rewards. Thus, the transfer price is not important to them. In this case, the accountant can preset the transfer price for all transfers to satisfy other needs of the accounting system, such as the need to minimize interdivisional profit elimination journal entries in

> **LEARNING OBJECTIVE 3**
>
> Determine how the different cost and price options can affect managerial decision making, planning, cost management, and performance evaluation.

---

[8] In certain situations (especially with multinational corporations), a transfer price can create differential tax effects. Tax and tariff implications usually are not covered at this level, however. The conclusion is still valid, though, if differential taxes and tariffs are added into the variable costs of transferring.

preparing consolidated financial statements for the company (a topic for Advanced Financial Accounting) or the need to trace cost variances to the proper RCs for performance evaluation.

In this example, Braxton is a profit center primarily selling motors to external customers, so all fixed manufacturing overhead should be "absorbed" (paid for) by externally sold motors. Both Braxton and Yard Equipment Company realize this. They would not be selling motors externally if they did not believe all fixed costs could be recovered and a satisfactory profit made. In other words, because Braxton is a profit center, and Yard Equipment Company has not required a long-term commitment to transfer motors to Clipper, all of Braxton's fixed costs should be recovered by normal external sales. Thus, the Braxton manager views the transfer decision as a special-order pricing problem, in which she calculates a minimally acceptable internal sales price (the floor in Exhibit 21–8).

Assume 100 motors were sold to external customers and 20 motors were transferred to Clipper. Using the floor as the transfer price results in the segmented contribution margin–based income statement illustrated in Exhibit 21–12 (based on the information presented in Exhibit 21–5). Transferring at the floor price allows Yard Equipment Company to see Braxton's real SM made by external sales and transfers. The Braxton manager just broke even on external sales. She should have made a $2,000 SM, but she had $2,000 in unfavorable production cost variances. She also lost another $200 on the 20 motors transferred because of the $10 per motor unfavorable variable production cost variances.

If the ceiling price had been used to transfer motors, this information would be much less clear. Transferring 20 motors at $275 each would result in an extra $2,000 in contribution margin and segment margin reported for transfers ($100 per motor from Exhibit 21–8 for each of the 20 motors transferred). Braxton really lost $200, but the accounting report would now show an SM

■EXHIBIT 21–12
Segmented Income Statement for Braxton Motors: Transfer Price at Floor of Transfer Pricing Matrix Range

| | | EXTERNAL SALES | | | |
| | | Budgeted | | Actual | |
	Units	Per Unit	Totals	Per Unit	Totals
Sales					
External	100	$300	$30,000	$300	$30,000
Transfers	20				
Total sales					
Variable costs:					
Production	120[a]	100	10,000	110	11,000
Other: External	100	90	9,000	90	9,000
Other: Transfers	20				
Total variable costs		<$190>	<$19,000>	<$200>	<$20,000>
Contribution margin		$110	$11,000	$100	$10,000
Fixed costs:					
Production			8,000		9,000
Other			1,000		1,000
Total fixed costs			<$9,000>		<$10,000>
Segment margin			$2,000		$–0–

Notes:
[a] Of the 120 units produced, 100 were for external sales ($10,000 @ $100 each), and 20 units were for transfers ($2,000 @ $100 each).

on transfers of $1,800! Thus, using the floor price for transfers will better satisfy management's need for performance evaluation information. Using the floor price should also provide a greater motivation for the Braxton manager to control her costs because cost overruns will not be "buried" in the SM reported on the transferred motors.

- *Reward systems based on a transfer's differential profit.* Yard Equipment Company can choose among three reward system alternatives within this option. The first reward system involves directly rewarding each manager for the transfer decision. This can take one of two forms. If Yard Equipment management predetermines the relative share of a transfer's differential profit each manager should receive, then the transfer price can be preset. For example, assume each manager will receive a bonus based on half of the transfer's differential profit. Then, the transfer price can be set at the midpoint of the range shown in Exhibit 21–8.

To illustrate, assume Braxton has sufficient surplus capacity. By setting the transfer price at $225, each manager will show a $50 greater CMU, half of the total for Yard Equipment Company. Since the Braxton manager incurred cost variances of $10 per motor, her reported CMU from the transfer will be only $40 per motor. The $10 cost overrun reduced the transfer's $100 anticipated differential profit to only $90. The accounting system should report this within the Braxton income statement because the $10 cost variance was her responsibility and should affect her rewards, not the Clipper manager's. The Braxton income statement is shown in Exhibit 21–13.

With the second reward system in this category, the relative share of each manager's direct reward from transferring may not be predetermined. In this type of reward system, Yard Equipment management wants the two managers to decide how to share the transfer's differential profit and reward. This means that the two managers will have to agree to a transfer price. The managers, through mutually setting the transfer price, will negotiate how

| TRANSFERS | | | | BRAXTON MOTORS TOTALS | | |
| Budgeted | | Actual | | | Cost Variances | |
Per Unit	Totals	Per Unit	Totals	Actual	Per Unit	Totals
				$30,000	$–0–	$–0–
$175	$3,500	$175	$3,500	3,500		
				$33,500	$–0–	$–0–
100	2,000	110	2,200	13,200	<10>	<1,200>
				9,000	–0–	–0–
75	1,500	75	1,500	1,500	–0–	–0–
<$175>	<$3,500>	<$185>	<$3,700>	<$23,700>	<$10>	<$1,200>
$–0–	$–0–	<$10>	<$200>	$9,800	<$10>	<$1,200>
				9,000		<1,000>
				1,000		–0–
				<$10,000>		<$1,000>
	$–0–		<$200>	<$200>	<$22>[b]	<$2,200>

[b] The segment margin cost variance total for Braxton is averaged over the motors sold externally only.

■EXHIBIT 21–13
**Segmented Income
Statement for Braxton
Motors: Transfer Price
at Midpoint of
Transfer Pricing
Matrix Range**

| | | EXTERNAL SALES | | | |
| | | Budgeted | | Actual | |
	Units	Per Unit	Totals	Per Unit	Totals
Sales					
External	100	$300	$30,000	$300	$30,000
Transfers	20				
Total sales					
Variable costs:					
Production	120	100	10,000	110	11,000
Other: External	100	90	9,000	90	9,000
Other: Transfers	20				
Total variable costs		<$190>	<$19,000>	<$200>	<$20,000>
Contribution margin		$110	$11,000	$100	$10,000
Fixed costs:					
Production			8,000		9,000
Other			1,000		1,000
Total fixed costs			<$9,000>		<$10,000>
Segment margin			$2,000		$–0–

Note: The segment margin cost variance total for Braxton is averaged over the motors sold externally only.

much of the transfer's differential profit each will report in his or her income statement.[9]

The third reward system is probably the most common way corporations reward profit centers. The managers' rewards are based on an aggregate divisional segment margin that includes both transfers and external sales. In this situation, the profit center manager who reports the highest segment margin gets the largest reward. As in the previous alternative, the two managers must negotiate a transfer price. Each manager, in attempting to maximize his or her segment margin, seeks to capture as much of the transfer's differential profit as possible. Thus, the Braxton manager negotiates for the highest transfer price possible, while the Clipper manager seeks the lowest transfer price he can get.

The pros and cons of requiring negotiation will be discussed in the next section, which also discusses transfer pricing policies actually in use. Exhibit 21–14 summarizes the reward systems and the recommended transfer pricing policies.

NEGOTIATION: "THE GOOD, THE BAD, AND THE UGLY".   If Yard Equipment Company uses either of the last two reward systems, the managers are placed in conflict with each other, which can lead to suboptimal decisions. This goal-congruence problem results if they choose not to transfer when they should simply because they cannot agree on a transfer price.

Why would the managers ever not decide to transfer when it would increase Yard Equipment Company's overall corporate profit? One reason is that they may not know the relevant costs for each profit center and therefore do not

[9] Reasons why Yard Equipment Company might want to use this and the next reward system are discussed in the last section of the chapter.

TRANSFERS				BRAXTON MOTORS TOTALS		
Budgeted		Actual			Cost Variances	
Per Unit	Totals	Per Unit	Totals	Actual	Per Unit	Totals
				$30,000	$–0–	$–0–
$225	$4,500	$225	$4,500	4,500		
				$34,500	$–0–	$–0–
100	2,000	110	2,200	13,200	<10>	<1,200>
				9,000	–0–	–0–
75	1,500	75	1,500	1,500	–0–	–0–
<$175>	<$3,500>	<$185>	<$3,700>	<$23,700>	<$10>	<$1,200>
$50	$1,000	$40	$800	$10,800	<$10>	<$1,200>
				9,000		<1,000>
				1,000		–0–
				<$10,000>		<$1,000>
	$1,000		$800	$800	<$22>	<$2,200>

know that transferring is the correct decision. This is a failure of the management accounting system. Many existing systems have been primarily designed for financial accounting needs, not for management's decision-making needs, thus this is a pervasive problem with traditional accounting systems.

In other cases, the profit center managers know the relevant costs for their own profit center but do not share that information with each other or with Yard Equipment headquarters. Why would they not share relevant information? Consider the Braxton manager's situation (Exhibits 21–5 and 21–8). If she has sufficient surplus capacity for the transfer, her floor price should be $175. However, she may be tempted to claim that her cost of a motor is $190 (the standard variable cost for external sales). By increasing the floor price, the range of transfer prices appears to be $190 to $275. The differential profit from transferring would then appear to be $85 instead of the real $100. If the managers share the $85 equally, they would agree to a $232.50 transfer price (the

Reward system option	Transfer price
■ Rewards not based on transfers' differential profit	Preset at floor
■ Rewards based on differential profit created by transfers	
1. Direct reward for transferring:	
a. Predetermined percentage	Preset transfer price using profit-sharing percentage
b. No predetermined percentage	None preset; managers must negotiate
2. Indirect reward based on aggregate divisional segment margins	None preset; managers must negotiate

■ EXHIBIT 21–14
Reward Systems and Transfer Pricing Policies

midpoint of the $190 to $275 range). In reality, the Braxton manager would get more of the transfer's differential profit, and thus a greater reward, than the Clipper manager. In this scenario, she would get one half of the transfer's apparent differential profit ($42.50), plus the $15.00 by which she overstated her cost. Her cost should have been $175, not $190. If she does not incur any cost variances, her share of the transfer's differential profit will be $57.50 per motor ($42.50 + $15.00, or $232.50 transfer price − $175.00 real cost). Meanwhile the Clipper manager receives only $42.50 of the transfer's differential profit.[10]

Obviously, if the Braxton manager could argue that her floor was even more than $190, she could obtain even more of the transfer's differential profit for herself. There are a number of motor "costs" she might use that are greater than her real relevant cost: the $180 standard absorptive manufacturing cost (Exhibit 21–2b), or the $280 budgeted average cost of externally sold motors ($190 variable cost + $90 allocation of total fixed costs from Exhibit 21–13). She might even claim that since she sells motors for $300 each, that is the minimum price she will accept from Clipper (or $275 allowing for the variable costs saved from an internal sale), hiding the fact that she has surplus capacity.

Product costs can be calculated in different ways to serve different purposes. It is often difficult to identify which costs are relevant to a particular decision situation faced by management. Withholding the relevant information from the rest of the "corporate family" and/or using the wrong information creates complex and serious ethical problems for the management accountant. The Institute of Management Accountants' *Statement of Management Accounting #1C: Standards of Ethical Conduct for Management Accountants* sections on competence, integrity, and objectivity may be violated if the Braxton Division's controller does not provide the correct information. There is no easy way to resolve the management accountant's conflict between professional competence and ethics on the one hand and the wishes of the Braxton manager on the other.

Some companies require corporate intervention (arbitration) to set the transfer price when the two managers cannot compromise on how to share the transfer's differential profit. Both arbitration and negotiation are time-consuming activities for all the management personnel involved, though. Another problem with negotiation is that divisional SMs become sensitive to the negotiating skills of the managers. But this problem is not unique to transfer pricing decisions. In many actual situations, profits are in part determined by the negotiating skills of profit center managers, regardless of whether the negotiations involve an internal or external sale.

Considering all the potential problems with negotiation, why would Yard Equipment Company use reward systems that require it? One reason is that the ability to negotiate successfully is a desirable profit center managerial skill. Requiring managers to negotiate mimics the external sales decision processes in which they primarily engage. One of the benefits from decentralizing is the managerial training ground provided by RCs.

A second reason is related to the purpose of decentralizing into profit centers in the first place. In some situations, corporate headquarters does not have the information needed for certain decisions; it only exists at the profit center level. Thus, decentralizing (allowing the divisional manager to act without prior consent from headquarters) results in better and quicker decisions. This reason is not valid for transfer decisions, though. Negotiation does not produce quicker decisions. Further, when negotiation is required because of the reward system used, then there is an increased likelihood for dysfunctional decisions. Finally,

---

[10] Remember that the transfer price is only a profit-sharing rule between the two managers. The CMU reported by each manager, based on the transfer price used, must always sum to the company total shown on the bottom line of the Transfer Pricing Matrix in Exhibit 21–8. In this case, Clipper would report a $42.50 per motor CMU and Braxton would report a $57.50 CMU. The sum is the transfer's $100.00 per motor differential profit for Yard Equipment Company.

this reason will disappear as decentralized enterprises implement client/server, interoperable ICBISs (see Chapter 20). Information sharing will replace private, local RC information.

Information sharing through interoperable ICBISs presents some interesting implications for the negotiation process. For example, the Clipper Division manager can purchase motors for $275 from a competitor of the Braxton Division. Braxton motors normally sell for $300. During negotiations, the Braxton manager may not be willing to accept a transfer price below $285 (the full capacity floor price of the Transfer Pricing Matrix in Exhibit 21–8) even if she has sufficient surplus capacity available.

Why would she not consider accepting a lower transfer price (down to the $175 surplus capacity floor price)? There are at least two possible explanations. First, the Braxton manager may believe that her competitor is offering an artificially low price to fill up his factory. If that competitor finds enough marginal business elsewhere, then this $275 external purchase cost may not be valid. Thus, the Braxton manager may be motivated to hold out for her normal CMU through a $285 transfer price. The second possible explanation for holding out for a $285 transfer price is that the manager believes that she can fill the Braxton factory to full capacity with other sales. If so, then she may not be motivated to accept a transfer price that will result in less CMU.[11]

Upper management wants the two managers to make the decision themselves because the relevant information exists on the divisional levels, and these managers are in the best position to evaluate their markets and set marketing strategies. Decentralization works best when information is at the local level and divisions are independent from each other. Requiring transfers may not be congruent with the corporation's reasons for creating the decentralized divisions.

As firms move toward becoming world-class manufacturers, however, the relevant transfer information should be as readily available to all parties as it is at the divisional level. New information technologies and networked, client/server interoperable ICBISs may overcome the need for decentralized decision making, at least for these types of transfer decisions.

With reward systems that require negotiation, the transfer decision becomes a two-stage process. First, the managers must decide whether to transfer, and then they have to agree on a profit-sharing transfer price. The decision to transfer *should be* based on whether the transfer creates a differential profit for Yard Equipment Company. Because the transfer price has nothing to do with whether Yard Equipment realizes a differential profit on the transfer, it *should be* irrelevant to the managers when making their joint decision to transfer. It becomes relevant to the two managers, however, when the amount of their individual rewards depends upon the transfer price. Thus, they do not consider the decision to transfer as a separate, first decision in a two-stage process. Instead, whether the transfer will occur depends on whether they can agree on a transfer price. Whenever divisional managers place their personal rewards and goals ahead of the corporation's, the possibility for suboptimal decisions exists. Upper management may have to deal with this goal-congruence problem if it chooses a reward system requiring negotiation.

Negotiating a transfer price, as a requirement for the decision to transfer, is incongruent with the firm's goal of transferring when corporate profitability can be increased (because the managers may choose not to transfer if they are unable to agree on a price). The two reward systems that require negotiation can only be justified by the belief that the marginal utility of other organizational

---

[11] See Rene Manes, "Birch Paper Company Revisited: An Exercise in Transfer Pricing," *Accounting Review,* July 1970, pp. 565–572; and Robert Swieringa and John Waterhouse, "Organizational Views of Transfer Pricing," *Accounting, Organizations and Society,* 1982, pp. 149–165.

goals (satisfied by requiring the negotiation process) is greater than the expected marginal utility from the transfer's differential profit possibly lost.[12]

This leads to the last transfer pricing policy found in practice. Many companies allow the profit center managers to decide whether to transfer, but dictate the use of a certain transfer price. Often the required transfer price is the external sales price, for example $300 for the motor (Exhibit 21–5). This market price-based policy is often justified because it is objective and simplifies the decision process. Of course, the Clipper manager may have little incentive to transfer if he will incur a higher cost.

Even if the transfer price were reduced to the ceiling of the range in Exhibit 21–8, the Clipper manager would not share in any of the transfer's differential profits created for Yard Equipment Company. Setting the transfer price at the ceiling results in all the transfer's differential profit being reported in Braxton's income statement. Why might the Clipper manager agree to a transfer when the ceiling price must be used? By using an internal supplier (Braxton versus an external supplier), he may obtain better control over motor quality and more reliable delivery schedules.

In summary, with the advent of multinational, world-class enterprises, optional transfers between decentralized profit centers are presenting the modern management accountant with many challenges. Designing a high-quality profit management system will require many knowledge areas, such as:

- Use of activity-based costing and management techniques to more accurately measure the costs of intermediate products.
- An understanding of the relevant profit elements that will influence these profit planning decisions.
- An understanding of the international arenas including cultural, political, and regulatory environments in which the divisions must operate.
- The ability to design client/server interoperable ICBISs so that the relevant information can be shared between decentralized divisions.
- The ability to design information displays and reports, in usable and simple formats, so that the managers can effectively and efficiently make goal congruent decisions.
- Knowledge of the reward systems in use and their effects on the transfer decision.
- And a keen sense of ethical conduct, especially in transfer situations that require negotiation.

There is little doubt that the setting of transfer pricing policies will continue to be one of the most controversial topics in modern profit management systems design.

SUMMARY OF LEARNING OBJECTIVES

The major goals of this chapter were to enable you to achieve three learning objectives:

Learning objective 1.   Distinguish between components made in cost centers and intermediate products made in profit centers.

Components made in cost centers are used by other RCs in making their products. Cost center managers do not sell components to external customers. Instead, they are required to transfer the components to other RCs that need them. An RC that sells to

---

[12] Marginal utility is the incremental benefit or worth of something. Here the argument is that the benefits in terms of better managerial skills from requiring negotiation are more important to Yard Equipment Company's upper management than the profits that might be lost if a transfer does not occur when it should.

outside customers receives sales revenues and contributes a profit to the overall corporation. In that case, the RC is a profit center. A profit center's product that can be sold externally or used by another RC in its production is called an intermediate product.

As this chapter has shown, determining a transfer pricing policy for profit centers making and selling intermediate products is more difficult than for cost centers that only make components for use in other RCs. Different organizational and accounting system goals are involved with intermediate profit center products than with cost center components. Thus, as the first step in understanding transfer pricing policies, cost centers making components must be distinguished from profit centers that make intermediate products.

Learning objective 2.   Understand the management accounting system's goals for transfer costing and transfer pricing.

The distinction between components transferred from cost centers and intermediate products transferred from profit centers also applies to transfer costing and transfer pricing. Transfer costing policies are for cost centers, which are required to transfer components to other RCs. Transfer pricing policies are for profit centers transferring intermediate products at their option.

A company wants cost center managers to meet their production schedules, and deliver quality components on time when needed. They should also control their costs; that is, not incur unfavorable cost variances. The accounting system should report information that allows management to determine whether the cost center manager incurred cost variances associated with a transfer. By doing this, the accounting system should assist the organization in motivating the cost center manager to control costs (an organizational goal-congruence objective).

The company wants profit center managers to sell products profitably. This involves, in part, choosing the most profitable customers and controlling costs so that budgeted profits are realized. The accounting system's role is to provide information that will help the profit center manager select the most profitable customer and assist in determining whether costs were controlled.

With respect to transfer pricing, a high-quality profit management system will report the relevant information needed to make the transfer decision. A Transfer Pricing Matrix display satisfies this goal. The system should also report profit variances associated with the transfer. This requires segmenting the selling division's income statement into external sales and transfers.

Learning objective 3.   Determine how the different cost and price options can affect managerial decision making, planning, cost management, and performance evaluation.

Transfer costs can be the actual production cost, the standard production cost, or a market price of the component. The cost can be the variable cost or the absorption cost. The chapter argued that the transfer costing policy should use standard absorptive manufacturing cost. This option provides the most meaningful information for management to use in determining whether cost variances occurred within the cost center. It also helps motivate the cost center manager to control costs. Using actual cost allows cost variances to be passed on to the RC receiving the component, reducing the motivation of the cost center manager to control costs. Using a market price makes it harder for management to identify cost variances within a cost center and creates pseudo profits that complicate the accounting system and performance evaluation.

In setting a transfer pricing policy, a number of possible transfer prices can be used. The correct transfer price depends upon the reward system used by upper management. First, though, the two profit center managers need to determine whether a transfer is profitable. When the selling division has surplus capacity, this involves comparing the cost of making the intermediate product against the cost of buying it from another supplier. When the supplying division is already producing at full capacity for normal customers, the comparison changes to consider the contribution margin per motor that the profit center is currently making. This process determines the minimum acceptable transfer price, which is compared with the cost of buying the intermediate product from an outside supplier (the maximum acceptable transfer price).

The calculation of a transfer's differential profitability can be further complicated if the transfer creates fixed costs, if there is insufficient capacity available in the supplying division, or if no other sources for the intermediate product exist. In all these situations, though, a Transfer Pricing Matrix can be created to calculate the transfer's differential profit for the company as a whole. The differential profit will always be the difference between the ceiling and floor of the range of transfer prices (Exhibit 21–8). When the ceiling is greater than the floor, the transfer creates differential profits, and the possible transfer prices that are acceptable to both managers are limited to those within the range.

With some reward systems, the transfer price can be preset. With others, it must be negotiated by the two profit center managers. The chapter recommended that the transfer price be preset at the floor price when the managers receive no special rewards for transferring. The selling division's income statement should be segmented between external sales and internal sales to promote cost control and identify cost variances within the RCs responsible.

If the managers receive a predetermined amount of a reward for making correct transfer decisions, the transfer price can be preset to allow for the proper profit-sharing ratios. This procedure stems from the realization that the transfer price only determines how much of the transfer's differential profit will be reported within each profit center's income statement.

If the managers must decide how much of a reward each will receive, they will have to negotiate the transfer price. Negotiation has its good, bad, and ugly points. The company will have to evaluate the trade-offs between using different reward systems

■■■ EXHIBIT 21–15
Transfer Policy Flowchart

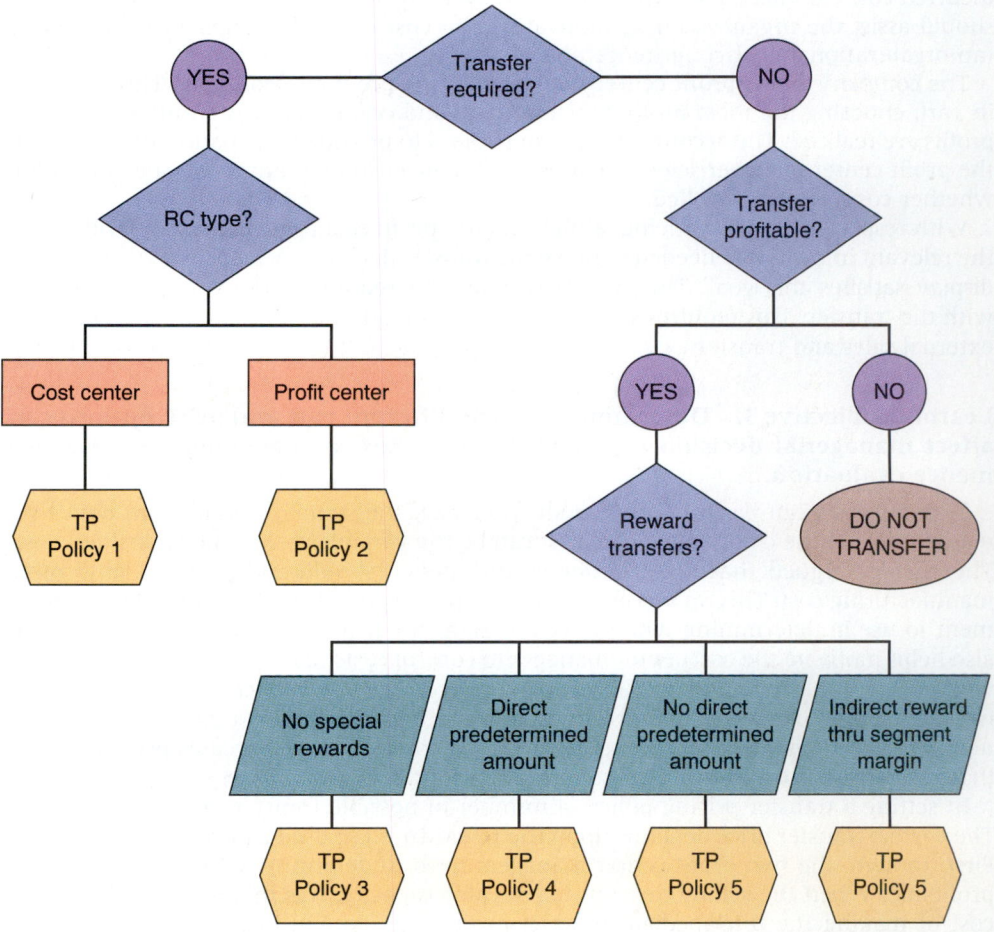

Transfer Policies:
1. Use Standard Absorptive Manufacturing Cost. Report Selling Division cost variances.
2. Same as 1 with transfers reported as deduction from COGS.
3. Preset at Floor. Segment Selling Division into external versus internal sales. Report cost variances for both profit centers.
4. Preset to yield percentages of shared profits. Segment Selling Division into external versus internal sales. Report cost variances for both profit centers.
5. Managers negotiate transfer price. Segment Selling Division into external versus internal sales. Report cost variances for both profit centers.

and requiring negotiation. Regardless of the choice, the management accountant should be able to develop a transfer pricing policy to match the reward system. The various policies discussed in this chapter were summarized in Exhibit 21–14 and are presented as a flowchart in Exhibit 21–15.

IMPORTANT TERMS

Ceiling transfer price   The lowest purchase price offered by an external supplier to a responsibility center that needs an intermediate product. This is the highest transfer price that the responsibility center manager will accept. Thus, it is the ceiling of the range of transfer prices in the Transfer Pricing Matrix.

Components   Parts that are produced within cost centers and are required to be transferred to other responsibility centers.

Floor transfer price   The lowest transfer price acceptable to the responsibility center supplying an intermediate product. It usually can be calculated by summing the internal variable cost to produce and deliver the intermediate product, the contribution margin per unit lost from normal sales that would have to be given up in a transfer, and the unitized differential fixed costs involved in the transfer.

Intermediate products   Products that can be sold to external customers or transferred to other responsibility centers as direct materials in that center's product.

Range of transfer prices   The set of mutually acceptable transfer prices for optional transfers between profit centers. It is bounded by the ceiling and floor transfer price options. The difference between these endpoints of the range determines the differential profitability from the transfer. This range also represents the set of possible transfer prices that both profit center managers could agree to.

Transfer   The process of moving a component or intermediate product from one responsibility center to another within a company. Stated another way, it is the exchange of goods or services between production responsibility centers of the same enterprise.

Transfer cost   The cost used in the accounting system to record required transfers of component parts from cost centers.

Transfer price   The price used in the accounting system to record optional transfers of intermediate products from profit centers.

Transfer Pricing Matrix   A presentation format for the relevant accounting information involved in an optional intermediate product transfer between profit centers. It can be used to calculate the transfer's differential profitability and to present the range of mutually acceptable transfer prices to both managers.

DEMONSTRATION PROBLEMS

■ **DEMONSTRATION PROBLEM 1**   *The Transfer Pricing Matrix and optional profit center transfers.*

Nessle Chocolate Corporation owns two profit center subsidiaries: Chocolate Bar Company and Nut Farm. Transfers are not required between subsidiaries because of Nessle's commitment to decentralization. Each profit center is evaluated based on its profit variances and rewarded for obtaining its target profit. Chocolate Bar Company normally buys nuts for its chocolate nut bar from a competitor of the Nut Farm. The following information about the two divisions is available:

NUT FARM DIVISION

Production data:
Current volume: 1,000 bushels sold to external customers
Capacity: 1,500 bushels could be produced in a month

Cost data:
Normal variable costs: Standard Costs

	Per Unit	Totals
Production costs	$10.00	$10,000
Other costs	9.00	9,000
Totals	$19.00	$19,000

Internal variable costs (for transfers):

Production costs	$ 8.00
Other costs	7.50
Totals	$15.50

Sales price: Bushels sold to outside customers at $30 each

CHOCOLATE BAR DIVISION

Purchase price per bushel from external supplier:	$27.50 each
Other variable costs of making chocolate nut bars:	14.00
Sales price for chocolate nut bars:	60.00

Required:

a. Prepare a Transfer Pricing Matrix for the managers so that they will have the relevant information for this transfer decision.

b. Should the managers agree to transfer?

c. If the ceiling of the range of transfer prices is used as the transfer price, how much of the differential profits created will appear in each profit center's net income?

d. Answer Requirement (c) if the floor is used.

e. Answer Requirement (c) if the midpoint of the range is used.

f. How will the use of each of the transfer price options in Requirements (c), (d), and (e) affect the profits of Nessle Chocolate Corporation?

SOLUTION TO DEMONSTRATION PROBLEM 1

a.

Range of transfer prices:	Transferred product made with selling division surplus capacity: (Exhibit 21-6)	Transferred product taken from normal customer sales: Full capacity situation (Exhibit 21-7)
CEILING: (determined by the "buying" division: Chocolate Bar Co.)	External purchase price: $27.50	External purchase price: $27.50
FLOOR: (determined by the "selling" division: Nut Farm)	Internal variable cost: $15.50	External sales price less variable costs saved by transferring: $26.50
Transfer's differential contribution margin per bushel of nuts: (for the "company": Nessle Chocolate)	Ceiling – Floor: $12.00	Ceiling – Floor: $1.00

b. Yes, they should agree to transfer. Nessle Chocolate Corporation will realize a differential profit of $12 per bushel if the Nut Farm has sufficient surplus capacity for the transfer. If the Nut Farm is already operating at full capacity for current sales, then the differential profit to Nessle will only be $1 per bushel.

c. If the ceiling is used, then all of the transfer's differential profit will appear in the selling division's (Nut Farm) segment margin. The buying division (Chocolate Bar Company) will see no change in its segment margin.

d. If the floor is used, all of the differential profit will appear in the buying division's segment margin (Chocolate Bar Company), while the Nut Farm will have no change in its segment margin.

e. The midpoint of the range of transfer prices is $21.50 per bushel if the Nut Farm has the surplus capacity to fill this order or $27.00 per bushel if the Nut Farm has no surplus capacity available. In either situation, the divisions will share equally in the transfer's differential profit ($6.00 per bushel each in the surplus capacity situation, and $0.50 per bushel each in the full capacity situation).

f. If the transfer happens (and in the absence of any cost variances), Nessle Chocolate

Corporation should realize an increase in pretax profits of $12 per bushel transferred in the surplus capacity situation or $1 per bushel in the full capacity situation. Nessle's differential profit is not changed if different transfer prices are used (in the absence of certain tax and tariff effects). The transfer price is just a profit-sharing rule between the two managers.

■**DEMONSTRATION PROBLEM 2**   *Managerial motivations and the range of acceptable transfer prices.*

a. Discuss how the two divisional managers of the Nessle Chocolate Corporation calculated their opportunity costs for the transfer situation above.
b. Why do these opportunity costs create a ceiling and floor for a range of transfer prices that would be acceptable to both managers?
c. In calculating the differential profits that the transfer can create, how does the Nessle Chocolate Corporation view each selling division situation?

SOLUTION TO DEMONSTRATION PROBLEM 2

a. As the buying division, the Chocolate Bar Company's manager has two alternatives: buying bushels of nuts from a competitor of the Nut Farm for $27.50, or transferring them from the Nut Farm. In the surplus capacity situation, the selling division (the Nut Farm) manager has to at least cover her variable costs for the transferred bushels, which is $15.50. If operating at full capacity for current external sales, she needs to maintain the same contribution margin per bushel that she already is receiving. Since $3.50 per bushel can be saved by transferring versus selling outside, she could pass this savings along to the buying division manager and still maintain her same CMU. The normal sales price is $30.00, which, less this savings of $3.50, results in a transfer price of $26.50 that will preserve her current contribution margin per bushel.

b. The external purchase cost for the Chocolate Bar Company is the ceiling of the range of mutually acceptable transfer prices because this manager can accept any transfer price up to this amount without his CMU going down. The Nut Farm manager, as the selling division, must receive a transfer price equal to or greater than her floor price calculated in (a). If the transfer price equals the floor, there will be no increase or decrease in her segment margin. If the transfer price is some amount above the floor, then that difference will be extra profit to her. Thus, she has no limit on how high the transfer price can be, just on how low it can go. Conversely, the buying division manager has a limit on how high the transfer price can go, but not on how low it can be. Any transfer price within the range created by these opportunity costs will be acceptable to each manager.

c. In the surplus capacity situation, the Nessle Chocolate Corporation views a transfer as a simple make-or-buy decision. It can make a bushel of nuts in the Nut Farm Division or buy it through the Chocolate Bar Company. It will want to transfer ("make") whenever that cost (the floor) is less than the cost of buying externally. Nessle views the full capacity situation as a sell-or-process-further decision. Bushels of nuts can be sold now or processed further into chocolate nut bars. If the money saved by processing further (transferring) is greater than the contribution margin per bushel currently being made by the Nut Farm, then Nessle will want a transfer.

▌REVIEW QUESTIONS

21.1 Define a transfer.
21.2 Distinguish between a transfer and a "normal" sale between two unrelated parties. Why is this an important distinction?
21.3 What is the distinction between components and intermediate products, and why is it important in choosing a transfer policy?
21.4 What is the objective of the management accounting system for transfers from a cost center?
21.5 What three managerial roles are involved in a transfer?
21.6 What are the information needs for each managerial role identified in Question 21.5 if the divisions are profit centers and transfers are optional? Consider the questions the manager wants answered in each case.

21.7 What are the responsibilities of a cost center manager who transfers components?

21.8 What are the responsibilities of profit center managers who receive transferred components?

21.9 What are the management accounting system's objectives for a transfer costing policy between a cost center and a profit center?

21.10 What are the three issues a management accountant must address in recommending a transfer costing policy?

21.11 Why should a transfer costing policy use the standard absorptive manufacturing cost of the transferred component as the transfer cost?

21.12 Why is standard absorptive manufacturing cost preferred over standard variable manufacturing cost as a transfer cost?

21.13 What is a "pseudo profit center," and how can a transfer costing system create one?

21.14 List two reasons why companies might want to create pseudo profit centers through the choice of a transfer costing policy.

21.15 When a profit center is required to transfer an intermediate product, why is standard absorptive manufacturing cost a good choice for the transfer price?

21.16 List the two goals for a transfer pricing policy when transfers are optional.

21.17 What is the ceiling transfer price within the Transfer Pricing Matrix?

21.18 What is the floor transfer price within the Transfer Pricing Matrix?

21.19 Why does the overall company view an optional transfer between profit centers as simply a make-or-buy decision when there is sufficient surplus capacity for the transfer within the selling division?

21.20 Explain why a range of mutually acceptable transfer prices exists whenever the transfer will generate a differential profit for the company.

21.21 In optional profit center transfers, why does the floor price change if the selling division does not have sufficient surplus capacity for the transfer?

21.22 The overall company views an optional transfer between profit centers as a sell-or-process-further decision when the selling division is currently at full capacity production. Why?

21.23 In optional transfers between profit centers, how does the transfer price affect the reported profits of each of the three parties involved?

21.24 In optional transfers between profit centers, what is the effect on each division's income statement from setting the transfer price at the ceiling of the range of transfer prices? At the floor? At the midpoint of the range?

21.25 List the four types of reward systems and the transfer price policy recommended for each in optional profit center transfers.

21.26 What are the costs and benefits from requiring a transfer price to be negotiated in optional profit center transfer situations?

| CHAPTER-SPECIFIC PROBLEMS

These problems require responses based directly on concepts and techniques presented in the text.

21.27 *Optional transfers between profit centers.* TAA, a multidivisional telecommunications corporation, has two completely independent profit centers considering a transfer. The Interstate Commerce Commission of the U.S. government has mandated that TAA subsidiaries operate within a decentralized environment. Thus, TAA cannot dictate transfers or impose a transfer pricing policy on the divisions. They must be free to decide whether they should transfer, and if so, they must negotiate a transfer price. Further, the TAA reward system must be based on the total divisional profits reported by the profit centers.

One of TAA's divisions, Southwestern Ringer, produces telephone sets that it sells for $30 each. The standard absorptive manufacturing cost is $24, which includes $6 per unit in fixed overhead. The fixed overhead is allocated over its annual sales forecast of 50,000 telephone sets. Its maximum production capacity is 75,000 sets annually.

Another division, Northeastern Tell, can use the telephone sets in an answering machine–telephone–radio product it markets. As an alternative to buying telephone sets from Southwestern, Northeastern can enter into a contract for the

20,000 sets needed from a Mexican company, OLA, Inc. OLA has quoted a price of $25 per set for the same quality telephone.

Required:
a. Determine whether a transfer should take place between Southwestern Ringer and Northeastern Tell.
b. Should a transfer occur if Southwestern can increase its sales and production volumes to 75,000 sets annually by dropping the sales price to $27.50?

21.28 *Managerial motivations and transfer pricing policies.* In the previous problem, the two divisional managers cannot agree on a transfer price. The Southwestern manager maintains that the transfer price should be his current sales price of $30 per telephone, because the ICC requires that the divisions act as independent entities. The Northeastern manager insists on the floor price, claiming that incremental production costs are only $18 and that it will not produce the 20,000 phones if Southwestern does not transfer them because there is no other market for the phones.

Required:
Although, as the corporate accountant for TAA, you cannot set a policy for interdivisional transfers, TAA management has asked you to evaluate the managers' claims and recommend a transfer price. Prepare a memo to the corporate vice president.

21.29 *Transfers with differential fixed costs.* Refer to Problem 21.27. Northeastern Tell wants its name imprinted on the telephone set. Its Mexican supplier has quoted a price of $31.00 per set. Southwestern Ringer will have to buy a stamping machine at a net cost of $20,000. Southwestern no longer can produce at full capacity by dropping its sales price to $27.50, so the manager has abandoned that idea.

Required:
Determine whether there should now be a transfer. What transfer price will result in the managers benefiting equally from the transfer?

21.30 *Limited capacity transfers.* Continuing the TAA example from the previous problem, the Northeastern marketing staff has decided against imprinting its name on the phone. However, they believe that if the color is changed to fuchsia, 30,000 specialty phone–answering machine–radios can be sold in the greater New York area. The Mexican supplier has quoted a price of $26.50 for an order of this size due to the higher cost of fuchsin. Southwestern already produces fuchsia-colored phones for its Los Angeles market and will incur no extra costs in changing the color.

Required:
Calculate whether this transfer should occur. If so, what transfer price will share the differential profits equally between the two managers?

21.31 *Imputing the ceiling price.* The Northeastern marketing staff has always been known for their creativity. Now they are considering changing the color of their specialty phone product to paisley. The Mexican supplier will not even bid on this, and no other supplier has been found. Northeastern believes that 22,500 of these specialty phone products can be sold at $200 each in the Atlantic City market. The costs to produce this product, other than the cost of the Southwestern phone set, are $183 each. Fortunately, Southwestern already produces a paisley phone for its San Francisco market. While this phone's cost structure is the same as Southwestern's other phones, it can only be sold for $20.

Required:
Determine whether a transfer is profitable for TAA. If so, suggest a transfer price that shares TAA's differential profit 75% for Northeastern and 25% for Southwestern.

21.32 *Optional profit center transfers.* Returning to the Nessle Chocolate Corporation demonstration problem, the Nut Farm management has just offered the California Pickers Union a new contract in the hopes of averting a labor strike. The new contract will increase standard direct labor costs by $2. New picking and sorting machinery promised in the contract will increase budgeted fixed production costs by $10,000 per year. Per bushel nut prices cannot be increased because of intense competition internationally. Chocolate Bar Company is not affected by the threatened strike as it has been importing nuts from a Brazilian supplier for $25.50 per bushel.

Required:
a. Should the Nut Farm and the Chocolate Bar Company managers agree to transferring nuts?
b. Assume the new President of the United States extends the Free Trade Agreement with Mexico to South American countries. With the elimination of the tariff on Brazilian nuts, the price per bushel will decrease $10. Should the two divisions transfer in this situation?

21.33 *Insufficient capacity for the transfer.* Continuing Problem 21.32, requirement (a), Chocolate Bar Company wants a transfer of 600 bushels. The Nut Farm manager, after consulting her sales manager, agrees that their normal business will not be lost in the long run by accepting this order.

Required:
Should the two managers agree to transfer? What transfer price will equally share the differential profit (if there is one) between them?

21.34 *Differential fixed costs and profit center transfers.* Use the original information from the Nessle Chocolate Corporation demonstration problems. Because the Food and Drug Administration has recently investigated one of its competitors, Chocolate Bar Company wants to change the size of the broken nut pieces used in its candy bar. Bigger pieces will require the purchase of a special nutcracker machine. The Nut Farm has agreed to buy this machine, which will only be used for transferred nuts, and the cost will be recaptured through this order.

Required:
a. If the transfer order is for 400 bushels, and the cost of the machine (after disposal) is $4,000, should the managers agree to transfer?
b. What are the midpoints of the range of acceptable transfer prices for both the surplus capacity and the full capacity situations?

21.35 *Limited capacity and variable cost savings.* National Industries is a highly decentralized corporation with independent operating divisions. Each division is evaluated and rewarded based on its total net income. One of the divisions, Windair, manufactures and sells air conditioners. It is projecting a sales forecast of 17,400 for next year.

Another division, Koolsource, makes and sells compressors. Its projected income statement for next year follows:

KOOLSOURCE DIVISION
PRO FORMA INCOME STATEMENT
FOR NEXT YEAR

	PER UNIT	TOTALS
Sales revenues	$100	$6,400,000
Less cost of goods sold:		
Direct materials	12	768,000
Direct labor	8	512,000
Variable overhead	10	640,000
Fixed overhead	11	704,000
Total COGS	<$ 41>	<$2,624,000>
Gross profit	$ 59	$3,776,000

Operating expenses:		
Variable selling expenses	$ 6	$ 384,000
Fixed selling expenses	4	256,000
Fixed administrative expenses	7	448,000
Total operating expenses	<$ 17>	<$1,088,000>
Pretax net income	$ 42	$2,688,000

Koolsource has the capacity to produce 75,000 compressors annually. Windair, currently purchasing from an outside source at $70, proposes that Koolsource transfer compressors to them at a transfer price of $50. The Windair manager justified the low bid based on some cost savings that should be realized if compressors are transferred. Because specifications for this compressor are slightly different from Koolsource's standard model, $1.50 per compressor of direct materials cost can be saved and no variable selling expenses will be incurred on compressors transferred.

Required:
a. Compute the estimated effect on Koolsource's net income if the 17,400 compressors are transferred at $50 each.
b. Determine whether it would be in National Industries' best interests for Koolsource to transfer compressors at $50 each.
c. What is the minimum transfer price you would accept as the Koolsource manager? Defend your answer.

[CMA adapted]

21.36 *Government contracting and imputed ceilings.* Gunco Corporation has two divisions, Ajax and Defco. Both are profit centers. One of the products Ajax manufactures is electrical fitting 1726, which is protected under patent and, thus, is not available from any other source. Its variable costs are $4.25 per unit, and its normal sales price is $7.50.

Defco has just been awarded an Air Force contract for the manufacture of a special brake unit. Because Defco was only operating at 50% capacity, it purposefully bid low to increase its chances of winning the contract in what, the manager believed, would be a very competitive process, due to the sagging state of the defense contracting and airline manufacturing industries. The brake's bid sheet shows:

Purchased parts from outside vendors	$22.50
Ajax electrical fitting 1726	5.00
Other variable costs	14.00
Standard variable manufacturing and delivery costs	$41.50
Indirect cost markup for fixed factory overhead, administration costs, and profit	8.00
Brake bid price	$49.50

Required:
a. Recommend whether or not Ajax should supply fitting 1726 to Defco.
b. Discuss whether a transfer is in Gunco's short-run economic interest.
c. Recommend to the Gunco president a transfer policy for situations such as this.

[CMA adapted]

THINK-TANK PROBLEMS

Although these problems are based on chapter material, reading extra material, reviewing previous chapters, and using creativity may be required to develop workable solutions.

21.37 *Considering the type of product and responsibility centers in choosing a transfer costing (pricing) policy.* What is the relationship between components and intermediate products with respect to cost centers and profit centers? Why is it important to consider the type of part, and the responsibility center transferring it, in choosing a transfer costing (pricing) policy?

21.38 *Actual versus standard costs in transfer costing.* Discuss the transfer costing policy issues dealing with the use of actual versus standard cost in transferring components. Include a numeric example to illustrate your points.

21.39 *Markups and transfer costing.* Discuss the transfer costing policy issues involved in using a "marked-up" transfer cost.

21.40 *Using market price for transfers.* Discuss the implications for the transferring division, the receiving division, and the overall company from using a transfer policy based on the external sales price of a part.

21.41 *Quality information as a goal for the transfer pricing policy.* Producing quality information is a "key role" for management accounting. In Chapter 1, five attributes of quality information were identified. Discuss the implications of each attribute when designing a transfer pricing policy.

21.42 *Ethics in optional profit center transfers.* In Chapter 1, four ethical standards of conduct were identified. Discuss the implications of these for the management accountant when designing a transfer pricing policy for optional profit center transfers.

21.43 *Transfers from a just-in-time producer.* Itsosweet Candy Corporation (ICC), a highly decentralized national manufacturer of confections, has just acquired a new subsidiary company, the Thomas Lollipop Company (TLC). One of the products TLC makes is a Valentine's Day lollipop. This heart-shaped lollipop contains two chocolate secret centers and has two sticks coming out of the bottom. Historically, TLC has purchased chocolate centers from a South American supplier, but chocolate prices have become very volatile over the past few years.

ICC has a subsidiary, Chocolate Forever Company (CFC), that can produce these secret centers for TLC. CFC is currently a cost center for ICC, with a flexible manufacturing process that produces chocolate products using JIT procedures. CFC estimates a standard absorptive manufacturing cost for secret centers to be $0.08. The standard fixed overhead cost is $0.03. A per-kanban setup cost of $50.00 is not included in the standard cost, however. Currently, TLC expects the purchase price of secret centers to remain somewhat stable at $0.06 each.

Required:
Recommend a transfer policy if ICC requires TLC to obtain secret centers from CFC.

Consider a second situation: The CFC plant manager presents a proposal to ICC to become a profit center. ICC agrees, but still requires that CFC supply secret centers to TLC whenever there are no kanbans for other chocolate products. The CFC manager sets a normal sales price for secret centers at $0.085, while budgeting a standard variable cost of $0.05 per secret center. Recommend a transfer policy for this situation. Does your recommendation change if the majority of CFC's output becomes secret centers transferred to TLC? With both recommendations, consider how the transfer policies are affected by a JIT supplying division.

21.44 *Transfers from a JIT profit center.* Continuing the situation in the previous problem, TLC argues that because of the volatility in South American chocolate prices, ICC should allow transfers to be optional, and any differential profits resulting from transfers should be shared between the TLC and CFC divisions. ICC agrees, but doesn't want to get involved in determining how the differential profits should be shared between the divisions because of its commitment to decentralized decision making. ICC rewards profit centers based on their aggregate divisional profit.

Required:
Recommend a transfer policy and a transfer price for this situation assuming the South American price remains stable. Should the two divisions be transferring secret centers? Would your answer change if the price of South American secret

centers dropped to $0.055 each? What if it dropped to $0.05? Now assume that TLC wants to issue a production kanban to CFC for 10,000 secret centers. What is the break-even South American price for secret centers?

21.45 *Negotiation failure.* Continuing the situation in the previous problems, assume the TLC and CFC managers are negotiating a transfer. The TLC manager demands a transfer price of $0.05. The CFC manager demands a transfer price of $0.06, the current South American price. Also assume that there will be no per-kanban setup costs for this transfer and that CFC has the surplus capacity for it. Play the role of each manager and "make your case" for that transfer price. Why is each manager motivated to argue for these transfer prices? Finally, play the role of the ICC vice president in charge of these two profit centers. In this role, what would you do?

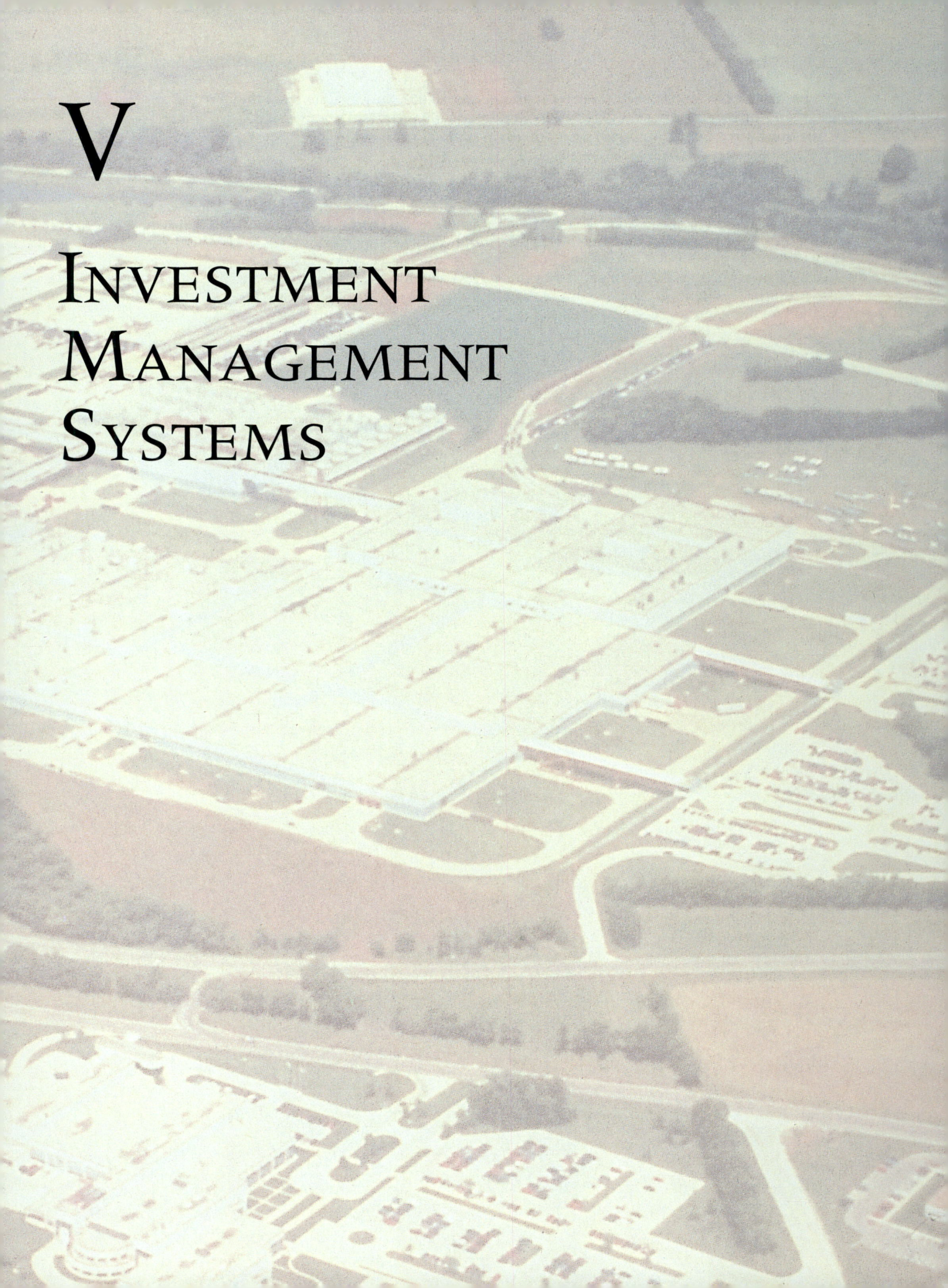

V

INVESTMENT MANAGEMENT SYSTEMS

Capital budgeting involves the investment of an enterprise's funds in specific capital projects that yield benefits in future years. These investment decisions are among the most important and difficult that managers make.

One of the challenges that management accountants face is to provide a systematic methodology to assist management in making appropriate investments in capital projects. The first section of Chapter 22 introduces a four-stage capital budgeting methodology that helps management accountants meet this challenge.

The first stage of the capital budgeting methodology answers the question, "What capital projects will help our enterprise move from where we are to where we want to be in accordance with our vision, mission statement, and strategic plan?" The capital budgeting methodology yields the best results only when it considers the best available capital project requests that have the potential of answering this question. Capital project requests are rated and scored in accordance with feasibility and benefit factors. Tangible and intangible benefits are converted to estimated cash inflows. Cost of each capital project is also estimated. At the end of the first stage of the capital budgeting methodology, inclusion of the capital projects in a Capital Projects Portfolio Statement does not mean that capital projects are approved for implementation. It only means that management has accepted them for planning purposes and financial analysis—the second stage of the capital budgeting methodology.

The capital budgeting financial analysis methods described in Chapter 23 include the following:

- Net present value (NPV) method
- Internal rate of return (IRR) method
- Present value index (PVI) method
- Payback period (PP) method
- Accounting rate of return (ARR) method

The purpose of financial analysis is to determine if a candidate capital project will provide sufficient returns to an enterprise and its owners to compensate them for their investment risk. A variety of possible outcomes can be incorporated into the financial analysis stage as an exercise in sensitivity analysis, which improves the breadth of information available for capital project selection.

The capital projects selected in stage two are ready for implementation, which is stage three. The first part of Chapter 24 presents three tools to safeguard capital projects from implementation failure:

- Gantt chart
- Program evaluation and review technique (PERT) network
- Implementation auditing

The last section of Chapter 24 covers postimplementation auditing, the fourth and final stage. The postimplementation audit reviews estimates and other factors to improve the capital budgeting methodology in the future. It also determines whether a project is functioning as planned. From this review, modifications are proposed that will make the project more profitable and beneficial.

22 THE CAPITAL BUDGETING METHODOLOGY AND ITS FIRST STAGE

Some capital projects are risky.

LEARNING OBJECTIVES

After studying this chapter, you should be able to:

1. Explain capital budgeting and define the capital budgeting methodology and list its stages.

2. Describe how planning for capital projects should be conducted.

3. Discuss why and how feasibility, benefits, and cash flows are estimated.

■ INTRODUCTION

A **capital project** is an asset or undertaking that is used to generate revenues or cost savings by providing benefits for more than one year. **Capital budgeting** allocates or rations funds for one or a mix of capital projects. The amount of these funds is usually sizable. This chapter suggests a capital budgeting methodology that systematizes capital budgeting decision making. ▬

THE PURPOSE OF CAPITAL BUDGETING

Because the long-term profitability of most enterprises depends on the nature and quality of their capital project investments, appropriate planning, evaluation, and implementation of high-return capital projects are imperative. Capital budgeting helps managers plan for the acquisition of capital projects that promise high returns.

> **LEARNING OBJECTIVE 1**
>
> Explain capital budgeting and define the capital budgeting methodology and list its stages.

▌ Types of Capital Budgeting Decisions

The impetus for capital budgeting decisions comes from many diverse sources. Sometimes these decisions are necessary to meet present needs of the enterprise such as the replacement of equipment. Or they may be the result of an organization's new vision and strategy. In some cases, they may be the result of expansion into a new market. Most capital budgeting decisions can be classified into one of the following capital project categories:

- *Legal and social responsibility.* Capital projects in this group are implemented due to legal requirements; examples include pollution control devices and worker safety facilities. Also, various capital projects are implemented for social responsibility (e.g., homeless shelters) and public relations reasons.
- *Replacement.* These capital projects ensure that the enterprise maintains the same productive capacity by replacing worn, damaged, or outdated equipment.
- *Strategic.* Capital projects in this category support management's vision of what the organization is to become, not what it is currently. Projects in this category reduce costs and generate revenues. They also expand capacity to accommodate the introduction of new products or services. Strategic capital projects involve long-term nonroutine investments that chart the strategic direction of the enterprise. The "new" organization may require implementation of some of the concepts and methods discussed in previous chapters, such as reengineering and continuous improvement, enterprisewide modeling, total quality management (TQM), just-in-time (JIT), material requirements planning (MRP), electronic data interchange (EDI), elimination of constraints, and increased throughput.

For manufacturing and for-profit service firms, long-term profitability is the objective of capital projects. For projects in the legal and social responsibility category, however, profitability may not be a consideration. But, even in this category, if the objective can be achieved in two or more ways, techniques are available to rank alternatives and thereby aid the decision-making process. The same can be said for replacement capital projects. In this and the two subsequent chapters, the concentration will be primarily on the strategic category of capital projects.

Should Caterpillar invest in a new product and facilities to manufacture it?

What Are the Consequences of Not Making Capital Budgeting Decisions?

Essentially, capital budgeting involves making choices. Given a range of choices, doing nothing represents an alternative course of action. Managers, however, often ignore the impact of taking no action by assuming that the status quo will be maintained. However, this is seldom the case. As Henry Ford said, "If you need a new machine and don't buy it, you pay for it without getting it."[1] The following material will help clarify what Henry Ford meant.

Capital assets are the engine of long-term growth and profitability. Time and again, companies that skimp on **capital investments** have found themselves unable to compete. Evidence abounds (e.g., see studies conducted by economists J. Bradford De Long and Lawrence Summers) that enterprises invest in capital assets *now* to ensure that they will be around *tomorrow*. William Wheeler, a partner in Coopers & Lybrand, believes that American industry needs to triple its capital spending: "If we don't start investing in the latest technology big time, we're going to end up being bypassed again." A Columbia University finance and law professor says, "Even when you are losing money, you've got to invest a fortune just to maintain market share." Robert Cizik of Cooper Industries says, "We're No. 1 in the world in files (Nicholson files). But, if I produced them the same way as five years ago, I'd be out of business. You've got to constantly update the capital base." A National Science Board study warns, "The United States is spending too little, not allocating it well, and utilizing it ineffectively."[2]

Exhibit 22–1 shows cash outflows during the early years and cash inflows during the later years. The traditional estimates show the net cash flows between line A and the zero baseline. What happens, however, if management

[1] Robert S. Kaplan, "Must CIM Be Justified by Faith Alone?" *Harvard Business Review*, March-April 1986, pp. 87–95.
[2] Edmund Faltermayer, "Invest or Die," *Fortune*, February 22, 1993, pp. 42–52.

■ EXHIBIT 22–1
Possible Effect of Not Making a Capital Investment and Trying to Maintain the Status Quo

Source: Allen H. Seed III, "Investment Justification of Factory Automation," in *Cost Accounting for the '90s: Responding to Technological Change* (Montvale, N.J.: Institute of Management Accountants, formerly the National Association of Accountants, 1988), p. 86. With permission.

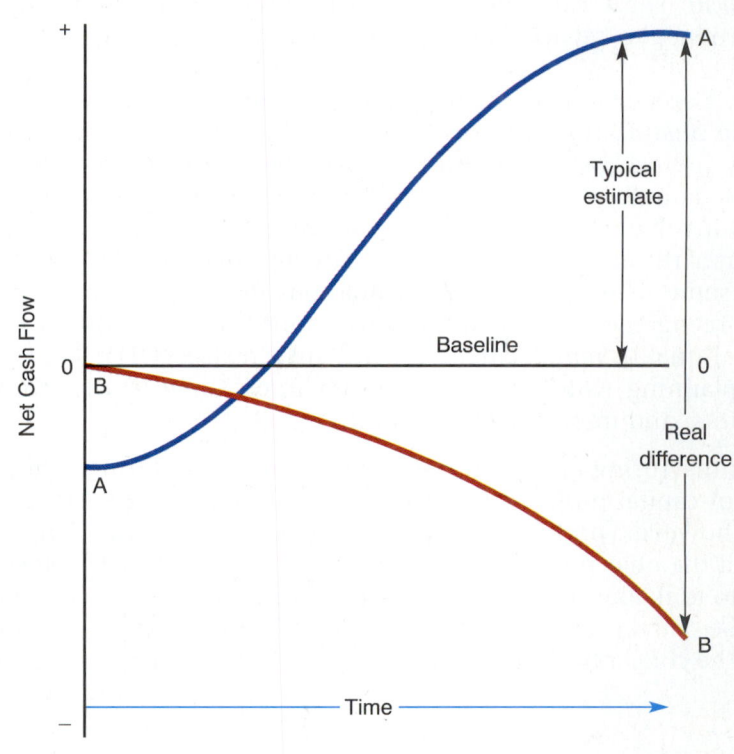

doesn't make capital investments? Most likely, the competition will step in and start taking away business. So the real difference is the difference between A and B, not between A and the baseline.[3]

The exhibit illustrates a concept called the moving baseline.[4] The **moving baseline** graphically shows that assuming the status quo will continue can lead to disastrous results, as indicated by line B. If management does not make capital investments, the enterprise will steadily lose ground in the marketplace and fail to generate cash flows. For example, the failure of American steel, railroad, and various manufacturing companies to upgrade their production facilities has proved to be a mistake. One can only imagine what the current status of these companies would be had they made the right kind of capital budgeting decisions. Today, with shorter product life cycles, rapid technological change, and stiff worldwide competition, capital budgeting decisions are even more difficult than in earlier times.

This analysis shows that in a competitive market nothing stands still. Competitors innovate, invest, and attempt to gain market share. Consequently, an enterprise must continually invest to stay even with or exceed the competition. Even in the maturity stage of the product life cycle (see Chapter 14), capital projects may have to be implemented to prevent sales of certain products from falling.

THE NEED FOR A CAPITAL BUDGETING METHODOLOGY

Because capital budgeting decisions are among the most important and difficult decisions that managers face, a methodology is recommended to assist managers in making the best decisions. The **capital budgeting methodology,** suggested in this book and shown in Exhibit 22–2, applies to all manufacturing, service, and not-for-profit organizations. It involves the following four stages:

- *Planning capital projects and estimating key variables.* In capital budgeting, probably not enough attention is paid to the linkage between strategic and operational goals of an enterprise and the planning and identification of capital projects. In the first stage, planning is conducted to generate capital projects that appear to support an enterprise's goals and strategic plan. Feasibility factors, benefits, and cash flows of each capital project are estimated. This first stage is the primary subject of this chapter.
- *Performing financial analysis of each candidate capital project.* In the second stage, capital budgeting financial analysis models are applied to evaluate projects to determine how financially attractive they are. This second stage is discussed in Chapter 23.
- *Scheduling, controlling, and managing development and implementation of each capital project.* This third stage involves the close monitoring of resources, costs, quality, and the capital project budget. In addition, a feedback loop is necessary to ensure that the project stays on schedule and is implemented in accordance with a target date. This third stage is presented in Chapter 24.
- *Conducting a postimplementation audit of each capital project.* In the fourth stage, the management accountant determines the amount of variance between earlier estimates and what actually occurred. The postimplementation audit is also treated in Chapter 24.

---

[3] Allen H. Seed III, "Investment Justification of Factory Automation," in *Cost Accounting for the 90s: Responding to Technological Change* (Montvale, N.J.: Institute of Management Accountants, formerly the National Association of Accountants, 1988), p. 85. With permission.

[4] Robert A. Howell, "The Controller's Responsibility in World-Class Manufacturing," in *Cost Accounting for the 90s: Responding to Technological Change* (Montvale, N.J.: Institute of Management Accountants, formerly the National Association of Accountants, 1988), pp. 160–162. With permission.

■■■ EXHIBIT 22–2
**Capital Budgeting
Methodology**

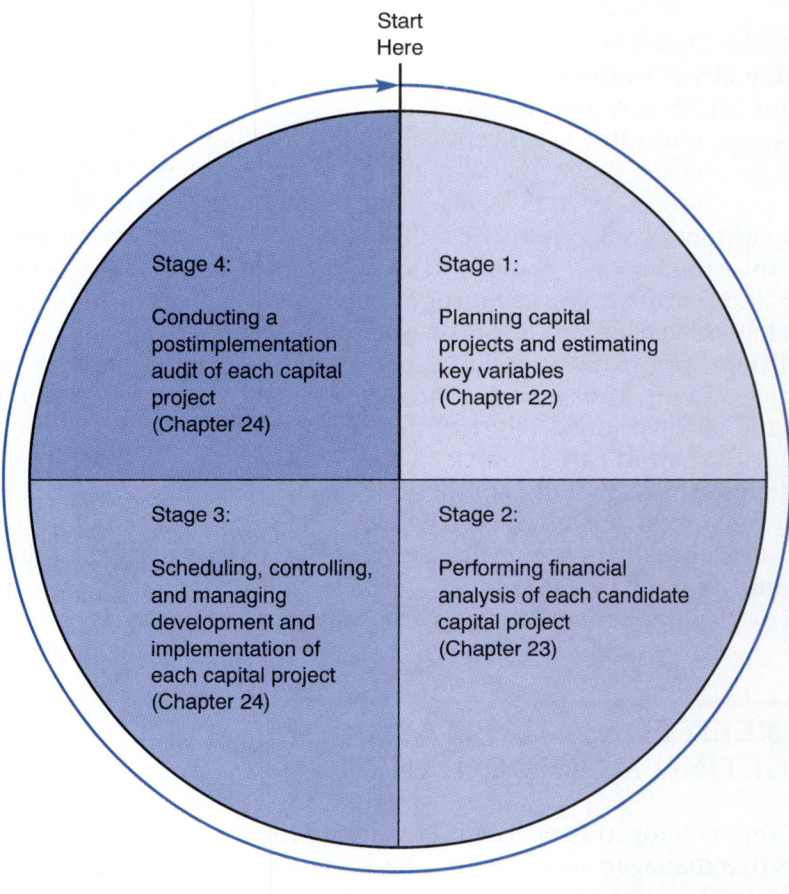

Start
Here

Stage 4:

Conducting a
postimplementation
audit of each capital
project
(Chapter 24)

Stage 1:

Planning capital
projects and estimating
key variables
(Chapter 22)

Stage 3:

Scheduling, controlling,
and managing
development and
implementation of
each capital project
(Chapter 24)

Stage 2:

Performing financial
analysis of each candidate
capital project
(Chapter 23)

**LEARNING
OBJECTIVE 2**

Describe how planning
for capital projects
should be conducted.

PLANNING FOR CAPITAL PROJECTS

Planning for capital projects is a process of generating capital project requests
that appear to support the vision of the enterprise. Providing the capital project
requests is the responsibility of managers throughout the enterprise.

Developing a Vision for the Future

For an enterprise to compete successfully, it must develop a vision of the future
that supports continuous improvement. If capital projects are not compatible
with the enterprise's vision,[5] they should be dropped from further consideration.

The first steps in any capital budgeting decision are to determine the enterprise's vision, then redesign and reengineer activities. Whether designing a new
activity or reengineering an existing one, management must determine which
tasks will be performed by people and which by machines. Management is
faced with an ever-widening range of choices, from activities requiring very
little automation to those requiring a great deal. Once the plan to improve the
activities is complete, various capital projects are requested and evaluated. Those
that can leverage an enterprise redesign by performing value-added activities
more effectively, efficiently, and economically should be selected. (A review of
Chapter 11 on activity-based management may be helpful at this point.)

To do otherwise is to use a "fire-ready-aim" approach instead of a "ready-

---

[5] Some managers prepare a vision statement to provide a futuristic sense of direction for an enterprise
and a mission statement that includes specific actions to be taken to make the vision a reality. In this
book, vision and mission statements are synonymous.

INSIGHTS & APPLICATIONS

Who Will Reengineer the Enterprise?

Reengineering is the radical redesign of an organization's activities and processes. Done properly, it produces extraordinary gains in lead time, productivity, quality, and profitability. Union Carbide used reengineering to cut $400 million out of fixed costs in three years. GTE's aim is to use reengineering to double revenues while reducing costs by 50 percent.

Reengineering starts fresh. It doesn't start with what exists followed by fine-tuning old activities. Reengineering starts *from the future* and works backward, unconstrained by existing activities. The organization is changed to match the vision of what it wants to become. "Don't fix stuff you shouldn't be doing in the first place," says Robert M. Tomasko, author of *Rethinking the Corporation.*

Your company wants to reengineer. It's going to turn itself inside out and glue itself back together—faster, smoother, leaner, and more competitive. Who's going to do it? Texas Instruments, Aetna Life and Casualty, and American Airlines are among a growing number of corporations that have created a *chief reengineering officer.*[6]

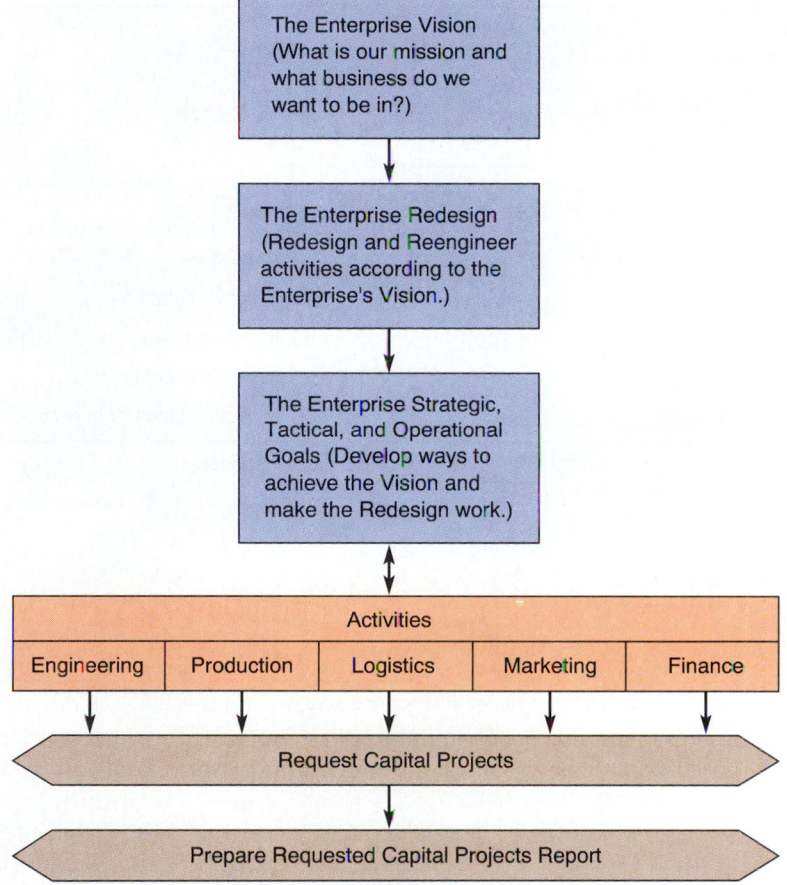

■EXHIBIT 22–3
Planning for Capital Projects

aim-fire" approach. Here "ready" and "aim" refer to the enterprise's vision, redesign, and goals, while "fire" means engaging capital budgeting decisions that support the "new" enterprise. The logical sequence in planning for capital projects is shown in Exhibit 22–3.

[6] Excerpted from Amy H. Johnson, "Who Will Steer You to the Future?" *Corporate Computing,* December 1992, pp. 23–24.

Requesting Capital Projects for the Enterprise

A **Capital Project Request Form,** illustrated in Exhibit 22–4, is used by managers of various activities, such as engineering, production, logistics, marketing, and finance, to request approval of capital projects they believe are necessary to support the enterprise. The Capital Project Request Form serves as a trigger for requesting funds for a capital project. Normally, these forms are submitted to upper management for general review and cursory evaluation. The requests are usually submitted two to six months in advance of the final commitment of capital funds, assuming the request is approved by senior management.

The **Requested Capital Projects Report,** shown in Exhibit 22–5, includes a list of capital projects that have been *tentatively* approved by a budget or steering committee. (Such a committee is usually composed of a group of managers who decide which capital projects will be implemented, postponed, or rejected. The committee also oversees capital project development and imple-

CAPITAL PROJECT REQUEST

■■EXHIBIT 22–4
Capital Project
Request Form

Project Name: _____

Dollar Amount Requested: _____

Capital Project Request Number: _____

Purpose of the capital project request

☐ Improve performance ☐ Expansion

☐ Reduce costs ☐ Improve safety

☐ Replacement ☐ Increase sales

☐ Improve quality ☐ Improve security

☐ Other (specify) _____ ☐ Improve customer service

Description of the proposed capital project

Justification of the proposed capital project

Originator: Date:

Approvals

Signature Title Date

■■ EXHIBIT 22–5
**Requested Capital
Projects Report**

Requested Capital Projects Report

Project name	Project number	Dollar amount requested
Riveting robot	124	$ 200,000
Injection mold	176	500,000
Mainframe computer	148	1,000,000
Manufacturing cell for Plant A	127	1,600,000
Fleet of trailer trucks	194	2,000,000
Modernization of Plant B	177	20,800,000
Total capital funds requested		$26,100,000

Approvals

Signature	Title	Date
_____	_____	_____
_____	_____	_____
_____	_____	_____

Note: Capital Project Request Forms are attached.

mentation and resolves conflicts.) This report is supported by individual Capital Project Request Forms. Capital projects are then subjected to further evaluation, as explained in the next section.

ESTIMATING FEASIBILITY, BENEFITS, AND CASH FLOWS

For capital project requests to qualify as candidates for financial analysis, they must achieve acceptable feasibility and benefit factor ratings. The projects that pass this screening process are assigned estimated cash flows necessary for financial analysis.

What Are Feasibility Factors?

What is the feasibility or likelihood of a capital project being a success? Or putting it negatively, what are the risks of failure inherent in a capital project? A thorough analysis of the feasibility factors of a capital project will significantly reduce the chance of failure and unpleasant surprises.

There are four **feasibility factors (TOES):**

- **T**echnical feasibility
- **O**perational feasibility
- **E**conomic feasibility
- **S**chedule feasibility

TECHNICAL FEASIBILITY.   Technical feasibility refers to the likelihood of the capital project working as advertised. Technical feasibility addresses the issue of whether the technical aspects of a proposed capital project are practical and achievable. Usually, technical feasibility is a more critical issue if the technology involved in the capital project is generally new or new to the enterprise. For example, will a new expert maintenance system help the maintenance crew uncover and fix maintenance problems more efficiently? Will the new local area network actually enable the company to replace a costly computer mainframe? Will robots reduce labor costs and improve quality? What about technical obsolescence? Will it occur faster than expected?

OPERATIONAL FEASIBILITY. **Operational feasibility** concerns whether existing procedures and employee skills are sufficient to develop, implement, and operate a proposed capital project. If not, can enough skills be acquired, people trained, and procedural changes made to make a capital project operational? Also, employees affected by a new capital project may be resistant to change. The importance of gaining user buy-in to a proposed capital project should not be underestimated. Users who have bought into a project will make the necessary changes, participate in development and implementation, and undergo disruption in their daily routine to ensure a capital project's success.

ECONOMIC FEASIBILITY. The **economic feasibility** factor raises a fundamental question: Will top management commit sufficient funds to acquire, develop, and implement a particular capital project in view of the competing requirements of other capital projects within the organization? Management typically discovers that the number of capital projects that meet the enterprise's needs exceeds the availability of funds. A new computer-integrated factory may be technically feasible for an enterprise, but top management's ability to support such a project economically may be doubtful.

Economic feasibility is not directly related to financial analysis (treated in the next chapter); that is, how financially attractive a project is. Rather, economic feasibility represents an enterprise's commitment to a capital project and its ability to fund that project. For example, a capital project may be very attractive from every viewpoint, but a company may not have the necessary economic resources available to support it. Or, for a myriad of reasons, top management may not be willing to support the project financially or otherwise. Unless an enterprise has a long-term commitment to acquire, implement, operate, and upgrade a capital project, the chance of its failure is high.

SCHEDULE FEASIBILITY. Any capital project is subject to development and implementation risks. **Schedule feasibility** determines if a proposed capital project will be developed and implemented within a specific timetable. This feasibility factor simply means that a capital project must be implemented by a target date. If not, the capital project will have to be modified or the target date changed. A large portion of Chapter 24 is devoted to methods of keeping a capital project on schedule.

What Are the Benefit Factors?

There are two kinds of **benefit factors:**

- Tangible benefits
- Intangible benefits

TANGIBLE BENEFITS. **Tangible benefits** can be traced directly to a capital project. Such benefits help achieve tactical and operational goals. For example, a new computerized order-entry system may reduce processing costs by 20 percent. Or a new manufacturing cell may reduce scrap and rework costs by 60 percent. Tangible benefits are capable of being appraised at an actual or approximate value.

INTANGIBLE BENEFITS. **Intangible benefits** cannot be easily traced to a capital project. Such benefits help achieve strategic goals, such as improving customer service. Measuring intangible benefits is more difficult than measuring tangible benefits because intangible benefits are not easy to perceive and are generally long term.

Tangible benefits	Intangible benefits
1. Reduce inventory costs	1. Improve delivery and service
2. Reduce labor costs	2. Increase product quality and reliability
3. Reduce scrap and rework costs	3. Improve production performance and lead time
4. Reduce material costs	4. Enhance production flexibility
5. Reduce material handling costs	5. Improve employee safety

EXHIBIT 22–6
Tangible and Intangible Benefits

Together, tangible and intangible benefits ensure that the enterprise will attain its vision and its strategic, tactical, and operational goals. Successful realization of these benefits is essential to ensuring the enterprise's success. Exhibit 22–6 lists a number of benefits most enterprises agree are important and thus strive to achieve, but this list is not exhaustive.

BENEFITS VERSUS COSTS.   Many managers tend to focus on the costs of a capital project rather than on evaluating its benefits, especially the intangible benefits. This tendency often leads to the least-cost decision. The least-cost capital projects, however, may prove to be the most expensive in the long run. The capital budgeting methodology emphasizes that a "benefits first, costs second" project evaluation strategy is more appropriate. Indeed, it is the tangible and intangible benefits of a capital project that provide the enterprise its competitive advantage.

Some authorities believe that intangible benefits cannot be measured financially. For example, they may question how a company can measure the monetary benefit of its investment in a day-care center for its employees' children. Admittedly, placing a monetary value on such benefits is difficult, but it can be done.

Presumably, the day-care center will help reduce absenteeism, employee turnover, and training, which will, in turn, improve production performance. If it can be established that absenteeism, employee turnover, and training are costing the company $5,000,000 annually and that 30 percent of these costs are due to the lack of day-care centers for employees, then a $1,500,000 ($5,000,000 × .30) cost savings can be estimated with a fairly high level of reliability.

Any capital budgeting decision is fraught with uncertainty. The objective of the capital budgeting methodology is to address and reduce this uncertainty in a rational, measured manner. Using the capital budgeting methodology, the day-care center project would be subjected to analysis and measurement, which should lead to elimination of bias, increased commitment throughout the enterprise, appropriate levels of funding, and scheduled implementation. Moreover, after such projects are implemented, audits are performed that help management evaluate the accuracy of the estimated benefits and costs. Knowing that postimplementation audits will be conducted may cause managers to be very careful in making estimates. Further, these postimplementation audits provide information that will help decrease uncertainty and increase capital budgeting skills in the future, resulting in reduced risk of failed projects.

Relating the Size of Capital Projects to Benefit Factors

One approach to determining the benefit factors is to relate the physical and financial size of a capital project under consideration to the benefits it is likely to produce, as illustrated in Exhibit 22–7. An example of a small investment is

■■■EXHIBIT 22–7
Benefits Relative to Capital Project Size

Source: Adapted from Robert A. Howell, ''The Controller's Responsibility in World-Class Manufacturing,'' in *Cost Accounting for the '90s: Responding to Technological Change* (Montvale, N.J.: Institute of Management Accountants, formerly the National Association of Accountants, 1988), p. 161. With permission.

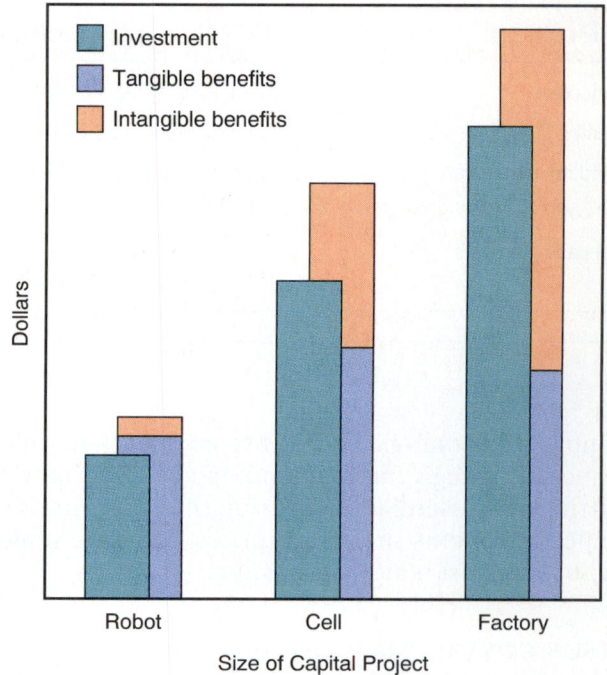

a robot; a mid-size investment would be a manufacturing cell; and a large investment, a total computer-integrated factory. Investments for such capital projects may range from a few hundred thousand dollars to over a billion dollars. For example, Caterpillar is investing $1.5 billion in a worldwide factory modernization program called ''Plant With a Future.''[7]

Generally, a smaller investment, such as the acquisition of a robot, provides mostly tangible benefits. For example, if a robot replaces a worker, the worker's wages and fringe benefits and the reduction in scrap resulting from worker error can be easily calculated.[8]

Normally, a larger capital investment, such as a manufacturing cell, provides a mix of tangible and intangible benefits. For larger, more integrated projects, the tangible and intangible benefits contribute toward increases in revenue as well as reductions in costs.

Relating the Size of Capital Projects to Cash Flows

Cash outflows occur from investment in a capital project and the cost of operating it over some period of time. **Cash inflows** stem from benefit factors. Cash flows, both inflows and outflows, related to capital project size are shown in Exhibit 22–8. Generally, a small capital project pays back relatively quickly. A larger capital project may take ten times longer to produce positive cash flows. Management may therefore be disinclined to make large, long-term investments in capital projects. On the other hand, managers must eventually secure the longer-term capital project investments if they are to stay in business. Such larger capital projects have longer lives, extended periods of returns, and also rely more heavily on intangible benefits.

[7] James A. Hendricks, Robert C. Bastian, and Thomas L. Sexton, ''Bundle Monitoring of Strategic Projects,'' *Management Accounting*, February 1992, p. 31. Reprinted from *Management Accounting.* Copyright by Institute of Management Accountants, Monvale, N.J.

[8] Robert A. Howell and Stephen R. Soucy, ''Capital Investment in the New Manufacturing Environment,'' in *World-Class Accounting for World-Class Manufacturing*, ed. Lamont F. Steedle (Montvale, N.J.: Institute of Management Accountants, formerly the National Association of Accountants, 1990), p. 156. With permission.

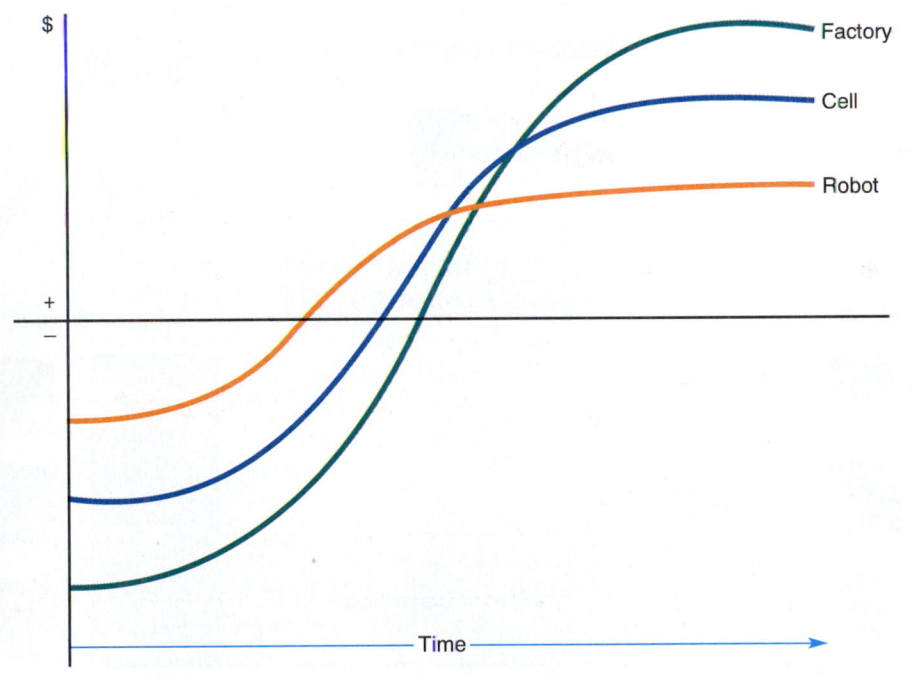

Amount of Incremental Cash Flows Related to Capital Project Size

ELICITING MANAGEMENT JUDGMENTS

To obtain better and more realistic estimates, managers' judgments about capital projects should be elicited in a systematic manner. The goal is to enhance objectivity and downplay subjectivity by translating managers' judgments and instincts into numbers. To perform realistic capital budgeting, the management accountant must be involved in the measurement or estimation of all feasibility factors and tangible and intangible benefits.

Management accountants must be concerned with the ambiguity that may occur whenever numbers are associated with judgment. Otherwise, they get "Garbage in, Garbage out" (GIGO). Nevertheless, in reality, judgment plays a major role in any decision-making process, from awarding gold medals at the Olympics to selecting capital projects for implementation.

Approaches to Gaining Consensus for Capital Projects

When evaluating the merits of capital projects, it is important to gain a consensus of judgments. This can present a difficult problem when people's knowledge and judgments differ. Two approaches can be used to resolve this problem:

- Joint investment decisions (JID) method
- Delphi method

JOINT INVESTMENT DECISIONS METHOD. The **joint investment decisions (JID) method** brings together managers, a facilitator, a scribe, and observers to provide agreed-on judgments. A typical JID layout is shown in Exhibit 22–9. The JID room is a separate room configured specifically for JID sessions. Managers sit at a U-shaped table. Separate tables are provided for the facilitator, scribe, and observers. White boards are used to capture dialogue. Flip charts may also be utilized, and flip chart paper may be hung on walls to keep the session on track and generate discussion. A workstation, or a PC, can capture questionnaire data and display results. The workstation is also used

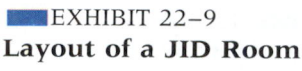

EXHIBIT 22–9
Layout of a JID Room

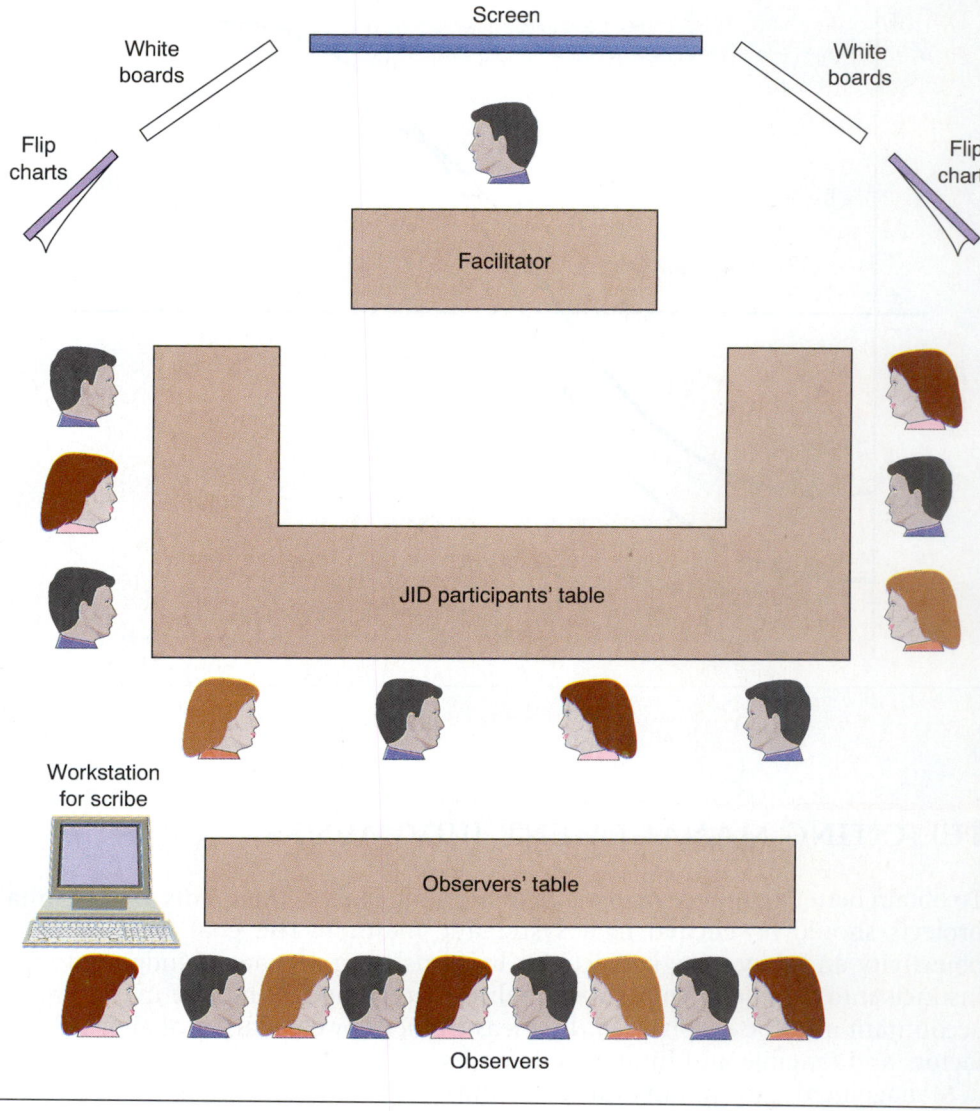

later to run the capital budgeting financial analysis models discussed in the next chapter.

No telephones, beepers, or other means of communicating with the outside world are allowed in the JID room. The objectives are to isolate the participants from day-to-day business activities and to *focus* on capital budgeting. The desirable outcome is a consensus on judgments relative to capital projects.

If managers' judgments differ, they are permitted to make a case for their position in an effort to reach a consensus. In reaching a consensus, managers must also follow established ground rules, such as majority vote or averaging the judgment measures to achieve a single number.

For the JID session to be effective, none of the participants can pull rank, no matter what their authority is outside the JID room. All egos must also be left behind. The facilitator must have the ability to encourage communication among participants, resolve conflicts, and keep the JID session focused. Generally, management accountants who understand group dynamics make good facilitators because they can remain independent and objective. When managers are reluctant to volunteer their judgments, an auction-type procedure may be helpful. The facilitator proposes a judgment value and asks managers to provide feedback.

The scribe's function is to record and document findings of the JID session. The observers serve a consultative role. They are present to answer technical questions that may arise. Examples of observers are equipment operators, engineers, market forecasters, computer experts, and vendor representatives.

JID sessions offer several advantages:

- Judgments are electronically documented, and participants receive immediate feedback.
- Judgments are extracted from multiple managers in parallel.
- Conflicts can be resolved *during* the sessions.
- Interactions among managers and consultants result in enriched understanding and more informed judgments.

At the same time, JID sessions have some disadvantages:

- Groupthink may occur in which participants tend to conform to the opinions prevailing in the group.
- Decision making may be politicized.
- Complete information may not be available during the session.
- Participants may be reluctant to disagree with their supervisors.
- Some participants may become engaged in protracted disagreements.

DELPHI METHOD.   The **Delphi method** employs a panel of managers to provide answers to a series of questionnaires. These questionnaires are used to elicit management judgments about the feasibility and benefits of a capital project under consideration.

Unlike the JID sessions, which are based on an open forum, the Delphi method is based on a closed group process in which people present their arguments and judgments while remaining anonymous. In Delphi, the participants review the questionnaire results and request adjustments without disclosing their identity.

The Delphi method is characterized by the following features:

- Selection of a panel of managers (i.e., experts) to be surveyed
- Anonymity of managers
- Repeated polling of managers with feedback of overall results to each manager after each successive round
- Statistical analysis of the degree of consensus achieved

Managers are chosen based on their expertise in a given field. Anonymity of the managers is maintained by administering the questionnaire to the managers by mail or by phone. In some situations, managers may participate in real-time by interacting via a computer-based network. The managers never meet during the Delphi, and their names are known only to the management accountant conducting the study.

The reason for anonymity is to avoid bias due to peer and superior influence and the "bandwagon" or "groupthink" effect. By maintaining the confidentiality of each participant, the Delphi method enables each participant to communicate more freely, allows more people to participate, and prevents unproductive disagreements.

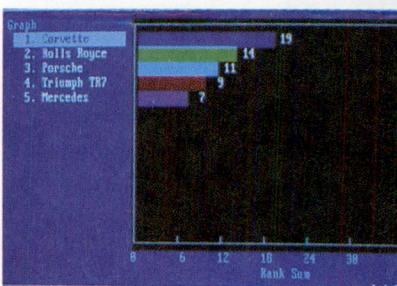

The managers are polled until a consensus is reached. The definition of consensus varies among organizations. The method of determining when the desired degree of agreement has been reached needs to be established before the Delphi process begins, however. For example, a consensus is reached when the majority of managers provide the same input values. In some companies, if a consensus is not reached after three rounds, the capital project under consideration is postponed or abandoned.

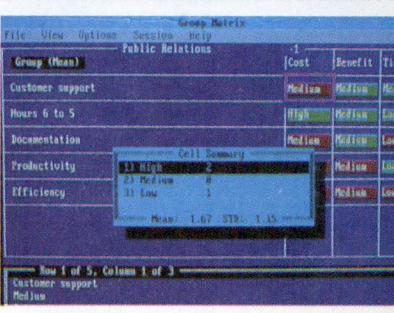

Group Systems V is a PC-based meeting system that enables participants to interact electronically. Courtesy of Ventana Corporation.

GROUP DECISION SUPPORT SYSTEMS.   By using group decision support (GDS) systems, as described in the accompanying *Insights & Applications* on the next page, Boeing has cut the time needed to complete a wide range of team

INSIGHTS & APPLICATIONS

Participants Talk through Keyboards

Group decision support (GDS) systems can support JID and Delphi methods. GDS systems are usually configured in a meeting room with PCs or workstations connected by a local area network. The microcomputers are arranged around a U-shaped table, with a facilitator station and projector screen at the front of the room. The microcomputers are used to provide each participant the ability to:

- Brainstorm
- Vote or provide ratings
- Make requests
- Analyze complaints

Responses can be in an open forum setting like JID, or a closed forum setting like Delphi. However, most responses, especially those involving brainstorming ideas, voting, and ratings, are communicated anonymously. Thus, ideas are more likely to be evaluated based on their merit, independent of the source. Criticism is less likely to be seen as a personal attack. Shy people are less afraid to participate, and extroverts are less able to dominate. By forcing the participants to write their comments, ideas tend to be more concise and more focused. Moreover, cross talk, side talk, and chitchat are reduced.

Management accountants participate in many group decisions, such as strategic planning, operating budgets, capital budgeting, reengineering, quality management, and so forth. GDS systems provide tools that help groups collaborate in these areas.

Vendors of GDS systems (sometimes referred to as "groupware") are Andersen Consulting (*CSTaR*), Collaborative Technologies (*VisionQuest*), Dickson, Anderson, and Associates (*SAMM*), IBM (*TeamFocus*), and Ventana Corporation (*GroupSystems*).[9]

---

projects by an average of 91 percent. Other users, such as IBM, Dell Computer, General Motors, Price Waterhouse, and J. P. Morgan, have also experienced similar results. When one considers that managers spend from 30 percent to more than 70 percent of the day in meetings, GDS systems promise some real savings in time *and* cost. It is probably safe to assume that people who work in industry and academe would gladly welcome a system that can improve the quality and productivity of meetings and move the group closer to the truth and a consensus.

The Feasibility and Benefit Factors Worksheet

Each management accountant must decide which method to use in eliciting management judgments about proposed capital projects. In any case, the objective is to provide a systematic, documented, and fair method for the first stage of the capital budgeting methodology.

Assuming that a consensus (as defined by each organization) is reached in either the JID or Delphi sessions, the results are entered in a **Feasibility and Benefit Factors Worksheet,** as illustrated in Exhibit 22–10. In this case, management is considering a small capital project, such as a robot.

RATING A SMALL CAPITAL PROJECT.   The Feasibility and Benefit Factors Worksheet provides overall feasibility and benefit ratings. For this particular capital project, management believes technical and operational feasibility factors (weighted at 30 and 40 percent, respectively) are more important than economic and schedule feasibility factors (20 and 10 percent), respectively. These relative weights are typical of small capital projects, which normally are less costly than large capital projects and have more predictable implementation schedules.

After the calculations are made, the overall feasibility factors rating is 9.3, which is excellent. Had the overall feasibility rating been lower than, say, 2.0,

A robot at Saturn.

[9] Adapted from Joseph G. Donelan, "Using Electronic Tools to Improve Meetings," *Management Accounting,* March 1993, pp. 42–45. Reprinted from *Management Accounting.* Copyright by Institute of Management Accountants, Monvale, N.J.

■ **EXHIBIT 22–10**
Derivation of Overall Rating of a Small Capital Project Based on Management Judgment

Feasibility and Benefit Factors Worksheet

Feasibility factors	Rating assigned by management	Weight assigned by management according to importance		Weighted value
1. Technical	9	30%		2.7
2. Operational	9	40		3.6
3. Economic	10	20	Overall	2.0
4. Schedule	10	10	feasibility	1.0
		100%	rating	9.3

Benefit factors	Rating assigned by management	Weight assigned by management according to importance		Weighted value
Tangible benefits:				
1. Reduce inventory costs	7	20%		1.4
2. Reduce labor costs	10	20		2.0
3. Reduce scrap and rework costs	9	40		3.6
4. Reduce material costs	8	15		1.2
5. Reduce material handling costs	8	5	Tangible benefit	0.4
		100%	rating	8.6
Intangible benefits:				
1. Improve delivery and service	1	30%		0.3
2. Increase product quality and reliability	8	30		2.4
3. Improve production performance and lead time	5	10		0.5
4. Enhance production flexibility	2	10		0.2
5. Improve employee safety	2	20	Intangible benefit	0.4
		100%	rating	3.8

Benefit category	Rating as determined above	Weight assigned by management to each category		Weighted rating
Tangible benefits	8.6	90%	Overall	7.74
Intangible benefits	3.8	10	benefit	0.38
		100%	rating	8.12

Rating scale is 1 to 10 with 10 as most important or excellent.

management might have decided to reject the capital project at this point and not consider it further. A capital project that has a weak overall feasibility rating will cause problems no matter what benefits and dollar values are assigned to it later.

If a capital project proves to be feasible, management's next step is to rate each benefit factor and assign weights to each benefit according to its importance. The weights assigned to each tangible and intangible benefit factor will normally not change regardless of the size or type of capital project being evaluated. The weighting represents the enterprise's vision, as well as its strategic, tactical, and operational goals.

Once a rating is calculated for both tangible and intangible benefits, both benefit category ratings are weighted. For example, a small capital project, such as a robot, truck, machine, or personal computer, simply does not possess the potential to produce a high level of intangible benefits. Thus, for a small capital project, the tangible benefits category will typically receive a weight of 90 percent or more, while 10 percent or less is assigned to the intangible benefits category. The overall benefit rating for this small capital project is a respectable 8.12 on a scale of 1 to 10, with 10 being most important. This rating means that the small capital project being evaluated in Exhibit 22–10 is a B-grade candidate that has the potential to provide the enterprise with some tactical and operational advantages.

A manufacturing cell at Caterpillar, Inc.

RATING A MID-SIZE CAPITAL PROJECT.   The Feasibility and Benefit Factors Worksheet for a mid-size capital project, shown in Exhibit 22–11, follows the same format as the worksheet for a small capital project. The ratings, however, may be significantly different because the capital project in question is not only different but larger. Economic and schedule feasibility factors are likely to be more important for a mid-size capital project because of its size and longer life. A mid-size capital project is also likely to possess more potential for intangible benefits than a smaller capital project.

In this case, the overall feasibility rating of 6.1 is not particularly strong, a grade of C− at best. Management may question the feasibility of the capital project at this point and reject or postpone it. In the example, management has decided to continue evaluating the project. The tangible benefit rating of 4.6 is not particularly strong, and the intangible benefit rating of 5.4 is moderate. Because a mid-size capital project generally possesses more potential for producing intangible benefits than a small capital project, the intangible benefits receive a weight of 40 percent, compared to 10 percent in Exhibit 22–10, while tangible benefits receive a weight of 60 percent. The overall rating for this mid-size capital project is a moderate 4.92.

A capital resource at Honda of America Manufacturing, Inc.

RATING A LARGE CAPITAL PROJECT.   Investment in large capital projects, such as fully automated factories, can easily exceed $100 million. Some very large projects can exceed $1 billion. The equipment involved is more complex, technically and operationally, than traditional pieces of stand-alone equipment. The benefits associated with such projects are usually more strategic and intangible. Enterprises make these kinds of capital investments to *completely* reengineer the enterprise in an effort to gain a competitive advantage.

The implementation schedule is much longer for large capital projects than for small and mid-size capital projects. GM's Saturn project, for example, required five years to implement. Returns to the enterprise also occur over a longer period of time, in the 10- to 20-year range. Such capital projects are more costly, longer term, and riskier and, therefore, require management's full attention in the analysis and rating process. The Feasibility and Benefit Factors Worksheet, demonstrated in Exhibit 22–12, provides an excellent tool for achieving this goal.

■ EXHIBIT 22–11
Derivation of Overall Rating of a Mid-Size Capital Project Based on Management Judgment

Feasibility and Benefit Factors Worksheet

Feasibility factors	Rating assigned by management	Weight assigned by management according to importance		Weighted value
1. Technical	9	10%		0.9
2. Operational	7	20		1.4
3. Economic	5	40	Overall	2.0
4. Schedule	6	30	feasibility	1.8
		100%	rating	6.1

Benefit factors	Rating assigned by management	Weight assigned by management according to importance		Weighted value
Tangible benefits:				
1. Reduce inventory costs	6	20%		1.2
2. Reduce labor costs	4	20		0.8
3. Reduce scrap and rework costs	4	40		1.6
4. Reduce material costs	4	15		0.6
5. Reduce material handling costs	8	5	Tangible benefit	0.4
		100%	rating	4.6
Intangible benefits:				
1. Improve delivery and service	6	30%		1.8
2. Increase product quality and reliability	5	30		1.5
3. Improve production performance and lead time	4	10		0.4
4. Enhance production flexibility	7	10		0.7
5. Improve employee safety	5	20	Intangible benefit	1.0
		100%	rating	5.4

Benefit category	Rating as determined above	Weight assigned by management to each category		Weighted rating
Tangible benefits	4.6	60%	Overall	2.76
Intangible benefits	5.4	40	benefit	2.16
		100%	rating	4.92

Rating scale is 1 to 10 with 10 as most important or excellent.

■■■ EXHIBIT 22–12

Derivation of Overall Rating of a Large Capital Project Based on Management Judgment

Feasibility and Benefit Factors Worksheet

Feasibility factors	Rating assigned by management	Weight assigned by management according to importance		Weighted value
1. Technical	7	20%		1.4
2. Operational	7	20		1.4
3. Economic	6	40	Overall	2.4
4. Schedule	5	20	feasibility	1.0
		100%	rating	6.2

Benefit factors	Rating assigned by management	Weight assigned by management according to importance		Weighted value
Tangible benefits:				
1. Reduce inventory costs	9	20%		1.8
2. Reduce labor costs	9	20		1.8
3. Reduce scrap and rework costs	9	40		3.6
4. Reduce material costs	8	15		1.2
5. Reduce material handling costs	8	5	Tangible benefit	0.4
		100%	rating	8.8
Intangible benefits:				
1. Improve delivery and service	9	30%		2.7
2. Increase product quality and reliability	9	30		2.7
3. Improve production performance and lead time	10	10		1.0
4. Enhance production flexibility	10	10		1.0
5. Improve employee safety	8	20%	Intangible benefit	1.6
		100%	rating	9.0

Benefit category	Rating as determined above	Weight assigned by management to each category		Weighted rating
Tangible benefits	8.8	40%	Overall	3.52
Intangible benefits	9.0	60	benefit	5.40
		100%	rating	8.92

Rating scale is 1 to 10 with 10 as most important or excellent.

In the worksheet, management has determined from a great deal of analysis that technical and operational feasibility factors should be assigned a rating of 7. Management believes that the technology is viable and that rigorous training programs will develop the skills necessary to make the new capital project operational. Because the cost of a large capital project is not as certain as that for a small capital project, management has rated the economic feasibility factor conservatively. The higher weight assigned to the economic feasibility factor reflects management's concern about the full cost involved. The time required to implement a large capital project is also more uncertain than that of a small capital project. Consequently, the schedule feasibility factor receives a conservative rating and a fairly high weight for a large capital project because management is concerned about the project's schedule for implementation.

The new capital project promises excellent tangible and intangible benefits, which are reflected in the ratings in the worksheet. Because the project has the potential to reap strategic-based benefits, especially those directed toward increasing revenues, the intangible benefit category receives a 60 percent weight, and the tangible benefit category receives a 40 percent weight.

The Prioritization Process

Each capital project is prioritized in accordance with its overall feasibility and benefit rating. This prioritization process is performed using a **priority grid,** as shown in Exhibit 22–13. Based on their overall ratings, capital projects can fall into one of four categories. Those in the low-potential category, with overall feasibility and benefit ratings of less than 2, are not worthy of further consideration and are thereby rejected. Those in the moderate-potential category, with overall feasibility and benefit ratings between 2 and 5, are worthy of further consideration, although they may be postponed until the next fiscal period. In Exhibit 22–13, the mid-size capital project (MS) with an overall feasibility rating of 6.1 and an overall benefit rating of 4.92 is such a project.

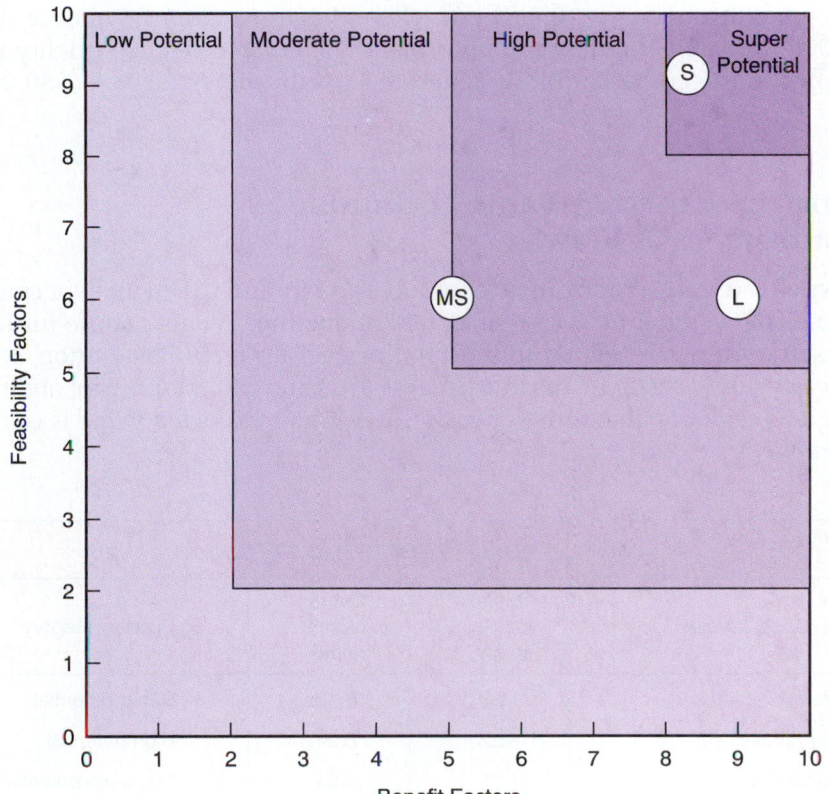

■■■ EXHIBIT 22–13
Priority Grid

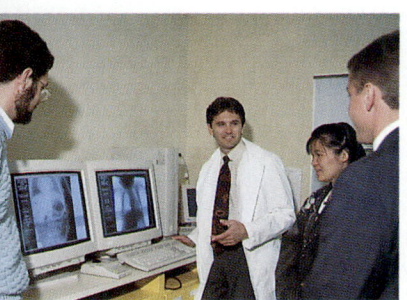

Acquisition of imaging equipment represents capital investments at hospitals.

Capital projects in the high-potential category, with overall feasibility and benefit ratings between 5 and 8, should be given immediate consideration. In Exhibit 22–13, the large capital project (L) with an overall feasibility rating of 6.2 and an overall benefit rating of 8.92 is such a capital project.

Finally, those capital projects that receive overall feasibility and benefit ratings of greater than 8 are also worthy of immediate attention. These are considered superpotential capital projects. In Exhibit 22–13, the small capital project (S) with an overall feasibility rating of 9.3 and an overall benefit rating of 8.12 is such a project.

The **Capital Projects Portfolio Statement,** illustrated in Exhibit 22–14, includes those capital projects that fall into the superpotential, high-potential, and moderate-potential categories. The Capital Projects Portfolio Statement contains the capital projects that have passed a major hurdle of the capital budgeting methodology. After associated cash flow estimates are made, they will be ready for financial analysis, as presented in Chapter 23.

▌ESTIMATING CASH FLOWS

An important part of capital budgeting is estimating the timing (i.e., pattern) and quantity of cash flows for each capital project being considered. Erroneous estimates may result in erroneous decisions regardless of the financial models used in Chapter 23.

Capital projects are supposed to reduce costs or generate revenue, or both. Decreasing costs and increasing revenues produces cash flows. But cash inflows produced by tangible and intangible benefits are difficult to estimate. The goal of the capital budgeting methodology, however, is to be approximately right rather than exactly wrong.

For example, what are the enterprise's current costs for scrap, rework, returns and allowances, field warranties, and quality inspections? In some enterprises, costs of quality may be as high as 30 percent of the cost of goods manufactured. If the annual cost of goods manufactured averages $800,000 and the present costs of quality average 20 percent, then the total costs of quality average $160,000 per year. If a new capital project will cut the costs of quality in half, then the estimated cash inflow generated by the investment is $80,000 per year.

▌Using the Expected Value Technique to Estimate Cash Flows

The **expected value technique** computes an amount called an expected value of a series of events. In the case of capital budgeting, events are the future cash inflows and outflows related to a capital project under consideration. Because these cash flows occur in the future and are thus uncertain, probabilities are assigned to each possible series of cash flows. Their expected value is calculated in three steps:

▌ EXHIBIT 22–14
Capital Projects Portfolio Statement

Capital project	Overall feasibility rating	Overall benefit rating	Priority category
Small project (S)	9.3	8.12	Super potential
Large project (L)	6.2	8.92	High potential
Mid-size project (MS)	6.1	4.92	Moderate potential

CAPITAL PROJECTS PORTFOLIO STATEMENT

- A probability is assigned to each event with the probabilities summing to 1.00.
- The weighted value of each event is computed by multiplying the value of each event by its corresponding probability.
- These products are summed to obtain the expected value of a series of events.

An example of how the expected value technique is applied is presented in Exhibit 22–15. Management is considering acquiring an electronic data interchange (EDI) system as part of its new integrated computer-based information system (ICBIS). After a great deal of analysis of both tangible and intangible benefits, management determines that the new capital project will both increase revenues and reduce costs. The total expected value of annual cash inflows from this project is estimated to be $536,000 ($126,000 increased revenues + $410,000 reduced costs).

The required capital investment outlay for the EDI system is $2,100,000. It is estimated that a major upgrade will not be needed for four years. Is the EDI project financially attractive? The methodology for answering this question is presented in the next chapter.

The Cash Flow Estimate Form

The **Cash Flow Estimate Form,** illustrated in Exhibit 22–16, is used to record and document cash flow data for the ICBIS. These data are used to perform financial analysis. Later, if the ICBIS is implemented, the form is used as a major document in conducting a postimplementation audit (the subject of Chapter 24) to determine how close the estimates were to actual values.

The emphasis in this chapter has been on estimating cash inflows that are generated by benefits of the capital project. Cash outflows occur because of the investment outlay and operating costs. Usually, the investment outlay can be calculated with a high degree of accuracy. The estimation of investment and operating costs has been addressed in other chapters (see Chapters 5, 7, and 14) and therefore will not be repeated in this chapter.

Increase in revenue	Probability of occurrence		Weighted value
$ 40,000	.05		$ 2,000
80,000	.20		16,000
120,000	.40		48,000
160,000	.25		40,000
200,000	.10		20,000
	1.00	Expected value	$126,000

Decrease in costs	Probability of occurrence		Weighted value
$100,000	.05		$ 5,000
200,000	.10		20,000
300,000	.15		45,000
400,000	.30		120,000
500,000	.20		100,000
600,000	.20		120,000
	1.00	Expected value	$410,000

	$126,000
	410,000
Total expected annual cash inflows from EDI systems project	$536,000

EXHIBIT 22–15
Estimating Cash Flows of EDI Systems Project

INSIGHTS & APPLICATIONS

Using Fuzzy Data to Make Estimates

In making capital project investment decisions, decision makers attempt to make trade-offs between expected return on investment and risk. These decision problems are characteristically complex. It is almost impossible for any decision maker to take full account of all the factors impinging on the decision simultaneously. It would be useful to find some way to consider explicitly both the preference structure of the decision makers and the uncertainties that characterize the investment situation. The use of probabilities and artificial intelligence not only provide quantitative measurements, but also capture the psychological preferences and risk attitudes of the decision makers.

FuziCalc (FuziWare, Inc., in Knoxville, Tennessee) is a hybrid spreadsheet and artificial intelligence engine that enables users to handle "fuzzy" (ambiguous) data and probabilities. With FuziCalc, users input "hard" numbers (e.g., last year's shoe sales) just as they would do in any other spreadsheet. FuziCalc also allows users to input fuzzy numbers (e.g., a range of probabilities of forthcoming shoe sales). After these numbers are entered, users can adjust them according to their beliefs and run what-if analyses. Once a consensus is reached, the spreadsheet component displays the values, such as estimated cash flows.[10]

[10] Adapted from Marc Ferranti, "Startup Tackles 'Fuzzy' Data," *PC Week*, May 3, 1993, pp. 40 and 46.

■ EXHIBIT 22–16
Cash Flow Estimate Form

Cash Flow Estimate Form				
Project name: ICBIS			Date: MM/DD/YY	
Estimators:		Name		Title
	Harry Cowan		Chief information officer (CIO)	
	Margaret Sherer		Management accountant	
	Marc Higgins		Systems analyst	
	Steve Ferranti		Manager of logistics	
	Krishna Mani		Financial accountant	

Investment outlay	Estimated	Actual	Variance
Initial cost	$5,000,000		
Sales tax	10,000		
Freight	20,000		
Installation	400,000		
Training	200,000		
Working capital	200,000		
Test runs	100,000		
Subtotal	$5,930,000		
Less trade in	<100,000>		
Total investment	$5,830,000		

Project's estimated cash flow	Period			
	1	2	3	4
Cash inflow	$ 2,000,000	$3,000,000	$4,000,000	$5,000,000
Cash outflow:				
Investment outlay	< 5,830,000>			
Operating costs	< 1,000,000>	< 1,200,000>	< 1,400,000>	< 1,600,000>
Estimated net cash flow	<$4,830,000>	$1,800,000	$2,600,000	$3,400,000

INSIGHTS & APPLICATIONS

Building a Vision

Without strategic information systems planning, an enterprise is prone to develop systems that are not goal-congruent. Insufficient methods of setting priorities for proposed systems projects, inappropriate allocation of resources, and unrealistic schedules contribute to the problem. Companies that don't perform strategic information systems planning can usually be recognized by their inability to meet schedules and budget targets, lack of project status awareness by workers and managers, and frequent duplication of effort.

Further, a truism in management is: If you don't plan a project, you will never be able to control it.

Without a vision and strategy, an enterprise can incur unnecessary costs and time delays in planning new capital projects, such as information systems. One company looked at support costs, throughput, customer support, and even workflow issues. Yet, despite such thorough analysis, the system failed. Why? The organization attempted to build the information system on those factors individually. In other words, there was no comprehensive vision and strategy for what was needed.

Another company, on the verge of producing significant new product lines, also needed a new information system. Unfortunately, politics got in the way of good systems planning and design and the end results were time delays, unwanted overlaps, and mass confusion.[11]

Because cash flows cannot be estimated with absolute certainty, managers responsible for capital budgeting decisions should be aware of the limitations and risks associated with using the cash flow estimates recorded in the Cash Flow Estimate Form. Managers are more likely to recognize these limitations if they are involved in the first stage of the capital budgeting methodology. Managers can also improve their estimating skills by studying the comparisons of actual costs and estimates supplied by postimplementation audits. This feedback can help managers make better estimates for future projects. Further, feedback from postimplementation audits will often point out the need for a coordinated vision and strategy, as declared in the above *Insights & Applications.*

SUMMARY OF LEARNING OBJECTIVES

The major goals of this chapter were to enable you to achieve three learning objectives:

Learning objective 1.   Explain capital budgeting and define the capital budgeting methodology and list its stages.

Correct capital budgeting decisions are vital to an enterprise's success. An enterprise that postpones these decisions will usually be unable to compete effectively.

The capital budgeting methodology is a four-stage cycle that enables management to make critical capital budgeting decisions in a systematic and coordinated fashion. It involves the following stages:

■ Planning capital projects and estimating key variables
■ Performing financial analysis of each candidate capital project
■ Scheduling, controlling, and managing development and implementation of each capital project
■ Conducting a postimplementation audit of each capital project

Learning objective 2.   Describe how planning for capital projects should be conducted.

An enterprise should make sure its "house is in order" before it considers any capital projects. To put its "house in order," the enterprise should establish a vision and strategic plan. The enterprise should be redesigned and reengineered to achieve the vision and ensure that strategic, tactical, and operational goals are met.

---

[11] Adapted from Hugh Ryan and John Santucci, "Building an Enterprise Information Architecture," *Infoworld,* March 22, 1993, pp. 57–60. The authors are partners with Andersen Consulting in Chicago.

Managers throughout the enterprise submit Capital Project Request Forms, which describe capital projects that the requesters believe support the enterprise's vision, redesign, and goals. Capital projects that are tentatively approved are included in a Requested Capital Projects Report.

Learning objective 3.   Discuss why and how feasibility, benefits, and cash flows are estimated.

Are the capital projects listed in the Requested Capital Projects Report feasible from a technical, operational, economic, and schedule viewpoint? Do the capital projects hold promise of producing tangible and intangible benefits? What are the cash flows relative to each capital project? Management's involvement helps to answer these questions.

Management judgments represent key elements in the planning stage. Two methods are commonly used to elicit these judgments:

- Joint investment decisions (JID) method
- Delphi method

Either method may be supported by a GDS system.

The JID method uses an open forum and group dynamics while the Delphi method uses anonymity to elicit management judgments. The Feasibility and Benefit Factors Worksheet is used to quantify and document these judgments. Associated with the worksheet is a priority grid that allows management to quickly visualize the potential of each capital project under consideration. Those capital projects that fall into the superpotential, high-potential, and moderate-potential categories are included in a Capital Projects Portfolio Statement.

Cash inflows stem from benefits. Normally, the greater the benefits, the greater the cash inflows. After subjecting capital projects to a systematic, rigorous evaluation, management will gain a great deal of knowledge about the benefits of each project. Consequently, management is able to assign probabilities for the expected value of cash inflows due to the benefits anticipated over the life of each capital project.

Cash outflows are incurred to acquire and operate the capital project over its life. Cost-estimating techniques covered in other chapters help determine these cash outflows.

The Cash Flow Estimate Form is used to record the estimated cash flow data. These cash flow data are the key elements used in performing financial analysis, the second stage of the capital budgeting methodology. The Cash Flow Estimate Form is also used to compare estimated cash flow data with actual cash flow data *after* the capital project is implemented.

IMPORTANT TERMS

Benefit factors   Include both tangible and intangible benefits that measure the level of potential usefulness of capital projects.

Capital budgeting   A process of allocating or rationing funds for one or a mix of capital projects.

Capital budgeting methodology   A four-stage cycle involving: (1) planning capital projects and estimating key variables, (2) performing financial analysis of each candidate capital project, (3) scheduling, controlling, and managing development and implementation of each capital project, and (4) conducting a postimplementation audit of each capital project.

Capital investments   Outlays of the enterprise's capital funds to yield benefits in future years.

Capital project   An asset or undertaking that is used to generate revenues or cost savings by providing benefits for more than one year.

Capital Projects Portfolio Statement   A document that lists the capital projects that fall into the superpotential, high-potential, and moderate-potential categories.

Capital Project Request Form   A document that enables managers to request capital projects that they believe will support the vision, redesign, and goals of the enterprise.

Cash Flow Estimate Form   A document that is used to record cash flow data assigned to each capital project.

Cash inflows   A stream or pattern of cash receipts flowing into an enterprise that are generated from benefits produced by a capital project.

Cash outflows   A stream or pattern of expenditures flowing out of an enterprise that are incurred for the acquisition and operation of a capital project.

Delphi method   A technique that uses an anonymous iterative process to elicit judgments from a panel of managers in order to obtain a consensus.

Economic feasibility   Refers to the likelihood that the capital project will be supported with the necessary capital funds.

Expected value technique   Measures the average value that would result from events in a distribution. It produces a sum of values weighted by the events' probabilities.

Feasibility and Benefit Factors Worksheet   A document that records estimates of the feasibility and benefits of a capital project.

Feasibility factors (TOES)   Four elements that measure the likelihood that a capital project will be implemented successfully. The feasibility factors are technical, operational, economic, and schedule.

Intangible benefits   Benefits that are difficult to trace directly to a capital project and are also difficult to measure with a high degree of accuracy.

Joint investment decisions (JID) method   A technique used to involve managers and specialists in the capital budgeting methodology. The JID method is especially useful in eliciting management judgments and reaching a consensus in an open forum.

Moving baseline   Shows how an enterprise's business conditions will change if it decides not to invest in capital projects and tries instead to maintain the status quo.

Operational feasibility   Indicates the likelihood that existing procedures and employee skills are sufficient to implement and make functional a capital project; if not, the environment can be changed to make the capital project functional.

Priority grid   A visual display of the priority ratings of all capital projects under consideration. It is divided into low-potential, moderate-potential, high-potential, and superpotential areas.

Requested Capital Projects Report   A document that lists all capital projects that have passed a preliminary, cursory evaluation.

Schedule feasibility   Refers to the likelihood that a capital project will be implemented within a predetermined time frame.

Tangible benefits   Benefits that are traced directly to a capital project and help achieve tactical and operational goals.

Technical feasibility   Refers to the likelihood that a capital project will work in accordance with certain mechanical, electrical, or design specifications.

▌DEMONSTRATION PROBLEMS

■ DEMONSTRATION PROBLEM 1   *Priortizing projects and estimating cash flows.*

Participants in a GDS system are considering three information system capital projects:

A. A cellular-based digital messaging system
B. An online payroll timekeeping system
C. An electronic data interchange (EDI) system

At the conclusion of the GDS system session, the following consensus was reached:

REQUESTED CAPITAL PROJECT	FEASIBILITY FACTORS				OVERALL FEASIBILITY FACTORS SCORE	BENEFITS		OVERALL BENEFIT FACTORS SCORE
	TECHNICAL	OPERATIONAL	ECONOMIC	SCHEDULE		TANGIBLE BENEFITS	INTANGIBLE BENEFITS	
A	7	1	1	7	4.0	2	1	1.5
B	9	6	9	8	8.0	9	5	7.0
C	8	6	8	6	7.0	9	9	9.0

The team members did not provide weights for individual factors as was done in the chapter. They felt that all factors should be weighted equally.

The attitudes and reasoning behind the ratings (also called votes in some GDS or groupware systems) include the following:

■ Although cellular-based messaging technology is feasible, the team members were uncomfortable with technology that transmits sensitive messages over the airwaves, which are subject to interception by unauthorized people. Encryption methods can be used, but the group was not convinced that this technology would be reliable and efficient. Economic commitment was spotty. Operationally, some people said that they would not carry the message transmitting and receiving device with them. They also indicated that such a system might be an invasion of privacy. The implementation schedule seemed reasonable, and the vendor gave assurances that the system would be implemented on time. The group, however, did not perceive any significant benefits. A few members thought that some slight gains in productivity would occur because of a decrease in the number of memos currently being generated.

■ The technology for online payroll timekeeping systems is relatively mature. Moreover, it has proven its reliability in a wide variety of enterprises. All the participants are strongly committed to its implementation, especially those people at the supervisory level who are currently wasting time preparing time sheets. To make the system operational, several short training sessions will have to be conducted. The vendor has installed a large number of systems. According to a survey of the vendor's clients, implementation occurred within a week to ten days of the target completion date.

The team members believed that the benefits of the project would spring primarily from reducing the amount of paperwork, errors, and input bottlenecks. Also, they thought that the timely capture of data would improve employee scheduling, cost accounting, and performance evaluation.

■ The technology for EDI is evolving, but it has proven to be reliable in a large number of companies, some of which have been using EDI for years. There is strong commitment by upper management to provide the funds necessary for the project's implementation. To make the system operational, comprehensive training programs will have to be developed. Moreover, all personnel will have to accept a new way of doing business. Evidence about meeting implementation schedules was spotty, but several vendors offer a "time is of the essence" clause in their sales agreements and substantial compensation for not meeting a stated schedule.

Management is convinced of the strategic value of EDI. A large portion of the team members were confident that the new system would produce substantial tangible and intangible benefits.

Another session was held to analyze further benefits of the EDI system. This session produced the following results:

BENEFITS	DECREASE IN COSTS	INCREASE IN REVENUE	PROBABILITY OF OCCURRENCE
Tangible benefits:			
Increased productivity	$ 500,000		.2
	800,000		.5
	1,400,000		.3
Increased throughput		$2,000,000	.1
		3,000,000	.2
		4,000,000	.7
Intangible benefit:		$1,000,000	.2
Service differentiation		2,000,000	.2
		3,000,000	.6

The EDI system is expected to have a useful life of five years before a major upgrade will be needed. The above data represent one year. The data for each year over the five-year period are the same.

Required:
a. Prepare a priority grid.
b. Calculate the expected cash inflow per year for the EDI project.

SOLUTION TO DEMONSTRATION PROBLEM 1

a.

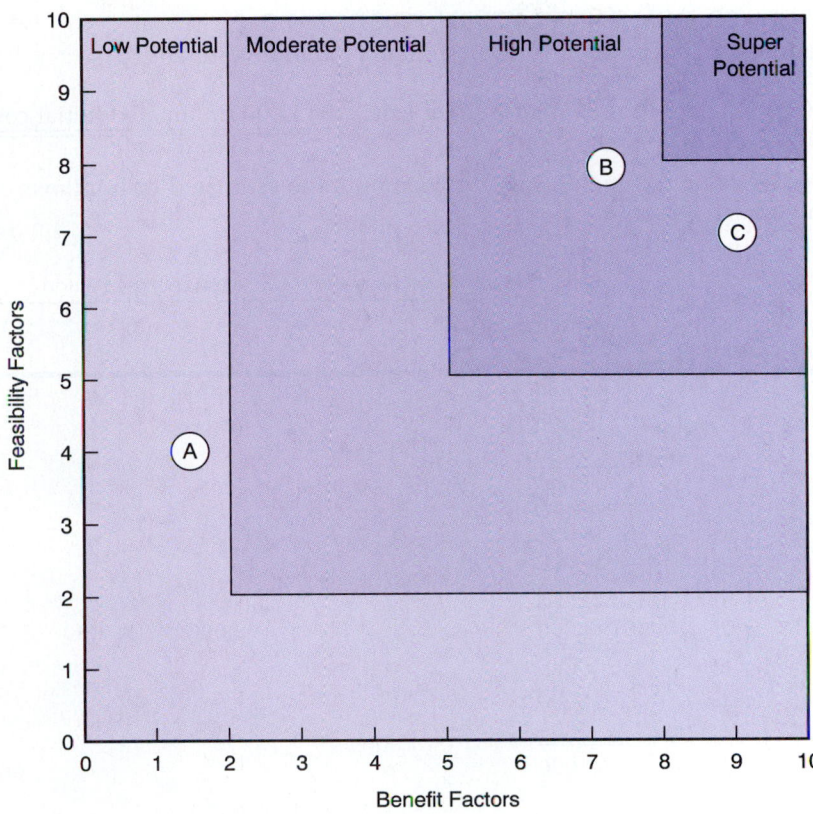

b.

BENEFITS	DECREASE IN COSTS	INCREASE IN REVENUE	PROBABILITY OF OCCURRENCE	WEIGHTED VALUE
Increased productivity	$ 500,000		.2	$ 100,000
	800,000		.5	400,000
	1,400,000		.3	420,000
Increased throughput		$2,000,000	.1	200,000
		3,000,000	.2	600,000
		4,000,000	.7	2,800,000
Service differentiation		1,000,000	.2	200,000
		2,000,000	.2	400,000
		3,000,000	.6	1,800,000
Expected cash inflow annually				$6,920,000

■ **DEMONSTRATION PROBLEM 2** *Expected value of building a new branch bank.*
First Interstate Bank is considering a capital project request to build a branch bank in the southwestern section of the city. The branch bank will occupy 5,000 square feet of floor space, and the cost estimating parameter is $87 per square foot. The useful life of the branch bank is five years before a major renovation will be needed.

 Estimated range of cash inflows for years 1 and 2 is $80,000, $60,000, and $30,000. Each value in this range has assigned probabilities of occurrence of .3, .5, and .2, respectively. For years 3 and 4, the estimated range of cash inflows is $290,000, $180,000, and $60,000 with assigned probabilities of occurrence of .2, .7, and .1, respectively. For year 5, the estimated range of cash inflows is $90,000, $70,000, and $40,000 with assigned probabilities of .2, .6, and .2, respectively.

Required:
Calculate the estimated initial investment and expected cash inflows for the branch bank capital project.

SOLUTION TO DEMONSTRATION PROBLEM 2
Using parametric cost estimating, the estimated initial investment is:

$87 per square foot $\times$ 5,000 square feet = $435,000 estimated initial cost

The expected value technique is used to compute the estimated cash inflows over the life of the branch bank:

RANGE OF ESTIMATED CASH INFLOWS	PROBABILITY OF OCCURRENCE	EXPECTED VALUE	ESTIMATED CASH INFLOW PER PERIOD				
			YEAR 1	YEAR 2	YEAR 3	YEAR 4	YEAR 5
$ 80,000	.3	$ 24,000					
60,000	.5	30,000					
30,000	.2	6,000					
Expected value for years 1 and 2		$ 60,000	60,000	60,000			
$290,000	.2	$ 58,000					
180,000	.7	126,000					
60,000	.1	6,000					
Expected value for years 3 and 4		$190,000			190,000	190,000	
$ 90,000	.2	$ 18,000					
70,000	.6	42,000					
40,000	.2	8,000					
Expected value for year 5		$ 68,000					68,000

❙ REVIEW QUESTIONS

22.1 What are capital projects? Explain the purpose of capital projects.

22.2 Capital budgeting (select all that apply):

a. is a process used to select a mix of projects.
b. assists managers in planning for acquisition of a capital asset.
c. rations funds.
d. is performed only by senior management.

22.3 Why should managers develop capital budgets?

22.4 Which of the following are capital budgeting decisions?

a. The purchase of ongoing supplies.
b. Implementation of JIT purchasing.
c. Continued enforcement of safety programs.
d. Replacement of worn equipment.

22.5 What are the three categories of capital projects?

22.6 Discuss how capital budgeting is linked to an enterprise's vision, mission statement, and strategic plan.

22.7 Reengineering corporate activities is an example of which category of capital projects?

22.8 What does the moving baseline illustrate? "We can avoid investing in capital projects and still maintain the status quo." Comment on this statement, including a reference to the moving baseline.

22.9 Why are capital budgeting decisions becoming more and more difficult?

22.10 What are the stages of the capital budgeting methodology?

22.11 In which stage of the capital budgeting methodology would one expect to develop cash flow estimates?

22.12 What is the purpose of the third stage (scheduling, controlling, and managing development and implementation of each capital project) of the capital budgeting methodology?

22.13 What is the first step in any capital budgeting decision?

22.14 Explain how ''fire-ready-aim'' and ''ready-aim-fire'' pertain to capital budgeting.

22.15 Why use a Capital Project Request Form?

22.16 What are five possible purposes for capital projects?

22.17 What are the four capital project feasibility factors? Explain their role in the capital budgeting methodology.

22.18 A company's ability and commitment to fund a capital project is an example of which capital budget feasibility factor?

22.19 When evaluating the capital budget from a schedule feasibility factor perspective, what does one hope to determine?

22.20 Explain the role that benefit factors play in the capital budgeting methodology.

22.21 Which of the following are tangible benefits?

    a. Reduced labor costs.
    b. Improved production flexibility.
    c. Increased product quality.
    d. Better delivery.
    e. Lower material costs.

22.22 Explain why the expected value technique is used to estimate cash flows.

22.23 ''The effectiveness of the capital budgeting methodology is questionable because predicting future cash inflows is often difficult and full of uncertainties.'' Do you agree with this statement? Explain why or why not.

22.24 What effect does the size of capital projects have on the capital budgeting methodology?

22.25 Define the joint investment decisions (JID) method and explain how it is used in the capital budgeting methodology.

22.26 Define the Delphi method and explain how it is used in the capital budgeting methodology.

22.27 Define group decision support (GDS) systems and explain how they are used in the capital budgeting methodology.

22.28 Explain the use of the Feasibility and Benefit Factors Worksheet.

22.29 Explain why capital projects of different sizes may be rated and scored differently.

22.30 Explain the purpose of a priority grid.

22.31 Define the Capital Projects Portfolio Statement and explain its purpose. If a capital project is listed in the statement, does that mean it has been accepted for implementation?

22.32 Explain how cash flows are estimated.

22.33 Define the Cash Flow Estimate Form and explain its purpose. Also, discuss how it is used during the postimplementation audit.

CHAPTER-SPECIFIC PROBLEMS

These problems require responses based directly on concepts and techniques presented in the text.

22.34 *Types of capital projects.* Following are some specific capital projects:

_____	Installation of smokestack scrubbers required by the Environmental Protection Agency (EPA).
_____	Development of facilities to accommodate the handicapped.
_____	Implementation of a fiber-optic telecommunications backbone to support reengineering of corporate activities.
_____	Implementation of a U-shaped manufacturing cell. The old manufacturing processes were set up in a sequential manner.
_____	Acquisition of a fleet of new trucks to replace the old fleet.

Required:

In the space provided, indicate the category into which each capital project falls: meeting legal and social responsibilities, replacing a present capital asset, or improving the strategic ability of the enterprise.

22.35 *Determining TOES feasibility and benefit factors.* Review the following random statements:

_____	We will be able to beat the competition by providing our customers with online tracking of their orders.
_____	At the present time, senior management is not willing to commit funds for the development of a new parking facility.
_____	This kind of equipment is too complex and sophisticated for our employees.
_____	The system will eliminate the need for data-entry clerks and reduce paperwork.
_____	We cannot wait a year for the project's implementation. We need it to be completed within six months.
_____	This project will be supported by technology that is the first release of the vendor.
_____	The new network will require the interconnection of disparate LANs.
_____	The new day-care center will increase employee morale.
_____	The new building will be designed by a top architect, and that will enhance the company's image.
_____	The new inventory management system will reduce inventory holding costs by 30% annually.

Required:

Indicate whether each statement illustrates a feasibility factor or a tangible or intangible benefit by inserting the appropriate letter in the space provided:

Technical feasibility factor	T
Operational feasibility factor	O
Economic feasibility factor	E
Schedule feasibility factor	S
Tangible benefit	TB
Intangible benefit	ITB

22.36 *Determining tangible and intangible factors.* Keith Howard, management accountant at Genco Engineering, has recently been assigned to develop a Feasibility and Benefit Factors Worksheet. Following is a list of benefit factors that Keith has compiled:

_____	Reduce inventory holding costs.
_____	Increase employee safety.
_____	Lower scrap and rework levels.
_____	Improve delivery and customer service.
_____	Reduce indirect labor costs.
_____	Improve quality of raw materials.
_____	Reduce production lead time.
_____	Improve timeliness of information for management decision making.
_____	Improve communications with vendors.

Required:

In the space provided, indicate whether each factor is a tangible (T) or intangible (I) benefit.

22.37 *Implementing group dynamics.* The study of how people interact in a group setting is called group dynamics. Group dynamics is becoming an important part of modern management accountants' expertise as they become a more and more integral part of the management team. Management accountants need to be able to harness the dynamics of groups in enterprises effectively because groups of people affect the success of many endeavors, such as capital budgeting.

Required:

Two major methods used to improve the effectiveness of group planning and decision making are the JID and Delphi methods. Describe both methods and identify how each can enhance the effectiveness of capital budgeting planning and decision making. Also, discuss how group decision support (GDS) systems facilitate each method.

22.38 *Using the Delphi method.* Kristy Paulsen, project leader for the Frud Cookie Company, is having a problem with cookie consistency. The test batch process worked great—the cookies did not break apart (spoilage) as they were packaged and taste tests exceeded expectations. However, now that the cookies are being produced on a conveyor system, there is a high percentage of spoilage. Kristy asks for your help, knowing that you have worked in several of the company's facilities and know many of the company's experts as well as being familiar with the corporate games. You decide that the best method to assist Kristy is to employ the Delphi method.

Required:
a. Explain the major features of the Delphi method.
b. Explain how the Delphi method avoids the "bandwagon effect."
c. Describe four drawbacks of the Delphi method.
d. Describe four benefits of the Delphi method.

22.39 *Expected value technique.* Buck Andrews has been a top performing sales representative for Corvas Company over the past eight years. John, the district sales manager, asks Buck how he is able to maintain consistently high performance. Buck replies, "Well, I always concentrate my sales efforts on those projects that have the best expected value, developing those projects that have potential for return and dropping projects with little or no return." Buck provides the following example projects:

	PROJECTS	POTENTIAL SALES AMOUNT	BUCK'S ESTIMATE OF SALES SUCCESS
A	Piroc Company	$ 25,000	70%
B	Bill Farmer	72,000	40
C	Delf, Inc.	53,000	55
D	Johnson, Ltd.	125,000	15
E	Comlo	18,000	85

Required:
a. Rank these projects in order of maximum expected value.
b. If you had to select two projects to pursue, using the expected value technique, which projects would you select?

22.40 *Using the JID method.* As a management accountant for Freeway Hydroponics, you suggest to Fred Freeway, the owner, that the company implement the JID method as a way to evaluate the various capital improvement projects the company is considering.

Required:
Fred Freeway asks you to:
a. Provide a sketch of the JID room.
b. Describe the layout of the JID room.
c. Explain the JID process.

Fred also asks you to:
d. Explain how you would develop JID method ground rules.
e. Explain how you would enforce the established ground rules.

THINK-TANK PROBLEMS

Although these problems are based on chapter material, reading extra material, reviewing previous chapters, and using creativity may be required to develop workable solutions.

22.41 *Applying the expected value technique.* Exquisite Foods, Inc. (EFI) sells premium foods to the middle-class market. Three independent marketing strategies are being considered to promote a new product, *Souffles for Microwaves,* to dual-career families. EFI's policy for promoting new products permits only one type of advertising campaign until the product is established.

■ *Strategy 1.* The first strategy concentrates on television and magazine advertising. EFI would hire a marketing consultant to prepare a 30-second video commercial and a magazine advertisement. The commercial would air during the evening to address the working market, while the magazine advertisement would be placed in magazines read by career-minded individuals. This advertising campaign would provide EFI with a $430,000 expected contribution from sales.

■ *Strategy 2.* This strategy promotes the product by offering $0.25 coupons in the Sunday newspaper supplements, with a projected 15% redemption rate on circulation of 1,000,000. EFI would hire a marketing consultant for $5,000 to design a one-quarter page, two-color coupon advertisement. The coupon would be distributed in the Sunday newspaper supplements at a cost of $205,000. Based on prior experience, EFI expects the following additional sales from this form of advertisement:

EXPECTED SALES	PROBABILITY
$500,000	10%
600,000	25
700,000	35
800,000	20
900,000	10

■ *Strategy 3.* This strategy involves offering a $0.50 mail-in rebate coupon attached to each box of *Souffles for Microwaves.* EFI would hire a marketing consultant for $5,000 to create a one-sixth page, one-color rebate coupon. Printing and attaching costs for the rebate coupon are $0.07 per package, and EFI is planning to include the rebate offer on 500,000 packages. Although 500,000 packages may be sold, only a 10% redemption rate is expected. EFI expects the following additional sales from this type of promotion:

EXPECTED SALES	PROBABILITY
$400,000	10%
450,000	30
500,000	35
550,000	20
600,000	5

Required:

a. EFI wishes to select the most profitable marketing alternative to promote *Souffles for Microwaves.* Recommend which of the three strategies EFI should adopt. Support your recommendation with appropriate calculations and analysis.

b. What selection criteria, other than profitability, should be considered in arriving at a decision on the choice of promotion alternatives?

[CMA adapted]

22.42 *The problem of trying to achieve interrelated goals.* Duval, Inc., is a large publicly held corporation whose product is well known throughout the United States. The corporation has always had good profit margins and excellent earnings. However, Duval has experienced a leveling of sales and a reduced market share in the past two years, resulting in a stabilization of profits rather than growth. Despite these trends, the firm has maintained an excellent cash and short-term investment position. The president has called a meeting of the treasurer and the vice presidents for sales and production to develop alternative strategies for improving Duval's performance. The four individuals form the nucleus of a well-organized management team that has worked together for several years to bring success to Duval.

The sales vice president suggests that sales levels can be improved by presenting the company's product in a more attractive and appealing package. He also recommends that advertising be increased and that the current price be maintained. This latter step would have the effect of a price decrease because the prices of most other competing products are rising.

The treasurer is skeptical of maintaining the present price when others are increasing prices, since this will curtail revenues unless this policy provides a competitive advantage. She also points out that the repackaging will increase costs at least in the near future because of the start-up costs of the new packing process. She does not favor increasing advertising outright because she is doubtful of the short-run benefit.

The sales vice president replies that increased, or at least redirected, advertising is necessary to promote the price stability and to take advantage of the new packaging; the combination would provide the company with a competitive advantage. The president adds that the advertising to be used—television, radio, newspaper, magazine—should be studied closely to determine which would be cost-effective. In addition, if television is used, attention must be directed to the type of programs to be sponsored—children's, family, sporting events, news specials, and so on.

The production vice president suggests several possible production improvements, such as a systems study of the manufacturing process to identify changes in the work flow that would cut costs. He suggests operating costs could be further reduced by the purchase of new equipment. The product could be improved by employing a better grade of raw materials and by engineering changes in the fabrication of the product. When queried by the president on the impact of the proposed changes, the production vice president indicated that the primary benefit would be product performance, but that appearance and safety would also be improved. The sales vice president and treasurer commented that this would result in increased sales.

The treasurer notes that all of the production proposals would increase costs, and this could result in lower profits. If profit performance is going to be improved, the price structure should be examined closely. She recommends that the current level of capital expenditures be maintained unless substantial cost savings can be obtained.

The treasurer further believes that expenditures for research and development should be decreased since previous outlays have not prevented a decrease in Duval's share of the market. The production vice president agrees that the research and development activities have not proven profitable, but thinks that this is because the research effort was applied in the wrong area. The sales vice president cautions against any drastic reductions because the packaging change will only provide a temporary advantage in the market; consequently, more effort will have to be devoted to product development.

Focusing on the use of liquid assets and the present high yield on securities, the treasurer suggests that the firm's profitability can be improved by shifting funds from the currently held short-term marketable securities to longer-term, higher-yield securities. She also points out that cost reductions would provide more funds for investments. She recognizes that the restructuring of the investments from short term to long term would hamper flexibility.

In his summarizing comments, the president observes that they have a good start and the ideas provide some excellent alternatives. He states, "I think we ought to develop these ideas further and consider other ramifications. For instance, what effect would new equipment and the systems study have on the labor force? Shouldn't we also consider the environmental impact of any plant and product change? We want to appear as a leader in our industry—not a follower.

"I note that none of you considered increased community involvement through such groups as the Chamber of Commerce and the United Fund.

"The factors you mentioned plus those additional points all should be considered as we reach a decision on the final course of action we will follow."

Required:

a. State explicitly the implied corporate goals being expressed by each of the following:
   1. Treasurer.
   2. Sales vice president.
   3. Production vice president.
   4. President.
b. After reviewing Chapters 11, 12, 14, and this chapter, prepare a comprehensive report stating:
   1. The goals in more precise, concrete terms.
   2. Specific methods that can be used to achieve these goals.
   3. A more systematic approach to developing capital projects and achieving goal congruency.

[CMA adapted]

22.43 ***Evaluating a capital project.*** Anne Hastings has just been hired as the new director of customer services for Uncle Sam Computer Systems, a mail-order computer software and hardware retailer. Dee Kandus, CEO, assigns Anne to upgrade the customer information system (CIS). Dee provided Anne the following information:

UNCLE SAM COMPUTER SYSTEMS
CAPITAL PROJECTS PORTFOLIO STATEMENT

PROJECT	FEASIBILITY RATING	BENEFIT RATING	PRIORITY CATEGORY
Phone answering system	8.9	6.7	High potential
Robotic assembly system	7.1	8.3	High potential
Upgraded mainframe	9.1	6.1	High potential
New packaging line	8.3	7.9	High potential

FEASIBILITY FACTORS	MANAGEMENT WEIGHTING
Technical	20%
Operational	30
Economic	40
Schedule	10

BENEFIT FACTORS	MANAGEMENT WEIGHTING
Tangible	10%
Intangible	90

TANGIBLE BENEFITS	MANAGEMENT WEIGHTING
Reduced inventory cost	10%
Reduced labor cost	30
Reduced scrap and rework	10
Reduced material cost	10
Reduced handling cost	40

INTANGIBLE BENEFITS	MANAGEMENT WEIGHTING
Improved delivery	30%
Improved product quality	25
Improved production performance	20
Improved production flexibility	15
Improved employee safety	10

Required:

a. After reviewing the information, state what you feel are the managerial areas of primary concern.
b. If you were in this situation, what other information would you need to make a CIS capital project recommendation?

22.44 *GDS features.* Group decision support (GDS) systems (or groupware) offer a comprehensive array of features that support almost any type of project that requires groups of people working together on collaborative projects.

Required:

Write a report stating what you believe to be the features of GDS systems.

22.45 *Converting a vision statement into an action plan.* Following is the vision statement of Washoe Health Systems (WHS) and Washoe Medical Center (WMC) of Reno, Nevada:

VISION STATEMENT

We see health care in the future being quite different from how we have known it in the past. Without question, the industry's advancement in providing state-of-the-art clinical and operational information to its organizations and medical staffs is a prerequisite for advancement in the next decade. Such information will have to be provided in an accurate and timely manner.

The use of advancing technology, as a crucial component to the art and science of medicine, must be anticipated and acted upon. Environmental and community issues will challenge health care organizations to provide cost-effective access to care in a well-coordinated fashion, to maximize the appropriateness and effectiveness of resources dedicated to patients and their families. Organizations will have to strive constantly to evaluate and enhance the coordination of care through the strengths of perpetual quality improvement.

Only the most acutely ill or injured persons will reside in the hospital. This will dictate which services will be offered within the hospital, and that value-added services must be emphasized, particularly on an outpatient basis.

Instrumental to this vision is management's and the medical staff's mutual accountability to one another to optimize health care provided. Fundamental to this process is collaborative innovation in current health care expectations and future advancements.

It is the belief of our organization that these concepts embody the future of health care, and we will be dedicated to:

- Information
- Technology
- Coordinated services
- Perpetual quality improvement
- Value-added services
- Collaboration
- Innovation

Required:

a. Review appropriate chapters in this text and describe how material in these chapters met the seven goals of the vision statement.
b. Create a capital budgeting planning team with some of your colleagues. Prepare several capital project requests that you believe support the vision statement. Using either the JID or Delphi method, estimate the feasibility and benefit factors of the capital projects. Based on these estimates, prepare a priority grid and a Capital Projects Portfolio Statement. Finally, using the expected value technique, prepare a Cash Flow Estimate Form for each capital project listed in the Capital Projects Portfolio Statement.

23

Capital Budgeting Methodology: The Financial Analysis Stage

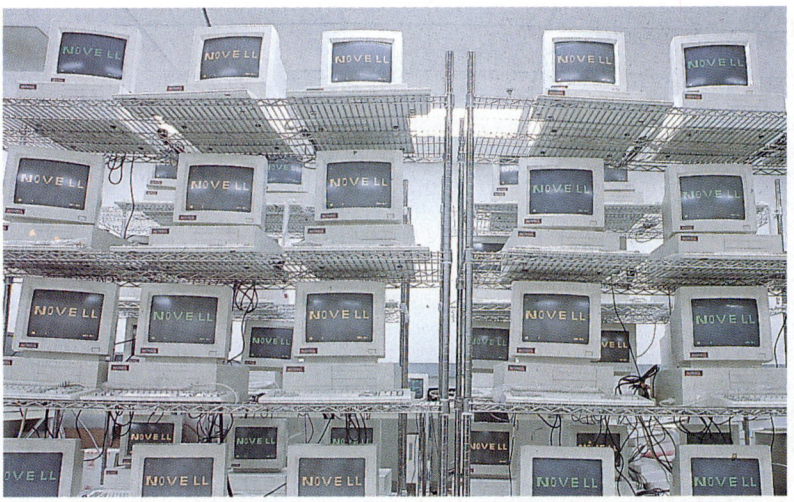

Novell invested in a SuperLab to ensure total quality. Courtesy of Novell, Inc.

LEARNING OBJECTIVES

After studying this chapter, you should be able to:

1. Discuss the discounted cash flow methods, and explain the net present value (NPV), internal rate of return (IRR), and present value index (PVI) methods.

2. Discuss the nondiscounted cash flow methods, which are the payback period (PP) method and the accounting rate of return (ARR) method.

3. Describe the impact of income taxes, purchasing versus leasing, and inflation on capital budgeting financial analysis.

4. Explain how sensitivity analysis assists managers in making capital budgeting decisions.

■ INTRODUCTION

Once the first stage of the capital budgeting methodology (covered in the previous chapter) has linked capital projects with an enterprise's vision and strategy, and estimated the quantity and timing of cash flows, the data are subjected to financial analysis. Using financial analysis methods (the second stage of the capital budgeting methodology), managers evaluate and compare alternative projects included in the Capital Projects Portfolio Statement. Such candidate capital projects will usually differ in the amount of initial investment required, terms of useful life, amount and timing of cash flows, salvage value, and cost of capital.

Two types of capital budgeting financial analysis methods are covered in this chapter:

- Discounted cash flow methods
- Nondiscounted cash flow methods ━━━

▌DISCOUNTED CASH FLOW METHODS

The main methods that managers use to financially analyze capital projects are called **discounted cash flow (DCF) methods,** which include the following:

- Net present value (NPV) method
- Internal rate of return (IRR) method
- Present value index (PVI) method

These methods rely on the **time value of money,** a concept that combines two basic principles:

- A dollar today is worth more than a dollar in the future (the idea of present value).
- The longer one waits for a dollar, the more uncertain the receipt is (the idea of risk).

Methods that incorporate the time value of money are dependent on a discount rate, which is based on cost of capital.

> **LEARNING OBJECTIVE 1**
>
> ──
>
> Discuss the discounted cash flow methods, and explain the net present value (NPV), internal rate of return (IRR), and present value index (PVI) methods.

▌The Cost of Capital and the Discount Rate

Most authorities lean toward some type of **weighted-average cost of capital,** which is viewed as a pool of capital investment funds that come from debt and equity sources. The correct weighted-average cost of capital is the one that reflects an enterprise's *expected* financing costs for its desired long-term capital structure mix. Under this approach, the weighted-average cost of capital reflects market conditions for securing incremental financing and enables an enterprise to evaluate its capital structure based on *future* events. New projects being evaluated must earn a rate of return equal to or higher than the marginal cost of capital in order to maintain or increase the value of an enterprise. Alternatively, weighted-average cost of capital based on historical capital sourcing values may not be relevant to future sources of investment funds.

Given a mix of debt, preferred stock, common stock, retained earnings, and recovered capital, a weighted-average cost of capital can be calculated. To do this, the cost of raising a dollar from each source in the capital investment pool is estimated and weighted according to its proportion in the mix.

To measure the cost of debt, the effective rate of interest that would have to be paid to acquire capital from *new* debt is used. The effective interest rate should be net of income taxes because interest is deductible for tax purposes.

Preferred stock usually has a contractual dividend rate. Consequently, this rate can be used to determine the effective cost of acquiring additional capital from the issuance of preferred stock. Unlike interest on debt, however, dividends are not deductible for income tax purposes. Thus, the effective rate is the annual contractual dividend per share divided by the estimated future share price.

The most troublesome aspect of calculating cost of capital is determining the cost of the common equity component of capital. Authorities do not agree on how this should be done. Some argue that the proper rate is the expected earnings per share divided by the current market value of the stock. Others contend that the cost of common equity funds is a function of expected dividends and expected share price. This theory must allow for an expected growth in dividend payments.

For capital resulting from retained earnings and capital recoveries (from depreciation), it must be recognized that shareholders do not pay income tax on undistributed assets. Presumably, shareholders would be willing to accept a smaller return on this source of capital than on common stock.

Exhibit 23–1 illustrates the cost of capital calculations for Cyberlink Corporation. The interest rate on debt is expected to be 10 percent, and debt is 20 percent of the sources of capital funds. Cyberlink's income tax rate is expected to be 40 percent over the next number of years. Preferred stock contributes up to 10 percent of capital funds, and its effective rate is expected to be 12 percent. Common stock comprises 40 percent of capital funds at an estimated future cost of 18 percent. Retained earnings and recovered capital provide 30 percent of capital funds at an estimated future cost of 16 percent. Based on the computations in the exhibit, Cyberlink's expected weighted-average cost of capital is 14.4 percent. This means that it will cost Cyberlink an average of 15 percent (rounded up) of each dollar annually to finance capital projects.

A **discount rate,** also referred to as a **hurdle rate,** should, in most cases, equal or exceed the enterprise's cost of capital. In other words, the discount rate is the *required* rate of return.

Some managers set the discount rate higher than the cost of capital because they recognize that indirect costs sometimes increase as the enterprise expands. Also, some capital projects are riskier than others because their outcome is more difficult to estimate. Managers will need some type of counterbalance or cushion for accepting the riskier alternatives. This cushion frequently takes the form of a higher discount rate. For example, in the case of Cyberlink, the discount rate for a low-risk project may be set at 12 percent (less than the cost of capital); for a moderate-risk project, 15 percent; for an average-risk project, 16 percent; for a high-risk project, 20 percent; and for an unchartered, super high-risk project, 30 percent or more. Because of the compounding nature of

---

■ EXHIBIT 23–1
Weighted-Average Cost of Capital for Cyberlink Corporation

Source of capital funds	Desired long-term proportion of total capital funds	Aftertax cost of financing	Weighted-average cost of capital
Debt	20%	6% (10% × 60%)*	1.2%
Preferred stock	10	12	1.2
Common stock	40	18	7.2
Retained earnings and recovered capital	30	16	4.8
Weighted-average cost of capital			14.4%

*Cyberlink's income tax rate is expected to be 40%; thus, its proportion of aftertax net income is 60%.

discounted cash flow methods, this method of adjusting for risk implicitly assumes that risk increases over time.

Managers exercise a significant amount of subjectivity in choosing the amount by which the discount rate will be increased to account for risk. In any capital budgeting decision, the estimation of costs, benefits, and cash flows, as well as risk, will always involve subjectivity. As the previous chapter pointed out, managers may also allow for risk in their estimates of feasibility factors and the amount and timing of cash flows. For example, the technology feasibility factor of a state-of-the-art capital project may be purposely weighted lower than a capital project involving traditional technology with which the organization is familiar. Or, the estimated future cash inflows of a risky project may be systematically reduced.

Another reason for raising the discount rate is the shareholder short-term mind-set for quick returns. American managers often feel pressure from fidgety shareholders to recoup investments fast. At public companies, the average holding period for stocks is *two* years. Consequently, the discount rates used to evaluate projects are higher than in other countries and much higher than their cost of capital. Higher discount rates do not encourage managers to make long-term capital investments.

DETERMINING THE PRESENT VALUE OF UNEQUAL CASH FLOWS USING A DISCOUNT RATE.   The Present Value of One Dollar Table in Exhibit 23–2 can be used to determine the present value of some lump-sum amount of cash in the future. The discount rates are shown at the top of the table, while the number of periods appear at the left. The value at which a discount rate and a number of periods intersect is the present value factor. For example, the value of $1.00 received three years from now at a discount rate of 14 percent is $0.675, or a present value factor of 0.675. To determine the present value of $1,750 received three years from now at a discount rate of 14 percent, the following calculation is performed:

$$\text{Present value} = \$1,750 \times .675$$
$$= \underline{\underline{\$1,181.25}}$$

To find the present value of two unequal cash inflows of $1,000 and $3,000 occurring in years 1 and 2, respectively, and discounted at 12 percent, the following computations are performed:

YEAR	CASH INFLOWS	PRESENT VALUE FACTOR (12%)	PRESENT VALUE
1	$1,000	.893	$ 893
2	3,000	.797	2,391
		Total present value	$3,284

DETERMINING THE PRESENT VALUE OF EQUAL CASH FLOWS.   Sometimes cash flows occur in equal amounts per period; this is termed an **annuity.** A Present Value of an Ordinary Annuity of One Dollar Table appears in Exhibit 23–3. In an ordinary annuity, the series of cash inflows occur at the end of the periods. If a capital project generates $2,000 of annual cash inflows for four years at a discount rate of 10 percent, then the present value of this annuity is $6,340 ($2,000 annuity × 3.170 present value factor).

The values in the Present Value of an Ordinary Annuity of One Dollar Table are cumulative values from the Present Value of One Dollar Table. For example, the $2,000 annuity is handled as if it were a series of *unequal* amounts as follows:

Discount Rates

Periods	2%	4%	6%	8%	10%	12%	14%	16%	18%	20%	22%	24%	26%	28%	30%	32%	40%
1	0.980	0.962	0.943	0.926	0.909	0.893	0.877	0.862	0.847	0.833	0.820	0.806	0.794	0.781	0.769	0.758	0.714
2	0.961	0.925	0.890	0.857	0.826	0.797	0.769	0.743	0.718	0.694	0.672	0.650	0.630	0.610	0.592	0.574	0.510
3	0.942	0.889	0.840	0.794	0.751	0.712	0.675	0.641	0.609	0.579	0.551	0.524	0.500	0.477	0.455	0.435	0.364
4	0.924	0.855	0.792	0.735	0.683	0.636	0.592	0.552	0.516	0.482	0.451	0.423	0.397	0.373	0.350	0.329	0.260
5	0.907	0.822	0.747	0.681	0.621	0.567	0.519	0.476	0.437	0.402	0.370	0.341	0.315	0.291	0.269	0.250	0.186
6	0.888	0.790	0.705	0.630	0.564	0.507	0.456	0.410	0.370	0.335	0.303	0.275	0.250	0.227	0.207	0.189	0.133
7	0.871	0.760	0.665	0.583	0.513	0.452	0.400	0.354	0.314	0.279	0.249	0.222	0.198	0.178	0.159	0.143	0.095
8	0.853	0.731	0.627	0.540	0.467	0.404	0.351	0.305	0.266	0.233	0.204	0.179	0.157	0.139	0.123	0.108	0.068
9	0.837	0.703	0.592	0.500	0.424	0.361	0.308	0.263	0.225	0.194	0.167	0.144	0.125	0.108	0.094	0.082	0.048
10	0.820	0.676	0.558	0.463	0.386	0.322	0.270	0.227	0.191	0.162	0.137	0.116	0.099	0.085	0.073	0.062	0.035
11	0.804	0.650	0.527	0.429	0.350	0.287	0.237	0.195	0.162	0.135	0.112	0.094	0.079	0.066	0.056	0.047	0.025
12	0.788	0.625	0.497	0.397	0.319	0.257	0.208	0.168	0.137	0.112	0.092	0.076	0.062	0.052	0.043	0.036	0.018
13	0.773	0.601	0.469	0.368	0.290	0.229	0.182	0.145	0.116	0.093	0.075	0.061	0.050	0.040	0.033	0.027	0.013
14	0.758	0.577	0.442	0.340	0.263	0.205	0.160	0.125	0.099	0.078	0.062	0.049	0.039	0.032	0.025	0.021	0.009
15	0.743	0.555	0.417	0.315	0.239	0.183	0.140	0.108	0.084	0.065	0.051	0.040	0.031	0.025	0.020	0.016	0.006
16	0.728	0.534	0.394	0.292	0.218	0.163	0.123	0.093	0.071	0.054	0.042	0.032	0.025	0.019	0.015	0.012	0.005
17	0.714	0.513	0.371	0.270	0.198	0.146	0.108	0.080	0.060	0.045	0.034	0.026	0.020	0.015	0.012	0.009	0.003
18	0.700	0.494	0.350	0.250	0.180	0.130	0.095	0.069	0.051	0.038	0.028	0.021	0.016	0.012	0.009	0.007	0.002
19	0.686	0.475	0.331	0.232	0.164	0.116	0.083	0.060	0.043	0.031	0.023	0.017	0.012	0.009	0.007	0.005	0.002
20	0.673	0.456	0.312	0.215	0.149	0.104	0.073	0.051	0.037	0.026	0.019	0.014	0.010	0.007	0.005	0.004	0.001
21	0.660	0.439	0.294	0.199	0.135	0.093	0.064	0.044	0.031	0.022	0.015	0.011	0.008	0.006	0.004	0.003	0.001
22	0.647	0.422	0.278	0.184	0.123	0.083	0.056	0.038	0.026	0.018	0.013	0.009	0.006	0.004	0.003	0.002	0.001
23	0.634	0.406	0.262	0.170	0.112	0.074	0.049	0.033	0.022	0.015	0.010	0.007	0.005	0.003	0.002	0.002	0.000
24	0.622	0.390	0.247	0.158	0.102	0.066	0.043	0.028	0.019	0.013	0.008	0.006	0.004	0.003	0.002	0.001	0.000
25	0.610	0.375	0.233	0.146	0.092	0.059	0.038	0.024	0.016	0.010	0.007	0.005	0.003	0.002	0.001	0.001	0.000
26	0.598	0.361	0.220	0.135	0.084	0.053	0.033	0.021	0.014	0.009	0.006	0.004	0.002	0.002	0.001	0.001	0.000
27	0.586	0.347	0.207	0.125	0.076	0.047	0.029	0.018	0.011	0.007	0.005	0.003	0.002	0.001	0.001	0.001	0.000
28	0.574	0.333	0.196	0.116	0.069	0.042	0.026	0.016	0.010	0.006	0.004	0.002	0.002	0.001	0.001	0.000	0.000
29	0.563	0.321	0.185	0.107	0.063	0.037	0.022	0.014	0.008	0.005	0.003	0.002	0.001	0.001	0.000	0.000	0.000
30	0.552	0.308	0.174	0.099	0.057	0.033	0.020	0.012	0.007	0.004	0.003	0.002	0.001	0.001	0.000	0.000	0.000

Discount Rates

EXHIBIT 23–3
Present Value of an Ordinary Annuity of One Dollar Table

Periods	2%	4%	6%	8%	10%	12%	14%	16%	18%	20%	22%	24%	26%	28%	30%	32%	40%
1	0.980	0.962	0.943	0.926	0.909	0.893	0.877	0.862	0.847	0.833	0.820	0.806	0.794	0.781	0.769	0.758	0.714
2	1.942	1.886	1.833	1.783	1.736	1.690	1.647	1.605	1.566	1.528	1.492	1.457	1.424	1.392	1.361	1.331	1.224
3	2.884	2.775	2.673	2.577	2.487	2.402	2.322	2.246	2.174	2.106	2.042	1.981	1.923	1.868	1.816	1.766	1.589
4	3.808	3.630	3.465	3.312	3.170	3.037	2.914	2.798	2.690	2.589	2.494	2.404	2.320	2.241	2.166	2.096	1.849
5	4.713	4.452	4.212	3.993	3.791	3.605	3.433	3.274	3.127	2.991	2.864	2.745	2.635	2.532	2.436	2.345	2.035
6	5.601	5.242	4.917	4.623	4.355	4.111	3.889	3.685	3.498	3.326	3.167	3.020	2.885	2.759	2.643	2.534	2.168
7	6.472	6.002	5.582	5.206	4.868	4.564	4.288	4.039	3.812	3.605	3.416	3.242	3.083	2.937	2.802	2.677	2.263
8	7.325	6.733	6.210	5.747	5.335	4.968	4.639	4.344	4.078	3.837	3.619	3.421	3.241	3.076	2.925	2.786	2.331
9	8.162	7.435	6.802	6.247	5.759	5.328	4.946	4.607	4.303	4.031	3.786	3.566	3.366	3.184	3.019	2.868	2.379
10	8.983	8.111	7.360	6.710	6.145	5.650	5.216	4.833	4.494	4.192	3.923	3.682	3.465	3.269	3.092	2.930	2.414
11	9.787	8.760	7.887	7.139	6.495	5.938	5.453	5.029	4.656	4.327	4.035	3.776	3.543	3.335	3.147	2.978	2.438
12	10.575	9.385	8.384	7.536	6.814	6.194	5.660	5.197	4.793	4.439	4.127	3.851	3.606	3.387	3.190	3.013	2.456
13	11.348	9.986	8.853	7.904	7.103	6.424	5.842	5.342	4.910	4.533	4.203	3.912	3.656	3.427	3.223	3.040	2.469
14	12.106	10.563	9.295	8.244	7.367	6.628	6.002	5.468	5.008	4.611	4.265	3.962	3.695	3.459	3.249	3.061	2.478
15	12.849	11.118	9.712	8.559	7.606	6.811	6.142	5.575	5.092	4.675	4.315	4.001	3.726	3.483	3.268	3.076	2.484
16	13.578	11.652	10.106	8.851	7.824	6.974	6.265	5.668	5.162	4.730	4.357	4.033	3.751	3.503	3.283	3.088	2.489
17	14.292	12.166	10.477	9.122	8.022	7.120	6.373	5.749	5.222	4.775	4.391	4.059	3.771	3.518	3.295	3.097	2.492
18	14.992	12.659	10.828	9.372	8.201	7.250	6.467	5.818	5.273	4.812	4.419	4.080	3.786	3.529	3.304	3.104	2.494
19	15.678	13.134	11.158	9.604	8.365	7.366	6.550	5.877	5.316	4.843	4.442	4.097	3.799	3.539	3.311	3.109	2.496
20	16.351	13.590	11.470	9.818	8.514	7.469	6.623	5.929	5.353	4.870	4.460	4.110	3.808	3.546	3.316	3.113	2.497
21	17.011	14.029	11.764	10.017	8.649	7.562	6.687	5.973	5.384	4.891	4.476	4.121	3.816	3.551	3.320	3.116	2.498
22	17.658	14.451	12.042	10.201	8.772	7.645	6.743	6.001	5.410	4.909	4.488	4.130	3.822	3.556	3.323	3.118	2.498
23	18.292	14.857	12.303	10.371	8.883	7.718	6.792	6.044	5.432	4.925	4.499	4.137	3.827	3.559	3.325	3.120	2.499
24	18.914	15.247	12.550	10.529	8.985	7.784	6.835	6.073	5.451	4.937	4.507	4.143	3.831	3.562	3.327	3.121	2.499
25	19.523	15.622	12.783	10.675	9.077	7.843	6.873	6.097	5.467	4.948	4.514	4.147	3.834	3.564	3.329	3.122	2.499
26	20.121	15.983	13.003	10.810	9.161	7.896	6.906	6.118	5.480	4.956	4.520	4.151	3.837	3.566	3.330	3.123	2.500
27	20.707	16.330	13.211	10.935	9.237	7.943	6.935	6.136	5.492	4.964	4.524	4.154	3.839	3.567	3.331	3.123	2.500
28	21.281	16.663	13.406	11.051	9.307	7.984	6.961	6.152	5.502	4.970	4.528	4.157	3.840	3.568	3.331	3.124	2.500
29	21.844	16.984	13.591	11.158	9.370	8.022	6.983	6.166	5.510	4.975	4.531	4.159	3.841	3.569	3.332	3.124	2.500
30	22.396	17.292	13.765	11.258	9.427	8.055	7.003	6.177	5.517	4.979	4.534	4.160	3.842	3.569	3.332	3.124	2.500

Year	Cash Inflows	Present Value Factor (10%)	Present Value
1	$2,000	.909	$1,818
2	2,000	.826	1,652
3	2,000	.751	1,502
4	2,000	.683	1,366
		3.169	$6,338

The $2 difference between the amount computed by the factor in the Present Value of an Ordinary Annuity of One Dollar Table ($6,340 = $2,000 × 3.170) and the amount computed by the sum of present value factors in the Present Value of One Dollar Table ($6,338 = $2,000 × each present value factor) is due to rounding. Both tables assume that cash inflows occur at the end of the year.

The Net Present Value Method

The **net present value (NPV) method** measures the difference in the present value of cash inflows and outflows associated with a capital project. Future cash flows are discounted to their present value using a desired discount rate. The basic decision rule for the NPV method is:

When NPV Is:	Decision:
>0	Accept project
<0	Reject project
=0	Indifferent

The accompanying cases help demonstrate the application of the NPV method.

In the Tahoe Ski Lodge case (see p. 1085), the capital project generated equal periodic cash inflows of $160,000. In many projects, however, the periodic cash inflows are unequal. This situation can be seen in the Gold Nugget case (see p. 1086).

The Internal Rate of Return Method

The **internal rate of return (IRR) method** (also called the **time-adjusted rate of return**) uses a specified rate of return as a hurdle rate against which the IRR is compared. The fundamental decision rule for the IRR method is:

When IRR Is:	Decision:
>specified hurdle rate	Accept project
<specified hurdle rate	Reject project
=specified hurdle rate	Indifferent

When the cash inflows are not uniform, as is usually the case, the rate is calculated by a trial-and-error process. Various rates are tried until the correct one is found. The correct rate is the one where the present value of the cash inflows is equal to the present value of the investment. The Euclid Machinery case on page 1087 illustrates the calculation of the IRR.

The Present Value Index Method

If capital projects involve different amounts of investment, it is useful to prepare a relative ranking of the capital projects by using a present value index (PVI), computed as follows:

$$PVI = \frac{\text{Present value of cash inflows}}{\text{Present value of cash outflows}}$$

INSIGHTS & APPLICATIONS

Tahoe Ski Lodge's NPV Analysis of a Project with Equal Net Cash Inflows and a Residual Value

Tahoe Ski Lodge is considering acquiring a new ski lift that will cost $500,000. The ski lift will last five years, and at the end of the five-year period, will have a $40,000 residual value. Use of the ski lift will increase cash inflows by $160,000 per year. Management at Tahoe requires a 16 percent target rate before taxes on all investment projects. Management also requires that capital budgeting decisions be based on NPV analysis.

These cash inflows represent a stream of periodic amounts that can be referred to as an annuity. The present value of an annuity is calculated by multiplying the periodic amount ($160,000 annually in this case) by the present value of an annuity of $1 for five periods discounted at 16 percent. From the 16 percent column for five periods in Exhibit 23–3, the discount factor is 3.274. The annuity of $160,000 annually is discounted to its present value of $523,840 ($160,000 annual cash inflow × 3.274 discount factor).

The residual value of $40,000 is another form of cash inflow that must be discounted to its present value and added to the present value of the project. The $40,000 must be discounted as a single amount, not as an annuity, because it will be received only at the end of the ski lift's useful life when it is sold. Therefore, the discount factor is found in the 16 percent column for five periods in Exhibit 23–2. The resulting discount factor is .476. The residual value of $40,000 is multiplied by .476, giving a present value of $19,040. This present value is added to the present value of the $160,000 annuity, giving a total present value of $542,880 ($523,840 present value of five periodic cash inflows of $160,000 + $19,040 present value of residual value of $40,000, both discounted at 16 percent). A summary of this analysis follows:

SKI LIFT PROJECT	PRESENT VALUE FACTOR (16%)	CASH INFLOWS	PRESENT VALUE OF CASH INFLOWS
Present value of equal cash inflows	3.274 ×	$160,000 per year =	$523,840
Present value of residual value	.476 ×	40,000 =	19,040
Present value of the project's total cash inflows			$542,880
Cash outflow (initial investment)			<500,000>
NPV of project			$ 42,880

According to the analysis, Tahoe Ski Lodge should purchase the new ski lift because it generates a net present value of $42,880 ($542,880 total present value of cash inflows − $500,000 initial investment), which is more than the desired 16 percent rate of return. In other words, Tahoe could spend up to $542,880 for the new ski lift and still obtain the 16 percent rate of return it desires. The net present value of $42,880, therefore, provides a "cushion" or "margin of error" for the company in estimating the benefits of the new project.

The **present value index (PVI) method,** also termed the **profitability index (PI)** and **cost/benefit ratio,** measures the ratio of the present value of cash inflows to the present value of cash outflows. The index will equal 1.0 when the present value of cash inflows equals the present value of cash outflows. A PVI of 1.30 indicates that for every dollar of present value invested in the project, the enterprise will receive cash inflows with a present value of $1.30. The higher a project's PVI, the more profitable that project is per investment dollar. The case on page 1088 illustrates how Maxximum Corporation uses the PVI in ranking two projects.

As the preceding analysis shows, if capital projects being compared involve different dollar amounts of investment, the project with a greater NPV may not be the more attractive project financially if it also requires a larger investment. For example, an NPV of $5,000 on an investment of $200,000 is not as financially attractive as an NPV of $4,000 on an investment of $50,000, provided

INSIGHTS & APPLICATIONS

Gold Nugget's NPV Analysis of a Project with Unequal Cash Inflows and Zero Residual Value

Gold Nugget is a large casino located on the east coast. The gaming manager is contemplating purchasing Big Winner, a giant computerized payday poker machine that randomly selects lucky winners when they cash their pay-

checks at Gold Nugget. Big Winner has multiple lighting features and sound effects and automatically dispenses prizes, such as jewelry, gift certificates, show tickets, and so forth, as soon as a lucky winner is announced. The machine will cost $100,000 and has zero residual value.

It is expected that the machine will generate the following cash inflows:

YEAR	CASH INFLOWS
1	$ 50,000
2	60,000
3	10,000
Total cash inflows	$120,000

Management's cutoff rate (i.e., discount rate or hurdle rate) for gaming investments is 14 percent; NPV analysis is required. The accountant at Gold Nugget prepared the following NPV analysis:

BIG WINNER PROJECT

PERIOD	PRESENT VALUE FACTOR (14%)	CASH INFLOWS	PRESENT VALUE OF CASH INFLOWS
1	.877	$50,000	$ 43,850
2	.769	60,000	46,140
3	.675	10,000	6,750

Total present value of cash inflows	$ 96,740
Investment	< 100,000>
NPV of project	<$ 3,260>

The NPV of the Big Winner project is negative $3,260, which means that its return is less than the 14 percent discount rate. Therefore, management at Gold Nugget rejected the project.

that the $150,000 difference in investments can be used to realize an NPV of at least $1,001 in other projects. In this case, the PVI should be used rather than the NPV dollar figure.

Ranking Independent Projects under Limited Investment Funds

Independent projects are capital projects that have no specific bearing on one another. For example, acquisition of a local area network is not related to the acquisition of a fleet of trucks.

Theoretically, an enterprise should invest in all independent capital projects with a positive NPV. Normally, however, an enterprise has limited capital and therefore cannot invest in all candidate projects. In such situations, managers should select those projects that maximize return on dollars invested. The PVI can be used to rank projects by following these steps:

- Rank all projects in descending order.
- Allocate the available investment funds to the projects in rank order until all funds are depleted. (It is assumed that partial investments are possible.)

Exhibit 23–4 on page 1088 illustrates how the PVI is used to rank projects. All capital projects will generate a positive NPV except Project E, which is

INSIGHTS & APPLICATIONS

Euclid's Use of the IRR Method

Euclid is considering the purchase of a machine for $200,000 that will reduce production costs by

$50,000, $80,000, $100,000, and $90,000 during year 1, year 2, year 3, and year 4, respectively. The machine has an estimated useful life of four years and has zero salvage value. Euclid's hurdle rate is 12 percent.

In the following computations, a 16 percent IRR is tried first. The present value of the cash inflows at 16 percent is $16,320 larger than the investment ($216,320 − $200,000). Therefore, the IRR is larger than 16 percent. Next, an 18 percent IRR is tried.

| | | 16% | | 18% | | 20% | |
YEAR	CASH INFLOWS	PRESENT VALUE FACTOR	PRESENT VALUE	PRESENT VALUE FACTOR	PRESENT VALUE	PRESENT VALUE FACTOR	PRESENT VALUE
1	$ 50,000	.862	$ 43,100	.847	$ 42,350	.833	$ 41,650
2	80,000	.743	59,440	.718	57,440	.694	55,520
3	100,000	.641	64,100	.609	60,900	.579	57,900
4	90,000	.552	49,680	.516	46,440	.482	43,380
			$216,320		$207,130		$198,450

Present value at 18%		$207,130	$207,130
Present value at 20%		198,450
Present value of investment			200,000
Difference		$ 8,680	$ 7,130

$$IRR = .18 + \frac{\$7,130}{\$8,680}(.20 - .18)$$

$$= .18 + .82(.02)$$

$$= .1964 \text{ or } 19.64\%$$

The results show that the 18 percent rate is still too low. With a 20 percent IRR, the present value is $1,550 less than the investment ($200,000 − $198,450). Thus, the true IRR is between 18 and 20 percent. By interpolating, the exact rate is 19.64 percent. The IRR of 19.64 percent is much larger than the 12 percent desired rate of return, or hurdle rate. So, the proposed investment is very attractive.

Euclid is also considering another capital project of $335,000 that provides uniform cash inflows of $100,000

for five years with zero salvage value. An approximation of the present value factor is calculated as follows:

$$IRR \text{ factor} = \frac{\$335,000}{\$100,000}$$

$$= \underline{\underline{3.350}}$$

Looking at the table in Exhibit 23–3 for five years, the present value for 14 percent is 3.433, and the factor for 16 percent is 3.274. Thus, the IRR with a factor of 3.350 would be very close to 15 percent.

rejected without further analysis. Investment in the other four projects requires a total of $65,000, but only $55,000 of investment funds are available. Which capital projects should be selected? Using the PVI, the projects should be ranked in descending order and funded as shown in the exhibit. Project D, with the highest PVI of 1.4, is funded first, followed by Project C and Project A. After these projects are funded, no funds remain and, consequently, Project B is not funded. By funding these projects, the enterprise achieves a total NPV of $15,000 ($12,000 NPV of D + $1,000 NPV of C + $2,000 NPV of A). A greater total NPV is not possible given the limited funds available. The PVI yields the return per investment dollar, and the greater the PVI, the greater the return per dollar invested. Therefore, selecting the projects with the highest PVI maximizes the NPV.

INSIGHTS & APPLICATIONS

Maxximum Corporation's Financial Analysis of Two Capital Projects Using the PVI and NPV Methods

Maxximum manufactures truck parts. Management is considering two new computer-controlled machining devices with the following present value of cash flows:

PERIOD	MACHINE A	MACHINE B
0	<$10,000>	<$30,000>
1	5,000	14,000
2	6,000	15,000
3	3,000	7,000

The NPV of each machine is:

$$NPV(A) = \$14,000 - \$10,000 = \$4,000$$
$$NPV(B) = \$36,000 - \$30,000 = \$6,000$$

Machine B is preferable under the NPV method. The PVI for machine A is:

$$\frac{\$5,000 + \$6,000 + \$3,000}{\$10,000} = 1.4$$

The PVI for machine B is:

$$\frac{\$14,000 + \$15,000 + \$7,000}{\$30,000} = 1.2$$

Machine A, however, is preferable under the PVI method. The PVI indicates that although machine B has the larger excess of present value over the amount to be invested, it is not as desirable as machine A in terms of the amount of present value per dollar invested.

▮ Ranking Mutually Exclusive Projects under Limited Investment Funds

With **mutually exclusive projects,** accepting one of a set of candidate capital projects causes all the others to be rejected. By accepting a particular project, the other projects in the set are excluded from further consideration because they would provide unneeded or redundant capability. Acquiring computer A from an array of computers that perform essentially the same functions is a mutually exclusive project. A replacement project, such as whether to keep an

▬▬EXHIBIT 23–4
Ranking Capital Projects with the PVI

	Five capital project opportunities		
Project	Present value of cash inflows	Present value of cash outflows (investment)	PVI
A	$22,000	$20,000	1.1
B	10,000	10,000	1.0
C	6,000	5,000	1.2
D	42,000	30,000	1.4
E	3,600	4,000	0.9*

* Reject: 0.9 < 1.0.

		Three capital projects selected for implementation		
Project	PVI	Investment required	Amount funded	Cumulative funding
D	1.4	$30,000	$30,000	$30,000
C	1.2	5,000	5,000	35,000
A	1.1	20,000	20,000	55,000
B	1.0	10,000	Not funded	—

old machine or acquire a new one, is another example. There may be some differences in capabilities and operating costs between the old and new machines, but if the company keeps the old machine, it will not acquire the new one; alternatively, if the new one is acquired, the old one will be sold. Therefore, the two machines are mutually exclusive.

When investment funds are unlimited, the project with the greatest NPV is selected from a set of mutually exclusive projects. When investment funds are limited, selecting a project in this manner may not produce the greatest *total* NPV.

Exhibit 23–5 illustrates a situation in which managers are evaluating Projects 1, 2, and 3. Projects 1 and 2 are mutually exclusive. Both are uninterruptible power supply systems for the company's computer system. Project 3 is a truck, which is an independent project.

If unlimited funds were available, management would select Project 2 over Project 1 and also invest in Project 3. If only $90,000 of investment funds were available, management would have two choices. It could invest all its funds in Project 2 with an NPV of $40,000, or it could invest in Projects 1 and 3, which have a combined NPV of $45,000. Investing in Projects 1 and 3 is the better choice.

It is also interesting to note that if the PVI had been used, Project 2 would have been selected, with a PVI of 1.44 compared to a PVI of 1.42 for Project 1. Clearly, this is not the wiser choice because the remaining $30,000 can be put to better use. Therefore, if investments are mutually exclusive, the NPV method may be a better approach to ranking projects. The PVI indicates the best return per dollar invested, but does not consider the alternative possibilities of unused funds.

Can a conclusion be drawn about ranking mutually exclusive projects? The problem with mutually exclusive projects is that they may rank differently with each of the discounted cash flow methods. One project may have the highest NPV, another the highest PVI, while another has the highest IRR. In most situations, however, the NPV is preferable to either the IRR or the PVI for ranking mutually exclusive projects.

Mutually exclusive capital projects.

Comparing Net Present Value and Internal Rate of Return When Analyzing Mutually Exclusive Projects

The choice of the NPV over the IRR is easy to demonstrate with a simple example. Assume an enterprise must choose between investing $1 that will return $2 in one year or investing $100,000 that will return $150,000 in one year. The IRRs of the projects are 100 percent and 50 percent, respectively, which makes the first alternative seem to be the better choice. Assuming the discount rate is 12 percent, the NPVs of the projects are $0.79 [($2.00 × 0.893) − $1.00] and $33,950 [($150,000 × 0.893) − $100,000], respectively. Selecting the first project based on the IRR criterion would lead to a return of $0.79 instead of $33,950. Therefore, the NPV is the better criterion when choosing between mutually exclusive projects. As the example shows, a manager concerned with the greatest absolute profitability should choose the project with the greatest NPV, not the largest IRR. The IRR is a percentage measure of profitability, while the NPV is an absolute measure.

Project	Investment	Present value	NPV
1	$60,000	$ 85,000	$25,000
2	90,000	130,000	40,000
3	30,000	50,000	20,000

■■ EXHIBIT 23–5
Required Investment for Two Mutually Exclusive Projects and One Independent Project

Generally, managers are more comfortable with the IRR method, though, because its results are in percentage terms. For example, a manager can say that a 20 percent IRR is desirable because it exceeds a hurdle rate of 15 percent and that a 5 percent IRR is undesirable. On the other hand, an NPV of $50,000 may not be as easy to interpret with respect to a desired discount rate.

The discount rate is the rate used to determine the NPV. If the NPV is zero, the discount rate equals the IRR. If the NPV is positive, the IRR is greater than the discount rate. If the NPV is negative, the IRR is less than the discount rate.

The NPV method assumes that cash inflows will be reinvested at the discount rate, while the IRR method assumes that the cash inflows will be reinvested at the rate earned by the project; that is, at the internal rate of return. If the project's cash inflows are not reinvested at the IRR, the ranking calculations obtained from the IRR method may be in error. In many situations, the NPV method may give more reasonable results because the reinvestment is assumed to be the cost of capital, a more likely scenario.

Under certain conditions, the NPV method indicates that a certain alternative has the highest NPV and therefore should be selected while the IRR method indicates another project is better because it produces the highest return. Such a situation occurs because the two methods make different assumptions about the *reinvestment* of cash inflows.

Two mutually exclusive capital projects are compared in Exhibit 23–6. The discount rate is 12 percent. Project A generates the higher NPV, and Project B produces a larger IRR. The NPV method assumes that cash inflows from Project B will be reinvested to earn 12 percent, the discount rate. Alternatively, the IRR method assumes that the cash inflows generated by Project B will be reinvested to earn 22.90 percent. If this is true, then Project B is the better alternative. Finding new capital projects that yield such high rates of return would be extremely difficult, however.

The problem arises because Projects A and B have unequal useful lives and cash inflows. One approach to resolving the problem of unequal project lives is to replace Project B at the end of two years with another project that covers the estimated useful life of Project A so there is a common termination date.

NONDISCOUNTED CASH FLOW METHODS

LEARNING OBJECTIVE 2

Discuss the nondiscounted cash flow methods, which are the payback period (PP) method and the accounting rate of return (ARR) method.

Nondiscounted cash flow methods include the following:

- Payback period method
- Accounting rate of return method

These methods ignore the time value of money and, therefore, do not use any present value techniques. Because they ignore the time value of money, many accountants consider these methods to be inferior to the discounted cash flow methods. Nevertheless, the payback period and accounting rate of return methods should still be studied for two reasons:

- Many organizations use these methods.
- Even in organizations where the use of discounted cash flow methods has increased, nondiscounted cash flow methods are also used in conjunction with them.

The Payback Period Method

The **payback period (PP) method** measures the number of years needed for a project to accumulate enough cash to pay for the initial cost of the investment. This span of time is termed the *payback period*. The shorter the payback period,

Comparing NPV and IRR When Mutually Exclusive Projects Are Involved

	Project A				Project B		
Year	Cash inflows	Present value factor (12%)	Present value	Year	Cash inflows	Present value factor (12%)	Present value
1	$2,000	.893	$1,786	1	$6,000	.893	$5,358
2	3,000	.797	2,391	2	3,200	.797	2,550
3	5,000	.712	3,560				
4	1,000	.636	636				
Present value of cash inflows			$8,373				$7,908
Present value of investment			<7,000>				<7,000>
Net present value			$1,373				$908
Internal rate of return			20.96%				22.90%

The internal rates of return for Projects A and B are calculated as follows:

Project A

		20%		22%	
Year	Cash inflows	Present value factor	Present value	Present value factor	Present value
1	$2,000	.833	$1,666	.820	$1,640
2	3,000	.694	2,082	.672	2,016
3	5,000	.579	2,895	.551	2,755
4	1,000	.482	482	.451	451
			$7,125		$6,862

Present value at 20%		$7,125	$7,125
Present value at 22%		6,862	
Present value of investment			7,000
Difference		$ 263	$ 125

$$\text{Internal rate of return} = .20 + \frac{\$125}{\$263}(.22 - .20)$$
$$= .20 + .48(.02)$$
$$= .2096 \text{ or } 20.96\%$$

Project B

		22%		24%	
Year	Cash inflows	Present value factor	Present value	Present value factor	Present value
1	$6,000	.820	$4,920	.806	$4,836
2	3,200	.672	2,150	.650	2,080
			$7,070		$6,916

Present value at 22%		$7,070	$7,070
Present value at 24%		6,916	
Present value of investment			7,000
Difference		$ 154	$ 70

$$\text{Internal rate of return} = .22 + \frac{\$70}{\$154}(.24 - .22)$$
$$= .22 + .45(.02)$$
$$= .2290 \text{ or } 22.90\%$$

INSIGHTS & APPLICATIONS

Metric Company's Use of the Payback Period Method

Metric Company manufactures instrumentation panels for small aircraft. Management is considering two machines, A and B. Machine A costs $323,000 and will reduce annual operating costs by $95,000. Machine B costs $396,000 and will reduce annual operating costs by $88,000. If managers at Metric accept or reject capital projects based on the PP method, which machine should be purchased?

$$\text{Machine A payback period} = \frac{\$323,000}{\$95,000} = 3.4 \text{ years}$$

$$\text{Machine B payback period} = \frac{\$396,000}{\$88,000} = 4.5 \text{ years}$$

According to the PP method calculations, Metric should purchase machine A, because it has a shorter payback period than machine B. But this may not be the wisest decision because the PP method does not measure the profitability of this decision, only its liquidity.

Additional information about the machines under consideration reveals that machine A has a useful life of four years and machine B has a useful life of eight years. It would take two purchases of machine A to provide the same length of service as a single purchase of machine B. Under these circumstances, machine B would be a significantly better investment than machine A, even though machine A has a shorter payback period. Machine A's total cash inflow is $380,000 ($95,000 annual cash inflow × 4 years of useful life), and machine B's total cash inflow is $704,000 ($88,000 annual cash inflow × 8 years of useful life). Therefore, machine B will give Metric an additional cash inflow of $324,000 based on the difference in the two machines' useful lives. Considering this additional information, management at Metric should select machine B.

the more desirable the investment. The PP method is expressed in years. The formula used in computing the payback period is:

$$\text{Payback period} = \frac{\text{Initial investment}}{\text{Expected annual cash inflows}}$$

This method is applied in the above Metric Company case.

When the cash inflows associated with a capital investment are uneven, the results from the payback formula are not directly comparable. Instead, the payback calculations take on a cumulative form. Each year's cash inflows are accumulated until the amount invested is recovered. This situation is demonstrated in the Hercules case on the next page.

The major strengths of the PP method, used in both even and uneven cash flow cases, is (1) its simplicity and (2) that it assists managers in weeding out capital projects not warranting further consideration. For example, some managers automatically reject a capital project if its payback period is more than five years. These managers may want a shorter payback period because the shorter the period, the sooner the investment will be recovered and the more accurate the forecasts are likely to be. Thus, the shorter the payback period, the less risk.

The weakness of the PP method is threefold. As already indicated in the Metric case, the PP method does not measure profitability and ignores cash inflows beyond the payback period. A further criticism of the PP method is that it does not consider the time value of money. A cash inflow to be received several years in the future is weighted equally with a cash inflow to be received today. Moreover, by taking a short-term perspective, management disregards long-term benefits and can place an enterprise in jeopardy with competitors.

Should the PP method be eliminated as a viable capital budgeting technique? Not necessarily. It can be useful to managers in making capital budgeting decisions so long as the managers fully understand its limitations.

INSIGHTS & APPLICATIONS

Hercules Construction Company's Payback Period Analysis

Hercules, a highway construction company, plans to buy an earth-moving machine costing $1,000,000. It is estimated that the machine will produce a total cash inflow of $1,600,000 over four years as follows:

YEAR	CASH INFLOWS	CUMULATIVE CASH INFLOWS
1	$400,000	$ 400,000
2	200,000	600,000
3	600,000	1,200,000
4	400,000	1,600,000

Because $600,000 will be received in the first two years, only $400,000 will remain to be recovered in year 3. Therefore, the payback period is two years and eight months [two years + ($400,000 / $600,000) of year 3].

The Accounting Rate of Return Method

The **accounting rate of return (ARR) method** (also called the **unadjusted rate of return** and the **book value rate of return**) relates the capital project's net income (income after income taxes) to the capital investment. The ARR is the ratio of the expected average aftertax net income to the investment required to generate this net income. The ARR is determined as follows:

$$ARR = \frac{\text{Average aftertax net income}}{\text{Investment (original or average)}}$$

The average aftertax net income is determined by adding the aftertax net income for each year of the project and then dividing this total by the number of years. Average aftertax net income can be approximated by subtracting average depreciation from average cash inflow. Assuming that all revenue earned in a period is collected and that depreciation is the only noncash expense, the approximation is exact.

The amount of investment can be the *original investment* or the *average investment*. If average investment is used, it is calculated as the original investment plus salvage value of the project, if any, divided by two.

The ARR method estimates the revenues that will be generated by the proposed capital project and then deducts from these revenues all estimated operating costs associated with them including depreciation and income taxes. The Vulcan case on the next page shows how these calculations are performed. In this case, average investment is used.

The Vulcan case used the average investment. The Cascade Industries case on page 1095 uses the original investment.

Although the ARR method measures profitability, it has a major weakness. It does not consider the time value of money. With ARR, a dollar received ten years from now is viewed as being just as valuable as a dollar received today. This defect becomes more significant the further one advances in time.

> **LEARNING OBJECTIVE 3**
>
> Describe the impact of income taxes, purchasing versus leasing, and inflation on capital budgeting financial analysis.

ADDITIONAL CAPITAL BUDGETING CONSIDERATIONS

Thus far, this chapter has provided basic treatment of discounted and nondiscounted cash flow methods. This section builds on the NPV method by incorporating the following additional considerations:

INSIGHTS & APPLICATIONS

Vulcan Machine Shop's Application of the ARR Method Using Average Investment

The superintendent at Vulcan Machine Shop is considering acquiring an automatic welding machine. This machine would aid in the fabrication of concrete mixing tanks, the sales of which would increase revenues by $100,000 per year. Cash operating costs and income taxes would be $68,000 per year. The automatic welding machine would cost $200,000 and have a ten-year life with no salvage value. Annual straight-line depreciation expense is $20,000 ($200,000 ÷ 10 years). The ARR for this project is computed as:

$$ARR = \frac{[\$100,000 - (\$68,000 + \$20,000)]}{\$200,000 \div 2}$$

$$= \frac{\$12,000}{\$100,000}$$

$$= \underline{12.00\%}$$

Soon after these calculations were made, it was learned that the machine would, in fact, have a salvage value of $30,000. The new annual depreciation is $17,000 [($200,000 − $30,000) ÷ 10 years]. The new ARR is:

$$ARR = \frac{[\$100,000 - (\$68,000 + \$17,000)]}{[(\$200,000 + \$30,000) \div 2]}$$

$$= \frac{\$15,000}{\$115,000}$$

$$= \underline{13.04\%}$$

Management at Vulcan rejected the proposal for purchasing the automatic welding machine because the ARR of 13.04 percent did not meet the minimum desired rate of return of 20.00 percent.

- Income taxes
- Purchasing versus leasing
- Inflation

Impact of Income Taxes on Capital Project Decisions

Clearly, aftertax cost is applicable to capital project financial analysis because it measures the actual amount of cash outflow resulting from expenditures. Therefore, it is necessary to place all financial analyses on an aftertax basis.

USING DEPRECIATION AS A TAX SHIELD.   An enterprise does not pay or receive any cash for depreciation. Depreciation expense, however, provides a **tax shield** that protects revenues against the payment of taxes. This tax shielding produces a tax benefit equal to the amount of the depreciation expense multiplied by the tax rate. For example, if the depreciation expense is $100,000 and the tax rate is 34 percent, then the tax benefit is $34,000 ($100,000 × .34). The impact of the tax shield is illustrated in Exhibit 23–7. Company D has a depreciation expense; Company E does not.

Notice that Company D's cash inflow exceeds Company E's by $40,800. To determine Company D's cash inflow, it is necessary to add the $120,000 depreciation deduction back to Company D's net income. This step is necessary because depreciation expense is a noncash deduction on the income statement. Although Company D's cash inflow is $40,800 greater than Company E's, its net income is $79,200 lower than Company E's ($264,000 − $184,800). How can this be? The higher cash inflow occurs because depreciation expense is acting as a tax shield. The reduction in tax payments, made possible by the depreciation tax shield, will always be equal to the amount of the depreciation expense deduction multiplied by the tax rate, as shown by the following formula:

INSIGHTS & APPLICATIONS

Cascade Industries' Application of the ARR Method Using the Original Investment

A drilling machine requires an initial outlay of $100,000. The life of the project is five years with the following cash inflows: $40,000, $50,000, $50,000, $40,000, $30,000. The machine will have zero salvage value after the five years, and all revenues earned within a year are collected in that year. The total cash inflow for the five years is $210,000, making the average cash inflow $42,000 ($210,000 ÷ 5 years). Average depreciation is $20,000 ($100,000 ÷ 5 years). The average net income is $22,000 ($42,000 − $20,000). Using the average net income and original investment, the ARR is 22 percent ($22,000 ÷ $100,000). If the average investment is used instead of the original investment, the ARR is 44 percent ($22,000 ÷ $50,000).

	Income Statements		
		Company D	Company E
Sales		$800,000	$800,000
Expenses:			
Cash operating costs		400,000	400,000
Depreciation expense		120,000	—
Total expenses		<520,000>	<400,000>
Net income before taxes		280,000	400,000
Income taxes (34%)		<95,200>	<136,000>
Net income		$184,800	$264,000

	Cash Flow Comparison		
Cash inflow from operations:			
Net income (from above)		$184,800	$264,000
Add noncash deduction for depreciation		120,000	—
Cash inflow		$304,800	$264,000
Greater amount of cash available to Company D		$40,800	

■■■EXHIBIT 23–7
The Impact of Depreciation Deductions on Tax Payments

$$\text{Tax savings from the depreciation tax shield} = \text{Tax rate} \times \text{Depreciation expense deduction}$$
$$= .34 \times \$120,000$$
$$= \underline{\$40,800}$$

CHOOSING DEPRECIATION METHODS.   Current tax laws require that the modified accelerated cost recovery system (MACRS) be used for tax depreciation purposes. MACRS specifies the amount allowable each year as a depreciation deduction (called "capital recovery" under MACRS). Estimates of future salvage values are ignored under MACRS. Any salvage or disposal price of the project is taxed at the same rate as ordinary income at the time of the sale.

As shown in Exhibit 23–8, eight different recovery periods are possible. These recovery periods do not necessarily reflect the estimated useful life of the assets included in each category. MACRS offers companies the option of using straight-

EXHIBIT 23–8
Modified Accelerated Cost Recovery System (MACRS)

Recovery period (years)	Recovery method	Examples of projects in recovery period class
3	200% declining balance	■ Light tools ■ Food processing devices
5	200% declining balance	■ Automobiles and light trucks ■ Computers, copiers, typewriters, and calculators
7	200% declining balance	■ Office furniture ■ Publishing equipment
10	200% declining balance	■ Barges and tugs ■ Oil refining equipment
15	150% declining balance	■ Cement manufacturing equipment ■ Sewage treatment plants
20	150% declining balance	■ Farm buildings
27.5	Straight-line	■ Residential rental properties
31.5	Straight-line	■ Nonresidential real property

line depreciation (called the alternative depreciation system, or ADS) within any recovery period class.

The accelerated depreciation method prescribed under MACRS for most property other than real estate is the 200 percent declining-balance method with a half-year convention (i.e., only a half-year's depreciation is allowed in the year of acquisition, and the other half-year is taken in the last year). Exhibit 23–9 lists the percentages of recovery for three-year property and five-year property. Because of the half-year convention, an additional year is added on to each property year category; that is, there are four depreciation percentages in the three-year category and six in the five-year category.

Exhibit 23–10 illustrates how this works. It is assumed that a company whose tax rate is 34 percent purchases a delivery truck at a cost of $20,000, an estimated useful life of six years, and an estimated residual value of $4,000. Under MACRS, the delivery truck is a five-year property and is depreciated for tax purposes using the 200 percent declining-balance method with a half-year convention. Under MACRS, estimated residual value is ignored. Depreciation expense for federal income tax purposes is calculated at the right side of the exhibit.

The cash inflow from activities performed by the delivery truck is estimated to be $8,000 annually. The bottom of the exhibit shows how the present value of the depreciation tax shield resulting from investing in the delivery truck is calculated. Annual cash savings from the tax shield are multiplied by the appropriate present value factors to obtain the present value of each annual cash inflow.

The positive NPV of $14,072 shown on the last line indicates that investment in the delivery truck is expected to return more than the company's required rate of return. It should also be noted that once the tax effects of the cash flows are computed and included in the calculations, the financial analysis proceeds the same way as for the methods presented earlier in this chapter. Income taxes are simply one more cash flow to consider when making a capital budgeting decision.

The choice of recovery method depends on the amount and timing of cash flows. If the enterprise will enjoy large cash inflows in the early years, the declining-balance method will be more beneficial. If, on the other hand, an enterprise is experiencing economic difficulties and will have little or no cash inflow in the early years, the straight-line method is better because it will stretch out the depreciation deductions rather than accelerate them.

EXHIBIT 23–9
Depreciation Percentages for Three-Year and Five-Year Property

MACRS

Three-Year Property	Five-Year Property
33.33%	20.00%
44.45	32.00
14.81	19.20
7.41	11.52
	11.52
	5.76

■■■ EXHIBIT 23–10
**Impact of
Depreciation Tax
Shield on Net Present
Value**

Depreciation tax shield computations

Year	Computation	Annual depreciation
1	$20,000 × 20.00%	$ 4,000
2	$20,000 × 32.00%	6,400
3	$20,000 × 19.20%	3,840
4	$20,000 × 11.52%	2,304
5	$20,000 × 11.52%	2,304
6	$20,000 × 5.76%	1,152
		$20,000

Net present value including the depreciation tax shield

	Year	Cash flow	Tax effects*	After-tax cash flow	Present value factor (16%)	Present value
Purchase truck	0	<$20,000>		<$20,000>	1.000	<$20,000>
Annual cash inflows	1–6	8,000	0.66	5,280	3.685	19,457
Salvage value	6	4,000	0.66	2,640	0.410	1,082
Tax shield:	1	4,000	0.34	1,360	0.862	1,172
	2	6,400	0.34	2,176	0.743	1,617
	3	3,840	0.34	1,306	0.641	837
	4	2,304	0.34	783	0.552	432
	5	2,304	0.34	783	0.476	373
	6	1,152	0.34	392	0.410	161
NPV of cash flows						$ 5,131

*Use (1 − tax rate) for taxable cash flows (e.g., revenues and expenses)

Purchasing versus Leasing

Capital budgeting *investment* decisions are judgments about which capital projects will be accepted for implementation. As already illustrated in this and the previous chapter, a number of methods are available to assist managers in making such decisions. If these methods produce favorable decisions, then optimal *financing* (i.e., acquisition) strategies must be determined. Common financing strategies involve purchase or lease decisions. Under certain situations, making or constructing the capital project is a third alternative.

In reality, a lease is just a substitute for a loan. Each lease payment implicitly contains a repayment of a portion of the loan and an interest charge.

For example, Protex Manufacturing has decided to acquire a computer numerical control machine with a five-year life at a purchase price of $500,000. Alternatively, the machine can be leased for $140,000 per year. The project has been accepted from previous NPV analysis. Now the optimal financing strategy—lease or purchase—must be determined. Protex can negotiate a loan at Central Bank for 10 percent. With a marginal tax rate of 40 percent, this loan has an aftertax cost of 6 percent [.10 × (1 − .40)]. Why discount cash flows at 6 percent rather than at Protex's discount rate, which would probably be higher than 6 percent? The company would use the 6 percent rather than the discount rate because *investment* decisions (which either accept or reject projects for implementation) and *financing* decisions are separate. Discount rates based on weighted-average cost of capital apply to investment decisions but not to financing decisions. The incremental cost of debt is the basic rate for discounting in financing decisions. Thus, in Exhibit 23–11, both sets of cash flows are

■■■EXHIBIT 23–11
Comparison of Purchasing and Leasing

Purchase

| Cost of project | | | | | | $500,000 |

Less present value of depreciation tax shield:

Year	Annual depreciation	Tax rate	Depreciation tax shield	Present value factor (6%)	Present value	
1	($500,000 × .200) = $100,000	.40	$40,000	.943	$37,720	
2	($500,000 × .320) = $160,000	.40	64,000	.890	56,960	
3	($500,000 × .192) = $96,000	.40	38,400	.840	32,256	
4	($500,000 × .115) = $57,500	.40	23,000	.792	18,216	
5	($500,000 × .115) = $57,500	.40	23,000	.747	17,181	
6	($500,000 × .058) = $29,000	.40	11,600	.705	8,178	<170,511>
				Net cost		$329,489

Lease

| Present value of aftertax lease payments ($140,000 × .60 × 4.212) | $353,808 |

discounted at 6 percent. Because the effective aftertax interest rate of the lease is higher than 6 percent, the purchase option is the wiser choice financially.

▌Adjusting for Inflation

Inflation is a decline in the general purchasing power of a monetary unit. Providers of both debt and equity funds demand higher rates when they expect significant inflation. Similarly, cash flows to be received in the future are less valuable due to inflation.

The discounted cash flow methods can be adjusted for inflation by increasing the discount rate and the expected cash flows by a factor to allow for the anticipated inflation. The inflation adjustment is made on the basis of some specific index that management believes to be applicable to the industry in which the enterprise operates.

Another option is to project all cash flows in terms of the current year's monetary unit without adjusting the discount rate or the cash flow projections for inflation. Whichever approach is used, management should use it *consistently*. Thus, *both* cash flows and the discount rate must be adjusted, or neither should be adjusted.

It might appear that both approaches will produce the same present value results. However, the results will be different because depreciation is deductible for tax purposes on the basis of *historical cost only*, not on the basis of historical cost adjusted for inflation.

The superior method adjusts both cash flows and the discount rate for inflation, as illustrated in Exhibit 23–12. Justrite Company is analyzing a machine that will help reduce its costs of quality, especially rework costs. The discount rate for all capital investments is 15 percent. This rate does not include an adjustment for inflation, which is expected to average 8 percent over the next five years. Justrite's income tax rate is 40 percent.

The new machine would be placed into service in early 1994. Costs-of-quality savings are estimated to be $250,000 annually over the next four years. However, the machine will require additional annual costs of supplies and power of $10,000 and $40,000, respectively, over the same time frame. Cost savings and additional costs are in current dollars.

▬▬EXHIBIT 23-12
Adjustment of Cash Flows and Discount Rate for Inflation—Justrite Company

Schedule showing the net aftertax annual cash inflows adjusted for inflation

	1994	1995	1996	1997
Costs-of-quality savings	$250,000	$250,000	$250,000	$250,000
Cost of additional supplies	<10,000>	<10,000>	<10,000>	<10,000>
Cost of additional power	<40,000>	<40,000>	<40,000>	<40,000>
Net cost savings	200,000	200,000	200,000	200,000
Inflation index	× 1.08	× 1.17	× 1.26	× 1.36
Inflation-adjusted net cost savings	216,000	234,000	252,000	272,000
Income taxes (40%)	<86,400>	<93,600>	<100,800>	<108,800>
Inflation-adjusted net aftertax cost savings	129,600	140,400	151,200	163,200
Depreciation tax shield	42,600	42,600	42,600	42,600
Net aftertax cash inflow adjusted for inflation	$172,200	$183,000	$193,800	$205,800

Net present value

Year	Net aftertax cash inflows adjusted for inflation	Present value factor (24%)*	Present value
0	<$426,000>	1.000	<$426,000>
1	172,200	.806	138,793
2	183,000	.650	118,950
3	193,800	.524	101,551
4	205,800	.423	87,053
		Net present value	$20,347

* Discount rate with the inflation factor of 8% is 24%:
$(1 + .15) (1 + .08) - 1 = .24$.

The new machine would be purchased and installed at the end of 1993 at a net cost of $426,000. If purchased, the machine would be depreciated using the straight-line method for both financial accounting and tax purposes. The machine would become obsolete in four years and have no salvage value at that time.

Management at Justrite incorporates inflation into capital budgeting decisions by adjusting the expected cash flows by an industry index. The adjusted aftertax cash flows are then discounted using an adjusted discount rate. The estimated year-end industry index values for each of the next five years are as follows:

YEAR	INDUSTRY INDEX
1993	1.00
1994	1.08
1995	1.17
1996	1.26
1997	1.36

Each element of cost savings is multiplied by the inflation index. The tax shield from the annual depreciation expense is not multiplied by the inflation factor, however, since this increase in value due to inflation is not allowed as a deduction by the Internal Revenue Service.

SENSITIVITY ANALYSIS

As the previous discussions have shown, estimates are used for various parameters, such as discount rates, cash flows, tax rates, useful lives, salvage values, and inflation indexes. The results of financial analysis are directly dependent on the parameter values used. Yet, since these parameter values are not known with certainty, it is quite possible that a change in a particular parameter's value might significantly affect the financial results. Conversely, a change in a particular parameter's value might not affect the results at all, or very little.

Sensitivity analysis is a process by which managers and management accountants determine how changes in parameter values affect the financial results. Sensitivity analysis helps managers determine the amount that parameter values must change before the decision will be affected. It is a what-if process. For example, sensitivity analysis addresses such questions as *what* is the effect on the decision to invest in the candidate project *if* the cash inflows are 10 percent less than expected and the salvage value is $20,000 more than estimated. Or, *what* is the effect (or financial results) *if* the discount rate is 2 percent higher than expected and the original investment is 14 percent less than estimated? The objective of management accountants is to present various possible results using numerous parameters so that management can evaluate and gain *insight* into a wide range of possibilities. Sensitivity analysis is the tool that enables management accountants to meet this objective.

The basic idea behind using sensitivity analysis in capital budgeting is to alter input parameter values and observe the effect on financial results. There are two broad classes of sensitivity analysis:

- Deterministic
- Probabilistic

The **deterministic class** involves altering parameters to specific or determined values and observing the specific results. The **probabilistic class** involves altering parameter values randomly within a specified probability distribution and observing the probability distribution and statistics (i.e., mean or expected value, standard deviation, and variance) of the results.

Common Approaches to Sensitivity Analysis

Four primary approaches are commonly used in sensitivity analysis:

- Graphical
- Spreadsheet
- Dedicated computer programs
- Monte Carlo Simulation

Before any of these approaches can be used, the financial analysis problem must first be defined in terms of mathematical equations, with specified input parameter values and output results. This collectively is often referred to as the mathematical model. A mathematical model can be created for any financial analysis situation, as well as for nonfinancial problems such as project timing. As an example, for a simple NPV analysis:

$$\text{NPV} = Y \times P - C$$

where Y is a yearly annuity amount, P is the present value percentage, and C is the original cost.

THE GRAPHICAL METHOD. The **graphical method** works best for simple models where only one or two input parameter values will be varied deterministically (others are held constant), and where there is a single output result of interest. Although it is possible to use this method for probabilistic analysis, it is not recommended.

The objective with the graphical method is to create a set of lines on a graph that represents the result value for various input values. The lines are typically generated by selecting two or more values of each input parameter, calculating the result values (by hand, with a calculator, or with a computer), plotting the values, and connecting the points.

The resulting shape and relation of the lines can tell managers a lot about the sensitivity of the parameters. Relatively flat lines indicate relative insensitivity, while sharply sloped lines indicate greater sensitivity. In other words, with a steeply sloping relationship, a small change in the input parameter value will cause a large change in the result. Further, lines grouped closely together indicate a relative insensitivity to changes in the parameter. Examples of these concepts are shown in Exhibit 23–13. It is important to realize, though, that the scale of the graph is very important when making relative comparisons of slopes and distances between lines. Caution is advised.

The previous example of Tahoe Ski Lodge's NPV calculation can be used to illustrate the graphical method. This example is shown on page 1102.

THE SPREADSHEET METHOD. The **spreadsheet method** is most appropriate for financial analysis problems that are too complex for the graphical method, but are simple enough to "program" into a computer spreadsheet. This method simply uses the ability of computer spreadsheets to recalculate results quickly for changes in any input parameter value. The effects of changes in input parameters can be quickly observed in any of the output result values.

When using spreadsheets, the previous results are "erased" when new values are entered. Therefore, it is important to keep a record of the results and input

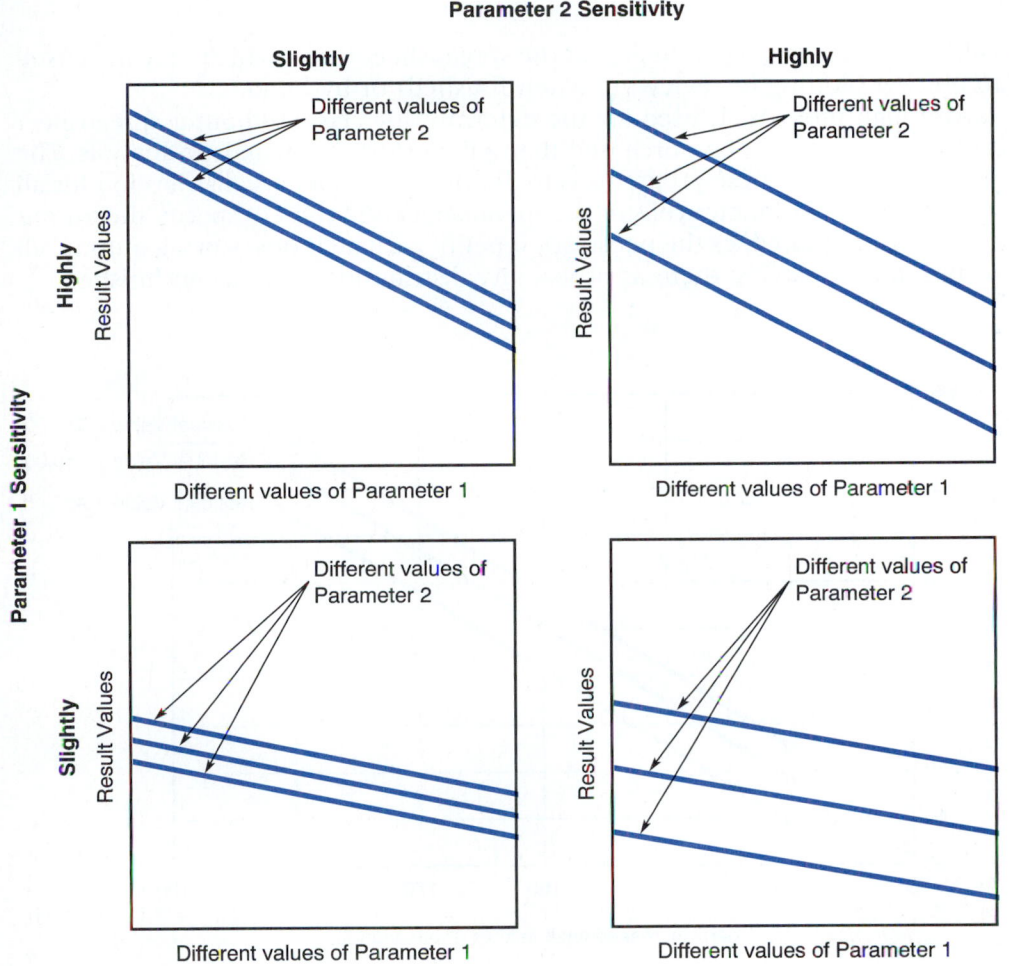

EXHIBIT 23–13
Examples of Possible Sensitivity Relationships with the Graphical Method

INSIGHTS & APPLICATIONS

Sensitivity Analysis of Tahoe Ski Lodge's NPV Calculation

LIFT COST	YEARLY CASH INFLOWS	RESIDUAL VALUE	NPV
$500,000	$140,000	$ –0–	<$ 41,640>
500,000	160,000	–0–	23,840
500,000	180,000	–0–	89,320
500,000	140,000	40,000	< 22,600>
500,000	160,000	40,000	42,880
500,000	180,000	40,000	108,360
500,000	140,000	65,000	< 10,700>
500,000	160,000	65,000	54,780
500,000	180,000	65,000	120,260

As previously given, the expected additional yearly cash inflows for a new ski lift are $160,000. The lift would cost $500,000 and have a useful life of five years and a salvage value of $40,000. These values result in an NPV of $42,880 at a discount rate of 16 percent.

Management at Tahoe Ski Lodge, however, is uncertain of the yearly increased cash inflows, thinking that they could be as high as $180,000 or as low as $140,000. Also, management believes the residual value of the lift could be $0, $40,000, or $65,000. With these deterministic values, NPVs were calculated, resulting in the following table:

These values were then plotted as shown in Exhibit 23–14. Note that the x-axis is the yearly increased cash inflows—from $130,000 to $190,000—and the three lines represent the three possible residual values. By choosing a residual value and a yearly cash flow value, the NPV can be read on the y-axis.

Examination of the graph indicates that the NPV is very sensitive to the yearly revenue, but not particularly sensitive to changes in the residual value. Since the project can more rapidly achieve a $0 NPV for higher values of yearly increased cash inflows, management should focus further analysis effort on refining the yearly cash inflow estimates and expend less effort on refining the residual value estimate.

values—either in a separate part of the spreadsheet itself (which may lend itself to quicker plotting or reviewing when finished) or by hand.

Although most often used for the deterministic class, computer spreadsheet add-on products can be purchased that will perform probabilistic analysis. The first step in using these programs is to define the probability distribution for all variable input parameter cells in the spreadsheet and then to specify the output cells. The program does the necessary repetitive calculations, storing output cell results and displaying them as probability distribution plots when finished.

■ EXHIBIT 23–14
Calculations and Plots of the Tahoe Ski Lodge Case

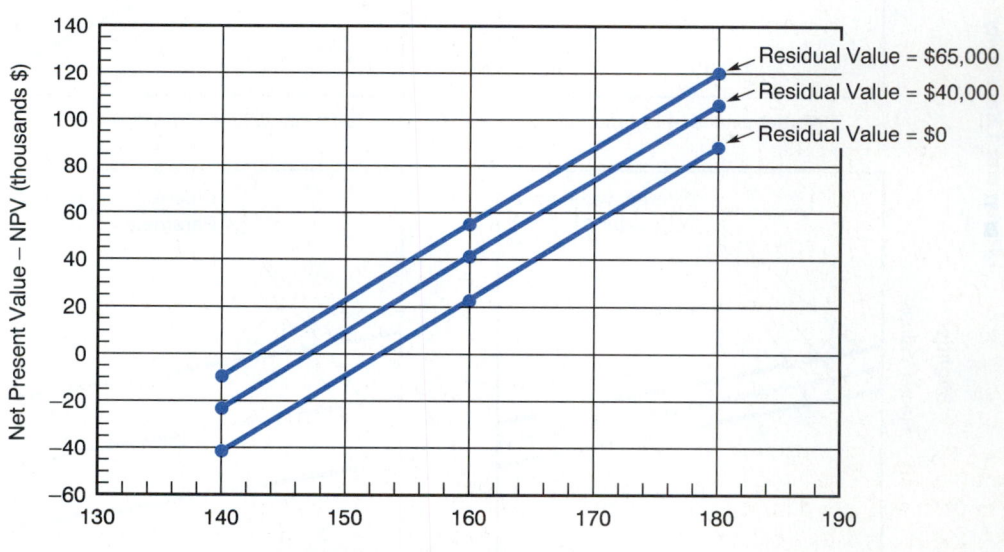

THE DEDICATED COMPUTER PROGRAM METHOD.   The **dedicated computer program method** is used for large complex problems with many input parameters and many desired output results. These programs are often custom designed for individual company requirements (e.g., future price forecasts, inflation forecasts, corporate tax structure, unique financial analysis methods), and used consistently throughout the enterprise.

THE MONTE CARLO SIMULATION METHOD.   The **Monte Carlo Simulation method** is a technique for probabilistic sensitivity analysis that is used in a wide variety of disciplines, including accounting, project management (illustrated in the next chapter), and scientific research. It can be used in any area where a mathematical model exists and input values can be derived from a probability distribution. The method involves randomly choosing input parameter values (usually more than one) based on specified probability distributions, performing the model calculations, and recording the output values. This process is typically performed thousands of times to ensure the accuracy of the simulation.

The accuracy of a Monte Carlo Simulation is greatly influenced by the number of iterations performed. As a general rule, the more iterations, the more accurate the results will be. Typically, the iterations continue until the random input parameter value distribution is representative of the desired probabilistic distribution and the output probability distributions are stable. Stability of the distributions is measured by examining the change in the mean, standard deviation, and variance of the distribution after each iteration. When the changes in these statistics become marginally small, the Monte Carlo iterations can stop. Due to the usually large number of iterations required for stability, Monte Carlo Simulations can require significant computation time, and the more complex simulations are routinely performed on the fastest supercomputers, though small and moderate simulations can be adequately and quickly performed on personal computers.

SUMMARY OF LEARNING OBJECTIVES

The major goals of this chapter were to enable you to achieve four learning objectives:

Learning objective 1.   Discuss the discounted cash flow methods, and explain the net present value (NPV), internal rate of return (IRR), and present value index (PVI) methods.

Discounted cash flow methods consider the time value of cash flows by discounting them to their present value using a discount rate based on the weighted-average cost of capital. The following capital budgeting financial analysis methods are based on discounted cash flow concepts:

- Net present value (NPV)
- Internal rate of return (IRR)
- Present value index (PVI)

The NPV technique calculates the expected net financial gain or loss from a capital project by discounting all estimated cash inflows and outflows to the present, using some predetermined discount rate. The IRR method calculates the rate at which the present value of estimated cash inflows from a capital project equals the present value of estimated cash outflows of the capital project. The PVI method calculates a ratio that compares the present value of cash inflows to the present value of the investment outlay. Because more profitable capital projects have higher indexes, an enterprise can rank its independent capital projects according to the PVI indexes.

The NPV, IRR, and PVI methods assist managers in deciding if capital projects are worthwhile financially. The decision rules for these methods are as follows:

METHOD	CONDITION	DECISION
NPV	>$0	Accept
IRR	>hurdle rate	Accept
PVI	>1.0	Accept

It is often argued that NPV is the most reasonable method, but many people who want to relate returns to a percentage figure find IRR easier to understand.

Learning objective 2.   Discuss the nondiscounted cash flow methods, which are the payback period (PP) method and the accounting rate of return (ARR) method.

Nondiscounted cash flow methods do not consider the time value of money. The following nondiscounted cash flow methods are widely used:

- Payback period (PP)
- Accounting rate of return (ARR)

The PP method calculates the amount of time needed to recoup the initial investment that the capital project requires. The ARR method divides the original or average investment into the estimated average annual income after depreciation and income taxes.

A summary of the capital budgeting financial analysis methods appears in Exhibit 23–15.

Learning objective 3.   Describe the impact of income taxes, purchasing versus leasing, and inflation on capital budgeting financial analysis.

Unless an enterprise is a tax-exempt organization, such as a government entity, income taxes should be considered in capital budgeting financial analysis. Tax-deductible cash expenditures must be converted to an aftertax basis by multiplying the expenditure by (1 − Tax rate). Only the aftertax amount is used in determining the desirability of a capital project. Similarly, taxable cash inflows must be placed on an aftertax basis by multiplying them by the same formula.

Although depreciation deductions do not involve a cash outflow, they represent tax deductions. These deductions shield income from taxation, resulting in less taxes being paid. These savings in income taxes are calculated by multiplying the depreciation deduction by the tax rate itself. Because accelerated depreciation methods provide the largest amount of tax shield early in the life of depreciable capital projects, they are normally superior to the straight-line method of depreciation. On the other hand, the straight-line method would be appropriate for start-up companies or companies that expect to experience low income or losses over the next several years.

A company that plans to acquire a capital project must determine how it will finance its acquisition and implementation. Two common methods used to finance acquisitions are purchasing and leasing. If a company purchases the project, funds can come from equity investment, debt, or other sources. When leasing, funds are provided by the lessor at some cost. Thus, the cost of leasing can be compared to the cost of owning to determine the least expensive method of financing an acceptable project.

Inflation is rampant in some countries. Inflation makes a dollar received in the future less valuable than a dollar on hand today. Inflation is generally incorporated into capital budgeting financial analysis by including an inflation factor in the discount rate. This inflation-adjusted discount rate is then used to estimate the future cash flows over the life of the project.

Learning objective 4:   Explain how sensitivity analysis assists managers in making capital budgeting decisions.

All capital investment decisions involve risk. Management can never be absolutely sure that the right capital projects are selected for implementation. This will not be known with any degree of certainty until several postimplementation audits are conducted. So, what can management accountants do to help deal with this risk and increase the level of certainty?

Up to this point, the management accountant has already set up a systematic way for management to participate in the capital budgeting methodology. In addition, promising capital projects were subjected to various financial analysis methods, such as the NPV and PVI. Conducting sensitivity analysis provides management with still another way to gain insight into the capital investment decisions that must be made. In almost any

Advantages	Disadvantages

Net Present Value (NPV)

Advantages	Disadvantages
■ Considers time value of money. ■ Considers cash flows over the entire life of the project. ■ When projects are *mutually exclusive,* NPV is generally the superior method to use in selecting the best project.	■ Discount rate may not be valid. ■ Timing and size of cash flows may not be reliable. ■ Difficult for some people to understand. ■ It is assumed that if the shorter-lived of two projects is selected, the cash inflows of that project will continue to earn the discount rate of return through the life of the longer-lived project. ■ If projects being compared involve different dollar amounts of investment, the project with more profitable dollars may not be the better project if it also requires a larger investment.

Internal Rate of Return (IRR)

Advantages	Disadvantages
■ Considers time value of money. ■ Considers cash flows over the entire life of the project. ■ Results in terms of a percentage may be more meaningful to managers than the NPV or PVI. ■ The percentage figure enables a reasonable ranking of projects that require different initial cash outlays and have unequal lives.	■ Hurdle rate may not be valid. ■ Timing and size of cash flows may not be reliable. ■ Difficult to calculate. ■ Projects are ranked for funding using the IRR rather than the absolute dollar return. ■ It is assumed that if the shorter-lived of two projects is selected, the cash inflows of that project will continue to earn the IRR through the life of the longer-lived project (generally not a reasonable assumption).

Present Value Index (PVI)

Advantages	Disadvantages
■ Same as NPV, except that it simplifies ranking of an optimum set of *independent* projects when the total capital budget is limited.	■ Same as NPV. ■ Gives relative answer but does not reflect absolute dollars of NPV. ■ It can be misleading on *mutually exclusive* projects that have different total initial investments.

Payback Period (PP)

Advantages	Disadvantages
■ It is simple to calculate and understand. ■ It may be used to select those capital projects yielding a quick return of cash, thus placing an emphasis on liquidity. ■ It signals the level of risk, i.e., shorter payback means lower risk.	■ It ignores the time value of money (discounted payback helps overcome this problem). ■ It ignores cash flows that may occur beyond the payback period. ■ It fails to consider salvage value that may exist after the payback period. ■ It does not favor profitable projects with longer payback periods.

Accounting Rate of Return (ARR)

Advantages	Disadvantages
■ Data for its calculation are relatively easy to obtain from the financial accounting system. ■ It considers income over the entire life of the project.	■ It ignores the time value of money. ■ It depends on averaging techniques that may yield inaccurate results, particularly when cash flows are unequal throughout a project's life.

decision-making process, conducting sensitivity analysis will enable the situation to be evaluated more thoroughly so that a better decision can be made.

IMPORTANT TERMS

Accounting rate of return (ARR) method (unadjusted rate of return and **book value rate of return)** Calculates the return from a capital project by dividing the average annual net income (after depreciation and income taxes) by the average investment or initial investment.

Annuity A series of equal cash flows (either inflows or outflows) per period.

Dedicated computer program method Customized software package for conducting specialized sensitivity analysis.

Deterministic class Involves altering parameters to specific or determined values and observing the specific results.

Discount rate (hurdle rate) Expected return on the capital funds invested at a given level of risk.

Discounted cash flow (DCF) methods The NPV, IRR, and PVI methods that determine the present value of future cash flows.

Graphical method A simple method of performing sensitivity analysis where only one or two input parameter values are varied deterministically.

Independent projects Capital projects that have no significant bearing on one another.

Internal rate of return (IRR) method (time-adjusted rate of return) The rate of return at which the present value of the net cash inflows minus the investment in the capital project equals zero.

Monte Carlo Simulation method A technique used to perform probabilistic sensitivity analysis in a wide variety of disciplines.

Mutually exclusive projects A set of candidate projects from which one is accepted.

Net present value (NPV) method The total cash inflows less the total cash outflows discounted by the discount rate to their current value.

Nondiscounted cash flow methods The payback period (PP) method and accounting rate of return (ARR) method.

Payback period (PP) method Measures how long in years it takes to recover in cash inflows an amount equal to the initial investment.

Present value index (PVI) method (profitability index [PI] and **cost/benefit ratio)** The ratio of the present value of a capital project's net cash inflows to the initial investment required.

Probabilistic class Involves altering parameter values randomly within a specified probability distribution and observing the probability distribution and statistics.

Sensitivity analysis A process by which managers and management accountants determine how changes in parameter values affect the financial results.

Spreadsheet method Used to conduct sensitivity analysis, usually on a deterministic class of parameters.

Tax shield A reduction in the amount of taxable income resulting from a depreciation deduction (or other deductions). The reduction in tax is calculated by multiplying the depreciation deduction by the prevailing tax rate.

Time value of money The value attributed to money as a result of its ability to earn a return over time. A dollar today is worth more than a dollar in the future, and the longer one waits for a dollar, the more uncertain the receipt is.

Weighted-average cost of capital A composite of the cost of the various sources of funds that comprise an enterprise's capital structure. It is the minimum rate of return that must be earned on new investments so as not to dilute shareholder interests.

DEMONSTRATION PROBLEMS

■ DEMONSTRATION PROBLEM 1 *Comprehensive analysis.*

Primerate Bank is considering the purchase of a local area network (LAN) for $800,000 that will reduce operating costs by $300,000, $400,000, $500,000, and $600,000 during

1994, 1995, 1996, and 1997, respectively. The LAN has an estimated life of four years with no salvage value. Primerate uses straight-line depreciation. The income tax rate is 40%, and Primerate's desired rate of return on capital project investments is 14%. The aftertax increase in net income and the cash flow from the proposed LAN investment are as follows:

	1994	1995	1996	1997
Increase in net income before taxes and depreciation	$300,000	$400,000	$500,000	$600,000
Depreciation	< 200,000>	< 200,000>	< 200,000>	< 200,000>
Net increase before taxes	100,000	200,000	300,000	400,000
Taxes (40%)	< 40,000>	< 80,000>	< 120,000>	< 160,000>
Net increase in net income after taxes	60,000	120,000	180,000	240,000
Depreciation	200,000	200,000	200,000	200,000
Cash savings	$260,000	$320,000	$380,000	$440,000

Required:
a. Calculate the internal rate of return (IRR) and give a brief description of it.
b. Calculate the net present value (NPV) and give a brief description of it.
c. Calculate the payback period and give a brief description of it.
d. Apply the payback period (PP) method in a way that will overcome its weakness of ignoring the time value of money.
e. Calculate the accounting rate of return (ARR) and give a brief description of it.

SOLUTION TO DEMONSTRATION PROBLEM 1

a.

PRIMERATE BANK
INTERNAL RATE OF RETURN
LAN PROJECT

		22%		24%		26%	
YEAR	COST SAVINGS	PRESENT VALUE FACTOR	PRESENT VALUE	PRESENT VALUE FACTOR	PRESENT VALUE	PRESENT VALUE FACTOR	PRESENT VALUE
1	$260,000	.820	$213,200	.806	$209,560	.794	$206,440
2	320,000	.672	215,040	.650	208,000	.630	201,600
3	380,000	.551	209,380	.524	199,120	.500	190,000
4	440,000	.451	198,440	.423	186,120	.397	174,680
			$836,060		$802,800		$772,720

Present value at 24%	$802,800	$802,800
Present value at 26%	772,720	
Present value of investment		800,000
Difference	$ 30,080	$ 2,800

$$IRR = .24 + \frac{\$ 2,800}{\$30,080}(.26 - .24)$$

$$= .24 + .09(.02)$$

$$= .2418 \text{ or } 24.18\%$$

The IRR is the actual discounted rate of return expected to be earned on the LAN. The process for computing the rate when the cash inflows are not uniform is based on trial and error. Various rates are tried until the correct one is found, usually by interpolation. The rate is correct when the present value of cash inflows is equal to the present value of cash outflows (e.g., investment).

If the IRR is greater than the discount rate (or hurdle rate), then the LAN is accepted. In this case, the return is 24.18%, which is much larger than the bank's discount rate of 14%.

b.

PRIMERATE BANK
NET PRESENT VALUE
LAN PROJECT

Present value of cash inflows:

YEAR	COST SAVINGS	PRESENT VALUE FACTOR (14%)	PRESENT VALUE
1	$260,000	.877	$228,020
2	320,000	.769	246,080
3	380,000	.675	256,500
4	440,000	.592	260,480
	Total present value of cash inflows		$991,080

Present value of cash outflow:
Investment, beginning of 1994   < 800,000>
          Net present value $191,080

Under the NPV method, the future cash inflows are discounted at the discount rate of 14%. The difference between the present value of the cash inflows and the present value of cash outflows (i.e., the investment) represents the NPV. The NPV of the LAN project is $191,080 and is accepted.

c.

PRIMERATE BANK
PAYBACK PERIOD
LAN PROJECT

YEAR	CASH INFLOWS	CUMULATIVE CASH INFLOWS	YEARS NEEDED
1	$260,000	$ 260,000	1.00
2	320,000	580,000	1.00
3	380,000	960,000	.58*
4	440,000	1,400,000	—
			2.58

$$*\text{Percentage of year needed} = \frac{\text{Cash needed to pay back investment}}{\text{Cash inflow for year}}$$

$$= \frac{\$800,000 \text{ investment} - \$580,000 \text{ cumulative cash flows}}{\$380,000}$$

$$= .58 \text{ of a year}$$

The payback period is the time it takes for the cumulative sum of the cash inflows to equal the initial cash outlay (i.e., the investment). For Primerate, the payback period for the LAN project is 2.58 years.

The PP method is widely used because it is easily calculated and understood. It has two weaknesses, however. First, it fails to measure profitability by ignoring all cash flows after the end of the payback period. Second, it does not consider the time value of money.

d.

PRIMERATE BANK
PAYBACK PERIOD USING DISCOUNTED CASH FLOWS
LAN PROJECT

YEAR	CASH INFLOWS	PRESENT VALUE FACTOR (14%)	PRESENT VALUE	CUMULATIVE CASH INFLOWS
1	$260,000	.877	$228,020	$228,020
2	320,000	.769	246,080	474,100

| 3 | 380,000 | .675 | 256,500 | 730,600* |
| 4 | 440,000 | .592 | 260,480 | 991,080 |

$$\text{*Payback period using a 14\% discount rate} = \frac{\text{Amount needed}}{\text{Total cash inflow in year 4}}$$

$$= \frac{\$800,000 - \$730,600}{\$260,480} + 3 \text{ years}$$

$$= 3.27 \text{ years}$$

This calculation eliminates the criticism that the payback period necessarily ignores the time value of money. Using the 14% discount rate and the present value of the cash inflows, the payback period is 3.27 years.

e.

**PRIMERATE BANK
ACCOUNTING RATE OF RETURN
LAN PROJECT**

$$\text{ARR} = \frac{\text{Average cash inflow} - \text{Depreciation}}{\text{Investment}}$$

where:

$$\text{Average cash inflow} = \$1,400,000 \div 4 \text{ years}$$
$$= \$350,000 \text{ per year}$$

$$\text{Depreciation} = \$800,000 \div 4 \text{ years}$$
$$= \$200,000 \text{ per year}$$

Therefore, the ARR using the original investment is:

$$\text{ARR} = \frac{\$350,000 - \$200,000}{\$800,000}$$

$$= 18.75\%$$

The ARR using the average investment as the denominator is:

$$\text{ARR} = \frac{\text{Average cash inflow} - \text{Depreciation}}{(\text{Investment} \div 2)}$$

$$= \frac{\$350,000 - \$200,000}{(\$800,000 \div 2)}$$

$$= 37.50\%$$

Under the ARR method, the expected annual net income is divided by the investment. The net income is the average net cash inflows minus depreciation.

The ARR can be calculated by dividing the average cash inflow by the original investment or by the average investment (investment plus salvage value divided by 2).

The ARR does not account for the time value of money. It is an averaging method, and if cash flows are not uniform during the life of the project, the degree of error can be substantial.

■**DEMONSTRATION PROBLEM 2**   *The tax effects of MACRS.*

The Comstock Company is considering purchasing a machine costing $10,000. The useful life of the machine is five years. Comstock's discount rate is 10%. Its income tax rate is 40%.

Required:
Calculate the NPV under the straight-line and MACRS methods using a half-year convention.

SOLUTION TO DEMONSTRATION PROBLEM 2

The depreciation tax shield is the amount by which income taxes are reduced because of depreciation expense. Calculating it is similar to calculating the tax effect of any deductible expense:

Depreciation tax shield = Annual depreciation deduction × Tax rate

Straight-Line Method

Year	Depreciation Expense	Tax Rate	Tax Shield	Present Value Factor (10%)	Present Value
1	$1,000	.40	$ 400.00	.909	$ 363.60
2	2,000	.40	800.00	.826	660.80
3	2,000	.40	800.00	.751	600.80
4	2,000	.40	800.00	.683	546.40
5	2,000	.40	800.00	.621	496.80
6	1,000	.40	400.00	.564	225.60
				Net present value	$2,894.00

MACRS Method

Year	Depreciation Expense	Tax Rate	Tax Shield	Present Value Factor (10%)	Present Value
1	$2,000	.40	$ 800.00	.909	$ 727.20
2	3,200	.40	1,280.00	.826	1,057.28
3	1,920	.40	768.00	.751	576.77
4	1,152	.40	460.80	.683	314.73
5	1,152	.40	460.80	.621	286.16
6	576	.40	230.40	.564	129.95
				Net present value	$3,092.09

As can be seen from this analysis, the NPV of the tax shield (i.e., tax savings) from MACRS is greater than that from the straight-line depreciation method.

■ DEMONSTRATION PROBLEM 3   *The lease-versus-purchase decision.*

Mercy Hospital's management accountant, Mary Balinsky, has just finished performing an NPV analysis for a $1,090,000 CAT scanner with a five-year useful life. Top management has agreed with Mary's recommendation and has asked her to analyze the alternative financing available.

After careful analysis, Mary has narrowed the financing of the project to two alternatives. The first alternative is a lease agreement with the manufacturer of the CAT scanner. The manufacturer is willing to lease the scanner to Mercy Hospital for five years. The lease agreement calls for Mercy to make annual payments of $250,000 at the beginning of each year.

The second alternative would be for Mercy to purchase the scanner outright from the manufacturer for $1,090,000. The hospital can claim an investment tax credit of $90,000 if it purchases the scanner. Preliminary negotiations with Mercy's bank indicate that the hospital would be able to finance the scanner acquisition with a 10% term loan.

If the scanner is purchased, Mercy plans to depreciate the scanner over five years using the straight-line method. Salvage value is zero.

All maintenance, taxes, and insurance costs are the same under both alternatives and are paid by Mercy. Mercy is subject to a 40% income tax rate.

Required:
a. Calculate the relevant present value cost of the purchasing alternative.
b. Calculate the relevant present value cost of the leasing alternative.
c. Financially, which is the better alternative?

SOLUTION TO DEMONSTRATION PROBLEM 3

a.

Purchase

Cost of project (cash outflow of $1,000,000 − $90,000 × present value factor of 1.000) = $1,000,000

Less present value of depreciation tax shield:

Present Value

YEAR	ANNUAL DEPRECIATION	TAX RATE	DEPRECIATION TAX SHIELD	PRESENT VALUE FACTOR (6%)	PRESENT VALUE
1	$200,000	0.4	$80,000	0.943	$75,440
2	200,000	0.4	80,000	0.890	71,200
3	200,000	0.4	80,000	0.840	67,200
4	200,000	0.4	80,000	0.792	63,360
5	200,000	0.4	80,000	0.747	59,760

Present value of purchase cost   < 336,960>

$ 663,040

b.

Lease

Time	AFTERTAX COST OF LEASE PAYMENT	PRESENT VALUE FACTOR (6%)	PRESENT VALUE
0	($250,000 × .60) = $150,000	1.000	$ 150,000
1–4	($250,000 × .60) = $150,000	3.465	519,750

Present value of lease payments $ 669,750

c. The purchase alternative is better financially because the present value of this alternative is $6,710 ($669,750 − $663,040) less than the present value cost of the purchase alternative.

■ **DEMONSTRATION PROBLEM 4**   *The graphical method of sensitivity analysis.* As presented in the text, the expected additional yearly revenue for a new automatic welding machine for Vulcan Machine Shop is $100,000. The yearly cash operating costs and income taxes are estimated at $68,000. The machine would cost $200,000, have a ten-year life, and have a salvage value of $30,000. A straight-line depreciation method is used. Management at Vulcan is uncertain of the yearly revenue, however, thinking that it could be as high as $125,000 or as low as $90,000. Also, management believes the salvage value of the machine could be $0, $30,000, or $50,000.

Required:
a. Create the mathematical model and perform a sensitivity analysis.
b. Show the results in graphical form.
c. Comment on the results.

SOLUTION TO DEMONSTRATION PROBLEM 4
a. The mathematical model for this problem is:

$$ARR = \frac{R - (OT + DE)}{(C + S) \div 2}$$

where:

R = Increased yearly revenue
OT = Yearly increased operating costs and taxes
C = Cost of the machine
S = Salvage value of the machine
DE = Yearly depreciation expense calculated by DE = $(C - S) \div L$
L = Life (years) of the machine

Calculating the various scenarios results in the following table:

MACHINE COST	REVENUES	COSTS AND TAXES	SALVAGE VALUE	ARR
$200,000	$ 90,000	$68,000	$ –0–	2.00
200,000	100,000	68,000	–0–	12.00
200,000	125,000	68,000	–0–	37.00
200,000	90,000	68,000	30,000	4.35
200,000	100,000	68,000	30,000	13.04
200,000	125,000	68,000	30,000	34.78
200,000	90,000	68,000	50,000	5.60
200,000	100,000	68,000	50,000	13.60
200,000	125,000	68,000	50,000	33.60

b. Note that the *x*-axis is the yearly revenue—from $80,000 to $130,000—and the three lines represent the three possible salvage values. By choosing a salvage value and a yearly revenue value, the ARR can be read on the *y*-axis.

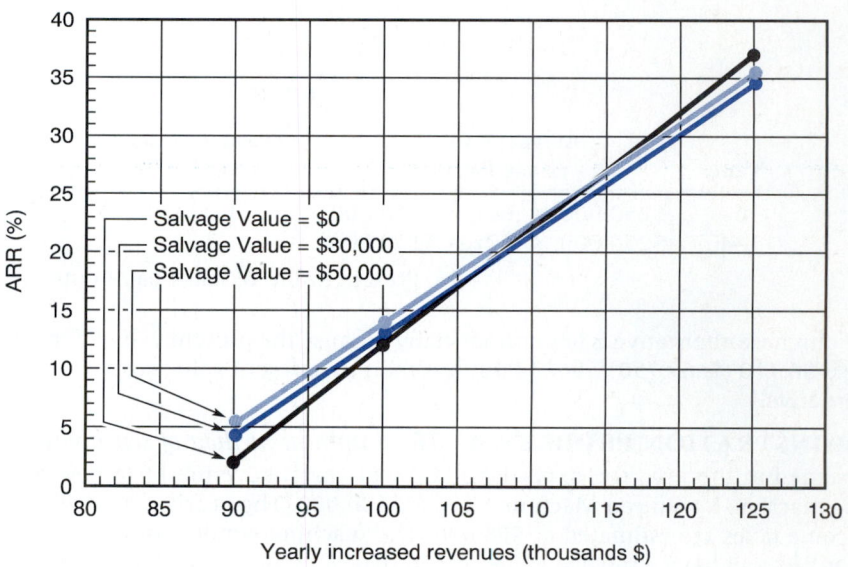

c. Examination of the graph indicates that the ARR is very sensitive to the yearly revenue, but not particularly sensitive to changes in the salvage value. Since the project can achieve the minimum desired rate of 20% for high values of yearly revenue, management should focus further analysis effort on refining the yearly revenue estimates and expend less effort on refining the salvage value estimate.

It can also be seen that the three lines are not parallel. This is a direct result of the formulation of the mathematical model. Since the salvage value is used in two different places, changes in this value will cause the slope to change.

■ **DEMONSTRATION PROBLEM 5**   *The spreadsheet method of sensitivity analysis.*
Management at Secure System is considering acquiring a machine that will manufacture a new automobile security device. The machine will cost $200,000 with a useful life of four years and no salvage value. There is some management disagreement as to the amount of net cash inflows the machine will produce. Estimates are $50,000, $70,000, and $90,000 annually. Cash inflows for each year are equal. Also, management believes the project should be analyzed assuming discount rates of 8, 10, and 12%, respectively.

Required:
Use sensitivity analysis to compute the NPV under each assumption.

SOLUTION TO DEMONSTRATION PROBLEM 5

Useful Life	Discount Rate	Initial Cash Outflow	Present Value of Cash Inflows		Net Present Value
4	8%	$200,000	$165,600 = ($50,000 × 3.312)		<$34,400>
4	10	200,000	158,500 = ($50,000 × 3.170)		< 41,500>
4	12	200,000	151,850 = ($50,000 × 3.037)		< 48,150>
4	8	200,000	231,840 = ($70,000 × 3.312)		31,840
4	10	200,000	221,900 = ($70,000 × 3.170)		21,900
4	12	200,000	212,590 = ($70,000 × 3.037)		12,590
4	8	200,000	298,080 = ($90,000 × 3.312)		98,080
4	10	200,000	285,300 = ($90,000 × 3.170)		85,300
4	12	200,000	273,330 = ($90,000 × 3.037)		73,330

Note: This type of problem is especially applicable to the spreadsheet method.

■**DEMONSTRATION PROBLEM 6**   *Sensitivity analysis with Monte Carlo Simulations.*

Zero Luggage Company is planning to introduce a new line of titanium briefcases. The estimated development costs are $110,000 with net cash inflows estimated at $85,000 and $50,000 for the two-year life of the product line. Management, knowing that these values could vary, performed further analysis and derived the following probability distributions:

Development Probability	Costs	Year 1 Probability	Cash Inflows	Year 2 Probability	Cash Inflows
0.1	$150,000	0.2	$100,000	0.2	$65,000
0.3	120,000	0.4	90,000	0.4	60,000
0.5	105,000	0.2	80,000	0.2	40,000
0.1	65,000	0.2	65,000	0.2	25,000

Required:
Assuming a discount rate of 14%:

a. Calculate the NPV for the original estimates.
b. Using Monte Carlo Simulation, calculate the mean of the iterations and the probability of the NPV being lower than $0.
c. Compare the results from Requirements (a) and (b) and comment. Make any assumptions you deem necessary.

SOLUTION TO DEMONSTRATION PROBLEM 6

a. The mathematical equation for the NPV is:

$$NPV = (0.877 \times Y1) + (0.769 \times Y2) - D$$

where:

$$NPV = \text{Net present value}$$
$$Y1 = \text{First-year cash inflow}$$
$$Y2 = \text{Second-year cash inflow}$$
$$D = \text{Initial development costs}$$

Using this equation, the original NPV would be:

$$NPV = (0.877 \times \$85,000) + (0.769 \times \$50,000) - \$110,000$$
$$NPV = \underline{\underline{\$2,995}}$$

b. The Monte Carlo sensitivity analysis was simplified by assuming step functions for each of the probability distributions. Then, a table of ten values for each parameter was created by using the probabilities. For example, for the development costs parameter, one of the ten values would be $150,000, three of the values would be $120,000, and so forth, resulting in the following:

Development Costs	Year 1 Cash Inflows	Year 2 Cash Inflows
$150,000	$100,000	$65,000
120,000	100,000	65,000
120,000	90,000	60,000
120,000	90,000	60,000
105,000	90,000	60,000
105,000	90,000	60,000
105,000	80,000	40,000
105,000	80,000	40,000
105,000	65,000	25,000
65,000	65,000	25,000

Then, for each Monte Carlo iteration, obtaining a random number for each parameter becomes a simple process of selecting one value from each column randomly. After obtaining the random parameter values, the NPV calculation was done. The NPV was saved for each iteration, and a cumulative mean value was calculated. The iterations were stopped when the cumulative mean value did not vary more than $250 and the cumulative variance did not vary more than $62,500 ($250 × $250) from iteration to iteration.

In all, 347 iterations were required, with the total number of NPVs below $0 being 151. Thus, the probability for the NPV being below $0 is:

$$\text{Probability} = 151 \div 347$$
$$= \underline{43.5\%}$$

The mean of the NPVs was $2,117.10.

The 43.5% probability that the project would have a negative NPV, even though the mean estimates show a positive NPV, might cause management to require further refinement of the parameter estimates and probability distributions before approving the project.

c. The mean values from Requirements (a) and (b) are somewhat different. This can be attributed to the limited number of iterations required to meet the cumulative mean and variance change limits. In a computerized Monte Carlo system, with a significantly smaller difference limit of $50, a total of 665 iterations were required for stabilization. The cumulative mean was $3,003.53—very close to the results in (a)—and the probability that the NPV would be less than $0 was 44.1%, not much of a change from that calculated in (b).

REVIEW QUESTIONS

23.1 The second stage of the capital budgeting methodology deals with:

a. Decisions affecting high-tech companies.
b. Financial analysis of long-term decisions.
c. Financial analysis of short-term decisions.
d. Capital asset tracking systems.

23.2 Present value is:

a. The sum of cash inflows discounted to time zero.
b. The sum of cash outflows discounted to time zero.
c. Both (a) and (b).
d. None of the above.

23.3 An enterprise's relevant weighted-average cost of capital:

a. Should be the same as the prime rate.
b. Should be unaffected by the enterprise's capital structure.
c. Is a weighted average of the enterprise's required future returns on debt and equity.

   d. Is a weighted average of common stock less paid-in capital.

23.4   The basis for measuring the cost of capital derived from debt and preferred stock, respectively, is the

   a. Pretax rate of interest for debt and stated annual dividend rate for preferred stock.
   b. Aftertax rate of interest for debt and stated annual dividend rate for preferred stock.
   c. Aftertax rate of interest for debt and stated annual dividend rate less the expected earnings per share for preferred stock.
   d. Pretax rate of interest for debt and stated annual dividend rate less the expected earnings per share for preferred stock.

23.5   The discount rate ordinarily used in present value calculations is:

   a. The prime rate.
   b. The savings bond rate.
   c. The Federal Reserve rate.
   d. The desired rate of return set by management.

23.6   Net present value is:

   a. The sum of discounted cash inflows plus discounted cash outflows.
   b. The sum of discounted cash outflows.
   c. The sum of discounted cash inflows less the sum of discounted cash outflows.
   d. The sum of discounted cash inflows.

23.7   The IRR and NPV methods usually produce identical rankings of candidate projects. Under certain conditions, however, dissimilar rankings can occur. When such differences occur, the method normally selected is:

   a. NPV because all reinvestment of funds occurs at the discount rate based on the cost of capital and because it takes into account the relative size of the original investment.
   b. IRR because all reinvestment of funds occurs at the discount rate that will make the NPV of the project equal to zero.
   c. NPV because all reinvestment of funds occurs at the discount rate that will make the NPV of the project equal to zero.
   d. IRR because all reinvestment of funds occurs at the rate of the cost of capital and because it takes into account the relative size of the original investment.

23.8   A manager at Coretop Company has questioned the accuracy of the NPV method because the present value factors are based on the assumption that cash flows occur at the end of the year. She argues that the cash flows actually occur uniformly throughout each year. What is your response to her?

   a. The NPV is totally accurate.
   b. The NPV is slightly understated but usable.
   c. The NPV gives a consistent 10% error of the estimate.
   d. The NPV is slightly overstated but usable.

23.9   A company is considering the purchase of a conveyor belt that will link to one of its major customers for just-in-time delivery of parts. The system will cost $900,000 and will have a life of seven years. It will provide a number of benefits, such as reduced transportation and storage costs, reduced handling costs, and increased revenue. The company's discount rate is 12%. What method should the management accountant select to evaluate the cost/benefit relationship of this capital project?

   a. CVP analysis.
   b. Regression analysis.
   c. EOQ analysis.
   d. NPV or IRR analysis.

23.10 Which of the following is an assumption regarding NPV computation?

    a. The life of all capital projects is less than the payback period.
    b. Reinvestment of the cash inflows will be made at the discount rate.
    c. All capital projects will generate long-term profits.
    d. The life of all projects is greater than five years.

23.11 Which of the following is a method of capital selection that considers the time value of money?

    a. IRR method.
    b. ARR method (based on original investment).
    c. ARR method (based on average investment).
    d. Linear programming.

23.12 The IRR method, as contrasted with the NPV method:

    a. Is considered better for analyzing lease financing.
    b. Is considered inferior because it fails to calculate compounded interest.
    c. Assumes that the rate of return on the reinvestment of the cash inflows is at the indicated rate of return of the project analyzed rather than at the discount rate.
    d. Uses average net income over the project's life.

23.13 Which of the following methods implies that cash inflows are reinvested at the rate of return earned by the capital project investment?

    a. ARR method.
    b. NPV method.
    c. IRR method.
    d. PVI method.

23.14 The present value index (PVI) is also called the cost/benefit ratio (or benefit/cost ratio). What are the benefits? Discuss what role Chapter 22 plays in providing data necessary to use the PVI or cost/benefit ratio, as well as the NPV, IRR, PP, and ARR methods.

23.15 The PVI is:

    a. Another term for profitability index (PI).
    b. The ratio of the present value to the original investment.
    c. Both (a) and (b).
    d. None of the above.

23.16 When the PVI for a project equals one:

    a. The NPV equals zero.
    b. The present value of project returns is less than the present value of the project cost.
    c. The IRR is less than the discount rate.
    d. The payback period is equal to one year.

23.17 A candidate project has an expected life of five years. In the computation of the NPV of the candidate project, salvage value would be:

    a. Included as a cash inflow at the future amount of the estimated salvage value.
    b. Included as a cash inflow at the present value of the estimated salvage value.
    c. Included as a cash inflow at the estimated salvage value.
    d. Excluded from NPV's computation.

23.18 Which of the following capital budgeting financial analysis methods assumes that funds are reinvested at the firm's cost of capital?

    a. NPV method.
    b. IRR method.

    c. ARR method.
    d. PP method.

23.19 An advantage of using the PP method of evaluating capital projects is that:

    a. It considers the time value of money.
    b. It is easy to apply and managers readily understand it.
    c. It incorporates inflation.
    d. It considers the full life of the project.

23.20 Deficiencies associated with using the PP method to evaluate capital projects include:

    a. The present value of cash inflows is ignored.
    b. Cash inflows of different time periods are treated equally.
    c. Disproportionate weight is given to cash flows occurring in the future.
    d. Cash flows after the payback period are ignored.
    e. All of the above.

23.21 The PP method measures:

    a. The total profitability of the project.
    b. How quickly investment dollars may be recovered.
    c. The cash inflow generated by the project's salvage value.
    d. The economic life of an investment.

23.22 Which of the following capital budgeting financial analysis methods has been criticized because it fails to consider investment profitability?

    a. NPV method.
    b. IRR method.
    c. PP method.
    d. ARR method.

23.23 A major criticism of the PP method is that it doesn't consider the time value of money. Explain how this criticism can be overcome.

23.24 Depreciation is incorporated in the discounted cash flow methods because it:

    a. Reduces the cash outlay for income taxes.
    b. Represents the initial cash outflow spread over the life of the project.
    c. Represents a hedge against inflation.
    d. Represents cash outflow that cannot be avoided.

23.25 Which of the following best describes the effect that changing from straight-line to accelerated depreciation will have on the financial analysis of a capital project?

    a. The calculations will be invalid because only the straight-line depreciation method can be used for tax purposes.
    b. The risk of the proposed investment will be larger than if the straight-line depreciation method is used.
    c. The NPV of the proposed investment will be larger than if the straight-line depreciation method is used.
    d. The cash inflows in each period after income tax effects will be smaller than with the straight-line depreciation method.

23.26 When applying one of the discounted cash flow methods to evaluate the desirability of a capital project, which of the following factors is generally not considered?

    a. The impact of inflation.
    b. The impact of income taxes.
    c. The timing and quantity of cash flows.
    d. The method of financing the project.

CHAPTER-SPECIFIC PROBLEMS

These problems require responses based directly on concepts and techniques presented in the text.

23.27 *Weighted-average cost of capital.* Excello Company is in the process of reengineering its activities based on activity-based management (ABM) analyses. The projects contained in the Capital Projects Portfolio Statement that support the reengineered activities involve nearly equal risk. They are independent of each other so that Excello may invest in a single project, any combination, or all of them. The capital outlay for each project is as follows:

Project A	$ 800,000
Project B	200,000
Project C	900,000
Project D	400,000
Total	$2,300,000

Excello intends to maintain a capital structure of 40% long-term debt and 60% equity, of which 80% is common stock and 20% retained earnings. The weighted-average cost of capital is 9% when historical values are used.

The expected annual cost of generating earnings available for the capital projects is 12%. Excello can issue long-term bonds at an annual interest rate of 10%. Issuance of common stock will cost 20%. Excello is subject to a 40% income tax rate.

Required:
a. Explain why new capital investments should be evaluted on the basis of future weighted-average cost of capital rather than a weighted-average cost of capital based on historical values.
b. Calculate the weighted-average cost of capital Excello should use in its discounted cash flow analysis.

23.28 *Using the PVI and NPV methods.* Seth Milam has collected the following data during the first stage of the capital budgeting methodology. These data relate to Projects Alpha and Beta, which are of equal risk.

PRESENT VALUE OF CASH FLOWS

YEAR	ALPHA	BETA
0	<$10,000>	<$30,000>
1	4,550	13,650
2	4,150	12,450
3	3,750	11,250

Required:
Which of the projects would be selected using the PVI and NPV methods?

23.29 *Capital rationing.* Arco has the opportunity to invest in the following independent projects:

PROJECT	REQUIRED INVESTMENT	NPV
A	$ 80,000	$2,000
B	100,000	1,000
C	40,000	1,200
D	80,000	1,500
E	92,000	2,200

Although Arco would like to invest in all five projects, it has only $240,000 of capital funds available.

Required:
Using the NPV and PVI methods, determine the combination of projects that

produces the greatest value to Arco's stockholders. Assume that the projects permit partial investment. Which method, the NPV or PVI, would you use to ration the capital funds of $240,000? Justify your answer.

23.30 *Calculating the payback period given unequal cash inflows.* A machine costing $2,000 produces total cash inflows of $3,000 over four years as follows:

YEAR	AFTERTAX CASH INFLOWS	CUMULATIVE CASH INFLOWS
1	$ 600	$ 600
2	800	1,400
3	1,000	2,400
4	600	3,000

Required:
Calculate the payback period.

23.31 *Calculating the payback period and accounting rate of return.* Hanley Company purchased a machine for $125,000. The machine will be depreciated $25,000 each year for five years. At the end of five years, it will have zero salvage value. The related cash flow from operations, net of income taxes, is expected to be $45,000 annually. Hanley's income tax rate is 40% for all years.

Required:
a. Calculate the payback period.
b. Calculate the accounting rate of return.

[AICPA adapted]

23.32 *Calculating the payback period given equal cash inflows.* Tarmack Company is considering the purchase of a machine for $350,000 with a life of five years and a salvage value of $50,000. The machine will be depreciated using the straight-line method. (Ignore the half-year convention.) The machine is expected to produce cash inflows from operations, net of income taxes, of $100,000 annually in each of the next five years.

Required:
Calculate the payback period.

23.33 *Calculating and comparing all the financial analysis methods.* Dynameg Corporation is trying to decide whether to select a mainframe-based centralized information system or a network-based distributed information system. Both systems will perform the same data processing tasks. Based on various tangible and intangible benefits, the annual cash inflows produced by these benefits are estimated to be $200,000 for the mainframe system and $100,000 for the network system. The original investment will require $500,000 for the mainframe and $217,000 for the network. The network has a life of four years and the mainframe five years.

Dynameg's discount rate is 10%. Neither capital project will have a salvage value at the end of its useful life. Both capital projects will be depreciated using the straight-line method. For the following calculations, ignore income taxes and the half-year convention.

Required:
a. Calculate the NPV for each investment.
b. Calculate the IRR (approximations are acceptable) for each investment.
c. Calculate the PVI for each investment.
d. Calculate the payback period for each investment.
e. Calculate the ARR for each investment. Use the original investment as the denominator.
f. Which project should be selected for implementation? Justify your answer.

23.34 *Considering income taxes.* Rockyford Company must replace some machinery. This machinery has zero book value, but its current market value is $1,800. One possibility is to invest in new machinery that will cost $40,000. This new machinery would produce estimated annual pretax operating cash savings of $12,500.

Assume the new machinery will have a useful life of four years and have depreciation of $10,000 each year for book and tax purposes. (Ignore the half-year convention.) It will have no salvage value at the end of four years. The investment in this new machinery would require an additional investment in working capital of $3,000.

If Rockyford accepts this investment proposal, the disposal of the old machinery and the investment in the new equipment will take place on December 31 of this year. The cash flows from the investment will occur during the next four calendar years.

Rockyford is subject to a 40% income tax rate for all ordinary income and capital gains and has a 10% aftertax cost of capital. All operating and tax cash flows are assumed to occur at year-end.

Required:
a. Calculate the present value of the aftertax cash inflow arising from the disposal of the old machinery.
b. Calculate the present value of the aftertax cash inflows for the next four years attributable to the operating cash savings.
c. Calculate the present value of the depreciation tax shield at the end of year 1.
d. Rockyford's additional investment in working capital of $3,000 required in the current year is:
    1. A sunk cost that is not recovered.
    2. Considered part of the original investment when determining the NPV.
    3. An item requiring amortization.
    4. Spread over the four-year life of the asset as a cash outflow.

[CMA adapted]

23.35 *Calculating the net present value under a depreciation tax shield.* Virtual Optical Disk Company is considering the purchase of a laser device for $400,000 that will reduce operating costs by $150,000, $200,000, $250,000, and $300,000 in years 1, 2, 3, and 4, respectively. Its useful life is four years, and Virtual uses the sum-of-the-years-digits (SYD) depreciation method. Virtual's income tax rate is 40%, and its discount rate is 12%.

Required:
Calculate the NPV of the laser device using the SYD method. Then calculate the NPV using the straight-line method. Which depreciation method produces the greater NPV and by how much?

23.36 *Selecting projects.* Mercken Industries is contemplating four projects, D, E, F, and G. The capital costs for the initiation of each project and its estimated aftertax cash inflows are listed below. Mercken's desired aftertax opportunity cost is 12%, and the company has a capital budget for the year of $450,000. Idle funds cannot be reinvested at greater than 12%.

	PROJECT D	PROJECT E	PROJECT F	PROJECT G
Initial cost	$200,000	$235,000	$190,000	$210,000

ANNUAL CASH FLOWS

	D	E	F	G
Year 1	$56,500	$90,000	$45,000	$40,000
Year 2	56,500	85,000	55,000	50,000
Year 3	56,500	75,000	65,000	60,000
Year 4	56,500	55,000	70,000	65,000
Year 5	56,500	50,000	75,000	75,000

	D	E	F	G
NPV	$3,683	$29,845	$27,345	<$7,845>
IRR	12.8%	17.6%	17.2%	10.6%
PVI	1.02	1.13	1.14	0.96

Required:
a. Which projects should Mercken select?
b. If Mercken was able to accept only one project, which one would it select?

[CMA adapted]

23.37 *Discounting cash flows using MACRS.* On January 1, 1994, Crane Comany will acquire a new asset that costs $400,000 and is anticipated to have a salvage value of $30,000 at the end of four years. The new asset:

- Qualifies as three-year property under the modified accelerated cost recovery system (MACRS).
- Will replace an old asset that currently has a tax base of $80,000 and can be sold now for $60,000.
- Will continue to generate the same operating revenues as the old asset ($200,000 per year). However, savings in operating costs will be experienced as follows: a total of $120,000 in each of the first three years and $90,000 in the fourth year.

Crane is subject to a 40% tax rate and rounds all computations to the nearest dollar. Assume that any gain or loss affects the taxes paid at the end of the year in which it occurred. The company uses the NPV method to analyze projects using the following factors and rates:

PERIOD	PRESENT VALUE OF $1 AT 14%	PRESENT VALUE OF $1 ANNUITY AT 14%	MACRS
1	.88	.88	33%
2	.77	1.65	45
3	.68	2.32	15
4	.59	2.91	7

Required:
a. What is the present value of the depreciation tax shield for the 1997 MACRS depreciation of Crane's new asset?
b. What is the discounted net-of-tax amount that should be factored into Crane's analysis for the disposal transaction?
c. What are the relevant discounted operating cash flows that should be factored into Crane's analysis?

[CMA adapted]

23.38 *Calculating the tax shield and payback period for a new machine.* Britelite Company is considering purchasing a new machine that will cost $120,000 and will have annual depreciation for tax purposes of $24,000 for five years. Cash inflows of $40,000 annually will be generated by the new machine.

Required:
If the tax rate is 40%, what is the payback period for the new machine?

23.39 *Considering mutually exclusive projects and income tax consequences.* Garrison Corporation is considering the replacement of an old machine that is currently being used. The old machine is fully depreciated but can be used by the corporation through 1997. If Garrison decides to replace the old machine, Picco Company has offered to purchase it for $60,000 on the replacement date. The old machine would have no salvage value in 1997.

If the replacement occurs, a new machine would be acquired from Hillcrest Industries on January 2, 1993. The purchase price of $1,000,000 for the new machine would be paid in cash at the time of replacement. Due to the increased efficiency of the new machine, estimated annual cash savings of $300,000 would be generated through 1997, the end of its expected useful life. The new machine is not expected to have any salvage value at the end of 1997.

All operating cash receipts, operating cash expenditures, and applicable tax payments and credits are assumed to occur at the end of the year. Garrison employs the calendar year for reporting purposes. Following are additional assumptions:

■ Garrison requires all investments to earn a 12% aftertax rate of return to be accepted.
■ Garrison is subject to an income tax rate of 40% on all income and gains (losses).
■ The new machine will have depreciation as follows:

YEAR	DEPRECIATION
1993	$ 250,000
1994	380,000
1995	370,000
	$1,000,000

Required:
a. Calculate the present value of the aftertax cash inflow associated with the salvage value of the old machine.
b. Before consideration of any depreciation tax shield, calculate the annual after-tax cash savings that arise from the increased efficiency of the new machine throughout its life.
c. Calculate the present value of the depreciation tax shield for 1994.
d. Assume that the new machine has a salvage value of $80,000 on December 31, 1997, instead of zero salvage value. Calculate the present value of the additional aftertax cash inflow.

[CMA adapted]

23.40 *Calculations of capital budgeting financial analysis methods.* Hazman Company plans to replace an old piece of equipment that is obsolete and expected to be unreliable under the stress of daily operations. The equipment is fully depreciated and will have no salvage value.

One piece of equipment being considered would provide annual cash savings of $7,000 before income taxes. The equipment would cost $18,000 and have annual depreciation of $3,600 for five years, for both book and tax purposes. It would have no salvage value at the end of five years.

The company is subject to a 40% tax rate and has a 14% aftertax cost of capital. Assume all operating revenues and expenses occur at the end of the year.

Required:
a. Calculate the aftertax payback period.
b. Calculate the aftertax ARR.
c. Calculate the aftertax NPV.
d. Calculate the aftertax PVI.
e. Calculate the aftertax IRR.

[CMA adapted]

23.41 *Analyzing alternative financing arrangements.* Crown Corporation has agreed to sell some used computer equipment to Bob Parsons, one of the company's employees, for $5,000. Crown and Parsons have been discussing alternative financing arrangements for the sale and the present and future values of each alternative.

Required:
Following are alternative financing arrangements:
a. Crown Corporation has offered to accept a $1,000 down payment and set up a note receivable for Parsons that calls for four $1,000 payments at the end of each of the next four years. If Crown uses a 6% discount rate, what would be the present value of the note receivable?
b. Parsons has agreed to the immediate down payment of $1,000 but would like the note for $4,000 to be payable in full at the end of the fourth year. Because of the increased risk associated with the terms of this note, Crown would apply an 8% discount rate. What would be the present value of this note?
c. If Parsons borrowed the $5,000 at 8% interest for four years from his bank

and paid Crown the full price of the equipment immediately, Crown would invest the $5,000 for three years at 7%. What would be the future value of this investment?

[CMA adapted]

23.42 *Analyzing the lease-versus-purchase decision.* LeToy Company produces a wide variety of children's toys, most of which are manufactured from stamped parts. The Production Department recommended that a new stamping machine be acquired. The Production Department further recommended that the company consider using the new stamping machine only for five years. Top management has concurred with the recommendation and has assigned Ann Mitchum of the Budget and Planning Department to supervise the acquisition and to analyze the alternative financing available.

After careful analysis and review, Mitchum has narrowed the financing of the project to two alternatives. The first alternative is a lease agreement with the manufacturer of the stamping machine. The manufacturer is willing to lease the equipment to LeToy for five years even though it has an economic useful life of ten years. The lease agreement calls for LeToy to make annual payments of $62,000 at the beginning of each year. The manufacturer (lessor) retains the title to the machine, and there is no purchase option at the end of five years. Investment credit is claimed by the lessor and does not flow through to LeToy (lessee). This agreement would be considered a lease by the Internal Revenue Service.

The second alternative would be for LeToy to purchase the equipment outright from the manufacturer for $240,000. LeToy can claim an investment tax credit of $16,000 if it purchases the equipment. Preliminary discussions with LeToy's bank indicate that the firm would be able to finance the asset acquisition with a 15% term loan.

LeToy would depreciate the equipment over five years using the sum-of-the-years-digits method. The market value of the equipment at the end of five years would be $45,000; consequently, LeToy would use a salvage value of $45,000 for depreciation purposes.

All maintenance, taxes, and insurance are the same under both alternatives and are paid by LeToy. LeToy requires an aftertax cutoff return of 18% for investment decisions and is subject to a 40% corporate income tax rate on both operating income and capital gains and losses.

Required:
a. Calculate the relevant present value cost of the leasing alternative for LeToy Company.
b. Calculate the relevant present value cost of the purchase alternative for LeToy Company.

THINK-TANK PROBLEMS

Although these problems are based on chapter material, reading extra material, reviewing previous chapters, and using creativity may be required to develop workable solutions.

23.43 *Comprehensive discussion of capital budgeting financial analysis methods.* Plasto Corporation is a manufacturer of plastic products. The company is embarking on a five-year modernization and expansion plan. Thus, management is identifying all of the capital projects that it should consider. Financial analyses will be prepared for each identified project. Plasto will not select and implement all of the projects because some may not be financially attractive and some are mutually exclusive. In addition, not all projects can be implemented because capital funds are limited.

All modernization and expansion projects would be completed in three years. The projects have varying lives, but none exceed seven years. Plasto's criteria for evaluating and selecting projects are maximization of return and quickness of investment recovery. The projects included in the Capital Projects Portfolio Statement are as follows:

PROJECT IDENTIFICATION AND DESCRIPTION	INVESTMENT	ESTIMATED LIFE IN YEARS
■ *Maintenance:* Extensive maintenance of current manufacturing facilities, including repairs and some replacement of equipment. This work must be completed in order to keep existing facilities in operation until reengineering and expansion projects are completed.	$ 2,000,000	3
■ *Reengineering:* Major reengineering of current manufacturing activities using general-purpose equipment.	6,000,000	5
■ *Reengineering:* Major reengineering of current manufacturing activities using special-purpose equipment (this project and the prior project are mutually exclusive).	8,500,000	5
■ *Make versus buy:* Construction of new facilities to manufacture parts and supplies used in making products. Parts and supplies are currently being purchased.	5,000,000	7
■ *Expansion:* Construction of new facilities to introduce new product NX-42.	10,000,000	7
■ *Expansion:* Construction of new facilities to introduce new product LV-221.	12,000,000	7

Required:

a. When attempting to determine if a project is profitable and should be implemented, Plasto should be sure that the project's:
   1. Return exceeds a hurdle rate specified by Plasto's management.
   2. Return exceeds the interest rate that is charged on any debt that is incurred to finance a capital project.
   3. Return exceeds the company's historical return on stockholders' equity.
   4. Payback is three years or less.

b. The overriding concern for Plasto's maintenance project should be to:
   1. Minimize the IRR.
   2. Minimize the present value of cash outlays.
   3. Maximize the payback period.
   4. Minimize the PVI.

c. Which of the following pairs of capital budgeting financial analysis methods would best satisfy Plasto's criteria for selecting capital projects?
   1. ARR and present value payback.
   2. NPV and PP.
   3. IRR and present value payback.
   4. ARR and IRR.

d. If Plasto is faced with capital rationing, the best general method of ranking the projects would be:
   1. Present value payback.
   2. PVI.
   3. NPV.
   4. IRR.
   5. Payback.

e. If Plasto must decide between the two mutually exclusive reengineering projects, the best general method of deciding between these projects would be:
   1. Present value payback.
   2. PVI.
   3. NPV.
   4. IRR.
   5. Payback

[CMA adapted]

23.44 *Analyzing mutually exclusive projects.* The Beta Corporation manufactures office equipment and distributes its products through wholesale distributors.

Beta Corporation recently learned of a patent on the production of a semiautomatic paper collator that can be obtained at a cost of $60,000 cash. The semiautomatic model is vastly superior to the manual model that the corporation now produces. At a cost of $40,000, the present equipment could be modified to accommodate the production of the new semiautomatic model. Such modifications would not affect the equipment's remaining useful life of four years or its salvage value of $10,000. Variable costs, however, would increase by $1 per unit. Fixed costs, other than relevant amortization charges, would not be affected. If the equipment is modified, the manual model cannot be produced.

The current income statement relative to the manual collator appears as follows:

Sales (100,000 units @ $4)		$400,000
Variable costs	$180,000	
Fixed costs*	120,000	
Total costs		< 300,000>
Net income before income taxes		100,000
Income taxes (40%)		< 40,000>
Net income after income taxes		$ 60,000

* All fixed costs are directly allocable to the production of the manual collator and include depreciation on equipment of $20,000, calculated on the straight-line basis with a useful life of ten years.

Market research has disclosed three important findings relative to the new semiautomatic model. First, a particular competitor will certainly purchase the patent if Beta does not. If this were to happen, Beta's sales of the manual collator would fall to 70,000 units per year. Second, if the selling price is not increased, Beta could sell approximately 190,000 units per year of the semiautomatic model. Third, because of the advances being made in this area, the patent will be completely worthless at the end of four years.

Because of the uncertainty of the current situation, the raw materials inventory has been almost completely exhausted. Regardless of the decision reached, substantial and immediate inventory replenishment will be required. The Engineering Department estimates that if the new model is to be produced, the average monthly raw materials inventory will be $20,000. If the old model is continued, the inventory balance will average $12,000 per month.

Required:
a. Prepare a schedule that shows the incremental aftertax cash flows for comparison of the two alternatives. Assume that Beta will use the sum-of-the-years-digits method for depreciating the costs of modifying the equipment. (Ignore MACRS and the half-life convention.)
b. Using the cash inflows in Requirement (a), if Beta has a cost of capital of 18%, will it decide to manufacture the semiautomatic collator?

INTEREST FACTORS FOR 18%

PERIOD	PRESENT VALUE OF $1	PRESENT VALUE OF $1 PER PERIOD RECEIVED AT END OF PERIOD	ACCUMULATED VALUE OF $1	ACCUMULATED VALUE OF $1 PER PERIOD RECEIVED AT END OF PERIOD
1	.85	.85	1.18	1.00
2	.72	1.57	1.39	2.18
3	.61	2.18	1.64	3.57
4	.52	2.70	1.94	5.21

c. Calculate the ARR for each project. Using this method, would you recommend that Beta manufacture the semiautomatic collator? Explain.
d. What additional analytical methods, if any, would you consider before presenting a recommendation to management? Why?

e. What concerns would you have about using the information given in the problem to reach a decision in this case?

[CMA adapted]

23.45 *Financing decision.* HMG Corporation is a for-profit health care provider, which operates three hospitals. One of these hospitals, Metrohealth, plans to acquire new X-ray equipment that management has already decided will be cost-beneficial and will enhance the technology available in the outpatient diagnostic laboratory. Before Metrohealth submits a purchase requisition for the equipment to corporate headquarters, Paul Monden, Metrohealth's management accountant, has to prepare an analysis comparing financing alternatives.

The new equipment is a Supraimage X-ray 400 machine priced at $1,000,000, including shipping and installation, and would be delivered January 1, 1984. Its annual depreciation expense will be $400,000, $240,000, $144,000, $108,000, and $108,000, respectively, over five years. The machine will have no salvage value at the end of five years.

Metrohealth is considering the following financing alternatives:

■ *Finance internally.* HMG Corporation would provide Metrohealth with the funds to purchase the equipment. The supplier would be paid on the day of delivery.
■ *Finance with a bank loan.* Metrohealth could obtain a bank loan to finance 90% of the equipment cost at 10% annual interest with five annual payments of $237,420 each due at the end of each year, with the first payment due on December 31, 1994. The loan amortization schedule follows. Metrohealth would provide the remaining $100,000, which would be paid upon delivery.

YEAR	BEGINNING BALANCE	PAYMENT	INTEREST	PRINCIPAL REDUCTION
1	$900,000	$237,420	$90,000	$147,420
2	752,580	237,420	75,258	162,162
3	590,418	237,420	59,042	178,378
4	412,040	237,420	41,204	196,216
5	215,824	237,420	21,582	215,838

■ *Lease from a lessor.* The equipment could be leased from MedLeasing with an initial payment of $50,000 due on equipment delivery and five annual payments of $220,000 each, commencing on December 31, 1994. At the option of the lessee, the equipment can be purchased at the fair market value at lease termination (the lessor is currently estimating a 30% residual value). The lease satisfies the requirements of an operating lease for both FASB and income tax purposes. Due to expected technological changes in medical equipment, Metrohealth is not planning to purchase the X-ray equipment at the end of the lease commitment.

Both HMG Corporation and Metrohealth have an effective income tax rate of 40%, an incremental borrowing rate of 10%, and an aftertax corporate hurdle rate of 12%. Income taxes are paid at the end of the year. Present value tables for several interest rates are as follows:

	PRESENT VALUE OF $1 RECEIVED AT THE END OF THE PERIOD				PRESENT VALUE OF AN ANNUITY OF $1 RECEIVED AT THE END OF EACH PERIOD (ORDINARY)			
PERIOD	6%	10%	12%	20%	6%	10%	12%	20%
1	.94	.91	.89	.83	.94	.91	.89	.83
2	.89	.83	.80	.69	1.83	1.74	1.69	1.53
3	.84	.75	.71	.58	2.67	2.49	2.40	2.11
4	.79	.68	.64	.48	3.47	3.17	3.04	2.59
5	.75	.62	.57	.40	4.21	3.79	3.61	2.99

Required:

a. Prepare a present value analysis as of January 1, 1994, of the expected aftertax cash inflows for each of the three financing alternatives available to Metrohealth for acquiring the new X-ray equipment. As part of your present value analysis:

1. Justify the discount rate(s) you employed.
2. Identify the financing alternative that is most advantageous to Metrohealth.

b. Discuss the qualitative factors Paul Monden should include for management consideration before a final decision is made regarding the financing of this new equipment.

[CMA adapted]

23.46 *Comprehensive lease analysis.* On December 29, 1994, Dallas Corporation leased 20 trucks to Reutzel Express Company under a six-year, noncancelable lease. Additional information regarding the lease and the trucks follows:

- The lease requires equal payments of $145,200 that are due on December 31 each year, and the first rent was paid December 31, 1994. These payments provide Dallas Corporation with a 12% return on the net investment; this implicit interest rate is known by Reutzel.
- The lease does not pass ownership of the trucks at the end of the lease, but Reutzel may purchase all of the trucks at the end of the lease for a total of $10,000. The estimated residual value of all of the trucks is $25,000 at the end of the lease term and $1,000 at the end of nine years.
- The fair value of the trucks is $674,000. The cost of the trucks to Dallas is $650,000, and each truck has an expected useful life of nine years.
- Reutzel's incremental borrowing rate is 14%.
- Reutzel pays the executory costs (insurance, taxes, and other fees not included in the annual lease payments) of $485 per year and depreciates all of its trucks using straight-line depreciation.
- The collectibility of the lease payments is reasonably predictable, and there are no important uncertainties surrounding the amount of unreimbursable costs yet to be incurred by Dallas.
- Present value factors for 12% are as follows:

PERIOD	PRESENT VALUE OF $1 RECEIVED AT THE END OF THE PERIOD	PRESENT VALUE OF AN ORDINARY ANNUITY OF $1	PRESENT VALUE OF AN ANNUITY DUE OF $1
6	0.51	4.11	4.60
9	0.36	5.33	5.97

- Present value factors for 14% are as follows:

PERIOD	PRESENT VALUE OF $1 RECEIVED AT THE END OF THE PERIOD	PRESENT VALUE OF AN ORDINARY ANNUITY OF $1	PRESENT VALUE OF AN ANNUITY DUE OF $1
6	0.46	3.89	4.43
9	0.31	4.95	5.64

Required:

a. 1. Explain the four criteria used to determine that a lease should be accounted for as a capital lease by the lessee.
   2. Identify which of these criteria are met by the lease between Dallas and Reutzel.
b. In general, what are the advantages of leasing to Reutzel?
c. Without prejudice to your response to previous requirements, assume that Reutzel recorded the lease on December 31, 1994, as a capital lease in the amount of $673,300. Prepare all the journal entries required to record the capital lease on the books of Reutzel for the fiscal year ended December 31, 1995.
d. Explain how the lease should be presented on Reutzel's Statement of Financial Position dated December 31, 1995. (Do not include footnote disclosure.)

[CMA adapted]

23.47 *Determining whether to make or buy.* Jonfran Company manufactures three different models of paper shredders including the waste container, which serves as the base. Although each model uses a different shredder head, the waste container is the same. The number of waste containers that Jonfran will need during the next five years is estimated as follows:

1994	50,000
1995	50,000
1996	52,000
1997	55,000
1998	55,000

The equipment used to manufacture the waste container must be replaced because it has broken and cannot be repaired. The new equipment would have a purchase price of $945,000 with terms of 2/10, n/30; company policy is to take all purchase discounts. The freight on the equipment would be $11,000, and installation costs would total $22,900. The equipment would be purchased in December 1993 and be placed into service on January 1, 1994. It would have a five-year economic life and would be treated as three-year property under the modified accelerated cost recovery system (MACRS). This equipment is expected to have a salvage value of $12,000 at the end of its economic life in 1998. The new equipment would be more efficient than the old equipment, resulting in a 25% reduction in both direct materials and variable overhead. The savings in direct materials would result in an additional onetime decrease in working capital requirements of $2,500 due to a reduction in direct materials inventories. This working capital reduction would be recognized at the time of equipment acquisition.

The old equipment is fully depreciated and is not included in the fixed overhead. The old equipment from the plant can be sold for a salvage amount of $1,500. Jonfran has no alternative use for the manufacturing space at this time, so if the waste containers are purchased, as discussed next, the old equipment would be left in place.

Rather than replace the equipment, one of Jonfran's production managers has suggested that the waste containers be purchased. One supplier has quoted a price of $27 per container. This price is $8 less than Jonfran's current manufacturing cost, which is as follows:

Direct materials		$10
Direct labor		8
Variable overhead		6
Fixed overhead:		
Supervision	$2	
Facilities	5	
General	4	11
Total manufacturing cost per unit		$35

Jonfran employs a plantwide fixed overhead rate in its operations. If the waste containers are purchased outside, the salary and benefits of one supervisor, included in the fixed overhead at $45,000, would be eliminated. There would be no other changes in the other cash and noncash items included in fixed overhead, except depreciation on the new equipment.

Jonfran is subject to a 40% income tax rate. Management assumes that all annual cash flows and tax payments occur at the end of the year. A 12% aftertax discount rate is used. The MACRS depreciation rates and the present values for 12 and 20% are as follows:

YEAR	MACRS THREE-YEAR RATE	PRESENT VALUE OF $1 RECEIVED AT THE END OF THE PERIOD 12%	20%	PRESENT VALUE OF AN ORDINARY ANNUITY OF $1 RECEIVED AT THE END OF EACH PERIOD 12%	20%
1	33.3%	.89	.83	.89	.83
2	44.5	.80	.69	1.69	1.53
3	14.8	.71	.58	2.40	2.11
4	7.4	.64	.48	3.04	2.59
5	—	.57	.40	3.61	2.99

Required:

a. Jonfran Company must decide whether to purchase the waste containers from an outside supplier or to purchase the equipment to manufacture the waste containers. Calculate the NPV of the estimated aftertax cash inflows at December 31, 1993, and determine which of these two options to pursue.

b. Companies often calculate the payback period for an investment. Without prejudice to your response in Requirement (a), assume that the capital cost is $1,000,000 and the aftertax cash inflows for 1994–1998 are as follows:

1994	$300,000
1995	350,000
1996	240,000
1997	200,000
1998	200,000

1. Explain why some companies calculate the payback period in addition to determining the NPV.
2. Calculate the payback period for this project using the assumed aftertax cash inflows.

[CMA adapted]

23.48 *Analyzing three alternative financing decisions.* Edwards Corporation is a manufacturing concern that produces and sells a wide range of products. The company not only mass-produces a number of products and equipment components but also is capable of producing special-purpose manufacturing equipment to customer specifications.

The firm is considering adding a new stapler to one of its product lines. More equipment will be required to produce the new stapler. Edwards has identified three alternative ways of acquiring the needed equipment:

■ Purchase general-purpose equipment
■ Lease general-purpose equipment
■ Build special-purpose equipment

Purchase of the special-purpose equipment has been ruled out because it would be prohibitively expensive.

The general-purpose equipment can be purchased for $125,000. The equipment has an estimated salvage value of $15,000 at the end of its useful life of ten years. At the end of five years, the equipment can be used elsewhere in the plant or be sold for $40,000.

Alternatively, the general-purpose equipment can be acquired under a five-year lease for $40,000 annually. The lessor will assume all responsibility for taxes, insurance, and maintenance.

Special-purpose equipment can be constructed by Edwards' Contract Equipment Department. Although the department is operating at a level that is normal for the time of year, it is below full capacity. The department could produce the equipment without interfering with its regular revenue-producing activities.

The estimated departmental costs for the construction of the special-purpose equipment are as follows:

Materials and parts	$ 75,000
Direct labor	60,000
Variable overhead (50% of DL$)	30,000
Fixed overhead (25% of DL$)	15,000
Total	$180,000

Corporation general and administrative costs average 20% of labor dollar content of factory production.

Engineering and management studies provide the following revenue and cost estimates (excluding lease payments and depreciation) for producing the new stapler, depending on the equipment used:

	GENERAL-PURPOSE EQUIPMENT		SELF-CONSTRUCTED EQUIPMENT
	LEASED	PURCHASED	
Unit selling price	$5.00	$5.00	$5.00
Unit production costs:			
Materials	1.80	1.80	1.70
Conversion costs:	1.65	1.65	1.40
Total unit production costs	3.45	3.45	3.10
Unit contribution margin	$1.55	$1.55	$1.90
Estimated unit volume	40,000	40,000	40,000
Estimated total contribution margin	$62,000	$62,000	$76,000
Other costs:			
Supervision	$16,000	$16,000	$18,000
Taxes and insurance	—	3,000	5,000
Maintenance	—	3,000	2,000
Total	$16,000	$22,000	$25,000

DISCOUNT FACTORS FOR
10% (ROUNDED)

PERIOD	PRESENT VALUE OF $1	PRESENT VALUE OF $1 PER PERIOD RECEIVED AT END OF PERIOD
1	.91	.91
2	.83	1.74
3	.75	2.49
4	.68	3.17
5	.62	3.79
6	.56	4.36
7	.51	4.87
8	.47	5.34
9	.42	5.76
10	.39	6.15

The company will depreciate the general-purpose machine over ten years using the sum-of-the-years-digits (SYD) method. At the end of five years, the accumulated depreciation will total $80,000. (The present value of this amount for the first five years is $62,100.) The special-purpose machine will be depreciated over five years using the SYD method. Its salvage value at the end of that time is estimated to be $30,000.

The company uses an aftertax cost of capital of 10%. Its marginal tax rate is 40%.

Required:
a. Calculate the NPV for each of the three alternatives that Edwards has at its disposal.
b. Should Edwards select any of the three options, and, if so, which one? Explain your answer.

[CMA adapted]

23.49 *Analyzing the impact of income taxes and inflation.* Catix Corporation is a divisionalized company, and each division has the authority to make capital expenditures up to $200,000 without approval of the corporate headquarters. The corporate controller has determined that the cost of capital for Catix Corporation is 12%. This rate does not include an allowance for inflation, which is expected to average 8% over the next five years. Catix pays income taxes at the rate of 40%.

The Electronics Division of Catix is considering the purchase of an automated assembly and soldering machine for use in the manufacture of its printed circuit boards. The machine would be placed in service in early 1994. The divisional controller estimates that if the machine is purchased, two positions will be eliminated, yielding a cost savings for wages and employee benefits. However, the machine would require additional supplies and power. The cost savings and additional costs in current 1993 prices are as follows:

Wages and employee benefits of the two positions eliminated ($25,000 each)	$50,000
Cost of additional supplies	3,000
Cost of additional power	10,000

The new machine would be purchased and installed at the end of 1993 at a net cost of $80,000. If purchased, the machine would be depreciated on a straight-line basis for both book and tax purposes. The machine will become technologically obsolete in four years and will have no salvage value at that time.

The Electronics Division compensates for inflation in capital expenditure analyses by adjusting the expected cash inflows by an estimated price level index. The adjusted aftertax cash inflows are then discounted using the appropriate discount rate. The estimated year-end index values for each of the next five years are as follows:

YEAR	YEAR-END PRICE INDEX
1993	1.00
1994	1.08
1995	1.17
1996	1.26
1997	1.36
1998	1.47

The Plastics Division of Catix compensates for inflation in capital expenditure analyses by adding the anticipated inflation rate to the cost of capital and then using the inflation-adjusted cost of capital to discount the project cash inflows. The Plastics Division recently rejected a project with cash inflows and economic life similar to those associated with the machine under consideration by the Electronics Division. The Plastics Division's analysis of the rejected project was as follows:

Net pretax cost savings	$37,000
Less incremental depreciation expenses	20,000
Increase in taxable income	$17,000
Increase in income taxes (40%)	6,800
Increase in aftertax income	$10,200
Add back noncash expense (depreciation)	20,000
Net aftertax annual cash inflow (unadjusted for inflation)	$30,200

Present value of net cash inflows using the sum of the cost of capital (12%) and the inflation rate (8%) or a minimum required return of 20%	$77,916
Investment required	< 80,000>
Net present value	<$ 2,084>

All operating revenues and expenditures occur at the end of the year. Appropriate discount tables are as follows:

PRESENT VALUE OF $1 RECEIVED
AT THE END OF PERIOD

PERIOD	8%	11%	12%	13%	20%	21%
1	0.93	0.90	0.89	0.89	0.83	0.83
2	0.86	0.81	0.80	0.78	0.69	0.68
3	0.79	0.73	0.71	0.69	0.58	0.56
4	0.74	0.66	0.64	0.61	0.48	0.47
5	0.68	0.59	0.57	0.54	0.40	0.39

PRESENT VALUE OF ANNUITY OF $1 RECEIVED
AT THE END OF EACH PERIOD

PERIOD	8%	11%	12%	13%	20%	21%
1	0.93	0.90	0.89	0.89	0.83	0.83
2	1.78	1.71	1.69	1.67	1.53	1.51
3	2.58	2.44	2.40	2.36	2.11	2.07
4	3.31	3.10	3.04	2.97	2.59	2.54
5	3.99	3.70	3.61	3.52	2.99	2.93

Required:
a. Using the price index provided, prepare a schedule showing the net aftertax annual cash inflows adjusted for inflation for the automated assembly and soldering machine under consideration by the Electronics Division.
b. Without prejudice to your answer in Requirement (a), assume that the net aftertax annual cash inflows adjusted for inflation for the project being considered by the Electronics Division are as follows:

	1994	1995	1996	1997
Net aftertax annual cash inflow adjusted for inflation	$30,000	$35,000	$37,000	$40,000

Calculate the NPV for Electronic Division's project.
c. Evaluate the methods used by the Plastics Division and the Electronics Division to compensate for expected inflation in capital expenditure analyses.

[CMA adapted]

23.50 *Capital budgeting and pricing.* Wardl Industries is a manufacturer of standard and custom-designed bottling equipment. Early in December 1993, Lyan Company asked Wardl to quote a price for a custom-designed bottling machine to be delivered on April 1, 1994. Lyan intends to make a decision on the purchase of such a machine by January 1 so Wardl would have the entire first quarter of 1994 to build the equipment.

Wardl's standard pricing policy for custom-designed equipment is 50% markup on full cost. Lyan's specifications for the equipment have been reviewed by Wardl's Engineering and Cost Accounting Departments, and they made the following estimates for raw materials and direct labor:

Raw materials	$256,000
Direct labor (11,000 DLhr at $15)	165,000

Manufacturing overhead is applied on the basis of direct labor hours. Wardl normally plans to run its plant with 15,000 direct labor hours per month and assigns overhead on the basis of 180,000 direct labor hours per year. The overhead application rate for 1994 of $9 per direct labor hour is based on the following budgeted manufacturing overhead costs for 1994:

Variable manufacturing overhead	$ 972,000
Fixed manufacturing overhead	648,000
Total manufacturing overhead	$1,620,000

The Wardl production schedule calls for 12,000 direct labor hours per month during the first quarter. If Wardl is awarded the contract for the Lyan equipment, production of one of its standard products will have to be reduced. This is necessary because production levels can only be increased to 15,000 direct labor hours each month on short notice. Furthermore, Wardl's employees are unwilling to work overtime.

Sales of the standard product equal to the reduced production will be lost, but there will be no permanent loss of future sales or customers. The standard product, whose production schedule will be reduced, has a unit sales price of $12,000 and the following cost structure:

Raw materials	$2,500
Direct labor (250 DLhr at $15)	3,750
Overhead (250 DLhr at $9)	2,250
Total cost	$8,500

Lyan needs the custom-designed equipment to increase its bottle-making capacity so that it will not have to buy bottles from an outside supplier. Lyan Company requires 5,000,000 bottles annually. Its present equipment has a maximum capacity of 4,500,000 bottles with a directly traceable cash outlay of $0.15 per bottle. Thus, Lyan has had to purchase 500,000 bottles from a supplier at $0.40 each. The new equipment would allow Lyan to manufacture its entire annual demand for bottles at a raw material cost savings of $0.01 for each bottle manufactured.

Wardl estimates that Lyan's annual bottle demand will continue to be 5,000,000 bottles over the next five years, the estimated economic life of the special-purpose equipment. Wardl further estimates that Lyan has an aftertax cost of capital of 15% and is subject to a 40% marginal income tax rate, the same rates as Wardl.

Required:
a. Wardl Industries plans to submit a bid to Lyan Company for the manufacture of the special-purpose bottling equipment.
   1. Calculate the bid Wardl would submit if it follows its standard pricing policy for special-purpose equipment.
   2. Calculate the minimum bid Wardl would be willing to submit on the Lyan equipment that would result in the same profits as planned for the first quarter of 1994.
b. Wardl wants to estimate the maximum price Lyan would be willing to pay for the special-purpose bottling equipment.
   1. Calculate the present value of the aftertax savings in directly traceable cash outlays that Lyan could expect to realize from the new special-purpose bottling equipment.
   2. Identify the other factors Wardl would have to incorporate in its estimate of the maximum price Lyan would be willing to pay for the equipment.

3. Describe how the cost savings (Requirement [b]1) and the other factors (Requirement [b]2) would be combined to calculate the estimate of the maximum price Lyan would be willing to pay for the equipment.

[CMA adapted]

23.51 *Monte Carlo sensitivity analysis.* NoClip Novelties has discovered a better method for attaching name badges, like those used at conventions and conferences, without using clips or pins that could damage clothing. By using an adhesive stick-on system, NoClip believes it can capture a significant part of the badge market. It is planning to use new technology and is somewhat uncertain about development costs. Development cost estimates are as follows:

Best case	$150,000
Worst case	330,000
Most likely case	240,000

Probabilities assigned to estimate cash inflows over four years, the life of the new project, are as follows:

YEAR 1 PERCENT-AGE	ESTIMATED CASH INFLOWS	YEAR 2 PERCENT-AGE	ESTIMATED CASH INFLOWS	YEAR 3 PERCENT-AGE	ESTIMATED CASH INFLOWS	YEAR 4 PERCENT-AGE	ESTIMATED CASH INFLOWS
0.1	$100,000	0.1	$150,000	0.2	$150,000	0.1	$110,000
0.2	90,000	0.3	110,000	0.4	110,000	0.1	90,000
0.1	85,000	0.5	100,000	0.3	80,000	0.6	70,000
0.2	70,000	0.1	75,000	0.1	55,000	0.2	40,000
0.1	65,000						
0.3	50,000						

Required:

a. Assuming the discount rate is 10%, set up the problem for a Monte Carlo sensitivity analysis based on the NPV for this project by determining the mathematical model and the parameters that are to be varied. Plot the probability distributions for each uncertain parameter.

b. Calculate the NPV for the best, worst, and most likely cases, using the means of all the uncertain parameters.

23.52 *Monte Carlo sensitivity analysis discussions.* The following graphs are selected results from a Monte Carlo sensitivity analysis on a CleanSweep Manufacturing proposal for creating a new product line:

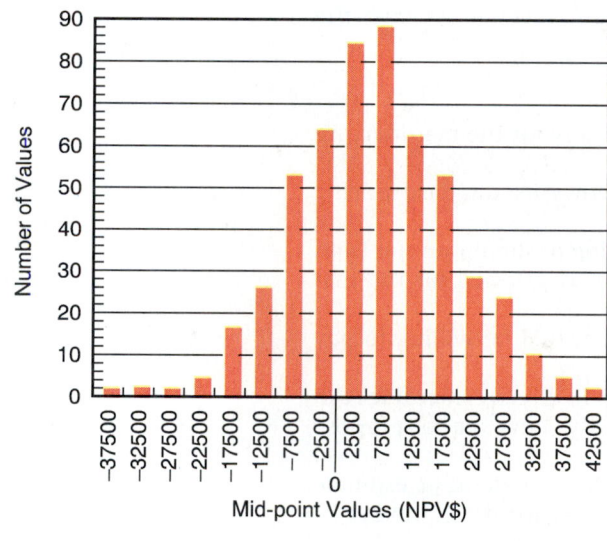

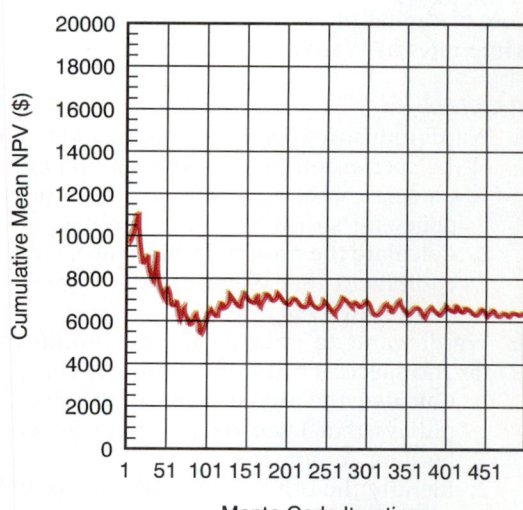

Required:

For the following, make any assumptions you deem necessary:

a. What is the minimum number of iterations required for the Monte Carlo Simulation? Discuss and justify your answer.

b. Should CleanSweep proceed with the new product line? Discuss and justify your answer.

24 CAPITAL PROJECT IMPLEMENTATION MANAGEMENT

LEARNING OBJECTIVES

After studying this chapter, you should be able to:

1. Describe the Gantt chart and its use.

2. Use the program evaluation and review technique (PERT) as a project management and modeling tool.

3. Explain why an implementation audit is conducted.

4. Discuss the reason for conducting a postimplementation audit, and describe the tools used in conducting such an audit.

Capital projects under development. Courtesy of Krump Construction Company.

■ INTRODUCTION

The capital projects selected in the second stage of the capital budgeting methodology are built by a contractor as presented in the *Insights & Applications* on page 1138; purchased from a vendor, such as a manufacturer of production equipment; or developed internally, such as an information system with various hardware (e.g., computers and telecommunications equipment) being purchased from vendors. In any case, the actual development and implementation of such projects often takes months or years to complete and requires sound project management. The aim of the project manager is threefold:

■ To coordinate people and activities
■ To keep the project progressing on schedule
■ To control project costs

According to some authorities, projects that are completed on time but over budget are 140 percent more profitable than projects that are completed on budget but six months late. For this reason, some companies and government entities give early-completion bonuses to project teams or contractors that complete their projects ahead of schedule. Consequently, accurately estimating a project's completion date and completing the project on or before that date are a vital part of project management.[1]

This chapter begins by describing two popular project management tools used by project managers:

■ Gantt chart
■ Program evaluation and review technique (PERT)[2]

Next, the process of auditing a capital project *while* it is being developed is examined. The last section of the chapter treats postimplementation auditing, the fourth and final phase of the capital budgeting methodology. ▬

▌GANTT CHART

LEARNING OBJECTIVE 1

Describe the Gantt chart and its use.

The **Gantt chart,** named after its developer Henry Gantt, is a bar chart that shows activities (also called tasks or phases) on the left side and units of time (e.g., days, weeks, and months) across the top or bottom, as shown in Exhibit 24–1. The letter "C" at the end of the "Actual" bar means that the activity is complete.

▌How to Construct a Gantt Chart

Gantt charts are simple to construct and use. To develop a Gantt chart, the project is divided into logical activities, and the start and completion times are estimated for each activity. Then, a bar chart is prepared showing each activity as a horizontal bar along a time scale. The bar representing each activity runs from the start date to the completion date for that activity.

Interstate Gas Company's capital project calls for a pipeline to be laid from a source of natural gas to plant A. A Gantt chart for this project is illustrated in

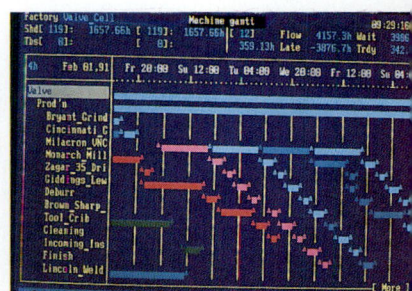

TACTIC The Scheduler Assistant helps decision makers perform what-if analysis through interactive Gantt chart capability. Courtesy of Waterloo Manufacturing Software.

---

[1] Avery L. Jenkins, "Managing the Variables of Project Management," *Digital Review,* June 3, 1991, p. 21.

[2] Most of the following project management computer software packages provide a Gantt, PERT, and work breakdown structure (WBS): Microsoft Project from Microsoft Corporation, CA-SuperProject for Windows from Computer Associates, Project Scheduler 6 from Scitor Corporation, Artemis Prestige for Windows from Lucas Management Systems, Open Plan 4.0 from Welcom Software Technology, PARISS Enterprise from Computer Aided Management, Primavera Project Planner 5.0 from Primavera Systems, Inc., and Project Workbench for Windows from Applied Business Technology Corporation.

INSIGHTS & APPLICATIONS

How Big Is It?

The International Falls, Minnesota, capital project is so large that it's hard to comprehend. The building that houses the new paper machine is almost three football fields long and as tall as an eight-story building; the paper machine itself is over two football fields long.

The equipment and materials for the entire expansion—about 1.5 million separate pieces, which would have filled tractor-trailers lined up for almost 20 miles—came from suppliers in 41 U.S. states and eight foreign countries.

Huge amounts of materials were required to complete the project:

- Concrete—enough for 409 miles of sidewalk
- Steel—10,800 tons (enough to make over 14,000 mid-size automobiles)

- Pipe—70 miles with almost 30,000 valves, fittings, and inserts
- Wiring—663 miles (equivalent to almost 10,000 miles of household extension cord)

Similarly, huge amounts of power and materials are used to run the paper machine and the associated pulp production facilities:

- Horsepower—70,000 horsepower (enough to power 800 automobiles)
- Steam—enough to heat about 50,000 average homes each day
- Water—28 million gallons a day (enough to supply 47,000 homes per day)
- Wood chips—300,000 cubic feet a day (would make a pile that is 1 foot wide, 1 foot high, and 57 miles long)

Adapted from "World-Class Act," *Insight* (Boise, Idaho: Published by the Corporate Communications Department for Boise Cascade, May 1991), pp. 2 and 3.

EXHIBIT 24–1
Gantt Chart

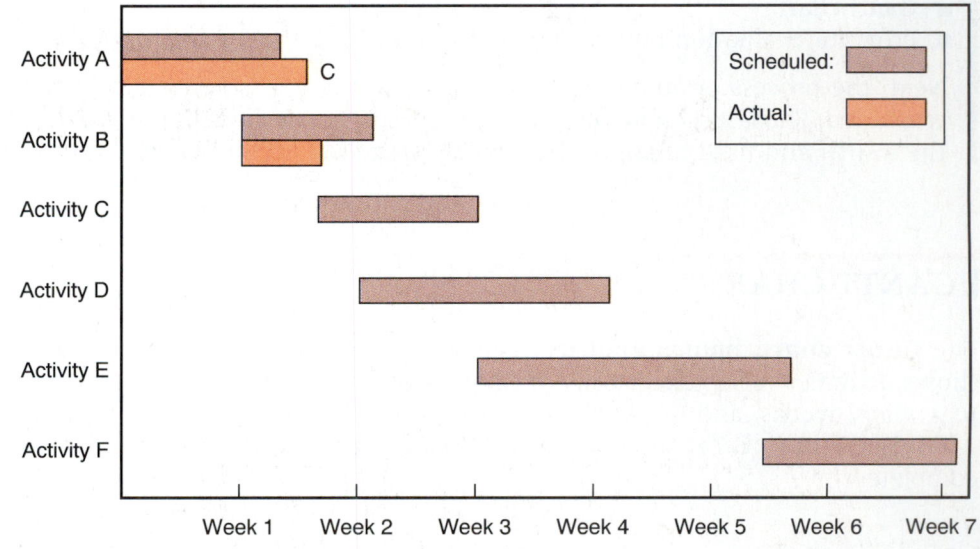

Exhibit 24–2. Once the pipeline project begins, the Gantt chart will be used to compare estimated performance against actual performance to determine whether the pipeline project is ahead of, behind, or on schedule.

Advantages of the Gantt Chart

An important advantage of the Gantt chart is its simplicity. People can quickly and easily comprehend a schedule for the entire project. The chart forces the project manager to think ahead and define activities. As the project progresses, actual completion times can be compared to estimated times. This project management tool requires no special devices or mathematics and can be used on small projects as well as large ones.

INSIGHTS & APPLICATIONS

Help for Managing Projects

Project management tools provide the power to maximize the capital budgeting methodology and move capital projects forward effectively and efficiently. Computerized project management tools automate scheduling to maintain peak efficiency throughout the project life cycle. Using work planning features, project managers can customize the work plan online, set tracking levels, and indicate task responsibilities.

Window-based packages make project management tools such as Gantt and PERT (program evaluation and review technique) charts easy to view and manipulate. Mike Brown, a manager at Walt Disney, credits project management software with saving the day for a significant project that involved downsizing a mainframe application.

"The project would have fallen apart if we hadn't watched it like a hawk," says Brown. "Our staff found that a user-friendly project management package made the difference in getting the system completed on time."[3]

Activities	Estimated time	
	Start	Complete
• Clear right-of-way	January 1	February 1
• Dig ditch	January 15	March 1
• Lay pipe	January 31	April 30
• Fill ditch	February 15	June 30

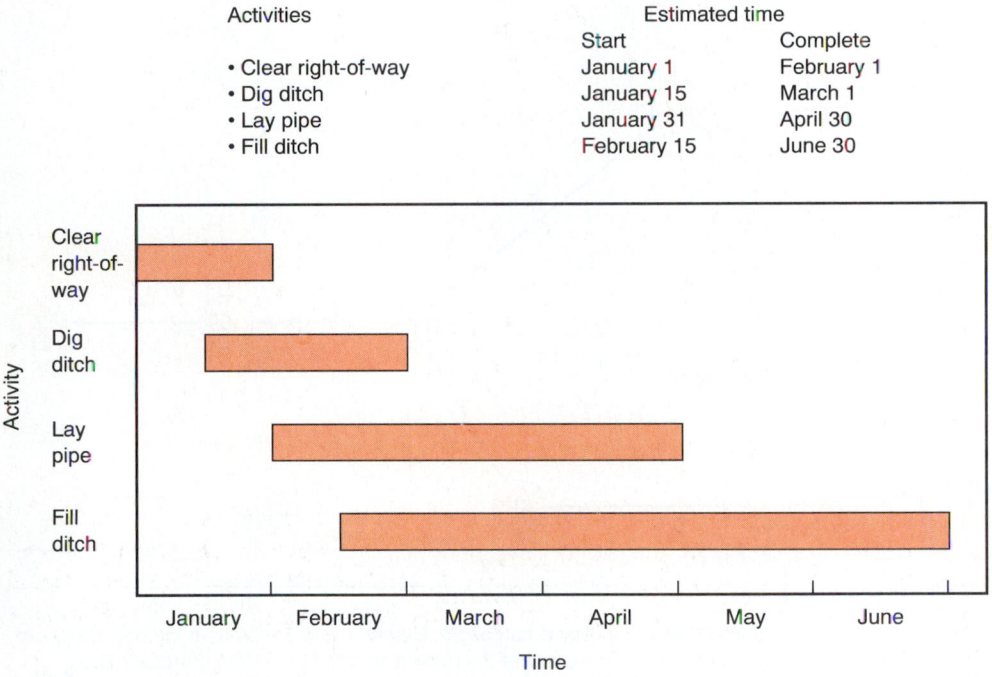

■ EXHIBIT 24–2
Gantt Chart for Pipeline Project

PROGRAM EVALUATION AND REVIEW TECHNIQUE

The **program evaluation and review technique (PERT)** is used to estimate, schedule, and manage a network of interdependent project activities. It is especially useful for managing large-scale, complex projects. In the past, PERT was more sophisticated than Gantt, because it incorporated probabilities, identified critical activities, and showed interdependencies among all activities. Today, computer-based Gantt systems include similar features.

Introducing Key Terms

Before presenting the steps for building a PERT network, it is necessary to introduce some key terms. To aid in visualizing these terms, a generic PERT

[3] Adapted from Lance B. Eliot, "Off-the-Shelf Help for Downsizing Jobs," *Corporate Computing*, p. 30.

network is displayed in Exhibit 24–3. An **event,** represented by a circle, indicates either the beginning or completion of an activity. An **activity** (also called a **task**), represented by an arrow, is the work and resources necessary to go from one event to the next. Before an event can begin, all activities flowing into it must be completed. Events in the network are numbered so that the event representing the completion of an activity always has a larger number than the event representing the beginning of the activity. Some authorities designate events by letters instead of numbers. Both identification systems produce the same results, and the text and problems in this chapter will use both systems.

The project is not complete until all the activities are completed. Before a given activity can begin, other activities must be completed.[4] These predecessor activities take on several forms, as shown in Exhibit 24–4. Note that activities that must occur consecutively are linked in a series, while activities that occur simultaneously are linked in parallel.

[4] Wayne L. Winston, *Operations Research: Applications and Algorithms,* 2d ed. (Boston: PWS-Kent, 1991), p. 399.

■■■ EXHIBIT 24–3
Generic PERT Network

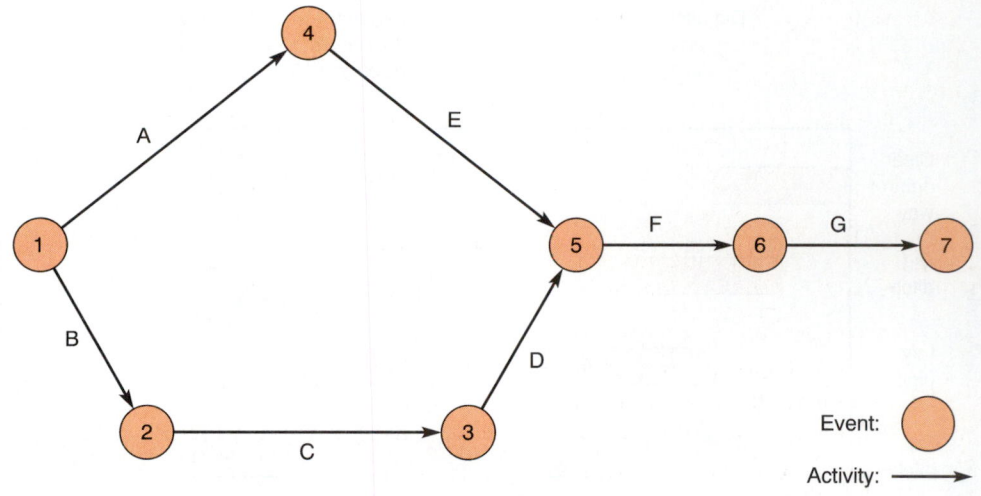

■■■ EXHIBIT 24–4
Forms of Predecessor Activities and Events

Activity A must be completed before Activity B can begin. Events 1 and 2 represent the beginning and completion of Activity A. Events 2 and 3 represent the beginning and completion of Activity B.

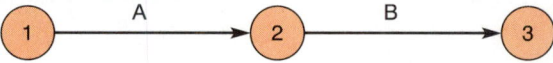

Activities A and B must be completed before Activity C can begin. Events 1 and 3 represent the beginning and completion of Activity A. Events 2 and 3 represent the beginning and completion of Activity B.

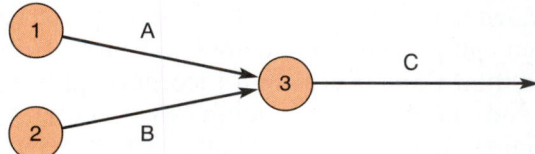

Activity A must be completed before Activity B or C can begin. Events 1 and 2 represent the beginning and completion of Activity A.

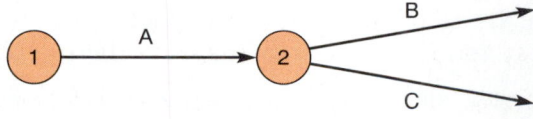

a. Violation of rules connecting activities and events.

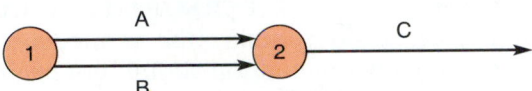

b. Use a dummy activity to correct violation.

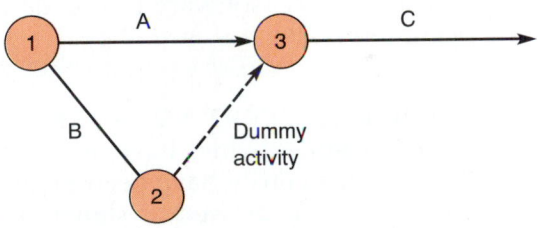

■ EXHIBIT 24–5
Use of a Dummy Activity

An activity can be represented by only one arrow, and two events can be connected by only one activity. These rules are violated in Exhibit 24–5a. Activities A and B are both predecessors of activity C, and both can begin at the same time. But events 1 and 2 cannot be connected by more than one activity. By using a **dummy activity,** which takes zero time and is indicated by a dashed arrow, both A and B can be represented as predecessor activities of activity C. The network in Exhibit 24–5b ensures that event 3 cannot begin until both activities A and B are completed. With these key terms in mind, we are now ready to describe the steps for building a PERT network.

▍Steps for Building a PERT Network

Building a PERT network involves a five-step process:

Step 1. Identify and list activities.
Step 2. Determine the proper sequence of activities and activities that can be performed simultaneously.
Step 3. Build the basic PERT network.
Step 4. Calculate expected activity times.
Step 5. Find the critical path.

STEP 1: IDENTIFY AND LIST ACTIVITIES.   The activities involved in development and implementation of a new information systems project are listed in Exhibit 24–6.

Activity code	Activity description	Immediate predecessor activity
A	Setting documentation standards	—
B	Designing software	—
C	Preparing site	—
D	Selecting additional personnel	—
E	Preparing documentation	A
F	Coding software	B
G	Installing equipment	C
H	Training personnel	D
I	Testing software	F, G
J	Testing total system	I
K	Converting system	E, J, H

■ EXHIBIT 24–6
Activities Necessary to Develop and Implement a New Information System

STEP 2: DETERMINE THE PROPER SEQUENCE OF ACTIVITIES AND ACTIVITIES THAT CAN BE PERFORMED SIMULTANEOUSLY. The last column in Exhibit 24–6 contains the immediate predecessor activities. For example, preparing documentation should not begin before the documentation standards have been set, coding of software cannot start until the software has been designed, and so forth. Several activities may be performed simultaneously, however. For example, software can be designed while documentation standards are being set.

STEP 3: BUILD THE BASIC PERT NETWORK. Now that the activity codes and immediate predecessor activities have been established and activities that can be performed simultaneously have been identified, a basic PERT network can be constructed. The basic network is shown in Exhibit 24–7.

STEP 4: CALCULATE EXPECTED ACTIVITY TIMES. The **expected activity time** is the estimated duration that an activity will take. To calculate the expected activity time, the project manager and his or her staff will provide three time estimates for each activity:

- **Optimistic time,** which is an estimate of the activity's duration under the most favorable conditions
- **Pessimistic time,** which is an estimate of the activity's duration under the least favorable conditions
- **Most likely time,** which is an estimate of the activity's duration under normal conditions

The purpose in making these three time estimates is to use them to calculate a single weighted-average time for each activity, using the following formula:

$$T_e = \frac{O + 4M + P}{6}$$

where:

■■■ EXHIBIT 24–7
Basic PERT Network Showing Activities and Events of the Information Systems Project

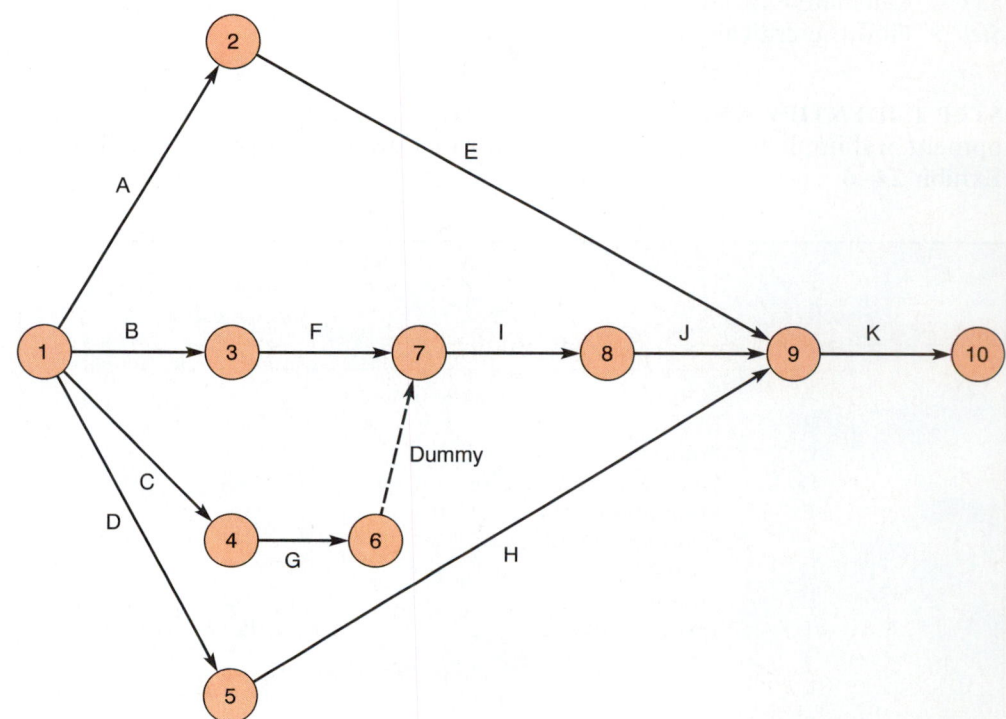

T_e = Expected activity time
O = Optimistic time estimate
P = Pessimistic time estimate
M = Most likely time estimate

This formula is used to calculate the expected activity times in Exhibit 24–8. The beginning and ending events of each activity have been numbered to aid identification. Remember that the number of the ending event must be larger than the number of the beginning event. This convention allows the activities to be identified by an ordered pair of numbers. For example, activity B could be identified as activity 1, 3. In some computer-based PERT systems, this is the conventional way of identifying activities. The expected activity times are included in the PERT network shown in Exhibit 24–9.

| Activity code | Events | | Estimated times | | | Expected activity time (T_e) |
	Begin	End	Optimistic (O)	Most likely (M)	Pessimistic (P)	
A	1	2	1	2	3	2
B	1	3	8	15	28	16
C	1	4	5	9	9	8.3
D	1	5	1	3	5	3
E	2	9	6	14	22	14
F	3	7	4	7	10	7
G	4	6	4	6	8	6
Dummy	6	7	0	0	0	0
H	5	9	5	10	21	11
I	7	8	10	16	34	18
J	8	9	4	6	8	6
K	9	10	4	6	8	6

■ EXHIBIT 24–8
Expected Activity Times in Weeks for the Information Systems Project

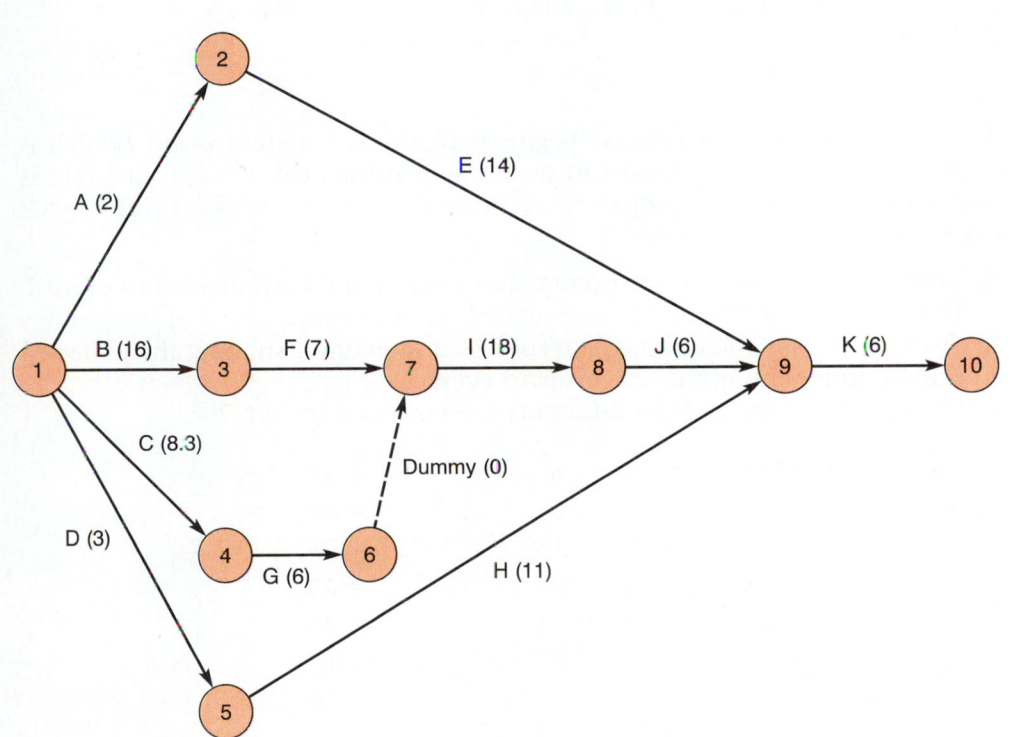

■ EXHIBIT 24–9
PERT Network with Expected Activity Times in Weeks of the Information Systems Project

STEP 5: FIND THE CRITICAL PATH. In order to complete a project, all events on the PERT network must be completed. Thus, the path that has the longest cumulative expected activity time through the network dictates the project's completion date. This path, which is called the **critical path,** encompasses every critical event and serves as an estimate of the minimum time needed to complete a project.

Two key values are needed to find the critical path:

- **Early event time** for event i, represented by $ET(i)$, is the earliest time at which event i can occur.
- **Late event time** for event i, represented by $LT(i)$, is the latest time at which event i can occur without delaying the completion of the project.

To calculate $ET(i)$:

1. Find each event prior to event i that is connected to event i by an arrow. These events are the immediate predecessors of event i.
2. To the ET of each immediate predecessor of event i, add the expected activity time connecting the immediate predecessor to event i.
3. $ET(i)$ equals the maximum of the sum calculated in step 2.

To find the ET for each event in the PERT network, begin with event 1, which represents the start of the project; therefore, $ET(1) = 0$. Then, since event 1 is the only immediate predecessor of event 2, and activity A has an expected activity time of 2, $ET(2) = ET(1) + 2 = 2$. The ETs for the other events are calculated as follows:

$$
\begin{aligned}
ET(3) &= ET(1) + 16 &&= 16 \\
ET(4) &= ET(1) + 8.3 &&= 8.3 \\
ET(5) &= ET(1) + 3 &&= 3 \\
ET(6) &= ET(4) + 6 &&= 14.3 \\
ET(7) &= \max \begin{cases} ET(3) + 7 &= 23 \\ ET(6) + 0 &= 14.3 \end{cases} &&= 23 \\
ET(8) &= ET(7) + 18 &&= 41 \\
ET(9) &= \max \begin{cases} ET(2) + 14 = 16 \\ ET(5) + 11 = 14 \\ ET(8) + 6 = 47 \end{cases} &&= 47 \\
ET(10) &= ET(9) + 6 &&= 53
\end{aligned}
$$

To calculate $LT(i)$, the process begins with the completion event (which is event 10) and works backward in descending numerical order until $LT(1)$ is determined. Because the project can be completed in 53 weeks, $LT(10) = 53$. $LT(i)$ is calculated as follows:

1. Determine each event that occurs after event i and is connected to event i. These events are the immediate successors of event i.
2. From the LT for each immediate successor to event i, subtract the expected activity time joining the successor to event i.
3. $LT(i)$ is the smallest of the differences determined in step 2.

$$
\begin{aligned}
LT(9) &= LT(10) - 6 &&= 47 \\
LT(8) &= LT(9) - 6 &&= 41 \\
LT(7) &= LT(8) - 18 &&= 23 \\
LT(6) &= LT(7) - 0 &&= 23 \\
LT(5) &= LT(9) - 11 &&= 36 \\
LT(4) &= LT(6) - 6 &&= 17 \\
LT(3) &= LT(7) - 7 &&= 16 \\
LT(2) &= LT(9) - 14 &&= 33
\end{aligned}
$$

$$LT(1) = \min \begin{cases} LT(2) - 2 & = 31 \\ LT(3) - 16 & = 0 \\ LT(4) - 8.3 & = 8.7 \\ LT(5) - 3 & = 33 \end{cases} = 0$$

Now that ET(i) and LT(i) have been calculated, the activities that have slack time and those that have zero slack time can be determined. **Total slack (TS)** for any activity is the maximum amount of time the activity can be delayed without affecting the completion time of the project. Subtracting ET(i) from LT(i) will give the total slack allowable for any activity, calculated as:

$$TS(i) = LT(i) - ET(i)$$

If an activity has zero TS, any delay in starting or completing the activity will delay the completion of the project. For example, increasing the duration of an activity with zero TS by four weeks will increase the length of the project by four weeks. Such an activity is *critical* to the on-time completion of the project. Therefore, the critical path is composed of critical activities. Exhibit 24–10 shows the critical path of the PERT network.

Activities that are not on the critical path have a certain amount of slack; that is, they may be started later and still allow the project, as a whole, to proceed on schedule. An activity's TS can be used as a measure of the flexibility in the duration of the activity. For example, activity A can take up to 31 weeks longer than its scheduled duration of 2 weeks without delaying the completion of the project.

An activity's **free slack (FS)** is the maximum amount of time the activity can be delayed without delaying the start of the next activity. Free slack will only occur on noncritical activities and will never exceed total slack.

■■■ EXHIBIT 24–10
PERT Network With Critical Path of the Information Systems Project

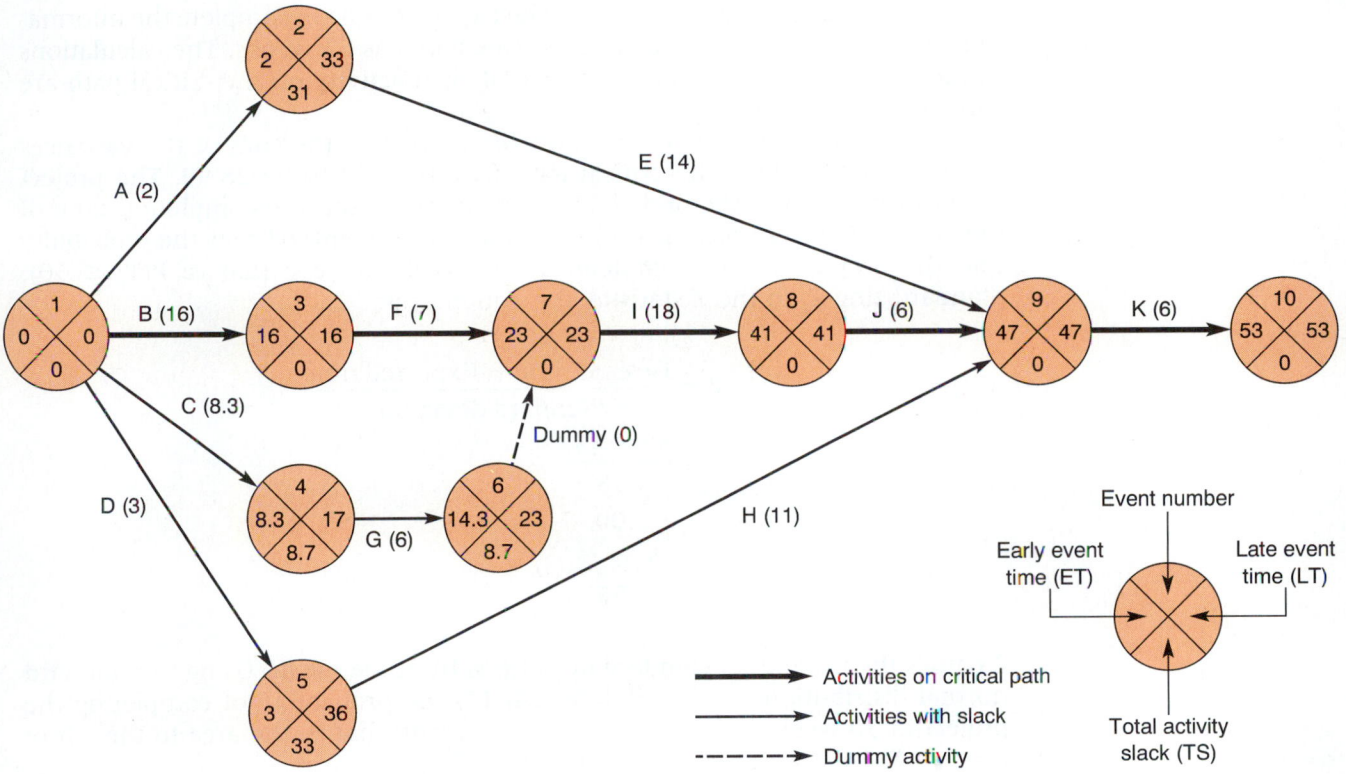

Suppose the occurrence of event i, or the duration of activity (i, j), is delayed by k units. Then, the earliest that event j can occur is $ET(i) + T_e(i, j) + k$. Thus, if $ET(i) + T_e(i, j) + k \leq ET(j)$, or $k \leq LT(j) - ET(i) - T_e(i, j)$, then event j is not delayed. If event j is not delayed, no other activities will be delayed beyond their earliest possible starting times. Therefore:

$$FS(i, j) = LT(j) - ET(i) - T_e(i, j)$$

Activity A:	$FS(1, 2) =$	33	$-$	0	$-$	2	$= 31$
Activity C:	$FS(1, 4) =$	17	$-$	0	$-$	8.3	$= 8.7$
Activity D:	$FS(1, 5) =$	36	$-$	0	$-$	3	$= 33$
Activity E:	$FS(2, 9) =$	47	$-$	2	$-$	14	$= 31$
Activity G:	$FS(4, 6) =$	23	$-$	8.3	$-$	6	$= 8.7$
Activity H:	$FS(5, 9) =$	47	$-$	3	$-$	11	$= 33$

Probability Concepts with PERT

PERT assumes that the time needed to perform each activity is a random variable described by a probability distribution. The time distribution that PERT assumes for an activity is a beta distribution. The mean, standard deviation (σ), and variance (σ^2), respectively, of the time for activity Z can be calculated by the following approximation formulas:

$$T_e(Z) = \frac{O + 4M + P}{6}$$

$$\sigma(Z) = \text{Standard deviation} = \frac{P - O}{6} \text{ or } \sqrt{\text{Variance}}$$

$$\sigma^2(Z) = \text{Variance} = \left[\frac{(P - O)}{6}\right]^2 \text{ or } \frac{(P - O)^2}{36}$$

The expected completion time of the project is the sum of all the expected activity times along the critical path. The expected time to complete the information systems project has already been calculated as 53 weeks. The calculations of the standard deviation and variance of each activity on the critical path are shown in Exhibit 24–11.

The variance of project completion (σ_p^2), which is the sum of the variances of the activities along the critical path, is estimated to be 28.99. The project manager can now make probabilistic statements about the completion time of the project. For example, the project manager may want to know the probability that the project will be completed in 50 weeks or less; that is: $P(T_p \leq 50)$. Standardizing T_p to the Z statistic, the equation is:

$$Z = \frac{\text{Desired time} - \text{Expected time}}{\text{Standard deviation}}$$

$$= \frac{50 - 53}{5.38}$$

$$= \frac{-3.00}{5.38}$$

$$= -0.5576$$

Z equals the number of standard deviations from the mean. Using the standard normal distribution table in Exhibit 24–12, the probability of completing the project in 50 weeks is approximately 29 percent; that is, the area to the left of $Z = -0.5576$ is about 0.2900 (1.0000 − 0.7100).

Activities on critical path	Expected times			Standard deviation $\sigma = \dfrac{P - O}{6}$	Variance $\sigma^2 = \dfrac{(P - O)^2}{36}$
	O	M	P		
B	8	15	28	$\dfrac{28 - 8}{6} = 3.33$	$\dfrac{(28 - 8)^2}{36} = 11.11$
F	4	7	10	$\dfrac{10 - 4}{6} = 1.00$	$\dfrac{(10 - 4)^2}{36} = 1.00$
I	10	16	34	$\dfrac{34 - 10}{6} = 4.00$	$\dfrac{(34 - 10)^2}{36} = 16.00$
J	4	6	8	$\dfrac{8 - 4}{6} = 0.667$	$\dfrac{(8 - 4)^2}{36} = 0.44$
K	4	6	8	$\dfrac{8 - 4}{6} = 0.667$	$\dfrac{(8 - 4)^2}{36} = 0.44$

$\sigma_p^2 = \Sigma(\text{variances of activities on critical path})$
$= \underline{\underline{28.99}}$

$\sigma_p = \sqrt{\Sigma(\text{variances of activities on critical path})}$
$= \sqrt{28.99}$
$= \underline{\underline{5.38 \text{ (approximately)}}}$

Note: σ_p is not equal to the sum of individual σ's.

█EXHIBIT 24–12
Areas under the Standard Normal Curve

To find the area under the normal curve, you must know how many standard deviations that point is to the right of the mean. Then, the area under the normal curve can be read directly from the normal table. For example, the total area under the normal curve for a point that is 1.60 standard deviations to the right of the mean is .94520. If Z equals −1.60, the area to the left of Z equals −1.60 is .05480, or 1 − .94520 = .05480.

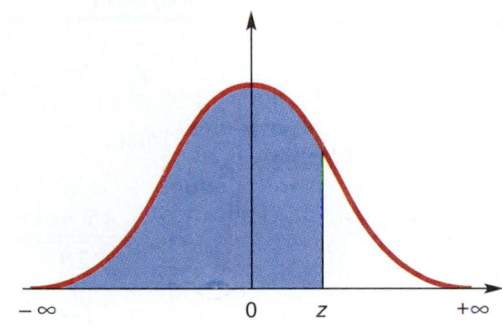

Z	.00	.01	.02	.03	.04	.05	.06	.07	.08	.09
.0	.5000	.5040	.5080	.5120	.5160	.5199	.5239	.5279	.5319	.5359
.1	.5398	.5438	.5478	.5517	.5557	.5596	.5636	.5675	.5714	.5753
.2	.5793	.5832	.5871	.5910	.5948	.5987	.6026	.6064	.6103	.6141
.3	.6179	.6217	.6255	.6293	.6331	.6368	.6406	.6443	.6480	.6517
.4	.6554	.6591	.6628	.6664	.6700	.6736	.6772	.6808	.6844	.6879
.5	.6915	.6950	.6985	.7019	.7054	.7088	.7123	.7157	.7190	.7224
.6	.7257	.7291	.7324	.7357	.7389	.7422	.7454	.7486	.7517	.7549
.7	.7580	.7611	.7642	.7673	.7704	.7734	.7764	.7794	.7823	.7852
.8	.7881	.7910	.7939	.7967	.7995	.8023	.8051	.8078	.8106	.8133
.9	.8159	.8186	.8212	.8238	.8264	.8289	.8315	.8340	.8365	.8389
1.0	.8413	.8438	.8461	.8485	.8508	.8531	.8554	.8577	.8599	.8621

Continued

—Continued

1.1	.8643	.8665	.8686	.8708	.8729	.8749	.8770	.8790	.8810	.8830
1.2	.8849	.8869	.8888	.8907	.8925	.8944	.8962	.8980	.8997	.9015
1.3	.9032	.9049	.9066	.9082	.9099	.9115	.9131	.9147	.9162	.9177
1.4	.9192	.9207	.9222	.9236	.9251	.9265	.9279	.9292	.9306	.9319
1.5	.9332	.9345	.9357	.9370	.9382	.9394	.9406	.9418	.9492	.9441
1.6	.9452	.9463	.9474	.9484	.9495	.9505	.9515	.9525	.9535	.9545
1.7	.9554	.9564	.9573	.9582	.9591	.9599	.9608	.9616	.9625	.9633
1.8	.9641	.9649	.9656	.9664	.9671	.9678	.9686	.9693	.9699	.9706
1.9	.9713	.9719	.9726	.9732	.9738	.9744	.9750	.9756	.9761	.9767
2.0	.9772	.9778	.9783	.9788	.9793	.9798	.9803	.9808	.9812	.9817
2.1	.9821	.9826	.9830	.9834	.9838	.9842	.9846	.9850	.9854	.9857
2.2	.9861	.9864	.9868	.9871	.9875	.9878	.9881	.9884	.9887	.9890
2.3	.9893	.9896	.9898	.9901	.9904	.9906	.9909	.9911	.9913	.9916
2.4	.9918	.9920	.9922	.9925	.9927	.9929	.9931	.9932	.9934	.9936
2.5	.9938	.9940	.9941	.9943	.9945	.9946	.9948	.9949	.9951	.9952
2.6	.9953	.9955	.9956	.9957	.9959	.9960	.9961	.9962	.9963	.9964
2.7	.9965	.9966	.9967	.9968	.9969	.9970	.9971	.9972	.9973	.9974
2.8	.9974	.9975	.9976	.9977	.9977	.9978	.9979	.9979	.9980	.9981
2.9	.9981	.9982	.9982	.9983	.9984	.9984	.9985	.9985	.9986	.9986
3.0	.9987	.9987	.9987	.9988	.9988	.9989	.9989	.9989	.9990	.9990
3.1	.9990	.9991	.9991	.9991	.9992	.9992	.9992	.9992	.9993	.9993
3.2	.9993	.9993	.9994	.9994	.9994	.9994	.9994	.9995	.9995	.9995
3.3	.9995	.9995	.9995	.9996	.9996	.9996	.9996	.9996	.9996	.9997
3.4	.9997	.9997	.9997	.9997	.9997	.9997	.9997	.9997	.9997	.9998

For another example, the project manager may ask, "What is the probability that activity I can be completed by week 45?" The following variances are associated with the pertinent critical path activities:

ACTIVITY	σ^2
B	11.11
F	1.00
I	16.00
Total	28.11

$$Z = \frac{45 - 41}{\sqrt{28.11}}$$

$$= \frac{4.00}{5.30}$$

$$= 0.7547$$

The area under the normal curve for $Z = 0.7547$ is approximately 0.7750. Therefore, the probability that activity I will be completed by week 45 is 77.5 percent.

CRASHING THE PROJECT

Frequently, the project manager will be required to complete the project in a time that is less than the normal critical path. For example, Kumar Davishar, project manager, is charged with the responsibility of constructing a bridge in

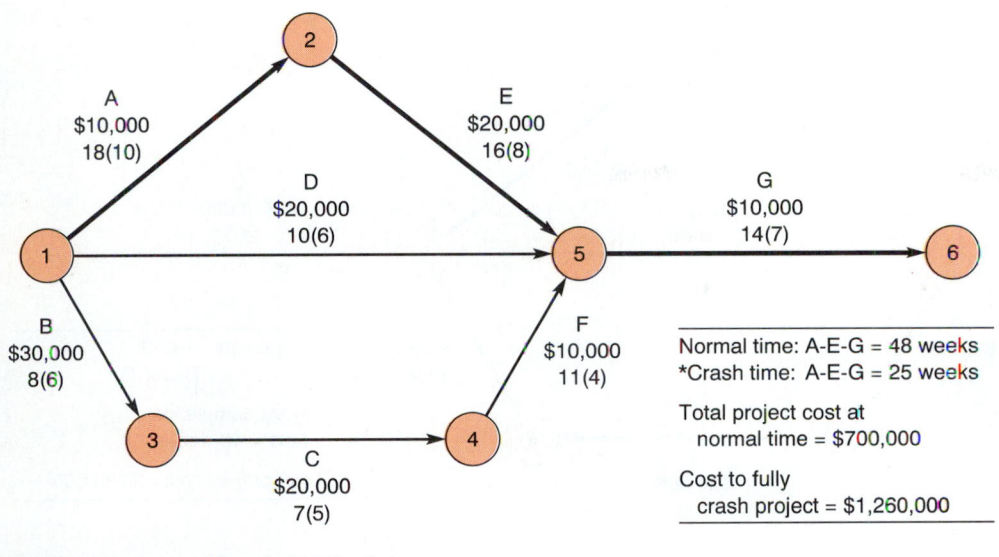

■■■EXHIBIT 24–13
**Initial PERT Network
for the Bridge Project**

Normal time: A-E-G = 48 weeks
*Crash time: A-E-G = 25 weeks

Total project cost at
  normal time = $700,000

Cost to fully
  crash project = $1,260,000

*Note: This is the time for a fully crashed A-E-G path.

less time than was originally estimated. To do this, Kumar will have to expand the project's resources by taking such steps as initiating overtime work, leasing additional equipment, and hiring more employees. This process is referred to as **crashing**.[5]

The PERT network for building the bridge is shown in Exhibit 24–13. The total cost at normal time for this project is $700,000. The normal time (in weeks) for each activity appears first, followed by the fully crashed time in parentheses. Below the activity codes are the incremental costs of crashing the activity; that is, the crash cost per week. For example, activity A can be reduced by 8 weeks at a cost of $10,000 per week, which means that crashing activity A fully would add $80,000 to the total project cost.

What if Kumar Davishar wants to know the least-cost schedule to complete the project in 40 weeks, 45 weeks, or any other time frame between 48 and 25 weeks. To reduce the total project time, the time needed to complete the critical path must also be reduced. Kumar also wants to do this at the lowest possible cost. Thus, he should choose the activity on the critical path that has the least cost of crashing.

Activities A and G both cost $10,000 per week to crash. In case of a tie, the activity that can reduce the project duration by the greatest amount should be chosen, in this case activity A. Now activity A is fully crashed from 18 weeks to 10 weeks. This adds $80,000 to the project cost ($10,000 × 8 weeks), giving a total project cost of $780,000 ($700,000 + $80,000).

The network is redrawn in Exhibit 24–14 to represent the crashing of activity A. The crashing of activity A has not only reduced the previous critical path, A–E–G, to 40 weeks, but it has made path B–C–F–G critical as well, with a total duration of 40 weeks. This is an example of how noncritical activities can become critical when activities are crashed.

Now activity G is the only activity that can reduce the project time alone. Therefore, it is chosen to crash next, from 14 weeks to 7 weeks, at a cost of $70,000 ($10,000 × 7 weeks). The new network with a project time of 33 weeks and a total project cost of $850,000 ($780,000 + $70,000) is presented in Exhibit 24–15.

Because activity F has the lowest crash cost remaining, it is chosen to crash

[5] Herbert Moskowitz and Gordon P. Wright, *Operations Research Techniques for Management* (Englewood Cliffs, N.J.: Prentice-Hall, 1979), pp. 722–732.

**PERT Network for the
Bridge Project after
Crashing Activity A**

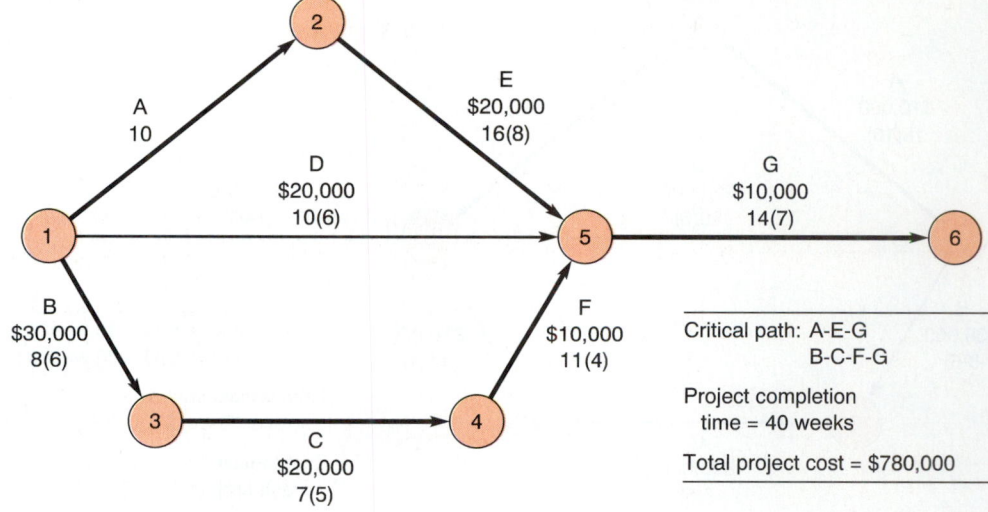

Critical path: A-E-G
             B-C-F-G

Project completion
   time = 40 weeks

Total project cost = $780,000

**PERT Network for the
Bridge Project after
Crashing Activity G**

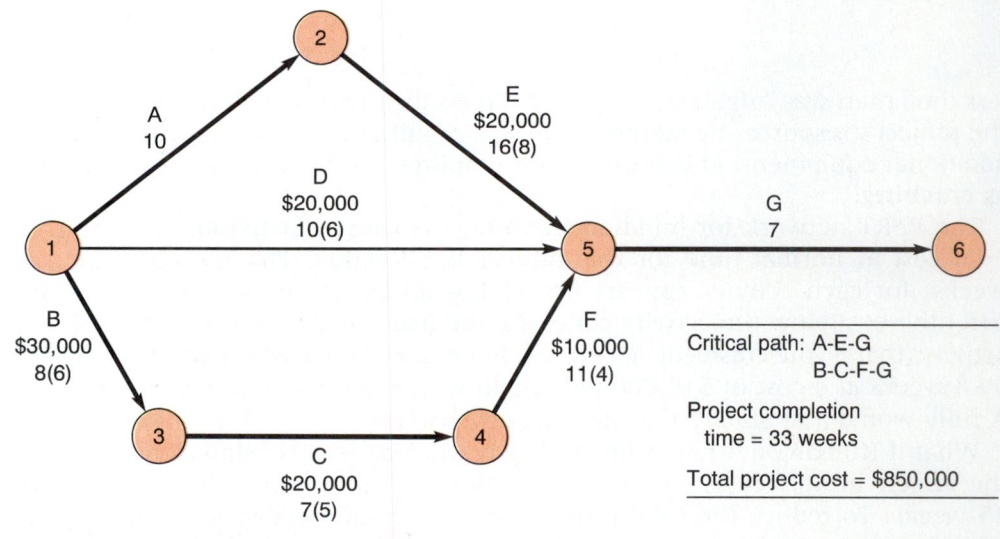

Critical path: A-E-G
             B-C-F-G

Project completion
   time = 33 weeks

Total project cost = $850,000

next. In addition, activity E is the only activity remaining on path A–E–G that has not been crashed. Crashing activity F (7 weeks) and partially crashing activity E (7 of the possible 8 weeks) increases the total project cost by $210,000 ($10,000 × 7 weeks and $20,000 × 7 weeks). The project time is reduced to 26 weeks, with a total project cost of $1,060,000. The resulting network is illustrated in Exhibit 24–16. Note that crashing activity E fully is not worthwhile because doing so would reduce critical path A–E–G to 25 weeks while critical path B–C–F–G remains at 26 weeks.

Fully crashing activity E becomes worthwhile, however, if critical path B–C–F–G can be reduced by one week. This can be accomplished by partially crashing activity C, which has the lowest crash cost. Thus, the final step is to crash activity E completely and partially crash activity C. This step costs $40,000 ($20,000 × 1 week and $20,000 × 1 week), making the total project cost of the crashed project $1,100,000, which is $160,000 ($1,260,000 − $1,100,000) less than crashing all the activities, as presented in Exhibit 24–13. Exhibit 24–17 illustrates the final network. Crashing activity B or D or crashing activity C further will not reduce project time. The results of the analysis are graphed in Exhibit 24–18, which shows the cost of crashing for any project completion time between a normal and a fully crashed schedule.

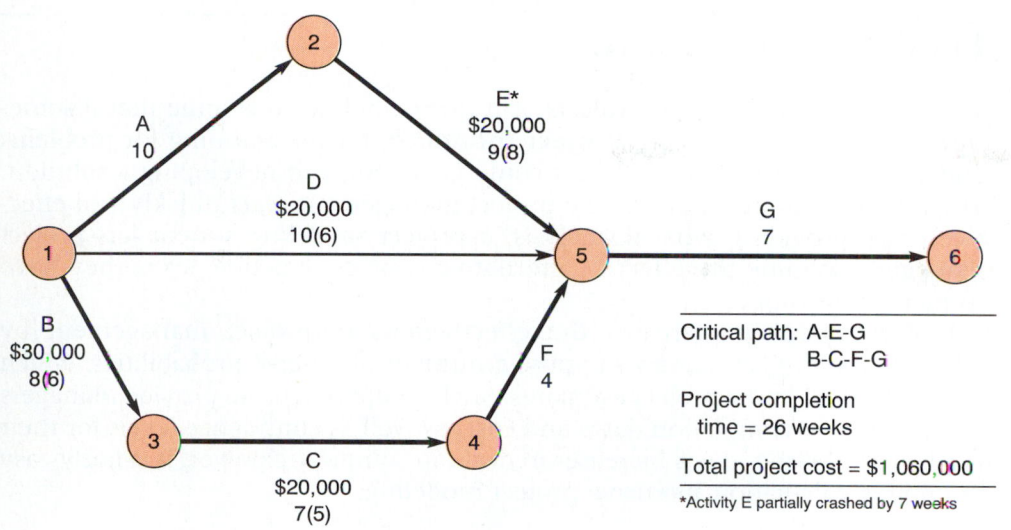

■ EXHIBIT 24–16
PERT Network for the Bridge Project after Crashing Activity F and Partially Crashing Activity E

Critical path: A-E-G
            B-C-F-G

Project completion
  time = 26 weeks

Total project cost = $1,060,000

*Activity E partially crashed by 7 weeks

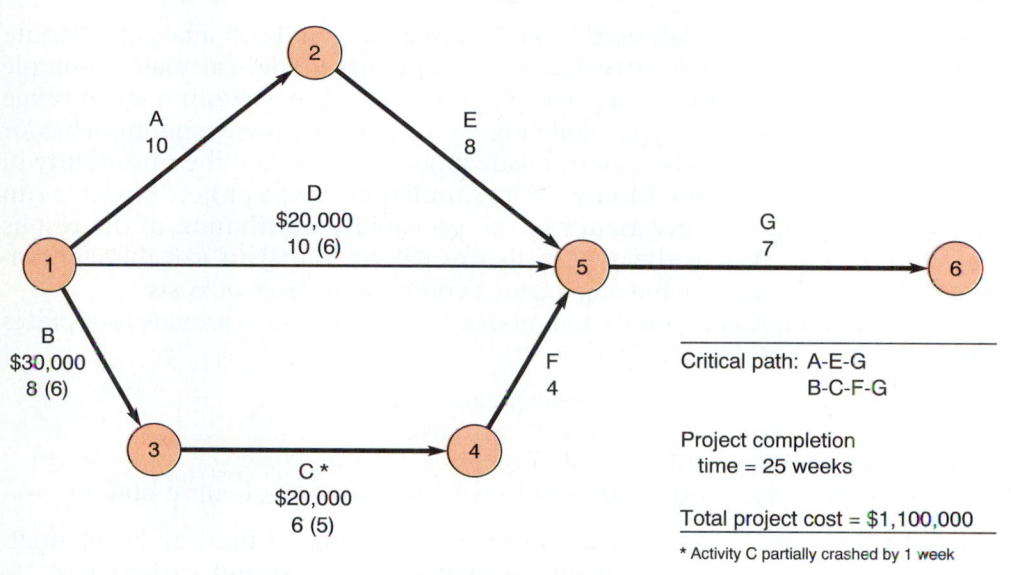

■ EXHIBIT 24–17
PERT Network for the Bridge Project after Completely Crashing Activity E and Partially Crashing Activity C

Critical path: A-E-G
            B-C-F-G

Project completion
  time = 25 weeks

Total project cost = $1,100,000

* Activity C partially crashed by 1 week

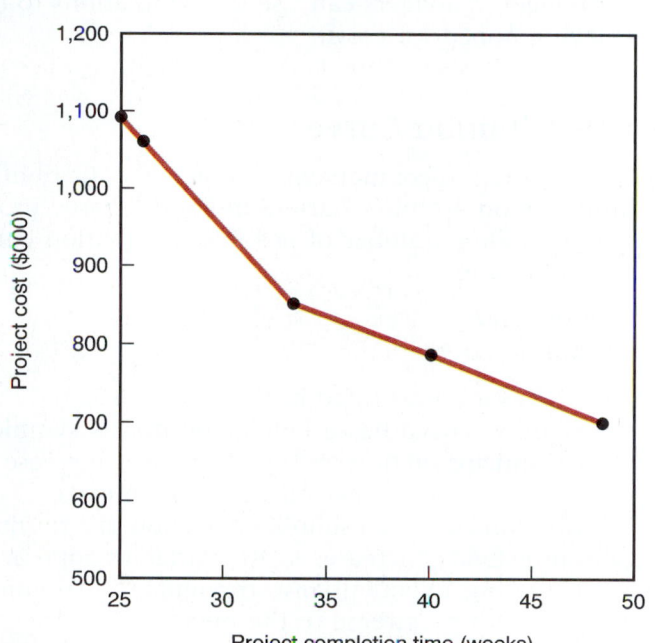

■ EXHIBIT 24–18
Bridge Project Cost Profile for Normal and Crashed Activities

PROJECT MODELING

When dealing with capital projects, it is normally best to assume that if something can go wrong, it will. **Project modeling** means planning for problems and working out in advance what could go wrong and developing a solution. Then, when a problem arises, the project manager can react quickly and effectively. By providing what-if analysis, a project modeling system lets project managers examine the effect of alternative courses of action *before* they have to make a decision.

Project modeling increases the effectiveness of project management by allowing the project manager to pose a number of what-if probabilities, which are vital to validating project estimates. Such an approach can provide managers with estimated completion dates and costs as well as confidence levels for their predictions. With today's increases in desktop computing power, it is fairly easy to employ calculation-intensive project modeling.

Monte Carlo Simulation

One of the popular models used in project modeling and risk analysis is Monte Carlo Simulation. The **Monte Carlo Simulation** model calculates multiple possible scenarios by randomly selecting a number from within a given range and applying it to the project modeling system. In this way, random behavior may be added to otherwise deterministic models to simulate the uncertainty in real-world situations. The Monte Carlo Simulation–based project model is run a great many times. The variance of the probability distribution of the results is determined as well as the average performance. Managers can thereby estimate the likelihood of achieving various completion dates or costs.

To run a Monte Carlo Simulation model, project managers provide four pieces of data:

- Earliest completion date the project can have
- Latest completion date the project can have
- Expected completion date of the project
- A probability distribution curve selected from a range of curve options

Monte Carlo Simulation can be applied to cost estimates in a similar manner. By providing the project modeling system with lowest and highest costs as well as the target budget, managers can use the simulations to determine the likelihood of achieving hoped-for costs.

Selecting a Distribution Curve

As might be expected, the project manager's choice of a distribution curve will have a strong influence on a Monte Carlo Simulation–based project modeling system. Although an endless number of possible distribution curves exist, the following two are dominant:

- Normal distribution curve
- Triangular distribution curve

These distribution curves are illustrated in Exhibit 24–19.

The normal distribution curve has a bell shape that is symmetric about its mean. Probabilities of anticipated time and cost outcomes increase exponentially as these variables approach their expected values, or means.

A triangular distribution curve is a simplified version of a normal distribution curve. Once again, probability increases as the variables approach their mean. But rather than increasing exponentially, triangular distribution probability increases linearly from either extreme to the mean.

Few guidelines exist to help project managers decide which distribution curve

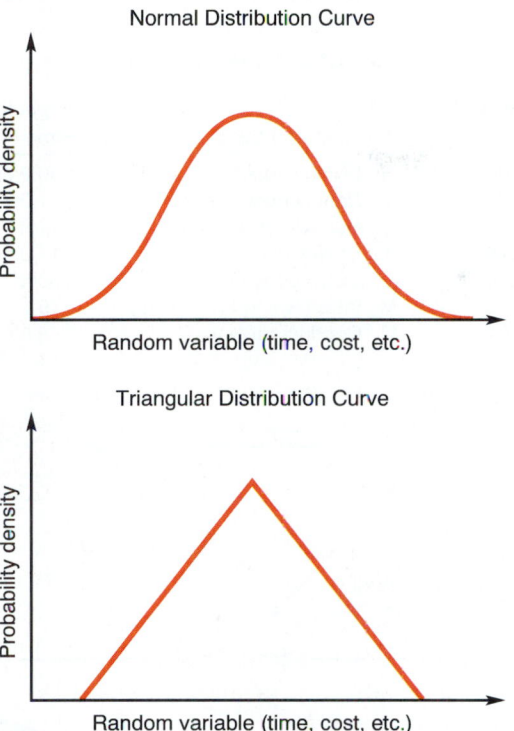

■ EXHIBIT 24–19
Normal and Triangular Distribution Curves

to use for a specific project. Therefore, the best approach is to apply various curves to similar projects that have been completed and observe which curve provides the greatest level of accuracy in matching those times and costs. If historical data are missing, a ''best guess'' regarding a distribution curve type is the only option. Experience will eventually dictate which curve type is most appropriate.[6]

Running the Iterations

A second factor influencing the accuracy of Monte Carlo Simulations is the number of iterations the project modeling system performs. As a general rule, the more iterations, the more accurate the results will be. In general, between 100 and 5,000 iterations must be performed to obtain optimum results.

Monte Carlo Simulation in Practice

Cynthia Kemp, senior project engineer for Hi-Vac Industries, has developed a PERT network to assist in managing the construction of a new assembly line. This PERT network and its tasks are illustrated in Exhibit 24–20. Note that Cynthia has calculated the variance, σ^2, for each activity as well as the expected time, T_e. The critical path is indicated by a bold line.

Although Cynthia's PERT diagram could have been created by hand, she decided to use a project management software package to prepare the diagram. By doing so, Cynthia saved time and effort in entering project task information; she only needed to enter it once. The project management software package then allowed her to ask any number of what-if questions regarding project time and cost with just a few keystrokes. She could, for example, crash one or more tasks to see how the network's critical path would change. Or she could ask the computer to determine the least costly way to crash the network by five days.

[6] Ibid., p. 23.

■ EXHIBIT 24–20
PERT Network to Assist in Managing the Construction of a New Assembly Line

Task		Expected Time (T_e)	Variance (σ^2)		Task		Expected Time (T_e)	Variance (σ^2)
A	Design line layout	14.0 days	16.00		H	Dummy task	0.0 days	0.00
B	Prepare equipment list	11.3	4.00		I	Print documentation	1.0	0.00
C	Prepare building interior	21.2	38.00		J	Run wiring simulation	11.2	4.70
D	Install false floor & ceiling	15.3	1.78		K	Draw wiring schematic	14.0	8.17
E	Write documentation	15.0	32.10		L	Install equipment	30.8	6.25
F	Acquire equipment	15.8	6.25		M	Install wiring & plumbing	9.2	0.70
G	Install air ductwork	13.2	10.04		N	Conduct training	8.8	0.70

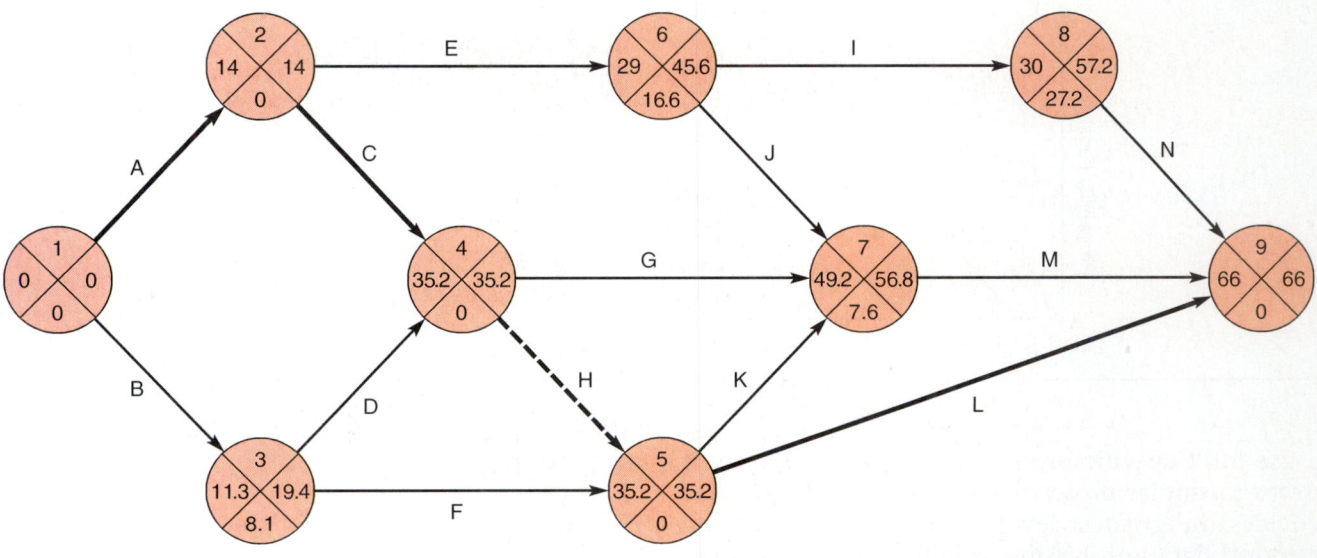

Cynthia's project management system integrates Monte Carlo Simulation with the package's PERT features. Ed, the plant manager, wants Cynthia to run such a simulation. He feels that by iterating the PERT network with randomly selected task times, the resulting project schedule will more accurately reflect actual conditions.

Cynthia loads her PERT data into the Monte Carlo module. The software asks her to enter parameters that define the probability distribution from which random values will be selected. She enters values for earliest, latest, and expected times for completion of the project. Cynthia is not sure what type of probability distribution to use or the number of iterations to run. Ed suggests using a normal distribution curve and running 1,000 iterations. He feels different distributions and iteration counts can be used in future projects until sufficient experience is gained to make a more educated choice. Cynthia makes the appropriate selections and runs the simulations.

The Monte Carlo Simulation takes about 15 minutes to run on Cynthia's computer. Exhibit 24–21 shows the software's output, a PERT network identical to the one in Exhibit 24–20. The PERT mean (expected) time of 66 days and variance of 60.27 are tabulated next to the results of the Monte Carlo Simulation. The PERT estimate of the project mean was low (optimistic) by only 1.5 percent $[((67.00 - 66.00) \div 67.00) \times 100]$, but the estimated variance was too high by 42 percent $[((60.27 - 42.39) \div 42.39) \times 100]$. In this case, this discrepancy was due to a considerable amount of slack along subcritical paths at each PERT event. Subcritical paths are paths that, while not actually critical, require nearly as much time as the critical path. If there is a large amount of

▰ EXHIBIT 24–21
PERT Network after Monte Carlo Simulation

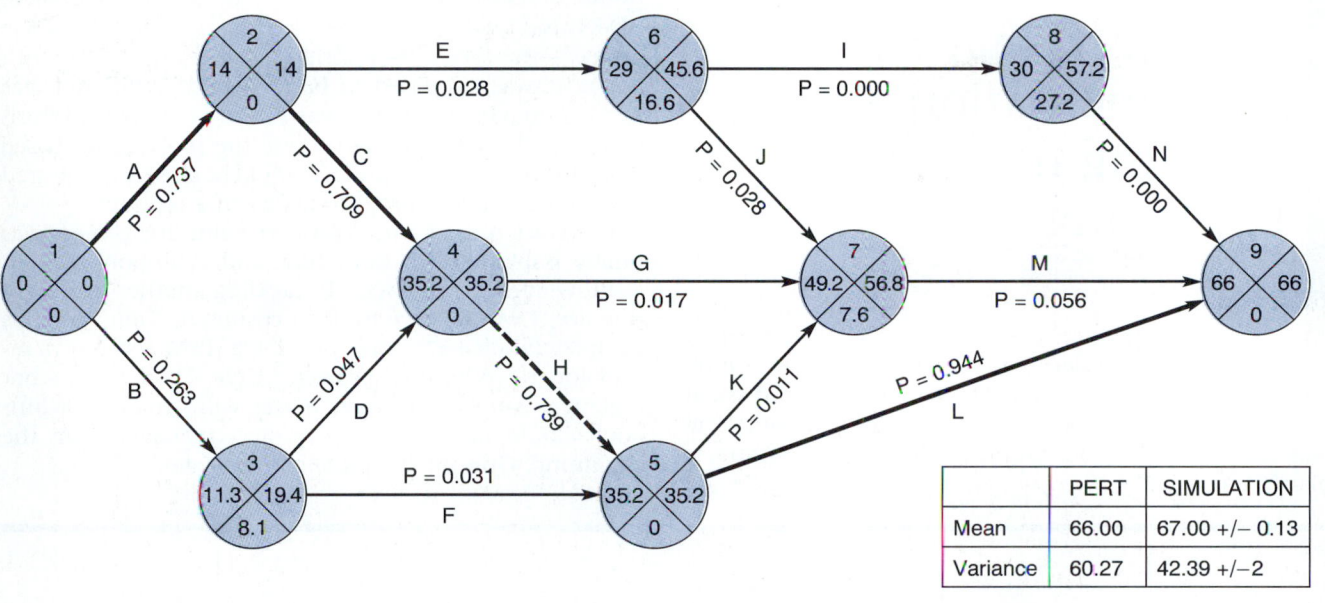

		PERT	SIMULATION
Mean		66.00	67.00 +/− 0.13
Variance		60.27	42.39 +/−2

slack along these paths, the probability of one of them actually becoming critical is relatively low, and the variance will be overstated by PERT, as in this case.

Finally, Cynthia gets one more type of information from the Monte Carlo Simulation output. Each task arrow now includes the probability of that task becoming part of the critical path. As an example, activity A shows a probability of 0.737, or 73.7 percent. This means that out of the 1,000 iterations run during the simulation, the critical path included activity A 737 times. On the other hand, activity K, with a probability of 0.011, fell onto the critical path only 11 times out of 1,000 simulation runs. These probabilities can help Cynthia's team concentrate on the tasks that are most likely to affect the completion time of the project.

▌ THE IMPLEMENTATION AUDIT

The **implementation audit** is a systematic review of capital projects conducted during the development and implementation stage of the capital budgeting methodology. Such audits have three purposes:

- Assessing performance and resolving problems *before* they surface
- Identifying opportunities for improvement
- Providing recommendations so that corrective action can be taken

Consequently, an implementation audit involves a great deal of fact-finding and analysis *while* the project is under development and implementation. If problems are identified at an early stage, the likelihood of the project being implemented on time, falling within budget, and meeting user requirements is increased substantially.

▌ Conducting the Implementation Audit

As part of its fact-finding and analysis, an implementation audit makes use of a wide variety of methods. The following methods are most commonly used:

LEARNING
OBJECTIVE 3

Explain why an implementation audit is conducted.

INSIGHTS & APPLICATIONS

A Project That Needed Implementation Auditing from the Beginning

There were beginning to be signs that development of the hot line project was out of control. About nine months into the project, Jan Massey of Whirlpool asked to see a project plan, but IBM couldn't provide one. She was stunned. "How do you develop a system without a plan?" she asked.

That was nothing compared with what happened next. About a year-and-a-half after the project was initiated, IBM was supposed to deliver the key component of the project—the *kernel*, as Whirlpool calls it. Up to a month before it was supposed to be delivered, Whirlpool was told it would be on time. It wasn't. An executive at Whirlpool, at this point, wanted to kill the project. But based on assurances that the project would be closely monitored by Jan Massey, the project was given a reprieve.

The crisis passed and Whirlpool's hot line project was finally implemented. Both IBM and Whirlpool officials acknowledge their flaws. "In tackling another project of this size, I would have to tell a customer, 'Don't trust us completely, please,'" says Bob Essig, IBM account manager for the Whirlpool project. "Unless both sides work together, you'll never have a win-win situation. Whirlpool should have had a co-project manager from the beginning. One-sided equations never work."[7]

- ■ Interviewing
- ■ Observing
- ■ Inspecting documented deliverables

INTERVIEWING. Interviewing is an exchange of information between the management accountant and the project manager (and others, such as project team members). It is a prime way to gather facts. Both open-ended and closed-ended questions may be used during the interview.

Open-ended questions are neutral and nonrestrictive. They give interviewees considerable freedom in answering questions and encourage them to disclose information previously unknown to the management accountant. "What are your feelings about using encryption devices in the new LAN project?" is an example of an open-ended question.

Closed-ended questions are specific and give the management accountant more control over the direction and progress of the interview. Closed-ended questions are limiting, however, in that they usually obtain only the information they ask for and do not invite interviewees to open up and reveal relevant information that the management accountant has not anticipated. "Should we use diskless workstations on the new LAN?" is an example of a closed-ended question. Closed-ended questions should never be leading or loaded, such as "Shouldn't we use diskless workstations on the new LAN?" "You agree with this report format, don't you?"

Is the new capital project being implemented as planned?

OBSERVING. Physical observation of the development and implementation of a capital project can be a useful way of identifying possible inefficiencies, delays, or problems. Observing permits the management accountant to determine what is being done, how it is being done, who does it, when it is done, how long it takes, where it is done, and why it is done. As Yogi Berra said: "You can observe a lot by watching." Examples of problems found by observing include poor cable installation procedures (e.g., kinks or sharp bends in cable, cable placed too close to power wiring), idle equipment on a construction project, excessive redesign work, and inability to schedule and coordinate work.

---

[7] Adapted from Jeffrey Rothfeder, "Crossed Wires," *Corporate Computing*, December 1992, pp. 158–165.

INSPECTING DOCUMENTED DELIVERABLES.   Documented deliverables provide information about the development and progress of the new project. For example, the work performed on a systems design proposal during a particular time period will be represented by a documented deliverable. In information systems development, documented deliverables are required when a stage in the systems development methodology is achieved. In a construction project, documented deliverables are prepared that include information on the cost and progress of the project to date.

Inspecting (sometimes called walk-throughs) these documented deliverables can uncover a host of inconsistencies and problems. For example, inspection of a systems design documented deliverable may reveal a number of design errors. Since most systems problems are caused by poor design, it is imperative that the systems design be thoroughly inspected before moving on to other stages, especially before converting to operations. Uncovering errors after the system is converted to operations is far more costly than discovering them earlier.

By inspecting the results of PERT networks or Gantt charts, management accountants can track a project's progress and cost. If, for example, a project's activity on the critical path is delayed ten days, then the schedule will slip ten days unless resources from slack activities are allocated to the critical activity. PERT also monitors actual costs against budgeted costs to check for cost overruns.

Implementation of a world-class paper machine at Boise Cascade.

Preparing the Implementation Audit Report

The implementation audit report is usually an *action* document that requires immediate attention. Therefore, its quick preparation and distribution to top management or some other designated recipient (e.g., a steering committee) are imperative. If the implementation audit report is delayed, it may be out-of-date by the time it is issued. Moreover, the opportunity to take corrective action may be restricted or gone altogether.

Normally, an exit conference with the auditee should be held to discuss the findings of the audit and suggested recommendations *before* the final version of the implementation audit report is prepared and distributed. Not only does such a meeting enhance the management accountant's rapport with the auditee, but it can also improve the overall quality of the audit report since misinterpretations and unreasonable recommendations are unlikely to go unchallenged. If an auditee disagrees with the audit report language, revisions can be made. The auditee should also be given a chance to provide written comments for inclusion in the audit report. For an example of how to prepare an implementation audit report, see the Highland Manufacturing case on the next page.

Auditing a capital project's progress continuously enables management to allocate resources more effectively, change tactics or strategies, or revise policies to bring a project that is off course back on track. In some instances, however, implementation audit results may indicate that the best decision is to scrap a particular project. If original estimates are substantially off and the project has no hope of achieving its estimated benefits, the cost of discontinuing the project may be less than the cost of investing additional resources to transform a boondoggle project into a success.

THE POSTIMPLEMENTATION AUDIT

Whereas an implementation audit monitors capital projects *while* they are under development and implementation, a **postimplementation audit** reviews cap-

LEARNING OBJECTIVE 4

Discuss the reason for conducting a postimplementation audit, and describe the tools used in conducting such an audit.

INSIGHTS & APPLICATIONS

Implementation Auditing of a New ICBIS for Highland Manufacturing Company

After performing net present value analysis, Highland Manufacturing selected a new integrated computer-based information system (ICBIS) to be developed and implemented for better integration of users throughout the company. The development costs are estimated to be $5,830,000. Joel Milam, management accountant at Highland, was chosen to audit the development and implementation of the new ICBIS. The project began July 1, 1994. As of July 15, 1994, a number of missteps had occurred.

"Was a systems plan prepared before the ICBIS was approved for development and implementation?" asked Joel.

"No, we were assigned to the project with very little guidance," said Shirley McGovern, project team leader. "I understand that it's budgeted at $5,830,000, but we're really starting from scratch as far as the development is concerned."

"Have you prepared a schedule and assigned your team members to specific activities?" asked Joel.

"No, not yet," said Shirley.

"Do you plan to follow a systems development methodology?" Joel asked.

"Yes," Shirley responded.

"What do you think about using a project management software package that provides you with the ability to break down activities and schedule them?" asked Joel.

"I really believe that such a system would help us throughout the development and implementation of this project," said Shirley.

"I have to prepare my first implementation audit report and submit it to the systems steering committee the first of next week," said Joel. "I'll prepare the first draft and go over it with you tomorrow. Should you want to include any comments, you are welcome to do so."

Joel's report is presented in Exhibit 24–22.

---

ital projects *after* they have been implemented to determine if they have lived up to their earlier estimates. The postimplementation audit analyzes what went right and what went wrong.

Purpose of the Postimplementation Audit

A sound postimplementation audit completes the life cycle of the capital budgeting methodology for a particular project. It compares actual results to original estimates made in the first stage of the capital budgeting methodology to point out variances.

A comparison will help management evaluate the reliability of estimates of costs and benefits given in support of a capital project. People requesting projects may be biased in favor of the projects they request. Such bias may result in overly optimistic estimates. People providing unreliable estimates should be required to explain major variances. Knowing in advance that postimplementation audits will be conducted may cause project sponsors and estimators to be more careful in developing their estimates.

Thus, postimplementation audits offer several benefits:

- Detecting strengths and weaknesses throughout the capital budgeting methodology
- Suggesting modifications to improve capital budgeting performance
- Identifying individuals who submit overly optimistic or pessimistic estimates
- Helping to avoid the same mistakes on similar future projects

Conducting the Postimplementation Audit

Normally, the postimplementation audit is conducted six months to one year after the capital project becomes operational. At this point, the capital project

Project:	Integrated computer-based information system	Date of report: 07/21/94
		Period covered: 07/01/94 thru 07/15/94

■ EXHIBIT 24–22
Implementation Audit Report for the New ICBIS

Purpose: To determine whether management has reasonable assurance that the project will be developed and implemented on time and within budget. Additionally, audit tasks will be performed to ensure that the project is being developed in compliance with management standards and policies and that user requirements are being met.

Scope: To assess overall development and implementation of the project in order to:

- Determine whether a proper systems development methodology is being followed and documented deliverables are being produced
- Ascertain whether proper security and accounting controls are being built into the system as it is being developed
- Judge the adequacy of testing procedures
- Review request for proposals (RFP) submitted to computer vendors
- Analyze proposals from computer vendors
- Monitor conversion procedures
- Evaluate training programs for users

Audit work performed: We have audited the activities of the project team. Our audit was conducted during the period from July 1, 1994 through July 15, 1994, and consisted of:

- Interviews with the project team leader
- Observations of project team activity
- Inspection of the capital budget
- Comparison of the capital budget to actual results

General evaluation: The project began July 1, 1994. To date, missteps have occurred due to the lack of a systems plan and uncertainty about which activities should be performed and in what sequence. Present arrangements for systematically scheduling and controlling the project are unsuitable. Serious breakdowns have occurred, and they will continue unless corrective action is taken immediately.

Recommendation: We recommend that a project management software package be acquired. Such a project management system will formalize a plan and schedule, coordinate activities, help control time and cost, and produce documented deliverables. A critical path of the project will be determined and closely monitored.

Comments by auditee: I have reviewed the recommendation and other contents of this audit report and agree with its contents.

Signed: _____
Shirley McGovern
Project leader

Signed: _____
Joel Milam
Management accountant

INSIGHTS & APPLICATIONS

Recognizing the Warning Signs of a Runaway System

Following are warning signs of a capital project out of control:

- Periodic reporting isn't occurring or is occurring less than once a month.
- Users aren't directly involved, aren't asked to sign off on key facets of the project, and aren't attending planning meetings.

- Staff lacks technical expertise or experience in related technologies.
- No testing, inadequate testing, or test reports that fail to produce corrective actions.
- Failure to document project status, accomplishments, and system components.[8]

Project management tools (e.g., Gantt and PERT) used during implementation auditing assist both the project manager and management accountant to maintain tight control and prevent runaway projects. This assistance includes:

- Online query analysis
- Extensive tracking
- Schedule and cost variances reporting
- What-if analyses
- Change request prioritization
- Resource allocation

---

under audit has had time to settle into a somewhat normal operating pattern. The audit will usually continue periodically (e.g., once a year) over the life of the capital project.

A postimplementation audit may be conducted by a team composed of user representatives, internal auditors, and management accountants. In some enterprises, however, an external consultant or independent auditor is brought in to conduct the audit to help increase objectivity and reduce any political ramifications that may exist among internal groups.

The following postimplementation audit areas merit the most attention:

- Feasibility factors
- Benefit factors
- Cash flows

AUDITING FEASIBILITY FACTORS. As discussed in Chapter 22, during the first stage of the capital budgeting methodology, managers assign ratings to the following feasibility factors:

- Technical
- Operational
- Economic
- Schedule

The results of auditing these feasibility factors are recorded in a **Feasibility Factors Audit Rating Checklist.** Exhibit 24–23 presents the checklist used to record the results of the postimplementation audit of Highland Manufacturing Company's new ICBIS. The checklist guides the audit team in reviewing the feasibility factors. Sample questions that the audit team addressed are disclosed in the checklist.

During the first stage of the capital budgeting methodology, management estimated the capital project's feasibility factors ratings at 7, 7, 9, and 9, respectively. During the postimplementation audit, the audit team discovered that the technical feasibility factor worked even better than was originally estimated, warranting a rating of 8. The other three feasibility factors have not fared as well, however. The users are not happy with the way the ICBIS was implemented because the training program was inadequate. But new training programs have been installed, and a turnaround in attitude is beginning to take

---

[8] Deborah Asbrand, ''Uncharted Waters Pose Risk of Runaway Projects,'' *Infoworld*, June 28, 1993, p. 67.

Feasibility Factors Audit Rating Checklist

■ EXHIBIT 24–23
**Feasibility Factors
Audit Rating
Checklist Used as a
Postimplementation
Audit Guide**

	Estimated rating	Audit rating	Variance
Technical feasibility	7	8	1 (F)
■ Is the technology supporting the operations as originally specified?			
■ Did the capital project have to be modified to make it fit the operation?			
■ Does the vendor provide sufficient technical assistance?			
Operational feasibility:	7	5	2 (U)
■ Are employees committed to working with the capital project?			
■ Are employees sufficiently trained to operate, maintain, and use the capital project?			
Economic feasibility:	9	5	4 (U)
■ Were adequate funds available for development or acquisition of the capital project?			
■ Are adequate funds available for operating and maintaining the capital project?			
Schedule feasibility:	9	6	3 (U)
■ Was the overall schedule of the capital project met?			
Total	32	24	8 (U)
Final score	(32/4) 8	(24/4) 6	(8/4) 2 (U)

Rating scale:
0   5   10
Poor Fair Excellent

place. Therefore, operational feasibility is rated 5. Economic feasibility is also rated 5 because adequate capital funds were not committed to the ICBIS, which required some design modifications. Currently, sufficient funds are available for operating and maintaining it. Schedule feasibility is rated 6. The target date for implementation of the ICBIS was late by three months. Part of the schedule problem, however, was due to the unanticipated modifications. The final audit rating is 6 compared to an earlier estimated rating of 8.

AUDITING BENEFIT FACTORS. The postimplementation audit of the feasibility factors is a formal process to determine how well the capital project is working, how it has been accepted, and whether adjustments or redesigns are needed. Another important reason for conducting a postimplementation audit is to compare actual benefits with those that were estimated during the first stage of the capital budgeting methodology. The **Benefit Factors Audit Rating Checklist,** illustrated in Exhibit 24–24, allows the audit team to do this.

As the checklist indicates, the estimated ratings for Highland's ICBIS were mediocre at best. There were many reasons for these low ratings, most of them revolving around management's skepticism that the ICBIS would provide significant benefits.

Those misgivings have proved to be unfounded. As both the Capital Project Request Form and several JID sessions (see Chapter 22 for a review of the

■■■ EXHIBIT 24–24
Benefit Factors Audit Rating Checklist Used as a Postimplementation Audit Guide

Benefit Factors Audit Rating Checklist

	Estimated rating	Audit rating	Variance
Tangible benefits:			
■ Reduce inventory costs	4	9	5 (F)
■ Reduce labor costs	5	9	4 (F)
■ Reduce scrap and rework costs	3	9	6 (F)
■ Reduce material costs	4	9	5 (F)
■ Reduce material handling costs	4	9	5 (F)
Tangible benefit rating	(20/5) 4	(45/5) 9	(25/5) 5 (F)
Intangible benefits:			
■ Improve delivery and service	2	10	8 (F)
■ Increase product quality and reliability	3	10	7 (F)
■ Improve production performance and lead time	2	10	8 (F)
■ Enhance production flexibility	4	10	6 (F)
■ Improve employee safety	4	10	6 (F)
Intangible benefit rating	(15/5) 3	(50/5) 10	(35/5) 7 (F)

Rating scale:

0	5	10
Poor	Fair	Excellent

Capital Project Request Form and JID) proposed, the ICBIS general design provides EDI linkage to major customers, suppliers, and carriers. The ICBIS is also based on an enterprisewide network that interconnects all the enterprise's activities, such as engineering, production, logistics, marketing, and accounting. The ICBIS includes activity-based costing (ABC), activity-based management (ABM), total quality management (TQM), flexible budgeting, an array of performance measurements, life cycle analysis and target costing methods, a completely integrated logistics system, and a revised responsibility accounting system. Thus far, the ICBIS has only been in operation for one year. Even though it had to be subjected to some design modifications and some people were unhappy with the early implementation and training programs, its ability to provide timely, accurate, and relevant information to management and other users has far exceeded earlier expectations.

The ABC and ABM systems have reduced material handling costs by 60 percent. The TQM system has reduced rework costs and external failure costs by 60 percent. Flexible budgeting has helped to reduce overhead. The performance measurements have had a substantial impact on all benefit factors, as have the new life cycle analysis and target costing methods. The integrated logistics system has reduced inventory, labor, and material handling costs, as well as improved delivery and service. The revised responsibility accounting system has also had an impact on all benefit factors. The postimplementation audit team is pleased with its findings and therefore has assigned high ratings to all benefit factors.

AUDITING CASH FLOWS. During the first stage (Chapter 22) of the capital budgeting methodology, the Cash Flow Estimate Form was used to record and document estimated cash flow data for the new ICBIS. The Cash Flow Estimate Form presented in Exhibit 24–25 is used during the postimplementation stage to disclose variances between estimated and actual cash flows for the first period. The initial cost of the ICBIS was estimated to be $5,000,000, but because of

■■■EXHIBIT 24–25
Cash Flow Estimate Form Including Postimplementation Audit Results

Cash Flow Estimate Form

Project name:	ICBIS		Date:	MM/DD/YY

Estimators:	Name	Title
	Harry Cowan	Chief information officer (CIO)
	Margaret Sherer	Management accountant
	Marc Higgins	Systems analyst
	Steve Ferranti	Manager of logistics
	Krishna Mani	Financial accountant

Investment outlay	Estimated	Actual	Variance	
Initial cost	$5,000,000	$4,500,000	$500,000	(F)
Sales tax	10,000	20,000	<10,000>	(U)
Freight	20,000	40,000	<20,000>	(U)
Installation	400,000	600,000	<200,000>	(U)
Training	200,000	100,000	100,000	(F)
Working capital	200,000	100,000	100,000	(F)
Test runs	100,000	50,000	50,000	(F)
Subtotal	$5,930,000	$5,410,000	$520,000	(F)
Less trade in	<100,000>	<20,000>	<80,000>	(U)
Total investment	$5,830,000	$5,390,000	$440,000	(F)

Cash flow from operations	Period			
	1	2	3	4
Estimated cash inflow	$2,000,000	$3,000,000	$4,000,000	$5,000,000
Estimated operating costs	<1,000,000>	<1,200,000>	<1,400,000>	<1,600,000>
Estimated net cash inflow	$1,000,000	$1,800,000	$2,600,000	$3,400,000
Actual cash inflow	$2,300,000			
Actual operating costs	<1,100,000>			
Actual net cash inflow	$1,200,000			
Net cash inflow variance	$ 200,000 (F)			

budget cutbacks forcing design modifications, the ICBIS actually had an initial cost of $4,500,000, giving a favorable variance of $500,000. Sales tax, freight, and installation costs were underestimated. Although costs for training, working capital, and test runs were overestimated, the postimplementation audit team, as well as users, learned that scrimping on training and testing will cost more in the long run. This issue was brought out while the audit team was auditing the operational feasibility factor. Consequently, favorable variances in areas such as installing, training, and testing may be misleading. In any event, the total *actual* investment is $5,390,000, which is $440,000 less than the $5,830,000 originally estimated.

The postimplementation audit team also audited the benefit factors and discovered that the actual cash inflow from benefits is $2,300,000 ($2,000,000 originally estimated) and cash outflow from operating costs is $1,100,000 ($1,000,000 originally estimated). Estimated net cash inflow of $1,000,000 ($2,000,000 − $1,000,000) less actual net cash inflow $1,200,000 ($2,300,000 − $1,200,000) yields a favorable net cash inflow variance of $200,000. The postimplementation audit team will audit the ICBIS again next year, which is period 2, along with other capital projects to determine if this year's findings represent a trend and to ascertain variances between estimated and actual cash inflows and outflows.

AUDITING ECONOMIC VALUE ADDED. A large number of companies, such as CSX, Briggs & Stratton, Coca-Cola, and AT&T, are using an evaluation tool called **economic value added (EVA).** Some predict that EVA will become the chief performance measurement of management's capital investment decisions. It takes into consideration the company's weighted-average cost of capital (discussed in Chapter 23) and aftertax operating profit.

Of course, nothing is new about an enterprise trying to earn more than its cost of capital. This is probably one of the oldest ideas in business as illustrated by return on investment (ROI) and residual income (RI) explained in Chapter 20. EVA is calculated in the following example.

Luminex Company has a capital base of $8,000,000, which is composed of 20 percent debt at a cost of 5 percent and 80 percent equity at a cost of 12 percent. Its operating profit is $1,800,000 and income taxes are $600,000. Luminex's EVA is calculated as follows:

	AFTERTAX OPERATING PROFIT	<MINUS>	COST OF CAPITAL	[EQUALS]	EVA
Operating profit	$1,800,000		$8,000,000		
Income taxes	<600,000>		× 10.6%*		
Aftertax operating profit	$1,200,000	−	$ 848,000	=	$352,000

* Weighted-average cost of capital:

	Capital Structure	Cost of Capital	Weighted Average
Debt	20%	5%	1.0%
Equity	80%	12%	9.6%
			10.6%

As can be seen, EVA is a simple and fundamental measurement of return on capital. It can be used as a valuable tool in evaluating capital project investments, especially over the long run. Managements can increase their EVA by:

- *Earning more profit without using more capital.* As pointed out in several places in this book, this may lead to disastrous consequences in the long run because such an objective may dissuade management from making strategic capital project investments.
- *Use less capital.* If this objective results from reengineering, reduction in non-value-added activities, and continuous improvement, then it will increase EVA based on positive initiatives. If, on the other hand, it results in arbitrary cost-cutting, then the enterprise will suffer in the long run.
- *Invest in high-return, strategic capital projects.* This is the objective of making capital investments. Use of the capital budgeting methodology combined with EVA-based evaluations assists management in achieving this objective.

SUMMARY OF LEARNING OBJECTIVES

The major goals of this chapter were to enable you to achieve four learning objectives:

Learning objective 1.   Describe the Gantt chart and its use.

A Gantt chart is a very simple project management tool in which every activity is represented by a horizontal bar on a time scale. The purpose of Gantt charts is to organize and clarify the use of activities (resources) in a time framework. They serve as excellent visual aids for allocating resources and scheduling time.

Learning objective 2. Use the program evaluation and review technique (PERT) as a project management and modeling tool.

PERT can be used to estimate the probability that a project will be completed by a given deadline. Each activity has a set of predecessor activities that must be completed before the activity begins. A PERT network is used to indicate the precedence relationships between activities, which are represented by arrows. Events, which mark the beginning and ending of activities, are represented by circles.

The first step in building a PERT network is to list each activity and identify the activities that immediately precede it. The second step is to determine the proper sequencing of serial and parallel activities. In the third step, the basic PERT network is constructed. Next, in the fourth step, expected activity times are calculated. The fifth and final step is to find the critical path.

Once the PERT network is finished, a number of probabilistic statements can be made with respect to the total time of the project and individual project activities. For example, the estimated completion date may be calculated as 200 days. The project manager may want to know the probability that the project will be completed in less than 200 days.

In some situations, the project manager must complete the project within a time frame that is less than the length of the initial critical path. In such a situation, the project must be crashed by applying additional resources to critical activities.

Paths outside the critical path cannot be ignored, especially those with small amounts of slack, because one of them may eventually turn critical when the project is crashed. Only critical path activities are crashed, but the path where these activities lie is not always the same. As activities are crashed, the critical path changes.

Project modeling allows project managers to simulate outcomes of PERT time and cost networks according to a number of what-if assumptions. One popular simulation method is the Monte Carlo Simulation. This type of simulation uses a computer to randomly select cost or time quantities and apply them to the PERT model. This allows the project manager to approximate real-world uncertainty.

Learning objective 3.   Explain why an implementation audit is conducted.

An implementation audit is performed to make sure that a capital project is implemented on time, within budget, in compliance with management standards and policies, and in accordance with user requirements. An implementation audit report discloses the purpose and scope of the audit. It also includes the results of audit work plus recommendations for corrective action.

Learning objective 4.   Discuss the reason for conducting a postimplementation audit, and describe the tools used in conducting such an audit.

After implementation, capital projects should be audited to see if they have lived up to their earlier estimates, and if not, why not? Were there feasibility problems? Did the benefits and cash inflows materialize? Was management too optimistic? Too pessimistic? What was done right? What was done wrong? How can mistakes be corrected for future capital budgeting?

The following are the primary tools used in conducting a postimplementation audit:

- Feasibility Factors Audit Rating Checklist
- Benefit Factors Audit Rating Checklist
- Cash Flow Estimate Form

These tools help determine how close early estimates are to what actually occurred. Economic value added (EVA) is a tool that can be used to measure management's effectiveness in making capital project investments, especially over the long run.

IMPORTANT TERMS

Activity   On a PERT network, a task that consumes resources in order to move from one event to another; it is designated by an arrow.

Benefit Factors Audit Rating Checklist   A device used during the postimplementation audit for comparing estimated benefit factors to actual benefit factors and recording the variances.

Crashing   Completing the project in a time that is less than the original initial critical path.

Critical path   The path on the PERT network with the longest cumulative activity time.

Dummy activity   A nonresource activity designated by a dashed arrow on the PERT network.

Early event time   The earliest time an event can occur.

Event   A circle on a PERT network that shows the beginning and ending of an activity or activities.

Expected activity time   The estimated duration an activity will take.

Feasibility Factors Audit Rating Checklist   A device used during the postimplementation audit for comparing estimated feasibility factors to actual feasibility factors and recording the variances.

Free slack (FS)   The maximum amount of time an activity can be delayed without delaying the start of the next activity.

Gantt chart   A bar chart, named after its developer Henry Gantt, that shows activities on the left side and units of time across the top or bottom.

Implementation audit   A systematic process of reviewing and monitoring capital projects during their development and implementation.

Late event time   The latest time an event can occur.

Monte Carlo Simulation   A model that calculates multiple possible scenarios by randomly selecting a number within a given range and applying it to the project modeling system.

Most likely time   An estimate of the activity's duration under normal conditions.

Optimistic time   An estimate of the activity's duration under the most favorable conditions.

Pessimistic time   An estimate of the activity's duration under the least favorable conditions.

Postimplementation audit   A process that reviews the actual results of capital projects over time to see how well these actual results compare to earlier estimates.

Program evaluation and review technique (PERT)   A network of activities and events of a project.

Project modeling   Planning for problems and working out in advance by simulation what could go wrong on a project and developing a solution.

Total slack (TS)   The maximum amount of time an activity can be delayed without affecting the completion time of the project.

DEMONSTRATION PROBLEMS

■ **DEMONSTRATION PROBLEM 1**   *Planning and scheduling with a Gantt chart.*

Fashions Galore, a retail store, is planning on moving to a larger building. The owner has requested that a Gantt chart be prepared identifying the major activities, time estimates for each activity, and their sequence.

After analysis of the move was made, it was determined that the first activity would be to locate the new building, which would require 8 weeks. Interviewing salespeople would start at the same time and would require 4 weeks. At the beginning of the fourth week, hiring and training of new salespeople would begin and require 10 weeks. Selecting and ordering fixtures would begin week 8 and require 6 weeks. Remodeling would also begin week 8 and require 11 weeks. Beginning week 14, fixtures would be received and would require 4 weeks for installation. Moving in would start week 19 and be completed week 20.

Required:
Prepare a Gantt chart for the preceding information.

SOLUTION TO DEMONSTRATION PROBLEM 1

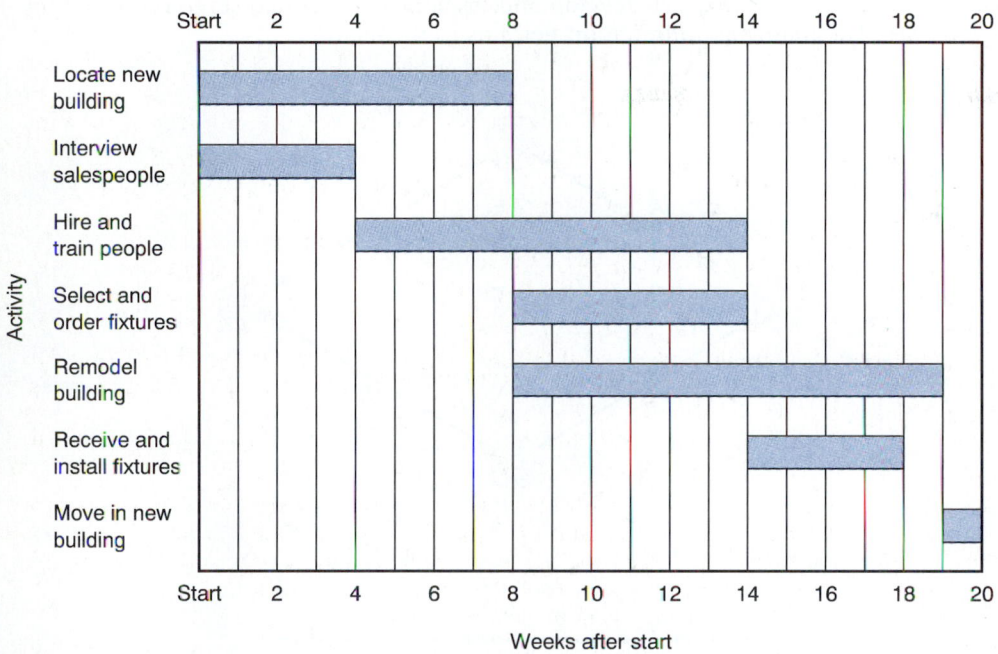

■ **DEMONSTRATION PROBLEM 2**   *Determining the critical path.*

Following is a PERT network showing expected time for each activity:

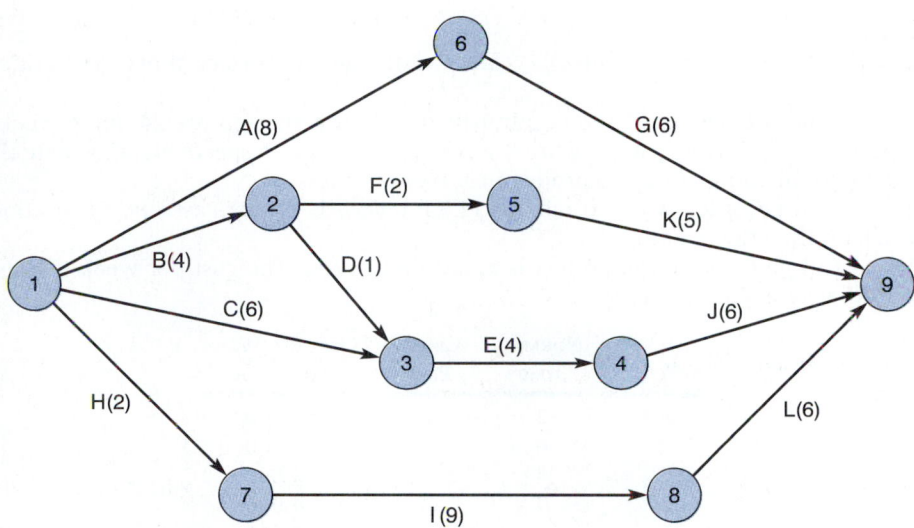

Required:

List all the paths in the network and determine which is the critical path.

SOLUTION TO DEMONSTRATION PROBLEM 2

PATH	TIME
1, 6, 9	14
1, 2, 5, 9	11
1, 2, 3, 4, 9	15
1, 3, 4, 9	16
1, 7, 8, 9	17

Path 1, 7, 8, 9 is the critical path because it has the longest time.

■ DEMONSTRATION PROBLEM 3   *Implementing a local area network (LAN).*
General Hospital is planning to develop and implement a LAN to serve its physicians
and nurses. The following information pertains to this plan:

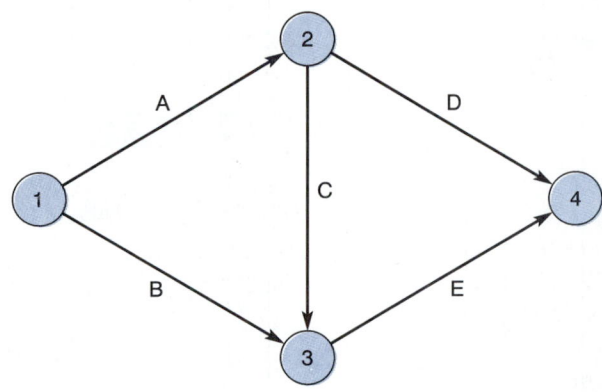

Activity	Activity Description	T_e
A	Acquire workstations	2 weeks
B	Install cable	8 weeks
C	Install software	4 weeks
D	Train users	3 weeks
E	Connect and test	2 weeks

Required:
a. Calculate the early event time (ET), late event time (LT), slack times, and critical
path.
b. Assume that the pessimistic and optimistic times for activity B are 24 and 6 weeks,
respectively. For activity E, they are 8 weeks and 1 week, respectively. Calculate the
probability of completing the project in 8 weeks or less.
c. Illustrate three other ways to label a PERT network. In at least one illustration,
designate the critical path.
d. The cost of performing the project is $2,200 per week. The cost per week to crash
and other relevant data follow:

Activity	Normal Time	Crash Time	Cost Per Week to Crash
A	2	1	$1,900
B	8	4	500
C	4	2	2,800
D	3	2	4,000
E	2	1	2,000

Calculate an optimum time-cost solution.

SOLUTION TO DEMONSTRATION PROBLEM 3

a.

Event	Early Event Time (ET)	Late Event Time (LT)	Slack
1	0	0	0
2	2	4	2
3	8	8	0
4	10	10	0

$$ET(1) = 0 \qquad\qquad = 0$$
$$ET(2) = 0 + 2 \qquad\quad = 2$$

$$ET(3) = \max \begin{cases} ET(2) + 4 = 6 \\ ET(1) + 8 = 8 \end{cases} = 8$$

$$ET(4) = \max \begin{cases} ET(2) + 3 = 5 \\ ET(3) + 2 = 10 \end{cases} = 10$$

$$LT(4) = 10 \qquad\qquad\qquad = 10$$

$$LT(3) = LT(4) - 2 \qquad\qquad = 8$$

$$LT(2) = \min \begin{cases} LT(4) - 3 = 7 \\ LT(3) - 4 = 4 \end{cases} = 4$$

$$LT(1) = \min \begin{cases} LT(2) - 2 = 2 \\ LT(3) - 8 = 0 \end{cases} = 0$$

The critical path is the one containing events 1, 3, and 4. Therefore, activities B and E will have to be closely monitored since neither has any slack.

b. The expected time to complete the LAN project is 10 weeks. The standard deviation (σ) and variance (σ^2) of activities B and E on the critical path are calculated as follows:

ACTIVITY	STANDARD DEVIATION (σ)	VARIANCE (σ^2)
B	$\dfrac{24 - 6}{6} = 3.00$	9.00
E	$\dfrac{8 - 1}{6} = 1.17$	$\underline{1.37}$
		$\sigma_p^2 = 10.37$
		$\sigma_p = 3.22$

To determine the probability that the project will be completed on or before week 8, the following calculations are required:

$$Z = \frac{8 - 10}{3.22}$$

$$= \frac{-2.00}{3.22}$$

$$= -0.6211$$

where Z equals the number of standard deviations from the mean. The area under the curve for Z = −0.6211 is approximately 0.2650. Therefore, the probability of completing the LAN project in 8 weeks is approximately 26.5%.

c. Events lettered with expected times on activities:

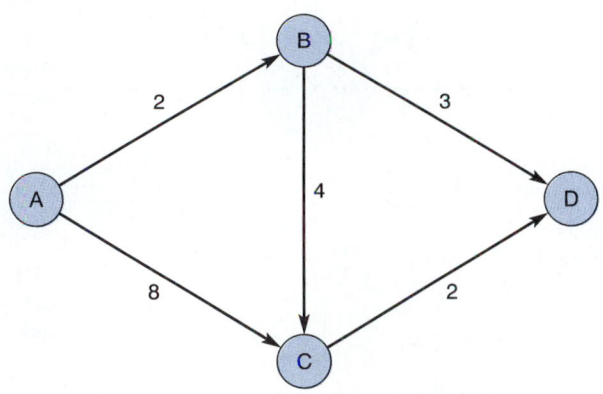

ACTIVITY	ACTIVITY DESCRIPTION	T_e
A–B	Acquire workstations	2 weeks
A–C	Install cable	8 weeks
B–C	Install software	4 weeks
B–D	Train users	3 weeks
C–D	Connect and test	2 weeks

Events numbered and activities lettered with expected times on activities in parentheses:

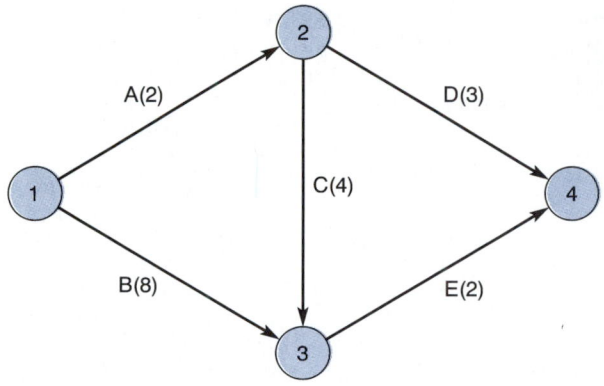

ACTIVITY	ACTIVITY DESCRIPTION	T_e
A	Acquire workstations	2 weeks
B	Install cable	8 weeks
C	Install software	4 weeks
D	Train users	3 weeks
E	Connect and test	2 weeks

Numbered events, lettered activities including expected times in parentheses, and critical path:

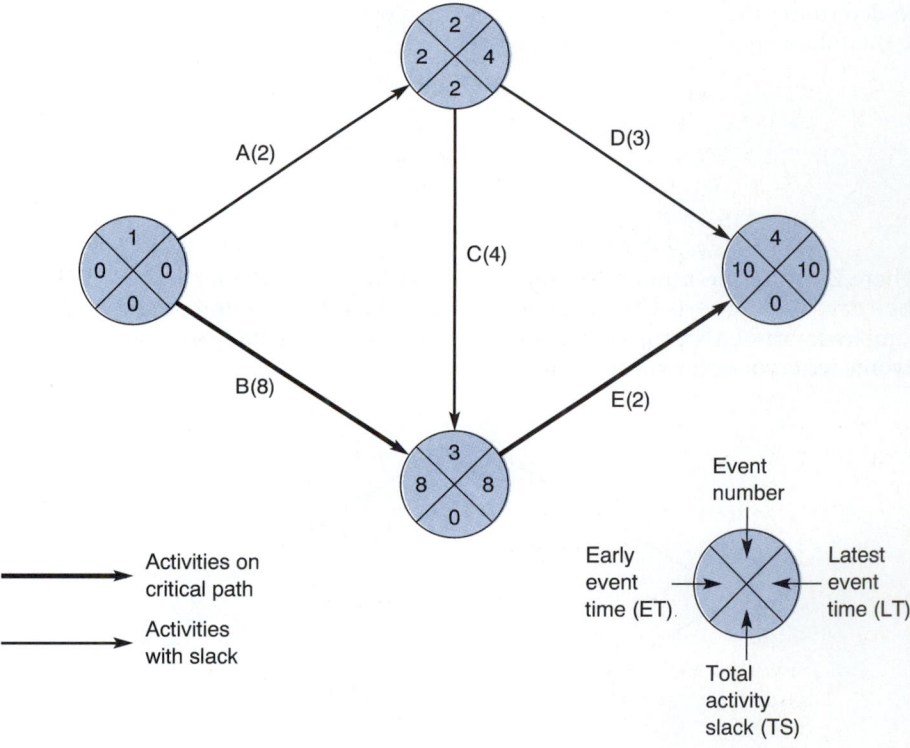

d. The critical path activities are ranked in order of lowest crashing cost and the number of weeks each can be crashed:

ACTIVITY	COST PER WEEK TO CRASH	AVAILABLE WEEKS
B	$ 500	4
E	2,000	1

The activity on the critical path with the lowest cost per week to crash ($500) is activity B. By crashing activity B for one week, thereby incurring an additional cost of $500, the project completion time can be reduced by one week to nine weeks.

Next, crashing activity B for a second week leaves the PERT network with two critical paths, A–C–E and B–E, both eight weeks in length. The remaining points for crashing and their costs are as follows:

PATH	ACTIVITY	COST PER WEEK TO CRASH
A–C–E	A	$1,900
	C	2,800
	E	2,000
B–E	B	500
	E	2,000

Which activity or activities should be crashed? Activity E might seem to be out of the question since it has the highest crash cost of $2,000. However, E is on both critical paths, so crashing it will reduce the project by one week for a cost of $2,000. The other option of reducing the least expensive activity on each path would cost $2,400 ($1,900 for A plus $500 for B). The project duration is now seven weeks.

At this point, no additional improvement is cost-effective. The cost to crash A is $1,900 and the cost to crash B is $500, for a total of $2,400, which would exceed the project costs of $2,200 per week.

The crashing sequence is summarized as follows:

	LENGTH AFTER CRASHING n WEEKS			
PATH	$n = 0$	1	2	3
A–C–E	8	8	8	7
B–E	10	9	8	7
Activity crashed		B	B	E
Cost		$500	$500	$2,000

■**DEMONSTRATION PROBLEM 4**   *Conducting an implementation audit.*
Refurbish It, Inc., has acquired a rundown building that was formerly occupied by a franchise restaurant outlet some ten years ago. The building has been unoccupied since that time and has had no general upkeep performed on it. A general contractor, hired by the company, began gutting the building three days ago. You, the management accountant at Refurbish It, have scheduled an implementation audit walk-through for tomorrow. You are currently finalizing the audit program checklist that you have developed to assist you in conducting the implementation audit.

Required:
a. Identify the three goals of your implementation audit.
b. Identify key items to look for during the physical on-site observation.
c. Identify key questions to ask the project contractor.
d. Identify key items to verify on documented deliverables.

SOLUTION TO DEMONSTRATION PROBLEM 4
a. The three goals of the implementation audit are:
   1. To assess the performance of the construction crew to date.
   2. To identify opportunities for improving the ongoing construction project.
   3. To provide recommendations for corrective action.
b. Key items to look for during the physical on-site observation include:
   1. Is electrical wiring adequately secured to prevent on-the-job injury?
   2. Are still usable equipment and fixtures being segregated and accounted for and not allowed to leave the job site?
   3. Are shipments of equipment and fixtures not being received until just prior to the installation date in order to prevent damage and theft?
   4. Is the construction crew arriving on time, not leaving early, and not taking excessive breaks?
c. Key questions to ask the contractor include:
   1. Have any problems with the construction project been encountered to date? If so, what if anything, can be done to help alleviate those problems?
   2. Is the project on schedule?

3. Are the building and tools/equipment being adequately safeguarded from after-hours pilferage and damage?

d. Key items to verify on documented deliverables include:

1. Do the percentage of completion, labor hours, and materials charged to date appear realistic and compatible with physical observations?
2. Have the shipments of tools, equipment, and fixtures received and observed at the job site been properly documented and accounted for on company records?
3. Is anything that was recorded as received missing from the job site?

■ DEMONSTRATION PROBLEM 5 *Conducting a postimplementation audit.*

A fully integrated computer system was installed at Allied Distributing Company approximately nine months ago and has been fully operational for seven months. As the company's management accountant, you have been asked to conduct a postimplementation audit to compare actual to expected results.

Required:

Prepare a Feasibility Factors Audit Rating Checklist and a Benefit Factors Audit Rating Checklist. Include at least two considerations for each of the four feasibility factor categories and each of the two benefit types.

SOLUTION TO DEMONSTRATION PROBLEM 5

FEASIBILITY FACTORS AUDIT RATING CHECKLIST

	ESTIMATED RATING	AUDIT RATING	VARIANCE
Technical feasibility:			
■ Is the system adequate to meet user needs?			
■ Can required system changes be made by a company employee or must a computer specialist be called in for even minor system changes?			
Operational feasibility:			
■ Is the system user-friendly?			
■ Have system users received adequate training?			
Economic feasibility:			
■ Were adequate funds committed to the computer system design, installation, and training?			
■ Are adequate funds committed to ongoing hardware maintenance and software upgrades?			
Schedule feasibility:			
■ Was the system installation completed on schedule?			
■ Were old systems phased out and the new system brought online within the projected downtime time frame?			

BENEFIT FACTORS AUDIT RATING CHECKLIST

	ESTIMATED RATING	AUDIT RATING	VARIANCE
Tangible benefits:			
■ Increases processing speed			
■ Reduces data-entry errors			
Intangible benefits:			
■ Improves accessibility of company information through use of online inquiry			

- Allows online communication between departments
- Improves customer service

REVIEW QUESTIONS

24.1 Describe how the Gantt chart is used as a project management tool. Discuss its major advantages and disadvantages.

24.2 Briefly discuss the five steps involved in building a PERT network.

24.3 Under what conditions is PERT the most useful tool in managing capital project activities?

24.4 If the optimistic time for completing an activity is 8 days, the most likely time is 12 days, and the pessimistic time is 22 days, the expected time for the activity would be:

a. 10 days.
b. 14 days.
c. 17 days.
d. 13 days.

24.5 In a PERT network, the optimistic time for a particular activity is 9 weeks, and the pessimistic time is 21 weeks. Which of the following is the best estimate of the standard deviation for the activity?

a. 2.
b. 6.
c. 9.
d. 12.

24.6 When using PERT, which of the following formulas can be used to calculate the expected time for an activity, given an optimistic time (O), a pessimistic time (P), and a most likely time (M)?

a. $(20 + 3M + 4P)/9$.
b. $(O - P)/2$.
c. $(O + 4M + P)/6$.
d. $(O + P)/2$.

24.7 When determining an optimum time-cost solution in PERT analysis, the first activity that should be crashed is the one:

a. with the most slack.
b. on the critical path with the lowest unit crash cost.
c. on the critical path with the maximum possible time reduction.
d. with the largest amount of slack.

24.8 What is the significance of the TS of an activity?

24.9 Discuss the implication of crashing a project (PERT system) on the project's resources.

24.10 Describe the purpose of project modeling, how it works, and its primary benefits.

24.11 The implementation audit occurs during the development and implementation stage of capital budgeting. Name the three purposes of such an audit.

24.12 What positive benefits can a project receive if an implementation audit successfully identifies problems during the early stages of the project?

24.13 Name the three most commonly used methods of gathering and analyzing facts during an implementation audit.

24.14 Explain why holding an exit conference with auditees is important.

24.15 What information should be included in an implementation audit report?

24.16 Identify at least three goals of a postimplementation audit.

24.17 The postimplementation audit compares actual to estimated results for what three major capital budgeting areas?

24.18 During what time frame after bringing a capital project online should a postimplementation audit be conducted?

24.19 When should a company consider bringing in an external consultant or auditor to conduct the postimplementation audit?

24.20 Which audit form/checklist should be used during the postimplementation audit to assist in determining the project's success and acceptance and whether any redesign work is required?

CHAPTER-SPECIFIC PROBLEMS

These problems require responses based directly on concepts and techniques presented in the text.

24.21 *Critical path and cost.* The following network diagram and table illustrate the time and costs associated with a particular project:

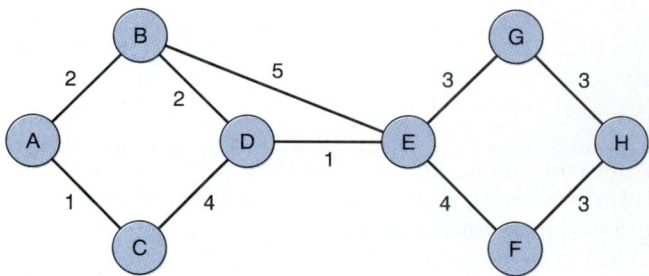

ACTIVITY	NORMAL ACTIVITY TIME	NORMAL ACTIVITY COST	TOTAL CRASHED TIME	CRASH ACTIVITY COST
A–B	2 weeks	$1,000	2 weeks	$ 1,000
A–C	1	800	1	800
B–D	2	1,500	2	1,500
B–E	5	5,100	3	10,200
C–D	4	2,500	3	3,500
D–E	1	600	1	600
E–F	4	1,700	4	1,700
E–G	3	1,200	2	2,600
F–H	3	1,400	2	2,100
G–H	3	1,300	3	1,300

Required:
a. Determine the project's critical path.
b. Compute the total cost of the project as planned.
c. Compute the incremental cost of completing the project in 12 weeks.

[CMA adapted]

24.22 *Calculating the probability of completing a project.* Neptune Marina is planning to install a new docking facility for its customers' boats. The expected completion time is 70 weeks. Erika Loomis, chief operating officer, desires a completion date 18 weeks sooner.

Required:
Calculate the probability of completing the project 18 weeks sooner, given a variance of 81.

24.23 *Determining expected time, critical path, and slack.* Because of continuing increases in enrollment, the School of Business building at Summa University has exceeded its capacity. To better serve students and faculty, the administration has provided the school with a choice among several underutilized buildings on campus that would meet the school's expansion needs.

After several committee meetings, eight major expansion project activities have been identified. Also, those people who will be involved in the expansion have been pooled to gather time estimates. From this work, the following data and PERT network have been prepared:

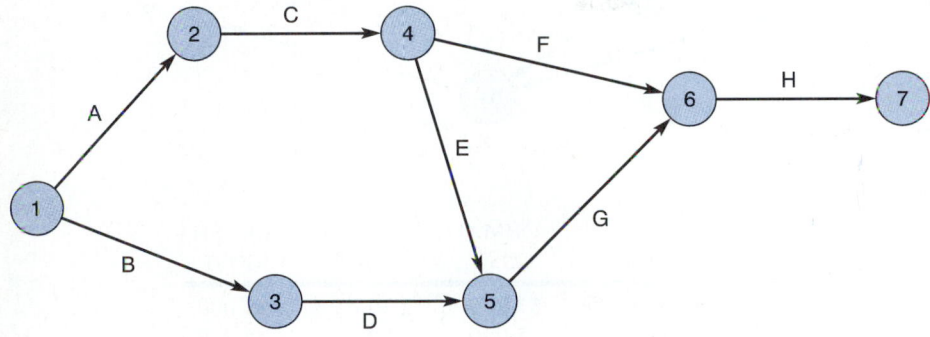

TIME ESTIMATES (WEEKS)

ACTIVITY	ACTIVITY DESCRIPTION	OPTIMISTIC	MOST LIKELY	PESSIMISTIC
A	Select building	1	2	3
B	Interview staff applicants	2	3	4
C	Develop remodeling plans	1	2	3
D	Select staff applicants	2	4	6
E	Remodel	1	4	7
F	Prepare parking spaces	1	3	5
G	Install facilities	2	5	8
H	Move in	1	2	3

Required:
Develop a PERT network indicating the critical path with a bold line. In each node (circle) include early event time (ET), late event time (LT), and slack. Also, calculate the amount of slack for all activities not on the critical path.

24.24 *Crashing a project.* California Building Corporation uses the PERT method to monitor construction jobs. The company is currently two weeks behind schedule on job 181, which is subject to a $10,500 per week completion penalty. Path A–B–C–F–G–H–I has a normal completion time of 20 weeks, and path A–D–E–F–G–H–I has a normal completion time of 22 weeks. The following activities can be crashed:

ACTIVITY	COST TO CRASH ONE WEEK	COST TO CRASH TWO WEEKS
B–C	$ 8,000	$15,000
D–E	10,000	19,600
E–F	8,800	19,500

California Building wants to reduce the normal completion time of job 181 and, at the same time, report the highest possible income for the year. California Building should crash:

a. Activity B–C one week and activity E–F one week.
b. Activity B–C two weeks.
c. Activity D–E one week and activity B–C one week.
d. Activity E–F two weeks.
e. Activity D–E one week and activity E–F one week.

[CMA adapted]

24.25 *Crashing a project.* The PERT network diagram and corresponding activity cost chart for a manufacturing project at Networks, Inc., are presented below. The numbers in the diagram are the expected times (in days) to perform each activity in the project.

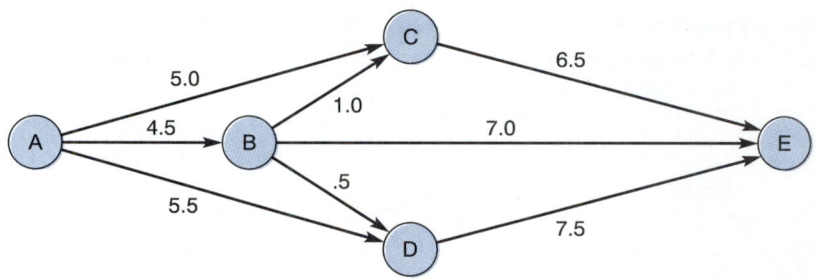

| | NORMAL | CRASH | CRASH |
ACTIVITY	COST	TIME	COST
A–B	$3,000	3.50 days	$4,000
A–C	5,000	4.50	5,250
A–D	4,000	4.00	4.750
B–E	6,000	5.00	7,000
C–E	8,000	5.00	9,200
D–E	6,000	6.00	6,750
B–C	2,500	.50	3,500
B–D	2,000	.25	2,500

Required:
a. Calculate total expected time on the critical path.
b. To keep costs at a minimum and decrease the completion time by one and one-half days, which activity or activities should Networks crash?

[CMA adapted]

24.26 *Conducting an implementation audit.* Steve Loomis, owner of the Donut Stop, has decided to install an espresso/cappuccino corner in his donut shop due to heavy demand for fancier coffees by his current patrons. Due to space limitations and the desire to make the espresso/cappuccino corner a customer focal point, Steve plans to extend one wall 15 feet and redecorate it in an old European style. Since he will have to close his business for the duration of the construction, he wants to make sure that the project is completed in a timely manner and that he is not overcharged. Steve has therefore requested that you, his son, observe the construction to ensure timely project completion and cost containment.

Required:
a. Identify key items you should look for during the physical observation.
b. Identify key questions to ask the contractor.
c. Identify key items to verify on documented deliverables.

24.27 *Conducting a postimplementation audit.* The Monthly Magazine Company is a mid-sized company employing about 100 employees in a single-story building. In an effort to reduce the costs of intercompany mail sorting and delivery, the company purchased an automated mail cart and placed it in service six months ago. The cart follows a set route through the building, stopping at each mail stop location to allow each area to retrieve and distribute its mail. The mail cart cost the company $25,000 (including tax, freight, and installation) and requires an ongoing maintenance and service contract of $3,000 annually. Test run costs were $3,000 and training $2,500. Estimated costs were $22,000, $3,000, $4,000, and $2,000, respectively. Use of the mail cart enabled the company to eliminate the position of mail runner, who was compensated $20,000 annually, including company benefits. Senior management has asked you to perform a postimplementation audit to compare actual and expected results from a cash flow standpoint. Actual cash flows for the first four years were <$12,000>, $17,000, $17,000, and $18,000.

Required:
Prepare a Cash Flow Estimate Form to reflect the postimplementation audit results.

THINK-TANK PROBLEMS

Although these problems are based on chapter material, reading extra material, reviewing previous chapters, and using creativity may be required to develop workable solutions.

24.28 *PERT network and crashing the project.* Silver Aviation assembles small aircraft for commercial use. The majority of Silver's business is with small freight airlines serving areas where the airport is too small to accommodate larger planes. The remainder of Silver's customers are commuter airlines and individuals who use planes in their businesses such as the owners of large ranches. Silver recently expanded its market into Central and South America, and the company expects to double its sales over the next three years.

Silver uses PERT to schedule work and keep track of all projects. The PERT diagram for the construction of a single cargo plane follows. The diagram shows that there are four alternative paths with the critical path being A–B–G–E–F–J–K.

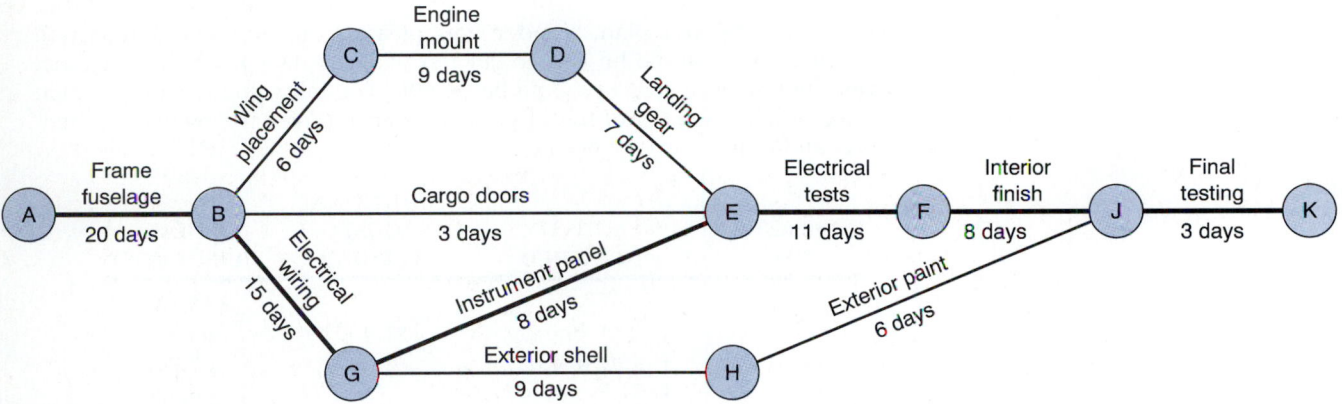

Bob Peterson, president of Coastal Airlines, has recently placed an order with Silver Aviation for five cargo planes. At the time of contract negotiations, Peterson agreed to a delivery time of 13 weeks (five working days per week) for the first plane with the balance of the planes being delivered at the rate of one every four weeks. Because of problems with some of the aircraft Coastal is currently using, Peterson has contacted Grace Vander, sales manager for Silver Aviation, to ask about improving the delivery date of the first cargo plane. Vander replied that she believed the schedule could be shortened by as much as ten working days or two weeks, but the cost of construction would increase as a result. Peterson said he would be willing to consider the increased costs, and they agreed to meet the following day to review a revised schedule that Vander would prepare.

Because Silver Aviation has assembled aircraft on an accelerated basis before, the company has compiled a list of crash costs for this purpose. Vander used the following to develop a plan to cut ten working days from the schedule at a minimum increase in cost to Coastal Airlines.

CRASH COST LISTING

ACTIVITY		EXPECTED ACTIVITY TIMES		DIRECT COST		ADDED CRASH COST PER REDUCED DAY
		REGULAR	CRASH	REGULAR	CRASH	
A–B	Frame fuselage	20 days	16 days	$12,000	$16,800	$1,200
B–C	Wing placement	6	5	3,600	5,000	1,400
C–D	Engine mount	9	7	6,600	8,000	700
D–E	Landing gear	7	5	5,100	6,700	800
B–E	Cargo doors	3	3	1,400	1,400	—
B–G	Electrical wiring	15	13	9,000	11,000	1,000
G–E	Instrument panel	8	6	5,700	8,300	1,300
E–F	Electrical tests	11	10	6,800	7,600	800
G–H	Exterior shell	9	7	4,200	5,200	500
F–J	Interior finish	8	7	3,600	4,000	400
H–J	Exterior paint	6	5	3,600	4,000	400
J–K	Final testing	3	2	3,500	4,400	900
				$65,100	$82,400	

Upon completing her plan, Vander was pleased that she could report to Peterson that Silver would be able to cut ten working days from the schedule. The associated increase in cost would be $6,600. The following is Vander's plan for the accelerated delivery of the cargo plane starting from the regularly scheduled days and cost.

COMPLETION TIME	ACTIVITY CRASHED	ADDITIONAL COST PER DAY	TOTAL DIRECT COST
65 days			$65,100
64	H–J by one day	$ 400	65,500
63	F–J by one day	400	65,900
61	G–H by two days	500	66,900
59	C–D by two days	700	68,300
58	E–F by one day	800	69,100
56	D–E by two days	800	70,700
55	B–G by one day	1,000	71,700

Required:
a. PERT is a form of network analysis.
   1. Explain how the expected times for each activity are derived in using PERT.
   2. Define the term "critical path" and explain why path ABGEFJK is the critical path in this situation.
b. Evaluate the accelerated delivery schedule prepared by Grace Vander.
   1. Explain why Vander's plan as presented is unsatisfactory.
   2. Revise the accelerated delivery schedule so that Coastal Airlines will take delivery of the first plane two weeks (ten working days) ahead of schedule at the least incremental cost to Coastal.
   3. Calculate the incremental costs Bob Peterson will have to pay for this revised accelerated delivery.

[CMA adapted]

24.29 *PERT network and crashing the project.* Barker Systems, founded by Janice Barker in 19X4, manufactures a highly sophisticated tracking system, FasTrac, which is used in conjunction with the Navy's PDQ2 water-to-water, antisubmarine missile guidance system.

FasTrac is largely hand-assembled from component parts in seven distinct steps at a manufacturing cost of $200,000 per unit. Barker Systems uses PERT to schedule and keep track of all projects. The following PERT chart shows the normal number of days required to complete a FasTrac unit:

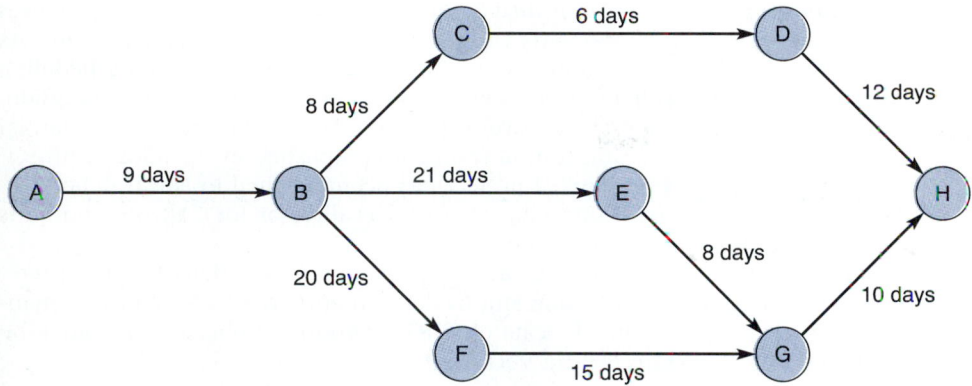

One Monday evening, Barker received a telephone call at her home from the PDQ2 missile staging base. Commander Grecon, procurement officer, requested delivery of a FasTrac unit ten days earlier than the normal delivery time, indicating the government would pay the additional costs associated with this accelerated delivery.

Barker called Howard Green, the company's production manager, and asked him to have a plan for meeting this delivery date, along with the incremental crash costs, ready for her review in the morning. Using the Crash Cost Listing presented next, Green prepared his plan for the accelerated delivery of a FasTrac unit, keeping in mind the need to minimize the cost impact.

CRASH COST LISTING

ACTIVITY	NORMAL TIME	CRASH TIME	CRASH COST PER REDUCED DAY
A–B	9 days	6 days	$10,500
B–C	8	6	1,000
C–D	6	5	1,000
D–H	12	8	6,000
B–E	21	20	3,000
E–G	8	6	4,500
G–H	10	9	4,000
B–F	20	16	5,000
F–G	15	12	2,000

Following is the plan Green presented to Barker for her evaluation. He was pleased that the necessary ten days could be eliminated at the cost of only $25,000.

ACCELERATED DELIVERY SCHEDULE

ACTIVITY CRASHED	DAYS CRASHED	TOTAL CRASH COST
B–C	2	$ 2,000
C–D	1	1,000
F–G	3	6,000
B–E	1	3,000
G–H	1	4,000
E–G	2	9,000
	10	$25,000

Required:
a. By preparing a schedule of paths, with their total days, from the PERT network for the normal production of Barker's FasTrac unit, identify the critical path and explain why it is the critical path.
b. Janice Barker found Howard Green's plan for the accelerated delivery to be unsatisfactory. Explain why it is unsatisfactory.
c. Revise the Accelerated Delivery Schedule so that the delivery time of the FasTrac unit can be ten days ahead of the normal schedule at the least incremental cost.

[CMA adapted]

24.30 *Discussing the advantages and disadvantages of PERT.* Caltron, Inc., produces computer-controlled components for a wide variety of military hardware. As a defense contractor, the company is often under severe time and scheduling constraints. The development of a new component, Vector-12, is no exception; the project has the potential for future contracts that could generate substantial revenue if development and testing can be accomplished in the allotted time.

The planning of the Vector-12 project has been assigned to Norm Robertson. This is Robertson's first assignment as a project director for Caltron, and he is eager to demonstrate his capabilities.

This project, like many of Caltron's projects, cuts across departments. Therefore, scheduling and coordination among departments are crucial. Caltron's management has long been an advocate of PERT. Therefore, Robertson prepared the following PERT diagram for the Vector-12 project:

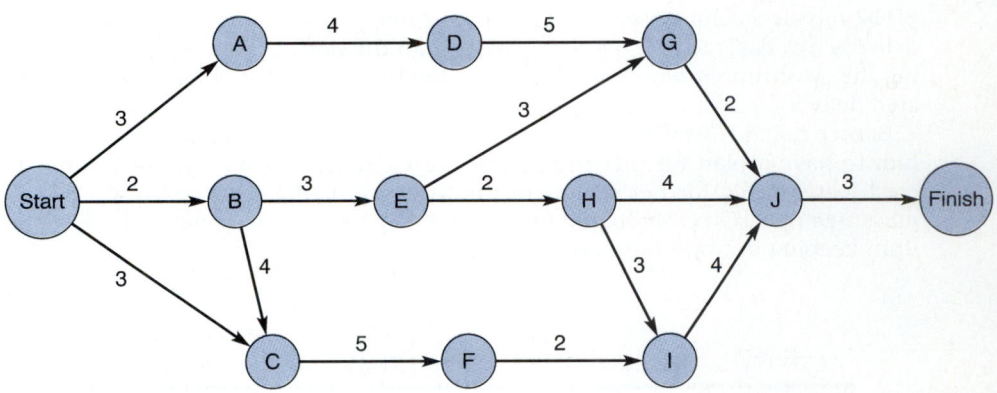

The numbers by the activity arrows represent the expected time in weeks required to complete each activity. The responsibility for the critical path, Start–B–C–F–I–J–Finish, is shared by two departments, Electromechanical Engineering (EME) and Fabrication (FAB). Resource Appropriation and Processing (RAP) is responsible for Start–A–D–G–J.

Robertson developed the PERT diagram with minimal input from the department directors affected. He did review the preliminary diagrams with the directors of EME and FAB. Robertson was unable to contact the director of RAP, Shiela Neill, and he neglected to talk with Neill when she returned to the office. The directors of EME and FAB offered suggestions to Robertson on how to revise the diagrams in terms of ordering activities and time estimates. They also indicated how Neill's activities would coordinate with their activities. However, none of the directors reviewed the final PERT diagram.

As the Vector-12 project entered its fourth week, Robertson requested progress reports from the department directors. Neill told Robertson that activity A–D would take 10–12 weeks. When Robertson asked Neill to explain the delay, Neill replied, "I could have told you there would be a problem, but you never asked for my input. The time for activity A–D is understated as is, and I cannot even start until activity B–E is completed by FAB."

Required:
a. Discuss the advantages and disadvantages of PERT as a means of organizing and coordinating projects.
b. Identify the specific reason that would cause Norm Robertson to be concerned about the delay in activity A–D.
c. Critique the way Norm Robertson developed the PERT diagram for the Vector-12 project.
d. Discuss the behavioral problems that could arise within Caltron as a consequence of the planning of the Vector-12 project.

[CMA adapted]

24.31 *Auditing implementation activities.* Janine Wilson has been assigned to implement an order-entry processing program for the new ICBIS. Her supervisor provided the following activities and related time for each activity:

Design program   50 hours
Code program   40 hours
Test program   70 hours
Document program   40 hours

After several days, Angela Milam, management accountant, interviews Janine to determine her progress. Janine reports the following:

ACTIVITY	ESTIMATED	ACTUAL	REMAINING
Design program	50	20	0
Code program	40	4	27
Test program	70	0	15
Document program	40	0	12

Required:
Discuss what reaction Angela Milam may have to this revised plan.

24.32 *Postimplementation audit of cost and benefit estimates.* You have plotted actual cost and benefit figures against those estimated early in the systems project as follows:

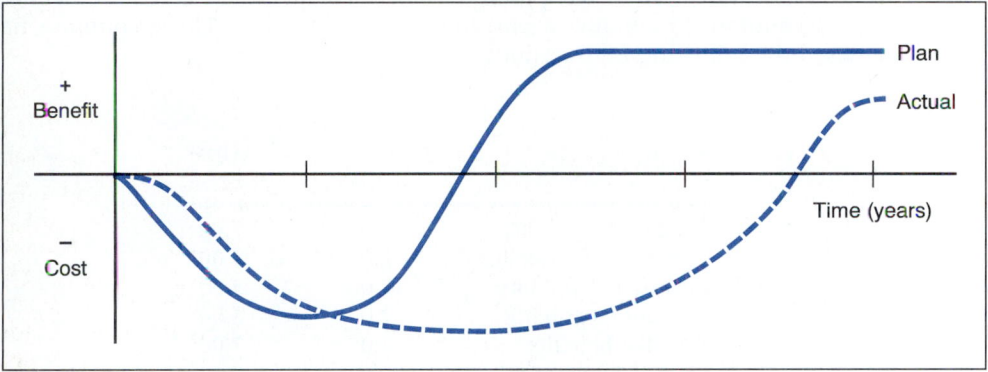

Required:
What does this graph say about meeting cost and benefit expectations?

24.33 *Conducting an implementation audit.* The Electric Company is currently in its sixth year of construction on a waste-to-energy plant, a new and promising energy generation technology. Unfortunately, an accident has just occurred in a competitor's fully functioning waste-to-energy plant, forcing its immediate shutdown. This has added fuel to public outcry that the new plants are emitting an excessive amount of particulates into the atmosphere and causing increased health problems in surrounding areas.

As management accountant at the Electric Company, you have been asked to conduct an implementation audit to assess the continued feasibility of the study. The following are your findings:

1. The project was 80% complete at the time of the accident. Due to the imposition of stricter construction requirements, however, the project is now only 50% complete and will require extensive rework to existing structures to meet code.
2. The project was expected to cost $75 million in total. Total actual costs incurred to date, however, have exceeded this estimate by more than 50% and are $115 million.
3. The partially completed plant represents about 40% of the Electric Company's total assets.
4. The corporate hierarchy allowed construction to progress with little attention given to cost overruns, quality of engineering, and construction delays on the part of the subcontractors.
5. The primary contractor has no collateral that could be won if the Electric Company pursues a lawsuit.
6. There is strong statewide opposition to waste-to-energy burning plants.
7. There is increasing public pressure on the State Public Service Commission to force the company to keep its rates as low as possible and to use proven and dependable technology in its plants.

Required:
What are your recommendations to senior management?

24.34 *Conducting a postimplementation audit.* The DLM Company installed a new production line over one year ago. One of the senior managers has just attended a seminar on the capital budgeting methodology in which the benefits of a postimplementation audit were touted. He has assigned the company's management accountant to conduct a postimplementation audit. The accountant has gathered the following information:

	ESTIMATED RATING	AUDIT RATING
Technical feasibility	8.00	7.00
Operational feasibility	7.00	9.00
Economic feasibility	7.00	5.00
Schedule feasibility	7.00	6.00
Tangible benefits	7.00	7.00
Intangible benefits	6.67	8.33

Required:
Prepare Feasibility and Benefits Factors Audit Rating Checklists. Make any assumptions needed to solve this problem.

24.35 *Postimplementation audit of systems performance.* Terminal response time is the time that the user must wait to begin a transaction after completing the previous one. Definition of a good response time depends on the application and user. Typically, data-entry applications are the most demanding, because little thought on the part of the user is required. Therefore, any delay between the completion of one transaction and the beginning of the next is considered a significant interruption in work flow. Skilled data-entry operators complain bitterly about terminal response time greater than 2.5 seconds. You have been using a hardware monitor as part of your postimplementation audit. The following graph displays an average online response time during one month of monitoring operations:

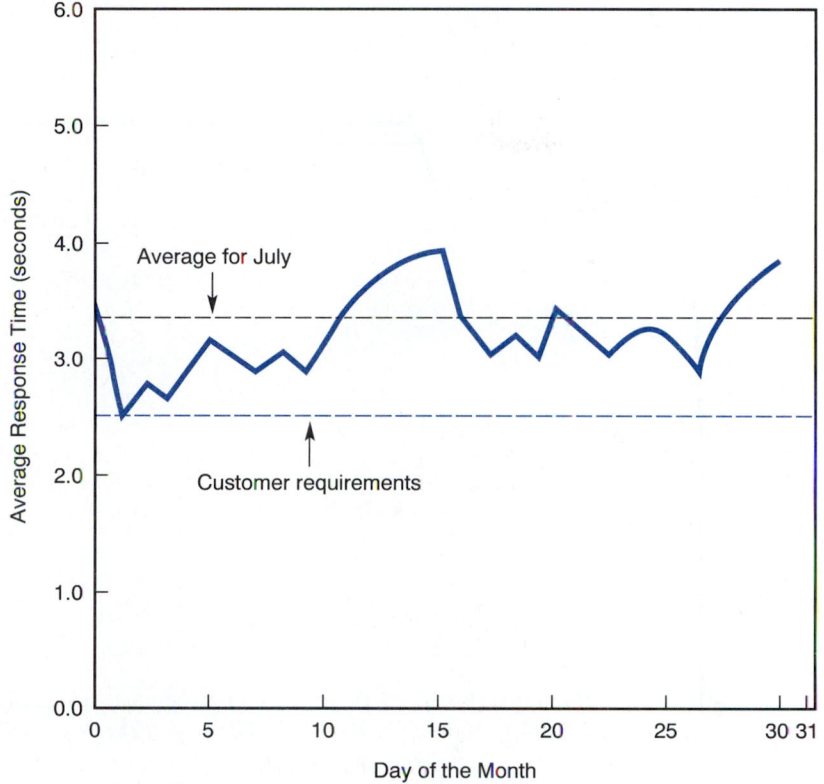

Required:

Based on the information displayed in the graph, prepare a response to be included in your postimplementation audit report. If the system you are reviewing is designed to support mostly data-entry operations, is the system adequate? What might be some feasible changes in the system that would make it more adequate?

24.36 *Postimplementation audit of systems performance.* The percentage of systems availability time is closely related to terminal response time. A low percentage of availability and poor terminal response time, however, may be symptoms of different problems. The percentage of systems availability is considered an important measure of systems performance.

The percentage of systems availability is calculated with the following equation:

$$\frac{\text{Percentage}}{\text{availability}} = \frac{(\text{Total scheduled availability} - \text{Downtime}) \times 100}{\text{Total scheduled availability}}$$

Total scheduled availability is the total number of hours the system is scheduled to operate within a given time period. The time period may be a day, week, month, or year. Downtime is the number of hours the system is unavailable for use during the same time period.

You have monitored the system for a month immediately following systems conversion. The results of this monitoring are presented in the following graph:

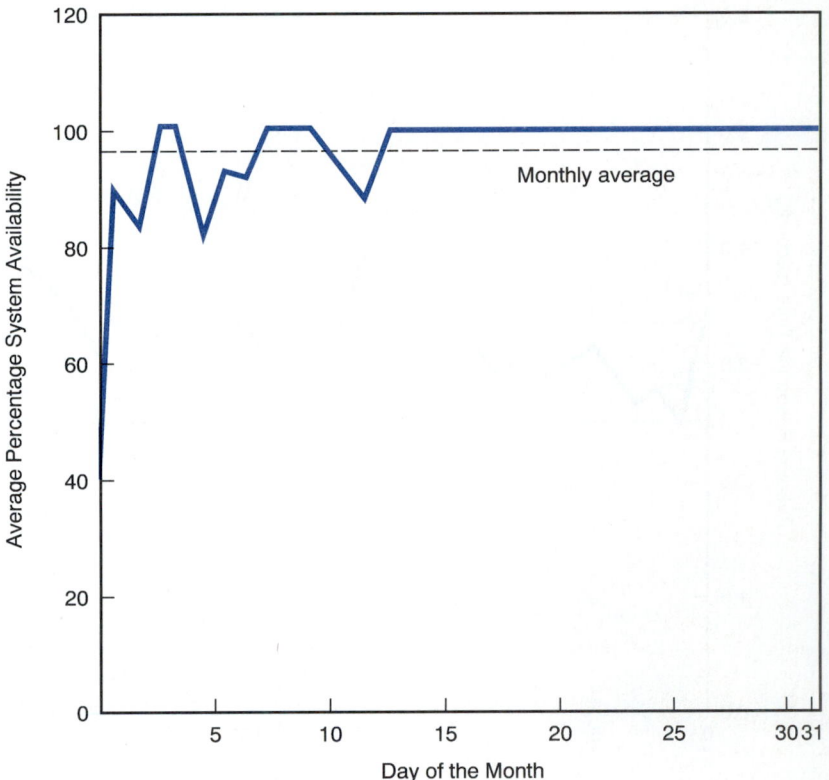

Required:

What assessment of the system's availability can you make from this graph? Make any assumptions that you deem appropriate and explain the reason or reasons behind the fluctuations in the first half of the month. Do you plan to continue monitoring the system next month? Why or why not?

24.37 *Postimplementation audit of systems performance.* The new order-entry system has been in operation for four months after direct conversion. During this time, orders have been reported late 35% of the time because of system malfunctions and user incompetency. Reruns are common, and the order-entry software has suffered 14 abnormal terminations. On the first three abnormal terminations, operators took over two days to restart the system.

Required:

Prepare a critique of this system's implementation. What should have been done to prevent these problems from occurring? Justify all of your answers and make any assumptions you deem necessary.

ACRONYM LIST

Management accountants tend to refer to many concepts by their acronyms, a practice that can initially be confusing for students. Although care has been taken to identify acronyms throughout the text, the following list may be helpful for reference. The number in parentheses after each term indicates the page where the acronym is introduced or the first significant discussion of the concept occurs. For full references to each term, see its entry in the Subject Index.

ABC   Activity-based costing (445)
ABM   Activity-based management (446)
ADS   Alternative depreciation system (1096)
ANSI   American National Standards Institute (191)
AOH   Actual overhead (152)
AOL   Abnormal output loss (244)
AP   Actual price (156)
AQ   Actual quantity (156)
AQp   Actual quantity purchased (335)
AQu   Actual quantity used (340)
ARR   Accounting rate of return (1093)
ATP   Available-to-promise (105)

BCAS   Backflush cost accounting system (367)
BEP   Break-even point (837)
BER   Break-even revenues (838)
BOM   Bill of materials (99)
BOP   Beginning of (accounting) period (417)

CAD   Computer-aided design (80)
CAE   Computer-aided engineering (80)
CAM   Computer-aided manufacturing (80)
CAM-I   Computer Aided Manufacturing-International (505)
CAS   Cost accounting system (129)

CASE   Computer-aided systems and software engineering (528)
CEO   Chief executive officer (932)
CER   Cost estimating relationship (677)
CIM   Computer-integrated manufacturing (79)
CM   Contribution margin (837)
CMA   Certified Management Accountant (23)
CMU   Contribution margin per unit (836)
COGM   Cost of goods manufactured (367)
COGS   Cost of goods sold (130)
COO   Chief operating officer (934)
CPA   Certified public accountant (14)
CSI   Construction Specification Institute (199)
CVP   Cost-volume-profit (834)
cwt   Hundredweight (615)

DBMS   Database management system (528)
DCF   Discounted cash flow (1079)
DFOH   Direct fixed overhead (405)
DL   Direct labor (129)
DLhr   Direct labor hour (150)
DM   Direct materials (129)
DOE   Design of experiment (77)
D:P   Delivery production (ratio) (520)
DVOH   Direct variable overhead (405)

EBQ   Economic batch quantity (623)
EDI   Electronic data interchange (108)
EOP   End of (accounting) period (417)
EOQ   Economic order quantity (620)
EPR   Economic production run (623)
ERD   Entity relationship diagram (92)
ET   Early event time (1144)
EUP   Equivalent units of production (228)
EVA   Economic value added (1164)

FASB   Financial Accounting Standards Board (14)
FDA   Food and Drug Administration (784)
FDDI   Fiber distributed data interface (191)
FGI   Finished goods inventory (130)
FICA   Federal Insurance Contributions Act (144)
FIFO   First-in, first-out (232)
FOH   Fixed overhead (129)
4GLS   Fourth-generation languages (528)
FS   Free slack (1145)
FUTA   Federal Unemployment Tax (145)

GAAP   Generally accepted accounting principles (14)
GDS   Group decision support (1055)
GIGO   Garbage in, garbage out (1053)

ICBIS   Integrated computer-based information system (19)
ICMA   Institute of Certified Management Accountants (25)
IL   Indirect labor (133)
IM   Indirect materials (133)
IMA   Institute of Management Accountants (25)
IRR   Internal rate of return (1084)
IRS   Internal Revenue Service (14)
ISO   International Organization for Standardization (553)

JE   Journal entry (137)
JID   Joint investment decision (1053)
JIT   Just-in-time (64)
JOCAS   Job order cost accounting system (130)

LAN   Local area network (63)
LCL   Lower control limit (575)

LIFO	Last-in, last-out (632)	POR	Predetermined overhead rate (152)	ST	Subject to (the following constraints) (751)
LINDO	Linear Interactive Discrete Optimizer (750)	PP	Payback period (1090)	SUB	Supplemental Unemployment Benefit (149)
LP	Linear programming (725)	PPB	Parts per billion (569)	SUTA	State Unemployment Tax (145)
LT	Late event time (1144)	PPM	Parts per million (568)	SWOT	Strengths, weaknesses, opportunities, threats (783)
LTE	Lead time efficiency (75)	PVI	Present value index (1085)		
MAC	Military Airlift Command (752)	QC	Quality control (235)		
MACRS	Modified accelerated cost recovery system (1095)	QFD	Quality function deployment (659)	TOC	Theory of constraints (695)
				TOES	Technical, operational, economic, and schedule (feasibility) (1049)
Mhr	Machine hour (150)			TOH	Total overhead (129)
MNE	Multinational enterprise (290)			TPM	Total preventive maintenance (77)
MRP	Material requirements planning (99)	RC	Responsibility center (932)		
		RI	Residual income (962)	TQM	Total quality management (77)
MRP II	Manufacturing resource planning (101)	RIP	Raw-in-process (367)	TS	Total slack (1145)
		RMI	Raw materials inventory (130)		
		ROA	Return on assets (509)		
NAA	National Association of Accountants (25)	ROI	Return on investment (509)	UC	Unit cost (194)
				UCL	Upper control limit (575)
NOL	Normal output loss (244)	SAMC	Standard absorptive manufacturing cost (281)		
NPV	Net present value (1084)				
NRV	Net realizable value (182)	SBA	Small Business Administration (784)	VOH	Variable overhead (129)
				VPI	Vendor performance index (513)
		SCA	Standard cost allowed (349)	VSAT	Very small aperture terminal (901)
OH	Overhead	SCAS	Standard cost accounting system (155)		
OLRT	Online real-time (938)				
		SEC	Securities and Exchange Commission (14)		
PCAS	Process cost accounting system (131)	SM	Segment margin (1010)	WA	Weighted average (232)
		SMA	Society of Management Accountants (25)	WAN	Wide area network (63)
PE	Professional engineer (25)			WBS	Work breakdown structure (199)
PERT	Program evaluation and review technique (1139)	SP	Standard price (155)	WCM	World-class manufacturing (50)
		SPC	Statistical process control (77)	WIP	Work-in-process/work-in-progress (8)
PI	Profitability index (1085)	SQA	Standard quantity allowed (155)		

Author Index

COMPANY INDEX

IMPORTANT TERMS INDEX

Subject Index

PHOTO CREDITS

Traditional Manufacturing Process

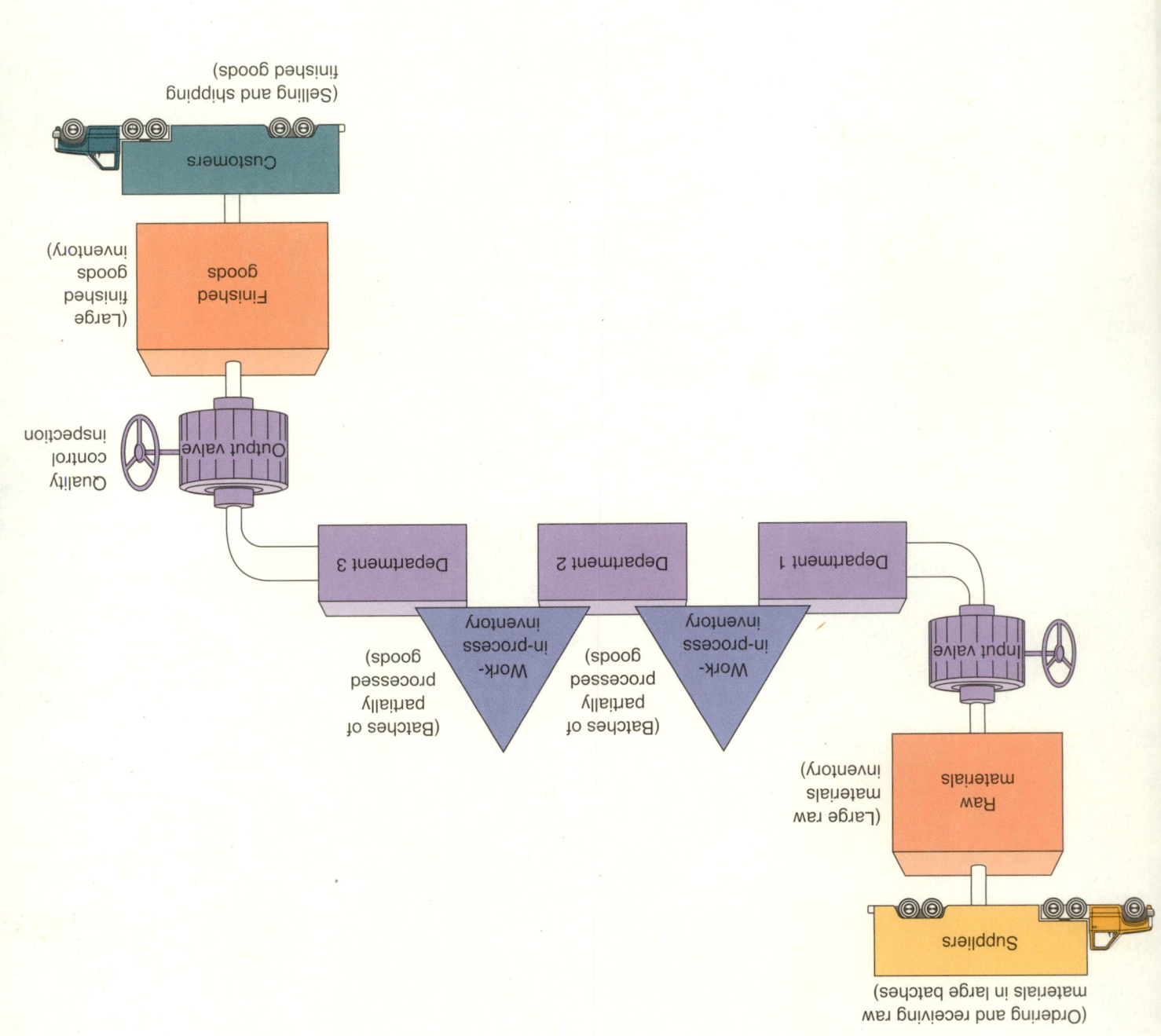